D0022692

OFFICIAL (ISC)²®
GUIDE TO THE
CISSP® CBK®

FOURTH EDITION

OTHER BOOKS IN THE (ISC)²® PRESS SERIES

Official (ISC)²® Guide to the CISSP® CBK®, Fourth Edition
Adam Gordon, Editor
ISBN: 978-1-4822-6275-9

Official (ISC)²® Guide to the HCISPP^SM CBK®
Steven Hernandez, Editor
ISBN: 978-1-4822-6277-3

Official (ISC)²® Guide to the CCFP^SM CBK®
Peter Stephenson, Editor
ISBN: 978-1-4822-6247-6

Official (ISC)²® Guide to the ISSAP® CBK®, Second Edition
Adam Gordon, Editor
ISBN: 978-1-4665-7900-2

Official (ISC)²® Guide to the CAP® CBK®, Second Edition
Patrick D. Howard
ISBN: 978-1-4398-2075-9

Official (ISC)²® Guide to the SSCP® CBK®, Second Edition
Harold F. Tipton, Editor
ISBN: 978-1-4398-0483-4

Official (ISC)²® Guide to the ISSAP® CBK®
Harold F. Tipton, Editor
ISBN: 978-1-4398-0093-5

Official (ISC)²® Guide to the ISSMP® CBK®
Harold F. Tipton, Editor
ISBN: 978-1-4200-9443-5

CISO Leadership: Essential Principles for Success
Todd Fitzgerald and Micki Krause, Editors
ISBN: 978-0-8493-7943-X

Official (ISC)²® Guide to the CISSP®-ISSEP® CBK®
Susan Hansche
ISBN: 978-0-8493-2341-X

OFFICIAL (ISC)²®
GUIDE TO THE
CISSP® CBK®
FOURTH EDITION

Edited by
Adam Gordon - CISSP-ISSAP, ISSMP, SSCP

CRC Press
Taylor & Francis Group
Boca Raton London New York

CRC Press is an imprint of the
Taylor & Francis Group, an **informa** business
AN AUERBACH BOOK

CRC Press
Taylor & Francis Group
6000 Broken Sound Parkway NW, Suite 300
Boca Raton, FL 33487-2742

© 2015 by Taylor & Francis Group, LLC
CRC Press is an imprint of Taylor & Francis Group, an Informa business

No claim to original U.S. Government works

Printed on acid-free paper
Version Date: 20150206

International Standard Book Number-13: 978-1-4822-6275-9 (Hardback)

Visit the Taylor & Francis Web site at
http://www.taylorandfrancis.com

and the CRC Press Web site at
http://www.crcpress.com

CISSP®

Contents

Domain 1 — Security & Risk Management

Domain 2 — Asset Security

Domain 3 — Security Engineering

Domain 4 — Communications & Network Security

Domain 5 — *Identity & Access Management*

Domain 6 — *Security Assessment & Testing*

Domain 7 — *Security Operations*

Domain 8—*Security in the Software Development Life Cycle*

CISSP®

Foreword

Foreword to the CISSP CBK Study Guide

As the dynamics of the information security industry evolve, so must the core components of the gold standard Certified Information Systems Security Professional (CISSP). Global subject matter experts reviewed the CISSP CBK and made significant changes to the content – in fact, 40% of the content is new. The ten domains of the CISSP have been reorganized into the following eight domains:

- **Security and Risk Management** – Apply security governance principles
- **Asset Security** – Classify information and supporting assets
- **Security Engineering** – Implement and manage an engineering lifecycle using security design principles
- **Communication and Network Security** – Apply secure design principles to network architecture
- **Identity and Access Management** – Control physical and logical access to assets
- **Security Assessment and Testing** – Design and validate assessment and test strategies
- **Security Operations** – Understand and apply foundational security operations concepts
- **Software Development Security** – Understand and apply security in the software development lifecycle

Advancements in technology continue to bring about the need for updates. We work tirelessly to ensure that our exam content is always relevant to the industry. I look forward to your feedback on the revamped CISSP exam, and congratulate you on taking the first step toward earning the certification that SC *Magazine* named "Best Professional Certification Program" for the fourth time.

Achieving the CISSP is the next step in advancing your career; not to mention, you'll gain access to unparalleled global continuing education resources, peer networking, mentoring, and a wealth of other opportunities. Becoming a member of (ISC)² elevates you into one of the largest communities of information security professionals in the world. Required by some of the world's most security conscious organizations and government entities, the CISSP validates that information security leaders possess the breadth of knowledge, skills, and experience required to credibly build and manage the security posture of their organizations/governments.

Through 100,000 credential holders, the CISSP continues to be recognized by the media and industry professionals as the benchmark for information security certification worldwide.

This *Official (ISC)² Guide to the CISSP CBK* is the best reference available, reflecting the most relevant topics in the ever-changing field of information security. It provides a robust and comprehensive guide to the new eight CISSP domains, with sub-topics on the issues that security professionals face today. Compiled and reviewed by CISSPs and luminaries around the world, this textbook provides an unrivaled study tool for the certification exam that is up-to-date and authoritative.

The road to becoming a CISSP is not easy and becomes even more challenging each year; but the end results are well worth all your efforts. Not only is the CISSP an objective measure of excellence, it has become the global standard for the information security profession. Managing security in today's operations without a CISSP is now tantamount to practicing medicine without a license.

Congratulations on your decision to broaden your horizons through the best security education and certification program in the world. Good luck!

— W. Hord Tipton, Former Executive Director, (ISC)²

CISSP®

Introduction

There are two main requirements that must be met in order to achieve the status of CISSP; one must take and pass the certification exam, and be able to demonstrate a minimum of 5 years of direct full-time security work experience in two or more of the 8 domains of the (ISC)² CISSP CBK. A firm understanding of what the 8 domains of the CISSP CBK are, and how they relate to the landscape of business is a vital element in successfully being able to meet both requirements and claim the CISSP credential. The mapping of the 8 domains of the CISSP CBK to the job responsibilities of the Information Security professional in today's world can take many paths, based on a variety of factors such as industry vertical, regulatory oversight and compliance, geography, as well as public versus private versus military as the overarching framework for employment in the first place. In addition, considerations such as cultural practices and differences in language and meaning can also play a substantive role in the interpretation of what aspects of the CBK will mean, and how they will be implemented in any given workplace.

It is not the purpose of this book to attempt to address all of these issues or provide a definitive proscription as to what is "the" path forward in all areas. Rather, it is to provide the official guide to the CISSP CBK, and in so doing, to lay out the information necessary to understand what the CBK is, and how it is used to build the foundation for the CISSP and its role in business today. To that end, it is important to begin any journey with a sense of place, specifically where you are, and where you want to end up; and as a result, what tools you will need to have in order to make the journey comfortable and successful. The most important tool that the intrepid traveler can have at their disposal is a compass, that trusty device that always allows one to understand in what direction they are heading, and get their bearings when necessary. The compass of the Information Security professional is their knowledge, experience, and understanding of the world around them. The thing that is amazing about a compass is that no matter where you stand on Earth, you can hold one in your hand and it will point toward the North Pole. While we do not need to know where the North Pole always is in Information Security, as a CISSP, you are expected to be able to provide guidance and direction to the businesses and users that you are responsible for. Being able to map the CISSP

CBK to your knowledge, experience, and understanding is the way that you will be able to provide that guidance, and to translate the CBK into actionable and tangible elements for both the business and its users that you represent.

1. The **Security and Risk Management** domain addresses the framework and policies, concepts, principles, structures, and standards used to establish criteria for the protection of information assets and to assess the effectiveness of that protection. It includes issues of governance, organizational behavior, and security awareness. Information security management establishes the foundation of a comprehensive and proactive security program to ensure the protection of an organization's information assets. Today's environment of highly interconnected, interdependent systems necessitates the requirement to understand the linkage between information technology and meeting business objectives. Information security management communicates the risks accepted by the organization due to the currently implemented security controls, and continually works to cost effectively enhance the controls to minimize the risk to the company's information assets. Security management encompasses the administrative, technical, and physical controls necessary to adequately protect the confidentiality, integrity, and availability of information assets. Controls are manifested through a foundation of policies, procedures, standards, baselines, and guidelines.

2. The **Asset Security** domain contains the concepts, principles, structures, and standards used to monitor and secure assets and those controls used to enforce various levels of confidentiality, integrity, and availability. Information security architecture and design covers the practice of applying a comprehensive and rigorous method for describing a current and/or future structure and behavior for an organization's security processes, information security systems, personnel and organizational sub-units, so that these practices and processes align with the organization's core goals and strategic direction.

3. The **Security Engineering** domain contains the concepts, principles, structures, and standards used to design, implement, monitor, and secure, operating systems, equipment, networks, applications, and those controls used to enforce various levels of confidentiality, integrity, and availability. Information security architecture and design covers the practice of applying a comprehensive and rigorous method for describing a current and/or future structure and behavior for an organization's security processes, information security systems, personnel and organizational sub-units, so that these practices and processes align with the organization's core goals and strategic direction.

4. The **Communication and Network Security** domain encompasses the structures, transmission methods, transport formats, and security measures used to provide confidentiality, integrity, and availability for transmissions over private and public communications networks and media. Network security is often described as the cornerstone of IT security. The network is a central asset, if not the most central, in most IT environments. Loss of network assurance (the combined properties of confidentiality, integrity, availability, authentication, and non-repudiation) on any level can have devastating consequences, while control of the network provides an easy and consistent venue of attack. Conversely, a well-architected and well-protected network will stop many attacks in their tracks.

5. Although ***Identity and Access Management*** is a single domain within the CISSP Common Body of Knowledge (CBK), it is the most pervasive and omnipresent aspect of information security. Access controls encompass all operational levels of an organization:

- ¤ ***Facilities*** – Access controls protect entry to, and movement around, an organization's physical locations to protect personnel, equipment, information, and, other assets inside that facility.

- ¤ ***Support Systems*** – Access to support systems (such as power, heating, ventilation and air conditioning (HVAC) systems; water; and fire suppression controls) must be controlled so that a malicious entity is not able to compromise these systems and cause harm to the organization's personnel or the ability to support critical systems.

- ¤ ***Information systems*** – Multiple layers of access controls are present in most modern information systems and networks to protect those systems, and the information they contain, from harm or misuse.

- ¤ ***Personnel*** – Management, end users, customers, business partners, and nearly everyone else associated with an organization should be subject to some form of access control to ensure that the right people have the ability to interface with each other, and not interfere with the people with whom they do not have any legitimate business.

The goals of information security are to ensure the continued Confidentiality-Integrity-Availability of an organization's assets. This includes both physical assets (such as buildings, equipment, and, of course, people) and information assets (such as company data and information systems.) Access controls play a key role in ensuring the confidentiality of systems and information. Managing access to physical and information assets is fundamental to preventing exposure of data by controlling who can see, use, modify, or destroy those assets. In addition, managing an entity's admittance and rights to specific enterprise resources ensures that valuable data and services are not abused, misappropriated, or stolen. It is also a key factor for many organizations that are required to protect personal information in order to be compliant with appropriate legislation and industry compliance requirements.

6. ***Security Assessment and Testing*** covers a broad range of ongoing and point-of-time based testing methods used to determine vulnerabilities and associated risk. Mature system development lifecycles include security testing and assessment as part of the development, operations and disposition phases of a system's life. The fundamental purpose of test and evaluation (T&E) is to provide knowledge to assist in managing the risks involved in developing, producing, operating, and sustaining systems and capabilities. T&E measures progress in both system and capability development. T&E provides knowledge of system capabilities and limitations for use in improving the system performance, and for optimizing system use in operations. T&E expertise must be brought to bear at the beginning of the system life cycle to provide earlier learning about the strengths and weaknesses of the system under development. The goal is early identification of technical, operational, and system deficiencies, so that appropriate and timely corrective actions can be developed prior to fielding the system. The creation of the test and evaluation strategy involves planning for technology development, including risk; evaluating the system design against mission requirements; and identifying where competitive prototyping and other evaluation techniques fit in the process.

7. The **Security Operations** domain is used to identify critical information and the execution of selected measures that eliminate or reduce adversary exploitation of critical information. It includes the definition of the controls over hardware, media, and the operators with access privileges to any of these resources. Auditing and monitoring are the mechanisms, tools and facilities that permit the identification of security events and subsequent actions to identify the key elements and report the pertinent information to the appropriate individual, group, or process. The Information Security professional should always act to Maintain Operational Resilience, Protect Valuable Assets, Control System Accounts and Manage Security Services Effectively. In the day to day operations of the business, maintaining expected levels of availability and integrity for data and services is where the Information Security professional impacts Operational Resilience. The day to day securing, monitoring, and maintenance of the resources of the business, both human and material, illustrate how the Information Security professional is able to Protect Valuable Assets. Providing a system of checks and balances with regards to privileged account usage, as well as system access, allows the Information Security professional to act to Control Systems Accounts in a consistent way. The use of change and configuration management by the Information Security professional, as well as reporting and service improvement programs (SIP), ensures that the actions necessary to Manage Security Services Effectively are being carried out.

8. The **Software Development Security** domain requires a security professional to be prepared to do the following:
   ◻ Understand and apply security in the software development lifecycle
   ◻ Enforce security controls in the development environment
   ◻ Assess the effectiveness of software security
   ◻ Assess software acquisition security

Although information security has traditionally emphasized system-level access controls, the security professional needs to ensure that the focus of the enterprise security architecture includes applications, since many information security incidents now involve software vulnerabilities in one form or another. Application vulnerabilities also allow an entry point to attack systems, sometimes at a very deep level. When examined, most major incidents, breaches and outages will be found to involve software vulnerabilities. Software continues to grow increasingly larger and more complex with each release. In addition, software is becoming standardized, both in terms of the programs and code used as well as the protocols and interfaces involved. Although this provides benefits in training and productivity, it also means that a troublesome characteristic may affect the computing and business environment quite broadly. Also, legacy code and design decisions taken decades ago are still involved in current systems and interact with new technologies and operations in ways that may open up additional vulnerabilities that the security professional may, or may not, even be aware of.

CISSP®

Editors

Adam Gordon – *Lead Editor*

With over 25 years of experience as both an educator and IT professional, Adam holds numerous Professional IT Certifications including CISSP, CISA, CRISC, CHFI, CEH, SCNA, VCP, and VCI. Adam holds his Bachelor's Degree in International Relations and his Master's Degree in International Political Affairs from Florida International University.

Adam has held a number of positions during his professional career including CISO, CTO, Consultant, and Solutions Architect. He has worked on many large implementations involving multiple customer program teams for delivery.

Adam has been invited to lead projects for companies such as Microsoft, Citrix, Lloyds Bank TSB, Campus Management, US Southern Command (SOUTHCOM), Amadeus, World Fuel Services, and Seaboard Marine.

Javvad Malik – *Lead Technical Editor*

Javvad Malik is a Senior Analyst in the 451 Enterprise Security Practice, providing in-depth, timely perspective on the state of enterprise security and emerging trends. Prior to joining 451 Research, he was an independent security consultant, with an extensive career spanning 12+ years working for some of the largest companies in the world.

Javvad is an active blogger, event speaker and possibly best known as one of the industry's most prolific video bloggers with his signature fresh and light-hearted perspective on security that speak to both technical and non-technical audiences alike. His articles regularly feature in online and print media, he is a coauthor of The Cloud Security Rules book and a volunteer member of the (ISC)² foundations Safe and Secure Online initiative. Javvad was a founder of the Security B-Sides London conference, in 2010 was named as a finalist for SC Magazine's Blogger of the Year award and in 2013 won the RSA Social Security Blogger award for the most entertaining blogger as well as winning best security video blogger and most entertaining blog at the European Security Blogger awards. You can follow him on Twitter as @ J4vv4D or on his website www.J4vv4D.com.

Steven Hernandez – *Technical Editor*

Steven Hernandez MBA, HCISPP, CISSP, CSSLP, SSCP, CAP, CISA, is a Chief Information Security Officer practicing in the U.S. Federal Government in Washington DC. Hernandez has over seventeen years of information assurance experience in a variety of fields including international healthcare, international heavy manufacturing, large finance organizations, educational institutions, and government agencies. Steven is an Honorary Professor at California State University San Bernardino and affiliate faculty at the National Information Assurance Training and Education Center located at Idaho State University. Through his academic outreach, he has lectured over the past decade on numerous information assurance topics including risk management, information security investment, and the implications of privacy decisions to graduate and postgraduate audiences. In addition to his credentials from (ISC)², Hernandez also holds six U.S. Committee for National Security Systems certifications ranging from systems security to organizational risk management. Steven also volunteers service to (ISC)²'s Government Advisory Board and Executive Writers Bureau. Steven enjoys relaxing and traveling with his wife, whose patience and support have been indispensable in his numerous information assurance pursuits.

Preface

Audience Voice

In the following domain discussions, three specific audience roles will be addressed as noted below:

1. ***The Security Architect*** – Responsible for the enterprise security architecture of the enterprise
2. ***The Security Practitioner*** – Responsible for the tactical and operational elements of the security infrastructure of the enterprise
3. ***The Security Professional*** – Responsible for the managerial oversight of the security elements of the enterprise

Each of these roles is important in its own right, and often will be found standing alone as a separate job within the enterprise. On occasion, one or more of these roles will be combined together within a single job role or function within the enterprise. The CISSP candidate will need to understand ALL three roles, and incorporate aspects of all of them in order to be successful as a member of the information security community.

Please make sure that as you read through the discussions within this domain that you take note of which voice, or voices, are being referenced with regards to actions and activities. Being able to understand what each of these roles is responsible for within the enterprise will be a valuable addition to the skills and knowledge that the CISSP candidate should have.

The Fourth Edition – What's New?

While there has been some reclassification of the domain names within the CISSP Common Body of Knowledge (CBK), the important thing to note is what has been introduced from a content perspective. With that in mind, here is a partial list of some of the new material you can expect to see:

- Within the *Security and Risk Management* domain
  - Compliance
  - Data Breaches
  - Conducting a Business Impact Analysis (BIA)
  - Implementation

- ¤ Continuous improvement
- ¤ Threat Modeling
- ¤ Determining potential attacks
- ¤ Performing a Reduction Analysis
- ¤ Technologies and processes used to remediate threats
- ¤ Integrating security risk considerations into acquisitions strategy and practice
- ¤ Third-Party assessments
- ¤ Minimum security requirements
- ¤ Service-Level requirements
- ¤ Appropriate levels of awareness, training, and education within an organization
- ¤ Periodic reviews for content relevancy
- ■ Within the *Asset Security* domain
  - ¤ Data owners
  - ¤ Data processes
  - ¤ Data Remanence
  - ¤ Baselines
  - ¤ Scoping and tailoring
  - ¤ Standards selection
- ■ Within the *Security Engineering* domain
  - ¤ Implementing and managing an engineering lifecycle using security design principles
  - ¤ Large scale parallel data systems
  - ¤ Cryptographic systems
  - ¤ Assessing and mitigating vulnerabilities in mobile systems
  - ¤ Embedded devices and cyber-physical systems
  - ¤ Data Rights Management (DRM)
  - ¤ Designing and implementing facility security
  - ¤ Wiring closets
- ■ Within the *Communications and Network Security* domain
  - ¤ Converged protocols
  - ¤ Software defined networks
  - ¤ Content distribution networks
  - ¤ Physical devices
  - ¤ Virtualized networks
- ■ Within the *Identity and Access Management* domain
  - ¤ Controlling physical and logical access to assets
  - ¤ Registration and proof of identity
  - ¤ Credential management systems
  - ¤ Integrating Identity as a Service
  - ¤ Integrating third-party identity services
  - ¤ Preventing or mitigating access control attacks

- Within the *Security Assessment and Testing* domain
  - ¤ Assessment and testing strategies
  - ¤ Security control testing
  - ¤ Log reviews
  - ¤ Code review and testing
  - ¤ Negative testing
  - ¤ Misuse case testing
  - ¤ Test coverage analysis
  - ¤ Interface testing
  - ¤ Collecting security process data
  - ¤ Account management
  - ¤ Management review
  - ¤ Key performance and risk indicators
  - ¤ Analyzing and reporting test output
- Within the *Security Operations* domain
  - ¤ Understanding the requirements for various investigation types
    - Operational
    - Criminal
    - Civil
    - Regulatory
    - Electronic Discovery (eDiscovery)
  - ¤ Continuous monitoring
  - ¤ Egress monitoring
  - ¤ Securing the provisioning of resources
  - ¤ Configuration Management
  - ¤ Physical assets
  - ¤ Virtual assets
  - ¤ Cloud assets
  - ¤ Application provisioning
  - ¤ Service Level Agreements (SLA)
  - ¤ Hardware and Software asset management
  - ¤ Mitigation
  - ¤ Lessons learned
  - ¤ Whitelisting/Blacklisting
  - ¤ Third-Party security services
  - ¤ Sandboxing
  - ¤ Honeypots/Honeynets
  - ¤ Antimalware
  - ¤ Testing a Disaster Recovery Plan
    - Read through
    - Walk through
    - Simulation
    - Parallel
    - Full interruption

- Within the *Software Development Security* domain
  - Integrated product teams
  - Code repositories
  - Application Program Interfaces (APIs)
  - Acceptance testing
  - Assessing software acquisition security

In addition, there have been nine new appendices added with useful forms and process that can help the security professional in their day-to-day job functions as well as a glossary with over 450 definitions. Finally there are almost 200 end of domain practice questions with the answers and rationale provided in Appendix A.

Domain 1
Security &
Risk Management

The "Security and Risk Management" domain of the Certified Information Systems Security Professional (CISSP)® Common Body of Knowledge (CBK)® addresses the framework and policies, concepts, principles, structures, and standards used to establish criteria for the protection of information assets and to assess the effectiveness of that protection. It includes issues of governance, organizational behavior, and security awareness.

Information security management establishes the foundation of a comprehensive and proactive security program to ensure the protection of an organization's information assets. Today's environment of highly interconnected, interdependent systems necessitates the requirement to understand the linkage between information technology and meeting business objectives. Information security management communicates the risks accepted by the organization due to the currently implemented security controls, and it continually works to cost effectively enhance the controls to minimize the risk to the company's information assets. Security management encompasses the administrative, technical, and physical controls necessary to adequately protect the confidentiality, integrity, and availability of information assets. Controls are manifested through a foundation of policies, procedures, standards, baselines, and guidelines.

Information security management practices that manage risk include such tools as risk assessment, risk analysis, data classification, and security awareness. Information assets are classified, and through risk assessment, the threats and vulnerabilities related to these assets are categorized, and the appropriate safeguards to mitigate risk of compromise can be identified and prioritized by the security professional.

Risk management minimizes loss to information assets due to undesirable events through identification, measurement, and control. It encompasses the overall security review, risk analysis, selection and evaluation of safeguards, cost–benefit analysis, management decision, and safeguard identification and implementation, along with ongoing effectiveness review. Risk management provides a mechanism to the organization

1

to ensure that executive management knows current risks, and informed decisions can be made to use one of the risk management principles: risk avoidance, risk transfer, risk mitigation, or risk acceptance, all described in more detail later in this chapter.

Security management is concerned with regulatory, customer, employee, and business partner requirements for managing data as they flow between the various parties to support the processing and business use of the information. Confidentiality, integrity, and availability of the information must be maintained throughout the process.

Business continuity planning (BCP) and disaster recovery planning (DRP) address the preparation, processes, and practices required to ensure the preservation of the organization in the face of major disruptions to normal organization operations. BCP and DRP involve the identification, selection, implementation, testing, and updating of processes and specific prudent actions necessary to protect critical organization processes from the effects of major system and network disruptions and to ensure the timely restoration of organization operations if significant disruptions occur.

This chapter describes a process for building an enterprise-wide business continuity (BC) program. It discusses the evolution of the industry regulations that have influenced or in some cases mandated that organizations build programs within their organization that will ensure the continuation of their organization "no matter what."

Finally, it discusses the interrelationship between information security and BC and other risk management areas such as physical security, records management, vendor management, internal audit, financial risk management, operational risk management, and regulatory compliance (legal and regulatory risk) in the context of the overall BC risk management framework shown in *Figure 1.1*.

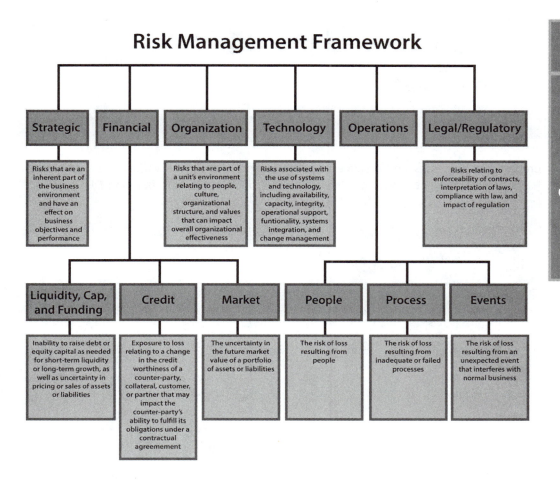

Figure 1.1 – **BC Risk Management Framework**

TOPICS

- The concepts of confidentiality, integrity, and availability
- Security governance principles
- Compliance
- Legal and regulatory issues
- Documented security policy, standards, procedures, and guidelines
- Business continuity requirements
- Personnel security policies
- Risk management concepts
- Threat modeling
- Integrating security risk considerations into acquisitions strategy and practice
- Security education, training, and awareness

OBJECTIVES

According to the (ISC)[2] Candidate Information Bulletin (Exam Outline), a CISSP candidate is expected to be able to:

- Understand and apply concepts of confidentiality, integrity, and availability.
- Apply security governance principles through compliance
- Understand legal and regulatory issues that pertain to information security in a global context.
- Develop and implement documented security policy, standards, procedures, and guidelines.
- Understand business continuity requirements.
- Contribute to personnel security policies.
- Understand and apply risk management concepts.
- Understand and apply threat modeling.
- Integrate security risk considerations into acquisitions strategy and practice.
- Establish and manage security education, training, and awareness.

Confidentiality, Integrity, and Availability

A well-structured, enterprise-wide information security program must ensure that the core concepts of availability, integrity, and confidentiality are supported by adequate security controls designed to mitigate or reduce the risks of loss, disruption, or corruption of information. Each of the security principles of the CIA triad is defined as follows:

Confidentiality

Confidentiality supports the principle of "least privilege" by providing that only authorized individuals, processes, or systems should have access to information on a need-to-know basis. The level of access that authorized individuals should have is at the level necessary for them to do their job. In recent years, much press has been dedicated to the privacy of information and the need to protect it from individuals who may be able to commit crimes by viewing the information. Identity theft is the act of assuming one's identity through knowledge of confidential information obtained from various sources.

An important measure that the security architect should use to ensure confidentiality of information is data classification. This helps to determine who should have access to the information (public, internal use only, or confidential). Identification, authentication, and authorization through access controls are practices that support maintaining the confidentiality of information. A sample control for protecting confidentiality is to encrypt information. Encryption of information limits the usability of the information in the event it is accessed by an unauthorized person.

Integrity

Integrity is the principle that information should be protected from intentional, unauthorized, or accidental changes. Information stored in files, databases, systems, and networks must be relied upon to accurately process transactions and provide accurate information for business decision making. Controls are put in place to ensure that information is modified through accepted practices.

Sample controls include management controls such as segregation of duties, approval checkpoints in the systems development life cycle (SDLC), and implementation of testing practices that assist in providing information integrity. Well-formed transactions and security of the update programs provide consistent methods of applying changes to systems. Limiting update capability to those individuals with a documented need to access limits the exposure to intentional and unintentional modification.

Availability

Availability is the principle that ensures that information is available and accessible to users when needed. The two primary areas affecting the availability of systems are

1. Denial-of-Service attacks
2. Loss of service due to a disaster, which could be man-made (e.g., poor capacity planning resulting in system crash, outdated hardware, and poor testing resulting in system crash after upgrade) or natural (e.g., earthquake, tornado, blackout, hurricane, fire, and flood).

In either case, the end-user does not have access to information needed to conduct business. The criticality of the system to the user and its importance to the survival of the organization will determine how significant the impact of the extended downtime becomes. The lack of appropriate security controls can increase the risk of viruses, destruction of data, external penetrations, or denial-of-service (DOS) attacks. Such events can prevent the system from being used by normal users.

Sample controls include an up-to-date and active anti-malicious code detection system, tested incident management plans, and disaster recovery planning or business continuity planning that ensure that the department functions using alternate processes when an outage to the computer system occurs for a defined period. Disaster recovery ensures that all or parts of information technology processing systems can be recovered. Disaster recovery and business continuity work together to minimize the impact of critical events on the enterprise.

When considering the design and implementation of a network, system, application, or management process, the security professional should understand the evaluation of the impact to confidentiality, integrity, and availability.

- The main question that the security architect needs to ask is "Will it **enhance** any of the core security principles?"
- The main question that the security practitioner needs to ask is "Will it **impact** any of the core security principles?"

Different security controls apply to different core security principles. An example would be the selection of a backup tape procedure. The software and hardware necessary to perform the backups would be most oriented toward the availability aspect of information security, whereas the selection of a security token utilizing strong, two-factor authentication would be most related to the enhancement of the confidentiality of information through improving authentication. An identity management system would be best deployed to support access control in order to ensure that only the appropriate personnel have update functions commensurate with their job supporting the integrity principle.

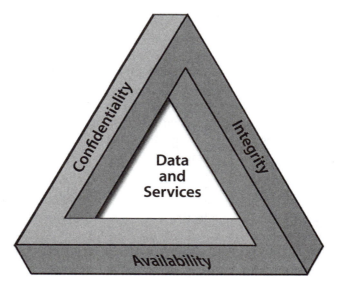

Figure 1.2 – **The CIA Triad**

Security Governance

Increased corporate governance requirements have caused companies to examine their internal control structures more closely to ensure that controls are in place and operating effectively. Organizations are increasingly competing in the global marketplace, which is governed by multiple laws and supported by various best practices (i.e., NIST, ITIL, ISO 27000, COSO, and COBIT). Appropriate information technology investment decisions must be made that are in alignment with the mission of the business. Information technology is no longer a back-office accounting function in most businesses, but rather it is a core operational necessity for the business, which must have the proper visibility to the board of directors and management's attention and oversight of the program.

This dependence on information technology mandates ensuring the proper alignment and understanding of the potential risks to the business. Substantial investments are made in these technologies (which must be appropriately managed), company reputations are at risk if insecure systems are deployed or found to be operating, and the trust in the systems needs to be demonstrated to all parties involved, including the shareholders, employees, business partners, and customers. Information security governance provides the mechanisms for the board of directors and management to have the proper oversight to manage the risk to the enterprise to an acceptable level.

The intent of governance is to guarantee that the appropriate information security activities are being performed to ensure that the risks are appropriately reduced, the information security investments are appropriately directed, and that executive management has visibility into the program and is asking the appropriate questions to determine the effectiveness of the program.

The IT Governance Institute (ITGI), in their publication entitled "Board Briefing on IT Governance, 2nd edition," defines IT governance as being "the responsibility of the board of directors and executive management. It is an integral part of enterprise governance and consists of the leadership and organizational structures and processes that ensure that the organization's IT sustains and extends the organization's strategies and objectives."[1]

The ITGI proposes that information security governance should be considered a part of IT governance and that the board of directors should:

- Be informed about information security
- Set direction to drive policy and strategy
- Provide resources to security efforts
- Assign management responsibilities
- Set priorities
- Support changes required
- Define cultural values related to risk assessment
- Obtain assurance from internal or external auditors
- Insist that security investments are made measurable and reported on for program effectiveness.

---

1   See the following: ITGI main website: http://www.itgi.org
     ITGI Board Briefing on IT Governance 2nd edition: http://www.isaca.org/restricted/Documents/26904_Board_Briefing_final.pdf

Additionally, the ITGI suggests that the management should:

- Write security policies with business input
- Ensure that roles and responsibilities are defined and clearly understood
- Identify threats and vulnerabilities
- Implement security infrastructures and control frameworks (standards, guidelines, baselines, and procedures)
- Ensure that policy is approved by the governing body
- Establish priorities and implement security projects in a timely manner
- Monitor breaches
- Conduct periodic reviews and tests
- Reinforce awareness education as critical
- Build security into the systems development life cycle

The security professional needs to work in partnership with management in order to ensure that these goals are achieved. These concepts are further delineated throughout this chapter.

Goals, Mission, and Objectives of the Organization

Information security management practices protect the assets of the organization through the implementation of physical, administrative, managerial, technical, and operational controls. Information assets must be managed appropriately to reduce the risk of loss to confidentiality, integrity, or availability. Just as financial assets are managed through finance departments, human assets (people) are managed and cared for by the human resources department and so are associated codes of conduct and employment policies and practices. Failure to protect information assets from loss, destruction, or unexpected alteration can result in significant losses of productivity, reputation, or financial loss. Information and the systems supporting the mission of an organization are assets that must be protected by the security professional.

Information security management validates that appropriate policies, procedures, standards, and guidelines are implemented to ensure business operations are conducted within an acceptable level of risk. Security exists to support and enable the vision, mission, and business objectives of the organization. Effective security management requires judgment based upon the risk tolerance of the organization, the costs to implement the security controls, and the benefit to the business. Although attaining 100% security of information is an admirable goal, in practice this is unrealistic. Even if this goal were attainable through an effective security program that includes all the best security practices for managing risk and a budget that would support all of the activities, it would not be long before a new vulnerability or exploit was discovered that could place the information at risk. As a result, a well-structured and managed program must be proactive and ongoing.

Because most organizations are in a competitive environment that requires continuous product innovation and reduction of administrative costs, funding information security at the "100% security level" is cost-prohibitive and impracticable for the organization. Therefore, effective security management requires risk management that includes a strong understanding of the business objectives of the organization, senior management's tolerance for risk, the costs of the various security alternatives, and, subsequently, the due diligence to match the appropriate security controls to the business initiatives. The security professionals who lead the information security program are relied upon for their knowledge of security and risk management principles. Senior management ultimately makes the final decision on the level of security expenditures and the risk it is willing to accept.

Security professionals should view their role as risk advisors to the organization, as they should not be the final decision makers when it comes to risk management. There may be situations where a risk is viewed as low, and therefore, senior management is willing to take a risk due to reasons that the security professional may not understand or be aware of. For example, the decision to accept operating in a regional office without a sprinkler system may be appropriate if the company has been operating in that office for ten years without a fire and management has undisclosed plans to relocate the office within the next six months.

Alternatively, there may be government mandates to comply with new regulations or audit findings that have a higher priority. Senior management must weigh all of the risks to the business, and choosing whether to implement specific security controls represents one of those risk management activities. This is why security professionals must be effective at communicating risks and possible security solutions. There will always be residual risk accepted by an organization, and effective security management will minimize this risk to a level that fits within the organization's risk tolerance or risk profile.

Security management is the glue that ensures that the risks are identified and an adequate control environment is established to mitigate the risks. Security management ensures the interrelationships among assessing risk, implementing policies and controls in response to the risks, promoting awareness of the expectations, monitoring the effectiveness of the controls, and using this knowledge as input to the next risk assessment. These relationships are shown in *Figure 1.3*.

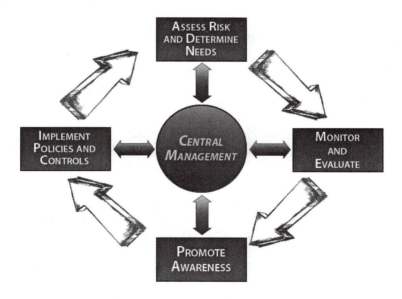

Figure 1.3 – **Security and Risk Management Relationships**

Organizational Processes

Understanding the mission of an organization and the processes that support it is critical for the success of a security program. In many ways, an organization is like a living thing. It may go through several phases of growth, decline, and illness during its lifetime. Understanding of the business transformational events and entities ensures the security professional maintains situational awareness of what is occurring in the boardroom and the management decisions being made on a day-to-day basis throughout the enterprise. For example, the following are common activities organizations undergo that may impact the security professional:

- **Acquisitions and Mergers** – Organizations combine for many reasons. Some mergers are friendly with both parties realizing a gain from the merger, while others may be described as "hostile." In either situation, the information security professional must be aware of the following items and plan accordingly:
  - Additional data types that may need more protection than the existing security program provides
  - Additional technology types that may need more protection than the existing security program provides
  - New staff and roles with enhanced requirements for security awareness and training
  - Threats from former employees or possibly threats the new organization will face that the old one did not
  - Vulnerabilities when systems are merged
  - Potentially new policies, standards, and procedures to support compliance with any laws, regulations, and requirements that the organization will need to be aware of
  - External business partners and interconnections that will need review and assessment
- **Divestitures and Spinoffs** – The opposite of an acquisition or a merger, a divesture may involve the spinoff of a part of an organization or possibly the complete liquidation of an existing organization. These are tense times in an organization, and the information security professional should be concerned with the following situations and plan accordingly:
  - Data loss and data leakage due to employees leaving for the spinoff or another company
  - System interconnections, protocols, and ports left open after the function they were serving is no longer applicable
  - Loss of visibility into the network and system logs if both organizations did not keep the appropriate security monitoring tools and capabilities in house
  - New threats from employees who may have been laid off or forced out of the organization
  - The need to revise policies, standards, and procedures to recognize any new governance bodies in the organization and reflect the organization change if applicable
  - The need to meet any divestiture imposed deadlines for data segregation or spinoff between organizations

- **Governance Committees** – A governance committee is responsible for recruiting and maintaining the governance board for an organization. The committee is also typically responsible for determining missing qualifications and characteristics needed to enhance the efficiency and effectiveness of the board. The security professional should learn how the board functions and, as much as possible, attempt to:
  - Ensure the committee understands at a high level the importance of information security and risk management.
  - Ensure committee recruitment exercises for new board members include requirements for information security and risk aptitude where needed.
  - Maintain a working relationship with committee members and be available to respond to specific risk, privacy, and information security questions as needed.

Security Roles and Responsibilities

Many different individuals within an organization contribute to successful information protection. Security is the responsibility of everyone within the company. Every end-user is responsible for understanding the policies and procedures that are applicable to his or her particular job function and adhering to any and all security control expectations. Users must have knowledge of their responsibilities and be trained to a level that is adequate to reduce the risk of loss to an acceptable level. Although the exact titles and scope of responsibility of the individuals may vary from organization to organization, the following roles support the implementation of security controls. An individual may be assigned multiple roles for the organization. It is important to provide clear definition and communication of roles and responsibilities including accountability through the distribution of policies, job descriptions, training, and management direction, as well as providing the foundation for execution of security controls by the workforce.

Today's Security Organizational Structure

There is no "one size fits all" for the information security department or the scope of the responsibilities. The location of where the security organization should report has also been evolving. In many organizations, the Information Systems Security Officer (ISSO) or Chief Information Security Officer (CISO) still reports to the Chief Information Officer (CIO) or the individual responsible for the information technology activities of the organization. This is due to the fact that many organizations still view the information security function as an information technology problem and not a core business issue.

Alternatively, the rationale for this may be due to the necessity to communicate in a technical language, which is understood by information technology professionals and not typically well understood by business personnel. Regardless of the rationale for the placement, placing the individual responsible for information security within the information technology organization could represent a conflict of interest because the IT department is motivated to deliver projects on time, within budget, and of high quality. Shortcuts may be taken on the security requirements to meet these constraints, if the security function is reporting to the individual making these decisions. The benefit of having the security function report to the CIO is that the security department is more likely to be engaged in the activities of the IT department and aware of the upcoming initiatives and security challenges.

There is a growing trend toward integrating the information and physical security functions. This is partially a result of the increased automation of physical controls and requirements on physical aspects of security to protect information. There has been less separation in these areas and more integration. This growing trend is for the security function to be treated as a risk management function and, as such, be located outside of the IT organization. This provides a greater degree of independence as well as the focus on risk management versus management of user IDs, password resets, and access authorization with the reporting relationship outside of the IT organization, which also introduces a different set of checks and balances on the security activities that are expected to be performed. The security function may report to some other function outside of information technology. The function should report as high in the organization as possible, preferably at the C-level. This ensures that the proper message is conveyed to senior management, the company employees view the appropriate authority of the department, and funding decisions can be made while considering the needs across the company.

Responsibilities of the Information Security Officer
The Information Security Officer is accountable for ensuring the protection of all of the business information assets from intentional and unintentional loss, disclosure, alteration, destruction, and unavailability. The security officer typically does not have the resources available to perform all of these functions and must depend upon other individuals within the organization to implement and execute the policies, procedures, standards, and guidelines to ensure the protection of information. In this capacity, the information security officer acts as the facilitator of information security for the organization.

The threat environment is constantly changing and, as such, it is incumbent upon the security officer to keep up with the changes. It is difficult for any organization to anticipate new threats, some of which come from the external environment and some from new technological changes. Prior to the September 11, 2001 terrorist attack in the United States, few individuals perceived that sort of attack as very likely. However, since then, many organizations have revisited their access control policies, physical security, and business continuity plans. More recently, the issues raised by the disclosures made by Edward Snowden have forced a reevaluation and reconsideration of security policy and practice throughout the world, for both the enterprise and the individual. New technologies, such as wireless, low-cost removable media (writeable DVDs and USB drives), and mobile computing devices such as laptops, tablets, and smartphones have created new threats to confidentiality and disclosure of information, which need to be addressed. Although the organization tries to write policies to last for two or three years without change, depending upon the industry and the rate of change, these may need to be revisited more frequently.

The security officer and his or her team are responsible for ensuring that the security policies, procedures, baselines, standards, and guidelines are written to address the information security needs of the organization. However, this does not mean that the security department must write all the policies by themselves. Nor should the policies be written solely by the security department without the input and participation of the other departments within the organization, such as legal, human resources, information technology, compliance, physical security, the business units, and others that have to implement the policies. Approval of policy must be done at the executive level. Typically standards, procedures, and baselines do not require that level of approval.

The security officer must stay abreast of emerging technologies to ensure that the appropriate solutions are in place for the company based upon its risk profile, corporate culture, resources available, and desire to be an innovator. Security solutions will be prioritized differently when an organization is a leader, or follower (mature product implementation) with regards to technology and security solutions. Failure to stay abreast of technology enhancements could increase the costs to the organization by maintaining older, less effective products. Approaches to satisfying accepted practices may range from active involvement in security industry associations to interaction with vendors to subscribing to industry research groups to simply reviewing printed material and Internet news.

Compliance is the process of ensuring adherence to security policies. A policy or standard for hardening of the company's firewalls is not very useful if the activity is not being performed. Governments are continuously passing new laws, rules, and regulations that establish requirements to protect nonpublic information or improve controls over critical processes with which the enterprise must be in compliance. Although many of the laws are overlapping with regards to security requirements, frequently the new laws will provide a more stringent requirement for a particular aspect of information security. Time frames to be in compliance with the law may not always come at the best time for the organization, nor may they line up with the budget funding cycles. The security officer must stay abreast of emerging regulatory developments to enable response in a timely manner. Planning and documentation are very critical with regards to proof of compliance. Periodic compliance, whether through internal or external inspection, ensures that the procedures, checklists, and baselines are documented and practiced. Compliance reviews are also necessary to ensure that end-users and technical staff are trained and have read the security policies.

Security officers are often responsible for implementing and operating computer incident response teams (CIRTs). CIRTs are groups of individuals with the necessary skills, including management, technical staff, infrastructure, and communications staff, for evaluating the incident, evaluating the damage caused by an incident, and providing the correct response to repair the system and collect evidence for potential prosecution or sanctions. CIRTs are activated depending upon the nature of the incident and the culture of the organization. Security incidents need to be investigated and followed up promptly because this is a key mechanism in minimizing losses from an incident and reducing the chance of a recurrence.

The security officer provides the leadership for the information security awareness program by ensuring that the program is delivered in a meaningful, understandable way to the intended audience. The program should be developed to grab the attention of the participants to convey general awareness of the security issues and what reporting actions are expected when the end-user notices security violations. When awareness is not promoted, the policies will not get communicated and there will be much less assurance that they will be practiced within the company. An effective awareness program will have multiple components and methods of delivery, be ongoing and be delivered throughout the year, not just as a one-time effort.

Security officers must be involved in the management teams and planning meetings of the organization to be fully effective. Project directions and decisions are made during these meetings, as well as the establishment of buy-in and prioritization for the security initiatives. These meetings will include board of director meetings (periodic updates), IT steering committees, manager meetings, and departmental meetings.

Central to the security officer's success within the organization is understanding the vision, mission, objectives/goals, and plans of the organization. This understanding increases the chances of success, allowing security to be introduced at the correct times during the project lifecycle, and better enables the organization to carry out the corporate mission. The security officer needs to understand the competitive pressures facing the organization, the strengths, weaknesses, threats, opportunities, and the regulatory environment within which the organization operates. All of this will increase the likelihood that appropriate security controls are applied to the areas with the greatest need and highest risk, thus resulting in an optimal allocation of the scarce security funding. The business strategies of each department are critical to their success. Integrating security into that strategy will determine the security officer's success.

Communicate Risks to Executive Management

The information security officer is responsible for understanding the business objectives of the organization, ensuring that a risk assessment is performed, taking into consideration the threats and vulnerabilities impacting the particular organization, and subsequently communicating the risks to executive management. The makeup of the executive management team will vary based on the type of industry or government entity, but typically it includes individuals with C-level titles, such as the Chief Executive Officer (CEO), Chief Operating Officer (COO), Chief Financial Officer (CFO), and Chief Information Officer (CIO). The executive team also includes the first-level reporting to the CEO, such as the VP of sales and marketing, VP of administration, general counsel, and the VP of human resources.

The executive team is interested in maintaining the appropriate balance between acceptable risk and ensuring that business operations are meeting the mission of the organization. In this context, executive management is not concerned with the technical details of the implementations but rather with what is the cost/benefit of the solution and what residual risk will remain after the safeguards are implemented. For example, the configuration parameters of installing a particular vendor's router are not as important as the answers to the following questions:

- What is the real perceived threat (problem to be solved)?
- What is the risk (impact and probability) to business operations?
- What is the cost of the safeguard?
- What will be the residual risk (risk remaining after the safeguard is properly implemented and sustained)?
- How long will the project take?
- Each of these must be evaluated along with the other items competing for resources (time, money, people, and systems).

The security officer has a responsibility to ensure that the information presented to executive management is based upon a real business need and the facts are represented clearly. Recommendations for specific controls should be risk based. Ultimately, it is the executive management of the organization that is responsible for information security. Presentations should be geared at a high level to convey the purpose of the technical safeguard and not be a rigorous detailed presentation of the underlying technology unless requested.

Reporting Model

The security officer and the information security organization should report as high in the organization as possible to:

1. Maintain visibility of the importance of information security.
2. Limit the distortion or inaccurate translation of messages that can occur due to hierarchical, deep organizations.

The higher up in the organization, the greater the ability to gain other senior management's attention to security and the greater the capability to compete for the appropriate budget and resources. Where the security officer's reports in the organization have been the subject of debate for several years and depend upon the culture of the organization, there is no one best model that fits all organizations but rather pros and cons associated with each placement choice. Whatever the chosen reporting model, there should be an individual chosen with the responsibility for ensuring information security at the enterprise-wide level to establish accountability for resolving security issues. The discussion in the next few sections should provide the perspective for making the appropriate choice for the target organization.

Business Relationships

Wherever the security officer reports, it is imperative that he or she establishes credible and good working relationships with business executive management, middle management, and the end-users. Information gathered and acted upon by executive management is obtained through their daily interactions with many individuals, not just other executives. Winning their support may be the result of influencing a respected individual within the organization, possibly several management layers below the executive. Similarly, the relationship between the senior executives and the security officer is important if the security strategies are to carry through to implementation. Establishing a track record of delivery and demonstrating the value of the protection to the business will build this relationship. If done properly, the security function becomes viewed as an enabler of the business versus a control point that slows innovation, provides roadblocks to implementation, and represents an overhead cost function. Reporting to an executive structure that understands the need and importance to the business for information security and is willing to work to actively represent security and battle for appropriate funding is critical to success.

Reporting to the CEO

Reporting directly to the CEO greatly reduces the filtering of messages that can occur if a message must pass through several layers, improves overall communication, as well as demonstrates to the organization the importance of information security. Firms that have high security needs, such as credit card companies, technology companies, and companies whose revenue stream depends highly upon Internet website commerce, such as eBay or Amazon, might utilize such a model. The downside to this model is that the CEO may be preoccupied with other business issues and may not have the interest or time to devote to information security issues.

The security professional needs to be aware of the fact that some organizations are required to report on incidents that meet certain conditions. For example, United States civilian government agencies are required to report any breach of personally identifiable information to the U.S. Computer Emergency Readiness Team (US-CERT) within an hour of discovery. Policies and procedures must be defined to determine how an incident is routed when criminal activity is suspected. Additionally, policies and procedures need to be in place to determine how an incident is escalated and should address:

- Does the media or an organization's external affairs group need to be involved?
- Does the organization's legal team need to be involved in the review?
- At what point does notification of the incident rise to the line management, middle management, senior management, the board of directors, or the stakeholders?
- What confidentiality requirements are necessary to protect the incident information?
- What methods are used for the reporting? If email is attacked, how does that impact the reporting and notification process?

Reporting to the Information Technology (IT) Department

In this model, the information security officer reports directly to the Chief Information Officer (CIO), director of information technology, the vice president of information technology, or whatever is the title for the head of the IT department. Most organizations have utilized this relationship because this was historically where the data security function was found in many companies. This was often due to security being viewed as only a technical problem. The advantage to this model is that the individual to which the security officer is reporting has an understanding of the technical issues often impacted by information security and typically has the clout with senior management to make the desired changes. It can also be beneficial because the information security officer and his department must spend a good deal of time interacting with other areas in the information systems department. This can build strength, trust, and appropriate awareness of project activities and issues.

The downside of the reporting structure is the conflict of interest. When the CIO must make decisions with respect to time to market, resource allocations, cost minimization, application usability, and project priorities, the ability exists to slight the information security function. The typical CIO's goals are more oriented toward delivery of application products to support the business in a timely manner. Often the perception is that security controls may slow the time to get products completed and money to implement. As a result, the security considerations may not be provided equal weight. It may also be useful to have a dotted line to another area of the organization, such as legal counsel too, so that conflicts of interest can be adjudicated.

Reporting to a lower level within the CIO organization should be avoided, as noted earlier; the more levels between the CEO and the information security officer, the more challenges arise that must be overcome. Levels further down in the organization may also have their own domains of expertise that they are focusing on, such as computer operations, applications programming, or computing or networking infrastructure.

Reporting to Corporate Security

Corporate security in most organizations is focused on the physical security of the enterprise. Often the individuals in this environment have backgrounds as former police officers, military, or were associated in some other manner with the criminal justice system. This alternative may appear logical; however, the individuals from these organizations historically come from different backgrounds. Physical security is focused on criminal justice, protection, safety, and investigation services, while information security professionals usually have different training in business and information technology. These disciplines intersect in some areas, but they are vastly different in others. A potential downside of being associated with the physical security group is that it could result in the perception of a police-type mentality. This could make it difficult to build effective business relationships with users. Establishing positive relationships with end-users can increase their willingness to listen and comply with policy and any implemented security controls. It can also increase user acceptance and support for the security department in reporting policy violations.

Reporting to the Administrative Services Department

The information security officer may report to the vice president of administrative services, which in some organizations may also include the physical security, employee safety, and HR departments. As it was described in the benefits of reporting to the CIO, there is only one level between the CEO and the information security department. This model can also be viewed as an enterprise function due to the association with the human resources department. It is an attractive model because it can provide focus on security for all forms of information (paper, oral, and electronic). Compared to the functions residing in the technology department, where the focus may tend to be more on just electronic information, there can be benefits. A downside can be that the leaders of this area would have a limited knowledge of information technology, and this could make it more difficult to understand both the business strategies and security requirements and to communicate technical solutions to senior executives and the CEO.

Reporting to the Insurance and Risk Management Department

Information-intensive organizations such as banks, stock brokerages, and research companies may benefit from this model. The Chief Risk Officer (CRO) is already concerned with the risks to the organization and the methods to control those risks through mitigation, acceptance, insurance, etc. The downside is that the risk officer may not be conversant in information systems technology, and the strategic focus of this function may give less attention to day-to-day operational security projects.

Reporting to the Internal Audit Department

This reporting relationship could be seen as a conflict of interest because the internal audit department is responsible for evaluating the effectiveness and implementation of the organization's control structure, including the activities of the information security department. It would be difficult for the internal audit to provide an independent viewpoint. The internal audit department may have adversarial relationships with other portions of the company due to the nature of its role (to uncover deficiencies in departmental processes), and through association, the security department may be perceived in a similar light. It is advisable that the security department establishes close working relationships with the internal audit department to facilitate the control environment. The internal audit manager most likely has a background in financial, operational, and general controls and may have difficulty relating to the technical activities of the information security department. On the positive side, both areas are focused on improving the controls of the company. The internal audit department does have a preferable reporting relationship for audit issues through a dotted-line relationship with the company's audit committee on the board of directors. It is advisable for the information security function to have a similar path to report security issues to the board of directors as well, either in conjunction with the internal audit department or on its own.

Reporting to the Legal Department

Attorneys are concerned with compliance with regulations, laws, and ethical standards, performing due diligence, and establishing policies and procedures that are consistent with many of the information security objectives. The company's general counsel also typically has the respect or ear of the CEO. In regulated industries, this may be a very good fit.

An advantage is that the distance between the CEO and the information security officer is one level. On the downside, due to the emphasis on compliance activities, the information security department may end up performing more compliance-checking activities (versus security consulting and support), which are typically the domain of internal audit.

Determining the Best Fit

As indicated earlier, each organization must view the pros and cons of each type of potential reporting relationship and develop the appropriate relationship based upon the company culture, type of industry, and what will provide the greatest benefit to the company. Optimal reporting relationships will minimize conflicts of interest, increase visibility, ensure funding is appropriately allocated, and ensure that communication is effective when the placement of the information security department is determined.

Budget

The information security officer prepares a budget to manage the information security program and ensures that security is included in the various other departmental budgets, such as the help/service desk, applications development, and the computing infrastructure. Security is much less expensive and easier to justify when it is built into the application design versus added as an afterthought at or after implementation. Estimates range widely over the costs of adding security later in the lifecycle; however, it is not just the added cost caused by not considering security through the development or acquisition lifecycle. It can be perceived as delaying implementation when the time necessary to properly implement security was not factored into the implementation timeline and delays occur. The security officer must work with the application development managers to ensure that security is considered in the project cost during each phase of development (analysis, design, development, testing, implementation, and post-implementation). For systems security certification, there should be at minimum walk-throughs held to ensure that the deliverables meet security requirements. To facilitate this best from an independence perspective, the security officer should not report to information system or application development management.

In addition to ensuring that new project development activities appropriately address security, one must also see that ongoing functions such as access administration, intrusion detection, incident handling, policy development, standards compliance, support of external auditors, and evaluations of emerging technology are appropriately funded. The security officer will rarely receive all the funding necessary to complete all of the projects for which he or she and his or her team have envisioned and must usually plan these activities over multiple years. The budgeting process requires examination of the current risks and ensuring that activities with the largest cost/benefit to the organization are implemented; this is also known as Risk Management. Projects greater than 12–18 months are generally considered to be long term and strategic in nature and typically require more funding and resources or are more complex

1

in their implementation. In the event these efforts require a longer time frame, pilot projects to demonstrate near-term results on a smaller scale are preferable. Organizations often lose patience with funding long-term efforts, as the initial management supporters may change, as well as some of the team members implementing the change. The longer the payback period, the higher the Rate of Return (ROR) expected by executive management. This is due primarily to the higher risk level associated with longer-term efforts.

The number of staff, level of security protection required, tasks to be performed, regulations to be met, staff qualification level, training required, and degree of metrics tracking are also parameters that drive funding requirements. For example, if an organization must meet government regulations to increase the number of individuals with security certifications, such as the CISSP or other industry standard security certifications, then the organization may feel an obligation to fund internal training seminars to prepare the individuals. This will need to be factored into the budget. This may also be utilized to attract and retain security professionals to the organization through increased learning opportunities. As another example, the time required in complying with government mandates and laws may necessitate increased staffing to provide the appropriate ongoing tracking and responses to audit issues.

Metrics
Measurements can be collected that provide information on long-term trends and illustrate the day-to-day workload. Measurement of processes provides the ability to improve the process. For example, measuring the number of help/service desk tickets for password resets can be translated into workload hours and may provide justification for the implementation of new technologies for the end-user to self-administer the password reset process. Tracking how viruses spread or the frequency of reporting may indicate a need for further education or improvement of the anti-virus management process. Many decisions need to be made when collecting metrics, such as who will collect the metrics, what statistics will be collected, when they will be collected, and what are the thresholds where variations are out of bounds and should be acted upon. An important first decision is to determine what metrics will be used to prove and whether the metric gathering effort will provide the necessary evidence or value desired.

Resources
When considering the overall resource management of an information security function, the information security professional should consider more than just budget to ensure the success of the information security program. In many organizations, the following resources may play a role in directly supporting the information security function:

- System Administrators
- Database Administrators
- Network Administrators
- Policy Officers
- Compliance Officers
- Legal Council
- Law Enforcement
- Quality Assurance Testers
- Help Desk/Service Desk Technicians

Additionally, the information security program is indirectly supported by several functions including but not limited to:

- Budget Officers
- Procurement Specialists
- Business Analysts
- Administrative Professionals
- Enterprise Architects
- Software Developers

The size, complexity, and mission of an organization greatly influence the resources available to the information security program and the information security officer. Understanding the mission of the organization and building relationships with supporting resources as described above often make the difference between a successful security program and an ineffectual one. The security officer rarely has the tools or the team to solely resolve an organization's most pressing challenges.

Information Security Strategies

Strategic, tactical, and operational plans are interrelated, and each provides a different focus toward enhancing the security of the organization. Planning reduces the likelihood that the organization will be reactionary toward the security needs. With appropriate planning, decisions on projects can be made with respect to whether they support the long- or short-term goals and have the priority that warrants the allocation of more security resources.

Strategic Planning

Strategic plans are aligned with the strategic business and information technology goals. These plans have a longer-term horizon (three to five years or more) to guide the long-term view of the security activities. The process of developing a strategic plan emphasizes thinking of the company environment and the technical environment a few years into the future. High-level goals are stated to provide the vision for projects to achieve the business objectives. These plans should be reviewed minimally on an annual basis or whenever major changes to the business occur, such as a merger, acquisition, establishment of outsourcing relationships, major changes in the business climate, introductions of new competitors, and so forth. Technological changes will be frequent during a five-year period, and so the plan should be adjusted. The high-level plan provides organizational guidance to ensure that lower-level decisions are consistent with executive management's intentions for the future of the company. For example, strategic goals may consist of the following:

- Establishing security policies and procedures
- Effectively deploying servers, workstations, and network devices to reduce downtime
- Ensuring that all users understand the security responsibilities and reward excellent performance
- Establishing a security organization to manage security enterprise-wide
- Ensuring effective risk management so that risks are effectively understood and controlled

Tactical Planning

Tactical plans provide the broad initiatives to support and achieve the goals specified in the strategic plan. These initiatives may include deployments such as establishing an electronic policy development and distribution process, implementing robust change control for the server environment, reducing vulnerabilities residing on the servers using vulnerability management, implementing a "hot site" disaster recovery program, or implementing an identity management solution. These plans are more specific and may consist of multiple projects to complete the effort. Tactical plans are shorter in length, such as 6–18 months to achieve a specific security goal of the company.

Operational and Project Planning

Specific plans with milestones, dates, and accountabilities provide the communication and direction to ensure that the individual projects are completed. For example, establishing a policy development and communication process may involve multiple projects with many tasks:

1. Conduct security risk assessment
2. Develop security policies and approval processes
3. Develop technical infrastructure to deploy policies and track compliance
4. Train end-users on policies
5. Monitor compliance

Depending upon the size and scope of the efforts, these initiatives may be steps or tasks as part of a single plan, or they may be multiple plans managed through several projects. The duration of these efforts is short term to provide discrete functionality at the completion of the effort. Traditional "waterfall" methods of implementing projects spend a large amount of time detailing the specific steps required to implement the complete project. Executives today are more focused on achieving some short-term, or at least interim, results to demonstrate the value of the investment along the way. Such demonstration of value maintains organizational interest and visibility to the effort, increasing the chances of sustaining longer-term funding. The executive management may grow impatient without realizing these early benefits, which is why regular communication targeted at managing expectations is a vital element to successful outcomes.

The Complete and Effective Security Program

Several frameworks and assessment methods are available to assess the completeness and effectiveness of an information security program. Some organizations have established an enterprise-wide security oversight committee, sometimes referred to as a "Security Council" to help guide and support these efforts within the enterprise. This group can serve as a steering committee to provide oversight and direction to the information security program. The vision of the Security Council must be clearly defined and understood by all members of the council.

Oversight Committee Representation

For maximum effectiveness, the oversight committee should consist of representatives from multiple organizational units. This will increase a sense of ownership for the security program enterprise-wide and improve support for the policies in the long term. The HR department is essential to provide knowledge of the existing code of conduct, employment and labor relations, termination and disciplinary action policies, and practices that are in place.

The legal department is needed to ensure that the language of the policies states what is intended and that applicable local, state, and federal laws are appropriately followed. The IT department provides technical input and information on current initiatives and the development of procedures and technical implementations to support the policies. The individual business unit representation is essential to understand how practical the policies may be in carrying out the mission of the business. Compliance department representation provides insight on ethics, contractual obligations, and investigations that may require policy creation. And finally, the security officer, who typically chairs the council, should represent the information security department and members of the security team for specialized technical expertise.

The oversight committee is a management committee and, as such, is populated primarily with management-level employees. It is difficult to obtain the time commitment required to review policies at a detailed level by senior management. Reviewing the policies at this level is a necessary step to achieve buy-in within management. However, it would not be good to use the senior management level in the early stages of development. Line management is very focused on their individual areas and may not have the organizational perspective necessary (beyond their individual departments) to evaluate security policies and project initiatives. Middle management appears to be in the best position to appropriately evaluate what is best for the organization, as well as possessing the ability to influence senior and line management to accept the policies. Where middle management does not exist, it is appropriate to include line management because they are typically filling both of these roles (middle and line functions) when operating in these positions.

Many issues may be addressed in a single Security Council meeting, which necessitates having someone record the minutes of the meeting. The chairperson's role in the meeting is to facilitate the discussion, ensure that all viewpoints are heard, and drive the discussions to decisions where necessary. It is difficult to perform that function at the same time as taking notes. Recording the meeting is also helpful to capture key points that may have been missed in the notes so that accurate minutes can be produced.

The relationship between the security department and the security oversight committee is a dotted-line relationship that may or may not be reflected on the organization chart. The value of the committee is in providing the business direction and increasing the awareness of the security activities that are impacting the organization on a continuous basis. How frequently the committee meets will depend upon the organizational culture (i.e., are monthly or quarterly oversight meetings held on other initiatives?), the number of security initiatives, and the urgency of decisions that need the input of the business units.

Security Council Vision Statement

A clear security vision statement should exist that is in alignment with, and supports, the organizational vision. Typically, these statements draw upon the security concepts of confidentiality, integrity, and availability to support the business objectives. Vision statements are not technical and focus on the advantages to the business. People will be involved in the council from management and technical areas and have limited time to participate, so the vision statement must be something that is viewed as worthwhile to sustain their continued involvement. The vision statement is a high-level set of statements that is brief, to the point, and achievable.

Mission Statement

Mission statements are objectives that support the overall vision. These become the road map to achieving the vision and help the council clearly view the purpose for its involvement. Some individuals may choose nomenclature such as goals, objectives, initiatives, etc. A sample mission statement is shown in *Figure 1.4*.

The Information Security Council provides management direction and a sounding board for the ACME Company's information security efforts to ensure that these efforts are:

- ✔ Appropriately prioritized
- ✔ Supported by each organizational unit
- ✔ Appropriately funded
- ✔ Realistic given ACME's information security needs
- ✔ Balance security needs to be made between cost, response time, ease of use, flexibility, and time to market

The Information Security Council takes an active role in enhancing our security profile and increasing the protection of our assets through:

- ✔ Approval of organization-wide information security initiatives
- ✔ Coordination of various workgroups so that security goals can be achieved
- ✔ Promoting awareness of security initiatives within their organizations
- ✔ Discussion of security ideas, policies, and procedures and their impact on the organization
- ✔ Recommendation of policies to the ACME Company IT Steering Committee
- ✔ Increased understanding of the threats, vulnerabilities, and safeguards facing our organization
- ✔ Active participation in policy, procedure, and standard review

The ACME Company information technology steering committee supports the information security council by:

- ✔ Developing the strategic vision for the deployment of information technology
- ✔ Establishing priorities, arranging resources in concert with the vision
- ✔ Approval of the recommended policies, standards, and guidelines
- ✔ Approving major capital expenditures

Figure 1.4 – **Sample Security Council mission statement**

Effective mission statements do not need to be lengthy because the primary concern is to communicate the goals so both technical and nontechnical individuals readily understand them. The primary mission of the Security Council will vary by organization. The vision and mission statements should also be reviewed on an annual basis to ensure that the council is still functioning according to the values expressed in the mission statement, as well as to ensure that new and replacement members are in alignment with the objectives of the council.

Security Program Oversight
By establishing this goal in the beginning, the members of the council begin feeling that they have some input and influence over the direction of the security program. This is important because many security decisions will impact the areas of operation of members of the committee. This also is the beginning of management's commitment, as the deliverables produced through the information security program now become recommended or approved by the Security Council versus the information security department. The main activities engaged in by the Security Council are listed below:

- ***Decide on Project Initiatives*** – Each organization has limited resources (time, money, and people) to allocate across projects to advance the business. The primary objective of information security projects is to reduce the organizational business risk through the implementation of reasonable controls. The council should take an active role in understanding the initiatives and the resulting business impact.
- ***Prioritize Information Security Efforts*** – Once the Security Council understands the proposed project initiatives and the associated positive impact to the business, its members can be involved with the prioritization of the projects. This may be in the form of a formal annual process or through the discussion and expressed support for individual initiatives.
- ***Review and Recommend Security Policies*** – Review of the security policies should include:
  - ¤ A line-by-line review of the policies
  - ¤ A general review of any standards
  - ¤ A cursory review of the procedures that are designed to support the policies
  - ¤ Monitor the security implementation plan to ensure it meets policy, standards, and baseline requirements

  Through this activity, three key concepts are implemented that are important to sustaining commitment:
  - ¤ Understanding of the policy is enhanced.
  - ¤ Practical ability of the organization to support the policy is discussed.
  - ¤ A sense of ownership is established to increase support of implementation activities.
- ***Review and Audit the Security Program*** – Auditors provide an essential role for maintaining and improving information security. They provide an independent view of the design, effectiveness, and implementation of controls. The results of audits generate findings that require management response and corrective action plans to resolve the issue and mitigate the risk. Auditors often request information prior to the start of the audit to facilitate the review. Some audits are performed at a high level without substantive testing, while other audits will identify test samples to determine if a control is implemented and followed.

The security department cooperates with the internal and external auditors to ensure that the control environment is adequate and functional.

- ■ ***Champion Organizational Security Efforts*** – Once the council understands and accepts the policies, it serves as the organizational champion behind the policies. Council members may have started by reviewing a draft of the policy created by the information systems security department, but the resulting product was only accomplished through their review, input, and participation in the process. Their involvement creates ownership of the deliverable and a desire to see the security policy or project succeed within the company.

- ■ ***Recommend Areas Requiring Investment*** – Members of the council have the opportunity to provide input from the perspective of their individual business units. The council serves as a mechanism for establishing broad support for security investments from this perspective. Resources within any organization are limited and allocated to the business units with the greatest need and the greatest perceived return on investment. Establishing this support enhances the budgetary understanding of the other business managers, as well as the chief financial officer, which is often essential to obtain the appropriate funding.

End-Users

The end-user is responsible for protecting information assets on a daily basis through adherence to the security policies that have been communicated. End-users are like windows in a building. Just like a window that allows all activity to be seen and monitored, their actions will expose weaknesses in a poorly designed and communicated compliance regime. For example, downloading unauthorized software, opening attachments from unknown senders, or visiting malicious websites could introduce malicious code (e.g., virus, Trojans, and spyware) into the environment. However, end-users can also be the front-line eyes and ears of the organization and report security incidents and unusual behavior to the appropriate roles for investigation. In order for the security professionals to create this culture, they must clearly define the expectations and acceptable behaviors associated with this role, as well as ensuring that these are documented and communicated clearly to every member of the enterprise.

Executive Management

Executive management maintains the overall responsibility for protection of the information assets of the enterprise. The business operations are dependent upon information being available, accurate, and protected from individuals without a need to know. Financial losses can occur if the confidentiality, integrity, or availability of this information is compromised. Executive Management must be aware of the risks that they are accepting for the organization. Risk must be identified through risk assessment and communicated clearly so that management can make informed decisions.

Information Systems Security Professional

Drafting of security policies, standards and supporting guidelines, procedures, and baselines is coordinated through these individuals. Guidance is provided for technical security issues, and emerging threats are considered with regards to the adoption of new policies. Activities such as interpretation of government regulations and industry trends and analysis of vendor solutions to include in the security architecture that advances the security of the organization are performed by this role.

Data/Information/Business Owners

A business executive or manager is typically responsible for an information asset. These are the individuals that assign the appropriate classification to information assets. They ensure that the business information is protected with appropriate controls. Periodically, the information owners need to review the classification and access rights associated with information assets. The owners, or their delegates, may be required to approve access to the information. Owners also need to determine the criticality, sensitivity, retention, backups, and safeguards for the information. Owners, or their delegates, are responsible for understanding the risks that exist with regards to the information that they control.

Data/Information Custodian/Steward

A data custodian is an individual or function that takes care of the information on behalf of the owner. These individuals ensure that the information is available to the end-users and is backed up to enable recovery in the event of data loss or corruption. Information may be stored in files, databases, or systems whose technical infrastructure must be managed by systems administrators. This group administers access rights to the information assets on behalf of the information owners.

Information Systems Auditor

IT auditors determine whether users, owners, custodians, systems, and networks are in compliance with the security policies, procedures, standards, baselines, designs, architectures, management direction, and other requirements placed on systems. The auditors provide independent assurance to the management on the appropriateness of the security controls. The auditor examines the information systems and determines whether they are designed, configured, implemented, operated, and managed in a way ensuring that the organizational objectives are being achieved. The auditors provide senior company management with an independent view of the controls in place and their effectiveness across the enterprise.

Business Continuity Planner

Business continuity planners develop contingency plans to prepare for any occurrence that could have the ability to impact the company's objectives negatively. Threats may include earthquakes, tornadoes, hurricanes, blackouts, changes in the economic/political climate, terrorist activities, fire, or other major actions potentially causing significant harm. The business continuity planner ensures that business processes can continue through the disaster and coordinates those activities with the business areas and information technology personnel responsible for disaster recovery.

Information Systems/Information Technology Professionals

These personnel are responsible for designing security controls into information systems, testing the controls, and implementing the systems in production environments through agreed upon operating policies and procedures. The information systems professionals work with the business owners and the security professionals to ensure that the designed solution provides security controls commensurate with the acceptable criticality, sensitivity, and availability requirements of the application.

Security Administrator

A security administrator manages the user access request process and ensures that privileges are provided to those individuals who have been authorized for access by application/system/data owners. This individual has elevated privileges and creates and deletes accounts and access permissions. The security administrator also terminates access privileges when individuals leave their jobs or transfer between company divisions. The security administrator maintains records of access request approvals and produces reports of access rights for the auditor during testing in an access controls audit to demonstrate compliance with the policies.

Network/Systems Administrator

A systems administrator (sysadmin/netadmin) configures network and server hardware and the operating systems running on them in order to ensure that the information accessible through these systems will be available when needed. The administrator maintains the computing infrastructure using tools and utilities such as patch management and software distribution mechanisms to install updates and test patches on organization computers. The administrator tests and implements system upgrades to ensure the continued reliability of the servers and network devices. The administrator provides vulnerability management through either commercial off the shelf (COTS) or non-COTS solutions to test the computing environment and mitigate vulnerabilities appropriately.

Physical Security

The individuals assigned to the physical security role establish relationships with external law enforcement, such as the local police agencies, state police, or the Federal Bureau of Investigation (FBI) to assist in investigations. Physical security personnel manage the installation, maintenance, and ongoing operation of the closed circuit television (CCTV) surveillance systems, burglar alarm systems, and card reader access control systems. Guards are placed where necessary as a deterrent to unauthorized access and to provide safety for the company employees. Physical security personnel interface with systems security, human resources, facilities, and legal and business areas to ensure that the practices are integrated.

Administrative Assistants/Secretaries

This role can be very important to information security; in many companies of smaller size, this may be the individual who greets visitors, signs packages in and out, recognizes individuals who desire to enter the offices, and serves as the phone screener for executives. These individuals may be subject to social engineering attacks, whereby the potential intruder attempts to solicit confidential information that may be used for a subsequent attack. Social engineers prey on the goodwill of the helpful individual to gain entry. A properly trained assistant will minimize the risk of divulging useful company information or of providing unauthorized entry.

Help Desk/Service Desk Administrator

As the name implies, the help/service desk is there to field questions from users that report system problems. Problems may include poor response time, potential virus infections, unauthorized access, inability to access system resources, or questions on the use of a program.

The help/service desk is also often where the first indications of security issues and incidents will be seen. A help/service desk individual would contact the computer security incident response team (CSIRT) when a situation meets the criteria developed by the team.[2] The help/service desk resets passwords, resynchronizes/reinitializes tokens and smart cards, and resolves other problems with access control.

These functions may alternatively be performed through self-service by the end-user, e.g., an intranet-based solution that establishes the identity of the end-user and resets the password, or by another area, such as the security administration, systems administrator, etc., depending upon the organizational structure and separation of duties principles in place. A help/service desk area is also a prime target for social engineering attacks and, as such, should receive additional attention in security awareness training.

Organizations may have other roles related to information security to meet particular needs. Individuals within the different roles will require different levels of training. The end-user may require basic security awareness training, including the activities that are acceptable, how to recognize that there may be a problem, and what the mechanism is for reporting the problem to the appropriate personnel for resolution. The security administrator will need more in-depth training on the access control packages to manage the logon IDs, accounts, and log file reviews. The systems/network administrator will need technical security training for the specific operating system (e.g., Windows, UNIX, Linux, etc.) or network components (e.g., firewall, routers, switches) to competently set the security controls. Establishing clear, unambiguous security roles has many benefits to the organization beyond providing information as to the responsibilities to be performed and who needs to perform them. These benefits include:

- Demonstrable executive management support for information security
- Increased employee efficiency by reducing confusion about who is expected to perform which tasks
- Team coordination to protect information as it moves from department to department
- Lower risks to company reputation/brand recognition due to security problems
- Capability to manage complex information systems and networks
- Personal accountability for information security
- Reduction of turf battles between departments
- Security objectives balanced with business objectives
- Support of disciplinary actions for security violations up to and including termination
- Facilitation of increased communication for resolution of security incidents
- Demonstrable compliance with applicable laws and regulations
- Shielding of management from liability and negligence claims
- Road map for auditors to determine whether necessary work is performed effectively and efficiently
- Continuous improvement efforts (i.e., ISO 9000)
- Overall risk management
- Provision of a foundation for determining the level of security and awareness training required

---

2   See the following for an overview of what a CSIRT is and the responsibilities it has within the enterprise: http://www.cert.org/incident-management/csirt-development/csirt-faq.cfm?

Information security is a team effort requiring the skill sets and cooperation of many different individuals. Executive management may have overall responsibility, and the security officer/director/manager may be assigned the day-to-day task of ensuring that the organization is complying with the defined security practices. However, every person in the organization has one or more roles to play in order to ensure proper and appropriate protection of the information assets within the organization.

Control Frameworks

To aid in ensuring security and privacy requirements are met, many organizations adopt control frameworks to provide a governance program that is:

1. ***Consistent*** – A governance program must be consistent in how information security and privacy is approached and applied. If two similar situations or requests result in different outcomes, stakeholders will lose faith in the integrity of the program and its usefulness.

2. ***Measurable*** – The governance program must provide a way to determine progress and set goals. Organizations who implement frameworks that can be measured are more likely to improve their security posture over time. Most control frameworks contain an assessment standard or procedure to determine compliance and in some cases risk as well.

3. ***Standardized*** – As with measurable above, a controls framework should rely on standardization so results from one organization or part of an organization can be compared in a meaningful way.

4. ***Comprehensive*** – The selected framework should cover the minimum legal and regulatory requirements of an organization and be extensible to accommodate additional organization-specific requirements.

5. ***Modular*** – A modular framework is more likely to withstand the changes of an organization since only the controls or requirements needing modification are reviewed and updated.

An example of a control framework is the United States National Institute of Standards and Technology's Special Publication 800-53r4.[3] SP 800-53r4 is a control framework made up of 285 controls in 19 families. The framework includes the ability to scope and tailor controls to an organization's specific mission or requirements. The 19 Control Families are listed below in *Table 1.1*:

CONTROL FAMILY
AC - Access Control
AT - Awareness and Training
AU - Audit and Accountability
CA - Security Assessment and Authorization
CM - Configuration Management
CP - Contingency Planning
IA - Identification and Authentication
IR - Incident Response
MA - Maintenance
MP - Media Protection

---

3   See the following: http://nvlpubs.nist.gov/nistpubs/SpecialPublications/NIST.SP.800-53r4.pdf

CONTROL FAMILY
PE - Physical and Environmental Protection
PL - Planning
PM - Program Management
PS - Personnel Security
RA - Risk Assessment
SA - System and Services Acquisition
SC - System and Communications Protection
SI - System and Information Integrity
PC - Privacy Controls

*Table 1.1 – **NIST SP800-53r4 19 Control Families***

NIST SP 800-53r4 is mandatory for United States federal agencies and their contractors. While frameworks such as these may seem daunting, they are designed to be applicable to almost every organization.

Another example is the International Standard Organization (ISO) 27001:2013 Standard.[4] Like NIST SP 800-53r4, ISO 27001:2013 is designed to cover organizations of all sizes and types. The annex A of ISO 27001:2013 contains the control framework with objectives and specifics about each control. ISO is a global framework adopted by numerous industries in most countries. Frameworks often map to each other as well. For example, NIST SP 800-53r4 has been mapped to the ISO 27001:2013 standard. While there is considerable overlap, there are some areas that are not an exact fit. *Figure 1.5* demonstrates a sample control framework comparison.

The security professional must exercise care and judgment when implementing a controls framework to ensure the proper fit for an organization.

Category	Subcategory	CRR Reference	RMM Reference	Informative References
Asset Management (AM): The data, personnel, devices, systems, and facilities that enable the organization to achieve business purposes are identified and managed consistent with their relative importance to business objectives and the organization's risk strategy.	**ID.AM-1:** Physical devices and systems within the organization are inventoried	AM:G2.Q1 (Technology)	ADM:SG1.SP1	• CCS CSC 1 • COBIT 5 BAI03.04, BAI09.01, BAI09.02, BAI09.05 • ISA 62443-2-1:2009 4.2.3.4 • ISA 62443-3-3:2013 SR 7.8 • ISO/IEC 27001:2013 A.8.1.1, A.8.1.2 • NIST SP 800-53 Rev. 4 CM-8
	ID.AM-2: Software platforms and applications within the organization are inventoried	AM:G2.Q1 (Technology)	ADM:SG1.SP1	• CCS CSC 2 • COBIT 5 BAI03.04, BAI09.01, BAI09.02, BAI09.05 • ISA 62443-2-1:2009 4.2.3.4 • ISA 62443-3-3:2013 SR 7.8 • ISO/IEC 27001:2013 A.8.1.1, A.8.1.2 • NIST SP 800-53 Rev. 4 CM-8
	ID.AM-3: Organizational communication and data flows are mapped	AM:G2.Q2	ADM:SG1.SP2	• CCS CSC 1 • COBIT 5 DSS05.02 • ISA 62443-2-1:2009 4.2.3.4 • ISO/IEC 27001:2013 A.13.2.1 • NIST SP 800-53 Rev. 4 AC-4, CA-3, CA-9
	ID.AM-4: External information systems are catalogued	AM:G2.Q1 (Technology)	ADM:SG1.SP1	• COBIT 5 APO02.02 • ISO/IEC 27001:2013 A.11.2.6 • NIST SP 500-291 3, 4 • NIST SP 800-53 Rev. 4 AC-20, SA-9

---

4   See the following: http://www.standards-online.net/27001en1/iso27001-2013.pdf

Category	Subcategory	CRR Reference	RMM Reference	Informative References
Asset Management (AM): The data, personnel, devices, systems, and facilities that enable the organization to achieve business purposes are identified and managed consistent with their relative importance to business objectives and the organization's risk strategy	**ID.AM-5:** Resources (e.g., hardware, devices, data, and software) are prioritized based on their classification, criticality, and business value	AM:G1.Q4	ADM:SG2.SP1	• COBIT 5 APO03.03, APO03.04, BAI09.02 • ISA 62443-2-1:2009 4.2.3.6 • ISO/IEC 27001:2013 A.8.2.1 • NIST SP 800-34 Rev. 1 IDENTIFY (ID) • NIST SP 800-53 Rev. 4 CP-2, RA-2, SA-14
	ID.AM-6: Cybersecurity roles and responsibilities for the entire workforce and third-party stakeholders (e.g., suppliers, customers, partners) are established	AM:MIL2.Q3	ADM:GG2.GP7	• COBIT 5 APO01.02, DSS06.03 • ISA 62443-2-1:2009 4.3.2.3.3 • ISO/IEC 27001:2013 A.6.1.1 • NIST SP 800-53 Rev. 4 CP-2, PM-11

Figure 1.5 – **NIST SP 800-53r4 and ISO 27001:2013 sample control comparison**
(Cyber Resilience Review (CRR): NIST Security Framework Crosswalk.
February 2014. U.S. Department of Homeland Security)[5]

Due Care

Due care is an important topic for the information security professional to understand. It is primarily a legal term used to describe the care a "reasonable person" would exercise under given circumstances. In other words, it is used to also describe what an individual's or organization's legal duty is considered to be. The lack of due care is often considered negligence, and in most countries it is actionable under law. If an organization is legally mandated to comply with regulations or information security requirements, knowingly or unknowingly neglecting those requirements could lead to legal exposure from a due care perspective.

Due Diligence

Due diligence is similar to due care with the exception that it is a preemptive measure made to avoid harm to other persons or their property. If performed correctly, due diligence leads to due care when needed and avoids other situations where due care may need to be exercised. Due diligence is a practice that should be adopted by the information security professionals as a core tenant of their career. Examples of due diligence in an organization include but are not limited to:

- Background checks of employees
- Credit checks of business partners
- Information system security assessments
- Risk assessments of physical security systems
- Penetration tests of firewalls
- Contingency testing of backup systems
- Threat intelligence services being used to check on the availability of company Intellectual Property (IP) posted to public forums and in the cloud

In each of the above examples, the organization is attempting to avoid a situation that may lead to harm to the organization or other individuals. While at times due diligence can be

---

5   http://www.us-cert.gov/sites/default/files/c3vp/csc-crr-nist-framework-crosswalk.pdf

expensive, the cost of a single data breach or lawsuit may be large enough to shut down an organization and destroy a career.[6]

According to NIST, the concept of Information Security Due Diligence can and should be framed with regards to managing the risk to organizational missions and business functions. "The security controls in NIST Special Publication 800-53r4 are designed to facilitate compliance with applicable federal laws, Executive Orders, directives, policies, regulations, standards, and guidance. Compliance is not about adhering to static checklists or generating unnecessary FISMA reporting paperwork. Rather, compliance necessitates organizations executing due diligence with regard to information security and risk management. Information security due diligence includes using all appropriate information as part of an organization-wide risk management program to effectively use the tailoring guidance and inherent flexibility in NIST publications so that the selected security controls documented in organizational security plans meet the mission and business requirements of organizations. Using the risk management tools and techniques that are available to organizations is essential in developing, implementing, and maintaining the safeguards and countermeasures with the necessary and sufficient strength of mechanism to address the current threats to organizational operations and assets, individuals, other organizations, and the Nation. Employing effective risk-based processes, procedures, and technologies will help ensure that all federal information systems and organizations have the necessary resilience to support ongoing federal responsibilities, critical infrastructure applications, and continuity of government." [7]

Compliance

The past 30 years have brought significant changes in the way organizations are structured and run. Entirely new business models have emerged, and old ones have been radically transformed. Productivity has soared, fueled by an endless stream of innovations in information and communications technology (ICT). Centuries-old paradigms for data collection, storage, and use have shifted. Until the early 1990s, it was fairly common for individual departments and divisions to collect, store, and use their own data in their own file cabinets or in departmental computers; as a result, information could not easily be shared with other groups. Rapid advances in the ability of different technologies to interoperate have made it easier for entities of all sizes to exchange information in an almost seamless fashion. Such information exchanges are integral to business efficiency, competitiveness, collaboration, and agility in the 21st century.

The massive and rapid flow of information over the Internet has played a key role in this transformation, by enabling applications that make use of intelligent data analysis, expanded sales and service channels, and other tools. These applications, along with diminishing storage costs, have made it easy for organizations and individuals to accumulate unprecedented amounts of data. This situation has raised awareness of the need to protect confidential data kept by organizations – including intellectual property, trade secrets and market data, and the personal data of customers, employees, and partners – against misuse and unauthorized

---

6   See the following, Burglary Triggers Medical Records Firm's Collapse: http://blogs.wsj.com/
      bankruptcy/2012/03/12/burglary-triggers-medical-records-firm%E2%80%99s-collapse/

7   http://nvlpubs.nist.gov/nistpubs/SpecialPublications/NIST.SP.800-53r4.pdf (Page 11).

disclosure or modification. In some cases, concerns have led to the enactment of laws and regulations that vary by industry or geography and the creation of specific industry standards.

Motivated by security threats and by the need to protect consumers' personal information from abuse, legislative bodies and government institutions have moved to regulate processing and transfer of personal information. Standards bodies and industry associations have followed suit by promoting or requiring the adoption of key security and privacy standards. These actions serve two key objectives: to spread awareness and use of best practices and to promote levels of self-regulation that might forestall the enactment of increasingly restrictive laws that could harm industries or commerce in general. Below is a sampling of these laws, regulations, and industry standards:

- In most European nations, the right to privacy is considered a basic human right. European Union member nations are required to enact laws that comply with the Data Protection Directive (DPD) 95/46/EC. The directive's guidelines are considered a baseline for national laws, and local legislative bodies in member nations may include provisions that go beyond it. Implementation of 95/46/EC is not limited to EU members; Iceland, Norway, and Lichtenstein are among the non-EU nations that have enacted privacy laws that comply with the directive.

- Many other nations have also enacted comprehensive privacy legislation. Examples include Australia's Privacy Act, Argentina's Personal Data Protection Law, and Canada's Personal Information Protection and Electronic Documents Act (PIPEDA).

- In the United States, privacy legislation has taken more of a sector-based approach. Different laws regulate how organizations collect, use, and protect the confidentiality of personally identifiable information (PII) in different sectors. Examples include the Health Insurance Portability and Accountability Act (HIPAA) for health-related PII and the Gramm-Leach-Bliley Act (GLBA) for credit-related PII. Concerns about data breaches that could lead to an increase in identity theft have led most states to enact data breach notification laws. Prompted by the same concerns, states such as Massachusetts and Nevada have also enacted laws that require adoption of encryption technologies to protect the sensitive personal information of state residents in different scenarios.

- The payment card industry (PCI) has taken steps to prevent credit card fraud and protect cardholders against identity theft. The PCI Security Standards Council (PCI SSC) requires all entities that want to hold, process, or transfer cardholder information to comply with the PCI Data Security Standard (PCI DSS). Among other provisions, the standard requires that an organization's compliance be assessed every year by an independent Qualified Security Assessor (QSA).

Organizations are left with the daunting and increasingly expensive task of determining which rules – including geographically based and industry-specific ones – apply to their national or globally dispersed activities. In some instances, they are forced to decide what constitutes a conflict between multiple compliance obligations and to determine how to address it. The issues are complex and depend on the type of data involved, the type of industry, where and how the data is collected, how it is used, and the residence of the individuals whose PII is collected.

Governance, Risk Management, and Compliance (GRC)

The combination of business and technology-related challenges and the requirement to meet regulatory compliance obligations is not unique to the area of information security and privacy. Such combinations are common in areas such as enterprise risk management, finance, operational risk management, and IT in general. An approach commonly known as governance, risk management, and compliance (GRC) has evolved to analyze risks and manage mitigation in alignment with business and compliance objectives.

- Governance ensures that the business focuses on core activities, clarifies who in the organization has the authority to make decisions, determines accountability for actions and responsibility for outcomes, and addresses how expected performance will be evaluated. All of this happens within a clearly defined context that might span a division, the entire organization, or a specific set of cross-discipline functions.

- Risk management is a systematic process for identifying, analyzing, evaluating, remedying, and monitoring risk. As a result of this process, an organization or group might decide to mitigate a risk, transfer it to another party, or assume the risk along with its potential consequences.

- Compliance generally refers to actions that ensure behavior complies with established rules as well as the provision of tools to verify that compliance. It encompasses compliance with laws as well the enterprise's own policies, which in turn can be based on best practices. Compliance requirements are not static, and compliance efforts should not be either.

GRC goes beyond merely implementing these three elements separately and finds ways to integrate them to increase effectiveness and efficiency and decrease complexity. GRC ensures than an organization acts in accordance with self-imposed rules, acceptable risk levels, and external regulations, as illustrated in *Figure 1.6*. Each circle in the figure represents one component of the GRC approach; each rectangle includes the description of that component's main objective. Each arrow shows the information exchanges among the three elements.

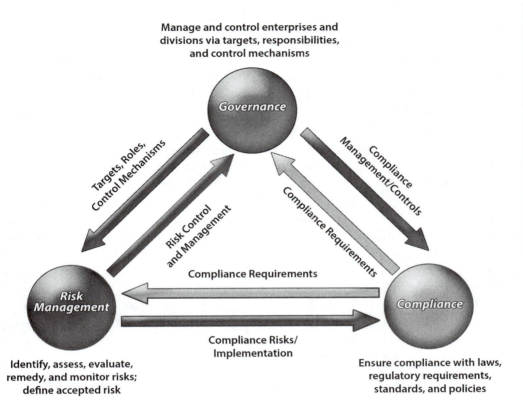

Figure 1.6 – **GRC overview** [8]

Organizations typically find it easier to focus on compliance first and then gradually expand efforts to include risk management and governance. It is important to note, however, that governance activities will happen, whether planned or not, and that lack of planned governance and rigorous risk management can have serious consequences for the business because of the issues associated with uncoordinated actions being carried out on behalf of the organization. With the lack of a clear strategic focus and senior level management guidance to coordinate and control these actions, an organization must assume large risk when aligning them to the business objectives with regards to due diligence and due care.

Legislative and Regulatory Compliance

Organizations operate in environments where laws, regulations, and compliance requirements must be met. Security professionals must understand the laws and regulations of the country and industry they are working in. An organization's governance and risk management processes must take into account these requirements from an implementation and a risk perspective. These laws and regulations often offer specific actions that must be met for compliance, or in some cases, what must be met for a "safe harbor" provision. A safe harbor provision is typically a set of "good faith" conditions that, if met, may temporarily or indefinitely protect the organization from the penalties of a new law or regulation.

---

8   http://www.giza-blog.de/content/binary/IT-Infrastructure_Compliance_Maturity_Model_Microsoft_Kranawetter_EN.pdf (Page 24)

For example, in the United States, federal executive agencies are required to adhere to the Federal Information Security Management Act (FISMA).[9] FISMA mandates the use of specific actions, standards, and requirements for agencies to ensure sensitive information and vital mission services are not disrupted, distorted, or disclosed to improper individuals. Agencies often take the requirements from FISMA and use them as the baseline for their information security policy and adopt the standards required by FISMA as their own. In doing so, they not only meet the requirements of the law but can also provide proof to external parties that they are making a good faith effort to comply with the requirements of the law.

Compliance stemming from legal or regulatory requirements is best addressed by ensuring an organization's policies, procedures, standards, and guidance are consistent with any laws or regulations that may govern it. Furthermore, it is advisable that specific laws and their requirements are sited in an organization's governance program and information security training programs. As a general rule, laws and regulations represent a "moral minimum," which must be adhered to and should never be considered wholly adequate for an organization without a thorough review. Additional requirements and specificity can be added to complement the requirements of law and regulation, but they should never conflict with them. For example, a law may require sensitive financial information to be encrypted, and an organization's policy could state that in accordance with the law all financial information will be encrypted. Furthermore, the agency may specify a standard strength and brand of encryption software to be used in order to achieve the required level of compliance with the law while also providing for the additional layers of protection that the organization wants in place.

Privacy Requirements Compliance

Privacy laws and regulations pose "confidentiality" challenges for the security professional. Personally identifiable information is becoming an extremely valuable commodity for marketers, as demonstrated by the tremendous growth of social networking sites based on demography and the targeted marketing activities that come with them. While valuable, this information can also become a liability for an organization that runs afoul of information privacy regulations and laws.

For example, the European Data Protection Directive only allows for the processing of personal data under specific circumstances such as:

1. When processing is necessary for compliance with a legal action.
2. When processing is required to protect the life of the subject.
3. When the subject of the personal data has provided consent.
4. When the processing is performed within the law and scope of "public interest."

The four requirements listed above reflect only a small portion of the directive. The directive further states what rights the subject has, such as objecting at any time to the processing of his or her personal data if the use is for direct marketing purposes. Recently, several Internet search companies and social media companies have been cited for not complying with this law. These organizations have been accused of using the personal data of the subject for direct marketing efforts without the subject's permission. The information security professional working in a marketing firm in the European Union must understand the impact of these requirements on how information will be processed, stored, and transmitted in his or her organization.

---

9   See the following: http://csrc.nist.gov/groups/SMA/fisma/
     http://www.whitehouse.gov/sites/default/files/omb/memoranda/2014/m-14-04.pdf

1

The "Directive 95/46 of the European Parliament and the Council of 24 October 1995 on the protection of individuals with regard to the processing of personal data and on the free movement of such data" (Data Protection Directive 95/46/EC) was established to provide a regulatory framework to guarantee secure and free movement of personal data across the national borders of the EU member countries, in addition to setting a baseline of security around personal information wherever it is stored, transmitted, or processed.[10] The Directive contains 33 articles in 8 chapters. The Directive went into effect in October 1998. This general Data Protection Directive has been complemented by other legal instruments, such as the e-Privacy Directive (Directive 2002/58/EC) for the communications sector.[11] There are also specific rules for the protection of personal data in police and judicial cooperation in criminal matters (Framework Decision 2008/977/JHA).[12]

The Data Protection Directive 95/46/EC defines the basics elements of data protection that member states must transpose into national law. Each state manages the regulation of data protection and its enforcement within its jurisdiction, and data protection commissioners from the EU states participate in a working group at the community level, pursuant to Article 29 of the Directive.

Personal data is defined in the Data Protection Directive 95/46/EC as any information that relates to an "identified or identifiable natural person." The Directive mandates that the data controller ensures compliance with the principles relating to data quality and provides a list of legitimate reasons for data processing. The data controller has information duties toward the data subject whenever personal data is collected directly from the person concerned or obtained otherwise. The data controller is also mandated to implement appropriate technical and organizational measures against unlawful destruction, accidental loss or unauthorized alteration, disclosure, or access.

Data subjects' individual rights, as established by the Directive, are: the right to know who the data controller is, the recipient of the data, and the purpose of the processing; the right to have inaccurate data rectified; a right of recourse in the event of unlawful processing; and the right to withhold permission to use data in some circumstances. For example, individuals have the right to opt-out free of charge from receiving direct marketing material. The EU Data Protection Directive contains strengthened protections concerning the use of sensitive personal data relating, for example, to health, sex life, or religious or philosophical beliefs as well.

Enforcement of the regulatory framework on the processing of personal data can either be through administrative proceedings of the supervisory authority or judicial remedies. Member states' supervisory authorities are endowed with investigative powers and effective powers of intervention, such as powers to order blocking, erasure, and destruction of data or to impose a temporary or definite ban on processing. Any person who has suffered damage as a result of an unlawful processing operation is entitled to receive compensation from the liable controller. The Data Protection Directive provides a mechanism by which transfers of personal data outside the territory of the EU have to meet a level of processing "adequate" to the one prescribed by the directive's provisions.

---

10   See the following for the full text of Directive 95/46/EC: http://eur-lex.europa.eu/legal-content/EN/TXT/?uri=CELEX:31995L0046

11   See the following for the full text of Directive 2002/58/EC: http://eur-lex.europa.eu/legal-content/EN/ALL/?uri=CELEX:32002L0058

12   See the following for the full text of Directive 2008/977/JHA: http://eur-lex.europa.eu/legal-content/EN/TXT/?qid=1405188191230&uri=CELEX:32008F0977

In January 2012, after the Lisbon Treaty gave the EU the explicit competence to legislate on the protection of individuals with regard to the processing of their personal data, the Commission proposed a reform package comprising a general data protection regulation to replace Directive 95/46/EC and a directive to replace Framework Decision 2008/977/JHA.

The Parliament's committee on Civil Liberties, Justice and Home Affairs adopted its reports on the basis of 4,000 amendments (to the Regulation) and 768 amendments (to the Directive). The Parliament adopted a position at first reading in March 2014. The key points of the Parliament's position in regards to the Regulation are:[13]

- A comprehensive approach to data protection, with a clear, single set of rules, which applies within and outside the Union;
- A clarification of the concepts used (personal data, informed consent, data protection by design, and default) and a strengthening of individuals' rights (e.g., as regards inter alia the right of access or the right to object to data processing);
- A more precise definition of the rules concerning the processing of personal data relating to some sectors (health, employment, and social security) or for some specific purposes (historical, statistical, scientific research, or archives-related purposes);
- A clarification and a strengthening of the regime of sanctions;
- A better and consistent enforcement of data protection rules (strengthened role of the corporate data protection officers, setting up of a European Data Protection Board, unified framework for all Data Protection Authorities, creation of a one-stop shop mechanism);
- A strengthening of the criteria for assessing the adequacy of protection offered in a third country.

The proposed directive deals with the processing of personal data in the context of prevention, investigation, detection, or prosecution of criminal offences or the execution of criminal penalties. Parliament's position on the directive contains key elements such as:

- A clear definition of the data protection principles (the exceptions that have to be duly justified);
- The conditions to be complied with as regards the processing (e.g., lawful, fair, transparent and legitimate processing, and explicit purposes) and the transmission of personal data;
- The setting up of an evaluation mechanism and of a data protection impact assessment;
- A clear definition of profiling;
- A strengthening of the regime for transferring personal data to third countries;
- A clarification of the monitoring and enforcement powers of the Data Protection Authorities;
- A new article on genetic data.

The security professionals need to stay up to date on the latest developments such as those being pursued by the Parliament with regards to processing and handling of personal information in order to ensure that the compliance activities that they engage in are directed towards supporting the required laws and regulations that are in force within the geographies that the enterprise operates within and that they are responsible for.

---

13 See the following for the full text of the adopted 12 March, 2014 by the Parliament, including all of the proposed amendments: http://www.europarl.europa.eu/sides/getDoc.do?type=TA&language=EN&reference=P7-TA-2014-0212
http://ec.europa.eu/prelex/detail_dossier_real.cfm?CL=en&DosId=201286

Global Legal and Regulatory Issues

Computer/Cyber Crime

With the proliferation of computer viruses, spyware, phishing and fraud schemes, and hacking activity from every location in the world, computer crime and security are certainly topics of concern when discussing computer ethics. Besides outsiders, or hackers, many computer crimes, such as embezzlement or planting of logic bombs, are committed by trusted personnel who have authorization to use company computer systems. Some examples of these types of crimes include the following:

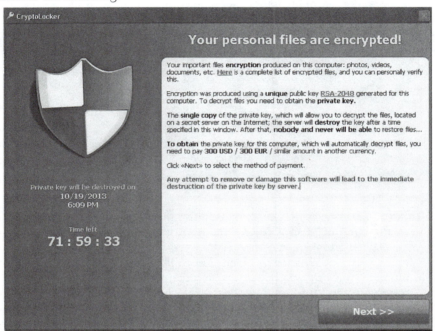

- **CryptoLocker Ransomware** – It spreads via email and propagates rapidly. The virus encrypts various file types and then a pop-up window appears on victims' computers that states their data has been encrypted. The only way to get it back is to send a specified monetary payment to the perpetrator. This ransomware provides the victim with a timeline to pay via a displayed countdown clock. If victims do not pay on time, they lose the ability to pay and risk having their data permanently encrypted and rendered unusable. Perpetrators are demanding a $300 to $700 payment sent to the perpetrator using various methods.

- **Child Pornography Scareware** – This scareware is transmitted when computer users visit an infected website. The victim's computer locks up and displays a warning that the user has violated U.S. federal law. Child pornography is either embedded in a banner image that appears on the victims' screen or revealed via an automatic browser redirecting them to a child pornography website. The scareware is used as an extortion technique by threatening prosecution for visiting or viewing these images. The victim is also informed that he or she has been recorded using audio, video, and other devices. The only way to unlock the computer is to pay the fine, which is usually between $300 and $5,000.

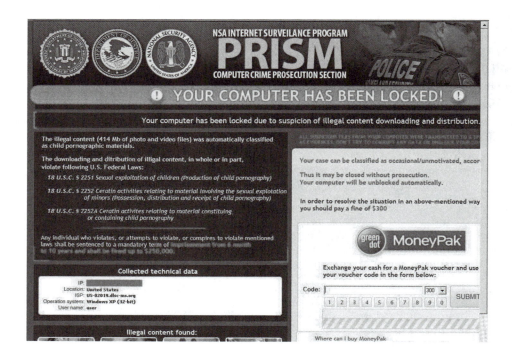

- **Citadel Ransomware** – The Citadel ransomware, named Reveton, displays a warning on the victims' computer purportedly from a law enforcement agency claiming that their computer had been used for illegal activities, such as downloading copyrighted software or child pornography. To increase the illusion they are being watched by law enforcement, the screen also displays the victim's IP address, and some victims even report activity from their webcam. Victims are instructed to pay a fine to the U.S. Department of Justice to unlock their computer. Many were told to pay the fines via prepaid cash services such as Ucash or Paysafecard. In addition to installing the ransomware, the Citadel malware continues to operate on the compromised computer to collect sensitive data that could potentially be used to commit a variety of financial frauds.

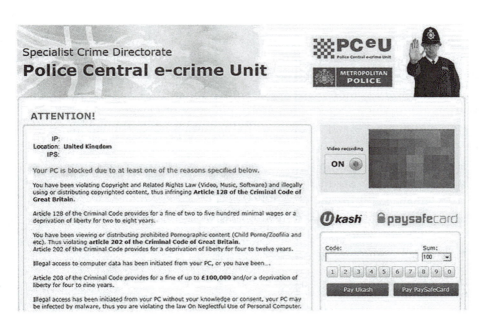

- **_Fake or Rogue Anti-Virus Software_** – In this scheme, victims are scared into purchasing anti-virus software that would allegedly remove viruses from their computers. A pop-up box appears that informs users that their computers are full of viruses and need to be cleaned. The pop-up message has a button victims can click to purchase anti-virus software that supposedly can immediately get rid of these viruses. If the victims click the pop-up to purchase the anti-virus software, they are infected with malware. In some instances, victims have been infected regardless of clicking on the pop-up box.

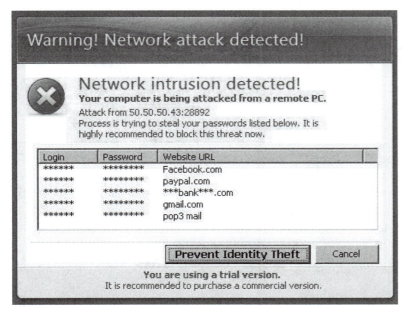

Cybercrime activities are globally diffused, financially-driven acts. Such computer-related fraud is prevalent, and it makes up around one-third of acts around the world. Another conspicuous portion of cybercrime acts is represented by computer content, including child pornography and piracy. Another significant portion of crime relates to acts against confidentiality, integrity, and accessibility of computer systems. That includes illegal access to a computer system, which accounts for another one-third of all acts.

When assessing the effect of cybercrime, the security professional will find it necessary to evaluate a series of factors such as:

- The loss of intellectual property and sensitive data.
- Opportunity costs, including service and employment disruptions.
- Damage to the brand image and company reputation.
- Penalties and compensatory payments to customers (for inconvenience or consequential loss) or contractual compensation (for delays, etc.).
- Cost of countermeasures and insurance.
- Cost of mitigation strategies and recovery from cyber-attacks.

Ponemon Institute's 2013 Cost of Cyber Crime study finds the average company in the U.S. experiences more than 100 successful cyber-attacks each year at a cost of $11.6M. That's an increase of 26% from 2012. Companies in other regions fared better, but they still experienced significant losses. The 2013 annual study was conducted in the United States, United Kingdom, Germany, Australia, Japan, and France and surveyed over 230 organizations.[14]

But the study also shows that companies who implement enabling security technologies reduced losses by nearly $4M, and those employing good security governance practices reduced costs by an average of $1.5M. Key findings include:

- The average annualized cost of cybercrime incurred per organization was $11.56 million, with a range of $1.3 million to $58 million. This is an increase of 26 percent, or $2.6 million, over the average cost reported in 2012.
- Organizations in defense, financial services, and energy and utilities suffered the highest cybercrime costs.
- Data theft caused major costs, 43% of the total external costs; business disruption or lost productivity accounts for 36% of external costs. While the incidence of data theft overall decreased by 2% from 2012 to 2013, business disruption increased by 18% over the same time period.
- Organizations experienced an average of 122 successful attacks per week, up from 102 attacks per week in 2012.
- The average time to resolve a cyber-attack was 32 days, with an average cost incurred during this period of $1,035,769, or $32,469 per day – a 55 percent increase over 2012's estimated average cost of $591,780 for a 24-day period.
- Denial-of-service, Web-based attacks, and insiders account for more than 55% of overall annual cybercrime costs per organization.
- Smaller organizations incur a significantly higher per-capita cost than larger organizations.
- Recovery and detection are the most costly internal activities.

---

14 See the following to download the global as well as country specific versions of the report:
    http://www.hpenterprisesecurity.com/ponemon-2013-cost-of-cyber-crime-study-reports

It should be clear from the summarized findings above that the security professionals have their work cut out for them with regards to the prevention of cybercrime and the impact that it can have on the enterprise. The security professional needs to be able to partner with the security architect and the security practitioner to work across the enterprise at every level in order to ensure that the best possible defenses are envisioned, designed, implemented, managed, monitored, and optimized in order to ensure that the risks and impacts from cybercrime are properly identified, analyzed, and communicated to the organization's senior management. Once senior management has understood and weighed the risks and communicated the risk appetite and position of the enterprise to the security professional, then those risks identified as being the ones that will be accepted should be acted upon as necessary based on the decisions made.

Licensing and Intellectual Property

Although no one expects an information systems security professional to be a legal expert on all areas of technology-related law – as with the various legal systems – a working knowledge of legal concepts directly related to information technology is required to fully understand the context, issues, and risks inherent with operation and management of information systems. Two general categories of information technology law have the largest impact on information systems: intellectual property and privacy regulations. This section only provides a brief summary of these concepts. Readers wishing to delve deeper into this area are strongly encouraged to refer to the relevant legislation and regulations in their respective countries.

Intellectual Property Laws

Intellectual property laws are designed to protect both tangible and intangible items and property. Although there are various rationales behind the state-based creation of protection for this type of property, the general goal of intellectual property law is to protect property from those wishing to copy or use it, without due compensation to the inventor or creator. The notion is that copying or using someone else's ideas entails far less work than what is required for the original development. According to the World Intellectual Property Organization (WIPO):

Intellectual property is divided into two categories: *Industrial property*, which includes inventions (patents), trademarks, industrial designs, and geographical indications of source; and *Copyright*, which includes literary and artistic works such as novels, poems and plays, films, musical works, artistic works such as drawings, paintings, photographs and sculptures, and architectural designs.[15]

Patent

Simply put, a patent grants the owner a legally enforceable right to exclude others from practicing the invention covered for a specific time (usually 20 years). A patent is the "strongest form of intellectual property protection." A patent protects novel, useful, and nonobvious inventions. The granting of a patent requires the formal application to a government entity. Once a patent is granted, it is published in the public domain to stimulate other innovations. Once a patent expires, the protection ends and the invention enters the public domain. WIPO, an agency of the United Nations, looks after the filing and processing of international patent applications.

---

15   http://www.wipo.int/about-ip/en/iprm/

Trademark

Trademark laws are designed to protect the goodwill an organization invests in its products, services, or image. Trademark law creates exclusive rights to the owner of markings that the public uses to identify various vendor or merchant products or goods. A trademark consists of any word, name, symbol, color, sound, product shape, device, or combination of these that is used to identify goods and distinguish them from those made or sold by others. The trademark must be distinctive and cannot mislead or deceive consumers or violate public order or morality. Trademarks are registered with a government registrar. International harmonization of trademark laws began in 1883 with the Paris Convention, which prompted the Madrid Agreement of 1891. In addition to patents, WIPO oversees international trademark law efforts, including international registration.

Copyright

A copyright covers the expression of ideas rather than the ideas themselves; it usually protects artistic property such as writing, recordings, databases, and computer programs. In most countries, once the work or property is completed or is in a tangible form, the copyright protection is automatically assumed. Copyright protection is weaker than patent protection, but the duration of protection is considerably longer (e.g., a minimum of 50 years after the creator's death or 70 years under U.S. copyright protection). Although individual countries may have slight variations in their domestic copyright laws, as long as the country is a member of the international Berne Convention, the protection afforded will be at least at a minimum level, as dictated by the convention; unfortunately, not all countries are members.[16]

Trade Secret

A trade secret refers to proprietary business or technical information, processes, designs, practices, etc., that are confidential and critical to the business (e.g., Coca-Cola's formula). The trade secret may provide a competitive advantage or, at the very least, allow the company to compete equally in the marketplace. To be categorized as a trade secret, it must not be generally known and must provide some economic benefit to the company. Additionally, there must be some form of reasonable steps taken to protect its secrecy. A trade secret dispute is unique because the actual contents of the trade secret need not be disclosed. Legal protection for trade secrets depends upon the jurisdiction. In some countries, it is assumed under unfair business legislation, and in others, specific laws have been drafted related to confidential information. In some jurisdictions, legal protection for trade secrets is practically perpetual and does not carry an expiry date, as is the case with patents. Trade secrets are often at the heart of industrial and economic espionage cases and are the proverbial crown jewels of some companies.

Licensing Issues

The issue of illegal software and piracy is such a large problem that it warrants discussion. More than one company has been embarrassed publicly, sued civilly, or criminally prosecuted for failing to control the use of illegal software or violating software licensing agreements. With high-speed Internet access readily available to most employees, the ability – if not the temptation – to download and use pirated software has greatly increased. According to a recent (2013) study by the Business Software Alliance (BSA) and International Data Corporation

---

16 Read more about the Berne convention here: http://www.wipo.int/treaties/en/ip/berne/trtdocs_wo001.html

(IDC), prevalence and frequency of illegal software is exceedingly high: The weighted average was 42% worldwide. The same study found that for every two dollars' worth of legal software purchased, one dollar's worth of software was pirated.[17] Though not all countries recognize the forms of intellectual property protection previously discussed, the work of several international organizations and industrialized countries seems somewhat successful in curbing the official sanctioning of intellectual property rights violations (e.g., software piracy).

There are several categories of software licensing including freeware, shareware, commercial, and academic. Within these categories, there are specific types of agreements. Master agreements and end-user licensing agreements (EULAs) are the most prevalent, though most jurisdictions have refused to enforce the shrink-wrap agreements that were commonplace at one time. Master agreements set out the general overall conditions of use along with any restrictions, whereas the EULA specifies more granular conditions and restrictions. The EULA is often a "click through" or radio button that the end-user must click on to begin the install, indicating that he or she understands the conditions and limitations and agrees to comply.

Various third parties have developed license metering software to ensure and enforce compliance with software licensing agreements. Some of these applications can produce an audit report and either disable software attempting to run in violation of an agreement (e.g., exceeding the number of devices running software concurrently) or produce an automated alert. The use of carefully controlled software libraries is also a recommended solution. Ignorance is no excuse when it comes to compliance with licensing conditions and restrictions. The onus is clearly on the organization to enforce compliance and police the use of software or face the possibility of legal sanctions, such as criminal prosecution or civil penalties.

Import/Export

Concerns about the inappropriate transfer of new information, technologies, and products with military applications outside the U.S. led to the passage of two laws in the late 1970s that control exports of selected technologies and products.

1. ***International Traffic In Arms Regulations (ITAR)*** – The Arms Export Control Act (Sec. 38) of 1976, as amended (P.L. 90-629), authorizes (22 U.S.C., Chapter 39, Subchapter III, Sec. 2778 entitled Control of Arms Exports and Imports) the President to:

    A. Designate those items which shall be considered as defense articles and defense services

    B. Control their import and the export.

The items so designated shall constitute the United States Munitions List (22 CFR Part 121) and are regulated through the U.S. Department of State, Office of Defense Trade Controls.

Defense articles (Sec. 120.6 & Part 121) include any item or technical data (recorded or stored in any physical form, models, mockups, or other items that reveal technical data) designated in the U.S. Munitions List. Of the 21 declared item categories controlled under ITAR, the following 19 are of potential interest to the information security professional, in particular those that may work in the aerospace and defense industries, due to the potential lateral applications of computer related technologies and information service technologies inherent in each of these categories and the technology represented by each:[18]

---

17   See the following for the 2013 study: http://globalstudy.bsa.org/2013/index.html

18   See the following for a full listing of the ITAR categories: http://fas.org/spp/starwars/offdocs/itar/p121.htm

I.   Firearms

II.   Artillery Projectors

III.   Ammunition

IV.   Launch Vehicles, Guided Missiles, Ballistic Missiles, Rockets, Torpedoes, Bombs and Mines

V.   Explosives, Propellants, Incendiary Agents, and Their Constituents

VI.   Vessels of War and Special Naval Equipment

VII.   Tanks and Military Vehicles

VIII.   Aircraft and Associated Equipment

IX.   Military Training Equipment

X.   Protective Personnel Equipment

XI.   Military Electronics

XII.   Fire Control, Range Finder, Optical and Guidance and Control Equipment

XIII.   Auxiliary Military Equipment

XIV.   Toxicological Agents and Equipment and Radiological Equipment

XV.   Spacecraft Systems and Associated Equipment

XVI.   Nuclear Weapons Design and Test Equipment

XVII.   Classified Articles, Technical Data and Defense Services Not Otherwise Enumerated

XVIII. Submersible Vessels, Oceanographic and Associated Equipment

XIX.   Miscellaneous Articles:

1. Defense articles not specifically enumerated in the other categories that have substantial military applicability and that have been specifically designed or modified for military purposes. The decision on whether any article may be included in this category shall be made by the Director of the Office of Defense Trade Controls.

- Technical data (Sec. 120.21) and defense services (Sec. 120.8) directly related to the defense articles.

2. ***Export Administration Regulations (EAR)*** – The Export Administration Act of 1979 authorized the President to regulate exports of civilian goods and technologies (equipment, materials, software, and technology, including data and know-how) that have military applications (dual-use items). Such controls have traditionally been temporary, and when it has lapsed, the President has declared a national emergency and maintained export control regulations under the authority of an executive order.

The items so designated constitute the United States Commerce Control List (15 CFR Part 774 2) and are regulated through the U.S. Department of Commerce, Bureau of Industry and Security. Of the 9 declared categories, the following are of interest to the information security professional in particular:[19]

- ***Category 4*** – Computers
- ***Category 5 Part 1*** – Telecommunications
- ***Category 5 Part 2*** – Information Security

---

19   See the following for a full listing of all of the EAR categories: http://www.bis.doc.gov/index.php/regulations/export-administration-regulations-ear

In addition, Section 734.3 paragraph (b) (3) of EAR exempts publicly available technology and software from controls, except for software controlled for "Encryption Item" reasons under Export Control Classification Number (ECCN) 5D002, Information Security – "Software", on the Commerce Control List and mass market encryption software with symmetric key length exceeding 64-bits controlled under ECCN 5D992, if it:

- Is already published or will be published;
- Arises during, or results from, fundamental research;
- Is educational; or
- Is included in certain patent applications

Therefore, it is essential for broad understanding and agreement of the following basic concepts related to export controls amongst security professionals operating in the United States or representing companies that do business with the United States or United States based companies:

1. The nature of the technology that is export controlled and how it is recognized,
2. What is an "export" (ITAR) or a "deemed export" (EAR),
3. The fundamental research exclusion and the meaning of "Public Domain", and
4. Whether or not there are:
   - Restrictions imposed on publication of scientific and technical information resulting from the project or activity, OR
   - Controls imposed on access and dissemination of information resulting from the research by federal funding agencies.

The security professional should also be aware of the Wassenaar Arrangement. The Wassenaar Arrangement has been established in order to contribute to regional and international security and stability by promoting transparency and greater responsibility in transfers of conventional arms and dual-use goods and technologies, thus preventing destabilizing accumulations.[20] Participating States seek, through their national policies, to ensure that transfers of these items do not contribute to the development or enhancement of military capabilities that undermine these goals and are not diverted to support such capabilities. The Participating States of the Wassenaar Arrangement are:

Argentina, Australia, Austria, Belgium, Bulgaria, Canada, Croatia, Czech Republic, Denmark, Estonia, Finland, France, Germany, Greece, Hungary, Ireland, Italy, Japan, Latvia, Lithuania, Luxembourg, Malta, Mexico, Netherlands, New Zealand, Norway, Poland, Portugal, Republic of Korea, Romania, Russian Federation, Slovakia, Slovenia, South Africa, Spain, Sweden, Switzerland, Turkey, Ukraine, United Kingdom, and United States.

The decision to transfer or deny transfer of any item is the sole responsibility of each Participating State. All measures with respect to the Arrangement are taken in accordance with national legislation and policies and are implemented on the basis of national discretion. With regards to the United States, the EAR listing discussed above reflects the same categories as those controlled under the Wassenaar Arrangement.

---

20 See the following for the complete listing of the Wassenaar Arrangement controls:
   http://www.wassenaar.org/controllists/index.html

Trans-Border Data Flow

The movement of information across national borders drives today's global economy. Cross-border data transfers allow businesses and consumers access to the best available technology and services, wherever those resources may be located around the world. The free-flow of data across borders benefits all industry sectors, from manufacturing to financial services, education, healthcare, and beyond. The seamless transfer of information is as critically important as it is inexorably linked to the growth and success of the global economy.

As information moves from one server to another or from one cloud to another, the location of the data and the hosting organization begins to matter. Information developed in one country, transmitted through another and finally stored in a third may be subject to three different jurisdictions and three different legal systems along the route of its journey from start to finish. In some situations even if information is stored in one country, if the organization who owns the server is a member of a different country, the latter may be able to gain jurisdiction over the information stored on the system in question.

There are many issues that the security professional will need to consider and be concerned with in this area. A few examples are listed below:

- Governments throughout the world are looking at new ways to identify their citizens and visitors to fight terrorism, to combat fraud, and to deliver services. This has prompted governments to consider identity cards, enhanced passports and other travel documents, and the use of biometrics in health cards, drivers' licenses, and other entitlement documents. These documents will leave data trails that may create risks in countries without adequate data protection.
- Corporations and governments, in a drive to reduce costs and become more efficient, are outsourcing activities, including the processing of personal information of their customers and citizens. The phenomenon is not new; the scale and speed and number of players having access to the data is unprecedented and shows little sign of abating. This has led to legitimate concerns about the security and misuse of information being transferred to countries without data protection legislation.
- Technologies and applications as diverse as search engines, radio frequency identification chips (RFIDs), Voice Over Internet Protocol (VOIP), Web logging, and wireless communications generate huge amounts of personal transactional information and create data trails that can survive long after the transaction or conversation has taken place. Requirements for data retention could ensure that much of this data will persist for years, split among various jurisdictions across the world.
- The fight against terrorism and the related concerns about public safety have prompted governments to put individuals under unprecedented scrutiny. Governments are demanding significant amounts of personal information about people entering their countries, developing assessment tools to detect suspicious patterns of travel and behavior, creating watch lists, and sharing this information with other countries. This raises significant concerns about the ability of individuals to exercise their information rights in the countries they visit.

Trans-border data flows are increasing exponentially, whether for processing purposes, to facilitate e-commerce, for law enforcement and national security purposes, or simply the result of people going about their daily lives. These trends are creating new and complex challenges for security professionals and other organizations charged with overseeing privacy and data protection laws.

Privacy

With the proliferation of technology and the increasing awareness that most of our personally identifiable information (PII) is stored online or electronically in some way, shape, or form, there is growing pressure to protect personal information.[21] Almost monthly, there are media reports worldwide of databases being compromised, files being lost, and attacks against businesses and systems that house personal, private information. This has spurred concerns over the proper collection, use, retention, and destruction of information of a personal or confidential nature. This public concern has prompted the creation of regulations intended to foster the responsible use and stewardship of personal information. In the context of this discussion, privacy is one of the primary areas in which business, in almost all industries, is forced to deal with regulations and regulatory compliance.

The actual enactment of regulations or, in some cases, laws dealing with privacy depend on the jurisdiction. Some countries have opted for a generic approach to privacy regulations, horizontal enactment (i.e., across all industries, including government), while others have decided to regulate by industry, vertical enactment (e.g., financial, health, publicly traded).

Regardless of the approach, the overall objective is to protect a citizen's personal information while at the same time balancing the business, governmental, and academic or research need to collect and use this information appropriately. Unfortunately, there is no one international privacy law, resulting in a mosaic of legislation and regulations. Some countries have been progressive in dealing with privacy and personal information, while others have yet to act in this area. Given the fact that the Internet has created a global community, our information and business transactions and operations may cross several different borders and jurisdictions – each with its own sovereign concerns, societal standards, and laws. Therefore, it is prudent to have a basic understanding of privacy principles and guidelines and keep up to date with the changing landscape of privacy regulations that may affect business as well as personal information.

Privacy can be defined as the rights and obligations of individuals and organizations with respect to the collection, use, retention, and disclosure of personal information. Personal information is a rather generic concept and encompasses any information that is about or on an identifiable individual. Although international privacy laws are somewhat different in respect to their specific requirements, they all tend to be based on core principles or guidelines. The Organization for Economic Cooperation and Development (OECD) has broadly classified these principles into the collection limitation, data quality, purpose specification, use limitation, security safeguards, openness, individual participation, and accountability.[22] The guidelines are as follows:

- There should be limits to the collection of personal data, and any such data should be obtained by lawful and fair means and, where appropriate, with the knowledge or consent of the data subject.
- Personal data should be relevant to the purposes for which they are to be used and, to the extent necessary for those purposes, should be accurate, complete, and kept up to date.

---

21 For more information on PII, see the following: http://csrc.nist.gov/publications/nistpubs/800-122/sp800-122.pdf

22 See the following: http://oecdprivacy.org/

- The purposes for which personal data is collected should be specified not later than at the time of data collection, and the subsequent use should be limited to the fulfillment of those purposes or such others as are not incompatible with those purposes and as are specified on each occasion of change of purpose.
- Personal data should not be disclosed, made available, or otherwise used for purposes other than those specified above except:
  - With the consent of the data subject.
  - By the authority of law.
- Personal data should be protected by reasonable security safeguards against such risks as loss or unauthorized access, destruction, use, modification, or disclosure of data.
- There should be a general policy of openness about developments, practices, and policies concerning personal data. Means should be readily available for establishing the existence and nature of personal data, and the main purposes of their use, as well as the identity and usual residence of the data controller.
- An individual should have the right:
  - To obtain from a data controller, or otherwise, confirmation of whether the data controller has data relating to him.
  - To have communicated to him, data relating to him:
    - Within a reasonable time.
    - At a charge, if any, that is not excessive.
    - In a reasonable manner.
    - In a form that is readily intelligible to him.
  - To be given reasons if a request made is denied and to be able to challenge such denial.
  - To challenge data relating to him and, if the challenge is successful, to have the data erased, rectified, completed, or amended.
  - A data controller should be accountable for complying with measures that give effect to the principles stated above.

It should be noted that the OECD is very cautious about not creating barriers to the legitimate trans-border flow of personal information. The OECD also cautions members to be aware of, and sensitive to, regional or domestic differences and safeguard personal information from countries that do not follow the OECD guidelines or an equivalent.[23]

Generally, these principles should form the minimum set of requirements for the development of reasonable legislation, regulations, and policy, and that nothing prevents organizations from adding additional principles. However, the actual application of these principles has proved more difficult and costly in almost all circumstances; there has been a vast underestimation of the impact of the various privacy laws and policies both domestically and with cross-border commerce. This is not an excuse to abandon, block, or fail to comply with applicable laws, regulations, or policies. However, security professionals need to appreciate that business practices have changed due to the need to be in compliance (often with international regulations) and that budgets must be appropriately increased to meet the demand.

---

23 For example, the difference within the EU between personal information and 'sensitive' personal information is something for the security professional to be aware of, but perhaps it may not be something that is addressed by an organization or its policies depending on where they do business.

Data Breaches

It is important for the security professionals of the world to have a sense of community and identity. Certifications such as the CISSP help to foster and create this community by allowing security professionals to share a sense of accomplishment at having attained an important milestone in their careers through certification, as well as by gaining access to a community shared amongst information security professionals. The main thing that helps to define a community is the culture that it represents and the shared values and points of reference that the culture is built upon. Common points of reference are important for all sorts of reasons, but especially so because they provide for the ability to agree on definitions and expectations with regards to things such as vocabulary. To that end, the following definitions of vocabulary terms are offered as noted:

- ***Incident*** – A security event that compromises the integrity, confidentiality, or availability of an information asset.
- ***Breach*** – An incident that results in the disclosure or potential exposure of data.
- ***Data Disclosure*** – A breach for which it was confirmed that data was actually disclosed (not just exposed) to an unauthorized party.

The incident and breach landscape is an ever-changing one. With the nature of interconnected systems today, an incident that starts out as a small breach, perhaps limited to one system, can quickly spread if unchecked to encompass entire global networks and data systems. The security professional needs to have a general sense of the kinds of breaches and data disclosures that are being faced by organizations around the world today in order to be prepared to react to the threats that they will encounter in the enterprise. The security professional and the security practitioner both also need to keep in mind that if incidents are identified quickly, and responded to in an efficient and effective manner, then those efforts may be able to prevent the incident from becoming a full blow breach.

While it is impossible to create a comprehensive and timely list of incidents, breaches, and data disclosure events, the following list represents the largest items on the list as of the first seven months of 2014, based on publically disclosed information.

eBay

The online retailer suffered one of the biggest data breaches yet reported by an online retailer. Attackers compromised a "small number of employee log-in credentials" between late February and early March to gain access to the company's network and, through it, compromised a database that contained customer names, encrypted passwords, email addresses, physical addresses, phone numbers, and dates of birth. The breach is thought to have affected the majority of the company's 145 million members, and many were asked to change their passwords as a result.

Michaels Stores

The point-of-sale systems at 54 Michaels and Aaron Brothers stores "were attacked by criminals using highly sophisticated malware" between May 2013 and January 2014. The company said up to 2.6 million payment card numbers and expiration dates at Michaels stores and 400,000 at Aaron Brothers could have been obtained in the attack. The company received confirmation of at least some fraudulent use.

Montana Department of Public Health and Human Services

After suspicious activity was noticed, officials conducted an investigation in mid-May that led to the conclusion that a server at the Montana Department of Public Health and Human Services had been hacked. The server held names, addresses, dates of birth, and social security numbers on roughly 1.3 million people, although the department said it has "no reason to believe that any information contained on the server has been used improperly or even accessed."

Variable Annuity Life Insurance Co.

A former financial adviser at the company was found in possession of a thumb drive that contained details on 774,723 of the company's customers. The drive was provided to the company by law enforcement as the result of a search warrant served on the former adviser. The thumb drive included full or partial social security numbers, but the insurance company said it did not believe any of the data had been used to access customer accounts.

Spec's

A 17-month-long "criminal attack" on the Texas wine retailer's network resulted in the loss of information of as many as 550,000 customers. The intrusion began in October 2012 and affected 34 of the company's stores across the state. It continued until as late as March 20 of 2014, and the company fears hackers got away with customer names, debit or credit card details, card expiration dates, card security codes, bank account information from checks, and possibly driver's license numbers.

St. Joseph Health System

A server at the Texas healthcare provider was attacked between December 16 and 18 of 2013. It contained "approximately 405,000 former and current patients', employees' and some employees' beneficiaries' information." This included names, social security numbers, dates of birth, medical information, and, in some cases, addresses and bank account information. As with many other hacks, an investigation was not able to determine if the data was accessed or stolen.

According to the Verizon Data Breach Investigation Report (DBIR) 2014, the following 8 categories are responsible for approximately 94% of all data breach activity tracked and reported globally through the study:[24]

- POS Intrusions – 14%
- Web App Attacks – 35%
- Insider Misuse – 8%
- Physical Theft/Loss - <1%
- Miscellaneous Errors – 2%
- Crimeware – 4%
- Card Skimmers – 9%
- Cyber-espionage – 22%

The Verizon data illustrates very clearly what the categories of threats were that the security professional needed to be concerned with during 2013 and early 2014, while the report's data was being gathered and analyzed. However, as you are reading this paragraph, the threat categories and risks associated with them that the security professional is facing today may be very different than those listed above, although there may be similarities as well.

---

24 See the following to download the Verizon DBIR 2014: http://www.verizonenterprise.com/DBIR/2014/

So what can the security professional do to create an ongoing awareness of and ability to defend against threats and risks such as those listed above, especially when there are newly emerging threat vectors and bad actors constantly cropping up? Perhaps looking towards the same community identified earlier in this discussion and relying on it to help create a sort of global early warning system for threat vectors that are emerging from the wild would provide valuable insights to the security professional? But how would one do something so audacious and achieve something so important but at the same time so elusive? How indeed.

A Brief Primer on VERIS & VCDB

The Vocabulary for Event Recording and Incident Sharing (VERIS) is designed to provide a common language for describing security incidents in a structured and repeatable manner. It takes the narrative of "who did what to what (or whom) with what result," and it translates it into the kind of data you see in the Verizon DBIR 2014. Get additional information on the VERIS community site; the full schema is available on GitHub.

Both are good companion references for the security professional to help with understanding terminology and context.

- www.veriscommunity.com
- www.github.com/vz-risk/veris

Launched in 2013, the VERIS Community Database (VCDB) project enlists the cooperation of volunteers in the security community in an attempt to record all publicly disclosed security incidents in a free and open dataset. Learn more about VCDB by visiting the website below:

- www.vcdb.org

Some additional resources that the security professional may find to be valuable are listed below:

- http://www.databreachtoday.com/news (Lists information for the U.S., U.K., Europe, India, and Asia)
- http://www.informationisbeautiful.net/visualizations/worlds-biggest-data-breaches-hacks/ (Infographic that constantly updates with information from data breaches occurring globally that represent losses greater than 30,000 records per breach)
- http://www.scmagazine.com/the-data-breach-blog/section/1263/
- http://datalossdb.org/

Relevant Laws and Regulations

Currently in the United States, a company's possession and use of consumer data is regulated by a patchwork of industry-specific federal laws and generally applicable state data protection and notification laws. At the federal level, the Gramm-Leach-Bliley Act ("GLBA") and the Health Insurance Portability and Accountability Act of 1996 ("HIPAA") are two prominent examples. The GLBA applies to financial institutions and provides for the implementation of standards to limit the purposeful disclosure of and protect against unauthorized access to consumers' "nonpublic personal information." The GLBA also mandates that a financial institution must provide to its consumers notice of its policies on sharing nonpublic personal information. HIPAA, on the other hand, sets national standards for the security of electronically protected health information. Additionally, HIPAA requires covered entities – i.e., healthcare providers, health plans, and healthcare clearinghouses – and business associates to give notice to consumers whose unsecured protected health information has been compromised due to a breach.

In addition to industry-specific federal laws, there are numerous state and territorial personal data protection laws. While these laws serve the same general purpose of protecting individuals from identity theft, some vary as to the obligations they impose. For example, once unencrypted personal information is shown to have been compromised, most state laws require that notice be provided to affected individuals or the company that owns the data, depending on who suffered the breach. Some states also require the company that owns the data to notify consumer reporting agencies in certain circumstances. In the same vein, some states require that notice be given to the state's attorney general or other state agency whenever any state resident must be notified of a data breach, and other states require such notice only if a certain number of state residents must be notified. However, the majority of states do not require any notice to the attorney general or other state agency.

On 25 August 2013, the EU's new breach notification Regulation for electronic communication service (ECS) providers came into force. The Regulation supplements an earlier Directive that instructed ECS companies to notify their competent national authority in accordance with national laws.

The Regulation defines a standard process across the entire Union: European ECS providers are required to provide notice of data breaches (defined in the Directive as the "accidental or unlawful destruction, loss, alteration, unauthorized disclosure of, or access to, personal data transmitted, stored or otherwise processed in connection with the provision of a publicly available electronic communications service in the Union"). It also states, "The provider shall notify the personal data breach to the competent national authority no later than 24 hours after the detection of the personal data breach, where feasible."[25]

The European Union Agency for Network and Information Security (ENISA) reviewed the existing measures and the procedures in EU Member States with regard to personal data breaches and published in 2011 a study on the technical implementation of the Art. 4 of the ePrivacy Directive (2002/58/EC), which included recommendations on how to plan and prepare for data breaches, how to detect and assess them, how to notify individuals and competent authorities, and how to respond to data breaches. A proposal of a methodology for personal data breach severity assessment was also included as an annex to the above mentioned recommendations, which was, however, not considered mature enough to be used at national level by the different Data Protection Authorities.

Against this background, the Data Protection Authorities of Greece and Germany in collaboration with ENISA developed, based on the above mentioned work, an updated methodology for data breach severity assessment that could be used both by DPAs as well as data controllers. The working paper draft for this project, Working Document, v1.0, December 2013, can be accessed at https://www.enisa.europa.eu/activities/identity-and-trust/library/deliverables/dbn-severity.

On September 26, 2013, the U.K. Information Commissioner's Office (ICO) published new breach notification guidance, applicable to telecom operators, Internet service providers (ISPs), and other public electronic communications service (ECS) providers.[26]

---

25   http://eur-lex.europa.eu/LexUriServ/LexUriServ.do?uri=OJ:L:2013:173:0002:0008:en:PDF

26   http://ico.org.uk/~/media/documents/library/Privacy_and_electronic/Practical_application/notification-of-pecr-security-breaches.pdf

The U.K. Privacy and Electronic Communications (EC Directive) Regulations 2003 (PECR) implementation contained wide-ranging rules on marketing and advertising by telephone, fax, email, and text message, as well as rules relating to cookies and security breaches. The breach notification requirements contained in the PECR apply to ECS providers (e.g., telecom providers and ISPs). In the event of a data breach, these entities must notify the ICO within 24 hours of becoming aware of the basic facts of the breach.

The Guidance sets out the breach requirements that must be provided to the ICO. A secure online form for all notifications is now available; previously, service providers were expected to complete a breach notification form and email it to the ICO.[27] The form is high level and anticipates that notifying organizations may be awaiting further details from an internal investigation. Organizations submitting an initial breach notification form are expected to submit a second notification form containing further details of the breach within three days. If a data breach is likely to adversely affect individuals, the organization must notify those individuals "without undue delay" in addition to notifying the ICO. Data breach logs also must be maintained and submitted to the ICO on a monthly basis. The ICO provides a template log to help service providers understand what information needs to be submitted to the ICO.

Based on the sampled diversity of approaches discussed above, the security professionals will need to clearly familiarize themselves with the appropriate laws and regulatory requirements based on the area of the world that they are practicing in. To that end, one of the best resources currently available to help the security professional stay up to date on the differences by geography with regards to data privacy laws is the International Compendium of Data Privacy Laws compiled by BakerHostetler.[28]

Understand Professional Ethics

The consideration of computer ethics fundamentally emerged with the birth of computers. There was concern right away that computers would be used inappropriately to the detriment of society, or that they would replace humans in many jobs, resulting in widespread job loss. To fully grasp the issues involved with computer ethics, it is important to consider the history. The following provides a brief overview of some significant events.

Consideration of computer ethics is recognized to have begun with the work of MIT professor Norbert Wiener during World War II in the early 1940s, when he helped to develop anti-aircraft cannons that were capable of shooting down fast warplanes. This work resulted in Wiener and his colleagues creating a new field of research that Wiener called cybernetics, the science of information feedback systems. The concepts of cybernetics, combined with the developing computer technologies, led Wiener to make some ethical conclusions about the technology called information and communication technology (ICT), in which Wiener predicted social and ethical consequences.

Wiener published the book The Human Use of Human Beings in 1950, which described a comprehensive foundation that is still the basis for computer ethics research and analysis.

---

27   https://report.ico.org.uk/security-breach/

28   The 2014 version can be found here: http://www.bakerlaw.com/files/Uploads/Documents/Data%20 Breach%20documents/International-Compendium-of-Data-Privacy-Laws.pdf

In the mid-1960s, Donn B. Parker, at the time with SRI International in Menlo Park, CA, began examining unethical and illegal uses of computers and documenting examples of computer crime and other unethical computerized activities. He published "Rules of Ethics in Information Processing" in Communications of the ACM in 1968, and headed the development of the first Code of Professional Conduct for the Association for Computing Machinery, which was adopted by the ACM in 1973.

During the late 1960s, Joseph Weizenbaum, a computer scientist at MIT in Boston, created a computer program that he called ELIZA that he scripted to provide a crude imitation of "a Rogerian psychotherapist engaged in an initial interview with a patient." People had strong reactions to his program, some psychiatrists fearing it showed that computers would perform automated psychotherapy. Weizenbaum wrote Computer Power and Human Reason in 1976, in which he expressed his concerns about the growing tendency to see humans as mere machines. His book, MIT courses, and many speeches inspired many thoughts and projects focused on computer ethics.

Walter Maner is credited with coining the phrase "computer ethics" in the mid-1970s when discussing the ethical problems and issues created by computer technology, and taught a course on the subject at Old Dominion University. From the late 1970s into the mid-1980s, Maner's work created much interest in university-level computer ethics courses. In 1978, Maner published the Starter Kit in Computer Ethics, which contained curriculum materials and advice for developing computer ethics courses. Many university courses were put in place because of Maner's work.

In the 1980s, social and ethical consequences of information technology, such as computer-enabled crime, computer failure disasters, privacy invasion using computer databases, and software ownership lawsuits, were being widely discussed in America and Europe.

James Moor of Dartmouth College published "What Is Computer Ethics?" in Computers and Ethics, and Deborah Johnson of Rensselaer Polytechnic Institute published Computer Ethics, the first textbook in the field in the mid-1980s. Other significant books about computer ethics were published within the psychology and sociology field, such as Sherry Turkle's The Second Self, about the impact of computing on the human psyche, and Judith Perrolle's Computers and Social Change: Information, Property and Power, about a sociological approach to computing and human values.

Maner Terrell Bynum held the first international multidisciplinary conference on computer ethics in 1991. For the first time, philosophers, computer professionals, sociologists, psychologists, lawyers, business leaders, news reporters, and government officials assembled to discuss computer ethics. During the 1990s, new university courses, research centers, conferences, journals, articles, and textbooks appeared, and organizations like Computer Professionals for Social Responsibility, the Electronic Frontier Foundation, and the Association for Computing Machinery-Special Interest Group on Computers and Society (ACM-SIGCAS) launched projects addressing computing and professional responsibility. Developments in Europe and Australia included new computer ethics research centers in England, Poland, Holland, and Italy. In the U.K., Simon Rogerson, of De Montfort University, led the ETHICOMP series of conferences and established the Centre for Computing and Social Responsibility.

Regulatory Requirements for Ethics Programs

When creating an ethics strategy, it is important to look at the regulatory requirements for ethics programs. These provide the basis for a minimal ethical standard upon which an organization can expand to fit its own unique organizational environment and requirements. An increasing number of regulatory requirements related to ethics programs and training now exist.

The 1991 U.S. Federal Sentencing Guidelines for Organizations (FSGO) outline minimal ethical requirements and provide for substantially reduced penalties in criminal cases when federal laws are violated if ethics programs are in place. Reduced penalties provide strong motivation to establish an ethics program. Effective November 1, 2004, the FSGO was updated with additional requirements:

In general, board members and senior executives must assume more specific responsibilities for a program to be found effective:

- Organizational leaders must be knowledgeable about the content and operation of the compliance and ethics program, perform their assigned duties exercising due diligence, and promote an organizational culture that encourages ethical conduct and a commitment to compliance with the law.
- The commission's definition of an effective compliance and ethics program now has three subsections:
  - **Subsection (a)** – The purpose of a compliance and ethics program
  - **Subsection (b)** – Seven minimum requirements of such a program,
  - **Subsection (c)** – The requirement to periodically assess the risk of criminal conduct and design, implement, or modify the seven program elements, as needed, to reduce the risk of criminal conduct

The purpose of an effective compliance and ethics program is to exercise due diligence to prevent and detect criminal conduct and otherwise promote an organizational culture that encourages ethical conduct and a commitment to compliance with the law. The new requirement significantly expands the scope of an effective ethics program and requires the organization to report an offense to the appropriate governmental authorities without unreasonable delay.

The U.S. Sarbanes–Oxley Act of 2002 introduced accounting reform and requires attestation to the accuracy of financial reporting documents:

- Section 103, "Auditing, Quality Control, and Independence Standards and Rules," requires the board to
  - Register public accounting firms
  - Establish, or adopt, by rule, "auditing, quality control, ethics, independence, and other standards relating to the preparation of audit reports for issuers"
- New Item 406(a) of Regulation S-K requires companies to disclose:
  - Whether they have a written code of ethics that applies to their senior officers
  - Any waivers of the code of ethics for these individuals
  - Any changes to the code of ethics
- If companies do not have a code of ethics, they must explain why they have not adopted one.

The U.S. Securities and Exchange Commission approved a new governance structure for the New York Stock Exchange (NYSE) in December 2003. It includes a requirement for companies to adopt and disclose a code of business conduct and ethics for directors, officers, and employees, and promptly disclose any waivers of the code for directors or executive officers. The NYSE regulations require all listed companies to possess and communicate, both internally and externally, a code of conduct or face delisting.

In addition to these, U.S. organizations must monitor new and revised regulations from U.S. regulatory agencies, such as the Food and Drug Administration (FDA), Federal Trade Commission (FTC), Bureau of Alcohol, Tobacco, Firearms and Explosives (ATF), Internal Revenue Service (IRS), and Department of Labor (DoL), and many others throughout the world such as the EU Data Protection Directives. Ethics plans and programs need to be established within the organization to ensure that the organization complies with all such regulatory requirements regardless of the country they reside.

Topics in Computer Ethics

When establishing a computer ethics program and accompanying training and awareness program, it is important to consider the topics that have been addressed and researched. The following topics, identified in most computer ethics textbooks are good to use as a basis.

Computers in the Workplace

Computers can pose a threat to jobs as people feel they may be replaced by them. However, the computer industry already has generated a wide variety of new jobs. When computers do not eliminate a job, they can radically alter it. In addition to job security concerns, another workplace concern is health and safety. It is a computer ethics issue to consider how computers impact health and job satisfaction when information technology is introduced into a workplace.

Computer Crime

With the proliferation of computer viruses, spyware, phishing and fraud schemes, and hacking activity from every location in the world, computer crime and security are certainly topics of concern when discussing computer ethics. Besides outsiders, or hackers, many computer crimes, such as embezzlement or planting of logic bombs, are committed by trusted personnel who have authorization to use company computer systems.

Privacy and Anonymity

One of the earliest computer ethics topics to arouse public interest was privacy. The ease and efficiency with which computers and networks can be used to gather, store, search, compare, retrieve, and share personal information make computer technology especially threatening to anyone who wishes to keep personal information out of the public domain or out of the hands of those who are perceived as potential threats. The variety of privacy-related issues generated by computer technology has led to reexamination of the concept of privacy itself.

Intellectual Property

One of the more controversial areas of computer ethics concerns the intellectual property rights connected with software ownership. Some people, like Richard Stallman, who started the Free Software Foundation, believe that software ownership should not be allowed at all. He claims that all information should be free, and all programs should be available for copying, studying, and modifying by anyone who wishes to do so. Others, such as Deborah Johnson, author of the first major textbook on computer ethics, argue that software companies or programmers would not invest weeks and months of work and significant funds in the development of software if they could not get the investment back in the form of license fees or sales.

Professional Responsibility and Globalization

Global networks such as the Internet and conglomerates of business-to-business network connections are connecting people and information worldwide. Such globalization issues that include ethics considerations include:

- Global laws
- Global business
- Global education
- Global information flows
- Information-rich and information-poor nations
- Information interpretation

The gap between rich and poor nations, and between rich and poor citizens in industrialized countries, is very wide. As educational opportunities, business and employment opportunities, medical services, and many other necessities of life move more and more into cyberspace, the gaps between the rich and the poor may become even worse, leading to new ethical considerations.

Common Computer Ethics Fallacies

Although computer education is starting to be incorporated in lower grades in elementary schools, the lack of early computer education for most current adults led to several documented generally accepted fallacies that apply to nearly all computer users. As technology advances, these fallacies will change; new ones will arise, and some of the original fallacies will no longer exist as children learn at an earlier age about computer use, risks, security, and other associated information.

There are more than described here, but Peter S. Tippett, developer of Norton Antivirus, identified the following computer ethics fallacies, which have been widely discussed and generally accepted as being representative of the most common.

Computer Game Fallacy

Computer users tend to think that computers will generally prevent them from cheating and doing wrong. Programmers particularly believe that an error in programming syntax will prevent it from working, so that if a software program does indeed work, then it must be working correctly and preventing bad things or mistakes from happening. Even computer users in general have gotten the message that computers work with exacting accuracy and will not allow actions that should not occur. Of course, what computer users often do not consider is that although the computer operates under very strict rules, the software programs are written by humans and are just as susceptible to allowing bad things to happen as people often are in their own lives. Along with this, there is also the perception that a person can do something with a computer without being caught, so that if what is being done is not permissible, the computer should somehow prevent them from doing it.

Law-Abiding Citizen Fallacy

Laws provide guidance for many things, including computer use. Sometimes users confuse what is legal with regard to computer use with what is reasonable behavior for using computers. Laws basically define the minimum standard about which actions can be reasonably judged, but such laws also call for individual judgment. Computer users often do not realize they also have a responsibility to consider the ramifications of their actions and to behave accordingly.

Shatterproof Fallacy

Many, if not most, computer users believe that they can do little harm accidentally with a computer beyond perhaps erasing or messing up a file. However, computers are tools that can harm, even if computer users are unaware of the fact that their computer actions have actually hurt someone else in some way. For example, sending an e-mail insult to a large group of recipients is the same as publicly humiliating them. Most people realize that they could be sued for libel for making such statements in a physical public forum, but may not realize they are also responsible for what they communicate and for their words and accusations on the Internet.

As another example, forwarding e-mail without permission of the author can lead to harm or embarrassment if the original sender was communicating privately without expectation of his or her message being seen by any others. Also, using e-mail to stalk someone, to send spam, and to harass or offend the recipient in some way also are harmful uses of computers. Software piracy is yet another example of using computers to, in effect, hurt others.

Generally, the shatterproof fallacy is the belief that what a person does with a computer can do minimal harm, and only affects perhaps a few files on the computer itself; it is not considering the impact of actions before doing them.

Candy-from-a-Baby Fallacy

Illegal and unethical activity, such as software piracy and plagiarism, are very easy to do with a computer. However, just because it is easy does not mean that it is right. Because of the ease with which computers can make copies, it is likely almost every computer user has committed software piracy of one form or another. The Software Publisher's Association (SPA) and Business Software Alliance (BSA) studies reveal software piracy costs companies multibillions of dollars. Copying a retail software package without paying for it is theft. Just because doing something wrong with a computer is easy does not mean it is ethical, legal, or acceptable.

Hacker Fallacy

Numerous reports and publications of the commonly accepted hacker belief is that it is acceptable to do anything with a computer as long as the motivation is to learn and not to gain or make a profit from such activities. This so-called hacker ethic is explored in more depth in the following section titled "Hacking and Hactivism".

Free Information Fallacy

A somewhat curious opinion of many is the notion that information "wants to be free," as mentioned earlier. It is suggested that this fallacy emerged from the fact that it is so easy to copy digital information and to distribute it widely. However, this line of thinking completely ignores the fact the copying and distribution of data are completely under the control and whim of the people who do it, and to a great extent, the people who allow it to happen.

Hacking and Hacktivism

Hacking is an ambivalent term, most commonly perceived as being part of criminal activities. However, hacking has been used to describe the work of individuals who have been associated with the open-source movement. Many of the developments in information technology have resulted from what has typically been considered as hacking activities. Manuel Castells considers hacker culture as the "informationalism" that incubates technological breakthrough, identifying hackers as "the actors in the transition from an academically and institutionally constructed milieu of innovation to the emergence of self-organizing networks transcending organizational control".

A hacker was originally a person who sought to understand computers as thoroughly as possible. Soon hacking came to be associated with phreaking, breaking into phone networks to make free phone calls, which is clearly illegal.

The Hacker Ethic

The idea of a hacker ethic originates in the activities of the original hackers at MIT and Stanford in the 1950s and 1960s. Stephen Levy, journalist and author of several books on computers, technology, and privacy, outlined the so-called hacker ethic as follows:

1. Access to computers should be unlimited and total.
2. All information should be free.
3. Authority should be mistrusted and decentralization promoted.
4. Hackers should be judged solely by their skills at hacking, rather than by race, class, age, gender, or position.
5. Computers can be used to create art and beauty.
6. Computers can change your life for the better.

The hacker ethic has three main functions:

1. It promotes the belief of individual activity over any form of corporate authority or system of ideals.
2. It supports a completely free-market approach to the exchange of and access to information.
3. It promotes the belief that computers can have a beneficial and life-changing effect.

Ethics Codes of Conduct and Resources

Several organizations and groups have defined the computer ethics their members should observe and practice. In fact, most professional organizations have adopted a code of ethics, a large percentage of which address how to handle information. To provide the ethics of all professional organizations related to computer use would fill a large book. The following are provided to give an opportunity to compare similarities between the codes and, most interestingly, to note the differences (and sometimes contradictions) in the codes followed by the various diverse groups.

The Code of Fair Information Practices

In 1973 the U.S. Secretary's Advisory Committee on Automated Personal Data Systems for the U.S. Department of Health, Education and Welfare recommended the adoption of the following Code of Fair Information Practices to secure the privacy and rights of citizens:

1. There must be no personal data record-keeping systems whose very existence is secret.
2. There must be a way for an individual to find out what information is in his or her file and how the information is being used.
3. There must be a way for an individual to correct information in his or her records.
4. Any organization creating, maintaining, using, or disseminating records of personally identifiable information must assure the reliability of the data for its intended use and must take precautions to prevent misuse.
5. There must be a way for an individual to prevent personal information obtained for one purpose from being used for another purpose without his or her consent.

Internet Activities Board (IAB)
(Now the Internet Architecture Board) and RFC 1087

RFC 1087 is a statement of policy by the Internet Activities Board (IAB) posted in 1989 concerning the ethical and proper use of the resources of the Internet. The IAB "strongly endorses the view of the Division Advisory Panel of the National Science Foundation Division of Network, Communications Research and Infrastructure," which characterized as unethical and unacceptable any activity that purposely

1. Seeks to gain unauthorized access to the resources of the Internet
2. Disrupts the intended use of the Internet
3. Wastes resources (people, capacity, computer) through such actions
4. Destroys the integrity of computer-based information or
5. Compromises the privacy of users

Computer Ethics Institute (CEI)

In 1991 the Computer Ethics Institute held its first National Computer Ethics Conference in Washington, D.C. The Ten Commandments of Computer Ethics were first presented in Dr. Ramon C. Barquin's paper prepared for the conference, "In Pursuit of a 'Ten Commandments' for Computer Ethics." The Computer Ethics Institute published them as follows in 1992:

1. Thou Shalt Not Use a Computer to Harm Other People.
2. Thou Shalt Not Interfere with Other People's Computer Work.
3. Thou Shalt Not Snoop around in Other People's Computer Files.
4. Thou Shalt Not Use a Computer to Steal.
5. Thou Shalt Not Use a Computer to Bear False Witness.
6. Thou Shalt Not Copy or Use Proprietary Software for Which You Have Not Paid.
7. Thou Shalt Not Use Other People's Computer Resources without Authorization or Proper Compensation.
8. Thou Shalt Not Appropriate Other People's Intellectual Output.
9. Thou Shalt Think about the Social Consequences of the Program You Are Writing or the System You Are Designing.
10. Thou Shalt Always Use a Computer in Ways That Insure Consideration and Respect for Your Fellow Humans.

National Conference on Computing and Values

The National Conference on Computing and Values (NCCV) was held on the campus of Southern Connecticut State University in August 1991. It proposed the following four primary values for computing, originally intended to serve as the ethical foundation and guidance for computer security:

1. Preserve the public trust and confidence in computers.
2. Enforce fair information practices.
3. Protect the legitimate interests of the constituents of the system.
4. Resist fraud, waste, and abuse.

The Working Group on Computer Ethics

In 1991, the Working Group on Computer Ethics created the following End User's Basic Tenets of Responsible Computing:

1. I understand that just because something is legal, it isn't necessarily moral or right.
2. I understand that people are always the ones ultimately harmed when computers are used unethically. The fact that computers, software, or a communications medium exists between me and those harmed does not in any way change moral responsibility toward my fellow humans.
3. I will respect the rights of authors, including authors and publishers of software as well as authors and owners of information. I understand that just because copying programs and data is easy, it is not necessarily right.
4. I will not break into or use other people's computers or read or use their information without their consent.
5. I will not write or knowingly acquire, distribute, or allow intentional distribution of harmful software like bombs, worms, and computer viruses.

National Computer Ethics and Responsibilities Campaign (NCERC)

In 1994, a National Computer Ethics and Responsibilities Campaign (NCERC) was launched to create an "electronic repository of information resources, training materials and sample ethics codes" that would be available on the Internet for IS managers and educators. The National Computer Security Association (NCSA) and the CEI cosponsored NCERC. The NCERC Guide to Computer Ethics was developed to support the campaign.

The goal of NCERC is to foster computer ethics awareness and education. The campaign does this by making tools and other resources available for people who want to hold events, campaigns, awareness programs, seminars, and conferences or to write or communicate about computer ethics. NCERC is a nonpartisan initiative intended to increase understanding of the ethical and moral issues unique to the use, and sometimes abuse, of information technologies.

(ISC)² Code of Professional Ethics

The following is an excerpt from the (ISC)² Code of Ethics preamble and canons, by which all (ISC)² members must abide. Compliance with the preamble and canons is mandatory to maintain membership and credentials. Professionals resolve conflicts between the canons in the order of the canons. The canons are not equal and conflicts between them are not intended to create ethical binds.

Code of Ethics Preamble

Safety of the commonwealth, duty to our principals, and to each other requires that we adhere, and be seen to adhere, to the highest ethical standards of behavior. Therefore, strict adherence to this Code is a condition of certification.

Code of Ethics Canons

Protect Society, the Commonwealth, and the Infrastructure

- Promote and preserve public trust and confidence in information and systems.
- Promote the understanding and acceptance of prudent information security measures
- Preserve and strengthen the integrity of the public infrastructure.
- Discourage unsafe practice.

Act Honorably, Honestly, Justly, Responsibly, and Legally

- Tell the truth; make all stakeholders aware of your actions on a timely basis.
- Observe all contracts and agreements, express or implied.
- Treat all constituents fairly. In resolving conflicts, consider public safety and duties to principals, individuals, and the profession in that order.
- Give prudent advice; avoid raising unnecessary alarm or giving unwarranted comfort. Take care to be truthful, objective, cautious, and within your competence.
- When resolving differing laws in different jurisdictions, give preference to the laws of the jurisdiction in which you render your service.

Provide Diligent and Competent Service to Principals

- Preserve the value of their systems, applications, and information.
- Respect their trust and the privileges that they grant you.
- Avoid conflicts of interest or the appearance thereof.
- Render only those services for which you are fully competent and qualified.

Advance and Protect the Profession

- Sponsor for professional advancement those best qualified. All other things equal, prefer those who are certified and who adhere to these canons. Avoid professional association with those whose practices or reputation might diminish the profession.
- Take care not to injure the reputation of other professionals through malice or indifference.
- Maintain your competence; keep your skills and knowledge current. Give generously of your time and knowledge in training others.

Support Organization's Code of Ethics

Peter S. Tippett has written extensively on computer ethics. He provided the following action plan to help corporate information security leaders to instill a culture of ethical computer use within organizations:

1. Develop a corporate guide to computer ethics for the organization.
2. Develop a computer ethics policy to supplement the computer security policy.
3. Add information about computer ethics to the employee handbook.
4. Find out whether the organization has a business ethics policy, and expand it to include computer ethics.

5.   Learn more about computer ethics and spreading what is learned.
6.   Help to foster awareness of computer ethics by participating in the computer ethics campaign.
7.   Make sure the organization has an E-mail privacy policy.
8.   Make sure employees know what the E-mail policy is.

Fritz H. Grupe, Timothy Garcia-Jay, and William Kuechler identified the following selected ethical bases for IT decision making

- **Golden Rule** – Treat others as you wish to be treated. Do not implement systems that you would not wish to be subjected to yourself. Is your company using unlicensed software although your company itself sells software?
- **Kant's Categorical Imperative** – If an action is not right for everyone, it is not right for anyone. Does management monitor call center employees' seat time, but not its own?
- **Descartes' Rule of Change (also called the Slippery Slope)** – If an action is not repeatable at all times, it is not right at any time. Should a Web site link to another site, "framing" the page, so users think it was created and belongs to the former?
- **Utilitarian Principle (also called Universalism)** – Take the action that achieves the most good. Put a value on outcomes and strive to achieve the best results. This principle seeks to analyze and maximize the IT of the covered population within acknowledged resource constraints. Should customers using a Web site be asked to opt in or opt out of the possible sale of their personal data to other companies?
- **Risk Aversion Principle** – Incur least harm or cost. When there are alternatives that have varying degrees of harm and gain, choose the one that causes the least damage. If a manager reports that a subordinate criticized him in an e-mail to other employees, who would do the search and see the results of the search?
- **Avoid Harm** – Avoid malfeasance or "do no harm." This basis implies a proactive obligation of companies to protect their customers and clients from systems with known harm. Does your company have a privacy policy that protects, rather than exploits customers?
- **No Free Lunch Rule** – Assume that all property and information belong to someone. This principle is primarily applicable to intellectual property that should not be taken without just compensation. Has a company used unlicensed software? Or hired a group of IT workers from a competitor?
- **Legalism** – Is it against the law? Moral actions may not be legal, and vice versa. Might a Web advertising exaggerate the features and benefits of products? Are web sites collecting information illegally on minors?
- **Professionalism** – Is an action contrary to codes of ethics? Do the professional codes cover a case and do they suggest the path to follow? When you present technological alternatives to managers who do not know the right questions to ask, do you tell them all they need to know to make informed choices?
- **Evidentiary Guidance** – Is there hard data to support or deny the value of taking an action? This is not a traditional "ethics" value but one that is a significant factor related to IT's policy decisions about the impact of systems on individuals and groups. This value involves probabilistic reasoning where outcomes can be predicted based on hard evidence based on research. Does management assume that they know PC users are satisfied with IT's service or has data been collected to determine what they really think?

- **Client/Customer/Patient Choice** – Let the people affected decide. In some circumstances, employees and customers have a right to self-determination through the informed consent process. This principle acknowledges a right to self-determination in deciding what is "harmful" or "beneficial" for their personal circumstances. Are workers subjected to monitoring in places where they assume that they have privacy?

- **Equity** – Will the costs and benefits be equitably distributed? Adherence to this principle obligates a company to provide similarly situated persons with the same access to data and systems. This can imply a proactive duty to inform and make services, data, and systems available to all those who share a similar circumstance. Has IT made intentionally inaccurate projections as to project costs?

- **Competition** – This principle derives from the marketplace where consumers and institutions can select among competing companies, based on all considerations such as degree of privacy, cost, and quality. It recognizes that to be financially viable in the market, it is necessary to have data about what competitors are doing and understand and acknowledge the competitive implications of IT decisions. When presenting a build or buy proposition to management, is it fully aware of the risk involved?

- **Compassion/Last Chance** – Religious and philosophical traditions promote the need to find ways to assist the most vulnerable parties. Refusing to take unfair advantage of users or others who do not have technical knowledge is recognized in several professional codes of ethics. Do all workers have an equal opportunity to benefit from the organization's investment in IT?

- **Impartiality/Objectivity** – Are decisions biased in favor of one group or another? Is there an even playing field? IT personnel should avoid potential or apparent conflicts of interest. Do you or any of your IT employees have a vested interest in the companies that you deal with?

- **Openness/Full Disclosure** – Are persons affected by this system aware of its existence, aware of what data are being collected, and knowledgeable about how it will be used? Do they have access to the same information? Is it possible for a Web site visitor to determine what cookies are used and what is done with any information they might collect?

- **Confidentiality** – IT is obligated to determine whether data it collects on individuals can be adequately protected to avoid disclosure to parties whose need to know is not proven. Have security features been reduced to hold expenses to a minimum?

- **Trustworthiness and Honesty** – Does IT stand behind ethical principles to the point where it is accountable for the actions it takes? Has IT management ever posted or circulated a professional code of ethics with an expression of support for seeing that its employees act professionally?

How a Code of Ethics Applies to CISSPs

In 1998, Michael Davis, a professor of Philosophy at the Illinois Institute of Technology, described a professional ethics code as a "contract between professionals." According to this explanation, a profession is a group of persons who want to cooperate in serving the same ideal better than they could if they did not cooperate. Information security professionals, for example, are typically thought to serve the ideal of ensuring the confidentiality, integrity, and availability of information and the security of the technology that supports the information use. A code of ethics would then specify how professionals should pursue their common ideals so that each may do his or her best to reach the goals at a minimum cost while appropriately addressing the issues involved.

The code helps to protect professionals from certain stresses and pressures (such as the pressure to cut corners with information security to save money) by making it reasonably likely that most other members of the profession will not take advantage of the resulting conduct of such pressures. An ethics code also protects members of a profession from certain consequences of competition, and encourages cooperation and support among the professionals.

Considering this, an occupation does not need society's recognition to be a profession. Indeed, it only needs the actions and activities among its members to cooperate to serve a certain ideal. Once an occupation becomes recognized as a profession, society historically has found reason to give the occupation special privileges (e.g., the sole right to do certain kinds of work) to support serving the ideal in question (in this case, information security) in the way the profession serves society.

Understanding a code of ethics as a contract between professionals, it can then be explained why each information security professional should not depend upon only his or her private conscience when determining how to practice the profession, and why he or she must take into account what a community of information security professionals has to say about what other information security professionals should do. What others expect of information security professionals is part of what each should take into account in choosing what to do within professional activities, especially if the expectation is reasonable. The ethics code provides a guide to what information security professionals may reasonably expect of one another, basically setting forth the rules of the game.

Just as athletes need to know the rules of football to know what to do to score, computer professionals also need to know computer ethics to know, for example, whether they should choose information security and risk reduction actions based completely and solely upon the wishes of an employer, or, instead, also consider information security leading practices and legal requirements when making recommendations and decisions.

A code of ethics should also provide a guide to what computer professionals may expect other members of our profession to help each other do. Keep in mind that people are not merely members of this or that profession. Each individual has responsibilities beyond the profession and, as such, must face his or her own conscience, along with the criticism, blame, and punishment of others, as a result of actions. These issues cannot be escaped just by making a decision because their profession told them to.

Information security professionals must take their professional code of ethics and apply it appropriately to their own unique environments. To assist with this, Donn B. Parker a consultant, information security researcher and fellow of the association for computing machinery describes the following five ethical principles that apply to processing information in the workplace, and also provides examples of how they would be applied.

1. **Informed consent.** Try to make sure that the people affected by a decision are aware of your planned actions and that they either agree with your decision, or disagree but understand your intentions.

   Example: An employee gives a copy of a program that she wrote for her employer to a friend, and does not tell her employer about it.

2. **Higher ethic in the worst case.** Think carefully about your possible alternative actions and select the beneficial necessary ones that will cause the least, or no, harm under the worst circumstances.

   Example: A manager secretly monitors an employee's email, which may violate his privacy, but the manager has evidence-based reason to believe that the employee may be involved in a serious theft of trade secrets.

3. **Change of scale test.** Consider that an action you may take on a small scale, or by you alone, could result in significant harm if carried out on a larger scale or by many others.

   Examples: A teacher lets a friend try out, just once, a database that he bought to see if the friend wants to buy a copy, too. The teacher does not let an entire classroom of his students use the database for a class assignment without first getting permission from the vendor. A computer user thinks it's okay to use a small amount of her employer's computer services for personal business, since the others' use is unaffected.

4. **Owners' conservation of ownership.** As a person who owns or is responsible for information, always make sure that the information is reasonably protected and that ownership of it, and rights to it, are clear to users.

   Example: A vendor, who sells a commercial electronic bulletin board service with no proprietary notice at log-on, loses control of the service to a group of hackers who take it over, misuse it, and offend customers.

5. **Users' conservation of ownership.** As a person who uses information, always assume others own it and their interests must be protected unless you explicitly know that you are free to use it in any way that you wish.

   Example: Hacker discovers a commercial electronic bulletin board with no proprietary notice at logon, and informs his friends, who take control of it, misuse it, and then uses it to offend other customers.

Develop and Implement Security Policy

Imagine the day-to-day operation of an organization without any policies. Individuals would have to make decisions about what is right or wrong for the company based upon their personal values or their own past experience. While many small companies and startups operate in this fashion, this could potentially create as many values as there are people in the organization. Policies establish the framework for the security program that ensures that everyone has a common set of expectations and communicates the management's goals and objectives.

Procedures, standards, guidelines, and baselines (illustrated in *Figure 1.7*) are components that support the implementation of the security policy. A policy without mechanisms supporting its implementation is analogous to an organization having a business strategy without action plans to execute the strategy. Policies communicate the management's expectations, which are fulfilled through the execution of procedures and adherence to standards, baselines, and guidelines.

Security officers and their teams have typically been charged with the responsibility of creating the security policies. The policies must be written and communicated appropriately to ensure that they can be understood by the end-users that will consume them. Policies that are poorly written, or written at too high of an education level (common industry practice is to focus the content for general users at the sixth- to eighth-grade reading level), will not be understood.

While security officers may be responsible for the development of the security policies, the effort should be collaborative to ensure that the appropriate business issues are addressed. The security officers will get better corporate support by including other areas in policy development. This helps to instill buy-in within these areas as they take on a greater ownership of the final product and reduces rework later should they need to provide vital input.

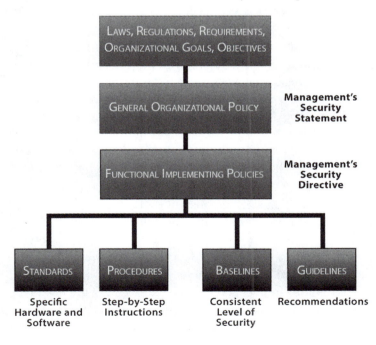

Figure 1.7 - **Relationships among policies, standards, procedures, baselines, and guidelines**

The security professional should consider inviting areas such as HR, legal, compliance, various IT areas, and specific business area representatives who represent critical business units to participate in the drafting process. When policies are developed solely within the IT department and then distributed without business input, they are likely to miss important business considerations.

Once policy documents have been created, the basis for ensuring compliance is established. Depending on the organization, additional documentation may be necessary to support policy. This support may come in the form of additional controls described in standards, baselines, or procedures to help personnel with compliance. An important step after documentation is to make the most current version of the documents readily accessible to those who are expected to follow them. Many organizations place the documents on their intranets or in shared file folders to facilitate their accessibility. Such placement of these documents plus awareness actions, training if needed, checklists, forms, and sample documents can make awareness and ultimately compliance more effective.

Business Continuity (BC) & Disaster Recovery (DR) Requirements

Project Initiation and Management

The first step in building the Business Continuity (BC) program is project initiation and management. During this phase, the following activities will occur:

- Obtain senior management support to go forward with the project
- Define a project scope, the objectives to be achieved, and the planning assumptions
- Estimate the project resources needed to be successful, both human resources and financial resources
- Define a timeline and major deliverables of the project

In this phase, the program will be managed like a project, and a project manager should be assigned to coordinate the team's activities.

Senior Leadership Support

Before the project can even start, it must have committed senior management support. Without that support, the project will fail. To convince leadership that the organization needs to build an enterprise-wide BC and DR plan, the planner must sell the importance of the program to the leadership.

Senior leadership in any organization has two major goals: Execute the mission and protect the organization. Business continuity and DR have little to do with executing the mission (unless the organization's mission is DR!) and everything to do with protecting the organization. It is still a hard sell because unless the organization actually has a disaster; the value of the time, money, and human resources required to build the plan is going to be suspect because it takes away from goal number one, executing the mission. So, why does an organization need BC and DR anyway? What possible value could they provide? We have to go back to the beginning in order to answer these questions.

It all started in the data center. Once computers became part of the enterprise landscape, even before the introduction of personal computers on individual desks, it quickly became clear that organizations could not return to manual processes if computers failed. The operational model had changed. The work people did with manual general ledgers in ledger books or with their hands in a manufacturing environment was now done more consistently, with fewer errors and many times faster, by computers. If those computer systems failed, there were not enough people to do the work nor did the people in the organization still have the skills to do it manually anymore. This was the start of the DR industry. Still today, the term "disaster recovery" commonly means recovery of the technology environment.

It took some time for many industries to realize that it really did not matter if the data center were recovered if there were no people to use it. That is when the term Business Continuity began to replace Disaster Recovery as a more accurate reflection of the goal of the industry – to enable the continuation of the work/mission of the organization as quickly and with as little disruption as possible.

To convince leadership of the need to build a viable Disaster Recovery Plan (DRP) and Business Continuity Plan (BCP), the planner needs to help them understand the risk they are accepting by not having one and the potential cost to the organization if a disaster were to occur. The risks to the organization are found in three areas: financial (how much money the organization stands to lose), reputational (how negatively the organization will be perceived by its customers and its shareholders), and regulatory (fines or penalties incurred, lawsuits filed against them). There is also the potential that the leaders of the organization could be held personally liable, financially and even criminally, if it is determined that they did not use due care to adequately protect the organization and its resources.

Financial risks can be quantified in many cases and are generally used to help determine how much should be spent on the recovery program. One of the ways financial risk can be calculated is using the formula $P * M = C$:

- ■ ***Probability of Harm (P)*** – the chance that a damaging event will occur, times the
- ■ ***Magnitude of Harm (M)*** – the amount of financial damage that would occur should a disaster happen =
- ■ ***Cost of Prevention (C)*** – the price of putting in place a countermeasure preventing the disaster's effects. The cost of countermeasures should not be more than the cost of the event.

Reputational risk is harder to quantify. For example, if a company cannot satisfy the needs of its customers when required, it is not hard for the customer to find someone else who will. Reputational risk is about how the company is perceived by its customers and stockholders. There are many examples of a negative impact to stock price in the wake of a crisis that is not managed properly. Effective BC and DR programs can be the difference between a company surviving an event and a company ceasing to exist.

Additional Benefits of the Planning Process
In many organizations, contingency planning is a necessity that has turned out to be beneficial in more ways than ever expected. Contingency planning helps to ensure an organization's viability during and following a disaster. Another benefit of contingency planning is significant improvements in the daily operations of many organizations.

Researching and documenting contingency plans can discover numerous Single Points of Failure (SPOF). A SPOF is any single input to a process that, if missing, would cause the process or several processes to be unable to function. Once identified, these SPOFs can often easily be eliminated or have their damaging potential reduced. Many organizations have also witnessed process improvements as a direct result of their contingency planning efforts, particularly while exercising their DR and BCPs.

There are many more benefits to contingency planning. Few other processes require that a data center staff or an organization think about what they do, how they do it, and how to make it better. Thinking about how to recover in a new environment, operating without the primary building, missing half the staff, or working without connectivity all lead to improved performance and resilience.

Develop and Document Project Scope and Plan

When one is seeking senior leadership approval, it is important to gain agreement on the scope and goals of the planning effort. Will the plan cover just the technology recovery or will it cover the organizational operations as well? Will it address only the technology in the data center or will it address all the technology used to run the organization? Will it address recovery of the main office only or will all the offices be considered?

Every company needs a technology recovery plan. Whether the company is a small organization that conducts all of its business on a laptop or a major corporation with multiple data centers, technology is an integral part of how business is conducted in today's world.

Planning for the recovery of the organization operations is also key to the survivability of the organization. Both the technology recovery and the organization recovery enable the organization to continue in the wake of an unexpected event. Another type of planning to consider is some type of workforce impairment event such as a pandemic, a labor strike, transportation issues, etc., where the building is fine, the data center is fine, but for some reason, the workforce is unable or unwilling to come to work.

The planner will need to agree with the senior leadership on the scope of the planning effort because that will define the project resources the planner will need, the timeline to complete the project, and the deliverables the leadership team can expect as the project progresses. Generally, building a plan where none currently exists within a medium sized organization (1,000 - 3,000 staff with two data centers) with an experienced planner and a commitment from leadership to support the effort would follow a timeline as outlined below:

- **Emergency Notification List** – 1 month
  - ¤ To respond to an emergency with any success, the planner must first be able to reach the people in the organization who can and will respond.
- **Vital Records Backup and Recovery** – Within the first 6 months
  - ¤ To be able to recover from a disaster situation, the planner must have access to all records needed to operate the organization.
- **Business Impact Analysis** – First 6 months
  - ¤ Identify organization functions, the capabilities of each organization unit to handle outages, and the priority and sequence of functions and applications to be recovered; identify resources required for recovery of those areas and interdependencies.

- **Strategy Development** – 6 to 9 months
  - ¤ Assessing various available strategies, performing cost benefit analysis, and making recommendations to leadership for approval.
- **Alternate Site Selection** – 9 to 12 months
  - ¤ Preparing Requests for Proposals (RFPs), performing site surveys, selecting vendor and/or build out and equip of internal site, and negotiating contracts.
- **Contingency Plan Development** – 12 months
  - ¤ Including: emergency response, restoring of critical systems, and organization functions to normal organization operations.
- **Testing, Plan Maintenance, and Periodic Audit** – Ongoing

Organizational Analysis
Senior leadership must support an organizational policy requiring compliance with the BCP/DRP development program to facilitate getting resources assigned from the various areas of the organization that will need to participate. The policy should state the following:

"The senior leaders of each functional area of the company are responsible for ensuring that a BCP exists for their area of responsibility, for the contents of the plan itself, and for affirming their concurrence with the plan annually by signing off on the plan document."

Conducting the Business Impact Analysis (BIA)
The next step in the planning process is to have the planning team perform a BIA. The BIA will help the company decide what needs to be recovered, and how quickly. Mission functions are typically designated with terms such as critical, essential, supporting, and nonessential to help determine the appropriate prioritization.

Identify and Prioritize

Critical Organization Functions
Generally speaking, organizations do not hire staff to perform nonessential tasks. Every function has a purpose, but some are more time sensitive than others when there is limited time or resources available to perform them. A bank that has suffered a building fire could easily stop its marketing campaign but would not be able to stop check processing and deposits made by its customers. The organization needs to look at every function in this same light. How long can the company not perform this function without causing significant financial losses, significant customer unhappiness or losses, or significant penalties or fines from regulators or lawsuits?

All organizational functions and the technology that supports them need to be classified based on their recovery priority. Recovery time frames for organizational operations are driven by the consequences of not performing the function. The consequences may be the result of contractual commitments not met resulting in fines or lawsuits, lost goodwill with customers, etc. *Figure 1.8* is a simple BIA form for classifying functions and determining their time sensitivity code, which is shown in *Figure 1.9*. To use this form, the planner will need to adjust the factors to reflect the organization being evaluated. The planner will need to define for the planning team what a low, medium, or high impact is in that organization in each of the impact areas, as well as the time before impact is realized.

	Impact Codes	Call Center	Customer Account Maintenance	Customer Monetary
Mail Zone		Z 45	Z 37	Z 38
Risk Code	F=Financial C=Customer R=Regulatory	C & F	C	C & F & R
Time Before Impact	0=Week 2 or more 1=Week 1 5=Up to 3 days 10=Day 1 20=4 hours 40=Immediate	40	1	10
Customer Impact	0=None 1=Low 3=Medium 5=High	5	3	3
Regulatory Impact	0=None 1=Low 3=Medium 5=High	1	0	3
Financial Impact	0=None 1=0 to10K 2=>10K but < 100K 3=>100K but <500K 4=>500K but <1 Mil 5=>1Mil	3	0	4
Rating Total	Sum of 1 through 4	**49**	**4**	**20**
Recovery Time Sensitivity Code		AAA	D	A
Alternate Site		Surviving sites then Smith Road	Work from Home	Smith Road

Figure 1.8 - **Sample BIA form**

Business Function Recovery Time Sensitive Codes

Rating Total of 45 or More =

AAA Immediate Recovery

Must be performed in at least two geographically dispersed locations that are fully equipped and staffed

Rating Total of 25 to 45 =

AA Up to 4 hours to recover

Must have a viable alternate site that can be staffed and functioning within the four hour timeframe required

Rating Total of 15 to 24 =

A Same day recovery

Must be operational the same business day and must therefore have a viable alternate site that can be staffed and functioning within the same business day

Rating Total of 10 to 14 =

B Up to 3 days

Can be suspended for up to 3 business days, but must have a viable alternate site that can be staffed and functioning by the fourth business day

Rating Total of 7 to 10 =

C Week 1

Can be suspended for up to a week, but must have a viable alternate site that can be staffed and functioning by the second week following an interruption

Rating Total of 0 to 6 =

D Week 2 or greater downtime allowable

Can be suspended for greater than one week - A maximum number of days should be identified for this function

Figure 1.9 – **Time Sensitivity Codes**

Determine Maximum Tolerable Downtime

All applications, like all organization functions, need to be classified as to their time sensitivity for recovery even if those applications do not support organization functions that are time sensitive. For applications, this is commonly referred to as Recovery Time Objective (RTO) or Maximum Tolerable Downtime (MTD). This is the amount of time the organization can function without that application before significant impact occurs.

Assess Exposure to Outages

Understanding the Organization

As part of the planning process, the planner will need to perform a risk assessment to determine which threats the organization has and where the planner will recommend spending mitigating dollars to attempt to reduce the impact of a threat.

There are three elements of risk: threats, assets, and mitigating factors. A threat is an event or situation that, if it occurred, would prevent the organization from operating in its normal manner, if at all. Threats are measured in probabilities such as "may happen 1 time in 10 years" and have a specified duration of time where the impact is felt.

External Threats and Vulnerabilities

The most common threat that impacts an organization's ability to function normally is power availability. Power outages cause more organization interruption events than any other type of event. The second most common type of event is water, either too much water (flooding, plumbing leak, broken pipes, and leaky roof) or not enough (water main break). Other common events are severe weather, cable cuts resulting in network outages, fires, labor disputes, transportation mishaps, and for the data center, hardware failures.

Internal Threats and Vulnerabilities

Internal outages are typically caused by the following actions:

- Equipment fails prematurely
  - Could be due to improper installation
  - Could also be due to improper environment
- Equipment fails due to wear and tear
  - Most equipment has a "mean time between failures" (MTBF) rating
  - Running equipment beyond the MTBF is risking failure
- Equipment goes down due to untested production changes or other human errors

Refer to the threat matrix in *Figure 1.10*. Reviewing the list of threats, one will notice that some of them are events that are fairly localized while others, like a hurricane, have a more regional impact. Threats to be considered include both natural hazards, such as tornados, earthquakes, and hurricanes, and man-made hazards, such as transportation mishaps, chemical spills, and sabotage.

Potential Threats

- Earthquake
- Hurricane
- Tornado
- Volcanic eruption
- Flood
- Power outage
- Falling aircraft
- Transport Mishap
    - Rail
    - Road
    - Boat
- Labor Strike
- Workforce illness (Pandemic)
- Scandal
- Severe weather

- Fire
- Smoke
- Denial of access from contamination
- Workplace Violence
- Civil disorder
- Water damage
- Bomb threats
- Sabotage/Vandalism
- Mechanical breakdown
- Hardware failure
- Software failure
- Computer virus/Worm
- Breach of confidential info
- Sudden loss or death of key leaders

Figure 1.10 – **Potential Threats**

Recovery Point Objectives (RPO)

Once all the organization functions have been identified and a recovery time frame determined, the planning team then needs to identify all the resources necessary to perform each of those functions. Resources include applications systems, minimum staff requirements, phone requirements, desktop requirements, internal and external interdependencies, etc.

The recovery priority for application systems is identified during this process. It is the organization that decides what application systems need to come back online when based on the recovery priority of the functions those applications support.

This technology review process is sometimes difficult for the organization to perform. The basic average desktop users know they click on this icon and this application system launches. They have little comprehension of where the application resides (mainframe, Web, server, or desktop), where the data resides (central storage, a network server, the cloud, or the desktop), or where the executable resides for that matter.

These are important considerations in building a recovery plan. If the application is collocated with the organization, then the recovery for that application must be part of the site recovery plan for that site. If it is not, then recovery could mean only providing network access to the application at the alternate site.

For both organization functions and applications, the organization also needs to determine the amount of work in process that may be at risk during an event. The data that is on employees' desks when a fire occurs would be lost forever if that information was not backed up somewhere else. The information stored in file cabinets, incoming mail in the mailroom, the backup tapes that have not yet left the building, are all also at risk.

The planning team needs to make decisions about all types of data because data is what runs the organization. How much data is it acceptable to lose? A minute's worth? An hour's worth? A whole business day? This is commonly referred to as the recovery point objective (RPO), the point in time that the planner will attempt to recover to. Backup policies and procedures for electronic data and hard copy data need to comply with the RPO established by the organization.

Manage Personnel Security

Individuals within an organization come to work every day to perform their jobs to the best of their ability. As such, these individuals have the appropriate intentions and seek out information on the best ways to perform their jobs, the training required, and what the expectations of their jobs are. The media has placed much attention on the external threat faced by the organization with regards to hackers; however, there is also the threat internally of erroneous or fraudulent transactions, which could cause information assets to be damaged or destroyed. Internal personnel are closest to the data and best understand the processes, along with control weaknesses, that currently exist. Job controls such as the segregation of duties, job description documentation, mandatory vacations, job and shift rotation, and need-to-know (least privilege) access need to be implemented by the security professional in order to minimize the risks to data from within the organization. The security practitioner may look to robust monitoring controls such as behavioral anomaly detection to detect patterns of unusual data access based on what a "normal" user's baseline may be as an additional layer of controls to further reinforce a defense in depth strategy in this area.

In addition, various activities should be performed prior to an individual starting in a position. Some will be performed by the security professional directly, while others may be performed with his or her input or oversight by other members of the organization. These activities may include developing job descriptions, contacting references, screening/investigating of the background of the individual, developing confidentiality and non-disclosure agreements, as well as determining policies on vendor, contractor, consultant, and temporary staff access.

Employment Candidate Screening

Hiring qualified, suitable, and trustworthy individuals depends upon implementing and adhering to personnel policies that screen out those whose past actions may indicate undesirable behavior. Lower employee morale can result in reduced compliance with controls. Increased staff turnover can also result in lower levels of staff expertise over time. Termination policies and procedures are necessary to ensure that terminated employees no longer have access to the system, and therefore do not have the opportunity to damage files or systems or disrupt company operations. These are also necessary to ensure that policy is consistently applied to personnel. Although most employees are hardworking, competent individuals with no intentions of wrongdoing, there can be a few people with less than desirable intentions. Poor personnel security increases the risks to information, making it imperative to implement the appropriate personnel security controls.

Job descriptions should contain the roles and responsibilities of the position and the education, experience, and expertise required to satisfactorily perform the job function. A well-written job description provides not only the basis for conversation with the applicant to determine if his or her skills are a good match but also the barometer by which ongoing performance reviews can be measured. Individual job goals stated within the performance reviews should mirror the job description. Failure to align the correct job description with a position could result in the individual lacking skills for the job requirements. To ensure that individuals possess the necessary skills on an ongoing basis, one should periodically reassess the job skills. Requirements for annual training, especially for those individuals requiring specialized security training, will ensure that the skills remain relevant and current. Roles and responsibilities as defined by policies can help identify specific security skills that are needed. The employee training and participation in professional activities should be monitored and encouraged. All job descriptions of the organization should have some reference to information security responsibilities because these responsibilities are shared across the organization. Specific technology, platform requirements, and certifications required for security staff should be noted within the job posting.

The access and duties of an individual for a particular department should be assessed to determine the sensitivity of the job position. The degree of harm that the individual can cause through misuse of the computer system, through disclosing information, disrupting data processing, sharing internal secrets, modifying critical information, or committing computer fraud should be input to the classification as well. Role-based access establishes roles for a job or class of jobs, indicating the type of information the individual is permitted to access. Job sensitivity may also be used to require more stringent policies related to mandatory vacations, job rotations, and access control policies. Excess controls for the sensitivity level of the position waste resources through the added expense, while fewer controls cause unacceptable risks.

Reference Checks

During the interviewing and hiring process, individuals attempt to determine the past work history of the applicant and his or her competencies, such as teamwork, leadership abilities, perseverance, ethics, customer service orientation, management skills, planning, and specific technical and analytical capabilities. Much of the information provided is obtained by observing the individual during the interview process or from the information he or she has provided through the targeted questions. It is not always possible to determine the true work orientation of the prospective employee without other collaborating information. There are essentially two kinds of reference checks: personal and work. Personal accounting for the character of the person and work associated with verifying the provided work history.

Personal reference checks involve contacting those individuals supplied by the prospective employee. Many employers are reluctant to provide personal references for fear of future litigation. As such, many employers may have policies that only allow information such as date of hire and date of termination to be released. No information on why a termination occurred is released other than potentially whether it was a friendly (employee choice) or unfriendly (company terminated) decision. This still does not necessarily provide a reflection on the employee behavior because it may have been the result of staff reduction having nothing to do with performance. After all, when a company provides a reference, it can be perceived as placing a stamp of approval on the performance or character of the employee, even though the person providing the reference really has no control over the future work performance of the employee. Many individuals will provide references to place them in the best possible light and may place individuals such as presidents, vice presidents, doctors, lawyers, ministers, and so forth on the list to create the appearance of greater integrity. Targeted questions will be used by an employer to ascertain the tendencies and capabilities of the candidate, such as leadership ability, oral and written communication skills, decision-making skills, ability to work with others, respect from peers, how the individual acted under stress, and managerial ability (budgeting, attracting talent, delivering projects). Multiple reference checks provide multiple perspectives and provide for corroboration of the desired behaviors. Employers need to balance the response of references with the knowledge that the references were provided by the applicant and may be biased in their opinions. Failure of a prospective employee to provide references may be an indicator of a spotty work record or the possibility of prior personnel actions/sanctions against the individual.

Background Investigations

Just as the personal reference checks provide the opportunity to obtain corroborating information on whether the applicant will potentially be a good addition to the company, background checks can uncover more information related to the ability of the organization to trust the individual. Organizations want to be sure of the individuals that they are hiring and minimize future lawsuits or exposure. Resumes are often filled with errors, accidental mistakes, or blatant lies to provide a perceived advantage to the applicant. Common falsifications include embellishment of skill levels, job responsibilities, and accomplishments, certifications held, and the length of employment. The background checks can greatly assist the hiring manager in determining whether he or she has an accurate representation of the skills, experience, and work accomplishments of the individual. Commercial businesses typically do not have the time and money to conduct meaningful, thorough investigations on their own and hire outside firms that specialize in the various background checks. Background checks can uncover:

- Gaps in employment
- Misrepresentation of job titles
- Job duties
- Salary
- Reasons for leaving a job
- Validity and status of professional certification
- Education verification and degrees obtained
- Credit history
- Driving records
- Criminal history
- Personal references
- Social security number verification

Benefits of Background Checks

The benefits of background checks in protecting the company are self-evident; however, the following benefits may also be realized:

- Risk mitigation
- Increased confidence that the most qualified candidate was hired versus the one who interviewed the best
- Lower hiring cost
- Reduced turnover
- Protection of assets
- Protection of the company's brand reputation
- Shielding of employees, customers, and the public from theft, violence, drugs, and harassment
- Insulation from negligent hiring and retention lawsuits
- Safer workplace by avoiding hiring employees with a history of violence
- Discouraging of applicants with something to hide
- Identify criminal activity

Timing of Checks

An effective background check program requires that all individuals involved in the hiring process support the program prior to the candidate being selected for hire. This requires that the human resources department, legal, hiring supervisors, and recruiters understand and execute the screening process. Once the individual is hired into the organization, it is much harder to obtain the information without having a specific cause for performing the investigation. Employees should also be periodically reinvestigated consistent with the sensitivity of their positions. This should also be documented in the appropriate policies, including a frequency schedule.

Types of Background Checks

Many different types of background checks can be performed depending upon the position that the individual may be hired for. A best practice would be to perform background checks on all of the company's employees and to require external agencies through contract agreements to perform background checks on the contractors, vendors, and anyone coming in contact with the company assets, systems, and information. If this is cost-prohibitive, the organization must decide on the positions on which it is most critical to conduct background checks. Banks, for example, are required to perform background checks on any employee who may come in contact with money. In a bank, this is obviously nearly every employee. The types of checks range from minimal checks to full background investigations. The types of individuals upon whom an organization may focus the checks or decide to provide more extensive checks include:

- Individuals involved in technology
- Individuals with access to confidential or sensitive information
- Employees with access to company proprietary or competitive data
- Positions working with accounts payable, receivables, or payroll
- Positions dealing directly with the public
- Employees working for healthcare industry-based organizations or organizations dealing with financial information
- Positions involving driving a motor vehicle
- Employees who will come in contact with children

There is a broad range of possible background checks available. The following are the most common background checks performed.

Credit History

Credit history is the primary vehicle used by financial institutions to ensure the repayment of consumer loans, credit cards, mortgages, and other types of financial obligations. Credit histories are used to screen for high default risks and to discourage default. Financial services firms use credit histories as primary leverage, providing a threat to place delinquent information on the individual's credit reports should he or she fall behind in payments. In the past, managers would run a credit report only on those individuals who were directly handling money; however, this has changed due to the interconnection of computers and the potential access to high-risk applications. Basic credit reports verify the name, address, social security number, and prior addresses of the applicant. These can be used to provide more extensive criminal searches or uncover gaps in employment. Detailed credit histories provide the employer with liens, judgments, and payment obligations that may give an indication as to the individual's ability to handle his or her financial obligations. However, these items must be evaluated in context because the individual may have previously slipped into financial trouble and then reorganized his or her financial life so that this would not present a risk to the prospective employer. Sometimes credit reports have limited or no information, which may be representative of a prospect's age (has not yet established a credit history), cash paid for purchases, assumption of a false identity, or a prospect's residence (lives in an area that relies on fringe lenders, which typically do not report to credit bureaus).

Employers need to ensure that they are using the information appropriately, according to their country's laws. In the United States, the Fair Credit Reporting Act (FCRA), laws under the Equal Employment Opportunity Commission (EEOC), and some state laws will govern the actions by the organization.[29] Legal counsel and human resources should be involved in the development of any policies and procedures related to the screening process.

Criminal History

Criminal records are more difficult to obtain than credit histories because credit histories are exchanged through a system among banks, retail establishments, financial services firms, and credit-reporting bureaus. With more than 3,000 legal jurisdictions in the United States, it is not feasible to search each jurisdiction. Starting with the county of residence and searching in other prior addresses will provide a reasonable background check for the applicant. Most background checks examine felonies and overlook misdemeanors (less serious crimes). Under the FCRA, employers can request full criminal records for the past seven years unless the applicant earns more than $75,000 annually, in which case there are no time restrictions. Important information to be searched includes state and county criminal records, sex and violent offender records, and prison parole and release records.

---

29   Please see the following for detailed information on the Fair Credit Reporting Act:
       http://www.consumer.ftc.gov/sites/default/files/articles/pdf/pdf-0111-fair-credit-reporting-act.pdf
       Please see the following for information about the Equal Employment Opportunity Commission:
       http://www.eeoc.gov/

Driving Records

Driving records should be checked for those employees who will be operating a motor vehicle on their job. These records can also reveal information about applicants who will not be driving vehicles as part of their employment, such as verification of the applicant's name, address, and social security number, and will include information on traffic citations, accidents, driving-under-the-influence arrests, convictions, suspensions, revocations, and cancellations. These may be indicators of a possible alcohol or drug addiction or a lack of responsibility.

Drug and Substance Testing

The use of illicit drugs is tested for by most organizations because drug use may result in lost productivity, absenteeism, accidents, employee turnover, violence in the workplace, and computer crimes. Individuals using drugs avoid applying or following through the process with companies that perform drug testing. There are many different screening tests available, such as screens for amphetamines, cocaine and PCP, opiates (codeine, morphine, etc.), marijuana (THC), phencyclidine, and alcohol. Independent labs are frequently employed by employers to ensure that proper testing is performed because businesses are not in the drug testing business. Labs employ safeguards to reduce the likelihood of false-positives or making a wrongful determination of drug use. In the United States, laws such as the Americans with Disabilities Act (ADA) may provide protections for individuals undergoing rehabilitation.[30]

Prior Employment

Verifying employment information such as dates employed, job title, job performance, reason for leaving, and if the individual is eligible for rehire can provide information as to the accuracy of the information provided by the applicant. This is not an easy process; as noted earlier, many companies have policies to not comment on employee performance and will only confirm dates of employment.

Education, Licensing, and Certification Verification

Diploma and degree credentials listed on the resume can be verified with the institution of higher learning. Degrees can be purchased through the Internet for a fee, without attendance in any classes, so care should be taken to ensure that the degree is from an accredited institution. Certifications in the technology field, such as the CISSP or other industry- or vendor-specific certifications, can be verified by contacting the issuing agency. State licensing agencies maintain records of state-issued licenses, complaints, and revocations of licenses.

Social Security Number Verification and Validation

That a number is indeed a social security number can be verified through a mathematical calculation, along with the state and year that the number may have been issued. Verification that the number was issued by the Social Security Administration, was not misused, was issued to a person who is not deceased, or that the inquiry address is not associated with a mail-receiving service, hotel or motel, state or federal prison, campground, or detention facility can be done through an inquiry to the Social Security Administration.

---

30   Please see the following for detailed information on the Americans with Disabilities Act: http://www.ada.gov/

Suspected Terrorist Watch List

Various services search the federal and international databases of suspected terrorists. Although the construction of these databases and the methods for identifying the terrorists are relatively new and evolving, industries of higher risk, such as the defense, biotech, aviation, and pharmaceutical industries, or those that conduct business with companies associated with known terrorist activities would benefit from checking these databases.

Employment Agreements and Policies

Employment agreements are usually signed by the employee before he or she starts the new job or during his or her first day. These agreements will vary from organization to organization as to the form and content, but their purpose is to protect the organization while the individual is employed, as well as after the employee has left employment by the organization. For example, non-disclosure agreements contain clauses to protect the company's rights to retain trade secrets or intellectual property that the employee may have had access to even after the employee's departure from the organization. Code of conduct, conflict of interest, gift-handling policies, and ethics agreements may be required to ensure that the employee handles the continued employment in a manner that will be in the best interests of the organization and reduce the liability of the organization to lawsuits for unethical behavior by its employees.

Ongoing supervision and periodic performance reviews ensure that the individuals are evaluated on their current qualifications and attainment of security goals. Performance ratings for all employees should cover compliance with security policies and procedures. Compensation and recognition of achievements should be appropriate to maintain high morale of the department. Monitoring ongoing skill capabilities, training, and experience requirements reduces the risk that inappropriate controls are being applied to information security. A variety of policies, agreements, and processes are considered best practices in managing employee risk. The ultimate goal is to ensure the employee can do the function he or she was hired for while minimizing the susceptibility, environments and enticement of fraud, theft, abuse, or waste. The following processes aid in ensuring an efficient and low risk workforce.

Job Rotation

Job rotations reduce the risk of collusion between individuals. Companies with individuals working with sensitive information or systems where there might be the opportunity for personal gain through collusion can benefit by integrating job rotation with segregation of duties. Rotating someone's position may uncover activities that the individual is performing outside of normal operating procedures, highlighting errors or fraudulent behavior. It may be difficult to implement in small organizations due to the particular skill set required for the position, and thus security controls and supervisory control will need to be relied upon. Rotating individuals in and out of jobs provides the ability to give backup coverage, succession planning, and job enrichment opportunities for those involved. It also provides diversity of skills to support a separation of duties policy.

Separation of Duties (SOD)

One individual should not have the capability to execute all of the steps of a particular process. This is especially important in critical business areas where individuals may have greater access and capability to modify, delete, or add data to the system. Failure to separate duties could result in individuals embezzling money from the company without the involvement of others. Duties are typically subdivided or split between different individuals or organizational groups to achieve separation. This separation reduces the chances of errors or fraudulent acts; each group serves as a balancing check on the others, and a natural control process occurs. Management is responsible for ensuring that the duties are well defined and separated within their business processes. Failure to do so can result in unintended consequences; for example:

- An individual in the finance department with the ability to add vendors to the vendor database, issue purchase orders, record receipt of shipment, and authorize payment could issue payments to falsified vendors without detection.
- An individual in the payroll department with the ability to authorize, process, and review payroll transactions could increase the salaries of coworkers without detection.
- A computer programmer with the ability to change production code could change the code to move money to a personal bank account and then conceal his or her actions by replacing the production code and hiding or creating false logging.
- A programmer with the authority to write code, move it to production, and run the production job, skipping internal systems development procedures, could implement erroneous, even malicious code either inadvertently or deliberately.

Some organizations utilize a two-dimensional segregation of duties matrix to determine what positions should be separated within a department. Each position is written along the axes of the matrix, with an *x* placed where the two responsibilities should not reside with the same individual. This *x* indicates where the job duties should be subdivided among different individuals. It is critical to separate the duties between the IS department and the business units, as well as between those areas within the IS organization. For example, the management of the user departments is responsible for providing the authorization of systems access for the access rights of their employees. The information systems department, more specifically the area responsible for security administration, is responsible for granting the access. On a periodic basis, this access is also reviewed and confirmed by the business management. Within the IT department, the security administrator would be separated from the business analyst, computer programmer, computer operator, and so forth. These duties, which should not be combined within one person or group, are referred to as incompatible duties. Incompatible duties may vary from one organization to another. The same individual should not typically perform the following functions:

- Systems administration
- Network management
- Data entry
- Computer operations
- Security administration
- Systems development and maintenance
- Security auditing
- Information systems management
- Change management

In smaller organizations, it may be difficult to separate the activities because there may be limited staff available to perform these functions. These organizations may have to rely on compensating controls, such as supervisory review or active monitoring, to mitigate the risk. Audit logging and after-the-fact review by a third party can provide an effective control in lieu of separating the job functions. Larger organizations need to ensure that appropriate separation, supervisory review, and development of formalized operational procedures are in place. The separated functions should be documented fully and communicated to the staff to ensure that only the assigned individuals will execute tasks associated with these functions. These actions can help prevent or detect erroneous work performed by the user. Larger-dollar-amount transactions should have more extensive supervisory review controls (i.e., director/vice president/president formal sign-off) before processing is permitted.

Individuals in the information systems department must be prohibited from entering data into the business systems. Data entry personnel must not be the same individuals verifying the data, and reconciliation of the information should not be performed by the individual entering the information. Separation of these duties introduces checks and balances on the transactions. As new applications are developed, mergers and acquisitions occur, and systems are replaced, care must be taken to ensure that the segregation of duties is maintained. Periodic management review ensures that the transaction processing environment continues to operate with the designed separation principles.

Least Privilege (Need to Know)

Least privilege refers to granting users only the accesses that are required to perform their job functions. Some employees will require greater access than others based upon their job functions. For example, an individual performing data entry on a mainframe system may have no need for Internet access or the ability to run reports regarding the information that he or she is entering into the system. Conversely, a supervisor may have the need to run reports but should not be provided the capability to change information in the database. Well-formed transactions ensure that users update the information in systems consistently and through the developed procedures. Information is typically logged from the well-formed transactions. This can serve as a preventive or deterrent control because the user knows that the information is being logged and a detective control can discover how information was modified after the fact. Security controls around these transactions are necessary to ensure that only authorized changes are made to the programs applying the transaction. Access privileges need to be defined at the appropriate level that provides a balance between supporting the business operational flexibility and adequate security. Defining these parameters requires the input of the business application owner to be effective.

Mandatory Vacations

Requiring mandatory vacations of a specified consecutive-day period can provide similar benefits to using job rotations. If work is reassigned during the vacation period, irregularities may surface through the transaction flow, communications with outside individuals, or requests to process information without following normal procedures. Some organizations remove access to the remote systems during this period as well to ensure that the temporarily replaced employee is not performing work.

Employee Termination Processes

Employees join and leave organizations every day. The reasons vary widely, due to retirement, reduction in force, layoffs, termination with or without cause, relocation to another city, career opportunities with other employers, or involuntary transfers. Terminations may be friendly or unfriendly and will need different levels of care as a result.

Friendly Terminations

Regular termination is when there is little or no evidence or reason to believe that the termination is not agreeable to both the company and the employee. A standard set of procedures, typically maintained by the human resources department, governs the dismissal of the terminated employee to ensure that company property is returned and all access is removed. These procedures may include exit interviews and return of keys, identification cards, badges, tokens, and cryptographic keys. Other property, such as laptops, cable locks, credit cards, and phone cards, is also collected. The user manager notifies the security department of the termination to ensure that access is revoked for all platforms and facilities. Some facilities choose to immediately delete the accounts, while others choose to disable the accounts for a policy defined period (for example, 30 days) to account for changes or extensions in the final termination date. The termination process should include a conversation with the departing associate about his or her continued responsibility for confidentiality of information.

Unfriendly Terminations

Unfriendly terminations may occur when the individual is fired, involuntarily transferred, laid off, or when the organization has reason to believe that the individual has the means and intention to potentially cause harm to the system. Individuals with technical skills and higher levels of access, such as the systems administrators, computer programmers, database administrators, or any individual with elevated privileges, may present higher risk to the environment. These individuals could alter files, plant logic bombs to create system file damage at a future date, or remove sensitive information. Other disgruntled users could enter erroneous data into the system that may not be discovered for several months. In these situations, immediate termination of systems access is warranted at the time of termination or prior to notifying the employee of the termination.

Managing the people aspect of security, from pre-employment to postemployment, is critical to ensure that trustworthy, competent resources are employed to further the business objectives that will protect company information. Each of these actions contributes to preventive, detective, or corrective personnel controls.

Vendor, Consultant, and Contractor Controls

Business partners and other third parties often bring personnel into an organization. Therefore the organization must ensure controls are in place to prevent the loss of sensitive information and also mitigate any damage these individuals could intentionally or unintentionally perform to an organization. Much like organizational employee screening, there are several approaches one may take depending on the nature of the relationship between the vendor and the organization.

- If the third party is infrequently on site or accessing systems but has administrative access, consider:
  - Escorting the individual while on site to monitor activities.

- Virtually monitoring the employee with screen sharing technology and recording all actions performed.
- Ensuring an appropriate non-disclosure agreement with specific sanctions has been signed by the individual and the individual's organization if applicable.
- Ensuring the third party identifies who the specified personnel gaining access are and verifying their identification upon access.

- If the third party is on site for a more permanent basis and has administrative access, consider:
  - Performing a background investigation and determining if any suitability issues arise.
  - Virtually monitoring the employee with screen sharing technology and recording all actions performed.
  - Ensuring an appropriate non-disclosure agreement with specific sanctions has been signed by the individual and the individual's organization if applicable.
  - Ensuring the third party identifies who the specified personnel gaining access are and verifying their identification upon access.

- Regardless of duration, if the third party has limited access to sensitive information, consider:
  - Virtually monitoring the employee with screen sharing technology and recording all actions performed.
  - Ensuring an appropriate non-disclosure agreement with specific sanctions has been signed by the individual and the individual's organization if applicable.

Ensure someone with a legal background is involved in any contractual negotiations and understands the requirements listed above. Many successful penetration tests involve short visits by "vendors" or "repair people" who are actually attackers. Careful screening of third parties can help ensure only suitable and authorized individuals gain access to facilities and systems. Contracts must specify the requirements the vendors must meet to ensure they can plan and budget accordingly.

Privacy

All individuals have an expectation of privacy. This expectation varies by culture and people, but the security professional must understand the limits of monitoring individuals within the law of a country. While it is generally considered acceptable to place CCTV cameras in public parking lots, most of the world would not approve of CCTV cameras in a private area such as a shower or locker room. While these examples are extreme, others fall into a "grey" area. Such examples include a home office. Does an organization have a right to monitor any space work is performed on their behalf, including a private home? Most privacy experts would side with a "no" answer for this question, but some security professionals or investigators may say "yes." This is largely due to a difference in perspective. The investigator is interested in collecting evidence, and the security professional is interested in ensuring the safety of the individual and security of the organization's information.

In most instances communication about the organization's privacy policies is key to ensuring privacy related complaints are minimized. Many organizations place conspicuous signs that state CCTV or other types of monitoring are being conducted in an area. While some may argue this is alerting an attacker, in reality the attackers already assume or know there are cameras in the area. If they did not, a notice may very well deter or dissuade them. Either way, notifying or being conspicuous about monitoring can have advantages.

Risk Management Concepts

Risk, as defined in the *American Heritage Dictionary*, is "the possibility of loss." *Random House Dictionary* defines risk management as "the technique or profession of assessing, minimizing, and preventing accidental loss to a business, as through the use of insurance, safety measures, etc." *Figure 1.11* illustrates the activities associated with the United States' National Institute of Standards and Technology (NIST) Risk Assessment Process. While this is a specific framework, it encompasses the general risk management process. The details of the various steps are detailed below.

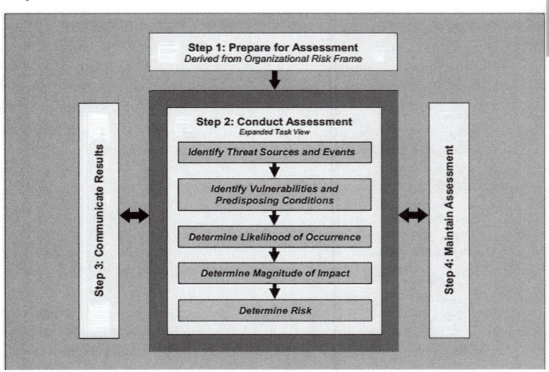

*Figure 1.11 – **The NIST Risk Assessment Process flowchart** [31]*

The first step in the risk assessment process is to prepare for the assessment. The objective of this step is to establish a context for the risk assessment. This context is established and informed by the results from the risk framing step of the risk management process. Risk framing identifies, for example, organizational information regarding policies and requirements for conducting risk assessments, specific assessment methodologies to be employed, procedures for selecting risk factors to be considered, scope of the assessments, rigor of analyses, degree of formality, and requirements that facilitate consistent and repeatable risk determinations across the organization. Organizations use the risk management strategy to the extent practicable to

---

31   http://csrc.nist.gov/publications/nistpubs/800-30-rev1/sp800_30_r1.pdf (Page 23).

obtain information to prepare for the risk assessment. Preparing for a risk assessment includes the following tasks:

- Identify the purpose of the assessment;
- Identify the scope of the assessment;
- Identify the assumptions and constraints associated with the assessment;
- Identify the sources of information to be used as inputs to the assessment; and
- Identify the risk model and analytic approaches (i.e., assessment and analysis approaches) to be employed during the assessment.

The second step in the risk assessment process is to conduct the assessment. The objective of this step is to produce a list of information security risks that can be prioritized by risk level and used to inform risk response decisions. To accomplish this objective, organizations analyze threats and vulnerabilities, impacts and likelihood, and the uncertainty associated with the risk assessment process. This step also includes the gathering of essential information as a part of each task and is conducted in accordance with the assessment context established in the Prepare step of the risk assessment process. The expectation for risk assessments is to adequately cover the entire threat space in accordance with the specific definitions, guidance, and direction established during the Prepare step. However, in practice, adequate coverage within available resources may dictate generalizing threat sources, threat events, and vulnerabilities to ensure full coverage and assessing specific, detailed sources, events, and vulnerabilities only as necessary to accomplish risk assessment objectives. Conducting risk assessments includes the following specific tasks:

- Identify threat sources that are relevant to organizations;
- Identify threat events that could be produced by those sources;
- Identify vulnerabilities within organizations that could be exploited by threat sources through specific threat events and the predisposing conditions that could affect successful exploitation;
- Determine the likelihood that the identified threat sources would initiate specific threat events and the likelihood that the threat events would be successful;
- Determine the adverse impacts to organizational operations and assets, individuals, other organizations, and the Nation resulting from the exploitation of vulnerabilities by threat sources (through specific threat events); and
- Determine information security risks as a combination of likelihood of threat exploitation of vulnerabilities and the impact of such exploitation, including any uncertainties associated with the risk determinations.

The specific tasks are presented in a sequential manner for clarity. However, in practice, some iteration among the tasks will be necessary and expected. Depending on the purpose of the risk assessment, organizations may find reordering the tasks advantageous. Whatever adjustments organizations make to the tasks described, risk assessments should meet the stated purpose, scope, assumptions, and constraints established by the organizations initiating the assessments.

The third step in the risk assessment process is to communicate the assessment results and share risk-related information. The objective of this step is to ensure that decision makers across the organization have the appropriate risk-related information needed to inform and guide risk decisions. Communicating and sharing information consists of the following specific tasks:

- Communicate the risk assessment results; and
- Share information developed in the execution of the risk assessment to support other risk management activities.

The fourth step in the risk assessment process is to maintain the assessment. The objective of this step is to keep current the specific knowledge of the risk organizations incur. The results of risk assessments inform risk management decisions and guide risk responses. To support the ongoing review of risk management decisions (e.g., acquisition decisions, authorization decisions for information systems and common controls, connection decisions), organizations maintain risk assessments to incorporate any changes detected through risk monitoring. Risk monitoring provides organizations with the means to, on an ongoing basis, determine the effectiveness of risk responses, identify risk-impacting changes to organizational information systems and the environments in which those systems operate, and verify compliance. Maintaining risk assessments includes the following specific tasks:

- Monitor risk factors identified in risk assessments on an ongoing basis and understand subsequent changes to those factors; and
- Update the components of risk assessments reflecting the monitoring activities carried out by organizations.

Organizational Risk Management Concepts

An organization will conduct a risk assessment (the term *risk analysis* is sometimes interchanged with risk assessment) to evaluate the following:

- Threats to its assets
- Vulnerabilities present in the environment
- The likelihood that a threat will be realized by taking advantage of an exposure (or probability and frequency when dealing with quantitative assessment)
- The impact that the exposure being realized will have on the organization
- Countermeasures available that can reduce the threat's ability to exploit the exposure or that can lessen the impact to the organization when a threat is able to exploit a vulnerability
- The residual risk (e.g., the amount of risk that is left over when appropriate controls are properly applied to lessen or remove the vulnerability)

An organization may also wish to document evidence of the countermeasure in a deliverable called an exhibit, or in some frameworks this is called "evidence." An exhibit can be used to provide an audit trail for the organization and, likewise, evidence for any internal or external auditors that may have questions about the organization's current state of risk.

Why undertake such an endeavor? Without knowing what assets are critical and which would be most at risk within an organization, one cannot possibly protect those assets appropriately. For example, if an organization is bound by HIPAA regulations but does not know to what extent electronic personally identifiable information may be at risk, the organization may make significant mistakes in securing that information, such as neglecting to protect against certain risks or applying too much protection against low-level risks.[32]

---

32   Please see the following for detailed information on HIPPA: http://www.hhs.gov/ocr/privacy/

Security and Audit Frameworks and Methodologies

Multiple frameworks and methodologies have been created to support security, auditing, and risk assessment of implemented security controls. These resources are valuable to assist in the design and testing of a security program. The following frameworks and methodologies have each gained a degree of acceptance within the auditing or information security community. Although several of them were not specifically designed to support information security, many of the processes within these practices help security professionals identify and implement controls to support confidentiality, integrity, and availability.

COSO [33]

The Committee of Sponsoring Organizations of the Treadway Commission (COSO) was formed in 1985 to sponsor the National Commission on Fraudulent Financial Reporting, which studied factors that lead to fraudulent financial reporting and produced recommendations for public companies, their auditors, the Securities Exchange Commission, and other regulators. COSO identifies five areas of internal control necessary to meet the financial reporting and disclosure objectives. These include:

1. Control environment
2. Risk assessment
3. Control activities
4. Information and Communication
5. Monitoring

The COSO internal control model has been adopted as a framework by some organizations working toward Sarbanes–Oxley Section 404 compliance.

ITIL [34]

The IT Infrastructure Library (ITIL) is a set of books published by the British government's Stationary Office between 1989 and 2014 to improve IT service management. The framework contains a set of best practices for IT core operational processes such as change, release, and configuration management, incident and problem management, capacity and availability management, and IT financial management. ITIL's primary contribution is showing how the controls can be implemented for the service management IT processes. These practices are useful as a starting point for tailoring to the specific needs of the organization, and the success of the practices depend upon the degree to which they are kept up to date and implemented on a daily basis. Achievement of these standards is an ongoing process, whereby the implementations need to be planned, supported by management, prioritized, and implemented in a phased approach.

COBIT [35]

Control Objectives for Information and Related Technology (COBIT) is published by the IT Governance Institute and integrates the following IT and risk frameworks:

- COBIT 5.0
- Val IT 2.0
- Risk IT
- IT Assurance Framework (ITAF)
- Business Model for Information Security (BMIS)

---

33 Please see the following for detailed information on COSO: http://www.coso.org/

34 Please see the following for detailed information on ITIL: http://www.itil-officialsite.com/

35 Please see the following for detailed information on COBIT: http://www.isaca.org/COBIT/Pages/default.aspx

The COBIT framework examines the effectiveness, efficiency, confidentiality, integrity, availability, compliance, and reliability aspects of the high-level control objectives. The framework provides an overall structure for information technology control and includes control objectives that can be utilized to determine effective security control objectives that are driven from the business needs. The Information Systems Audit and Control Association (ISACA) dedicates numerous resources to the support and understanding of COBIT.

ISO 27002:2013 (Formerly Known as ISO17799/BS7799)

The BS 7799/ISO 17799 standards can be used as a basis for developing security standards and security management practices. The U.K. Department of Trade and Industry (DTI) Code of Practice (CoP) for information security, which was developed with the support of the industry in 1993, became British Standard 7799 in 1995. BS 7799 was subsequently revised in 1999 to add certification and accreditation components, which became Part 2 of BS 7799. Part 1 of BS 7799 became ISO 17799 and was published as ISO 17799:2005 as the first international information security management standard by the International Organization for Standardization (ISO) and International Electrotechnical Commission (IEC). ISO 17799 was modified in June 2005 and renamed ISO/IEC 17799:2005. It was modified again and renamed ISO/IEC 27002:2005. This was again modified and updated as ISO/IEC 27002:2013.

It contains over 100 detailed information security controls based upon the following 14 areas:

1. Information security policy
2. Organization of information security
3. Human resources security
4. Asset management
5. Access control
6. Cryptography
7. Physical and environmental security
8. Operations security
9. Communications and operations management
10. Systems acquisition, development, and maintenance
11. Supplier relationships
12. Information security incident management
13. Information security aspects of business continuity management
14. Compliance

Risk Assessment Methodologies

NIST SP 800–30r1, 800-39, and 800–66r1 [36]

These methodologies are qualitative methods established for the use of the United States federal government and the global general public, but they are particularly used by regulated industries, such as healthcare. SP 800–66r1 is written specifically with HIPAA clients in mind (though it is possible to use this document for other regulated industries as well). 800-39 focuses on organizational risk management, and 800-30r1 focuses on information system risk management.

---

36 See the following for the most current versions of all NIST Special Publications: http://csrc.nist.gov/publications/PubsSPs.html

CRAMM

As described on the CRAMM (CCTA Risk Analysis and Management Method) website, residing on Siemens Insight Consulting's website, "CRAMM provides a staged and disciplined approach embracing both technical (e.g., IT hardware and software) and nontechnical (e.g., physical and human) aspects of security. To assess these components, CRAMM is divided into three stages: asset identification and valuation, threat and vulnerability assessment, and countermeasure selection and recommendation." [37] The implementation of this methodology is much like the other methods listed in this chapter.

Failure Modes and Effect Analysis [38]

Failure modes and effect analysis was born in hardware analysis, but it can be used for software and system analysis. It examines potential failures of each part or module and examines effects of failure at three levels:

1. Immediate level (part or module)
2. Intermediate level (process or package)
3. System-wide

The organization would then "collect total impact for failure of given modules to determine whether modules should be strengthened or further supported."

FRAP [39]

The Facilitated Risk Analysis Process (FRAP) makes a base assumption that a narrow risk assessment is the most efficient way to determine risk in a system, business segment, application, or process. The process allows organizations to prescreen applications, systems, or other subjects to determine if a risk analysis is needed. By establishing a unique prescreening process, organizations will be able to concentrate on subjects that truly need a formal risk analysis. The process has little outlay of capital and can be conducted by anyone with good facilitation skills.

OCTAVE [40]

As defined by its creator, Carnegie Mellon University's Software Engineering Institute, OCTAVE "is a self-directed information security risk evaluation." OCTAVE is defined as a situation where people from an organization manage and direct an information security risk evaluation for their organization. The organization's people direct risk evaluation activities and are responsible for making decisions about the organization's efforts to improve information security. In OCTAVE, an interdisciplinary team, called the analysis team, leads the evaluation.

Figure 1.12 illustrates that the OCTAVE approach is driven by operational risk and security practices. Technology is examined only in relation to security practices.

---

37   Please see the following for the quoted overview of the CRAMM methodology: http://www.cramm.com

38   Please see the following for detailed information on Failure Modes and Effects Analysis: http://asq.org/learn-about-quality/process-analysis-tools/overview/fmea.html

39   Please see the following for detailed information on FRAP: http://csrc.nist.gov/nissc/2000/proceedings/papers/304slide.pdf

40   Please see the following for detailed information on OCATVE: http://www.cert.org/octave/

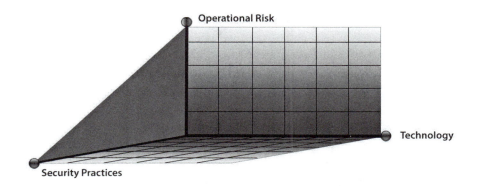

Figure 1.12 – **The Octave approach is driven by operational risk and security practices.**

The OCTAVE criteria are a set of principles, attributes, and outputs. Principles are the fundamental concepts driving the nature of the evaluation. They define the philosophy that shapes the evaluation process. For example, self-direction is one of the principles of OCTAVE. The concept of self-direction means that people inside the organization are in the best position to lead the evaluation and make decisions.

The requirements of the evaluation are embodied in the attributes and outputs. Attributes are the distinctive qualities, or characteristics, of the evaluation. They are the requirements that define the basic elements of the OCTAVE approach and what is necessary to make the evaluation a success from both the process and organizational perspectives. Attributes are derived from the OCTAVE principles. For example, one of the attributes of OCTAVE is that an interdisciplinary team (the analysis team) staffed by personnel from the organization leads the evaluation. The principle behind the creation of an analysis team is self-direction.

Finally, outputs are the required results of each phase of the evaluation. They define the outcomes that an analysis team must achieve during each phase. It is recognized that there is more than one set of activities that can produce the outputs of OCTAVE. It is for this reason that one does not specify one set of required activities.

Security Officers Management and Analysis Project (SOMAP)
The Security Officers Management and Analysis Project (SOMAP) is a Swiss nonprofit organization with a primary goal to run an open information security management project and maintain free and open tools and documentation under the GNU license. SOMAP has created a handbook and a guide and a risk tool to help with understanding risk management. In the SOMAP risk assessment guide, the qualitative and quantitative methodologies are discussed. SOMAP identifies the importance of choosing the best methodology based on the goals of the organization.

SOMAP illustrates risk assessment workflow as illustrated in *Figure 1.13* More information, including the handbook, guide, and available tools, can be obtained from http://www.somap.org.

Figure 1.13 – **The SOMAP Risk Assessment Workflow**

Spanning Tree Analysis

Spanning tree analysis "creates a 'tree' of all possible threats to or faults of the system. 'Branches' are general categories such as network threats, physical threats, component failures, etc." When conducting the risk assessment, organizations "prune 'branches' that do not apply."

VAR (Value at Risk)

In a paper presented by Jeevan Jaisingh and Jackie Rees of the Krannert Graduate School of Management at Purdue University, a new methodology for information security risk assessment titled Value at Risk (VAR) was introduced. The VAR methodology provides a summary of the worst loss due to a security breach over a target horizon. Many of the information security risk assessment tools are qualitative in nature and are not grounded in theory. VAR is identified as a theoretically based, quantitative measure of information security risk. Many believe that when organizations use VAR, they can achieve the best balance between risk and cost of implementing security controls. Many organizations identify an acceptable risk profile for their company. Determine the cost associated with this risk so that when the dollar value at risk for the organization exceeds that dollar amount, the organization can be alerted to the fact that an increased security investment is required. The VAR framework for information security risk assessment appears in *Figure 1.14.*

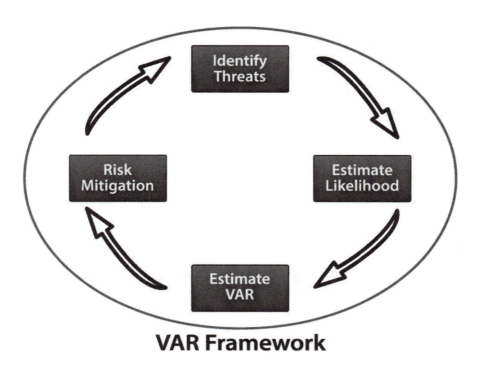

VAR Framework

Figure 1.14 – **The VAR Framework for information Security Risk Assessment**

Qualitative Risk Assessments

Organizations have the option of performing a risk assessment in one of two ways: qualitatively or quantitatively. Qualitative risk assessments produce valid results that are descriptive versus measurable. A qualitative risk assessment is typically conducted when:

- The risk assessors available for the organization have limited expertise in quantitative risk assessment; that is, assessors typically do not require as much experience in risk assessment when conducting a qualitative assessment.
- The time frame to complete the risk assessment is short.
- Implementation is typically easier.
- The organization does not have a significant amount of data readily available that can assist with the risk assessment, and as a result, descriptions, estimates, and ordinal scales (such as high, medium, and low) must be used to express risk.
- The assessors and team available for the organization are long-term employees and have significant experience with the business and critical systems.

The following methods are typically used during a qualitative risk assessment:

- Management approval to conduct the assessment must be obtained prior to assigning a team and conducting the work. Management is kept apprised during the process to continue to promote support for the effort.
- Once management approval has been obtained, a risk assessment team can be formed. Members may include staff from senior management, information security, legal or compliance, internal audit, HR, facilities/safety coordination, IT, and business unit owners, as appropriate.

The assessment team requests documentation, which may include, dependent upon scope:

- Information security program strategy and documentation
- Information security policies, procedures, guidelines, and baselines
- Information security assessments and audits
- Technical documentation, to include network diagrams, network device configurations and rule sets, hardening procedures, patching and configuration management plans and procedures, test plans, vulnerability assessment findings, change control and compliance information, and other documentation as needed
- Applications documentation, to include software development life cycle, change control and compliance information, secure coding standards, code promotion procedures, test plans, and other documentation as needed
- Business continuity and disaster recovery plans and corresponding documents, such as business impact analysis surveys
- Security incident response plan and corresponding documentation
- Data classification schemes and information handling and disposal policies and procedures
- Business unit procedures, as appropriate
- Executive mandates, as appropriate
- Other documentation, as needed

The team sets up interviews with organizational members for the purposes of identifying vulnerabilities, threats, and countermeasures within the environment. All levels of staff should be represented, to include:

- Senior management
- Line management
- Business unit owners
- Temporary or casual staff (i.e., interns)
- Business partners, as appropriate
- Remote workers, as appropriate
- Any other staff deemed appropriate to task

It is important to note that staff across all business units within scope for the risk assessment should be interviewed. It is not necessary to interview every staff person within a unit; a representative sample is usually sufficient.

Once interviews are completed, the analysis of the data gathered can be completed. This can include matching the threat to a vulnerability, matching threats to assets, determining how likely the threat is to exploit the vulnerability, and determining the impact to the organization in the event an exploit is successful. Analysis also includes a matching of current and planned countermeasures (i.e., protection) to the threat–vulnerability pair.

When the matching is completed, risk can be calculated. In a qualitative analysis, the product of likelihood and impact produces the level of risk. The higher the risk level, the more immediate is the need for the organization to address the issue, to protect the organization from harm.

Once risk has been determined, additional countermeasures can be recommended to minimize, transfer, or avoid the risk. When this is completed, the risk that is left over – after countermeasures have been applied to protect against the risk – is also calculated. This is the residual risk, or risk left over after countermeasure application.

Quantitative Risk Assessments

As an organization becomes more sophisticated in its data collection and retention and staff becomes more experienced in conducting risk assessments, an organization may find itself moving more toward quantitative risk assessment. The hallmark of a quantitative assessment is the numeric nature of the analysis. Frequency, probability, impact, countermeasure effectiveness, and other aspects of the risk assessment have a discrete mathematical value in a pure quantitative analysis.

Often, the risk assessment an organization conducts is a combination of qualitative and quantitative methods. Fully quantitative risk assessment may not be possible because there is always some subjective input present, such as the value of information. Value of information is often one of the most difficult factors to calculate.

It is clear to see the benefits, and the pitfalls, of performing a purely quantitative analysis. Quantitative analysis allows the assessor to determine whether the cost of the risk outweighs the cost of the countermeasure. Purely quantitative analysis, however, requires an enormous amount of time and must be performed by assessors with a significant amount of experience. Additionally, subjectivity is introduced because the metrics may also need to be applied to qualitative measures. If the organization has the time and manpower to complete a lengthy and complex accounting evaluation, this data may be used to assist with a quantitative analysis; however, most organizations are not in a position to authorize this level of work.

Three steps are undertaken in a quantitative risk assessment: initial management approval, construction of a risk assessment team, and the review of information currently available within the organization. Single Loss Expectancy (SLE) must be calculated to provide an estimate of loss. SLE is defined as the difference between the original value and the remaining value of an asset after a single exploit. The formula for calculating SLE is as follows:

SLE = *Asset Value (in $)* × *Exposure Factor*
(loss due to successful threat exploit, as a %)

Losses can include lack of availability of data assets due to data loss, theft, alteration, or denial of service (perhaps due to business continuity or security issues).

Next, the organization would calculate the Annualized Rate of Occurrence (ARO). ARO is an estimate of how often a threat will be successful in exploiting a vulnerability over the period of a year.

When this is completed, the organization calculates the Annualized Loss Expectancy (ALE). The ALE is a product of the yearly estimate for the exploit (ARO) and the loss in value of an asset after an SLE. The calculation follows:

ALE = *SLE x ARO*

Note that this calculation can be adjusted for geographical distances using the Local Annual Frequency Estimate (LAFE) or the Standard Annual Frequency Estimate (SAFE).

Given that there is now a value for SLE, it is possible to determine what the organization should spend, if anything, to apply a countermeasure for the risk in question. Remember that no countermeasure should be greater in cost than the risk it mitigates, transfers, or avoids. Countermeasure cost per year is easy and straightforward to calculate. It is simply the cost of the countermeasure divided by the years of its life (i.e., use within the organization). Finally, the organization is able to compare the cost of the risk versus the cost of the countermeasure and make some objective decisions regarding its countermeasure selection.

Identify Threats and Vulnerabilities

Identify Vulnerabilities

NIST Special Publication 800–30 Rev. 1, page 9, defines a vulnerability as "an inherent weakness in an information system, security procedures, internal controls, or implementation that could be exploited by a threat source."[41]

In the field, it is common to identify vulnerabilities as they are related to people, processes, data, technology, and facilities. Examples of vulnerabilities could include:

■ Absence of a receptionist, mantrap, or other physical security mechanism upon entrance to a facility

■ Inadequate integrity checking in financial transaction software

■ Neglecting to require users to sign an acknowledgment of their responsibilities with regard to security, as well as an acknowledgment that they have read, understand, and agree to abide by the organization's security policies

■ Patching and configuration of an organization's information systems are done on an *ad hoc* basis and, therefore, are neither documented nor up to date

Unlike a risk assessment, vulnerability assessments tend to focus on the technology aspects of an organization, such as the network or applications. Data gathering for vulnerability assessments typically includes the use of software tools, which provide volumes of raw data for the organization and the assessor. This raw data includes information on the type of vulnerability, its location, its severity (typically based on an ordinal scale of high, medium, and low), and sometimes a discussion of the findings.

Assessors who conduct vulnerability assessments must be expert in properly reading, understanding, digesting, and presenting the information obtained from a vulnerability assessment to a multidisciplinary, sometimes nontechnical audience. Why? Data that are obtained from the scanning may not truly be a vulnerability. False-positives are findings that are reported when no vulnerability truly exists in the organization (i.e., something that is occurring in the environment has been flagged as an exposure when it really is not); likewise, false-negatives are vulnerabilities that should have been reported and are not. This sometimes occurs when tools are inadequately "tuned" to the task, or the vulnerability in question exists outside the scope of the assessment.

Some findings are correct and appropriate but require significant interpretation for the organization to make sense of what has been discovered and how to proceed in remediation (i.e., fixing the problem). This task is typically suited for an experienced assessor or a team whose members have real-world experience with the tool in question. It is important for the security practitioner to understand that prioritization of the findings and assessment of their potential impact needs to be done by one or more qualified individuals, as opposed to attempting to automate this process. The reason for this is that many automated tools will assign ratings or rankings that are not consistent with the organization's view, based on the BIA. For instance, if the organization interprets vulnerability "A" as a low impact, low priority vulnerability due to the outcome of the BIA, but the tool ranks vulnerability "A" as a high priority, medium impact vulnerability, then resources may be inappropriately tasked to remediate a vulnerability that is not important to the organization.

---

41 http://csrc.nist.gov/publications/nistpubs/800-30-rev1/sp800_30_r1.pdf

Identify Threats

The National Institute of Standards and Technology (NIST), in Special Publication (SP) 800–30 Rev. 1, pages 7 – 8, defines threats as "any circumstance or event with the potential to adversely impact organizational operations and assets, individuals, other organizations, or the Nation through an information system via unauthorized access, destruction, disclosure, or modification of information, and/or denial of service". In the OCTAVE framework, threats are identified as the source from which assets in the organization are secured (or protected).

NIST, in Special Publication (SP) 800-30 Rev.1, page 8, defines a threat-source as either:
   1. Intent and method targeted at the intentional exploitation of a vulnerability or
   2. A situation and method that may accidentally trigger a vulnerability.

Threat sources can be grouped into a few categories. Each category can be expanded with specific threats, as follows:

   - **Human** – Malicious outsider, malicious insider, (bio) terrorist, saboteur, spy, political or competitive operative, loss of key personnel, errors made by human intervention, cultural issues.
   - **Natural** – Fire, flood, tornado, hurricane, snow storm, earthquake.
   - **Technical** – Hardware failure, software failure, malicious code, unauthorized use, use of emerging services, such as wireless, new technologies.
   - **Physical** – Closed-circuit TV failure due to faulty components, perimeter defense failure.
   - **Environmental** – Hazardous waste, biological agent, utility failure.
   - **Operational** – A process (manual or automated) that affects confidentiality, integrity, or availability.

Many specific threats exist within each category; the organization will identify those sources as the assessment progresses, utilizing information available from groups such as (ISC)² and SANS and from government agencies such as the National Institute of Standards and Technology (NIST), the Federal Financial Institutions Examination Council (FFIEC), the Department of Health and Human Services (HHS), and others.

Selecting Tools and Techniques for Risk Assessment

It is expected that an organization will make a selection of the risk assessment methodology, tools, and resources (including people) that best fit its culture, personnel capabilities, budget, and timeline. Many automated tools, including proprietary tools, exist in the field. Although automation can make the data analysis, dissemination, and storage of results easier, it is not a required part of risk assessment. If an organization is planning to purchase or build automated tools for this purpose, it is highly recommended that this decision be based on an appropriate timeline and resource skill sets for creation, implementation, maintenance, and monitoring of the tool(s) and data stored within, long term.

Risk Assessment/Analysis

Risk assessment processes may vary between frameworks and industries, but the basic approach and formulas remain largely the same. Risk is a function of threats, vulnerabilities, likelihood, and impact. Risk assessments may also be qualitative, quantitative, or a hybrid of the two. Qualitative risk assessments define risk in relative terms such as "high," "moderate," or "low". Quantitative risk assessments attempt to provide specific measurements and impacts with dollar figures representing the expected loss. In many cases, these methods are combined to get the best of both worlds.

Likelihood Determination

It is important to note that likelihood is a component of a qualitative risk assessment. Likelihood, along with impact, determines risk. Likelihood can be measured by the capabilities of the threat and the presence or absence of countermeasures. Initially, organizations that do not have trending data available may use an ordinal scale, labeled high, medium, and low, to score likelihood rankings. Another method is presented in *Figure 1.15(a) and (b)*.

Once a value on the ordinal scale has been chosen, the selection can be mapped to a numeric value for computation of risk. For example, the selection of high can be mapped to the value of 1. Medium can likewise be mapped to 0.5, and low can be mapped to 0.1. As the scale expands, the numeric assignments will become more targeted.

Determination of Impact

Impact can be ranked much the same way as likelihood. The main difference is that the impact scale is expanded and depends upon definitions rather than ordinal selections. Definitions of impact to an organization often include loss of life, loss of dollars, loss of prestige, loss of market share, and other facets. Organizations need to take sufficient time to define and assign impact definitions for high, medium, low, or any other scale terms that are chosen.

Likelihood and Consequences Rating

Likelihood		Consequence	
Rare *(Very Low)*	E	**Insignificant** *(Low - No Business Impact)*	1
Unlikely *(Low)*	D	**Minor** *(Low - Minor Business Impact, some loss of confidence)*	2
Moderate *(Medium)*	C	**Moderate** *(Medium - Business is Interrupted, loss of confidence)*	3
Likely *(High)*	B	**Major** *(High - Business is Disrupted, major loss of confidence)*	4
Almost Certain *(Very High)*	A	**Catastrophic** *(High - Business cannot continue)*	5

Figure 1.15(a) – **Likelihood Qualification – How to Arrive at a Likelihood Rating**

How to Qualify Likelihood	Rating
Skill *High Skill Level Required ⇨ Low or No Skill Required*	*1=High Skill Required ⇨* *5=No Skill Required*
Ease of Access *Very Difficult to Do ⇨ Very Simple to Do*	*1=Very Difficult ⇨ 5=Simple*
Incentive *High Incentive ⇨ Low Incentive*	*1=Low or No Incentive ⇨* *5=High Incentive*
Resource *Requires Expensive or Rare Equipment ⇨ No Resources Required*	*1=Rare/Expensive ⇨* *5=No Resource Required*
Total *Add Rating and Divide by 4*	*1=E 2=D 3=C 4=B 5=A*

*Figure 1.15(b) –***Qualified Likelihood Rating**

Once the terms are defined, impact can be calculated. If an exploit has the potential to result in the loss of life (such as a bombing or bioterrorist attack), then the ranking will always be high. In general, groups such as the National Security Agency view loss of life as the highest-priority risk in any organization. As such, it may be assigned the top value in the impact scale. An example: 51 to 100 = high; 11 to 50 = medium; 0 to 10 = low.

Determination of Risk

Risk is determined as the byproduct of likelihood and impact. For example, if an exploit has a likelihood of 1 (high) and an impact of 100 (high), the risk would be 100.[42] As a result, 100 would be the highest exploit ranking available. These scenarios (high likelihood, high impact) should merit immediate attention from the organization.

As the risk calculations are completed, they can be prioritized for attention, as required. Note that not all risks will receive the same level of attention, based on the organization's risk tolerance and its strategy for mitigation, transfer, or avoidance of risk. *Figure 1.16* shows another view of risk.

---

42   This can be represented by the following formula: (Likelihood * Impact = Risk or L*I = R)

	Consequence				
Likelihood	*Insignificant*	*Minor*	*Moderate*	*Major*	*Catastrophic*
	1	*2*	*3*	*4*	*5*
A (Almost Certain)	H	H	E	E	E
B (Likely)	M	H	H	E	E
C (Possible)	L	M	H	E	E
D (Unlikely)	L	L	M	H	E
E (Rare)	L	L	M	H	H
E	**Extreme Risk:** *Immediate action required to mitigate the risk or decide to not proceed*				
H	**High Risk:** *Action should be taken to compensate for the risk*				
M	**Moderate Risk:** *Action should be taken to monitor the risk*				
L	**Low Risk:** *Routine acceptance of the risk*				

Figure 1.16 – **Rating Likelihood and Consequences**

Risk Avoidance

Risk avoidance is the practice of coming up with alternatives so that the risk in question is not realized. For example, have you ever heard a friend or parents of a friend complain about the costs of insuring an underage driver? How about the risks that many of these children face as they become mobile? Some of these families will decide that the child in question will not be allowed to drive the family car but will rather wait until he or she is of legal age (i.e., 18 years of age) before committing to owning, insuring, and driving a motor vehicle.

In this case, the family has chosen to avoid the risks (and any associated benefits) associated with an underage driver, such as poor driving performance or the cost of insurance for the child. Although this choice may be available for some situations, it is not available for all. Imagine a global retailer who, knowing the risks associated with doing business on the Internet, decides to avoid the practice. This decision will likely cost the company a significant amount of its revenue (if, indeed, the company has products or services that consumers wish to purchase). In addition, the decision may require the company to build or lease a site in each of the locations, globally, for which it wishes to continue business. This could have a catastrophic effect on the company's ability to continue business operations.

Risk Transfer

Risk transfer is the practice of passing on the risk in question to another entity, such as an insurance company. Let us look at one of the examples that were presented above in a different way. The family is evaluating whether to permit an underage driver to use the family car. The family decides that it is important for the youth to be mobile, so it transfers the financial risk of a youth being in an accident to the insurance company, which provides the family with auto insurance.

It is important to note that the transfer of risk may be accompanied by a cost. This is certainly true for the insurance example presented earlier, and it can be seen in other insurance instances, such as liability insurance for a vendor or the insurance taken out by companies to protect against hardware and software theft or destruction. This may also be true if an organization must purchase and implement security controls in order to make their organization less desirable to attack.

It is important to remember that not all risk can be transferred. While financial risk is simple to transfer through insurance, reputational risk may almost never be fully transferred. If a banking system is breached, there may be a cost in the money lost, but what about the reputation of the bank as a secure place to store assets? How about the stock price of the bank and the customers the bank may lose due to the breach? Another area that security professionals need to consider with regards to risk transfer is cloud services. Many companies assume that because of contractual hosting agreements with the cloud service provider, that they are in effect transferring the risks associated with managing and maintaining the platform and infrastructure to the provider. While elements of the risks are being transferred and assumed by the provider, elements of the risk are not, and they still are the responsibility of the customer.

Risk Mitigation

Risk mitigation is the practice of the elimination of or the significant decrease in the level of risk presented. Examples of risk mitigation can be seen in everyday life and are readily apparent in the information technology world.

For example, to lessen the risk of exposing personal and financial information that is highly sensitive and confidential, organizations put countermeasures in place, such as firewalls, intrusion detection/prevention systems, and other mechanisms, to deter malicious outsiders from accessing this highly sensitive information. In the underage driver example, risk mitigation could take the form of driver education for the youth or establishing a policy not allowing the young driver to use a cell phone while driving or not letting the youth of a certain age have more than one friend in the car as a passenger at any given time.

Risk Acceptance

In some cases, it may be prudent for an organization to simply accept the risk that is presented in certain scenarios. Risk acceptance is the practice of accepting certain risk(s), typically based on a business decision that may also weigh the cost versus the benefit of dealing with the risk in another way.

For example, an executive may be confronted with risks identified during the course of a risk assessment for his or her organization. These risks have been prioritized by high, medium, and low impact to the organization. The executive notes that in order to mitigate or transfer the low-level risks, significant costs could be involved. Mitigation might involve the hiring of additional highly skilled personnel and the purchase of new hardware, software, and office equipment, while transference of the risk to an insurance company would require premium payments. The executive then further notes that minimal impact to the organization would occur if any of the reported low-level threats were realized. Therefore, he or she (rightly) concludes that it is wiser for the organization to forego the costs and accept the risk. In the young driver example, risk acceptance could be based on the observation that the youngster has demonstrated the responsibility and maturity to warrant the parent's trust in his or her judgment.

The decision to accept risk should not be taken lightly nor without appropriate information to justify the decision. The cost versus benefit, the organization's willingness to monitor the risk long term, and the impact it has on the outside world's view of the organization must all be taken into account when deciding to accept risk. When one is accepting risk, the business decision to do so must be documented.

It is important to note that there are organizations that may also track containment of risk. Containment lessens the impact to an organization when an exposure is exploited through distribution of critical assets (i.e., people, processes, data, technologies, and facilities).

Risk Assignment

"Who is assigned and responsible for risk?" is a very serious question, with an intriguing answer: It depends. Ultimately, the organization (i.e., senior management or stakeholders) owns the risks that are present during operation of the company. Senior management, however, may rely on business unit (or data) owners or custodians to assist in identification of risks so that they can be mitigated, transferred, or avoided. The organization also likely expects that the owners and custodians will minimize or mitigate risk as they work, based upon policies, procedures, and regulations present in the environment. If expectations are not met, consequences such as disciplinary action, termination, or prosecution will usually result.

Here is an example: A claims processor is working with a medical healthcare claim submitted to his organization for completion. The claim contains electronic personally identifiable healthcare information for a person the claims processor knows. Although he has acknowledged his responsibilities for the protection of the data, he calls his mother, who is a good friend of the individual who filed the claim. His mother in turn calls multiple people, who in turn contact the person who filed the claim. The claimant contacts an attorney, and the employee and company are sued for the intentional breach of information.

Several things are immediately apparent from this example. The employee is held immediately accountable for his action in intentionally exploiting a vulnerability (i.e., sensitive information was inappropriately released, according to United States federal law – Health Insurance Portability and Accountability Act of 1996 (HIPAA)). While he was custodian of the data (and a co-owner of the risk), the court also determined that the company was co-owner of the risk and hence also bore the responsibility for compensating the victim (in this example, the claimant).

Once the findings from the assessment have been consolidated and the calculations have been completed, it is time to present a finalized report to senior management. This can be done in a written report or through a presentation. Any written reports should include an acknowledgment to the participants, a summary of the approach taken, findings in detail (in either tabulated or graphical form), recommendations for remediation of the findings, and a summary. Organizations are encouraged to develop their own formats, to make the most of the activity as well as the information collected and analyzed.

Countermeasure Selection

One of the most important steps for the organization is to appropriately select countermeasures to apply to risks in the environment. Many aspects of the countermeasure must be considered to ensure that they are a proper fit to the task. Considerations for countermeasures or controls include:

- Accountability (can be held responsible)
- Auditability (can it be tested?)
- Trusted source (source is known)
- Independence (self-determining)
- Consistently applied
- Cost-effective
- Reliable
- Independence from other countermeasures (no overlap)
- Ease of use
- Automation
- Sustainable
- Secure
- Protects confidentiality, integrity, and availability of assets
- Can be "backed out" in event of issue
- Creates no additional issues during operation
- Leaves no residual data from its function

From this list it is clear that countermeasures must be above reproach when deployed to protect an organization's assets.

It is important to note that once risk assessment is completed and there is a list of remediation activities to be undertaken, an organization must ensure that it has personnel with appropriate capabilities to implement the remediation activities as well as to maintain and support them. This may require the organization to provide additional training opportunities to personnel involved in the design, deployment, maintenance, and support of security mechanisms within the environment.

In addition, it is crucial that appropriate policies with detailed procedures and standards that correspond to each policy item be created, implemented, maintained, monitored, and enforced throughout the environment. The organization should assign resources that can be accountable to each task and track tasks over time, reporting progress to senior management and allowing time for appropriate approvals during this process.

Implementation of Risk Countermeasures

A security professional, security architect, and security practitioner all go into a bar …

Sound silly? Of course it does; you know why? Because they would never have gone into the bar before sending in an intern to see if it was safe!!!

Now, the reality of that silly story is actually important, even though it is often times overlooked by many of us. We all know that it is common sense to "look before you leap", and yet many times we find ourselves in situations that could have been made much better, or avoided all together, if we had only done exactly that.

When a security architect sits down to start pondering how to design the enterprise security architecture, he or she should be thinking about many things, such as what framework(s) should I use as points of reference? What business issues do I need to take into account? Who are my stakeholders? Why am I only addressing this and not that area of the business? How will I be able to integrate this system design into the overall architecture? Where will the SPOFs be in this architecture? The challenge for the architect is to try and coordinate all of those streams of thought and channel them into a process that will let him or her design a coherent and strong enterprise security architecture.

When a security practitioner sits down to start deploying the enterprise security architecture, he or she should be thinking about many things, such as what tool(s) should I use to set up and deploy these systems? Who are the end-users of this system going to be? Why am I only being given "x" amount of time to get this done? How will I be able to integrate this system design into my existing network? Where will I manage this from? The challenge for the practitioner is to try and coordinate all of those streams of thought and channel them into a process that will let him or her deploy a coherent and strong enterprise security architecture.

When a security professional sits down to start pondering how to manage the enterprise security architecture, he or she should be thinking about many things, such as what are the metrics that I have available to manage these systems? Who do I need to partner with to ensure successful operation of the system? Why are we not addressing this or that concern? How will I be able to communicate the appropriate level of information regarding the system to each of my user audiences? Where will I find the time to be able to do this? The challenge for the professional is to try and coordinate all of those streams of thought and channel them into a process that will let him or her manage a coherent and strong enterprise security architecture.

All three security actors are vital, and each contributes to the success of the enterprise security architecture, or its failure, in his or her own ways. However, all three also share many things in common. They all need to be focused on doing their job so that the others can do theirs. They all need to ensure that the communication regarding their part of the puzzle is bi-directional, clear, and concise with regards to issues and concerns with the architecture. Most importantly, they all need to use common sense to assess and evaluate not just the portions of the architecture that they are responsible for but all of the actions that are engaged in to interact with the entire architecture. It is the use of common sense that often is the difference between success and failure in anything, and security is no different.

For all three security actors, common sense will mean several things: situational awareness, paying attention to details, not assuming, etc. It will also mean that they must become experts at understanding and managing risk; each in his or her own area but, at the same time, with an eye towards a common goal. That goal is to manage risk in such a way that it does not negatively impact the enterprise. That goal is shared by everyone that interacts with the architecture at any level for any reason in some way. The end-users need to use systems in such a way that they do not expose them to threats and vulnerabilities due to their behavior. The system administrators need to ensure that the systems are kept up to date with regards to security patching to ensure that all known vulnerabilities are being mitigated within the system. Senior management needs to provide the appropriate resources to ensure that the systems can be maintained as needed to ensure safe operating conditions for all users.

The identification and management of risk through the deployment of countermeasures is the common ground that all system users, regardless of role or function, share in the enterprise. Let's look at some examples:

Mobile Applications
- ■ **Risks** – lost or stolen devices, malware, multi-communication channel exposure, weak authentication.
- ■ **Countermeasures** – meeting mobile security standards, tailoring security audits to assess mobile application vulnerabilities, secure provisioning, control and monitoring of application data on personal devices.

Web 2.0
- ■ **Risks** – securing social media, content management, security of third-party technologies and services.
- ■ **Countermeasures** – security API, CAPTCHA, unique security tokens, and transaction approval workflows.

Cloud Computing Services
- ■ **Risks** – multi-tenant deployments, security of cloud computing deployments, third-party risk, data breaches, denial of service, and malicious insiders.
- ■ **Countermeasures** – cloud computing security assessment, compliance-audit assessment on cloud computing providers, due diligence, encryption in transit and at rest, and monitoring.

Each of the security actors will have to identify and understand the risks he or she faces within his or her area of the enterprise and move to deploy countermeasures that are appropriate to address them. The thing that will be most important to ensure the relative success of these individual efforts is the ability to document and communicate effectively ALL of the efforts being undertaken by area and platform in order to ensure that as complete a picture as possible of the current state of risk within the enterprise is always available. This "risk inventory" should be made available through some form of centrally managed enterprise content management platform that will allow for secure remote access when required. It should also deploy a strong version control and change management functionality to ensure that the information contained within it is accurate and up to date at all times. Access control needs to be integrated into this system as well to ensure that role- or job-based access can be granted as appropriate to users.

Types of Controls

In the development of an access control architecture for an enterprise, it is necessary to fully understand the different categories and types of potential controls. This section will describe those different categories and discuss how each fits into the overall access control universe. This will also establish a foundation for later discussion on access control technology, practices, and processes.

There are literally hundreds of different access approaches, control methods, and technologies, both in the physical world and in the virtual electronic world. Each method addresses a different type of access control or a specific access need. For example, access control solutions may incorporate identification and authentication mechanisms, filters, rules, rights, logging and monitoring, policy, and a plethora of other controls. However, despite the diversity of access control methods, all access control systems can be categorized into seven primary categories. The seven main categories of access control are:

1. **Directive** – Controls designed to specify acceptable rules of behavior within an organization
2. **Deterrent** – Controls designed to discourage people from violating security directives
3. **Preventive** – Controls implemented to prevent a security incident or information breach
4. **Compensating** – Controls implemented to substitute for the loss of primary controls and mitigate risk down to an acceptable level
5. **Detective** – Controls designed to signal a warning when a security control has been breached
6. **Corrective** – Controls implemented to remedy circumstance, mitigate damage, or restore controls
7. **Recovery** – Controls implemented to restore conditions to normal after a security incident

Figure 1.17 shows a continuum of controls relative to the timeline of a security incident:

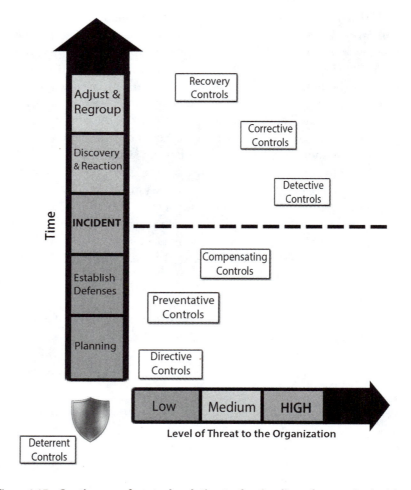

Figure 1.17 – **Continuum of controls relative to the timeline of a security incident**

Directive Controls

Directive controls, sometimes referred to as administrative controls, provide guidance to personnel as to the expected behavior with respect to security within the organization. Directive controls provide users with the general guidelines they must follow if they are to be permitted access to information or systems. Directive controls are not only applicable to an organization's employees, but contractors, guests, vendors, and anyone else who will have access to the organization's information systems must additionally abide by them.

The most common examples of directive controls are the organization's security policies and procedures. These documents provide the basis for information security throughout the organization and provide personnel with the model that must be adhered to as they perform their work. Although directive controls are generally implemented in the form of documented statements of organizational intent, they should not be considered optional or modifiable by organization personnel.

Directive controls have the weight of law within the organization and should be as strongly followed and enforced as any technical or procedural limitation. Many organizations compile their directive controls into a single acceptable use policy (AUP). The AUP provides a concise listing of the proper (and, in many cases improper) procedures, behaviors, and processes that all personnel must follow in order to gain and maintain access to information and systems within the organization. It is considered a best practice for all employees to agree to and sign the AUP before being granted access to any organizational resource. If the employee is unable (or unwilling) to abide by the terms of the AUP, no access will be granted. Many organizations require their employees to sign the AUP annually, either as part of the regular security awareness training or as part of the annual performance review process.

Deterrent Controls

Access controls act as a deterrent to threats and attacks by the simple fact that the existence of the control is enough to keep some potential attackers from attempting to circumvent the control. This is often because the effort required to circumvent the control is far greater than the potential reward if the attacker is successful, or, conversely, the negative implications of a failed attack (or getting caught) outweigh the benefits of success. For example, if one forces the identification and authentication of a user, service, or application, and all that it implies, the potential for incidents associated with the system is significantly reduced because an attacker will fear association with the incident. If there are no controls for a given access path, the number of incidents and the potential impact become infinite. Controls inherently reduce exposure to risk by applying oversight for a process. This oversight acts as a deterrent, curbing an attacker's appetite in the face of probable repercussions.

The best example of a deterrent control is demonstrated by employees and their propensity to intentionally perform unauthorized functions, leading to unwanted events. When users begin to understand that by authenticating into a system to perform a function, their activities are logged and monitored, it reduces the likelihood they will attempt such an action. Many threats are based on the anonymity of the threat agents, and any potential for identification and association with their actions is avoided at all costs. It is this fundamental reason why access controls are the key target of circumvention by attackers. Deterrents also take the form of potential punishment if users do something unauthorized. For example, if the organization policy specifies that an employee installing an unauthorized wireless access point will be fired, that should deter most employees from installing wireless access points.

The effect deterrent controls have on a potential attacker will vary with both the type of control and the motivation of the attacker. For example, many organizations post a warning message to computer users during the login process indicating that their activities may be monitored. While this may deter a casual user from performing unauthorized activities, it will not stop a determined attacker from his goals. Likewise, implementing a multifactor authentication mechanism on an application will greatly reduce system compromises through such mechanisms as password guessing, but a sophisticated attacker may then turn to the use of a vulnerability scanning tool to determine if the system can be compromised through a host or network vulnerability. As the sophistication and the determination of an attacker rises, so does the sophistication and cost of an effective deterrent to prevent that attacker from attempting his attack.

Preventative Controls

Preventative access controls keep a user from performing some activity or function. Preventative controls differ from deterrent controls in that the control is not optional and cannot (easily) be bypassed. Deterrent controls work on the theory that it is easier to obey the control rather than to risk the consequences of bypassing the control. In other words, the power for action resides with the user (or the attacker). Preventative controls place the power of action with the system - obeying the control is not optional. The only way to bypass the control is to find a flaw in the control's design or implementation.

Compensating Controls

Compensating controls are introduced when the existing capabilities of a system do not support the requirement of a policy. Compensating controls can be technical, procedural, or managerial. Although an existing system may not support the required controls, there may exist other technology or processes that can supplement the existing environment, closing the gap in controls, meeting policy requirements, and reducing overall risk. For example, the access control policy may state that the authentication process must be encrypted when performed over the Internet. Adjusting an application to natively support encryption for authentication purposes may be too costly. Secure Socket Layer (SSL), an encryption protocol, can be employed and layered on top of the authentication process to support the policy statement. Other examples include a separation of duties environment, which offers the capability to isolate certain tasks to compensate for technical limitations in the system and ensure the security of transactions. In addition, management processes, such as authorization, supervision, and administration, can be used to compensate for gaps in the access control environment.

Keep in mind that it is not possible to completely eliminate the risk in a given area while still allowing functionality. The use of compensating controls allows an organization to reduce that risk down to a level that is acceptable, or at least more manageable. Finally, compensating controls can be temporary solutions to accommodate a short-term change or support the evolution of a new application, business development, or major project. Changes and temporary additions to access controls may be necessary for application testing, data center consolidation efforts, or even to support a brief business relationship with another company.

The critical points to consider when addressing compensating controls are:

- Do not compromise stated policy requirements.
- Ensure that the compensating controls do not adversely affect risk or increase exposure to threats.
- Manage all compensating controls in accordance with established practices and policies.
- Compensating controls designated as temporary should be removed after they have served their purpose, and another, more permanent control should be established.

Detective Controls

Detective controls are those that provide notification to appropriate personnel if the deterrent, preventative, and compensating controls are not able to thwart an attack. Detective controls warn when something has happened and are the earliest point in the post-incident timeline.

Access controls are a deterrent to threats and can be aggressively utilized to prevent harmful incidents through the application of least privilege. However, the detective nature of access controls can provide significant visibility into the access environment and help organizations manage their access strategy and related security risk. As mentioned previously, strongly managed access privileges provided to an authenticated user offer the ability to reduce the risk exposure of the enterprise's assets by limiting the capabilities that authenticated user has. However, there are few options to control what a user can perform once privileges are provided. For example, if a user is provided write access to a file and that file is damaged, altered, or otherwise negatively impacted (either deliberately or unintentionally), the use of applied access controls will offer visibility into the transaction. The control environment can be established to log activity regarding the identification, authentication, authorization, and use of privileges on a system. This can be used to detect the occurrence of errors, the attempts to perform an unauthorized action, or to validate when provided credentials were exercised. The logging system as a detective device provides evidence of actions (both successful and unsuccessful) and tasks that were executed by authorized users.

Detection aspects of access control can range from evidentiary, such as post incident investigations, to real-time alerting of inappropriate activities. This philosophy can be applied to many different characteristics of the security environment. Access detection can be triggered by intrusion detection systems (IDSs), virus controls, applications, Web filtering, network operations, administration, logs and audit trails, and security management systems. Visibility into the environment is a key factor in ensuring a comprehensive security posture and the ability to promptly detect problems in the environment.

Corrective Controls

When a security incident occurs, elements within the security infrastructure may require corrective actions. Corrective controls are actions that seek to alter the security posture of an environment to correct any deficiencies and return the environment to a secure state. A security incident signals the failure of one or more directive, deterrent, preventative, or compensating controls. The detective controls may have triggered an alarm or notification, but now the corrective controls must work to stop the incident in its tracks. Corrective controls can take many forms, all depending on the particular situation at hand or the particular security failure that needs to be addressed.

The sheer number of corrective actions possible makes them difficult to successfully quantify. They can range from "quick fix" changes like new firewall rules, router access control list updates, and access policy changes to more long-term infrastructure changes such as the introduction of certificates for wireless 802.1x authentication, movement from single-factor to multifactor authentication for remote access, or the introduction of smart cards for authentication. The difficulty in quantification is founded on the fact that access controls are universal throughout the environment. Nevertheless, it is important that a consistent and comprehensive management capability exists that can coordinate and employ corrective changes throughout the enterprise to enable policy compliance.

Recovery Controls

Any changes to the access control environment, whether in the face of a security incident or to offer temporary compensating controls, need to be accurately reinstated and returned to normal operations. There are several situations that may affect access controls, their applicability, status, or management. Events can include system outages, attacks, project changes, technical demands, administrative gaps, and full-blown disaster situations. For example, if an application is not correctly installed or deployed, it may adversely affect controls placed on system files or even have default administrative accounts unknowingly implemented upon install. Additionally, an employee may be transferred, quit, or be on temporary leave that may affect policy requirements regarding separation of duties. An attack on systems may have resulted in the implantation of a Trojan horse program, potentially exposing private user information, such as credit card information and financial data. In all of these cases, an undesirable situation must be rectified as quickly as possible and controls returned to normal operations.

Access Control Types

The access control categories discussed in the previous section serve to classify different access control methods based on where they fit into the access control time continuum shown in *Figure 1.17*. However, another way to classify and categorize access controls is by their method of implementation. For any of the access control categories, the controls in those categories can be implemented in one of three ways, as:

- **Administrative Controls** – Sometimes called Management Controls, these are procedures implemented to define the roles, responsibilities, policies, and administrative functions needed to manage the control environment.
- **Logical (Technical) Controls** – These are electronic hardware and software solutions implemented to control access to information and information networks.
- **Physical Controls** – These are controls to protect the organization's people and physical environment, such as locks, fire management, gates, and guards. Physical controls may be called "operational controls" in some contexts.

The categories discussed earlier can be mapped against these three access control types to demonstrate various control examples and options as shown in *Figure 1.18*.

	Administrative	*Technical*	*Physical*
Directive	- Policy	- Configuration Standards	- Authorized Personnel Only Signs - Traffic Lights
Deterrent	- Policy	- Warning Banner	- Beware of Dog Sign
Preventative	- User Registration Procedure	- Password Based Login	- Fence
Detective	- Review Violation Reports	- Logs	- Sentry - CCTV
Corrective	- Termination	- Unplug, isolate, and terminate connection	- Fire Extinguisher
Recovery	- DR Plan	- Backups	- Rebuild
Compensating	- Supervision - Job Rotation - Logging	- CCTV - Keystroke Logging	- Layered Defense

Figure 1.18 – **Control examples for types and categories**

The figure shows how elements of an access control solution or device can be represented in the form of categories to ensure that all aspects that define the capabilities of access control are met. The value of this matrix is that it can be applied by the security architect, practitioner, and professional to the entire organization, a specific domain within the environment, or a single access path, such as employee remote access.

Physical Controls
Physical security covers a broad spectrum of controls to protect the physical assets (primarily the people) in an organization. Physical controls are sometimes referred to as "operational" controls in some risk management frameworks. These controls range from doors, locks, and windows to environment controls, construction standards, and guards. Typically, physical security is based on the notion of establishing security zones or concentric areas within a facility that require increased security as you get closer to the valuable assets inside the facility. Security zones are the physical representation of the defense-in-depth principle. Typically, security zones are associated with rooms, offices, floors, or smaller elements, such as a cabinet or storage locker. The design of the physical security controls within the facility must take into account the protection of the asset as well as the individuals working in that area. For example, the fire control and suppression systems must account for the health and safety of personnel in potential fire zones. One must consider fires, floods, explosions, civil unrest, or other man-made or natural disasters when planning the physical layout of a facility. Emergency strategies must be included in the physical controls to accommodate the safe exiting of personnel and adherence to safety standards or regulations. Adequate exits and emergency evacuation routes

must be available in all areas, and sensitive areas or information must be able to be secured quickly in case those areas must be evacuated. Human safety is the most important priority in all decisions regarding physical security.

The physical access controls in each zone should be commensurate with the level of security required for that zone. For example, an employee may work in the data center of a large financial institution – a very sensitive area. The employee may have a special badge to access the parking lot and the main entrance where guards are posted and recording access. To access the specific office area, he or she may need a different badge and PIN to dis-engage the door lock. Finally, to enter the data center, he or she must combine the card and PIN with a biometric device that must be employed to gain access. As one gets closer and closer to the valuable asset – the data center – the protections get progressively stronger.

The most prevalent and visible aspect of physical security is often the perimeter of a facility. A typical perimeter should be without gaps or areas that can be easily broken into or entered undetected. The perimeter starts with the surrounding grounds. Hills, ditches, retention walls, fences, concrete posts, and high curbs can all act as deterrents to attack. Depending on the sensitivity of the facility, guards, attack dogs, and other aggressive measures can be applied. The construction of the facility may include special walls, reinforced barriers, and even certain foliage strategically placed near doors, windows, and utilities. All this can be augmented by cameras, alarms, locks, and other essential controls.

However, security is not the only consideration when designing a facility. The overall design of the facility must balance the function of the building with the security needs of the organization. For example, a company's headquarters building will need good security to protect private areas, stored records, and personnel against malicious acts. But it must also serve as the company's face to the public and present a welcoming atmosphere to visitors. Protections at such a facility might include guards at the front desk (unarmed), locked doors, and badge readers to restrict entry. However, the company's data center facility would most likely have much more stringent measures to keep intruders out, such as a tall razor-wire fence, armed guards, biometric entry controls, and mantrap doors. As with all architecture, form follows function.

If an organization leases space in a facility (as opposed to owning the facility), there may be limits on what modifications can be made to accommodate the company's security needs. Any special security requirements must be negotiated with the facility's owner before the lease agreement is signed. If the organization is sharing the facility with other tenants, additional thought must be given to security and access control measures because much of the facility (those portions not occupied by the organization) will be accessible to non-organization personnel. Areas of special concern to the information security professional will include heating ventilation and air conditioning (HVAC) equipment, electrical power panels, and wiring closets – all of which may be readily accessible to contractors and other tenants of the facility.

Finally, the oversight of physical controls must adhere to the same basic principles of other forms of controls: separation of duties and least privilege. For example, it may be necessary to segment the job role of various guards to ensure that no single point of failure or collusion potentially allows threat agents to enter unchecked.

Physical Entry

Secure areas should be protected by appropriate entry controls to ensure that only authorized personnel are allowed access. The provisioning of credentials must take into consideration the needs of the individual, his or her job function, and the zone accessed. As discussed previously, the person requiring access must successfully pass an investigative process prior to being provided access. In defining physical entry controls, one should consider the following:

- Visitors should be appropriately cleared prior to entry and supervised while on the premises. Moreover, the date, time, and escort should be recorded and validated with a signature. Visitors should only be provided access to the areas that do not contain sensitive information or technologies and should be provided with instructions concerning security actions and emergency procedures.

- Access to controlled areas, such as information processing centers and where sensitive data may reside, should be restricted to authorized persons only. Authentication controls, such as badges, swipe cards, smart cards, proximity cards, PINs, and (potentially) biometric devices, should be employed to restrict access.

- Everyone within the controlled perimeter must wear some form of identification and should be encouraged to challenge others not wearing visible identification. Be aware, however, that most cultures encourage politeness and deference in social interactions, particularly where strangers are involved. Challenging an unknown person does not come easily to many people, and this may be a large culture change for most organizations. Awareness and education programs on this topic are advised.

- Different styles of identification should be employed to allow others to quickly ascertain the role of an individual. For example, employees may be given white badges and visitors given blue badges. This makes it easier to identify who is an employee and who is not to ensure that all nonemployees are escorted in the building. In another example, a red ID badge may signify access to the fourth floor of an office building. If someone appeared on the fourth floor wearing a blue badge, others would be able to determine appropriate actions. Action may include verifying they are escorted, notifying security, or escorting them to the nearest exit.

- All access rights and privileges should be regularly reviewed and audited. This should include random checks on seemingly authorized users, control devices, approval processes, and training of employees responsible for physical security.

There may be an occasional need for temporary facility access to sensitive areas for visitors, contractors, or maintenance personnel. Preparations and procedures should be defined in advance for these situations; special identification should be required for all temporary personnel, and they should be escorted by facility personnel at all times. This will make it easier for regular facility personnel to identify the temporary visitors in unauthorized areas and ensure that they are not able to cause any damage to the facility or obtain any confidential information.

Administrative Controls

Administrative controls represent all the actions, policies, processes, and management of the control system. These include any aspect of the access control environment that is necessary to oversee and manage the confidentiality, availability, and integrity of the access controls and manage the people who use it, set policy on use, and define standards for operations.

Administrative controls can be broad and can vary depending on organizational needs, industry, and legal implications. Nevertheless, they can be broken into six major groups:

- Policies and procedures
- Personnel security, evaluation, and clearances
- Security policies
- Monitoring
- User management
- Privilege management

Policies and Procedures

The first aspect of administrative (managerial) oversight is the operations management of the control environment and how it should align with the enterprise architecture. Access control is realized by aligning the capabilities of many systems and processes, collaborating to ensure that threats are reduced and incidents prevented. Therefore, other operational elements of the environment must be addressed in some fashion within the access control strategy. These include but are not limited to:

- Vulnerability management and patch management
- Product lifecycle management
- Network management

When changes to the environment are required to accommodate a need, they must be defined, approved, tested, applied, verified, deployed, audited, and documented. Changes can be minor, such as a static route being added to a network, or more significant, such as the redesign of a storage solution. Every organization must have a change control process to ensure that there is a formalized methodology for making and documenting changes to the environment.

Given the scope of access control, it is important that the change control process includes aspects of the access strategy and policy. In some cases, this is obvious, such as adding a new virtual private network (VPN) gateway for remote access. Clearly this will affect the access control environment. Some changes, such as network redesign, which can affect various established access paths to information, are much less obvious but can have significant impacts to access controls.

Many organizations have business continuity and disaster recovery (BCP/DRP) plans to ensure that the organization can maintain critical operations in case of a catastrophic event or failure. BCP/DRP plans can be simplistic, such as ensuring there are regular backups performed, or highly complex solutions incorporating multiple data centers. The scope and complexity of the BCP/ DRP plan are typically defined by the business environment, risks, and system criticality.

Regardless of the type of BCP/DRP plan, the availability of access controls during an event is essential and must be incorporated into the plan. For example, if a system failure occurs and an alternate system is temporarily employed without the expected, original controls, the exposure to critical data can be significant. All too often, security is a secondary consideration in disaster recovery operations. If an event was to occur, a company could have its most valuable assets completely exposed. However, critical systems are most important in the context of BCP/DRP. Therefore, a system included in the BCP/DRP plan is important, and the information on that system is valuable.

The first step that the security architect, practitioner, and professional all need to take in some way is to ensure that the security measures incorporated into the BCP/DRP plans are defining the access controls for the temporary systems, services, and applications to be used during disaster recovery. This includes the access control system itself. For example, a RADIUS server may seem unimportant on the surface, but its absence in a disaster could be detrimental to security. In addition, a disaster scenario, by definition, is an unusual event with many extenuating arrangements that will need to be made to enable the organization to continue its work. Subsequently, there may be different access needs defined than what the organization would normally have in place or need. The notion of "acceptable security" may be very different during a disaster than it would be under ordinary circumstances, so proper planning and consideration of alternative access control needs and methods must be considered and incorporated into the BCP/DRP plan.

Traditional networks and applications are typically engineered to provide a high level of performance to users, systems, and services. The network is the cardiovascular system of most companies, and if its performance is low, the productivity of the organization will suffer. The same holds true for the access control environment. If it takes a user an excessive amount of time to log on, this could have a negative impact to operations and potentially encourage users to find ways to bypass the access control system. To reduce the time associated with usage of access controls, the performance optimization processes for the network and system environments should include the base lining and ongoing monitoring of the performance of controls overseeing authentication and access.

Like change control, configuration management represents the administrative tasks performed on a system or device to ensure optimal operations. Configurations can be temporary or permanent to address a multitude of the organization's operations and security needs, and configuration management of devices, systems, services, and applications can greatly affect the access control environment. Changes to a system's configuration must take into account what, if any, impacts on user access may occur after the configuration is modified.

Given the common separation of the security group from the IT group, it is not uncommon for the IT group to make a seemingly innocuous modification to a system configuration and impact the access controls associated with that system. Therefore, it is important to ensure that the resources responsible for configuration management, such as network administrators, system owners, and application developers, are aware of the security control environment and the importance of their domain of influence on the security of the organization. This often ties in closely with any change management processes an organization might have in place, so it is a natural fit for processes to be enacted that tie in access control considerations as part of any change management or configuration management program.

Vulnerability management will typically include activities such as identifying system vulnerabilities, recommending potential remediation, and implementing system patches to accommodate a security issue, update a system service, or add features to a system or application. When patches are installed, there may be key system modifications made that can negatively affect the security of the system, server, or application. Patches must be applied through the change control system to provide a comprehensive record of system modifications and accurate documentation. Ensuring that the current state of a system is well documented allows organizations to gain more visibility into the status of their environment in the event a new vulnerability is published. This promotes rapid assessments to evaluate potential risks in the face of an attack or vulnerability. In addition, data from the change control system utilized during the application of patches offer documentation of the current state of a system that can be consulted prior to applying new patches or installing new software.

A key attribute of vulnerability management is the importance of minimizing the time for deploying patches or other system updates in order to mitigate a vulnerability. Vulnerabilities surface in a multitude of ways. For example, a vulnerability may be published by a vendor who has discovered a security issue and provides a patch. Usually, at this point, both attackers and organizations are made aware of the vulnerability. While companies are exercising due diligence in applying fixes, attackers are developing methods and tools to exploit the vulnerability. In contrast, an incident may have occurred that exposes the vulnerability in a system and constitutes an immediate threat. The most dangerous example of this kind of threat is zero day/zero hour attacks, where an attacker identifies and exploits the vulnerability before that vulnerability is known to the vendor or the general user community. The attackers can exploit the vulnerability on a massive scale, understanding that time is on their side. It is very common for attackers to discover a vulnerability, develop tools and tactics to exploit it, then execute those exploits before anyone knows of the vulnerability or how to defend against it. Vulnerable organizations must find alternative measures to compensate for the threat while vendors rush to produce a patch, each consuming time as the attacks expand.

Given the complexity of each potential scenario, time is always a critical element in protecting assets. The ability to use time effectively to deploy a patch or employ compensating controls until a patch is published directly corresponds to the level of risk and the overall security posture of the organization. Emphasis on efficient testing and deployment of system patches or compensating controls should be at the core of any vulnerability management program.

However, time must be balanced against effective deployment. Initially, the documentation provided by the configuration management and change control processes can be investigated to determine which systems are vulnerable and represent the greatest risk, then prioritized accordingly. As the process continues, other affected systems are addressed by a manual or automated (or combination) patch management process that is used to deploy the update throughout the organization. The vulnerability management program must then verify that the patch was, in fact, implemented as expected. Although this may seem inherent to the objective, it cannot be assumed. In the case of manual deployment, users and system owners may not respond accordingly or in a timely fashion. Even if timely deployment is executed, the patch may have failed. This is somewhat compensated for in automated deployment; nevertheless, both scenarios require validation of an effective installation.

The installation of a patch or control does, by itself, represent the complete mitigation of an identified vulnerability. Many systems are unique to a specific environment, representing the potential that a change mitigating one vulnerability unintentionally introduces another. Or, in some cases, it is assumed that the implementation of a patch or control eliminated the vulnerability altogether. Therefore, a vulnerability management system must not only address the testing, deployment, and verification that the patch was implemented as expected, but it should also include testing to ensure that the target vulnerability was mitigated and new problems were not introduced by the process. In the final analysis, vulnerability management is a comprehensive and integral process that every security program must develop, maintain, and test regularly.

In every organization, there comes a time to upgrade or replace devices and systems. Reasons for the upgrade vary but can include product obsolescence, the availability of newer technology with previously unavailable desirable features, or the need for advanced operational capabilities. Baselines must be established within the access control architecture that define the minimum access control requirements for all new systems to ensure that appropriate and acceptable controls are established. By doing so, the organization has a clear foundation by which to evaluate products for implementation without sacrificing security or expected controls. Do not assume that all new products have the security capabilities the organization needs. Each organization's needs vary, and each environment may be different from that for which the product was designed. It is important to test all new products for access control functionality.

Finally, many networks are supported by a separate management network that allows administrators to manage devices without affecting the production environment. This is another form of separation of duties, where the production network and the management network have separate purposes, separate network connectivity, and separate access and control requirements. Given the ability to change aspects of the network environment, one must have strong access controls established on the management network to reduce risk to systems and network devices. If network management is performed using the same network as general production traffic, strong authentication and authorization are required to ensure that unauthorized personnel cannot modify network devices.

Personnel Security, Evaluation, and Clearances

One of the more overlooked aspects of access control is a review of the requirements of people requesting access to a resource. Prior to granting access of any kind, one should check the credentials of the person requesting the access for validity and thoroughly evaluate his need for access. This does not mean that every user needs to have a complete background check prior to checking her email. Clearly, the level of validation of an individual should be directly proportional to the sensitivity of the assets and the level of permissions available to the user. Nevertheless, it is critical that processes exist to evaluate users and ensure that they are worthy of the level of trust that is requested and, ultimately, granted.

First and foremost, security requirements – at some level – should be included in all defined job roles and responsibilities. Job roles defined by the organization should have alignment to defined policies and be documented appropriately. They should include any general responsibilities for adhering to security policies, as well as any specific responsibilities concerning the protection of particular assets related to the given role.

Once the security requirements for a role are defined and clearly documented, the process for validation of individuals to obtain credentials for a role can be defined and exercised. The definition of a screening process is typically related to the sensitivity of the assets being accessed. However, there may be contractual demands, regulatory compliance issues, and industry standards that define how a person is screened to reach a certain level of access. The best example of this type of screening comes from the military and the allocation of clearances. Depending on the clearance level requested, a person may be subjected to intense background checks, friend and family interviews, credit checks, employment history, medical history, polygraph examinations, and a plethora of other potentially unpleasant probing. Of course, once the applicant attains clearance, it translates to a level of trustworthiness and, therefore, access.

A typical organization will need only a standard process and some additional factors in the light of applicable legal requirements or regulations. These may include a credit check and criminal background checks that simply assure management that an applicant has not falsified information during the application process. Typical aspects of staff verification may include but are not limited to the following:

- Satisfactory character references
- Confirmation of claimed academic and professional qualifications
- Independent identity validation, such as a passport
- A credit check for those requiring access to financial systems
- Federal, state, and local law enforcement records check
- An online search of publicly available information on social media sites

The relevance of credit checks and other personal history can be valuable in determining a person's propensity for unlawful acts. Personal or financial problems, changes in behavior or lifestyle, recurring absences, and evidence of stress or depression might lead an employee to fraud, theft, error, or other security implications. The type of background check performed may vary based on the type of employee and his or her placement in the organization.

In the event the employee is temporary, the access provided must take into consideration the potential exposure of proprietary information given the transient position. Organizations that use staffing agencies to supply temporary help should require those agencies to perform employee validation checks and provide a reliability report on the temporary workers supplied to the organization. The requirements for background checks should be incorporated into the underlying contract with the staffing agency, and its implementation should be reviewed and audited on a regular basis. Management should also evaluate the supervision and provisioning of access to new or inexperienced staff. It should not be necessary to provide a new employee with the keys to the kingdom until he or she has satisfied a probationary period.

Employees should also be periodically reevaluated to ensure that significant changes to key elements about them or their lives have not occurred that would alter their security worthiness. Also, it is important to remember that all information collected about an individual is private and confidential and should be afforded security controls like any other sensitive material. Finally, confidentiality or non-disclosure agreements should be read and signed annually by all employees to ensure there is no doubt on the part of employees that the information they will have access to is confidential, secret, protected, and valuable to the organization.

Security Policies
The organization's requirements for access control should be defined and documented in its security policies. Access rules and rights for each user or group of users should be clearly stated in an access policy statement. The access control policy should minimally consider:

- Statements of general security principles and their applicability to the organization.
- Security requirements of individual enterprise applications, systems, and services.
- Consistency between the access control and information classification policies of different systems and networks.
- Contractual obligations or regulatory compliance regarding protection of assets.
- Standards defining user access profiles for organizational roles.
- Details regarding the management of the access control system.

Monitoring

The ability to monitor the access control environment effectively is essential to the overall success and management of the security program. It is one thing to apply controls, but it is another to validate their effectiveness and ongoing status. The capacity for ensuring that controls are properly employed and working effectively and for being aware of unauthorized activity is enabled by the existence of monitoring and logging within the environment.

Systems should be monitored to detect any deviation from established access control policies and record all successful and unsuccessful authentication processes, credential assertion, user management, rights usage, and access attempts. The procedures and technology should also monitor the ongoing status of controls to ensure conformity to policies and expectations. This last point is typically overlooked and represents a significant liability, due to the potential to mask or hide unauthorized activities. For example, if the control activities are monitored, yet the status of controls is not, attackers can disable various controls, grant themselves access, and then re-enable the controls without detection. The logging and monitoring of the activities will then not raise any suspicion because they are now valid operations, thanks to the attacker.

Systems and activity logs are (typically) electronic records of any activity that has occurred within a system or application. They provide the documented record of what has happened and can be extremely useful when investigating an operational or security incident. Logs and their contents are important to security management and maintenance of an effective access control solution. A log can include:

- User IDs used on systems, services, or applications.
- Dates and times for logon and logoff.
- System identities, such as IP address, host name, or media access control (MAC) address. It may also be possible to determine the network location of a device through local area network (LAN) logging, wireless access point identification, or remote-access system identification, if applicable.
- Logging of both successful and rejected authentication and access attempts. Knowing when and where people are utilizing their rights can be very helpful to determine if those rights are necessary for a job role or function. It is also helpful to know where access rights are denied to have a better understanding of what a user is trying to do. This can help determine if you have a user who does not have adequate rights to perform his or her job.

Audit logs should be retained for a specified period, as defined by organizational need and (potentially) regulatory requirements. In the latter case, this is preordained and not open to interpretation. However, there are cases where no legal or regulatory demands exist. If this is the case, the retention time will probably be defined by organizational policy and the size of available storage. The security of the logs is critical. If a log can be altered to erase unauthorized activity, there is little chance for discovery, and if discovered, there may be no evidence. Logs must also be protected from unauthorized reading as well as writing because they can contain sensitive information such as passwords (for instance, when users accidentally type the password into a user ID prompt). Log security is also critical if the logs are needed as evidence in a legal or disciplinary proceeding. If logs are not secure and can be proven as such before, during, and after an event, the logs may not be accepted as valid legal evidence due to the potential for tampering. The fundamental approach to logs is that they must be an accurate reflection of system activity and, as such, must be secured and maintained for an appropriate period of time in order to provide a reference point for future investigative activity.

Once the events are properly logged, it is necessary to periodically review the logs to evaluate the impact of a given event. Typically, system logs are voluminous, making it difficult to isolate and identify a given event for identification and investigation. To preserve potential evidence, many organizations will make a copy of the log (preserving the original) and use suitable utilities and tools to perform automated interrogation and analysis of the log data. There are several tools available that can be very helpful in analyzing a log file to assist administrators in identifying and isolating activity. Once again, separation of duties plays an important role in reviewing logs. Logs should never be initially reviewed or analyzed by the "subject" of the logs. For example, a system administrator should not perform the log review for a system he or she manages. Otherwise, it may be possible for the person to "overlook" evidence of his or her unauthorized activity or intentionally manipulate the logs to eliminate that evidence. Therefore, it is necessary to separate those being monitored from those performing the review.

User Access Management

An organization must have a formal procedure to control the allocation of credentials and access rights to information systems and services. The procedure should cover all stages in the lifecycle of user access, from the initial registration of new users to the final decommissioning of accounts that are no longer required. To provide access to resources, the organization must first establish a process for creating, changing, and removing users from systems and applications. These activities should be controlled through a formal process, based on policy, which defines the administrative requirements for managing user accounts. The process should define expectations, tasks, and standards concerning the user management. For example, elements of the process should include:

- Approval of user access, including information from human resources, the user's manager, or a business unit that has approved the creation of the user account. The owner of the system who is providing information or services should concur with the approval request. Approval processes should also address the modification of user accounts and their removal.
- Standards defining unique user IDs, their format, and any application-specific information. Additionally, information about the user should be included in the credential management system to ensure the person is clearly bound to the user ID defined within the system.
- A process for checking that the level of access provided is appropriate to the role and job purpose within the organization and does not compromise defined segregation of duties requirements. This is especially important when a user's role and job function change. A process must exist to evaluate existing privileges compared to the new role of the user and ensure changes are made accordingly.
- Defining and requiring users to sign a written statement indicating that they understand the conditions associated with being granted access and any associated liabilities or responsibilities. It is important to understand that user confirmation should occur whenever there is a change in rights and privileges, not simply upon creation of the account.
- A documentation process to capture system changes and act as a record of the transaction. Keeping a log of the administrative process and relative technical information is essential to an effective access control system. The information will be used in assessments, audits, change requests, and as evidence for investigative purposes.

- Access modification and revocation procedures to ensure that users who have left the organization or changed job roles have their previously held access privileges immediately removed to ensure elimination of duplications and removal of dormant accounts.
- Specific actions that may be taken by management if unauthorized access is attempted by a user or other forms of access abuse are identified. This must be approved by the organization's human resources and legal departments.

A more in-depth look at user management will be found later in this book when the "Identity and Access Management" domain is discussed.

In addition to overall user management, it is necessary to define policies, procedures, and controls regarding passwords. The use of passwords is a common practice for validating a user's identity during the authentication process. Given that, in most traditional authentication solutions, the password is the only secret in the transaction, one should take great care in considering how passwords are created and managed by users and systems.

A process governing user password should consider the following:

- Users should be required to sign a statement agreeing to keep their passwords safe and confidential and to not share, distribute, or write down their passwords.
- All temporary passwords should be permitted to be used only once – to reset the user's password to something that only he or she knows.
- Passwords should never be stored unprotected and in clear text.
- Passwords should have length requirements and require the use of various characters and formats to increase their complexity and reduce their susceptibility to brute force and guessing attacks.
- Passwords should be changed regularly.
- Accounts should be locked for a period of time if excessive failed password attempts occur (typically within three to five tries).
- A history of passwords should be maintained to prevent users from repeating old passwords as they are changed.
- Passwords should not be disclosed to support personnel, and those personnel should not ask users for their passwords.

There is some debate over the security realized by a username and password combination used for authentication. For example, depending on the system, a longer, more complex password can actually make it more prone to compromise if it results in the user writing it down. The potential for exposure of passwords, poor password selection by users, and the sheer number of passwords most users need to track lay the foundation for potential compromises.

However, alternatives to passwords can be expensive, cumbersome, and annoying to end-users, potentially negating any security or business benefit they may provide. Before moving away from the use of passwords toward an alternative technology or method, the security professional must always consider the value of the information or system that the passwords are protecting. Current password technology and processes (including the use of minimum complexity standards, lockouts, and reuse restrictions) will provide the organization with a certain minimal level of security protection. If, in the opinion of the organization, that level of protection is sufficient to protect the resources behind the password, then password technology is sufficient. If, however, the organization feels that password protection does not adequately protect the resources behind the password, then it must seek out alternative authentication methodologies.

Nevertheless, and despite all the negative connotations passwords have in the security space, passwords are today's de facto baseline standard. The best approach to ensure consistency and control is:[43]

- Clearly defined password policies
- Well-implemented system controls
- Understanding of the technical considerations
- Comprehensive user training
- Continuous auditing

Privilege Management

The importance of access privileges demands that their allocation, administration, and use should have specific processes and considerations. The lack of effective privilege management can result in core failures in otherwise sophisticated access control systems. Many organizations will focus exclusively on identification, authentication, and modes of access. Although all these are critical and important to deterring threats and preventing incidents, the provisioning of rights within the system is the next layer of control. The typical cause of problems in the allocation of rights is due primarily to the vast number of access options available to administrators and managers. The complexity of potential access configurations leads to inadequate and inconsistent security. This aspect of privilege management demands clear processes and documentation that defines and guides the allocation of system rights.

In the development of procedures for privilege management, careful consideration should be given to the identification and documentation of privileges associated with each system, service, or application, and the defined roles within the organization to which they apply. This involves identifying and understanding the available access rights that can be allocated within a system, aligning those to functions within the system, and defining user roles that require the use of those functions. Finally, user roles need to be associated with job requirements. A user may have several job requirements, forcing the assignment of several roles and resulting in a collection of rights within the system. Be careful, however, of the consequences of aggregate access rights. Many systems have rules of precedence that dictate how access rules are applied. Should a rule that restricts access conflict with, and be overridden by, a rule that allows access, the unintended consequence is that the user will be granted more access permission than was intended. Remember the primary mantra of least privilege: Only rights required to perform a job should be provided to a user, group, or role.

An authorization process and a record of all privileges allocated should be maintained. Privileges should not be granted until the authorization process is complete and validated. If any significant or special privileges are needed for intermittent job functions, these should be performed using an account specifically allocated for such a task, as opposed to those used for normal system and user activity. This enables the access privileges assigned to the special account to be tailored to the needs of the special function rather than simply extending the

---

43 Keeping an eye on the future, things such as geo location, mobile device identity, behavioral patterns, etc. are things that companies are trying to bake into the authentication process as an add-on to passwords. The security professional will need to evaluate these, their effectiveness and determine suitability as they become options for use in the organization.

access privileges associated with the user's normal work functions. For example, an administrator of a UNIX system might have three accounts: one for daily routines, another for specific job requirements, and "root" (the all-omniscient access ID on UNIX systems) for rare occurrences where complete system access must be utilized.

Logical (Technical) Controls

Logical controls are those mechanisms employed within the digital and electronic infrastructure of an organization that enforce that organization's security policy. Given the pervasive nature of technology, logical access controls may take on a wide variety of forms and implementations. Logical controls can include elements such as firewalls, filters, operating systems, applications, and even routing protocols. Logical controls can be broadly categorized in the following groups:

- Network access
- Remote access
- System access
- Application access
- Malware control
- Encryption

Network Access

Network access controls are those employed within the communication infrastructure to restrict who may connect to, and use, that infrastructure. Usually, this is implemented through access control lists, remote-access solutions, virtual local area networks (VLANs), access control protocols, and security devices like firewalls and intrusion detection or intrusion prevention systems. The role of network access controls is usually to limit communications between two networks or resources. For example, a firewall will limit what protocols and protocol features are permitted from a given source to a defined destination.

However, there are other network-level controls that can be used to employ security services that increase the level of access management in the environment. The most common example is a proxy system: a device or service that is located in the middle of the communication between a user and an application and employs controls that monitor and regulate the traffic between the user and the application. Proxy systems can apply specific logic in managing service-level communications within the network. For example, a proxy system may control access to Web-based services via the hypertext transfer protocol (HTTP). Just as a firewall would block specific ports, a proxy system would block or control certain aspects of the HTTP session to limit exposure. Many proxy systems are used to authenticate sessions for internal users attempting to access the Internet and potentially filter out unwanted website activity, such as Java applets, active server page (ASP) code, plug-ins, or access to inappropriate websites.

VLANs can be utilized to segment traffic and limit the interaction from one network to another. VLANs are used in situations where many systems are on the same physical network, but they need to be logically separated to enforce the access control requirements of the organization. Conversely, VLANs can be used to virtually connect systems in multiple physical locations to appear as if they are all on the same logical network segment.

Wireless networks can also employ several access control mechanisms, such as MAC filtering, multiple forms of authentication, encryption, and limitations on network access.

Network Access Control (NAC) provides the ability to restrict access to systems based on one or more network-wide policies defined by the system administrator. Prior to allowing a system to join the network, the NAC service queries the target system to ensure it is adhering to established policies. Policies can be as simple as ensuring an anti-virus package is present on the system or as complex as validating the system is up to date with security patches. In the event the system does not meet the required security policy, it may be denied access or redirected to a secure area of the network for further testing or to allow the user to implement the necessary changes required prior to gaining full access the network.

Remote Access

In today's environment, users working from outside the traditional office space make up a significant portion of the user community. Remote access solutions offer services to remote users requiring access to systems and data. One of the more commonly utilized technical solutions is the virtual private network (VPN). VPNs allow users to authenticate themselves and establish a secure communications channel over an insecure medium like the Internet. Typically, a VPN device is placed on the organization's Internet connection or behind a firewall to allow remote users to access the network, authenticate, and establish a protected session with various internal systems.

VPN access controls typically use authentication mechanisms in combination with encryption methods. For example, a VPN solution can be configured to permit access by users with the appropriate specific (company branded) client software or version of a browser, limit access to certain portions of the network, limit the types of services permissible, and control session time windows. In addition, because the connection is occurring over an insecure and publicly accessible network like the Internet, most VPN solutions employ multifactor authentication to positively identify the user.

System Access

The term "system" comprises a wide variety of technologies and components, but the definition most often used is one or more computers that provide a service or assist in a process. When most people think of a system, they think of their personal computer, and that provides a good model for discussing system access controls. The most prevalent system access control is the user ID and password combination. Almost all modern systems have this unless it has been specifically disabled for a particular reason. The user ID/password combination may be replaced in some systems by other forms of authentication, such as a smartcard or a one-time password token. Nevertheless, all these methods serve the same purpose: to restrict system access to authorized users.

All computer systems have an underlying operating system that controls all its functions and regulates how the various components of the system interact. There are literally hundreds of different operating systems, but most users (including security professionals) work primarily in one of the three major publicly available operating systems: Microsoft Windows®, Apple's OS, and UNIX (including the many variants of Linux). Mobile operating systems such as Google's Android and Apple's iOS are also operating systems security professionals must be familiar with. Each of these operating systems has internal controls and layers built in that manage access control between components of the system. In particular, they all tightly control programs that directly access the hardware components of the system, such as the kernel (the part of the system that interfaces between the OS and the system hardware) and various device drivers that allow application programs to use devices like keyboards and printers. The ability to directly manipulate the system hardware is a powerful tool and must be tightly controlled by the operating system to prevent misuse by malicious programs.

Finally, almost all operating systems have some sort of file system to store information for later retrieval. The file system will also have controls to restrict who may access various files and directories. Some of these controls are imposed by the operating system itself, while others may be assigned by individual users to protect their personal files. These controls are very important to ensure that information is not disclosed to unauthorized individuals who may have access to the system.

Application Access

Applications will usually employ user and system access controls to deter threats and reduce exposure to security vulnerabilities. However, applications can also incorporate mechanisms to supplement other controls and ensure secure operations. For example, applications can monitor user sessions, apply inactivity time-outs, validate data entry, and limit access to specific services or modules based on user rights and defined user roles. Moreover, the application itself can be designed and developed to reduce exposure to buffer overflows, race conditions (where two or more processes are waiting for the same resource), and loss of system integrity.

The architecture of an application plays a significant role in its ability to thwart attack. Object-oriented programming, multitier architectures, and even database security are important to controlling what services are provided to users and what tasks can be performed. Access controls associated with all aspects of an application are important to sound security. Many applications are complicated and offer a wide range of services and access to potentially sensitive information. Additionally, applications may be critical to the operational needs of the business. Therefore, their sensitivity to disruption must be considered when designing or using the access control features of the application.

Applications can also be segmented into modules or layers to further enforce access control policies. For example, a typical email application can be segmented into modules for composing a message, managing address book information, connecting to network resources, and managing mail delivery and retrieval. Doing this allows the application designer to specify how each module can be accessed, what services each module will present to the user and to other applications, and what privileges each provides to the user. For example, the address book management module may be accessible from an email application but not by any other application to prevent the possibility of a virus examining and using a user's address book. It is important to manage the interaction between application modules within an application as well as the interaction between these modules and other applications to ensure that malicious users or programs do not try to use them to perform unauthorized activities. A more detailed discussion of application security issues is found in the "Software Development Security" domain.

Malware Control

Malicious code, such as viruses, worms, Trojans, spyware, and even spam, represents potential security threats to the enterprise. Weaknesses in systems, applications, and services offer opportunities for worms and viruses to infiltrate an organization, causing outages or damage to critical systems and information. Technical controls can be applied to reduce the likelihood of impact from such malicious programs. The most prevalent of these controls are anti-virus systems that can be employed on the network perimeter, servers, and end-user systems to detect and potentially eliminate viruses, worms, or other malicious programs. Other technical solutions include file integrity checks and intrusion prevention systems that can detect when a system service or file is modified, representing a risk to the environment. The security practitioner will also want to be aware of technologies such as application and process whitelisting, sandboxing, forensic file analysis as well as integration of one or more of these technologies with real time intelligence feeds from vendors.

Cryptography

Encryption has an important role in the "Security and Risk Management" domain. Encryption can be used to ensure the confidentiality of information or authenticate information to ensure integrity. These two characteristics are highly leveraged in the identification and authentication processes associated with access control. Authentication protocols will employ encryption to protect the session from exposure to intruders; passwords are typically hashed (put through a one-way mathematical function that cannot be reversed) to protect them from disclosure, and session information may be encrypted to support the continued association of the user to the system and services used. Encryption can also be used to validate a session. For example, a server can be configured such that if session information is not encrypted, the resulting communication is denied. The most predominant aspect of cryptography in access control is the employment of cryptographic mechanisms to ensure the integrity of authentication protocols and processes.

Encryption can also be used as a compensating control to improve security when the available access control functions are not granular enough to provide adequate security. For example, it may be necessary for several employees of a company to share a particularly sensitive financial spreadsheet. Unfortunately, all of these people are located in different offices in different parts of the country, and the only way for them to share this file is to use the company's general shared drive that was set up for all employees to transfer information between offices. While access to the drive is restricted to only internal company users, there is no way to specify that only particular users can access a specific file. In this case, the file can be encrypted and the key to decrypt the file can be disclosed only to the employees who need to see the spreadsheet. This will allow the file to be placed on the general shared drive while still restricting access to only those who need to see the file.

Cryptography is commonly used within applications to protect sensitive data. Information such as credit card numbers may be encoded so that they are not visible (except perhaps the last few digits) to personnel who do not need to see the entire number. Examples of this may be seen in reports or printouts, in the storage of such information in a database, or in the layout of a screen that is displayed to the user. Consider the use of encryption in those situations where the available access controls are not sufficient to provide the appropriate granularity of protection for sensitive information.

Controls Assessment/Monitoring and Measuring

Security control assessments are not about checklists, simple pass-fail results, or generating paperwork to pass inspections or audits. Rather, security controls assessments are the principal vehicle used to verify that the implementers and operators of information systems are meeting their stated security goals and objectives. The assessment results provide organizational officials with:

- Evidence about the effectiveness of security controls in organizational information systems;

- An indication of the quality of the risk management processes employed within the organization; and
- Information about the strengths and weaknesses of information systems that are supporting organizational missions and business functions in a global environment of sophisticated and changing threats.

The findings produced by assessors are used to determine the overall effectiveness of the security controls associated with an information system (including system-specific, common, and hybrid controls) and to provide credible and meaningful inputs to the organization's risk management process. A well-executed assessment helps to: (i) determine the validity of the security controls contained in the security plan and subsequently employed in the information system and its environment of operation; and (ii) facilitate a cost-effective approach to correcting weaknesses or deficiencies in the system in an orderly and disciplined manner consistent with organizational mission/business needs.

The concepts of tailoring and supplementation may be used by the security professional. Tailoring involves scoping the assessment procedures to more closely match the characteristics of the information system and its environment of operation. The tailoring process gives organizations the flexibility needed to avoid assessment approaches that are unnecessarily complex or costly while simultaneously meeting the assessment requirements established by applying the fundamental concepts in their risk management framework. Supplementation involves adding assessment procedures or assessment details to adequately meet the risk management needs of the organization (e.g., adding organization-specific details such as system/platform-specific information for selected security controls). Supplementation decisions should be made in consultation with the senior management of the organization in order to maximize flexibility in developing security assessment plans when applying the results of risk assessments in determining the extent, rigor, and level of intensity of the assessments.

The selection of appropriate security controls for an information system is an important task that can have major implications on the operations and assets of an organization as well as the welfare of individuals. Security controls are the management, operational, and technical safeguards or countermeasures prescribed for an information system to protect the confidentiality, integrity (including non-repudiation and authenticity), and availability of the system and its information. Once employed within an information system, security controls are assessed to provide the information necessary to determine their overall effectiveness: that is, the extent to which the controls are implemented correctly, operating as intended, and producing the desired outcome with respect to meeting the security requirements for the system. Understanding the overall effectiveness of the security controls implemented in the information system and its environment of operation is essential in determining the risk to the organization's operations and assets, to individuals, and to other organizations resulting from the use of the system.

A sample security control assessment table is shown below in *Figure 1.19*. The assessor would use a table such as this one to list and then assess the current state of every control being evaluated for the assessment. Once the assessment table had been completed by the assessor, the results of the assessment would be correlated and then would need to be reported to senior management based on the method discussed and agreed to at the beginning of the assessment, either in a written report or through a presentation or briefing.

Security Control Family: *Access Control (AC)*

Security Control Number	Security Control Name	Security Control and Enhancements	Base Applicability			Security Control Type	Last Date Security Control Assessed	Assessor Information	Assessed Security Control Effectiveness	Assessment Steps Used	Assessment Evidence
			L	M	H						
AC-1	Access Control Policy and Procedures	*The organization develops, disseminates, and periodically reviews/updates:* - A formal documented, access control policy that addresses purpose, scope, roles, responsibilities, management commitment, coordination among organizational entities, and compliance. - Formal documented procedures to facilitate the implementation of the access control policy and associated access controls.	X	X	X						

Figure 1.19 – **Security Controls Assessment table**

As part of an effective risk management program, an organization should employ a variety of methods to determine the effectiveness of its access controls. Vulnerability assessment, control assessment, and penetration testing are all valuable methods of determining the effectiveness of an organization's access controls and their ability to mitigate risk.

Vulnerability Assessment

When seeking to determine the security position of an organization, the security professional will eventually turn to a vulnerability assessment to help identify specific areas of weakness that need to be addressed. A vulnerability assessment is the use of various tools and analysis methodologies to determine where a particular system or process may be susceptible to attack or misuse. Most vulnerability assessments concentrate on technical vulnerabilities in systems or applications, but the assessment process is equally as effective when examining physical or administrative business processes.

To begin the vulnerability assessment process, the assessor must have a good understanding of the business, its mission, and the system or application to be assessed. While it is possible to simply run an automated tool against the target system to produce a list of potential problems, understanding first what the system does and its relationship to the overall business process will assist the analyst in determining the overall risk of any discovered vulnerabilities. In addition, the security analyst must have a good understanding of the known and potential threats to the system as specifically identified by the business or by the assessor's general knowledge of the security landscape. A vulnerability in the absence of a validated threat will rate lower on the criticality scale when compared to a vulnerability that has a known threat poised to strike against it.

Threat and vulnerability information can come from many sources. The first place to begin is by discussing the system with the appropriate business owners and other interested stakeholders. They are the closest to both the system and the business landscape the system operates in, and they will have a good understanding of security issues they have had previously or similar problems that competitors or others in the industry may have faced. In addition, including appropriate business stakeholders in the vulnerability assessment process will build a better sense of partnership between the business group and the security team.

Once the business aspect of the system has been addressed, the analyst can turn to various sources of security industry information, including known vulnerability databases such as the U.S. Government's National Vulnerability Database (NVD), published vendor vulnerability information, and security mailing lists.[44] If the assessor is using one or more automated tools, those tools will include many known vulnerabilities as part of their internal scanning database.

The next step is to examine the existing controls in place to protect the system or process. This includes any directive, preventative, deterrent, and detective controls that are in place in the organization. These controls may be specific to the system or business function or may be part of the organization's general control environment, such as security policies and standards, firewalls, anti-virus systems, intrusion detection/prevention systems, and available authentication and access controls. The analyst will then match these existing controls against the known threats previously identified to determine if the existing control systems counteract the identified threats. Whatever gaps remain after this analysis will need to be addressed.

---

44 See the following: http://nvd.nist.gov/
    https://www.owasp.org/index.php/Main_Page

In most situations, the assessor will turn to the use of a variety of automated tools to assist in the vulnerability assessment process. These tools contain extensive databases of specific known vulnerabilities as well as the ability to analyze system and network configuration information to predict where a particular system might be vulnerable to different types of attacks. There are many different types of tools currently available to address a wide variety of vulnerability assessment needs. Some tools will examine a system from the viewpoint of the network, seeking to determine if a system can be compromised by a remote attacker exploiting available services on a particular host system. These tools will test for open ports listening for connections, known vulnerabilities in common services, and known operating system exploits.

These tools will also often attempt to determine if a system has the latest security patches in place. Other tools will examine individual applications to determine if they are susceptible to application exploits like buffer overflow, improper input handling, database manipulation attacks, or common Web-based vulnerabilities. Because the vulnerability landscape is constantly evolving as new exploits are discovered and others are patched, the security manager must establish a process to ensure that any scanning tools used for vulnerability analysis are kept up to date so as to always have the latest information against which to test.

Once the vulnerability scanning is complete, the security analyst must examine the results for accuracy. It is rare that the results from a scanning tool are completely accurate. False positives are common because the tool may have incorrectly identified a target system or incorrectly analyzed the result data from the probes it performed. In addition, the analyst must match the scan results against what is already known about the business function of the system being analyzed. For example, many testing tools will report the use of the anonymous FTP service as a vulnerability because this can be seen as a potential security problem. However, if the system in question is being officially operated as an anonymous FTP server for the organization, that result, although correct, would not be considered a vulnerability to the organization.

The security analyst must combine the information gathered during the discussions with the business areas with the information obtained from the scanning tools to make a final analysis of the actual vulnerabilities that must be addressed by the organization. It is also common to rate those vulnerabilities on some type of criticality scale (high/medium/low or 1–5 ratings are common) to give the organization a sense of the level of concern and immediacy to place on each particular finding. Many tools will give a ranking for each vulnerability. The assessor must remember those ratings are based on harm to the system and not the organization. The assessor must make the determination of risk to the organization based on input from the tools rather than relying solely on the ratings from the tool. Many organizations will also establish time limits for remediation actions – shorter time limits for more critical vulnerabilities and longer ones for less critical problems.

Once the final analysis is complete, the assessor should discuss the findings with the business area to determine the appropriate course of remediation action to take. The actions should be based on the criticality of each reported vulnerability, the cost to remediate, the potential compensating controls that can be enacted, and the impact the remediation will have on the system and the business function that the system serves. In some circumstances, the business group may elect to accept the risk of continued operation with the known vulnerability due to the cost of corrective measures or other business considerations. No matter what the resolution is, the assessor should ensure that all concerned understand – and agree to – the remediation plan.

Assuming that an application or system group will always address all items in the report in a timely manner is a mistake. The system group will have a multitude of projects and deadlines they need to address, of which the vulnerability report is but one. The assessor may be asked and should continuously follow up with the system group to ensure they are addressing the vulnerabilities as agreed.

Vulnerability analysis is an important part of the security management process, and it is one that many organizations do not address consistently or effectively. It is a key component in the risk management process and, if performed effectively, can dramatically reduce the organization's overall risk and susceptibility to current, and future, security problems. Vulnerability analysis and management is also a core component in building an effective continuous monitoring program.

Penetration Testing

The next level in vulnerability assessments seeks to exploit existing vulnerabilities to determine the true nature and impact of a given vulnerability. Penetration testing goes by many names, such as ethical hacking, tiger teaming, red teaming, and vulnerability testing. It is the use of exploitive techniques to determine the level of risk associated with a vulnerability or collection of vulnerabilities in an application or system. The primary goal of penetration testing is to simulate an attack on a system or network to evaluate the risk profile of an environment. This includes understanding the level of skill required, the time needed to exploit a given vulnerability, and the level of impact, such as depth of access and attainable privileges.

Penetration testing can be employed against any system or service. However, because of the time, expense, and resources required to properly execute a penetration test, most companies seek penetration testing to focus on Internet systems and services, remote-access solutions, and critical applications.

The key to successful and valuable penetration testing is clearly defined objectives, scope, stated goals, agreed-upon limitations, and acceptable activities. For example, it may be acceptable to attack an FTP server but not to the point where the system is rendered useless or data are damaged. Having a clear framework and management oversight during a test is essential to ensure that the test does not have adverse effects on the target company and the most value is gained from the test.

Penetration Test Strategies

Strategies for penetration testing, based on specific objectives to be achieved, are a combination of the source of the test, how the company's assets are targeted, and the information (or lack thereof) provided to the tester. One of the first steps in establishing the rules of engagement for a penetration test is determining the amount of information to provide the tester about the target. No matter the scope or scale of a test, how information flows initially will set in motion other attributes of planning, ultimately defining factors by which the value of the test will be measured. Usually some form of information is provided by the target, and only in the most extreme cases is absolutely no information offered. Some cannot be avoided, such as the name of the company, while others can be easily kept from the testers without totally impeding the mechanics of the test.

External testing refers to attacks on the organization's network perimeter using procedures performed from outside the organization's systems, for example, from the Internet. To conduct the test, the testing team begins by targeting the company's externally visible servers or devices, such as the domain name server (DNS), email server, Web server, or firewall.

Internal testing is performed from within the organization's technology environment. The focus is to understand what could happen if the network perimeter was successfully penetrated or what an organization insider could do to penetrate specific information resources within the organization's network.

In a blind testing strategy, the testing team is provided with only limited information concerning the organization's information systems configuration. The penetration testing team must use publicly available information (such as the company website, domain name registry, and Internet discussion boards) to gather information about the target and conduct its penetration tests. Blind testing can provide information about the organization that may have been otherwise unknown, but it can also be more time consuming and expensive than other types of penetration testing (such as targeted testing) because of the effort required by the penetration testing team to research the target. However, in blind testing the "attackers" (the test team) have little or no knowledge about the target company, but the "defenders" (the company's IT and security teams) know the attack is coming and are prepared to defend against it.

Double-blind testing presents a more real-life attack scenario because the organization's IT and security teams are not notified or informed before the test and are "blind" to the planned testing activities. In addition to testing the strength of a network or application, double-blind testing can test the organization's security monitoring and incident identification, escalation, and response procedures. In double-blind testing engagements, very few people within the organization are made aware of the testing, perhaps only the project sponsor, and double-blind testing requires careful monitoring by the project sponsor to ensure that the testing procedures and the organization's incident response procedures can be terminated when the objectives of the test have been achieved or the test threatens to affect production systems or networks.

In a targeted testing environment (often referred to as the "lights on" approach), both the organization's IT team and the penetration testing team are made aware of the testing activities and are provided with information concerning the target and the network design. A targeted testing approach may be more efficient and cost-effective when the objective of the test is focused more on the technical setting, or on the design of the network, than on the organization's incident response and other operational procedures. A targeted test typically takes less time and effort to complete than blind testing, but it may not provide as complete a picture of an organization's security vulnerabilities and response capabilities.

There are three basic categories of penetration test separated by how much information is provided to the tester or test team: zero knowledge, partial knowledge, and full knowledge. In zero knowledge testing, the tester is provided no information about the target's network or environment. The tester is simply left to his abilities to discover information about the company and use it to gain some form of access. This is also called black box or closed testing, depending on who is scoping the test. Zero knowledge testing is particularly appropriate when executing a test from outside the organization because this is the position most attackers will be in when they start to attack an organization.

In a partial knowledge test scenario, the tester is provided with some knowledge about the environment. The information provided is high-level public (or near-pubic) information that would be trivial for a real attacker to find without much effort, including phone numbers and IP addresses to be tested, domain information, and application names. It is assumed that a competent attacker would be able to obtain this level of information rather quickly, so this information is given to the tester to speed up the testing process a bit. The interesting aspect of getting some information and not all is the assumption of scope. Organizations can use limited information to define boundaries of the test as opposed to simply providing all the initial data to support the test. For example, exposing the organization's IP address range is an attempt to speed up the gathering of easily obtained information, while exposing the fact that the network has intrusion detection systems can shape the way the tester goes about performing the test.

Full knowledge testing provides every possible piece of information about the environment to the tester. This type of test is typically employed when there is greater focus on what can be done as opposed to what can be discovered. The assumption is that an attacker can easily discover what is in the environment and the test needs to focus on how much damage can be done with that information. This is particularly appropriate when testing for internal penetrations. In that situation, the tester is taking the role of an informed insider (e.g., an employee or contractor) with existing inside knowledge of the environment, architecture, and information paths. The insider has all the knowledge he or she needs to find the target. The question the tester needs to answer is whether the target's defenses will withstand such an attack.

The organization must determine the area of the organization or the service to be tested. This is important when defining the scope of the test because it will determine the boundaries and limits of acceptable testing practices. More than one target may be defined for a test, but each must be well defined and clearly understood by all involved.

Application Security Testing

The objective of application security testing is to evaluate the controls within an application and its information process flow. Topics to be evaluated may include the application's use of encryption to protect the confidentiality and integrity of information, the authentication of users, the integrity of the Internet user's session with the host application, and the management of the current processing state between parts of the application. Application testing will test the flow of information through the application and its susceptibility to interception or alteration. It will also test how the application handles input data and determine if user input can harm or crash the application. Finally, application testing will test for a wide range of common (as well as some uncommon) attack scenarios to gauge the level of resistance an application has to attacks of varying levels of sophistication.

Denial-of-Service (DoS) Testing

The goal of DoS testing is to evaluate the system's susceptibility to attacks that will render it inoperable or unable to provide needed services to the organization or external users. Decisions regarding the extent of DoS testing to be incorporated into a penetration testing exercise will depend on the relative importance of ongoing, continued availability of the information systems and related processing activities. When deciding to perform DoS testing, one must ensure that these tests are not performed on live production systems unless that is a specific objective of the test and all system and information owners know about, and approve, this course of action.

The potential for system disruption beyond a simple crash is very high with DoS testing, potentially leading to extended down time, angry customers, or lost revenue. In addition, the security assessor needs to make sure that everyone knows that a DoS test is being performed so that nobody (including system owners, users, and help desk staff) is caught unaware. Because DoS testing presents such a risk to systems, many testers will perform the attack steps leading up to the DoS but stop short of actually crashing the system. This saves a great deal of response and recovery time while still exposing a potentially risky situation on the system.

War Dialing

War dialing is a technique for systematically calling a range of telephone numbers in an attempt to identify modems, remote-access devices, and maintenance connections for computers that may exist within an organization's network. Well-meaning users can inadvertently expose the organization to significant vulnerability by connecting a modem to the organization's information systems or network devices. Once a modem or other access device has been identified, analysis and exploitation techniques are performed to assess whether this connection can be used to penetrate the organization's information systems network. In the Internet age, it may be difficult to understand that modems are still a primary source of network connectivity for many purposes, but they are still out there and there are plenty of them, very often connected to administrative ports on equipment for use by system administrators for emergency access, maintenance, or recovery purposes. Organizations would be wise not to underestimate their reach into the infrastructure or their potential for creating vulnerabilities in the environment.

Wireless Network Testing

The introduction of wireless networks, whether through formal, approved network architecture or the inadvertent actions of well-meaning users, creates additional security exposures. Attackers have become proficient in identifying wireless network access points within an organization simply by driving by, or walking around, office buildings with their wireless network equipment; this is sometimes referred to as war driving. The goal of wireless network testing is to identify security gaps or flaws in the design, implementation, or operation of the organization's wireless network. War driving also provides an advantage to attackers, who may be able to access and penetrate a network through the wireless connection even though they are not on the property of the organization they are breaking in to. The security professional needs to view the existence of one or more wireless connections on a corporate network to the equivalent of having a live network jack in the parking lot of the company.

Social Engineering

Often used in conjunction with blind and double-blind testing, social engineering refers to techniques using social interaction, typically with the organization's employees, suppliers, and contractors, to gather enough information to be able to penetrate the organization's physical premises or systems. Such techniques could include posing as a representative of the IT department's help desk and asking users to divulge their user account and password information, posing as an employee and gaining physical access to restricted areas that may house sensitive information, or intercepting mail, courier packages, or even searching through trash for sensitive information on printed materials (also known as dumpster diving). Social engineering activities can test a less technical, but equally important, security component: the ability of the organization's people to contribute to (or prevent) unauthorized access to information and information systems.

PBX and IP Telephony Testing

Beyond war dialing, phone systems (traditional "POTS" service, corporate ISDN, and new IP-based telephone services) have traditionally been a highly vulnerable, yet often overlooked, method of gaining access to corporate resources. Attackers can gain access to voicemail systems to gather information and monitor activity. Moreover, phone systems can be manipulated to permit an attacker to make long-distance calls free and undetected, potentially furthering an attack on other organizations. It is also not uncommon for security services to leave secret information (e.g., passwords and account information) on voicemail systems, relying on the authentication mechanisms of the voicemail service to provide protection. If an attacker compromises the voicemail service, that information can be compromised.

IP telephony, or voice-over-IP (VoIP), is the use of traditional Internet protocol (IP) data networks to handle voice traffic. It can also include the integration of phone systems with network applications, databases, and other services, such as email or workflow collaboration systems. While IP telephony systems share many of the same security vulnerabilities as traditional phone services, their integration with the IP protocol gives them an additional susceptibility to network-level attacks. Tests can be performed against these technologies to gain a better understanding of the risks the organization may face when combining voice and data on a single network or whether a DoS attack on the data network would also render the VoIP system inoperable. The potential threat profile represented by combining the threats associated with IP networks and those of telephone systems is one that the security professional should take seriously.

Penetration Test Methodology

A methodology is an established collection of processes that are performed in a predetermined order to ensure the job, function, or, in this case, security test is accurately executed. There are many ways of performing a penetration test, perhaps as many as there are testers. However, there is a basic and logical methodology that has become a "best practice" for performing such tests:

1. **Reconnaissance/Discovery** – Identify and document information about the target.
2. **Enumeration** – Gain more information with intrusive methods.
3. **Vulnerability Analysis** – Map the environment profile to known vulnerabilities.
4. **Execution** – Attempt to gain user and privileged access.
5. **Document Findings** – Document the results of the test.

Step 1: Reconnaissance

As is the case with most military and espionage campaigns, penetration tests typically begin with a reconnaissance phase. Reconnaissance is the search for any available information on the target to assist in planning or executing the test. The search can include quick ping sweeps to see what IP addresses on a network will respond, scouring news groups on the Internet in search of disgruntled employees divulging useful information, or rummaging through the trash to find inside information on the business or the technical environment (also known as dumpster diving). The ultimate goal of the reconnaissance phase is to gather as much information on the target as possible. This may include physical and virtual layouts, building and network topography, organizational strengths and weaknesses, operational patterns, technology in use, and practically anything else the tester may think will be useful in the coming attack. Reconnaissance can also include theft, lying to people, monitoring networks, impersonations, or even leveraging falsified friendships to collect data about a target. The search for information is only limited by the extremes to which a company and the tester are willing to go. The rule of thumb in the reconnaissance phase is that no piece of information is too small to be useful.

Step 2: **Enumeration**

Also known as network or vulnerability discovery, enumeration is the process of obtaining information directly from the target systems, applications, and networks. An interesting point to understand is that the enumeration phase represents a point within the penetration testing project where the line between a passive attack and an active attack begins to blur. At this point, the tester is not just gathering information anymore; he or she is sending network probes or otherwise communicating with systems and network devices in order to gather more information. Some of these devices may be fragile or susceptible to even the slightest nudge from the tester. When one is setting up the test parameters, the enumeration phase should be thoroughly reviewed with the operations, support, and security teams to ensure there are no surprise alerts generated as a result of the test.

To build an accurate picture of a company's environment, one should refer to the several tools and techniques available to compile a list of information obtained from the systems. Most notably, port scanning is the most common and easily executed basic test to start with. A port scan is the manipulation of the basic communication setup between two networked systems to determine what services are being offered on the target system. Collecting information about available systems and services is the first step in formulating an attack plan. From here, the tester can build on the information found during the reconnaissance phase and define a path to attempt to compromise the system.

Step 3: **Vulnerability Analysis**

The information gathered by the reconnaissance and enumeration phases will yield a great deal of valuable information about the target environment. The next step is to analyze that data to determine potential vulnerabilities that may be exploited to successfully attack the target. This calls for a logical and pragmatic approach to analyzing data. During the enumeration phase, the tester performs an analysis of the information collected (or provided), looking for relationships between systems, networks, and applications that may lead to exposures that can be exploited. The vulnerability analysis phase is a practical process of comparing the information collected with known vulnerabilities.

Most information about potential vulnerabilities can be collected from openly available sources, such as the Internet, public websites, hacker periodicals and mailing lists, news groups, vendor bug and patch data, and even the personal experience of the tester. These can be used to analyze information gleaned from the target to seek options for exploitation. All this information, properly analyzed, can be used to formulate a successful attack.

Because each organization and environment is different, the tester (and the attacker) must analyze the information carefully to identify potential avenues of attack that will work against that potential environment. The use of easily obtained reconnaissance and analysis tools can help this effort a great deal. Such tools will systematically explore and analyze multiple categories of potential vulnerabilities, such as Web exploits, data handling exploits, buffer overflows, misconfigured systems, trust relationships, authentication errors, and even missing patches or system updates. The analysis of potential vulnerabilities is critical because it will pinpoint precise areas of weakness in the environment and optimize the tester's time when attempting to penetrate a system.

Step 4: **Execution**

A great deal of planning and evaluation should be performed during the earlier testing phases to ensure that the test focuses on the areas of greatest vulnerability and criticality, ensuring ultimately that core business systems can be better protected. This planning must lead to the actual execution of some form of attack scenarios. Exploiting systems and applications can be as easy as running an automated tool or as intricate as manually executing specific steps to get a desired result. No matter the level of difficultly of the test, good testers follow a specific pattern during the exploitation phase of a test to ensure consistent and successful results.

During a penetration test, the details considered in the planning, reconnaissance, and analysis phases come to fruition and affect the outcome of every action taken by the tester. A sound methodology is needed to translate all the planning into an attack scenario to meet the objectives within the specified period and within the defined scope. The attack process is typically broken up into multiple threads of execution and groups of test scenarios. A thread is a collection of tasks that must be performed in a specific order to achieve a specific attack goal. Threads can be a single step or multiple steps used to gain access or compromise a system. Every thread is different, but many have similar steps that they share in common. Therefore, threads can be combined into groups to create a collection of access strategies. Groups are then reviewed, compared, and optimized to support a comprehensive attack strategy using different threads in a structured manner.

Each test should be evaluated at multiple points throughout the process to ensure that the expected outcome is being met. Occasionally during a test, the tester will need to diverge from the established plan due to unexpected circumstances or an unexpected reaction from the target. Each divergence from the plan is appraised to make two fundamental determinations:

- Are the test objectives of the thread or group not being met or are the test's results conflicting with the company's assumptions and stated goals? The objective is to ensure that each test falls within the bounds of what was established and agreed upon. On the other hand, if the test begins to produce results that were not considered during the planning, enumeration, and vulnerability analysis phases, the engagement needs to be reconsidered, or at minimum, the planning phase needs to be revisited. Meeting expectations is a primary goal of testing, and in the world of ethical hacking, it can represent a fundamental challenge when not planned properly or not executed to the plan.
- Is a system reacting in an unexpected manner, which is having an impact on the test? Live systems in a dynamic environment do not always react as predicted or expected. Keeping alert for unexpected responses from systems ensures that the target has not been negatively affected and the set scope and boundaries of the test have not been exceeded.

Step 5: **Document Findings**

The goal of penetration testing is to gain awareness and a detailed understanding of the state of the security environment. Information is collected throughout the test, producing information that can be used to draw conclusions and articulate findings. The tester will need to collate and analyze that information, document findings in a clear and concise manner, and provide an analysis of the results that can be used to improve the overall security profile of the environment. The goal of the document is to clearly present the findings, tactics used, and tools employed, and to produce an analysis of information collected from the test. Specific areas to cover in the documentation and analysis include but are not limited to:

- Vulnerabilities discovered in the target system(s)
- Gaps in security measures
- Intrusion detection and response capabilities
- Observation of log activity and analysis
- Suggested countermeasures

Although penetration testing is complex and potentially expensive to perform, it is well worth the effort to an organization that is serious about improving its security and maintaining strong controls against attacks.

Tangible and Intangible Asset Valuation

All information has value. Value is typically represented by information's cost and its perceived value internally and externally to organization. It is important to remember that over time, however, information may lose its value. Additionally, information may lose value if it is modified, improperly disclosed, or has not had its proper value calculated. It is of utmost importance, then, to periodically attempt to properly value information assets.

How, then, is information value to be determined? Similar to risk analysis, information valuation methods may be descriptive (subjective) or metric (objective) based. Subjective methods include the creation, dissemination, and collection of data from checklists or surveys. An organization's policies or the regulatory compliance requirements that it must follow can also help to determine information's worth. Metric or statistical measures may provide a more objective view of information valuation due to the fact that they are based on specific quantitative measurements as opposed to qualitative. Each of these methods has its uses within an organization.

One of the methods that uses consensus relative to valuation of information is the consensus/modified Delphi method. Participants in the valuation exercise are asked to comment anonymously on the task being discussed. This information is collected and disseminated to a participant other than the original author. This participant comments upon the observations of the original author. The information gathered is discussed in a public forum, and the best course is agreed upon by the group (consensus).

Risk assessment also takes into account special circumstances under which assets may require additional protection, such as with regulatory compliance. Many times, these regulatory requirements are the means to completion of an appropriate risk assessment for the organization because meeting the compliance objectives requires the risk assessment to be done.

Because no organization has limitless dollars, resources, and time, it can be difficult to persuade senior executives to undertake risk assessment, even in the face of regulatory requirements. How, then, might they be persuaded? One of the principle outcomes of risk assessment is the definition and identification of threats, vulnerabilities, and countermeasures present (or desired) within the organization. It would then be useful to "reuse" the data gathered during the risk assessment for other security initiatives, such as business continuity, security incident response, disaster recovery, and others. The act of reusing data gathered during a risk assessment, when possible and appropriate, can save the organization dollars, time, and resources and can be demonstrated to senior management as a tangible value, or return on investment (ROI).

Tangible Asset Valuation

Tangible assets are those which have a physical presence. These assets are valued based on the original cost of the assets minus depreciation. These assets are often depreciated to zero for accounting purposes. For risk assessment purposes, the information security professional needs to be aware of the original cost as well as the replacement cost of the items in question. As suppliers and vendors come into and leave the market, the cost of replacing a specific appliance, server, or type of lock may change due to supply and demand. Additionally, assets originally depreciated may gain in value if the supply is less than the demand. Certain assets may also become outdated, and new assets may be required to replace the functionality or utility they provided. Ways to determine tangible asset value include:

- Original cost minus depreciation
- Actual market value through market research
- Consider online auction sites that show what others are actually buying the asset for.
- Call vendors and get updated quotes for replacement cost comparison.
- Cost of switching to a competing asset or capability

Intangible Asset Valuation

Intangible assets are not physical. Examples of intangible property include, but are not limited to:

- Trademarks
- Patents
- Copyrights
- Business processes
- Brand recognition
- Intellectual property

Intangible assets may also be further classified as definite or indefinite:

- A definite intangible asset is an intangible asset with a definite expiration period. An example of a definite intangible asset is a patent. The patent has value only as long as it is enforceable. Once the patent expires, it no longer has value.
- An indefinite intangible asset is an intangible asset with an indefinite expiration period. An example would be an organization's brand. The brand is expected to be maintained and preserved into the foreseeable future.

Intangible assets can be quite difficult to determine a value for. What is the value of the "CISSP®" trademark? It is valuable to the members who hold the credential, and it has a value to (ISC)² the organization that owns the trademark. But what is the total value of the trademark? For someone to approximate the value of an intangible asset, the following methods are considered generally acceptable:

- **Cost** – The cost to create and to replace the asset. This approach must be used cautiously because rarely does the value of intangible assets only equal the creation or acquisition cost.
- **Capitalization of Historic Profits** – If getting a patent, creating a brand, or developing a new process directly led to increased profits, those profits can be considered part of the overall value of the asset.

145

- **Cost Avoidance or Savings** – If acquiring the trademark of a product service allowed an organization to avoid paying royalties, those savings can be considered part of the asset's value.

The security professional should seek the aid of a financial expert when attempting to determine the intangible value of an asset. These are some of the most complex and valuable assets an organization has and require thorough valuation efforts.

Continuous Improvement

Among the most widely used tools for continuous improvement is a four-step quality model – the plan-do-check-act (PDCA) cycle, also known as Deming Cycle or Shewhart Cycle:

- **Plan** – Identify an opportunity and plan for change.
- **Do** – Implement the change on a small scale.
- **Check** – Use data to analyze the results of the change and determine whether it made a difference.
- **Act** – If the change was successful, implement it on a wider scale and continuously assess your results. If the change did not work, begin the cycle again.

Other widely used methods of continuous improvement – such as Six Sigma, Lean, and Total Quality Management – emphasize employee involvement and teamwork; measuring and systematizing processes; and reducing variation, defects, and cycle times.

Continuous or Continual?

The terms continuous improvement and continual improvement are frequently used interchangeably. But some quality practitioners make the following distinction:

- **Continual improvement:** a broader term preferred by W. Edwards Deming to refer to general processes of improvement and encompassing "discontinuous" improvements – that is, many different approaches, covering different areas.
- **Continuous improvement:** a subset of continual improvement, with a more specific focus on linear, incremental improvement within an existing process. Some practitioners also associate continuous improvement more closely with techniques of statistical process control.

Statistical process control (SPC) procedures can help with the monitoring of process behavior.

A control chart helps you record data and lets you see when an unusual event (e.g., a very high or low observation compared with "typical" process performance) occurs. Control charts attempt to distinguish between two types of process variation:

- Common cause variation, which is intrinsic to the process and will always be present.
- Special cause variation, which stems from external sources and indicates that the process is out of statistical control.

Other process-monitoring tools have been developed as well, including:

- **Cumulative Sum (CUSUM) charts** – The ordinate of each plotted point represents the algebraic sum of the previous ordinate and the most recent deviations from the target.
- **Exponentially Weighted Moving Average (EWMA) charts** – Each chart point represents the weighted average of current and all previous subgroup values, giving more weight to recent process history and decreasing weights for older data.

Risk Management Frameworks

The underlying premise of enterprise risk management is that every entity exists to provide value for its stakeholders. All entities face uncertainty, and the challenge for management is to determine how much uncertainty to accept as it strives to grow stakeholder value. Uncertainty presents both risk and opportunity, with the potential to erode or enhance value. Enterprise risk management enables management to effectively deal with uncertainty and associated risk and opportunity, enhancing the capacity to build value. Value is maximized when management sets strategy and objectives to strike an optimal balance between growth and return goals and related risks, and efficiently and effectively deploys resources in pursuit of the entity's objectives. Enterprise risk management encompasses:

- ■ ***Aligning Risk Appetite and Strategy*** – Management considers the entity's risk appetite in evaluating strategic alternatives, setting related objectives, and developing mechanisms to manage related risks.
- ■ ***Enhancing Risk Response Decisions*** – Enterprise risk management provides the rigor to identify and select among alternative risk responses – risk avoidance, reduction, sharing, and acceptance.
- ■ ***Reducing Operational Surprises and Losses*** – Entities gain enhanced capability to identify potential events and establish responses, reducing surprises and associated costs or losses.
- ■ ***Identifying and Managing Multiple and Cross-Enterprise Risks*** – Every enterprise faces a myriad of risks affecting different parts of the organization, and enterprise risk management facilitates effective response to the interrelated impacts and integrated responses to multiple risks.
- ■ ***Seizing Opportunities*** – By considering a full range of potential events, management is positioned to identify and proactively realize opportunities.
- ■ ***Improving Deployment of Capital*** – Obtaining robust risk information allows management to effectively assess overall capital needs and enhance capital allocation.

These capabilities inherent in enterprise risk management help management achieve the entity's performance and profitability targets and prevent loss of resources. Enterprise risk management helps ensure effective reporting and compliance with laws and regulations, and it helps avoid damage to the entity's reputation and associated consequences. Overall, enterprise risk management helps an entity get to where it wants to go and avoid pitfalls and surprises along the way.

Events – Risks and Opportunities

Events can have negative impacts, positive impacts, or both. Events with a negative impact represent risks, which can prevent value creation or erode existing value. Events with positive impact may offset negative impacts or represent opportunities. Opportunities are the possibility that an event will occur and positively affect the achievement of objectives, supporting value creation or preservation. Management channels opportunities back to its strategy or objective-setting processes, formulating plans to seize the opportunities.

Enterprise Risk Management Defined

Enterprise risk management deals with risks and opportunities affecting value creation or preservation, defined as follows:

The definition reflects certain fundamental concepts. Enterprise risk management is:
- A process, ongoing and flowing through an entity.
- Effected by people at every level of an organization.
- Applied in a strategy setting.
- Applied across the enterprise, at every level and unit, and includes taking an entity level portfolio view of risk.
- Designed to identify potential events that, if they occur, will affect the entity and to manage risk within its risk appetite.
- Able to provide reasonable assurance to an entity's management and board of directors.
- Geared to achievement of objectives in one or more separate but overlapping categories.

This definition is purposefully broad. It captures key concepts fundamental to how companies and other organizations manage risk, providing a basis for application across organizations, industries, and sectors. It focuses directly on achievement of objectives established by a particular entity and provides a basis for defining enterprise risk management effectiveness.

Achievement of Objectives
Within the context of an entity's established mission or vision, management establishes strategic objectives, selects strategy, and sets aligned objectives cascading through the enterprise. This enterprise risk management framework is geared to achieving an entity's objectives, set forth in four categories:
- **Strategic** – High-level goals, aligned with and supporting its mission
- **Operations** – Effective and efficient use of its resources
- **Reporting** – Reliability of reporting
- **Compliance** – Compliance with applicable laws and regulations

This categorization of entity objectives allows a focus on separate aspects of enterprise risk management. These distinct but overlapping categories – a particular objective can fall into more than one category – address different entity needs and may be the direct responsibility of different executives. This categorization also allows distinctions between what can be expected from each category of objectives.

Because objectives relating to reliability of reporting and compliance with laws and regulations are within the entity's control, enterprise risk management can be expected to provide reasonable assurance of achieving those objectives.

Achievement of strategic objectives and operations objectives, however, is subject to external events not always within the entity's control; accordingly, for these objectives, enterprise risk management can provide reasonable assurance that management, and the board in its oversight role, are made aware, in a timely manner, of the extent to which the entity is moving toward achievement of the objectives.

Components of Enterprise Risk Management

Enterprise risk management consists of eight interrelated components. These are derived from the way management runs an enterprise and are integrated with the management process. These components are:

- **Internal Environment** – The internal environment encompasses the tone of an organization and sets the basis for how risk is viewed and addressed by an entity's people, including risk management philosophy and risk appetite, integrity and ethical values, and the environment in which they operate.
- **Objective Setting** – Objectives must exist before management can identify potential events affecting their achievement. Enterprise risk management ensures that management has in place a process to set objectives and that the chosen objectives support and align with the entity's mission and are consistent with its risk appetite.
- **Event Identification** – Internal and external events affecting achievement of an entity's objectives must be identified, distinguishing between risks and opportunities. Opportunities are channeled back to management's strategy or objective setting processes.
- **Risk Assessment** – Risks are analyzed, considering likelihood and impact, as a basis for determining how they should be managed. Risks are assessed on an inherent and a residual basis.
- **Risk Response** – Management selects risk responses – avoiding, accepting, reducing, or sharing risk – developing a set of actions to align risks with the entity's risk tolerances and risk appetite.
- **Control Activities** – Policies and procedures are established and implemented to help ensure the risk responses are effectively carried out.
- **Information and Communication** – Relevant information is identified, captured, and communicated in a form and time frame that enable people to carry out their responsibilities. Effective communication also occurs in a broader sense, flowing down, across, and up the entity.
- **Monitoring** – The entirety of enterprise risk management is monitored and modifications are made as necessary. Monitoring is accomplished through ongoing management activities, separate evaluations, or both.

Enterprise risk management is not strictly a serial process, where one component affects only the next. It is a multidirectional, iterative process in which almost any component can and does influence another.

What is a Risk Management Framework?[45]

A risk management framework is defined by the Australian Standard as:

A set of components that provide the foundations and organizational arrangements for designing, implementing, monitoring, reviewing and continually improving risk management throughout the organization.

The Standard notes that the framework can include:

- The policy, objectives, mandate, and commitment to manage risk.
- The organizational arrangements include plans, relationships, accountabilities, resources, processes, and activities and should be embedded within the organization's overall strategic and operational policies and practices.

---

45   See the following for more information on AS/NZS ISO 31000:2009: http://infostore.saiglobal.com/store/Details.aspx?ProductID=1378670

Purpose of a Risk Management Framework

The purpose of establishing an organizational risk management framework is to ensure that key risks are effectively identified and responded to in a manner that is appropriate to:

- The nature of the risks faced by the organization.
- The organization's ability to accept and/or manage risks.
- The resources available to manage risks within the organization.
- The organization's culture.

Ultimately, risk needs to be managed so that the organization maximizes its ability to meet its strategic objectives as well as associated operational targets and goals. Some examples of risk management frameworks are:

The Risk IT Framework - ISACA [46]

The Risk IT Framework fills the gap between generic risk management frameworks and detailed (primarily security-related) IT risk management frameworks. It provides an end-to-end, comprehensive view of all risks related to the use of IT and a similarly thorough treatment of risk management, from the tone and culture at the top to operational issues. In summary, the framework will enable enterprises to understand and manage all significant IT risk types, building upon the existing risk related components within the current ISACA frameworks (i.e., COBIT and Val IT).

ISO 31000 - Risk management [47]

Risks affecting organizations can have consequences in terms of economic performance and professional reputation, as well as environmental, safety, and societal outcomes. Therefore, managing risk effectively helps organizations to perform well in an environment full of uncertainty. ISO 31000 is a family of standards relating to risk management codified by the International Organization for Standardization. The purpose of ISO 31000:2009 is to provide principles and generic guidelines on risk management. ISO 31000 seeks to provide a universally recognized paradigm for practitioners and companies employing risk management processes to replace the myriad of existing standards, methodologies, and paradigms that differed between industries, subject matters, and regions. ISO also designed its ISO 21500 Guidance on Project Management standard to align with ISO 31000:2009. [48]

ISO 31000:2009, Risk Management [49]

ISO 31000:2009, Risk Management – "Principles and Guidelines", provides principles, a framework, and a process for managing risk. It can be used by any organization regardless of its size, activity, or sector. Using ISO 31000 can help organizations increase the likelihood of

---

46 See the following for more information on the ISACA Risk IT Framework: http://www.isaca.org/Knowledge-Center/Research/ResearchDeliverables/Pages/The-Risk-IT-Framework.aspx

47 See the following for more information on the ISO 31000 series of Standards: http://www.iso.org/iso/iso31000

48 See the following for an overview of the ISO 21500 Guidance on Project Management Standard: http://www.iso.org/iso/home/news_index/news_archive/news.htm?refid=Ref1662

49 ISO 31000:2009 has been received as a replacement to the existing standard on risk management, AS/NZS 4360:2004 (In the form of AS/NZS ISO 31000:2009). Whereas the Standards Australia approach provided a process by which risk management could be undertaken, ISO 31000:2009 addresses the entire management system that supports the design, implementation, maintenance, and improvement of risk management processes.

achieving objectives, improve the identification of opportunities and threats, and effectively allocate and use resources for risk treatment.

However, ISO 31000 cannot be used for certification purposes, but it does provide guidance for internal or external audit programs. Organizations using it can compare their risk management practices with an internationally recognized benchmark, providing sound principles for effective management and corporate governance.

Managing Risk
ISO 31000:2009 provides a list on how to deal with risk:
1. Avoiding the risk by deciding not to start or continue with the activity that gives rise to the risk.
2. Accepting or increasing the risk in order to pursue an opportunity.
3. Removing the risk source.
4. Changing the likelihood.
5. Changing the consequences.
6. Sharing the risk with another party or parties (including contracts and risk financing).
7. Retaining the risk by informed decision.

Related Standards
Below are two additional standards that also relate to risk management.
- **ISO Guide 73:2009, Risk Management** – Vocabulary complements ISO 31000 by providing a collection of terms and definitions relating to the management of risk.
- **ISO/IEC 31010:2009, Risk Management** – Risk assessment techniques focus on risk assessment. Risk assessment helps decision makers understand the risks that could affect the achievement of objectives as well as the adequacy of the controls already in place. ISO/IEC 31010:2009 focuses on risk assessment concepts, processes, and the selection of risk assessment techniques.

Enterprise Risk Management – Integrated Framework (2004) [50]
In response to a need for principles-based guidance to help entities design and implement effective enterprise-wide approaches to risk management, COSO issued the Enterprise Risk Management – Integrated Framework in 2004. This framework defines essential Enterprise Risk Management (ERM) components, discusses key ERM principles and concepts, suggests a common ERM language, and provides clear direction and guidance for enterprise risk management. The guidance introduces an enterprise-wide approach to risk management as well as concepts such as risk appetite, risk tolerance, and portfolio view.

The NIST Risk Management Framework (RMF)
The NIST Risk Management Framework (RMF), described in NIST Special Publication 800-37 Revision 1, Guide for Applying the Risk Management Framework to Federal Information Systems: a Security Life Cycle Approach, is a methodology for implementing risk management

---

50   See the following for overview information on the COSO ERM – Integrated Framework:
     http://www.coso.org/-erm.htm

at the information systems tier.[51] The RMF (depicted in *Figure 1.20*) identifies six distinct steps that provide a disciplined and structured process to integrate information security risk management activities into the system development life cycle. The RMF addresses security concerns of organizations related to the design, development, implementation, operation, and disposal of information systems and the environments in which those systems operate.

According to NIST, SP 800-37 Revision 1, developed by the Joint Task Force Transformation Initiative Working Group, transforms the traditional Certification and Accreditation (C&A) process into the six-step Risk Management Framework (RMF). The revised process emphasizes:

1. Building information security capabilities into federal information systems through the application of state-of-the-practice management, operational, and technical security controls.

2. Maintaining awareness of the security state of information systems on an ongoing basis though enhanced monitoring processes.

3. Providing essential information to senior leaders to facilitate decisions regarding the acceptance of risk to organizational operations and assets, individuals, other organizations, and the Nation arising from the operation and use of information systems.

The RMF has the following characteristics:

■ Promotes the concept of near real-time risk management and ongoing information system authorization through the implementation of robust continuous monitoring processes;

■ Encourages the use of automation to provide senior leaders the necessary information to make cost-effective, risk-based decisions with regard to the organizational information systems supporting their core missions and business functions;

■ Integrates information security into the enterprise architecture and system development life cycle;

■ Provides emphasis on the selection, implementation, assessment, and monitoring of security controls, and the authorization of information systems;

■ Links risk management processes at the information system level to risk management processes at the organization level through a risk executive (function); and

■ Establishes responsibility and accountability for security controls deployed within organizational information systems and inherited by those systems (i.e., common controls).

The risk management process changes the traditional focus of C&A as a static, procedural activity to a more dynamic approach that provides the capability to more effectively manage information system-related security risks in highly diverse environments of complex and sophisticated cyber threats, ever-increasing system vulnerabilities, and rapidly changing missions.

The Risk Management Framework (RMF), illustrated in *Figure 1.20*, provides a disciplined and structured process that integrates information security and risk management activities into the system development life cycle.

---

51 See the following for NIST SP 800-37 Revision 1: http://csrc.nist.gov/publications/nistpubs/800-37-rev1/sp800-37-rev1-final.pdf

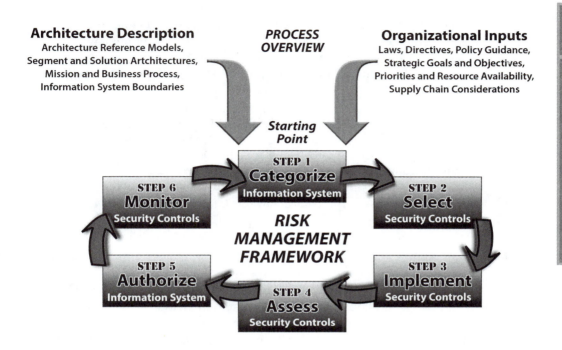

Figure 1.20 – **NIST Risk Management Framework**

The RMF steps include:

- Categorize the information system and the information processed, stored, and transmitted by that system based on an impact analysis.

- Select an initial set of baseline security controls for the information system based on the security categorization, tailoring and supplementing the security control baseline as needed based on an organizational assessment of risk and local conditions.

- Implement the security controls and describe how the controls are employed within the information system and its environment of operation.

- Assess the security controls using appropriate assessment procedures to determine the extent to which the controls are implemented correctly, operating as intended, and producing the desired outcome with respect to meeting the security requirements for the system.

- Authorize information system operation based on a determination of the risk to organizational operations and assets, individuals, other organizations, and the Nation resulting from the operation of the information system and the decision that this risk is acceptable.

- Monitor the security controls in the information system on an ongoing basis including assessing control effectiveness, documenting changes to the system or its environment of operation, conducting security impact analyses of the associated changes, and reporting the security state of the system to designated organizational officials.

In March of 2014, the United States Department of Defense issued the Department of Defense Instruction Number 8510.01, entitled "Risk Management Framework (RMF) for DoD Information Technology (IT)."[52] As stated in the instruction, the purpose is to:

A. Reissues and renames DoD Instruction (DoDI) 8510.01 (Reference (a)) in accordance with the authority in DoD Directive (DoDD) 5144.02 (Reference (b)).

B. Implements References (c) through (f) by establishing the RMF for DoD IT (referred to in this instruction as "the RMF"), establishing associated cybersecurity policy, and assigning responsibilities for executing and maintaining the RMF. The RMF replaces the DoD Information Assurance Certification and Accreditation Process (DIACAP) and manages the life-cycle cybersecurity risk to DoD IT in accordance with References (g) through (k).

C. Redesignates the DIACAP Technical Advisory Group (TAG) as the RMF TAG.

D. Directs visibility of authorization documentation and reuse of artifacts between and among DoD Components deploying and receiving DoD IT.

E. Provides procedural guidance for the reciprocal acceptance of authorization decisions and artifacts within DoD, and between DoD and other federal agencies, for the authorization and connection of information systems (ISs).

While many security professionals may not be working in areas that would require them to directly implement the NIST RMF as specified in the DoD Instruction above, general knowledge and awareness of the NIST RMF will be important for the security professionals to develop as they pursue risk management in general across the enterprise.

---

52 http://www.dtic.mil/whs/directives/corres/pdf/851001_2014.pdf

TRY IT FOR YOURSELF

The following is a collection of resources that the security professional can use in order to better understand the various aspects of risk management. The templates and assessments can be found in Appendix B.

Conducting a Risk Assessment

The Risk Assessment template will allow the security professionals to go through the process of identifying and cataloguing the various risks that will be important for them to manage in their organizations.

Conducting a Potential Breach Assessment

The potential breach assessment template will allow the security professionals to go through the process of identifying potential breaches that will be important for them to manage in their organizations. Once a breach has been clearly identified and investigated, the security professionals can then catalogue it using the breach register template.

Risk Management Plan Document Template Pack

A. *Sample Risk Management Plan*

The sample Risk Management Plan template will allow the security professional to go through the high level process of documenting the risk management plan for the enterprise.

This plan template needs to be used in conjunction with the sample Risk Management Log and the sample Risk Management Procedures template documents.

B. *Sample Risk Management Log*

The sample Risk Management Log template will allow the security professional to go through the operational process of documenting all of the risks that have been identified and are being actively managed within the enterprise.

This log template needs to be used in conjunction with the sample Risk Management Procedures template document.

C. *Sample Risk Management Procedures*

The sample Risk Management Procedures template provides the guidance required for the security professional to go through the operational process of documenting all of the risks that have been identified and are being actively managed within the enterprise.

This procedure template needs to be used in conjunction with the sample Risk Management Log template document.

Threat Modeling

Threat modeling enables informed decision making about application security risk. In addition to producing a model, typical threat modeling efforts also produce a prioritized list of security improvements to the concept, requirements, design, or implementation.

As part of the design phase of the Software Development Life Cycle (SDLC), threat modeling allows software architects to identify and mitigate potential security issues early, when they are relatively easy and cost-effective to resolve. Therefore, it helps reduce the total cost of development.

Threat modeling is a procedure for optimizing Network/Application/Internet Security by identifying objectives and vulnerabilities and then defining countermeasures to prevent, or mitigate the effects of, threats to the system. A threat is a potential or actual undesirable event that may be malicious (such as DoS attack) or incidental (failure of a Storage Device). Threat modeling is a planned activity for identifying and assessing application threats and vulnerabilities.

A basic threat modeling process consists of the following steps. The process of exploring the search space is iterative and constantly refined based on what you have done so far. So, for example, starting with all possible vulnerabilities is usually pointless because most of them are not attackable by the threat agents, protected by a safeguard, or do not lead to a consequence.

- **Assessment Scope** – Identifying tangible assets like databases of information or sensitive files is usually easy. Understanding the capabilities provided by the application and valuing them is more difficult. Less concrete things such as reputation and goodwill are the most difficult to measure, but they are often the most critical.
- **Identify Threat Agents and Possible Attacks** – A key part of the threat model is a characterization of the different groups of people who might be able to attack an application. These groups should include insiders and outsiders, performing both inadvertent mistakes and malicious attacks.
- **Understand Existing Countermeasures** – The model must include any and all existing countermeasures already deployed within the enterprise.
- **Identify Exploitable Vulnerabilities** – Once you have an understanding of the security in the application, you can then analyze for new vulnerabilities. The focus needs to be on vulnerabilities that connect the possible attacks that you have identified to the negative consequences that you have identified.
- **Prioritized Identified Risks** – Prioritization is everything in threat modeling because there are always lots of risks that simply do not rate any attention. For each threat, you estimate a number of likelihood and impact factors to determine an overall risk or severity level.
- **Identify Countermeasures to Reduce Threat** – The last step is to identify countermeasures to reduce the risk to acceptable levels, based on the risk appetite of the enterprise.

The security architect and the security professional will both want to ensure that they understand the basic concepts involved with threat modeling in order to be able to ensure that they are applying them when engaging in identification of risk and vulnerability activities. In order to get some practical experience with a threat modeling solution, take a look at the following:

Going Hands-On with Threat Modeling – *Resources to Use*
Microsoft has built and provided, for free, a threat modeling tool and many associated supporting resources that the security architect and security professional may want to acquaint themselves with as a starting point to gain some practical experience with threat modeling. The resources may be found here:

http://www.microsoft.com/security/sdl/adopt/threatmodeling.aspx

http://www.microsoft.com/security/sdl/video/Default.aspx#

http://www.microsoft.com/en-us/download/details.aspx?id=42518

Determining Potential Attacks and Reduction Analysis

What is a Social Engineering Attack?
In a social engineering attack, an attacker uses human interaction (social skills) to obtain or compromise information about an organization or its computer systems. An attacker may seem unassuming and respectable, possibly claiming to be a new employee, repair person, or researcher and even offering credentials to support that identity. However, by asking questions, he or she may be able to piece together enough information to infiltrate an organization's network. If an attacker is not able to gather enough information from one source, he or she may contact another source within the same organization and rely on the information from the first source to add to his or her credibility.

What Is a Pretexting Attack?
Pretexting is the act of creating and using an invented scenario (the pretext) to engage a targeted victim in a manner that increases the chance the victim will divulge information or perform actions that would be unlikely in ordinary circumstances. An elaborate lie, it most often involves some prior research or setup and the use of this information for impersonation (e.g., date of birth, social security number, last bill amount) to establish legitimacy in the mind of the target.

What Is a Phishing Attack?
Phishing is a form of social engineering. Phishing attacks use email or malicious websites to solicit personal information by posing as a trustworthy organization. For example, an attacker may send email seemingly from a reputable credit card company or financial institution that

requests account information, often suggesting that there is a problem. When users respond with the requested information, attackers can use it to gain access to the accounts.

Phishing attacks may also appear to come from other types of organizations, such as charities. Attackers often take advantage of current events and certain times of the year, such as:

- Natural disasters
- Epidemics and health scares
- Economic concerns
- Major political elections
- Holidays

Phone phishing (or "vishing") uses a rogue interactive voice response (IVR) system to recreate a legitimate-sounding copy of a bank or other institution's IVR system. The victim is prompted (typically via a phishing email) to call in to the "bank" via a (ideally toll free) number provided in order to "verify" information. A typical system will reject log-ins continually, ensuring the victim enters PINs or passwords multiple times, often disclosing several different passwords. More advanced systems transfer the victim to the attacker posing as a customer service agent for further questioning.

What Is a Baiting Attack?
In this attack, the attacker leaves a malware infected CD-ROM or USB flash drive in a location sure to be found (bathroom, elevator, sidewalk, parking lot), gives it a legitimate looking and curiosity-piquing label, and simply waits for the victim to use the device.

What Is a Tailgating Attack?
An attacker, seeking entry to a restricted area secured by unattended, electronic access control, (e.g., by RFID card) simply walks in behind a person who has legitimate access. Following common courtesy, the legitimate person will usually hold the door open for the attacker. The legitimate person may fail to ask for identification for any of several reasons or may accept an assertion that the attacker has forgotten or lost the appropriate identity token. The attacker may also fake the action of presenting an identity token.

Countermeasures that can be applied via Reduction Analysis are discussed below for both the individual as well as the organization. The security architect, security practitioner, and security professional all will need to play an active part in any systems built and deployed to address these kinds of concerns throughout the enterprise.

How Does an Individual Avoid Being a Victim?
- Be suspicious of unsolicited phone calls, visits, or email messages from individuals asking about employees or other internal information. If an unknown individual claims to be from a legitimate organization, try to verify his or her identity directly with the company.
- Do not provide personal information or information about your organization, including its structure or networks, unless you are certain of a person's authority to have the information.
- Do not reveal personal or financial information in email, and do not respond to email solicitations for this information. This includes following links sent in email.

- Do not send sensitive information over the Internet before checking a website's security.
- Pay attention to the URL of a website. Malicious websites may look identical to a legitimate site, but the URL may use a variation in spelling or a different domain (e.g., .com vs. .net).
- If you are unsure whether an email request is legitimate, try to verify it by contacting the company directly. Do not use contact information provided on a website connected to the request; instead, check previous statements for contact information. Information about known phishing attacks is also available online from groups such as the Anti-Phishing Working Group (http://www.antiphishing.org).
- Install and maintain anti-virus software, firewalls, and email filters to reduce some of this traffic.
- Take advantage of any anti-phishing features offered by your email client and Web browser.

How Can Organizations Reduce Their Security Risks?

- Establishing frameworks of trust on an employee/personnel level (i.e., specify and train personnel when/where/why/how sensitive information should be handled).
- Identifying which information is sensitive and evaluating its exposure to social engineering and breakdowns in security systems (building, computer system, etc.).
- Establishing security protocols, policies, and procedures for handling sensitive information.
- Training employees in security protocols relevant to their position. (e.g., in situations such as tailgating, if a person's identity cannot be verified, then employees must be trained to politely refuse.).
- Performing unannounced, periodic tests of the security framework.
- Reviewing the above steps regularly; no solutions to information integrity are perfect.
- Using a waste management service that has dumpsters with locks on them, with keys to them limited only to the waste management company and the cleaning staff. Locating the dumpster either in view of employees, such that trying to access it carries a risk of being seen or caught, or behind a locked gate or fence where the person must trespass before he or she can attempt to access the dumpster.

Technologies & Processes to Remediate Threats

Implementing a continuous IT and security risk management strategy requires all business units (e.g., internal audit, compliance, and security departments) to work together and effectively communicate on the organization's compliance, technology, and risk management efforts. Before a major risk management strategy is undertaken, however, managers and auditors need to understand the company's existing risk culture and threats to its business operations. This will enable auditors to provide recommendations that are in line with the organization's risk management needs. For instance, the presence of weak internal controls may lead to a network security breach that could expose confidential information and other data assets to unauthorized personnel. Worse, this breach could lead to a significant business disruption that impacts the organization's bottom line, reputation, and shareholder value.

Besides requiring all business units to work together during the strategy's implementation, the organization must migrate to a business paradigm in which all employees are accountable for their work and are aware of their duties. Organizations that hold employees accountable are better positioned to manage risks and comply with internal policies and external regulations. Furthermore, organizations that continuously check their compliance activities and manage risks on an ongoing basis can use their resources more effectively, thus lowering operation costs and freeing up resources to create more revenue-generating opportunities and adding new value to its services.

Once IT auditors understand the organization's risk culture and IT infrastructure, they can provide recommendations that enhance existing risk management efforts and compliance. For instance, auditors can recommend that traditional security practices be updated and supplemented with real-time vulnerability assessments, monitoring, and alerts; policy monitoring and enforcement; compliance monitoring; and user training. Such capabilities can enable auditors and management to access information that will help to prevent, detect, and respond to IT security incidents more effectively.

The security architect, security practitioner, and the security professional all need to play a part in the enterprise's strategy to deploy the most effective technology and processes to remediate threats. There is a myriad of potential designs and systems that could be deployed depending on the specifics of the threats being addressed. It may be an Intrusion Prevention System (IPS) or Intrusion Detection System (IDS), which are discussed in more detail in the "Security Operations" domain. It could be the use of Cryptography or Digital Rights Management (DRM) technology, which is discussed in the "Security Engineering" domain; or perhaps the use of VLANs and SSL/TLS, which are discussed in the "Communication and Network Security" domain. Whatever it may be, the right choices need to be made by the security architects as they plan the design of the systems. The security practitioners need to make the right choices as they implement and operate the systems day to day, while the security professionals need to ensure that they are able to clearly understand the systems so that they can produce the appropriate policies to manage and oversee it.

The following references will provide some guidance to all three security actors as they look to carry out their responsibilities in this area:

- *NIST SP 800-40 Revision 3: Guide to Enterprise Patch Management Technologies*
  http://nvlpubs.nist.gov/nistpubs/SpecialPublications/NIST.SP.800-40r3.pdf
- *NIST SP 800-52 Revision 1: Guidelines for the Selection, Configuration, and Use of Transport Layer Security (TLS) Implementations*
  http://nvlpubs.nist.gov/nistpubs/SpecialPublications/NIST.SP.800-52r1.pdf
- *NIST SP 800-61 Revision 2: Computer Security Incident Handling Guide*
  http://nvlpubs.nist.gov/nistpubs/SpecialPublications/NIST.SP.800-61r2.pdf
- *NIST SP 800-81-2 Secure Domain Name System (DNS) Deployment Guide*
  http://nvlpubs.nist.gov/nistpubs/SpecialPublications/NIST.SP.800-81-2.pdf
- *NIST SP 800-82 Revision 1: Guide to Industrial Control Systems (ICS) Security*
  http://nvlpubs.nist.gov/nistpubs/SpecialPublications/NIST.SP.800-82r1.pdf
- *NIST SP 800-83 Revision 1: Guide to Malware Incident Prevention and Handling for Desktops and Laptops*
  http://nvlpubs.nist.gov/nistpubs/SpecialPublications/NIST.SP.800-83r1.pdf
- *Open Web Application Security Project (OWASP) Top Ten for 2013*
  https://www.owasp.org/index.php/Category:OWASP_Top_Ten_Project#tab=OWASP_Top_10_for_2013
- *Open Web Application Security Project (OWASP) Developer Guide*
  https://www.owasp.org/index.php/Category:OWASP_Guide_Project

1

Acquisitions Strategy and Practice

Hardware, Software, and Services

Supply chain risks often are characterized in terms of tangible property exposures such as fires and natural catastrophes. Physical damage to buildings, machinery, and transportation infrastructure, however, are not the only potential causes of supply chain disruptions. Information and communication technologies are vulnerable to hardware and software failures, as well as to damage caused by hackers and malware writers. Significant cyber-related supply chain disruptions are rare, but a large-scale cyber event holds the potential to be as damaging as a major natural catastrophe. Organizations should implement a supply chain risk management program to proactively address these exposures. They also should consider insurance specifically designed for cyber-related risks, including supply chain risks.

"Supply chain" typically implies the movement of physical items, but in a world where digital assets often exceed the value of physical assets, the concept of supply chain needs to be expanded to include information and services. Organizations of all types rely on the Internet and various software tools and service providers to order and pay for supplies, to trade information with business partners and to transact business with customers. Interruption of those processes potentially can be even more disruptive than damage to transportation infrastructure. Organizations whose products are largely digital can be crippled if their information suppliers or digital infrastructure vendors are unable to perform.

When an organization purchases products or services with inadequate built-in security, the risks persist throughout the lifespan of the item purchased. The lasting effect of inadequate security in acquired items is part of what makes acquisition reform so important to achieving cybersecurity and resiliency. Purchasing products and services that have appropriate cybersecurity designed and built in may have a higher up-front cost in some cases, but doing so reduces total cost of ownership by providing risk mitigation and reducing the need to fix vulnerabilities in fielded solutions.

Increasingly, organizations are relying on network connectivity, processing power, data storage, and other information and communications technology (ICT) functions to accomplish their missions. The networks that the modern enterprise relies on today are often acquired and sustained through purchases of commercial ICT products and services. These capabilities greatly benefit the enterprise but have also, in some cases, made it more vulnerable to cyber-attacks and exploitation.

Resilience to cyber risks has become a topic of core strategic concern for business and government leaders worldwide and is an essential component of an enterprise risk management strategy.

The security professionals need guidance as to how to proceed. How do they source and acquire secure systems? Where do they turn to find trusted partners as they look to outsource? When is the right time to start planning a move to the cloud? Where will the next threat emerge from?

The recommendations below are designed to be considered as one part of the enterprise's comprehensive response to cyber risks. The recommendations focus on driving consistency in interpretation and application of procurement rules and incorporation of cybersecurity into the technical requirements of acquisitions. The recommendations are summarized as follows:

1. **Institute baseline cybersecurity requirements as a condition of contract award for appropriate acquisitions.**

   For acquisitions that present cyber risks, the enterprise should only do business with organizations that meet appropriate baseline requirements in both their own operations and in the products and services they deliver. The baseline should be expressed in the technical requirements for the acquisition and should include performance measures to ensure the baseline is maintained and risks are identified.

2. **Address cybersecurity through relevant training.**

   As with any change to practice or policy, there is a concurrent need to train the relevant workforces to adapt to the changes. Incorporate acquisition cybersecurity into required training curricula for appropriate workforces. Require organizations that do business with the enterprise to receive training about the acquisition cybersecurity requirements of the organization's contracts.

3. **Develop common cybersecurity definitions for acquisitions.**

   Unclear and inconsistently defined terms lead, at best, to suboptimal outcomes for both efficiency and cybersecurity. Increasing the clarity of key cybersecurity terms in acquisitions will increase efficiency and effectiveness for enterprise.

4. **Institute an acquisition cyber risk management strategy.**

   From an enterprise-wide cybersecurity perspective, identify a hierarchy of cyber risk criticality for acquisitions. To maximize consistency in application of procurement rules, develop and use "overlays" for similar types of acquisition, starting with the types of acquisitions that present the greatest cyber risk.[53]

5. **Include a requirement to purchase from Original Equipment Manufacturers (OEMs), their authorized resellers, or other "trusted" sources, whenever available, in appropriate acquisitions.**

   In certain circumstances, the risk of receiving inauthentic or otherwise nonconforming items is best mitigated by obtaining required items only from OEMs, their authorized resellers, or other trusted sources. The cyber risk threshold for application of this limitation of sources should be consistent across the enterprise.

6. **Increase the organizational accountability for cyber risk management.**

   Identify and modify acquisition practices that contribute to cyber risk. Integrate security standards into acquisition planning and contract administration. Incorporate cyber risk into enterprise risk management and ensure key decision makers are accountable for managing risks of cybersecurity shortfalls in a fielded solution.

---

53 An overlay is a fully specified set of security requirements and supplemental guidance that provide the ability to appropriately tailor security requirements for specific technologies or product groups, circumstances and conditions, and/or operational environments.

Significant supply chain disruptions caused by cyber-related events, fortunately, are still uncommon. That should not be an excuse for complacency, however. The risks are very real. Disruptions can occur at any point on the chain. The following scenarios could occur at any time.

- A virus infecting the systems of a key supplier destroys essential records, forcing the supplier to shut down its systems for several days to eradicate the infection. Once the systems are back online, customers are required to resubmit their orders, causing further delays.
- A malicious attack on a trucking company disrupts its dispatch, freight management, and logistic systems, resulting in delays in shipments of vital parts.
- A successful attack on a large commodities exchange interrupts the flow of essential materials and causes increased price volatility throughout numerous markets.

Supply chains are often understood in terms of manufacturing processes, but "supplies" also can be digital. In addition to damage to suppliers and transporters, security professionals should be concerned about the digital infrastructure that supports modern commerce. Almost every business today relies on third parties such as Internet service providers and Web hosting services to support supply chain activities. Interruption of services provided through this digital infrastructure could be extremely disruptive – potentially even more disruptive in the short run than damage to physical infrastructure caused by a natural catastrophe.

The risk of supply chain disruptions caused by system malfunctions, hackers, or viruses should be managed much the same as other supply chain risks. Supplier diversification is essential: Relying on a single supplier is simply asking for trouble. Additionally, the quality of cyber defenses should be a criterion when evaluating potential suppliers.

For critical suppliers, a system security audit may be justified. Companies also should consider insurance for their contingent business interruption exposures. First party cyber insurance policies may provide coverage for extra expense, business interruption, and contingent business interruption losses due to a cyber-attack. Organizations should work with their brokers to assure that their insurance programs provide the coverage appropriate to their supply chain exposures.

Manage Third-Party Governance

With the growing adoption of cloud computing, the security professional must understand the contractual and governance implications of managing the risks associated with the use of a third-party service provider. With regards to the cloud, third-party solutions can be viewed in three ways:

1. Infrastructure as a service (IaaS)
2. Platform as a service (PaaS)
3. Software as a Service (SaaS)

Infrastructure as a Service (IaaS) focuses on providing "bare metal" or basic computing resources such as processors, memory, storage, or transmission media to a customer. The customer is responsible for proving an operating system, data, applications, databases, and the majority of the security controls. Platform as a Service (PaaS) offerings typically provide and operating system or a database to the customer. The customer has little visibility into the hardware layer and shares a security control balance with the provider with the customer responsible for the application and data. Finally, Software as a Service (SaaS) means the customer is only providing the data for the most part and the provider is responsible for the vast majority of the security controls.

When partnering with a third party, the security professional must be cautious to ensure service level agreements (SLAs) are not confused with the assurance provided by due diligence actives such as on-site assessments, document exchanges, and process or policy reviews. SLAs are an important concept in any third-party governance program or contract. SLAs define the agreed upon level of performance and compensation or penalty between the provider and the customer. However, simply having an SLA defined and in place does not mean that the provider will always be in compliance with the SLA. For example, assume a provider is selling processing time to customer one for one U.S. dollar an hour. The SLA that the customer has with the provider states that if processing is not available, they will penalize the provider one U.S. dollar an hour. Therefore, the net cost to the provider for an hour of down time is two U.S. dollars. One for the lost revenue and one for the penalty. Should the provider be less than honest and another customer offers to pay five U.S. dollars per an hour for the processing power, the provider may use customer one's processing power and still make a net gain of three U.S. dollars. This is a very simple example, but one that illustrates that SLAs do not equate to assurance.

Assurance can only be gained through inspection, review, and assessment. A security professional may be asked to review the security documentation of a third-party system and then perform an assessment to determine its compliance with a specific control framework or regulation. The assessment gives the security professional and the customer an opportunity to view the system provider as it really is. Findings such as a very high utilization rate with no firewalls may indicate a provider who is very inexpensive and has many customers but may have cut some corners on security to save costs. The security professional must ensure the assessment or inspection covers the information security and privacy areas that are deemed to be most important to the organization.

Additionally, organizations must be cautious about the countries and individuals who own, operate, and have jurisdiction over the third-party provider's system. Individuals who may not be suitable to access the customer's information may have access if proper controls are not implemented. Furthermore, sensitive organizational information may be released to a non-friendly government without the consent or knowledge of the organization. Working with legal counsel, the security professional has a duty to determine what legal exposure an organization may face depending on a third-party system's hosting country.

Minimum Security and Service-Level Requirements

Requirements gathering is an essential part of any project and a foundational element of project management. Understanding fully what a project will deliver is critical to its success. This may sound like common sense, but surprisingly it's an area that is often given far too little attention.

Many projects start with a list of requirements that are provided by one or more parties, only to find out later that the customers' needs have not been properly understood.

One way to avoid this problem is by producing a statement of requirements. This document is a guide to the main requirements of the project. It provides:

- A succinct requirement specification for management purposes.
- A statement of key objectives.
- A description of the environment in which the system will work.
- Background information and references to other relevant material.
- Information on major design constraints.

The contents of the statement of requirements should be stable or change relatively slowly. Once you have created your statement of requirements, ensure the customer and all other stakeholders agree to it and understand that this and only this will be delivered. Finally, ensure you have cross-referenced the requirements in the statement of requirements with those in the project definition report to ensure there is no mismatch.

Rules for Successful Requirements Gathering

To be successful at requirements gathering, the security architect should follow these rules:

- Do not assume you know what the customer wants; ask.
- Involve the users from the start.
- Define and agree to the scope of the project.
- Ensure requirements are specific, realistic, and measurable.
- Gain clarity if there is any doubt.
- Create a clear, concise, and thorough requirements document and share it with the customer.
- Confirm your understanding of the requirements with the customer (play them back).
- Avoid talking technology or solutions until the requirements are fully understood.
- Get the requirements agreed upon with the stakeholders before the project starts.
- Create a prototype if necessary to confirm or refine the customers' requirements.

Common mistakes that can easily be made while gathering and processing requirements include:

- Basing a solution on complex or cutting edge technology and then discovering that it cannot easily be rolled out to the 'real world.'
- Not prioritizing the user requirements.
- Not enough consultation with real users and practitioners.
- Solving the 'problem' before you know what it is.
- Lacking a clear understanding and making assumptions rather than asking.

Requirements gathering is about creating a clear, concise, and agreed upon set of customer requirements that will allow the security architect to provide exactly what the customer is looking for. Correctly capturing and documenting the requirements is the first step for the security architect. Once this has been done, the security architect will need to draft the Service Level Agreement (SLA) based on the requirements. The SLA will then be used to manage the service lifecycle and to specify the responsibilities for the customer and the service provider. The SLA is measured and reported on by the Service Level Report, which is produced to compare the agreed to and actually achieved service levels, and it also includes information on the usage of services, ongoing measures for service improvement, and any exceptional events.

Service Level Requirements (SLR)

The Service Level Requirements document contains the requirements for a service from the client viewpoint, defining detailed service level targets, mutual responsibilities, and other requirements specific to a certain group of customers. The SLR document evolves into a draft Service Level Agreement.

The Service Level Requirements document contains the requirements of the IT service from the client viewpoint; it is an input for the Service Specification Sheet and the Service Level Agreement, which further expand the following items:

- Name of the service
- Service description (short description of the service)
- Users of the IT service on the client side
- Breakdown of the offered service into service groups (e.g., along Infrastructure Components or IT Applications lines)
- Handling of service interruptions (by telephone, by remote access, on site?)
- User services (user administration, installation, etc.)
- Availability requirements, number of interruptions allowed
- Availability thresholds (xx.xx %)
- Downtimes for maintenance (number of allowed downtimes, pre-notification periods)
- Procedure for announcing interruptions to the service (planned/unplanned)
- Performance requirements
- Required capacity (lower/upper limit) for the service
- Allowed workload/usage of the service
- Response times from applications
- Reaction and resolution times (according to priorities, definition of priorities; e.g., for the classification of incidents)
- Requirements for the maintenance of the service in the event of a disaster

	Questions	Reason for the Question	Example / Sample Values	Responses	Comments
1	What are the core business hours for this system?	Need to ensure that the support level correlates with this information.	24 x 7 8am - Midnight x 7 9am - 5pm x 5 Others?		
2	What is the preferred time frame for reporting and batch processing?	Allows for processing windows to be established. Depending on the chosen solution, the system may/may not be available, or responsiveness may be reduced due to additional load.	24 x 7 8am - Midnight x 7 9am - 5pm x 5 Others?		
3	What is the preferred time frame for planned outages to perform general system maintenance?	Allows for maintenance window to be negotiated and agreed upon with support groups/vendors.	24 x 7 8am - Midnight x 7 9am - 5pm x 5 Others?		
4	What are the peak periods of usage for this system? Identify any known peak hour or peak day periods.	This information needs to be captured before determining the detailed system requirements because it identifies the nature of the system loading.	Mon - Fri 9:00-17:00 Mon - Fri 11:00-15:00 Others?		

Table 1.2 – **A Sample of an SLR document**

Service Level Agreement (SLA)

An agreement between an IT service provider and a customer, the SLA describes the IT service, documents service level targets, and specifies the responsibilities of the IT service provider and the customer. A single SLA may cover multiple services or multiple customers.

Service Level Report

The Service Level Report gives insight into a service provider's ability to deliver the agreed service quality. To this purpose, it compares the agreed to and actually achieved service levels, and it also includes information on the usage of services, ongoing measures for service improvement, and any exceptional events. A Service Level Report is issued by the service provider for its customers, IT management, and other Service Management processes. A similar report is also created by an external service supplier to document its achieved service performance.

Security Education, Training, and Awareness

Policies define what the organization needs to accomplish at a high level and serve as management's intention with regards to information security. Security awareness can be defined as helping establish an understanding of the importance and how to comply with security policies within the organization. Given today's complex business environments, most organizations perceive value in promoting an awareness of security within their environments. There are many methods by which an organization can educate its members regarding security. These methods, as well as observations about their implementation, follow. Security awareness addresses the why of policy. If end-users understand the why, they are more apt to follow the policy. Generally, people follow policy more consistently if they understand why policy exists and how to comply.

Formal Security Awareness Training

Security awareness training is a method by which organizations can inform employees about their roles, and expectations surrounding their roles, in the observance of information security requirements. Additionally, training provides guidance surrounding the performance of particular security or risk management functions, as well as providing information surrounding the security and risk management functions in general. Finally, educated users aid the organization in the fulfillment of its security program objectives, which may also include audit objectives for organizations that are bound by regulatory compliance (such as HIPAA, the Sarbanes–Oxley Act, the Gramm–Leach–Bliley Act, or any other type of regulation).

Training Topics

Security is a broad discipline, and as such, there are many topics that could be covered by security awareness training. Topics that can be investigated within the security awareness curriculum include:

- Corporate security policies
- The organization's security program
- Regulatory compliance requirements for the organization
- Social engineering
- Business continuity
- Disaster recovery

- Emergency management, to include hazardous materials, biohazards, and so on
- Security incident response
- Data classification
- Information labeling and handling
- Personnel security, safety, and soundness
- Physical security
- Appropriate computing resource use
- Proper care and handling of security credentials, such as passwords
- Risk assessment
- Accidents, errors, or omissions

A well-rounded security curriculum will include specialty classes and awareness aids for individuals performing specialized roles within the organization, such as those in IT, accounting, and others. The training may also align with job functions, roles, and responsibilities. The organization must also keep in mind that special attention should be paid to aligning training with security risk management activities. In doing so, the training may result in partial or complete offset of the risk within the organization.

Creating a Security Awareness Course

The following creates an outline for a security awareness course surrounding a corporate security policy. Assuming that this is the first formal course the organization has conducted, it is likely that personnel have not been formally introduced to the policy. This introduction would be an appropriate place to begin. A curriculum may proceed as follows:

What Is a Corporate Security Policy?

This item allows the organization to explain, in detail, a security measure it is undertaking to protect its environment.

Why Is Having a Corporate Security Policy Important?

This item provides the opportunity to share with employees that it is everyone's responsibility to protect the organization, its people, and its assets. This is also an appropriate place for senior management to voice their support of the corporate security policy and the security management effort in general.

How Does This Policy Fit into My Role at the Organization?

Many employees are concerned about the effect that security may have on them. Some fear that they will not be able to accomplish tasks on time; others fear that their role may change. This is the right time to indicate to employees that although security considerations may add a bit to job performance, it is more than likely that they are already performing many of the security responsibilities set forth in the security policy. The policy adds formalization to the ad hoc security functions in practice; that is, these ad hoc practices are now documented and may be enhanced as well.

What about People Who Say They Do Not Have Any Security Functions Present in Their Current Role?

It is important to point out that these functions may be present in an ad hoc fashion, but that any process performed over time becomes at least partly automatic. This leads to decreased time to performance, in reality, over time. The instructor may ask the student whether there was a time in recent memory when he or she was asked to perform a new function as part of his or her job. The instructor can then point out that this is a similar situation.

Do I Have to Comply?

It is crucial for an organization to agree that all employees, including senior management, must comply with corporate security policies. If there are exceptions to the rule, then the policy may become unenforceable. This puts the organization in the position of having wasted dollars, time, and resources in the crafting of a policy with no "teeth."

What Are the Penalties for Noncompliance?

It is equally critical that an organization spells out in common and easily understood terms what the penalty is for noncompliance with a corporate security policy. Policies may indicate in the body of the policy that all personnel, contractors, and business associates are expected to adhere to the policies, or this may be covered as an overall statement for all policies. Typically, failure to do so results in disciplinary action, up to and including termination or prosecution.

At this point, there are likely to be questions about what may happen in the event of an accidental violation. It is important to reiterate to the students that security violations (or incidents) should be reported immediately so that the impact to the organization can be minimized.

What Is the Effect of This Corporate Policy on My Work (Will It Make Things Harder)?

This item was discussed in detail above; the instructor may tie this back to impact on the individual's role.

What Type of Things Should I Be Looking For?

At this point, the employee's questions have been answered, relative to their responsibility to comply with the corporate security policy. This would be an appropriate time to discuss the policy's contents with the students. This can be done as a lecture, by example, or in a "spot the security problem" format.

When teaching a course of this type, the instructor should be sure to address topics that apply to all staff, including senior management, line management, business unit users, temporary or seasonal staff, contractors, business associates, and so on.

Awareness Activities and Methods – Creating the Culture of Awareness in the Organization

There is a variety of methods that can be used to promote security awareness. Some of the more common methods include:

- Formalized courses, as mentioned above, delivered either in a classroom fashion using slides, handouts, or books, or online through training websites suited to this purpose.

- Use of posters that call attention to aspects of security awareness, such as password protection, physical security, personnel security, and others.
- Business unit walk-throughs to aid workers in identification of practices that should be avoided (such as posting passwords on post-it notes in a conspicuous place on the desktop) and practices that should be continued (such as maintaining a clean desk or using a locked screensaver when away from the computer).
- Use of the organization's intranet to post security reminders or to host a weekly or monthly column about information security happenings within the organization.
- Appointment of a business unit security awareness mentor to aid with questions, concerns, or comments surrounding the implementation of security within the environment; these individuals would interact together and with the organization's security officer. These mentors could also interact with the organization's internal audit, legal, information technology, and corporate business units on a periodic (monthly or quarterly) basis.
- Sponsor an enterprise-wide security awareness day, complete with security activities, prizes, and recognition of the winners.
- Sponsor an event with an external partner, such as Information Systems Security Association (ISSA), Information Systems Audit and Control Association (ISACA), SysAdmin, Audit, Network, Security (SANS) Institute, International Information Systems Security Certification Consortium ((ISC)²), or others; allow time for staff members to fully participate in the event.
- Provide trinkets for the users within the organization that support security management principles.
- Consider a special event day, week, or month that coincides with other industry or world awareness events such as Global Security Awareness Week (annually in September) and Security Awareness Month (typically annually in October).
- Provide security management videos, books, websites, and collateral for employees to use for reference.

It is important to note that activities should be interesting and rewarding for the organization's people. To facilitate this interest, the program should be adaptable, and the content and format of the awareness materials should be subject to change on a periodic basis.

Job Training

Unlike general security awareness training, security training assists personnel with the development of their skill sets relative to performance of security functions within their roles. A typical security curriculum in a mature organization will include specialty classes for individuals performing specialized roles within the organization, such as those in IT, accounting, and others.

Even within these business units, specialized training will occur. For example, in the IT area, it would be advisable for network staff responsible for maintenance and monitoring of the firewalls, intrusion detection/prevention systems, and syslog servers to be sufficiently trained to perform these duties. Say senior management determined that there were no funds available for training. What would be the result? Typically, motivated staff will receive some on-the-job learning; however, it may not be sufficient to perform the job duties adequately.

As a result, the organization is breached and sensitive information is stolen. Who would be at fault in this case? Senior management is always ultimately responsible in the organization for information security objectives. Senior management failed, in this case, to adequately protect the environment by refusing to properly train staff in their respective security duties. Any legal ramifications would fall squarely upon management's shoulders.

However, assume that the personnel in question indicated to management that although no paid training was available, they felt comfortable that they could perform the security functions for which they were responsible. To demonstrate, they performed the requisite functions for IT management to demonstrate capability. All is well until the organization is breached some months later, and confidential information is stolen. Senior management returns to information systems management and asks the director to investigate. During his or her investigation, he or she discovers that patching has not occurred for the past three months. When the staff was asked about the incident, no satisfactory answer could be given. Who would be responsible for the breach in that event? Again, senior management is always ultimately responsible for information security within the organization; however, senior management held the network team accountable for failing to maintain patching levels and promptly fired them from their positions. Ensuring that a resource is properly trained can assist an organization in assigning accountability for the satisfactory completion of security tasks for which they are responsible.

The organization must also keep in mind that training should be closely aligned with security risk management activities. In doing so, the training may result in a partial or complete offset of the risk within the organization.

Performance Metrics

It is important for the organization to track performance relative to security for the purposes of both enforcement and enhancement of security initiatives under way. It is also important for the organization to ensure that users acknowledge their security responsibilities by signing off after each class that they have heard and understand the material and will agree to be bound by the organization's security program, policies, procedures, plans, and initiatives. Measurement can include periodic walk-throughs of business unit organizations, periodic quizzes to keep staff up to date, and so on.

Summary

The "Security and Risk Management" domain addresses the framework and policies, concepts, principles, structures, and standards used to establish criteria for the protection of information assets and to assess the effectiveness of that protection. It includes issues of governance, organizational behavior, and security awareness.

Information security management helps the security professional to establish the foundation of a comprehensive and proactive security program to ensure the protection of an organization's information assets. Today's environment of highly interconnected, interdependent systems necessitates the requirement to understand the linkage between information technology and meeting business objectives. Information security management communicates the risks accepted by the organization due to the currently implemented security controls and continually works to cost effectively enhance the controls to minimize the risk to the company's information assets. Security management encompasses the administrative, technical, and physical controls necessary to adequately protect the confidentiality, integrity, and availability of information assets. Controls are manifested through a foundation of policies, procedures, standards, baselines, and guidelines.

Information security management practices that manage risk include such tools as risk assessment, risk analysis, data classification, and security awareness. Information assets are classified, and through risk assessment, the threats and vulnerabilities related to these assets are categorized, and the appropriate safeguards to mitigate risk of compromise can be identified and prioritized by the security professional.

Risk management minimizes loss to information assets due to undesirable events through identification, measurement, and control. It encompasses the overall security review, risk analysis, selection and evaluation of safeguards, cost–benefit analysis, management decision, and safeguard identification and implementation, along with ongoing effectiveness review. Risk management provides a mechanism to the organization to ensure that executive management knows current risks, and informed decisions can be made to use one of the risk management principles: risk avoidance, risk transfer, risk mitigation, or risk acceptance.

Security management is concerned with regulatory, customer, employee, and business partner requirements for managing data as they flow between the various parties to support the processing and business use of the information. Confidentiality, integrity, and availability of the information must be maintained throughout the process.

Business continuity planning (BCP) and disaster recovery planning (DRP) addresses the preparation, processes, and practices required to ensure the preservation of the organization in the face of major disruptions to normal organization operations. BCP and DRP involve the identification, selection, implementation, testing, and updating of processes and specific prudent actions necessary to protect critical organization processes from the effects of major system and network disruptions and to ensure the timely restoration of organization operations if significant disruptions occur.

This chapter has described a process for building an enterprise-wide business continuity (BC) program. It discusses the evolution of the industry regulations that have influenced or in some cases mandated that organizations build programs within their organization that will ensure the continuation of their organization "no matter what."

Finally, it discussed the interrelationship between information security and BC and other risk management areas such as physical security, records management, vendor management, internal audit, financial risk management, operational risk management, and regulatory compliance (legal and regulatory risk) in the context of the overall BC risk management framework.

Domain 1: Review Questions

1. Within the realm of IT security, which of the following combinations best defines risk?

    A.   Threat coupled with a breach

    B.   Threat coupled with a vulnerability

    C.   Vulnerability coupled with an attack

    D.   Threat coupled with a breach of security

2. When determining the value of an intangible asset which is be **BEST** approach?

    A.   Determine the physical storage costs and multiply by the expected life of the company

    B.   With the assistance of a finance of accounting professional determine how much profit the asset has returned

    C.   Review the depreciation of the intangible asset over the past three years.

    D.   Use the historical acquisition or development cost of the intangible asset

3. Qualitative risk assessment is earmarked by which of the following?

    A.   Ease of implementation and it can be completed by personnel with a limited understanding of the risk assessment process

    B.   Can be completed by personnel with a limited understanding of the risk assessment process and uses detailed metrics used for calculation of risk

    C.   Detailed metrics used for calculation of risk and ease of implementation

    D.   Can be completed by personnel with a limited understanding of the risk assessment process and detailed metrics used for the calculation of risk

4. Single loss expectancy (SLE) is calculated by using:

    A.   Asset value and annualized rate of occurrence (ARO)

    B.   Asset value, local annual frequency estimate (LAFE), and standard annual frequency estimate (SAFE)

    C.   Asset value and exposure factor

    D.   Local annual frequency estimate and annualized rate of occurrence

5. Consideration for which type of risk assessment to perform includes all of the following:

    A.   Culture of the organization, likelihood of exposure and budget

    B.   Budget, capabilities of resources and likelihood of exposure

    C.   Capabilities of resources, likelihood of exposure and budget

    D.   Culture of the organization, budget, capabilities and resources

6. Security awareness training includes:

    A.   Legislated security compliance objectives

    B.   Security roles and responsibilities for staff

    C.   The high-level outcome of vulnerability assessments

    D.   Specialized curriculum assignments, coursework and an accredited institution

7. What is the minimum and customary practice of responsible protection of assets that affects a community or societal norm?

    A.   Due diligence

    B.   Risk mitigation

    C.   Asset protection

    D.   Due care

8. Effective security management:

    A.   Achieves security at the lowest cost

    B.   Reduces risk to an acceptable level

    C.   Prioritizes security for new products

    D.   Installs patches in a timely manner

9. Availability makes information accessible by protecting from:

    A.   Denial of services, fires, floods, hurricanes, and unauthorized transactions

    B.   Fires, floods, hurricanes, unauthorized transactions and unreadable backup tapes

    C.   Unauthorized transactions, fires, floods, hurricanes and unreadable backup tapes

    D.   Denial of services, fires, floods, and hurricanes and unreadable backup tapes

10. Which phrase best defines a business continuity/disaster recovery plan?

    A. A set of plans for preventing a disaster.

    B. An approved set of preparations and sufficient procedures for responding to a disaster.

    C. A set of preparations and procedures for responding to a disaster without management approval.

    D. The adequate preparations and procedures for the continuation of all organization functions.

11. Which of the following steps should be performed first in a business impact analysis (BIA)?

    A. Identify all business units within an organization

    B. Evaluate the impact of disruptive events

    C. Estimate the Recovery Time Objectives (RTO)

    D. Evaluate the criticality of business functions

12. Tactical security plans are **BEST** used to:

    A. Establish high-level security policies

    B. Enable enterprise/entity-wide security management

    C. Reduce downtime

    D. Deploy new security technology

13. Who is accountable for implementing information security?

    A. Everyone

    B. Senior management

    C. Security officer

    D. Data owners

14. Security is likely to be most expensive when addressed in which phase?

    A. Design

    B. Rapid prototyping

    C. Testing

    D. Implementation

1

Security & Risk Management

177

15. Information systems auditors help the organization:

    A.   Mitigate compliance issues

    B.   Establish an effective control environment

    C.   Identify control gaps

    D.   Address information technology for financial statements

16. The Facilitated Risk Analysis Process (FRAP)

    A.   makes a base assumption that a broad risk assessment is the most efficient way to determine risk in a system, business segment, application or process.

    B.   makes a base assumption that a narrow risk assessment is the most efficient way to determine risk in a system, business segment, application or process.

    C.   makes a base assumption that a narrow risk assessment is the least efficient way to determine risk in a system, business segment, application or process.

    D.   makes a base assumption that a broad risk assessment is the least efficient way to determine risk in a system, business segment, application or process.

17. Setting clear security roles has the following benefits:

    A.   Establishes personal accountability, reduces cross-training requirements and reduces departmental turf battles

    B.   Enables continuous improvement, reduces cross-training requirements and reduces departmental turf battles

    C.   Establishes personal accountability, establishes continuous improvement and reduces turf battles

    D.   Reduces departmental turf battles, Reduces cross-training requirements and establishes personal accountability

18. Well-written security program policies are **BEST** reviewed:

    A.   At least annually or at pre-determined organization changes

    B.   After major project implementations

    C.   When applications or operating systems are updated

    D.   When procedures need to be modified

1

19. An organization will conduct a risk assessment to evaluate

    A.   threats to its assets, vulnerabilities not present in the environment, the likelihood that a threat will be realized by taking advantage of an exposure, the impact that the exposure being realized will have on the organization, the residual risk

    B.   threats to its assets, vulnerabilities present in the environment, the likelihood that a threat will be realized by taking advantage of an exposure, the impact that the exposure being realized will have on another organization, the residual risk

    C.   threats to its assets, vulnerabilities present in the environment, the likelihood that a threat will be realized by taking advantage of an exposure, the impact that the exposure being realized will have on the organization, the residual risk

    D.   threats to its assets, vulnerabilities present in the environment, the likelihood that a threat will be realized by taking advantage of an exposure, the impact that the exposure being realized will have on the organization, the total risk

20. A security policy which will remain relevant and meaningful over time includes the following:

    A.   Directive words such as shall, must, or will, technical specifications and is short in length

    B.   Defined policy development process, short in length and contains directive words such as shall, must or will

    C.   Short in length, technical specifications and contains directive words such as shall, must or will

    D.   Directive words such as shall, must, or will, defined policy development process and is short in length

21. The ability of one person in the finance department to add vendors to the vendor database and subsequently pay the vendor violates which concept?

    A.   A well-formed transaction

    B.   Separation of duties

    C.   Least privilege

    D.   Data sensitivity level

22. Collusion is best mitigated by:

    A.   Job rotation

    B.   Data classification

    C.   Defining job sensitivity level

    D.   Least privilege

23. Data access decisions are best made by:

    A.   User managers

    B.   Data owners

    C.   Senior management

    D.   Application developer

24. Which of the following statements **BEST** describes the extent to which an organization should address business continuity or disaster recovery planning?

    A.   Continuity planning is a significant organizational issue and should include all parts or functions of the company.

    B.   Continuity planning is a significant technology issue and the recovery of technology should be its primary focus.

    C.   Continuity planning is required only where there is complexity in voice and data communications.

    D.   Continuity planning is a significant management issue and should include the primary functions specified by management.

25. Business impact analysis is performed to **BEST** identify:

    A.   The impacts of a threat to the organization operations.

    B.   The exposures to loss to the organization.

    C.   The impacts of a risk on the organization.

    D.   The cost efficient way to eliminate threats.

26. During the risk analysis phase of the planning, which of the following actions could **BEST** manage threats or mitigate the effects of an event?

    A.   Modifying the exercise scenario.

    B.   Developing recovery procedures.

    C.   Increasing reliance on key individuals

    D.   Implementing procedural controls.

27. The **BEST** reason to implement additional controls or safeguards is to:

    A.   deter or remove the risk.

    B.   identify and eliminate the threat.

    C.   reduce the impact of the threat.

    D.   identify the risk and the threat.

28. Which of the following statements **BEST** describes organization impact analysis?

    A.   Risk analysis and organization impact analysis are two different terms describing the same project effort.

    B.   A organization impact analysis calculates the probability of disruptions to the organization.

    C.   A organization impact analysis is critical to development of a business continuity plan.

    D.   A organization impact analysis establishes the effect of disruptions on the organization.

29. The term "disaster recovery" refers to the recovery of:

    A.   organization operations.

    B.   technology environment.

    C.   manufacturing environment.

    D.   personnel environments.

30. Which of the following terms **BEST** describes the effort to determine the consequences of disruptions that could result from a disaster?

    A.   Business impact analysis.

    B.   Risk analysis.

    C.   Risk assessment.

    D.   Project problem definition

31. The elements of risk are as follows:

    A.   Natural disasters and manmade disasters

    B.   Threats, assets and mitigating controls

    C.   Risk and business impact analysis

    D.   business impact analysis and mitigating controls

32. Which of the following methods is not acceptable for exercising the business continuity plan?

    A.   Table-top exercise.

    B.   Call exercise.

    C.   Simulated exercise.

    D.   Halting a production application or function.

Security & Risk Management

1

33. Which of the following is the primary desired result of any well-planned business continuity exercise?

    A. Identifies plan strengths and weaknesses.

    B. Satisfies management requirements.

    C. Complies with auditor's requirements.

    D. Maintains shareholder confidence

34. A business continuity plan is best updated and maintained:

    A. Annually or when requested by auditors.

    B. Only when new versions of software are deployed.

    C. Only when new hardware is deployed.

    D. During the configuration and change management process.

35. Which of the following is **MOST** important for successful business continuity?

    A. Senior leadership support.

    B. Strong technical support staff.

    C. Extensive wide area network infrastructure.

    D. An integrated incident response team.

36. A service's recovery point objective is zero. Which approach **BEST** ensures the requirement is met?

    A. RAID 6 with a hot site alternative.

    B. RAID 0 with a warm site alternative

    C. RAID 0 with a cold site alternative

    D. RAID 6 with a reciprocal agreement.

37. The (ISC)² code of ethics resolves conflicts between canons by:

    A. there can never be conflicts between canons.

    B. working through adjudication.

    C. the order of the canons.

    D. vetting all canon conflicts through the board of directors.

Domain 2
Asset Security

The Asset Security domain contains the concepts, principles, structures, and standards used to monitor and secure assets and those controls used to enforce various levels of confidentiality, integrity, and availability. Information security architecture and design covers the practice of applying a comprehensive and rigorous method for describing a current and/or future structure and behavior for an organization's security processes, information security systems, personnel and organizational sub-units, so that these practices and processes align with the organization's core goals and strategic direction.

Operations security can be challenging for the security professionals, depending on their background and experience. Operations security is primarily concerned with the protection and control of information processing assets in centralized and distributed environments. Operations security is a quality of other services and is also a set of services in its own right.

Information Security Governance and Risk Management addresses the frameworks and policies, concepts, principles, structures, and standards used to establish criteria for the protection of information assets, as well as to assess the effectiveness of that protection. It includes issues of governance, organizational behavior, and security awareness.

Information security management establishes the foundation of a comprehensive and proactive security program to ensure the protection of an organization's information assets. Today's environment of highly interconnected, interdependent systems necessitates the requirement to understand the linkage between information technology and meeting business objectives. Information security management communicates the risks accepted by the organization due to the currently implemented security controls, and it continually works to cost effectively enhance the controls to minimize the risk to the company's information assets. Security management encompasses the administrative, technical, and physical controls necessary to adequately protect the confidentiality, integrity, and availability of information assets. Controls are manifested through a foundation of policies, procedures, standards, baselines, and guidelines.

TOPICS

- Classify information and supporting assets
  - Sensitivity
  - Criticality
- Determine and maintain ownership
  - Data owners
  - System owners
  - Business/Mission owners
- Protect Privacy
  - Data owners
  - Data processes
  - Data remanence
- Ensure appropriate retention
  - Media
  - Hardware
  - Personnel
- Determine data security controls
  - Data at Rest
  - Data in Transit
  - Baselines
  - Scoping and tailoring
  - Standards selection
  - Cryptography
- Establish handling requirements
  - Markings
  - Labels
  - Storage
  - Destruction of sensitive information

OBJECTIVES

According to the (ISC)^2 Candidate Information Bulletin (Exam Outline), a CISSP candidate is expected to:

- Classify information and supporting assets
- Determine and maintain ownership
- Protect Privacy
- Ensure appropriate retention
- Determine data security controls
- Establish handling requirements

2

Asset Security

Data Management: Determine and Maintain Ownership

Data management is a process involving a broad range of activities from administrative to technical aspects of handling data. Good data management practices include:

- A data policy that defines strategic long-term goals and provides guiding principles for data management in all aspects of a project, agency, or organization.
- Clearly defined roles and responsibilities for those associated with the data, in particular of data providers, data owners, and custodians.
- Data quality procedures (e.g., quality assurance, quality control) at all stages of the data management process. Verification and validation of accuracy of the data.
- Documentation of specific data management practices and descriptive metadata for each dataset.
- Adherence to agreed upon data management practices.
- Carefully planned and documented database specifications based on an understanding of user requirements and data to be used.
- Defined procedures for updates to the information system infrastructure (hardware, software, file formats, storage media), data storage and backup methods, and the data itself.
- Ongoing data audit to monitor the use and assess effectiveness of management practices and the integrity of existing data. Data storage and archiving plan and testing of this plan (disaster recovery).
- Ongoing and evolving data security approach of tested layered controls for reducing risks to data.
- Clear statements of criteria for data access and, when applicable, information on any limitations applied to data for control of full access that could affect its use.
- Clear and documented published data that is available and useable to users, with consistent delivery procedures.

Data Policy

A sound data policy defines strategic long-term goals for data management across all aspects of a project or enterprise. A data policy is a set of high-level principles that establish a guiding framework for data management. A data policy can be used to address strategic issues such as data access, relevant legal matters, data stewardship issues and custodial duties, data acquisition, and other issues. Because it provides a high-level framework, a data policy should be flexible and dynamic. This allows a data policy to be readily adapted for unanticipated challenges, different types of projects, and potentially opportunistic partnerships while still maintaining its guiding strategic focus.

Issues to be considered by the security practitioner when establishing a data policy include:

- ***Cost*** – Consideration should be given to the cost of providing data versus the cost of providing access to data. Cost can be both a barrier for the user to acquire certain datasets as well as for the provider to supply data in the format or extent requested.

2

Asset Security

- **Ownership and Custodianship** – Data ownership should be clearly addressed. Intellectual property rights can be owned at different levels; e.g., a merged dataset can be owned by one organization even though other organizations own the constituent data. If the legal ownership is unclear, the risk exists for the data to be improperly used, neglected, or lost.

- **Privacy** – Clarification of what data is private and what data is to be made available in the public domain needs to occur. Privacy legislation normally requires that personal information be protected from others. Therefore, clear guidelines are needed for the inclusion, usage, management, storage, and maintenance of personal information in datasets.

- **Liability** – Liability involves how protected an organization is from legal recourse. This is very important in the area of data and information management, especially where damage is caused to an individual or organization as a result of misuse or inaccuracies in the data. Liability is often dealt with via end-user agreements and licenses. A carefully worded disclaimer statement can be included in the metadata and data retrieval system so as to free the provider, data collector, or anyone associated with the dataset of any legal responsibility for misuse or inaccuracies in the data.

- **Sensitivity** – There is a need to identify any data that is regarded as sensitive. Sensitive data is any data that if released to the public, would result in an adverse effect (harm, removal, destruction) on the attribute in question or to a living individual. A number of factors need to be taken into account when determining sensitivity, including type and level of threat, vulnerability of the attribute, type of information, and whether it is already publicly available.

- **Existing Law & Policy Requirements** – Consideration should be given to laws and policies related to data and information as they apply. Existing legislation and policy requirements may have an effect on the enterprise's data policy.

- **Policy and Process** – Consideration should be given to legal requests for data and policies that may need to be put in place to allow for the timely processing of and, if appropriate, response to the request. In addition, if one or more policies already exist, then they have to be examined and assessed to decide whether they will be sufficient or if they may need to be modified in some way to be fully integrated with any new processes being created. The policy and process used to provide access to data based on a legal request have to be designed and implemented in such a way that they do not violate access controls or any existing policies that mandate how secure access may be granted under such circumstances, ensuring that only the data subject to the request is made available and that unrelated data is not exposed.

Roles and Responsibilities

Data management is about individuals and organizations as much as it is about information technology, database practices, and applications. In order to meet data management goals and standards, all involved parties must understand their associated roles and responsibilities.

The objectives of delineating data management roles and responsibilities are to:

- Clearly define roles associated with functions.
- Establish data ownership throughout all phases of a project.
- Instill data accountability.
- Ensure that adequate, agreed-upon data quality and metadata metrics are maintained on a continuous basis.

Data Ownership

Information has a life that consists of creation, use, and finally destruction. Several important information security activities surround the lifecycle of information to protect it, ensure it is available to only those who require access to it, and finally to destroy it when it is no longer needed. Several concepts of information ownership need to be understood by the information security professionals as part of their duties.

When information is created, someone in the organization must be directly responsible for it. Often this is the individual or group that created, purchased, or acquired the information to support the mission of the organization. This individual or group is considered the "information owner." The information owner typically has the following responsibilities:

- Determine the impact the information has on the mission of the organization.
- Understand the replacement cost of the information (if it can be replaced).
- Determine who in the organization or outside of it has a need for the information and under what circumstances the information should be released.
- Know when the information is inaccurate or no longer needed and should be destroyed.

A key aspect of good data management involves the identification of the owner(s) of the data. Data owners generally have legal rights over the data, along with copyright and intellectual property rights. This applies even where the data is collected, collated, or disseminated by another party by way of contractual agreements, etc. Data ownership implies the right to exploit the data and, in situations where the continued maintenance becomes unnecessary or uneconomical, the right to destroy it. Ownership can relate to a data item, a merged dataset, or a value-added dataset.

It is important for data owners to establish and document the following (if applicable):

- The ownership, intellectual property rights, and copyright of their data
- The statutory and non-statutory obligations relevant to their business to ensure the data is compliant
- The policies for data security, disclosure control, release, pricing, and dissemination
- The agreement reached with users and customers on the conditions of use, set out in a signed memorandum of agreement or license agreement, before data is released

Data Custodianship

Data custodians are established to ensure that important datasets are developed, maintained, and are accessible within their defined specifications. Designating a person or role as being charged with overseeing these aspects of data management helps to ensure that datasets do not become compromised. How these aspects are managed should be in accordance with the defined data policy applicable to the data, as well as any other applicable data stewardship specifications. Some typical responsibilities of a data custodian may include:

- Adherence to appropriate and relevant data policy and data ownership guidelines
- Ensuring accessibility to appropriate users, maintaining appropriate levels of dataset security
- Fundamental dataset maintenance, including but not limited to data storage and archiving
- Dataset documentation, including updates to documentation
- Assurance of quality and validation of any additions to a dataset, including periodic audits to assure ongoing data integrity

2

Asset Security

Custodianship is generally best handled by a single role or entity that is most familiar with a dataset's content and associated management criteria. For the purposes of management and custodianship feasibility in terms of resources (time, funding, hardware/software), it may be appropriate to develop different levels of custodianship service, with different aspects potentially handled by different organizations.

Specific roles associated with data custodianship activities may include:

- Project Leader
- Data Manager
- GIS Manager
- IT Specialist
- Database Administrator
- Application Developer
- Collection and Capture

Data Quality

Quality as applied to data has been defined as fitness for use or potential use. Many data quality principles apply when dealing with species data and with the spatial aspects of those data. These principles are involved at all stages of the data management process, beginning with data collection and capture. A loss of data quality at any one of these stages reduces the applicability and uses to which the data can be adequately put. These include:

- Data capture and recording at the time of gathering
- Data manipulation prior to digitization (label preparation, copying of data to a ledger, etc.)
- Identification of the collection (specimen, observation) and its recording
- Digitization of the data
- Documentation of the data (capturing and recording the metadata)
- Data storage and archiving
- Data presentation and dissemination (paper and electronic publications, Web-enabled databases, etc.)
- Using the data (analysis and manipulation)

All of these affect the final quality or fitness for use of the data and apply to all aspects of the data. Data quality standards may be available for:

- Accuracy
- Precision
- Resolution
- Reliability
- Repeatability
- Reproducibility
- Currency
- Relevance
- Ability to audit
- Completeness
- Timeliness

Quality control (QC) is an assessment of quality based on internal standards, processes, and procedures established to control and monitor quality, while quality assurance (QA) is an assessment of quality based on standards external to the process and involves reviewing of the activities and quality control processes to insure final products meet predetermined standards of quality. While quality assurance procedures maintain quality throughout all stages of data development, quality control procedures monitor or evaluate the resulting data products.

Although a dataset containing no errors would be ideal, the cost of attaining 95%-100% accuracy may outweigh the benefit. Therefore, at least two factors are considered when setting data quality expectations:

1. Frequency of incorrect data fields or records
2. Significance of error within a data field

Errors are more likely to be detected when dataset expectations are clearly documented and what constitutes a 'significant' error is understood. The significance of an error can vary both among datasets and within a single dataset. For example, a two-digit number with a misplaced decimal point (e.g., 10 vs. 1.0) may be a significant error, while a six-digit number with an incorrect decimal value (e.g., 1000.00 vs. 1000.01), may not. However, one incorrect digit in a six-digit asset serial number could indicate a different asset class.

QA/QC mechanisms are designed to prevent data contamination, which occurs when a process or event introduces either of two fundamental types of errors into a dataset:

1. Errors of commission include those caused by data entry or transcription or by malfunctioning equipment. These are common, fairly easy to identify, and can be effectively reduced up front with appropriate QA mechanisms built into the data acquisition process, as well as QC procedures applied after the data has been acquired.
2. Errors of omission often include insufficient documentation of legitimate data values, which could affect the interpretation of those values. These errors may be harder to detect and correct, but many of these errors should be revealed by rigorous QC procedures.

Data quality is assessed by applying verification and validation procedures as part of the quality control process. Verification and validation are important components of data management that help ensure data is valid and reliable. The United States Environmental Protection Agency defines data verification as the process of evaluating the completeness, correctness, and compliance of a dataset with required procedures to ensure that the data is what it purports to be. Data validation follows data verification, and it involves evaluating verified data to determine if data quality goals have been achieved and the reasons for any deviations. While data verification checks that the digitized data matches the source data, validation checks that the data makes sense. Data entry and verification can be handled by personnel who are less familiar with the data, but validation requires in-depth knowledge about the data and should be conducted by those most familiar with the data.[1]

Principles of data quality need to be applied at all stages of the data management process (capture, digitization, storage, analysis, presentation, and use). There are two keys to the improvement of data quality – prevention and correction. Error prevention is closely related to both the collection of the data and the entry of the data into a database. Although considerable effort can and should be given to the prevention of error, the fact remains that errors in large datasets will continue to exist and data validation and correction cannot be ignored.

---

1   See the following: http://www.epa.gov/QUALITY/qs-docs/g8-final.pdf

Documentation is the key to good data quality. Without good documentation, it is difficult for users to determine the fitness for use of the data and difficult for custodians to know what and by whom data quality checks have been carried out. Documentation is generally of two types, and provision for them should be built into the database design. The first is tied to each record and records what data checks have been done and what changes have been made and by whom. The second is the metadata that records information at the dataset level. Both are important, and without them, good data quality will be compromised.

Data Documentation and Organization

Data documentation is critical for ensuring that datasets are useable well into the future. Data longevity is roughly proportional to the comprehensiveness of their documentation. All datasets should be identified and documented to facilitate their subsequent identification, proper management and effective use, and to avoid collecting or purchasing the same data more than once.

The objectives of data documentation are to:

- Ensure the longevity of data and their re-use for multiple purposes.
- Ensure that data users understand the content context and limitations of datasets.
- Facilitate the discovery of datasets.
- Facilitate the interoperability of datasets and data exchange.

One of the first steps in the data management process involves entering data into an electronic system. The following data documentation practices may be implemented during database design and data entry to facilitate the retrieval and interpretation of datasets not only by the data collector but also by those who may have future interest in the data.

Dataset Titles and File Names

Dataset titles and corresponding file names should be descriptive, as these datasets may be accessed many years in the future by people who will be unaware of the details of the project or program. Electronic files of datasets should be given a name that reflects the contents of the file and includes enough information to uniquely identify the data file.

File names may contain information such as project acronym or name, study title, location, investigator, year(s) of study, data type, version number, and file type. The file name should be provided in the first line of the header rows in the file itself. Names should contain only numbers, letters, dashes, and underscores – no spaces or special characters. In general, lowercase names are less software and platform dependent and are preferred. For practical reasons of legibility and usability, file names should not be more than 64 characters in length and, if well-constructed, could be considerably less; file names that are overly long will make it difficult to identify and import files into analytical scripts. Including a data file creation date or version number enables data users to quickly determine which data they are using if an update to the dataset is released.

File Contents

In order for others to use the data, they must understand the contents of the dataset, including the parameter names, units of measure, formats, and definitions of coded values. At the top of the file, include several header rows containing descriptors that link the data file to the dataset (for example, the data file name, dataset title, author, today's date, date the data within the file was last modified, and companion file names). Other header rows should describe the content of each column, including one row for parameter names and one for parameter units. For those datasets that are large and complex and may require a lot of descriptive information about dataset contents, that information may be provided in a separate linked document rather than as headers in the data file itself.

- **Parameters** – The parameters reported in datasets need to have names that describe their contents, and their units need to be defined so that others understand what is being reported. Use commonly accepted parameter names. A good name is short, unique (at least within a given dataset), and descriptive of the parameter contents. Column headings should be constructed for easy importing by various data systems. Use consistent capitalization and use only letters, numerals, and underscores – no spaces or decimal characters – in the parameter name. Choose a consistent format for each parameter and use that format throughout the dataset. When possible, try to use standardized formats, such as those used for dates, times, and spatial coordinates.

  All cells within each column should contain only one type of information (e.g., either text, numbers, etc.). Common data types include text, numeric, date/time, Boolean (Yes/No or True/False), and comments, used for storing large quantities of text.

- **Coded Fields** – Coded fields, as opposed to free text fields, often have standardized lists of predefined values from which the data provider may choose. Data collectors may establish their own coded fields with defined values to be consistently used across several data files. Coded fields are more efficient for the storage and retrieval of data than free text fields.

- **Missing Values –** There are several options for dealing with a missing value. One is to leave the value blank, but this poses a problem as some software do not differentiate a blank from a zero, or a user might wonder if the data provider accidentally skipped a column. Another option is to put a period where the number would go. This makes it clear that a value should be there, although it says nothing about why the data is missing. One more option is to use different codes to indicate different reasons why the data is missing.

Metadata

Metadata, defined as data about data, provides information on the identification, quality, spatial context, data attributes, and distribution of datasets, using a common terminology and set of definitions that prevent loss of the original meaning and value of the resource. Discovering that a resource exists, what data was collected and how it was measured and recorded, and how to access it would be a difficult undertaking without descriptive metadata.

Data Standards

Data standards describe objects, features, or items that are collected, automated, or affected by activities or the functions of organizations. In this respect, data need to be carefully managed and organized according to defined rules and protocols. Data standards are particularly important in any situation where data and information need to be shared or aggregated.

Benefits of data standards include:

- More efficient data management (including updates and security)
- Increased data sharing
- Higher quality data

- Improved data consistency
- Increased data integration
- Better understanding of data
- Improved documentation of information resources

When adopting and implementing data standards, one should consider the following different levels of standards:

- International
- National
- Regional
- Local

Where possible, adopt the minimally complex standard that addresses the largest audience. The security practitioner should be aware that standards are continually updated, so the necessity of maintaining compliance with as few as possible is desirable.

Data Lifecycle Control

Good data management requires the whole lifecycle of data to be managed carefully. This includes:

- Data specification and modeling processing and database maintenance and security
- Ongoing data audit, to monitor the use and continued effectiveness of existing data
- Archiving, to ensure data is maintained effectively, including periodic snapshots to allow rolling back to previous versions in the event that primary copies and backups are corrupted

Data Specification and Modeling

The majority of the work involved in building databases occurs long before using any database software. Successful database planning takes the form of a thorough user requirements analysis, followed by data modeling. Understanding user requirements is the first planning step. Databases must be designed to meet user needs, ranging from data acquisition through data entry, reporting, and long-term analysis. Data modeling is the methodology that identifies the path to meet user requirements. The focus should be to keep the overall model and data structure as simple as possible while still adequately addressing project participant's business rules and project goals and objectives.

Detailed review of protocols and reference materials on the data to be modeled will articulate the entities, relationships, and flow of information. Data modeling should be iterative and interactive. The following broad questions are a good starting point:

- What are the database objectives?
- How will the database assist in meeting those objectives?
- Who are the stakeholders in the database? Who has a vested interest in its success?
- Who will use the database and what tasks do those individuals need the database to accomplish?
- What information will the database hold?
- What are the smallest bits of information the database will hold and what are their characteristics?

- Will the database need to interact with other databases and applications? What accommodations will be needed?
- What length of time will the data be required to be held for?
- What will be the dependencies on the database?
- What will the database decommissioning process be?

The conceptual design phase of the database lifecycle should produce an information/data model. An information/data model consists of written documentation of concepts to be stored in the database, their relationships to each other, and a diagram showing those concepts and their relationships. In the database design process, the information/data model is a tool to help the design and programming team understand the nature of the information to be stored in the database, not an end in itself. Information/data models assist in communication between the people who are specifying what the database needs to do (data content experts) and the programmers and database developers who are building the database. Careful database design and documentation of that design are important not only in maintaining data integrity during use of a database, but they are also important factors in the ease and extent of data loss in future migrations (including reduction of the risk that inferences made about the data now will be taken at some future point to be original facts). Therefore, information/data models are also vital documentation when it comes time to migrate the data and user interface years later in the lifecycle of the database. Information/data models may be as simple as a written document or drawing, or they may be complex and constructed with the aid of design tools.

Database Maintenance

Technological obsolescence is a significant cause of information loss, and data can quickly become inaccessible to users if stored in out-of-date software formats or on outmoded media. Effective maintenance of digital files depends on proper management of a continuously changing infrastructure of hardware, software, file formats, and storage media. Major changes in hardware can be expected every 1-2 years, and in software every 1-3 years. As software and hardware evolve, datasets must be continuously migrated to new platforms, or they must be saved in formats that are independent of specific platforms or software (e.g., ASCII delimited files).

A database or dataset should have carefully defined procedures for updating. If a dataset is live or ongoing, this will include such things as additions, modifications, and deletions, as well as frequency of updates. Versioning will be extremely important when working in a multi-user environment. Management of database systems requires good day-to-day system administration. Database system administration needs to be informed by a threat analysis and should employ means of threat mitigation, such as regular backups, highlighted by that analysis.

Data Audit

Good data management requires ongoing data audits to monitor the use and continued effectiveness of existing data. A data or information audit is a process that involves:

1. Identifying the information needs of an organization/program and assigning a level of strategic importance to those needs.

2. Identifying the resources and services currently provided to meet those needs mapping information flows within an organization (or program) and between an organization and its external environment, and analyzing gaps, duplications, inefficiencies, and areas of over-provision that enable the identification of where changes are necessary.

An information audit not only counts resources but also examines how they are used, by whom, and for what purpose. The information audit examines the activities and tasks that occur in an organization and identifies the information resources that support them. It examines not only the resources used but also how they are used and how critical they are to the successful completion of each task. Combining this with the assignment of a level of strategic significance to all tasks and activities enables the identification of the areas where strategically significant knowledge is being created. It also identifies those tasks that rely on knowledge sharing or transfer and those that rely on a high quality of knowledge. Benefits of a data audit include:

Awareness of data holdings

- Promote capacity planning
- Facilitate data sharing and reuse
- Monitor data holdings and avoid data leaks

Recognition of data management practices

- Promote efficient use of resources and improved workflows
- Increase ability to manage risks – data loss, inaccessibility, compliance
- Enable the development/refinement of a data strategy

Data Storage and Archiving

Data storage and archiving address those aspects of data management related to the housing of data. This element includes considerations for digital/electronic data and information as well as relevant hardcopy data and information. Without careful planning for storage and archiving, many problems arise that result in the data becoming out of date and possibly unusable as a result of not being property managed and stored.

Some important physical dataset storage and archiving considerations for electronic/digital data include:

- ***Server Hardware and Software*** – What type of database will be needed for the data? Will any physical system infrastructure need to be set up or is the infrastructure already in place? Will a major database product be necessary? Will this system be utilized for other projects and data? Who will oversee the administration of this system?

- ***Network Infrastructure*** – Does the database need to be connected to a network or to the Internet? How much bandwidth is required to serve the target audience? What hours of the day does it need to be accessible?

- ***Size and Format of Datasets*** – The size of a dataset should be estimated so that storage space can properly be accounted for. The types and formats should be identified so that no surprises in the form of database capabilities and compatibility will arise.

- ***Database Maintenance and Updating*** – A database or dataset should have carefully defined procedures for updating. If a dataset is live or ongoing, this will include such things as additions, modifications, and deletions, as well as frequency of updates. Versioning will be extremely important when working in a multi-user environment.

- ***Database Backup and Recovery Requirements*** – The requirements for the backing up or recovery of a database in case of user error, software/media failure, or disaster, should be clearly defined and agreed upon to ensure the longevity of a dataset. Mechanisms, schedules, frequency and types of backups, and appropriate recovery plans should be specified and planned.

This can include types of storage media for onsite backups and whether off-site backing up is necessary.

Archiving of data should be a priority data management issue. Organizations with high turnovers of staff and data stored in a distributed manner need sound documenting and archiving strategies built into their information management chain. Snapshots (versions) of data should be maintained so that rollback is possible in the event of corruption of the primary copy and backups of that copy.

In addition, the security professional needs to consider the costs associated with the deployment and management of the data throughout its lifecycle in the organization. For instance, the hardware cost for a deployment of a dataset managed on a Microsoft SQL server cluster or an Oracle server cluster will be higher if that deployment is done onsite versus through a cloud provider via an IaaS solution. However, the operational costs associated with providing access to the dataset over the lifecycle of its use will be potentially higher for the cloud-based deployment then for the onsite deployment. It is up to the security architect and the security professional to work together to document and help the organization understand the costs issues associated with the security solution but also the overall costs associated with platform choices due to security considerations.

Longevity and Use

Data Security

Security involves the system, processes, and procedures that protect a database from unintended activity. Unintended activity can include misuse, malicious attacks, inadvertent mistakes, and access made by individuals or processes, either authorized or unauthorized. Physical equipment theft or sabotage is another consideration. Accidents and disasters (such as fires, hurricanes, earthquakes, or even spilled liquids) are another category of threat to data security. Efforts should be made by the security practitioner to stay current on new threats so that a database and its data are not put at risk. Appropriate measures and safeguards should be put in place for any feasible threats.

Security should be implemented in layers using a defense in depth architecture and should never rely on a single method. Several methods should be used: for example, uninterruptible power supply, mirrored servers (redundancy), backups, backup integrity testing, physical access controls, network administrative access controls, firewalls, sensitive data encryption, up-to-date-software security patches, incident response capabilities, and full recovery plans. Where possible, any implemented security features should be tested to determine their effectiveness.

Risk management is the process that allows Information Technology (IT) managers to balance the operational and economic costs of protective measures with gains in mission capability by protecting the IT systems and data that support their enterprises' missions. Risk management encompasses three processes:

1. Risk Assessment
2. Risk Mitigation
3. Evaluation and Assessment

Minimizing negative impact on an enterprise and the need for a sound basis in decision making are the fundamental reasons enterprises implement a risk management process for their IT systems.

Risk assessment is the first process in the risk management methodology. Enterprises use risk assessment to determine the extent of the potential threat and the risk associated with an IT system throughout its system development life cycle. The output of this process helps to identify appropriate controls for reducing or eliminating risk during the risk mitigation process. Risk is a function of the likelihood of a given threat-source's exercising of a particular potential vulnerability and the resulting impact of that adverse event on the enterprise. To determine the likelihood of a future adverse event, one must analyze threats to an IT system in conjunction with the potential vulnerabilities and the controls in place for the IT system. Impact refers to the magnitude of harm that could be caused. The level of impact is governed by the potential mission impacts and in turn produces a relative value for the IT assets and resources affected (e.g., the criticality and sensitivity of the IT system components and data).

Risk mitigation, the second process of risk management, involves prioritizing, evaluating, and implementing the appropriate risk-reducing controls recommended from the risk assessment process. Because the elimination of all risk is usually impractical or close to impossible, it is the responsibility of senior management and functional and business managers to use the least-cost approach and implement the most appropriate controls to decrease mission risk to an acceptable level, with minimal adverse impact on the enterprise's resources and mission.

In most enterprises, the information system itself will continually be expanded and updated, its components changed, and its software applications replaced or updated with newer versions. In addition, personnel changes will occur and security policies are likely to change over time. These changes mean that new risks will surface and risks previously mitigated may again become a concern. Thus, the risk management process is ongoing and evolving.

Data Access, Sharing, and Dissemination

Data and information should be readily accessible to those who need them or those who are given permission to access them. Some issues to address with access to data and a database system include:

- Relevant data policy and data ownership issues regarding access and use of data
- The needs of those who will require access to the data
- Various types and differentiated levels of access needed and as deemed appropriate
- The cost of actually providing data versus the cost of providing access to data
- Format appropriate for end-users
- System design considerations, including any data (if any) that requires restricted access to a subset of users
- Issues of private and public domain in the context of the data being collected
- Liability issues should be included in the metadata in terms of accuracy, recommended use, use restrictions, etc.
- A carefully worded disclaimer statement can be included in the metadata so as to free the provider, data collector, or anyone associated with the dataset of any legal responsibility for misuse or inaccuracies in the data.
- Where the data is when at rest, and if there are legal or jurisdictional issues specific or peculiar to that geography that must be taken into account.

- Where the data moves through when on the wire (in transit), and if there are legal or jurisdictional issues specific or peculiar to that geography that must be taken into account.
- Where the data is when being consumed, and if there are legal or jurisdictional issues specific or peculiar to that geography that must be taken into account.
- The need for single-access or multi-user access and subsequent versioning issues associated with multi-user access systems
- Intentional obfuscation of detail to protect sensitive data

Whether certain data is made available or not, and to whom, is a decision of the data owner(s) and/or custodian. Decisions to withhold data should be based solely on privacy, commercial-in-confidence, national security considerations, or legislative restrictions. The decision to withhold needs to be transparent, and the criteria on which the decision is made need to be based on a stated policy position.

An alternative to denying access to certain data is to generalize or aggregate it to overcome the basis for its sensitivity. Many enterprises will supply statistical data that has been derived from the more detailed data collected by surveys. Some enterprises will supply data that has lower spatial resolution than the original data collected to protect sensitive data. It is important that users of data be made aware that certain data has been withheld or modified because this can limit processes or transactions they are involved in and the quality or utility of the information product produced. One remedy is for data custodians to make clear in publicly available metadata records and as explicit statements on data products that there are limitations applied to the data supplied or shown that could affect fitness for use.

Data Publishing

Information publishing and access need to be addressed when implementing integrated information management solutions. Attention to details, such as providing descriptive data headings, legends, metadata/documentation, and checking for inconsistencies, helps ensure that the published data actually makes sense, is useable to those accessing it, and that suitable documentation is available so users can determine whether the data may be useful and pursue steps to access it.

Establish Handling Requirements

Marking, Handling, Storing, and Destroying of Sensitive information

As with physical assets, it is important that classified information assets are clearly marked and labeled. Ideally, the computing systems will in turn enforce those labels uniformly. This, however, is commonly only done in systems using mandatory access control (MAC). Systems based on discretionary access control (DAC) do not typically enforce labels uniformly, and labels may be lost as information assets are transferred from one system to another.

Information assets are harder to value because they may not have a declared value on the organization's financial statements. Such assets include all forms of information, including the many types of intellectual property. Even asset ownership can be harder to resolve in the case of information assets: It could be the creator of the asset or the organization who ultimately owns it.

Unlike physical assets, information assets can also be harder to delineate. Information assets with different values to the organization may exist on the same systems, but they may need to be protected very differently. To help guide the valuation and protection of information assets, information classification is often used.

2

Asset Security

Information classification refers to the practice of differentiating between different types of information assets and providing some guidance as to how sensitive information will need to be protected. Traditional information classification schemes were based on confidentiality requirements. Assets (objects) would be classified according to their confidentiality (such as Top Secret, Secret, or Public), and subjects would be granted clearances based on a matching set of clearance levels. Modern information classification schemes pull in multiple criteria including confidentiality, integrity, and availability requirements.[2]

In both cases, the goal of information classification is to group similar assets together and protect them based on common classification levels. This allows protection solutions to be used across multiple assets with similar value to the organization and with similar security requirements. This helps to achieve economies-of-scale as well as ensuring that managing those solutions is more cost-effective.

Information classification also includes the processes and procedures to declassify information. For example, declassification may be used to downgrade the sensitivity of information. Over the course of time, information once considered sensitive may decline in value or criticality. In these instances, declassification efforts should be implemented to ensure that excessive protection controls are not used for non-sensitive information. Marking, handling, and storage requirements will likely be reduced when declassifying information. Organizations should have declassification practices well documented for use by individuals assigned to this task.

Media
Media storing sensitive information requires physical and logical controls. The security professional must continually bear in mind that media lacks the means for digital accountability when the data is not encrypted. For this reason, extensive care must be taken when handling sensitive media. Logical and physical controls, such as marking, handling, storing, and declassification, provide methods for the secure handling of sensitive media.

Marking
Organizations should have policies in place regarding the marking of media. Storage media should have a physical label identifying the sensitivity of the information contained. The label should clearly indicate if the media is encrypted. The label may also contain information regarding a point of contact and a retention period. When media is found or discovered without a label, it should be immediately labeled at the highest level of sensitivity until the appropriate analysis reveals otherwise. The security practitioner and the security professional both need to exercise common sense with regards to the use of a media marking policy. Specifically, they need to understand that not all organizations have the kind of data that would benefit from this kind of a control mechanism and that it may be a cumbersome and ineffective approach to achieving an end result that may be better sought through other means, such as security awareness training regarding appropriate data management techniques. The need for media marking typically is strongest in organizations where sensitive IP and confidential data must be stored and shared amongst multiple people. If the security architect can design centrally managed and controlled Enterprise Content

---

2   Read more about the United States Civilian Government information classification here:
     http://csrc.nist.gov/publications/nistpubs/800-60-rev1/SP800-60_Vol1-Rev1.pdf

Management (ECM) systems paired with Data Leakage Protection technology (DLP), then the entire threat vector that media marking is designed to address may be able to be handled in a totally different way as well.

Handling

Only designated personnel should have access to sensitive media. Policies and procedures describing the proper handling of sensitive media should be promulgated. Individuals responsible for managing sensitive media should be trained on the policies and procedures regarding the proper handling and marking of sensitive media. Security professionals should never assume that all members of the organization are fully aware of or that they understand security policies. It is also important that logs and other records are used to track the activities of individuals handling backup media. Manual processes, such as access logs, are necessary to compensate for the lack of automated controls regarding access to sensitive media.

Storing

Sensitive media should not be left lying about where a passerby could access it. Whenever possible, backup media should be encrypted and stored in a security container, such as a safe or strong box with limited access. Storing encrypted backup media at an off-site location should be considered for disaster recovery purposes. Sensitive backup media stored at the same site as the system should be kept in a fire-resistant box whenever possible. In every case, the number of individuals with access to media should be strictly limited, and the separation of duties and job rotation concepts should be implemented where it is cost-effective to do so.

Destruction [3]

Media that is no longer needed or is defective should be destroyed rather than simply disposed of. A record of the destruction should be used that corresponds to any logs used for handling media. Security practitioners should implement object reuse controls for any media in question when the sensitivity is unknown rather than simply recycling it.

Record Retention [4]

Information and data should be kept only as long as it is required. Organizations may have to keep certain records for a period as specified by industry standards or in accordance with laws and regulations. Hard- and soft-copy records should not be kept beyond their required or useful life. Security practitioners should ensure that accurate records are maintained by the organization regarding the location and types of records stored. A periodic review of retained records is necessary to reduce the volume of information stored and ensure that only relevant information is preserved.

Record retention policies indicate how long an organization must maintain copies of information. For example, financial transactions related to a fraud case may need to be retained indefinitely or until ten years after a court judgment. Other information such as

---

3   Read more about media destruction recommendations at: http://csrc.nist.gov/publications/ nistpubs/800-88/NISTSP800-88_with-errata.pdf

4   There is a new NIST standard under development, Draft NIST SP800-88 Revision 1: http://csrc.nist.gov/ publications/drafts/800-88-rev1/sp800_88_r1_draft.pdf
Read more about records retention here: http://www.acc.com/vl/public/ProgramMaterial/loader. cfm?csModule=security/getfile&pageid=20

system logs may need to be retained for six months or longer to ensure appropriate forensics and incident response capabilities can use the information to reconstruct a past event. The security professional must ensure:

- The organization understands the retention requirements for different types of data throughout the organization.
- The organization documents in a records schedule the retention requirements for each type of information.
- The systems, processes, and individuals of the organization retain information in accordance with the schedule but not longer.

A common mistake in records retention is finding the longest retention period and applying it to all types of information in an organization without analysis. This not only wastes storage but also adds considerable "noise" when searching or processing information in search of relevant records. Records and information no longer mandated to be retained should be destroyed in accordance with the policies of the enterprise and any appropriate legal requirements that may need to be taken into account.

The security professional needs to be aware of developments locally, nationally, and internationally that could potentially have an impact on the issues surrounding data protection, user privacy, and data retention. For instance, the May 2014 ruling by the European Court of Justice that anyone — people living in Europe and potentially those living outside the region — could ask search engines to remove links to online information if they believed the links breached their right to privacy could have all sorts of potential consequences and concerns that security professionals may need to consider and address, or at the very least provide guidance about both within the enterprise and beyond it.[5]

In its full ruling of 13 May 2014, the EU Court said:

a. **On the territoriality of EU rules:** Even if the physical server of a company processing data is located outside Europe, EU rules apply to search engine operators if they have a branch or a subsidiary in a Member State that promotes the selling of advertising space offered by the search engine;

b. **On the applicability of EU data protection rules to a search engine:** Search engines are controllers of personal data. Google can therefore not escape its responsibilities before European law when handling personal data by saying it is a search engine. EU data protection law applies and so does the right to be forgotten.

c. **On the "Right to be Forgotten":** Individuals have the right - under certain conditions - to ask search engines to remove links with personal information about them. This applies where the information is inaccurate, inadequate, irrelevant, or excessive for the purposes of the data processing (paragraph 93 of the ruling). The court found that in this particular case, the interference with a person's right to data protection could not be justified merely by the economic interest of the search engine. At the same time, the Court explicitly clarified that the right to be forgotten is not absolute but will always need to be

---

5 See the following:
  1. Full ruling opinion: http://goo.gl/bMJJoF
  2. Press release announcing ruling from the Court of Justice of the European Union: http://curia.europa.eu/jcms/upload/docs/application/pdf/2014-05/cp140070en.pdf
  3. Fact Sheet summarizing opinion's pertinent issues: http://ec.europa.eu/justice/data-protection/files/factsheets/factsheet_data_protection_en.pdf

balanced against other fundamental rights, such as the freedom of expression and of the media (paragraph 85 of the ruling). A case-by-case assessment is needed considering the type of information in question, its sensitivity for the individual's private life, and the interest of the public in having access to that information. The role the person requesting the deletion plays in public life might also be relevant.

The intricate and complex nature of the issues that security architects, security practitioners, and professionals will be faced with as a result of this ruling in particular may not be well understood for a long time after the ruling. Due to the difficulties involved in creating the response mechanisms required to attempt to be in compliance with the requirements of the ruling, many organizations will need to examine the ways that they create, consume, and collect data of all types. Security professionals will need to be prepared to take the lead in many of these activities and assessments in order to ensure that the needs of the organization as well as the rights of the individual are safeguarded and addressed in the most appropriate ways possible.

Data Remanence

Data remanence is the residual physical representation of data that has been in some way erased. After storage media is erased, there may be some physical characteristics that allow data to be reconstructed. The security practitioner needs to understand the differences in architecture and function of the modern storage systems being used in the enterprise today in order to effectively deal with the issues posed by data remanence.

On a hard disk drive (HDD), the data is magnetically written onto the drive by altering the magnetic field of the hard drive platter. HDDs are mechanical – the read/write head must physically move and the platter must rotate to access the location with the right data. Because data is recorded magnetically, the magnetic field of the platter can be altered to record new data, overwriting and erasing the previous data.

Solid state drives (SSD) use flash memory to store data. Flash memory electrically stores bits of data in many arrays of memory cells. Unlike an HDD, mechanically moving pieces are not required to access the stored data. Rather, the data is accessible directly from the stored location via the drive's flash translation layer. This enables data to be retrieved faster, especially when compared to the seek time of an HDD.

Data remanence on HDDs is caused by the failure of the methods/mechanisms used to "clean" the HDD when it is time to remove the current data in use on the drive to fully remove all information and references to it from the drive media. There are three commonly accepted countermeasures employed to address data remanence in HDDs.

Clearing

Clearing is the removal of sensitive data from storage devices in such a way that there is assurance that the data may not be reconstructed using normal system functions or software file/data recovery utilities. The data may still be recoverable but not without special laboratory techniques.

Purging

Purging or sanitizing is the removal of sensitive data from a system or storage device with the intent that the data cannot be reconstructed by any known technique.

Destruction

The storage media is made unusable for conventional equipment. Effectiveness of destroying the media varies. Destruction using appropriate techniques is the most secure method of preventing retrieval.

The specific methods used with the three countermeasures listed above are as follows:

- **Overwriting** – A common method used to counter data remanence is to overwrite the storage media with new data. This is often called wiping or shredding a file or disk. The simplest overwrite technique writes the same data everywhere, often just a pattern of all zeroes. In an attempt to counter more advanced data recovery techniques, specific overwrite patterns and multiple passes have often been prescribed. These may be generic patterns intended to eradicate any trace signatures; for example, the seven-pass pattern: 0xF6, 0x00, 0xFF, random, 0x00, 0xFF, random. One challenge with overwrites is that some areas of the disk may be inaccessible due to media degradation or other errors.

- **Degaussing** – Erasure via degaussing may be accomplished in two ways: In AC erasure, the medium is degaussed by applying an alternating field that is reduced in amplitude over time from an initial high value (i.e., AC powered); in DC erasure, the medium is saturated by applying a unidirectional field (i.e., DC powered or by employing a permanent magnet). While many types of older magnetic storage media can be safely degaussed, degaussing renders the magnetic media of modern HDDs completely unusable and damages the storage system. This is due to the devices having an infinitely variable read/write head positioning mechanism that relies on special servo control data that is meant to be permanently embedded into the magnetic media. This servo data is written onto the media a single time at the factory using special-purpose servo writing hardware.

  The servo patterns are normally never overwritten by the device for any reason and are used to precisely position the read/write heads over data tracks on the media, to compensate for sudden jarring device movements, thermal expansion, or changes in orientation. Degaussing indiscriminately removes not only the stored data but also the servo control data, and without the servo data the device is no longer able to determine where data is to be read or written on the magnetic medium. The medium must be low-level formatted to become usable again; with modern hard drives, this is generally not possible without manufacturer-specific and often model-specific service equipment.

- **Encryption** – Encrypting data before it is stored on the media can mitigate concerns about data remanence. If the decryption key is strong and carefully controlled, it would be very difficult for an untrusted party to recover any data from the HDD. Even if the key is stored on the media, the key can be overwritten very quickly and thoroughly in comparison to the entire dataset stored on the HDD. This process is called a crypto-erase.

Media Destruction

Thorough destruction of the underlying storage media is the most certain way to counter data remanence.

Specific destruction techniques include:

- Physically breaking the media apart (e.g., by grinding or shredding)
- Chemically altering the media into a non-readable, non-reverse-constructible state (e.g., through incineration or exposure to caustic/corrosive chemicals)
- Phase transition (e.g., liquefaction or vaporization of a solid disk)
- For magnetic media, raising its temperature above the Curie temperature [6]

SSDs use flash memory for data storage and retrieval. Flash memory differs from magnetic memory in one key way: Flash memory cannot be overwritten. When existing data on an HDD is changed, the drive overwrites the old data with the new data. This makes overwriting an effective way of erasing data on an HDD. However, when changes are made to existing data on an SSD, the drive writes that data, along with the new changes, to a different location rather than overwriting the same section. The flash translation layer then updates the map so that the system finds the new, updated data rather than the old data. Because of this, an SSD can contain multiple iterations of the same data, even if those iterations are not accessible by conventional means. This is what causes data remanence on SSDs.

SSDs have a unique set of challenges that require a specialized set of data destruction techniques. Unlike HDDs, overwriting is not effective for SSDs. Because the flash translation layer controls how the system is able to access the data, it can effectively "hide" data from data destruction software, leaving iterations of the data un-erased on different sections of the drive. Instead, SSD manufacturers include built-in sanitization commands that are designed to internally erase the data on the drive. The benefit of this is that the flash translation layer does not interfere with the erasure process. However, if these commands were improperly implemented by the manufacturer, this erasure technique will not be effective.

Another technique, called cryptographic erasure or crypto-erase, takes advantage of the SSD's built-in data encryption. Most SSDs encrypt data by default. When the encryption key is erased, the data will then be unreadable. However, this approach relies again on being able to effectively erase data despite interference by the flash translation layer. If the flash translation layer masks the presence of any data pertaining to the encryption, the "encrypted" drive may still be readable.

Due to the unique complexities of SSDs, the best data destruction method is, in fact, a combination of all these techniques – crypto-erase, sanitization, and targeted overwrite passes. SSDs require the careful attention of a committed data destruction expert, who can tune these erasure techniques to effectively prevent data remanence on SSDs.[7]

---

6 The Curie temperature is the critical point where a material's intrinsic magnetic alignment changes direction. See the following for information on the Curie point: http://en.wikipedia.org/wiki/Curie_point

7 See the following for a full explanation of why an approach that uses multiple methods to address the data remanence issue on SSD drives is recommended: "SAFE: Fast, Verifiable Sanitization for SSDs, Or: Why encryption alone is not a solution for sanitizing SSDs": http://cseweb.ucsd.edu/users/swanson/papers/TR-cs2011-0963-Safe.pdf

The use of cloud-based storage today also presents a data remanence challenge for the security practitioner. As more and more data is being moved to cloud-based storage systems, the ability to address data security issues in general can become much more difficult for the enterprise. Among the many challenges that face the security practitioner in this area is the ability to authoritatively certify that data has been successfully destroyed upon decommissioning of cloud-based storage systems. Due to the fact that a third party owns and operates the system, and the enterprise is effectively renting storage space, there is little to no visibility into the management and security of the data in many cases.

While the challenge is a big one for the enterprise, the use of PaaS-based architectures can actually provide a solution for the issues raised by data remanence in the cloud. The security practitioner and the cloud vendor have to be willing to work together to architect a PaaS solution that addresses the daunting issues of media and application level encryption via a platform offering. There are many parts that have to be properly set up and synchronized for this solution to work, such as messaging, data transactionality, data storage and caching, and framework APIs. In addition, the platform has to be set up in such a way, with appropriate safeguards available to ensure that no unencrypted data is ever written to physical media at any time during the data lifecycle, including data in transit.

There are several standards pertaining to data lifecycle management in general, and data remanence is in particular what the security practitioner may want to become familiar with. The NIST Guidelines for Media Sanitization, Draft Special Publication 800-88 Revision 1, is the most recent version of the guidance provided by NIST in this area.[8] It was updated in September of 2012, replacing the original guidance published in September of 2006. The United States Air Force Systems Security Instruction 8580, dated 17 November, 2008 on Remanence Security.[9] This replaced Air Force System Security Instruction 5020, dated 20 August, 1996 on Remanence Security. The United States Department of Defense, Defense Security Service National Industrial Security Program (DSS NISPOM).[10] The Communications Security Establishment Canada, Clearing and Declassifying Electronic Data Storage Devices– ITSG-06, published July 2006.[11] The United States National Security Agency (NSA) Central Security Service (CSS) Media Destruction Guidance.[12] The New Zealand Information Security Manual, 2010.[13] The Australian Government Department of Defense Intelligence and Security, Information Security Manual 2014.[14]

8   See the following: http://csrc.nist.gov/publications/drafts/800-88-rev1/sp800_88_r1_draft.pdf

9   See the following: http://www.altus.af.mil/shared/media/document/afd-111108-041.pdf

10   See the following for the current DSS NISPOM Library: http://www.dss.mil/isp/fac_clear/download_nispom.html

11   See the following: http://www.cse-cst.gc.ca/its-sti/publications/itsg-csti/itsg06-eng.html

12   See the following: http://www.nsa.gov/ia/mitigation_guidance/media_destruction_guidance/

13   See the following: http://www.gcsb.govt.nz/newsroom/nzism/NZISM_2010_Version_1.0.pdf

14   See the following: http://www.asd.gov.au/publications/Information_Security_Manual_2014_Controls.pdf

Classify Information and Supporting Assets

Clearly the information owner must work with the information security program and officer to ensure the protection, availability, and destruction requirements can be met. To standardize the types of information and protection requirements, many organizations use classification or categorization to sort and mark the information. Classification is concerned primarily with access, while categorization is primarily concerned with impact.

Classification is most often referred to when discussing military or government information; however several organizations may use systems that are similar in function. The purpose of a classification system is to ensure information is marked in such a way that only those with an appropriate level of clearance can have access to the information. Many organizations will use the terms "confidential", "close hold" or "sensitive" to mark information. These markings may limit access to specific members such as board members or possibly certain sections of an organization such as the Human Resources area.

Categorization is the process of determining the impact of the loss of confidentiality, integrity, or availability of the information to an organization. For example, public information on a webpage may be low impact to an organization as it requires only minimal uptime. It does not matter if the information is changed and it is globally viewable by the public. However, a startup company may have a design for a new clean power plant that, if it was lost or altered, may cause the company to go bankrupt as a competitor may be able to manufacture and implement the design faster. This type of information would be categorized as "high" impact.

Several classification and categorization systems exist. The information security professional should minimally be familiar with a few and understand which are common in the country and industry they practice. For an example of classification systems, see:

- Canada's "Security of Information Act"[15]
- China's Law on "Guarding State Secrets"[16]
- The United Kingdom's "Official Secrets Acts"[17]

An excellent example of categorization may be found in the United States' National Institute of Standards and Technology's (NIST) Federal Information Processing Standard (FIPS) 199 and NIST's Special Publication SP800-60 "Guide for Mapping Types of Information and Information Systems to Security Categories".[18] The United States federal civilian government is required to categorize information using these standards and guidelines.

Classification and categorization is used to help standardize the defense baselines for information systems and the level of suitability and trust an employee may need to access information. By consolidating data of similar categorization and classification, organizations can realize economy of scale in implementing appropriate security controls. Security controls are then tailored for specific threats and vulnerabilities.

---

15 http://laws-lois.justice.gc.ca/eng/acts/O-5/

16 http://www.asianlii.org/cn/legis/cen/laws/gssl248/

17 http://www.legislation.gov.uk/ukpga/1989/6/section/8

18 See the following for the FIPS 199 Standard: http://csrc.nist.gov/publications/fips/fips199/FIPS-PUB-199-final.pdf
    See the following for the NIST SP800-60 Standard: http://csrc.nist.gov/publications/nistpubs/800-60-rev1/SP800-60_Vol1-Rev1.pdf

Data classification entails analyzing the data that the organization retains, determining its importance and value, and then assigning it to a category. Data that is considered "secret," whether contained in a printed report or stored electronically, needs to be classified so that it can be handled properly. IT administrators and security administrators can guess how long data should be retained and how it should be secured, but unless the organization has taken the time to classify its data, it may not be secured correctly or retained for the required time period.

When classifying data, the security practitioner needs to determine the following aspects of the policy:

1. Who has access to the data? Define the roles of people who can access the data. Examples include accounting clerks who are allowed to see all accounts payable and receivable but cannot add new accounts, and all employees who are allowed to see the names of other employees (along with managers' names, and departments, and the names of vendors and contractors working for the company). However, only HR employees and managers can see the related pay grades, home addresses, and phone numbers of the entire staff. And only HR managers can see and update employee information classified as private, including Social Security numbers (SSNs) and insurance information.

2. How the data is secured. Determine whether the data is generally available or, by default, off limits. In other words, when defining the roles that are allowed to have access, you also need to define the type of access—view only or update capabilities—along with the general access policy for the data. As an example, many companies set access controls to deny database access to everyone except those who are specifically granted permission to view or update the data.

3. How long the data is to be retained. Many industries require that data be retained for a certain length of time. For example, the finance industry requires a seven-year retention period. Data owners need to know the regulatory requirements for their data, and if requirements do not exist, they should base the retention period on the needs of the business.

4. What method(s) should be used to dispose of the data? For some data classifications, the method of disposal will not matter. But some data is so sensitive that data owners will want to dispose of printed reports through cross-cut shredding or another secure method. In addition, they may require employees to use a utility to verify that data has been removed fully from their PCs after they erase files containing sensitive data to address any possible data remanence issues or concerns.

5. Whether the data needs to be encrypted. Data owners will have to decide whether their data needs to be encrypted. They typically set this requirement when they must comply with a law or regulation such as the Payment Card Industry Data Security Standard (PCI-DSS).

6. What use of the data is appropriate? This aspect of the policy defines whether data is for use within the company, is restricted for use by only selected roles, or can be made public to anyone outside the organization. In addition, some data has legal usage definitions associated with it. The organization's policy should spell out any such restrictions or refer to the legal definitions as required.

Proper data classification also helps the organization comply with pertinent laws and regulations. For example, classifying credit card data as private can help ensure compliance with the PCI Data Security Standard. One of the requirements of this standard is to encrypt credit card information. Data owners who correctly defined the encryption aspect of their organizations' data classification policy will require that the data be encrypted according to the specifications defined in this standard.[19]

What Classifications Should Be Used?

The general guideline is that the definition of the classification should be clear enough so that it is easy to determine how to classify the data. In other words, there should be little, if any, overlap in the classification definitions. Also, it is helpful to use a term for the title of the classification that indicates the type of data that falls into the particular category.

Here are some examples of categorizing data by title:

- **Private** – Data that is defined as private, such as SSNs, bank accounts, or credit card information.
- **Company Restricted** – Data that is restricted to a subset of employees.
- **Company Confidential** – Data that can be viewed by all employees but is not for general use.
- **Public** – Data that can be viewed or used by employees or the general public.

Who Decides Data's Classification?

The individual who owns the data should decide the classification under which the data falls. The data owner is best qualified to make this decision because he or she has the most knowledge about the use of the data and its value to the organization.

One example of how data classification may be implemented is to look at the role of the database administrator. The database administrator can be a good checkpoint to ensure that data is classified and protected properly. Data owners set the classification, but the classification may be poorly communicated or forgotten by programmers developing in-house written applications. When new files are created, the Database Administrator (DBA) can review the classification to ensure that programmers understand the type of data with which they are working. When new files are moved from the development environment to production, DBAs can perform a final check to ensure the default access on the file is being set appropriately, given the data's classification.

Finally, data owners should review their data's classification at least annually to ensure that the data remains correctly classified. If any discrepancies are uncovered during the review, they need to be documented by the data owner and then reviewed with the data custodian(s) responsible for the data in question in order to establish the following:

1. Understand why the deviation has occurred, under what circumstances, and for what reason(s).
2. Under whose authority was the change in classification carried out?
3. What documentation, if any, exists to substantiate the change in classification?

All information must eventually come to an end. Organizations often hoard old information, assuming it will be valuable at some point when really most information outlives its value and usefulness in a matter of years or months. Organizations should document retention schedules for information in their administrative policies. These schedules should mandate

---

19   See the following for the PCI Data Security Standard version 3.0: https://www.pcisecuritystandards.org/documents/PCI_DSS_v3.pdf

2

Asset Security

the destruction of information after a set date, period, or non-use trigger. The advantages of taking this approach are:

- Storage costs are reduced.
- Only relevant information is kept and this can speed up searching and indexing.
- Litigation holds and eDiscovery are less likely to encounter erroneous, pre-decisional, or deliberative information.

Asset Management

Inventory management is about capturing the basics of what assets are on hand, where they reside, and who owns them. It's about maintaining an accurate, up-to-date view of owned hardware and software assets so that at any time you can see an actual state of the components that comprise your infrastructure.

Configuration management adds a relationship dynamic, such that you can associate each item with other items in the inventory. In configuration management, classes and components, upstream and downstream, and parent/child relationships establish relationships between each configuration item (CI). Furthermore, it involves processes around planning and identifying CI structures, having a controlled environment for changing CIs, and being able to report on the status of CIs.

IT asset management (ITAM) is a much broader discipline, adding several dimensions of management and involving a much broader base of stakeholders. First, it introduces the financial aspects of assets, including cost, value, and contractual status. In a broader sense, ITAM also refers to the full lifecycle management of IT assets, from point of acquisition or procurement through disposition, which together account for a comprehensive expected state. ITAM is designed to manage the physical, contractual, and financial aspects of those assets.

Inventory, configuration, and IT asset management build upon one another. The security practitioner should consider implementing inventory management before undertaking configuration management or ITAM, although some processes in configuration management and ITAM can be implemented simultaneously, depending on the process and organizational maturity of the organization. Successfully implementing inventory, configuration, and IT asset management requires planning and forethought. All three should undergo careful requirements planning to minimize overlap in functionality or data collection requirements as the processes broaden and mature within the enterprise.

Undertaken in an evolutionary approach, building a centralized inventory repository with configuration information forms the basis for a configuration management database (CMDB). A CMDB is a logical entity with key integration points, and it supports and enables processes in service delivery, service support, IT asset management, and other IT disciplines. The CMDB should hold the relationship among all system components, including incidents, problems, known errors, changes, and releases. The CMDB also contains information about incidents, known errors and problems, and enterprise data about employees, suppliers, locations, and business units. The CMDB enables powerful insight into the current and ever-changing profile of the infrastructure. Tightly integrated with service management processes as advocated by ITIL (the IT Infrastructure

Library), inventory, configuration, and IT asset management can be powerful and highly impactful activities that help IT organizations reduce costs, improve service, and mitigate risk.[20]

There are three primary enablers to success for implementing one or all of these disciplines:

1. A single, centralized, and relational repository: Implicit in configuration and IT asset management are the relational attributes of assets to components, contracts, operational status, financial impact, and upstream/downstream relationships. Because the data from all three build upon one another, starting with a repository that's capable of managing complex relationships will save time and money in the long run.

2. Organizational alignment and defined processes: These three disciplines touch many organizations. Within IT, the applications delivery group, infrastructure, desktop support, and network operations are just a few of the groups that will rely on inventory and configuration information. IT asset management extends tangible benefits to people in contracts, procurement, and finance; thus alignment with cross-organizational people and processes makes sense. It behooves the security practitioner to align requirements and understand all processes that will influence the initiatives, thus allowing them to benefit from a coordinated implementation of tools, technologies, and interdepartmental processes.

3. Scalable technologies and infrastructure: Significant value can be gained from deploying inventory, configuration, and ITAM on an enterprise-wide basis. The service impact and risk mitigation benefits will impact all areas of the enterprise. Therefore, planning and executing with enterprise-class scalable tools and technologies is the approach that the security practitioner should consider.

The value of inventory, configuration, and IT asset management extends throughout the IT organization and by extension the customers that IT supports. Well-conceived planning and implementation will improve quality of IT services to the business community, reduce costs of those services, and mitigate financial and operational risks associated with IT systems and the business processes they support.

Asset management is a foundation of information security. If an organization cannot account for its hard drives, servers, or systems, it has no way of knowing if a data breach has occurred. Asset systems can also be used to drive access control systems such as Network Authentication/Access Control (NAC).[21] Software and equipment are the two major areas of asset management the information security professional should review.

---

20 See the following for information about ITIL: http://www.axelos.com/

21 Network Access Control (NAC) is a security registration system for the enterprise network. NAC ensures the integrity of the overall network and minimizes the potential for computer security vulnerabilities. Before a computer or other network device is granted access to the network, it must be registered through the NAC system.

    Security vulnerabilities may include malware, missing security patches, or other malicious threats. If a computer is compromised with one of these vulnerabilities it will be quarantined and prevented from accessing network services. The owner of the computer may be contacted and provided with steps to remove the malware or other security threats, or the system may be remediated automatically using a pre-established baseline for comparison.

    The first time a computer attempts to access the network, access is restricted and directed to the NAC registration page. Computer registration is a simple process that takes only a few minutes. Once registration is complete, access will be granted. A computer may be required to re-register with the NAC system if it has not been active on the network for a preset period of time, or when a significant vulnerability threatens to compromise the network.

Software Licensing

Software is an important asset in need of protection. Original copies of licensed software must be controlled by the organization to prevent copyright infringement. Unscrupulous individuals within an organization may make illegal copies of software for their personal use, or an IT administrator may inadvertently exceed the number of permitted licenses. Security practitioners should assist their organizations in providing appropriate physical controls to prevent illegal duplication and distribution of licensed software. All software copies should be managed by a software or media librarian who is responsible for maintaining control over software assets, both physically and as information assets. Inventory scans of installed software should also be conducted by the organization to identify unauthorized installations or license violations.

Equipment Lifecycle

All equipment has a useful life in the organization. Often, IT equipment will be depreciated by the accounting department until its value is zero. IT equipment may also become unsuitable if it is no longer capable of performing required tasks or if support is no longer available for it. This is one of the reasons that many organizations have opted for strategies that involve leasing equipment where possible. This is also one of the reasons behind the popularity and growth of cloud-based platforms and services such as PaaS, IaaS, and SaaS. The information security professional must ensure that appropriate information security activities take place throughout the lifecycle of the equipment. The following illustrates common activities that the information security professional should engage in throughout the equipment lifecycle:

- Defining Requirements
    - Ensure relevant security requirements are included in any specifications for new equipment
    - Ensure appropriate costs have been allocated for security features required
    - Ensure new equipment requirements fits into the organizational security architecture
- Acquiring and Implementing
    - Validate security features are included as specified
    - Ensure additional security configurations, software, and features are applied to the equipment
    - Ensure the equipment is followed through any security certification or accreditation process as required
    - Ensure the equipment is inventoried
- Operations and Maintenance
    - Ensure the security features and configurations remain operational
    - Review the equipment for vulnerabilities and mitigate if discovered
    - Ensure appropriate support is available for security related concerns
    - Validate and verify inventories to ensure equipment is in place as intended
    - Ensure changes to the configuration of the system are reviewed through a security impact analysis and vulnerabilities are mitigated
- Disposal and Decommission
    - Ensure equipment is securely erased and then either destroyed or recycled depending on the security requirements of the organization
    - Ensure inventories are accurately updated to reflect the status of decommissioned equipment

Protect Privacy

The law of privacy can be traced as far back as 1361, when the Justices of the Peace Act in England provided for the arrest of peeping toms and eavesdroppers. Various countries developed specific protections for privacy in the centuries that followed. In 1776, the Swedish Parliament enacted the "Access to Public Records Act," which required that all government-held information be used for legitimate purposes. In 1792, the Declaration of the Rights of Man and the Citizen declared that private property is inviolable and sacred. France prohibited the publication of private facts and set stiff fines in 1858. In 1890, American lawyers Samuel Warren and Louis Brandeis wrote a seminal piece on the right to privacy as a tort action, describing privacy as "the right to be left alone."

The modern privacy benchmark at an international level can be found in the 1948 Universal Declaration of Human Rights, which specifically protected territorial and communications privacy. Article 12 states:

"No-one should be subjected to arbitrary interference with his privacy, family, home or correspondence, nor to attacks on his honour or reputation. Everyone has the right to the protection of the law against such interferences or attacks." [22]

Laws for the protection of privacy have been adopted worldwide. Their objectives vary: Some have attempted to remedy past injustices under authoritarian regimes, others seek to promote electronic commerce, and many ensure compliance with pan-European laws and enable global trade. Regardless of the objective, data protection laws tend to converge around the principle that individuals should have control over their personal information.

Interest in the right to privacy increased in the 1960s and 1970s with the advent of information technology. The surveillance potential of powerful computer systems prompted demands for specific rules governing the collection and handling of personal information. The genesis of modern legislation in this area can be traced to the first data protection law in the world, enacted in the Land of Hesse in Germany in 1970.[23] The idea of creating a special data protection law came about as a result of the passing of the Hessisches Datenschutzgesetz, on September 30, 1970. The purpose was to protect all digitized material of public agencies within their responsibilities against disclosure, misuse, alteration, or deletion by civil servants. A brand new role was called for as well: the data protection officer (Datenschutzbeauftragter). This role was to be responsible for ensuring the confidential handling of citizen's data. This was followed by national laws in Sweden (1973), the United States (1974), Germany (1977), and France (1978).[24]

Two crucial international instruments evolved from these laws: the Council of Europe's 1981 Convention for the Protection of Individuals with regard to the Automatic Processing of Personal Data and the Organization for Economic Cooperation and Development's 1980

---

22   See the following: http://www.hrweb.org/legal/udhr.html

23   The original body of the law, in German, may be found here: http://www.datenschutz.rlp.de/
downloads/hist/ldsg_hessen_1970.pdf
A summary of the background and history of the law, in German, can be found here:
http://de.wikipedia.org/wiki/Hessisches_Datenschutzgesetz

24   A translated version in English may be found here: http://translate.google.com/
translate?hl=en&sl=de&u=http://de.wikipedia.org/wiki/Hessisches_Datenschutzgesetz&prev=/
search%3Fq%3Dhessisches%2Bdatenschutzgesetz%26biw%3D667%26bih%3D589
An excellent analysis of these laws is found in David Flaherty, "Protecting Privacy in surveillance societies", University of North Carolina Press, 1989.

Guidelines Governing the Protection of Privacy and Transborder Data Flows of Personal Data.[25] These rules describe personal information as data that are afforded protection at every step, from collection to storage and dissemination.[26, 27]

Although the expression of data protection requirements varies across jurisdictions, all require that personal information must be:

- Obtained fairly and lawfully
- Used only for the original specified purpose
- Adequate, relevant, and not excessive to purpose
- Accurate and up to date
- Accessible to the subject
- Kept secure
- Destroyed after its purpose is completed

On November 4, 2010, the European Commission set out a strategy to strengthen EU data protection rules (IP/10/1462 and MEMO/10/542). The goals were to protect individuals' data in all policy areas, including law enforcement, while reducing red tape for business and guaranteeing the free circulation of data within the EU. The Commission invited reactions to its ideas and also carried out a separate public consultation to revise the EU's 1995 Data Protection Directive (95/46/EC).[28] The strategy was translated into a comprehensive reform of the EU's Data Protection Directive on January 25, 2012, with the proposal of a formal framework for data protection reform.[29]

The proposals focus on how to modernize the EU framework for data protection rules through a series of key goals:

1. Strengthening individuals' rights so that the collection and use of personal data is limited to the minimum necessary. Individuals should also be clearly informed in a transparent way on how, why, by whom, and for how long their data is collected and used. People should be able to give their informed consent to the processing of their personal data (for example, when surfing online) and should have the "right to be forgotten" when their data is no longer needed or they want their data to be deleted.

2. Enhancing the Single Market dimension by reducing the administrative burden on companies and ensuring a true level-playing field.

---

25 For the Council of Europe's 1981 Convention for the Protection of Individuals with regard to the Automatic Processing of Personal Data, see the following: http://conventions.coe.int/Treaty/en/Treaties/Html/108.htm For the Organization for Economic Cooperation and Development's 1980 Guidelines Governing the Protection of Privacy and Transborder Data Flows of Personal Data see the following: http://www.oecd.org/internet/ieconomy/oecdguidelinesontheprotectionofprivacyandtransborderflowsofpersonaldata.htm

26 The OECD's Privacy Guidelines were updated for the first time since 1980 in late 2013. Information regarding the update may be found here: http://www.oecd.org/sti/ieconomy/privacy.htm The full text of the updates may be found here: http://www.oecd.org/sti/ieconomy/2013-oecd-privacy-guidelines.pdf

27 The full OECD Privacy framework for 2013 may be found here: http://www.oecd.org/sti/ieconomy/oecd_privacy_framework.pdf

28 See the following for Directive 95/46/EC of the European Parliament and Council of 24 October 1995 on the protection of individuals with regard to the processing of personal data and on the free movement of such data: http://eur-lex.europa.eu/legal-content/en/ALL/?uri=CELEX:31995L0046

29 See the following for the Draft Report on the proposal for a regulation of the European Parliament and of the Council on the protection of individual with regard to the processing of personal data and on the free movement of such data, dated December 17, 2012: http://www.europarl.europa.eu/meetdocs/2009_2014/documents/libe/pr/922/922387/922387en.pdf

3. Revising data protection rules in the area of police and criminal justice so that individuals' personal data is also protected in these areas. Under the Lisbon Treaty, the EU now has the possibility to lay down comprehensive and coherent rules on data protection for all sectors, including police and criminal justice. Under the review, data retained for law enforcement purposes should also be covered by the new legislative framework. The Commission is also reviewing the 2006 Data Retention Directive, under which companies are required to store communication traffic data for a period of between six months and two years.[30]

4. Ensuring high levels of protection for data transferred outside the EU by improving and streamlining procedures for international data transfers.

5. More effective enforcement of the rules, by strengthening and further harmonizing the role and powers of Data Protection Authorities.

EU data protection rules aim to protect the fundamental rights and freedoms of natural persons and in particular the right to data protection, as well as the free flow of data. This general Data Protection Directive has been complemented by other legal instruments, such as the e-Privacy Directive for the communications sector. There are also specific rules for the protection of personal data in police and judicial cooperation in criminal matters (Framework Decision 2008/977/JHA).[31]

The right to the protection of personal data is explicitly recognized by Article 8 of the EU's Charter of Fundamental Rights and by the Lisbon Treaty.[32] The Treaty provides a legal basis for rules on data protection for all activities within the scope of EU law under Article 16 of the Treaty on the Functioning of the European Union.[33]

The European Commission's Directive on Data Protection went into effect in October of 1998, and it prohibits the transfer of personal data to non-European Union countries that do not meet the European Union (EU) "adequacy" standard for privacy protection. While the United States and the EU share the goal of enhancing privacy protection for their citizens, the United States takes a different approach to privacy from that taken by the EU.

In order to bridge these differences in approach and provide a streamlined means for U.S. organizations to comply with the Directive, the U.S. Department of Commerce in consultation with the European Commission developed a "Safe Harbor" framework, the U.S.-EU Safe Harbor program.[34]

2

Asset Security

---

30 See the following for the full text of the Directive 2006/24/EC Of The European Parliament And Of The Council, March 15 2006 on the retention of data generated or processed in connection with the provision of publically available electronic communications services or of public communications networks: http://eur-lex.europa.eu/LexUriServ/LexUriServ.do?uri=CELEX:32006L0024:EN:HTML

31 See the following for Council Framework Decision 2008/977/JHA of November 27, 2008 on the protection of personal data processed in the framework of police and judicial cooperation in criminal matters, as part of Acts Adopted Under Title VI Of The EU Treaty: http://www.aedh.eu/plugins/fckeditor/userfiles/file/Protection%20des%20données%20personnelles/Council%20framework%20decision%202008%20977%20JHA%20of%2027%20november%202008.pdf

32 See the following for the Charter Of Fundamental Rights Of The European Union (2010/C 83/02): http://eur-lex.europa.eu/LexUriServ/LexUriServ.do?uri=OJ:C:2010:083:0389:0403:en:PDF

33 See the following for the Treaty on the Functioning of the European Union (TFEU): http://www.eudemocrats.org/fileadmin/user_upload/Documents/D-Reader_friendly_latest%20version.pdf

34 See the following for the U.S. – EU Safe Harbor website: http://export.gov/safeharbor/eu/eg_main_018365.asp

The U.S. Department of Commerce in consultation with the Federal Data Protection and Information Commissioner of Switzerland developed a separate "Safe Harbor" framework to bridge the differences between the two countries' approaches to privacy and provide a streamlined means for U.S. organizations to comply with Swiss data protection law.[35]

There are many questions that arise with regards to the structure, focus, implementation, management, and observance of the Safe Harbor framework. Some of the most common ones are listed below: [36]

- How will data controllers in Europe know which companies in the U.S. can receive data? The Department of Commerce holds a list of organizations that have joined the "safe harbor". The list is publicly available at the Department of Commerce's website and is kept regularly up to date.

- Will "harborites" be the only U.S. companies that can receive personal data from the EU? No. Some other transfers may benefit from exemptions under Article 26(1) of the Directive (e.g., if data subjects have given their unambiguous and informed consent, or if the transfer is made to fulfill a contract involving the data subject). In addition, Article 26(2) allows data to be transferred to destinations where adequate protection is not generally guaranteed and where the exporter can show that adequate safeguards are in place (for example, in the form of a contract with the importer).

  The contract between the exporter and the importer of data can either be tailored to the specific transfer, in which case it will have to be approved beforehand by national data protection authorities, or it can rely on standard contractual clauses adopted by the Commission to this effect and available at http://www.eu.int/comm/privacy. Generally speaking, these clauses do not need prior approval from national data protection commissioners. In cases where prior authorization is still required by a Member State, it will be granted automatically.

- How will U.S. companies get on to the "safe harbor" list? By self-certification. Companies are obliged to declare that they conform to the "safe harbor" principles when they sign up, but this is not compulsorily subject to any independent verification. After they self-certify, companies are subject to the oversight and possible enforcement actions of the Federal Trade Commission or the U.S. Department of Transportation for unfair and deceptive practices. Organizations are also required to identify an independent dispute resolution body so by consulting the list, anybody who has a problem knows where to go to make a complaint.

- How will we be sure that data transferred to U.S. companies within the "safe harbor" will not be passed to others outside the "safe harbor" where data is not protected? One of the rules of the "safe harbor" is that transfers of data to a third party can only be made if the individual has first been given the opportunity to opt-out. The only exception to this rule is when the disclosure is made to a third party acting as an agent under instructions from the "harborite". In this case, the disclosure can be made either to other

---

35 See the following for the U.S. – Swiss Safe Harbor website: http://export.gov/safeharbor/swiss/index.asp

36 See the following for the Article 29 Working Party for Data Protection FAQ section regarding how will the "safe harbor" arrangement for personal data transfers to the US work?: http://ec.europa.eu/justice/policies/privacy/thridcountries/adequacy-faq1_en.htm

"harborites" or to companies that have undertaken contractual obligations to observe similar standards.

■ Isn't the safe harbor a voluntary system? Signing up is indeed voluntary: Companies will only join if they want to. But the rules are binding for those who sign up.

■ Who will make sure that the rules are in fact observed? Companies in the "safe harbor" may have their compliance checked annually by an independent body, but this is not obligatory, in order not to discourage small and medium-sized enterprises from signing up. Companies not opting for independent verification must conduct effective self-verification. Beyond that, enforcement will largely be complaint driven, initially through alternative dispute resolution mechanisms. These bodies will investigate and try to resolve complaints in the first place. If "harborites" fail to comply with their rulings, these cases will be notified to the Federal Trade Commission or the Department of Transportation, depending on the sector, which have legal powers and can impose effective sanctions to oblige them to comply. Serious cases of non-compliance will result in companies being struck off the Department of Commerce's list. This means that they will no longer receive data transfers from the EU under the "safe harbor" arrangement.

■ What role will the Federal Trade Commission play? The FTC Act makes it illegal in the U.S. to make misrepresentations to consumers or to commit deceptive acts that are likely to mislead reasonable consumers in a material way. Announcing a particular set of privacy policies and practices and then not abiding by them is likely to amount to misrepresentation or deception. The FTC has strong enforcement powers, including the capacity to impose heavy fines. Moreover, getting on the wrong side of the FTC brings bad publicity and often triggers a stream of private legal actions. The FTC thus backs up the private sector programs. It is not there to take up large numbers of individual cases, but it has undertaken to give priority to referrals of non-compliance with self-regulatory guidelines received from privacy programs or from the EU's data protection authorities. The FTC's powers can be used in the same way to ensure that the private sector bodies involved in dispute resolution abide by their undertakings

■ What about the sectors that are excluded from the FTC's jurisdiction? The FTC covers commerce in general, but some sectors are excluded from its jurisdiction (financial services, transport, telecommunications, etc.). These sectors could in future also be covered by the "safe harbor" to the extent that other public bodies with similar powers to the FTC undertake to pursue companies in sectors under their jurisdiction for non-compliance with the principles. For the time being, only the U.S. Department of Transportation has chosen to come forward with the necessary information to allow the Commission to recognize it as a government enforcement body in addition to the FTC. This allows airlines to join the "safe harbor". The Commission expects to be able to recognize other U.S. government enforcement bodies in due course.

Regarding financial services (banking, insurance, etc.), the talks between the Commission and the Department of Commerce on the "safe harbor" coincided with important legislative developments in the U.S., establishing new rules, inter alia for data protection, notably for banks (the Gramm/Leach/Bailey Act). It was agreed to suspend talks on data transfers from the

2

Asset Security

EU in these sectors and to resume them after the implementation of the new act with a view to extending the benefits of the "safe harbor" to financial services. The Commission's services remain ready to engage in discussions with the U.S. authorities concerning arrangements for those sectors currently excluded from the scope of the Safe Harbor, in particular financial services.

Ensure Appropriate Retention

Media, Hardware, and Personnel

Different types of data have different data retention requirements. In establishing information governance and database archiving policies, the security practitioner should take a holistic approach:

- Understand where the data exists. The enterprise cannot properly retain and archive data unless knowledge of where data resides and how different pieces of information relate to one another across the enterprise is available to the security practitioner.
- Classify and define data. Define what data needs to be archived and for how long, based on business and retention needs.
- Archive and manage data. Once data is defined and classified, archive data appropriately, based on business access needs. Manage that archival data in a way that supports the defined data retention policies.

To build an effective overall archiving and data retention strategy, the security practitioner should consider the following guidelines:

- Involve all stakeholders in the process of aligning the business and legal requirements for the data retention policies, along with the technology infrastructure required to execute them. Define clear lines of accountability and responsibility while ensuring that IT, business units, and compliance groups work together.
- Establish common objectives for supporting archiving and data retention best practices within the organization. Make sure business users are appropriately involved and informed about how information will be managed and how their business requirements for data access will be met.
- Monitor, review, and update documented data retention policies and archiving procedures. Continue to improve archive processes to support your ongoing business objectives for providing appropriate service levels while supporting retention compliance requirements.

Eight basic steps can guide an organization in developing a sound record retention policy:

1. Evaluate statutory requirements, litigation obligations, and business needs
2. Classify types of records
3. Determine retention periods and destruction practices
4. Draft and justify record retention policy
5. Train staff
6. Audit retention and destruction practices
7. Periodically review policy
8. Document policy, implementation, training, and audits

An organization likely will decide that it needs to retain a large variety of records. To enable the organization to access the records when needed, the organization must classify the records into helpful categories. Certain records are legally required to be retained for given time periods. An organization may choose to retain those records just as long as required and then destroy them, or it may determine, for business reasons, that such records should be retained for some longer period. In any event, if the records are relevant to some anticipated or ongoing litigation, they may not be destroyed.

Those same considerations exist for all records. If there is no legal obligation to retain a record, the organization is free to choose the length of time it wishes to retain a record, except that no record may be destroyed if it is relevant for anticipated or ongoing litigation.

For every type of record, an organization must, in consultation with appropriate staff, determine the proper retention period. Certain records may have an infinite retention period, such as an organization's articles of incorporation. Others may be appropriate to destroy immediately, such as junk mail.

With guidelines established, the organization should then draft its record retention policy, outlining the classification of records, retention and destruction schedules, parties responsible for retention and destruction, and procedures to be used for destruction. In addition to record management procedures and rules, the policy should include an explicit justification for those procedures and rules. The justification should set out the sound business rationale for keeping certain records and destroying others. Among other appropriate grounds, the rationale may reference the business interests of the following: organizing records in a fashion that makes them easier to access, limiting the records retained to as few as possible to make searching for records as quick and inexpensive as possible, limiting the records retained to save on storage expense, and limiting records retained to lessen the burden of keeping backup copies as protection against catastrophic loss.

Training must be part of retention policy implementation. Every employee must be taught the importance of retaining records in accordance with the policy. The organization should stress that every record of the business, whether it is created or received in the office, while traveling, at home, or anywhere else, is subject to the policy. The security professional needs to be responsible for helping the organization to accurately assess and measure the training being delivered around the retention policy in order to gauge its effectiveness. Equally important is the notion that individual employees should not destroy any record, except those that the policy specifically permits employees to destroy.

The security practitioner should provide guidance to the organization so that it understands the importance of training employees as soon as the record retention policy is adopted. In addition, every new employee should be trained as part of the employee's initial training. Furthermore, the policy should set a schedule for continuing refresher training to ensure that employees remain vigilant with respect to their record retention obligations.

The security practitioner should conduct periodic audits to ensure that records are being retained and destroyed appropriately. Paper files and electronic storage media should be checked to ensure that records are not retained past their scheduled destruction dates. Hard drives may be spot-checked to ensure that improper efforts have not been made to delete records. The particular process used to audit compliance depends on the types of records that an organization generates and the storage methods used. In addition, the issue of data

2

Asset Security

being shared outside of the organization with federated partners and suppliers must also be considered by the security professional, as this data will have to be subjected to similar auditing and spot-checking on site.

A record retention policy should not be entirely static. An organization's business need for different types of records may evolve. New laws or regulations governing record retention may apply to the organization. Laws or regulations may be altered or repealed. Feedback from organization employees or officers may show that records need to be categorized differently or that other alterations would be beneficial. Changes in the policy should be accompanied by appropriate training, depending on the nature of a particular change.

It is crucial that an organization document all aspects of record retention policy implementation. The policy itself must be written and communicated to all those affected by it. Furthermore, the policy should be accompanied by a log that shows all training efforts, auditing processes and results, and record destruction schedules and actions.

Company "X" Data Retention Policy

Key Principles

This data retention policy outlines how Company "X" operates with regard to data storage, retention, and destruction. It pays particular attention to the requirements laid down in the U.K. Data Protection Act of 1998. [37]

The key principles of this policy are:

- Data must be stored securely and appropriately having regard to the sensitivity and confidentiality of the data.
- Appropriate measures are put in place to prevent unauthorized access and processing of the data, or accidental loss or damage to the data.
- Data is retained for only as long as necessary.
- Data is disposed of appropriately and securely to ensure the data does not fall into the hands of unauthorized personnel.

Storage

Data and records are stored securely to avoid misuse or loss.

Any data file or record that contains personal data or personal sensitive data is considered as confidential.

Examples of how we approach storage are:

- We only use secure data centers that prevent unauthorized physical access to our hardware.
- We only use our own hardware; we do not rent or share servers.
- Access to the hardware and maintenance is restricted to appropriately trained and authorized Company "X" employees.
- Only employees who are required to assist in meeting our obligations in providing services have access to the data. These employees have a full understanding of the obligations and their duty of confidentiality and the care required in the handling of the data.

We password protect all databases.

---

37   See the following: http://www.legislation.gov.uk/ukpga/1998/29/contents

We encrypt data transferred between our Web servers and a client's browser using reputable SSL certificates to a maximum of 256 bytes, with initial key exchange at 2048 bytes. The actual level on transfer depends on the capability of the user's browser.

We do not keep the Personal Data or Sensitive Personal Data on any laptop or other removable drive. In the event Personal Data or Personal Sensitive Data had to be stored on a laptop or removable drive, then the data would be encrypted to a level in line with industry best practice and standards available at that time.

Our secure data centers are located in Mumfield and Wakelane. We do not disclose the exact location on this public document because by doing so in part compromises security.

We do not and will not transfer Personal Data or Personal Sensitive Data to a country or territory outside the European Economic Area unless that country or territory ensures an adequate level of protection for the rights and freedoms of data subjects.

Retention

The Data Protection Act requires that personal data processed for any purpose "shall not be kept for longer than necessary for that purpose."

In terms of the data stored, we regard the following aspects to be personal:

- A mobile phone number
- First and last name
- Customer identification number (CIN)
- Content of the communications sent and received

The maximum period of retention is regarded as 5 years. If there is no communication sent to or received from a user in 5 years, then all personal data in regard to that user will be deleted.

No data file or record will be retained for more than 5 years after it is closed unless a good reason can be demonstrated.

Destruction and Disposal

All information of a confidential or sensitive nature must be securely destroyed when no longer required.

The procedure for the destruction of confidential or sensitive records is as follows:

- Electronic files are deleted in such a way that they cannot be retrieved by simply undoing the last action or restoring the item from the Recycle Bin.
- Destruction of backup copies is also dealt with in the same manner.
- Prior to disposal, data storage devices are wiped to the standards defined by the NIST SP 800-88 Revision 1, Guidelines for Media Sanitization.[38]

The sample data retention policy provided above helps the security practitioner to frame the conversation with regards to retention in the enterprise. Without a clearly articulated policy that can be communicated to all employees, implemented, monitored for effectiveness, managed for compliance, and audited for assurance, the security practitioner will not be able to safeguard the enterprise and ensure that proper processes are being followed with regards to asset management.

---

38   See the following: http://csrc.nist.gov/publications/drafts/800-88-rev1/sp800_88_r1_draft.pdf

2

Asset Security

By classifying these objects, the security practitioner, in partnership with the enterprise, can begin to define the rules for managing them at different stages in the information lifecycle. Ask yourself the following questions:

- Who needs access to archived data and why? How fast do they need it?
- Do access requirements change as the archives age?
- How long do we need to keep the archived data? When should it be disposed of or deleted?

To effectively define and classify business information for retention and disposal, consider the following best practices:

- Promote cross-functional ownership. Typically, business units own their data and set the data retention policies, while IT owns the infrastructure and controls data management processes. Accordingly, business managers are responsible for defining who can touch the data and what they can do with it. IT must implement a technology infrastructure that supports these policies.

  Promoting a cross-functional ownership for archiving, retention, and disposal policies provides a great indicator of project success because then all groups have a vested interest in a positive outcome. These retention policy definitions can then be saved to a glossary to be leveraged throughout the data lifecycle, providing the proper context and metadata to define, manage, and validate retention policies.

- Plan and practice data retention and orderly disposal. After all stakeholders have signed off on the archiving and data retention policies, IT can develop a plan to implement those policies. Consider solutions that manage enterprise-wide retention policies for both structured and unstructured data, supporting the defensible disposal of unneeded information in addition to the retention of information based on its business value, regulatory, or legal obligations. Also, think about solutions that generate notification reports and identify which archives are nearing expiration.

By focusing in three distinct areas (media, hardware, and personnel), the security practitioner can ensure that retention is being addressed in a formal manner, aligned with the policies of the enterprise, and meant to ensure confidentiality, integrity, and availability of data as required. Some examples of retention policies are as follows:

- European Document Retention Guide 2013: A Comparative View Across 15 Countries To Help You Better Understand Legal Requirements And Records Management Best Practices. Iron Mountain, January 2013.[39]
- State of Florida Electronic Records and Records Management Practices, November 2010.[40]
- The Employment Practices Code, Information Commissioner's Office, U.K., November 2011.[41]

---

39 See the following: http://www.project-consult.de/files/Iron%20Mountain%20Guide%202013%20 European%20Retention%20Periods.pdf

40 See the following: http://dlis.dos.state.fl.us/barm/handbooks/electronic.pdf

41 See the following: http://ico.org.uk/Global/~/media/documents/library/Data_Protection/Detailed_ specialist_guides/the_employment_practices_code.ashx

- Wesleyan University, Information Technology Services Policy Regarding Data Retention for ITS-Owned Systems, September 2013.[42]
- Visteon Corporation, International Data Protection Policy, April 2013.[43]
- Texas State Records Retention Schedule (Revised 4th edition), effective July 4, 2012. [44]

TRY IT FOR YOURSELF

A sample template that will allow the security practitioner to review in detail what a retention policy statement and supporting documentation may look like is provided as Appendix C. The template will walk you through the stages of a retention policy for a mythical company that is involved in the financial services industry. Defining a retention policy documents clear responsibilities for all those involved with retention activities.

Download the template and go through the sections in order to understand how a retention policy is structured.

Determine Data Security Controls

Data at Rest

The protection of stored data is often a key requirement for an organization's sensitive information. Backup tapes, off-site storage, password files, and many other types of sensitive information need to be protected from disclosure or undetected alteration. This is done through the use of cryptographic algorithms that limit access to the data to those that hold the proper encryption (and decryption) keys. (Note: Because password files are hashed instead of encrypted, there are no keys to decrypt them.) Some modern cryptographic tools also permit the condensing or compressing of messages, saving both transmission and storage space.

Description of Risk

Malicious users may gain unauthorized physical or logical access to a device, transfer information from the device to an attacker's system, and perform other actions that jeopardize the confidentiality of the information on a device.

Recommendations

Removable media and mobile devices must be properly encrypted following the guidelines below when used to store covered data. Mobile devices include laptops, tablets, wearable tech, and smartphones.

---

42 See the following: http://www.wesleyan.edu/its/policies/dataretention.html

43 See the following: http://www.visteon.com/utils/media/privacy.pdf

44 See the following: https://www.tsl.texas.gov/slrm/recordspubs/rrs4.html

1. Develop and test an appropriate Data Recovery Plan.
2. Use compliant encryption algorithm and tools.
   a. Whenever possible, use Advanced Encryption Standard (AES) for the encryption algorithm because of its strength and speed. For more information, refer to NIST's Guide to Storage Encryption Technologies for End-User Devices.[45]
3. When creating a password, follow strong password requirements. Do not use the same password from other systems. Passwords MUST:
   a. Contain nine characters or more
   b. Contain characters from two of the following three character classes:
      - Alphabetic (e.g., a-z, A-Z)
      - Numeric (i.e., 0-9)
      - Punctuation and other characters (e.g., !@#$%^&*()_+|~-=\`{} []:";'<>?,./)
4. Use a secure password management tool to store sensitive information such as passwords and recovery keys.
   a. Where passwords need to be shared with other users, ensure that passwords are sent separately from the encrypted file. E.g., call the person to verbally communicate the password.
   b. Do not write down the password and store it at the same location as the storage media (e.g., post-it note with the password next to the encrypted USB drive)
5. After the covered data is copied to a removable media,
   a. Verify that the removable media works by following instructions to read the encrypted covered data.
   b. If applicable, securely delete unencrypted covered data following secure deletion guidelines.
6. Removable media (e.g., CD, hard disks) should be labeled with the following information:
   a. Title. For example, "Project ABC"
   b. Data owner. For example, "Snoopy Dog"
   c. Encryption date. For example, "12/1/15"
7. When unattended, the removable media should be stored in a secured and locked location (e.g., cabinets, lock boxes, etc.) where access is limited to users on a need-to-know basis.
8. Document the physical location of removable media, along with the label information (specified above) for tracking and future reference.

Compliant Encryption Tools

The various tools to encrypt data can be divided into 3 broad categories: Self-Encrypting USB Drives, Media Encryption Software, and File Encryption Software.

■ **Self-Encrypting USB Drives** – Portable USB drives that embed encryption algorithms within the hard drive, thus eliminating the need to install any encryption software. The limitation of such devices is that the files are only encrypted when residing on the encrypted USB drive, which means files

---

45 See the following: http://csrc.nist.gov/publications/nistpubs/800-111/SP800-111.pdf

copied from the USB drive to be sent over email or other file sharing options will not protected.

- **Media Encryption Software** – Software that is used to encrypt otherwise unprotected storage media such as CDs, DVDs, USB drives, or laptop hard drives. The flexibility of this software allows protection to be applied to a greater selection of storage media. However, the same limitation on collaboration applies to media encryption software as it does to Self-Encrypting USB Drives.

- **File Encryption Software** – Allows greater flexibility in applying encryption to specific file(s). When using File Encryption Software properly, resource owners can share encrypted files over email or other file sharing mechanisms while maintaining protection. To share encrypted files, ensure that passwords are shared securely following the recommendations in item 4 above.

The following is a sample list of tools that comply with removable media encryption requirements:

Tools Category	Tool Options	Best For
Self-Encrypting USB Drives	- Imation S250 - Imation D250 - Kingston DataTraveler 4000 & 6000	- Small group of users (less than 5) - Minimal file sharing or collaboration required - Small or moderate size of data - Minimal technical support resources
Media Encryption Software	- Apple Disk Utilities/File Vault - Symantec PGP Whole Disk Encryption	- Small group of users (less than 5) - Minimal file sharing or collaboration required - Large data size
File Encryption Software	- 7zip (using AES 256 bit encryption)	- Moderate to large group of users (greater than 5) - Files must be worked on collaboratively by users in geographically distributed locations - Moderate or large data size

Table 2.1 – **Sample list of tools that comply with removable media encryption requirements**

Data in Transit

One of the primary purposes throughout history has been to move messages across various types of media. The intent was to prevent the contents of the message from being revealed even if the message itself was intercepted in transit. Whether the message is sent manually, over a voice network, or via the Internet, modern cryptography provides secure and confidential methods to transmit data and allows the verification of the integrity of the message so that any changes to the message itself can be detected. Advances in quantum cryptography also theorize the detection of whether a message has even been read in transit.

2

Asset Security

Link Encryption

Data are encrypted on a network using either link or end-to-end encryption. In general, link encryption is performed by service providers, such as a data communications provider on a Frame Relay network. Link encryption encrypts all of the data along a communications path (e.g., a satellite link, telephone circuit, or T-1 line). Because link encryption also encrypts routing data, communications nodes need to decrypt the data to continue routing. The data packet is decrypted and re-encrypted at each point in the communications channel. It is theoretically possible that an attacker compromising a node in the network may see the message in the clear. Because link encryption also encrypts the routing information, it provides traffic confidentiality better than end-to-end encryption. Traffic confidentiality hides the addressing information from an observer, preventing an inference attack based on the existence of traffic between two parties.

End-to-End Encryption

End-to-end encryption is generally performed by the end-user within an organization. The data are encrypted at the start of the communications channel or before and remain encrypted until they are decrypted at the remote end. Although data remain encrypted when passed through a network, routing information remains visible. It is possible to combine both types of encryption. See *Figure 2.1*.

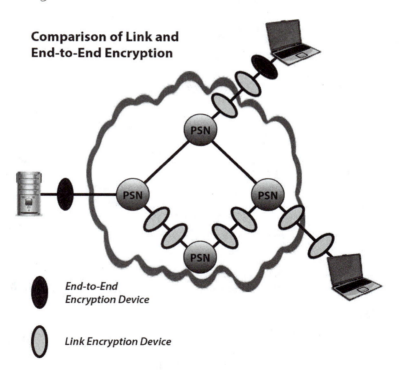

Comparison of Link and End-to-End Encryption

End-to-End Encryption Device

Link Encryption Device

Figure 2.1 - **Comparaison of Link and End-to-End encryption**

Description of Risk

Malicious users may intercept or monitor plaintext data transmitting across an unencrypted network and gain unauthorized access to that, jeopardizing the confidentiality of the sensitive data.

Recommendations

Covered data must be encrypted when transmitted across any network to protect against eavesdropping of network traffic by unauthorized users. In cases where source and target endpoint devices are within the same protected subnet, covered data transmission must still be encrypted as recommended below due to the potential for high negative impact of a covered data breach. The types of transmission may include client-to-server, server-to-server communication, as well as any data transfer between core systems and third-party systems.

Email is not considered secure and must not be used to transmit covered data unless additional email encryption tools are used.

When attempting to secure data in transit, the security practitioner should consider the following recommendations to design secure transmission of data.

1. Where the covered device is reachable via Web interface, Web traffic must be transmitted over Secure Sockets Layer (SSL), using only strong security protocols, such as SSLv3, and Transport Layer Security v1.1 or v1.2 (TLS).
2. Covered data transmitted over email must be secured using cryptographically strong email encryption tools such as PGP or S/MIME. Alternatively, prior to sending the email, users should encrypt covered data using compliant File Encryption tools and attach it to email for transmission.
3. Non-Web covered data traffic should be encrypted via application level encryption
4. Where an application database resides outside of the application server, all connections between the database and application should also be encrypted using FIPS compliant cryptographic algorithms.
5. Where application level encryption is not available for non-Web covered data traffic, implement network level encryption such as IPSec or SSH tunneling.
6. Encryption should be applied when transmitting covered data between devices in protected subnets with strong firewall controls.

Examples of insecure network protocols and their secure alternatives include:

Action	Instead of this ...	Use these ...
Web Access	HTTP	HTTPS
File Transfer	FTP, RCP	FTPS, SFTP, SCP
Remote Shell	telnet	SSH3
Remote Desktop	VNC	radmin, RDP

Table 2.2 – **Examples of insecure network protocols and their secure alternatives**

2

Asset Security

227

Picking Encryption Algorithms

When selecting algorithms to encrypt covered data, keep these considerations in mind:

- For the same encryption algorithm, a longer encryption key length generally provides stronger protection.
- Long, complex passphrases are stronger than shorter passphrases.
- Passphrases MUST:
  - *a.* Contain fifteen characters or more
  - *b.* Contain characters from two of the following three character classes:
    - Alphabetic (e.g., a-z, A-Z)
    - Numeric (i.e., 0-9)
    - Punctuation and other characters (e.g., !@#$%^&*()_+|~-=\`{} []:";'<>?,./)
- Strong encryption generally consumes more CPU resources than weak encryption.

Wireless Connection

When connecting to wireless networks to access a system handling covered data, only connect to wireless networks employing cryptographically strong wireless encryption standards such as WPA2. Encryption mechanisms described in the section above must also be applied in addition to strong wireless network encryption to ensure end-to-end protection.

Baselines

Effective network security demands an integrated defense-in-depth approach. The first layer of a defense-in-depth approach is the enforcement of the fundamental elements of network security. These fundamental security elements form a security baseline, creating a strong foundation on which more advanced methods and techniques can subsequently be built.

The following questions should be considered by the security practitioner when applying baseline security:

- Which parts of the enterprise or systems can be protected by the same baseline?
- Should the same baseline be applied throughout the whole enterprise?
- What security level should the baseline aim at?
- How will the controls forming the baseline(s) be determined?

The use of one baseline level will reduce the cost of implementing controls considerably, and everyone within the enterprise can rely on the same level of security being present.

The objective of baseline protection is to establish a minimum set of safeguards to protect all or some of the IT systems of the enterprise. By the security practitioner using this approach, it is possible to apply baseline protection enterprise-wide and, additionally use detailed risk analysis reviews to protect IT systems at high risk or systems critical to the business.

The appropriate baseline protection can be achieved through the use of safeguard catalogues and checklists that suggest a set of safeguards to protect an IT system against the most common threats. The level of baseline security can be adjusted to the needs of the enterprise. A detailed assessment of threats, vulnerabilities, and risks is not necessary. Instead, all that has to be done to apply baseline protection is to select those parts of the safeguard catalogue that are relevant for the IT system considered. After the security professional identifies the safeguards already in place, a comparison is made with those safeguards listed in the baseline catalogue. Those that are not already in place, and are applicable, should be implemented.

Baseline catalogues may specify safeguards to be used in detail, or they may suggest a set of security requirements to be addressed with whatever safeguards appropriate to the system under consideration. Both approaches have advantages. One of the objectives of the baseline approach is consistency of security safeguards throughout the enterprise, which can be achieved by both approaches.

Several documents are already available that provide sets of baseline safeguards.[46] Also, sometimes a similarity of environments can be observed among companies within the same industrial sector. After the examination of the basic needs, it may be possible for baseline safeguard catalogues to be used by a number of different organizations. For example, catalogues of baseline safeguards could be obtained from:[47]

- International and national standards organizations.
- Industry sector standards or recommendations.
- Some other company, preferably with similar business objectives and of comparable size.

An enterprise may also generate its own baseline, established commensurate with its typical environment and with its business objectives. There are several advantages with this approach, such as:

- Only a minimum amount of resources is needed for risk analysis and management for each safeguard implementation, and thus less time and effort is spent on selecting security safeguards.
- Baseline safeguards may offer a cost-effective solution, as the same or similar baseline safeguards can be adopted for many systems without great effort if a large number of the enterprise's systems operates in a common environment and if the security needs are comparable.

One such example of this approach can be found by examining the United States Government Configuration Baseline (USGCB).[48] The purpose of the USGCB initiative is to create security configuration baselines for Information Technology products widely deployed across the federal agencies. The USGCB baseline evolved from the Federal Desktop Core Configuration mandate. The USGCB is a federal government-wide initiative that provides guidance to agencies on what should be done to improve and maintain effective configuration settings focusing primarily on security.

2

Asset Security

---

46   See the following for the NIST Special Publication 800-70 Revision 2, National Checklist Program for IT Products – Guidelines for Checklist Users and Developers: http://csrc.nist.gov/publications/nistpubs/800-70-rev2/SP800-70-rev2.pdf

47   See the following for examples of different approaches to baseline security in both the public and private sectors: https://www.gov.uk/government/publications/security-policy-framework
http://www.cse-cst.gc.ca/its-sti/publications/itsg-csti/index-eng.html
http://www.cisco.com/c/en/us/td/docs/solutions/Enterprise/Security/CiscoSCF.html
http://usgcb.nist.gov/
http://msdn.microsoft.com/en-us/library/aa720329(v=vs.71).aspx
http://www.scotland.gov.uk/Resource/Doc/925/0105599.pdf
http://benchmarks.cisecurity.org/downloads/
https://cio.gov/wp-content/uploads/downloads/2013/05/Federal-Mobile-Security-Baseline.pdf
http://www.ucl.ac.uk/informationsecurity/itsecurity/knowledgebase/securitybaselines
http://www.isaca.org/Knowledge-Center/Research/ResearchDeliverables/Pages/COBIT-Security-Baseline-An-Information-Security-Survival-Kit-2nd-Edition1.aspx

48   See the following for general information about the USGCB: http://usgcb.nist.gov/usgcb_faq.html

Another example can be found in the Estonian Information System's Authority IT baseline security system ISKE.[49] ISKE is an information security standard developed for the Estonian public sector, which is mandatory for state and local government organizations that handle databases. ISKE is based on a German information security standard – IT Baseline Protection Manual (IT-Grundschutz in German) – which has been adapted to suit the Estonian situation. ISKE is implemented as a three level baseline system, meaning that three different sets of security measures for three different security requirements have been developed and are available for implementation, based on the needs of the entity managing the databases in question and the type(s) of data that the database contains.

This section introduces some generally accepted principles that address information security from a very high-level viewpoint. These principles are fundamental in nature and rarely changing. They are not stated here as security requirements but are provided as useful guiding references for developing, implementing, and understanding security policies and baselines for use in the enterprise. The principles listed below are by no means exhaustive.

- ***Information System Security Objectives*** – Information system security objectives or goals are described in terms of three overall objectives: Confidentiality, Integrity, and Availability. Security policies, baselines, and measures are developed and implemented according to these objectives.
- ***Prevent, Detect, Respond, and Recover*** – Information security is a combination of preventive, detective, response, and recovery measures. Preventive measures are for avoiding or deterring the occurrence of an undesirable event. Detective measures are for identifying the occurrence of an undesirable event. Response measures refer to coordinated response to contain damage when an undesirable event (or incident) occurs. Recovery measures are for restoring the confidentiality, integrity, and availability of information systems to their expected state.
- ***Protection of Information While Being Processed, In Transit, and In Storage*** – Security measures should be considered and implemented as appropriate to preserve the confidentiality, integrity, and availability of information while it is being processed, in transit, and in storage.
- ***External Systems are Assumed to be Insecure*** – In general, an external system or entity that is not under your direct control should be considered insecure. Additional security measures are required when your information assets or information systems are located in, or interfacing with, external systems. Information systems infrastructure could be partitioned using either physical or logical means to segregate environments with different risk levels.
- ***Resilience for Critical Information Systems*** – All critical information systems need to be resilient to withstand major disruptive events, with measures in place to detect disruption, minimize damage, and rapidly respond and recover.
- ***Auditability and Accountability*** – Security requires auditability and accountability. Auditability refers to the ability to verify the activities in an information system. Evidence used for verification can take form of audit trails, system logs, alarms, or other notifications. Accountability refers to the ability to audit the actions of all parties and processes that interact with information systems. Roles and responsibilities should be clearly defined, identified, and authorized at a level commensurate with the sensitivity of information.

---

49   See the following for more information regarding ISKE: https://www.ria.ee/iske-en

Scoping and Tailoring

"In developing standards and guidelines required by FISMA, NIST consults with other federal agencies and offices as well as the private sector to improve information security, avoid unnecessary and costly duplication of effort, and ensure that NIST publications are complementary with the standards and guidelines employed for the protection of national security systems. In addition to its comprehensive public review and vetting process, NIST is collaborating with the Office of the Director of National Intelligence (ODNI), the Department of Defense (DOD), and the Committee on National Security Systems (CNSS) to establish a common foundation for information security across the federal government. A common foundation for information security will provide the Intelligence, Defense, and Civil sectors of the federal government and their contractors more uniform and consistent ways to manage the risk to organizational operations and assets, individuals, other organizations, and the Nation that results from the operation and use of information systems. A common foundation for information security will also provide a strong basis for reciprocal acceptance of security authorization decisions and facilitate information sharing. NIST is also working with public and private sector entities to establish specific mappings and relationships between the security standards and guidelines developed by NIST and the International Organization for Standardization and International Electrotechnical Commission (ISO/IEC) 27001, Information Security Management System (ISMS)." [50]

The above quote helps the security practitioner to understand the impact of scoping and tailoring with regards to information security. NIST, among many other entities today, engages in scoping and tailoring in order to produce the valuable guidance that they provide to the many organizations globally that consume their Special Publications.

Scoping guidance provides an enterprise with specific terms and conditions on the applicability and implementation of individual security controls. Several considerations can potentially impact how baseline security controls are applied by the enterprise. System security plans should clearly identify which security controls employed scoping guidance and include a description of the type of considerations that were made. The application of scoping guidance must be reviewed and approved by the authorizing official for the information system in question.

Tailoring involves scoping the assessment procedures to more closely match the characteristics of the information system and its environment of operation. The tailoring process gives enterprises the flexibility needed to avoid assessment approaches that are unnecessarily complex or costly while simultaneously meeting the assessment requirements established by applying the fundamental concepts of a risk management framework. Supplementation involves adding assessment procedures or assessment details to adequately meet the risk management needs of the organization (e.g., adding organization-specific details such as system/platform-specific information for selected security controls). Supplementation decisions are left to the discretion of the organization in order to maximize flexibility in developing security assessment plans when applying the results of risk assessments in determining the extent, rigor, and level of intensity of the assessments.

---

50   NIST Special Publication 800-53A Revision 1, Guide for Assessing the Security Controls in Federal Information Systems and Organizations: Building Effective Security Assessment Plans. June 2010 (Page 6)

The security practitioner needs to be aware of the value that scoping, tailoring, and supplementation can bring to the security architectures being planned and assessed for the enterprise. The use of scoping and tailoring to properly narrow the focus of the architecture will ensure that the appropriate risks are identified and addressed. The use of supplementation will allow the architecture to stay flexible over time and grow to address the needs of the enterprise that arise during operation of the architecture, once it is implemented fully.

TRY IT FOR YOURSELF

A sample template that will allow the security practitioner to try his or her hand at scoping and tailoring is provided as *Appendix C*. The template will walk you through the stages of creating a security approach for a project. Defining a security approach for a project provides a line of site from business requirements through team members and components all the way to implemented security controls. It documents clear responsibilities for implementation, certification, and accreditation of the system security and provides a framework for communicating security-based impacts on other development and project management activities. This security approach defines from a security perspective how systems associated with the project will be characterized, categorized, and managed.

Download the template and go through the sections in order to practice how to scope and tailor a security approach for a project.

Standards Selection

The security practitioner needs to be familiar with a wide range of standards and the organizations and entities that are responsible for them. These range from United States based entities such as NIST to transnational entities such as the European Network and Information Security Agency (ENISA), the International Telecommunications Union (ITU), and the International Standards Organization (ISO). The following is a list of many of the leading standards bodies and the standards that they are responsible for.

United States Resources

U.S. Department of Defense Policies

Department of Defense Instruction 8510.01 (DoDI 8510.01)

DoD Instruction 8510.01 establishes the Defense Information Assurance Certification & Accreditation Process (DIACAP) for authorizing the operation of DoD Information Systems, for managing the implementation of IA capabilities and services, and for providing visibility of accreditation decisions regarding the operation of DoD Information Systems, including core enterprise services- and Web services-based software systems and applications.

DoDI 8510.01 URL:
http://www.dtic.mil/whs/directives/corres/pdf/851001_2014.pdf

United States National Security Agency (NSA) IA Mitigation Guidance
The NSA provides guidance on Information Assurance security solutions so that customers can benefit from NSA's unique and deep understanding of risks, vulnerabilities, mitigations, and threats. Available mitigation guidance includes security configuration, trusting computing, and system level IA guidance.

NSA IA Mitigation Guidance Website:
http://www.nsa.gov/ia/mitigation_guidance/index.shtml

National Institute of Standards and Technology (NIST) Computer Security Division
The National Institute of Standards and Technology (NIST) is the U.S. federal technology agency that works with industry to develop and apply technology, measurements, and standards. The NIST Computer Security Division (CSD) focuses on providing measurements and standards to protect information systems against threats to the confidentiality of information, integrity of information and processes, and availability of information and services in order to build trust and confidence in Information Technology systems. The NIST CSD maintains an online Computer Security Resource Center that can be accessed at:

http://csrc.nist.gov/index.html.

NIST Publications Series

Federal Information Processing Standards (FIPS)
Federal Information Processing Standards (FIPS) is the official series of publications relating to standards and guidelines adopted under the Federal Information Security Management Act (FISMA) of 2002. FIPS publications provide standards guidance on topics such as minimum security requirements, standards for security categorization for federal information and information systems, personal identity verification and digital signature standards, among others. The complete library of FIPS publications can be found at:

http://csrc.nist.gov/publications/PubsFIPS.html

FIPS Publication 199
FIPS Publication 199, Standards for Security Categorization of Federal Information and Information Systems provides standards for categorizing information and information systems. Security categorization standards provide a common framework and understanding for expressing security that promotes effective management and oversight of information security programs and consistent reporting to oversight offices on the adequacy and effectiveness of information security policies, procedures, and practices. Document URL:

http://csrc.nist.gov/publications/fips/fips199/FIPS-PUB-199-final.pdf

2

Asset Security

FIPS Publication 200

FIPS Publication 200, Minimum Security Requirements for Federal Information and Information Systems, was created in response to the need for each U.S. federal agency to develop, document, and implement an enterprise-wide program to provide information security for the information and information systems that support the operations and assets of the agency, and it outlines minimum security requirements for U.S. Federal information and information systems. Document URL:

http://csrc.nist.gov/publications/fips/fips200/FIPS-200-final-march.pdf

Special Publications (SP) 800 Series

The Special Publications (SP) 800 series presents documents of general interest to the computer security community and reports on research, guidelines, and outreach efforts in computer security, and its collaborative activities with industry, government, and academic organizations. SPs 800-37, 800-53, and 800-60 are highlighted here for reference. The complete text of all SP 800 documents can be downloaded at:

http://csrc.nist.gov/publications/PubsSPs.html

SP 800-37, Guide for Applying Risk Management Framework to Federal Information Systems

NIST Special Publication 800-37, Guide for Applying the Risk Management Framework to Federal Information Systems, establishes a common framework to improve information security, strengthen risk management processes, and encourage reciprocity among federal agencies. This publication introduces guidelines for a six-step Risk Management Framework. See Risk Management Framework for additional information. Document URL:

http://csrc.nist.gov/publications/nistpubs/800-37-rev1/sp800-37-rev1-final.pdf

SP 800-53, Security and Privacy Controls for Federal Information Systems and Organizations

NIST Special Publication 800-53, Security and Privacy Controls for Federal Information Systems and Organizations, provides guidelines for selecting and specifying security controls for organizations and information systems supporting the executive agencies of the federal government. The guidelines apply to all components of an information system that process, store, or transmit federal information. Document URL:

http://csrc.nist.gov/publications/drafts/800-53-rev4/sp800-53-rev4-ipd.pdf

SP 800-60, Guide for Mapping Types of Information and Information Systems to Security Categories

NIST Special Publication 800-60, Guide for Mapping Types of Information and Information Systems to Security Categories, provides guidelines recommending the types of information and information systems to be included in each category of potential security impact. This guideline is intended to help agencies consistently map security impact levels to types of information (e.g., privacy, medical, proprietary, financial, contractor sensitive, trade secret, investigation) and information systems (e.g., mission critical, mission support, administrative). Document URL:

http://csrc.nist.gov/publications/nistpubs/800-60-rev1/SP800-60_Vol1-Rev1.pdf

Additional NIST Resources

Risk Management Framework

The management of organizational risk is a key element in an organization's information security program and provides an effective framework for selecting the appropriate security controls for an information system. The NIST Risk Management Framework is a risk-based approach to security control selection and specification and is comprised of activities related to managing organizational risk. These activities are paramount to an effective information security program and can be applied to both new and legacy information systems. See Special Publication 800-37 for additional information. Risk Management Framework Website:

http://csrc.nist.gov/groups/SMA/fisma/framework.html

National Checklist Program (NCP)

The National Checklist Program (NCP) is the U.S. government repository of publicly available security checklists (or benchmarks) that provide detailed low level guidance on setting the security configuration of operating systems and applications. The checklist repository can be found at:

http://web.nvd.nist.gov/view/ncp/repository

International Resources

10 Steps to Cybersecurity

Published by CESG, the guidance provided by the 10 Steps to Cybersecurity offers practical steps that organizational leaders can direct to be taken to improve the protection of networks and the information carried upon them. 10 Steps to Cybersecurity also directs readers to The 20 Critical Controls developed by CSIS, which is also referenced in this guide, for further guidance. Document URL:

https://www.gov.uk/government/uploads/system/uploads/attachment_data/file/73128/12-1120-10-steps-to-cyber-security-executive.pdf

Cybersecurity Strategy of the European Union

Published by the European Commission, the cybersecurity strategy An Open, Safe, and Secure Cyberspace represents the EU's comprehensive vision on how best to prevent and respond to cyber disruptions and incidents. Specific actions are aimed at enhancing cyber resilience of information systems, reducing cybercrime and strengthening EU international cybersecurity policy and cyber defense.

The EU international cyberspace policy promotes the respect of EU core values, defines norms for responsible behavior, and advocates the application of existing international laws in cyberspace, while assisting countries outside the EU with cybersecurity capacity-building, and promoting international cooperation in cyber issues. Document URL:

http://eeas.europa.eu/policies/eu-cyber-security/cybsec_comm_en.pdf

European Network and Information Security Agency (ENISA)

The European Network and Information Security Agency (ENISA) is a center of network and information security expertise for the EU, its Member States, the private sector, and Europe's citizens. ENISA works with these groups to develop advice and recommendations

2

Asset Security

on good practice in information security. It assists EU Member States in implementing relevant EU legislation and works to improve the resilience of Europe's critical information infrastructure and networks. ENISA seeks to enhance existing expertise in EU Member States by supporting the development of cross-border communities committed to improving network and information security throughout the EU. More information about ENISA and its work can be found at:

http://www.enisa.europa.eu

National Cyber Security Strategies: An Implementation Guide

The National Cyber Security Strategies implementation guide developed by ENISA introduces a set of concrete actions, which if implemented will lead to a coherent and holistic national cybersecurity strategy. It also proposes a national cybersecurity strategy lifecycle, with a special emphasis on the development and execution phase. Policy makers will find practical recommendations on how to control the overall development and improvement processes and how to follow up on the status of national cybersecurity affairs within their country. Document URL:

http://www.enisa.europa.eu/activities/Resilience-and-CIIP/national-cyber-security-strategies-ncsss/national-cyber-security-strategies-an-implementation-guide

International Organization for Standardization (ISO)

ISO is a developer of voluntary International Standards in collaboration with its partners in international standardization, the IEC (International Electrotechnical Commission) and the ITU (International Telecommunication Union), particularly in the field of information and communication technologies. ISO Website:

http://www.iso.org/iso/home.html

ISO/IEC 27001

ISO/IEC 27001 covers all types of organizations including government agencies, and it specifies the requirements for establishing, implementing, operating, monitoring, reviewing, maintaining, and improving a documented Information Security Management System within the context of the organization's overall business risks. It specifies requirements for the implementation of security controls customized to the needs of individual organizations and is designed to ensure the selection of adequate and proportionate security controls that protect information assets and give confidence to interested parties. ISO/IEC Standards are under copyright and cannot be redistributed without purchase. ISO/IEC 27001 is available for purchase at:

http://www.iso.org/iso/catalogue_detail?csnumber=42103

ISO/IEC 27002

In conjunction with ISO/IEC 27001, ISO/IEC 27002 establishes guidelines and general principles for initiating, implementing, maintaining, and improving information security management in an organization. The objectives outlined provide general guidance on the commonly accepted goals of information security management. The control objectives and controls in ISO/IEC 27002 are intended to be implemented to meet the requirements identified by a risk assessment. ISO/IEC Standards are under copyright and cannot be redistributed without purchase. ISO/IEC 27002 is available for purchase at:

http://www.iso.org/iso/catalogue_detail?csnumber=50297

International Telecommunications Union-Telecommunications (ITU-T) Standardization

The International Telecommunication Union is a specialized agency of the United Nations responsible for issues that concern information and communication technologies. The Study Groups of ITU's Telecommunication Standardization Sector (ITU-T) assemble global experts to produce international standards known as ITU-T Recommendations that act as defining elements in the global infrastructure of information and communication technologies (ICTs). ITU-T Standardization Sector Webpage:

http://www.itu.int/en/ITU-T/Pages/default.aspx

Recommendations X.800 – X.849

The X.800 series of ITU-T Recommendations defines a security baseline against which network operators can assess their network and information security status in terms of readiness and ability to collaborate with other entities to counteract information security threats. The complete text of all X.800 series recommendations can be downloaded at:

http://www.itu.int/rec/T-REC-X/e

Recommendation X.1205

Recommendation ITU-T X.1205 provides a definition for cybersecurity and taxonomy of security threats from an organization point of view. Cybersecurity threats and vulnerabilities including the most common hacker's tools are presented, and threats are discussed at various network layers. Available cybersecurity technologies are discussed as well as network protection principles, such as defense in depth and access management with application to cybersecurity. Risk management strategies and techniques are presented, including the value of training and education in protecting the network. Document URL:

http://www.itu.int/rec/T-REC-X.1205-200804-I/en

National Cyber Security Framework Manual

The National Cyber Security Framework Manual provides detailed background information and in-depth theoretical frameworks to help the reader understand the various facets of National Cyber Security, according to different levels of public policy formulation. The four levels of government - political, strategic, operational, and tactical/technical - have their own perspectives on National Cyber Security, and each is addressed in individual sections within the Manual. Additionally, the Manual gives examples of relevant institutions in National Cyber Security, from top-level policy coordination bodies down to cyber crisis management structures and similar institutions. Document URL:

http://www.ccdcoe.org/publications/books/NationalCyberSecurityFrameworkManual.pdf

Based on the previous listings, the security practitioners have many options to choose from as they seek the guidance of authoritative parties, best practices, and standards to help guide them. While there are many avenues to explore and many voices to be heard, the following offer three examples for the security practitioners of the importance of selecting the appropriate standards to help guide them in their professional practice. The need to understand the scope of the security needs to be addressed, as well as the business requirements to be supported, and the resources available to accomplish the tasks at hand are all part of the formula for success that the security practitioner must learn to master.

2

Asset Security

The National Institute of Standards and Technology (NIST) is responsible for publishing a variety of guides for implementing security controls, performing audits, and certifying systems. Some of these guides are very specific, such as recommended settings to harden Windows servers, and others are very generic, such as how to audit change management procedures. Many of these NIST standards have been adopted by auditors as the model for network management. In the U.S. government, many FISMA audits specifically reference NIST guidelines.

The Center for Strategic & International Studies (CSIS) 20 Critical Security Controls initiative provides a unified list of twenty critical controls that have been identified through a consensus of federal and private industry security professionals as the most critical security issues seen in the industry. The CSIS team includes officials from the NSA, U.S. Cert, DoD JTF-GNO, the Department of Energy Nuclear Laboratories, Department of State, DoD Cyber Crime Center, and the commercial sector. The CSIS controls do not introduce any new security requirements, but they organize the requirements into a simplified list to aid in determining compliance and ensure that the most important areas of concern are addressed.

In 2013, the stewardship and sustainment of the Controls was transferred to the Council on CyberSecurity (the Council), an independent, global non-profit entity committed to a secure and open Internet.

The CSIS initiative is designed to help the federal government prioritize resources and consolidate efforts to reduce costs and ensure that the critical security issues are addressed. The five "critical tenets" of the CSIS initiative, as listed on the SANS website, are as follows:[51]

1. **Offense Informs Defense** – Use knowledge of actual attacks that have compromised systems to provide the foundation to build effective, practical defenses. Include only those controls that can be shown to stop known real-world attacks.

2. **Prioritization** – Invest first in controls that will provide the greatest risk reduction and protection against the most dangerous threat actors and that can be feasibly implemented in your computing environment.

3. **Metrics** – Establish common metrics to provide a shared language for executives, IT specialists, auditors, and security officials to measure the effectiveness of security measures within an organization so that required adjustments can be identified and implemented quickly.

4. **Continuous Monitoring** – Carry out continuous monitoring to test and validate the effectiveness of current security measures.

5. **Automation** – Automate defenses so that organizations can achieve reliable, scalable, and continuous measurements of their adherence to the controls and related metrics.

The current list of Critical Security Controls – Version 5 are as follows:[52]

1. Inventory of Authorized and Unauthorized Devices
2. Inventory of Authorized and Unauthorized Software
3. Secure Configurations for Hardware and Software on Mobile Devices, Laptops, Workstations, and Servers

---

51   See the following: https://www.sans.org/media/critical-security-controls/CSC-5.pdf

52   See the following: http://www.sans.org/critical-security-controls

4. Continuous Vulnerability Assessment and Remediation

5. Malware Defenses

6. Application Software Security

7. Wireless Access Control

8. Data Recovery Capability

9. Security Skills Assessment and Appropriate Training to Fill Gaps

10. Secure Configurations for Network Devices such as Firewalls, Routers, and Switches

11. Limitation and Control of Network Ports, Protocols, and Services

12. Controlled Use of Administrative Privileges

13. Boundary Defense

14. Maintenance, Monitoring, and Analysis of Audit Logs

15. Controlled Access Based on the Need to Know

16. Account Monitoring and Control

17. Data Protection

18. Incident Response and Management

19. Secure Network Engineering

20. Penetration Tests and Red Team Exercises

Paired with the Critical Security Controls, NIST has also created the Security Content Automation Protocol (SCAP). SCAP is a suite of specifications that standardize the format and nomenclature by which software flaw and security configuration information is communicated, both to machines and humans. SCAP is a multi-purpose framework of specifications that support automated configuration, vulnerability and patch checking, technical control compliance activities, and security measurement. Goals for the development of SCAP include standardizing system security management, promoting interoperability of security products, and fostering the use of standard expressions of security content.

SCAP version 1.2 is comprised of eleven component specifications in five categories:[53]

1. ***Languages*** – The SCAP languages provide standard vocabularies and conventions for expressing security policy, technical check mechanisms, and assessment results. The SCAP language specifications are Extensible Configuration Checklist Description Format (XCCDF), Open Vulnerability and Assessment Language (OVAL®), and Open Checklist Interactive Language (OCIL™).

2. ***Reporting Formats*** – The SCAP reporting formats provide the necessary constructs to express collected information in standardized formats. The SCAP reporting format specifications are Asset Reporting Format (ARF) and Asset Identification. Although Asset Identification is not explicitly a reporting format, SCAP uses it as a key component in identifying the assets that reports relate to.

3. ***Enumerations*** – Each SCAP enumeration defines a standard nomenclature (naming format) and an official dictionary or list of items expressed using that nomenclature. The SCAP enumeration specifications are Common Platform Enumeration (CPE™), Common Configuration Enumeration (CCE™), and Common Vulnerabilities and Exposures (CVE®).

---

53 See the following: http://csrc.nist.gov/publications/nistpubs/800-126-rev2/SP800-126r2.pdf

4. ***Measurement and Scoring Systems*** – In SCAP, this refers to evaluating specific characteristics of a security weakness (for example, software vulnerabilities and security configuration issues) and, based on those characteristics, generating a score that reflects their relative severity. The SCAP measurement and scoring system specifications are Common Vulnerability Scoring System (CVSS) and Common Configuration Scoring System (CCSS).

5. ***Integrity*** – A SCAP integrity specification helps to preserve the integrity of SCAP content and results. Trust Model for Security Automation Data (TMSAD) is the SCAP integrity specification.

SCAP utilizes software flaw and security configuration standard reference data. This reference data is provided by the National Vulnerability Database (NVD), which is managed by NIST and sponsored by the Department of Homeland Security (DHS).

The U.S. federal government, in cooperation with academia and private industry, is adopting SCAP and encourages its use in support of security automation activities and initiatives. SCAP has achieved widespread adoption by major software manufacturers and has become a significant component of large information security management and governance programs. The protocol is expected to evolve and expand in support of the growing needs to define and measure effective security controls, assess and monitor ongoing aspects of that information security, and successfully manage systems in accordance with risk management frameworks such as NIST Special Publication 800-534, Department of Defense (DoD) Instruction 8500.2, and the Payment Card Industry (PCI) framework.

By detailing the specific and appropriate usage of the SCAP 1.2 components and their interoperability, NIST encourages the creation of reliable and pervasive SCAP content and the development of a wide array of products that leverage SCAP.

Framework for Improving Critical Infrastructure Cybersecurity

Recognizing that the national and economic security of the United States depends on the reliable functioning of critical infrastructure, the president issued Executive Order 13636, Improving Critical Infrastructure Cybersecurity, in February 2013.[54] It directed NIST to work with stakeholders to develop a voluntary framework – based on existing standards, guidelines, and practices - for reducing cyber risks to critical infrastructure.

NIST released the first version of the Framework for Improving Critical Infrastructure Cybersecurity on February 12, 2014.[55] The Framework, created through collaboration between industry and government, consists of standards, guidelines, and practices to promote the protection of critical infrastructure. The prioritized, flexible, repeatable, and cost-effective approach of the Framework helps owners and operators of critical infrastructure to manage cybersecurity-related risk.

Building from standards, guidelines, and practices, the Framework provides a common taxonomy and mechanism for organizations to:

- Describe their current cybersecurity posture;
- Describe their target state for cybersecurity;

---

54   See the following: http://www.whitehouse.gov/the-press-office/2013/02/12/executive-order-improving-critical-infrastructure-cybersecurity

55   See the following: http://www.nist.gov/cyberframework/upload/cybersecurity-framework-021214-final.pdf

- Identify and prioritize opportunities for improvement within the context of a continuous and repeatable process;
- Assess progress toward the target state;
- Communicate among internal and external stakeholders about cybersecurity risk.

The Framework is a risk-based approach to managing cybersecurity risk and is composed of three parts: the Framework Core, the Framework Implementation Tiers, and the Framework Profiles. Each Framework component reinforces the connection between business drivers and cybersecurity activities. These components are explained below.

1. ***The Framework Core*** is a set of cybersecurity activities, desired outcomes, and applicable references that are common across critical infrastructure sectors. The Core presents industry standards, guidelines, and practices in a manner that allows for communication of cybersecurity activities and outcomes across the organization from the executive level to the implementation/operations level. The Framework Core consists of five concurrent and continuous Functions—Identify, Protect, Detect, Respond, Recover. When considered together, these Functions provide a high-level, strategic view of the lifecycle of an organization's management of cybersecurity risk. The Framework Core then identifies underlying key Categories and Subcategories for each Function, and it matches them with example Informative References such as existing standards, guidelines, and practices for each Subcategory.

2. ***Framework Implementation Tiers ("Tiers")*** provide context on how an organization views cybersecurity risk and the processes in place to manage that risk. Tiers describe the degree to which an organization's cybersecurity risk management practices exhibit the characteristics defined in the Framework (e.g., risk and threat aware, repeatable, and adaptive). The Tiers characterize an organization's practices over a range, from Partial (Tier 1) to Adaptive (Tier 4). These Tiers reflect a progression from informal, reactive responses to approaches that are agile and risk-informed. During the Tier selection process, an organization should consider its current risk management practices, threat environment, legal and regulatory requirements, business/mission objectives, and organizational constraints.

3. ***A Framework Profile ("Profile")*** represents the outcomes based on business needs that an organization has selected from the Framework Categories and Subcategories. The Profile can be characterized as the alignment of standards, guidelines, and practices to the Framework Core in a particular implementation scenario. Profiles can be used to identify opportunities for improving cybersecurity posture by comparing a "Current" Profile (the "as is" state) with a "Target" Profile (the "to be" state). To develop a Profile, an organization can review all of the Categories and Subcategories and, based on business drivers and a risk assessment, determine which are most important; they can add Categories and Subcategories as needed to address the organization's risks. The Current Profile can then be used to support prioritization and measurement of progress toward the Target Profile, while factoring in other business needs including cost-effectiveness and innovation. Profiles can be used to conduct self-assessments and communicate within an organization or between organizations.

2

Asset Security

241

The United States Department of Homeland Security's Critical Infrastructure Cyber Community C³ Voluntary Program helps align critical infrastructure owners and operators with existing resources that will assist their efforts to adopt the Cybersecurity Framework and manage their cyber risks.[56]

The security practitioner has to be able to choose from among the many standards that exist in order to apply the most beneficial guidance for the enterprise architecture that he or she is looking to create.

---

56   See the following: http://www.dhs.gov/ccubedvp

Summary

Asset Security covers a wide range of topics focused on the concepts, principles, structures, and standards used to monitor and secure assets and those controls used to enforce various levels of confidentiality, integrity, and availability across IT services throughout the enterprise. Security practitioners focused on asset security must use and apply standards to ensure that the systems under their protection are maintained and supported properly. Security practitioners understand the different security frameworks, standards, and best practices leveraged by numerous methodologies, and how they may be used together to provide stronger systems. Information Security Governance and Risk Management has enabled information technology to be used safely, responsibly, and securely in environments never before possible. The ability to establish strong system protections based on standards and policy and to assess the level and efficacy of that protection through auditing and monitoring is vital to the success of asset security. Today's environment of highly interconnected, interdependent systems necessitates the requirement to understand the linkage between information technology and meeting business objectives. Information security management communicates the risks accepted by the organization due to the currently implemented security controls and continually works to cost effectively enhance the controls to minimize the risk to the company's information assets.

2

Asset Security

Domain 2: Review Questions

1. In the event of a security incident, one of the primary objectives of the operations staff is to ensure that

   A. the attackers are detected and stopped.

   B. there is minimal disruption to the organization's mission.

   C. appropriate documentation about the event is maintained as chain of evidence.

   D. the affected systems are immediately shut off to limit to the impact.

2. Good data management practices include:

   A. Data quality procedures at all stages of the data management process, verification and validation of accuracy of the data, adherence to agreed upon data management practices, ongoing data audit to monitor the use and assess effectiveness of management practices and the integrity of existing data.

   B. Data quality procedures at some stages of the data management process, verification and validation of accuracy of the data, adherence to agreed upon data management practices, ongoing data audit to monitor the use and assess effectiveness of management practices and the integrity of existing data.

   C. Data quality procedures at all stages of the data management process, verification and validation of accuracy of the data, adherence to discussed data management practices, ongoing data audit to monitor the use and assess effectiveness of management practices and the integrity of existing data.

   D. Data quality procedures at all stages of the data management process, verification and validation of accuracy of the data, adherence to agreed upon data management practices, intermittent data audit to monitor the use and assess effectiveness of management practices and the integrity of existing data.

3. Issues to be considered by the security practitioner when establishing a data policy include:

   A. Cost, Due Care and Due Diligence, Privacy, Liability, Sensitivity, Existing Law & Policy Requirements, Policy and Process

   B. Cost, Ownership and Custodianship, Privacy, Liability, Sensitivity, Future Law & Policy Requirements, Policy and Process

   C. Cost, Ownership and Custodianship, Privacy, Liability, Sensitivity, Existing Law & Policy Requirements, Policy and Procedure

   D. Cost, Ownership and Custodianship, Privacy, Liability, Sensitivity, Existing Law & Policy Requirements, Policy and Process

2

Asset Security

4. The information owner typically has the following responsibilities:

   A. Determine the impact the information has on the mission of the organization, understand the replacement cost of the information, determine who in the organization or outside of it has a need for the information and under what circumstances the information should be released, know when the information is inaccurate or no longer needed and should be archived.

   B. Determine the impact the information has on the mission of the organization, understand the replacement cost of the information, determine who in the organization or outside of it has a need for the information and under what circumstances the information should be released, know when the information is inaccurate or no longer needed and should be destroyed.

   C. Determine the impact the information has on the policies of the organization, understand the replacement cost of the information, determine who in the organization or outside of it has a need for the information and under what circumstances the information should not be released, know when the information is inaccurate or no longer needed and should be destroyed.

   D. Determine the impact the information has on the mission of the organization, understand the creation cost of the information, determine who in the organization or outside of it has a need for the information and under what circumstances the information should be released, know when the information is inaccurate or no longer needed and should be destroyed.

5. QA/QC mechanisms are designed to prevent data contamination, which occurs when a process or event introduces either of which two fundamental types of errors into a dataset: (**choose TWO**)

   A. Errors of commission

   B. Errors of insertion

   C. Errors of omission

   D. Errors of creation

6. Some typical responsibilities of a data custodian may include: (**Choose ALL that apply**)

   A. Adherence to appropriate and relevant data policy and data ownership guidelines.

   B. Ensuring accessibility to appropriate users, maintaining appropriate levels of dataset security.

   C. Fundamental dataset maintenance, including but not limited to data storage and archiving.

   D. Assurance of quality and validation of any additions to a dataset, including periodic audits to assure ongoing data integrity.

7. The objectives of data documentation are to: (**Choose ALL that apply**)

    A. Ensure the longevity of data and their re-use for multiple purposes

    B. Ensure that data users understand the content context and limitations of datasets

    C. Facilitate the confidentiality of datasets

    D. Facilitate the interoperability of datasets and data exchange

8. Benefits of data standards include:

    A. more efficient data management, decreased data sharing, higher quality data, improved data consistency, increased data integration, better understanding of data, improved documentation of information resources

    B. more efficient data management, increased data sharing, higher quality data, improved data consistency, increased data integration, better understanding of data, improved documentation of information resources

    C. more efficient data management, increased data sharing, medium quality data, improved data consistency, decreased data integration, better understanding of data, improved documentation of information resources

    D. more efficient data management, increased data sharing, highest quality data, improved data consistency, increased data integration, better understanding of data, improved documentation of information metadata

9. When classifying data, the security practitioner needs to determine the following aspects of the policy: (**Choose ALL that apply**)

    A. who has access to the data

    B. what methods should be used to dispose of the data

    C. how the data is secured

    D. whether the data needs to be encrypted

10. The major benefit of information classification is to

    A. map out the computing ecosystem

    B. identify the threats and vulnerabilities

    C. determine the software baseline

    D. identify the appropriate level of protection needs

11. When sensitive information is no longer critical but still within scope of a record retention policy, that information is **BEST**

    A. Destroyed

    B. Re-categorized

    C. Degaussed

    D. Released

2

Asset Security

12. What are the **FOUR** phases of the equipment lifecycle?

    A. Defining requirements, acquiring and implementing, operations and maintenance, disposal and decommission

    B. Acquiring requirements, defining and implementing, operations and maintenance, disposal and decommission

    C. Defining requirements, acquiring and maintaining, implementing and operating, disposal and decommission

    D. Defining requirements, acquiring and implementing, operations and decommission, maintenance and disposal

13. Which of the following **BEST** determines the employment suitability of an individual?

    A. Job rank or title

    B. Partnership with the security team

    C. Role

    D. Background investigation

14. The best way to ensure that there is no data remanence of sensitive information that was once stored on a DVD-R media is by

    A. Deletion

    B. Degaussing

    C. Destruction

    D. Overwriting

15. Which of the following processes is concerned with not only identifying the root cause but also addressing the underlying issue?

    A. Incident management

    B. Problem management

    C. Change management

    D. Configuration management

16. Before applying a software update to production systems, it is **MOST** important that

    A. Full disclosure information about the threat that the patch addresses is available

    B. The patching process is documented

    C. The production systems are backed up

    D. An independent third party attests the validity of the patch

Domain 3
Security Engineering

The Security Engineering domain contains the concepts, principles, structures, and standards used to design, implement, monitor, and secure operating systems, equipment, networks, applications, and those controls used to enforce various levels of confidentiality, integrity, and availability. Information security architecture and design covers the practice of applying a comprehensive and rigorous method for describing a current and/or future structure and behavior for an organization's security processes, information security systems, personnel and organizational sub-units, so that these practices and processes align with the organization's core goals and strategic direction. Cryptography examines the principles, means, and methods of applying mathematical algorithms and data transformations to information to ensure its integrity, confidentiality, and authenticity. Physical security focuses on the threats, vulnerabilities, and countermeasures that can be utilized to physically protect an enterprise's resources and sensitive information. These resources include people, the facility in which they work, and the data, equipment, support systems, media, and supplies they utilize. Physical security describes measures that are designed to deny access to unauthorized personnel (including attackers) from physically accessing a building, facility, resource, or stored information, and guidance on how to design structures to resist potentially hostile acts. In addition to preventing unauthorized personnel from accessing information, a focus on physical security makes it possible to ensure protection for users from hazards like fire as well as providing for clearly marked safe passages out of the facility. Explaining the "what," "why," and "how" of this domain will help frame the rest of the chapter.

What?

Security architecture:

- Provides the framework and foundation to enable secure communication, protect information resources, and ensure that where required, IT delivery is confidential, available, and with integrity.

- Identifies the basic services needed to provide security for current and future systems.

- ■ Models the rules of behavior as well as the technologies required to securely and effectively protect assets.

- ■ Documents these evolving models to connect the business drivers to the technical implementation of controls.

- ■ Is typically built using standardized methodologies founded on industry frameworks and international standards.

Why?

The security architect faces a trade off when examining the "why" of security architectures. On the one hand, a security architecture can require a considerable investment in time and resources to build and implement properly. At the same time, a well thought out security architecture, one that addresses business and IT security alignment, as well as being standards based and widely communicated about and trained on within the enterprise, will yield many potential benefits. These benefits can include:

- ■ Better coordination of investment in security technologies and practices

- ■ Improved long-term planning for capital investment and operating budgets

- ■ Interoperability with other components of system and enterprise architecture

- ■ Greater adaptability, scalability, and coherence of security services

- ■ Standardization of common functions across multiple systems

- ■ Consistent application of security practices and solutions, including compliance with regulations

- ■ Providing the means to ensure that the implementation of security controls is correct and verifiable

How?

There are many methodologies for developing an IT and security architecture. This chapter will discuss some examples of frameworks, models, and standards frequently used in secure design. Although most security architectures are built on common themes, they vary depending on the needs of the organization that sponsored them. Successful integration is predicated on the acceptance and adoption of the stakeholders and customers of the architecture. This is accomplished by ensuring that the security architecture addresses the business requirements of a system. Those requirements will often be different depending on the scope of the design effort: System security architecture will focus on requirements for individual systems, while enterprise security architecture (ESA) will focus on multiple systems throughout the enterprise. The basic principles of secure design and the common methodologies and techniques used to create, implement, and verify these designs will be focused on. Finally, key concepts in system security architecture and ESA will be addressed. The security professional needs to understand how security architecture and design is performed and how different levels of architecture work together to secure information assets.

System security architecture is focused on designing security services within individual computing systems. Modern computing systems are complex creatures, comprised of a myriad of moving parts: computing platform hardware, firmware, operating system (OS), utilities, and a variety of specialized applications. Each moving part may either have a native control, the ability to implement a control, or none of the above.

In general, a well-architected solution will be able to combine security functions from each of the moving parts into a cohesive design. At the same time, it will need to strike a balance between security and the other needs of the computing system. This can be a very difficult balance to achieve. Because security components can consume considerable resources, control is frequently sacrificed in favor of improved functionality, usability, or performance. It is a security architect's challenge to find the balance and ensure that necessary controls are implemented as designed. This is most important because the ability to be successful when designing and building an enterprise security architecture "begins at the beginning, and ends at the end". Specifically, the security architect needs to understand that the ability to envision security and incorporate it from the very beginning of the planning cycle, through the design and build phases, all the way to the end of the lifecycle when an architecture is retired, is what equates to success. If security is an afterthought or is left till late in the implementation of the architecture, as opposed to being considered from the very beginning of the process, then security will never be as thorough nor as impactful as if it was "built-in" from the beginning.

There is a wide variety of computing platforms available, and each platform will take a different approach to providing security services. The architecture of these platforms is fundamental to the ways that they approach security requirements. Most computing platforms will offer a wide variety of security controls to help protect sensitive assets that are being generated, transmitted, or stored by the system. The security architect may be responsible for determining what security controls will be implemented, or he or she may be responsible for deciding what native controls will be used for a particular system in the enterprise.

The security architect must understand the basic building blocks that make up modern computing systems as well as some characteristics that distinguish types of systems from each other. Most importantly, he or she should be aware of the different ways that security can be implemented at the system level and be able to choose which mechanisms would be most appropriate in a given scenario.

3

Security Engineering

TOPICS

- Implement and manage an engineering lifecycle using security design principles
- Fundamental concepts of security models
- Controls and countermeasures based upon information systems security standards
- Security capabilities of information systems
- Assess and mitigate the vulnerabilities of security architectures, designs, and solution elements
  - Client-based (e.g., applets, local caches)
  - Server-based (e.g., data flow control)
  - Database security
  - Large scale parallel data systems
  - Distributed systems (e.g., cloud computing, grid computing, peer to peer)
  - Cryptographic systems
- Vulnerabilities in Web-based systems
- Vulnerabilities in mobile systems
- Vulnerabilities in embedded devices and cyber-physical systems (e.g., network-enabled devices)
- Cryptography
  - Cryptographic lifecycle
  - Cryptographic types (e.g., symmetric, asymmetric, elliptic curves)
  - Public key infrastructure (PKI)
  - Key management practices
  - Digital signatures
  - Digital rights management (DRM)
  - Non-repudiation
  - Integrity (hashing and salting)
  - Methods of cryptanalytic attacks (e.g., brute force, cipher-text only, known plaintext)
- Apply secure principles to site and facility design
- Facility security
  - Wiring closets
  - Server room
  - Media and storage facilities
  - Evidence storage
  - Restricted and work area security (e.g., operations center)
  - Data center security
  - Utilities and HVAC considerations
  - Water issues (e.g., leakage, flooding)
  - Fire prevention, detection, and suppression

OBJECTIVES

According to the (ISC)[2] Candidate Information Bulletin (Exam Outline), a CISSP candidate is expected to:

- Understand the engineering lifecycle and apply security design principles

- Understand the fundamental concepts of security models

- Select controls and countermeasures based upon information systems security standards

- Understand the security capabilities of information systems

- Assess and mitigate the vulnerabilities of:
  - Security architectures, designs, and solution elements
  - Web-based systems
  - Mobile systems
  - Embedded devices and cyber-physical systems

- Apply cryptography

- Apply secure principles to site and facility design

- Design and implement facility security

3

Security Engineering

The Engineering Lifecycle Using Security Design Principles

According to one definition, systems engineering is "an interdisciplinary approach to translating users' needs into the definition of a system, its architecture and design through an iterative process that results in an effective operational system. Systems engineering applies over the entire life cycle, from concept development to final disposal." [1]

Systems engineering models and processes usually organize themselves around the concept of a lifecycle. The International Council on Systems Engineering (INCOSE) systems engineering process is a widely recognized representation of classical systems engineering.[2] ISO/IEC 15288:2008 is an international systems engineering standard covering processes and lifecycle stages. It defines a set of processes divided into four categories: technical, project, agreement, and enterprise. Example lifecycle stages can include concept, development, production, utilization, support, and retirement. For example, the U.S. Department of Defense uses the following phases: materiel solution analysis, technology development, engineering and manufacturing development, production and deployment, and operations and support.

While the detailed views, implementations, and terminology used to articulate the system's engineering lifecycle differ, they all share fundamental elements, depicted in Figure 3.1 by the V-model. The left side of the V represents concept development and the decomposition of requirements into functions and physical entities that can be architected, designed, and developed. The right side of the V represents integration of these entities and their ultimate transition into the field, where they are operated and maintained.

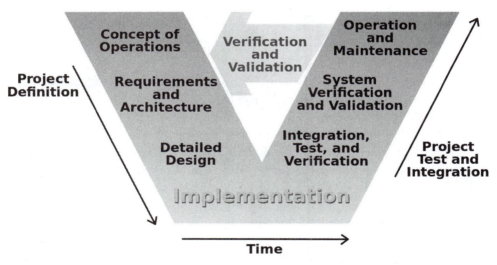

Figure 3.1 – **The V-model is a graphical representation of the system's development life cycle. It summarizes the main steps to be taken in conjunction with the corresponding deliverables within a computerized system validation framework. The V represents the sequence of steps in a project lifecycle. It describes the activities to be performed and the results that have to be produced during product development.**

---

1   See the following: Committee on Pre-Milestone A Systems Engineering, 2009, *Pre-Milestone A and Early-Phase Systems Engineering: A Retrospective Review and Benefits for Future Air Force Acquisition,* The National Academies Press. http://www.nap.edu/catalog.php?record_id=12065

2   See the following for information about INCOSE: http://www.incose.org/

There are often iterative cycles, skipped phases, overlapping elements, etc. that will occur within the lifecycle. Additionally, important processes and activities apply to more than one phase in a system lifecycle. Risk identification and management is one example of such a cross cutting process.

Key system engineering technical process topics include:

- Requirements Definition
- Requirements Analysis
- Architectural Design
- Implementation
- Integration
- Verification
- Validation
- Transition

Key system engineering management process topics include:

- Decision Analysis
- Technical Planning
- Technical Assessment
- Requirements Management
- Risk Management
- Configuration Management
- Interface Management
- Technical Data Management

Securing information and systems against the full spectrum of threats requires the use of multiple, overlapping protection approaches addressing the people, technology, and operational aspects of information systems. This is due to the highly interactive nature of the various systems and networks and to the fact that any single system cannot be adequately secured unless all interconnecting systems are also secured. The security architects need to understand that unless they are given the unique opportunity to design, build, and implement an architecture from the beginning, in the process "ripping and replacing" what exists in favor of what they are building, then the systems that they are working with and integrating into the architecture are fraught with their own issues, concerns, and problems. These things may or may not be apparent, and they may or may not be addressed by the architecture that the security architect is proposing or implementing.

By using multiple, overlapping protection mechanisms, the failure or circumvention of any individual protection approach will not leave the system unprotected. Through user training and awareness, well-crafted policies and procedures, and redundancy of protection mechanisms, layered protections enable effective protection of information technology for the purpose of achieving the required objectives of the security architecture, balanced against the enterprise's appetite for risk.

The "Generally Accepted Principles and Practices for Securing Information Technology Systems" (NIST SP 800-14) provides a foundation upon which organizations can establish and review information technology security programs. The eight Generally Accepted System Security Principles in SP 800-14 are designed to provide an organization-level perspective when creating new systems, practices, or policies. SP 800-14 lays out eight principles and 14 practices that provide an organizational-level perspective for information technology security.[3]

The Common Criteria provides a structured methodology for documenting security requirements, documenting and validating security capabilities, and promoting international cooperation in the area of IT security. Use of the Common Criteria "protection profiles" and "security targets" greatly aids in the development of products and systems that have IT security functions. The rigor and repeatability of the Common Criteria methodology provides for thorough definition of user security needs. Security targets provide system integrators with key information needed in the procurement of components and implementation of secure IT systems.[4]

In order to come up with an approach that would be more consistent and offer the proper level of guidance, NIST compiled a set of engineering principles for system security. These principles provide a foundation upon which a structured approach to the design, development, and implementation of IT security capabilities can be constructed. While the primary focus of these principles is the implementation of technical controls, these principles highlight the fact that, to be effective, a system security design should also consider non-technical issues, such as policy, operational procedures, and user education and training. These principles are detailed in NIST SP 800-27 Rev A, the Engineering Principles for Information Technology Security (A Baseline for Achieving Security), Revision A.[5]

The five life cycle planning phases used in NIST SP 800-27 Rev A are defined in the Generally Accepted Principles and Practices for Securing Information Technology Systems, SP 800-14, as noted below:

- **Initiation** – During the initiation phase, the need for a system is expressed and the purpose of the system is documented. Activities include conducting an impact assessment in accordance with FIPS-199.[6]

- **Development/Acquisition** – During this phase, the system is designed, purchased, programmed, developed, or otherwise constructed. This phase often consists of other defined cycles, such as the system development cycle or the acquisition cycle. Activities include determining security requirements, incorporating security requirements into specifications, and obtaining the system.

- **Implementation** – During implementation, the system is tested and installed or fielded. Activities include installing/turning on controls, security testing, certification, and accreditation.

- **Operation/Maintenance** – During this phase, the system performs its work. Typically, the system is also being modified by the addition of hardware and software and by numerous other events. Activities include security operations and administration, operational assurance, and audits and monitoring.

---

3   See the following for the complete NIST SP 800-14 publication: http://csrc.nist.gov/publications/ nistpubs/index.html

4   See the following for information on the Common Criteria: http://www.commoncriteriaportal.org/

5   See the following for the complete NIST SP 800-27 Rev A publication: http://csrc.nist.gov/publications/ nistpubs/index.html

6   See the following for the Federal Information Processing Standards Publication - Standards for Security Categorization of Federal Information and Information Systems (FIPS Pub 199): http://csrc.nist.gov/ publications/fips/fips199/FIPS-PUB-199-final.pdf

3

Security Engineering

- **Disposal** – The disposal phase of the IT system lifecycle involves the disposition of information, hardware, and software. Activities include moving, archiving, discarding, or destroying information and sanitizing the media.

NIST SP 800-27 Rev A creates 33 IT security principles that are grouped into the following 6 categories:
- Security Foundation
- Risk Based
- Ease of Use
- Increase Resilience
- Reduce Vulnerabilities
- Design with Network in Mind

The 33 IT security principles are broken down by category:

Security Foundation
- *Principle 1:* Establish a sound security policy as the "foundation" for design
- *Principle 2:* Treat security as an integral part of the overall system design
- *Principle 3:* Clearly delineate the physical and logical security boundaries governed by the associated security policies
- *Principle 4:* Ensure that developers are trained in how to develop secure software

Risk Based
- *Principle 5:* Reduce risk to an acceptable level
- *Principle 6:* Assume that external systems are insecure
- *Principle 7:* Identify potential trade-offs between reducing risk and increased costs and decrease in other aspects of operational effectiveness
- *Principle 8:* Implement tailored system security measures to meet organizational security goals
- *Principle 9:* Protect information while being processed, in transit, and in storage
- *Principle 10:* Consider custom products to achieve adequate security
- *Principle 11:* Protect against all likely classes of "attacks"

Ease of Use
- *Principle 12:* Where possible, base security on open standards for portability and interoperability
- *Principle 13:* Use common language in developing security requirements
- *Principle 14:* Design security to allow for regular adoption of new technology, including a secure and logical technology upgrade process
- *Principle 15:* Strive for operational ease of use

Increase Resilience
- *Principle 16:* Implement layered security (Ensure no single point of vulnerability)
- *Principle 17:* Design and operate an IT system to limit damage and to be resilient in response
- *Principle 18:* Provide assurance that the system is, and continues to be, resilient in the face of expected threats
- *Principle 19:* Limit or contain vulnerabilities

- *Principle 20:* Isolate public access systems from mission critical resources (e.g., data, processes, etc.)
- *Principle 21:* Use boundary mechanisms to separate computing systems and network infrastructures
- *Principle 22:* Design and implement audit mechanisms to detect unauthorized use and to support incident investigations
- *Principle 23:* Develop and exercise contingency or disaster recovery procedures to ensure appropriate availability

Reduce Vulnerabilities

- *Principle 24:* Strive for simplicity
- *Principle 25:* Minimize the system elements to be trusted
- *Principle 26:* Implement least privilege
- *Principle 27:* Do not implement unnecessary security mechanisms
- *Principle 28:* Ensure proper security in the shutdown or disposal of a system
- *Principle 29:* Identify and prevent common errors and vulnerabilities

Design with Network in Mind

- *Principle 30:* Implement security through a combination of measures distributed physically and logically
- *Principle 31:* Formulate security measures to address multiple overlapping information domains
- *Principle 32:* Authenticate users and processes to ensure appropriate access control decisions both within and across domains
- *Principle 33:* Use unique identities to ensure accountability

The 33 NIST principles help the security practitioner to understand and appreciate the scope and depth of the security design principles that have to be interwoven into any engineering lifecycle in order to appropriately identify and address the various areas of concern with regards to Confidentiality, Integrity, and Availability. The challenge that the NIST principles by themselves present to the security architect is one of context and sufficiency with regards to integration within the broader context of the lifecycle architecture.

This challenge manifests itself because often the security architecture is treated as a separate architecture domain within the enterprise architecture while needing to be fully integrated in it. The focus of the security practitioner should be the enforcement of the security policies of the enterprise without inhibiting value.

Security architectures generally have the following characteristics:

- Security architecture has its own discrete security methodology.
- Security architecture composes its own discrete views and viewpoints.
- Security architecture addresses non-normative flows through systems and among applications.
- Security architecture introduces its own normative flows through systems and among applications.
- Security architecture introduces unique, single-purpose components in the design.
- Security architecture calls for its own unique set of skills and competencies of the enterprise and IT architects.

The security practitioner needs to understand how to identify the key issues and concerns that the engineering lifecycle must address for the enterprise. Once they are identified, then they must be clearly defined and agreed upon by the stakeholders in the enterprise. When the stakeholders have agreed, then security design principles can be used by the architect to ensure that all known and identified threats, vulnerabilities, and risks have been addressed as part of the security architecture being included in the lifecycle.

There are many examples of secure development lifecycle frameworks such as the Cisco Secure Development Lifecycle, Microsoft's Trustworthy Computing Security Development Lifecycle, the Center's for Medicare and Medicaid Services Technical Reference Architecture standards, and the Building Security in Maturity Model-V (BSIMM-V).[7]

In addition, there is ISO/IEC 21827:2008, the Systems Security Engineering - Capability Maturity Model (SSE-CMM), which describes the essential characteristics of an organization's security engineering process that must exist to ensure good security engineering.[8] ISO/IEC 21827:2008 does not prescribe a particular process or sequence, but it captures practices generally observed in industry. The model is a standard metric for security engineering practices covering the following:

- The entire lifecycle, including development, operation, maintenance, and decommissioning activities;
- The whole organization, including management, organizational, and engineering activities;
- Concurrent interactions with other disciplines, such as system, software, hardware, human factors and test engineering;
- System management, operation, and maintenance;
- Interactions with other organizations, including acquisition, system management, certification, accreditation, and evaluation.

Fundamental Concepts of Security Models

Creating and maintaining a good security architecture can be a difficult task. The primary role of the security architect is to translate business requirements into solutions that provide security for key assets. Since both the assets requiring protection and the organization's preferred approach to protecting them may be different, each design will be unique. A strong design will require that the architect understands both the assets to be protected and management's priorities. The architect must also be prepared to adjust the design over time as key assets or priorities change as well as verify that his or her designs have been implemented correctly.

---

7   See the following for more information: Cisco Secure Development Lifecycle: http://www.cisco.com/web/about/security/cspo/csdl/process.html
    Microsoft Trustworthy Computing Security Development Lifecycle: http://msdn.microsoft.com/en-us/library/ms995349.aspx
    Center for Medicare and Medicaid Services Technical Reference Architecture standards: http://www.cms.gov/Research-Statistics-Data-and-Systems/CMS-Information-Technology/Technical-Reference-Architecture-Standards/
    BSIMM-V: http://bsimm.com/

8   See the following for ISO/IEC 21827:2008: https://www.iso.org/obp/ui/#iso:std:iso-iec:21827:ed-2:v1:en

Common System Components

Modern computing systems are comprised of layers of hardware, firmware, and software that work together to provide computing services. Although the security architect may not need to be a specialist in system architecture, he or she should understand some of the most common system components as well as their respective roles. Given their importance for system security, the focus of discussion will be on four main components: processors, storage, peripherals, and the OS.

Each has specialized roles in the architecture. Processors are the brains of a computer system that perform calculations while solving problems and performing system tasks. Storage devices provide both long- and short-term storage of information. Peripherals (scanners, printers, modems, etc.) are devices that either input data or receive the data output by the processors. The OS provides the glue that binds all these elements together as well as providing the interface for applications, utilities, and the end-user. Security functions are often distributed across these components where most appropriate to ensure that the system can secure information assets most effectively.

Processors [9]

Processing is the conversion of inputted raw data into useful output. Traditionally, processing was performed exclusively by a single processing unit (the central processing unit or CPU), responsible for ensuring that system instructions were performed and that interactions between memory, storage, and input/output devices were controlled. While this continues to be the case in smaller embedded systems, it is more common to find multiple processors that share the responsibility for processing in a computing system. While CPUs continue to play the most important role, there are also specialized processing units for graphics (graphics processing units or GPUs) and numerous coprocessors, including those used to offload cryptographic functions from the CPUs.

Traditionally, the CPU managed all of the system's devices as well as doing the actual data processing. In modern systems, the CPU still plays an important role but is no longer the sole source of processing power. It is paired with a computer's motherboard, which provides the supporting chipset that controls access to memory, storage, and input/output devices such as mice, keyboards, monitors, and other communications devices. The CPU, motherboard, and memory operate together, with the memory holding data and the next set of program instructions as the CPU uses its current instructions to perform calculations on the data.

Processors perform four main tasks: fetching, decoding, executing, and storing. When the CPU requires data, it retrieves it from memory. The CPU fetches information from memory, i.e., instructions and data; it decodes the instructions to decipher next steps; it executes the instructions, e.g., calculating numbers; and it stores the results of the instruction. Then the cycle repeats until there are no further instructions to be executed.

---

9   See the following for an overview of the CPU and the parts that make it up: http://education-portal.com/academy/lesson/central-processing-unit-cpu-parts-definition-function.html#lesson
See the following for the IEEE special report "25 Microchips That Shook the World":
http://spectrum.ieee.org/static/25chips
See the following for a comprehensive historical reference on the semiconductor:
http://www.computerhistory.org/semiconductor/resources.html

This simple process is sufficient for a system that is only running a single, serial set of instructions, but it may not be the most efficient way to provide processing to a complex program or many programs that must share a common processor. Ideally, the processor should be able to weave multiple sets of instructions together to make sure that they are taking full advantage of any processing power.

One way to take advantage of the capabilities of a processor is to split programs into multiple, cooperating processes. A multitasking system switches from one process to another quickly to speed up processing. To the user, it appears to be simultaneous execution even though only one process is running at any given time on the CPU. However, there needs to be a mechanism in place that will allow the OS to start running an application with the probability, but not the certainty, that the application will sooner or later return control to the OS.

Another way to achieve higher performance can be realized by increasing the number of processors in a system where each processor can assume some of the load. Powerful computers such as servers have several processors handling different tasks, although there must be one processor to control the flow of instructions and data through the supplementary processors. This type of system is called a multiprocessing system.

Another common way to get higher performance is to split programs into threads. As the name implies, threads are a series of instructions that can be treated as a running thread. Normally, as a program is executing, a processor runs each line of code in sequence. However, there are times when a subsequent step is not dependent upon the completion of a previous step. If the programmer requests a new thread to be generated for the later step, the CPU can be asked to do something else at the same time the application continues doing its current task. An example might be a spreadsheet calculation running at the same time that the main application asks a user for input.

Multithreading, then, is the concept whereby the OS time slices the threads and gives one thread some time on the CPU, then switches to another thread and lets it run for a while. This routine continues until the first thread has its turn again. In essence, the threads are split up and given to the CPU in an interleaved manner. Each thread operates as though it has exclusive access to the CPU, even though it runs only for a short time and then stops until it runs again in a short time.

While multitasking, multiprocessing, and multithreading have obvious advantages, they can lead to some potential security vulnerabilities. It is vital that the system provides means to protect multiple processes, tasks, and threads from the other processes/tasks/threads that may contain bugs or exhibit unfriendly actions. Techniques need to be implemented to measure and control resource usage. For example, when a system is running many different tasks, being able to measure each task's total resource usage is a desired piece of managing security in such a system. This information needs to be gathered without incurring a significant performance penalty and without changing the manner that tasks are written and executed. If this type of functionality is not available, a task might assign and seize enough memory to result in a denial-of-service attack, a crash, or a system slowdown. The bottom line, even though there are many advantages to implementing multiprocessing, multitasking, and multithreading, is that the more subtasks a system creates, the more things can go awry.

The security architects need to be aware of some of the main issues inherent in CPU security in order to ensure that they are making informed decisions as they deploy systems into the enterprise. Some of the key features that processors should have in order to address security concerns at multiple levels are as follows:

- Tamper detection sensors
- Crypto acceleration
- Battery backed logic with a physical mesh
- The ability to customize a device with secure boot capabilities
- Secure memory access controller with on-the-fly encrypt and decrypt capabilities
- Static and differential power analysis (SPA/DPA) countermeasures
- Smart card UART controllers

One example of how these safeguards can be built into a secure chip architecture can be found in Freescale's C29x crypto coprocessor. The C29x is engineered to help the world's top data center equipment manufacturers efficiently scale to handle dramatic increases in secure network traffic. The device enables multi-chip, single PCI-E card solutions providing more than 120,000 RSA 2,048 operations/second. Silicom has created a new C29x PCI-E card. This solution offers industry-leading encryption performance to accelerate public key processing in servers, data centers, and security appliances. In addition, Green Hills Software has ported its security-certified INTEGRITY RTOS (Real Time Operating System) to the C29x coprocessor. This combination creates an ideal solution for secure key management applications, which requires highly "trusted" architectures to ensure encryption keys are secure in such applications as online banking and video-on-demand servers.

In addition, there is also the question of how cloud-based solutions such as Desktop as a Service (DaaS) and more broadly virtualization will impact the discussion around CPU security. The security architect needs to be aware of these issues and take them into account when planning his or her architectures. For example, in June of 2012, Vulnerability VU#649219 was logged and released by the US CERT. The vulnerability report was titled: "SYSRET 64-bit operating system privilege escalation vulnerability on Intel CPU hardware." The following is an excerpt from the Vulnerability Note:[10]

Overview

Some 64-bit operating systems and virtualization software running on Intel CPU hardware are vulnerable to a local privilege escalation attack. The vulnerability may be exploited for local privilege escalation or a guest-to-host virtual machine escape.

Intel claims that this vulnerability is a software implementation issue, as their processors are functioning as per their documented specifications. However, software that fails to take the Intel-specific SYSRET behavior into account may be vulnerable.

Description

A ring3 attacker may be able to specifically craft a stack frame to be executed by ring0 (kernel) after a general protection exception (#GP). The fault will be handled before the stack switch, which means the exception handler will be run at ring0 with an attacker's chosen RSP causing a privilege escalation.

---

10   See the following for the full Vulnerability Note from the US-CERT: http://www.kb.cert.org/vuls/id/649219

Details from Xen

CVE-2012-0217 / XSA-7 - 64-bit PV guest privilege escalation vulnerability

A vulnerability that can allow a 64-bit PV guest kernel running on a 64-bit hypervisor to escalate privileges to that of the host by arranging for a system call to return via sysret to a non-canonical RIP. Intel CPUs deliver the resulting exception in an undesirable processor state.

Details from FreeBSD

FreeBSD-SA-12:04.sysret: Privilege escalation when returning from kernel

FreeBSD/amd64 runs on CPUs from different vendors. Due to varying behavior of CPUs in 64 bit mode a sanity check of the kernel may be insufficient when returning from a system call. Successful exploitation of the problem can lead to local kernel privilege escalation, kernel data corruption and/or crash.

Details from Microsoft

User Mode Scheduler Memory Corruption Vulnerability - MS12-042 - Important

An elevation of privilege vulnerability exists in the way that the Windows User Mode Scheduler handles system requests. An attacker who successfully exploited this vulnerability could run arbitrary code in kernel mode. An attacker could then install programs; view, change, or delete data; or create new accounts with full administrative rights.

Mitigating Factors for User Mode Scheduler Memory Corruption Vulnerability

Mitigation refers to a setting, common configuration, or general best practice, existing in a default state that could reduce the severity of exploitation of a vulnerability. The following mitigating factors may be helpful in your situation:

- An attacker must have valid logon credentials and be able to log on locally to exploit this vulnerability. The vulnerability could not be exploited remotely or by anonymous users.
- This vulnerability only affects Intel x64-based versions of Windows 7 and Windows Server 2008 R2.
- Systems with AMD or ARM-based CPUs are not affected by this vulnerability.

Details from Red Hat

RHSA-2012:0720-1 & RHSA-2012:0721-1: It was found that the Xen hypervisor implementation as shipped with Red Hat Enterprise Linux 5 did not properly restrict the syscall return addresses in the sysret return path to canonical addresses. An unprivileged user in a 64-bit para-virtualized guest, which is running on a 64-bit host that has an Intel CPU, could use this flaw to crash the host or, potentially, escalate their privileges, allowing them to execute arbitrary code at the hypervisor level. (CVE-2012-0217, Important)

Impact

A local authenticated attacker may exploit this vulnerability for operating system privilege escalation or for a guest-to-host virtual machine escape.

While this vulnerability was widespread across multiple vendor platforms, it did not affect all vendors that provided virtualization solutions. Any architecture that was built upon the selection of an AMD chip as the CPU of choice would not have been exposed to this vulnerability. The security architect would not have been able to know this ahead of time and would have made a choice regarding the CPU without any idea that the choice made had a 50% chance of exposing the information stored on those systems to a potential security threat. While the chances of this particular threat being used to attack a system may or may not have been high at the time, the fact still remains that the security architect would bear ultimate responsibility for this threat and its impact on the systems affected.

Memory and Storage

In general, system architecture will focus heavily on memory and how memory is managed. Valuable or critical information assets are stored in memory. Sensitive or important programs are executed from memory. This makes memory the key for any system security architecture, and it may explain why most security components within computing systems are so heavily focused on it. There are a few main types of memory, each requiring different approaches for protection.

Primary Storage

As data waits for processing by the processors, it sits in a staging area called primary storage. Whether implemented as memory, cache, or registers (part of the CPU), and regardless of its location, primary storage stores data that has a high probability of being requested by the CPU, so it is usually faster than long-term, secondary storage. The location where data is stored is denoted by its physical memory address. This memory register identifier remains constant and is independent of the value stored there. Some examples of primary storage devices include random-access memory (RAM), synchronous dynamic random-access memory (SDRAM), and read-only memory (ROM). RAM is volatile: When the system shuts down, it flushes the data in RAM although recent research has shown that data may still be retrievable.[11] Contrast this to ROM, which is nonvolatile storage that retains data even when electrical power is shut off.

The closer data is to the CPU, the faster it can be retrieved and thus processed. Data is sent to the CPU through various input devices (keyboards, modems, etc.), cache, main memory, and disk storage devices. As the data travels to the CPU, it moves from storage devices (disks, tapes, etc.) to main memory (RAM), then to cache memory, finally arriving at the CPU for processing (*Figure* 3.2). The further data are from the CPU, the longer the trip takes. In fact, if one were to compare speed of access to data, retrieving data from disk storage takes the longest, retrieval from RAM is faster than disk storage, and cache memory retrieval takes the least amount of time. Cache memory can be described as high-speed RAM on the same chip as the processor. Optimally designed caches can reduce the memory access time because data moves from the slower RAM to the faster cache then to the CPU. This process speeds up the CPU's access to the data and thus improves the performance of program execution.

---

11   See the following for the original research paper on the phenomena of DRAM data remanence, entitled "Lest We Remember: Cold Boot Attacks on Encryption Keys". http://citpsite.s3-website-us-east-1.amazonaws.com/oldsite-htdocs/pub/coldboot.pdf

See the following for the original publications and research papers that identified RAM data remanence as a potential security issues:

Anderson R. Security engineering: a guide to building dependable distributed systems. 1st ed. Wiley; January 2001.

Gutmann P. Secure deletion of data from magnetic and solid-state memory. Proc. 6th USENIX Security Symposium, pp. 77–90, July 1996.

Gutmann P. Data remanence in semiconductor devices. Proc. 10th USENIX Security Symposium, pp. 39–54, August 2001.

3

Security Engineering

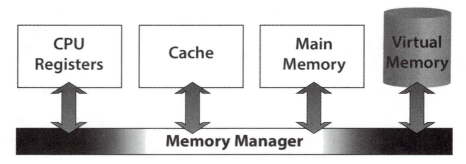

Figure 3.2 – **Common types of memory in most computing systems. One of the main tasks of memory management is to ensure that information is in an appropriate area of memory when it is needed as well as manage how information is moved between the different types of memory available to the memory manager.**

Memory Protection[12]

The main purpose of memory protection is to prevent a process from accessing memory that has not been allocated to it. There are several methods used to achieve memory protection. The three most common ones are segmentation, paging, and protection keying. Segmentation refers to dividing a computer's memory into segments. A reference to a memory location includes a value that identifies a segment and an offset within that segment. Paging divides the memory address space into equal-sized blocks called pages. A page table maps virtual memory to physical memory. Page tables make it easier to allocate additional memory, as each new page can be allocated from anywhere in physical memory. It is impossible for an application to access a page that has not been explicitly allocated to it because every memory address either points to a page allocated to that application or generates an interrupt called a page fault. Unallocated pages, and pages allocated to any other application, do not have any addresses from the application point of view. A protection key mechanism divides physical memory up into blocks of a particular size, each of which has an associated numerical value called a protection key. Each process also has a protection key value associated with it. When memory is accessed, the hardware checks that the current process's protection key matches the value associated with the memory block being accessed; if not, then an exception occurs.

Memory protection for computer security includes additional techniques such as address space layout randomization (ASLR) and executable space protection. ASLR involves randomly arranging the positions of key data areas of a program, including the base of the executable and the positions of the stack, heap, and libraries in a process's memory address space. Address space layout randomization is based upon the low chance of an attacker guessing the locations of randomly placed areas. Security is increased by increasing the search space.[13] Executable space protection is the marking of memory regions as non-executable, implying

---

12 See the following for in-depth documentation on memory protection techniques on Intel platforms:
    http://www.intel.com/content/www/us/en/processors/architectures-software-developer-manuals.html

13 See the following for an overview of ASLR:
    A. http://www.cs.berkeley.edu/~dawnsong/papers/syscall-tr.ps
    B. https://www.usenix.org/legacy/event/sec05/tech/full_papers/bhatkar/bhatkar.pdf
    C. http://www.cs.columbia.edu/~angelos/Papers/instructionrandomization.pdf
    D. http://www.stanford.edu/~blp/papers/asrandom.pdf

that any attempt to execute machine code in these regions will cause an exception. Many 64-bit operating systems implement executable space protection with ASLR in some form to prevent certain kinds of buffer overflow attacks from taking place, such as return-to-libc and return-to-plt attacks.[14]

Secondary Storage

Secondary storage holds data not currently being used by the CPU and is used when data must be stored for an extended period of time using high-capacity, nonvolatile storage. Computer systems use multiple media types for storing information as both raw data and programs. This media differs in storage capacity, speed of access, permanency of storage, and mode of access. Fixed disks may store up to terabytes in personal computers and up to hundreds of petabytes in large systems.

Fixed-disk data access is done randomly and is slower than RAM access. However, data stored on fixed disks is permanent in that it does not disappear when power is turned off, although data can be erased and modified. Dismountable media devices can be removed for storage or shipping and include floppy diskettes, which are randomly accessed; magnetic tapes, with gigabytes of storage and either sequential or random access (DLT, SDLT, 8-mm DAT); optical compact disks (CDs), with 650 to 870 MB of storage per CD; high-capacity DVDs and Blu-rays, with 50 to 125 GB of storage. Both CDs and DVDs use random access. External hard drives and USB drives range from a few GB to Terabytes of information and are random access based.

Virtual Memory

Most OSs have the ability to simulate having more main memory than is physically available in the system. This is done by storing part of the data on secondary storage, such as a disk. This can be considered a virtual page. If the data requested by the system is not currently in main memory, a page fault is taken. This condition triggers the OS handler. If the virtual address is a valid one, the OS will locate the physical page, put the right information in that page, update the translation table, and then try the request again. Some other page might be swapped out to make room. Each process may have its own separate virtual address space along with its own mappings and protections.

One of the reasons that virtual memory was developed is that computer systems have a limited amount of physical memory, and often that amount of RAM is insufficient to simultaneously run all of the programs that users want to use. For example, with the Windows OS loaded and an email program, along with a Web browser and word processor, physical memory may be insufficient to hold all of the data. If there were no such entity as virtual memory, the computer would not be able to load any more applications. With virtual memory, the OS looks for data in RAM that has not been accessed recently and copies it onto the hard disk. The cleared space is now available to load additional applications (but within the same physical memory constraints). This process occurs automatically, and the computer functions as though it has almost unlimited RAM available. Because hard disks are cheaper than RAM chips, virtual memory provides a good, cost-effective solution.

---

14   See the following for an overview of the return-to-libc and return-to-plt attacks: http://www.exploit-db.com/download_pdf/17131
       http://www.exploit-db.com/wp-content/themes/exploit/docs/17286.pdf

There are potential downsides to using virtual memory, especially if it is not configured correctly. To take advantage of virtual memory, the system must be configured with a swap file. This swap or page file is the hard disk area that stores the data contained in the RAM. These pages of RAM, called page frames, are used by the OS to move data back and forth between the page file and RAM.

When it comes to accessing data, the read and write speeds of a hard drive are drastically slower than RAM access. In addition, because hard drives are not designed to constantly access tiny bits of data, if a system relies too much on virtual memory, there may be a negative impact on performance. One solution is to install sufficient RAM to run all tasks simultaneously. Even with sufficient physical memory, the system may experience a small hesitation as tasks are changed. However, with the appropriate amount of RAM, virtual memory functions well. On the other hand, with an insufficient amount of RAM, the OS continuously has to swap data between the hard disk and RAM. This thrashing of data between the disk and RAM will also slow down a computer system.

Firmware

Firmware is the storage of programs or instructions in ROM. Typically, this software is embedded into hardware and is used to control that hardware. Because ROM is nonvolatile, these programs and instructions will not change if power is shut off, but instead they become a permanent part of the system. User manipulation of the firmware should not be permitted.

Usually, firmware is upgradeable and is stored in electrically erasable programmable read-only memory (EEPROM). This is handy in those instances where firmware may have bugs and an upgrade will fix the problems. The hardware itself is not upgradeable without substituting portions of it. Therefore, vendors attempt to store as many important controls as possible in the firmware in case changes need to be made. From the vendor's perspective, if a bug is discovered, it is preferable to notify the affected clients to upgrade the firmware than to replace the product. Examples of devices with firmware are computer systems, peripherals, and accessories such as USB flash drives, memory cards, and mobile phones.

Peripherals and Other Input/Output (I/O) Devices

Data needs to be inputted and processed and output generated. The data is transferred between numerous locations – from disk to CPU or from the CPU to memory or from memory to the display adapter. It would be unrealistic to have discrete circuits between every pair of entities. For instance, throughput would be too slow. However, when a bus concept is implemented, a shared set of wires connects all the computer devices and chips. Certain wires transmit data; others send control and clocking signals. Addresses identifying specific devices or memory locations are transmitted, and when a device's address is transmitted, the corresponding device then transfers data across the wires to the CPU, RAM, display adapter, etc.

Data is the raw information fed to the computer, and programs are the collection of instructions that provide directions to the computer. To tell a system what tasks to perform, commands are entered into the system by the user. For ease of use, input takes various forms. Commands and responses can be entered locally via a keyboard or mouse, with menus and icons, or remotely from another system or peripheral.

The result of computer processing is considered output. This output is in binary or hexadecimal numbers, but for users to understand the output, it takes the form of alphanumeric characters and words that are interpreted by humans as video, audio, or printed text. Thus, output devices may be computer displays, speaker systems, laser printers, and all-in-one devices. Inputs are the signals received through an interface, and outputs are the signals sent from the interfaces. A person (or another computer system) communicates with the computer by using these interfaces (I/O devices). In summary, the CPU and main memory, working in tandem, are the core processes of a computer, and the transfer of information from or to that duo, for example, retrieving from and storing data to a disk drive, is considered to be I/O.

Software programs called drivers control the input and output devices and the communication channels that are used for system I/O. Drivers enable the OS to control and communicate with hardware. Different signals require different interfaces that differ according to the communications channel of the I/O device. For example, a Universal Serial Bus (USB) device communicates through a USB cable attached to a USB port. The current USB standard supports higher speeds and large numbers of peripheral devices, such as removable disk drives, mice, printers, and keyboards.

Operating Systems

The Operating System is the software that controls the operation of the computer from the moment it is turned on or booted. The OS controls all input and output to and from the peripherals, as well as the operation of other programs, and allows the user to work with and manage files without knowing specifically how the data is stored and retrieved. In multiuser systems, the OS will manage user access to the processor and peripherals and schedule jobs.

The system kernel is the core of an OS, and one of its main functions is to provide access to system resources, which include the system's hardware and processes. The kernel supplies the vital services: It loads and runs binary programs, schedules the task swapping, which allows computer systems to do more than one thing at a time, allocates memory, and tracks the physical location of files on the computer's hard disks. The kernel provides these services by acting as an interface between other programs operating under its control and the physical hardware of the computer; this insulates programs running on the system from the complexities of the computer. For example, when a running program needs access to a file, it does not simply open the file. Instead, it issues a system call asking the kernel to open the file. The kernel takes over and fulfills the request, then notifies the program of the success or failure of the request. To read data from the file requires another system call. If the kernel determines the request is valid, it reads the requested block of data and passes it back to the program.

How They Work Together

A program is a set of instructions, along with the information necessary to process those instructions. When a program executes, it spawns a process or an instance of that program. This process then requests any necessary resources (usually called handles or descriptors).

The OS allocates the required resources, such as memory, to run the program. A process progresses through phases from its initial entry into the system until it completes or exits. From the process's point of view, it is either running or not, and the status of each process is maintained in a process table.

When a process requests resources, it creates one or more independent threads. There is not a parent/child relationship between threads as there is for processes. This is because threads may be created and joined by many different threads in the process. Threads can be created by any thread, joined by any other, and have different attributes and options. A thread can be considered a lightweight process.

Upon creation, a process is allocated a virtual address space as well as control of a resource (a file, I/O device, etc.). This process (or task) has protected access to processors, other processes, files, and I/O resources. As it is executing, it becomes a lightweight process or thread. This thread is either running or ready to run. If it is not running, its context is saved. When it is executing, a thread has access to the memory space and resources of its processes. Thus, it takes less time to create a new thread than a process because the newly created thread uses the current process's address space.

Communication overhead between threads is minimized because the threads share everything. Because address space is shared, data produced by one thread is immediately available to all other threads. Similar to multiple processes running on some systems, there can also be multiple threads running (when it is multithreading). Once the process has completed, all threads are closed by the OS, and allocated resources are freed up and can be reallocated to other executing processes as needed.

Enterprise Security Architecture

Security architecture refers to the set of disciplines used to design solutions to address security requirements at a solution or system level. Enterprise Security Architecture (ESA) implements the building blocks of information security infrastructure across the entire organization. Rather than focus on individual functional and nonfunctional components in an individual application, it focuses on a strategic design for a set of security services that can be leveraged by multiple applications, systems, or business processes.

ESA is focused on setting the long-term strategy for security services in the enterprise. Its primary purpose is to establish the priorities for security services development and provide that input into information security program planning. It focuses on the design and implementation of common security services and the enforcement of security zones of control. These approaches are used to help ensure that enterprise security services are both effective and cost-sensitive.

Key Goals and Objectives

While ESA can be applied in many different ways, it is focused on a few key goals:

- **It represents a simple, long-term view of control:** With the heterogeneity of possible solutions, duplications and inefficiencies are endemic to many security architectures. To ensure that the organization gets the right level of control to address the most common risks, a good architecture must be comprehensive but also simple. It must also avoid unnecessary duplication of services or complexities that could compromise the business benefits of the security services. It must be able to address control requirements as they evolve over time.

- **It provides a unified vision for common security controls:** By providing this common services model, the architecture looks at security controls from a holistic view, identifying potential gaps in those controls and providing a long-term plan for improvement. As such, it is a fundamental part of good security management practices.

- **It leverages existing technology investments:** Any proposed security should reuse existing technologies that are already deployed in the enterprise whenever practical. By focusing on what the organization has already deployed, the architecture can take full advantage of the internal skill sets, licensing, and agreements to minimize the need for training or staff augmentation.
- **It provides a flexible approach to current and future threats and also the needs of core functions:** If done well, the implementation of the architecture should be flexible enough to provide safeguards and countermeasures for current and emerging threats. It also, however, has to be flexible enough to allow the core applications within the organization to operate and integrate as intended.

The result should be an architecture that supports and integrates with:

1. An effective security program that recognizes that all information is not equal or constant in terms of value and risk over time.
2. An efficient security program that applies the right technology to protect the most critical assets combined with quality processes that reduce the risks to acceptable business levels. This is achieved through some form of evaluation process.
3. A high quality security program that includes regular management reviews and technology assessments to ensure controls are working as intended and providing feedback so that technology and processes can adapt to changes in value and risks over time. This is measured and monitored as part of a system assurance program.

Intended Benefits

While every design may be different, all ESAs strive to:

- Provide guidance to IT architects and senior management and enable these decision makers to make better security-related investment and design decisions;
- Establish future-state technology architecture for the security environment focused on a limited set of proposed security services;
- Support, enable, and extend security policies and standards;
- Describe general security strategies used to guide security-related decisions at technical architecture and solution levels;
- Leverage industry standards and models to ensure security best practices are being applied;

Present and document the various elements of the security architecture in order to ensure proper linkage and alignment with other architecture domains;

- Define technology security architecture in relationship with other technology domains;
- Provide an understanding of the impact on the security posture (better, worse, no change) of development and implementation within the other domains;
- Manage IT solution risk consistently across the project, while leveraging industry best practices;
- Reduce costs and improve flexibility by implementing reusable, common security services; and
- Provide a secure mechanism for end-of-life and decommissioning solutions when necessary.

3

Security Engineering

Defining and Maintaining Enterprise Security Architecture

ESA starts with a basic understanding of the overall strategic direction of the organization, and the IT delivery strategies that are used to support them. Key business drivers and technology positions are also documented. Current policies and standards are used as input to requirement gathering (particularly with legal or regulatory compliance). As security hinges on the question of access of subjects (active parties asking for information) to objects (passive parties providing information), effort is made to capture common types of users, types of sensitive or critical assets, and how access between the two should be mitigated. To capture high-level priorities, generally accepted security and security architecture principles are discussed and documented. Other requirements are obtained through interviews with key stakeholders, documentation reviews, and current IT security management processes and procedures. All of these inputs are then used to provide a comprehensive set of requirements for security services. The success of any design can then be measured against its alignment with these standards.

Once these requirements have been documented, they are then used to derive a set of architectural models. A security architect starts with conceptual target models describing a number of sets of common security services. These services are defined according to their intended users, the systems and data they access, and how security must be applied in the contexts of use scenarios. Target models include high-level logical models for each set of common security services as well as walkthroughs using those models, combining user groups and scenarios. At the beginning, the security architect may choose to develop a limited set of target models intended to address the most critical business problems. Further models may be added in the future.

Component models and physical models are considerably more granular, addressing security components within individual systems. Component models describe security functionality in terms of generic components, component flows, and nodes. Physical models showing security services in context are also developed during implementation. These types of models are developed as part of projects focused on the deployment of new services and incorporated into the ESA during development. As decisions are made, they are captured as architectural decisions. These are separate documents describing the issue at hand, the options that were considered, and the rationale for decisions that were made. This ensures that all decisions are open to continuous review.

While models assist in framing the final shape of the ESA, it is important that they be grounded in a practical, ordered set of transition activities that will move the organization from the current environment to the future state. With the development of the models, the current security controls environment is documented. A gap analysis is then performed, and steps to address those gaps are prioritized based on business priorities and interdependencies. These are then articulated into a strategic roadmap, showing how those gaps will be addressed over an extended period, typically three to five years.

The security architect has to be prepared to address any issues, risks, and planned updates that may come up during the development of the designs. For example, a threat/risk assessment provides a method of quantifying the risks associated with IT and can be used to help validate the abilities of new security controls and countermeasures to address the identified risks. If new vulnerabilities have been discovered or introduced, it also provides a way to determine if changes are required to the overall ESA.

With a firm idea of the current threat/risk environment, security architects can set priorities for the solution-level design and implementation, and security designs can be revalidated to ensure that the high-level requirements and models can be kept up to date.

Common Security Services

A number of security functions are suitable as foundations for common security services in the enterprise. Most ESAs distinguish between different types of services. The following is a sample taxonomy of services that may be used as building blocks in ESA.

- **Boundary Control Services** – These services are concerned with how and whether information is allowed to flow from one set of systems to another, or from one state to another. Boundary control systems are intended to enforce security zones of control by isolating entry points from one zone to another (choke points). As such, they provide a set of common points to access or transmit information across security zones. These systems will include the typical range of secure networking devices – firewalls, border routers, proxies, and other boundary services – intended to protect more trusted/sensitive assets from less trusted/sensitive assets.

- **Access Control Services** – These services focus on the identification, authentication, and authorization of subject entities (whether human or machine) as they are deployed and employed to access the organization's assets. As a strategic set of services, they are intended to normalize identification and promote shared authentication throughout the enterprise. In general, these services will promote reduced-sign-on (RSO) or single-sign-on (SSO), but they will also include RSO or SSO services themselves as common services.[15] It will also include a number of other services surrounding the creation, handling, and storage of credentials in the enterprise. On the authorization side, these services focus on what valid user entities are allowed and not allowed to do within the enterprise given a set of rules enforced through automated systems. They will offer coarse-grained (system-level) authorization services that can be leveraged by other domains in the enterprise architecture.

- **Integrity Services** – Integrity services focus on the maintenance of high-integrity systems and data through automated checking to detect and correct corruption. As a set of common services, these can be leveraged by the enterprise at various levels, but many are intended for systems that can be accessed directly by untrusted or less trusted user entities or systems. Integrity services typically focus on antivirus, content filtering, file integrity services, whitelisting, and intrusion prevention systems (IPS).

---

15 SSO defines a system where the end-user logs in once to access their workstation. This initial authentication could be an ID/Password challenge or some passwordless challenge such as using physical or biometric means of authentication. Subsequent application access will not challenge the user for further authentication. The challenge still exists, but it is handled by some type of software layer that knows the user's credentials and is populating them on behalf of the user.

   RSO is significantly different. The concept of RSO is that the number of ID/Password combinations an end-user will need to remember is "reduced". In other words, the end-user will need to authenticate to his or her workstation AND to each application; however, the ID/Password will be guaranteed to be the same on each challenge.

3

Security Engineering

273

- **Cryptographic Services** – While cryptography is a common security tool used by many systems, cryptographic services focus on common services that can be deployed and reused by a variety of systems. This will involve a modest public key infrastructure (PKI) as well as the continued use of PKI functions through external providers. This may also include common hashing and encryption services, tools, and technologies.
- **Audit and Monitoring Services** – These services will focus on the secure collection, storage, and analysis of audited events through centralized logging as well as the events themselves through intrusion detection systems (IDS) and similar services. Services will include log collection, collation, and analysis services through the deployment of security event information management (SEIM) solutions. Given the centralized infrastructure required, this is also the suitable place to consider centralized management systems.

Security Zones of Control

Maintaining a consistent and manageable level of risk is a significant challenge in a complex and largely distributed environment. Easy access to networks complicates the picture, especially when publicly accessible networks such as the Internet or outsourced environments are involved. The security architects need to be aware of the fact that their actions and choices can lead to a trade-off between security (applying mechanisms to lower risk) and user accessibility and that they should do whatever they can to minimize this impact while maintaining the integrity of the architecture. Some information is highly sensitive or valuable and other information is much less so (e.g., public information on webpages about historical buildings). The challenge is to apply the appropriate amount of security control without greatly affecting access to information.

The following questions help to understand the complexity:

- How are information assets protected in relation to the environment within which they exist?
- What is the appropriate level of authentication required to access the information asset? Is there a difference when accessing the asset over an untrusted network? Are there similar requirements inside the internal networks?
- How will confidentiality be protected? Does the required confidentiality level change depending on where or how the asset is accessed?
- How must the availability of protected resources be assured? Will access controls have a positive or negative effect on them?
- Are there assets with high integrity requirements? How will the integrity of assets be maintained as many entities are given access to them?
- How can the architect decide how to apply these trade-offs when the information assets may have such different characteristics?

One method of addressing these questions is with security zones of control. A security zone of control is an area or grouping within which a defined set of security policies and measures are applied to achieve a specific level of security. Zones are used to group together those entities with similar security requirements and levels of risk and ensure each zone is adequately segregated from another zone.

The separation of the zones ensures that the capability of accessing or modifying information and systems in a more secure zone does not leak through to a less secure zone. Access between the zones is tightly controlled with control mechanisms such as firewalls, authentication services, and proxy services. The security zones of control become crucial, high-level design constructs in the security architecture. The following diagram (*Figure 3.3*) from the U.S. National Institute of Standards and Technology (NIST) illustrates this concept using a subsystem guard (Joint Task Force Transformation Initiative Feb, 2010).[16]

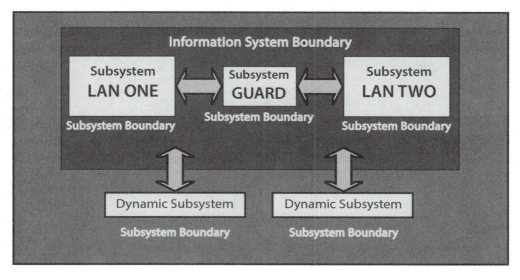

Figure 3.3 - **An example of a Subsystem guard**

Common Architecture Frameworks

No two security architects will likely produce the same design or approach the problem in the same way. To help one security architect understand the designs produced by another, any design must be created using standardized methodologies that will allow other security architects (as well as business owners, auditors, and others) to validate their design processes and deliverables. This will require the security architect to be transparent about the methods he or she is using. To ease the acceptance of their designs, security architects can take advantage of common architecture frameworks used across multiple industries and disciplines.

An architecture framework is a structure that can be used for developing a broad range of different architectures. It describes a method for designing a target state as an integrated set of systems or system components, and it provides a set of tools to ease architecture development and a common vocabulary. It also frequently include a set of recommended standards and operational practices. They may also include information on compliant vendor products, modules, or components that can be used as design elements within the framework. The following describes some common architecture frameworks used in enterprise architecture and a few for security architecture in particular.

---

16   Joint Task Force Transformation Initiative, First. United States National Institute of Standards and Technology, "NIST Special Publication 800-37 Revision 1 | Guide for Applying the Risk Management Framework to Federal Information Systems, A Security Life Cycle Approach." Last modified Feb, 2010. http://csrc.nist.gov/publications/nistpubs/800-37-rev1/sp800-37-rev1-final.pdf (Page 13)

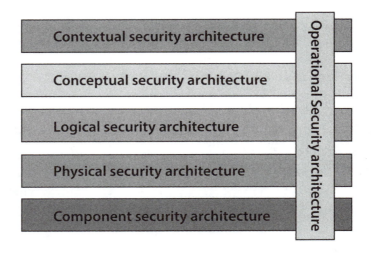

Figure 3.4 - **The SABSA Model for Security Architecture at a high level. It takes a very similar approach to the Zachman Framework by describing any architecture with different levels of detail and for different audiences.**

(Available online at http://www.sabsa-institute.org/the-sabsa-method/the-sabsa-model.aspx. **With permission)**

Zachman Framework [17]

In the 1980s, John Zachman, a contributor to the federal enterprise architecture framework (FEAF) effort, developed a common context for understanding a complex architecture. His Zachman Framework allows for the communication and collaboration of all entities in the development of the architecture. While not specific to security architecture, it provides a logical structure for integrating the various perspectives such as the plan, design, and build aspects. As Zachman himself explained, "The Framework, as it applies to enterprises, is a logical structure for identifying and organizing the descriptive representations (models) that are important in the management of enterprises and to the development of the systems, both automated and manual, that comprise them."

Sherwood Applied Business Security Architecture (SABSA) Framework [18]

Intended to follow the same basic outline provided by Zachman, SABSA is a holistic lifecycle for developing security architecture that begins with assessing business requirements and subsequently creating a "chain of traceability" through the phases of strategy, concept, design, implementation, and metrics. It represents any architecture using six layers, each representing a different perspective for the design and construction and use of the target system (see *Figure 3.4*).

---

17 Read more about the Zachman framework at: http://www.zachman.com/about-the-zachman-framework http://www.eacoe.org/index.shtml

18 Read more about the SABSA framework here: http://www.sabsa-institute.org/the-sabsa-method/the-sabsa-model.aspx

The Open Group Architecture Framework (TOGAF) [19]

Originally inspired by earlier frameworks from the U.S. Department of Defense, the Open Group started to develop TOGAF in the mid-1990s. It is an open framework for organizations wishing to design and build enterprise architecture. TOGAF (*Figure* 3.5) provides a common set of terms, an architecture development method (ADM) that describes the step-by-step process employed by TOGAF architects, an architecture content framework (ACF) to describe standard building blocks and components as well as numerous reference models. It also provides advice on how organizations may best incorporate TOGAF into their enterprises.

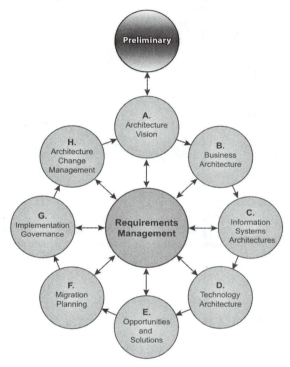

Figure 3.5 – **The TOGAF Architecture Development Method. It highlights the critical role that requirements analysis plays in each step of the model.**

(From Marley, S., Architectural Framework, NASA /SCI, 2003.)

IT Infrastructure Library (ITIL) [20]

ITIL was developed by the Central Computer and Telecommunications Agency (CCTA) under the auspices of the British government as a collection of best practices for IT governance. ITIL defines the organizational structure and skill requirements of an IT organization as well as the set of operational procedures and practices that direct IT operations and infrastructure, including information security operations. ITIL continues to evolve. What sets the current version of ITIL apart is the strong focus on end-to-end service delivery and management. ITIL v4 comprises five main activities or tasks: service strategy, service design, service transition, service operations, and continuous service improvement.

---

19   Read more about the TOGAF framework here: http://www.opengroup.org/togaf/

20   Read more about ITIL here: http://www.itil-officialsite.com/AboutITIL/WhatisITIL.aspx

3

Security Engineering

Each of these activities is addressed in a separate volume within ITIL. *Figure 3.6* illustrates the five main "books" that comprise ITILv4 and how they relate to each other:

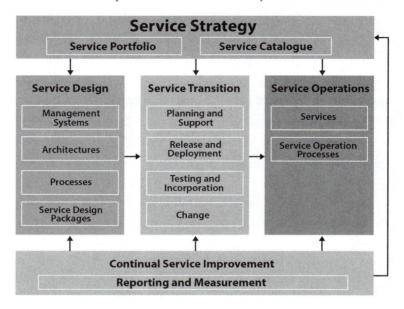

Figure 3.6 - **ITIL Version 4 summary. Note that ITIL constantly feeds back the results of more detailed architecture work in the service strategy, and continuous service improvement identifies opportunities for evolution across other parts of ITIL.**

- ***Service Strategy*** – addresses new business needs by describing the range of services that are or will be deployed. The service portfolio includes all of the services that are provided by IT. These may include services that are entirely internal to the IT organization as well as services provided to its customers. The service catalogue is a limited subset of the service portfolio containing only services for customers of IT. These services are a particular focus within ITIL because success or failure is generally measured by the ability to service the customer. Service strategy provides requirements for most other activities under ITIL, including service design, service transition, and service operations. Changes to service strategy may either originate from changes to business requirements or through Continual Service Improvement.

- ***Service Design*** – focuses on creating the services described within the service portfolio. In addition to the service design packages that describe the design of individual services and the metrics and service levels that will be used to govern them, this component within ITIL also focuses on management systems and architectures that guide or constrain design as well as the design processes that are in place. Service design packages are the key deliverable from service design because these packages are the primary input into service transition.

- ***Service Transition*** – is primarily concerned with translating designs into operational services through a standard project management structure. It is also responsible for managing change to existing services. Planning and support focuses on providing the necessary structure for service transition, particularly when multiple services are being deployed. Release and deployment represents the core set of processes that guide the deployment of new or updated services through a phased deployment. Testing and incorporation addresses the need to ensure that newly deployed services meet the service design and service strategy requirements and that the service has been properly incorporated within the production environment. Change provides the structure and processes for change management. Once the services have been deployed, they are transferred into steady-state service operations. The key to this component in ITIL are the service operation processes that provide structure to service delivery and ensure that metrics are being captured.

These metrics are a key input into Continual Service Improvement. Through reporting and measurement, each service is validated against its individual key performance indicators and service levels. Based on the need to provide improvement, this ITIL component provides feedback into all other aspects of service management. It may propose recommendations to changes within the service strategy. It may recommend changes to any aspect of service design. It may provide input to the way that services are deployed or tested through service transition. Finally, it may provide input to service operations processes in service operations.

Types of Security Models

Most security models will focus on defining allowed interactions between subjects (active parties) and objects (passive parties) at a particular moment in time. For example, consider a simple example of a user trying to access a file on a computing system. As the active party, the user would be the subject while the file would be considered the object. The following types of security model approach the problem in slightly different ways.

- **State Machine Model** [21]– State describes a system at a point in time. A state machine model, then, describes the behavior of a system as it moves between one state and another, from one moment to another. Typically, it uses mathematics to describe system states and the transition functions that define allowed or unpermitted actions. When it is used in security modeling, the purpose is to define which actions will be permitted at any point in time to ensure that a secure state (a point in time when things are secure) is preserved. The role of time in a state machine model is very important. According to its rule set, which is determined by a security policy, a model system's secure state can only change at distinct points in time, such as when an event occurs or a clock triggers it. Thus, upon its initial start-up, the system checks to determine if it is in a secure state. Once the system is determined to be in a secure state, the state machine model will ensure that every time the system is accessed, it will be accessed only in accordance with the security policy rules. This process will guarantee that the system will transition only from one secure state to another secure state.

- **Multilevel Lattice Models** [22]– A multilevel security model describes strict layers of subjects and objects and defines clear rules that allow or disallow interactions between them based on the layers they are in. These are often described using lattices, or discrete layers with minimal or no interfaces

---

21   Read more about state machine models here: http://openlearn.open.ac.uk/mod/oucontent/view. php?id=397581&section=9.1

22   Read more about Multilevel Lattice Security here: http://dimacs.rutgers.edu/Workshops/Lattices/slides/ meadows.pdf

between them. Most lattice models define a hierarchical lattice with layers of lesser or greater privilege. Subjects are assigned security clearances that define what layer they are assigned to, and objects are classified into similar layers. Related security labels are attached to all subjects and objects. According to this type of model, the clearance of the subject is compared with the classification of the data to determine access. They will also look at what the subject is trying to do to determine whether access should be allowed.

■ ***Noninterference Models*** [23] – May be considered a type of multilevel model with a high degree of strictness, severely limiting any higher-classified information from being shared with lower-privileged subjects even when higher-privileged subjects are using the system at the same time. In other words, these models not only address obvious and intentional interactions between subjects and objects, but they also deal with the effects of covert channels that may leak information inappropriately. The goal of a noninterference model is to help ensure that high-level actions (inputs) do not determine what low-level users can see (outputs). Most of the security models presented are secured by permitting restricted flows between high- and low-level users. A noninterference model maintains activities at different security levels to separate these levels from each other. In this way, it minimizes leakages that may happen through covert channels because there is complete separation between security levels. Because a subject at a higher security level has no way to interfere with the activities at a lower level, the lower-level subject cannot get any information from the higher level.

■ ***Matrix-Based Models*** – While lattice-based models tend to treat similar subjects and objects with similar restrictions, matrix-based models focus on one-to-one relationships between subjects and objects. The best known example is the organization of subjects and objects into an access control matrix. An access control matrix is a two-dimensional table that allows for individual subjects and objects to be related to each other. It lists the subjects (such as users or processes) down the left-hand side and all the resources and functions across the top in the table. A matrix is a concise way to represent the capabilities that subjects have when accessing particular objects. To make this easier, an individual subject may be put into groups or roles, and the matrix is built according to role or group membership. This provides ease of management and simplification. Most matrix-based models provide more than simple binary rules (such as allow or deny). Sometimes, it is beneficial to specify how the access will be performed or what capabilities the subject will require. Perhaps some subjects are allowed read only, while others can read and write. The list of access methods will be what is appropriate to the organization. Typical access methods for content are read, write, edit, and delete. Recording this type of information requires extending the access control matrix to include the appropriate permissions in each cell. It is important to note that this model does not describe the relationship between subjects in the model, such as if one subject created another or gave another subject access rights.

---

23 Read more about Noninterference Models here: http://www.cs.cornell.edu/andru/cs711/2003fa/reading/1990mclean-sp.pdf

- **Information Flow Models** [24] – While most models are concerned with subject-to-object relationships, information flow models focus on how information is allowed or not allowed between individual objects. Information flow models are used to determine if information is being properly protected throughout a given process. They may be used to identify potential covert channels, unintended information flow between compartments in compartmented systems. For example, although compartment A has no authorized path to do so, it may send information to compartment B by changing a variable or condition that B can see. This usually involves cooperation between the owners of the compartments in a manner that is not intended or anticipated by the managers of the system. Alternatively, compartment B may simply gather intelligence about compartment A by observing some condition that is influenced by A's behavior.

Examples of Security Models

There are hundreds of security models. The following are few examples that have had a major impact on the ways that security services have been developed over the years.

Bell–LaPadula Confidentiality Model [25]

The Bell–LaPadula model is perhaps the most well-known and significant security model, in addition to being one of the oldest models used in the creation of modern secure computing systems. Like the Trusted Computer System Evaluation Criteria (or TCSEC), it was inspired by early U.S. Department of Defense security policies and the need to prove that confidentiality could be maintained. In other words, its primary goal is to prevent disclosure as the model system moves from one state (one point in time) to another.

It starts by describing four basic components in defining the main actors and how they are distinguished from each other. Subjects are the active parties, while objects are the passive parties. To help determine what subjects will be allowed to do, they are assigned clearances that outline what modes of access (read, write, or read/write) they will be allowed to use when they interact with objects assigned a classification level. The model system uses labels to keep track of clearances and classifications, and it implements a set of rules to limit interactions between different types of subjects and objects.

Using this set of basic components, the Bell–LaPadula model explores the rules that would have to be in place if a subject is granted a certain level of clearance and a particular mode of access. They describe these as different properties, depending on whether the subject in question has the ability to read, write, or read/write objects in the model system. In the simple security property (*Figure* 3.7), Bell and LaPadula considered a subject with the ability to read information (but not write it).

---

24   Read more about Information flow models here: http://users.cis.fiu.edu/~smithg/papers/sif06.pdf

25   Read more about Bell-La Padula here: http://www.acsac.org/2005/papers/Bell.pdf

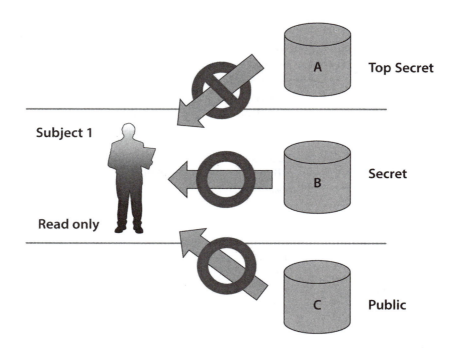

*Figure 3.7-***The Simple Security Property according to Bell-LaPadula**
Subject 1 has been assigned a clearance level of secret and the ability to read only from a set of
objects. In order to prevent disclosure, the subject may read information from objects classified
as public or secret but is prevented from reading information classified as top secret.

To prevent disclosure, that subject would be able to read information from objects at a similar classification level or at lower levels but would be barred from reading any information from objects classified at a higher level of confidentiality. For example, if an employee has a government security clearance of secret, he or she may be allowed to read secret and documents classified at lower levels. The employee would not be allowed to read top secret information as this would result in disclosure.

In the "* property" (so named as the story goes because the authors never replaced the asterisk with another term in the manuscript before it was published),[26] the same subject has the ability to write information but not read it (*Figure* 3.8).

To prevent disclosure, the subject would be able to write information to objects at a similar classification level or higher levels but would be barred from writing any information to objects classified at a lower level of confidentiality. This can seem very odd at first glance, but remember that the goal is to prevent disclosure. Writing something at a higher level will not result in disclosure, even if it makes it impossible for the original subject to read it! It also has some practical value in some cases. For example, an organization's president may wish a set of subordinate officers to make reports to their superiors in such a way that they cannot read each other's reports while still allowing their superiors to read and collate information across reports from their subordinates.

---

26   http://www.acsac.org/2005/papers/Bell.pdf (page 3)

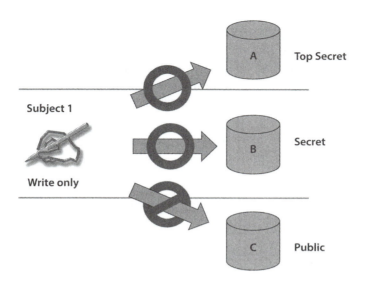

Figure 3.8 - **The * Property according to Bell–LaPadula**
Subject 1 has been assigned a clearance level of secret and the ability to write only to a set of objects. In order to prevent disclosure, the subject may write information to objects classified as secret or top secret but is prevented from writing information classified as public.

In the strong * property (*Figure* 3.9), they consider the same subject with the ability to read or write to objects in the model system. To be mathematically certain that the subjects could never disclose information, they must be restricted to objects at a similar classification level and not be allowed to interact with any other objects in the model system.

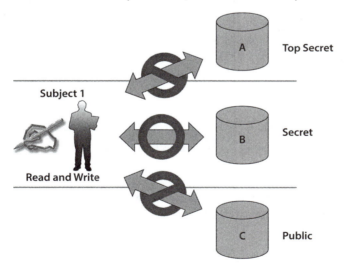

Figure 3.9 - **The Strong * Property according to Bell–LaPadula**
Subject 1 has been assigned a clearance level of secret and the ability to read or write to a set of objects. In order to prevent disclosure, the subject may only access information classified at their own level, in this case objects classified as secret.

3

Security Engineering

Bell–LaPadula is not without its limitations. It is only concerned with confidentiality and makes no mention of other properties (such as integrity and availability) or more sophisticated modes of access. These have to be addressed through other models. More importantly, it does not address important confidentiality goals such as need-to-know, or the ability to restrict access to individual objects based on a subject's need to access them. Since Bell–LaPadula does not provide a mechanism for a one-to-one mapping of individual subjects and objects, this also needs to be addressed by other models.

Biba Integrity Model [27]

Like Bell–LaPadula, Biba is also a lattice-based model with multiple levels. It also uses the same modes of access (read, write, and read/write) and also describes interactions between subjects and objects. Where Biba differs most obviously is that it is an integrity model: It focuses on ensuring that the integrity of information is being maintained by preventing corruption. At the core of the model is a multilevel approach to integrity designed to prevent unauthorized subjects from modifying objects. Access is controlled to ensure that objects maintain their current state of integrity as subjects interact with them. Instead of the confidentiality levels used by Bell– LaPadula, Biba assigns integrity levels to subjects and objects depending on how trustworthy they are considered to be. Like Bell–LaPadula, Biba considers the same modes of access but with different results. *Figure 3.10* compares the BLP and Biba models.

Property	BLP Model	Biba Model
ss-property	A subject cannot read/ access an object of a higher classification (no read up)	A subject cannot observe an object of a lower integrity level (no read down)
*-property	A subject can only save an object at the same or higher classification (no write down)	A subject cannot modify an object of a higher integrity level (no write up)
Invocation property	Not Used	A subject cannot send logical service requests to an object of a higher integrity
Source – Hare, C., Policy development, in Information Security Management Handbook, 6th edn., Tipton, H.F. and Krause, M., Eds., Auerbach Publications. New York 2007. 47&		

*Figure 3.10 - **BLP and Biba Model Properties***

In the simple integrity property (*Figure 3.11* and *Figure 3.12*), a given subject has the ability to read information from different types of objects with differing levels of integrity or accuracy. In this case, less accurate information than what the subject would expect could result in corruption so the subject must not be allowed to read from less accurate objects but can read from objects that are more accurate than the subject needs.

---

27 Read more about the Biba Integrity Model here: http://www.dtic.mil/cgi-bin/GetTRDoc?AD=ADA166920 (Page 27).

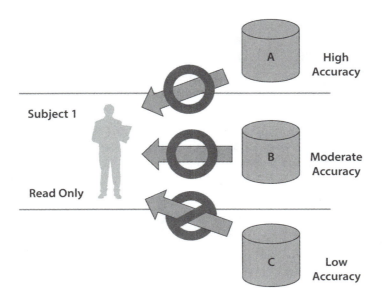

Figure 3.11 - **The Simple Integrity Property according to Biba**
In this example, Subject 1 has information that is moderately accurate and can read from a set
of objects with varying degrees of accuracy. In order to prevent corruption, the subject may be
able to read information with the same or higher level of accuracy but not information that is less
accurate because that may compromise the integrity of the information it already possesses.

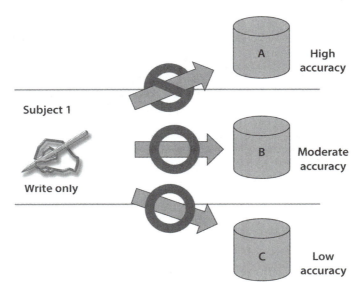

Figure 3.12 - **The Simple Integrity Property according to Biba**
In this example, Subject 1 has information that is moderately accurate and can write to a set of objects
with varying degrees of accuracy. In order to prevent corruption, the subject may be able to write
information with the same or lower level of accuracy but not information that is more accurate because
that may compromise the integrity of the information in the more accurate object (Object A).

For example, consider a subject that wishes to add two numbers together. The subject needs information that is reasonably accurate to two decimal places and has different values to choose from. Some of these values are accurate to more than two decimal places. Some are less accurate. To prevent corruption, the subject must only use information that is at least as accurate as two decimal places; information that is only accurate to one decimal place must not be used or corruption may occur.

In the * integrity property, a given subject has the ability to write information to different types of objects with differing levels of integrity or accuracy. In this case, the subject must be prevented from corrupting objects that are more accurate than it is. The subject should then be allowed to write to objects that are less accurate but not to objects that are more accurate. To allow otherwise may result in corruption. Biba also addresses the problem of one subject getting a more privileged subject to work on their behalf. In the invocation property, Biba considers a situation where corruption may occur because a less trustworthy subject was allowed to take advantage of the capabilities of a more trustworthy subject by invoking their powers. According to Biba, this must be prevented or corruption could occur.

Clark–Wilson Integrity Model [28]

As it turns out, Biba only addresses one of three key integrity goals. The Clark–Wilson model improves on Biba by focusing on integrity at the transaction level and addressing three major goals of integrity in a commercial environment. In addition to preventing changes by unauthorized subjects, Clark and Wilson realized that high-integrity systems would also have to prevent undesirable changes by authorized subjects and to ensure that the system continued to behave consistently. It also recognized that it would need to ensure that there is constant mediation between every subject and every object if such integrity was going to be maintained.

To address the second goal of integrity, Clark and Wilson realized that they needed a way to prevent authorized subjects from making changes that were not desirable. This required that transactions by authorized subjects be evaluated by another party before they were committed on the model system. This provided separation of duties where the powers of the authorized subject were limited by another subject given the power to evaluate and complete the transaction. This also had the effect of ensuring external consistency (or consistency between the model system and the real world) because the evaluating subject would have the power to ensure that the transaction matched what was expected in reality.

To address internal consistency (or consistency within the model system itself), Clark and Wilson recommended a strict definition of well-formed transactions. In other words, the set of steps within any transaction would need to be carefully designed and enforced. Any deviation from that expected path would result in a failure of the transaction to ensure that the model system's integrity was not compromised.

To control all subject and object interactions, Clark–Wilson establishes a system of subject–program–object bindings such that the subject no longer has direct access to the object. Instead, this is done through a program with access to the object. This program arbitrates all access and ensures that every interaction between subject and object follows a defined set of rules. The program provides for subject authentication and identification and limits all access to objects under its control.

---

28 Read more about the Clark-Wilson model here: http://www.cs.clemson.edu/course/cpsc420/material/ Policies/Integrity%20Policies.pdf

Lipner Model

Lipner combines elements of Bell–LaPadula and Biba together with the idea of job functions or roles in a novel way to protect both confidentiality and integrity. The Lipner implementation, published in 1982, describes two ways of implementing integrity. One uses the Bell–LaPadula confidentiality model, and the other uses both the Bell–LaPadula model and the Biba integrity model together. Both methods assign security levels and functional categories to subjects and objects. For subjects, this translates into a person's clearance level and job function (e.g., user, operator, applications programmer, or systems programmer). For objects, the sensitivity of the data or program and its functions (e.g., test data, production data, application program, or system program) are defined according to its classification.

Lipner's first method, using only the Bell–LaPadula model, assigns subjects to one of two sensitivity levels – system manager and anyone else – and to one of four job categories. Objects (i.e., file types) are assigned specific classification levels and categories. Most of the subjects and objects are assigned the same level; therefore, categories become the most significant integrity (i.e., access control) mechanism. The applications programmers, systems programmers, and users are confined to their own domains according to their assigned categories, thus preventing unauthorized users from modifying data (the first integrity goal).

Lipner's second method combines Biba's integrity model with Bell–LaPadula. This combination of models helps to prevent the contamination of high-integrity data by low-integrity data or programs. The assignment of levels and categories to subjects and objects remains the same as for Lipner's first method. Integrity levels are used to avoid the unauthorized modification of system programs; integrity categories are used to separate domains that are based on functional areas (e.g., production or research and development). This method prevents unauthorized users from modifying data and prevents authorized users from making improper data modifications.

Lipner's methods were the first to separate objects into data and programs. The importance of this concept becomes clear when viewed in terms of implementing the Clark–Wilson integrity model; because programs allow users to manipulate data, it is necessary to control which programs a user may access and which objects a program can manipulate.

Brewer–Nash (The Chinese Wall) Model

This model focuses on preventing conflict of interest when a given subject has access to objects with sensitive information associated with two competing parties. The principle is that users should not access the confidential information of both a client organization and one or more of its competitors. At the beginning, subjects may access either set of objects. Once, however, subjects access an object associated with one competitor, they are instantly prevented from accessing any objects on the opposite side. This is intended to prevent the subject from sharing information inappropriately between the two competitors even unintentionally. It is called the Chinese Wall Model because, like the Great Wall of China, once on one side of the wall, a person cannot get to the other side. It is an unusual model in comparison with many of the others because the access control rules change based on subject behavior.

Graham–Denning Model

Graham–Denning is primarily concerned with how subjects and objects are created, how subjects are assigned rights or privileges, and how ownership of objects is managed. In other words, it is primarily concerned with how a model system controls subjects and objects at a very basic level where other models simply assumed such control.

The Graham–Denning access control model has three parts: a set of objects, a set of subjects, and a set of rights. The subjects are composed of two things: a process and a domain. The domain is the set of constraints controlling how subjects may access objects. Subjects may also be objects at specific times. The set of rights governs how subjects may manipulate the passive objects. This model describes eight primitive protection rights called commands that subjects can execute to have an effect on other subjects or objects. The model defines eight primitive protection rights:

1. **Create Object** – The ability to create a new object
2. **Create Subject** – The ability to create a new subject
3. **Delete Object** – The ability to delete an existing object
4. **Delete Subject** – The ability to delete an existing subject
5. **Read Access Right** – The ability to view current access privileges
6. **Grant Access Right** – The ability to grant access privileges
7. **Delete Access Right** – The ability to remove access privileges
8. **Transfer Access Right** – The ability to transfer access privileges from one subject or object to another subject or object

Harrison–Ruzzo–Ullman Model

This model is very similar to the Graham–Denning model, and it is composed of a set of generic rights and a finite set of commands. It is also concerned with situations in which a subject should be restricted from gaining particular privileges. To do so, subjects are prevented from accessing programs or subroutines that can execute a particular command (to grant read access for example) where necessary.

Capturing and Analyzing Requirements

Regardless of the framework used, the security architect needs to establish the business requirements from key stakeholders and reviewers before any design work can proceed. This may require the architect to work closely with sponsoring executives, business line management, business process owners, and IT management to capture and document the major requirements. Because these requirements will determine the success or failure of any design, it is important that they are firmly established at the beginning and agreed upon by the stakeholders.

A security architect should start with establishing key principles and guidelines for the design. Principles are defined as fundamental statements of belief, mandatory elements that will restrict the overall design and establish the key priorities for protection. To act as trustworthy guides to design, these must be negotiated with their sponsors and key stakeholders so that everyone understands the motivations and implications of the chosen principles. Not all potential principles end up being mandatory, and they may become optional guidelines instead. As the design effort progresses, the architect should refer back to the chosen principles and guidelines to ensure continued alignment with them.

The security architect will also need to establish detailed requirements in addition to any principles or guidelines. There are two main types of requirements: functional and nonfunctional requirements (*Figure 3.13*).

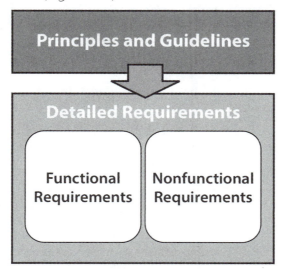

Figure 3.13 - **Different levels of requirements**
Principles and guidelines provide the high-level requirements for secure design by setting the design priorities while functional and non-functional requirements are more detailed. Together they are used to establish the goals and objectives for the design.

- **Functional Requirements –** address what the design must do or accomplish. This includes what types of controls need to be included, what assets must be protected, what common threats must be addressed, and what vulnerabilities have been found. In other words, functional requirements will guide what security services will be included in the design.
- **Nonfunctional Requirements –** focus on the qualities of the services, including any requirements for reliability and performance.

These detailed requirements can be captured in a number of different ways, depending on the scope of the architecture and the level of detail required. Paradoxically, requirements will need to be more detailed the smaller the scope, in order to allow it to be examined and validated more thoroughly. For example, the requirements for a design limited to a single system will be highly detailed to allow for improved ability to verify the design and to provide solid guidance to implementers of the system. On the other hand, requirements for ESA tend to be more general to provide greater flexibility.

Vulnerability assessments, risk assessments, and threat modeling may be used to capture detailed requirements. In some cases, detailed requirements will be captured by others and passed along to the security architect. Detailed product evaluation criteria requirements may be documented by product consumers. These detailed requirements are then passed along to product vendors for architecture and implementation. Third-party evaluation labs may then be employed to examine the product against the requirements and to certify whether or not it addresses the requirements and how much assurance the consumer should have that the product will perform the tasks required. Principles, guidelines, and detailed requirements must be signed off by an appropriate authority such as an executive sponsor or senior leader if they are to be used to guide the next phase: the creation of security designs.

Creating and Documenting Security Architecture

Once the requirements have been captured and signed off on, the security architect can get down to the business of creating suitable designs based on those requirements. This will require the architect to be able to provide designs that appeal to a wide variety of stakeholders with varying degrees of depth and technical detail. It may also need to be presented in a variety of different deliverables, including technical specifications, modeling documents, presentations, and executive summaries.

Following the SABSA framework, a complete security architecture will be represented by six layers of designs. Each layer is a view intended to provide a different level of detail. *Figure 3.14* summarizes the six layers of views according to SABSA.

The security architect will be expected to produce all or some of these different layers depending on the scope of the architecture and the need for the design. In many cases, system security architecture will focus most on logical, physical, and component security architecture, while ESA may focus more heavily on contextual, conceptual, and logical security architectures. It will depend on their design goals. Because ESA tends to focus on long-term strategic planning, there is less need for the detail and precision required by system security architecture.

Contextual security architecture	*The Business view:* Assets to be protected in context
Conceptual security architecture	*The Architect's view:* High-level view of services to protect the assets
Logical security architecture	*The Designer's view:* Node-level view of the services showing how services will be deployed and how they relate to each other at a high level
Physical security architecture	*The Builder's view:* Detailed, node-level view of all services and how they will be deployed against physical assets
Component security architecture	*The Tradesman's view:* Component view of individual security services
Operational security architecture	*The Facility Manager's view:* Security Operations view of all security services in scope

Figure 3.14 – **The different layers of security architecture using the SABSA model**
(From Sherwood, J., Clark, A., and Lynas, D., Enterprise Security Architecture: A Business-Driven Approach, CMP, San Francisco, CA, 2005. With permission.)

Given the amount of effort that may be required, security architects may rely on a variety of reference architectures to provide a starting point for their designs. Reference architectures provide templates for secure design based on industry best practices and recommended deployment models. The architects may also make use of a variety of modeling tools and languages to document their designs, including variations on the unified modeling language

(UML) and systems modeling language (SysML).[29] They will also illustrate how security services will work through the usage scenarios and walkthroughs.

They may also rely on a number of international standards and best practices as well as regulations and legislation that mandate good practices for information security. They can have a profound effect not only in shaping security requirements but also in how security architecture is developed.

Information Systems Security Evaluation Models

Once the design work is completed, any security architecture needs to be carefully evaluated to ensure that it has effectively addressed the documented requirements. This may be as simple as a peer review or may require a complex series of tests to ensure that the design is sound. Where it is necessary to prove that the design is correct, formal security models and verification techniques may be issued. Alternatively, vendor products may be evaluated using international, standardized, product evaluation criteria or can be tested in its intended deployment environment and certified before being run in production.

The following reviews each one of these approaches. Each provides different ways to verify that the security architecture is correct and meets the security requirements, although they are used in very different situations. They also have an impact on how security requirements and security architecture is documented and described.

Common Formal Security Models

Security policy documents the security requirements of an organization. Subsequently, a security model is a specification that describes the rules to be implemented to support and enforce the security policy. A formal security model describes and verifies the ability to enforce security policy in mathematical or measurable terms. A number of security models have been proposed over the years, and many have become fundamental models that have been used to design security services for many systems deployed today. The security policy can be thought of as the "what" (what are the requirements for security), while the security model can be thought of as the "how" (how are those requirements translated into implementable and auditable technical specifications). Given the demands of formal verification, most models are focused on system-level security architecture at the component level. In most cases, it would be too difficult or too time consuming to formally verify all aspects of large scale security architectures.

Evaluation Criteria

In most cases, formal security models have limited value in the real world and are narrowly focused on a small number of system components where formal verification is practical or desirable. Verifying their correct implementation will only give the architect a limited view of the security in a complex computing platform, so other mechanisms must be reviewed to verify the implementation of secure design in real-world vendor products. Vendors and their consumers need some assurance that security requirements have been met and will continue to be met over time. The aim of system assurance is to verify that a system enforces a desired set of security goals. To accomplish this, they need a common way to describe security requirements, evaluate products against them in a consistent and repeatable manner, and report on the results.

---

29   See the following for an overview introduction to the UML and SysML languages: http://www.eng. umd.edu/~austin/enes489p/lecture-slides/2012-MA-UML-and-SysML.pdf

A number of product evaluation criteria have been published over the years to help verify that a system enforces a desired set of security goals. These criteria provide a shared mechanism to allow certified third-party evaluation labs to evaluate vendor products against a set of security requirements and publish their findings. Each criteria has taken different approaches to this task with later criteria building on the lessons learned through the use of earlier criteria.

Although there have been many product evaluation criteria developed in the last three decades, three are the focus of this chapter: TCSEC, ITSEC, and the Common Criteria. Before we can explore the evaluation criteria, we must first understand the basics of certification and accreditation.

Certification and Accreditation

A primary way to determine how well a system meets its security requirements is to perform an analysis of the system within its intended deployment environment. The objective is to determine how well a system measures up to a preferred level of security in the real world and then make a decision whether or not to proceed with its use in the enterprise. During the certification phase, the product or system is tested to see whether it meets the documented requirements (including any security requirements). It considers the system in context, including the other systems around it, the network it is running on, and its intended use. At the beginning of the process, the evaluation criteria must be chosen. With the criteria known, the certification process will test the system's hardware, software, and configuration in a production-like environment. The results of the evaluation become a baseline, which will be used to compare against the set of specific security requirements. If the certification is positive, the system enters the next phase of the evaluation.

In the accreditation phase, management evaluates the capacity of a system to meet the needs of the organization. If management determines that the needs of the system satisfy the needs of the organization, they will formally accept the evaluated system, usually for a defined period of time or set of conditions. If the configuration is changed or the accreditation expires, the new configuration must be certified. Recertification must normally be performed either when the time period elapses or when significant configuration changes are made.

Product Evaluation Models

When evaluating product security, the security architect has several pre-defined frameworks to choose from. Some frameworks such as the Trusted Computer System Evaluation Criteria were designed for classified systems, while others such as Common Criteria are more generic and global in nature. The security architect must understand the industry, data types, and mission of the organization he or she is serving to determine the best evaluation model.

Trusted Computer System Evaluation Criteria (TCSEC)

First published in 1983 and updated in 1985, the TCSEC, frequently referred to as the Orange Book, was a United States Government Department of Defense (DoD) standard that sets basic standards for the implementation of security protections in computing systems. Primarily intended to help the DoD find products that met those basic standards, TCSEC was used to evaluate, classify, and select computer systems being considered for the processing, storage, and retrieval of sensitive or classified information on military and government systems. As such, it was strongly focused on enforcing confidentiality with no focus on other aspects of security such as integrity or availability. Although it has since been superseded by the common criteria, it influenced the development of other product evaluation criteria, and some of its basic approach and terminology continues to be used. *Figure 3.15* is a summary of Orange Book evaluation criteria divisions.

TCSEC differs most from other evaluation criteria by being both very specific and very prescriptive. Rather than provide a flexible set of security requirements, TCSEC defined very specific types of security controls that should be implemented in secure and defined levels of secure systems based on their ability to implement them. A great deal of emphasis was placed on the ability to enforce security in ways that could be formally verified to be correct and reliable. The more rigid and formal the system's enforcement of security policy, the higher the rating that the system could receive.

Evaluation Division	Evaluation Class	Degree of Trust
A - Verified Protection	*A1* - Verified Design	Highest
B - Mandatory Protection	*B3* - Security Domains *B2* - Structured Protection *B1* - Labeled Security Protection	
C - Discretionary Protection	*C2* - Controlled Access Protection *C1* - Discretionary Security Protection	
D - Minimal Protection	*D1* - Minimal Protection	Lowest

Source –
Herman, D.S., The common criteria for IT Security evaluation, in Information Security Management Handbook, 6th edn., Tipton, H.F. and Krause, M., Eds., Auerbach Publications. New York 2007. 1489

Figure 3.15 – **Summary of Orange Book Evaluation Criteria Divisions**

To assist with the evaluation of secure products, TCSEC introduced the idea of the Trusted Computing Base (TCB) into product evaluation. In essence, TCSEC starts with the principle that there are some functions that simply must be working correctly for security to be possible and consistently enforced in a computing system. For example, the ability to define subjects and objects and the ability to distinguish between them is so fundamental that no system could be secure without it. The TCB then are these fundamental controls implemented in a given system, whether that is in hardware, software, or firmware.

Each of the TCSEC levels describes a different set of fundamental functions that must be in place to be certified to that level. *Figure 3.16* describes the high-level requirements that any TCB would need to meet to achieve each division or class (essentially a subdivision).

The most important thing to note is the move from DAC to MAC between the C levels and B levels. Most commercial, general-purpose computing systems were never intended for MAC and could only achieve a C2 rating. The more rigid requirements for the higher B and A levels also had the effect of limiting the size and scope of the systems being evaluated, and they made it highly impractical for them to be used in the development of highly complex, distributed systems.

Division	Class	Description
D	–	Evaluated but does not meet security requirements
C	C1	Discretionary Security Protection: ■ *Basic Discretionary Access Control (DAC)*
	C2	Controlled Access Protection: ■ *Improved DAC* ■ *Individual accountability through login procedures and audit trails* ■ *Resource isolation* ■ *Essential system documentation and user manuals*

B	B1	Labeled Security Protection:
		■ *Mandatory Access Control (MAC) over some subjects and objects*
		  - *Informal statement of the security policy model*
		  - *Data sensitivity labels and label exportation*
		■ *All discovered flaws must be removed or otherwise mitigated*

	B2	Structured Protection: ■ *DAC and MAC enforcement extended to all subjects and objects* ■ *Security policy model clearly defined and formally documented* ■ *Covert storage channels are identified and analyzed* ■ *Objects are carefully structured into protection-critical and non-protection-critical* ■ *Design and implementation enable more comprehensive testing and review* ■ *Authentication mechanisms are hardened from compromise* ■ *Trusted management segregates administrator and operator privileges* ■ *Strict configuration management*
	B3	Security Domains: ■ *Can satisfy reference monitor requirements* ■ *Structured to exclude code not essential to security policy enforcement* ■ *Significant system engineering directed toward minimizing complexity* ■ *Trusted management provides security administrator function* ■ *Audits all security-relevant events* ■ *Automated imminent intrusion detection, notification, and response* ■ *Trusted system recovery procedures* ■ *Covert timing channels are identified and analyzed*
A	A1	Verified Design: ■ *Functionally identical to B3 but more formal design and verification*

Figure 3.16 - **High-Level TCB Requirements**

Information Technology Security Evaluation Criteria (ITSEC)

ITSEC was not widely accepted outside of the United States due to some of its perceived limitations and relative inflexibility. It inspired a number of other national product evaluation criteria as a result. This lack o international standardization put a great deal of pressure on product vendors because they essentially had to build and document the same products in different ways to meet different criteria. From lessons learned from the use of TCSEC and other national product evaluation criteria, a more harmonized approach was proposed by a number of European nations and later ratified by the European Community.

In contrast to TCSEC, security requirements are not as proscribed in ITSEC. Instead, the consumer or the vendor has the ability to define a set of requirements from a menu of possible requirements into a Security Target (ST), and vendors develop products (the Target of Evaluation or ToE) and have them evaluated against that target. While it still assigned levels, it provided two sets of levels: functional levels and assurance levels. Unlike TCSEC, it also addressed a wider range of security needs, including integrity and availability requirements.

Functional levels (F1 to F10) are intended to describe the functional strength of a system under evaluation similar to what TCSEC did with its levels. They are really provided for guidance only because adherence to them was not a strict requirement and the consumers or vendors could still define their own.

Where ITSEC was significantly different from TCSEC is in the assignment of assurance levels (or E levels). Assurance can be defined as the level of confidence that the evaluator has that the product not only meets the functional requirements, but that it will continue to meet those requirements. In other words, it is really a statement of how much assurance the evaluator has that the product is trustworthy. To this end, ITSEC defined six different levels of assurance, each more difficult to achieve than the last. *Figure 3.17* outlines the requirements for E1 through E6:

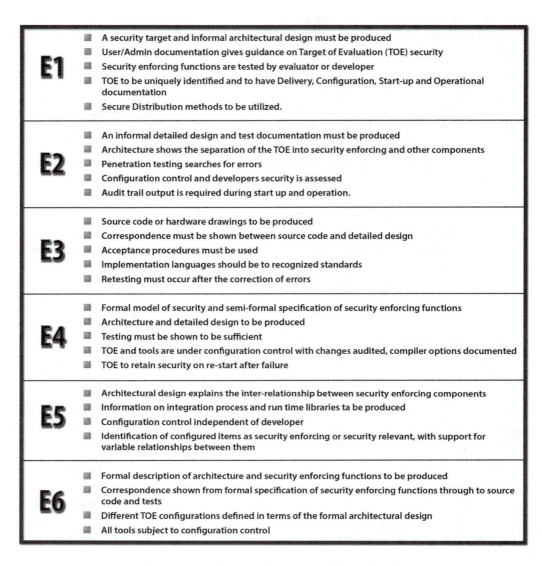

Figure 3.17 - **ITSEC Requirements E1 through E6** [30]

In order to achieve a higher E-level, vendors would need to be prepared to provide more formal architecture and documentation, and the product would need to be tested more carefully and thoroughly. Higher E-levels are intended then to provide the consumer with higher degrees of assurance. When picking between products with similar functionality, one should use assurance levels to pick the more appropriate option.

The Common Criteria [31]

Although ITSEC provided some international harmonization, it was not universally adopted, and vendors continued to have to develop their products with multiple criteria in mind. The publication of the Common Criteria as the ISO/IEC 15408 standard provided the first truly international product evaluation criteria. It has largely superseded all other criteria, although there continue to be products in general use that were certified under TCSEC, ITSEC, and other criteria. It takes a very similar approach to ITSEC by providing a flexible set of functional and assurance requirements, and like ITSEC, it is not very proscriptive as TCSEC had been. Instead, it is focused on standardizing the general approach to product evaluation and providing mutual recognition of such evaluations all over the world.

While flexibility can be desirable, it does make it difficult for vendors to develop products to a common set of requirements or for consumers to evaluate two or more products against a predefined common baseline. To help with this, common criteria introduced protection profiles (PP). These are a common set of functional and assurance requirements for a category of vendor products deployed in a particular type of environment. For example, the "Software based Personal Firewall for Home Internet Use" PP provides functional and assurance requirements that should be common to all such firewall systems. This could then be used as the basis for vendor development and subsequent product evaluation.

In many cases, however, these protection profiles may not be specific enough or may not cover the specific situation required by the consumer, so they may still choose to develop their own. The vendor product (referred to as a ToE) is then examined against this specific profile by a third-party evaluation lab using a common evaluation methodology (CEM).

Short Name	Long Name	Level of Confidence
EAL1	Functionally tested	Lowest
EAL 2	Structurally tested	
EAL3	Methodically tested and checked	
EAL4	Methodically designed, tested, and reviewed	Medium
EAL5	Semi-formally designed and tested	
EAL6	Semi-formally verified design and tested	

Source –
Herrman, D.S. The common criteria for IT security evaluation, in Information Security Management Handbook, 6th edn., Tipton, H.F. and Krause, M. Eds., Auerbach Publications, New York, 2007, 1496.

Figure 3.18 - **Standard EAL Packages**

---

31   See the following for the most up to date information on the Common Criteria: https://www. commoncriteriaportal.org/
See the following for the ISO/IEC 15408:2009 standard: http://standards.iso.org/ittf/ PubliclyAvailableStandards/index.html

The result of that evaluation is a report that outlines whether the ToE met the requirements identified by the profile or not. It also assigns the evaluation an Evaluation Assurance Level (EAL) as shown in *Figure 3.18*. The EAL level is intended to provide the consumers or the vendors with some idea of how confident they should be in the results of the evaluation, based on how much information was available to the evaluation lab and how carefully the system was examined. The EALs are as follows:

- **EAL 1:** The product is functionally tested; this is sought when some assurance in accurate operation is necessary, but the threats to security are not seen as serious.
- **EAL 2:** Structurally tested; this is sought when developers or users need a low to moderate level of independently guaranteed security.
- **EAL 3:** Methodically tested and checked; this is sought when there is a need for a moderate level of independently ensured security.
- **EAL 4:** Methodically designed, tested, and reviewed; this is sought when developers or users require a moderate to high level of independently ensured security.
- **EAL 5:** Semi-formally designed and tested; this is sought when the requirement is for a high level of independently ensured security.
- **EAL 6:** Semi-formally verified, designed, and tested; this is sought when developing specialized TOEs for high-risk situations.
- **EAL 7:** Formally verified, designed, and tested; this is sought when developing a security TOE for application in extremely high-risk situations.

EALs are frequently misunderstood to provide a simple means to compare security products with similar levels. In fact, products may be very different even if they are assigned the same EAL level because their functionality may have little in common.

Industry and International Security Implementation Guidelines

Some industries and organizations are required to adhere to security standards or guidelines when implementing systems. These requirements and specifications should be captured by the security architect when defining the organization's macro security architecture. For example, if an organization accepts payment by credit cards, they will be expected to conform to the security requirements of Payment Card Industry Data Security Standard (PCI-DSS). While these standards rarely are sufficient for a secure system, they represent the minimum mandatory requirements a security architect must address if applicable.

ISO/IEC 27001 and 27002 Security Standards [32]

The International Organization for Standardization (ISO) is the world's largest developer and publisher of international standards. ISO is a nongovernment organization of the national standards institutes of 157 countries, one member per country, with a Central Secretariat in Geneva, Switzerland that coordinates the system. Its mission is to form a bridge between the public and private sectors, enabling consensus to be reached on solutions that meet both the requirements of business and the broader needs of society. The 27000 series of standards addresses information security practices.

The security standards 27001 and 27002 are universally recognized as the standards for sound security practices. Both standards were inspired by the earlier British Standard 7799 (BS7799). The first part of BS7799 inspired the publication of ISO/IEC 17799, which was

---

32   Read more about the ISO 27000 series here: http://www.27000.org/

renumbered as ISO/IEC 27002 in 2005. In turn, the second part of BS7799 strongly influenced the development of ISO/IEC 27001. Although they share common origins, these standards approach information security management in very different ways.

ISO/IEC 27001:2013 is focused on the standardization and certification of an organization's information security management system (ISMS). An ISMS (*Figure 3.19*) is defined as the governance structure supporting an information security program. It addresses the tone at the top, roles, and responsibilities, and it maps business drivers to the implementation of appropriate controls vis-à-vis the risk management process. The following illustrates the elements common to a generic ISMS:

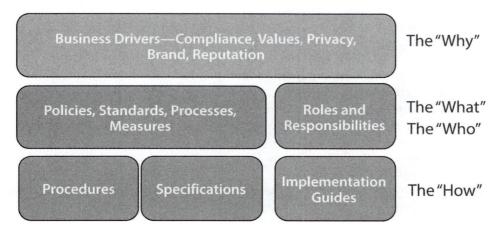

Figure 3.19 - **A generic Information Security Management System**

It starts with key business drivers and determines how the organization will respond
to them and how responsibility will be shared within the organization.

ISO/IEC 27001:2013 provides instructions on how to apply the ISMS concept and to construct, run, sustain, and advance information security management. The core of the standard is focused on five key areas:

1. General requirements of the ISMS
2. Management responsibility
3. Internal ISMS audits
4. Management review of the ISMS
5. ISMS improvement

ISO/IEC 27002:2013 is often used in tandem with 27001:2013. Rather than focus on security governance, it provides a "Code of Practice for Information Security Management," which lists security control objectives and recommends a range of specific security controls according to industry best practice. Unlike 27001:2013, this standard is more of a guideline than a standard, leaving it up to the organization to decide what level of control is appropriate, given the risk tolerance of the specific environment under the scope of the ISMS. The recommended control objectives are the "how" – they demonstrate the implementation of operational controls. A well-rounded information security program will likely include services that address each of these control objectives. ISO/IEC 27002:2013 includes the following 14 focus areas:[33]

---

33   See the following for: https://www.iso.org/obp/ui/#iso:std:iso-iec:27002:ed-2:v1:en

1. **Information Security Policies** – Provide management guidance and support for information security.
2. **Organization of Information Security** – Provides a formal and defined security mechanism within an organization that includes information processing facilities and information assets accessed or maintained by third parties.
3. **Human Resource Security** – Provides security aspects for employees joining, moving, and leaving an organization.
4. **Asset Management** – Protects the organization's assets by ensuring valuable data assets are identified and receive appropriate protection.
5. **Access Control** – Limits access to data, mobile communications, telecommunications, and network services, as well as detects unauthorized activities.
6. **Cryptography** – Provides the ability to protect the confidentiality, integrity, and authenticity of information.
7. **Physical and Environmental Security** – Prevents unauthorized physical access, damage, and interference to facilities and data.
8. **Operations Security** – Ensures the proper and secure operation of data processing facilities by protecting software, communications, data, and the supporting infrastructure.
9. **Communications Security** – Ensures proper data exchange between organizations.
10. **Information Systems Acquisitions, Development, and Maintenance** – Implements security controls into operations and development systems to ensure the security of application system's software and data.
11. **Supplier Relationships** – Implements security controls to protect corporate information and assets that are accessible by suppliers and ensure that suppliers provide the agreed upon level of service and security.
12. **Information Security Incident Management** – Implements procedures to detect and respond to information security incidents.
13. **Information Security Aspects of Business Continuity Management** – Mitigates an incident's impact on critical business systems.
14. **Compliance** – Ensures adherence to criminal and civil laws and statutory, regulatory, or contractual obligations, complies with organizational security policies and standards, and provides for a comprehensive audit process.

Each of these control objectives also includes numerous clauses describing specific controls along with recommendations on how they should be implemented in a typical enterprise.

Both standards can be used to guide security architecture and design. The big difference lies with certification. An organization's ISMS may be certified by a licensed third-party assessor under ISO/IEC 27001:2013, but their control practices cannot be. The certification process allows the assessors to capture the essential elements of the organization's ISMS and publish their findings in the form of a statement of applicability. This document is intended not only to highlight the ISMS but also to allow different organizations to compare their ISMSs. For this reason, ISO/IEC 27001:2013 certification is commonly used by service organizations to share information regarding the ISMS with current and potential customers.

Control Objects for Information and Related Technology (COBIT)

The COBIT is a framework for IT management that was created by the Information Systems Audit and Control Association (ISACA) and the IT Governance Institute (ITGI) in the early 1990s. COBIT provides a set of generally accepted processes to assist in maximizing the benefits derived using information technology (IT) and developing appropriate IT governance. It describes security controls as recommended by the IT auditing community and is often thought of as the base minimum security services that every IT organization will need to implement. It is also frequently used as the basis for both internal and external audits.

The most recent version of COBIT (version 5) documents five principles that drive control objectives categorized in seven enablers. See *Figure 3.20*:

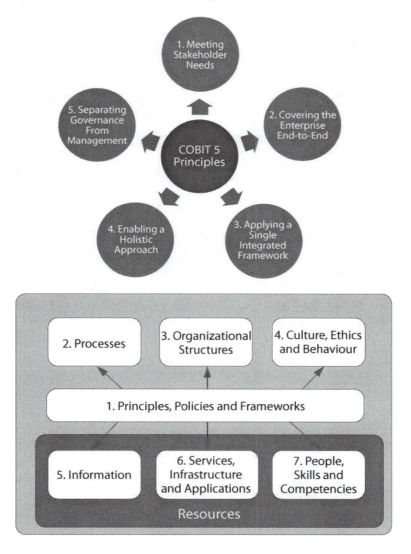

Figure 3.20 - **COBIT's 5 Principles and 7 Enablers** [34]

---

34   ISACA. n.d. http://www.isaca.org/popup/Pages/framefig12large.aspx (accessed May 1, 2014).

COBIT is frequently used by security architects as a menu of core security services that must be implemented, and design documents will frequently use the COBIT structure to document security services. This can ease the effort required to provide audit support and allow current control gaps to be addressed as part of the architecture.

Payment Card Industry Data Security Standard (PCI-DSS)

PCI-DSS was developed by the PCI Security Standards Council to enhance payment card data security. Much like COBIT and ISO 27002, the PCI- DSS provides the security architect with a framework of specifications to ensure the safe processing, storing, and transmission of cardholder information. PCI-DSS is focused on compliance with the standard that includes prevention, detection, and reaction to security incidents.

PCI-DSS is targeted towards merchants and service providers but is mandated for the systems involved in handling an organization's payment card services.[35] Six goals are further defined through twelve broad requirements as seen in *Figure 3.21.*

Goals	PCI-DSS Requirements
Build and Maintain a Secure Network	1. Install and maintain a firwall configuration to protect cardholder data 2. Do not use vendor-supplied defaults for system passwords and other security parameters
Protect Cardholder Data	3. Protect stored cardholder data 4. Encrypt transmission of cardholder data across open, public networks
Maintain a Vulnerability Management Progtram	5. Use and regualary update anti-virus sofware or programs 6. Develp and maintain secure systems and applications
Implement Strong Access Control Measures	7. Restrict access to cardholder data by business need to know 8. Assign unique ID to each person with computer access 9. Restrict physical access to cardholder data
Regularly Monitor and Test Networks	10. Track and montior all access to network resources and cardholder data 11. Regularly test security systems and processes
Maintain an Information Security Policy	12. Maintain a policy that addresses information secruity for all personnel

*Figure 3.21 - **PCI DSS requirements**[36]*

---

35   PCI Security Standards Council, First. "PCI-DSS Quick Reference Guide." Last modified Oct, 2010. https://www.pcisecuritystandards.org/documents/PCI SSC Quick Reference Guide.pdf (Page 34).

36   Read more about PCI-DSS here: https://www.pcisecuritystandards.org/security_standards/documents. php?view=&association=PCI+DSS&language=

Each requirement has several sub-objectives that must be met. For example, under the category Protect Cardholder Data and Requirement 4, "Encrypt transmission of cardholder data across open, public networks," the following objectives apply:

- **4.1** – Use strong cryptography and security protocols such as SSL/TLS, SSH, or IPSec to safeguard sensitive cardholder data during transmission over open, public networks (e.g., Internet, wireless technologies, Global System for Mobile communications [GSM], General Packet Radio Service [GPRS]). Ensure wireless networks transmitting cardholder data or connected to the cardholder data environment use industry best practices (e.g., IEEE 802.11i) to implement strong encryption for authentication and transmission. The use of WEP as a security control is prohibited.
- **4.2** – Never send unprotected Primary Account Numbers (PANs) by end-user messaging technologies.

If security architects were required to comply with PCI-DSS, they would look at existing secure infrastructure to determine if it were suitable from an encryption perspective to support the requirement. If not, they would research the best approach for either enhancing the existing infrastructure or acquiring suitable infrastructure. The recommendations made by the security architect must be correct as they will be implemented by the organization and assessed by an independent party to determine if the requirements are truly met. If flaws are found or the infrastructure does not encrypt and protect as required, the architect may be faulted and the organization will need to revisit the infrastructure enhancement or acquisition. These mistakes prove to be costly and disrupt the mission of the organization. Understanding the architectural requirements and implementing them correctly saves considerable amounts of waste and rework.

Security Capabilities of Information Systems

While the requirements of security frameworks may seem daunting from an implementation perspective, there are a wide range of techniques and technologies available that the system security architect may choose. The challenge for the security architect is to provide security without compromising the primary function of the system. This can be extremely difficult in some types of computing environments where processing power is scarce and any security features may cause unacceptable delays in normal processing. At the same time, there are a wide variety of techniques available to protect systems across the many layers of hardware, firmware, and software that make up modern computing platforms.

Access Control Mechanisms

All systems need to be able to distinguish between individual subjects and objects managed by the system and make appropriate decisions concerning how they will be allowed to interact with each other. The system will need some way to assign identifiers to both subjects and objects and to authenticate all subjects before they are allowed to access resources on the system. This is one of the most fundamental controls required on a secure system, and its correct operation is a requirement for many other security controls. For this reason, it is one of the key elements in a TCB that may be the subject of careful verification using security models and product evaluation criteria.

When no subject can gain access to any object without authorization, this is referred to as complete mediation. Complete mediation is normally the responsibility of the security kernel implementing the reference monitor concept. A reference monitor will examine all attempts by subjects to access objects to determine if it should be allowed or not. It consults with the security kernel database, which stores access controls lists and logs its decision into a secure audit log. Ideally, this function will be as simple as possible to allow for easier modeling, implementation, and formal verification. A reference monitor is considered to be in place only when such mediation is complete.

Secure Memory Management

From a security perspective, memory and storage are the most important resources in any computing system. If data in memory is damaged or corrupted, the system may not function or may function in inappropriate ways. If data in memory is disclosed, sensitive or confidential information may be revealed to less privileged subjects or unprivileged attackers. At the same time, few resources are more available – physically and logically – than memory, putting it constantly in harm's way.

Ideally, it would be possible to easily separate memory used by subjects (such as running processes and threads) from objects (such as data in storage). Unfortunately for security architects, most modern computing systems share a common approach to computing memory where subjects and objects share a common pool of memory, leaving it up to the system to distinguish between areas of memory that will be executed from areas of memory that will be used for storage only. This is one of the reasons why buffer overflows are so successful. With a common pool of memory, the security architect must resort to a variety of techniques to keep subjects isolated from objects and from each other. These techniques include the use of processor states, layering, and data hiding.

Technologies such as address space layout randomization (ASLR) involve randomly arranging position of data areas in memory to help protect against hard coded values in malware and viruses. While most modern operating systems support ASLR, the security architect must ensure programs and applications are designed and configured to take advantage of this security control.

Processor States

Processors and their supporting chipsets provide one of the first layers of defense in any computing system. In addition to providing specialized processors for security functions (such as cryptographic coprocessors), processors also have states that can be used to distinguish between more than less privileged instructions. Most processors support at least two states: a supervisor state and a problem state. In supervisor state (also known as kernel mode), the processor is operating at the highest privilege level on the system, and this allows the process running in supervisor state to access any system resource (data and hardware) and execute both privileged and non-privileged instructions. In problem state (also known as user mode), the processor limits the access to system data and hardware granted to the running process.

This is an extremely useful function for a variety of reasons. It allows the processor to give priority to processes that have access to supervisor state over those which do not. It also enables the processor to apply limitations on resources (which requires processor power in itself) only when it has to. Thus, processes that need rapid and relatively unlimited access to memory can get it, while processes that do not can be restricted when need be.

The use of processor states also has some important limitations. It requires that any process in supervisor state be highly trustworthy and isolated from processes that are not. A malicious process running in supervisor state has very little restrictions placed upon it and can be used to cause a lot of damage. Ideally, access to supervisor state is limited only to core OS functions that are abstracted from end-user interaction through other controls, but this is not always the case. For example, device drivers that control input/output devices are typically installed by end-users but are often granted access to supervisor state to help them run faster. This may allow a malformed driver to be used to compromise the system unless other controls are in place to mitigate this risk.

Layering

One of the ways that privileged parts of the system are protected is through the use of discrete layers that control interactions between more privileged and less privileged processes on the system. In computer programming, layering is the organization of programming into separate functional components that interact in some sequential and hierarchical way, with each layer usually having an interface only to the layer above it and the layer below it. This helps to ensure that volatile or sensitive areas of the system are protected from unauthorized access or change.

One of the most common ways this is done uses ring protection (*Figure* 3.22). It is frequently represented as a series of concentric rings where the innermost ring is assigned the lowest number and the outermost ring is assigned the highest number. For example, in a ring architecture with four rings, the innermost ring would be Ring 0 with the outermost ring being Ring 4. In ring protection, privilege level controls prevent direct memory access from less privileged to more privileged rings while memory access from more privileged to less privileged levels is permitted. Mechanisms called control gates manage transfers from a less privileged level to a more privileged ring. The most privileged ring (Ring 0 in our example) is associated with core system functions like the most sensitive parts of the OS kernel, while the lowest privileged ring (Ring 3 in our example) is associated to end-user applications.

The rings are used to control interactions between different execution domains (or the range of objects available to a given subject) with different levels of privilege. This is done through the use of application programming interfaces (API) and similar mechanisms that allow less privileged processes to call on the services of more privileged processes in a different ring.

Process Isolation

Process isolation can also be used to prevent individual processes from interacting with each other, even when they are assigned to the same ring when ring protection is used. This can be done by providing distinct address spaces for each process and preventing other processes from accessing that area of memory. Naming distinctions is also used to distinguish between different processes. Virtual mapping is also used to assign randomly chosen areas of actual memory to a process to prevent other processes from finding those locations easily. Encapsulation of processes as objects can also be used to isolate them. Because an object includes the functions for operating on it, the details of how it is implemented can be hidden. The system can also ensure that shared resources are managed to ensure that processes are not allowed to access shared resources in the same time slots.

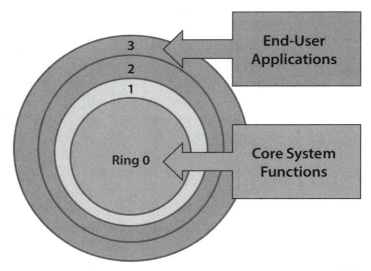

Figure 3.22 - **One example of ring protection in action** The x86 architecture defines four rings (numbered 0 through 3) where more privileged functions, usually limited to kernel functions and some device drivers, are assigned to Ring 0 while less privileged applications are assigned to outer rings.

Functions assigned to lower rings can access all other higher rings, but applications assigned to Ring 3 can only access functions outside their own ring through very restricted gates or interfaces.

Data Hiding

Data hiding maintains activities at different security levels to separate these levels from each other. This assists in preventing data at one security level from being seen by processes operating at other security levels.

Abstraction

Abstraction involves the removal of characteristics from an entity in order to easily represent its essential properties. For example, it is easier for a system administrator to grant group rights to a group of 25 people called "Human Resources" than to grant 25 individual rights to each HR member. Abstraction negates the need for users to know the particulars of how an object functions. They only need to be familiar with the correct syntax for using an object and the nature of the information that will be presented as a result.

Cryptographic Protections

Cryptography can be used in a variety of ways to protect sensitive system functions and data. By encrypting sensitive information and limiting the availability of key material, data can be hidden from less privileged parts of the system. For example, secure file systems make heavy use of cryptography to encrypt large amounts of data in storage to prevent it from being disclosed inappropriately. A Trusted Platform Module (TPM) is an example of a specialized cryptoprocessor that provides for the secure generation, use, and storage of cryptographic keys.[37] Because each TPM is unique, it may also be used to provide hardware authentication using its keys.

---

37 For more information about Trusted Platform Modules, please see the following: http://www. trustedcomputinggroup.org/resources/tpm_main_specification

Host Firewalls and Intrusion Prevention

While firewalls and IPS are normally associated with network partitioning and the enforcement of security zones of control, they are also frequently used to protect individual hosts from attack. Software or hardware-based firewalls can be implemented within individual hosts to control traffic to and from a particular system. Similarly, host intrusion prevention can be used to validate network traffic directed at a host and block it from executing if it is found to be malicious.

Audit and Monitoring Controls

Secure systems must also have the ability to provide administrators with evidence of their correct operation. This is performed using logging subsystems that allow for important system, security, and application messages to be recorded for analysis. More secure systems will provide considerable protection to ensure that these logs cannot be tampered with, including secure export of such logs to external systems.

Host Intrusion Detection Systems (HIDS) and *Network Intrusion Detection Systems (NIDS)* may also be considered as types of audit and monitoring controls. HIDS subsystems examine the operation of the system to detect anomalous events and alert security administrators accordingly. They will frequently analyze logs, running processes, and common services/daemons that may come under attack to determine if the system continues to be secure. NIDS performs similar functions but at the network layer.

Virtualization

Virtualization offers numerous advantages from a security perspective. Virtual machines are typically isolated in a sandbox environment and if infected can quickly be removed or shut down and replaced by another virtual machine. Virtual machines also have limited access to hardware resources and therefore help protect the host system and other virtual machines. Virtual machines do require strong configuration management control and versioning to ensure known good copies are available for restoration if needed. They are also subject to all the typical requirements of hardware-based systems including anti-malware software, encryption, HIDS, firewalls, and patching. Given the existing requirements, plus the required overhead for the VM host, systems with consistent high resource utilization may not benefit through virtualization. Additionally, more malware and viruses are becoming virtual machine aware.[38] They are able to detect when they are in a virtual machine and "break out" to the host system. The security architect must be aware of these tradeoffs and plan accordingly for the system and enterprise security architecture.

Vulnerabilities of Security Architectures

While every system is different, insecure systems tend to suffer from the same sorts of threats and vulnerabilities. Common vulnerabilities include poor memory management, the existence of covert channels, insufficient system redundancy, poor access control, and poor protection for key system components such as hardware resources and core OS functions. Common threats to system availability, integrity, and confidentiality include hardware failure, misuse of system privileges, buffer overflows and other memory attacks, denial of service, reverse engineering, and system hacking.

---

38   Read more about virtual machine aware malware here: http://www.kb.cert.org/vuls/id/649219

Because many vulnerabilities result from insecure design and most threats are well known, it is the responsibility of the security architects to ensure that their designs are addressing security requirements appropriately while also ensuring that the system can continue to perform its intended function. A look at the Verizon Data Breach Investigations Report for 2014 will help to frame this conversation for the security architect.[39]

Web applications were associated with 3,937 security incidents and 490 confirmed data breaches in 2013. Many of the attacks analyzed by Verizon were targeting popular blogging platforms or content management systems from Joomla, Wordpress, and Drupal. In order to address some of these concerns, the security architect would need to have knowledge of blog sites and content management systems being deployed throughout the enterprise. The "shadow IT" phenomenon that allows many IT functions to devolve into the hands of non-IT practitioners has to be of concern to the security architect in this regard. If there are systems being maintained in production environments without the knowledge of the IT function within the enterprise and more importantly without the appropriate controls that the IT function would implement, then these kind of attacks can become a significant threat for the enterprise.

Verizon said human error was at the core of 412 confirmed data breaches in 2013 and associated with more than 16,000 security incidents. Process failures, a lack of communication, and poor controls mitigating business partner risk were associated with many of the incidents. Public sector organizations, administrative, and healthcare firms were the most affected by human error, according to the analysis. The top three errors were mis-delivery of information, publishing mistakes, and disposal errors. Properly implemented and configured data loss prevention technology may be the best way to proactively address employee mistakes. Security architects should implement more efficient processes and set enforceable security policies to control them.

Cyber-espionage activity was associated with 511 security incidents and 306 confirmed data breaches, according to the Verizon report. Basic security best practices are the key to successfully repelling these attacks. Network segmentation, proactive log management, and two-factor authentication could help stop lateral movement if an attacker is already inside and attempting to get to sensitive systems. The security architect should ensure that the foundation of the defense in depth strategy used to secure the enterprise is built on a solid architecture, one that incorporates best practices and accomplishes the basics of a well-defined security architecture first and foremost in order to ensure that as many threats as possible may be mitigated through the use of time proven strategies and techniques.

Point-of-sale (POS) systems suffered 198 data breaches in 2013 according to Verizon. Weak and default passwords on point-of-sale systems were consistently targeted by attackers. BlackPOS, a common memory-scraping malware, was a top technique used by credit card data thieves, Verizon said. Security architects need to lock down their POS systems and should consider application whitelisting and the use of updated antivirus solutions on these systems to counteract these threats.

Lost or stolen devices are consistently ranked as a top concern of IT security pros and chief information security officers. Lost laptops and other devices accounted for more than 9,000 security incidents and 116 confirmed data breaches in 2013 according to the Verizon report.

---

39   See the following to download a copy of the 2014Verizon Data Breach Investigation report: http://www. verizonenterprise.com/DBIR/2014/

Information assets are lost much more than they are stolen, by a 15-to-1 difference, Verizon said. Security architects need to implement device encryption, encourage users to keep devices with them at all times and implement an effective backup strategy to address these threats.

The abuse of privileges by an employee, contractor, or partner was associated with more than 11,600 security incidents and 112 confirmed data breaches in 2013. Verizon said it is watching a trend of insider espionage targeting internal data and trade secrets. Because most insider attacks happened within the office network, security architects should build additional controls around systems containing sensitive data. They also must review user account activity and quickly disable former employees' user accounts as part of an overall access control lifecycle.

Crimeware, mainly financially driven attacks using automated attack toolkits, is a common problem faced by nearly every industry, and Verizon found crimeware associated with more than 12,000 security incidents and 50 data breaches in 2013. The Zeus and SpyEye Trojan families spread quickly by organized cybercriminal networks that use spam messages and malicious links to trick people into downloading the dangerous malware. The malware is designed to steal account credentials and drain bank accounts. Many infections happen by simply visiting an attack website or downloading a malicious file. Security architects need to deploy browser security patches and apply updates to browser plug-ins. Java should be disabled or uninstalled if it is not needed. In addition, the use of at least two-factor authentication would thwart many attacks that use stolen credentials.

Distributed denial-of-service attacks, designed to cripple the network or bring down websites and Web applications, are being carried out by attackers that are compromising servers in public and private cloud data centers to increase the bandwidth of their attacks. Verizon analyzed more than 1,100 total security incidents in 2013. Security architects should have a plan in place and consider the use of an Internet service provider DDoS mitigation service and also consider isolating IP address spaces not in active use.

There were more than 7,200 security incidents that do not fit into a common incident pattern, according to the Verizon report. Nearly all of these attacks were external and were browser-based threats, using a combination of hacking, phishing, and malware. Three-quarters of all incidents involved compromised Web servers, and they usually represented mass attacks, in which hundreds of servers are hijacked to host malware for drive-by attacks or phishing sites.

The security architects should use a variety of resources and data points to gather a picture of the threats facing their networks. Resources such as the Verizon Data Breach Investigations Report are valuable because they present findings across a large variety of industries and architectures. Some additional resources that the security architect may find helpful in this regard are listed below:

The Secunia Vulnerability Review 2014

http://secunia.com/?action=fetch&filename=secunia_vulnerability_review_2014.pdf

The Symantec Internet Security Threat Report 2014

http://www.symantec.com/content/en/us/enterprise/other_resources/b-istr_main_report_
v19_21291018.en-us.pdf

The Sophos Security Threat Report 2014

http://www.sophos.com/en-us/medialibrary/PDFs/other/sophos-security-threat-report-2014.pdf

The Cisco 2014 Annual Security Report

https://www.cisco.com/web/offer/gist_ty2_asset/Cisco_2014_ASR.pdf

Price Waterhouse Coopers the Global State of Information Security Survey 2014

http://www.pwc.com/gx/en/consulting-services/information-security-survey/index.jhtml

Trustwave's 2014 Security Pressures Report

http://www2.trustwave.com/rs/trustwave/images/2014%20Trustwave%20Security%20Pressures%20Report.pdf

Websense 2014 Threat Report

http://www.websense.com/assets/reports/report-2014-threat-report-en.pdf

Systems

Poorly designed systems are ripe for attack. The security architects must familiarize themselves with well-known attacks and vulnerabilities in their industry and the types of systems they work with. They should also possess an understanding of what kinds of threats and capabilities exist concerning the organization's mission and system. Countless attacks exist; however, some of the most challenging in terms of secure architecture are emanations, state attacks, and covert channels.

Emanations

System emanations are unintentional electrical, mechanical, optical, or acoustical energy signals that contain information or metadata about the information being processed, stored, or transmitted in a system.[40] One of the earliest public descriptions released by the U.S. National Security Agency describes it as:

"Any time a machine is used to process classified information electrically, the various switches, contacts, relays, and other components in that machine may emit radio frequency or acoustic energy. These emissions, like tiny radio broadcasts may radiate through free space for considerable distances-a half mile or more in some cases.

Or they may be induced on nearby conductors like signal lines, power lines, telephone lines, or water pipes and be conducted along those paths for some distance-and here we may be talking of a mile or more.

When these emissions can be intercepted and recorded, it is frequently possible to analyze them and recover the intelligence that was being processed by the source equipment. The phenomenon affects not only cipher machines, but any information-processing equipment-teletypewriters, duplicating equipment, intercoms, facsimile, computers–you name it. But it has special significance for crypto-machines because it may reveal not only the plaintexts of individual messages being processed but also that carefully guarded information about the internal machine processes. Thus, conceivably, the machine could be radiating information which could lead to the reconstruction of our daily changing keying variables–and from a

---

40 Read more about optical emanations here: http://applied-math.org/acm_optical_tempest.pdf

Comsec viewpoint, that is absolutely the worst thing that can happen to us. This problem of compromising radiation we have given the cover name TEMPEST." [41]

Governments, intelligence organizations, and militaries have spent years and countless resources researching emanations. Their research has focused on how to capture them and use or protect against them. TEMPEST is a set of standards designed to shield buildings and equipment to protect them against eavesdropping and passive emanations gathering attempts. One of the more common approaches was the "Red/Black" separation of equipment.

The Red/Black separation requirements meant installing physical security controls such as shielding between normal unclassified (non-sensitive) circuits and equipment and the classified ones. Once it was implemented and certified, the operators must ensure the smallest of changes to the controls were reported because something as small as moving a component a few millimeters can invalidate the installation.

While this may initially seem to apply only to the counter intelligence situations, the prudent security architect will understand today's competitive market place and the possibility of industrial espionage and the criminal element. As the price of emanations monitoring capability goes down, the incentive to use it by dishonest individuals to steal intellectual property and other assets increases. For example, a research paper by Dmitri Asonov and Rakesh Agrawal describes an emanation attack on an automatic teller machine (ATM).[42] Asonov and Agrawal proposed that the sound (audible emanation) from the ATM pad was different for each key pressed. They studied the keypad and determined they could "listen in" at distances of 15 meters and greater. As a result, they were able to determine about 79% of the key presses accurately. This means an attacker would be able to determine the banking PIN of a person, at a distance, without installing any additional equipment on the ATM. Many security architecture frameworks would miss this vulnerability. A security architect designing banking systems with ATMs would need to take this vulnerability into account and possibly specify the keypad be made of a different material or determine a way to muffle or distort the sound.

State Attacks

State attacks are also known as "race conditions," which attempt to take advantage of how a system handles multiple requests. For example, during a logon process, the process is started at the kernel level of the processor and then demoted to the standard level. Should a user login and then quickly interrupt the login process by pressing the escape key before the processor has time to demote the level, he or she would have successfully accomplished a state attack. The attacker escalated his or her privilege in violation of the system security policy by exploiting the timing of the login process.

Race conditions are also caused by poorly written code and the adoption of applications without assessing the security posture of the system and how it will integrate into the existing environment. A time of check to time of use (TOC/TOU) is a common race condition bug in programming. The attack involves changing the system between the checking of a condition and the action that results from the check. While the coder and system developer are typically

---

41   US NSA, First. "TEMPEST: A Signal Problem." Last modified Sept, 27, 2007. http://www.nsa.gov/ public_info/_files/cryptologic_spectrum/tempest.pdf (Pages 1-2)

42   See the following for the original paper: http://rakesh.agrawal-family.com/papers/ssp04kba.pdf

the roles involved in ensuring race conditions cannot exist, the security architect should be aware of the condition and ensure the selected control framework can test for the condition.

Covert Channels

Covert channels are communications mechanisms hidden from the access control and standard monitoring systems of an information system. Covert channels may use irregular methods of communication such as the free space sections of a disk or even the timing of processes to transmit information. The TCSEC identifies two types of covert channels:

- **Storage channels** that communicate via a stored object
- **Timing channels** that modify the timing of events relative to each other

The only way to mitigate covert channels is through the secure design of an information system. The security architect must understand how covert channels function and strive to eliminate them in any design that has associated requirements.

Technology and Process Integration

Different computing platforms have traditionally taken slightly different approaches to system and security architecture. The following describes the high-level architecture of common computing platforms and how they have addressed security concerns.

Mainframes and Other Thin Client Systems

The term mainframe originally referred to the very large computer systems housed in steel-framed boxes, and it was used to differentiate them from the smaller mini- or microcomputers. These mainframes were used in Fortune 1000 companies to process commercial applications and were also employed by federal, state, and local governments. The term has been used in numerous ways over the years, but most often it describes the successive families of large-scale systems built by IBM and other companies.

Historically, a mainframe was associated with centralized rather than distributed computing. This means that most processing occurs within a large centralized system while clients (or terminals in the mainframe world) are limited to simple interaction and emulation. This type of thin client architecture puts the majority of processing and memory resources within the mainframe itself while peripherals (such as secondary storage and printing) are treated as separate, discrete systems. Centralizing processing power also has the effect of centralizing the responsibility for security, although discrete peripherals may also implement their own security features.

In today's modern mainframe environment, they are less likely to be used as discrete computing platforms. Instead, the base system is used to host a wide variety of other OSs as virtual hosts. By consolidating multiple vendor platforms and providing scalability, mainframes are an effective way to minimize costs. Multiple OSs can be running on a mainframe, most notably numerous instances of Linux. Other uses include data warehousing systems, Web applications, financial applications, and middleware. Mainframes provide reliability, scalability, and maintainability, with the lower total cost of ownership (TCO) and credible disaster recovery.

Mainframes are not the only systems to provide a highly centralized model for processing. Other thin client systems have emerged to provide a similar centralized processing environment, limiting the client to keyboard and mouse emulation, graphics processing, and basic networking functions. This has the benefit of centralizing most functions (including most security functions) while allowing the client to focus on user interaction and networking.

For example, central server-based processing can be combined with diskless workstations or other types of hardware thin clients. A diskless workstation is a computer without a hard drive in it and sometimes without a DVD drive or a USB port. The workstation has a network card and video card, and it may also have other expansion cards, such as a sound card. It relies on services provided by network servers for most of its operation, such as booting and running applications. This puts greater pressure on the central server infrastructure while minimizing the processing power required at the workstation level. Software-based thin client applications provide similar advantages. For example, an Internet browser may be considered a thin client.

From a security perspective, the advantage of this type of architecture is that it focuses the design and implementation of security services in a single, centralized environment. This can make it easier to design, implement, and verify security services as well as maintain them. Because patches and updates only need to be patched in a central location, most security vulnerabilities can be dealt with quickly and efficiently. At the same time, unpatched vulnerabilities will be inherited across the entire system. This makes any vulnerability much more pervasive and dangerous than in other computing platforms. It also requires very careful control of privileged and non-privileged subjects operating at the same time to ensure that one cannot interfere or leak information to the other.

Middleware

Middleware is a connectivity software that enables multiple processes running on one or more machines to interact. These services are collections of distributed software that are present between the application running on the OS and the network services, which reside on a network node. The main purpose of middleware services is to help solve many application connectivity and interoperability problems.

In essence, middleware is a distributed software layer that hides the intricacies and heterogeneous distributed environment consisting of numerous network technologies, computer architectures, OS, and programming languages. Some of the services provided are directory services, transaction tracking, data replication, and time synchronization, services that improve the distributed environment. Some examples are workflow, messaging applications, Internet news channels, and customer ordering through delivery.

In recent years, considerable attention has been placed on middleware as a foundation for Service Oriented Architectures (SOA).[43] Organizations are recognizing that continued reliance on legacy systems impedes business imperatives such as growth, speed to market, business, and IT alignment. Moreover, upgrading to newer technologies is an expensive proposition, especially in a struggling economy. With these challenges in mind, organizations are migrating to a more usable and efficient IT architecture, which enables their customers to more closely interact with the company through Internet-based Web applications. In a SOA, disparate entities make their resources available to an entire population in a standardized way. In other words, SOA is a model for distributed computing, wherein applications call other applications over the network. Functionality is distributed over the network, utilizing the ability to find the functionality and the ability to connect to it.

---

43 Read more about SOA vulnerabilities and mitigations here: http://www.nsa.gov/ia/_files/factsheets/ SOA_security_vulnerabilities_web.pdf

Security Engineering

3

The SOA provides for modularity, flexibility, and reusability. Moreover, it allows for consistent and collaborative governance, security, and management, including policy enforcement, authentication, encryption, and digital signature implementations, with the caveat that the security is designed and implemented correctly. The availability of middleware interfaces, however, can make them common targets for attack as many of the SOAs were not developed with end-to-end security as a requirement.

Embedded Systems

Embedded systems are used to provide computing services in a small form factor with limited processing power. They embed the necessary hardware, firmware, and software into a single platform that can be used to provide a limited range of computing services, usually around a single application. They typically feature a limited OS with the base minimum functionality required to meet its functional requirements. Other constrained devices such as mobile phones, media players, and networking devices such as routers and wireless devices take a similar approach.

From the security architect perspective, embedded systems have a number of potential advantages and disadvantages. Security services tend to be simple, testable, and verifiable, making the task of ensuring that security has been designed and implemented correctly much simpler. Unfortunately, security in such systems is typically limited to a few basic security features to help protect memory and privileged access to memory. While they may be able to support a wide range of security services, they have very limited processing power that must be shared by the core functions and security components. This frequently results in less-than-robust security features, particularly when richer functionality is the primary business driver. It is also frequently more difficult to patch security vulnerabilities in constrained embedded devices.[44] This is why the security architect needs to consider where security needs to be placed and how it needs to be addressed BOTH inside and outside of the embedded system, as well as how much trust can be placed in the integrity of the embedded system from an architecture standpoint.

Pervasive Computing and Mobile Devices

The number of mobile devices has grown considerably in the past four or five years. Products vary from sophisticated mobile phones, such as fourth-generation (4G) handsets, to full-featured "ultrabooks" and tablets.

These devices can now manage personal information, such as contacts, appointments, and to-do lists. Current tablets and cell phones connect to the Internet, function as global positioning system (GPS) devices, and run multimedia software. They can also support a wireless Bluetooth network and wireless wide area networks (WANs). They have memory card slots that accept flash media that can serve as additional storage for files and applications. Most all devices provide audio and video support, incorporating MP3 players, a microphone, a speaker, and headphone jacks along with a built-in digital camera. Integrated security features such as a biometric fingerprint reader can also be included.

These devices share common security concerns with other resource-constrained devices. In many cases, security services have been sacrificed to provide richer user interaction when

---

44   Read more about embedded device security here: http://www.csoonline.com/article/704346/embedded-system-security-much-more-dangerous-costly-than-traditional-soft-ware-vulnerabilities
HD Moore's paper on UPnP: https://community.rapid7.com/docs/DOC-2150

processing power is very limited. Their mobility has made them a prime vector for data loss because they can be used to transmit and store information in ways that may be difficult to control. As a result, the security architect needs to be able to address a long list of threats and vulnerabilities across a wide array of device platforms and form factors in the enterprise. The following list sums up the key areas and actions that the security architect should focus on:

1. Mobile Devices Need Antimalware Software
2. Secure Mobile Communications
3. Require Strong Authentication, Use Password Controls
4. Control Third-party Software
5. Create Separate, Secured Mobile Gateways
6. Choose (or Require) Secure Mobile Devices, Help Users Lock Them Down
7. Perform Regular Mobile Security Audits, Penetration Testing

For example, how would a security architect take the items on this list and integrate them into a coherent strategy for management of mobile devices in the enterprise? The easiest answer is to create a security policy that addresses some or many of the items on the list. The harder answer involves the steps required to draft, review, implement, communicate, train, manage, optimize, enforce, audit, and update the policy over time within the enterprise. What would be involved in crafting a security policy to address the use of mobile devices in the enterprise? A policy would include some of the bullet points listed below:

GENERAL MOBILE DEVICE BEST PRACTICES

■ Use a passcode/passphrase/pattern to lock the device after inactivity; typically no more than 10 minutes of inactivity should trigger this.

■ Encrypt the device if the option is available, using the highest encryption possible (minimum 128-bit). If encryption is unavailable, never store highly confidential data on the device.

■ When choosing between unsecured Wi-Fi and 3G/4G/CDMA service, always opt for the cellular data service, as it is typically significantly more secure than unsecured Wi-Fi. If accessing sensitive/protected data, never use unsecured Wi-Fi unless you have access to a VPN client.

■ Use a VPN if the device will support it.

■ Report stolen/lost devices as soon as possible. Note your device serial number, ESN (Electronic Serial Number, if applicable), and other identifying information for your own records and to facilitate law enforcement or other recovery.

■ Utilize remote wipe capabilities if possible, based on platform.

■ Carefully select applications to install on the device, taking into account the type of data the application will access, whether or not the application is believed to be secure, and whether or not the vendor typically collects information from users through the application (leading to possible data leakage).

■ It is recommended to avoid use of Remote Desktop programs via a mobile device.

■ Disable options and applications that you do not use.

■ If Bluetooth is enabled, do not allow the device to be discovered automatically, and secure it with a password to prevent unauthorized access.

■ Never leave the mobile device unattended.

■ Utilize antivirus/anti-malware software if supported.

- Regularly back up data – preferably in an encrypted fashion.
- Update the device's software per the manufacturer's instructions. Typically updates tend to fix security holes and improve device functionality.
- Limit use of the device by third parties to protect your personal data and facilitate accountability for potential misuse.
- Turn off GPS and data when not being used.
- Do not jailbreak the mobile device.

IPAD/IPOD/IPHONE SPECIFIC BEST PRACTICES

Use of configuration templates to set up the device on the enterprise network and to enforce suggested policies on the device, including:

- Use of a passcode (strength dependent on the potential data the device may contain)
- Allow device wipe if 10 failed passcode attempts
- Use of Cisco AnyConnect VPN – Available in the Apple App Store
- Encryption of device configuration profile
- Forced encryption of device backups
- If multiple users will be accessing the device, the native mail program should not be used to protect the primary user's email account.
- If the device is no longer in use, ensure that all of the data on it is wiped, and it is disposed of properly.

Another resource for the security architect to take a look at would be NIST Special Publication 800-124 Revision 1, "Guidelines for Managing the Security of Mobile Devices in the Enterprise".[45] The Guidelines provide a comprehensive overview of the current state of centralized mobile device management technologies, including an overview of the components, architectures, and capabilities of these technologies and offer recommendations for selecting, implementing, and using such technologies.

Other key recommendations for organizations seeking to implement and maintain a sound mobile device security program include:

- Instituting a mobile device security policy that is documented in the system security plan and that defines:
  1. The types of enterprise resources that may be accessed via mobile devices;
  2. The types of mobile devices that are permitted to access the organization's resources;
  3. The degree of access of the various classes of mobile devices (organization-provided mobile devices vs. personally-owned mobile devices) and how provisioning should be handled;
  4. How the organization's centralized mobile device management servers are administered and how policies in those servers are updated; and
  5. All other requirements for mobile device management technologies.

---

45   See the following: http://www.nist.gov/customcf/get_pdf.cfm?pub_id=913427

- Developing system threat models for mobile devices and the organization resources that are accessed through mobile devices before designing and deploying mobile device solutions.

- Considering the merits of each security service provided by mobile device solutions, determine which services are needed for the organization's environment, and then designing and acquiring one or more solutions that collectively provide the necessary security services.

- Implementing and testing a pilot of the enterprise mobile device solution before putting the solution into production by:
    1. Evaluating connectivity, protection, authentication, application functionality, solution management, logging, and performance for each type of mobile device;
    2. Updating/configuring all components with the latest patches following sound security practices;
    3. Implementing a mechanism for automatic detection of jailbroken or rooted mobile devices; and
    4. Ensuring that the mobile device solution doesn't unexpectedly fall back to insecure default settings.

- Securing each organization-issued mobile device before allowing a user to access it by:
    1. Fully securing to a known good state already deployed to other organization-provided mobile devices with an unknown security profile, and
    2. Deploying supplemental security controls such as anti-virus software and data loss prevention solutions, as needed based on potential risk.

- Regularly maintaining mobile device security by employing operational processes such as the ones listed below and performing periodic assessments (vulnerability scans, penetration testing, reviewing logs) to confirm that the organization's mobile device policies, processes, and procedures are being followed:
    1. Keeping an active inventory of each mobile device, its users, and applications;
    2. Deleting applications that have been installed but subsequently assessed as being too risky for use or revoking access to such applications;
    3. Scrubbing sensitive data from organization-issued devices before re-issuing them to other enterprise users;
    4. Checking for, acquiring, testing, and deploying upgrades and patches;
    5. Ensuring that each mobile device infrastructure component has its clock synched to a common time source;
    6. Reconfiguring access control features as needed;
    7. Detecting and documenting anomalies, such as unauthorized configuration changes to mobile devices.

Lastly, Appendix XX to the Guidelines lists the major controls from the NIST Special Publication 800-53, "Security and Privacy Controls for Federal Information Systems and Organizations, Revision 4" that are applicable to enterprise mobile device security, and Appendix C provides a list of mobile device security resources.[46]

---

46 See the following: http://nvlpubs.nist.gov/nistpubs/SpecialPublications/NIST.SP.800-53r4.pdf

317

TRY IT FOR YOURSELF

A sample template that will allow the security practitioner to review in detail what a mobile device usage policy may look like is provided as Appendix D. The 2 page template will walk you through the stages of a usage policy for a mythical company. Defining a usage policy documents clear responsibilities for all those involved with mobile device activities.

Download the template and go through the sections in order to understand how a mobile device policy is structured.

Single Point of Failure (SPOF)

As technology such as virtualization makes technology more efficient and manageable, the security architect must also understand how single points of failure can arise. Using the example of virtualization, if one were to compare the before and after states from a point of failure perspective, it would seem virtualization often adds a single point of failure to many enterprises. Before virtualization, servers were typically individual hardware components all separate from one another. If the email server went down, it would rarely mean the network attached storage server would go down as well. If these systems were virtualized and ran on the same host, that host becomes a single point of failure for both systems. If the host goes down, all guests running on the host will go down as well. The security architect must identify single points of failure and determine alternatives so stakeholders can make informed decisions regarding the acceptance of the risk or mitigation strategies.

Just how does a security architect go about identifying single points of failure? How does the security architect determine what alternatives will be acceptable as mitigation strategies? This is often the hard part, as there are no easy and standardized answers that are applicable to every situation. There are best practices that the security architect can use such as building redundancy into mission critical systems and the use of High Availability and Fault Tolerance technologies to ensure system survivability during a failure or outage scenario of some kind. In addition, the security architect should ensure that a Risk Analysis and Business Impact Analysis have been done for all major systems, thus ensuring that the valuation of the systems to the business is clearly understood, as well as the potential threats and vulnerabilities that an individual system may face during daily operations. The security architect should also carry out a single point of failure audit, and the results should be cross-referenced against the outcomes of the Risk Analysis and the Business Impact Analysis, thus ensuring that mission critical systems, processes, and people are identified as well as ensuring that all of the supporting components and sub-systems that may form dependencies for or with the main systems are also identified. This is a critical activity because without a thorough understanding of the system architecture, and specifically the dependencies that the architecture has, there is no way to properly address any single points of failure identified.

Because single points of failure can occur throughout the architecture, it is best to look at each area separately and identify common SPOFs. Most IT organizations are being asked to do more with less. This may mean reducing the size of the servers or utilizing virtual environments. For example, if a clustered virtualized infrastructure is being deployed within the enterprise, then there will be many potential SPOFs that the security architect needs to consider and manage as part of the enterprise security architecture. Let's discuss the following technologies and how they can have their SPOFs reduced within the context of a clustered architecture:

- Data Connectivity
- Network Connectivity
- Cluster Communication
- Application Availability
- OS Availability
- Infrastructure

Data Connectivity

This section will cover how to ensure that your application has redundant connectivity to the storage devices. For Data Connectivity, we will examine the connection from the server to the storage.

The first level of redundancy is to have at least two Host Bus Adapters (HBAs) or storage paths and make use of multi-pathing software.

Another common SPOF in this area is having these multiple HBA connections from the server to a single SAN switch. If the single SAN switch were to fail or go offline for any reason, all paths to the storage would fail. Another common variation is having a single SAN switch, which has a single connection to the array. It is best to ensure that each SAN switch is connected to a different front-end port on the array. Having multiple paths at each point in the infrastructure allows for a failure without causing an outage.

Network Connectivity

In this section, we will discuss how to ensure the network is available and identify any potential SPOFs. In understanding your network and taking an end-to-end view, there are typically a large number of paths a packet of data can traverse to get from one machine to another. There can be multiple SPOFs within this stack. A typical configuration issue is a single Network Interface Card (NIC) for the public network. If that single NIC was to be disconnected or the network switch port was to fail, then that server would no longer be able to communicate across the network. The security architect would need to deploy systems that have the ability to configure two different NIC ports, both available on the public network, and when the primary NIC fails the Virtual IP (VIP) address that is associated with the application can migrate from one physical NIC to another in the same box. This reduces the time the application will be unavailable as it is no longer necessary to bring the application and associated infrastructure offline on one server and then bring them online on another.

Cluster Communication

Cluster Communication refers to how to ensure that the clustering solution detects failure and communicates between cluster nodes. Clustering technologies need to both pass state information, as well as do node arbitration in the case of cluster communication loss. When one is configuring the cluster, it is recommend that more than one heartbeat network is configured. These connections pass along resource and service group state information between the nodes in the cluster. If a single heartbeat link is configured and that NIC goes down, then the cluster has to determine which of the nodes are able to communicate to avoid a split-brain condition. A split-brain condition is when more than one cluster is formed from the original cluster nodes using the same resources or applications. Many clustering solutions have methods to ensure only one cluster is formed when the heartbeat communication is fragmented. They can use different methods that are adaptable to each enterprise's unique environment. For example, SCSI-3 Persistent Reservations can be used to ensure that there is no possibility of data corruption. If a server has a limited number of NICs, then the cluster software should have the ability to use the public network in a low priority mode. Instead of a constant flow of state information, the public NIC will be used infrequently to determine status and pass along some information. Having multiple paths for cluster communication prevents a network SPOF from bringing down the cluster.

Application Availability

Some applications have High Availability (HA) built into them, and they can allow multiple systems to access different instances of the application at the same time. In general, several typical limitations present themselves as SPOFs with application HA tools. The largest amount of time in moving an application from one server to another during a failover event is migrating the file systems between servers. With a Clustered File System (CFS), multiple systems can all have the file systems mounted so that when a failover event occurs only the application and VIP need to be moved to another cluster node. Additionally, the cluster should provide the ability to restart an application on the same system to avoid this issue as well. For applications that have HA embedded within them, the cluster software can still provide a benefit through the control of the application and startup order dependencies. In addition, the application itself can be restarted if it was to fail, and a monitoring system will be notified if there was an issue.

OS Availability

In this section, we will talk about how the cluster software can be used to protect an Operating System. Most cluster software has the ability to work with several types of virtualization including Solaris LDOMs and Zones, HP-UX IVM, AIX WPAR, and LPAR as well as VMware and Microsoft's Hyper-V. OS Virtualization allows for one operating system to migrate as a service between different physical systems. Each virtualization technology is different and several have the ability to move between physical servers with limited or no downtime. Clustering software can determine if a VM goes offline and migrate the VM as well as the applications to another physical server to startup.

Infrastructure

There are many external influences to consider when protecting a running application. Most are considered when planning for a data center; for example, utilizing a UPS prevents against power outage. What would happen if the fire suppression system went off in the server room? Are the cluster nodes in different parts of the data center? Are they connected to different UPSs? By ensuring that your application can continue to function if an event occurs and takes out one box you are also looking for SPOFs in your infrastructure.

In summary, a High Availability application can provide quick automated failure detection and take action when necessary, but the entire environment needs to be architected properly to ensure that the failure of one component does not impact the availability of the application.

Clustering software can migrate applications from one node to another in case of failure, but if both servers are on the same circuit breaker and somehow it is tripped, the cluster will not be able to ensure the application stays online. In addition, all infrastructure outside of the cluster should be inspected for SPOFs as well, allowing for a thorough understanding of any dependencies that may also need to be addressed so that they do not negatively impact the survivability of the system.

Client-Based Vulnerabilities

The client platform is increasingly a staging ground for more advanced attacks towards servers and services. Additionally, client platforms are also more diverse and mobile with tablets and smartphones becoming dominate devices for information access. Most tablets and smartphones rely on apps or applets to interface the device with a service or server. The security architect must be aware of what the organization's mobile (smartphones, tablets, and removable media) and stationary (standard workstations and thin clients) system environment consists of. The architect must also either determine or make certain assumptions regarding the security posture of the end device data and services reach. For example, the European Network and Information Security Agency (ENISA) warned banks in 2012 to stop assuming customer's computers were free of malware and viruses. They further suggested banks consider offline verification before allowing large transactions.[47]

Desktops, Laptops, and Thin Clients

The security architect must take into account the basis of the client's machines when designing security architecture. Refer to the ENISA example. If the architect knows customers need to use the bank's website, but the architect cannot force the customer to use a "clean" workstation, then the architect must design security with the assumption the client is infected. This could take the form of one time pad tokens or a variety of security measures to ensure loss and exposure is limited to the customer and the bank. The client level security architecture of an organization should ensure the organization's client systems minimally include:

- A supported and licensed operating system is running.
- Updated, verified, and supported anti-malware and anti-virus capabilities are installed. [48]
- A host-based intrusion detection system is installed.
- The whole drive or sensitive information on the drive is encrypted with strong encryption.
- Whenever possible, the client operates in a "limited" account that does not have administrative privileges.
- Whenever possible, the client system is part of a continuous monitoring program that monitors for vulnerabilities and patches them when needed without the need for interaction of the end-user.

---

47   See the following: http://www.enisa.europa.eu/media/press-releases/eu-cyber-security-agency-enisa-201chigh-roller201d-online-bank-robberies-reveal-security-gaps

48   For those that would like to have a definition of anti-malware and anti-virus, let's start with the differences between "viruses" and "malware." Viruses are a specific type of malware (designed to replicate and spread), while malware is a broad term used to describe all sorts of unwanted or malicious code. Malware can include viruses, spyware, adware, nagware, trojans, worms, and more. Anti-malware then is software designed to address malware infestations in a device. Anti-virus software is designed to address virus outbreaks or infections in a device.

- Changes to the operating system or new software are validated through an assessment process to determine any security impacts.

Mobile Devices

Tablets and smartphones are increasingly being used in the professional environment as the client platform of choice. Due to their intuitive interfaces, ease of portability, and size, mobile devices have become the platform of choice for many organizations and individuals. Additionally, many users are demanding organizations allow their personal device onto the organization's network and systems in a "bring your own device" or BYOD movement. The security architect needs to be aware of cultural shifts such as the BYOD movement and realign the security architecture of an organization accordingly while keeping the architecture aligned with business needs.

The majority of mobile devices available were not explicitly built for enterprise security or control. In many cases, they were designed with the average end-user in mind, and functionality was the top priority. The security architect must understand the devices the end-users are using and how to protect sensitive information on them. The architects could consider all of the following options when defining a mobile device security architecture, and they should also ensure that they check with whatever legal function exists in the enterprise or become familiar with whatever the current standards and laws are that are in force regarding privacy, personally identifiable information (PII), and mobile device management within their locale:

- Integration with a mobile device management (MDM) system, which allows for:
  - ▢ Remote
    - Whole device wipe
    - Account management
    - GPS/WIFI/Cellular location of the device
    - OS, application, and firmware updates
    - Application management
    - Device authentication and enrollment
    - Information archive with integrity validation for legal hold situations
  - ▢ Secure
    - Web browser
    - Virtual private network (VPN) with Web filtering or proxying
    - Organization application "store"
  - ▢ Whole device encryption with key escrow
  - ▢ "Jailbreak" or "root" access detection
- Secure encrypted container technology for organizational system access, which includes:
  - ▢ Automatic deletion of any organizational information downloaded to the device
  - ▢ VPN for container traffic
  - ▢ Secure Web browser for container
  - ▢ Secure application "store" for container
  - ▢ "Jailbreak" or "root" access detection

Server-Based Vulnerabilities

Servers present an enticing target for attackers. While hosting sensitive information and processing an organization's mission sensitive tasks, a server also supports several options, which makes an attacker's attempts more effective. The security architect should consider the following when designing server security architecture:

- Determine how remote access will be established to the server:
  - Many servers are located in data centers physically away from the operations of an organization. This requires the security architect to determine the most secure way to access the server for administration and changes.
  - The security architect should consider out of band communications such as separate networks for administration of large groups or servers. Where physical separation is not practical, logical separation should be considered.
  - Strong, multifactor authentication including one-time pads should be used to help prevent the use of brute force attacks and key logging.
  - Built-in remote access services should be evaluated to determine if they are sufficient to provide secure remote access. If they are not, they should be disabled.
- Determine how configuration management will be performed:
  - Identify the individual, group, or process responsible for change management and configuration management in the organization.
    - Ensure they are capable of monitoring and patching the server on an ongoing basis. If not, the security architect should recommend a monitoring and patching solution.
    - Identify the vulnerability management capability within the organization. If none exists, the security architect should recommend a vulnerability scanning and tracking solution.
    - Determine how updated code or new versions of software will be deployed on the server. Does a mature system development life cycle include a development, test, stage, and production promotion approach? If not the security architect should recommend a system development life cycle approach that suits the organization.
- Determine the business continuity requirements and ensure the server security architecture includes backups, fail over sites, and notification processes as determined by the mission the server supports.

Data Flow Control

The security architect must be familiar with how data flows into and out of systems. This is most often accomplished using a data flow diagram (DFD). *Figure 3.23* shows an example from the U.S. National Institute of Standards and Technology for the process of analyzing a website's link structure. The diagram breaks down the basic operations into data, processes, and windows a user or operator might see. The diagram also delineates the timing of different groups by website, session, analysis, and visualization. The security architect is interested in the controls between the various components that enforce the data flow to only the required recipients and how the communication is protected if required. The concept of least privilege should be employed to ensure data only flows to authorized recipients and processes. The architect should also review any technologies in use such as PERL, the parser, and the visualization tool kit to ensure they are supported under the existing security architecture and if not ensure they can be or find alternatives.

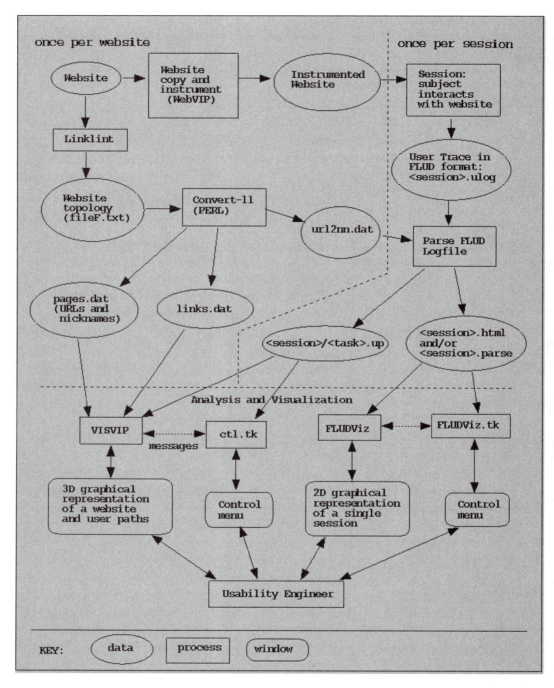

Figure 3.23 – **NIST Data Flow diagram** [49]

Database Security

Database vulnerabilities go beyond vulnerabilities in the server platform to how the data stored within the database is controlled. The security architect must be aware of several topics surrounding database security including inference, aggregation, data mining, and warehousing.

Warehousing

A data warehouse is a repository for information collected from a variety of data sources. Because of the compilation of information from many sources, data warehouses eliminate the organization's original information structures and access controls to enable sharing of that information to more levels of employees. The data stored in a data warehouse is not used for operational tasks but rather for analytical purposes. The data warehouse combines all of the data from various databases into one large data container. Because the data is collected into one central location for analysis, instead of several smaller databases, the combined data can be used by executives to make business decisions. The security architect needs to keep in mind that the old adage about "the sum being greater than the individual parts" applies here. Specifically, the focus of the security architect needs to be not just on the architecture of the data warehouse nor just on the usability of the tools used to extract and analyze data. Rather, the entire ecosystem that comprises the data warehouse needs to be considered and addressed in some way by the security architect, as the sum of the ecosystem supporting and creating the data warehouse is much bigger, and potentially much more valuable to a hacker, than the individual parts making up the data warehouse. For example, a hacker may or may not be interested in one component making up the data warehouse, such as the back end storage system or the reporting engine, but the hacker will be very interested in what those two individual parts are able to combine to create, which will be formatted, highly focused, summarized reports of data contained within the warehouse.

A current term associated with data warehouses is data marts. Data marts are smaller versions of data warehouses. While a data warehouse is meant to contain all of an organization's information, a data mart may contain the information from just a division or only about a specific topic. In most instances, the creation of a data mart is less time consuming, and thus the data can be available for analysis sooner than if a data warehouse was created.

The following tasks illustrate a simplified process of building a data warehouse:

- Feed all data into a large, high-availability, and high-integrity database that resides at the confidentiality level of the most sensitive data.
- Normalize the data. Regardless of how the data is characterized in each system, it must be structured the same when moved into the data warehouse. For example, one database could categorize birth date as "month/day/year," another as "day/month/year," and still another as "year/month/day." The data warehouse must normalize the various data categories into only one category. Normalization will also remove redundancies in the data.
- Mine the data for correlations to produce metadata.
- Sanitize and export the metadata, results of analysis of the data, to its intended users.
- Feed all new incoming data and the metadata into the data warehouse.

In traditional database administration, rules and policies are implemented to ensure the confidentiality and integrity of the database, such as defining user views and setting access permissions. Security is even more critical for data warehouses. From a security architecture perspective, rules and policies must be in place to control access to the data. This includes items such as defining the user groups and the type of data each group can access and outlining the user's security responsibilities and procedures. Another danger of data warehouses is if the physical or logical security perimeter of the database servers were breached, the unauthorized user could gain access to all of the organization's data. The security architect must ensure data flow diagrams and access controls are carefully examined to determine if information leakage or breach may be an issue.

In addition to confidentiality controls, security for the data also includes the integrity and availability of the information. For example, if the data warehouse were accidentally or intentionally destroyed, a valuable repository of the organization's historical and compiled data would also be destroyed. To avoid such a total loss, the security architect must ensure appropriate plans for backups are defined and developed, as well as the security architecture for recovery options such as hardware and software applications.

Inference

Inference is the ability to deduce (infer) sensitive or restricted information from observing available information. Essentially, users may be able to determine unauthorized information from what information they can access and may never need to directly access unauthorized data. For example, if a user is reviewing authorized information about patients, such as the medications they have been prescribed, the user may be able to determine the illness. Inference is one of the hardest threats to control, and the security architect will need to apply a deep understanding of the business models surrounding an organization's mission to mitigate this risk. In order to gain this level of understanding, the security architects need to ensure that they plan to spend adequate time with the data owner, process owner, and/or business owner, as well as users to "walk a mile in their shoes." Specifically, what the security architect needs to accomplish through the investment of this time is to gain a better understanding of the usage scenarios that each stakeholder brings to the system in question and what the intricacies of those scenarios are in order to perform a risk analysis against them, and as a result, he or she will gain a better understanding of the potential threats and vulnerabilities to be addressed as part of any defenses that may be planned and implemented.

Aggregation

Aggregation is combining non-sensitive data from separate sources to create sensitive information. For example, a user takes two or more publicly available pieces of data and combines them to form a classified piece of data that then becomes unauthorized for that user. Thus, the combined data sensitivity can be greater than the sensitivity of individual parts. For years, mathematicians have been struggling unsuccessfully with the problem of determining when the aggregation of data results in data at a higher classification. The security architect must work with the data architect to understand the fields and types of information present in a database. The security architect must understand the possible combinations of information including which combinations may result in an escalation of sensitivity.

Data Mining

Data mining is a process of discovering information in data warehouses by running queries on the data. A large repository of data is required to perform data mining. Data mining is used to reveal hidden relationships, patterns, and trends in the data warehouse. Data mining is based on a series of analytical techniques taken from the fields of mathematics, statistics, cybernetics, and genetics. The techniques are used independently and in cooperation with one another to uncover information from data warehouses.

There are several advantages to using data-mining including the ability to provide better information to managers that outlines the organization's trends, its customers, and the competitive marketplace for its industry. There are also disadvantages, especially for security. The detailed data about individuals obtained through data mining might risk a violation of privacy. The risk increases when private information is stored on the Web or an unprotected area of the network, and thus it becomes available to unauthorized users. In addition, the integrity of the data may be at risk. Because a large amount of data must be collected, the chance of errors through human data entry may result in inaccurate relationships or patterns. These errors are referred to as data contamination. The security architect should reference integrity models such as Clark-Wilson and Biba when determining data mining security procedures.

Large Scale Parallel Data Systems

As computer systems become more pervasive and computation spreads over the network, parallel processing issues become engrained into a variety of applications. In computer security, intrusion detection and prevention are outstanding challenges. In the case of network intrusion detection, data is collected at distributed sites and must be analyzed rapidly for signaling intrusion. The infeasibility of collecting this data at a central location for analysis requires effective parallel and distributed algorithms. In the area of cryptography, some of the most spectacular applications of Internet-based parallel computing have focused on factoring extremely large integers.

Embedded systems increasingly rely on distributed control algorithms for accomplishing a variety of tasks. A modern automobile consists of large numbers of processors communicating to perform complex tasks for optimizing handling and performance. In such systems, traditional parallel and distributed algorithms are frequently used.

According to IDC, from 2005 to 2020 the digital universe will grow by a factor of 300 – from 130 exabytes to more than 5,200 gigabytes for every man, woman, and child in 2020. Between now and 2020, the digital universe will double every two years.[50] Where we are today versus where we have come from is a very telling narrative with regards to large scale parallel data systems and the reason that they have come into existence in the first place, big data.

The first warning about the growth of knowledge as a storage and retrieval problem came in 1944, when Fremont Rider, a Wesleyan University librarian, estimated that American University Libraries were doubling in size every sixteen years. Given this growth rate, Rider estimated that the Yale Library in 2040 would have "approximately 200,000,000 volumes, which will occupy over 6,000 miles of shelves ... [requiring] a cataloging staff of over six thousand persons."[51]

In 1948, Claude Shannon published "A Mathematical Theory of Communication," which established a framework for determining the minimal data requirements to transmit information over noisy (imperfect) channels.[52] It followed Nyquist's "Certain Factors Affecting

---

50   IDC IVIEW - THE DIGITAL UNIVERSE IN 2020: Big Data, Bigger Digital Shadows, and Biggest Growth in the Far East. December 2012. By John Gantz and David Reinsel. http://idcdocserv.com/1414 (Page 1).

51   Freemont Rider, The Scholar and the Future of the Research Library, New York, 1944. Pages 10 -12.

52   http://cm.bell-labs.com/cm/ms/what/shannonday/shannon1948.pdf

Telegraph Speed," which enabled us to sample analog signals and represent them digitally, which is the foundation of modern data processing.[53]

In 1956, the concept of virtual memory was developed by German physicist Fritz-Rudolf Güntsch as an idea that treated finite storage as infinite. Storage, managed by integrated hardware and software to hide the details from the user, permitted us to process data without being subjected to hardware memory constraints. Within approximately ten years, the formalized constructs and architectures required to design, develop, and implement centralized computing systems had emerged.

In 1970, Edgar F. Codd, a mathematician working at the IBM Research Lab, published a paper showing how information stored in large databases could be accessed without knowing how the information was structured or where it resided in the database.[54] This gave rise to the Relational Database, which provided a level of data independence that allowed users to access information without having to master details of the physical structure of a database.

In 1985, Barry Devlin and Paul Murphy defined an architecture for business reporting and analysis, which became a foundation of data warehousing. At the heart of that architecture, and data warehousing in general, is the need for high-quality, consistent storage of historically complete and accurate data.[55] In 1992, Crystal Reports created the first simple database report using Windows. These reports allowed businesses to create a single report from a variety of data sources with minimum written code. In 1996, R.J.T. Morris and B.J. Truskowski published their article, "The Evolution of Storage Systems".[56]

In July of 1997, the term "big data" was used for the first time in an article by NASA researchers Michael Cox and David Ellsworth. The pair claimed that the rise of data was becoming an issue for current computer systems. This was also known as the "problem of big data".[57] In August of 1997, Michael Lesk published "How much information is there in the world?" He concluded that "There may be a few thousand petabytes of information all told; and the production of tape and disk will reach that level by the year 2000. So in only a few years, (a) we will be able [to] save everything–no information will have to be thrown out, and (b) the typical piece of information will never be looked at by a human being." [58]

In 1999, Peter Lyman and Hal R. Varian published the first study that quantified, in computer storage terms, the total amount of new and original information created in the world annually. The study was titled "How Much Information?" [59] In February of 2001, Gartner Analyst Doug Laney published "3D Data Management: Controlling Data Volume, Velocity, and Variety," which led to the definition of the "3V's" that form the basis of the dimensions of big data as we know it today.[60]

---

53 http://alcatel-lucent.com/bstj/vol03-1924/articles/bstj3-2-324.pdf

54 http://www.seas.upenn.edu/~zives/03f/cis550/codd.pdf

55 http://9sight.com/EBIS_Devlin_&_Murphy_1988.pdf

56 http://signallake.com/innovation/morris.pdf

57 http://www.nas.nasa.gov/assets/pdf/techreports/1997/nas-97-010.pdf

58 http://www.lesk.com/mlesk/ksg97/ksg.html

59 http://www2.sims.berkeley.edu/research/projects/how-much-info/

60 http://blogs.gartner.com/doug-laney/files/2012/01/ad949-3D-Data-Management-Controlling-Data-Volume-Velocity-and-Variety.pdf

In 2004, Google published a paper on a process called MapReduce.[61] The MapReduce framework provides a parallel processing model and associated implementation to process large amounts of data. With MapReduce, queries are split and distributed across parallel nodes and processed in parallel (the Map step). The results are then gathered and delivered (the Reduce step). The framework became very successful, so an implementation of the MapReduce framework was adopted by an Apache open source project named Hadoop. Hadoop was created in 2006, and it brought about an open source solution for storing and processing data that enabled distributed parallel processing of huge amounts of data across inexpensive servers that both store and process the data and can scale without limits.[62]

In December of 2008, a group of computer science researchers published a paper titled "Big Data Computing: Creating Revolutionary Breakthroughs in Commerce, Science, and Society." The article states: "Big-data computing is perhaps the biggest innovation in computing in the last decade. We have only begun to see its potential to collect, organize, and process data in all walks of life. A modest investment by the federal government could greatly accelerate its development and deployment."[63]

In May of 2009, Gartner predicts that enterprise data would grow by 650% over the next 5 years. In response, Jon Reed says "if a Google type of company can present a way of pulling together all this unstructured information in a cloud-based environment, and then somehow connect that to a structured platform – uniting the unstructured and structured information – then that's a big, big thing."[64] In 2011, the top Business Intelligence trends emerged with cloud computing, data visualization, predictive analysis, and big data leading the way.[65]

The article "Critical Questions for Big Data", published in the Information, Communications, and Society Journal in March of 2012, defines big data as "a cultural, technological, and scholarly phenomenon that rests on the interplay of:

1. **Technology** – Maximizing computation power and algorithmic accuracy to gather, analyze, link, and compare large datasets.

2. **Analysis** – Drawing on large datasets to identify patterns in order to make economic, social, technical, and legal claims.

3. **Mythology** – The widespread belief that large datasets offer a higher form of intelligence and knowledge that can generate insights that were previously impossible, with the aura of truth, objectivity, and accuracy."[66]

In 2013, we see the rise of features such as the ability to perform federated queries that give users the ability to take a query and provide solutions based on information from many different sources, and the ability to generate reports from in-memory databases, which will provide faster and more predictable performance. In 2014, while 47% of organizations surveyed by Gartner plan to move their core ERP systems to the cloud within five years, Cloud ERP is actually accelerating at an even faster-than-predicted rate due to two-tier ERP strategies that

---

61 http://static.googleusercontent.com/media/research.google.com/en/us/archive/mapreduce-osdi04.pdf

62 http://www.cloudera.com/content/dam/cloudera/Resources/PDF/Olson_IQT_Quarterly_Spring_2010.pdf

63 http://www.cra.org/ccc/files/docs/init/Big_Data.pdf

64 http://www.cio.com/article/508023/The_Future_of_ERP_Part_II

65 http://blogs.enterprisemanagement.com/shawnrogers/2011/01/11/top-10-trends-in-business-intelligence-and-analytics-for-2011/

66 http://www.tandfonline.com/doi/pdf/10.1080/1369118X.2012.678878

3

Security Engineering

extend a company's legacy ERP system while allowing them to move into new markets and scale at a faster rate.[67]

The world's effective capacity to exchange information through telecommunication networks was 281 petabytes in 1986, 471 petabytes in 1993, 2.2 exabytes in 2000, 65 exabytes in 2007, and it is predicted that the amount of traffic flowing over the Internet will reach 667 exabytes annually by 2014.[68] It is estimated that one-third of the globally stored information is in the form of alphanumeric text and still image data, which is the format most useful for most big data applications.[69]

Most computing systems, such as cluster computing, grid computing, cloud computing, the Internet, telecommunication networks, Cyber-Physical Systems (CPS), and Machine-to-Machine communication networks (M2M), are parallel and distributed systems. While providing improved expandability, manageability, efficiency, and reliability, parallel and distributed systems increase their security weaknesses to an unprecedented scale. As the system devices are widely connected, their vulnerabilities are shared by the entire system. The security architect needs to be aware of the "force multiplier" effects that these systems bring to the enterprise with regards to vulnerabilities, threats, and risk, as well as the challenges they pose to confidentiality, integrity, and availability of data. The distributed nature of these systems coupled with the growing reliance of the enterprise on them to store and manage any type of data that exists and the lack of an integrated solution to manage the data and the systems with a common set of policies and controls poses significant challenges for the traditional elements of systems architecture, as well as the areas of access control and identity management.

The big data phenomenon is driven by the intersection of three trends:

- Mountains of data that contain valuable information
- The abundance of cheap commodity computing resources
- "Free" analytics tools (very low to non-existent barriers to acquire)

The last item often raises security concerns when one is talking about the security of big data environments. Without knowing where many of these tool sets have come from, how they are architected, and who is behind them, as well as how they are being deployed and utilized within the enterprise, the security architect is faced with a significant challenge with regards to data confidentiality and integrity. The addition of distributed computing architectures such as cloud-based systems that allow end point access to data on demand, from anywhere that a network connection can be accessed, adds to the myriad of challenges being faced by security architects.

These systems use many nodes for distributed data storage and management. They store multiple copies of data across multiple nodes. This provides the benefits of fail-safe operation in the event any single node fails, and it means the data queries move to the data, where processing resources are available. It is this distributed cluster of data nodes cooperating with each other to handle data management and data queries that makes big data so potentially valuable for enterprise architectures, but at the same time it presents such unique challenges to the security of the enterprise.

---

67   http://www.forbes.com/sites/louiscolumbus/2014/02/07/why-cloud-erp-adoption-is-faster-than-gartner-predicts/

68   http://www.sciencemag.org/content/332/6025/60

69   http://martinhilbert.net/WhatsTheContent_Hilbert.pdf

The essential characteristics of big data, the things that allow it to handle data management and processing requirements that outstrip previous data management systems, such as volume, data velocity, distributed architecture and parallel processing, are what make securing these systems all the more difficult. The clusters are somewhat open and self-organizing, and they allow users to communicate with multiple data nodes simultaneously. Validating which data nodes and which clients should have access to information is difficult. The elastic nature of big data means new nodes are automatically meshed into the cluster, sharing data and query results to handle client tasks.

The security architect faces challenges in the areas of trust, privacy, and general security. In the area of trust related issues, items such as key verification, mitigation of trust-based DoS attacks, and content leakage detection within trusted networks may need to be addressed. Privacy issues may include remote authentication schemes for wireless network access to data, traffic masking to obfuscate data, anonymization of large scale datasets, and decentralized access control solutions for cloud-based data access. General security challenges may span a wide range of issues and concerns such as response mechanisms in the face of fast spreading/fast acting intrusion vectors, the existence of inconsistent authorization policies and/or user credentials within distributed databases accessed by cloud-based systems, and the concerns associated with securely, efficiently, and flexibly sharing data using public key cryptosystems.

Distributed Systems

Distributed systems are the opposite of centralized systems like mainframes and thin client implementations. Traditional client/server architectures are the most common example of a distributed system. In a traditional client/server architecture, responsibilities for processing have been balanced between centralized servers providing services to multiple clients and client machines that focus on user interaction and standalone processing where appropriate. For the most part, servers are responsible for serving, meaning that they provide services that will be leveraged by the clients in the environment. Clients are the primary consumers of server services, while also hosting services of their own primarily for their own individual use.

In distributed environments, users log into their own computer and data is saved locally or remotely at various sites. There is no central authority that administers user authentications and accounts or manages data storage. No central server is necessary, although servers may have an assortment of roles in such systems. Distributed environments support a wide range of diverse software applications, real-time data access, and varied media formats and data storage. In addition, distributed systems support diverse devices, such as desktops and laptop computers, cell phones, or other kinds of handheld devices. Finally, because there may be a wide range of resources accessed, updated, and stored, there needs to be a way to track user interactions with the system.

A distributed environment will typically need to share common protocols and interfaces. For example, file-sharing networks use a common or universal file format (e.g., network file system [NFS]) to allow an unknown array of files to be stored, recognized, and exchanged by any authorized user on the network. For more functional software, such as gaming or instant messaging, all involved users must have a common software application. This software is obtained in diverse ways, including propagating software around the network from one user to another.

3

Security Engineering

Peer-to-peer systems are another type of distributed environment. These support peer-to-peer exchanges of data and software, typically with the minimal involvement of a centralized authority. Rather, each individual, or peer, logs on and is connected to all other peers in a network. This permits the viewing and exchanging of files with any other peer. Although many peer-to-peer implementations use central servers to set up the interconnected network of users, many peer-to-peer implementations use dynamic peer discovery. This enables them to discover all other peers connected to the system and running the same software. This collection of interconnected users provides a new type of functionality that does not need a central authority to negotiate transactions or store data.

One challenge of distributed systems is the need to coordinate resources that may be distributed on numerous systems. This is accomplished through common structures such as a central naming repository, which generates universally unique identifiers (UUIDs). When a user requests a resource, a search is done within a potentially large network to find a particular resource, thus requiring a precise specification of the resource.

However, authorization may be the biggest challenge, as there is no central authority to trust. It is also significantly more difficult to control security vulnerabilities in a distributed environment, although such vulnerabilities may be less pervasive. Each system has some responsibility for enforcing security and protecting themselves from compromise.

Grid Computing

Grid computing is the sharing of CPU and other resources across a network in such a manner that all machines function as one large computer. Grid computers are often used for processor intensive tasks, which are suitable to be processed by parallel tasks. Grid computing is often confused with "cluster computing." Both involve using two or more computers to solve problems, but grid computing is heterogeneous while cluster computing is homogenous. Grid computers can have different operating systems, hardware, and software. Grid systems are also associated with multi-tasking (a desktop computer may be part of a grid with spare CPU resources and also serve normal desktop functions), whereas a cluster is devoted to a single task. Finally, clusters are most often physically close together with a fast bus or network connecting the nodes, while a grid is geographically dispersed.

Given the dispersed and shared nature of grid computing, the security architect involved in the design of a grid system should keep in mind some of the vulnerabilities this leads to:

- Unless dedicated private communication lines are funded between nodes, much of the traffic for the grid will flow over public Internet conduits. Encryption of information between nodes or the use of VPN technology may provide mitigation for this vulnerability.
- Given the geographic distance a grid has between nodes, user authentication may be completely logical. Therefore, strong logical authentication controls must be implemented to ensure only authorized users access the grid. Consider specifying Kerberos, PKI, or multifactor authentication methods as part of the grid's security architecture.
- Grid node software must be examined if joining a grid and designed security if hosting a grid. Special attention should be directed towards how the grid application isolates grid computing activity from other system activities.

Cloud Computing

Cloud computing is a vague and ambiguous term. Many vendors market their product as cloud although it may not match what another vendor considers cloud. For the sake of discussion, cloud computing has been formally defined by U.S. NIST as:

> *".. a model for enabling ubiquitous, convenient, on-demand network access to a shared pool of configurable computing resources (e.g., networks, servers, storage, applications, and services) that can be rapidly provisioned and released with minimal management effort or service provider interaction. This cloud model is composed of five essential characteristics, three service models, and four deployment models."* [70]

NIST defines the five essential characteristics of cloud computing as:

- **On-Demand Self-Service** – A consumer can unilaterally provision computing capabilities, such as server time and network storage, as needed automatically without requiring human interaction with each service provider.

- **Broad Network Access** – Capabilities are available over the network and accessed through standard mechanisms that promote use by heterogeneous thin or thick client platforms (e.g., mobile phones, tablets, laptops, and workstations).

- **Resource Pooling** – The provider's computing resources are pooled to serve multiple consumers using a multi-tenant model, with different physical and virtual resources dynamically assigned and reassigned according to consumer demand. There is a sense of location independence in that the customer generally has no control or knowledge over the exact location of the provided resources but may be able to specify location at a higher level of abstraction (e.g., country, state, or datacenter). Examples of resources include storage, processing, memory, and network bandwidth.

- **Rapid Elasticity** – Capabilities can be elastically provisioned and released, in some cases automatically, to scale rapidly outward and inward commensurate with demand. To the consumer, the capabilities available for provisioning often appear to be unlimited and can be appropriated in any quantity at any time.

- **Measured Service** – Cloud systems automatically control and optimize resource use by leveraging a metering capability at some level of abstraction appropriate to the type of service (e.g., storage, processing, bandwidth, and active user accounts). Resource usage can be monitored, controlled, and reported, providing transparency for both the provider and consumer of the utilized service." [71]

NIST identifies three service models that represent different types of cloud services available:

- **Software as a Service (SaaS)** – The capability provided to the consumer is to use the provider's applications running on a cloud infrastructure. The applications are accessible from various client devices through either a thin client interface, such as a Web browser (e.g., Web-based email), or a program

---

70   Mell, Peter, and Timothy Grance. US National Institute of Standards and Technology, "The NIST Definition of Cloud Computing." Last modified Sept 2011. http://csrc.nist.gov/publications/nistpubs/800-145/SP800-145.pdf (Page 2-3)

71   Mell, Peter, and Timothy Grance. US National Institute of Standards and Technology, "The NIST Definition of Cloud Computing." Last modified Sept 2011. http://csrc.nist.gov/publications/nistpubs/800-145/SP800-145.pdf (Page 2-3)

interface. The consumer does not manage or control the underlying cloud infrastructure including network, servers, operating systems, storage, or even individual application capabilities, with the possible exception of limited user-specific application configuration settings.

- **Platform as a Service (PaaS)** – The capability provided to the consumer is to deploy onto the cloud infrastructure consumer-created or acquired applications created using programming languages, libraries, services, and tools supported by the provider. The consumer does not manage or control the underlying cloud infrastructure including network, servers, operating systems, or storage, but he or she has control over the deployed applications and possibly configuration settings for the application-hosting environment.

- **Infrastructure as a Service (IaaS)** – The capability provided to the consumer is to provision processing, storage, networks, and other fundamental computing resources where the consumer is able to deploy and run arbitrary software, which can include operating systems and applications. The consumer does not manage or control the underlying cloud infrastructure but has control over operating systems, storage, and deployed applications, and possibly limited control of select networking components (e.g., host firewalls). [72]

Finally, NIST describes four different deployment models:

- **Private Cloud** – The cloud infrastructure is provisioned for exclusive use by a single organization comprising multiple consumers (e.g., business units). It may be owned, managed, and operated by the organization, a third party, or some combination of them, and it may exist on or off premises.

- **Community Cloud** – The cloud infrastructure is provisioned for exclusive use by a specific community of consumers from organizations that have shared concerns (e.g., mission, security requirements, policy, and compliance considerations). It may be owned, managed, and operated by one or more of the organizations in the community, a third party, or some combination of them, and it may exist on or off premises.

- **Public Cloud** – The cloud infrastructure is provisioned for open use by the general public. It may be owned, managed, and operated by a business, academic, or government organization, or some combination of them. It exists on the premises of the cloud provider.

- **Hybrid Cloud** – The cloud infrastructure is a composition of two or more distinct cloud infrastructures (private, community, or public) that remain unique entities but are bound together by standardized or proprietary technology that enables data and application portability (e.g., cloud bursting for load balancing between clouds)." [73]

As more organizations are leveraging SaaS, PaaS, and IaaS, the security architect must be aware of the limited ability he or she has to define specific security controls and functions. As cloud computing moves from infrastructure to platform to software, the responsibility to implement effective security controls shifts away from the organization and towards the

---

72   Mell, Peter, and Timothy Grance. US National Institute of Standards and Technology, "The NIST Definition of Cloud Computing." Last modified Sept 2011. http://csrc.nist.gov/publications/nistpubs/800-145/SP800-145.pdf (Page 2-3)

73   Mell, Peter, and Timothy Grance. US National Institute of Standards and Technology, "The NIST Definition of Cloud Computing." Last modified Sept 2011. http://csrc.nist.gov/publications/nistpubs/800-145/SP800-145.pdf (Page 3.)

cloud service provider. Therefore, as cloud service models are being designed, the security architect must understand which controls may be modified or added and which may need compensating controls.

For example, assume an online retailer has decided to use Infrastructure as a Service to store their credit card holder's information. The retailer has several PCI-DSS requirements they must adhere to including encrypting the cardholder's information when in storage. As the cloud service provider is not offering encrypted storage, the security architect may advise encrypting the information prior to transmission of the cloud storage service. If the retailer instead decided to use a SaaS option in the form of a pre-designed and ready to use storefront software, the approach would be different. The security architect would ensure as part of the contracting process the retailer has passed a PCI-DSS assessment and has appropriate encryption of cardholder information in place.

Cryptographic Systems

Encryption Concepts

It is important the security professional understands several key cryptographic concepts and definitions. These terms should be thoroughly understood by the information security professional and are used frequently in the operational environment of most organizations' security function.

Key Concepts and Definitions

- **Key Clustering** – When different encryption keys generate the same ciphertext from the same plaintext message.
- **Synchronous** – Each encryption or decryption request is performed immediately.
- **Asynchronous** – Encrypt/Decrypt requests are processed in queues. A key benefit of asynchronous cryptography is utilization of hardware devices and multiprocessor systems for cryptographic acceleration.
- **Hash Function** – A hash function is a one-way mathematical operation that reduces a message or data file into a smaller fixed length output, or hash value. If one compares the hash value computed by the sender with the hash value computed by the receiver over the original file, unauthorized changes to the file can be detected, assuming they both used the same hash function. Ideally there should never be more than one unique hash for a given input and one hash exclusively for a given input.
- **Digital Signatures** – Provide authentication of a sender and integrity of a sender's message. A message is input into a hash function. Then the hash value is encrypted using the private key of the sender. The result of these two steps yields a digital signature. The receiver can verify the digital signature by decrypting the hash value using the signer's public key, then perform the same hash computation over the message, and then compare the hash values for an exact match. If the hash values are the same, then the signature is valid.
- **Asymmetric** is a term used in cryptography in which two different but mathematically related keys are used, where one key is used to encrypt and another is used to decrypt. This term is most commonly used in reference to Public Key Infrastructure (PKI).

3

Security Engineering

- A **Digital Certificate** is an electronic document that contains the name of an organization or individual, the business address, the digital signature of the certificate authority issuing the certificate, the certificate holder's public key, a serial number, and the expiration date. The certificate is used to identify the certificate holder when conducting electronic transactions.

- **Certificate Authority (CA)** is an entity trusted by one or more users as an authority in a network that issues, revokes, and manages digital certificates.

- **Registration Authority (RA)** performs certificate registration services on behalf of a CA. The RA, a single purpose server, is responsible for the accuracy of the information contained in a certificate request. The RA is also expected to perform user validation before issuing a certificate request.

- **Plaintext** or **Cleartext** is the message in its natural format. Plaintext is human readable and is extremely vulnerable from a confidentiality perspective.

- **Ciphertext** or **Cryptogram** is the altered form of a plaintext message, so as to be unreadable for anyone except the intended recipients. An attacker seeing ciphertext would be unable to easily read the message or to determine its content.

- The **Cryptosystem** represents the entire cryptographic operation. This includes the algorithm, the key, and key management functions.

- **Encryption** is the process of converting the message from its plaintext to ciphertext. It is also referred to as enciphering. The two terms are used interchangeably in the literature and have similar meanings.

- **Decryption** is the reverse process from encryption. It is the process of converting a ciphertext message into plaintext through the use of the cryptographic algorithm and key that was used to do the original encryption. This term is also used interchangeably with the term decipher.

- The **Key** or **Cryptovariable** is the input that controls the operation of the cryptographic algorithm. It determines the behavior of the algorithm and permits the reliable encryption and decryption of the message. There are both secret and public keys used in cryptographic algorithms.

- **Nonrepudiation** is a security service by which evidence is maintained so that the sender and the recipient of data cannot deny having participated in the communication. Individually, it is referred to as the "nonrepudiation of origin" and "nonrepudiation of receipt."

- An **Algorithm** is a mathematical function that is used in the encryption and decryption processes. It may be quite simple or extremely complex.

- **Cryptanalysis** is the study of techniques for attempting to defeat cryptographic techniques and, more generally, information security services.

- **Cryptology** is the science that deals with hidden, disguised, or encrypted communications. It embraces communications security and communications intelligence.

- **Collision** occurs when a hash function generates the same output for different inputs.

- **Key Space** represents the total number of possible values of keys in a cryptographic algorithm or other security measure, such as a password. For example, a 20-bit key would have a key space of 1,048,576.

- **Work Factor** represents the time and effort required to break a protective measure.

■ An **Initialization Vector (IV)** is a non-secret binary vector used as the initializing input algorithm for the encryption of a plaintext block sequence to increase security by introducing additional cryptographic variance and to synchronize cryptographic equipment.

■ **Encoding** is the action of changing a message into another format through the use of a code. This is often done by taking a plaintext message and converting it into a format that can be transmitted via radio or some other medium, and it is usually used for message integrity instead of secrecy. An example would be to convert a message to Morse code.

■ **Decoding** is the reverse process from encoding – converting the encoded message back into its plaintext format.

■ **Transposition** or **Permutation** is the process of reordering the plaintext to hide the message. Transposition may look like this:

Plaintext	Transposition Algorithm	Ciphertext
HIDE	REORDER SEQUENCE 2143	IHED

■ **Substitution** is the process of exchanging one letter or byte for another. This operation may look like this:

Plaintext	Substitution Process	Ciphertext
HIDE	Shift alphabet three places	KLGH

■ The **SP-Network** is the process described by Claude Shannon used in most block ciphers to increase their strength. SP stands for substitution and permutation (transposition), and most block ciphers do a series of repeated substitutions and permutations to add confusion and diffusion to the encryption process. An SP-network uses a series of S-boxes to handle the substitutions of the blocks of data. Breaking a plaintext block into a subset of smaller S-boxes makes it easier to handle the computations.

■ **Confusion** is provided by mixing (changing) the key values used during the repeated rounds of encryption. When the key is modified for each round, it provides added complexity that the attacker would encounter.

■ **Diffusion** is provided by mixing up the location of the plaintext throughout the ciphertext. Through transposition, the location of the first character of the plaintext may change several times during the encryption process, and this makes the cryptanalysis process much more difficult.

■ The **Avalanche Effect** is an important consideration in all cryptography used to design algorithms where a minor change in either the key or the plaintext will have a significant change in the resulting ciphertext. This is also a feature of a strong-hashing algorithm.

Foundational Concepts

The information security professional must also be familiar with the fundamental concepts and methods related to cryptography. Methods and concepts range from different ways of using cryptographic technologies to encrypt information to different standard encryption systems used in industry.

High Work Factor

The average amount of effort or work required to break an encryption system, that is to say decrypt a message without having the entire encryption key or to find a secret key given all or part of a ciphertext, is referred to as the work factor of the cryptographic system. This is measured in some units such as hours of computing time on one or more given computer systems or a cost in dollars of breaking the encryption. If the work factor is sufficiently high, the encryption system is considered to be practically or economically unbreakable, and it is sometimes referred to as "economically infeasible" to break. Communication systems using encryption schemes that are economically infeasible to break are generally considered secure. The work factor required to break a given cryptographic system can vary over time due to advancements in technology, such as improvements in the speed and capacity of computers. For example, while a 40-bit secret key encryption scheme can currently be broken by a fast personal computer in less than a year or by a room full of personal computers in a short amount of time, future advances in computer technology will likely substantially reduce this work factor.

Methods of Cryptography

Several common methods of cryptography exist including stream-based and block ciphers. The information security professional must have a basic understanding of both to ensure further understanding of encryption implementations.

Stream-Based Ciphers

There are two primary methods of encrypting data: the stream and block methods. When a cryptosystem performs its encryption on a bit-by-bit basis, it is called a stream-based cipher. This is the method most commonly associated with streaming applications, such as voice or video transmission Wireless Equivalent Privacy, or WEP, uses a streaming cipher, RC4, but it is not considered secure due to number of weaknesses that expose the encryption key to an attacker - weak key size among other well-known vulnerabilities in WEP implementation. Newer wireless cryptography implements block ciphers such as Advanced Encryption Standard (AES), discussed later, which provide stronger security. The cryptographic operation for a stream-based cipher is to mix the plaintext with a keystream that is generated by the cryptosystem. The mixing operation is usually an exclusive-or (XOR) operation – a very fast mathematical operation.

As seen in *Figure 3.24*, the plaintext is XORed with a seemingly random keystream to generate ciphertext. It is seemingly random because the generation of the keystream is usually controlled by the key. If the key could not produce the same keystream for the purposes of decryption of the ciphertext, then it would be impossible to ever decrypt the message.

Plaintext	Encryption Keystream	Ciphertext
A	XOR randomly generated keystream	$
0101 0001	0111 0011	=0010 0010

Figure 3.24 – **Cryptographic operation for a Stream-Based cipher**

The exclusive-or process is a key part of many cryptographic algorithms. It is a simple binary operation that adds two values together. If the two values are the same, 0 + 0 or 1 + 1, then the output is always a 0; however, if the two values are different, 1 + 0 or 0 + 1, then the output is a 1.

From the example above, the following operation is the result:

	Input plaintext		0101 0001
+	Keystream	+	0111 0011
	Output of XOR		0010 0010

A stream-based cipher relies primarily on substitution – the substitution of one character or bit for another in a manner governed by the cryptosystem and controlled by the cipher key. For a stream-based cipher to operate securely, it is necessary to follow certain rules for the operation and implementation of the cipher:

1. **Keystream should not be linearly related to the cryptovariable** – knowledge of the keystream output value does not disclose the cryptovariable (encryption/decryption key).
2. **Statistically Unpredictable** – given n successive bits from the keystream, it is not possible to predict the n + 1st bit with a probability different from 1/2.
3. **Statistically Unbiased** – there should be as many 0s as 1s, as many 00s as 01s, 10s, 11s, etc.
4. Long periods without repetition.
5. **Functional Complexity** – each keystream bit should depend on most or all of the cryptovariable bits.

The keystream must be strong enough to not be easily guessed or predictable. In time, the keystream will repeat, and that period (or length of the repeating segment of the keystream) must be long enough to be difficult to calculate. If a keystream is too short, then it is susceptible to frequency analysis or other language-specific attacks. The implementation of the stream-based cipher is probably the most important factor in the strength of the cipher – this applies to nearly every crypto product and, in fact, to security overall. Some important factors in the implementation are to ensure that the key management processes are secure and cannot be readily compromised or intercepted by an attacker.

Block Ciphers

A block cipher operates on blocks or chunks of text. As plaintext is fed into the cryptosystem, it is divided into blocks of a preset size – often a multiple of the ASCII character size – 64, 128, 192 bits, etc. Most block ciphers use a combination of substitution and transposition to perform their operations. This makes a block cipher relatively stronger than most stream-based ciphers but more computationally intensive and usually more expensive to implement. This is also why many stream-based ciphers are implemented in hardware, whereas a block-based cipher is implemented in software.

3

Security Engineering

Initialization Vectors (IV) – Why They Are Needed

Because messages may be of any length, and because encrypting the same plaintext using the same key always produces the same ciphertext as described below, several "modes of operation" have been invented, which allow block ciphers to provide confidentiality for messages of arbitrary length (See *Figure 3.25* for block cipher mode descriptions). The use of various modes answers the need for unpredictability into the keystream such that even if the same key is used to encrypt the same message, the ciphertext will still be different each time.

Mode	How It Works	Usage
Electronic Code Book (ECB)	In ECB mode, each block is encrypted independently, allowing randomly accessed files to be encrypted and still accessed without having to process the file in a linear encryption fashion.	Any file with non-repeating blocks (less than 64 bits in length), such as transmission of a DES key or short executables.
Cipher Block Chaining (CBC)	In CBC mode, the result of encrypting one block of data is fed back into the process to encrypt the next block of data.	Data at rest, such as stand-alone encrypted files on users' hard drives.
Cipher Feedback (CFB)	In CFB mode, the cipher is used as a keystream generator rather than for confidentiality. Each block of keystream comes from encrypting the previous block of ciphertext.	Retired due to the delay imposed by encrypting each block of keystream before proceeding.
Output Feedback (OFB)	In OFB mode, the keystream is generated independently of the message	Retired due to Avalanche problems. Was uses in Pay-Per-View applications.
Counter (CTR)	Uses the formula Encrypt (Base+N) as a keystream generator where Base is a starting 64 bit number and N is a simple incrementing function.	Used where high speed or random access encryption is needed. Examples are WPA2 and the Content Scrambling System.

Source –

Tiller, J.S., Message authentication, in Information Security Management Handbook, 5th ed., Tipton, H.F. and Krause, M., Eds., Auerbach Publications, New York, 2004. With permission.

Figure 3.25 – **Basic Block Cipher Modes**

To illustrate why an IV is needed when using block ciphers, consider how they are used in various modes of operation using block ciphers. The simplest mode is the Electronic Code Book (ECB) mode where the plaintext is divided into blocks and each block is encrypted separately. However, in the Cipher-Block Chaining (CBC) mode, each block of plaintext is XORed with the previous ciphertext block before being encrypted. In the ECB mode, the same plaintext will encrypt to the same ciphertext for the same key. This reveals patterns in the code.

In the CBC mode, each block is XORed with the result of the encryption of the previous block. This hides patterns. However, two similar plaintexts that have been encrypted using the same key will yield the same ciphertext up to the block containing the first difference. This problem can be avoided by adding an IV block, which starts the keystream randomization process for the first real block, to the plaintext. This will make each ciphertext unique, even when similar plaintext is encrypted with the same key in the CBC mode. There is no need for the IV to be secret, in most cases, but it is important that it is never reused with the same key. Reusing an IV leaks some information about the first block of plaintext and about any common prefix shared by the two messages. Therefore, the IV must be randomly generated at encryption time.

Key Length

Key length is another important aspect of key management to consider when generating cryptographic keys. Key length is the size of a key, usually measured in bits or bytes, which a cryptographic algorithm used in ciphering or deciphering protected information. As discussed earlier, keys are used to control how an algorithm operates so that only the correct key can decipher the information. The resistance to successful attacks against the key and the algorithm, aspects of their cryptographic security, is of concern when choosing key lengths. An algorithm's key length is distinct from its cryptographic security. Cryptographic security is a logarithmic measure of the fastest known computational attack on the algorithm, also measured in bits. The security of an algorithm cannot exceed its key length. Therefore, it is possible to have a very long key and yet it provides low security. As an example, three-key (56 bits per key) Triple DES (i.e., Triple Data Encryption Algorithm aka TDEA) can have a key length of 168 bits but, due to the meet-in-the-middle attack (discussed later), the effective security that it provides is at most 112 bits. However, most symmetric algorithms are designed to have security equal to their key length. A natural inclination is to use the longest key possible, which may make the key more difficult to break. However, the longer the key, the more computationally expensive the encrypting and decrypting process can be. The goal is to make breaking the key cost more (in terms of effort, time, and resources) than the worth of the information or mission being protected and, if possible, not a penny more (to do more would not be economically sound).

Block Size

The block size of a block cipher, like key length, has a direct bearing on the security of the key. Block ciphers produce a fixed length block of ciphertext. However, since the data being encrypted are arbitrary number of bytes, the ciphertext block size may not come out to be a full block. This is solved by padding the plaintext up to the block size before encryption and unpadding after decryption. The padding algorithm is to calculate the smallest nonzero number of bytes, say N, which must be suffixed to the plaintext to bring it up to a multiple of the block size.

Encryption Systems

Various systems exist to encrypt and decrypt information. Many share common characteristics such as the ability to use a null cipher and substitution cipher. Many of these characteristics were implemented to enhance use cases and interoperability. The security architect, professional, and practitioner all should have a working knowledge of the concepts inherent in encryption systems and a general high-level understanding of the major encryption systems. The minute details of how any one of these systems may be architected, tested, implemented, managed, monitored, optimized, and over time maintained are beyond the scope of this discussion, as there are many variables that the security professional needs to account for that will be unique to his or her implementation of such a system based on business need as well as local laws and standards.

Null Cipher

A null cipher option may be used in cases where the use of encryption is not necessary, but yet the fact that no encryption is needed must be configured in order for the system to work. In such cryptographic systems, various encryption options are configurable including the option to not use encryption. Null cipher is used when testing/debugging, low security is needed, or when using authentication-only communications. For example, certain implementations of cryptographic schemes such as IPSec and SSL may offer the choice to authenticate only and not encrypt.

The term null cipher is also a reference to an ancient form of ciphering where the plaintext is mixed together with non-cipher material. Today, it is regarded as a type of steganography, discussed later, which can be used to hide ciphertext. A simple example is

> *"Interesting Home Addition to Expand behind Eastern Dairy Transport Intersection Meanwhile Everything."*

If the first letter of each word is used, the message decodes into the secret message

> *"I Hate Bed Time."*

Substitution Ciphers

The substitution cipher involves the simple process of substituting one letter for another based upon a cryptovariable. Substitution involves shifting positions in the alphabet of a defined number of characters. Many old ciphers were based on substitution, including the Caesar cipher and ROT-13. [74]

Playfair Cipher

The playfair cipher was used well into the twentieth century and was a key element of the cryptographic systems used by the Allies in the Second World War.

The sender and the receiver agreed on a key word - for example, Triumph.

A table was then constructed using that word and then the rest of the alphabet – skipping over the letters already appearing in the key and using I and J as the same letter. For the sake of clarity, the key word is highlighted in the table so that it can be easily found.

---

74 Chris Hare, Cryptography 101, Data Security Management, 2002.

T	R	I/J	U	M
P	H	A	B	C
D	E	F	G	K
L	N	O	Q	S
V	W	X	Y	Z

If the sender wanted to encrypt the message "Do not accept offer," it would be encrypted by first grouping the plaintext in two letter blocks and spacing the repeated letters in the plaintext with a filler letter, e.g., X.

The plaintext would then be:

```
DO NO TA CX CX EP TO FX FX ER
```

The table is read by looking at where the two letters of the block intersect. For example, if the first block, DO, was made into a rectangle, the letters at the other two corners of the rectangle would be FL, that is, the ciphertext for the block DO. The box created by the letters DO is in a border for clarity. The next plaintext block is NO, and because both of those letters are on the same row and the ciphertext of the next letters (in this case, NO) would be encrypted as OQ. If the input block had been OS, then the row would wrap and the output ciphertext would be QL, using the next letter after the O, and the next letter after the S being the L from the beginning of the row.

The letters FX fall in the same column, and for letters that fall in the same row, the same applies – use the next lower letter and wrap to the top of the column if necessary. The block FX would be encrypted as either OI or OJ.

Transposition Ciphers

All of the above cryptosystems are based on the principle of substitution - that is, to substitute or exchange one value or letter for another. Cryptosystems that use transposition or permutation are instrumental for the information security professional to understand. These systems rely on concealing the message through the transposing of or interchanging the order of the letters.

3

Security Engineering

The Rail Fence

In the simple transposition cipher known as the rail fence, the message is written and read in two or more lines. To send the message "Purchase gold and oil stocks," one would write the message in alternating diagonal rows as shown:

P	R	H	S	G	L	A	D	I	S	O	K	
	U	C	A	E	O	D	N	O	L	T	C	S

The ciphertext would read as follows:

PRHSGLADIGOKUCAEODNOLTCS

The problem with such a system is that because the letters are the same as the plaintext, no substitution has taken place, just a reordering of the letters; the ciphertext is still susceptible to frequency analysis and other cryptographic attacks.

Rectangular Substitution Tables

The use of rectangular substitution tables was an early form of cryptography. The sender and receiver decided on the size and structure of a table to hold the message and then the order in which to read the message.

Using the same plaintext as the previous example ("Purchase gold and oil stocks") and placing it in a rectangular substitution block results in the following:

P	U	R	C	H
A	S	E	G	O
L	D	A	N	D
O	I	L	S	T
O	C	K	S	

Reading the table in a top-down manner would produce the following ciphertext:

PALOOUSDICREALKCGNSSHODT

Of course, the sender and receiver could agree on reading the table any way – bottom up, diagonally – that suited them.

Monoalphabetic and Polyalphabetic Ciphers

The Caesar cipher is a simple substitution algorithm that merely shifted the plaintext over three places to create the ciphertext. This was a monoalphabetic system – the substitution was one alphabet letter for another. In the case of the Caesar cipher, the replacement alphabet was offset by three places:

A	B	C	D	E	F	G	H	I	J	K	...	Z
D	E	F	G	H	I	J	K	L	M	N	...	C

There is also the scrambled alphabet. In this case, the substitution alphabet is a scrambled version of the alphabet. It could look like this, for example:

A	B	C	D	E	F	G	H	I	J	K	...	Z
M	G	P	U	W	I	R	L	O	V	D	...	K

Using the scrambled alphabet above, one can see that the plaintext of BAKE would be substituted as GMDW. The problem with monoalphabetic ciphers, however, is that they are still subject to the characteristics of the plaintext language – an E, for example, would be substituted as a W throughout the ciphertext. That would mean the letter W in the ciphertext would appear as frequently as an E in plaintext. That makes a cryptanalytic attack of a monoalphabetic system fairly simple.

The use of several alphabets for substituting the plaintext is called a polyalphabetic cipher. It is designed to make the breaking of a cipher by frequency analysis more difficult. Instead of substituting one alphabet for another, the ciphertext is generated from several possible substitution alphabets.

For Example:

Plaintext	A	B	C	D	E	F	G	H	I	J	K	...	Z
Substitution 1	M	G	P	U	W	I	R	L	O	V	D	...	K
Substitution 2	V	K	P	O	I	U	Y	T	J	H	S	...	A
Substitution 3	L	P	O	I	J	M	K	H	G	T	U	...	F
Substitution 4	N	B	V	C	X	Z	A	S	D	E	Y	...	W

Using this table, substitute the plaintext FEED as IIJC, using the substitution alphabets in sequence. The power of using multiple alphabets in this example is evident, as the repeated E in the plaintext is substituted for different results in the ciphertext. The ciphertext has a repeated I, and yet that is for different plaintext values.

3

Security Engineering

Blais de Vigenère

Blais de Vigenère, a Frenchman, developed the polyalphabetic cipher using a key word and 26 alphabets, each one offset by one place. This is shown in the following table. The top row of the table would be the plaintext values and the first column of the table the substitution alphabets.

	A	B	C	D	E	F	G	H	I	J	K	L	...	Z
A	A	B	C	D	E	F	G	H	I	J	K	L	...	Z
B	B	C	D	E	F	G	H	I	J	K	L	M	...	A
C	C	D	E	F	G	H	I	J	K	L	M	N	...	B
D	D	E	F	G	H	I	J	K	L	M	N	O	...	C
E	E	F	G	H	I	J	K	L	M	N	O	P	...	D
F	F	G	H	I	J	K	L	**M**	N	O	P	Q	...	E
G	G	H	I	J	K	L	M	N	O	P	Q	R	...	F
H	H	I	J	K	L	M	N	O	P	Q	R	S	...	G
I	I	J	K	L	M	N	O	P	Q	R	S	T	...	H
J	J	K	L	M	N	O	P	Q	R	S	T	U	...	I
K	K	L	M	N	O	P	Q	R	S	T	U	V	...	J
L	L	M	N	O	P	Q	R	S	T	U	V	W	...	K
...	...	...	...	...	...	...	...	...	...	...	...	...	...	...
Z	Z	A	B	C	D	E	F	G	H	I	J	K	...	Y

The sender and the receiver of the message would agree on a key to use for the message; in this case, one could use the word FICKLE as the key. Just as in the running cipher shown below, one would repeat the key for the length of the plaintext.

To encrypt the message "HIKE BACK," it would be constructed as follows:

Plaintext	H	I	K	E	B	A	C	K
Key	F	I	C	K	L	E	F	I
Ciphertext	M	Q	M	O	M	E	H	S

The ciphertext is found by finding where the H of the plaintext – the top row of the table – intersects with the F row of the ciphertext. Again, one sees the power of a polyalphabetic system where repeated values in the plaintext do not necessarily give the same ciphertext values, and repeated ciphertext values correspond to different plaintext inputs.

Modular Mathematics and the Running Key Cipher

The use of modular mathematics and the representation of each letter by its numerical place in the alphabet are the key to many modern ciphers:

A	B	C	D	E	F	G	H	I	J	K	L	M	N	O	P	Q	...	Z
0	1	2	3	4	5	6	7	8	9	10	11	12	13	14	15	16	...	25

The English alphabet would be calculated as "mod 26" because there are 26 letters in the English alphabet. The use of mod 26 means that whenever the result of a mathematical operation is equal to or greater than 26, 26 is subtracted from the total as often as needed until it is less than 26.

Using the above values, the cryptographic operation operates as follows:

$$Ciphertext = plaintext + key \ (mod \ 26).$$

$$This \ is \ written \ as \ C = P + K \ (mod \ 26).$$

$$Ciphertext \ is \ the \ value \ of \ the \ plaintext + the \ value \ of \ the \ key \ (mod \ 26).$$

For example, the plaintext letter N has a value of 13 (it is the 13th letter in the alphabet using the table above). If the key to be used to encrypt the plaintext is a Q with a value of 16, the ciphertext would be 13 + 16, or the 29th letter of the alphabet. Because there is no 29th letter in the English alphabet, 26 is subtracted (hence the term mod 26) and the ciphertext becomes the letter corresponding to the number 3, a D.

Running Key Cipher

In the example below, the use of a running key cipher is demonstrated. In a running key cipher, the key is repeated (or runs) for the same length as the plaintext input. The key of FEED is selected to encrypt the plaintext CHEEK. The key is repeated as long as necessary to match the length of the plaintext input. To demonstrate this in the following table, the encryption of the word CHEEK and the key of FEED are used. The numbers under the letters represent the value or position of that letter in the alphabet.

Plaintext:					
CHEEK	C	H	E	E	K
	2	7	4	4	10
Key:					
FEED	F	E	E	D	F
	5	4	4	3	5

The key is repeated for the length of the plaintext.

The ciphertext is computed as follows:

Plaintext Key	D	O	N	O	T	N	E	G
	K	S	O	S	D	F	S	H
Value of Plaintext	3	14	13	14	19	13	4	6
Value of Key	10	18	14	18	3	5	18	7
Ciphertext Value	13	32[1]	27[2]	6	22	18	22	13
Ciphertext	N	G	B	G	W	S	W	N

1 – (mod 26)=6
2 – (mod 26)=1

One-Time Pads

The only cipher system asserted as unbreakable, that is as long as it is implemented properly, is the one-time pad. These are often referred to as Vernam ciphers after the work of Gilbert Vernam, who proposed the use of a key that could only be used once and that must be as long as the plaintext but never repeats.

The one-time pad uses the principles of the running key cipher, using the numerical values of the letters and adding those to the value of the key; however, the key is a string of random values the same length as the plaintext. It never repeats, compared to the running key that may repeat several times. This means that a one-time pad is not breakable by frequency analysis or any other cryptographic attacks.

Message Integrity Controls (MICs)

An important part of electronic commerce and computerized transactions today is the assurance that a message has not been modified, is indeed from the person that the sender claims to be, and that the message was received by the correct party. This is accomplished through cryptographic functions that perform in several manners, depending on the business needs and level of trust between the parties and systems.

Traditional cryptography, such as symmetric algorithms, does produce a level of message authentication. If two parties share a symmetric key, and they have been careful not to disclose that key to anyone else, then when they transmit a message from one to another, they have assurance that the message is indeed from their trusted partner. In many cases, they would also have some degree of confidence in the integrity of the message because any errors or modifications of the message in transit would render the message undecipherable. With chaining-type algorithms, any error is likely to destroy the remainder of the message.

Asymmetric algorithms also provide message authentication. Some, such as RSA, El Gamal, and ECC, have message authentication and digital signature functionality built into the implementation. These work with open messages and secure and signed messages using asymmetric key cryptography.

Symmetric Cryptography

To this point, some of the history of cryptography and some of the methods of cryptography has been covered. The following describes how cryptographic principles are actually used today in real implementations. There are two primary forms of cryptography in use today: symmetric and asymmetric cryptographies. Symmetric algorithms operate with a single cryptographic key that is used for both encryption and decryption of the message. For this reason, it is often called single, same, or shared key encryption. It can also be called secret or private key encryption because the key factor in secure use of a symmetric algorithm is to keep the cryptographic key secret.

Some of the most difficult challenges of symmetric key ciphers are the problems of key management. Because the encryption and decryption processes both require the same key, the secure distribution of the key to both the sender (or *encryptor*) of the message and the receiver (or *decryptor*) is a key factor in the secure implementation of a symmetric key system. The cryptographic key cannot be sent in the same channel (or transmission medium) as the data, so out-of-band distribution must be considered. Out of band means using a different channel to transmit the keys, such as courier, fax, phone, or some other methods (*Figure 3.26*).

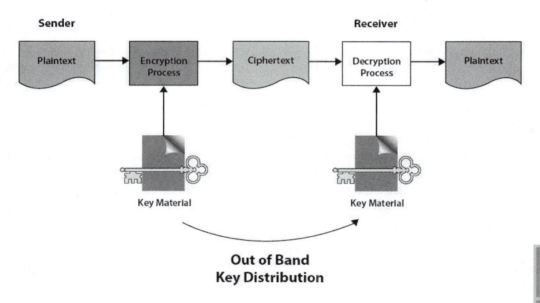

Figure 3.26 - **Out-of-Band key distribution**

The advantages of symmetric key algorithms are that they are usually very fast, secure, and cheap. There are several products available on the Internet at no cost to the user who uses symmetric algorithms.

The disadvantages include the problems of key management, as mentioned earlier, but also the limitation that a symmetric algorithm does not provide many benefits beyond confidentiality, unlike most asymmetric algorithms, which also provide the ability to establish nonrepudiation, message integrity, and access control. Symmetric algorithms can provide a form of message integrity; the message will not decrypt if changed. Symmetric algorithms also can provide a measure of access control; without the key, the file cannot be decrypted.

This limitation is best described by using a physical security example. If 10 people have a copy of the key to the server room, it can be difficult to know who entered that room at 10 p.m. yesterday. There is limited access control in that only those people with a key are able to enter; however, it is unknown which one of those 10 actually entered. The same occurs with a symmetric algorithm; if the key to a secret file is shared between two or more people, then there is no way of knowing who the last person to access the encrypted file was. It would also be possible for a person to change the file and allege that it was changed by someone else. This would be most critical when the cryptosystem is used for important documents such as electronic contracts. If a person that receives a file can change the document and allege that that was the true copy he had received, repudiation problems arise.

Examples of Symmetric Algorithms

Algorithms and systems such as the Caesar cipher, the Spartan scytale, and the Enigma machine are all examples of symmetric algorithms. The receiver needed to use the same key to perform the decryption process as he had used during the encryption process. The following covers many of the modern symmetric algorithms.

The Data Encryption Standard (DES)

The Data Encryption Standard was based on the work of Harst Feistal.[75] Harst Feistal had developed a family of algorithms that had a core principle of taking the input block of plaintext and dividing it in half. Then each half was used several times through an exclusive-or operation to alter the other half, providing a type of permutation as well as substitution.

DES became the standard in 1977 when it was adopted by several agencies of the U.S. federal government for deployment across all U.S. government departments for nonclassified but sensitive information. DES is used extensively even today in many financial, virtual private network (VPN), and online encryption systems. DES has been replaced as the standard by the AES, which is based on the Rijndael algorithm. The origin of DES was the Lucifer algorithm developed by Feistal; however, Lucifer had a 128-bit key. The algorithm was modified to make it more resistant to cryptanalysis, and the key length was reduced to 56 bits so that it could be fit onto a single chip. DES operates on 64-bit input blocks and outputs ciphertext into 64-bit blocks. There are 16 identical stages of processing, termed rounds. Before the main rounds, the block is divided into two 32-bit halves (because it is a Feistal cipher) and processed alternately using a 56-bit key.

When one is looking at a DES key, it is 64 bits in length; however, every eighth bit (used for parity) is ignored. Therefore, the effective length of the DES key is 56 bits. Because every bit has a possible value of either 1 or 0, it can be stated that the effective key space for the DES key is 2^{56}. This gives a total number of keys for DES to be 7.2×1016. However, the modes of operation discussed next are used by a variety of other block ciphers, not just in DES. Originally, there were four modes of DES accepted for use by the U.S. federal government (NIST); in later years, the CTR mode was also accepted (*Table 3.25*).

---

75 It is also spelled Horst in other publications. The work of Feistal was the implementation of the research done by Claude Shannon in 1945.

Basic Block Cipher Modes

The following basic block cipher modes operate in a block structure.[76]

- **Electronic Codebook Mode –** The ECB is the most basic block cipher mode (*Figure* 3.27). It is called codebook because it is similar to having a large codebook containing every piece of 64-bit plaintext input and all possible 64-bit ciphertext outputs. When a plaintext input is received by ECB, it operates on that block independently and produces the ciphertext output. If the input was more than 64 bits long and each 64-bit block was the same, then the output blocks would also be the same. Such regularity would make cryptanalysis simple. For that reason, as seen in *Table 3.25*, ECB is only used for very short messages (less than 64 bits in length), such as transmission of a key. As with all Feistal ciphers, the decryption process is the reverse of the encryption process.

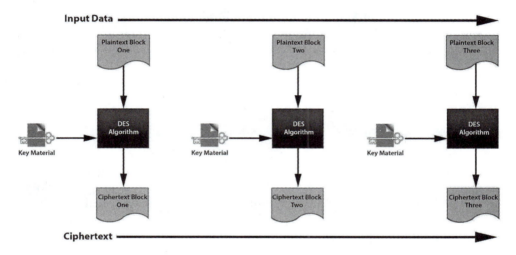

Figure 3.27 – **Electronic codebook is a basic mode used by block ciphers**

- **Cipher Block Chaining Mode –** The CBC mode is stronger than ECB in that each input block will produce a different output – even if the input blocks are identical. This is accomplished by introducing two new factors in the encryption process – an IV and a chaining function that XORs each input with the previous ciphertext. (Note: Without the IV, the chaining process applied to the same messages would create the same ciphertext.) The IV is a randomly chosen value that is mixed with the first block of plaintext. This acts just like a seed in a stream-based cipher. The sender and the receiver must know the IV so that the message can be decrypted later. The function of CBC can be seen in *Figure 3.28*.

  The initial input block is XORed with the IV, and the result of that process is encrypted to produce the first block of ciphertext. This first ciphertext block is then XORed with the next input plaintext block. This is the chaining process, which ensures that even if the input blocks are the same, the resulting outputs will be different.

---

76   See the following for a current list of block cipher modes approved by the U.S. government: http://csrc. nist.gov/groups/ST/toolkit/BCM/current_modes.html

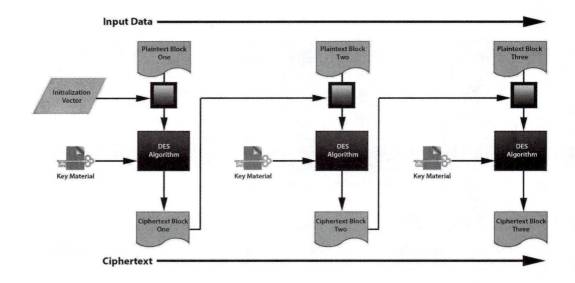

Figure 3.28 - **Cipher Block chaining mode.**

The Stream Modes of DES

The following modes of DES operate as a stream; even though DES is a block mode cipher, these modes attempt to make DES operate as if it were a stream mode algorithm. A block-based cipher is subject to the problems of latency or delay in processing. This makes them unsuitable for many applications where simultaneous transmission of the data is desired. In these modes, DES tries to simulate a stream to be more versatile and provide support for stream-based applications.

- **Cipher Feedback Mode** – In the CFB mode, the input is separated into individual segments, the size of which can be 1-bit, 8-bit, 64-bit, or 128-bit (the four sub-modes of CFB)*; it is usually of 8 bits because that is the size of one character (*Figure 3.29*). When the encryption process starts, the IV is chosen and loaded into a shift register. It is then run through the encryption algorithm. The first 8 bits that come from the algorithm are then XORed with the first 8 bits of the plaintext (the first segment). Each 8-bit segment is then transmitted to the receiver and also fed back into the shift register. The shift register contents are then encrypted again to generate the keystream to be XORed with the next plaintext segment. This process continues until the end of the input. One of the drawbacks of this, however, is that if a bit is corrupted or altered, all of the data from that point onward will be damaged.

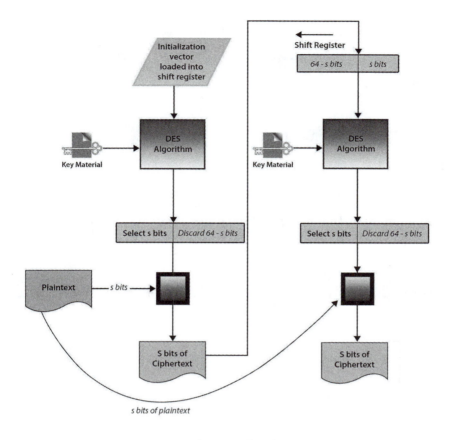

Figure 3.29 – **Cipher Feedback mode of DES**

■ ***Output Feedback Mode*** **–** The OFB mode is very similar in operation to the CFB except that instead of using the ciphertext result of the XOR operation to feed back into the shift register for the ongoing keystream, it feeds the encrypted keystream itself back into the shift register to create the next portion of the keystream (*Figure 3.30*).

Because the keystream and message data are completely independent (the keystream itself is chained, but there is no chaining of the ciphertext), it is now possible to generate the entire keystream in advance and store it for later use.

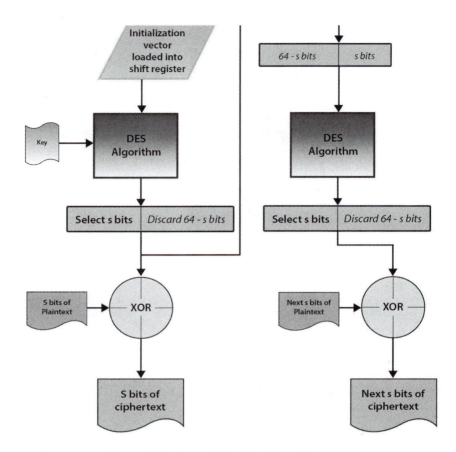

Figure 3.30 - **Output feedback mode of DES**

■ ***Counter Mode*** – The CTR mode is used in high-speed applications such as IPSec and ATM (*Figure 3.31*). In this mode, a counter – a 64-bit random data block – is used as the first IV. A requirement of CTR is that the counter must be different for every block of plaintext, so for each subsequent block, the counter is incremented by 1. The counter is then encrypted just as in OFB, and the result is used as a keystream and XORed with the plaintext. Because the keystream is independent from the message, it is possible to process several blocks of data at the same time, thus speeding up the throughput of the algorithm.

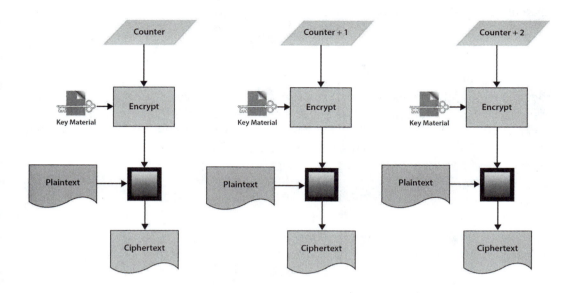

Figure 3.31 – **Counter mode is used in high-speed applications such as IPSec and ATM**

Advantages and Disadvantages of DES

Initially, DES was considered unbreakable, and early attempts to break a DES message were unrealistic. (A computer running at one attempt per millisecond would still take more than 1000 years to try all possible keys.) However, DES is susceptible to a brute force attack. Because the key is only 56 bits long, the key may be determined by trying all possible keys against the ciphertext until the true plaintext is recovered. The Electronic Frontier Foundation (www.eff.org) demonstrated this several years ago. However, it should be noted that they did the simplest form of attack – a known plaintext attack; they tried all possible keys against a ciphertext, knowing what they were looking for (they knew the plaintext). If they did not know the plaintext (did not know what they were looking for), the attack would have been significantly more difficult. Regardless, DES can be deciphered using today's computing power and enough stubborn persistence. There have also been criticisms of the structure of the DES algorithm. The design of the S-boxes used in the encryption and decryption operations was secret, and this can lead to claims that they may contain hidden code or untried operations.

Double DES

The primary complaint about DES was that the key was too short. This made a known plaintext brute force attack possible. One of the first alternatives considered to create a stronger version of DES was to double the encryption process, hence the name Double DES. However, this turned out to not be such a good approach, as more serious vulnerabilities in double DES have emerged. The intention of double DES was to create an algorithm that would be equivalent in strength to a 112-bit key (two 56-bit keys). Unfortunately, this was not the case because of the "meet in the middle" attack, which is why the lifespan of double DES was very short.

3

Security Engineering

Meet in the Middle

The most effective attack against double DES was just like the successful attacks on single DES, based on doing a brute force attack against known plaintext (*Figure* 3.32).[77] The attacker would encrypt the plaintext using all possible keys and create a table containing all possible results. This intermediate cipher is referred to as "m" for this discussion. This would mean encrypting using all 2^{56} possible keys. The table would then be sorted according to the values of m. The attacker would then decrypt the ciphertext using all possible keys until he found a match with the value of m. This would result in a true strength of double DES of approximately 2^{56} (twice the strength of DES, but not strong enough to be considered effective), instead of the 2^{112} originally hoped.[78]

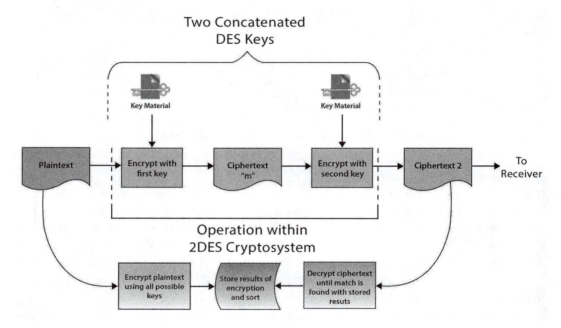

Figure 3.32 - **Meet-in-the-Middle attack on 2DES**

Triple DES (3DES)

The defeat of double DES resulted in the adoption of triple DES as the next solution to overcome the weaknesses of single DES. Triple DES was designed to operate at a relative strength of 2^{112} using two different keys to perform the encryption. This effectively rendered a key with a 168 bit strength. There are several different modes that Triple DES can be implemented through, but the four explained above are the most common and of the most concern to the security professional.

---

77 In a known plaintext attack, the attacker has both the plaintext and the ciphertext, but he does not have the key, and the brute-force attack was an attack trying all possible keys. See "Attacks on hashing algorithms and message authentication codes" Section for more details on this.

78 Note that most cryptographers consider the strength of single DES to be 2^{55}, not 2^{56} as might be expected. Because double DES is approximately twice the strength of DES, it would be considered to be 2^{56}.

Advanced Encryption Standard

In 1997, the National Institute of Standards and Technology (NIST) in the United States issued a call for a product to replace DES and 3DES. The requirements were that the new algorithm would be at least as strong as DES, have a larger block size (because a larger block size would be more efficient and more secure), and overcome the problems of performance with DES. DES was developed for hardware implementations and is too slow in software. 3DES is even slower, and thus it creates a serious latency in encryption as well as significant processing overhead.

After considerable research, the product chosen to be the new AES was the Rijndael algorithm, created by Dr. Joan Daemon and Dr. Vincent Rijmen of Belgium. The name Rijndael was merely a contraction of their surnames. Rijndael beat out the other finalists: Serpent, of which Ross Anderson was an author; MARS, an IBM product; RC6, from Ron Rivest and RSA; and TwoFish, developed by Bruce Schneier. The AES algorithm was obliged to meet many criteria, including the need to be flexible, implementable on many types of platforms, and free of royalties.

What follows is a deeper discussion about AES and how it works. While it is important for the security architect and professional to have an understanding of ALL of the components of any systems that they are tasked with interacting with, it is also important to have an appropriate perspective with regards to certain aspects of those systems, such as the mathematics that underlie the implementation of the algorithm and the intricacies of how the algorithm is implemented. Unless the security architects specialize in cryptographic system design, they may never have a need to get to the technical level of understanding of that which is discussed below. If the security professionals do not have a need to implement a system that uses cryptography, then they will not have a need to deeply immerse themselves in the intricacies of the architecture discussed below. What both of these security roles will require however is the ability to have a basic understanding of algorithms, such as AES, and most importantly the knowledge of who to call on within the enterprise or perhaps outside the enterprise in order to get the appropriate amount of guidance if necessary.

Counter Mode with Cipher Block Chaining Message Authentication Code Protocol (CCMP)

CCMP is an encryption protocol that forms part of the 802.11i standard for wireless local area networks. The CCMP protocol is based on AES encryption using the CTR with CBC-MAC (CCM) mode of operation. CCMP is defined in the IETF RFC 3610 and is included as a component of the 802.11i IEEE standard.[79]

How CCMP Works

AES processing in CCMP must use AES 128-bit key and 128-bit block size. Per United States' Federal Information Processing Standard (FIPS) 197 standard, the AES algorithm (a block cipher) uses blocks of 128 bits, cipher keys with lengths of 128, 192, and 256 bits, as well as a number of rounds 10, 12, and 14 respectively.[80] CCMP use of 128-bit keys and a 48-bit IV minimizes vulnerability to replay attacks. The CTR component provides data privacy. The Cipher Block Chaining Message Authentication Code component produces a message integrity code (MIC) that provides data origin authentication and data integrity for the packet payload data.

---

79   See the following: http://tools.ietf.org/html/rfc3610

80   See the following: http://csrc.nist.gov/publications/fips/fips197/fips-197.pdf

The 802.11i standard includes CCMP. AES is often referred to as the encryption protocol used by 802.11i; however AES itself is simply a block cipher. The actual encryption protocol is CCMP. It is important to note here that, although the 802.11i standard allows for TKIP encryption Robust Security Network (RSN) is part of the 802.11i IEEE standard and negotiates authentication and encryption algorithms between access points and wireless clients. This flexibility allows new algorithms to be added at any time and supported alongside previous algorithms. The use of AES-CCMP is mandated for RSNs. AES-CCMP introduces a higher level of security from past protocols by providing protection for the MAC protocol data unit (MPDU) and parts of the 802.11 MAC headers. This protects even more of the data packet from eavesdropping and tampering.

Rijndael

The Rijndael algorithm can be used with block sizes of 128, 192, or 256 bits. The key can also be 128, 192, or 256 bits, with a variable number of rounds of operation depending on the key size. Using AES with a 128-bit key would do 10 rounds, whereas a 192-bit key would do 12 and a 256-bit key would do 14. Although Rijndael supports multiple block sizes, AES only supports one block size (subset of Rijndael). AES is reviewed below in the 128-bit block format. The AES operation works on the entire 128-bit block of input data by first copying it into a square table (or array) that it calls state. The inputs are placed into the array by column so that the first four bytes of the input would fill the first column of the array.

Following is input plaintext when placed into a 128-bit state array:

1st byte	5th byte	9th byte	13th byte
2nd byte	6th byte	10th byte	14th byte
3rd byte	7th byte	11th byte	15th byte
4th byte	8th byte	12th byte	16th byte

The key is also placed into a similar square table or matrix.

The Rijndael operation consists of four major operations.

1. **Substitute Bytes** – Use of an S-box to do a byte-by-byte substitution of the entire block.
2. **Shift Rows** – Transposition or permutation through offsetting each row in the table.
3. **Mix Columns** – A substitution of each value in a column based on a function of the values of the data in the column.
4. **Add Round Key** – XOR each byte with the key for that round; the key is modified for each round of operation.

Substitute Bytes

The substitute bytes operation uses an S-box that looks up the value of each byte in the input and substitutes it with the value in the table. The S-box table contains all possible 256 8-bit word values, and a simple cross-reference is done to find the substitute value using the first half of the byte (4-bit word) in the input table on the x-axis and the second half of the byte on the y-axis. Hexadecimal values are used in both the input and S-box tables.

Shift Row Transformation

The shift row transformation step provides blockwide transposition of the input data by shifting the rows of data as follows. If one starts with the input table described earlier, the effect of the shift row operation can be observed. Please note that by this point, the table will have been subjected to the substitute bytes operation, so it would not look like this any longer, but this table will be used for the sake of clarity.

	Columns			
Rows	1st byte	5th byte	9th byte	13th byte
	2nd byte	6th byte	10th byte	14th byte
	3rd byte	7th byte	11th byte	15th byte
	4th byte	8th byte	12th byte	16th byte

The first row is not shifted.

1st byte	5th byte	9th byte	13th byte

The second row of the table is shifted one place to the left.

6th byte	10th byte	14th byte	2nd byte

3

Security Engineering

The third row of the table is shifted two places to the left.

11th byte	15th byte	3rd byte	7th byte

The fourth row of the table is shifted three places to the left.

16th byte	4th byte	8th byte	12th byte

The final result of the shift rows step would look as follows:

1	5	9	13
6	10	14	2
11	15	3	7
16	4	8	12

Mix Column Transformation

The mix column transformation is performed by multiplying and XORing each byte in a column together, according to the table in *Figure 3.33*.

1	5	9	13
6	10	14	2
11	15	3	7
16	4	8	12

⊕

02	03	01	01
01	02	03	01
01	01	02	03
03	01	01	01

State table   Exclusive OR   Mix Columns table

*Figure 3.33 – **Mix Column Transformation***

The *Figure* 3.33 table is the result of the previous step, so when the first column (shaded in the state table) with the first row is worked using multiplication and XOR in the mix column table (shaded), the computation of the mix columns step for the first column would be

```
(1*02)  (6*03)  (11*01)  (16*01)
```

The second byte in the column would be calculated using the second row in the mix column table as

```
(6*01)  (11*02)  (16*03)  (1*01)
```

Add Round Key

The key is modified for each round by first dividing the key into 16-bit pieces (4 4-bit words) and then expanding each piece into 176 bits (44 4-bit words). The key is arrayed into a square matrix, and each column is subjected to rotation (shifting the first column to the last; 1, 2, 3, 4 would become 2, 3, 4, 1) and then the substitution of each word of the key using an S-box. The result of these first two operations is then XORed with a round constant to create the key to be used for that round. The round constant changes for each round, and its values are predefined. Each of the above steps (except for the mix columns, which is only done for nine rounds) are done for 10 rounds to produce the ciphertext. AES is a strong algorithm that is not considered breakable at any time in the near future and is easy to deploy on many platforms with excellent throughput.

International Data Encryption Algorithm (IDEA)

IDEA was developed as a replacement for DES by Xuejai Lai and James Massey in 1991. IDEA uses a 128-bit key and operates on 64-bit blocks. IDEA does eight rounds of transposition and substitution using modular addition and multiplication, and bitwise exclusive-or (XOR).

CAST

CAST was developed in 1996 by Carlisle Adams and Stafford Tavares. CAST-128 can use keys between 40 and 128 bits in length and will do between 12 and 16 rounds of operation, depending on key length. CAST-128 is a Feistal-type block cipher with 64-bit blocks. CAST-256 was submitted as an unsuccessful candidate for the new AES. CAST-256 operates on 128-bit blocks and with keys of 128, 192, 160, 224, and 256 bits. It performs 48 rounds and is described in RFC 2612.

Secure and Fast Encryption Routine (SAFER)

All of the algorithms in SAFER are patent-free. The algorithms were developed by James Massey and work on either 64-bit input blocks (SAFER-SK64) or 128-bit blocks (SAFER-SK128). A variation of SAFER is used as a block cipher in Bluetooth.

Blowfish

Blowfish is a symmetrical algorithm developed by Bruce Schneier. It is an extremely fast cipher and can be implemented in as little as 5K of memory. It is a Feistal-type cipher in that it divides the input blocks into two halves and then uses them in XORs against each other. However, it varies from the traditional Feistal cipher in that Blowfish does work against both halves, not just one. The Blowfish algorithm operates with variable key sizes, from 32 up to 448 bits on 64-bit input and output blocks.

Twofish

Twofish was one of the finalists for the AES. It is an adapted version of Blowfish developed by a team of cryptographers led by Bruce Schneier. It can operate with keys of 128, 192, or 256 bits on blocks of 128 bits. It performs 16 rounds during the encryption/decryption process.

3

Security Engineering

361

RC5

RC5 was developed by Ron Rivest of RSA and is deployed in many of RSA's products. It is a very adaptable product that is useful for many applications, ranging from software to hardware implementations. The key for RC5 can vary from 0 to 2040 bits; the number of rounds it executes can be adjusted from 0 to 255, and the length of the input words can also be chosen from 16-, 32-, and 64-bit lengths. The algorithm operates on two words at a time in a fast and secure manner.

RC5 is defined in RFC 2040 for four different modes of operation:

- RC5 block cipher is similar to DES ECB, producing a ciphertext block of the same length as the input.
- RC5-CBC is a cipher block chaining form of RC5, using chaining to ensure that repeated input blocks would not generate the same output.
- RC5-CBC-Pad combines chaining with the ability to handle input plaintext of any length. The ciphertext will be longer than the plaintext by at most one block.
- RC5-CTS is called ciphertext stealing and will generate a ciphertext equal in length to a plaintext of any length.

RC4

RC4, a stream-based cipher, was developed in 1987 by Ron Rivest for RSA Data Security and has become the most widely used stream cipher, being deployed, for example, in WEP and SSL/TLS. RC4 uses a variable length key ranging from 8 to 2048 bits (1 to 256 bytes) and a period of greater than 10^{100}. In other words, the keystream should not repeat for at least that length.

If RC4 is used with a key length of at least 128 bits, there are currently no practical ways to attack it; the published successful attacks against the use of RC4 in WEP applications are related to problems with the implementation of the algorithm, not the algorithm itself.

Advantages and Disadvantages of Symmetric Algorithms

Symmetric algorithms are very fast and secure methods of providing confidentiality and some integrity and authentication for messages being stored or transmitted. Many algorithms can be implemented in either hardware or software and are available at no cost to the user.

However, there are serious disadvantages to symmetric algorithms – key management is very difficult, especially in large organizations. The number of keys needed grows rapidly with every new user according to the formula n (n − 1)/2, where n is the number of users. An organization with only 10 users, all wanting to communicate securely with one another, requires 45 keys (10*9/2). If the organization grows to 1000 employees, the need for key management expands to nearly a half million keys.

Symmetric algorithms also are not able to provide nonrepudiation of origin, access control, and digital signatures, except in a very limited way. If two or more people share a symmetric key, then it is impossible to prove who altered a file protected with a symmetric key. Selecting keys is an important part of key management. There needs to be a process in place that ensures that a key is selected randomly from the entire keyspace and that there is some way to recover a lost or forgotten key.

Because symmetric algorithms require both users (the sender and the receiver) to share the same key, there can be challenges with secure key distribution. Often, the users must use an out-of-band channel such as in person, mail, fax, telephone, or courier to exchange secret keys. The use of an out-of-band channel should make it difficult for an attacker to seize both the encrypted data and the key. The other method of exchanging the symmetric key is to use an asymmetric algorithm.

Asymmetric Cryptography

Due to the practical limitations of symmetric cryptography, asymmetric cryptography attempts to provide the best of all worlds. While initially more key management is required, the fundamentals of asymmetric cryptography provide an extensible and elastic framework in which to deploy cryptographic functions for integrity, confidentiality, authentication, and nonrepudiation.

Asymmetric Algorithms

Whereas symmetric algorithms have been in existence for several millennia, the use of asymmetric (or public key) algorithms is relatively new. These algorithms became commonly known when Drs. Whitfield Diffie and Martin Hellman released a paper in 1976 called "New Directions in Cryptography." [81] The Diffie–Hellman paper described the concept of using two different keys (a key pair) to perform the cryptographic operations. The two keys would be linked mathematically, but they would be mutually exclusive. For most asymmetric algorithms, if one half of this key pair was used for encryption, then the other key half would be required to decrypt the message.

When a person wishes to communicate using an asymmetric algorithm, she would first generate a key pair. Usually this is done by the cryptographic application or the PKI without user involvement to ensure the strength of the key generation process. One half of the key pair is kept secret, and only the key holder knows that key. For this reason, it is often called the private key. The other half of the key pair can be given freely to anyone that wants a copy. In many companies, it may be available through the corporate website or access to a key server. That is why this half of the key pair is often referred to as the public key. Asymmetric algorithms are one-way functions, that is, a process that is much simpler to go in one direction (forward) than to go in the other direction (backward or reverse engineering). The process to generate the public key (forward) is fairly simple, and providing the public key to anyone who wants it does not compromise the private key because the process to go from the public key to the private key is computationally infeasible.

Confidential Messages

Because the keys are mutually exclusive, any message that is encrypted with a public key can only be decrypted with the corresponding other half of the key pair, the private key. Therefore, as long as the key holder keeps her private key secure, there exists a method of transmitting a message confidentially. The sender would encrypt the message with the public key of the receiver. Only the receiver with the private key would be able to open or read the message, providing confidentiality. See *Figure 3.34.*

---

81   Whit Diffie and Martin Hellman, New directions in cryptography, IEEE Transactions on Information Theory, IT-22, 1976.

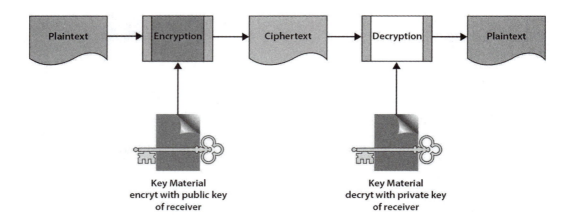

Figure 3.34 – **Using Public Key cryptography to send a confidential message**

Open Message

Conversely, when a message is encrypted with the private key of a sender, it can be opened or read by anyone who possesses the corresponding public key. When a person needs to send a message and provide proof of origin (nonrepudiation), he can do so by encrypting it with his own private key. The recipient then has some guarantee that, because she opened it with the public key from the sender, the message did, in fact, originate with the sender. See *Figure 3.35.*

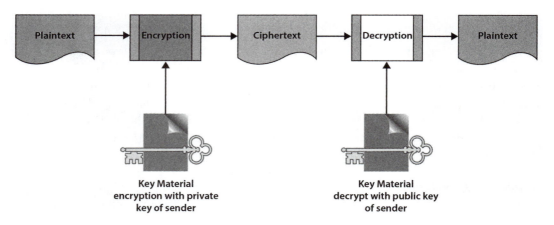

Figure 3.35 – **Using public key cryptography to send a message with proof of origin**

Confidential Messages with Proof of Origin

By encrypting a message with the private key of the sender and the public key of the receiver, one is able to send a message that is confidential and has proof of origin. See *Figure 3.36.*

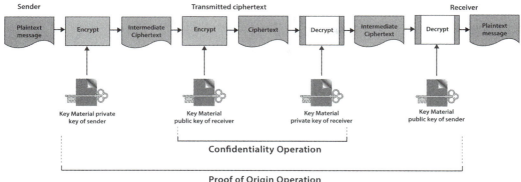

Figure 3.36 - **Using public key cryptography to send a message that is confidential and has a proof of origin**

RSA

RSA was developed in 1978 by Ron Rivest, Adi Shamir, and Len Adleman when they were at MIT. RSA is based on the mathematical challenge of factoring the product of two large prime numbers. A prime number can only be divided by 1 and itself. Some prime numbers include 2, 3, 5, 7, 11, 13, and so on. Factoring is defined as taking a number and finding the numbers that can be multiplied together to calculate that number. For example, if the product of a*b = c, then c can be factored into a and b. As 3*4 = 12, then 12 can be factored into 3, 4 and 6, 2 and 12, and 1. The RSA algorithm uses large prime numbers that when multiplied together would be incredibly difficult to factor. Successful factoring attacks have been executed against 512-bit numbers (at a cost of approximately 8000 MIPS years), and successful attacks against 1024-bit numbers appear increasingly possible in the near term; the U.S. government organization NIST recommended moving away from 1024-bit RSA key size by the end of 2010.[82] The recommendation in part is stated as follows:

"If information is initially signed in 2009 and needs to remain secure for a maximum of 10 years (i.e., from 2009 to 2019), a 1024 bit RSA key would not provide sufficient protection between 2011 and 2019 and, therefore, it is not recommended that 1024-bit RSA be used in this case." RSA is the most widely used public key algorithm and operates on blocks of text according to the following formula:

$$C = P^e \bmod n$$

The ciphertext is computed from the plaintext to the exponent e mod n.

Attacking RSA

The three primary approaches to attack the RSA algorithm are to use brute force, trying all possible private keys; mathematical attacks, factoring the product of two prime numbers; and timing attacks, measuring the running time of the decryption algorithm.

---

82   See chart on page 5, NIST SP 800–131A "Transitions: Recommendation for Transitioning the Use of Cryptographic Algorithms and Key Lengths". http://csrc.nist.gov/publications/nistpubs/800-131A/sp800-131A.pdf

Diffie–Hellmann Algorithm

Diffie–Hellmann is a key exchange algorithm. It is used to enable two users to exchange or negotiate a secret symmetric key that will be used subsequently for message encryption. The Diffie–Hellmann algorithm does not provide for message confidentiality, but it is extremely useful for applications such as Public Key Infrastructure (PKI). Diffie–Hellmann is based on discrete logarithms. This is a mathematical function based first on finding the primitive root of a prime number. Using the primitive root, one can put together a formula as follows:

$$b \le a^i \bmod p \quad 0 \pounds i \pounds (p - 1)$$

Where i is the discrete log (or index) for a mod p.

El Gamal

The El Gamal cryptographic algorithm is based on the work of Diffie–Hellmann, but it included the ability to provide message confidentiality and digital signature services, not just session key exchange. The El Gamal algorithm was based on the same mathematical functions of discrete logs.

Elliptic Curve Cryptography (ECC)

One branch of discrete logarithmic algorithms is based on the complex mathematics of elliptic curves. These algorithms, which are too complex to explain in this context, are advantageous for their speed and strength. The elliptic curve algorithms have the highest strength per bit of key length of any of the asymmetric algorithms. The ability to use much shorter keys for ECC implementations provides savings on computational power and bandwidth. This makes ECC especially beneficial for implementation in smart cards, wireless, and other similar application areas. Elliptic curve algorithms provide confidentiality, digital signatures, and message authentication services.

Advantages and Disadvantages of Asymmetric Key Algorithms

The development of asymmetric key cryptography revolutionized the cryptographic community. Now it was possible to send a message across an untrusted medium in a secure manner without the overhead of prior key exchange or key material distribution. It allowed several other features not readily available in symmetric cryptography, such as the nonrepudiation of origin, access control, data integrity, and the nonrepudiation of delivery.

The problem was that asymmetric cryptography is extremely slow compared to its symmetric counterpart. Asymmetric cryptography was a product that was extremely problematic in terms of speed and performance and would be impractical for everyday use in encrypting large amounts of data and frequent transactions. This is because asymmetric is handling much larger keys and computations – making even a fast computer work harder than if it were only handling small keys and less complex algebraic calculations. The ciphertext output from asymmetric algorithms may be much larger than the plaintext. This means that for large messages, they are not effective for secrecy; however, they are effective for message integrity, authentication, and nonrepudiation.

Hybrid Cryptography

The solutions to many of the problems with symmetric encryption lie in developing a hybrid technique of cryptography that combined the strengths of both symmetric cryptography, with its great speed and secure algorithms, and asymmetric cryptography, with its ability to securely exchange session keys, message authentication, and nonrepudiation. Symmetric cryptography is best for encrypting large files. It can handle the encryption and decryption processes with little impact on delivery times or computational performance.

Asymmetric cryptography can handle the initial setup of the communications session through the exchange or negotiation of the symmetric keys to be used for this session. In many cases, the symmetric key is only needed for the length of this communication and can be discarded following the completion of the transaction, so the symmetric key in this case will be referred to as a session key. A hybrid system operates as shown in *Figure 3.37*. The message itself is encrypted with a symmetric key, SK, and is sent to the recipient. The symmetric key is encrypted with the public key of the recipient and sent to the recipient. The symmetric key is decrypted with the private key of the recipient. This discloses the symmetric key to the recipient. The symmetric key can then be used to decrypt the message.

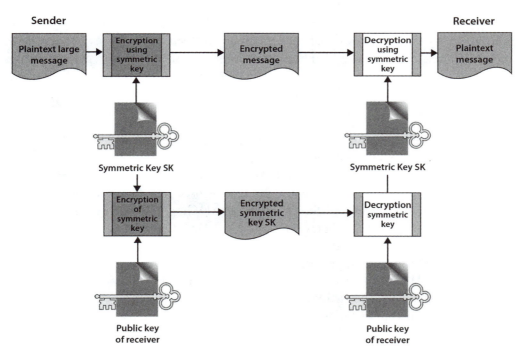

Figure 3.37 – Hybrid system using asymmetric algorithm for bulk data encryption and an asymmetric algorithm for distribution of the symmetric key

Message Digests

A message digest is a small representation of a larger message. Message digests are used to ensure the authentication and integrity of information, not the confidentiality.

Message Authentication Code

A MAC (also known as a cryptographic checksum) is a small block of data that is generated using a secret key and then appended to the message. When the message is received, the recipient can generate her own MAC using the secret key and thereby know that the message has not changed either accidentally or intentionally in transit. Of course, this assurance is only as strong as the trust that the two parties have that no one else has access to the secret key. A MAC is a small representation of a message and has the following characteristics:

- A MAC is much smaller than the message generating it.
- Given a MAC, it is impractical to compute the message that generated it.
- Given a MAC and the message that generated it, it is impractical to find another message generating the same MAC.

In the case of DES-CBC, a MAC is generated using the DES algorithm in CBC mode, and the secret DES key is shared by the sender and the receiver. The MAC is actually just the last block of ciphertext generated by the algorithm. This block of data (64 bits) is attached to the unencrypted message and transmitted to the far end. All previous blocks of encrypted data are discarded to prevent any attack on the MAC itself. The receiver can just generate his own MAC using the secret DES key he shares to ensure message integrity and authentication. He knows that the message has not changed because the chaining function of CBC would significantly alter the last block of data if any bit had changed anywhere in the message. He knows the source of the message (authentication) because only one other person holds the secret key. If the message contains a sequence number (such as a TCP header or X.25 packet), he knows that all messages have been received and not duplicated or missed.

HMAC

A MAC based on DES is one of the most common methods of creating a MAC; however, it is slow in operation compared to a hash function. A hash function such as MD5 does not have a secret key, so it cannot be used for a MAC. Therefore, RFC 2104 was issued to provide a hashed MACing system that has become the process used now in IPSec and many other secure Internet protocols, such as SSL/TLS. Hashed MACing implements a freely available hash algorithm as a component (black box) within the HMAC implementation. This allows ease of the replacement of the hashing module if a new hash function becomes necessary. The use of proven cryptographic hash algorithms also provides assurance of the security of HMAC implementations. HMACs work by adding a secret key value to the hash input function along with the source message. The HMAC operation provides cryptographic strength similar to a hashing algorithm, except that it now has the additional protection of a secret key, and it still operates nearly as rapidly as a standard hash operation.

Software and System Vulnerabilities and Threats

Software and systems will continue to suffer from vulnerabilities. Web-based applications, clients, servers, and the technologies supporting them continue to require remediation actions. Sound design through a secure architecture can help mitigate and eliminate vulnerabilities before they develop.

Web-Based

In essence, Web applications are subject to all of the threats and protection mechanisms discussed elsewhere. However, Web applications are specifically vulnerable because of their accessibility.

Specific protections that may be helpful include having a particular assurance sign-off process for Web servers, hardening the operating system used on such servers (removing default configurations and accounts, configuring permissions and privileges correctly, and keeping up to date with vendor patches), extending Web and network vulnerability scans prior to deployment, passively assessing IDS and advanced intrusion prevention system (IPS) technology, using application proxy firewalls, and disabling any unnecessary documentation and libraries.

Ensure administrative interfaces are removed or secured appropriately. Only allow access from authorized hosts or networks, and then use strong (possibly multifactor) user authentication. Do not hard code the authentication credentials into the application itself, and ensure the security of the credentials using certificates or similar high trust authenticators. Use account lockout and extended logging and audit, and protect all authentication traffic with encryption. Ensure that the interface is at least as secure as the rest of the application, and most often secure it at a higher level.

Because of the accessibility of Web systems and applications, input validation is critical. Application proxy firewalls are appropriate in this regard, but ensure that the proxies are able to deal with problems of buffer overflows, authentication issues, scripting, submission of commands to the underlying platform (which includes issues related to database engines, such as SQL commands), encoding issues (such as Unicode), and URL encoding and translation. In particular, the proxy firewall may have to address issues of data submission to in-house and custom software, ensuring validation of input to those systems. (This level of protection will have to be custom programmed for the application.)

XML

Extensible Markup Language (XML) is a World Wide Web Consortium (W3C) standard for structuring data in a text file so that both the format of the data and the data can be shared on intranets and the Web. A markup language, such as the Hypertext Markup Language (HTML), is simply a system of symbols and rules to identify structures (format) in a document. XML is called extensible because the symbols are unlimited and can be defined by the user or author. The format for XML can represent data in a neutral format that is independent of the database, application, and the underlying DBMS.

XML became a W3C standard in 1998, and many believe it is the de facto standard for integrating data and content. It offers the ability to exchange data and bridge different technologies, such as object models and programming languages. Because of this advantage, XML is expected to transform data and documents of current DBMSs and data access standards (e.g., ODBC, JDBC, etc.) by Web-enabling these standards and providing a common data format. Another, and probably more important, advantage is the ability to create one underlying XML document and display it in a variety of different ways and devices. The security architect must be aware of XML's fundamental structure and how it allows an attacker to manipulate the XML parser. As in database security, the security architect must understand that XML is vulnerable to injection attacks. When reviewing the XML parser

3

Security Engineering

for an application, the architect must ensure input is validated and "normal" parameters are established in the design phases.

SAML

The Security Assertion Markup Language is an XML-based standard used to exchange authentication and authorization information. SAML was developed by the security services technical committee of the Organization of the Advancement of Structured Information Standards (OASIS). SAML is designed to allow federated systems with different identity management systems to interact through simplified sign-on and single sign-on exchanges. OASIS cites the following as advantages of SAML:[83]

- **Platform Neutrality** – SAML abstracts the security framework away from platform architectures and particular vendor implementations. Making security more independent of application logic is an important tenet of Service-Oriented Architecture.

- **Loose Coupling of Directories** – SAML does not require user information to be maintained and synchronized between directories.

- **Improved Online Experience for End-Users** - SAML enables single sign-on by allowing users to authenticate at an identity provider and then access service providers without additional authentication. In addition, identity federation (linking of multiple identities) with SAML allows for a better-customized user experience at each service while promoting privacy.

- **Reduced Administrative Costs for Service Providers** – Using SAML to "reuse" a single act of authentication (such as logging in with a username and password) multiple times across multiple services can reduce the cost of maintaining account information. This burden is transferred to the identity provider.

- **Risk Transference** – SAML can act to push responsibility for proper management of identities to the identity provider, which is more often compatible with its business model than that of a service provider.

While SAML is inherently designed to be secure, the security architect must ensure the implementation does not weaken the security of the language. For example, when passing SAML assertions, if a system were to leave out the identifier of the authorization request or the identity of the recipient, an attacker could be able to access a user's account without authorization.[84]

Another item for the security architect to consider in this regard is the OpenID Connect standard.[85] OpenID Connect is an interoperable authentication protocol based on the OAuth 2.0 family of specifications.[86] It uses straightforward REST/JSON message flows with a design goal of "making simple things simple and complicated things possible."

---

83   See the following: https://www.oasis-open.org/committees/download.php/13525/sstc-saml-exec-overview-2.0-cd-01-2col.pdf (Page 3)

84   See the following for more information: http://www.kb.cert.org/vuls/id/612636

85   The OpenID Connect standard was officially launched on February 26th, 2014. See the following for more information: http://openid.net/2014/02/26/the-openid-foundation-launches-the-openid-connect-standard/

86   OAuth 2.0, is a framework, specified by the IETF in RFCs 6749 and 6750 (published in 2012) designed to support the development of authentication and authorization protocols. It provides a variety of standardized message flows based on JSON and HTTP; OpenID Connect uses these to provide Identity services.

OpenID Connect has many architectural similarities to OpenID 2.0, and in fact the protocols solve a very similar set of problems. However, OpenID 2.0 used XML and a custom message signature scheme that in practice sometimes proved difficult for developers to get right, with the effect that OpenID 2.0 implementations would sometimes mysteriously refuse to interoperate. OAuth 2.0, the substrate for OpenID Connect, outsources the necessary encryption to the Web's built-in TLS (also called HTTPS or SSL) infrastructure, which is universally implemented on both client and server platforms. OpenID Connect uses standard JSON Web Token (JWT) data structures when signatures are required. This makes OpenID Connect dramatically easier for developers to implement, and in practice it has resulted in much better interoperability.

OpenID Connect lets developers authenticate their users across websites and apps without having to own and manage password files. For the app builder, it provides a secure, verifiable answer to the question: "What is the identity of the person currently using the browser or native app that is connected to me?"

OpenID Connect allows for clients of all types, including browser-based JavaScript and native mobile apps, to launch sign-in flows and receive verifiable assertions about the identity of signed-in users.

```
(Identity, Authentication) + OAuth 2.0 = OpenID Connect
```

OWASP

The Open Web Application Security Project (OWASP) is a nonprofit focused on improving the security of software. OWASP develops numerous free and useful products of interest to the security architect including:

- **OWASP Top 10 Project** – Provides OWASP's opinion of the top ten Web-based application security flaws and how to mitigate them.[87]
- **OWASP Guide Project** – Aimed at architects, this is a comprehensive manual for designing secure Web applications and services.[88]
- **OWASP Software Assurance Maturity Model (SAMM)** – SAMM is a framework used to design software that is secure and tailored to an organization's specific risks.[89]
- **OWASP Mobile Project** – Provides a resource for developers and architects to develop and maintain secure mobile applications.[90]

Given the prevalence of Web-based and cloud-based solutions, OWASP provides an accessible and thorough framework with processes for Web application security. The security architect should be thoroughly familiar with OWASP's work and how it may apply to the mission he or she serves.

---

87 See the following for the current OWASP Top 10 Project information: https://www.owasp.org/index.php/Category:OWASP_Top_Ten_Project

88 See the following for the current OWASP Guide Project information: https://www.owasp.org/index.php/Category:OWASP_Guide_Project

89 See the following for the current information on OWASP SAMM: http://www.opensamm.org/

90 See the following for the current OWASP Mobile Project information: https://www.owasp.org/index.php/OWASP_Mobile_Security_Project

3

Security Engineering

Vulnerabilities in Mobile Systems

Over the past two decades, we have witnessed significant technology advances in mobile devices, from the personal data assistants (PDAs) of the late 1990s and early 2000s to the multifunctional smartphones of today. These advances have extended the virtual boundaries of the enterprise, blurring the lines between home and office by providing constant access to email, enabling new mobile business applications and allowing the access to, and storing of, sensitive company data on any device at any time.

When the first BlackBerry smartphone was released in the early 2000s, corporations soon recognized the benefits of remote email and calendar access and began providing smartphones with network access to a large percentage of their workforce, effectively establishing the idea of 24-hour connectivity. The popularity of smartphones extended beyond business users with the release of Apple's iPhone and later devices running Android and the Windows Phone operating systems. Features expanded beyond just email and Web browsing; mobile devices now have the ability to take photos, run custom applications, view rich content websites with Flash and JavaScript, connect to other devices and networks wirelessly, establish virtual private network connections, and act as data traffic conduits for other devices (known as tethering). Tablet PCs, such as the iPad, Surface, and Galaxy, are redefining the concept of the smart device and blurring the line between mobile devices and computers.

With the increase in mobile device capabilities and subsequent consumer adoption, these devices have become an integral part of how people accomplish tasks, both at work and in their personal lives. Although improvements in hardware and software have enabled more complex tasks to be performed on mobile devices, this functionality has also increased the attractiveness of the platform as a target for attackers. Android's "open application" model has led to multiple instances of malicious applications with hidden functionality that surreptitiously harvest user data.[91] Similarly, third-party Android application markets in China, Eastern Europe, and the Middle East have been identified as hosting applications with administrative remote command execution capability.

The first detected Android malware surfaced in August 2010, and since then, well over 300 distinct malware families have been found and identified on the platform. Sophisticated at avoiding detection and removal, there has been great innovation in how Android malware seeks to avoid and counter detection methods. Ginmaster is a case in point. First discovered in China in August 2011, this Trojanized program is injected into many legitimate apps that are also distributed through third-party markets. In 2012, Ginmaster began resisting detection by obfuscating class names, encrypting URLs and C&C instructions, and moving towards the polymorphism techniques that have become commonplace in Windows malware. In 2013, Ginmaster's developers implemented far more complex and subtle obfuscation and encryption, making this malware harder to detect or reverse engineer.[92]

Many organizations are concerned about data integrity, and increased regulation and data protection requirements have placed further obligations on organizations to properly secure data that interacts with mobile devices. As a result, higher levels of security and data protection assurance are required. The challenge is that these levels may be more than vendors or the

---

91   See the following: http://googlemobile.blogspot.com/2011/03/update-on-android-market-security.html
      http://www.csc.ncsu.edu/faculty/jiang/pubs/OAKLAND12.pdf

92   See the following: http://www.virusbtn.com/pdf/conference_slides/2013/Yu-VB2013.pdf

platforms themselves are currently able to provide. Another challenge faced by the security practitioner is that the benefits and rewards of using mobile devices are sometimes counteracted by fraud and security risks. As an example, security researchers have identified several iPhone and Android security vulnerabilities that allowed users to bypass device restrictions and install their own firmware through the "jailbreaking" or "rooting" of devices.[93] This may result in the users' ability to bypass many of the restrictions that prevent malicious software from running on the device.

Apple, RIM, Microsoft, and Google all support different operating systems and software development kits (SDKs) that developers use to create applications. Each of these platforms has a different security model that affects how developers address security within their applications. And each language has its own pitfalls and exposures that must be considered when developing an application. Restrictions on JavaScript or persistent session data have also led developers to place sensitive information and session information within the URL of every request to the server. In addition, network bandwidth limitations may encourage developers to create mobile device-formatted sites that cache additional information from webpages, potentially exposing this information if the device is compromised.

In Q4 of 2012, a global study by Forrester Research Inc. found that 74% of employees use personal smartphones for business tasks. The global study also found that 44% of employees use smartphones for work in coffee shops or other public places, and 47% use them while travelling.[94] As a result of these kinds of trends, the security practitioner needs to examine the current state of mobile device deployment and use within the enterprise. Understanding and effectively managing system vulnerabilities are fundamental and critical steps in any security management program. For example, the first four Critical Controls for Effective Cyber Defense (formerly the SANS Top 20 Security Controls) involve identification and inventory of devices and software, hardening of configurations, and regular and automated system vulnerability assessment and mitigation.[95] These controls also represent much of the first phase of the U.S. Department of Homeland Security's Continuous Diagnostics and Mitigation (CDM) Program.[96]

The challenges presented by mobile platforms are numerous and varied, but they can be examined and identified by breaking them down into functional units, or categories, as follows.

Risks from Remote Computing

Organizations often assume that remote users are secure because they access the corporate network through a virtual private network (VPN). Yet while VPNs provide a tunneled connection that allows only authenticated users to access the corporate intranet, they are not a complete, end-to-end solution. VPNs do not ensure that remote and mobile devices are free from software and configuration vulnerabilities, which could be used to propagate viruses or

---

93 See the following for a summary of issues and concerns with regards to "JailBroken" or "Rooted" Devices: https://www.owasp.org/index.php/Mobile_Jailbreaking_Cheat_Sheet

94 Forrsights Workforce Employee Survey, Q4 2012, Forrester Research, Inc. See the following: http://www.forrester.com/Forrsights+Workforce+Employee+Survey+Q4+2012/-/E-SUS1671

95 See the following: https://www.sans.org/media/critical-security-controls/cag4-1.pdf

96 See the following: http://www.dhs.gov/cdm
    http://www.us-cert.gov/cdm

3

Security Engineering

worms. These examples of malware are easily introduced, and as a result, remote machines can expose critical network assets to these vulnerabilities.

One example of a VPN-related breach was the 2008 incident at Heartland Payment Systems. The payment processing system was breached, in part, through the use of a VPN connection. First, a SQL injection attack allowed hackers to take control of a system inside Heartland but not within the transaction processing environment itself. The attackers then used the compromised internal system to execute an elevation of privilege attack. They were able to do this because systems such as workstations were not secured to the same level as systems that hosted sensitive data, such as the payment processing systems.[97]

A similar incident affected Google, Adobe, Microsoft, Yahoo, and approximately 30 tech companies in January 2010.[98] Following the incident, Google instructed its users to make emergency changes to VPN settings due to highly sophisticated and targeted attacks suspected to be from China. The attacks later were said to be directed at un-patched browser flaws.[99] The timing of the VPN configuration change led some to conclude there was a relationship between internal systems with un-patched software and VPN access to internal networks and sensitive data.[100] Segmentation, proxies, and filtering, as well as monitoring, may have prevented this breach. Patching and/or upgrading of the browser also may have prevented it. Ironically, three months after the attack, Google suggested that its users in China consider using VPN technology to bypass perimeter security and to ensure ongoing access to Google services in mainland China.

End point device risks can include the following issues:

- **Trusted Clients** – Who is on the other end of the device and what are their intentions?

- **Network Architectures** – Where is the infrastructure located to control and manage mobile device access? Typically it is in the LAN instead of in the DMZ, presenting opportunities for hackers to penetrate all the way into the LAN through APT attacks and RAT-based malware introduction. In addition, is there a robust and fully implemented patch management solution in place across the enterprise to address the potentiality of vulnerabilities due to exploits available in unpatched infrastructure? [101]

- **Policy Implementation** – Incorrect, insufficient, or weakly implemented controls can be easily bypassed by hackers and malware.

- **Stolen or Lost Devices** – Physical access control poses a significant challenge when devices containing sensitive data are not fully under the control and management of the enterprise security apparatus.

---

97 See the following: http://www.wired.com/images_blogs/threatlevel/2009/08/gonzalez.pdf

98 See the following: http://www.sophos.com/en-us/security-news-trends/security-trends/operation-aurora.aspx
    http://chenxiwang.wordpress.com/2010/01/21/why-google-and-microsoft-were-at-fault-for-the-attack-not-cloud-computing/

99 See the following: https://technet.microsoft.com/library/security/979352

100 See the following: http://googleblog.blogspot.com/2010/01/new-approach-to-china.html

101 See the following: http://nvlpubs.nist.gov/nistpubs/SpecialPublications/NIST.SP.800-40r3.pdf
    http://www.infoworld.com/d/security/cisco-fixes-remote-access-vulnerabilities-in-cisco-secure-access-control-system-234354

Risks from Mobile Workers

Mobile employees take their laptops home and on the road, then work from their new location in much the same way they would in the office. However, now they are without the protection of the corporate firewall and other security protection devices traditionally deployed to protect the enterprise LAN. This leaves their systems exposed to viruses, worms, and other types of malware, increasing the risk that these machines will later be used by attackers to access the network illegally. These machines eventually return to the corporate network, literally walking past the network firewall, and they are allowed to connect as trusted devices. If infected, a machine can easily become a conduit for introducing malicious code into the corporate environment. Mobile worker risks can include the following issues:

- **Platform Proliferation –** With the average employee now using two or three different mobile devices to access the corporate network, IT and security departments face the challenge of having to implement and manage mobile security across an almost limitless range of devices and operating systems, including Android, iOS, Windows Phone, Windows Mobile, BlackBerry, and Symbian.

- **Home Based PC and Multi-Device Synch Solutions –** This can introduce an additional risk of data leakage. Even though the employees may only be interested in backing up their personal files and photos, they could also be downloading corporate data and passwords from their mobile device onto their home computer as part of the sync process. If the employee's home computer has already been infected by Trojans or spyware, this could compromise the security of corporate data. Furthermore, if the computer has unpatched vulnerabilities, cybercriminals can easily access the mobile data that is backed up, stored, or synced onto the computer regardless of the security software that is actually running on the mobile device.

The list below categorizes some of the potential attack vectors for mobile devices:

- SMS
- Wi-fi
- Bluetooth
- Infra-red
- USB
- Web browser
- Email client
- Third-party applications
- "Jail-broken" phones
- Operating system vulnerabilities
- Physical access

The following list categorizes some of the potential examples for possible targets for attackers:

- **SMS**
  - SMS messages on the device can be forwarded to the attacker, or the attacker can search them for valuable information.
  - Many commerce sites, including financial institutions, communicate one time passwords or credential information through SMS as an out-of-band channel.
  - SMS can be utilized as a means to perform transactions that can lead to an attacker being able to perform unauthorized transactions from the device.

- **Email**
  - □ If the device is being used to send or retrieve email messages, the messages can be forwarded or searched by an attacker. This includes private as well as corporate email messages.
  - □ Email messages could likely contain sensitive company information as well as other private information such as credentials from password reset links.
- **Phone**
  - □ Low-level access to the hardware of mobile devices through mobile operating systems can provide an attacker the ability to record or listen to voice conversations.
- **Video/Photo**
  - □ Low-level access to the hardware of mobile devices through mobile operating systems can provide an attacker the ability to activate the internal camera to record video or take photos from the phone to provide detailed views of the device's surroundings.
- **Social Networking**
  - □ Social networking applications running on a smartphone can be utilized to propagate malware through the trust of the users associated with the compromised account.
  - □ Impersonation carried out as the associated account can allow the retrieval of personal information about the users and their social contacts.
- **Location Information**
  - □ Most mobile phones provide location information (for example, using built-in GPS or GSM antenna info), so it may be possible for an attacker to query this information on the device to determine where the device is located.
- **Voice Recording**
  - □ Low-level access to the hardware of mobile devices through mobile operating systems can provide an attacker the ability to activate the internal microphone to record any sound or voice close to the mobile phone, including phone calls.
- **Documents**
  - □ The attacker can retrieve documents stored on the device, including attachments from emails.
  - □ Document types can include PDF files, Microsoft Office files, credentials, encryption certificates, internal videos or internal e-books, among others.
- **Credentials**
  - □ Cached credentials may be stored insecurely inside third-party applications.

One example of the challenges facing security practitioners and architects today in the area of assessing and mitigating mobile systems vulnerabilities can be seen when examining a small but important difference between two mobile phone devices and how they approach implementing device-based encryption.

Windows Phone 8/8.1 BitLocker encryption is not automatically enabled on an unmanaged device when a screen-lock passcode is created, unlike iPhones. Specifically, Windows Phone 8/8.1 devices are not encrypted at all until activating Exchange ActiveSync (EAS). Device encryption can only be invoked on devices using remotely provisioned management policy (via EAS or a MDM). On the other hand, iPhone offers on-the-fly device and file encryption as soon as one creates a screen lock password.

To protect personal information on a Windows Phone, Microsoft has said users should set up a numeric PIN code. If the phone is lost, stolen, or malicious users attempt to brute force their way into the device, the device can be automatically be wiped (provided that the device has been registered, as noted below). To prevent attacks on the Windows Phone storage, Microsoft offers a few different options. First, when the phone is attached to a PC using USB, access to the data is gated based on successful entry of the user's PIN. Second, an offline attack affecting physical removable storage is addressed by fixing storage media to the device itself. Finally, users can register their Windows Phone devices, which will enable them to locate, ring, lock, or even erase the device when the phone is lost or stolen, according to Microsoft.[102]

The security practitioner needs to consider many variables when examining the threats, vulnerabilities, and risks associated with mobile systems in the enterprise. Guidance may be provided by standards such as those listed below:

- NIST SP 800-40 Revision 3, Guide to Enterprise Patch Management Technologies[103]
- NIST SP 800-121 Revision 1, Guide to Bluetooth Security[104]
- NIST SP 800-124 Revision 1, Guidelines for Managing the Security of Mobile Devices in the Enterprise[105]

Vulnerabilities in Embedded Devices and Cyber-Physical Systems

Intelligent, connected devices are all around us today. Smartphones are ubiquitous, and smart vehicles, smart buildings, and even smart appliances are moving closer to mainstream. While manufacturers are embedding intelligence into these devices and connecting them to the Internet to make them more useful, this level of sophistication also renders them targets for exploitation and security attacks. So what is the security architect to do? Take the following two examples:

Daniel Crowley and David Bryan, researchers with Trustwave SpiderLabs who presented at the Black Hat conference in 2013, demonstrated the ease of hacking a home system in a video interview with SC magazine using VeraLite, a $180 home automation gateway sold by Mi Casa Verde.

As Crowley explained, the VeraLite "has a Web interface but also UPnP (Universal Plug and Play Protocol) interface, which doesn't take a username and password. You can go on the network, ask if there are UPnP devices; it will respond and tell you all the things it can do.

---

102 See the following: http://www.windowsphone.com/en-US/how-to/wp8/settings-and-personalization/find-a-lost-phone

103 http://nvlpubs.nist.gov/nistpubs/SpecialPublications/NIST.SP.800-40r3.pdf

104 http://csrc.nist.gov/publications/nistpubs/800-121-rev1/sp800-121_rev1.pdf

105 http://nvlpubs.nist.gov/nistpubs/SpecialPublications/NIST.SP.800-124r1.pdf

If I have access to your home network, then I have access to your home." He said this shortly before using a couple of keystrokes to open a door lock sitting on the table in front of him.

VeraLite is not alone. Crowley and Bryan said they had tested 10 different products, "and only found one or two that we couldn't manage to break. Most didn't have any security controls at all." [106]

The second example has to do with the case of 300 BMWs stolen in England in 2013 and 2014 because hackers were able to breach a technology port in the car that gave them access to each car's key fob digital ID.

There was no authentication required to program the fob. BMW left this system 'open' to make life easier for its dealer networks, but unfortunately it only made their cars easier to steal.[107]

The security architect has a difficult battle to wage in this arena, as the clear bias seems to be that usability and ease of access are winning out over common sense security protocols and procedures; likewise for the security professionals who will be tasked with managing many of these systems as they continue to be implemented, both in the enterprise and also in the home. It seems that here as well, the common sense approaches to security that are time tested and proven to work are being shunted aside in favor of ease of access and "functionality" at the end-user level. What about Cyber Physical Systems? Are they being architected and deployed and managed with the same lack of attention to security that is being observed in the consumer space?

Cyber Physical Systems (CPS) are smart networked systems with embedded sensors, processors, and actuators that are designed to sense and interact with the physical world (including the human users) and support real-time, guaranteed performance in safety-critical applications. In CPS systems, the joint behavior of the "cyber" and "physical" elements of the system is critical - computing, control, sensing, and networking are deeply integrated into every component, and the actions of components and systems must be carefully orchestrated.

A partial list of industrial areas where CPS offerings may be found is below:

- Transportation
- Manufacturing
- Healthcare
- Energy
- Agriculture
- Defense
- Building Controls
- Emergency Response Systems

There are several challenges faced by CPS-based architectures today. Two in particular are of interest to the security practitioner and architect: Cybersecurity and Interoperability. Cybersecurity is important due to the fact that many of the attacks tacking place against traditional infrastructures such as websites, databases, and networks can easily be adapted and replicated to attack CPS solutions such as smart power grids and transportation networks. These kinds of attacks can have dire consequences if carried out successfully. Interoperability

---

106 http://www.scmagazine.com/video-hacking-home-automation-systems/article/305416/#

107 http://cars.uk.msn.com/news/new-bmws-at-risk-of-theft

is important because of the need to address the fact that CPSs can operate across a myriad of systems to carry out complex tasks.

Some of the connected and core technologies needed to integrate and manage CPS offerings are as follows:

- **Abstractions, Modularity, and Composability** – to enable CPS system elements to be combined and reused while retaining safety, security, and reliability.

- **Systems-Engineering Based Architectures and Standards** – to enable efficient design and development of reliability systems while ensuring interoperability and integration with legacy systems.

- **Adaptive and Predictive Hierarchical Hybrid Control** – to achieve tightly-coordinated and synchronized actions and interactions in systems that are intrinsically synchronous, distributed, and noisy.

- **Integration of Multi-Physics Models and Models of Software** – to enable co-design of physical engineered and computational elements with predictable system behaviors.

- **Distributed Sensing, Communications, and Perception** – to enable flexible, reliable, and high performance distributed networks of CPS that provide an accurate and reliable model of the world and enable time-aware and time-critical functionality.

- **Diagnostics and Prognostics** – to identify, predict, and prevent or recover from faults in complex systems.

- **Cybersecurity** – to guarantee safety by guarding against malicious attacks on CPS systems.

- **Validation, Verification, and Certification** – to speed up the design cycle for bringing innovations to market while ensuring high confidence in system safety and functionality.

- **Autonomy and Human Interaction** – to develop models of autonomous CPS systems and humans interacting with them to facilitate model-based design of reactive systems that are used by humans.[108]

The security practitioner and architect both have to play a role in understanding and managing the emerging CPS solutions found in the enterprise today. In addition to traditional IT security mechanisms for prevention such as authentication, encryption, firewalls, and detection such as intrusion detection systems and forensics, there is a need for new CPS security mechanisms to be designed and integrated into the enterprise. The security architect should work hand in hand with the practitioner to ensure that the necessary attention is focused on the development and integration of solutions that address CPS security. There are many areas to consider, but three stand out in particular.

The first is risk assessment: The security architect should consider questions such as, "Where should I allocate my budget to minimize potential physical damages to my systems?" A second area is bad data detection mechanisms. These mechanisms should not assume random, independent failures, but they should consider detection of sophisticated attackers. One particular problem needing to be addressed in this area is bad topology detection mechanisms. Replacing sensed data

---

108 "Cyber Physical Systems (CPS) Vision Statement" – Working Draft (5/8/14) Page 4. Available here: http://www.nitrd.gov/nitrdgroups/images/6/6a/Cyber_Physical_Systems_%28CPS%29_Vision_Statement.pdf

with false data, which would be a form of a deception attack, is a very generic attack that can be extended to any smart grid application, as all of them are based on correct sensor measurements. As a result, it is important to develop intrusion detection mechanisms or reputation management systems for smart grid applications where not all received data can be trusted. The third approach is to architect resiliency/survivability of the system to attacks. A promising direction is to design the topology of the power distribution network to withstand malicious commands to circuit breakers trying to change and disconnect the network due to the use of APTs or other malware vectors used to take control of the system by bad actors.

Industrial systems and critical infrastructures are often monitored and controlled by simple computers called Industrial Control Systems (ICS). ICS are based on standard embedded systems platforms, and they often use commercial off-the-self software. ICS are used to control industrial processes such as manufacturing, product handling, production, and distribution. Well-known types of ICS include supervisory control and data acquisition (SCADA) systems, distributed control systems (DCS), and programmable logic controllers (PLC).

SCADA systems historically distinguish themselves from other ICS by being the largest subgroup of ICS systems and large scale processes that can include multiple sites and large distances. A Supervisory Control and Data Acquisition (SCADA) system can be typically viewed as an assembly of interconnected equipment used to monitor and control physical equipment in industrial environments. They are widely used to automate geographically distributed processes such as electricity power generation, transmission and distribution, oil and gas refining and pipeline management, water treatment and distribution, chemical production and processing, rail systems, and other mass transit.

The following is a top ten list of threats for automation and process control systems and Industrial Control System Security: [109]

No.	Threat	Explanation
1	Unauthorized use of remote maintenance access points	Maintenance access points are deliberately created external entrances to the ICS network and are often insufficiently secure.
2	Online attacks via office or enterprise networks	Office IT is usually linked to the network in several ways. In most cases, network connections from offices to the ICS network also exist, so attackers can gain access via this route.
3	Attacks on standard components used in the ICS network	Standard IT components (commercial off-the-shelf (COTS)) such as systems software, application servers, or databases often contain flaws or vulnerabilities, which can be exploited by attackers. If these standard components are also used in the ICS network, the risk of a successful attack on the ICS network increases.
4	(D)DoS Attacks	(Distributed) Denial-of-Service attacks can impair network connections and essential resources and cause systems to fail – in order to disrupt the operation of an ICS, for instance.

---

109 See the following: http://www.insys-icom.com/bausteine.net/f/10564/KB_en_INSYS_icom_IT-Security_V04_final_RTO.pdf?fd=0

No.	Threat	Explanation
5	Human error and sabotage	Intentional deeds – whether by internal or external perpetrators – are a massive threat to all protection targets. Negligence and human error are also a great threat, especially in relation to the protection targets confidentiality and availability.
6	Introducing malware via removable media and external hardware	The use of removable media and mobile IT components of external staff always entails great risk of malware infection.
7	Reading and writing news in the ICS network	Most control components currently use clear text protocols, so communication is unprotected. This makes it relatively easy to read and introduce control commands.
8	Unauthorized access to resources	Internal perpetrators and subsequent attacks following initial external penetration have it especially easy if services and components in the process network do not utilize authentication and authorization methods or if the methods are insecure.
9	Attacks on network components	Attackers can manipulate network components in order to carry out man-in-the-middle attacks or to make sniffing easier, for example.
10	Technical malfunctions or force majeure	Outages resulting from extreme weather or technical malfunctions can occur at any time – risk and potential damage can only be minimized in such cases.

There have been several incidents since 1999 that highlight the importance of these kinds of threats to embedded systems.

Incident: Gasoline Pipeline Rupture

In June 1999, a 16 inch diameter steel pipeline owned by The Olympic Pipe Line Company ruptured and released about 237,000 gallons of gasoline into a creek that flowed through Whatcom Falls Park in Bellingham, Washington. About 1 1/2 hours after the rupture, the gasoline ignited and burned about 1 1/2 miles along the creek. Two 10-year-old boys and an 18-year-old young man died as a result of the accident. Eight additional injuries were documented. A single-family residence and the city of Bellingham's water treatment plant were severely damaged. Olympic estimated that total property damages were at least $45 million.

One of the causes of the accident was Olympic Pipe Line Company's practice of performing database development work on the SCADA system while the system was being used to operate the pipeline. Shortly before the rupture, new records for pump vibration data were entered into the SCADA historical database. The records were created by a pipeline controller who had been temporarily assigned as a computer system administrator. According to the accident report, the database updates led to the system's becoming non-responsive at a critical time during pipeline operations.[110]

Malicious Control System Cybersecurity Attack – Maroochy Water Services, Australia

Vitek Boden worked for Hunter Watertech, an Australian firm that installed SCADA (Supervisory Control And Data Acquisition) radio-controlled sewage equipment for the Maroochy Shire Council in Queensland, Australia. Boden applied for a job with the

---

110 See the following: http://www.ntsb.gov/doclib/reports/2002/PAR0202.pdf
    http://www.historylink.org/index.cfm?DisplayPage=output.cfm&file_id=5468

Maroochy Shire Council, apparently after he walked away from a "strained relationship" with Hunter Watertech. The Council decided not to hire him. Consequently, Boden decided to get even with both the Council and his former employer. He packed his car with stolen radio equipment attached to a computer. He drove around the area on at least 46 occasions from February 28 to April 23, 2000, issuing radio commands to the sewage equipment he had helped to install. Boden caused 800,000 liters of raw sewage to spill out into local parks, rivers, and even the grounds of a Hyatt Regency hotel. "Marine life died, the creek water turned black, and the stench was unbearable for residents," said a representative of the Australian Environmental Protection Agency.[111] Boden coincidentally got caught when a policeman pulled him over for a traffic violation after one of his attacks. A judge sentenced him to two years in jail and ordered him to reimburse the Council for cleanup. Boden's attack became the first widely known example of someone maliciously breaking into a control system.[112]

Incident: Virus Attacks Train Signaling System

In August 2003, a computer virus was blamed for bringing down train signaling systems throughout the eastern U.S. The signaling outage briefly affected the entire CSX system, which covers 23 states east of the Mississippi River. The virus infected the computer system at CSX Corp's Jacksonville, Fla. headquarters, shutting down signaling, dispatching, and other systems. The cause was believed to be a virus known as SoBig, adding to havoc caused by the Blaster worm, which debuted one week earlier. A derivative of Blaster brought down Air Canada's check-in systems during the same timeframe.[113]

The security practitioner and the security architect both need to be aware of the threats, vulnerabilities, and risks associated with operating embedded systems within the enterprise. The security architect needs to consider all appropriate standards and guidance that may be available on systems design, while the security practitioner needs to be aware of best practices associated with management, maintenance, operations, and securing of these systems. Risk management also must be considered by both the architect and the practitioner, as well as business impact.

The following standards are particularly relevant for the cybersecurity of ICT systems in non-nuclear critical energy infrastructure:

The ISO 27000 series should be mentioned first. It describes operational and technical requirements for information security management. The ISO 27001 standard for information security management provides the foundation, which is developed in more detail in ISO standard 27002. Higher numbered standards specify sector-specific implementations.

ISO 27032:2012 specifically targets the problems arising from the complex interaction of Internet security, network security, and application security. Therefore, it discusses controls for all cyberspace stakeholders (consumer and provider organizations). It is unique in that it explicitly

---

111 See the following: http://www.theregister.co.uk/2001/10/31/hacker_jailed_for_revenge_sewage/

112 See the following for a complete analysis of this incident: http://csrc.nist.gov/groups/SMA/fisma/ics/documents/Maroochy-Water-Services-Case-Study_report.pdf

113 See the following: http://www.informationweek.com/computer-virus-brings-down-train-signals/d/d-id/1020446?

targets topics such as controls against social engineering attacks, cybersecurity readiness, and awareness. Most importantly, it includes a framework for information sharing and coordination.[114]

IEC 62351 directly targets information security for power system control operations. It primarily implements standards for security affecting the communication protocols defined by the IEC TC 57 working group, specifically the IEC 60870-5 series, the IEC 60870-6 series, the IEC 61850 series, the IEC 61970 series, and the IEC 61968 series.[115] These standards are mainly applicable for manufacturers. The M/490 SGIS110 group is working to expand these standards to include specific technical aspects for smart grid cybersecurity.[116]

The IEC 62443 series (derived from ISA-99) covers security for Industrial Automation and Control Systems (IACS).[117] The focus is on operational best practices. The standard is driven by vendors and end-users from different industrial sectors, including major oil and gas companies. It targets asset owners, system integrators, and component providers with separate substandards. IEC 62443 tries to include and align with existing standards – in particular with NISTIR 7628 and ISO 27001/2.

NIST Special Publication 800-39, Managing Information Security Risk – Organization, Mission, and Information System View,[118] for the ISMS framework, references the ISO 27000 standards as well as ISO 31000 and ISO 27005 (risk management). It recommends a unifying risk management approach.

NISTIR 7628 (Guidelines for Smart Grid Cyber Security) targets cybersecurity for electric power infrastructure. The report focuses on security requirements.[119] Part 1 lists high-level security requirements and heavily references other NIST standards for specific requirements. It identifies seven domains in the smart grid (Operations, Distribution, Transmission, etc.) and defines logical interface categories (e.g., interfaces between control systems within the same organization and within different organizations). Security requirements (e.g., integrity, authentication, bandwidth, real-time requirements) are then applied to these interface categories.

Most of the security requirements in NISTIR 7628 are covered by ISO 27001, 27002, and IEC 62351. Appendix A of the Catalog of Control System Security Recommendations contains additional cross-references to the security measures in the following standards: FIPS 140-2, NERC CIP, and IEEE 1402 (Guide for Electric Power Substation Physical and Electronic Security).[120]

---

114 See the following: http://www.iso.org/iso/catalogue_detail?csnumber=44375

115 See the following: http://www.iec.ch/smartgrid/standards/
   http://iectc57.ucaiug.org/wg15public/Public%20Documents/White%20Paper%20on%20Security%20
   Standards%20in%20IEC%20TC57.pdf

116 See the following: http://ec.europa.eu/energy/gas_electricity/smartgrids/doc/xpert_group1_security.pdf

117 See the following: https://www.isa.org/isa99/
   http://isa99.isa.org/Documents/Committee_Meeting/(2012-05)%20Gaithersburg,%20MD/ISA-99-
   Security_Levels_Proposal.pdf

118 See the following: http://csrc.nist.gov/publications/nistpubs/800-39/SP800-39-final.pdf

119 See the following: http://www.nist.gov/smartgrid/upload/nistir-7628_total.pdf

120 See the following: http://ieeexplore.ieee.org/xpl/articleDetails.jsp?arnumber=836296

The North American Electric Reliability Corporation (NERC) has created the NERC Critical Infrastructure Protection (CIP) cybersecurity standards. There are separate standards from CIP-002 through CIP-009 for building a comprehensive cybersecurity framework. CIP compliance has been mandatory for power suppliers since the Energy Policy Act of 2005. Audits started in 2011. CIP also uses a risk-based approach and focuses specifically on the "Cyber Critical Assets" group in the Bulk Electric System. The current Standards that are subject to enforcement are listed below:[121]

- CIP-002-3 Critical Cyber Asset Identification
- CIP-003-3 Security Management Controls
- CIP-004-3a Personnel and Training
- CIP-005-3a Electronic Security Perimeter
- CIP-006-3c Physical Security of BES Cyber Systems
- CIP-007-3a Systems Security Management
- CIP-008-3 Incident Reporting and Response Planning
- CIP-009-3 Recovery Plans for BES Cyber Systems

NIST SP 800-53 (Recommended Security Controls for Federal Information Systems and Organizations) provides security control selection for U.S. federal information systems based on a risk management framework. It also provides a set of baseline security controls as a minimum standard. Rev. 4 includes an appendix for ICS security controls.[122]

NIST SP 800-82 Revision 1 (Guide to Industrial Control Systems Security) focuses specifically on SCADA systems and PLC/DCS.[123] It shows threats and vulnerabilities along with mitigating measures. SP 800-39 is referenced for the overall framework.

The Application and Use of Cryptography

The History of Cryptography

Cryptography has been around for many years, and yet the basic principles of cryptography have not changed. The core principle of most cryptographic systems is that they take a plaintext message and, through a series of transpositions or substitutions, convert it to ciphertext, as shown in *Figure 3.38*.

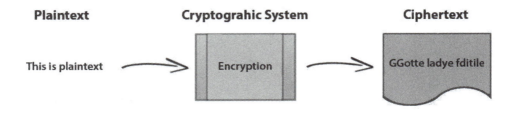

Figure 3.38 - **The Cryptographic Process**

---

121 See the following: http://www.nerc.com/pa/Stand/Pages/CIPStandards.aspx

122 See the following: http://nvlpubs.nist.gov/nistpubs/SpecialPublications/NIST.SP.800-53r4.pdf

123 See the following: http://nvlpubs.nist.gov/nistpubs/SpecialPublications/NIST.SP.800-82r1.pdf

The Early (Manual) Era

There is evidence of cryptographic-type operations going back thousands of years. In one case, there is an example in Egypt of one set of hieroglyphics that were encrypted with a simple substitution algorithm. The Spartans were known for the Spartan scytale – a method of transmitting a message by wrapping a leather belt around a tapered dowel. Written across the dowel, the message would be undecipherable once it was unwrapped from the dowel. The belt could then be carried to the recipient, who would be able to read the message as long as he had a dowel of the same diameter and taper.

There are further examples of the use and development of cryptographic methods throughout the past two centuries. Julius Caesar used the Caesar cipher – a simple substitution cipher that shifted the alphabet three positions. Developments in cryptographic science continued throughout the Middle Ages with the work of Leon Battista Alberti, who invented the idea of a cryptographic key in 1466, and the enhanced use of polyalphabetic ciphers by Blais de Vigenère. Their work will be examined in more detail when reviewing the methods of cryptography.

The Mechanical Era

From a paper-and-pencil world, cryptography developed into the mechanical era with the advent of cipher disks and rotors to simplify the manual processes of cryptography. Devices developed during this era were in regular use well into the twentieth century. These include the German Enigma machine, the Confederate Army's Cipher Disk, and the Japanese Red and Purple machines. During this era, tools and machines were developed that greatly increased the complexity of cryptographic operations, as well as enabling the use of much more robust algorithms. Many of these devices introduced a form of randomization to the cryptographic operations and made the use of cryptographic devices available to nontechnical people.

One core concept developed in this era was the performance of the algorithm on the numerical value of a letter rather than the letter itself. This was a natural transition into the electronic era, where cryptographic operations are normally performed on binary or hex values of letters rather than on the written letter. For example, the alphabet could be written as follows:

$$A = 0, \ B = 1, \ C = 3 \ . \ . \ . \ Z = 25$$

This was especially integral to the one-time pad and other cipher methods that were developed during this era.

The Modern Era

Today's cryptography is far more advanced than the cryptosystems of yesterday. Organizations are able to both encrypt and break ciphers that could not even have been imagined before human civilization had the power of computers. Today's cryptosystems operate in a manner so that anyone with a computer can use cryptography without even understanding cryptographic operations, algorithms, and advanced mathematics. However, it is still important to implement a cryptosystem in a secure manner. In fact, the majority of attacks against cryptosystems are not the result of weaknesses in cryptographic algorithms but rather poor or mismanaged implementations. As cryptographic algorithms in use today are examined, many of the advances of yesterday are being built into the functions of today. Randomization, transposition, and cryptographic keys will be explained.

3

Security Engineering

385

Emerging Technology

Quantum Cryptography [124]

A fundamental difference between traditional cryptography and quantum cryptography is that traditional cryptography primarily uses difficult mathematical techniques as its fundamental mechanism. Quantum cryptography, on the other hand, uses physics to secure data. Whereas traditional cryptography stands firm due to strong math, quantum cryptography has a radically different premise in that the security should be based on known physical laws rather than on mathematical difficulties.

Quantum cryptography (also known as *quantum key distribution*, or QKD) is built on quantum physics. Perhaps the most well-known aspect of quantum physics is the uncertainty principle of Werner Heisenberg. His basic claim is that a person cannot know both a particle's position and momentum with unlimited accuracy at the same time.

Specifically, quantum cryptography is a set of protocols, systems, and procedures by which it is possible to create and distribute secret keys. Quantum cryptography can be used to generate and distribute secret keys, which can then be used together with traditional crypto algorithms and protocols to encrypt and transfer data. It is important to note that quantum cryptography is not used to encrypt data, transfer encrypted data, or store encrypted data.

The need for asymmetric key systems arose from the issue of key distribution. The challenge is that users need a secure channel to set up a secure channel. Quantum cryptography solves the key distribution problem by allowing the exchange of a cryptographic key between two remote parties with complete security, as dictated via the laws of physics. Once the key exchange takes place, conventional cryptographic algorithms are used. For that reason, many prefer the term QKD to quantum cryptography.[125]

When used in a practical setting, the following is a basic overview of how quantum cryptography can be used:

1. Two remote parties need to exchange data electronically in a highly secure manner.

2. They choose standard crypto algorithms, protocols, systems, and transport technologies to exchange the data in an encrypted form.

3. They use a quantum cryptography channel to generate and exchange the secret keys needed by the algorithms.

4. They use the secret keys generated with quantum cryptography and the classical algorithms to encrypt the data.

5. They exchange the encrypted data using the chosen classical protocols and transfer technologies.

Within quantum cryptography, there are two unique channels. One is used for the transmission of the quantum key material via single-photon light pulses. The other channel carries all message traffic, including the cryptographic protocols, encrypted user traffic, and

---

124 See the following: Ben Rothke, An overview of quantum cryptography, in Information Security Management Handbook, 3rd ed., Vol. 3, Tipton, Harold F. and Krause, Micki, Eds., Auerbach Publications, New York, 2006, pp. 380–381.

125 See the following for the announcement of the first successful test of Quantum Key Distribution (QKD) technology over a live "lit" fiber network: http://www.homelandsecuritynewswire.com/dr20140425-major-step-toward-stronger-encryption-technology-announced

more. Within the laws of quantum physics, once a photon has been observed, its state is changed. This makes quantum cryptography perfect for security because any time that someone tries to eavesdrop on a secure channel, this will cause a disturbance to the flow of the photons. This can easily be identified to provide extra security.

Quantum algorithms are orders of magnitude better than current systems. It is theorized that quantum factorization can factor a number a million times longer than that used for RSA in a millionth of the time. In addition, it can crack a DES cipher in less than four minutes. The increased speed of a quantum computer comes from forming a superposition of numbers. Quantum computers are theoretically able to perform calculations on various superpositions simultaneously, which creates the effect of a massive parallel computation.[126]

While still mainly theoretical, quantum computing and quantum key distribution will likely provide the next leap in encryption technology. Just as there is a massive distinction between the belts the Spartans used and the super computers of today, quantum key distribution could be a leap of the same magnitude.

Core Information Security Principles

Cryptography addresses the principles, means, and methods of disguising information to ensure its integrity, confidentiality, and authenticity. Unlike the other security principles, cryptography does not completely support the standard of availability.

Availability

Many access control systems use cryptography to limit access to systems through the use of passwords. Many token-based authentication systems use cryptographic-based hash algorithms to compute one-time passwords. Denying unauthorized access prevents an attacker from entering and damaging the system or network, thereby denying access to authorized users.

Confidentiality

Cryptography provides confidentiality through altering or hiding a message so that ideally it cannot be understood by anyone except the intended recipient.

Integrity

Cryptographic tools provide integrity checks that allow a recipient to verify that a message has not been altered. Cryptographic tools cannot prevent a message from being altered, but they are effective to detect either intentional or accidental modification of the message. Cryptographic functions use several methods to ensure that a message has not been changed or altered. These include hash functions, digital signatures, and message authentication codes (MACs). The main concept is that the recipient is able to detect any change that has been made to a message, whether accidentally or intentionally.

Additional Features of Cryptographic Systems

In addition to the three core principles of information security listed above, cryptographic tools provide several more benefits.

---

126 See the following for a general overview of Quantum Computing: http://www.militaryaerospace.com/ articles/print/volume-24/issue-7/technology-focus/from-theory-to-reality-quantum-computing-enters-the-defense-industry.html

See the following for an overview of the application of Quantum Computing in the defense industry: http://www.militaryaerospace.com/articles/2014/03/lockheed-quantum-computing. html?cmpid=EnlEmbeddedComputingMarch102014

Nonrepudiation

In a trusted environment, the authentication of the origin can be provided through the simple control of the keys. The receiver has a level of assurance that the message was encrypted by the sender, and the sender has trust that the message was not altered once it was received. However, in a more stringent, less trustworthy environment, it may be necessary to provide assurance via a third party of who sent a message and that the message was indeed delivered to the right recipient. This is accomplished through the use of digital signatures and public key encryption. The use of these tools provides a level of nonrepudiation of origin that can be verified by a third party.

Once a message has been received, what is to prevent the recipient from changing the message and contesting that the altered message was the one sent by the sender? The nonrepudiation of delivery prevents a recipient from changing the message and falsely claiming that the message is in its original state. This is also accomplished through the use of public key cryptography and digital signatures and is verifiable by a trusted third party.

Authentication

Authentication is the ability to determine if someone or something is what it declares to be. This is primarily done through the control of the keys because only those with access to the key are able to encrypt a message. This is not as strong as the nonrepudiation of origin, which will be reviewed shortly.

Access Control

Through the use of cryptographic tools, many forms of access control are supported – from log-ins via passwords and passphrases to the prevention of access to confidential files or messages. In all cases, access would only be possible for those individuals that had access to the correct cryptographic keys.

Data at Rest

The protection of stored data is often a key requirement for an organization's sensitive information. Backup tapes, off-site storage, password files, and many other types of sensitive information need to be protected from disclosure or undetected alteration. This is done through the use of cryptographic algorithms that limit access to the data to those that hold the proper encryption (and decryption) keys. (*Note*: Because password files are hashed and salted instead of encrypted, there are no keys to decrypt them.) Some modern cryptographic tools also permit the condensing or compressing of messages, saving both transmission and storage space.

Data in Transit

One of the primary purposes throughout history has been to move messages across various types of media. The intent was to prevent the contents of the message from being revealed even if the message itself was intercepted in transit. Whether the message is sent manually, over a voice network, or via the Internet, modern cryptography provides secure and confidential methods to transmit data and allows the verification of the integrity of the message, so that any changes to the message itself can be detected. Advances in quantum cryptography also theorize the detection of whether a message has even been read in transit.

Link Encryption

Data are encrypted on a network using either link or end-to-end encryption. In general, link encryption is performed by service providers, such as a data communications provider on a

Frame Relay network. Link encryption encrypts all of the data along a communications path (e.g., a satellite link, telephone circuit, or T-1 line). Because link encryption also encrypts routing data, communications nodes need to decrypt the data to continue routing. The data packet is decrypted and re-encrypted at each point in the communications channel. It is theoretically possible that an attacker compromising a node in the network may see the message in the clear. Because link encryption also encrypts the routing information, it provides traffic confidentiality better than end-to-end encryption. Traffic confidentiality hides the addressing information from an observer, preventing an inference attack based on the existence of traffic between two parties.

The Cryptographic Lifecycle

All cryptographic functions and implementations have a useful life. As computational power increases and the ability to analyze cryptographic systems becomes more refined, cryptographic systems are constantly evaluated to ensure they still meet the security requirements originally specified. Information security professionals must stay abreast of current trends and discoveries in the cryptographic domain to ensure they provide accurate and timely assessments and recommendations. A cryptographic function or implementation is considered "broken" or no longer effective when one of the following conditions is met:

- For a hashing function:
  - Collisions or hashes can be reliably reproduced in an economically feasible fashion without the original source.
  - When an implementation of a hashing function allows a side channel attack.
- For an encryption system:
  - A cipher is decoded without access to the key in an economically feasible fashion.
  - When an implementation of an encryption system allows for the unauthorized disclosure of information in an economically feasible fashion.

Cryptographic system lifecycle phases are generally described in terms of strong, weakened, and compromised. The United States National Institute of Standards and Technology uses the following terms to describe algorithms and key lengths in its special publication 800-131A:[127]

- "Acceptable is used to mean that the algorithm and key length is safe to use; no security risk is currently known.
- Deprecated means that the use of the algorithm and key length is allowed, but the user must accept some risk. The term is used when discussing the key lengths or algorithms that may be used to apply cryptographic protection to data (e.g., encrypting or generating a digital signature).
- Restricted means that the use of the algorithm or key length is deprecated, and there are additional restrictions required to use the algorithm or key length for applying cryptographic protection to data (e.g., encrypting).
- Legacy-use means that the algorithm or key length may only be used to process already protected information (e.g., to decrypt ciphertext data or to verify a signature), but there may be risk in doing so. Methods for mitigating this risk should be considered."

---

127 See the following: http://csrc.nist.gov/publications/nistpubs/800-131A/sp800-131A.pdf

Algorithm/Protocol Governance

As cryptographic algorithms and protocols age, they become compromised and replacements need to be put in place. This is a challenge as many organizations must determine how to migrate existing information systems and their cryptographic elements to new platforms. The information security professional must ensure governance processes are in place to support an organization's use of cryptography. The policies, standards, and procedures relating to cryptography should minimally address:

- Approved cryptographic algorithms and key sizes.
- Transition plans for weakened or compromised algorithms and keys.
- Procedures for the use of cryptographic systems in the organization and standards indicating what information and processes are subject to cryptographic requirements.
- Key generation, escrow, and destruction.
- Incident reporting surrounding the loss of keys or the compromise of cryptographic systems.

Issues Surrounding Cryptography

The power of cryptography is increasingly misused by those with criminal intentions and is subject to export and law enforcement requirements. As part of risk analysis, it is important for the security professional to understand how cryptography can be misused so that appropriate security mitigation can be applied. An example of misuse is the cryptologic time bomb. This is the case where, for example, a disgruntled employee or a rogue criminal organization installs a computer program that is designed to encrypt a company's computer files using strong encryption – using a key that only the attacker knows. The attacker will either attempt to hold the computer files until a ransom is paid or until some painful consequence occurs to the victim company. The same issues apply to ransomware used by criminals to hold a computer system hostage until some sort of payment has been made.

Another issue with the potential misuse of cryptography is in the protection of intellectual property. Cryptographic protection is implemented for preventing software and media piracy. Although cryptography is used to allow or deny access to the video game market and DVDs, there are some general concerns expressed by privacy advocates about how such applications of cryptography could have macroeconomic effects if not used ethically. One scenario that could play out would be the case where a company could use encryption to create a new form of censorship based on the ability to track and identify electronic information. Such a system could be used to secretly inventory a computer anywhere on the Internet then make a catalog of software/hardware on a machine available for action by a third party, for example, barring someone with decryption software from playing a copy-protected DVD. So-called digital rights management systems (DRMS) require a design and governance that can be used to both protect intellectual property and individual privacy while ensuring an individual's fair use of the intellectual property. Some governments impose restrictions on the use, export, or import of cryptographic hardware and software having high work factors.

International Export Controls

Most countries have some regulations regarding the use or distribution of cryptographic systems. Usually, this is to maintain the ability of law enforcement to do their jobs and to keep strong cryptographic tools out of the hands of criminals. Cryptography is considered in most countries to be on par with munitions, a weapon of war, and is managed through laws written to control the distribution of military equipment. Some countries do not allow any cryptographic tools to be used by their citizens; others have laws that control the use of cryptography, usually based on key length. This is because key length is one of the most understandable methods of gauging the strength of a cryptosystem.

International export controls are employed by governments to limit the shipment of products containing strong cryptography to countries that that government feels is trustworthy enough to use in a friendly way. For example, in the United States, the governmental agencies responsible for regulating and enforcing strong cryptography product shipment to other countries are the National Security Agency, the U.S. Department of State, and the U.S. Department of Commerce.[128] In the United States, the process offers an opportunity for these agencies to determine if there is technology that should not be exported. Most countries' concern over their national security related to cryptography is established as specific technologies that would be detrimental to their national defense and, therefore, need to be controlled through export regulations. As a result of export controls, many vendors market two versions of their products, one that has strong encryption and another that has weaker encryption that is sold in other countries.

Law Enforcement

Privacy is a key issue in countries with a strong culture of freedom of speech and protection from unreasonable search and seizure, such as the United States. In some countries, this is not an issue as the laws require all organizations and individuals to provide law enforcement with their cryptographic keys, use weak keys, or not allow private use of encryption.

Electronic surveillance has become a powerful tool in the law enforcement arsenal. However, in the European Union and several other countries, finding a way to guarantee law enforcement, the ability to legally access encrypted information without damaging the commercial viability of commercial cryptography, or the civil liberties of citizens is an enormous technological and legislative challenge.

In many countries, there is a general public acceptance of the use of telephone and mail interception via a warrant with the goal of protecting society. However, there is a general aversion to similar warranted access for encrypted communications. Additionally, security technology vendors do not like the idea of having to "build in" key recovery backdoors into their products for law enforcement. This is seen as both expensive and unpopular with customers.

In the case of cloud-based technology platforms, the security architect has much to consider. The move to place more and more corporate data into some form of cloud-based solution, whether private, public, or hybrid, has meant that more and more cloud vendors are taking on the role of security architect and front line responder with regards to the security aspects of the cloud architecture. Many vendors offer the option for some form of "menu driven" encryption selections within their architectures, or an "a la carte" option for the addition of encryption, while the customers may or may not have the option to add on their own encryption solution and manage the encryption keys themselves.

Encryption is becoming more of a generic technology, integrated into an ever increasing number of applications and products. Voice and data are increasingly converging onto a single,

---

128 See the following: http://www.bis.doc.gov/licensing/exportingbasics.htm

Internet Protocol (IP) based transport network. Technology has reached the point where voice/data can be transmitted via Internet telephony, encrypted mobile phones, or stored on computers using disk encryption. The main technologic methods for lawful access to private data are key escrow, where a third party, possibly a government entity or service provider, holds a copy of the cryptographic keys, and brute force, where massive computer resources attack the key.

Public Key Infrastructure (PKI)

A PKI is a set of system, software, and communication protocols required to use, manage, and control public key cryptography. It has three primary purposes: publish public keys/certificates, certify that a key is tied to an individual or entity, and provide verification of the validity of a public key.

The Certification Authority (CA) "signs" an entity's digital certificate to certify that the certificate content accurately represents the certificate owner. There can be different levels of assurance implied by the CA signing the certificate similar to forms of the physical identification of an individual that can imply differing levels of trust. In the physical world, a credit card with a name on it has a differing level of authentication value than, say, a government-issued ID card. Any entity can claim to be anything it wants, but if the entity wants to provide a high level of assurance, it should provide identifying content in its certificate that is easily confirmed by third parties that are trusted by all parties involved. In the digital world, a Dun and Bradstreet number, credit report, or perhaps another form of trusted third party reference would be provided to the CA before certifying by signing the entity's certificate with a marking indicating the CA asserts a high level of trust of the entity. Now all the entities that trust the CA can now trust that the identity provided by a certificate is trustworthy.

The functions of a CA may be distributed among several specialized servers in a PKI. For example, server RAs may be used to provide scalability and reliability of the PKI. RA servers provide the facility for entities to submit requests for certificate generation. The RA service is also responsible for ensuring the accuracy of certificate request content.

The CA can revoke certificates and provide an update service to the other members of the PKI via a certificate revocation list (CRL), which is a list of non-valid certificates that should not be accepted by any member of the PKI. The use of public key (asymmetric) cryptography has enabled more effective use of symmetric cryptography as well as several other important features, such as greater access control, nonrepudiation, and digital signatures.

So often, the biggest question is, who can be trusted? How does one know that the public key being used to verify Terry's digital signature truly belongs to Terry, or that the public key being used to send a confidential message to Pat is truly Pat's and not that of an attacker who has set himself up in the middle of the communications channel?

Public keys are by their very nature public. Many people include them on signature lines in emails, or organizations have them on their Web servers so that customers can establish confidential communications with the employees of the organization, who they may never even meet. How does one know an imposter or attacker has not set up a rogue Web server and is attracting communications that should have been confidential to his site instead of the real account, as in a phishing attack?

Setting up a trusted public directory of keys is one option. Each user must register with the directory service, and a secure manner of communications between the user and the directory would be set up. This would allow the user to change keys – or the directory to force the change of keys. The directory would publish and maintain the list of all active keys and also delete or revoke keys that are no longer trusted. This may happen if a person believes that her private key has been compromised, or she leaves the employ of the organization. Any person wanting to communicate with a registered user of the directory could request the public key of the registered user from the directory.

An even higher level of trust is provided through the use of public key certificates. This can be done directly. Pat would send a certificate to Terry or through a CA, which would act as a trusted third party and issue a certificate to both Pat and Terry containing the public key of the other party. This certificate is signed with the digital signature of the CA and can be verified by the recipients. The certification process binds identity information and a public key to an identity. The resultant document of this process is the public key certificate. A CA will adhere to the X.509 standards. This is part of the overall X.500 family of standards applying to directories. X.509 version 3 of the standard is the most common. *Figure 3.39* shows an example of a certificate issued by Verisign. An X.509 certificate looks as follows:

Field	Description of Contents
Algorithm used for the signature	Algorithm used to sign the certificate
Issuer name	X.500 name of CA
Period of Validity	Start Date/End Date
Subject's name	Owner of the public key
Subject's Public Key Information (algorithm, parameters, key)	Public key and algorithm used to create it
Issuer unique identifier	Optional field used in case the CA used more than one X.500 name
Subject's unique identifier	Optional field in case the public key owner has more than one X.500 name
Extensions	
Digital signature of CA	Hash of the certificate encrypted with the private key of the CA

Figure 3.39 - **A X.509 certification issued by Verisign**

Key Management Processes

Perhaps the most important part of any cryptographic implementation is key management. Control over the issuance, revocation, recovery, distribution, and the history of cryptographic keys is of utmost importance to any organization relying on cryptography for secure communications and data protection.

The information security professional should know the importance of Kerckhoff's law. Auguste Kerckhoff wrote, "a cryptosystem should be secure even if everything about the system, except the key, is public knowledge." [129] The key, therefore, is the true strength of

---

129 See the following: http://underbelly.blog-topia.com/2005/01/kerckhoffs-law.html

the cryptosystem. The size of the key and the secrecy of the key are perhaps the two most important elements in a crypto implementation.

Claude Shannon, the famous twentieth-century military cryptographer, wrote, "the enemy knows the system." The secrecy of the algorithm, the deftness of the cryptographic operations, or the superiority of our technology to protect our data and systems cannot be relied on solely. Always consider that the adversary knows the algorithms and methods used and act accordingly. A symmetric algorithm shares the same key between the sender and the receiver. This often requires out-of-band transmission of the keys – distribution through a different channel and separate from the data. Key management also looks at the replacement of keys and ensures that new keys are strong enough to provide for the secure use of the algorithm. Users will often choose weak or predictable passwords and store them in an insecure manner. This same tendency would affect the creation of cryptographic keys if the creation was left to the user community.

People also forget passwords, necessitating the resetting of access to the network or a workstation; however, in the cryptographic world, the loss of a key means the loss of the data itself. Without some form of key recovery, it would be impossible to recover the stored data that were encrypted with a lost key.

Advances in Key Management
Key management has become increasingly important due to critical business requirements for secure information sharing and collaboration in high risk environments. As a result, developers are seeing the need to embed security, particularly cryptography, directly into the application or network device. However, the complexity and specialized nature of cryptography means increased risk if not implemented properly. To meet this challenge, a number of standardized key management specifications are being developed and implemented for use as a sort of key management "plug-in" for such products.

XML (Extensible Markup Language), the flexible data framework that allows applications to communicate on the Internet, has become the preferred infrastructure for e-commerce applications. All of those transactions require trust and security, making it mission-critical to devise common XML mechanisms for authenticating merchants, buyers, and suppliers to each other and for digitally signing and encrypting XML documents such as contracts and payment transactions. XML-based standards and specifications have been in development for use in the field of key management systems. Such specifications and standards are then implemented within Web services libraries, provided by vendors or by open source collaborative efforts.

One such specification is the XML Key Management Specification 2.0 (XKMS).[130] This specification defines protocols for distributing and registering public keys, suitable for use in conjunction with XML Digital Signatures[131] and XML Encryption.[132] XKMS, while very focused on key management, works in conjunction with other specifications that define protocols and services necessary to establishing and maintaining the trust needed for secure

---

130 "XML Key Management Specification (XKMS 2.0)", W3C, 28 June 2005, Available online: http://www.w3.org/TR/xkms2/ Last Accessed: 5 MAY 2014

131 "XML Signature Syntax and Processing (Second Edition)", W3C, 10 June 2008, Available online: http://www.w3.org/TR/xmldsig-core/ Last Accessed: 5 May 2014

132 "XML Encryption Syntax and Processing", W3C, 10 December 2002, Available online: http://www.w3.org/TR/xmlenc-core/ Last Accessed: 5 MAY 2014

Web transactions.[133] These basic mechanisms can be combined in various ways to accommodate building a wide variety of security models using a variety of cryptographic technologies. A goal of XKMS implementation is based on the assumption that simplicity helps developers avoid mistakes and, as such, increases the security of applications. The XKMS protocol consists of pairs of requests and responses. XKMS protocol messages share a common format that may be carried within a variety of protocols. However, XKMS messages transported via SOAP over HTTP are recommended for interoperability.

The two parts of the XML Key Management Specification 2.0 are the XML Key Information Service Specification (X-KISS) and the XML Key Registration Service Specification (X-KRSS). First, X-KISS describes a syntax that allows a client (i.e., application) to delegate part or all of the tasks required to process XML Signature < ds:KeyInfo > elements to a Trust service. A key objective of the protocol design is to minimize the complexity of applications that use XML Digital Signatures. By becoming a client of the trust service, the application is relieved of the complexity and syntax of the underlying PKI used to establish trust relationships, which may be based upon a different specification such as X.509/PKIX, SPKI, PGP, Diffie–Hellman, Elliptic Curve, and can be extended for other algorithms. The < ds:KeyInfo > element in a XML Digital Signature is an optional element that enables the recipient to obtain cryptography key-related data needed to validate the signature. The < ds:KeyInfo > element may contain the key itself, a key name, X.509 certificate, a PGP key identifier, chain of trust, revocation list info, in-band key distribution or key agreement data, and so on. As an option, a link to the location where the full < ds:KeyInfo > dataset can be found can also be provided.

For example, if using certificates, DSA, RSA, X.509, PGP, SPKI are values that can be used in the < ds:KeyInfo > element of an XML Digital Signature. An application (client of the XKMS) would learn what public key cryptographic algorithm is being used for the transaction by reading from a directory server the < ds:KeyInfo > element of an XML Digital Signature using the X-KISS protocol of XKMS 2.0.

Secondly, X-KRSS describes a protocol for registration of public key information. The key material can be generated by the X-KRSS, on request to support easier key recovery, or manually. The registration service can also be used to subsequently recover a private key. An application may request that the Registration Service (X-KRSS) binds information to a public key. The information bound may include a name, an identifier, or other attributes defined by the implementation. After first registering a key pair, the key pair is then usable along with the X-KISS or a PKI such as X.509v3.

The XKMS service shields the client application from the complexities of the underlying PKI such as:

- Handling of complex syntax and semantics (e.g., X.509v3).
- Retrieval of information from directory/data repository infrastructure
- Revocation status verification
- Construction and processing of trust chains

---

133 For example, Security Assertion Markup Language (SAML) for communicating user authentication, entitlement, and attribute information and WS-Security et al. For more details see: http://www.oasis-open.org/home/index.php

3

Security Engineering

Additional information about the signer's public signing key ("< ds:KeyInfo >") can be included inside the signature block, which can be used to help the verifier determine which public key certificate to select.

Information contained in the < ds:KeyInfo > element may or may not be cryptographically bound to the signature itself. Therefore, < ds:KeyInfo> element data can be replaced or extended without invalidating the digital signature. For example, Valerie signs a document and sends it to Jim with a <ds:KeyInfo > element that specifies only the signing key data. On receiving the message, Jim retrieves additional information required to validate the signature and adds this information into the < ds:KeyInfo > element when he passes the document on to Yolanda (see *Figure 3.40*).

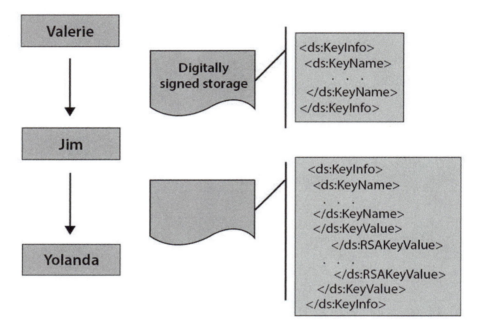

Figure 3.40 - **The XKMS service shields the client application from the complexities of the underlying PKI**

The X-KISS Locate service resolves a < ds:Keyinfo > element but does not require the service to make an assertion concerning the validity of the binding between the data in the < ds:Keyinfo > element. The XKMS service can resolve the < ds:Keyinfo > element using local information store or may relay the request to other directory servers. For example, the XKMS service might resolve a < ds:RetrievalMethod > element (*Figure 3.41*) or act as a gateway to an underlying PKI based on a non-XML syntax (e.g., X.509v3).

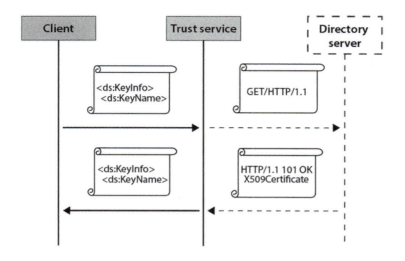

Figure 3.41 - **The SKMS service might resolve a <ds: Retrieval Method> element**

REAL WORLD EXAMPLE: ENCRYPTION

Terry wants to send an encrypted email to Pat but does not know Pat's encryption key. Terry can use both the S/MIME and PGP secure email formats. Terry's client uses Distinguished Names (DNs) to locate the XKMS service that provides a Locate service for keys bound to the domain example.com then sends an XKMS Locate request to the discovered XKMS service for a key bound to Pat@example.com and the S/MIME or PGP protocol. The application then verifies that the certificate obtained meets its trust criteria by standard certificate validation to a trusted root.

Pat receives the signed document from Terry, which specifies Terry's X.509v3 certificate but not the key value. Pat's email client is not capable of processing X.509v3 certificates but can obtain the key parameters from the XKMS service by means of the Locate service. Pat's email client sends the < ds:Keyinfo > element to the location service requesting that the corresponding < KeyValue > element be returned. The location service does not report the revocation status or the trust level of the certificate. However, the service takes the X.509v3 certificate from the < ds:Keyinfo> element and sends the key values.

Standards for Financial Institutions

ANSI X9.17 was developed to address the need of financial institutions to transmit securities and funds securely using an electronic medium. Specifically, it describes the means to ensure the secrecy of keys. The ANSI X9.17 approach is based on a hierarchy of keys. At the bottom of the hierarchy are data keys (DKs). Data keys are used to encrypt and decrypt messages. They are given short lifespans, such as one message or one connection. At the top of the hierarchy are master key-encrypting keys (KKMs).

KKMs, which must be distributed manually, are afforded longer lifespans than data keys. Using the two-tier model, the KKMs are used to encrypt the data keys. The data keys are then distributed electronically to encrypt and decrypt messages. The two-tier model may be enhanced by adding another layer to the hierarchy. In the three-tier model, the KKMs are not used to encrypt data keys directly but to encrypt other key-encrypting keys (KKs). The KKs, which are exchanged electronically, are used to encrypt the data keys.

Segregation of Duties

Another aspect of key management is maintaining control over sensitive cryptographic keys that enforce the need to know principle as part of a business process. For example, in many business environments, employees are required to maintain separation or segregation of duties. In other words, in such environments no one person is allowed to have full control over all phases of an entire transaction without some level of accountability enforcement. The more negotiable the asset under protection, the greater the need for the proper segregation of duties. Especially in the area of cryptography, this is a business concern. Imagine the damage that could be done by a single dishonest person if allowed unchecked access to cryptographic keys that, for example, unlock high risk, high value, or high liquidity information such as customer financial accounts.

The segregation of duties is used as a cross-check to ensure that misuse and abuse of assets, due to innocent mistake or malicious intent, can be efficiently detected and prevented. This is an important confidentiality and integrity principle that is often misunderstood, judging by news reports of embezzlement schemes, primarily by employee insiders, that go undetected for long amounts of time. The segregation of duties is primarily a business policy and access control issue. However, it may not be possible for smaller organizations, due to personnel constraints, to perform the segregation of all duties, so other compensating controls may have to be used to achieve the same control objective. Such compensating controls include monitoring of activities, audit trails, and management supervision. Two mechanisms, which are necessary to implement high integrity cryptographic operations environments where separation of duties is paramount, are dual control and split knowledge.

Dual Control

Dual control is implemented as a security procedure that requires two or more persons to come together and collude to complete a process. In a cryptographic system, the two (or more) persons would each supply a unique key, that when taken together, performs a cryptographic process. Split knowledge is the other complementary access control principle to dual control.

Split Knowledge

Split knowledge is the unique concept of "what each must bring" and then joining that knowledge together when implementing dual control. For example, a box containing petty cash is secured by one combination lock and one keyed lock. One employee is given the combination to the combo lock and another employee has possession of the correct key to the keyed lock. In order to get the cash out of the box, both employees must be present at the cash box at the same time. One cannot open the box without the other. This is the aspect of dual control.

On the other hand, split knowledge is exemplified here by the different objects (the combination to the combo lock and the correct physical key), both of which are unique and necessary, that each brings to the meeting. Split knowledge focuses on the uniqueness of separate objects that must be joined together. Dual control has to do with forcing the collusion of at least two or more persons to combine their split knowledge to gain access to an asset. Both split knowledge and dual control complement each other and are necessary functions that implement the segregation of duties in high integrity cryptographic environments (see *Figure 3.42*).

In cryptographic terms, one could say dual control and split knowledge are properly implemented if no one person has access to or knowledge of the content of the complete cryptographic key being protected by the two processes. The sound implementation of dual control and split knowledge in a cryptographic environment necessarily means that the quickest way to break the key would be through the best attack known for the algorithm of that key. The principles of dual control and split knowledge primarily apply to access to plaintext keys. Access to cryptographic keys used for encrypting and decrypting data or access to keys that are encrypted under a master key (which may or may not be maintained under dual control and split knowledge) do not require dual control and split knowledge.

Bad Examples	Problem	How to Make Dual Control Split Knowledge "Compliant"
Splitting a key "in half" to form two parts	Dual control but no split knowledge (assuming two people each with a unique key half). One person could determine the key by brute forcing the other key half space.	Each person maintains control of his or her half of the key. Protect each half with a unique pin or passphrase.
Storing key components on two cryptographic tokens with no further user authentication.	No enforcement of split knowledge (i.e., no unique authentication method for individual accountability)	Each person maintains control of his individual token/smartcard. Protect each smart card with unique pin/passphrase.
Storing a key on a single smartcard (or cryptographic token) that requires one or more passphrases to access.	No dual control enforcement. Single card cannot be maintained by two or more persons.	Distribute cryptographic token to each person. Protect token with unique pin/ passphrase.

Figure 3.42 - **Split knowledge and dual control complement each other and are necessary functions that implement segregation of duties in high-integrity cryptographic environments**

3

Security Engineering

Dual control and split knowledge can be summed up as the determination of any part of a key being protected must require the collusion between two or more persons with each supplying unique cryptographic materials that must be joined together to access the protected key. Any feasible method to violate the axiom means that the principles of dual control and split knowledge are not being upheld.

There are a number of applications that implement aspects of dual control and split knowledge in a scalable manner. For example, a PGP commercial product based on the OpenPGP standard has features for splitting public keys that are not part of the OpenPGP standard.[134] These features use Blakely–Shamir secret sharing. This is an algorithm that allows the user to take a piece of data and break it into N shares, of which K of them are needed to retrieve the original data. Using a simple version of this approach, the user could break the data into three shares, two of which are needed to get the data back. In a more complex version, the user could require 3 of 6 or even 5 of 12 shares to retrieve the original data, with each key share protected with a unique passphrase known only to the key holder.

Such a solution uses the basic form of secret sharing and shares the private key. This process permits a key pair to be controlled by a group of people, with some subgroup required to reconstitute and use the key. Other systems are based on key holders answering a series of questions in order to recover passwords needed to unlock a protected plaintext key.

To recreate the key under protection, a user can create a set of questions that contain some information only the user would know. The key is split to those questions, with some set of them being required to synthesize the key. Not only does the user provide individualized security questions that are unique to each key holder but also decides how many of the questions need to be answered correctly to retrieve the key under protection, by having it reconstructed from the split parts.

Creation and Distribution of Keys

Creation of Keys

The details of key creation using various algorithms were discussed earlier in this chapter. However, from a key management perspective, there are a number of issues that pertain to scalability and cryptographic key integrity.

Automated Key Generation

Mechanisms used to automatically generate strong cryptographic keys can be used to deploy keys as part of key lifecycle management. Effective automated key generation systems are designed for user transparency as well as complete cryptographic key policy enforcement.

Truly Random

For a key to be truly effective, it must have an appropriately high work factor. That is to say, the amount of time and effort (work by an attacker) needed to break the key must be sufficient so that it at least delays its discovery for as long as the information being protected needs to be kept confidential. One factor that contributes to strong keys, which have a high work factor, is the level of randomness of the bits that make up the key.

---

134 Callas, Jon, "OpenPGP Message Format", IETF, Available Online: http://www.ietf.org/rfc/rfc2440.txt
   Last Accessed: 4 April 2014

Random

As discussed earlier, cryptographic keys are essentially strings of numbers. The numbers used in making up the key need to be unpredictable so that an attacker cannot easily guess the key and then expose the protected information. Thus, the randomness of the numbers that comprise a key plays an important role in the lifecycle of a cryptographic key. In the context of cryptography, randomness is the quality of lacking predictability. Randomness intrinsically generated by a computer system is also called pseudo randomness. Pseudo randomness is the quality of an algorithm for generating a sequence of numbers that approximates the properties of random numbers. Computer circuits and software libraries are used to perform the actual generation of pseudo random key values. Computers and software libraries are well known as weak sources of randomness.

Computers are inherently designed for predictability not randomness. Computers are so thoroughly deterministic that they have a hard time generating high-quality randomness. Therefore, special purpose built hardware and software called "random number generators," or RNGs, are needed for cryptography applications. The U.S. federal government provides recommendations on deterministic random number generators through the NIST.[135] An international standard for random number generation suitable for cryptographic systems is sponsored by the International Organization for Standardization as ISO 18031.[136] A rigorous statistical analysis of the output is often needed to have confidence in such RNG algorithms. A random number generator based solely on deterministic computation done solely by a computer cannot be regarded as a true random number generator sufficient in lack of predictability for cryptographic applications because its output is inherently predictable.

There are various methods for ensuring the appropriate level of randomness in pseudo random keys. The approach found in most business level cryptographic products use computational algorithms that produce long sequences of apparently random results, which are in fact completely determined by a shorter initial value, known as a seed or key. The use of initialization vectors and seed values that are concatenated onto computer generated keys increases the strength of keys by adding additional uniqueness to a random key material. The seed value or initialization vector is the number input as a starting point for an algorithm. The seed or IV can be created either manually or by an external source of randomness, such as radio frequency noise, randomly sampled values from a switched circuit, or other atomic and subatomic physical phenomenon. To provide a degree of randomness intermediate between specialized hardware on the one hand and algorithmic generation on the other, some security related computer software requires the user to input a lengthy string of mouse movements or keyboard input.

Regarding manually created seed or initialization values, many may be familiar with this process if they have ever set up a wireless network with encryption using a WEP/WPA key. In most cases, when configuring wireless encryption on a wireless adapter or router, the user is asked to enter a password or variable length "key" that is used by the wireless device to create cryptographic keys for encrypting data across the wireless network. This "key" is really a seed or initialization value that will be concatenated to the computer generated key portion that

---

135 NIST, "Recommendation for Random Number Generation Using Deterministic Random Bit Generators, SP800–90", Available Online: http://csrc.nist.gov/publications/nistpubs/800–90/SP800–90revised_March2007.pdf Last Accessed: 4 April 2014.

136 "Security Techniques – Random Bit Generation, ISO/IEC 18031:2005", ISO, Available Online: http://www.iso.org Last Accessed: 4 April 2014.

together comprise the keying material to generate a key consisting of appropriate amount of pseudo randomness to make it hard for an attacker to easily guess and thus "breaking" the key.

The important role randomness plays in key creation is illustrated by the following example. One method of generating a two-key encryption key set making a private component and a public component is comprised of the following steps:

1. Generate a first pseudo random prime number;
2. Generate a second pseudo random prime number;
3. Produce a modulus by multiplying the first pseudo random prime number by a second pseudo random prime number;
4. Generate a first exponent by solving a first modular arithmetic equation;
5. Generate a second exponent that is a modular inverse to the first exponent by solving a second modular arithmetic equation and securely storing either the first exponent or the second exponent in at least one memory location.

Key Length

Key length is another important aspect of key management to consider when generating cryptographic keys. Key length is the size of a key, usually measured in bits or bytes, which a cryptographic algorithm used in ciphering or deciphering protected information. Keys are used to control how an algorithm operates so that only the correct key can decipher the information. The resistance to successful attack against the key and the algorithm, aspects of their cryptographic security, is of concern when choosing key lengths. An algorithm's key length is distinct from its cryptographic security. Cryptographic security is a logarithmic measure of the fastest known computational attack on the algorithm, also measured in bits.

The security of an algorithm cannot exceed its key length. Therefore, it is possible to have a very long key, and yet it provides low security. As an example, three-key (56 bits per key) Triple DES can have a key length of 168 bits, but, due to the meet-in-the-middle attack, the effective security that it provides is at most 112 bits. However, most symmetric algorithms are designed to have security equal to their key length. A natural inclination is to use the longest key possible, which may make the key more difficult to break. However, the longer the key, the more computationally expensive the encrypting and decrypting process can be. The goal is to make breaking the key cost more (in terms of effort, time, and resources) than the worth of the information being protected and, if possible, not a penny more (to do more would not be economically sound).

Asymmetric Key Length

The effectiveness of asymmetric cryptographic systems depends on the hard to solve nature of certain mathematical problems such as prime integer factorization. These problems are time consuming to solve but usually faster than trying all possible keys by brute force. Thus, asymmetric algorithm keys must be longer for equivalent resistance to attack than symmetric algorithm keys.

RSA Security claims that 1024-bit RSA keys are equivalent in strength to 80-bit symmetric keys, 2048-bit RSA keys to 112-bit symmetric keys, and 3072-bit RSA keys to 128-bit symmetric keys. RSA claims that 2048- bit keys are sufficient until 2030. An RSA key length of 3072 bits should be used if security is required beyond 2030.[137] NIST key management guidelines further suggest that 15,360-bit RSA keys are equivalent in strength to 256-bit symmetric keys.[138]

ECC can secure with shorter keys than those needed by other asymmetric key algorithms. NIST guidelines state that elliptic curve keys should be twice the length of equivalent strength symmetric key algorithms. For example, a 224-bit elliptic curve key would have roughly the same strength as a 112-bit symmetric key. These estimates assume no major breakthroughs in solving the underlying mathematical problems that ECC is based on.

Key Wrapping and Key Encrypting Keys

One role of key management is to ensure that the same key used in encrypting a message by a sender is the same key used to decrypt the message by the intended receiver. Thus, if Terry and Pat wish to exchange encrypted messages, each must be equipped to decrypt received messages and to encrypt sent messages. If they use a cipher, they will need appropriate keys. The problem is how to exchange whatever keys or other information are needed so that no one else can obtain a copy.

One solution is to protect the session key with a special purpose long- term use key called a key encrypting key (KEK). KEKs are used as part of key distribution or key exchange. The process of using a KEK to protect session keys is called key wrapping. Key wrapping uses symmetric ciphers to securely encrypt (thus encapsulating) a plaintext key along with any associated integrity information and data. One application for key wrapping is protecting session keys in untrusted storage or when sending over an untrusted transport. Key wrapping or encapsulation using a KEK can be accomplished using either symmetric or asymmetric ciphers. If the cipher is a symmetric KEK, both the sender and the receiver will need a copy of the same key. If using an asymmetric cipher, with public/private key properties, to encapsulate a session key, both the sender and the receiver will need the other's public key.

Protocols such as SSL, PGP, and S/MIME use the services of KEKs to provide session key confidentiality, integrity, and sometimes to authenticate the binding of the session key originator and the session key itself to make sure the session key came from the real sender and not an attacker.

Key Distribution

Keys can be distributed in a number of ways. For example, two people who wish to perform key exchange can use a medium other than that through which secure messages will be sent. This is called "out-of-band" key exchange. If the two or more parties will send secure messages via email, they may choose to meet up with each other or send via courier. The concept of "out-of-band" key exchange is not very scalable beyond a few people.

A more scalable method of exchanging keys is through the use of a PKI key server. A key server is a central repository of public keys of members of a group of users interested in exchanging keys to facilitate electronic transactions. Public key encryption provides a means to allow members of a group to conduct secure transactions spontaneously. The receiver's public key certificate, which contains the receiver's public key, is retrieved by the sender from

---

137 Kaliski, Burt, TWIRL and RSA Key Size, RSA Labs, Available Online: http://www.rsa.com/rsalabs/node.asp?id=2004 Last Accessed: 6 April 2014.

138 "Recommendation for Key Management -SP800–57", NIST, Available Online: http://csrc.nist.gov/publications/nistpubs/800–57/SP800–57-Part1.pdf Last Accessed: 6 April 2014.

the key server and is used as part of a public key encryption scheme, such as S/MIME, PGP, or even SSL to encrypt a message and send it. The digital certificate is the medium that contains the public key of each member of the group and makes the key portable, scalable, and easier to manage than an out-of-band method of key exchange.

Key Distribution Centers

Recall the formula used before to calculate the number of symmetric keys needed for users: $n(n - 1)/2$. This necessitates the setup of directories, public key infrastructures, or key distribution centers.

The use of a key distribution center (KDC) for key management requires the creation of two types of keys. The first are master keys, which are secret keys shared by each user and the KDC. Each user has his own master key, and it is used to encrypt the traffic between the user and the KDC. The second type of key is a session key, created when needed, used for the duration of the communications session, and then discarded once the session is complete. When a user wants to communicate with another user or an application, the KDC sets up the session key and distributes it to each user for use. An implementation of this solution is found in Kerberos. A large organization may even have several KDCs, and they can be arranged so that there are global KDCs that coordinate the traffic between the local KDCs.

Because master keys are integral to the trust and security relationship between the users and hosts, such keys should never be used in compromised situations or where they may become exposed. For encrypting files or communications, separate non-master keys should be used. Ideally, a master key is never visible in the clear; it is buried within the equipment itself, and it is not accessible to the user.

Key Storage and Destruction

The proper storing and changing of cipher keys are important aspects of key management and are essential to the effective use of cryptography for security. Ultimately, the security of information protected by cryptography directly depends on the protection afforded by the keys. All keys need to be protected against modification, and secret and private keys need to be protected against unauthorized disclosure. Methods for protecting stored keying material include trusted, tamperproof hardware security modules, passphrase protected smart cards, key wrapping the session keys using long-term storage KEKs, splitting cipher keys and storing in physically separate storage locations, protecting keys using strong passwords/passphrases, key expiry, and the like.

In order to guard against a long-term cryptanalytic attack, every key must have an expiration date after which it is no longer valid. The key length must be long enough to make the chances of cryptanalysis before key expiration extremely small. The validity period for a key pair may also depend on the circumstances in which the key is used. A signature verification program should check for expiration and should not accept a message signed with an expired key. The fact that computer hardware continues to improve makes it prudent to replace expired keys with newer, longer keys every few years. Key replacement enables one to take advantage of any hardware improvements to increase the security of the cryptosystem. Additional guidance for storage of cipher keys include: [139]

---

139 "Guideline for Implementing Cryptography In the Federal Government", NIST, Available Online: http://csrc.nist.gov/publications/nistpubs/800-21-1/sp800-21-1_Dec2005.pdf Last Accessed 5 May 2014

- All centrally stored data that is related to user keys should be signed or have a MAC applied to it (MACed) for integrity and encrypted if confidentiality is required (all user secret keys and CA private keys should be encrypted). Individual key records in a database – as well as the entire database – should be signed or MACed and encrypted. To enable tamper detection, each individual key record should be signed or MACed so that its integrity can be checked before allowing that key to be used in a cryptographic function.

- Backup copies should be made of central/root keys because the compromise or loss of those components could prevent access to keys in the central database and possibly deny system users the ability to decrypt data or perform signature verifications.

- Provide key recovery capabilities. There must be safeguards to ensure that sensitive records are neither irretrievably lost by the rightful owners nor accessed by unauthorized individuals. Key recovery capabilities provide these functions.

- Archive user keys for a sufficiently long crypto period. A crypto period is the time during which a key can be used to protect information; it may extend well beyond the lifetime of a key that is used to apply cryptographic protection (where the lifetime is the time during which a key can be used to generate a signature or perform encryption). Keys may be archived for a lengthy period (on the order of decades) so that they can be used to verify signatures and decrypt ciphertext.

The security architect, professional, and practitioner should all be prepared to address some of the following issues with regards to long term archiving of keys and data:

- What is to be done with data that is protected with keys committed to archival storage? Should this data be decrypted and re-encrypted with other keys that are being managed actively through a key management system?

- What if the key has been compromised? What is the risk exposure for the data encrypted with the compromised key?

- Who will be responsible for the long term archival of the data and keys? Is this a specified role in the enterprise separate from the current key management system?

- How will long term key/data archival storage differ from shorter term secure storage and management in the current systems being used today? Will Disaster Recovery Planning and Business Continuity Planning be extended to include the long term data archives?

- When will access be granted to the long term data archives and how? Under what conditions will access be granted, and what policies will govern usage of the data and the keys?

Among the factors affecting the risk of exposure are: [140]

1. The strength of the cryptographic mechanisms (e.g., the algorithm, key length, block size, and mode of operation)

2. The embodiment of the mechanisms (e.g., FIPS 140-2 Level 4 implementation or software implementation on a personal computer)

3. The operating environment (e.g., secure limited access facility, open office environment, or publicly accessible terminal)

---

140 "Recommendations for Key Management, SP800–57",NIST, Available Online: http://csrc.nist.gov/publications/nistpubs/800–57/sp800–57-Part1-revised2_Mar08–2007.pdf Last Accessed 3 May 2014

4. The volume of information flow or the number of transactions
5. The security life of the data
6. The security function (e.g., data encryption, digital signature, key production or derivation, key protection)
7. The re-keying method (e.g., keyboard entry, re-keying using a key loading device where humans have no direct access to key information, remote re-keying within a PKI)
8. The key update or key derivation process
9. The number of nodes in a network that share a common key
10. The number of copies of a key and the distribution of those copies
11. The threat to the information (e.g., whom is the information is protected from, and what are their perceived technical capabilities and financial resources to mount an attack?)

In general, short crypto periods enhance security. For example, some cryptographic algorithms might be less vulnerable to cryptanalysis if the adversary has only a limited amount of information encrypted under a single key. Caution should be used when deleting keys that are no longer needed. A simple deletion of the keying material might not completely obliterate the information. For example, erasing the information might require overwriting that information multiple times with other non-related information, such as random bits or all zero or one bits. Keys stored in memory for a long time can become "burned in." This can be mitigated by splitting the key into components that are frequently updated as shown in *Figure 3.43*.

Key Type	Cryptoperiod	
	Originator Usage Period (OUP)	Recipient Usage Period
1. Private Signature Key	1-3 Years	
2. Public Signature Key	Several Years (Depends on Key Size)	
3. Symmetric Authentication Key	$\leq$ 2 Years	$\leq$ OUP + 3 Years
4. Private Authentication Key	1-2 Years	
5. Public Authentication Key	1-2 Years	
6. Symmetric Data Encryption Keys	$\leq$ 2 Years	$\leq$ OUP + 3 Years
7. Symmetric Key Wrapping Keys	$\leq$ 2 Years	$\leq$ OUP + 3 Years
8. Symmetric and Asymmetric RNG Keys	Upon Reseeding	
9. Symmetric Master Key	About 1 Year	
10. Private Transport Key	$\leq$ 2 Years	
11. Public Key Transport Key	1-2 Years	

Figure 3.43 - Recommended Crypto Periods for key types

On the other hand, where manual key distribution methods are subject to human error and frailty, more frequent key changes might actually increase the risk of exposure. In these cases, especially when very strong cryptography is employed, it may be more prudent to have fewer, well-controlled manual key distributions rather than more frequent, poorly controlled manual key distributions. Secure automated key distribution, where key generation and exchange are protected by appropriate authentication, access and integrity controls may be a compensating control in such environments.

Users with different roles should have keys with lifetimes that take into account the different roles and responsibilities, the applications for which the keys are used, and the security services that are provided by the keys (user/data authentication, confidentiality, data integrity, etc.). Reissuing keys should not be done so often that it becomes excessively burdensome; however, it should be performed often enough to minimize the loss caused by a possible key compromise.

Handle the deactivation/revocation of keys so that data signed prior to a compromise date (or date of loss) can be verified. When a signing key is designated as "lost" or "compromised," signatures generated prior to the specified date may still need to be verified in the future. Therefore, a signature verification capability may need to be maintained for lost or compromised keys. Otherwise, all data previously signed with a lost or compromised key would have to be re-signed.

Cost of Certificate Replacement/Revocation

In some cases, the costs associated with changing digital certificates and cryptographic keys are painfully high. Examples include decryption and subsequent re-encryption of very large databases, decryption and re-encryption of distributed databases, and revocation and replacement of a very large number of keys; e.g., where there are very large numbers of geographically and organizationally distributed key holders. In such cases, the expense of the security measures necessary to support longer crypto periods may be justified; e.g., costly and inconvenient physical, procedural, and logical access security; and use of cryptography strong enough to support longer crypto periods even where this may result in significant additional processing overhead.

In other cases, the crypto period may be shorter than would otherwise be necessary; for example, keys may be changed frequently in order to limit the period of time the key management system maintains status information. On the other hand, a user losing his or her private key would require that the lost key be revoked so that an unauthorized user cannot use it. It would be a good practice to use a master decryption key (additional decryption key in PGP) or another key recovery mechanism to guard against losing access to the data encrypted under the lost key. Another reason to revoke a certificate is when an employee leaves the company or, in some cases, when changing job roles, as in the case of someone moving to a more trusted job role, which may require a different level of accountability, access to higher risk data, and so on.

Key Recovery

A lost key may mean a crisis to an organization. The loss of critical data or backups may cause widespread damage to operations and even financial ruin or penalties. There are several methods of key recovery, such as common trusted directories or a policy that requires all cryptographic keys to be registered with the security department. Some people have even been using steganography to bury their passwords in pictures or other locations on their machine to prevent someone from finding their password file. Others use password wallets or other tools to hold all of their passwords.

One method is multiparty key recovery. A user would write her private key on a piece of paper and then divide the key into two or more parts. Each part would be sealed in an envelope. The user would give one envelope each to trusted people with instructions that the envelope was only to be opened in an emergency where the organization needed access to the user's system or files (disability or death of the user). In case of an emergency, the holders of the envelopes would report to human resources, where the envelopes could be opened and the key reconstructed. The user would usually give the envelopes to trusted people at different management levels and different parts of the company to reduce the risk of collusion.

Key recovery should also be conducted with the privacy of the individual in mind. If a private individual used encryption to protect the confidentiality of some information, it may be legally protected according to local laws. In some situations, a legal order may be required to retrieve the key and decrypt the information.

Key Escrow

Key escrow is the process of ensuring a third party maintains a copy of a private key or key needed to decrypt information. Key escrow also should be considered mandatory for most organization's use of cryptography because encrypted information belongs to the organization and not the individual; however, often an individual's key is used to encrypt the information. There must be explicit trust between the key escrow provider and the parties involved, as the escrow provider now holds a copy of the private key and could use it to reveal information. Conditions of key release must be explicitly defined and agreed upon by all parties.

Digital Signatures

A digital signature is intended to be comparable to a handwritten signature on an important document such as a contract. It is important to note that a digital signature is a mathematical representation and conveys specific meaning in binary data, and it is not the same as a "digitized signature." A digitized signature is a representation of a handwritten personal signature that can be created using a scanner or fax machine.

The purpose of a digital signature is to provide the same level of accountability for electronic transactions where a handwritten signature is not possible. A digital signature will provide assurance that the message does indeed come from the person who claims to have sent it, it has not been altered, both parties have a copy of the same document, and the person sending the document cannot claim that he did not send it. A digital signature will usually include a date and time of the signature, as well as a method for a third party to verify the signature.

What is a digital signature? It is a block of data (a pattern of bits, usually a hash) that is generated based on the contents of the message sent and encrypted with the sender's private key. It must contain some unique value that links it with the sender of the message that can be verified easily by the receiver and by a third party, and it must be difficult to forge the digital signature or create a new message with the same signature.

Digital Signature Standard (DSS)

The DSS was proposed in 1991 as FIPS 186 using the Secure Hashing Algorithm (SHA). It has since been updated several times, most recently in July of 2013, when it was issued as FIPS 186-4 and expanded to include the Digital Signature Algorithm (DSA) based on RSA and ECC.[141] Contrasted with RSA, a digital signature is based on a public key (asymmetric) algorithm, but it does not provide for confidentiality of the message through encryption and is not used for key exchange.

The DSS uses two methods of creating the signature: the RSA method and the DSS approach. In both cases, the operation starts with the creation of a hash of the message. The RSA approach then encrypts the hash with the private key of the sender, thus creating the signature. The DSS approach is to sign the hash using the DSA. The DSA is based on the

---

141 See the following: http://nvlpubs.nist.gov/nistpubs/FIPS/NIST.FIPS.186-4.pdf

discrete logarithmic algorithms used in El Gamal and Schnorr. The DSA chooses a random number to create a private and public key pair and encrypts the hash value with the private key and a universal key to create a two-part signature.

A digital signature can be created by encrypting the entire message with the private key of the sender; however, in most cases this is not practical because of the computational impact of encrypting a message using asymmetric algorithms. Therefore, in most cases the digital signature is created by encrypting a hash of the message with the sender's private key. If further confidentiality is needed, then the message can be encrypted with a symmetric algorithm; however, it is best to create the signature before encrypting the message – then the signature authenticates the message itself and not the ciphertext of the message.

Once a digital signature is created, it is appended to the message and sent to the receiver. The receiver decrypts the signature with the public key of the sender and can verify the message has not been altered and can establish the nonrepudiation of origin of the signature.

Uses of Digital Signatures

Digital signatures have become invaluable in protecting the integrity of financial transactions, e-commerce, and email. They are also used by software vendors to ensure that software has not been compromised through the introduction of viruses or other manipulation. This is especially important when downloading a patch via the Internet to ensure that the patch is from a legitimate site, as well as ensuring the integrity of the download.

Digital signatures are used to sign digital certificates. A digital certificate is an electronic document that asserts authenticity and data integrity that is tied to a sender. A hash computation is performed over the certificate content; the hash value is then encrypted using the private key of the sender and then embedded into the certificate. The recipient decrypts the embedded hash value using the sender's public key. The receiver then uses the public key of the sender to verify the sender authenticity by performing the same hash computation over the certificate content as was done by the sender. If the hash results are the same, then sender authentication and data integrity of the certificate has been established. In many parts of the world, digital signatures have become recognized by the government and courts as a verifiable form of authentication.

Digital Rights Management (DRM)

DRM is defined as a broad range of technologies that grant control and protection to content providers over their own digital media. From the content's point of view, there are three key components to its lifecycle: the creation of content, the distribution and upkeep of content, and the use of content. A good DRM scheme should account for all three components and effectively define the interactions between the user, the permissions, and the content itself.

When content is created, the system needs to immediately ensure that rights are validated, assigned to their owners, and approved for use by authorized parties. In the distribution and storage of content, the system needs to have proper access to the content and metadata, and it manages the licensing and authorization. After content has been traded, the system must enforce the rights associated with the content by providing proper permissions to access, use, and modify as required.[142]

---

142 See the following: Jean-Marc Boucqueau, "Digital Rights Management", 3rd IEEE International Workshop on Digital Rights Management Impact on Consumer Communications, January 11 2007.

A main issue for DRM is the lack of standardized technologies. Furthermore, many traditional DRM technologies have been plagued by usability and legal problems, or they suffer from attacks that render them completely useless. As a result, many publishers in the industry developed their own proprietary software to meet the individual needs of DRM in today's media standards.

In October of 1998, the U.S. Senate passed an amendment to United States copyright law criminalizing the production and distribution of technology that would allow consumers to thwart technical copy-restriction methods. Essentially, the Digital Millennium Copyright Act, as it is known, makes it a crime to circumvent anti-piracy measures and outlaws the manufacture, sale, or distribution of code-cracking devices used to illegally copy software.[143]

The DMCA is a long and complex instrument, but what security practitioners need to be concerned with is section 1201: the "anti-circumvention" provisions. They make it illegal to circumvent an "effective means of access control" that restricts a copyrighted work. The companies that make DRM and the courts have interpreted this very broadly, enjoining people from publishing information about vulnerabilities in DRM, from publishing the secret keys hidden in the DRM, and from publishing instructions for getting around the DRM solutions. This poses a significant issue for the security practitioner because the DMCA's injunction against publishing weaknesses in DRM means that its vulnerabilities remain unpatched for longer than in comparable systems that are not covered by the DMCA. That means that any system with DRM will on average be more dangerous for its users than one without DRM protections operating.

For example, in 2005, Sony-BMG music shipped a DRM called the "Sony Rootkit" on 51m audio CDs. When one of these CDs was inserted into a PC, it automatically and undetectably changed the operating system so that it could no longer see files or programs that started with "SYS." The rootkit infected millions of computers, including over 200,000 U.S. military and government networks, before its existence became public. However, various large and respected security organizations have said that they knew about the Sony Rootkit months before the disclosure, but they did not publish any information regarding it because they feared punishment under the DMCA. Meanwhile, virus-writers immediately began renaming their programs to begin with SYS because these files would be invisible to virus-checkers if they landed on a computer that had been compromised by Sony's DRM Rootkit.

The DMCA has spread to other territories, through World Intellectual Property Organization (WIPO) treaties. In the EU, there is the Directive 2001/29/EC (Directive 2001/29/EC of the European Parliament and the Council of 22 May 2001), better known as the EU Copyright Directive (EUCD), which entered into force on June 22, 2001. It aims to harmonize the divergent European copyright regimes and to implement the WCT and WPPT. [144]

In Canada, there is Bill C-11, The Copyright Modernization Act. Bill C-11 received Royal Assent on June 29, 2012, and most of its provisions were brought into force on November 7, 2012. Sub-Section (f), Digital Locks, states that "Technological protection measure" (also known as "digital locks") are defined under two categories:

■ Any effective technology, device, or component that controls access to a work ("access control"), and

---

143 See the following: http://www.gpo.gov/fdsys/pkg/PLAW-105publ304/html/PLAW-105publ304.htm

144 See the following: http://cyber.law.harvard.edu/media/eucd_materials

- Any effective technology, device, or component that restricts one from exercising the exclusive rights of a copyright owner or remuneration rights, i.e., that control the reproduction or copying of a work ("copying control").

Bill C-11 prohibits the circumvention of any access control installed on a work, performer's performance fixed in a sound recording, or a sound recording, even if the work subject to the digital lock is legally acquired.

The digital lock prohibitions in the Act could potentially "trump" or prevail over various exceptions in the Copyright Act, e.g., the fair dealing or educational exceptions." [145]

There are several different types of DRM solutions that have been prevalent over the years.

- **Always-On DRM** – This is a fairly common form of DRM solution. The software or content being protected through the DRM system is only available when the system is connected to the Internet, allowing the DRM system to "check-in" and validate that it is operating. This kind of system is typically found in video games.
- **USB Key** – This is also a fairly easy to implement DRM solution. The software or content being protected through the DRM system is only available when the USB Key is plugged in and available to the system. The key benefit to this system is that DRM protected content can be used on multiple computers and be made available, provided the USB key is plugged in.
- **Digital Watermark** – This technology is used as part of a DRM solution, primarily with printed media and audio/video content. This solution is used to verify the integrity of the protected content.
- **Fingerprinting** – This technology verifies the integrity of a protected file as well, by assigning each user of the file a uniquely redundant part of the file. If any modification(s) to the file take place, the file integrity check shows them and can then identify the user responsible for the modification(s) based on the unique ID of each file assigned to each user.

Non-Repudiation

Non-repudiation is a service that ensures the sender cannot deny a message was sent and the integrity of the message is intact. NIST's SP 800-57 Recommendation for Key Management – Part 1: General (Revision 3) defines non-repudiation as:

> " A service that is used to provide assurance of the integrity and origin of data in such a way that the integrity and origin can be verified by a third party as having originated from a specific entity in possession of the private key of the claimed signatory. In a general information security context, assurance that the sender of information is provided with proof of delivery and the recipient is provided with proof of the sender's identity, so neither can later deny having processed the information." [146]

Non-repudiation can be accomplished with digital signatures and PKI. The message is signed using the sender's private key. When the recipient receives the message, he or she may use the sender's public key to validate the signature. While this proves the integrity of the message, it does not explicitly define the ownership of the private key. A certificate authority must have an association between the private key and the sender (meaning only the sender has the private key) for the non-repudiation to be valid.

---

145 See the following: http://copyright.ubc.ca/copyright-legislation/bill-c-11-the-copyright-modernization-act/

146 http://csrc.nist.gov/publications/nistpubs/800-57/sp800-57_part1_rev3_general.pdf (Page 25 & 32).

Hashing [147]

The hash function accepts an input message of any length and generates, through a one-way operation, a fixed-length output. This output is referred to as a hash code, or sometimes it is called a message digest. It uses a hashing algorithm to generate the hash, but it does not use a secret key.

There are several ways to use message digests in communications, depending on the need for the confidentiality of the message, the authentication of the source, the speed of processing, and the choice of encryption algorithms. The requirements for a hash function are that they must provide some assurance that the message cannot be changed without detection and that it would be impractical to find any two messages with the same hash value.

Five key properties of a hash function are:

    1.   ***Uniformly Distributed*** – The hash output value should not be predictable.

    2.   ***Weak Collision Resistant*** – Difficult to find a second input value that hashes to the same value as another input.

    3.   ***Difficult to Invert*** – Should be one way, should not be able to derive hash input x by reversing the hash function on output, y.

    4.   ***Strong Collision Resistant*** – Difficult to find any two inputs that hash to the same value

    5.   ***Deterministic*** – Given an input x, it must always generate the same hash value, y.

Simple Hash Functions

A hash operates on an input of any length (there are some limitations, but the message sizes are huge) and generates a fixed-length output. The simplest hash merely divides the input message into fixed-size blocks and then XORs every block. The hash would therefore be the same size as a block.

```
Hash = block 1 block 2 block 3 … end of message
```

MD5 Message Digest Algorithm

MD5 was developed by Ron Rivest at MIT in 1992. It is the most widely used hashing algorithm and is described in RFC 1321.[148] MD5 generates a 128-bit digest from a message of any length. It processes the message in 512-bit blocks and does four rounds of processing. Each round contains 16 steps. The likelihood of finding any two messages with the same hash code is estimated to be 2^{64}, and the difficulty of finding a message with a given digest is estimated to be 2^{128}. One common use of MD5 is to verify the integrity of digital evidence used in forensic investigations and ensure that the original media has not been altered since seizure. In the past two years, there have been several attacks developed against MD5 where it is now possible to find collisions through analysis. This is leading to many professionals recommending the abandonment of MD5 for use in secure communications, such as digital signatures. MD4 was developed in 1990 and revised in 1992. It only does three rounds of processing and fewer mathematical operations per round. It is not considered strong enough for most applications today. It also generated a 128-bit output. It is a predecessor to MD5.

---

147   See the following for the NIST Special Publication 800-107 Revision-1 Recommendation for Applications Using Approved Hash Algorithms: http://csrc.nist.gov/publications/nistpubs/800-107-rev1/sp800-107-rev1.pdf

148   See the following: http://www.ietf.org/rfc/rfc1321.txt

Secure Hash Algorithm (SHA) and SHA-1

The original SHA was developed by NIST in the United States in 1993 and issued as Federal Information Processing Standard (FIPS) 180. A revised version (FIPS 180-1) was issued in 1995 as SHA-1 (RFC 3174).[149] SHA was based on the MD4 algorithm, whereas SHA-1 follows the logic of MD5. SHA-1 operates on 512-bit blocks and can handle any message up to 264 bits in length. The output hash is 160 bits in length. The processing includes four rounds of operations of 20 steps each. Recently, there have been several attacks described against the SHA-1 algorithm despite it being considerably stronger than MD5. NIST has issued FIPS 180-4, which recognizes SHA-1, SHA-224, SHA-256, SHA-384, SHA-512, SHA-512/224, and SHA 512/256 as a part of the Secure Hash Standard. The output lengths of the digests of these vary from 160 to 512 bits.[150]

SHA-3

In November 2007, NIST issued an invitation for candidate algorithms for new hash algorithms for use in U.S. federal government cryptographic systems. NIST is conducting an open, public process to identify suitable candidates for the new hash algorithm, which is needed because of recent advances in the cryptanalysis of hash functions. NIST selected finalists in 2010 and announced the winner, Keccak, on October 2, 2012.[151] The new hash algorithm will be named SHA-3, and it will augment the hash algorithms currently specified in FIPS 180-4, the Secure Hash Standard.[152]

HAVAL

HAVAL was developed at the University of Wollongong in Australia. It combines a variable length output with a variable number of rounds of operation on 1024-bit input blocks. The output may be 128, 160, 192, 224, or 256 bits, and the number of rounds may vary from three to five. That gives 15 possible combinations of operation. HAVAL operates 60% faster than MD5 when only three rounds are used and is just as fast as MD5 when it does five rounds of operation.

RIPEMD-160

The European RACE Integrity Primitives Evaluation project developed the RIPEMD-160 algorithm in response to the vulnerabilities found in MD4 and MD5. The original algorithm (RIPEMD-128) has the same vulnerabilities as MD4 and MD5 and led to the improved RIPEMD-160 version. The output for RIPEMD-160 is 160 bits, and it operates similarly to MD5 on 512-bit blocks. It does twice the processing of SHA-1, performing five paired rounds of 16 steps each for 160 operations.

Attacks on Hashing Algorithms and Message Authentication Codes

There are two primary ways to attack hash functions: through brute force attacks and cryptanalysis. Over the past few years, research has been done on attacks on various hashing algorithms, such as MD-5 and SHA-1. Both cases are susceptible to cryptographic attacks. A brute force attack relies on finding a weakness in the hashing algorithm that would allow

---

149 See the following: http://www.ietf.org/rfc/rfc3174.txt

150 See the following: http://csrc.nist.gov/publications/fips/fips180-4/fips-180-4.pdf

151 See the following: http://csrc.nist.gov/groups/ST/hash/sha-3/winner_sha-3.html
For information on the KECCAK sponge function family, see the following: http://keccak.noekeon.org/

152 See the following for a copy of the proposed draft standard for FIPS PUB 202: SHA-3 Standard: Permutation-Based Hash and Extendable-Output Functions, initially published for review in April of 2014: http://csrc.nist.gov/publications/drafts/fips-202/fips_202_draft.pdf

3

Security Engineering

an attacker to reconstruct the original message from the hash value (defeat the one-way property of a hash function), find another message with the same hash value, or find any pair of messages with the same hash value (which is called collision resistance). Oorschot and Weiner developed a machine that could find a collision on a 128-bit hash in about 24 days.[153]

Cryptanalysis is the art and science of defeating cryptographic systems and gaining access to encrypted messages even when the keys are unknown. Side-channel attacks are examples of cryptanalyses. These attacks do not attack the algorithms but rather the implementation of the algorithms. Cryptanalysis is responsible for the development of "rainbow tables," which are used to greatly reduce the computational time and power needed to break a cipher at the expense of storage. A freely available password cracking program called "cain and abel" comes with rainbow tables preloaded.[154]

Rainbow tables are pre-computed tables or lists used in cracking password hashes. Tables are designed for specific algorithms, such as MD5 and SHA-1, and can be purchased on the open market. "Salted" hashes provide a defense against rainbow tables. In cryptographic terms, "salt" is made of random bits and is an input to the one-way hash function with target plaintext as the only other input. The salt is stored with the resulting hash so hashing will use the same salt and get the same results. As the rainbow table did not include the salt when it was created, its values will never match the salted values.

The security architect may also want to consider the value of slow hashing functions and their ability to deter attackers. For example, let's assume that a PC can be programmed to calculate roughly one billion hashes per second. The next question that has to be addressed is what kind of passwords would we use that power against? Assume that we use an 8 character password. To test whether or not this password would be safe from a brute force attack using our PC, we must consider the following:

- If the password can contain lowercase and uppercase letters, along with numbers, that would equate to 62 possible characters (26+26+10).
- An 8 character string has 62^8 possible variations. This is approximately 218 trillion, in case you do not have a calculator handy!
- At a rate of one billion hashes per second, our password would be found by a brute force attack in approximately 60 hours using only a single PC.
- If we switched out our 8 character password for a 6 character one, then the rate for solving it drops to under one minute with a single PC.

So, where does the slow hashing function come in? Well, instead of that PC running at one billion hashes per second, imagine that we used a hashing function that could only run one million times per second on the same PC. This would extend the time that a brute force attack would take against our 8 character password by 1,000 times, or put another way, 60 hours would turn into approximately 7 years. The trick is to use a hashing algorithm that supports what is called a cost parameter. The cost parameter is what makes the hashing algorithm a "slow" algorithm. Blowfish supports a cost parameter. The cost parameter is the base-2 logarithm of how many iterations the algorithm will run for. In Blowfish this number can range between 04 and 31. The lower the number set for the cost parameter, the slower the algorithm runs.

In addition to Blowfish, there are also the bcrypt and scrypt functions that could be used as well to achieve the same results. Bcrypt has been around for far longer than scrypt, and both have

---

153 Read more about Oorschot and Weiner here: http://people.scs.carleton.ca/~paulv/papers/JoC97.pdf

154 More information about Cain and Abel may be found here: http://www.oxid.it/cain.html

their advantages and disadvantages. For an interesting take on why bcrypt may be a better choice than scrypt, the interested security professional should take a look at the following blog entry:

http://blog.ircmaxell.com/2014/03/why-i-dont-recommend-scrypt.html

The Birthday Paradox

The birthday paradox has been described in textbooks on probability for several years. It is a surprising mathematical condition that indicates the ease of finding two people with the same birthday from a group of people. If one considers that there are 365 possible birthdays (not including leap years and assuming that birthdays are spread evenly across all possible dates), then one would expect to need to have roughly 183 people together to have a 50% probability that two of those people share the same birthday. In fact, once there are more than 23 people together, there is a greater than 50% probability that two of them share the same birthday. Consider that in a group of 23 people, there are 253 different pairings ($n(n-1)/2$). Once 100 people are together, the chance of two of them having the same birthday is greater than 99.99%.

So why is a discussion about birthdays important in the middle of hashing attacks? Because the likelihood of finding a collision for two messages and their hash values may be a lot easier than may have been believed.

It would be very similar to the statistics of finding two people with the same birthday. One of the considerations for evaluating the strength of a hash algorithm must be its resistance to collisions. The probability of finding a collision for a 160-bit hash can be estimated at either 2^{160} or $2^{160}/2$, depending on the level of collision resistance needed.

This approach is relevant because a hash is a representation of the message and not the message itself. Obviously, the attacker does not want to find an identical message; he wants to find out how to (1) change the message contents to what he wants it to read or (2) cast some doubt on the authenticity of the original message by demonstrating that another message has the same value as the original. The hashing algorithm must be resistant to a birthday-type attack that would allow the attacker to feasibly accomplish his goals.

Methods of Cryptanalytic Attacks

Any security system or product is subject to compromise or attack. The following explains common attacks against cryptography systems.

Ciphertext-Only Attack

The ciphertext-only attack is one of the most difficult because the attacker has so little information to start with. All the attacker starts with is some unintelligible data that he suspects may be an important encrypted message. The attack becomes simpler when the attacker is able to gather several pieces of ciphertext and thereby look for trends or statistical data that would help in the attack. Adequate encryption is defined as encryption that is strong enough to make brute force attacks impractical because there is a higher work factor than the attacker wants to invest into the attack. Moore's law states that available computing power doubles

3

Security Engineering

every 18 months.[155] Experts suggest this advance may be slowing; however, encryption strength considered adequate today will probably not be sufficient a few years from now due to advances in CPU and GPU technology and new attack techniques.[156] Security professionals should consider this when defining encryption requirements.

Known Plaintext

For a known plaintext attack, the attacker has access to both the ciphertext and the plaintext versions of the same message. The goal of this type of attack is to find the link – the cryptographic key that was used to encrypt the message. Once the key has been found, the attacker would then be able to decrypt all messages that had been encrypted using that key. In some cases, the attacker may not have an exact copy of the message; if the message was known to be an e-commerce transaction, the attacker knows the format of such transactions even though he does not know the actual values in the transaction.

Chosen Plaintext

To execute the chosen attacks, the attacker knows the algorithm used for the encrypting, or even better, he may have access to the machine used to do the encryption and is trying to determine the key. This may happen if a workstation used for encrypting messages is left unattended. Now the attacker can run chosen pieces of plaintext through the algorithm and see what the result is. This may assist in a known plaintext attack. An adaptive chosen plaintext attack is where the attacker can modify the chosen input files to see what effect that would have on the resulting ciphertext.

Chosen Ciphertext

This is similar to the chosen plain text attack in that the attacker has access to the decryption device or software and is attempting to defeat the cryptographic protection by decrypting chosen pieces of ciphertext to discover the key. An adaptive chosen ciphertext would be the same, except that the attacker can modify the ciphertext prior to putting it through the algorithm. Asymmetric cryptosystems are vulnerable to chosen ciphertext attacks. For example, the RSA

---

155 In 1965, Gordon Moore made the following observation:
"The complexity for minimum component costs has increased at a rate of roughly a factor of two per year. Certainly over the short term this rate can be expected to continue, if not to increase. Over the longer term, the rate of increase is a bit more uncertain, although there is no reason to believe it will not remain nearly constant for at least 10 years. That means by 1975, the number of components per integrated circuit for minimum cost will be 65,000."

His reasoning was based on an empirical relationship between device complexity and time, observed over three data points. He used this to justify that by 1975, devices with as many as 65,000 components would become feasible on a single silicon chip occupying an area of only about one-fourth of a square inch. This projection turned out to be accurate with the fabrication of a 16K CCD memory with about 65,000 components in 1975. In a subsequent paper in 1975, Moore attributed the relationship to exponential behavior of die sizes, finer minimum dimensions, and "circuit and device cleverness". He went on to state that:

There is no room left to squeeze anything out by being clever. Going forward from here we have to depend on the two size factors - bigger dies and finer dimensions."

He revised his rate of circuit complexity doubling to 18 months and projected from 1975 onwards at this reduced rate. This curve came to be known as "Moore's Law". Formally, Moore's Law states that circuit complexity doubles every eighteen months. By relating component density and increases in die-size to the computing power of a device, Moore's law has been extended to state that the amount of computing power available at a given cost doubles approximately every 18 months.

156 Read more about the slowing of Moore's law here: http://news.cnet.com/8301-10784_3-9780752-7.html

algorithm is vulnerable to this type of attack. The attacker would select a section of plaintext, encrypt it with the victim's public key, then decrypt the ciphertext to get the plaintext back. Although this does not yield any new information to the attacker, the attacker can exploit properties of RSA by selecting blocks of data, when processed using the victim's private key, yields information that can be used in cryptanalysis. The weakness with asymmetric encryption in chosen ciphertext attacks can be mitigated by including a random padding in the plaintext before encrypting the data. Security vendor RSA Security recommends modifying the plaintext by using a process called optimal asymmetric encryption padding (OAEP). RSA encryption with OAEP is defined in PKCS #1 v2.1.[157]

Differential Cryptanalysis

Also called a side channel attack, this more complex attack is executed by measuring the exact execution times and power required by the crypto device to perform the encryption or decryption. By measuring this, it is possible to determine the value of the key and the algorithm used.

Linear Cryptanalysis

This is a known plaintext attack that uses linear approximations to describe the behavior of the block cipher. Linear cryptanalysis is a known plaintext attack and uses a linear approximation to describe the behavior of the block cipher. Given sufficient pairs of plaintext and corresponding ciphertext, one can obtain bits of information about the key, and increased amounts of data will usually give a higher probability of success.

There have been a variety of enhancements and improvements to the basic attack. For example, there is an attack called differential-linear cryptanalysis, which combines elements of differential cryptanalysis with those of linear cryptanalysis.

Implementation Attacks

Implementation attacks are some of the most common and popular attacks against cryptographic systems due to their ease and reliance on system elements outside of the algorithm. The main types of implementation attacks include:

- Side-Channel Analysis
- Fault Analysis
- Probing Attacks

Side-Channel Attacks are passive attacks that rely on a physical attribute of the implementation such as power consumption/emanation. These attributes are studied to determine the secret key and the algorithm function. Some examples of popular side-channels include timing analysis and electromagnetic differential analysis.

Fault Analysis attempts to force the system into an error state to gain erroneous results. By forcing an error, gaining the results, and comparing it with known good results, an attacker may learn about the secret key and the algorithm.

Probing Attacks attempt to watch the circuitry surrounding the cryptographic module in hopes that the complementary components will disclose information about the key or the algorithm. Additionally new hardware may be added to the cryptographic module to observe and inject information.

---

157 See the following: http://www.rsa.com/rsalabs/node.asp?id=2125

Replay Attack

This attack is meant to disrupt and damage processing by the attacker, through the re-sending of repeated files to the host. If there are no checks such as time-stamping, use of one time tokens, or sequence verification codes in the receiving software, the system might process duplicate files.

Algebraic

Algebraic attacks are a class of techniques that rely for their success on block ciphers exhibiting a high degree of mathematical structure. For instance, it is conceivable that a block cipher might exhibit a group structure. If this were the case, it would then mean that encrypting a plaintext under one key and then encrypting the result under another key would always be equivalent to single encryption under some other single key. If so, then the block cipher would be considerably weaker, and the use of multiple encryption cycles would offer no additional security over single encryption.

Rainbow Table

Hash functions map plaintext into a hash. Because the hash function is a one-way process, one should not be able to determine the plaintext from the hash itself. To determine a given plaintext from its hash, refer to these two ways to do that:

1.   Hash each plaintext until matching hash is found; or
2.   Hash each plaintext, but store each generated hash in a table that can used as a look up table so hashes do not need to be generated again.

A rainbow table is a lookup table of sorted hash outputs. The idea here is that storing pre-computed hash values in a rainbow table that one can later refer to saves time and computer resources when attempting to decipher the plaintext from its hash value.

Frequency Analysis [158]

This attack works closely with several other types of attacks. It is especially useful when attacking a substitution cipher where the statistics of the plaintext language are known. In English, for example, some letters will appear more often than others will, allowing an attacker to assume that those letters may represent an E or S.

Birthday Attack

Because a hash is a short representation of a message, given enough time and resources, another message would give the same hash value. However, hashing algorithms have been developed with this in mind so that they can resist a simple birthday attack. The point of the birthday attack is that it is easier to find two messages that hash to the same message digest than to match a specific message and its specific message digest. The usual countermeasure is to use a hash algorithm with twice the message digest length as the desired work factor (e.g., use 160 bit SHA-1 to have it resistant to 2^{80} work factor).

Factoring Attacks

This attack is aimed at the RSA algorithm. Because that algorithm uses the product of large prime numbers to generate the public and private keys, this attack attempts to find the keys through solving the factoring of these numbers.

---

158 Read more about Frequency Analysis and Claude Shannon's work at: http://www.schneier.com/crypto-gram-9812.html

Social Engineering for Key Discovery

This is the most common type of attack and usually the most successful. All cryptography relies to some extent on humans to implement and operate. Unfortunately, this is one of the greatest vulnerabilities and has led to some of the greatest compromises of a nation's or organization's secrets or intellectual property. Through coercion, bribery, or befriending people in positions of responsibility, spies or competitors are able to gain access to systems without having any technical expertise.

Dictionary Attack

The dictionary attack is used most commonly against password files. It exploits the poor habits of users who choose simple passwords based on natural words. The dictionary attack merely encrypts all of the words in a dictionary and then checks whether the resulting hash matches an encrypted password stored in the SAM file or other password file.

Brute Force

Brute force is trying all possible keys until one is found that decrypts the ciphertext. This is why key length is such an important factor in determining the strength of a cryptosystem. With DES only having a 56-bit key, in time the attackers were able to discover the key and decrypt a DES message. This is also why SHA-256 is considered stronger than MD5; because the output hash is longer and, therefore, more resistant to a brute force attack. Graphical Processor Units (GPUs) have revolutionized brute force hacking methods. Where a standard CPU might take 48 hours to crack an eight character mixed password, a modern GPU can crack it in less than ten minutes. GPUs have a large number of "Arithmetic/Logic Units" (ALUs) and are designed to perform repetitive tasks continuously. These characteristics make them ideal for performing brute force attack processes. Due to the introduction of GPU based brute force attacks, many security professionals are evaluating password length, complexity, and multifactor considerations.

Reverse Engineering

This attack is one of the most common. A competing firm buys a crypto product from another firm and then tries to reverse engineer the product. Through reverse engineering, it may be able to find weaknesses in the system or gain crucial information about the operations of the algorithm.

Attacking the Random Number Generators

This attack was successful against the SSL installed in Netscape several years ago. Because the random number generator was too predictable, it gave the attackers the ability to guess the random numbers so critical in setting up initialization vectors or a nonce. With this information in hand, the attacker is much more likely to run a successful attack.

Temporary Files

Most cryptosystems will use temporary files to perform their calculations. If these files are not deleted and overwritten, they may be compromised and lead an attacker to the message in plaintext.

3

Security Engineering

Site and Facility Design Considerations

A physical security program is designed to prevent the interruption of operations and provide for the security of information, assets, and personnel. Operational interruptions can occur from natural or environmental catastrophes like hurricanes, tornados, and floods as well as from industrial accidents like fires, explosions, or toxic spills, and intentional acts of sabotage, vandalism, or theft.

During the design phase of a site, it should be the standard operational procedure for a security professional to review all aspects of construction to include land use, site planning, stand-off distance, controlled access zones, entry control and vehicular access, signage, parking, loading docks and service access, security lighting, and site utilities. Integrating security requirements into a comprehensive approach necessitates achieving a balance among many objectives such as reducing risk, architectural aesthetics, creating a safe work environment, and hardening of physical structures for added security.

It is important to remember that the nature of any threat is always changing. In other words, having direction is the best approach in dealing with physical security. Do not be reactive and start throwing money into security systems. Be insightful in identifying necessary security needs, and put a plan together along with a budget in order to achieve the overall objective.

In addition to the traditional problems of violence and crime, security professionals must now contend with international terrorism, environmental damage, energy disruptions, and potential pandemics. To these protracted and almost universal problems, one can add the prospect of unexpected and often violent natural events like earthquakes, floods, hurricane, fires, or tornadoes.

The Security Survey

Before any project begins, there must be an assessment made in order to put together an operational plan and a practical approach to securing the facility. This security assessment can also be called a security survey, a vulnerability assessment, or a risk analysis.

No one with any common sense starts a project without a plan. A ship's captain would never leave port without navigational tools, maps, global positioning systems, and a crew that was seasoned. The same goes for security professionals who will need the tools to initiate a security assessment. It makes no sense to simply deploy cameras around the organization without sound justification; this would be a waste of resources and money.

A security assessment is a comprehensive overview of the facility including physical security controls, policy, procedures, and employee safety. A good assessment requires the security professional to determine specific protection objectives. These objectives include threat definition, target identification, and facility characteristics.

The first question a security professional should be asking is, "What is the threat?" Then start down the list of the potential threats to the organization or facility. Is it vandals, hackers, terrorists, internal employees, corporate spies, or a combination? Stating the threat will identify how adversaries can impact assets and will provide the guidance to developing a sound physical protection system.

Target Identification

What is the most valuable asset that needs to be protected? Assets can be personnel, property, equipment, or information. To identify assets to be protected, one should prioritize the assets or establish a matrix and identify the asset in conjunction with probability of attack, along with the question, what would be the impact and consequence of the loss of the asset? *Figure 3.44* illustrates a threat matrix.

Asset	Probability of Attack	Consequence of Loss
Data Center Server	Medium	Very High
Portable Laptops (critical staff)	High	High
Copy Machine	Low	Low
Portable Laptops (non-essential personnel)	High	Low
PCU	Medium	High
Classified Containers	Low	High

Figure 3.44 - **A Threat Matrix**

Facility Characteristic

There are several things to look at from the standpoint of whether the facility is an existing structure or is new construction. The security professional will either be reviewing architectural drawings or doing a walkthrough of the facility. In the case of an existing structure, it is recommended that a team of security personnel walk the facility. Having several eyes on the project will assist in developing a good evaluation.

Walking with a team of security professionals through a facility will provide a static presentation of how to protect the facility. However, one of the best ways to build a comprehensive approach toward protecting the facility is by doing on-site interviews. Everyone has an opinion on security, and it is often that the best insight and information on what needs to be protected and how it should be protected comes from interviewing the staff. One such astute and insightful person is the overnight security officer. He often has nothing but time and walks the facility without interruption, seeing things that are only clearly visible at night.

The American Institute of Architects has established key security concerns that need to be addressed while performing the security assessment.[159]

1. Facility security control during and after hours of operation
2. Personnel and contract security policies and procedures
3. Personnel screening
4. Site and building access control
5. Video surveillance, assessment, and archiving
6. Natural surveillance opportunities
7. Protocols for responding to internal and external security incidents
8. Degree of integration of security and other building systems

---

159 Grassie, Richard P. "Vulnerability Analysis and Security Assessment." AIA Best Practices, Last modified February 2007. http://www.aia.org/aiaucmp/groups/ek_members/documents/pdf/aiap016650.pdf

9. Shipping and receiving security
10. Property identification and tracking
11. Proprietary information security
12. Computer network security
13. Workplace violence prevention
14. Mail screening operations, procedures, and recommendations
15. Parking lot and site security
16. Data center security
17. Communications security
18. Executive protection
19. Business continuity planning and evacuation procedures

Once these areas are reviewed and a thorough facilities evaluation and staff interview is completed, it is time to develop and outline a physical protection system for the facility.

Vulnerability Assessment

The assessment of any vulnerability of a facility or building should be done within the context of the defined threats and the value of the organization's assets. That is, each element of the facility should be analyzed for vulnerabilities to each threat, and a vulnerability rating should be assigned based on the criteria below. It would be foolish to install $10,000 worth of security equipment in order to protect $100 worth of assets. It should be noted that a vulnerability assessment might change the value rating of assets due to the identification of critical nodes or some other factor that makes the organization's assets more valuable. *Figure 3.45* is a sample vulnerability matrix.

Main Facility	Vulnerability
Front Entrance	Medium
Receptionist	High
Access Control	Low
Response to Alarms	High
Closed Circuit Television	Medium
Classified Containers	Low

Figure 3.45 - **A Sample Vulnerability Matrix**

- **Very High –** One or more major weaknesses have been identified that make the organization's assets extremely susceptible to an aggressor or hazard.
- **High –** One or more significant weaknesses have been identified that make the organization's assets highly susceptible to an aggressor or hazard.
- **Medium High –** An important weakness has been identified that makes the organization's assets very susceptible to an aggressor or hazard.
- **Medium –** A weakness has been identified that makes the organization's assets fairly susceptible to an aggressor or hazard.
- **Medium Low –** A weakness has been identified that makes the organization's assets somewhat susceptible to an aggressor or hazard.
- **Low –** A minor weakness has been identified that slightly increases the susceptibility of the organization's assets to an aggressor or hazard.
- **Very Low –** No weaknesses exist.

Site Planning

The single most important goal in planning a site is the protection of life, property, and operations. A security professional needs to make decisions in support of this purpose, and these decisions should be based on a comprehensive security assessment of the threats and hazards so that planning and design countermeasures are appropriate and effective in the reduction of vulnerability and risk.

There is a natural conflict between making a facility as convenient as possible for operation and maintaining a secure facility. If it were only up to security in designing a facility, it would look like the fortified castle shown in *Figure 3.46*. However, with most applications and design requirements, there needs to be cooperation between several departments. Convenience and accessibility should be considered during the different phases of the design review; however, the requirement for security should never be sacrificed for convenience. Proper security controls will reduce the flow rate and ease of entering and leaving a facility. These issues must be addressed in the initial planning to facilitate additional egress points or administrative requirements.

Once a process has been established, and there is buy-in from the organizational leadership, the acceptance of normal operations becomes the organizational standard. When there are changes to the design after the fact and personnel are used to doing something a certain way, there will be reluctance, questions, and push back.

To maximize safety and security, a design team should implement a holistic approach to site design that integrates security and function to achieve a balance among the various design elements and objectives. Even if resources are limited, significant value can be added to a project by integrating security considerations into the more traditional design tasks in such a way that they complement the design.

Figure 3.46 - **Facility designed by a security professional** *(Courtesy of Bosch Security Systems)*

The movement of people and materials throughout a facility is determined by the design of its access, delivery, and parking systems. Such systems should be designed to maximize efficiency while minimizing conflicts between the entry and exiting of vehicles and pedestrians. Designers should begin with an understanding of the organization's requirements based on an analysis of how the facility will be used.

Roadway Design

There is not a facility that does not have roadways and vehicular traffic. The idea of streets is often not thought of as a way to curtail unauthorized access or prevent sabotage and structural damage to the facility. Streets are generally designed to minimize travel time and maximize safety, with the end result typically being a straight path between two or more endpoints.

Although a straight line may be the most efficient course, designers should consider a roadway system to minimize vehicle velocity, thus using the roadway itself as a protective measure. This is accomplished through the use of several strategies.

First, straight-line or perpendicular approaches to the facility should not be used because this gives a vehicle the opportunity to gather the speed necessary to ram and penetrate buildings. This can also occur by accident when a gas pedal sticks and the driver panics. Instead, approaches should be parallel to the perimeter of the building, with natural earthen berms, high curbs, trees, or other measures used to prevent vehicles from departing the roadway. Existing streets can be retrofitted with barriers, bollards, swing gates, or other measures to force vehicles to travel in a serpentine path. Again, high curbs and other measures should be installed to keep vehicles from departing the roadway in an effort to avoid these countermeasures.

Crime Prevention through Environmental Design (CPTED) [160]

Crime Prevention through Environmental Design (CPTED) is a crime reduction technique that has several key elements applicable to the analysis of the building function and site design against physical attack. It is used by architects, city planners, landscapers, interior designers, and security professionals with the objective of creating a climate of safety in a community by designing a physical environment that positively influences human behavior.

CPTED concepts have been successfully applied in a wide variety of applications including streets, parks, museums, government buildings, houses, and commercial complexes.

The CPTED process provides direction to solve the challenges of crime with organizational (people), mechanical (technology and hardware), and natural design (architecture and circulation flow) methods.

CPTED concepts can be integrated into expansion or reconstruction plans for existing buildings as well as plans for new buildings. Applying CPTED concepts from the beginning usually has minimal impact on costs, and the result is a safer facility.

Landscape design features should be used to create the desired level of protection without turning the facility into a fortress. Elements such as landforms, water features, and vegetation are among the building blocks of attractive and welcoming spaces, and they can also be powerful tools for enhancing security. During site planning, it would be beneficial to consider and install these techniques from a cost savings approach. The earth movers, graders, and landscapers have all been budgeted, so why not use CPTED techniques to supplement security concerns? Stands of trees, natural earthen berms, and similar countermeasures generally

160 For more information about CPTED, please see the following: http://www.cpted.net/

cannot replace setbacks, but they can offer supplementary protection. With careful selection, placement, and maintenance, landscape elements can provide visual screening that protects employee gathering areas and other activities from surveillance without creating concealment for covert activity.

However, dense vegetation in close proximity to a building can screen illicit activity and should be avoided. Additionally, thick ground cover or vegetation over four inches tall can be a security disadvantage; in setback clear zones, vegetation should be selected and maintained with the elimination of concealment opportunities in mind. Similarly, measures to screen visually detractive components such as transformers, trash compactors, and condensing units should be designed to minimize concealment opportunities for people and weapons.

The New Zealand Ministry of Justice's The Seven Qualities for Well-Designed, Safer Places offers this advice: [161] Avoid using elements that create a poor image or a fortress-like appearance. Integrate any necessary security.

Figure 3.47- **Building designed with crime prevention in mind** *(Courtesy of Bosch Security Systems)*

- Treating gates and grilles as public art
- Making perimeter fences look attractive by allowing visibility through the fences, including simple design motifs or combining them with a hedge of thorny shrub varieties can 'target harden' boundary treatment
- Using open grilled designs or internal shutters instead of roller-shutter blinds
- Using different grades of toughened or laminated glass as a design alternative to various types of grille (*Figure 3.47*).

---

161 See the following: http://www.justice.govt.nz/publications/global-publications/n/national-guidelines-for-crime-prevention-through-environmental-design-in-new-zealand-part-1-seven-qualities-of-safer-places-part-2-implementation-guide-november-2005/the-seven-qualities-for-well-designed-safer-places

3

Security Engineering

Many CPTED crime prevention techniques are common sense approaches. For example, businesses are encouraged to direct all visitors through one entrance that offers contact with a receptionist who can determine the purpose of the visit and the destination and also provide sign in/sign out and an ID badge prior to building access. These measures are nothing new to the retail business world. This approach encourages employees to make personal contact with everyone entering the store in order to keep track of people who want to be invisible and do not want to attract the attention of store employees while they perpetrate crimes.

Other CPTED concepts include the idea that a standard front with windows overlooking sidewalks and parking lots is more effective than encircling the facility with cyclone fences and barbed wire. A communal area with picnic seating, in which activities happen frequently, has a greater deterrent effect. Trees also help, as they make shared areas feel safer. Access matters too; defensible spaces should have single egress points so that potential intruders are afraid of being trapped. For example, closed circuit television (CCTV) cameras best deter crime in facilities such as parking lots where there is a single exit.

Windows

Because of the ease with which most windows can be entered or broken into, it makes them targets for most intruders; so they need to be addressed as a potential vulnerability in the facility defenses. A standard home's installed glass windows can be shattered relatively easily when hit with force. Not only will the glass break but also it will leave sharp fragments that can cause severe lacerations.

Window systems such as glazing, frames, and anchorage to supporting walls on the exterior façade of a building should be used to mitigate the hazardous effects of flying glass during an explosion event. In an effort to protect occupants, the security professional should integrate the features of the glass, the connection of the glass to the frame, and anchoring of the frame to the building structure to achieve a balanced installation.

It is recommended that windows should not be placed adjacent to doors because, if the window is broken, the door can be reached and unlocked. Consider using laminated glass in place of conventional glass and placing window guards, such as grills, screens, or meshwork, across window openings to protect against covert entry. Windows on the ground level should not have the ability to open and should be protected with bars and alarm systems. The alarms available for a window include a magnetic switch, which when the magnets are separated, as when the window is opened, an alarm will sound. Windows up to the fourth floor should have this protection installed. Also, consider using steel window frames securely fastened or cement grouted into the surrounding structure.

Types of Glass

Tempered Glass

Tempered glass is similar to the glass installed in car windshields. It will resist breakage and will disintegrate into small cubes of crystals with no sharp edges. Tempered glass is used in entrance doors and adjacent panels.

Wired Glass

Wired glass provides resistance to impact from blunt objects. The wire mesh is imbedded into the glass thereby providing limited protection.

Laminated Glass

Laminated glass (*Figure* 3.48) is recommended for installation in street-level windows, doorways, and other access areas. It is made from two sheets of ordinary glass bonded to a middle layer of resilient plastic. When it is struck, it may crack but the pieces of glass tend to stick to the plastic inner material.

Bullet Resistant (BR) Glass

Bullet resistant glass (*Figure* 3.49) is typically installed in banks and high-risk areas. There are different layers of BR glass with the standard being 1 ¼-inch thick, which provides protection from a 9mm round.

Figure 3.48 - **Laminated glass is recommended for installation in street-level windows, doorways, and other access areas**
(Courtesy of Bosch Security Systems)

Figure 3.49 - **Bullet resistant (BR) glass is typically installed in banks and high-risk areas**
(Courtesy of Bosch Security Systems)

3

Security Engineering

Glass Break Sensors

Glass break sensors are a good intrusion detection device for buildings with a lot of glass windows and doors with glass panes. Glass as an exterior protection barrier can be easily defeated. Windows can be quickly and easily broken. There are several basic types of glass break sensors: Acoustic sensors listen for an acoustic sound wave that matches the frequency of broken glass, and shock sensors feel the shock wave when glass is broken. The use of dual-technology glass break sensors – both acoustic and shock wave – is most effective. The reason is that if only acoustic sensors are used and an employee pulls the window blinds up, it can set off a false alarm; but if it is set to a dual-alarm system, both acoustic and shock sensors will need to be activated before an alarm is triggered. There is not a significant price difference between a simple acoustic sensor and combination sensors (acoustic and shock). For the nominal component price increase, which is a fraction of the total installed cost, the increased capability can justify the higher price.

Garages

If the facility has an underground parking garage or an attached parking structure, the security professional must understand two primary safety threats: crime and vehicles hitting pedestrians.

Start by utilizing signage that can direct vehicles and pedestrians to the exits or the entrance to the facility. CCTV cameras should be used for monitoring events, and emergency call boxes should be placed throughout the garage. Installing bright lights is one of the most effective deterrents to both accidents and attacks. Lighting levels of at least 10 to 12 foot-candles over parked cars and 15 to 20 foot-candles in walking and driving aisles is recommended.

It is also advisable to install high lighting levels to illuminate the exterior of the parking facility, particularly in areas that experience high pedestrian traffic. As a rule, exterior lights should be placed approximately 12 feet above ground, and they should point downward to illuminate wide areas along the ground. Another method for increasing visibility is to paint the walls of the structure white to reflect light. Lighting fixtures should also be strategically placed to bounce light off the walls and reduce dark corners where criminals or attackers could hide.

If the garage is under the facility, elevators or walk-ups should all empty into the lobby, outside of the controlled space. Having all employees and visitors pass through the controlled receptionist area will maintain the integrity of the facility. In this way, the elevators going into the core of the building will only be accessible from the lobby and not from the garage levels.

Location Threats

Natural Threats

Natural hazards typically refer to events such as earthquakes, floods, tornado, and hurricanes. This requires preparation for these natural hazards by establishing a communication system in order to get information to employees and upper management. Information and periodic emergency training exercises are the best ways to be prepared and thereby reduce fear and anxiety. Organizations can also reduce the impact of disasters by flood proofing, installing emergency power systems, and securing items that could shake loose in an earthquake.

Types of Natural Threats

According to the United States Federal Emergency Management Agency (FEMA) "Are You Ready?" series, specific natural threats [162] include hurricanes, tornados, earthquakes, forest fires, mudslides, and floods. The security architects need to understand the types of natural threats that they may have to deal with depending on where they are located. Regardless of the specific threats that they may encounter, the security architects need to ensure that the Disaster Recovery Planning and Business Continuity Planning functions within the enterprise have taken notice of the natural threats potentially able to threaten the business and that the appropriate Risk Assessments, Risk Analysis, and Business Impact Analysis have been carried out regarding these natural threats. In addition, the need to keep those plans updated with accurate and timely information regarding changes in potential threats due to seasonal weather patterns, dependent events occurring elsewhere, and any other variables that may impact the plans should to be accounted for as well.

Man-Made Threats

Threats from fire can be potentially devastating and can affect an organization beyond the physical damage. Not only fire but also heat, smoke, and water can cause irreversible damage. The fire protection system should maintain life safety protection and allow for safe evacuation from the building. A facilities fire protection water system should be protected from a single point of failure. The incoming line should be encased, buried, or located 50 feet away from high-risk areas. The interior mains should be looped and sectionalized. Water can be the main fire suppression tool; however, it will cause extreme damage to electronic equipment.

Fire requires three elements to burn: heat, oxygen, and a fuel source. Fire extinguishers and fire suppression systems fight fires by removing one of the three elements. Fire extinguishers are divided into four categories, based on different types of fires:

- **Class A** – Extinguishers are for ordinary combustible materials such as paper, wood, cardboard, and most plastics. The numerical rating on this type of extinguisher indicates the amount of water it holds and the amount of fire it can extinguish.
- **Class B** – Fires involve flammable or combustible liquids such as gasoline, kerosene, grease, and oil. The numerical rating for a class B extinguisher indicates the approximate number of square feet of fire it can extinguish.
- **Class C** – Fires involve electrical equipment, such as appliances, wiring, circuit breakers, and outlets. Never use water to extinguish class C fires – the risk of electrical shock is far too great! Class C extinguishers do not have a numerical rating. The C classification means the extinguishing agent is nonconductive.
- **Class D** – Fire extinguishers are commonly found in a chemical laboratory. They are for fires that involve combustible metals, such as magnesium, titanium, potassium, and sodium. These types of extinguishers neither have numerical rating nor are they given a multipurpose rating. They are designed for class D fires only.

---

162 See the following: http://training.fema.gov/EMIWeb/is/is22.asp

Utility Concerns

Electrical

The primary security involvement dealing with electrical systems is to guarantee essential power to facility services, especially those required for daily operations and life safety. They should also consider the following recommendations:

- Emergency and normal electric panels, conduits, and switchgear should be installed separately, at different locations, and as far apart as possible. Electric distribution should also run at separate locations.
- Emergency generators should be located away from loading docks, entrances, and parking. More secure locations include the roof, protected grade level, and protected interior areas.
- Main fuel storage for generators should be located away from loading docks, entrances, and parking. Access should be restricted and protected to include locks on caps and seals.

Communications

Communication devices are also an integral part of the core facility utilities. Security professionals should consider having a second telephone service to maintain communications in case of an incident. For most operations, specific employees should be provided cellular telephones, or the organization should maintain a phone list of all critical employees and their cell phone numbers. In addition, a base radio communications system with a repeater antenna should be installed and portable radios distributed on floors. This system is usually operated by building guards, and the radio communications system can be used in cases of emergencies. A standard radio system can use more than one channel for operational purposes.

Utilities

Utility systems can suffer significant damage when subjected to the shock of extensive environmental hazards. Some of these utilities may be critical for safety of the facility. To minimize the possibility of critical failure due to hazards, apply the following measures:

- Where possible, provide underground, concealed, and protected utilities.
- Consider quick connects for portable utility backup systems if redundant sources are not available.
- Protect drinking water supplies from waterborne contaminants by securing access points, such as manholes. If warranted, maintain routine water testing to help detect waterborne contaminants.
- Minimize signs identifying critical utilities. Provide fencing to prevent unauthorized access, and use landscape planting to conceal aboveground systems.
- Locate petroleum, oil, and lubricants storage tanks and operations buildings down slope from all other occupied buildings. Locate fuel storage tanks at least 100 feet from buildings.
- Locate utility systems at least 50 feet from loading docks, front entrances, and parking areas.

Design and Implement Facility Security

The security architect and the security practitioner both play a role in the design and implementation of secure facilities. The architect needs to understand how to use risk assessments, risk analysis, and business impact analysis of the various design elements being considered to fully assess whether or not these elements will make a defense in depth architecture and design possible or whether they will detract from it instead. The security practitioner will need to use the same tools and approaches as the architect and focus them on the individual systems that they are asked to operate and manage within the enterprise. Together, these approaches can lead to secure designs as well as secure systems provided that they work together, mutually reinforcing one another.

The use of the methods already discussed such as CPTED can yield good results when examining how to site and design secure facilities. The addition of security perimeters and automated monitoring systems, such as CCTV and PIDAS fencing, can also enhance the security of a facilities design. The deployment of guards and mantraps as well as smart card access controls for all doors and computer systems can enhance the operational security of the facility, as well as the safety of those working inside and the confidentiality and integrity of the information stored within.

There is guidance available to the security architect and the practitioner from many areas and industries with regards to secure facility design. The underlying issues that have to be addressed first are the business purpose or reason(s) being addressed through the architecture and system(s) in question. Without a thorough understanding of the specific objectives to be achieved by the design and operation of the systems, the architect and practitioner will not be able to do their respective jobs effectively.

For example, in addition to the Federal Emergency Management Agency (FEMA) risk reduction publications that provide background information for performing risk assessments and guidance for protective design approaches, different branches of the federal government developed design criteria for the protection of federal facilities. The most prominent of these agency design criteria are the Interagency Security Committee (ISC) physical security criteria, the Department of Defense Protective Design Center (DOD-PDC), the Veterans Administration (VA), and the Department of State (DOS).

FEMA has published extensive guidance under its Risk Management Series (RMS), which is directed at providing design guidance for mitigating multi-hazard events. The series includes a large cadre of man-made disaster publications directed at strengthening the building inventory to reduce the potential impact from the forces that might be anticipated in a terrorist assault. The objective of the series is to reduce physical damage to structural and nonstructural components of buildings and related infrastructure and to reduce resultant casualties from impact by conventional bombs, chemical, biological, and radiological (CBR) agents, earthquakes, floods, and high winds. The intended audience includes architects and engineers working for private institutions, building owners/operators/managers, and state and local government officials working in the building sciences community.[163]

3

Security Engineering

---

163 See the following: http://www.fema.gov/what-mitigation/security-risk-management-series-publications

A sampling of the FEMA RMS publications are below:

- **FEMA 426** – Reference Manual to Mitigate Potential Terrorist Attacks Against Buildings, 2nd Edition (2011)
- **FEMA 427** – Primer for Design of Commercial Buildings to Mitigate Terrorist Attacks (2004)
- **FEMA 428** – Primer to Design Safe School Projects in Case of Terrorist Attacks and School Shootings, 2nd Edition (2012)
- **FEMA 429** – Insurance, Finance, and Regulation Primer for Terrorism Risk Management in Buildings (2003)
- **FEMA 430** – Site and Urban Design for Security: Guidance Against Potential Terrorist Attacks (2007)
- **FEMA 452** – A How-To Guide to Mitigate Potential Terrorist Attacks Against Buildings (2005)
- **FEMA 453** – Safe Rooms and Shelters: Protecting People Against Terrorist Attacks (2006)
- **FEMA 455** – Handbook for Rapid Visual Screening of Buildings to Evaluate Terrorism Risks (2009)
- **FEMA 459** – Incremental Protection for Existing Commercial Buildings from Terrorist Attack: Providing Protection to People and Buildings (2009)

Implementation and Operation of Facilities Security

Communications and Server Rooms

Securing the Area

Communication rooms or closets must maintain a high level of security. Access must be controlled into this area, and only authorized personnel should be allowed to work on this equipment. No matter what transmission mode or media is selected, it is important that a method for securing communications be included. This includes physical protection, such as providing a rigid metallic conduit for all conductors, as well as technical protection, such as encrypting communication transmissions.

What is Cable Plant Management?

Cable plant management is the design, documentation, and management of the lowest layer of the OSI network model-the physical layer. The physical layer is the foundation of any network, whether it is data, voice, video or alarms, and it defines the physical media upon which signals or data is transmitted through the network.

Approximately 70% of your network is composed of passive devices such as cables, cross-connect blocks, and patch panels. Documenting these network components is critical to keeping a network finely tuned. The physical medium can be copper cable (e.g., cat 6), coaxial cable, optical fiber (e.g., single or multimode), wireless or satellite. The physical layer defines the specifics of implementing a particular transmission medium. It defines the type of cable, frequency, terminations, etc. The physical layer is relatively static. Most change in the network occurs at the higher levels in the OSI model.

Key components of the cable plant include the entrance facility, equipment room, backbone cable, backbone pathway, telecommunication room, and horizontal distribution system.

Entrance Facility

The service entrance is the point at which the network service cables enter or leave a building. It includes the penetration through the building wall and continues to the entrance facility. The entrance facility can house both public and private network service cables. The entrance facility provides the means for terminating the backbone cable. The entrance facility generally includes electrical protection, ground, and demarcation point.

Equipment Room

The equipment room serves the entire building and contains the network interfaces, uninterruptible power supplies, computing equipment (e.g., servers, shared peripheral devices, and storage devices), and telecommunication equipment (e.g., PBX). It may be combined with the entrance facility.

Backbone Distribution System

A backbone distribution system provides connection between entrance facilities, equipment rooms, and telecommunication rooms. In a multi-floor building, the backbone distribution system is composed of the cabling and pathways between floors and between multiple telecommunication rooms. In a campus environment, the backbone distribution system is composed of the cabling and pathways between buildings.

Telecommunication Room

The telecommunication room (TR) typically serves the needs of a floor. The TR provides space for network equipment and cable terminations (e.g., cross-connect blocks and patch panels). It serves as the main cross-connect between the backbone cabling and the horizontal distribution system.

Horizontal Distribution System

The horizontal distribution system distributes the signals from the telecommunication room to the work areas. The horizontal distribution system consists of:

- Cables
- Cross-connecting blocks
- Patch panels
- Jumpers
- Connecting hardware
- Pathways (supporting structures such as cable trays, conduits, and hangers that support the cables from the telecommunication room to the work areas)

Protection from Lightning

A lightning strike to a grounding system produces an elevated ground or ground potential rise (GPR). Any equipment bonded to this grounding system and also connected to wire-line communications will most likely be damaged from outgoing currents seeking remote ground. Personnel working at this equipment are susceptible to harm because they will be in the current path of this outgoing current. The equipment damage from a lightning strike may not be immediate. Sometimes the equipment is weakened by stress and primed for failure at some future time. This is called latent damage and leads to premature "mean time before failure" (MTBF) of the equipment.

The best engineering design, for open ended budgets, is the use of dielectric fiber optic cable for all communications. Obviously, a fiber optic cable is non-conductive, provided that it is an all dielectric cable with no metallic strength members or shield, making isolation no longer a requirement. This is because physical isolation is inherent in the fiber optic product itself. This all dielectric fiber optic cable must be placed in a PVC conduit to protect it from rodents.

However, if budgets are tight, the engineering design solution to protect this equipment is to isolate the wire-line communications from remote ground. This is accomplished using optical isolators or isolation transformers. This equipment is housed together, mounted on a non- conducting surface in a non-conducting cabinet, and is called the high voltage interface (HVI).

The HVI isolates the equipment during a GPR and prevents any current flow from a higher potential grounding system to a lower potential grounding system. This totally protects any equipment from damage or associated working personnel from harm. No ground shunting device ever made, no matter how fast acting, will ever completely protect equipment from a GPR. Ground shunting devices are connected to the elevated ground and during a GPR offer an additional current path in the reverse direction from which they were intended to operate. Obviously, this flow of current, even away from the equipment, will immediately cause equipment damage and harm to working personnel.

Server Rooms

A server room needs a higher level of security than the rest of the facility. This should encompass a protected room with no windows and only one controlled entry into the area. Remember that once servers are compromised, the entire network is at risk. While some server attacks are merely annoying, others can cause serious damage. In order to protect the organization, it is paramount to protect your servers. Physical access to a system is almost a guaranteed compromise if performed by a motivated attacker.[164] Therefore, server room security must be comprehensive and constantly under review.

Rack Security

It would be unusual for everyone in a room full of racks to have the need to access every rack; rack locks can ensure that only the correct people have access to servers and only telecommunications people have access to telecommunications gear. "Manageable" rack locks that can be remotely configured to allow access only when needed – to specific people at specific times – reduce the risk of an accident, sabotage, or unauthorized installation of additional equipment that could cause a potentially damaging rise in power consumption and rack temperature.

Restricted and Work Area Security

Depending on the configuration and operations structure of the data center, administrators and operators can be within the secured portion of the data center or can be in an auxiliary area. In most cases the latter is true, for the simple fact that there just isn't enough room within the data center to maintain equipment and personnel. Additionally, server rooms are noisy and cold, not ideal conditions for human beings.

---

164 See the following for a discussion of the Ten Immutable Laws of Security V2.0: http://technet.microsoft.com/en-us/library/hh278941.aspx

Individuals who maintain sensitive information must present the common sense attitude of being security minded within the confines of the facility. Not everyone who works on sensitive information needs to be inside a secured room. For areas not considered a high security area, there are still requirements to maintain a responsible profile. Store and maintain sensitive information in security containers, which can be a filing cabinet with locking bars and a padlock. Maintain a clean desk approach, which encourages personnel to lock up information when they are finished for the day.

Maintain strong password protection for workstations. Never have computer screens facing toward the window without blinds or some type of protective film. Privacy filters and screen protectors keep prying eyes off sensitive work. Have a shredding company destroy trash containing all proprietary and customer confidential information. This will eliminate outsiders from obtaining confidential information through dumpster diving.

Restricted Work Areas

In highly restricted work areas such as government SCIFs, there is a requirement to increase the security blanket to ensure tighter access to these areas. The physical security protection for a SCIF is intended to prevent as well as detect visual, acoustical, technical, and physical access by unauthorized persons. An organization may not be required to maintain government-classified information; however, the company's livelihood and your employment is tied to proprietary information that requires the same level of security.

SCIF walls will consist of 3 layers of 5/8 inch drywall and will be from true floor to true ceiling. There will typically be only one SCIF entrance door, which will have an X-09 combination lock along with access control systems. According to the United States Director of Central Intelligence Directive 1/21 DCID1-21, all SCIF perimeter doors must be plumbed in their frames and the frame firmly affixed to the surrounding wall.[165] Door frames must be of sufficient strength to preclude distortion that could cause improper alignment of door alarm sensors, improper door closure, or degradation of audio security. All SCIF primary entrance doors must be equipped with an automatic door closer.

Basic HVAC requirements have any duct penetration into the secured area that is over 96 square inches include man bars to prevent a perpetrator from climbing through the ducts.

White noise or sound masking devices need to be placed over doors, in front of plenum, or pointed toward windows to keep an adversary from listening to classified conversations. Some SCIFs use music or noise that sounds like a constant flow of air to mask conversation. All access control must be managed from within the SCIF. Intrusion detection is sent out to a central station with the requirement that a response force will respond to the perimeter of the SCIF within 15 minutes.

Data Center Security

When discussing the need to secure the data center, security professionals immediately think of sabotage, espionage, or data theft. While the need is obvious for protection against intruders and the harm caused by intentional infiltration, the hazards from the ordinary activity of personnel working in the data center present a greater day-to-day risk for most facilities. For example, personnel within the organization need to be segregated from access areas where they have no "need to know" for that area. The security director would typically have physical

---

165 See the following: http://www.fas.org/irp/offdocs/dcid1-21.pdf

access to most of the facility but has no reason to access financial or HR data. The head of computer operations might have access to computer rooms and operating systems but not the mechanical rooms that house power and HVAC facilities. It comes down to not allowing wandering within the organization.

As data centers and Web hosting sites grow, the need for physical security at the facility is every bit as great as the need for cybersecurity of networks. The data center is the brains of the operation, and as such only specific people should be granted access. The standard scenario for increased security at a data center would consist of the basic security-in-depth: progressing from the outermost (least sensitive) areas to the innermost (most sensitive) areas. Security will start with entry into the building, which will require passing a receptionist or guard, then using a proximity card to gain building entry. For access into the computer room or data center, it will now require the same proximity card along with a PIN (*Figure 3.50*), plus a biometric device. Combining access control methods at an entry control point will increase the reliability of access for authorized personnel only. Using different methods for each access level significantly increases security at inner levels because each is secured by its own methods plus those of outer levels that must be entered first. This would also include internal door controls.

Figure 3.50 - **A Card Reader with PIN and biometric features for additional security**
(Courtesy of Boom Edam)

For a data center, the use of an internal mantrap or portal would provide increased entry and exit control. A portal (*Figure 3.51*) allows only one person in at a time and will only open the inner door once the outer door is closed. The portal can have additional biometrics within the device that must be activated before the secured side door opens.

Figure 3.51 - **A Secure Portal allows only one person in at a time and will only open the inner door once the outer door is closed** *(Courtesy of Bosch Security Systems)*

The "two-person" rule is a strategy where two people must be in an area together, making it impossible for a person to be in the area alone. Two-man rule programming is optional with many access control systems. It prevents an individual cardholder from entering a selected empty security area unless accompanied by at least one other person. Use of the two-person rule can help eliminate insider threats to critical areas by requiring at least two individuals to be present at any time. It is also used for life safety within a security area; if one person has a medical emergency, there will be assistance present.

Utilities and HVAC Considerations

Utilities and Power

Because they often host mission-critical servers, data centers are built with both battery and generator backups. If the power cuts out, the batteries take over, just as they might in a home user's uninterruptible power supply. The generators also begin and start producing power before the batteries fail. Areas that contain backup generators and power supplies need similar protection. This area can be controlled with key access or a card access reader, and electric door strikes can be installed for entry into this area. This area is also a person-specific area; there is no need to give everyone access to the generator room. This room will maintain backup power for the entire facility in the event of a power outage emergency.

Uninterruptible Power Supply (UPS)

This is a battery backup system, which maintains a continuous supply of electric power to connected equipment by supplying power from a separate source when utility power is not available. A UPS has internal batteries to guarantee that continuous power is provided to the equipment even if the power source stops providing power. Of course, the UPS can only provide power for a while, typically a few minutes, but that is often enough to ride out power company glitches or short outages. Even if the outage is longer than the battery lifetime of the UPS, this provides the opportunity to execute an orderly shutdown of the equipment.

Generator

Generator power should be activated automatically in the event of a utility failure by the transfer switch. The data center load is maintained by the UPS units; however, often this is a short time as the generator should be active and up to speed within 10 seconds of a power failure. A generator (*Figure 3.52*) is typically run on diesel fuel and can be located outside of the facility or inside a parking garage. The generator room needs to be protected from unauthorized access either by access control devices or key-locked doors. The generator will operate as long as fuel is supplied. Some generators have a 300-gallon capacity and a facilities manager will have a contract with a local distributor to supply fuel. Most operation centers have more than one generator and test them once a month. If it is located outside, it needs protective barriers placed around it to protect it from a vehicle running into it.

Figure 3.52 - **A Backup Generator is activated automatically in the event of a utility failure by the transfer switch** *(Courtesy of Bosch Security Systems)*

HVAC

HVAC stands for heating, ventilation, and air-conditioning. Heat can cause extensive damage to computer equipment by causing processors to slow down and stop execution or even cause solder connections to loosen and fail. Excessive heat degrades network performance and causes downtime. Data centers and server rooms need an uninterrupted cooling system. Generally, there are two types of cooling: latent and sensible.

Latent cooling is the ability of the air-conditioning system to remove moisture. This is important in typical comfort-cooling applications, such as office buildings, retail stores, and other facilities with high human occupancy and use. The focus of latent cooling is to maintain a comfortable balance of temperature and humidity for people working in and visiting such a facility. These facilities often have doors leading directly to the outside and a considerable amount of entrance and exit by occupants.

Sensible cooling is the ability of the air-conditioning system to remove heat that can be measured by a thermometer. Data centers generate much higher heat per square foot than typical comfort-cooling building environments, and they are typically not occupied by large numbers of people. In most cases, they have limited access and no direct means of egress to the outside of the building except for seldom used emergency exits.

Data centers have a minimal need for latent cooling and require minimal moisture removal. Sensible cooling systems are engineered with a focus on heat removal rather than moisture removal and have a higher sensible heat ratio; they are the most useful and appropriate choice for the data center. Cooling systems are dove tailed into the power supply overhead. If there is a power interruption, this will affect the cooling system. For the computers to continue operation, they need to be cooled. Portable air-conditioning units can be used as a backup in case of HVAC failure, but good design should ensure cooling systems are accounted for as backup devices.

Air Contamination

Over the past several years, there has been an increasing awareness dealing with anthrax and airborne attacks. Harmful agents introduced into the HVAC systems can rapidly spread throughout the structure and infect all persons exposed to the circulated air.

To avoid air contamination, place intakes at the highest practical level in the facility. For protection against malicious acts, the intakes should also be covered by screens so that objects cannot be tossed into the intakes or into air wells from the ground. Such screens should be sloped to allow thrown objects to roll or slide off the screen, away from the intake. Many existing buildings have air intakes that are located at or below ground level. For those that have wall-mounted or below-grade intakes close to the building, the intakes can be elevated by constructing a plenum or external shaft over the intake.

The following is a list of guidelines necessary to enhance security in this critical aspect of facility operations:

- Restrict access to main air intake points to persons who have a work-related reason to be there.
- Maintain access rosters of pre-approved maintenance personnel authorized to work on the system.
- Escort all contractors with access to the system while on site.
- Ensure that all air intake points are adequately secured with locking devices.

All buildings have air intake points that either are roof-mounted, exterior wall-mounted, or in a free-standing unit on the ground outside of the building. Due to "sick building syndrome," where one person infects several with a cold or flu through a building HVAC system, many governments require all new buildings to mix a certain percentage of fresh air in with re-circulated air in the HVAC system. The volume of fresh air taken in is based on the square footage of the building and the number of employees working inside.

One method of reducing the risk of biological agents circulating throughout a building is installation of UV light filters in the HVAC system's supply and return ducts. UV light inhibits the growth and reproduction of germs, bacteria, viruses, fungi, and mold. UV light is the portion of the electromagnetic spectrum that lies beyond the "purple" or visible edge of the spectrum. The sun acts as a natural outdoor air purification system, controlling airborne bacteria with UV rays. UV light penetrates the microorganism and breaks down molecular bonds causing cellular or genetic damage. The germs are either killed or sterilized, leaving them unable to reproduce. In either case, live bacterial counts can be significantly reduced and kept under control.

3

Security Engineering

Water Issues

Along with excessive heat, water is a detriment to computer equipment. A data center may have a gas suppression fire system, but what about the floors above? Are they on a standard water sprinkler system and what would happen if the sprinklers are activated or begin leaking? Proper planning moves equipment away from water pipes that might burst, basements that might flood, or roofs that might leak. However, there are other water leaks that are more difficult to recognize and detect. Blocked ventilation systems can cause condensation if warm, moist air is not removed quickly. If vents are located above or behind machines, condensation can form small puddles that no one sees. Stand-alone air conditioners are especially vulnerable to water leaks if condensation is not properly removed. Even small amounts of water near air intakes will raise humidity levels and fill servers with moisture.

Fire Prevention, Detection, and Suppression

To protect the server room from fire, the organization needs to have smoke detectors installed and linked to a panel with enunciators that will warn people that there is smoke in the room. Also, it should be linked to a fire suppression system that can help put out the fire with no damage to equipment from the gas itself.

Fire Detection

A smoke detector is one of the most important devices to have due to its ability to warn of a pending fire, coupled with a good signaling device.

A detector in proper working condition will sound an alarm and give all occupants a chance to make it out alive. There are two main categories of smoke detectors: optical detection (photoelectric) and physical process (ionization). Photoelectric detectors are classified as either beam or refraction. Beam detectors operate on the principle of light and a receiver. Once enough smoke enters the room and breaks the beam of light, the alarm is sounded. The refraction type has a blocker between the light and the receiver. Once enough smoke enters the room, the light is deflected around the beam to the signal. Finally, we have the ionization type detector; these detectors monitor the air around the sensors constantly. Once there is enough smoke in the room, the alarm will sound.

There are three main types of fire detectors: flame detectors, smoke detectors, and heat detectors. There are two main types of flame detectors, and they are classified as infrared (IR) and ultraviolet (UV) detectors. IR detectors primarily detect a large mass of hot gases that emit a specific spectral pattern in the location of the detector; these patterns are sensed with a thermographic camera and an alarm is sounded. Additional hot surfaces in the room may trigger a false response with this alarm. UV flame detectors detect flames at speeds of 3–4 milliseconds due to the high-energy radiation emitted by fires and explosions at the instant of their ignition. Some of the false alarms of this system include random UV sources such as lightning, radiation, and solar radiation that may be present in the room.

There are heat detectors, which include fixed temperature or rate of rise detectors. The user will set a predetermined temperature level for the alarm to sound. If the room temperature rises to that setting, the alarm will sound. Rate of rise temperature will detect a sudden change of temperature around the sensor. Usually this setting is at around 10–15 degrees per minute. Nothing more is required of the consumer except routine checks for battery life and operation status. Heat detectors should not be used to replace smoke detectors; each component in fire safety serves its purpose and should be taken seriously. The combination of devices and the knowledge of procedures are the only way to achieve success during a possible fire.

Fire Suppression

All buildings should be equipped with an effective fire suppression system, providing the building with around the clock protection. Traditionally, fire suppression systems employed arrays of water sprinklers that would douse a fire and surrounding areas. Sprinkler systems are classified into four different groups: wet, dry, pre-action, and deluge.

- **Wet Systems** – Have a constant supply of water in them at all times; once activated, these sprinklers will not shut off until the water source is shut off.
- **Dry Systems**– Do not have water in them. The valve will not release until the electric valve is stimulated by excess heat.
- **Pre-Action Systems** – Incorporate a detection system, which can eliminate concerns of water damage due to false activations. Water is held back until detectors in the area are activated.
- **Deluge Systems** – Operate in the same function as the pre-action system except all sprinkler heads are in the open position.

Water may be a sound solution for large physical areas such as warehouses, but it is entirely inappropriate for computer equipment. A water spray can irreparably damage hardware more quickly than encroaching smoke or heat. Gas suppression systems operate to starve the fire of oxygen. In the past, Halon was the choice for gas suppression systems; however, Halon leaves residue, depletes the ozone layer, and can injure nearby personnel.[166]

There are several gas suppression systems that are recommended for fire suppression in a server room or anywhere electronic equipment is employed:

- **Aero-K** – Uses an aerosol of microscopic potassium compounds in a carrier gas released from small canisters mounted on walls near the ceiling. The Aero-K generators are not pressurized until fire is detected. The Aero-K system uses multiple fire detectors and will not release until a fire is "confirmed" by two or more detectors (limiting accidental discharge). The gas is non-corrosive, so it does not damage metals or other materials. It does not harm electronic devices or media such as tape or discs. More important, Aero-K is nontoxic and does not injure personnel.

- **FM-200** – Is a colorless, liquefied compressed gas. It is stored as a liquid and dispensed into the hazard as a colorless, electrically non-conductive vapor that is clear and does not obscure vision. It leaves no residue and has acceptable toxicity for use in occupied spaces at design concentration. FM-200 does not displace oxygen and, therefore, is safe for use in occupied spaces without fear of oxygen deprivation.

---

166 The Montreal Protocol on Substances that Deplete the Ozone Layer was designed to reduce the production and consumption of ozone depleting substances in order to reduce their abundance in the atmosphere and thereby protect the earth's fragile ozone layer. The original Montreal Protocol was agreed on 16 September 1987 and entered into force on 1 January 1989.
See the following: http://ozone.unep.org/new_site/en/Treaties/treaties_decisions-hb.php?sec_id=5

3

Security Engineering

Summary

Security Architecture and Design covers a wide range of topics focused on designing security into computing systems and across IT services throughout the enterprise. The security architect is expected to understand a number of key security architecture concepts and apply them against a number of common scenarios. Security architects capture and analyze requirements, design security services based on those requirements, and verify the effectiveness of those designs. Security architects understand the different architecture frameworks, standards, and best practices leveraged by numerous frameworks and methodologies, and how they may be used together to provide stronger designs. Cryptography has enabled information technology use in environments never before possible. The move towards telework and the secure communications required for remote work would not be possible without the advances in cryptography. Cryptography provides the information security professional with a rich menu of methods, devices, software, and techniques to help ensure the confidentiality, integrity, authentication, and nonrepudiation of information. While advances in computing power have rendered some cryptographic tools weakened or comprised, security professionals and researchers are constantly developing new tools to enhance security. Cryptography will continue to play a vital role in the advancement of privacy, security, commerce, and communications for the foreseeable future.

Domain 3: Review Questions

1. A holistic lifecycle for developing security architecture that begins with assessing business requirements and subsequently creating a 'chain of traceability' through phases of strategy, concept, design, implementation and metrics is characteristic of which of the following frameworks?

    A. Zachman

    B. SABSA

    C. ISO 27000

    D. TOGAF

2. While an Enterprise Security Architecture (ESA) can be applied in many different ways, it is focused on a few key goals. Identify the proper listing of the goals for the ESA:

    A. It represents a simple, long term view of control, it provides a unified vision for common security controls, it leverages existing technology investments, it provides a fixed approach to current and future threats and also the needs of peripheral functions

    B. It represents a simple, long term view of control, it provides a unified vision for common security controls, it leverages new technology investments, it provides a flexible approach to current and future threats and also the needs of core functions

    C. It represents a complex, short term view of control, it provides a unified vision for common security controls, it leverages existing technology investments, it provides a flexible approach to current and future threats and also the needs of core functions

    D. It represents a simple, long term view of control, it provides a unified vision for common security controls, it leverages existing technology investments, it provides a flexible approach to current and future threats and also the needs of core functions

3. Which of the following can **BEST** be used to capture detailed security requirements?

    A. Threat modeling, covert channels, and data classification

    B. Data classification, risk assessments, and covert channels

    C. Risk assessments, covert channels, and threat modeling

    D. Threat modeling, data classification, and risk assessments

4. Which of the following security standards is internationally recognized as the standards for sound security practices and is focused on the standardization and certification of an organization's Information Security Management System (ISMS)?

    A.   ISO 15408

    B.   ISO 27001

    C.   ISO 9001

    D.   ISO 9146

5. Which of the following describes the rules that need to be implemented to ensure that the security requirements are met?

    A.   Security kernel

    B.   Security policy

    C.   Security model

    D.   Security reference monitor

6. A two-dimensional grouping of individual subjects into groups or roles and granting access to groups to objects is an example of which of the following types of models?

    A.   Multilevel lattice

    B.   State machine

    C.   Non-interference

    D.   Matrix-based

7. Which of the following models ensures that a subject with clearance level of 'Secret' has the ability to write only to objects classified as 'Secret' or 'Top Secret' but is prevented from writing information classified as 'Public'?

    A.   Biba-Integrity

    B.   Clark–Wilson

    C.   Brewer–Nash

    D.   Bell–LaPadula

8. Which of the following is unique to the Biba Integrity Model?

    A.   Simple property

    B.   * (star) property

    C.   Invocation property

    D.   Strong * property

9. Which of the following models is **BEST** considered in a shared data-hosting environment so that the data of one customer is not disclosed to a competitor or other customers sharing that hosted environment?

    A. Brewer–Nash

    B. Clark–Wilson

    C. Bell–LaPadula

    D. Lipner

10. Which of the following security models is primarily concerned with how the subjects and objects are created and how subjects are assigned rights or privileges?

    A. Bell–LaPadula

    B. Biba-Integrity

    C. Chinese Wall

    D. Graham–Denning

11. Which of the following ISO standards provides the evaluation criteria that can be used to evaluate security requirements of different products with different functions?

    A. 15408

    B. 27000

    C. 9100

    D. 27002

12. In the Common Criteria, the common set of functional and assurance requirements for a category of vendor products deployed in a particular type of environment are known as

    A. Protection Profiles

    B. Security Target

    C. Trusted Computing Base

    D. Ring Protection

13. Which of the following evaluation assurance level that is formally verified, designed and tested is expected for high risk situation?

    A. EAL 1

    B. EAL 3

    C. EAL 5

    D. EAL 7

3

Review Questions

14. Formal acceptance of an evaluated system by management is known as

    A. Certification

    B. Accreditation

    C. Validation

    D. Verification

15. Which stage of the Capability Maturity Model (CMM) is characterized by having organizational processes that are proactive?

    A. Initial

    B. Managed

    C. Defined

    D. Optimizing

16. Which of the following **BEST** provides a method of quantifying risks associated with information technology when validating the abilities of new security controls and countermeasures to address the identified risks?

    A. Threat/risk assessment

    B. Penetration testing

    C. Vulnerability assessment

    D. Data classification

17. The TCSEC identifies two types of covert channels, what are they? (**Choose TWO**)

    A. Storage

    B. Boundary

    C. Timing

    D. Monitoring

18. Which of the following is the main reason for security concerns in mobile computing devices?

    A. The 3G/4G protocols are inherently insecure

    B. Lower processing power

    C. Hackers are targeting mobile devices

    D. The lack of anti-virus software.

19. In decentralized environments device drivers that enable the OS to control and communicate with hardware need to be securely designed, developed and deployed because they are

    A. typically installed by end-users and granted access to the supervisor state

    B. typically installed by administrators and granted access to user mode state

    C. typically installed by software without human interaction.

    D. integrated as part of the operating system.

20. A system administrator grants rights to a group of individuals called "Accounting" instead of granting rights to each individual. This is an example of which of the following security mechanisms?

    A. Layering

    B. Data hiding

    C. Cryptographic protections

    D. Abstraction

21. Asymmetric key cryptography is used for the following:

    A. Encryption of data, Access Control, Steganography

    B. Steganography, Access control, Nonrepudiation

    C. Nonrepudiation, Steganography, Encryption of Data

    D. Encryption of Data, Nonrepudiation, Access Control

22. Which of the following supports asymmetric key cryptography?

    A. Diffie–Hellman

    B. Rijndael

    C. Blowfish

    D. SHA-256

23. What is an important disadvantage of using a public key algorithm compared to a symmetric algorithm?

    A. A symmetric algorithm provides better access control.

    B. A symmetric algorithm is a faster process.

    C. A symmetric algorithm provides nonrepudiation of delivery.

    D. A symmetric algorithm is more difficult to implement.

3

Review Questions

24. When a user needs to provide message integrity, what option is **BEST**?

    A. Send a digital signature of the message to the recipient

    B. Encrypt the message with a symmetric algorithm and send it

    C. Encrypt the message with a private key so the recipient can decrypt with the corresponding public key

    D. Create a checksum, append it to the message, encrypt the message, and then send to recipient

25. A CA provides which benefits to a user?

    A. Protection of public keys of all users

    B. History of symmetric keys

    C. Proof of nonrepudiation of origin

    D. Validation that a public key is associated with a particular user

26. What is the output length of a RIPEMD-160 hash?

    A. 160 bits

    B. 150 bits

    C. 128 bits

    D. 104 bits

27. ANSI X9.17 is concerned primarily with

    A. Protection and secrecy of keys

    B. Financial records and retention of encrypted data

    C. Formalizing a key hierarchy

    D. The lifespan of key-encrypting keys (KKMs)

28. When a certificate is revoked, what is the proper procedure?

    A. Setting new key expiry dates

    B. Updating the certificate revocation list

    C. Removal of the private key from all directories

    D. Notification to all employees of revoked keys

29. Which is true about link encryption?

    A. Link encryption is advised for high-risk environments, provides better traffic flow confidentiality, and encrypts routing information.

    B. Link encryption is often used for Frame Relay or satellite links, is advised for high-risk environments and provides better traffic flow confidentiality.

    C. Link encryption encrypts routing information, is often used for Frame Relay or satellite links, and provides traffic flow confidentiality.

    D. Link encryption provides better traffic flow confidentiality, is advised for high-risk environments and provides better traffic flow confidentiality.

30. NIST identifies three service models that represent different types of cloud services available, what are they?

    A. Software as a Service (SaaS), Infrastructure as a Service (IaaS) and Platform as a Service (PaaS)

    B. Security as a Service (SaaS), Infrastructure as a Service (IaaS) and Platform as a Service (PaaS)

    C. Software as a Service (SaaS), Integrity as a Service (IaaS) and Platform as a Service (PaaS)

    D. Software as a Service (SaaS), Infrastructure as a Service (IaaS) and Process as a Service (PaaS)

31. The process used in most block ciphers to increase their strength is

    A. Diffusion

    B. Confusion

    C. Step function

    D. SP-network

32. Which of the following **BEST** describes fundamental methods of encrypting data:

    A. Substitution and transposition

    B. 3DES and PGP

    C. Symmetric and asymmetric

    D. DES and AES

3

Review Questions

33. Cryptography supports all of the core principles of information security except

    A. Availability

    B. Confidentiality

    C. Integrity

    D. Authenticity

34. A way to defeat frequency analysis as a method to determine the key is to use

    A. Substitution ciphers

    B. Transposition ciphers

    C. Polyalphabetic ciphers

    D. Inversion ciphers

35. The running key cipher is based on

    A. Modular arithmetic

    B. XOR mathematics

    C. Factoring

    D. Exponentiation

36. The only cipher system said to be unbreakable by brute force is

    A. AES

    B. DES

    C. One-time pad

    D. Triple DES

37. The main types of implementation attacks include: (**Choose ALL that apply**)

    A. Fault analysis

    B. Known plaintext

    C. Probing

    D. Linear

38. Which is the **BEST** choice for implementing encryption on a smart card?

    A. Blowfish

    B. Elliptic Curve Cryptography

    C. TwoFish

    D. Quantum Cryptography

39. An e-mail with a document attachment from a known individual is received with a digital signature. The e-mail client is unable to validate the signature. What is the **BEST** course of action?

    A.   Open the attachment to determine if the signature is valid.

    B.   Determine why the signature can't be validated prior to opening the attachment.

    C.   Delete the e-mail

    D.   Forward the e-mail to another address with a new signature.

40. The vast majority of Virtual Private Networks use

    A.   SSL/TLS and IPSec.

    B.   El Gamal and DES.

    C.   3DES and Blowfish

    D.   TwoFish and IDEA.

3

Review Questions

Domain 4
Communications & Network Security

The Communication and Network Security domain encompasses the structures, transmission methods, transport formats, and security measures used to provide confidentiality, integrity, and availability for transmissions over private and public communications networks and media. Network security is often described as the cornerstone of IT security. The network is a central asset, if not the most central, in most IT environments. Loss of network assurance (the combined properties of confidentiality, integrity, availability, authentication, and non-repudiation) on any level can have devastating consequences, while control of the network provides an easy and consistent venue of attack. Conversely, a well-architected and well-protected network will stop many attacks in their tracks.

Network security, like all security controls and safeguards, is most effective when applied proactively. Waiting for impacts to materialize and applying controls and safeguards under crisis conditions will always cost more and be less effective than planned and managed deployments of network security policy, procedures, and technologies. The challenge associated with proactivity is that it requires a solid business case: Why should resources be applied without evidence of a need (such as a loss or breach)? In addition to a business case, the right mix of skills, knowledge, and capability is required to build, maintain, and monitor a resilient network. Security architects use high-level requirements and regulations to help design and in some cases implement network controls. The security practitioner is on the front lines of implementation, operation, and monitoring the network for performance and security. The security professional focuses on the overarching risk of control failure or shortcomings due to the threat environment and whatever vulnerabilities may exist throughout the network. These roles together address the challenge of securing resources and manage risk. Throughout this chapter, risks that can be quantitatively and qualitatively measured through established metrics will be used to support a proactive business case.

In the past, the focus of the security professional would have been on the network's perimeter defenses through the deployment and use of firewalls and similar tools. As the disappearance of "traditional" network boundaries becomes a business requirement facilitated through hastened introduction of new technologies, cloud computing, and the convergence of technologies onto an IP backbone, a constant struggle exists between ease of use and security. It is a fundamental tenet of secure design that the inside of a network must be as resilient as its perimeter, that tools alone are ineffective if not combined with proper process, and that the availability of a network is a critical measure of the success of its design. Increasingly, attacks on the network are aimed not only at disrupting availability but also at compromising the knowledge and "semantic" assets of the network through stealthy confidentiality and integrity attacks. A network with high uptime is a boon to an attacker who is trying to exfiltrate information out of an organization.

This chapter focuses on the Open System Interconnect (OSI) model as a point of reference and Transmission Control Protocol/Internet Protocol (TCP/IP) as the most commonly used protocol stack. Other protocol stacks will be discussed and reviewed as needed. Excellent books and Internet resources exist to teach the basics of networking, and this chapter covers basic network concepts insofar as they are required for the self-sufficiency of this book and useful for obtaining an understanding of network security concepts.

It is not possible to give a complete and comprehensive overview of all possible attack scenarios. For the purposes of this chapter, we focus on the most important security risks and those that will be instructive for the security professional, in order to facilitate their ability to gain an understanding of network security concepts and enable them to enhance their understanding and gain in-depth knowledge through self-study.

TOPICS

- ■ Secure design principles
  - □ OSI and TCP/IP models
  - □ IP networking
  - □ Implications of multilayer protocols (e.g.,DNP3)
  - □ Converged protocols (e.g., FCoE, MPLS, VoIP, iSCI)
  - □ Software-defined networks
  - □ Wireless networks
  - □ Cryptography used to maintain communications security

- ■ Securing network components
  - □ Operation of hardware
    - – Modem
    - – Switches
    - – Routers
    - – Wireless access points
  - □ Transmission media
    - – Wired
    - – Wireless
    - – Fiber
  - □ Network access control devices
    - – Firewalls
    - – Proxies
  - □ Endpoint security
  - □ Content distribution networks
  - □ Physical devices

- ■ Secure communication channels
  - □ Voice
  - □ Multimedia collaboration
    - – Remote meeting technology
    - – Instant messaging
  - □ Remote access
    - – VPN
    - – Screen scraper
    - – Virtual application/Desktop
    - – Telecommuting
  - □ Data communication (e.g., VLAN, TLS/SSL)
  - □ Virtualized networks (e.g., SDN, virtual SAN, guest operating systems, PVLAN)

- ■ Prevent or mitigate network attacks (e.g., DDoS, spoofing)

OBJECTIVES

4

According to the (ISC)^2 Candidate Information Bulletin (Exam Outline), a CISSP candidate is expected to:

- Apply secure design principles to network architecture.

- Actively secure network components.

- Design and establish secure communication channels.

- Prevent or mitigate network attacks.

Secure Network Architecture and Design

Network communication is usually described in terms of layers. Several layering models exist; the most commonly used are:

- The OSI reference model, structured into seven layers (physical layer, data-link layer, network layer, transport layer, session layer, presentation layer, application layer) [1]
- The TCP/IP or Department of Defense (DoD) model (not to be confused with the TCP/IP protocols), structured into four layers (link layer, network layer, transport layer, application layer) [2]

One feature that is common to both models and highly relevant from a security perspective is encapsulation. This means that not only do the different layers operate independently from each other, but they are also isolated on a technical level. Short of technical failures, the contents of any lower or higher layer protocol are inaccessible from any particular layer. This function of the models allows the security architects to ensure that their designs can provide both confidentiality and integrity. It also allows the security practitioner to implement those designs and operate them effectively, knowing that data flowing up and down the model's layers is being safeguarded. The security professional can manage the network knowing that the data that is in transit across it is being protected. We are going to focus on the OSI model because it is the model that is implemented most widely, and it is the one that the security professionals need to have an understanding of as a baseline for being able to do their job.

OSI and TCP/IP

The seven-layer OSI (Open System Interconnect) model was defined in 1984 and published as an international standard, ISO/IEC 7498–1. [3] The last revision to this standard was in 1994. Although sometimes considered complex, it has provided a practical and widely accepted way to describe networking. In practice, some layers have proven to be less crucial to the concept (such as the presentation layer), while others (such as the network layer) have required more specific structure, and applications overlapping and transgressing layer boundaries exist. [4]

---

1   See the following for a high level overview of the OSI reference model: http://en.wikipedia.org/wiki/OSI_model

2   See the following for a high level overview of the TCP/IP model: http://en.wikipedia.org/wiki/TCP/IP_model

3   See the following: http://www.ecma-international.org/activities/Communications/TG11/s020269e.pdf

4   See the following for the original paper by Hubert Zimmermann that lays out the OSI Reference Model Architecture based on the work of the ISO SC16, the working group established to create the OSI model in 1977. "OSI Reference Model – The ISO Model of Architecture for Open Systems Interconnection": http://citeseerx.ist.psu.edu/viewdoc/download?doi=10.1.1.136.9497&rep=rep1&type=pdf

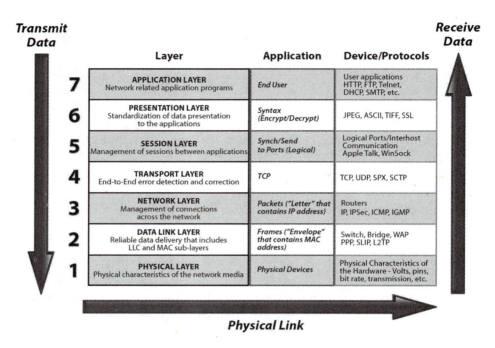

Transmit Data

Receive Data

	Layer	Application	Device/Protocols
7	**APPLICATION LAYER** Network related application programs	*End User*	User applications HTTP, FTP, Telnet, DHCP, SMTP, etc.
6	**PRESENTATION LAYER** Standardization of data presentation to the applications	*Syntax (Encrypt/Decrypt)*	JPEG, ASCII, TIFF, SSL
5	**SESSION LAYER** Management of sessions between applications	*Synch/Send to Ports (Logical)*	Logical Ports/Interhost Communication Apple Talk, WinSock
4	**TRANSPORT LAYER** End-to-End error detection and correction	*TCP*	TCP, UDP, SPX, SCTP
3	**NETWORK LAYER** Management of connections across the network	*Packets ("Letter" that contains IP address)*	Routers IP, IPSec, ICMP, IGMP
2	**DATA LINK LAYER** Reliable data delivery that includes LLC and MAC sub-layers	*Frames ("Envelope" that contains MAC address)*	Switch, Bridge, WAP PPP, SLIP, L2TP
1	**PHYSICAL LAYER** Physical characteristics of the network media	*Physical Devices*	Physical Characteristics of the Hardware - Volts, pins, bit rate, transmission, etc.

Physical Link

Figure 4.1 – **The Seven Layer OSI Reference Model**

- **Layer 1 –** The Physical layer describes the networking hardware, such as electrical signals and network interfaces and cabling.
- **Layer 2 –** The Data Link layer describes data transfer between machines, for instance, by an Ethernet.
- **Layer 3 –** The Network layer describes data transfer between networks, for instance, by the Internet Protocol (IP).
- **Layer 4 –** The Transport layer describes data transfer between applications, flow control, and error detection and correction, for instance, by TCP.
- **Layer 5 –** The Session layer describes the handshake between applications, for instance, authentication processes.
- **Layer 6 –** The Presentation layer describes the presentation of information, such as ASCII syntax.
- **Layer 7 –** The Application layer describes the structure, interpretation, and handling of information. In security terms, it is relevant because it relies on all underlying layers.

Each layer processes messages in a modular fashion, without concern for how the other layers on the same host process the message. For example, the layer that interacts directly with applications (layer 7) can communicate with its remote peer without knowing how the data is routed over the network (layer 3) or the hardware that is required (layers 1 and 2). When an application transmits data over a network, the data enters the top layer and moves to each successive lower level (moving down the stack) until it is transmitted over the network at layer 1. The remote host receives the data at layer 1 and moves to successive higher layers (moves up the stack) until it reaches layer 7 and then to the host's application.

Layer 1: Physical Layer

Physical topologies are defined at this layer. Because the required signals depend on the transmitting media (e.g., required modem signals are not the same as ones for an Ethernet network interface card), the signals are generated at the physical layer. Not all hardware consists of layer 1 devices. Even though many types of hardware, such as cables, connectors, and modems, operate at the physical layer, some operate at different layers. Routers and switches, for example, operate at the network and data-link layers, respectively.

Layer 2: Data Link Layer

The data link layer prepares the packet that it receives from the network layer to be transmitted as frames on the network. This layer ensures that the information that it exchanges with its peers is error free. If the data link layer detects an error in a frame, it will request that its peer resend that frame. The data link layer converts information from the higher layers into bits in the format that is expected for each networking technology, such as Ethernet, Token Ring, etc. Using hardware addresses, this layer transmits frames to devices that are physically connected only. As an analogy, consider the path between the end nodes on the network as a chain and each link as a device in the path. The data link layer is concerned with sending frames to the next link.

The Institute of Electrical and Electronics Engineers (IEEE) data link layer is divided into two sublayers:

- **Logical Link Control (LLC)** – Manages connections between two peers. It provides error and flow control and control bit sequencing.
- **Media Access Control (MAC)** – Transmits and receives frames between peers. Logical topologies and hardware addresses are defined at this sublayer. An Ethernet's 48-bit hardware address is often called a MAC address as a reference to the name of the sublayer.

Layer 3: Network Layer

It is important to clearly distinguish between the functions of the network and data link layers. The network layer moves information between two hosts that are not physically connected. On the other hand, the data link layer is concerned with moving data to the next physically connected device. Also, whereas the data link layer relies on hardware addressing, the network layer uses logical addressing that is created when hosts are configured.

- **Internet Protocol (IP)** – From the TCP/IP suite is the most important network layer protocol. IP has two functions:
- **Addressing** – IP uses the destination IP address to transmit packets through networks until the packets' destination is reached.
- **Fragmentation** – IP will subdivide a packet if its size is greater than the maximum size allowed on a local network.

IP is a connectionless protocol that does not guarantee error-free delivery. Layer 3 devices, such as routers, read the destination layer 3 address (e.g., destination IP address) in received packets and use their routing table to determine the next device on the network (the next hop) to send the packet. If the destination address is not on a network that is directly connected to the router, it will send the packet to another router.

Routing tables are built either statically or dynamically. Static routing tables are configured manually and change only when updated. Dynamic routing tables are built automatically when routers periodically share information that reflects their view of the network, which changes as routers go on and offline. When traffic congestion develops, this allows the routers to effectively route packets as network conditions change. Some examples of other protocols that are traditionally considered to work at layer 3 are as follows:

Routing Information Protocol (RIP) versions 1 and 2

The RIP v1 standard is defined in RFC 1058.[5] Routing Information Protocol (RIP) is a standard for exchange of routing information among gateways and hosts. RIP is most useful as an "interior gateway protocol". RIP uses distance vector algorithms to determine the direction and distance to any link in the internetwork. If there are multiple paths to a destination, RIP selects the path with the least number of hops. However, because hop count is the only routing metric used by RIP, it does not necessarily select the fastest path to a destination.

RIP v1 allows routers to update their routing tables at programmable intervals. The default interval is 30 seconds. The continual sending of routing updates by RIP v1 means that network traffic builds up quickly. To prevent a packet from looping infinitely, RIP allows a maximum hop count of 15. If the destination network is more than 15 routers away, the network is considered unreachable and the packet is dropped.

The RIP v2 standard is defined in RFC 1723 and updated for cryptographic authentication by RFC 4822.[6] RIP v2 provides the following advances over RIP v1:

- Carries a subnet mask.
- Supports password authentication security.
- Specifies the next hop address.
- Does not require that routes be aggregated on the network boundary.

Open Shortest Path First (OSPF) versions 1 and 2

The OSPF v1 standard is defined in RFC 1131.[7] Open Shortest Path First is an interior gateway routing protocol developed for IP networks based on the shortest path first or link-state algorithm. Routers use link-state algorithms to send routing information to all nodes in an internetwork by calculating the shortest path to each node based on a topography of the Internet constructed by each node. Each router sends that portion of the routing table (keeps track of routes to particular network destinations) that describes the state of its own links, and it also sends the complete routing structure (topography).

The advantage of shortest path first algorithms is that their use results in smaller, more frequent updates everywhere. They converge quickly, thus preventing such problems as routing loops and Count-to-Infinity (when routers continuously increment the hop count to a particular network). This makes for a more stable network. The disadvantage of shortest path first algorithms is that they require large amounts of CPU power and memory.

---

5   See the following: http://tools.ietf.org/html/rfc1058

6   See the following: http://tools.ietf.org/html/rfc1723
     http://tools.ietf.org/html/rfc4822

7   See the following: http://tools.ietf.org/pdf/rfc1131.pdf

4

OSPF v2 is defined in RFC 1583 and updated by RFC 2328.[8] It is used to allow routers to dynamically learn routes from other routers and to advertise routes to other routers. Advertisements containing routes are referred to as Link State Advertisements (LSAs) in OSPF. OSPF routers keep track of the state of all the various network connections (links) between itself and a network it is trying to send data to. This is the behavior that makes it a link-state routing protocol.

OSPF supports the use of classless IP address ranges and is very efficient. OSPF uses areas to organize a network into a hierarchal structure; it summarizes route information to reduce the number of advertised routes and thereby reduce network load and uses a designated router (elected via a process that is part of OSPF) to reduce the quantity and frequency of Link State Advertisements.

OSPF selects the best routes by finding the lowest cost paths to a destination. All router interfaces (links) are given a cost. The cost of a route is equal to the sum of all the costs configured on all the outbound links between the router and the destination network, plus the cost configured on the interface that OSPF received the Link State Advertisement on.

Internet Control Message Protocol (ICMP)

Internet Control Message Protocol (ICMP) is documented in RFC 792.[9] ICMP messages are classified into 2 main categories:

1. ICMP Error Messages
2. ICMP Query Messages

ICMP's goals are to provide a means to send error messages for non-transient error conditions and to provide a way to probe the network in order to determine general characteristics about the network. Some of ICMP's functions are to:

1. **Announce Network Errors** – Such as a host or entire portion of the network being unreachable, due to some type of failure. A TCP or UDP packet directed at a port number with no receiver attached is also reported via ICMP.

2. **Announce Network Congestion** – When a router begins buffering too many packets, due to an inability to transmit them as fast as they are being received, it will generate ICMP Source Quench messages. Directed at the sender, these messages should cause the rate of packet transmission to be slowed.

3. **Assist Troubleshooting** – ICMP supports an Echo function, which just sends a packet on a round trip between two hosts. Ping, a common network management tool, is based on this feature. Ping will transmit a series of packets, measuring average round trip times and computing loss percentages.

4. **Announce Timeouts** – If an IP packet's TTL field drops to zero, the router discarding the packet will often generate an ICMP packet announcing this fact. TraceRoute is a tool that maps network routes by sending packets with small TTL values and watching the ICMP timeout announcements.

---

8   See the following: RFC 1583: http://tools.ietf.org/html/rfc1583
    RFC 2328: http://tools.ietf.org/html/rfc2328

9   See the following: http://tools.ietf.org/html/rfc792

Internet Group Management Protocol (IGMP)

IGMP is used to manage multicasting groups, which are a set of hosts anywhere on a network that are interested in a particular multicast. Multicast agents administer multicast groups, and hosts send IGMP messages to local agents to join and leave groups. There are three versions of IGMP, as highlighted below:[10]

- **Version 1** – Multicast agents periodically send queries to a host on its network to update its database of multicast groups' membership. Hosts stagger their replies to prevent a storm of traffic to the agent. When replies no longer come from a group, agents will stop forwarding multicasts to that group.
- **Version 2** – This version extends the functionality of version 1. It defines two types of queries: a general query to determine membership of all groups and a group-specific query to determine the membership of a particular group. In addition, a member can notify all multicast routers that it wishes to leave a group.
- **Version 3** – This version further enhances IGMP by allowing hosts to specify from which sources they want to receive multicasts.

For a listing of protocols associated with layer 3 of the OSI model, see the following:

- **IPv4/IPv6** – Internet Protocol
- **DVMRP** – Distance Vector Multicast Routing Protocol
- **ICMP** – Internet Control Message Protocol
- **IGMP** – Internet Group Multicast Protocol
- **IPsec** – Internet Protocol Security
- **IPX** – Internetwork Packet Exchange
- **DDP** – Datagram Delivery Protocol
- **SPB** – Shortest Path Bridging

Layer 4: Transport Layer

The transport layer creates an end-to-end transport between peer hosts. User Datagram Protocol (UDP) and Transmission Control Protocol (TCP) are important transport layer protocols in the TCP/IP suite. UDP does not ensure that transmissions are received without errors, and therefore it is classified as a connectionless, unreliable protocol. This does not mean that UDP is poorly designed. Rather, the application will perform the error checking instead of the protocol.

Connection-oriented reliable protocols, such as TCP, ensure integrity by providing error-free transmission. They divide information from multiple applications on the same host into segments to be transmitted on a network. Because it is not guaranteed that the peer transport layer receives segments in the order that they were sent, reliable protocols reassemble received segments into the correct order. When the peer layer receives a segment, it responds with an acknowledgment. If an acknowledgment is not received, the segment is retransmitted. Lastly, reliable protocols ensure that each host does not receive more data than it can process without loss of data.

---

10   See the following for the RFC for IGMP Version 3: http://tools.ietf.org/html/rfc4604

TCP data transmissions, connection establishment, and connection termination maintain specific control parameters that govern the entire process. The control bits are listed as follows:

- **URG –** Urgent Pointer field significant
- **ACK –** Acknowledgement field significant
- **PSH –** Push Function
- **RST –** Reset the connection
- **SYN –** Synchronize sequence numbers
- **FIN –** No more data from sender

These control bits are used for many purposes; chief among them is the establishment of a guaranteed communication session via a process referred to as the TCP three way handshake, as described below:

1. First, the client sends a SYN segment. This is a request to the server to synchronize the sequence numbers. It specifies its initial sequence number (ISN), which is incremented by 1, and that is sent to the server. To initialize a connection, the client and server must synchronize each other's sequence numbers.

2. Second, the server sends an ACK and a SYN in order to acknowledge the request of the client for synchronization. At the same time, the server is also sending its request to the client for synchronization of its sequence numbers. There is one major difference in this transmission from the first one. The server transmits an acknowledgement number to the client. The acknowledgement is just proof to the client that the ACK is specific to the SYN the client initiated. The process of acknowledging the client's request allows the server to increment the client's sequence number by one and uses it as its acknowledgement number.

3. Third, the client sends an ACK in order to acknowledge the request from the server for synchronization. The client uses the same algorithm the server implemented in providing an acknowledgement number. The client's acknowledgment of the server's request for synchronization completes the process of establishing a reliable connection.

For a listing of protocols associated with layer 4 of the OSI model, see below:

- **ATP –** AppleTalk Transaction Protocol
- **DCCP –** Datagram Congestion Control Protocol
- **FCP –** Fiber Channel Protocol
- **RDP –** Reliable Datagram Protocol
- **SCTP –** Stream Control Transmission Protocol
- **SPX –** Sequenced Packet Exchange
- **SST –** Structured Stream Transport
- **TCP –** Transmission Control Protocol
- **UDP –** User Datagram Protocol
- **UDP Lite –** User Datagram Protocol Lite
- **μTP –** Micro Transport Protocol

Layer 5: Session Layer

This layer provides a logical, persistent connection between peer hosts. A session is analogous to a conversation that is necessary for applications to exchange information. The session layer is responsible for creating, maintaining, and tearing down the session. Three modes are offered:

1. **Full Duplex** – Both hosts can exchange information simultaneously, independent of each other.

2. **Half Duplex** – Hosts can exchange information but only one host at a time.

3. **Simplex** – Only one host can send information to its peer. Information travels in one direction only.

For a listing of protocols associated with layer 5 of the OSI model, see below:

- **ADSP** – AppleTalk Data Stream Protocol
- **ASP** – AppleTalk Session Protocol
- **H.245** – Call Control Protocol for Multimedia Communication
- **iSNS** – Internet Storage Name Service
- **PAP** – Password Authentication Protocol
- **PPTP** – Point-to-Point Tunneling Protocol
- **RPC** – Remote Procedure Call Protocol
- **RTCP** – Real-time Transport Control Protocol
- **SMPP** – Short Message Peer-to-Peer
- **SCP** – Session Control Protocol
- **SOCKS** – the SOCKS Internet protocol, see Internet socket
- **ZIP** – Zone Information Protocol

Layer 6: Presentation Layer

The applications that are communicating over a network may represent information differently, such as using incompatible character sets. This layer provides services to ensure that the peer applications use a common format to represent data. For example, if a presentation layer wants to ensure that Unicode-encoded data can be read by an application that understands the ASCII character set only, it could translate the data from Unicode to a standard format. The peer presentation layer could translate the data from the standard format into the ASCII character set. The presentation layer has a complex architecture that includes:

Services

- Data conversion
- Character code translation
- Compression
- Encryption and decryption

Sublayers

The presentation layer can be composed of two sublayers: common application service element (CASE) and specific application service element (SASE).

CASE

The common application service element sublayer provides services for the application layer and requests services from the session layer. It provides support for common application services, such as:

- **ACSE** – Association Control Service Element
- **ROSE** – Remote Operation Service Element
- **CCR** – Commitment Concurrency and Recovery
- **RTSE** – Reliable Transfer Service Element

SASE

The specific application service element sublayer provides application specific services (protocols), such as:

- **FTAM** – File Transfer, Access and Manager
- **VT** – Virtual Terminal
- **MOTIS** – Message Oriented Text Interchange Standard
- **CMIP** – Common Management Information Protocol
- **MMS** – Manufacturing Messaging Service
- **RDA** – Remote Database Access
- **DTP** – Distributed Transaction Processing

Protocols

In many widely used applications and protocols, no distinction is made between the presentation and application layers. For example, HyperText Transfer Protocol (HTTP), generally regarded as an application layer protocol, has presentation layer aspects such as the ability to identify character encoding for proper conversion, which is then done in the application layer.

Layer 7: Application Layer

This layer is the application's portal to network-based services, such as determining the identity and availability of remote applications. When an application or the operating system transmits or receives data over a network, it uses the services from this layer. Many well-known protocols, such as Hypertext Transfer Protocol (HTTP), File Transfer Protocol (FTP), and Simple Mail Transfer Protocol (SMTP), operate at this layer. It is important to remember that the application layer is not the application, especially when an application has the same name as a layer 7 protocol. For example, the FTP command on many operating systems initiates an application called FTP, which eventually uses the FTP protocol to transfer files between hosts. While some protocols are easily ascribed to a certain layer based on their form and function, others are very difficult to place precisely. An example of a protocol that falls into this category would be the Border Gateway Protocol.

Border Gateway Protocol (BGP)

BGP was created to replace the Exterior Gateway Protocol (EGP) protocol to allow fully decentralized routing. This allowed the Internet to become a truly decentralized system. BGP performs inter-domain routing in Transmission-Control Protocol/Internet Protocol (TCP/IP) networks. BGP is a protocol for exchanging routing information between gateway hosts (each with its own router) in a network of autonomous systems. BGP is often the protocol used between gateway hosts on the Internet. The routing table contains a list of known routers, the addresses they can reach, and a cost metric associated with the path to each router so that the best available route is chosen.

Hosts using BGP communicate using the Transmission Control Protocol (TCP) and send updated router table information only when one host has detected a change. Only the affected part of the routing table is sent. BGP-4, the latest version, lets administrators configure cost metrics based on policy statements.[11]

Many consider BGP an application that happens to affect the routing table. There are also those that would consider BGP a routing protocol as opposed to an application that affects the routing table. BGP creates and uses code attached to sockets. Does that mean that it should be considered an application? In the case of BGP when viewed in a traffic sniffer, there is a layer 4 header between the IP Header and the Routing Protocol header. Does that mean that we can say that BGP is an application that transports routing information at layer 4?

Perhaps a more appropriate way to classify a protocol is to look at the services it provides. BGP clearly provides services to the network layer, not the traditional transport services, but rather, BGP provides control information about how the network layer operates. This could allow us to move BGP down to the network layer.

This perspective is especially useful for management, control, and supervisory protocols that can be seen as applications of other protocols, and yet providing the necessary control, management, and supervisory information to the managed infrastructure that is on lower layers than the application layer. From this viewpoint, while BGP is truly just an application running over TCP, it is intimately tied into the operation of the network layer because it provides the necessary information about how the network layer should operate. That means that we could say that BGP is implemented as an application layer protocol, but with respect to its function, it is a network layer protocol.

As a security practitioner, you should understand how BGP works in real networks. Below are several links to simulators available online that can be used to model BGP and how it works:

- BGPlay, a HTML widget that presents a graphical visualization of BGP routes and updates for any real AS on the Internet.
  - Link is: https://stat.ripe.net/widget/bgplay
- SSFnet, SSFnet network simulator includes a BGP implementation developed by BJ Premore.
  - Link is: http://www.ssfnet.org/homePage.html
- C-BGP, a BGP simulator able to perform large scale simulation trying to model the ASes of the Internet or modelling ASes as large as Tier-1.
  - Link is: http://c-bgp.sourceforge.net/
- NetViews, a Java application that monitors and visualizes BGP activity in real time.
  - Link is: http://netlab.cs.memphis.edu/projects_netviews.html

For a listing of protocols associated with layer 7 of the OSI model, see below:

- **DHCP** – Dynamic Host Configuration Protocol
- **DHCPv6** – Dynamic Host Configuration Protocol v6
- **DNS** – Domain Name System
- **HTTP** – Hypertext Transfer Protocol

---

11 See the following: http://tools.ietf.org/html/rfc4271

- **IMAP** – Instant Message Access Protocol
- **IRC** – Internet Relay Chat
- **LDAP** – Lightweight Directory Access Protocol
- **XMPP** – Extensible Messaging and Presence Protocol
- **SMTP** – Simple Mail Transfer Protocol
- **FTP** – File Transfer Protocol
- **SFTP** – Secure File Transfer Protocol

TCP/IP Reference Model

The U.S. Department of Defense developed the TCP/IP model, which is very similar to the OSI model but with fewer layers as shown in *Figure 4.2*. The link layer provides physical communication and routing within a network. It corresponds to everything required to implement an Ethernet. It is sometimes described as two layers, a physical layer and a link layer. In terms of the OSI model, it covers layers 1 and 2. The network layer includes everything that is required to move data between networks. It corresponds to the IP protocol but also Internet Control Message Protocol (ICMP) and Internet Group Management Protocol (IGMP). In terms of the OSI model, it corresponds to layer 3.

The transport layer includes everything required to move data between applications. It corresponds to TCP and UDP. In terms of the OSI model, it corresponds to layer 4. The application layer covers everything specific to a session or application, in other words, everything relating to the data payload. In terms of the OSI model, it corresponds to layers 5 through 7. Owing to its coarse structure, it is not well suited to describe application-level information exchange.

As with the OSI model, data that is transmitted on the network enters the top of the stack, and each of the layers, with the exception of the physical layer, encapsulates information for its peer at the beginning and sometimes the end of the message that it receives from the next highest layer. On the remote host, each layer removes the information that is peer encapsulated before the remote layer passes the message to the next higher layer. Also, each layer processes messages in a modular fashion, without concern for how the other layers on the same host process the message.

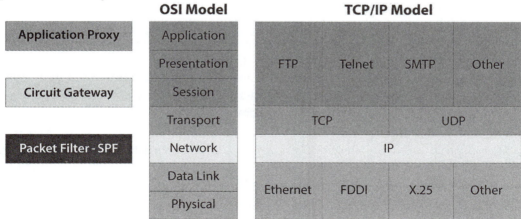

Figure 4.2 – **The TCP/IP Reference Model, with comparison to OSI stack**
(From Held, G., A Practical Guide to Content Delivery Networks, Auerbach Publications, Boca Raton, FL, 2006. With permission.)

IP Networking

Internet protocol (IP) is responsible for sending packets from the source to the destination hosts. Because it is an unreliable protocol, it does not guarantee that packets arrive error free or in the correct order. That task is left to protocols on higher layers. IP will subdivide packets into fragments when a packet is too large for a network.

Hosts are distinguished by the IP addresses of their network interfaces. The address is expressed as four octets separated by a dot (.), for example, 216.12.146.140. Each octet may have a value between 0 and 255. However, 0 and 255 are not used for hosts. The latter is used for broadcast addresses, and the former's meaning depends on the context in which it is used. Each address is subdivided into two parts: the network number and the host. The network number, assigned by an external organization, such as the Internet Corporation for Assigned Names and Numbers (ICANN), represents the organization's network. The host represents the network interface within the network.

Originally, the part of the address that represented the network number depended on the network's class. As shown in *Table 4.1*, a Class A network used the leftmost octet as the network number, Class B used the leftmost two octets, etc.

Class	Range of First Octet	Number of Octets for Network Number	Number of Hosts in Network
A	1 – 127	1	16,777,216
B	128 – 191	2	65,536
C	192 – 223	3	256
D	224 – 239	Multicast	
E	240 – 255	Reserved	

Table 4.1 – **Network Classes**

The part of the address that is not used as the network number is used to specify the host. For example, the address 216.12.146.140 represents a Class C network. Therefore, the network portion of the address is represented by the 216.12.146, and the unique host address within the network block is represented by 140.

127, which is the Class A network address block, is reserved for a computer's loopback address. Usually the address 127.0.0.1 is used. The loopback address is used to provide a mechanism for self-diagnosis and troubleshooting at the machine level. This mechanism allows a network administrator to treat a local machine as if it were a remote machine and ping the network interface to establish whether or not it is operational.

The explosion of Internet utilization in the 1990s caused a shortage of unallocated IPv4 addresses. To help remedy the problem, Classless Inter-Domain Routing (CIDR) was implemented. CIDR does not require that a new address be allocated based on the number of hosts in a network class. Instead, addresses are allocated in contiguous blocks from the pool of unused addresses.

To ease network administration, networks are typically subdivided into subnets. Because subnets cannot be distinguished with the addressing scheme discussed so far, a separate mechanism, the subnet mask, is used to define the part of the address that is used for the subnet. Bits in the subnet mask are 1 when the corresponding bits in the address are used for the subnet. The remaining bits in the mask are 0. For example, if the leftmost three octets (24 bits) are used to distinguish subnets, the subnet mask is 11111111 11111111 11111111 00000000. A string of 32 1s and 0s is very unwieldy, so the mask is usually converted to decimal notation: 255.255.255.0. Alternatively, the mask is expressed with a slash (/) followed by the number of 1s in the mask. The above mask would be written as /24.

IPv6

After the explosion of Internet usage in the mid-1990s, IP began to experience serious growing pains. It was obvious that the phenomenal usage of the Internet was stretching the protocol to its limit. The most obvious problems were a shortage of unallocated IP addresses and serious shortcomings in security. IPv6 is a modernization of IPv4 that includes:

1. A much larger address field: IPv6 addresses are 128 bits, which supports 2 hosts. Suffice it to say that we will not run out of addresses.

2. Improved security: As we will discuss below, IPSec must be implemented in IPv6. This will help ensure the integrity and confidentiality of IP packets and allow communicating partners to authenticate with each other.

3. A more concise IP packet header: Hosts will require less time to process each packet, which will result in increased throughput.

4. Improved quality of service: This will help services obtain an appropriate share of a network's bandwidth.

Transmission Control Protocol (TCP)

The Transmission Control Protocol provides connection-oriented data management and reliable data transfer. TCP and UDP map data connections through the association of port numbers with services provided by the host. TCP and UDP port numbers are managed by the Internet Assigned Numbers Authority (IANA). A total of 65,536 (2^{16}) ports exist. These are broken into three ranges:

- **Well-Known Ports** – Ports 0 through 1023 are considered to be well known. Ports in this range are assigned by IANA and, on most systems, can only be used by privileged processes and users.

- **Registered Ports** – Ports 1024 through 49151 can be registered with IANA by application developers but are not assigned by them. The reason for choosing a registered instead of a well- known port can be that on most systems, the user may not have the privileges to run an application on a well-known port.

- **Dynamic or Private Ports** – Ports 49152 through 65535 can be freely used by applications; one typical use for these ports is initiation of return connections for requested data or services.

Attacks against TCP include sequence number attacks, session hijacking, and SYN floods. More information about attacks can be found later in this chapter.

User Datagram Protocol (UDP)

The User Datagram Protocol provides a lightweight service for connectionless data transfer without error detection and correction. For UDP, the same considerations for port numbers as described for TCP in the section on Transmission Control Protocol apply. A number of protocols within the transport layer have been defined on top of UDP, thereby effectively splitting the transport layer into two. Protocols stacked between layers 4 and 5 include Real-time Protocol (RTP) and Real-time Control Protocol (RTCP) as defined in RFC 3550,

MBone, a multicasting protocol, Reliable UDP (RUDP), and Stream Control Transmission Protocol (SCTP) as defined in RFC 2960. As a connectionless protocol, UDP services are easy prey for spoofing attacks.

Internet–Intranet

The Internet, a global network of independently managed, interconnected networks, has changed life on earth. People from anywhere on the globe can share information almost instantaneously using a variety of standardized tools such as Web technologies or email.

An intranet, on the other hand, is a network of interconnected internal networks within an organization, which allows information to be shared within the organization and sometimes with trusted partners and suppliers. For instance, during a project, staff in a global company can easily access and exchange documents, thereby working together almost as if they were in the same office. As with the Internet, the ease with which information can be shared comes with the responsibility to protect it from harm. Intranets will typically host a wide range of organizational data. For this reason, access to these resources is usually coupled with existing internal authentication services even though they are technically on an internal network, such as a directory service coupled with multi-factor authentication.

Extranet

An extranet differs from a DMZ (demilitarized network zone) in the following way: An extranet is made available to authenticated connections that have been granted an access account to the resources in the extranet. Conversely, a DMZ will host publicly available resources that must support unauthenticated connections from just about any source, such as DNS servers and email servers. Due to the need for companies to share large quantities of information, often in an automated fashion, typically one company will grant the other controlled access to an isolated segment of its network to exchange information through the use of an extranet.

Granting an external organization access to a network comes with significant risk. Both companies have to be certain that the controls, both technical and nontechnical (e.g., operational and policy), effectively minimize the risk of unauthorized access to information. Where access must be granted to external organizations, additional controls such as deterministic routing can be applied upstream by service providers. This sort of safeguard is relatively simple to employ and has significant advantages because the ability for malicious entities to target an extranet for compromise leading to internal network penetration is abbreviated.

Companies that access extranets often treat the information within these networks and their servers as "trusted:" confidential and possessing integrity (uncorrupted and valid). However, these companies do not have control of each other's security profile. Who knows what kind of trouble a user can get into if he or she accesses supposedly trusted information through an extranet from an organization whose network has been compromised? To mitigate this potential risk, security architects and practitioners need to demand that certain security controls are in place before granting access to an extranet.

4

Dynamic Host Configuration Protocol (DHCP)

System and network administrators are busy people and hardly have the time to assign IP addresses to hosts and track which addresses are allocated. To relieve administrators from the burden of manually assigning addresses, many organizations use the Dynamic Host Configuration Protocol (DHCP) to automatically assign IP addresses to workstations (servers and network devices usually are assigned static addresses).

Dynamically assigning a host's IP configuration is fairly simple. When a workstation boots, it broadcasts a DHCPDISCOVER request on the local LAN, which could be forwarded by routers. DHCP servers will respond with a DHCPOFFER packet, which contains a proposed configuration, including an IP address. The DHCP client selects a configuration from the received DHCPOFFER packets and replies with a DHCPREQUEST. The DHCP server replies with a DHCPACK (DHCP acknowledgment), and the workstation adapts the configuration. Receiving a DHCP-assigned IP address is referred to as receiving a lease.

A client does not request a new lease every time it boots. Part of the negotiation of IP addresses includes establishing a time interval for which the lease is valid and timers that reflect when the client must attempt to renew the lease. This timer is referred to as a Time to Live counter, or just simply as the TTL. As long as the timers have not expired, the client is not required to ask for a new lease. Within the DHCP servers, administrators create address pools from which addresses are dynamically assigned when requested by a client. In addition, they can assign specific hosts to have static (i.e., permanent) addresses through the use of client reservations.

Because the DHCP server and client do not always authenticate with each other, neither host can be sure that the other is legitimate. For example, in a DHCP network, an attacker can plug his or her workstation into a network jack and receive an IP address, without having to obtain one by guessing or through social engineering. Also, a client cannot be certain that a DHCPOFFER packet is from a DHCP server instead of an intruder masquerading as a server.

To counteract these concerns, in June 2001 the IETF published RFC 3118, which specifies how to implement Authentication for DHCP Messages.[12] This standard describes an enhancement that replaces the normal DHCP messages with authenticated ones. Clients and servers check the authentication information and reject messages that come from invalid sources. The technology involves the use of a new DHCP option type, the Authentication option, and operating changes to several of the leasing processes to use this option. Although these vulnerabilities are not trivial, the ease of administration of IP addresses usually makes the risk from the vulnerabilities acceptable, except in very high security environments. Ultimately, the security architect will need to weigh the risks associated with using DHCP without an authentication option and decide how best to proceed.

Internet Control Message Protocol (ICMP)

The Internet Control Message Protocol (ICMP) is used for the exchange of control messages between hosts and gateways and is used for diagnostic tools such as ping and traceroute. ICMP can be leveraged for malicious behavior, including man-in-the-middle and denial-of-service attacks.

---

12   See the following: http://tools.ietf.org/html/rfc3118

Ping of Death [13]

Ping is a diagnostic program used to determine if a specified host is on the network and can be reached by the pinging host. It sends an ICMP echo packet to the target host and waits for the target to return an ICMP echo reply. Amazingly, an enormous number of operating systems would crash or become unstable upon receiving an ICMP echo greater than the legal packet limit of 65,536 bytes. Before the ping of death became famous, the source of the attack was difficult to find because many system administrators would ignore a seemingly harmless ping in their logs.

ICMP Redirect Attacks [14]

A router may send an ICMP redirect to a host to tell it to use a different, more effective default route. However, an attacker can send an ICMP redirect to a host telling it to use the attacker's machine as a default route. The attacker will forward all of the redirected traffic to a router so that the victim will not know that his or her traffic has been intercepted. This is a good example of a man-in-the-middle attack. Some operating systems will crash if they receive a storm of ICMP redirects. The security practitioner should have several tools in his or her toolbox to be able to model and interact with attacks such as the ICMP redirect attack in order to better understand them. One such tool that will be very effective is called Scapy.

Scapy is a powerful interactive packet manipulation program. It is able to forge or decode packets of a wide number of protocols, send them on the wire, capture them, match requests and replies, and much more. It can easily handle most classical tasks like scanning, tracerouting, probing, unit tests, attacks, or network discovery (it can replace hping, 85% of nmap, arpspoof, arp-sk, arping, tcpdump, tethereal, p0f, etc.). It also performs very well at a lot of other specific tasks that most other tools cannot handle, like sending invalid frames, injecting your own 802.11 frames, combining technics (VLAN hopping+ARP cache poisoning, VOIP decoding on WEP encrypted channel, etc.)

You can find Scapy here: http://www.secdev.org/projects/scapy/

Ping Scanning

Ping scanning is a basic network mapping technique that helps narrow the scope of an attack. An attacker can use one of many tools such as Very Simple Network Scanner for Windows based platforms and NMAP for Linux and Windows based platforms to ping all of the addresses in a range. [15] If a host replies to a ping, then the attacker knows that a host exists at that address.

Traceroute Exploitation

Traceroute is a diagnostic tool that displays the path a packet traverses between a source and destination host. Traceroute can be used maliciously to map a victim network and learn about its routing. In addition, there are tools, such as Firewalk, that use techniques similar to

---

13   See the following: http://insecure.org/sploits/ping-o-death.html

14   See the following: http://www.sans.org/reading-room/whitepapers/threats/icmp-attacks-illustrated-477

15   See the following to download:
      Very Simple Network Scanner for Windows: http://www.softpedia.com/progDownload/Very-Simple-Network-Scanner-Download-112841.html
      NMAP for Linux / Windows: http://nmap.org/download.html

those of traceroute to enumerate a firewall rule set.[16] The firewalk tool stopped being actively developed and maintained as of version 5.0 in 2003. The functionality of the firewalk tool has been subsumed into NMAP as part of the rule set that can be configured for use.[17]

What the firewalk host rule tries to do is to discover firewall rules using an IP TTL expiration technique known as firewalking. To determine a rule on a given gateway, the scanner sends a probe to a metric located behind the gateway, with a TTL one higher than the gateway. If the probe is forwarded by the gateway, then we can expect to receive an ICMP_TIME_ EXCEEDED reply from the gateway next hop router, or eventually the metric itself if it is directly connected to the gateway. Otherwise, the probe will time out.

It starts with a TTL equal to the distance to the target. If the probe times out, then it is resent with a TTL decreased by one. If we get an ICMP_TIME_EXCEEDED, then the scan is over for this probe. Every "no-reply" filtered TCP and UDP ports are probed. As for UDP scans, this process can be quite slow if lots of ports are blocked by a gateway close to the scanner. The scan parameters can be controlled using the firewalk.* optional arguments.

Remote Procedure Calls

Remote procedure calls (RPCs) represent the ability to allow for the executing of objects across hosts, with a client sending a set of instructions to an application residing on a different host on the network. Generically, several (mutually incompatible) services in this category exist, such as distributed computing environment RPC (DCE RPC) and Sun's Open Network Computing RPC (ONC RPC, also referred to as SunRPC or simply RPC). It is important to note that RPC does not in fact provide any services on its own; instead, it provides a brokering service by providing (basic) authentication and a way to address the actual service. Common Object Request Broker Architecture (CORBA) and Microsoft Distributed Component Object Model (DCOM) can be viewed as RPC-type protocols. Security problems with RPC include its weak authentication mechanism, which can be leveraged for privilege escalation by an attacker.

Directory Services

Domain Name Service (DNS)

Domain Name System is one of the most prominent and the most visible of all network services. The reason for this is DNS's role in creating the system that supports the use and resolution of email and World Wide Web (WWW) addresses, which have become a ubiquitous element of our everyday life. By virtue of this fact, DNS has become a prominent target of attack, aggravating weaknesses inherent in the protocol. By manipulating DNS, it is certainly possible to divert, intercept, or prevent the vast majority of end-user communications without having to resort to attacking any end-user devices, or endpoints.

---

16   See the following for the last available build (version 5.0) of firewalk: http://packetfactory.openwall.net/ projects/firewalk/

17   See the following to download the firewalk host rule script for NMAP: http://nmap.org/nsedoc/scripts/ firewalk.html

As shown in *Figure 4.3*, the Domain Name System as a whole is a distributed, hierarchical database. Through its caching architecture, it possesses a remarkable degree of robustness, flexibility, and scalability. This resiliency is due to the fact that the use of a multi-tiered resolver hierarchy for redundancy and security allows for one or more DNS resolvers to go offline while still maintaining the integrity of the system as a whole.

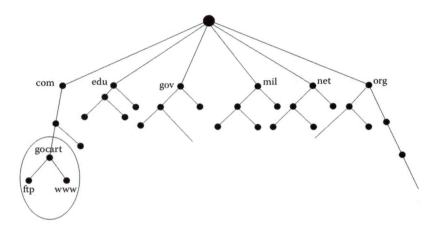

Figure 4.3 – The DNS database structure (From Held, G., ABCs of IP Addressing, Auerbach Publications, Boca Raton, FL, 2002. With permission.)

DNS's central element is a set of hierarchical name (domain) trees, starting from a so-called top-level domain (TLD). A number of so-called root servers manage the authoritative list of TLD servers. To resolve any domain name, each Domain Name Server in the world must hold a list of these root servers.

Ports	53/TCP, 53/UDP
Definition	RFC 882
	RC 1034
	RFC 1035

Table 4.2 – **DNS Quick Reference**

Various extensions to DNS have been proposed, to enhance its functionality and security, for instance, by introducing authentication through the use of DNSSEC, multicasting, or service discovery.[18]

Lightweight Directory Access Protocol (LDAP) [19]

LDAP is a client/server-based directory query protocol loosely based upon X.500, commonly used for managing user information. As opposed to DNS, for instance, LDAP is a front end and not used to manage or synchronize data per se.

Back ends to LDAP can be directory services, such as NIS (see Network Information Service (NIS), NIS +), Microsoft's Active Directory Service, Sun's iPlanet Directory Server (renamed to Sun Java System Directory Server), and Novell's eDirectory.

LDAP provides only weak authentication based on host name resolution. It would therefore be easy to subvert LDAP security by breaking DNS (see section on Domain Name Service).

Ports	389/TCP, 389/UDP
Definition	RFC 1777

Table 4.3 – **LDAP Quick Reference**

---

18   The following list of RFCs provides the details for all of the updated functionality that has been proposed for DNS:
RFC 1101: DNS Encoding of Network Names and Other Types
RFC 1183: New DNS RR Definitions
RFC 1706: DNS NSAP Resource Records
RFC 1982: Serial Number Arithmetic
RFC 2181: Clarifications to the DNS Specification
RFC 2308: Negative Caching of DNS Queries (DNS NCACHE)
RFC 4033: DNS Security Introduction and Requirements
RFC 4034: Resource Records for the DNS Security Extensions
RFC 4035: Protocol Modifications for the DNS Security Extensions
RFC 4470: Minimally Covering NSEC Records and DNSSEC On-line Signing
RFC 4592: The Role of Wildcards in the Domain Name System
RFC 5155: DNS Security (DNSSEC) Hashed Authenticated Denial of Existence
RFC 5452: Measures for Making DNS More Resilient against Forged Answers
RFC 6014: Cryptographic Algorithm Identifier Allocation for DNSSEC
RFC 6604: xNAME RCODE and Status Bits Clarification
RFC 6672: DNAME Redirection in the DNS
RFC 6840: Clarifications and Implementation Notes for DNS Security (DNSSEC)
RFC 6944: Applicability Statement: DNS Security (DNSSEC) DNSKEY Algorithm Implementation Status

19   See the following RFCs for LDAPv3 information:
The technical specification detailing version 3 of the Lightweight Directory Access Protocol (LDAP), an Internet Protocol, consists of this document and the following documents:
LDAP: Lightweight Directory Access Protocol (LDAP): Technical Specification Road Map[RFC4510]
LDAP: The Protocol [RFC4511] LDAP: Directory Information Models [RFC4512]
LDAP: Authentication Methods and Security Mechanisms [RFC4513]
LDAP: String Representation of Distinguished Names [RFC4514]
LDAP: String Representation of Search Filters [RFC4515]
LDAP: Uniform Resource Locator [RFC4516]
LDAP: Syntaxes and Matching Rules [RFC4517]
LDAP: Internationalized String Preparation [RFC4518] LDAP: Schema for User Applications [RFC4519]

LDAP communication is transferred in cleartext and therefore is easily intercepted. One way for the security architect to address the issues of weak authentication and cleartext communication would be through the deployment of LDAP over SSL, providing authentication, integrity, and confidentiality.

Network Basic Input Output System (NetBIOS)

The NetBIOS application programming interface (API) was developed in 1983 by IBM. NetBIOS was later ported to TCP/IP (NetBIOS over TCP/IP, also known as NetBT). Under TCP/IP, NetBIOS runs over TCP on ports 137 and 138 and over UDP on port 139. In addition, it uses port 135 for remote procedure calls (see Remote Procedure Calls).

Ports	135/UDP
	137/TCP
	138/TCP
	139/UDP
Definition	RFC 1001
	RFC 1002

Table 4.4 - **NetBIOS Quick Reference**

Network Information Service (NIS), NIS +

NIS and NIS + are directory services developed by Sun Microsystems, which are mostly used in UNIX environments. They are commonly used for managing user credentials across a group of machines, for instance, a UNIX workstation cluster or client/server environment, but they can be used for other types of directories as well.

NIS

NIS uses a flat namespace in so-called domains. It is based on RPC and manages all entities on a server (NIS server). NIS servers can be set up redundantly through the use of slave servers. NIS is known for a number of security weaknesses. The fact that NIS does not authenticate individual RPC requests can be used to spoof responses to NIS requests from a client. This would, for instance, enable an attacker to inject fake credentials and thereby obtain or escalate privileges on the target machine. Retrieval of directory information is possible if the name of a NIS domain has become known or is guessable, as any of the clients can associate themselves with a NIS domain. A number of guides have been published on how to secure NIS servers. The basic steps that the security architect and practitioner would need to take are the following: Secure the platform a NIS server is running on, isolate the NIS server from traffic outside of a LAN, and configure it so the probability for disclosure of authentication credentials, especially system privileged ones, is limited.

NIS +

NIS + uses a hierarchical namespace. It is based on Secure RPC (see Remote Procedure Calls). Authentication and authorization concepts in NIS + are more mature; they require authentication for each access of a directory object. However, NIS + authentication in itself will only be as strong as authentication to one of the clients in a NIS + environment, as NIS + is built on a trust relationship between different hosts. The most relevant attacks against a correctly configured NIS + network come from attacks against its cryptographic security. NIS + can be run at different security levels; however, most levels available are irrelevant for an operational network.[20]

Common Internet File System (CIFS)/Server Message Block (SMB)

CIFS/SMB is a file-sharing protocol prevalent on Windows systems. A UNIX/Linux implementation exists in the free Samba project. SMB was originally designed to run on top of the NetBIOS protocol (see Network Based Input Output System); it can, however, be run directly over TCP/IP.

Ports	445/TCP
	See also NetBIOS (Network Basic Input Output System)
Definition	Proprietary

Table 4.5 - **CIFS/SMB Quick Reference**

CIFS is capable of supporting user-level and tree/object-level (share-level) security. Authentication can be performed via challenge/response authentication as well as by transmission of credentials in cleartext. This second provision has been added largely for backward compatibility in legacy Windows environments.

The main attacks against CIFS are based upon obtaining credentials, be it by sniffing for cleartext authentication or by cryptographic attacks.

Network File System (NFS)

Network File System is a client/server file-sharing system common to the UNIX platform. It was originally developed by Sun Microsystems, but implementations exist on all common UNIX platforms, including Linux, as well as Microsoft Windows. NFS has been revised several times, including updates to NFS Versions 2 and 3. NFS version 2 was based on UDP, and version 3 introduced TCP support. Both are implemented on top of RPC (see Remote Procedure Calls). NFS versions 2 and 3 are stateless protocols, mainly due to performance considerations. As a consequence, the server must manage file locking separately.

---

20 Because the services provided by NIS+ are security-critical, NIS+ is designed to operate securely. An aspect of this design is the concept of "security levels", which determine the amount of scrutiny given to incoming RPC NIS requests. There are three security levels, numbered 0 through 2. In level 0, the NIS+ server (rpc.nisd) performs no authentication to determine the legitimacy of incoming requests. This option is provided for debugging purposes. In level 1, RPC AUTH_UNIX (client-presented UIDs and GIDs) are used to authenticate requests. In level 2, the most secure level, AUTH_DES is used to cryptographically authenticate incoming requests. Unfortunately, even when the system is operating in security level 2, which should mandate cryptographic authentication for all requests, the rpc.nisd daemon provides several RPC calls that are not authenticated. These calls allow a remote client to obtain sensitive system status information from the NIS+ server. The information available to a remote attacker includes NIS+ configuration information (including the security level of the server and a list of directory objects served by it), as well as the ability to determine valid process IDs on the NIS+ server. Additionally, one of the RPC calls available to remote clients can allow an attacker to disable logging on the NIS+ server, as well as to manipulate the NIS+ caches. This may allow attackers to degrade or deny service on NIS+ servers. The ability to use NIS+ to remotely ascertain valid process IDs is serious because it allows an attacker the ability to predict certain random numbers generated by Unix applications. Frequently, Unix applications generate random numbers using the process ID and the current time, either directly or as a seed to a random number generator.

Ports	See RPC (Section "Directory services")
Definition	RFC 1094
	RFC 1813
	RFC 3010

Table 4.6- **NFS Quick Reference**

Secure NFS (SNFS) offers secure authentication and encryption using Data Encryption Standard (DES) encryption. In contrast to standard NFS, secure NFS (or rather secure RPC) will authenticate each RPC request. This will increase latency for each request as the authentication is performed and introduces a light performance premium, mainly paid for in terms of computing capacity. Secure NFS uses DES encrypted time stamps as authentication tokens. If server and client do not have access to the same time server, this can lead to short-term interruptions until server and client have resynchronized themselves.

NFS version 4 is a stateful protocol that uses TCP port 2049. UDP support (and dependency) has been discontinued. NFS version 4 implements its own encryption protocols on the basis of Kerberos and has discontinued use of RPC. Foregoing RPC also means that additional ports are no longer dynamically assigned, which enables use of NFS through firewalls. Another approach that the security architect could consider as part of his or her design is to plan for the securing of NFS where it must be deployed, by tunneling NFS through Secure Shell (SSH), which can be integrated with operating system authentication schemes.

Simple Mail Transfer Protocol (SMTP) & Enhanced Simple Mail Transfer Protocol (ESMTP)

Using port 25/TCP, SMTP is a client/server protocol utilized to route email on the Internet. Information on mail servers for Internet domains is managed through DNS, using mail exchange (MX) records.ww Although SMTP takes a simple approach to authentication, it is robust in the way it deals with unavailability; an SMTP server will try to deliver email over a configurable period.

From a protocol perspective, SMTP's main shortcomings are the complete lack of authentication and encryption. Identification is performed by the sender's email address. A mail server will be able to restrict sending access to certain hosts, which should be on the same network as the mail server, as well as set conditions on the sender's email address, which should be one of the domains served by this particular mail server. Otherwise, the mail server may be configured as an open relay, although this is not a recommended practice traditionally because it poses a variety of security concerns and may get the server placed on ban lists of anti-spam organizations.

To address the weaknesses identified in SMTP, an enhanced version of the protocol, ESMTP, was defined. ESMTP is modular in that client and server can negotiate the enhancements used. ESMTP does offer authentication, among other things, and allows for different authentication mechanisms, including basic and several secure authentication mechanisms.

A quick summary comparison of SMTP and ESMTP can be seen in the following table:

SMTP	ESMTP
Stands for Simple Mail Transfer Protocol	Stands for Extended Simple Mail Transfer Protocol
First command in SMTP session:	First command in ESMTP session:
HELO sayge.com	EHLO sayge.com
RFC 821	RFC 1869
SMTP 'MAIL FROM' and 'RCPT TO' allows size only of 512 characters including <CRLF>.	ESMTP 'MAIL FROM' and 'RCPT TO' allows size greater than 512 characters.
SMTP alone cannot be extended with new commands.	ESMTP is a framework that has enhanced capabilities, allowing it to extend existing SMTP commands.

File Transfer Protocol (FTP)

Before the advent of the World Wide Web and proliferation of Hypertext Transfer Protocol (HTTP), which is built on some of its features, FTP was *the* protocol for publishing or disseminating data over the Internet.

Ports	20/TCP (data stream)
	21/TCP (control stream)
Definition	RFC 959

Table 4.7 - **FTP Quick Reference**

FTP is a stateful protocol that requires two communication channels. One control channel is on port 21 under TCP, over which state information is exchanged, and a data channel is on port 20, through which payload information is transmitted. In its original form, FTP uses simple username/password authentication, and credentials as well as all data are transmitted in cleartext (visible to anyone able to intercept or "sniff" the traffic). This makes the protocol subject to a wide range of attacks against confidentiality, integrity, and availability.

Although this authentication weakness can be addressed through the use of encryption, this approach carries with it the need for additional requirements to be imposed on the client. These requirements and methods are briefly outlined below:

1. **Secure FTP with TLS** is an extension to the FTP standard that allows clients to request that the FTP session be encrypted. This is done by sending the "AUTH TLS" command. The server has the option of allowing or denying connections that do not request TLS. This protocol extension is defined in the proposed standard RFC 4217.

2. **SFTP, the "SSH File Transfer Protocol"**, is not related to FTP except that it also transfers files and has a similar command set for users. SFTP, or secure FTP, is a program that uses Secure Shell (SSH) to transfer files. Unlike standard FTP, it encrypts both commands and data. It is functionally similar to FTP, but because it uses a different protocol, standard FTP clients cannot be used to talk to an SFTP server.

Communications & Network Security

3. ***FTP over SSH*** refers to the practice of tunneling a normal FTP session over an SSH connection. Because FTP uses multiple TCP connections, it is particularly difficult to tunnel over SSH. With many SSH clients, attempting to set up a tunnel for the control channel (the initial client-to-server connection on port 21) will protect only that channel; when data is transferred, the FTP software at either end will set up new TCP connections (data channels), which bypass the SSH connection and thus have no confidentiality or integrity protection.

FTP offers two principal modes of data transfer: ASCII and binary. In ASCII mode, a conversion of layer 6 representation, depending on the target platform, is performed, whereas this conversion is omitted in binary mode.

Transfer Modes

Although the control channel is always opened by the client, there are two different modes for the data channel:

■ ***Active mode (PORT mode)*** – Where the server initiates the data connection to the client. This mode has obvious drawbacks in firewalled environments, as incoming connections to the client can (and should) be blocked. A number of firewall products still support active mode.

■ ***Passive mode (PASV mode)*** – Where the client initiates the data connection to the server. Even though RFC 959 does not mandate implementation of passive FTP, the majority of FTP servers offer this type of connection.

Anonymous FTP

Before the advent and proliferation of HTTP, publication of information to an unspecific user group was fulfilled by FTP services offering guest authentication to anyone who so desired. These services were called anonymous FTP due to the fact that the guest user would be mapped to the FTP log-in ID "anonymous," whereas the user would pseudo-authenticate (and thereby identify) himself with his email address. In practice, the user could have been using any password or email address, whereas using one's true email address would still have been considered common courtesy.

Although Web browsers still support the (social) protocol as such, the use of anonymous FTP has widely fallen by the wayside. There are three main reasons.

1. With HTTP, anonymous publication of information can be handled in a much more efficient and seamless manner.
2. Disclosure of email addresses on the part of the user (or a requirement to do so) is widely regarded as an unsafe and privacy-violating practice that will expose the user to address harvesting by spammers.
3. Guest access can expose the FTP server to security risks.

Trivial File Transfer Protocol (TFTP)

TFTP is a simplified version of FTP, which is used when authentication is not needed and quality of service is not an issue. TFTP runs on port 69 over UDP. It should therefore only be used in trusted networks with low latency.

Ports	69/UDP
Definition	RFC 1350

Table 4.8 - **TFTP Quick Reference**

In practice, TFTP is used mostly in LANs for the purpose of pulling packages, for instance, in booting up a diskless client or when using imaging services to deploy client environments.

Hypertext Transfer Protocol (HTTP)

HTTP is the layer 7 foundation of the World Wide Web (WWW). HTTP, originally conceived as a stateless, stripped-down version of FTP, was developed at the European Organization for Nuclear Research (CERN) to support the exchange of information in Hypertext Markup Language (HTML).

Ports	80/TCP; other ports are in use, especially for proxy services
Definition	RFC 1945
	RFC 2109
	RFC 2616

Table 4.9 - **HTTP Quick Reference**

HTTP's popularity caused the deployment of an unprecedented number of Internet facing servers; many were deployed with out-of-the-box, vendor-preset configurations. Often these settings were geared at convenience rather than security. As a result, numerous previously closed applications were suddenly marketed as "Web enabled." By implication, not much time was spent on developing the Web interface in a secure manner, and authentication was simplified to become a browser-based style.

HTTP will work from within most networks, shielded or not, and thereby lends itself to tunneling an impressive number of other protocols, even though HTTP neither supports quality of service nor bidirectional communication natively— although workarounds were quickly developed to deal with Quality of Service (QoS) concerns and bidirectional communication needs.

HTTP does not natively support encryption and has a fairly simple authentication mechanism based on domains, which in turn are normally mapped to directories on a Web server. Although HTTP authentication is extensible, it is most often used in the classic username/password style.

HTTP Proxying

Anonymizing Proxies

Because HTTP is transmitting data in cleartext and generates a slew of logging information on Web servers and proxy servers, the resulting information can be readily used for illegitimate activities, such as industrial espionage. To address this significant concern, the security practitioner can use any of the commercial and free services available that allow for the anonymization of HTTP requests. These services are mainly geared at the privacy market but have also attracted a criminal element seeking to obfuscate activity. A relatively popular free service is Java Anonymous Proxy, or JAP, also referred to as project AN.ON, or Anonymity.Online. JAP is referred to as JonDo within the commercially available solution JonDonym anonymous proxy server.[21]

---

21   See the following: http://jap.inf.tu-dresden.de/index_en.html

Open Proxy Servers

Like open mail relays, open proxy servers allow unrestricted access to GET commands from the Internet. They can therefore be used as stepping stones for launching attacks or simply to obscure the origin of illegitimate requests. More importantly, an open proxy server bears an inherent risk of opening access to protected intranet pages from the Internet. (A misconfigured firewall allowing inbound HTTP requests would need to be present on top of the open proxy to allow this to happen.)

As a general rule, HTTP proxy servers should not allow queries from the Internet. For the security architect, it is a best practice to separate application gateways (sometimes implemented as reverse proxies) from the proxy for Web browsing because both have very different security levels and business importance. (It would be even better to implement the application gateway as an application proxy and not an HTTP proxy, but this is not always possible.)

Content Filtering

In many organizations, the HTTP proxy is used as a means to implement content filtering, for instance, by logging or blocking traffic that has been defined as or is assumed to be nonbusiness related for some reason. Although filtering on a proxy server or firewall as part of a layered defense can be quite effective to prevent virus infections (though it should never be the only protection against viruses), it will be only moderately effective in preventing access to unauthorized services (such as certain remote-access services or file sharing), as well as preventing the download of unwanted content.

HTTP Tunneling

HTTP tunneling is technically a misuse of the protocol on the part of the designer of such tunneling applications. It has become a popular feature with the rise of the first streaming video and audio applications and has been implemented into many applications that have a market need to bypass user policy restrictions. Usually, HTTP tunneling is applied by encapsulating outgoing traffic from an application in an HTTP request and incoming traffic in a response. This is usually not done to circumvent security but rather to be compatible with existing firewall rules and allow an application to function through a firewall without the need to apply special rules or additional configurations. Many of the most prevalent and successful malicious software packages including viruses, worms, and especially botnets will use HTTP as the means to transmit stolen data or control information from infected hosts through firewalls.

Suitable countermeasures that the security practitioner should consider include filtering on a firewall or proxy server and assessing clients for installations of unauthorized software. However, a security professional will have to balance the business value and effectiveness of these countermeasures with the incentive for circumvention that a restriction of popular protocols will create.

Implications of Multi-Layer Protocols

Multi-layer protocols have ushered in an era of new vulnerabilities that were once unthinkable. In the past, several "networked" solutions were developed to provide control and communications with industrial devices. These often proprietary protocols evolved over time and eventually merged with other networking technologies such as Ethernet and Token Ring. Several vendors now use the TCP/IP stack to channel and route their own protocols. These protocols are used to control coils, actuators, and machinery in multiple industries such as energy, manufacturing, construction, fabrication, mining, and farming to name a few. Insecurities in these systems often have real world visibility and impact. Given the fact that the life expectancy of many of the devices under control is 20 years or longer, it is easy to see how systems can become outdated. Often, critical infrastructure such as power grids are controlled using multi-layer protocols. The following table from the Idaho National Laboratory illustrates some of the differences and related challenges of control systems vs. standard information technology.[22]

SECURITY TOPIC	INFORMATION TECHNOLOGY	CONTROL SYSTEMS
Anti-virus/Mobile Code	– Common – Widely used	– Uncommon/ impossible to deploy effectively
Support Technology Lifetime	– 2-3 Years – Diversified vendors	– Up to 20 years – Single vendor
Outsourcing	– Common – Widely Used	– Operations are often outsourced, but not diverse to various providers
Application of Patches	– Regular – Scheduled	– Rare, Unscheduled – Vendor specific
Change Management	– Regular – Scheduled	– Highly managed and complex
Time Critical Content	– Generally delays accepted	– Delays are unacceptable
Availability	– Generally delays accepted	– 24x7x365 (continuous)
Security Awareness	– Moderate in both private and public sector	– Poor except for physical
Security Testing/Audit	– Part of a good security program	– Occasional testing for outages
Physical Security	– Secure (server rooms, etc.)	– Remote/Unmanned – Secure

---

22   http://www.inl.gov/technicalpublications/Documents/3375141.pdf (Page 8)

SCADA

The term most often associated with multi-layer protocols is Supervisory Control and Data Acquisition or SCADA. Another term used in relation with multi-layer protocols is "Industrial Control System" or ICS. In general, SCADA systems are designed to operate with several different communication methods including modems, WANS, and various networking equipment. The following figure shows a general layout of a SCADA system:[23]

As the figure demonstrates, a great complexity of devices and information exist in SCADA systems. Most SCADA systems minimally contain the following:

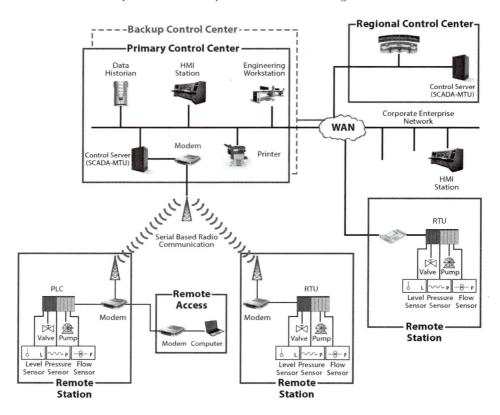

Figure 4.4 – **Diagram of a Generic SCADA ICS**

- **Control Server** – A control server hosts the software and often the interfaces used to control actuators, coils, and PLCs through subordinate control modules across the network.
- **Remote Terminal Unit (RTU)** – The RTU supports SCADA remote stations often equipped with wireless radio interfaces and is used in situations where land based communications may not be possible.
- **Human-Machine Interface (HMI)** – The HMI is the interface where the humans (operators) can monitor, control, and command the controllers in the system.
- **Programmable Logic Controller (PLC)** – The PLC is a small computer that controls relays, switches, coils, counters, and other devices.

---

23   http://csrc.nist.gov/publications/nistir/ir7442/NIST-IR-7442_2007CSDAnnualReport.pdf

■ ***Intelligent Electronic Devices (IED)*** – The IED is a sensor that can acquire data and also provide feedback to the process through actuation. These devices allow for automatic control at the local level.

■ ***Input/Output (IO) Server*** – The IO server is responsible for collecting process information from components such as IEDs, RTUs, and PLCs. They are often used to interface third-party control components such as custom dashboards with a control server.

■ ***Data Historian*** – The data historian is like the Security Event and Incident Management (SEIM) for industrial control systems. It is typically a centralized database for logging process information from a variety of devices.

Given the unique design of SCADA systems, and the critical infrastructures that they control, it is little wonder they are a new focus of attacks. Security architects and practitioners responsible for implementing or protecting SCADA systems should be aware of the following types of attacks:

■ Network Perimeter Vulnerabilities
■ Protocol Vulnerabilities throughout the Stack
■ Database Insecurities
■ Session Hijacking and Man-in-the-middle Attacks
■ Operating System and Server Weaknesses
■ Device and Vendor "Backdoors"

In late October of 2013, U.S. based researchers identified 25 zero-day vulnerabilities in industrial control SCADA software from 20 suppliers that are used to control critical infrastructure systems. Attackers could exploit some of these vulnerabilities to gain control of electrical power and water systems. The vulnerabilities were found in devices that are used for serial and network communications between servers and substations. Serial communication has not been considered as an important or viable attack vector up until now, but breaching a power system through serial communication devices can be easier than attacking through the IP network because it does not require bypassing layers of firewalls. In theory, an intruder could exploit the vulnerabilities simply by breaching the wireless radio network over which the communication passes to the server.

Another issue that the security professional needs to contend with is the inability of anti-virus software to address the threats facing SCADA/ICS environments. The Flame virus, for example, avoided detection from 43 different anti-virus tools and took more than two years to detect. What the security practitioner needs to do, instead of continuing to rely on the traditional enterprise tools that may work well for desktops and servers, is to have tools in place that allow them to identify threats, respond, and expedite forensic analysis in real time within these complicated systems. For the security practitioner to achieve this, continuous monitoring of all log data generated by IT systems is required to automatically baseline normal, day-to-day activity across systems and identify any and all anomalous activity immediately.

It was announced in March of 2014 that more than 7,600 different power, chemical, and petrochemical plants may still be vulnerable to a handful of SCADA vulnerabilities. A researcher at Rapid 7, the Boston-based firm responsible for the popular pen testing software Metasploit, and an independent security researcher discovered three bugs in Yokogawa Electric's CENTUM CS3000 R3 product. The Windows-based software is primarily used by infrastructure in power plants, airports, and chemical plants across Europe and Asia. The vulnerabilities are essentially a series of buffer overflows, heap based and stack based, that could open the software up to attack. All of them affect computers where CENTUM CS 3000, software that helps operate and monitor industrial control systems, is installed. With the first one, an attacker could send a specially crafted sequence of packets to BKCLogSvr.exe and trigger a heap-based buffer overflow, which in turn could cause a DoS and allow the execution of arbitrary code with system privileges. The second would involve a similar situation; a special packet could be sent to BKHOdeq.exe and cause a stack-based buffer overflow, allowing execution of arbitrary code with the privileges of the CENTUM user. Lastly, another stack-based buffer overflow, this involving the BKBCopyD. exe service, could allow the execution of arbitrary code as well.[24]

In April of 2014, attackers were able to compromise a utility in the United States through an Internet-connected system that gave the attackers access to the utility's internal control system network. The utility had remote access enabled on some of its Internet-connected hosts, and the systems were only protected by simple passwords. Officials at the ICS-CERT, an incident response and forensics organization inside the Department of Homeland Security that specializes in ICS and SCADA systems, said that the public utility was compromised "when a sophisticated threat actor gained unauthorized access to its control system network." The attacker apparently used a simple brute force attack to gain access to the Internet-facing systems at the utility and then compromised the ICS network. "After notification of the incident, ICS-CERT validated that the software used to administer the control system assets was accessible via Internet facing hosts. The systems were configured with a remote access capability, utilizing a simple password mechanism; however, the authentication method was susceptible to compromise via standard brute forcing techniques," ICS-CERT said in a published report.[25]

The security of industrial control systems and SCADA systems has become a serious concern in recent years as attackers and researchers have begun to focus their attention on them. Many of these systems, which control mechanical devices, manufacturing equipment, utilities, nuclear plants, and other critical infrastructure, are connected to the Internet, either directly or through networks, and this has drawn the attention of attackers looking to do reconnaissance or cause trouble on these networks. Researchers have been sharply critical of the security in the SCADA and ICS industries, saying it's "laughable" and has no formal security development lifecycle. The ICS-CERT report states that the systems in the compromised utility probably were the target of a number of attacks. "It was determined that the systems were likely exposed to numerous security threats and previous intrusion activity was also identified." The investigators were able to identify the issues and found that the attackers likely had not done any damage to the ICS system at the utility.

In the same report, ICS-CERT detailed a separate compromise at an organization that also had a control system connected to the Internet. Attackers were able to compromise the ICS system, which operates an unspecified mechanical device, but did not do any real damage. "The device was directly Internet accessible and was not protected by a firewall or authentication access controls. At the time of compromise, the control system was mechanically disconnected from the device for scheduled maintenance," the report says. "ICS-CERT provided analytic assistance and determined that the actor had access to the system over an extended period of

---

24 See the following for the full text of the Yokogawa Security Advisory Report: http://www.yokogawa.com/dcs/security/ysar/YSAR-14-0001E.pdf

25 http://ics-cert.us-cert.gov/sites/default/files/Monitors/ICS-CERT_Monitor_%20Jan-April2014.pdf

time and had connected via both HTTP and the SCADA protocol. However, further analysis determined that no attempts were made by the threat actor to manipulate the system or inject unauthorized control actions."

The security architect and practitioner should familiarize themselves with the latest alerts released by the ICS-CERT. These can be found here:

https://ics-cert.us-cert.gov/alerts/

Security professionals should also consider the following list as a starting point for defensive actions that can be used to help secure SCADA/ICS systems:

- Minimize network exposure for all control system devices. In general, locate control system networks and devices behind firewalls and isolate them from the business network.
- When remote access is required, employ secure methods, such as Virtual Private Networks (VPNs), recognizing that VPNs may have vulnerabilities and should be updated to the most current version available. Also recognize that VPN is only as secure as the connected devices.
- Remove, disable, or rename any default system accounts wherever possible.
- Implement account lockout policies to reduce the risk from brute forcing attempts.
- Establish and implement policies requiring the use of strong passwords.
- Monitor the creation of administrator level accounts by third-party vendors.
- Apply patches in the ICS environment, when possible, to mitigate known vulnerabilities.

Modbus

Modbus and Fieldbus are standard industrial communication protocols designed by separate groups. The focus of the design around these protocols is not security; rather it is uptime and control of devices. Many of these protocols send information in cleartext across transmission media. Additionally, many of these protocols and the devices they support require little or no authentication to execute commands on a device. The security architect and practitioner need to work together to ensure that strict logical and physical controls are implemented to ensure these protocols are encapsulated and isolated from any public or open network.

Converged Protocols

What is IP Convergence?

Security architects and practitioners have long desired a single network that would allow them to transfer both voice and data securely. The ability to provide timely access to information is now a key asset for the enterprise. Enterprise networks that are based on Internet Protocol network technology are in the forefront of answering businesses' requirement for a useful and cost-effective network that can serve as the backbone for all enterprise communication needs. Along with meeting the challenges posed by the physical integration of the network, one should also ensure that the aggregated flow of traffic meets the quality and functionality requirements for the network as well.

The core aspects that dictate the implementation and deployment of an IP convergent network include integrating discrete network elements, staying up to date with IP and its associated protocols, and having systems in place to manage voice, data, and video traffic for multimedia applications.

The benefits of IP convergence that the security architect and practitioner can bring to the enterprise through the design, deployment, and management of a converged network infrastructure are as follows:

1. Excellent support for multimedia applications. Improved connectivity means that devices can be assigned specific tasks; the number of devices required is less, which makes installation, deployment, management, and usage easier.

2. A converged IP network is a single platform on which interoperable devices can be run in innovative ways. Since IP is an open standard, it is vendor independent and this helps in fostering interoperability and improving network efficiency in terms of time and cost. The sphere of IP convergence encompasses networks, devices, and different technologies and systems that can be operated as a unified infrastructure.

3. A converged IP network is easier to manage because of the uniform setup in which the system resources operate. Training users to use the network resources is also easy.

4. An enterprise can achieve flexibility in terms of molding its communication patterns to its management practices. This is a dynamic process that can be continually improved with collaboration from network partners. What this results in is the right information to the right person at the right time, leading to improved decision making.

5. IP networks have proven to be remarkably scalable, and this has been one of the prime reasons that even large enterprises have gone ahead with implementing IP. Applications that run on IP networks are available all over the world; in fact, most new business applications include built-in IP support.

6. An IP convergent network is capable of making use of the developments in class of service differentiation and QoS-based routing. This leads to better utilization of resources and also allows for capacity redundancy to take care of an increase in the number of users.

7. A uniform environment requires fewer components in the network. Smoother maintenance and management result from this and in turn lead to improved processes. Affordable deployment results from the elimination of multiple networks operating in parallel, and manageability improves. In a converged environment, fewer platforms need to be tested, and gateways between networks are eliminated.

8. Business applications have different tolerance levels for transit delays, dropped packets, and error rates. IP architecture is capable of handling these so that the QoS reflects the requirements of the different applications.

9. Device integration has the potential to simplify end-to-end security management and at the same time make it more robust.

10. A converged IP network offers a business tremendous cost savings in terms of hardware and space utilization. It opens up more markets that can be reached, more products that can be introduced, increases employee productivity and mobility, and enables even smaller companies to compete with larger ones because of faster information relay.

Implementation

The first and most apparent result of integrating discrete network elements is that with a reduction in the number of nodes in a network, the operating and maintenance costs go down. Connectivity and wiring costs - whether to the user's work station or to the provider's facility - are reduced. A converged IP network means that there are always opportunities available for efficient bandwidth utilization. Routing Public Switched Telephone Network (PSTN) traffic over an IP network is one sure way of improving network capacity utilization. For a long time, the ability to reliably route and send facsimiles over an IP network has presented many challenges, but recent advances have made it possible to transfer faxes as IP packets, and they present another excellent avenue for maximizing IP network capacity.

The TCP/IP protocol stack is already being used by enterprises for communication. The advent of VoIP has played a big role in pushing companies to evolve toward implementing IP networks. Converging communications technology through IP protocol means that you can link subsystems and networks that include shared Ethernet LANs, dedicated WAN links, and ATM networks. IP convergence also implies that various legacy technologies can be used together, resulting in a consistent and uniform experience at the user interface, where a single device is used to access applications like telephony and video. Thus, IP convergence also leads to application or device convergence.

Using separate, single-purpose networks for data, management, and storage can be more complex and costly than required for IT organizations or infrastructure deployments. Network convergence is a more economical solution: It simplifies data center infrastructure by consolidating block-based storage and traditional IP-based data communications networks onto a single converged Ethernet network.

Traditional data center designs include separate, heterogeneous network devices for different types of data. Many data centers support three or more types of networks that serve these purposes:

- Block storage data management
- Remote management
- Business-centric data communications

Each network and device adds to the complexity, cost, and management overhead. Converged networks can simplify typical topologies by reducing the number of physical components. This convergence leads to simplified management and improvements in quality of service (QoS).

There have been many attempts to create converged networks over the past decade. Fibre Channel Protocol (FCP) is a lightweight mapping of SCSI to the Fibre Channel (FC) layers 1 and 2 transport protocol. Fibre Channel carries not only FCP traffic but also IP traffic, to create a converged network. The cost of FC and the acceptance of Ethernet as the standard for LAN communications prevented widespread FC use except for data center SANs for enterprise businesses.

- ***InfiniBand (IB)*** technology provides a converged network capability by transporting inter-processor communication, LAN, and storage protocols. The two most common storage protocols for IB are SCSI Remote Direct Memory Access Protocol (SRP) and iSCSI Extensions for RDMA (iSER). These protocols use the RDMA capabilities of IB. SRP builds a direct SCSI to RDMA mapping layer and protocol, and iSER copies data directly to the SCSI I/O buffers without intermediate data copies. These protocols are lightweight but not as streamlined as FC. Widespread deployment was impractical because of the perceived high cost of IB and the complex gateway and routers needed to translate from these IB-centric protocols and networks to native FC storage devices. High Performance Computing environments that have adopted IB as the standard transport network use SRP and iSER protocols.

- **Internet SCSI (iSCSI)** was an attempt to bring a direct SCSI to TCP/IP mapping layer and protocol to the mass Ethernet market. Proponents of iSCSI wanted to drive down cost and to deploy SANs over existing Ethernet LAN infrastructure. iSCSI technology was very appealing to the small and medium business market because of the low-cost software initiators and the ability to use any existing Ethernet LAN.
- **FC over IP (FCIP)** and **Internet FC Protocol (iFCP)** map FCP and FC characteristics to LANs, MANs, and WANs. Both of these protocols map FC framing on top of the TCP/IP protocol stack. FCIP is a SAN extension protocol to bridge FC SANs across large geographical areas. It is not for host-server or target-storage attachment. The iFCP protocol lets Ethernet-based hosts attach to FC SANs through iFCP-to-FC SAN gateways. These gateways and protocols were not widely adopted except for SAN extension because of their complexity, lack of scalability, and cost.

Now that 10 GbE is becoming more widespread, FCoE is the next attempt to converge block storage protocols onto Ethernet. FCoE takes advantage of 10 GbE performance and compatibility with existing Fibre Channel protocols. It relies on an Ethernet infrastructure that uses the IEEE Data Center Bridging (DCB) standards. The DCB standards can apply to any IEEE 802 network, but most often the term DCB refers to enhanced Ethernet. The DCB standards define four new technologies:

- **Priority-based Flow Control (PFC)** – 802.1Qbb allows the network to pause different traffic classes.
- **Enhanced Transmission Selection (ETS)** – 802.1Qaz defines the scheduling behavior of multiple traffic classes, including strict priority and minimum guaranteed bandwidth capabilities. This should enable fair sharing of the link, better performance, and metering.
- **Quantized Congestion Notification (QCN)** – 802.1Qau supports end-to-end flow control in a switched LAN infrastructure and helps eliminate sustained, heavy congestion in an Ethernet fabric. Before the network can use QCN, you must implement QCN in all components in the Converged Enhanced Ethernet (CEE) data path (Converged Network Adapters (CNAs), switches, and so on). QCN networks must also use PFC to avoid dropping packets and ensure a lossless environment.
- **Data Center Bridging Exchange Protocol (DCBX)** – 802.1Qaz supports discovery and configuration of network devices that support PFC, ETS, and QCN.

Fibre Channel over Ethernet (FCoE)

In legacy Ethernet networks, dropped frames occur under collision or congestion situations. The networks rely on upper layer protocols such as TCP to provide end-to-end data recovery. FCoE is a lightweight encapsulation protocol and lacks the reliable data transport of the TCP layer. Therefore, FCoE must operate on DCB-enabled Ethernet and use lossless traffic classes to prevent Ethernet frame loss under congested network conditions.

FCoE on a DCB network mimics the lightweight nature of native FC protocols and media. It does not incorporate TCP or even IP protocols. This means that FCoE is a layer 2 (non-routable) protocol just like FC. FCoE is only for short-haul communication within a data center. The main advantage of FCoE is that switch vendors can easily implement logic for converting FCoE on a DCB network (FCoE/DCB) to native FC in high-performance switch silicon. FCoE encapsulates FC frames inside of Ethernet frames. FCoE has several advantages:

- Uses existing OS device drivers. (Because the same vendors make devices used on CNAs and native FC HBAs, they use a common FC/FCoE driver architecture.)
- Uses the existing Fibre Channel security and management model.
- Makes storage targets that are provisioned and managed on a native FC SAN transparently accessible through an FCoE Fibre Channel Forwarder (FCF).

However, there are also some challenges with FCoE:

- Must be deployed using a DCB-enabled Ethernet network.
- Requires CNAs and new DCB-enabled Ethernet switches between the servers and FCFs (to accommodate DCB).
- Is a non-routable protocol and used only within the data center.
- Requires an FCF device to connect the DCB network to the legacy FC SANs and storage.
- Requires validating a new fabric infrastructure that converges LAN communications and FC traffic over DCB-enabled Ethernet. Validating the network ensures that you have applied proper traffic class parameters to meet your IT organizations' business objectives and service level agreements.

In one-hop architecture, converged traffic goes from a server to a switch that splits it to Ethernet and Fibre Channel. In two-hop architecture, converged traffic goes to a second switch before the split. The more switch hops there are in a DCB-enabled network, the more difficult it is to keep the network operating at peak efficiency while minimizing congestion.

Multihop FCoE technology can be used to extend convergence beyond the access layer to a fully converged network. This design creates a single, highly available, highly scalable network that has the flexibility and agility to support any traffic type. Using multihop FCoE, the physical infrastructure is shared, but SAN A and B separation is maintained with the use of dedicated FCoE links between the access and aggregation layers of the network. These dedicated links run Fabric Shortest Path First (FSPF), with no dependency on Ethernet forwarding protocols such as Spanning Tree Protocol, virtual PortChannel (vPC), or Transparent Interconnection of Lots of Links (TRILL). As an option, FCoE in the Cisco Nexus 7000 Series can be run in a separate storage VDC, providing isolation from non-storage processes running on the switch. This approach maintains the operation model and isolation requirements of Fibre Channel even within a converged network design.

The goal of FCoE is to consolidate input/output (I/O) and reduce switch complexity as well as to cut back on cable and interface card counts. Adoption of FCoE been slow, however, due to a scarcity of end-to-end FCoE devices and reluctance on the part of many organizations to change the way they implement and manage their networks.

Traditionally, organizations have used Ethernet for TCP/IP networks and Fibre Channel for storage networks. Fibre Channel supports high-speed data connections between computing devices that interconnect servers with shared storage devices and between storage controllers and drives. FCoE shares Fibre Channel and Ethernet traffic on the same physical cable or lets organizations separate Fibre Channel and Ethernet traffic on the same hardware.

FCoE uses a lossless Ethernet fabric and its own frame format. It retains Fibre Channel's device communications but substitutes high-speed Ethernet links for Fibre Channel links between devices. FCoE works with standard Ethernet cards, cables, and switches to handle Fibre Channel traffic at the data link layer, using Ethernet frames to encapsulate, route, and transport FC frames across an Ethernet network from one switch with Fibre Channel ports and attached devices to another, similarly equipped switch.

FCoE is often compared to iSCSI, an Internet Protocol (IP)-based storage networking standard.

Internet Small Computer System Interface (iSCSI)

iSCSI is Internet SCSI (Small Computer System Interface), an Internet Protocol (IP)-based storage networking standard for linking data storage facilities, developed by the Internet Engineering Task Force (IETF) as RFC 3270.[26] By carrying SCSI commands over IP networks, iSCSI is used to facilitate data transfers over intranets and to manage storage over long distances. Because of the ubiquity of IP networks, iSCSI can be used to transmit data over local area networks (LANs), wide area networks (WANs), or the Internet and can enable location-independent data storage and retrieval.

In essence, iSCSI allows two hosts to negotiate and then exchange SCSI commands using Internet Protocol (IP) networks. By doing this, iSCSI takes a high-performance local storage bus and emulates it over a wide range of networks, creating a storage area network (SAN). Unlike some SAN protocols, iSCSI requires no dedicated cabling; it can be run over existing IP infrastructure. As a result, iSCSI is often seen as a low-cost alternative to Fibre Channel, which requires dedicated infrastructure except in its FCoE (Fibre Channel over Ethernet) form. However, the performance of an iSCSI SAN deployment can be severely degraded if not operated on a dedicated network or subnet (LAN or VLAN), due to competition for a fixed amount of bandwidth.

Although iSCSI can communicate with arbitrary types of SCSI devices, system administrators typically deploy it to allow server computers (such as database servers) to access disk volumes on storage arrays. iSCSI SANs often have one of two objectives:

- ■ ***Storage Consolidation*** – Organizations move disparate storage resources from servers around their network to central locations, often in data centers; this allows for more efficiency in the allocation of storage because the storage

---

26 See the following: http://www.ietf.org/rfc/rfc3720.txt
    Below is a list of the additional RFCs relating to iSCSI:
    RFC 3721 - Internet Small Computer Systems Interface (iSCSI) Naming and Discovery
    RFC 3722 - String Profile for Internet Small Computer Systems Interface (iSCSI) Names
    RFC 3723 - Securing Block Storage Protocols over IP (Scope: The use of IPsec and IKE to secure iSCSI, iFCP, FCIP, iSNS and SLPv2.)
    RFC 3347 - Small Computer Systems Interface protocol over the Internet (iSCSI) Requirements and Design Considerations
    RFC 3783 - Small Computer Systems Interface (SCSI) Command Ordering Considerations with iSCSI
    RFC 3980 - T11 Network Address Authority (NAA) Naming Format for iSCSI Node Names
    RFC 4018 - Finding Internet Small Computer Systems Interface (iSCSI) Targets and Name Servers by Using Service Location Protocol version 2 (SLPv2)
    RFC 4173 - Bootstrapping Clients using the Internet Small Computer System Interface (iSCSI) Protocol
    RFC 4544 - Definitions of Managed Objects for Internet Small Computer System Interface (iSCSI)
    RFC 4850 - Declarative Public Extension Key for Internet Small Computer Systems Interface (iSCSI) Node Architecture
    RFC 4939 - Definitions of Managed Objects for iSNS (Internet Storage Name Service)
    RFC 5048 - Internet Small Computer System Interface (iSCSI) Corrections and Clarifications
    RFC 5047 - DA: Datamover Architecture for the Internet Small Computer System Interface (iSCSI)
    RFC 5046 - Internet Small Computer System Interface (iSCSI) Extensions for Remote Direct Memory Access (RDMA)

itself is no longer tied to a particular server. In a SAN environment, a server can be allocated a new disk volume without any changes to hardware or cabling.

- **Disaster Recovery** – Organizations mirror storage resources from one data center to a remote data center, which can serve as a hot standby in the event of a prolonged outage. In particular, iSCSI SANs allow entire disk arrays to be migrated across a WAN with minimal configuration changes, in effect making storage "routable" in the same manner as network traffic.

How iSCSI Works:

When an end-user or application sends a request, the operating system generates the appropriate SCSI commands and data request, which then go through encapsulation and, if necessary, encryption procedures. A packet header is added before the resulting IP packets are transmitted over an Ethernet connection. When a packet is received, it is decrypted (if it was encrypted before transmission) and disassembled, separating the SCSI commands and request. The SCSI commands are sent on to the SCSI controller and from there to the SCSI storage device. Because iSCSI is bidirectional, the protocol can also be used to return data in response to the original request.

Multi-Protocol Label Switching (MPLS)

Multi-Protocol Label Switching (MPLS) is best summarized as a layer 2.5 networking protocol. In the traditional OSI model, layer 2 covers protocols like Ethernet and SONET, which can carry IP packets but only over simple LANs or point-to-point WANs. Layer 3 covers Internet-wide addressing and routing using IP protocols. MPLS sits between these traditional layers, providing additional features for the transport of data across the network.

In a traditional IP network, each router performs an IP lookup ("routing"), determines a next-hop based on its routing table, and forwards the packet to that next-hop. Every router does the same, each making its own independent routing decisions, until the final destination is reached. MPLS does "label switching" instead. The first device does a routing lookup, just like before, but instead of finding a next-hop, it finds the final destination router. And it finds a pre-determined path from "here" to that final router. The router applies a "label" (or "shim") based on this information. Future routers use the label to route the traffic without needing to perform any additional IP lookups. At the final destination router, the label is removed, and the packet is delivered via normal IP routing.

So What Is the Advantage of Label Switching?

Originally, it was intended to reduce IP routing lookups. When Classless Inter-Domain Routing (CIDR) was introduced, it had unintended consequences. CIDR introduced the concept of "longest prefix matching" for IP routing. Longest prefix match lookups have historically been very difficult to do. The classic software algorithm for routing lookups was called a PATRICIA trie, which required many memory accesses just to route a single packet. Exact matches were comparatively much easier to implement in hardware. Most early hardware routing "cheated" by doing the first lookup in software, then did hardware-based exact matching for future packets in the "flow". Label switching (or "tag switching") lookups use exact matching. The idea was to have only the first router do an IP lookup, then all future routes in the network could do exact match "switching" based on a label. This would reduce load on the core routers, where high-performance was the most difficult to achieve, and distribute the routing lookups across lower speed edge routers.

Modern Application Specific Integrated Circuits (ASICs) have eliminated this issue... mostly. Today, commodity ASICs can do many tens of millions of IP routing lookups per second, relatively cheaply and easily. However, they still make up a significant portion of the cost of a router. Exact matching is still much cheaper and easier to implement. A layer 2 only Ethernet switch that does exact matching may be a quarter of the cost and 4x the capacity of a similar device with layer 3 capabilities.

So Why Do Security Professionals Still Care about MPLS?

Three reasons:

1. **Implementing Traffic-Engineering** – The ability to control where and how traffic is routed on your network, to manage capacity, prioritize different services, and prevent congestion.

2. **Implementing Multi-Service Networks** – The ability to deliver data transport services, as well as IP routing services, across the same packet-switched network infrastructure.

3. Improving network resiliency with **MPLS Fast Reroute**.

How Does MPLS Work?

MPLS Label Switched Path (LSP) is one of the most important concepts for the actual use of MPLS. It is essentially a unidirectional tunnel between a pair of routers, routed across an MPLS network. An LSP is required for any MPLS forwarding to occur. MPLS Router Roles/ Positions are:

- **Label Edge Router (LER) or "Ingress Node"** – The router that first encapsulates a packet inside an MPLS LSP. Also the router that makes the initial path selection.

- **Label Switching Router (LSR) or "Transit Node"** – A router that only does MPLS switching in the middle of an LSP.

- **Egress Node** – The final router at the end of an LSP, which removes the label.

MPLS router roles may also be expressed as "P" or "PE." These are terms that come from the description of VPN services.

- **P – Provider Router** – A core/backbone router that is doing label switching only. A pure P router can operate without any customer/Internet routes at all. This is common in large service provider networks.

- **PE – Provider Edge Router** – A customer facing router that does label popping and imposition. Typically, it has various edge features for terminating multiple services:
  - Internet
  - L3VPN
  - L2VPN/Pseudowires
  - VPLS

- **CE – Customer Edge** – The customer device a PE router talks to.

For someone to use an LSP, it must be signaled across your routers. An LSP is a network-wide tunnel, but a label is only a link-local value. An MPLS signaling protocol maps LSPs to specific label values. There are two main MPLS routing protocols in use today:

1. **Label Distribution Protocol (LDP)** – A simple non-constrained (does not support traffic engineering) protocol.

2. ***Resource Reservation Protocol with Traffic Engineering (RSVP-TE)*** – A more complex protocol, with more overhead, but which also includes support for traffic-engineering via network resource reservations.

Most complex networks will actually need to use both protocols. LDP is typically used by MPLS VPN (data transport) services. But RSVP-TE is necessary for traffic engineering features. Most networks will configure LDP to tunnel inside RSVP.

MPLS labels can also be stacked multiple times. The top label is used to control the delivery of the packet. When the destination is reached, the top label is removed (or "popped"), and the second label takes over to direct the packet further. Some common stacking applications are:

- VPN/Transport services, which use an inner label to map traffic to specific interfaces, and an outer label to route through the network.
- "Bypass" LSPs, which can protect a bundle of other LSPs to redirect traffic quickly without having to completely re-signal every LSP, in the event of a router failure.

There are two ways to terminate an LSP:

1. ***Implicit Null*** – Also called "Penultimate Hop Popping" (PHP). This is just a long way of saying "remove the label on the next-to-last hop."
2. ***Explicit Null*** – Preserve the label all the way to the very last router.

What's the difference? Implicit null is an optimization technique. Since the label is already removed on the next-to-last router, the last router can more easily begin to route the packet after it exits the LSP. Otherwise, the packet has to make two trips through the last router: one pass through the forwarding path to pop the label, and another pass to route the packet based on the underlying information.

MPLS Pseudowires

Layer 2 Pseudowire or VLL (Virtual Leased Line) is an emulated layer-2 point-to-point circuit, delivered over MPLS. They can be used to interconnect two different types of media such as Ethernet to Frame Relay. They are also useful for migrating legacy transport (e.g., ATM) to an MPLS network. However, they can be difficult to load balance, due to lack of visibility into the packet. The payload is unknown, so you cannot hash on the IP header inside for instance. Historically, there have been two competing methods for signaling:

- ***LDP-signaled*** – The simpler of the two methods, and more commonly implemented.
- ***BGP-signaled/L2VPN*** – More complex but with auto-discovery support for multi-point.

MPLS L3VPNs

An L3VPN is an IP based VPN. Networks build virtual routing domains (VRFs) on their edge routers. Customers are placed within a VRF and exchange routes with the provider router in a protected routing-instance, usually BGP or IGP. They can support complex topologies and interconnect many sites. They are usually load-balancing hash friendly because they have exposed IP headers. But they can add a significant load to the service provider infrastructure because the PE device must absorb the customer's routing table, consuming

Routing Information Base (RIB) and Forwarding Information Base (FIB) capacity.[27] MPLS L3VPNs are typically seen in enterprise environments as opposed to smaller networks. They are signaled via BGP within the provider network.

MPLS VPLS

VPLS (Virtual Private LAN Service) creates an Ethernet multipoint switching service over MPLS. It is used to link a large number of customer endpoints in a common broadcast domain. MPLS VPLS avoids the need to provision a full mesh of layer 2 circuits. It emulates the basic functions of a layer 2 switch:

- Unknown unicast flooding
- Mac learning
- Broadcasts

Typically, it is considered load-balancing friendly because the L2 Ethernet headers are examined and used, unlike L2 pseudowires where they are passed transparently.

MPLS Fast Reroute

MPLS Fast Reroute improves convergence during a failure by pre-calculating backup paths for potential link or node failures. In a normal IP network, the best path calculation happens on-demand when a failure is detected. It can take several seconds to recalculate best paths and push those changes to the router hardware, particularly on a busy router.

A transient routing loop may also occur, as every router in the networks learns about the topology change. With MPLS Fast Reroute, the next best path calculation happens before the failure actually occurs. The backup paths are pre-programmed into the router FIB awaiting activation, which can happen in milliseconds following failure detection. Because the entire path is set within the LSP, routing loops cannot occur during convergence, even if the path is briefly suboptimal.

---

27 A forwarding information base (FIB), also known as a forwarding table, is most commonly used in network bridging, routing, and similar functions to find the proper interface to which the input interface should send a packet to be transmitted by the router.

In contrast to routing information bases (RIB), also known as routing tables, FIBs are optimized for fast lookup of destination addresses. Earlier implementations cached only a subset of the routes most frequently used in actual forwarding, and this worked reasonably well for enterprises where there is a meaningful most-frequently-used subset. Routers used for accessing the entire Internet, however, experienced severe performance degradation in refreshing a small cache, and various implementations moved to having FIBs in one-to-one correspondence with the RIB.

RIBs are optimized for efficient updating by routing protocols and other control plane methods, and they contain the full set of routes learned by the router.

FIBs may also be implemented with fast hardware lookup mechanisms, such as ternary content addressable memory (TCAM). TCAM, however, is quite expensive, and it tends to be used more in edge routers with relatively small numbers of routes than in routers that must carry full Internet routing tables, with supplementary internal routes.

The RIB consists of at least three information fields:
1. The network id: i.e., the destination network id
2. Cost: i.e., the cost or metric of the path through which the packet is to be sent
3. Next hop: The next hop, or gateway, is the address of the next station to which the packet is to be sent on the way to its final destination

Voice over Internet Protocol (VoIP)

Voice over Internet Protocol (VoIP) is a technology that allows you to make voice calls using a broadband Internet connection instead of a regular (or analog) phone line. Some VoIP services may only allow you to call other people using the same service, but others may allow you to call anyone who has a telephone number - including local, long distance, mobile, and international numbers. Also, while some VoIP services only work over your computer or a special VoIP phone, other services allow you to use a traditional phone connected to a VoIP adapter. In other words, VoIP is simply the transmission of voice traffic over IP-based networks. VoIP is also the foundation for more advanced unified communications applications such as Web and video conferencing. The Internet Protocol (IP) was originally designed for data networking. The success of IP in becoming a world standard for data networking has led to its adaptation to voice networking.

There are many kinds of VoIP systems that are in use today. Using voice chat in Lync, Google Talk, Yahoo messenger, Face Time, or Skype could be regarded as VoIP; but these are all proprietary systems. To talk to someone using Face Time, the person at the other end also needs to have Face Time installed. The same applies to Yahoo and to Skype. They use their own special system that is not open and will not connect to other systems easily.

True VoIP systems are based on the use of the Session Initiation Protocol (SIP), which is the recognized standard. Any SIP compatible device can talk to any other. Any SIP based IP-phone can call another right over the Internet; you do not need any additional equipment or even a phone provider. Just plug your SIP phone into an Internet connection, configure it, and then dial the other person right over the Internet.

In all VoIP systems, your voice is converted into packets of data and then transmitted to the recipient over the Internet and decoded back into your voice at the other end. To make it quicker, these packets are compressed before transmission with certain codecs, almost like zipping a file on the fly. There are many codecs with different ways of achieving compression and managing bitrates; thus each codec has its own bandwidth requirements and provides different voice quality for VoIP calls.

VoIP systems employ session control and signaling protocols to control the signaling, set-up, and tear-down of calls. They transport audio streams over IP networks using special media delivery protocols that encode voice, audio, video with audio codecs, and video codecs as digital audio by streaming media. Various codecs exist that optimize the media stream based on application requirements and network bandwidth; some implementations rely on narrowband and compressed speech, while others support high fidelity stereo codecs. Some popular codecs include μ-law and a-law versions of G.711, G.722, which is a high-fidelity codec marketed as HD Voice by Polycom, a popular open source voice codec known as iLBC, a codec that only uses 8 kbit/s each way called G.729, and many others.

What is VoIP?: Some Useful Terms

Understanding these terms is a first step for the security professional toward learning the potential of this technology:

- **VoIP** refers to a way to carry phone calls over an IP data network, whether on the Internet or your own internal network. A primary attraction of VoIP is its ability to help reduce expenses because telephone calls travel over the data network rather than the phone company's network.

- **IP telephony** encompasses the full suite of VoIP enabled services including the interconnection of phones for communications, related services such as billing and dialing plans, and basic features such as conferencing, transfer, forward, and hold. These services might previously have been provided by a PBX.
- **IP communications** includes business applications that enhance communications to enable features such as unified messaging, integrated contact centers, and rich-media conferencing with voice, data, and video.
- **Unified communications** takes IP communications a step further by using such technologies as Session Initiation Protocol (SIP) and presence along with mobility solutions to unify and simply all forms of communications, independent of location, time, or device.

Voice over IP has been implemented in various ways using both proprietary protocols and protocols based on open standards. Examples of the VoIP protocols are:

- H.323
- Media Gateway Control Protocol (MGCP)
- Session Initiation Protocol (SIP)
- H.248 (also known as Media Gateway Control (Megaco))
- Real-time Transport Protocol (RTP)
- Real-time Transport Control Protocol (RTCP)
- Secure Real-time Transport Protocol (SRTP)
- Session Description Protocol (SDP)
- Inter-Asterisk eXchange (IAX)
- Jingle XMPP VoIP extensions
- Skype protocol
- Teamspeak

The H.323 protocol was one of the first VoIP protocols that found widespread implementation for long-distance traffic, as well as local area network services. However, since the development of newer, less complex protocols such as MGCP and SIP, H.323 deployments are increasingly limited to carrying existing long-haul network traffic. In particular, the Session Initiation Protocol (SIP) has gained widespread VoIP market penetration.

Session Initiation Protocol (SIP) [28]

As its name implies, SIP is designed to manage multimedia connections. It is not a comprehensive protocol suite and leaves much of the actual payload data transfer to other protocols, for instance, Real-Time Transport Protocol (RTP). SIP is designed to support digest authentication structured by realms, similar to HTTP (basic username/password authentication has been removed from the protocol as of RFC 3261).[29] In addition, SIP provides integrity protection through MD5 hash functions. SIP supports a variety of encryption mechanisms, such as TLS.

---

28   See the following: http://www.ietf.org/rfc/rfc2543.txt

29   See the following: http://www.ietf.org/rfc/rfc3361.txt

Privacy extensions to SIP, including encryption and caller ID suppression, have been defined in extensions to the original Session Initiation Protocol (RFC 3325).[30] On a related note, a SIP client may also act as a server that can receive requests from another machine. The security practitioner should consider this as a general risk for the machine the software is deployed to because as with any server software, there is a risk of security gaps such as buffer overflows that can be exploited over the network.

Ports	5060/TCP, 5060/UDP
Definition	RFC 2543
	RFC 3261
	RFC 3325

Table 4.10 - **SIP Quick Reference**

Packet Loss

Packet loss occurs in every kind of network. All network protocols are designed to cope with the loss of packets in one way or another. The TCP protocol, for example, guarantees packet delivery by sending redelivery requests for the lost packets. Real-Time Transport Protocol (RTP) employed by the VoIP protocol does not provide delivery guarantee, and VoIP must implement the handling of lost packets. While a data transfer protocol can simply request redelivery of a lost packet, VoIP has no time to wait for the packet to arrive. In order to maintain call quality, lost packets are substituted with interpolated data.

A technique called Packet Loss Concealment (PLC) is used in VoIP communications to mask the effect of dropped packets. There are several techniques that may be used by different implementations. Zero substitution is the simplest PLC technique that requires the least computational resources. These simple algorithms generally provide the lowest quality sound when a significant number of packets are discarded. Waveform substitution is used in older protocols, and it works by substituting the lost frames with artificially generated, substitute sound. The simplest form of substitution simply repeats the last received packet. Unfortunately, waveform substitution often results in unnatural, "robotic" sound when a long burst of packets is lost.

The more advanced algorithms interpolate the gaps, producing the best sound quality at the cost of using extra computational resources. The best implementation can tolerate up to 20% of packets lost without significant degradation of voice quality. While some PLC techniques work better than others, no masking technique can compensate for a significant loss of packets. When bursts of packets are lost due to network congestion, noticeable degradation of call quality occurs. In VoIP, packets can be discarded for a number of reasons, including network congestion, line errors, and late arrival. The network architect and security practitioner need to work together in order to select the right Packet Loss Concealment technique that best matches the characteristics of a particular environment, as well as to ensure that they implement measures to reduce packet loss on the network.

---

30   See the following: http://www.ietf.org/rfc/rfc3325.txt

Jitter

Jitter is a specific VoIP Quality of Service issue that may affect the quality of the conversation if it goes out of control. Unlike network delay, jitter does not occur because of the packet delay, but because of a variation of packet delays. As VoIP endpoints try to compensate for jitter by increasing the size of the packet buffer, jitter causes delays in the conversation. If the variation becomes too high and exceeds 150ms, callers notice the delay and often revert to a walkie-talkie style of conversation.

There are several steps to be taken to reduce jitter both on the network level and in the VoIP end points such as VoIP software, IP phones, or dedicated VoIP ATA's (adaptors) or FXS/FXO gateways. By definition, reducing the delays on the network helps keep the buffer under 150ms even if a significant variation is present. While the reduced delay does not necessarily remove the variation, it still effectively reduces the degree to which the effect is pronounced and brings it to the point where it's unnoticeable by the callers. Prioritizing VoIP traffic and implementing bandwidth shaping also helps reduce the variation of packet delay. At the endpoint, it is essential to optimize jitter buffering. While greater buffers reduce and remove the jitter, anything over 150ms noticeably affects the perceived quality of the conversation. Adaptive algorithms to control buffer size depending on the current network conditions are often quite effective. Fiddling with packet size (payload) or using a different codec often helps control jitter as well.

While jitter is caused by network delays more often than by the endpoints themselves, certain systems such as VoIP soft phones may introduce significant and unpredictable variations in packet delays. While someone is deploying VoIP endpoints or examining call quality problems within existing VoIP infrastructure, it is very important to isolate the cause of jitter.

Sequence Errors

Data packets travel independently of one another and are subject to various delays depending on the exact route they take. Out-of-sequence packets are not considered a problem for data transfers because data transfer protocols can re-order packets and reconstruct data without corruption. Due to the time sensitive nature of voice communications, VoIP systems are required to handle out-of-sequence packets in quite a different manner.

Some VoIP systems discard packets received out of order, while other systems discard out-of-order packets if they exceed the size of the internal buffer, which in turn causes jitter. Sequence errors can also cause significant degradation of call quality. Sequence errors may occur because of the way packets are routed. Packets may travel along different paths through different IP networks, causing different delivery times. As a result, lower numbered packets may arrive at the endpoint later than higher numbered ones. The packets are usually received in the buffer, allowing the endpoint to rearrange out-of-order frames and reconstruct the original signal. However, the size of internal buffer is limited to control jitter, and significant variance in the orderly delivery of packets may cause the endpoints to discard frames, resulting in both jitter and dropped packet issues. Routing VoIP calls through consistent routes to avoid spreading packets from the same call over different paths allows for significant reduction in sequencing errors.

Codec Quality

A codec is software that converts audio signals into digital frames and vice versa. Codecs are characterized by different sampling rates and resolutions. Different codecs employ different compression methods and algorithms, using different bandwidth and computational requirements. Choosing the best codec for particular network conditions may considerably increase the quality of voice calls. If the network has low effective bandwidth, choosing the lossless G.711 codec would be a big mistake because the quality of the calls would suffer due to bandwidth limitations and lost packets rather than codec quality. If there is less than 80 Kbit/s of available bandwidth, picking a low-bitrate, high-compression G.729 or G.723 codec is much more appropriate. Note that while a local area network (LAN) may provide high bandwidth, external calls may be subject to a bandwidth bottleneck upstream.

ADSL and cable network providers often limit upstream bandwidth, which results in upstream congestion if multiple VoIP calls are carried concurrently. In this case, low-bandwidth codecs may provide better results. G.711 (PCM), a high-bandwidth codec, provides the best audio quality yet consumes the most bandwidth (about 80 Kbit/s with overhead). G.729a (CS-ACELP), G.723.1 (MP-MLQ), and G.726 (ADPCM) offer varying conversation quality, sorted by decreasing relative quality. The codec choice will not take place automatically. You have to specify and prioritize codecs available to the particular VoIP system. The network architect and the security professional both need to understand that choosing the right codec may significantly improve conversation quality.

Although the possibility of transmitting voice over Internet connections has existed for a long time, the widespread acceptance of broadband home access has created a market for Voice-over-IP solutions. In essence, Internet and telephony are switching roles—while previously the telephone network was a ubiquitous commodity that would carry Internet dial-up traffic, the Internet is taking over the role of the principal commodity.

Increasingly, VoIP is replacing internal corporate telephony networks. While the benefits, such as negligible connection cost at a comparable initial investment and a larger degree of configurability, are obvious, VoIP networks are impacted by security risks in ways that would have left traditional telephony systems unaffected, such as being assailable by viruses and hacking and being dependent on electric power at all communication endpoints. In addition, VoIP systems are significantly more complex and need higher expertise to operate. For public services, questions of interconnectivity and interoperability come into focus. From a legal perspective, the situation is still unclear as to whether VoIP networks should be regulated in the same way as the public switched telephone network (PSTN).

One common requirement that the security architect needs to be aware of is the availability of gateways to public emergency services such as 911 when employing VoIP services. Due to the ability of VoIP devices to technically function from any IP address, they can be highly mobile, following their users anywhere they go. This presents a serious challenge for emergency response services because IP addresses do not come with geo-spatial coordinates (longitude/latitude or even street address); therefore, a central VoIP support desk has to be maintained to inform emergency responders of the location of a given VoIP phone–based customer's records and billing information. For large, corporate deployments of VoIP services, a means of tracking VoIP devices and mapping these devices to physical location is a key part of overall service management and often a regulatory requirement related to workplace health and safety.

Another common requirement is access for lawful interception, which, while legitimate from a public policy perspective, raises concerns from a security perspective because of the potential design of backdoors into existing systems, which could then be exploited by third parties. However, the more pressing issue with lawful interception has to do with the provision of intercept services for legitimate purposes. VoIP traffic is still IP traffic and mixes with all the other IP traffic on a network. To intercept VoIP calls requires powerful and sophisticated network analysis tools that can extract VoIP packets from a potential torrent of data flowing at gigabit speeds, re-assemble these packets, and extract the media stream within them, all in real time. The security architect, practitioner, and professional all will need to be aware of this issue, and contribute their expertise to an overall offering that can be designed, deployed, and managed successfully within the enterprise.

Deployment of VoIP services may raise security concerns for its carrier network, for instance, with regard to enabling interconnectivity with other VoIP applications in a secure manner. Last but not least, the security architect and practitioner need to ensure that a form of backup communication channel is available with any VoIP installation, to have independent communication channels available in case of a disaster or network outage.

Wireless

A wireless network is any type of computer network that uses wireless data connections for connecting network nodes. A wireless local-area network (LAN) uses radio waves to connect devices such as laptops to the Internet and to your business network and its applications. When you connect a laptop to a WiFi hotspot at a cafe, hotel, airport lounge, or other public place, you are connecting to that business's wireless network.

The enterprise can experience many benefits from a wireless network being deployed, including:

- **Convenience** – Users are able to access network resources from any location within the wireless network's coverage area or from any Wi-Fi hotspot.
- **Mobility** – Users are no longer tied to their desks, as they were with a wired connection. They can go online from anywhere within the coverage area of the network.
- **Productivity** – Wireless access to the Internet and to the enterprise's key applications and resources helps users to get their jobs done quickly and encourages collaboration.
- **Easy Setup** – The network team does not have to string cables, so installation can be quick and cost-effective.
- **Expandable** – It is easy to expand wireless networks with existing equipment, while a wired network might require additional wiring.
- **Cost** – Because wireless networks eliminate or reduce wiring costs, they can cost less to operate than wired networks.

Types of Wireless Technologies

Wi-Fi

Primarily associated with computer networking, Wi-Fi uses the IEEE 802.11 specification to create a wireless local-area network that may be secure, such as an office network, or public, such as a coffee shop. Usually a Wi-Fi network consists of a wired connection to the Internet, leading to a wireless router that transmits and receives data from individual devices, connecting them not only to the outside world but also to each other. Wi-Fi range is generally wide enough for most homes or small offices, and for larger campuses or homes, range extenders may be placed strategically to extend the signal. Over time, the Wi-Fi standard has evolved, with each new version faster than the last. Current devices usually use the 802.11n or 802.11ac versions of the spec, but backwards compatibility ensures that an older laptop can still connect to a new Wi-Fi router. However, to see the fastest speeds, both the computer and the router must use the latest 802.11 version.

Bluetooth

While both Wi-Fi and cellular networks enable connections to anywhere in the world, Bluetooth is much more local, with the stated purpose of "replacing the cables connecting devices," according to the official Bluetooth website. That's precisely what Bluetooth does; it connects iPods to car stereos, wireless keyboards and mice to laptops, or cell phones to the ubiquitous hands-free earpieces. Bluetooth uses a low-power signal with a maximum range of 50 feet but with sufficient speed to enable transmission of high-fidelity music and streaming video. As with other wireless technologies, Bluetooth speed increases with each revision of its standard but requires up-to-date equipment at both ends to deliver the highest possible speed. Also, the latest Bluetooth revisions are capable of using maximum power only when it's required, preserving battery life.

WiMAX

While over-the-air data is fast becoming the realm of cellular providers, dedicated wireless broadband systems also exist, offering fast Web surfing without connecting to cable or DSL. One well-known example of wireless broadband is WiMAX. Although WiMAX can potentially deliver data rates of more than 30 megabits per second, providers offer average data rates of 6 Mbps and often deliver less, making the service significantly slower than hard-wired broadband. The actual data rates available to someone using WiMAX can vary widely with their distance from the transmitter.

Types of Wireless Networks

Wireless PAN

Wireless personal area networks (WPANs) interconnect devices within a relatively small area that is generally within a person's reach. For example, both Bluetooth radio and invisible infrared light provides a WPAN for interconnecting a headset to a laptop. Wi-Fi PANs are becoming commonplace as equipment designers start to integrate Wi-Fi into a variety of consumer electronic devices. Intel "My WiFi" and Windows 7 "virtual Wi-Fi" capabilities have made Wi-Fi PANs simpler and easier to set up and configure.

Wireless LAN

A wireless local area network (WLAN) links two or more devices over a short distance using a wireless distribution method, usually providing a connection through an access point for Internet access. The use of spread-spectrum or OFDM technologies may allow users to move around within a local coverage area and still remain connected to the network.

Products using the IEEE 802.11 WLAN standards are marketed under the Wi-Fi brand name. Fixed wireless technology implements point-to-point links between computers or networks at two distant locations, often using dedicated microwave or modulated laser light beams over line of sight paths. It is often used in cities to connect networks in two or more buildings without installing a wired link.

Wireless Mesh Network

A wireless mesh network is a wireless network made up of radio nodes organized in a mesh topology. Each node forwards messages on behalf of the other nodes. Mesh networks can "self-heal," automatically re-routing around a node that has lost power.

Wireless MAN

Wireless metropolitan area networks are a type of wireless network that connects several wireless LANs. WiMAX is a type of Wireless MAN and is described by the IEEE 802.16 standard.

Wireless WAN

Wireless wide area networks are wireless networks that typically cover large areas, such as between neighboring towns and cities, or city and suburb. These networks can be used to connect branch offices of a business or as a public Internet access system. The wireless connections between access points are usually point-to-point microwave links using parabolic dishes on the 2.4 GHz band, rather than omnidirectional antennas used with smaller networks. A typical system contains base station gateways, access points, and wireless bridging relays. Other configurations are mesh systems where each access point acts as a relay also. When combined with renewable energy systems such as photovoltaic solar panels or wind systems, they can be stand-alone systems.

Cellular Network

A cellular network or mobile network is a radio network distributed over land areas called cells, each served by at least one fixed-location transceiver, known as a cell site or base station. In a cellular network, each cell characteristically uses a different set of radio frequencies from all their immediate neighboring cells to avoid any interference.

When joined together, these cells provide radio coverage over a wide geographic area. This enables a large number of portable transceivers (e.g., mobile phones, pagers, etc.) to communicate with each other and with fixed transceivers and telephones anywhere in the network via base stations, even if some of the transceivers are moving through more than one cell during transmission.

Although originally intended for cell phones, with the development of smartphones, cellular telephone networks routinely carry data in addition to telephone conversations. The Global System for Mobile Communications (GSM) network is divided into three major systems: the switching system, the base station system, and the operation and support system. The cell phone connects to the base system station which then connects to the operation and support station; it then connects to the switching station where the call is transferred to where it needs to go. GSM is the most common standard and is used for a majority of cell phones. The Personal Communications Service (PCS) is a radio band that can be used by mobile phones in North America and South Asia.

4

Spread Spectrum

Spread spectrum is a method commonly used to modulate information into manageable bits that are sent over the air wirelessly. Essentially, spread spectrum refers to the concept of splitting information over a series of radio channels or frequencies. Generally, the number of frequencies is in the range of about 70, and the information is sent over all or most of the frequencies before being demodulated, or combined at the receiving end of the radio system.

Two kinds of spread spectrum are available:

- Direct-sequence spread spectrum (DSSS)
- Frequency-hopping spread spectrum (FHSS)

DSSS typically has better performance, while FHSS is typically more resilient to interference. A commonly used analogy to understand spread spectrum is that of a series of trains departing a station at the same time. The payload is distributed relatively equally among the trains, which all depart at the same time. Upon arrival at the destination, the payload is taken off each train and is collated. Duplications of payload are common to spread spectrum so that when data arrives excessively corrupted, or fails to arrive, the redundancies inherent to this architecture provide a more robust data link.

Direct-Sequence Spread Spectrum (DSSS)

Direct-sequence spread spectrum is a wireless technology that spreads a transmission over a much larger frequency band, and with corresponding smaller amplitude. By spreading the signal over a wider band, the signal is less susceptible to interference at a specific frequency. In other words, the interference affects a smaller percentage of the signal. During transmission, a pseudorandom noise code (PN code) is modulated with the signal. The sender and receiver's PN code generators are synchronized so that when the signal is received, the PN code can be filtered out.

Frequency-Hopping Spread Spectrum (FHSS)

This wireless technology spreads its signal over rapidly changing frequencies. Each available frequency band is subdivided into sub-frequencies. Signals rapidly change (hop) among these sub-frequencies in an order that is agreed upon between the sender and receiver. The benefit of FHSS is that the interference at a specific frequency will affect the signal during a short interval. Conversely, FHSS can cause interference with adjacent DSSS systems.

Orthogonal Frequency Division Multiplexing (OFDM)

A signal is subdivided into sub-frequency bands or tones, and each of these bands is manipulated so that they can be broadcasted together without interfering with each other. In an OFDM system, each tone is considered to be orthogonal (independent or unrelated) to the adjacent tones and, therefore, does not require a guard band. Because OFDM is made up of many narrowband tones, narrowband interference will degrade only a small portion of the signal and has no or little effect on the remainder of the frequency components.

Vectored Orthogonal Frequency Division Multiplexing (VOFDM)

In addition to the standard OFDM principles, the use of spatial diversity can increase the system's tolerance to noise, interference, and multipath. This is referred to as vectored OFDM, or VOFDM. Spatial diversity is a widely accepted technique for improving performance in multipath environments. Because multipath is a function of the collection of bounced signals, that collection is dependent on the location of the receiver antenna. If two or more antennae are placed in the system, each would have a different set of multipath signals. The effects of each channel would vary from one antenna to the next, so carriers that may be unusable on one antenna may become usable on another.

Frequency Division Multiple Access (FDMA)

Frequency division multiple access is used in analog cellular only. It subdivides a frequency band into sub-bands and assigns an analog conversation to each sub-band. FDMA was the original "cellular" phone technology and has been de-commissioned in many locations in favor of GSM or CDMA-based technologies.

Time Division Multiple Access (TDMA)

Time division multiple access multiplexes several digital calls (voice or data) at each sub-band by devoting a small time slice in a round-robin to each call in the band. Two sub-bands are required for each call, one in each direction between sender and receiver.

Wireless Security Issues

Open System Authentication

Open System Authentication is the default authentication protocol for the 802.11 standard. It consists of a simple authentication request containing the station ID and an authentication response containing success or failure data. Upon successful authentication, both stations are considered mutually authenticated. It can be used with WEP (Wired Equivalent Privacy) protocol to provide better communication security; however it is important to note that the authentication management frames are still sent in cleartext during the authentication process. WEP is used only for encrypting data once the client is authenticated and associated. Any client can send its station ID in an attempt to associate with the Access Point (AP). In effect, no authentication is actually done.

Shared Key Authentication

Shared Key Authentication is a standard challenge and response mechanism that makes use of WEP and a shared secret key to provide authentication. Upon encrypting the challenge text with WEP using the shared secret key, the authenticating client will return the encrypted challenge text to the access point for verification. Authentication succeeds if the access point decrypts the same challenge text.

Ad-Hoc Mode

Ad-hoc mode is one of the networking topologies provided in the 802.11 standard. It consists of at least two wireless endpoints where there is no access point involved in their communication. Ad-hoc mode WLANs are normally less expensive to run because no APs are needed for their communication. However, this topology cannot scale for larger networks and lacks some security features like MAC filtering and access control.

Infrastructure Mode

Infrastructure mode is another networking topology in the 802.11 standard. It consists of a number of wireless stations and access points. The access points usually connect to a larger wired network. This network topology can scale to form large networks with arbitrary coverage and complex architectures.

4

Wired Equivalent Privacy Protocol (WEP)

Wired Equivalent Privacy (WEP) Protocol is a basic security feature in the IEEE 802.11 standard, intended to provide confidentiality over a wireless network by encrypting information sent over the network. A key scheduling flaw has been discovered in WEP, so it is now considered to be insecure because a WEP key can be cracked in a few minutes with the aid of automated tools.

Wi-Fi Protected Access (WPA) and Wi-Fi Protected Access 2 (WPA2)

Wi-Fi Protected Access (WPA) is a wireless security protocol designed to address and fix the known security issues in WEP. WPA provides users with a higher level of assurance that their data will remain protected by using the Temporal Key Integrity Protocol (TKIP) for data encryption. 802.1x authentication has been introduced in this protocol to improve user authentication.

Wi-Fi Protected Access 2 (WPA2), based on IEEE 802.11i, is a new wireless security protocol that allows only authorized users to access a wireless device, with features supporting stronger cryptography (e.g., Advanced Encryption Standard or AES), stronger authentication control (e.g., Extensible Authentication Protocol or EAP), key management, replay attack protection, and data integrity.

In July 2010, a security vendor claimed their organization had discovered a vulnerability in the WPA2 protocol, named "Hole 196".[31] By exploiting the vulnerability, an internally authenticated Wi-Fi user could decrypt the private data of other users and inject malicious traffic into the wireless network. After a thorough investigation, it turned out that such an attack cannot actually recover, break, or crack any WPA2 encryption keys (AES or TKIP). Instead, attackers could only masquerade as Access Points and launch a man-in-the-middle attack when clients attached to them. In addition, if the security architect does his or her job properly, such an attack would not be able to succeed in a properly configured environment in the first place. If the client isolation feature is enabled on all access points, wireless clients are not allowed to talk with each other when they are attached to the same access point. As a result of this simple security configuration setting being applied, an attacker is unable to launch a man-in-the-middle attack against other wireless users.

TKIP was initially designed to be used with WPA, while the stronger algorithm AES was designed to be used with WPA2. Some devices may allow WPA to work with AES, while some others may allow WPA2 to work with TKIP. In November 2008, a vulnerability in TKIP was uncovered that would allow an attacker to be able to decrypt small packets and inject arbitrary data into a wireless network. Thus, TKIP encryption is no longer considered to be secure. The security architect should consider using the stronger combination of WPA2 with AES encryption.

Low deployment costs make wireless networks attractive to users. However, the easy availability of inexpensive equipment also gives attackers the tools to launch attacks on the network. The design flaws in the security mechanisms of the 802.11 standard also give rise to a number of potential attacks, both passive and active. These attacks enable intruders to eavesdrop on, or tamper with, wireless transmissions.

---

31 See the following: http://community.arubanetworks.com/t5/Community-Tribal-Knowledge-Base/
Analysis-of-quot-Hole-196-quot-WPA2-Attack/ta-p/25382

A "Parking Lot" Attack

Access points emit radio signals in a circular pattern, and the signals almost always extend beyond the physical boundaries of the area they are intended to cover. Signals can be intercepted outside of buildings, or even through the floors in multi-story buildings. As a result, attackers can implement a "parking lot" attack, where they actually sit in the organization's parking lot and try to access internal hosts via the wireless network. If a network is compromised, the attacker has achieved a high level of penetration into the network. They are now through the firewall and have the same level of network access as trusted employees within the enterprise.

An attacker may also fool legitimate wireless clients into connecting to the attacker's own network by placing an unauthorized access point with a stronger signal in close proximity to wireless clients. The aim is to capture end-user passwords or other sensitive data when users attempt to log on to these rogue servers.

Shared Key Authentication Flaw

Shared key authentication can easily be exploited through a passive attack by eavesdropping on both the challenge and the response between the access point and the authenticating client. Such an attack is possible because the attacker can capture both the plaintext (the challenge) and the ciphertext (the response).

WEP uses the RC4 stream cipher as its encryption algorithm. A stream cipher works by generating a keystream (i.e., a sequence of pseudo-random bits) based on the shared secret key, together with an initialization vector (IV). The keystream is then XORed against the plaintext to produce the ciphertext. An important property of a stream cipher is that if both the plaintext and the ciphertext are known, the keystream can be recovered by simply XORing the plaintext and the ciphertext together, in this case the challenge and the response. The recovered keystream can then be used by the attacker to encrypt any subsequent challenge text generated by the access point to produce a valid authentication response by XORing the two values together. As a result, the attacker can be authenticated to the access point.

Service Set Identifier (SSID) Flaw

Access points come with vendor provided default SSIDs programmed into them. If the default SSID is not changed, it is very likely that an attacker will be able to successfully attack the device due to the use of the default configuration. In addition, SSIDs are embedded in management frames that will be broadcast in cleartext from the device, unless the access point is configured to disable SSID broadcasting or is using encryption. By conducting analysis on the captured network traffic from the air, the attacker could be able to obtain the network SSID and may be able to perform further attacks as a result.

The Vulnerability of Wired Equivalent Privacy Protocol (WEP)

Data passing through a wireless LAN with WEP disabled (which is the default setting for most products) is susceptible to eavesdropping and data modification attacks. However, even when WEP is enabled, the confidentiality and integrity of wireless traffic is still at risk because a number of flaws in WEP have been revealed, which seriously undermine its claims to security. In particular, the following attacks on WEP are possible:

- Passive attacks to decrypt traffic based on known plaintext and chosen ciphertext attacks;

- Passive attacks to decrypt traffic based on statistical analysis of ciphertexts;
- Active attacks to inject new traffic from unauthorized mobile stations;
- Active attacks to modify data; or
- Active attacks to decrypt traffic, based on tricking the access point into redirecting wireless traffic to an attacker's machine.

Attack on Temporal Key Integrity Protocol (TKIP)

The TKIP attack uses a mechanism similar to the WEP attack, in that it tries to decode data one byte at a time by using multiple replays and observing the response over the air. Using this mechanism, an attacker can decode small packets like ARP frames in about 15 minutes. If Quality of Service (QoS) is enabled in the network, the attacker can further inject up to 15 arbitrary frames for every decrypted packet. Potential attacks include ARP poisoning, DNS manipulation, and Denial of Service. Although this is not a key recovery attack and it does not lead to compromise of TKIP keys or decryption of all subsequent frames, it is still a serious attack and poses risks to all TKIP implementations on both WPA and WPA2 networks.

Cryptography Used to Maintain Communications Security

Cryptography is a discipline that embodies principles, means, and methods for the transformation of data in order to hide its information content, establish its authenticity, prevent its undetected modification, prevent its repudiation, and/or prevent its unauthorized use. It is one of the technological means to provide security for data on information and communications systems. Cryptography can be used to protect the confidentiality of data, such as financial or personal data, whether that data is in storage or in transit. Cryptography can also be used to verify the integrity of data by revealing whether data has been altered and identifying the person or device that sent it.

The importance of information and communications systems for society and the global economy is intensifying with the increasing value and quantity of data that is transmitted and stored on those systems. At the same time, those systems and data are also increasingly vulnerable to a variety of threats, such as unauthorized access and use, misappropriation, alteration, and destruction. Proliferation of computers, increased computing power, interconnectivity, decentralization, growth of networks, and the number of users, as well as the convergence of information and communications technologies, while enhancing the utility of these systems, also increase system vulnerability.

Security of information and communications systems involves the protection of the availability, confidentiality, and integrity of those systems and the data that is transmitted and stored on them. Availability is the property that data, information, and information and communications systems are accessible and useable on a timely basis in the required manner. Confidentiality is the property that data or information is not made available or disclosed to unauthorized persons, entities, and processes. Integrity is the property that data or information has not been modified or altered in an unauthorized manner. The relative priority and significance of availability, confidentiality, and integrity vary according to the information or communication systems and the ways in which those systems are used. The quality of security for information and communication systems and the data that is stored and transmitted on them depends not only on the technical measures, including the use of both hardware and software tools, but also on good managerial, organizational, and operational procedures.

Cryptography is an important component of secure information and communications systems, and a variety of applications have been developed that incorporate cryptographic methods to provide data security. Cryptography is an effective tool for ensuring both the confidentiality and the integrity of data, and each of these uses offers certain benefits. However, the widespread use of cryptography raises a number of important issues. Although there are legitimate governmental, commercial, and individual needs and uses for cryptography, it may also be used by individuals or entities for illegal activities, which can affect public safety, national security, the enforcement of laws, business interests, consumer interests, or privacy. Governments, together with industry and the general public, are challenged to develop balanced policies to address these issues.

Historically, cryptography has been used to encode information to conceal secret messages from unauthorized parties. Cryptography uses an algorithm to transform data in order to render it unintelligible to anyone who does not possess certain secret information (the cryptographic "key") necessary for decryption of the data. Today, the increased calculation power arising from the development of digital computing makes it possible to use complex mathematical algorithms for encryption of data.

The development of information and communications technologies that allow vast quantities of data to be transmitted, copied, and stored quickly and easily has prompted a growing concern for the protection of privacy and the confidentiality of data, including personal data, government administrative records, and business and financial information. Effective cryptography is an essential tool in a network environment for addressing these concerns.

Public Key Cryptography

In the mid-1970s, a new development in cryptography introduced the "public key" concept, which allows parties to exchange encrypted data without communicating a shared secret key in advance. Rather than sharing one secret key, this new design uses two mathematically related keys for each communicating party: a "public key" that is disclosed to the public and a corresponding "private key" that is kept secret. A message that is encrypted with a public key can only be decrypted by the corresponding private key. In this way, a confidential communication encrypted with the recipient's public key and decrypted with the recipient's private key could only be understood by the recipient of the message.

An important application for public key cryptography is "digital signature," which can be used to verify the integrity of data or the authenticity of the sender of data. In this case, the private key is used to "sign" a message, while the corresponding public key is used to verify a "signed" message. Public key cryptography offers the benefits of confidential transmissions and digital signature in an open network environment in which parties do not know one another in advance.

Public key cryptography plays an important role in developing information infrastructures. Much of the interest in information and communications networks and technologies centers on their potential to accommodate electronic commerce; however, open networks such as the Internet present significant challenges for making enforceable electronic contracts and secure payments. In connection with certifying the integrity of data, public key cryptography offers technological solutions for both of these problems by providing mechanisms for establishing the validity of a claimed identity of a user, device, or another entity in an information system ("authentication") and for limiting the ability of an individual or entity to effectively deny having performed a particular action related to data ("non-repudiation").

Digital Signature

There is a tremendous potential for fraud in the electronic world. Transactions take place at a distance without the benefit of physical clues that permit identification, making impersonation easy. The ability to make perfect copies and undetectable alterations of digitized data complicates the matter. Traditionally, hand-written signatures serve to determine the authenticity of an original document. In the electronic world, the concept of an "original" document is problematic, but a digital signature can verify data integrity and provide authentication and non-repudiation functions to certify the sender of the data. If a document itself has been altered in any way after it has been "signed," the digital signature will so demonstrate. Similarly, once a document is "signed" with a cryptographic key, the digital signature provides proof that the document was "signed" by the purported author, and the sender cannot easily deny having sent the document or claim that the information has been altered during transmission.

Cryptography can also provide technical solutions for the protection of intellectual property in digital form. For example, a digital signature together with a verifiable time-stamp can give authors some control over their work, by tying an electronic document to the issuer and ensuring that the document is not modified without detection. The same technology can be applied to ensuring the authenticity and integrity of documents archived electronically.

Electronic Payments

Secure payment systems are necessary in order for electronic commerce on open networks to flourish. Cryptography can be used to protect the confidentiality of a message containing a credit card number and to confirm that the message was indeed sent by the cardholder. While this method is currently being used, it leaves the credit card number vulnerable to improper use after the message containing it has been decrypted. Another design involves verifiable security mechanisms for the transaction to occur electronically, which are not simply based on the exchange of a credit card number – such as independent confirmation by digital signature – as well as an authorization process that is not tied to any proprietary network so that purchases can be made on open networks.

Several schemes for other kinds of electronic payment systems are in various stages of development, including a number of different "digital money" systems. Digital money systems use cryptography to create a unique electronic representation that is redeemable for payment or that can constitute legal tender that is storable, transferable, and unforgeable. Most of these systems operate much like credit cards, debit cards, or checks, offering varying degrees of traceability and anonymity; others act more like "digital cash," accommodating completely anonymous transactions like coins do.

Certifying Public Key Relationships

Affirming the relationship between an individual or entity and its associated public key is important to guard against impersonation in an electronic environment. In order for public key systems to work in the public domain, not only must the public key be freely accessible, but also senders and receivers must have a reliable way of determining that public keys are truly the keys of those parties with whom they wish to interact. This can be accomplished directly if the parties know one another in advance, or alternatively a formal mechanism to "certify" keys could be established. With that in mind, two basic types of solutions have emerged: an informal "web of trust" arrangement based on pre-existing relationships between parties, and a more formalized approach based on "certificate authorities."

The informal web of trust operates when keys are validated from person to person or from organization to organization in the context of established relationships. In this way, confidence in the relationship between an individual or entity and its associated public key extends from parties that have a direct relationship to those that do not because credentials are established through many individual instances of trust.

The other basic type of solution to address this problem is a public key infrastructure where certificate authorities authenticate public keys. A certificate authority is a "trusted" entity that provides information about the identity of a keyholder in the form of an authenticated "key certificate." The certificate is used to verify the identity of the parties exchanging encrypted information over a network. Certificate authorities can also perform other functions, such as notary and time-stamp services. Certificate authorities can be established by either the public or private sector, and they may operate either "in-house" for an individual organization or for the public at large.

Furthermore, the certificate authority itself must be reliable, so the certifier may need to be certified. This issue could be addressed by both a hierarchy of certificate authorities and a system of cross-certified certificate authorities. At the international level, independent international management frameworks for public key certification may be useful. The distinction between the web of trust and certificate authority methods becomes less clear when organizations that provide certificate functions cross-certify one another.

Special Issues for Consideration with Cryptographic Policy

User Trust

Increasingly, individuals, enterprises, and governments are affected by electronic information and communications systems, and there is an increasing dependence on their uninterrupted proper functioning. Concomitant with this is a mounting need for confidence that these systems will continue to be reliable and secure. Lack of security or lack of confidence in the security of these systems may hinder the development and use of new information and communication technologies.

Just as in the real world – where credit cards are forged, and cash is stolen – the "virtual world" will never be completely secure. While security methods and services should be trustworthy so that the users of information and communications systems can have confidence in them, ultimately, electronic transactions involve a calculated risk. The question then becomes not are transactions absolutely secure, but are they sufficiently secure?

Uncertainties may be met and confidence fostered by building consensus about use of information and communications systems. The challenge for the security professional is threefold: developing and implementing the technology; planning for avoiding and meeting the failures of the technology; and gaining public support and approval of use of the technology. It is also important for users to understand the legal framework that governs their use of cryptography, particularly in light of the "borderless" nature of information and communications networks.

4

User Choice

Solutions to protect against the diverse threats to information and communications systems and the data that is stored and transmitted on them can take a number of different forms. There is considerable choice of cryptographic methods available to meet a wide variety of user requirements for systems and data security, including both hardware and software solutions, which can stand alone or be integrated into related products and which can offer a certain level of strength and complexity depending on the algorithm and the product. Cryptographic methods can be designed to provide any combination of mechanisms to achieve confidentiality, authentication or non-repudiation, and to ensure data integrity. Users will choose different kinds of cryptographic methods for different purposes and to fulfil different data and systems security requirements. Furthermore, where systems for management of keys are developed, they too will offer a variety of functions for users to choose from.

Some governments have implemented regulations – and others may do so in the future – on the use of cryptography, including export controls, rules concerning key management systems, or requirements for minimum levels of protection for certain kinds of data. These regulations may have an impact on the kinds of cryptographic methods that are available for users to choose from. However, it is commonly agreed that, within these limitations, it is important for a wide variety of cryptographic methods to be available to meet the diverse needs for data and systems security. Broad options for choice of cryptographic methods will encourage the development of a wide range of offerings.

Standardization

Standardization is an important ingredient of security mechanisms. In the rapid-paced development of the information infrastructure, standards for security mechanisms, including cryptographic methods, emerge quickly, whether they be de-facto, through market dominance, or through national or international standards-setting bodies. It is important for governments and industry to work together to provide the necessary architecture and standards so that information and communications systems can reach their full potential. A common description of an effective standards-setting process is one that is industry-led, voluntary, consensus-based, and international.

For cryptography to function effectively as a security measure for information and communications systems, networks, and infrastructures, it is important that cryptographic methods be interoperable, mobile, and portable at the global level. Interoperability means the technical ability of multiple cryptographic methods to function together. Mobility means the technical ability of cryptographic methods to function in multiple information and communications infrastructures. Portability means the technical ability of cryptographic methods to be adapted and function in multiple systems. National and international standards for cryptographic methods can help to facilitate the development of these technical abilities.

Protection of Privacy

The respect of privacy and the confidentiality of personal information are important values in most societies. However, privacy is now at greater risk because in the emerging information and communications infrastructure neither open networks nor many types of private networks were designed with confidentiality of communications and storage of data in mind. However, cryptography forms the basis for a new generation of privacy enhancing technologies. The use of effective cryptography in a network environment can help protect the privacy of personal information and the secrecy of confidential information. The failure to use cryptography in an environment where data is not completely secure can put a number of interests at risk, including public safety and national security. In some cases, such as where national law calls for maintaining the confidentiality of data or protecting critical infrastructures, governments may require the use of cryptography of a minimum strength.

At the same time, the use of cryptography to ensure the integrity of data in electronic transactions can also have implications for privacy. The use of networks for all kinds of transactions will increasingly generate vast quantities of data that can be easily and cheaply stored, analyzed, and reused. When these operations require proof of identity, the transactional data will leave detailed and perhaps irrefutable trails of an individual's commercial activity, as well as paint a picture of private, non-commercial activities such as political associations, participation in online discussions, and access to specific types of information in online libraries or other databases. The key certification process also has implications for privacy because data can be collected when a certification authority binds an individual to a key pair.

All communication over the Internet uses the Transmission Control Protocol/Internet Protocol (TCP/IP). TCP/IP allows information to be sent from one computer to another through a variety of intermediate computers and separate networks before it reaches its destination.

The great flexibility of TCP/IP has led to its worldwide acceptance as the basic Internet and intranet communications protocol. At the same time, the fact that TCP/IP allows information to pass through intermediate computers makes it possible for a third party to interfere with communications in the following ways:

- **Eavesdropping** – Information remains intact, but its privacy is compromised. For example, someone could learn your credit card number, record a sensitive conversation, or intercept classified information.
- **Tampering** – Information in transit is changed or replaced and then sent on to the recipient. For example, someone could alter an order for goods or change a person's resume.
- **Impersonation** – Information passes to a person who poses as the intended recipient. Impersonation can take two forms:
- **Spoofing** – A person can pretend to be someone else. For example, a person can pretend to have the email address jdoe@security.net, or a computer can identify itself as a site called www.security.net when it is not. This type of impersonation is known as spoofing.
- **Misrepresentation** – A person or organization can misrepresent itself. For example, suppose the site www.buystuff.com pretends to be an electronics store when it is really just a site that takes credit card payments but never sends any goods.

Normally, users of the many cooperating computers that make up the Internet or other networks do not monitor or interfere with the network traffic that continuously passes through their machines. However, many sensitive personal and business communications over the Internet require precautions that address the threats listed above. Fortunately, a set of well-established techniques and standards known as public-key cryptography make it relatively easy to take such precautions.

Public-key cryptography facilitates the following tasks:

- ***Encryption*** and ***Decryption*** allow two communicating parties to disguise information they send to each other. The sender encrypts, or scrambles, information before sending it. The receiver decrypts, or unscrambles, the information after receiving it. While in transit, the encrypted information is unintelligible to an intruder.

- ***Tamper Detection*** allows the recipient of information to verify that it has not been modified in transit. Any attempt to modify data or substitute a false message for a legitimate one will be detected.

- ***Authentication*** allows the recipient of information to determine its origin - that is, to confirm the sender's identity.

- ***Non-repudiation*** prevents the sender of information from claiming later that the information was never sent.

Encryption and Decryption

Encryption is the process of transforming information so it is unintelligible to anyone but the intended recipient. Decryption is the process of transforming encrypted information so that it is intelligible again. A cryptographic algorithm, also called a cipher, is a mathematical function used for encryption or decryption. In most cases, two related functions are employed, one for encryption and the other for decryption.

With most modern cryptography, the ability to keep encrypted information secret is based not on the cryptographic algorithm, which is widely known, but on a number called a key that must be used with the algorithm to produce an encrypted result or to decrypt previously encrypted information. Decryption with the correct key is simple. Decryption without the correct key is very difficult and in some cases impossible for all practical purposes.

Symmetric-Key Encryption

With symmetric-key encryption, the encryption key can be calculated from the decryption key and vice versa. With most symmetric algorithms, the same key is used for both encryption and decryption.

Implementations of symmetric-key encryption can be highly efficient so that users do not experience any significant time delay because of the encryption and decryption. Symmetric-key encryption also provides a degree of authentication because information encrypted with one symmetric key cannot be decrypted with any other symmetric key. Thus, as long as the symmetric key is kept secret by the two parties using it to encrypt communications, each party can be sure that it is communicating with the other as long as the decrypted messages continue to make sense.

Symmetric-key encryption is effective only if the symmetric key is kept secret by the two parties involved. If anyone else discovers the key, it affects both confidentiality and authentication. A person with an unauthorized symmetric key not only can decrypt messages sent with that key but can encrypt new messages and send them as if they came from one of the two parties who were originally using the key.

Symmetric-key encryption plays an important role in the SSL protocol, which is widely used for authentication, tamper detection, and encryption over TCP/IP networks.

517

Public-Key Encryption

The most commonly used implementations of public-key encryption are based on algorithms patented by RSA Data Security. Therefore, this section describes the RSA approach to public-key encryption.

Public-key encryption (also called asymmetric encryption) involves a pair of keys-a public key and a private key-associated with an entity that needs to authenticate its identity electronically or to sign or encrypt data. Each public key is published, and the corresponding private key is kept secret. Data encrypted with your public key can be decrypted only with your private key.

In general, to send encrypted data to someone, you encrypt the data with that person's public key, and the person receiving the encrypted data decrypts it with the corresponding private key.

Compared with symmetric-key encryption, public-key encryption requires more computation and is therefore not always appropriate for large amounts of data. However, it's possible to use public-key encryption to send a symmetric key, which can then be used to encrypt additional data. This is the approach used by the SSL protocol.

Data encrypted with your private key can be decrypted only with your public key. This would not be a desirable way to encrypt sensitive data, however, because it means that anyone with your public key, which is by definition published, could decrypt the data. Nevertheless, private-key encryption is useful because it means you can use your private key to sign data with your digital signature-an important requirement for electronic commerce and other commercial applications of cryptography. Client software can then use your public key to confirm that the message was signed with your private key and that it has not been tampered with since being signed.

Key Length and Encryption Strength

In general, the strength of encryption is related to the difficulty of discovering the key, which in turn depends on both the cipher used and the length of the key. For example, the difficulty of discovering the key for the RSA cipher most commonly used for public-key encryption depends on the difficulty of factoring large numbers, a well-known mathematical problem.

Encryption strength is often described in terms of the size of the keys used to perform the encryption: In general, longer keys provide stronger encryption. Key length is measured in bits. For example, 128-bit keys for use with the RC4 symmetric-key cipher supported by SSL provide significantly better cryptographic protection than 40-bit keys for use with the same cipher. Roughly speaking, 128-bit RC4 encryption is 3×10^{26} times stronger than 40-bit RC4 encryption.

Different ciphers may require different key lengths to achieve the same level of encryption strength. The RSA cipher used for public-key encryption, for example, can use only a subset of all possible values for a key of a given length, due to the nature of the mathematical problem on which it is based. Other ciphers, such as those used for symmetric key encryption, can use all possible values for a key of a given length rather than a subset of those values. Thus, a 128-bit key for use with a symmetric-key encryption cipher would provide stronger encryption than a 128-bit key for use with the RSA public-key encryption cipher. This difference explains why the RSA public-key encryption cipher must use a 512-bit key (or longer) to be considered cryptographically strong, whereas symmetric key ciphers can achieve approximately the same level of strength with a 64-bit key. Even this level of strength may be vulnerable to attacks in the near future.

Because the ability to surreptitiously intercept and decrypt encrypted information has historically been a significant military asset, the U.S. government restricts export of cryptographic software, including most software that permits use of symmetric encryption keys longer than 40 bits.

Digital Signatures

Tamper detection and related authentication techniques rely on a mathematical function called a one-way hash (also called a message digest). A one-way hash is a number of fixed length with the following characteristics:

- The value of the hash is unique for the hashed data. Any change in the data, even deleting or altering a single character, results in a different value.
- The content of the hashed data cannot, for all practical purposes, be deduced from the hash, which is why it is called "one-way."

It is possible to use your private key for encryption and your public key for decryption. Although this is not desirable when you are encrypting sensitive information, it is a crucial part of digitally signing any data. Instead of encrypting the data itself, the signing software creates a one-way hash of the data, then uses your private key to encrypt the hash. The encrypted hash, along with other information, such as the hashing algorithm, is known as a digital signature.

The recipient of some signed data will get two items: the original data and the digital signature, which is a one-way hash (of the original data) that has been encrypted with the signer's private key. To validate the integrity of the data, the receiving software first uses the signer's public key to decrypt the hash. It then uses the same hashing algorithm that generated the original hash to generate a new one-way hash of the same data. Information about the hashing algorithm used is sent with the digital signature. Finally, the receiving software compares the new hash against the original hash. If the two hashes match, the data has not changed since it was signed. If they do not match, the data may have been tampered with since it was signed, or the signature may have been created with a private key that does not correspond to the public key presented by the signer.

If the two hashes match, the recipient can be certain that the public key used to decrypt the digital signature corresponds to the private key used to create the digital signature. Confirming the identity of the signer, however, also requires some way of confirming that the public key really belongs to a particular person or other entity.

The significance of a digital signature is comparable to the significance of a handwritten signature. Once you have signed some data, it is difficult to deny doing so later-assuming that the private key has not been compromised or out of the owner's control. This quality of digital signatures provides a high degree of non-repudiation: That is, digital signatures make it difficult for the signer to deny having signed the data. In some situations, a digital signature may be as legally binding as a handwritten signature.

Certificates and Authentication

A certificate is an electronic document used to identify an individual, a server, a company, or some other entity and to associate that identity with a public key. Like a driver's license, a passport, or other commonly used personal IDs, a certificate provides generally recognized proof of a person's identity. Public-key cryptography uses certificates to address the problem of impersonation.

To get a driver's license, you typically apply to a government agency, such as the Department of Motor Vehicles, which verifies your identity, your ability to drive, your address, and other information before issuing the license. To get a student ID, you apply to a school or college, which performs different checks (such as whether you have paid your tuition) before issuing the ID. To get a library card, you may need to provide only your name and a utility bill with your address on it.

Certificates work much the same way as any of these forms of identification. Certificate authorities (CAs) are entities that validate identities and issue certificates. They can be either independent third parties or organizations running their own certificate-issuing server software. The methods used to validate an identity vary depending on the policies of a given CA, just as the methods to validate other forms of identification vary depending on who is issuing the ID and the purpose for which it will be used. In general, before issuing a certificate, the CA must use its published verification procedures for that type of certificate to ensure that an entity requesting a certificate is in fact who it claims to be.

The certificate issued by the CA binds a particular public key to the name of the entity the certificate identifies (such as the name of an employee or a server). Certificates help prevent the use of fake public keys for impersonation. Only the public key certified by the certificate will work with the corresponding private key possessed by the entity identified by the certificate.

In addition to a public key, a certificate always includes the name of the entity it identifies, an expiration date, the name of the CA that issued the certificate, a serial number, and other information. Most importantly, a certificate always includes the digital signature of the issuing CA. The CA's digital signature allows the certificate to function as a "letter of introduction" for users who know and trust the CA but do not know the entity identified by the certificate.

Authentication is the process of confirming an identity. In the context of network interactions, authentication involves the confident identification of one party by another party. Authentication over networks can take many forms. Certificates are one way of supporting authentication.

Network interactions typically take place between a client, such as browser software running on a personal computer, and a server, such as the software and hardware used to host a website. Client authentication refers to the confident identification of a client by a server (that is, identification of the person assumed to be using the client software). Server authentication refers to the confident identification of a server by a client (that is, identification of the organization assumed to be responsible for the server at a particular network address).

Client and server authentication are not the only forms of authentication that certificates support. For example, the digital signature on an email message, combined with the certificate that identifies the sender, provide strong evidence that the person identified by that certificate did indeed send that message. Similarly, a digital signature on an HTML form, combined with a certificate that identifies the signer, can provide evidence, after the fact, that the person identified by that certificate did agree to the contents of the form. In addition to authentication, the digital signature in both cases ensures a degree of non-repudiation; that is, a digital signature makes it difficult for the signer to claim later not to have sent the email or the form.

Client authentication is an essential element of network security within most intranets or extranets. The sections that follow contrast two forms of client authentication:

- ***Password-Based Authentication*** – Almost all server software permits client authentication by means of a name and password. For example, a server might require a user to type a name and password before granting access to the server. The server maintains a list of names and passwords; if a particular name is on the list, and if the user types the correct password, the server grants access.

- ***Certificate-Based Authentication*** – Client authentication based on certificates is part of the SSL protocol. The client digitally signs a randomly generated piece of data and sends both the certificate and the signed data across the network. The server uses techniques of public-key cryptography to validate the signature and confirm the validity of the certificate.

Password-Based Authentication

The basic steps involved in authenticating a client by means of a name and password assumes the following:

- The user has already decided to trust the server, either without authentication or on the basis of server authentication via SSL.
- The user has requested a resource controlled by the server.
- The server requires client authentication before permitting access to the requested resource.

These are the steps:

1. In response to an authentication request from the server, the client displays a dialog box requesting the user's name and password for that server. The user must supply a name and password separately for each new server the user wishes to use during a work session.

2. The client sends the name and password across the network, either in the clear or over an encrypted SSL connection.

3. The server looks up the name and password in its local password database and, if they match, accepts them as evidence authenticating the user's identity.

4. The server determines whether the identified user is permitted to access the requested resource and, if so, allows the client to access it.

With this arrangement, the user must supply a new password for each server, and the administrator must keep track of the name and password for each user, typically on separate servers.

Proper implementation does not store passwords in plaintext. Instead it concatenates the password with a random per-user value (a so called "salt") and stores the hash value of the result along with the salt. This makes certain kinds of brute force attacks more difficult.

As shown in the next section, one of the advantages of certificate-based authentication is that it can be used to replace the first three steps in the password-based authentication process with a mechanism that allows the user to supply just one password (which is not sent across the network) and allows the administrator to control user authentication centrally.

Certificate-Based Authentication

Let's discuss how client authentication works using certificates and the SSL protocol. To authenticate a user to a server, a client digitally signs a randomly generated piece of data and sends both the certificate and the signed data across the network. For the purposes of this discussion, the digital signature associated with some data can be thought of as evidence provided by the client to the server. The server authenticates the user's identity on the strength of this evidence.

In addition, this discussion assumes that the user has already decided to trust the server and has requested a resource, and that the server has requested client authentication in the process of evaluating whether to grant access to the requested resource. Further, it also assumes that the client has a valid certificate that can be used to identify the client to the server. Certificate-based authentication is generally considered preferable to password-based authentication because it is based on wheat the user has (the private key) as well as what the user knows (the password that protects the private key). However, it's important to note that these two assumptions are true only if unauthorized personnel have not gained access to the user's machine or password, the password for the client software's private key database has been set, and the software is set up to request the password at reasonable frequent intervals.

Neither password-based authentication nor certificate-based authentication address security issues related to physical access to individual machines or passwords. Public-key cryptography can only verify that a private key used to sign some data corresponds to the public key in a certificate. It is the user's responsibility to protect a machine's physical security and to keep the private-key password secret.

These are the steps:

1. The client software maintains a database of the private keys that correspond to the public keys published in any certificates issued for that client. The client asks for the password to this database the first time the client needs to access it during a given session - for example, the first time the user attempts to access an SSL-enabled server that requires certificate-based client authentication. After entering this password once, the user does not need to enter it again for the rest of the session, even when accessing other SSL-enabled servers.

2. The client unlocks the private-key database, retrieves the private key for the user's certificate, and uses that private key to digitally sign some data that has been randomly generated for this purpose based on input from both the client and the server. This data and the digital signature constitute "evidence" of the private key's validity. The digital signature can be created only with that private key and can be validated with the corresponding public key against the signed data, which is unique to the SSL session.

3. The client sends both the user's certificate and the evidence (the randomly generated piece of data that has been digitally signed) across the network.

4. The server uses the certificate and the evidence to authenticate the user's identity.

At this point, the server may optionally perform other authentication tasks, such as checking that the certificate presented by the client is stored in the user's entry in an LDAP directory. The server then continues to evaluate whether the identified user is permitted to access the requested resource. This evaluation process can employ a variety of standard authorization mechanisms, potentially using additional information in an LDAP directory, company databases, and so on. If the result of the evaluation is positive, the server allows the client to access the requested resource.

As you can see by comparing the two processes, certificates replace the authentication portion of the interaction between the client and the server. Instead of requiring a user to send passwords across the network throughout the day, single sign-on requires the user to enter the private-key database password just once, without sending it across the network. For the rest of the session, the client presents the user's certificate to authenticate the user to each new server it encounters. Existing authorization mechanisms based on the authenticated user identity are not affected.

How Certificates Are Used

Types of Certificates

The security professional needs to ensure that he or she is familiar with the five kinds of certificates that are commonly used with most products:

- **Client SSL certificates** – Used to identify clients to servers via SSL (client authentication). Typically, the identity of the client is assumed to be the same as the identity of a human being, such as an employee in an enterprise. Client SSL certificates can also be used for form signing and as part of a single sign-on solution.
  - ¤ *Example:* A bank gives a customer a client SSL certificate that allows the bank's servers to identify that customer and authorize access to the customer's accounts. A company might give a new employee a client SSL certificate that allows the company's servers to identify that employee and authorize access to the company's servers.
- **Server SSL certificates** – Used to identify servers to clients via SSL (server authentication). Server authentication may be used with or without client authentication. Server authentication is a requirement for an encrypted SSL session.
  - ¤ *Example:* Internet sites that engage in e-commerce usually support certificate-based server authentication, at a minimum, to establish an encrypted SSL session and to assure customers that they are dealing with a website identified with a particular company. The encrypted SSL session ensures that personal information sent over the network, such as credit card numbers, cannot easily be intercepted.
- **S/MIME certificates** – Used for signed and encrypted email. As with client SSL certificates, the identity of the client is typically assumed to be the same as the identity of a human being, such as an employee in an enterprise. A single certificate may be used as both an S/MIME certificate and an SSL certificate. S/MIME certificates can also be used for form signing and as part of a single sign-on solution.
  - ¤ *Example*: A company deploys combined S/MIME and SSL certificates solely for the purpose of authenticating employee identities, thus permitting signed email and client SSL authentication but not encrypted email. Another company issues S/MIME certificates solely for the purpose of both signing and encrypting email that deals with sensitive financial or legal matters.
- **Object-Signing certificates** – Used to identify signers of program code, scripts, or other signed files.

□ *Example:* A software company signs software distributed over the Internet to provide users with some assurance that the software is a legitimate product of that company. Using certificates and digital signatures in this manner can also make it possible for users to identify and control the kind of access downloaded software has to their computers.

■ **Certificate Authority (CA) certificates** – Used to identify CAs. Client and server software use CA certificates to determine what other certificates can be trusted.

□ *Example:* The CA certificates stored in a program or application determine what other certificates that copy of the program can authenticate. An administrator can implement some aspects of corporate security policies by controlling the CA certificates stored in each user's copy of an application.

SSL Protocol

The Secure Sockets Layer (SSL) protocol is a set of rules governing server authentication, client authentication, and encrypted communication between servers and clients. SSL is widely used on the Internet, especially for interactions that involve exchanging confidential information such as credit card numbers.

SSL requires a server SSL certificate, at a minimum. As part of the initial "handshake" process, the server presents its certificate to the client to authenticate the server's identity. The authentication process uses public-key encryption and digital signatures to confirm that the server is in fact the server it claims to be. Once the server has been authenticated, the client and server use techniques of symmetric-key encryption, which is very fast, to encrypt all the information they exchange for the remainder of the session and to detect any tampering that may have occurred.

Servers may optionally be configured to require client authentication as well as server authentication. In this case, after server authentication is successfully completed, the client must also present its certificate to the server to authenticate the client's identity before the encrypted SSL session can be established.

Signed and Encrypted Email

Many email programs support digitally signed and encrypted email using a widely accepted protocol known as Secure Multipurpose Internet Mail Extension (S/MIME). Using S/MIME to sign or encrypt email messages requires the sender of the message to have an S/MIME certificate.

An email message that includes a digital signature provides some assurance that it was in fact sent by the person whose name appears in the message header, thus providing authentication of the sender. If the digital signature cannot be validated by the email software on the receiving end, the user will be alerted.

The digital signature is unique to the message it accompanies. If the message received differs in any way from the message that was sent - even by the addition or deletion of a comma - the digital signature cannot be validated. Therefore, signed email also provides some assurance that the email has not been tampered with. This kind of assurance is known as non-repudiation. In other words, signed email makes it very difficult for the sender to deny having sent the message. This is important for many forms of business communication.

S/MIME also makes it possible to encrypt email messages. This is also important for some business users. However, using encryption for email requires careful planning. If the recipient of encrypted email messages loses his or her private key and does not have access to a backup copy of the key, for example, the encrypted messages can never be decrypted.

Form Signing

Many kinds of e-commerce require the ability to provide persistent proof that someone has authorized a transaction. Although SSL provides transient client authentication for the duration of an SSL connection, it does not provide persistent authentication for transactions that may occur during that connection. S/MIME provides persistent authentication for email, but e-commerce often involves filling in a form on a webpage rather than sending an email.

The Red Hat Linux technology known as form signing addresses the need for persistent authentication of financial transactions. Form signing allows a user to associate a digital signature with Web-based data generated as the result of a transaction, such as a purchase order or other financial document. The private key associated with either a client SSL certificate or an S/MIME certificate may be used for this purpose.

When a user clicks the Submit button on a Web-based form that supports form signing, a dialog box appears that displays the exact text to be signed. The form designer can either specify the certificate that should be used or allow the user to select a certificate from among the client SSL and S/MIME certificates that are installed in Communicator. When the user clicks OK, the text is signed, and both the text and the digital signature are submitted to the server. The server can then use a Red Hat utility called the Signature Verification Tool to validate the digital signature.

Single Sign-On

Network users are frequently required to remember multiple passwords for the various services they use. For example, a user might have to type a different password to log into the network, collect email, use directory services, and access various servers. Multiple passwords are an ongoing headache for users, system administrators, and security professionals. Users have difficulty keeping track of different passwords, tend to choose poor ones, and tend to write them down in obvious places. Administrators and security professionals must keep track of a separate password database on each server and deal with potential security problems related to the fact that passwords are sent over the network routinely and frequently.

Solving this problem requires some way for a user to log in once, using a single password, and get authenticated access to all network resources that user is authorized to use, without sending any passwords over the network. This capability is known as single sign-on.

Both client SSL certificates and S/MIME certificates can play a significant role in a comprehensive single sign-on solution. A user can log in once, using a single password to the local client's private-key database, and get authenticated access to all SSL-enabled servers that user is authorized to use without sending any passwords over the network. This approach simplifies access for users because they do not need to enter passwords for each new server. It also simplifies network management because administrators can control access by controlling lists of certificate authorities (CAs) rather than much longer lists of users and passwords.

In addition to using certificates, a complete single sign-on solution must address the need to interoperate with enterprise systems, such as the underlying operating system, that rely on passwords or other forms of authentication.

Object Signing

Object signing uses standard techniques of public-key cryptography to let users get reliable information about code they download in much the same way they can get reliable information about shrink-wrapped software.

Most importantly, object signing helps users and network administrators implement decisions about software distributed over intranets or the Internet, for example, whether to allow Java applets signed by a given entity to use specific computer capabilities on specific users' machines.

The "objects" signed with object signing technology can be applets or other Java code, JavaScript scripts, plug-ins, or any kind of file. The "signature" is a digital signature. Signed objects and their signatures are typically stored in a special file called a JAR file.

Software developers and others who wish to sign files using object-signing technology must first obtain an object-signing certificate.

Contents of a Certificate

The contents of certificates are organized according to the X.509 v3 certificate specification, which has been recommended by the International Telecommunications Union (ITU), an international standards body, since 1988.

Users do not usually need to be concerned about the exact contents of a certificate. However, system administrators and security professionals working with certificates may need some familiarity with the information provided here.

Distinguished Names

An X.509 v3 certificate binds a distinguished name (DN) to a public key. A distinguished name is a series of name-value pairs, such as uid=Sdog, that uniquely identify an entity, that is, the certificate subject.

For example, this might be a typical DN for an employee of ISC²:

```
uid=Sdog, e=Sdog@isc2.org,cn=Snoopy Dog,o=ISC2,c=US
```

The abbreviations before each equal sign in this example have these meanings:
- **Uid** – user ID
- **e** – email address
- **cn** – the user's common name
- **o** – organization
- **c** – country

DNs may include a variety of other name-value pairs. They are used to identify both certificate subjects and entries in directories that support the Lightweight Directory Access Protocol (LDAP).

The rules governing the construction of DNs can be quite complex and are beyond the scope of this discussion. For comprehensive information about DNs, see "A String Representation of Distinguished Names" at the following URL:

http://www.ietf.org/rfc/rfc1485.txt

A Typical Certificate

Every X.509 certificate consists of two sections:

The **data** section includes the following information:

- The version number of the X.509 standard supported by the certificate.
- The certificate's serial number. Every certificate issued by a CA has a serial number that is unique among the certificates issued by that CA.
- Information about the user's public key, including the algorithm used and a representation of the key itself.
- The DN of the CA that issued the certificate.
- The period during which the certificate is valid (for example, between 10:00 p.m. on September 3, 2014 and 10:00 p.m. September 3, 2016)
- The DN of the certificate subject (for example, in a client SSL certificate this would be the user's DN), also called the subject name.
- Optional certificate extensions, which may provide additional data used by the client or server. For example, the certificate type extension indicates the type of certificate (whether it is a client SSL certificate, a server SSL certificate, a certificate for signing email, and so on). Certificate extensions can also be used for a variety of other purposes.

The **signature** section includes the following information:

- The cryptographic algorithm, or cipher, used by the issuing CA to create its own digital signature.
- The CA's digital signature, obtained by hashing all of the data in the certificate together and encrypting it with the CA's private key.

Here are the data and signature sections of a certificate in human-readable format:

```
Certificate:
Data:
Version: v3 (0x2)
Serial Number: 3 (0x3)
Signature Algorithm: PKCS #1 MD5 With RSA Encryption
Issuer: OU=ABC123 Certificate Authority, O=ABC123, C=US
Validity:
Not Before: Friday Aug 18 18:36:25 2000
Not After: Sun Aug 18 18:36:25 2002
Subject: CN=Snoopy Dog, OU=Dog House, O=ABC123, C=US
Subject Public Key Info:
Algorithm: PKCS #1 RSA Encryption
Public Key:
Modulus:
00:ca:fa:79:98:8f:19:f8:d7:de:e4:49:80:48:e6:2a:2a:86:
ed:27:40:4d:86:b3:05:c0:01:bb:50:15:c9:de:dc:85:19:22:
43:7d:45:6d:71:4e:17:3d:f0:36:4b:5b:7f:a8:51:a3:a1:00:
98:ce:7f:47:50:2c:93:36:7c:01:6e:cb:89:06:41:72:b5:e9:
73:49:38:76:ef:b6:8f:ac:49:bb:63:0f:9b:ff:16:2a:e3:0e: 9d:
3b:af:ce:9a:3e:48:65:de:96:61:d5:0a:11:2a:a2:80:b0:
7d:d8:99:cb:0c:99:34:c9:ab:25:06:a8:31:ad:8c:4b:aa:54: 91:f4:15
Public Exponent: 65537 (0x10001)
Extensions:
```

```
Identifier: Certificate Type
Critical: no
Certified Usage:
SSL Client
Identifier: Authority Key Identifier
Critical: no
Key Identifier:
f2:f2:06:59:90:18:47:51:f5:89:33:5a:31:7a:e6:5c:fb:36: 26:c9
Signature:
Algorithm: PKCS #1 MD5 With RSA Encryption
Signature:
6d:23:af:f3:d3:b6:7a:df:90:df:cd:7e:18:6c:01:69:8e:54:65:fc:06:
30:43:34:d1:63:1f:06:7d:c3:40:a8:2a:82:c1:a4:83:2a:fb:2e:8f:fb: f0
:6d:ff:75:a3:78:f7:52:47:46:62:97:1d:d9:c6:11:0a:02:a2:e0:cc: 2a:
75:6c:8b:b6:9b:87:00:7d:7c:84:76:79:ba:f8:b4:d2:62:58:c3:c5:
b6:c1:43:ac:63:44:42:fd:af:c8:0f:2f:38:85:6d:d6:59:e8:41:42:a5:
4a:e5:26:38:ff:32:78:a1:38:f1:ed:dc:0d:31:d1:b0:6d:67:e9:46:a8: d:c4
```

Here is the same certificate displayed in the 64-byte-encoded form interpreted by software:

```
-----BEGIN CERTIFICATE-----
MIICKzCCAZSgAwIBAgIBAzANBgkqhkiG9w0BAQQFADA3MQswCQYDVQQGEwJVUzER
MA8GA1UEChMITmV0c2NhcGUxFTATBgNVBAsTDFN1cHJpeWEncyBDQTAeFw05NzEw
MTgwMTM2MjVaFw05OTEwMTgwMTM2MjVaMEgxCzAJBgNVBAYTAlVTMREwDwYDVQQK
EwhOZXRzY2FwZTENMAsGA1UECxMEUHViczEXMBUGA1UEAxMOU3Vwcml5YSBTaGV0

dHkwgZ8wDQYJKoZIhvcNAQEFBQADgY0AMIGJAoGBAMr6eZiPGfjX3uRJgEjmKiqG

7SdATYazBcABu1AVyd7chRkiQ31FbXFOGD3wNktbf6hRo6EAmM5/R1AskzZ8AW7L

iQZBcrXpc0k4du+2Q6xJu2MPm/8WKuMOnTuvzpo+SGXelmHVChEqooCwfdiZywyZ
NMmrJgaoMa2MS6pUkfQVAgMBAAGjNjA0MBEGCWCGSAGG+EIBAQQEAwIAgDAfBgNV

HSMEGDAWgBTy8gZZkBhHUfWJM1oxeuZc+zYmyTANBgkqhkiG9w0BAQQFAAOBgQBt

I6/z07Z635DfzX4XbAFpjlRl/AYwQzTSYx8GfcNAqCqCwaSDKvsuj/vwbf91o3j3

UkdGYpcd2cYRCgKi4MwqdWyLtpuHAH18hHZ5uvi00mJYw8W2wUOsY0RC/a/IDy84
hW3WWehBUqVK5SY4/zJ4oTjx7dwNMdGwbWfpRqjd1A==
-----END CERTIFICATE-----
```

How CA Certificates Are Used to Establish Trust

Certificate authorities (CAs) are entities that validate identities and issue certificates. They can be either independent third parties or organizations running their own certificate-issuing server software. Any client or server software that supports certificates maintains a collection of trusted CA certificates. These CA certificates determine which other certificates the software can validate - in other words, which issuers of certificates the software can trust. In the simplest case, the software can validate only certificates issued by one of the CAs for which it has a certificate. It is also possible for a trusted CA certificate to be part of a chain of CA certificates, each issued by the CA above it in a certificate hierarchy.

4

CA Hierarchies

In large organizations, it may be appropriate to delegate the responsibility for issuing certificates to several different certificate authorities. For example, the number of certificates required may be too large for a single CA to maintain; different organizational units may have different policy requirements; or it may be important for a CA to be physically located in the same geographic area as the people to whom it is issuing certificates.

It is possible to delegate certificate-issuing responsibilities to subordinate CAs. The X.509 standard includes a model for setting up a hierarchy of CAs.

In this model, the root CA is at the top of the hierarchy. The root CA's certificate is a self-signed certificate: That is, the certificate is digitally signed by the same entity, the root CA that the certificate identifies. The CAs that are directly subordinate to the root CA have CA certificates signed by the root CA. CAs under the subordinate CAs in the hierarchy have their CA certificates signed by the higher-level subordinate CAs.

Security architects have a great deal of flexibility in terms of the way they set up their CA hierarchies.

Certificate Chains

CA hierarchies are reflected in certificate chains. A certificate chain is a series of certificates issued by successive CAs. A certificate chain traces a path of certificates from a branch in the hierarchy to the root of the hierarchy. In a certificate chain, the following occur:

- Each certificate is followed by the certificate of its issuer.
- Each certificate contains the name (DN) of that certificate's issuer, which is the same as the subject name of the next certificate in the chain.
- Each certificate is signed with the private key of its issuer. The signature can be verified with the public key in the issuer's certificate, which is the next certificate in the chain.

Verifying a Certificate Chain

Certificate chain verification is the process of making sure a given certificate chain is well-formed, valid, properly signed, and trustworthy. The following procedure is typically used for forming and verifying a certificate chain, starting with the certificate being presented for authentication:

- The certificate validity period is checked against the current time provided by the verifier's system clock.
- The issuer's certificate is located. The source can be either the verifier's local certificate database (on that client or server) or the certificate chain provided by the subject (for example, over an SSL connection).
- The certificate signature is verified using the public key in the issuer's certificate.

If the issuer's certificate is trusted by the verifier in the verifier's certificate database, verification stops successfully here. Otherwise, the issuer's certificate is checked to make sure it contains the appropriate subordinate CA indication in the certificate type extension, and chain verification returns to step 1 to start again but with this new certificate.

Managing Certificates

The set of standards and services that facilitate the use of public-key cryptography and X.509 v3 certificates in a network environment is called the public key infrastructure (PKI). PKI management is a complex topic made up of the following areas:

- Issuing Certificates
- Certificates and the LDAP Directory
- Key Management
- Renewing and Revoking Certificates
- Registration Authorities

Issuing Certificates

The process for issuing a certificate depends on the certificate authority that issues it and the purpose for which it will be used. The process for issuing non-digital forms of identification varies in similar ways. For example, if you want to get a generic ID card (not a driver's license) from the Department of Motor Vehicles in Florida, the requirements are straightforward: You need to present some evidence of your identity, such as a utility bill with your address on it and a student identity card. If you want to get a regular driving license, you also need to take a driving test when you first get the license, and a written test when you renew it. If you want to get a commercial license for an eighteen-wheeler, the requirements are much more stringent. If you live in some other state or country, the requirements for various kinds of licenses will differ.

Similarly, different CAs have different procedures for issuing different kinds of certificates. In some cases, the only requirement may be your email address. In other cases, your UNIX or Windows username and password may be sufficient. At the other end of the scale, for certificates that identify people who can authorize large expenditures or make other sensitive decisions, the issuing process may require notarized documents, a background check, and a personal interview.

Depending on an organization's policies, the process of issuing certificates can range from being completely transparent for the user to requiring significant user participation and complex procedures. In general, processes for issuing certificates should be highly flexible, so organizations can tailor them to their changing needs.

Certificates and the LDAP Directory

The Lightweight Directory Access Protocol (LDAP) for accessing directory services supports great flexibility in the management of certificates within an organization. System administrators can store much of the information required to manage certificates in an LDAP-compliant directory. For example, a CA can use information in a directory to prepopulate a certificate with a new employee's legal name and other information. The CA can leverage directory information in other ways to issue certificates one at a time or in bulk, using a range of different identification techniques depending on the security policies of a given organization. Other routine management tasks, such as key management and renewing and revoking certificates, can be partially or fully automated with the aid of the directory.

Information stored in the directory can also be used with certificates to control access to various network resources by different users or groups. Issuing certificates and other certificate management tasks can thus be an integral part of user and group management for the security practitioner.

Key Management

Before a certificate can be issued, the public key it contains and the corresponding private key must be generated. Sometimes it may be useful to issue a single person one certificate and key pair for signing operations and another certificate and key pair for encryption operations. Separate signing and encryption certificates make it possible to keep the private signing key on the local machine only, thus providing maximum non-repudiation, and to back up the private encryption key in some central location where it can be retrieved in case the user loses the original key or leaves the company.

Keys can be generated by client software or generated centrally by the CA and distributed to users via an LDAP directory. There are trade-offs involved in choosing between local and centralized key generation. For example, local key generation provides maximum non-repudiation, but it may involve more participation by the user in the issuing process. Flexible key management capabilities are essential for most organizations. The security architect needs to take these considerations into account as he or she looks to design a PKI solution for the enterprise that will be used to help secure communications through the use of digital certificates.

Key recovery, or the ability to retrieve backups of encryption keys under carefully defined conditions, can be a crucial part of certificate management (depending on how an organization uses certificates). Key recovery schemes usually involve an m of n mechanism (also known as constant-weight code): For example, m of n managers within an organization might have to agree, and each contribute a special code or key of their own, before a particular person's encryption key can be recovered. This kind of mechanism ensures that several authorized personnel must agree before an encryption key can be recovered.

Renewing and Revoking Certificates

Like a passport, a certificate specifies a period of time during which it is valid. Attempts to use a certificate for authentication before or after its validity period will fail. Therefore, mechanisms for managing certificate renewal are essential for any certificate management strategy. For example, an administrator may wish to be notified automatically when a certificate is about to expire so that an appropriate renewal process can be completed in plenty of time without causing the certificate's subject any inconvenience. The renewal process may involve reusing the same public-private key pair or issuing a new one.

A passport can be suspended even if it has not expired. Similarly, it is sometimes necessary to revoke a certificate before it has expired; for example, if an employee leaves a company or moves to a new job within the company.

Certificate revocation can be handled in several different ways. For some organizations, it may be sufficient to set up servers so that the authentication process includes checking the directory for the presence of the certificate being presented. When an administrator revokes a certificate, the certificate can be automatically removed from the directory, and subsequent authentication attempts with that certificate will fail even though the certificate remains valid in every other respect. Another approach involves publishing a certificate revocation list (CRL) to the directory at regular intervals and checking the list as part of the authentication process. For some organizations, it may be preferable to check directly with the issuing CA each time a certificate is presented for authentication. This procedure is sometimes called real time status checking. Many organizations are using the Online Certificate Status Protocol (OCSP) as well.[32]

OCSP is used for obtaining the revocation status of an X.509 digital certificate. It was created as an alternative to the use of certificate revocation lists (CRL), specifically addressing certain problems associated with using CRLs in a public key infrastructure (PKI). OCSP can be vulnerable to replay attacks, where a signed, 'good' response is captured by a malicious intermediary and replayed to the client at a later date after the subject certificate may have been revoked. OCSP overcomes this by allowing a nonce to be included in the request that must be included in the corresponding response. However, since most OCSP responders and clients do not support or use the nonce extension and Certificate Authorities (CAs) issue responses with a validity period of multiple days, the replay attack is still a threat to validation systems. The security practitioner, the security professional, and the security architect all need to be aware of the risk issue associated with the deployment of OCSP. The security architect needs to consider the risk from the architectural and design perspectives, and he or she may decide to implement the use of the nonce in order to effectively mitigate the risk as part of the design for the organization's PKI system. The security practitioner needs to consider the risk from the operational and implementation perspectives and will need to ensure that the PKI system is built according to the security architect's design requirements that the nonce be supported and used with OCSP in the organization's PKI system. In addition, the security practitioner will also need to ensure that monitoring is implemented to validate that the nonce is being used for all OCSP transactions through the system. The security professional will need to design policies and procedures, in partnership with the security practitioner, to ensure that the use of the nonce with OCSP is clearly articulated within the organization. In addition, the security professional will need to work in partnership with the security practitioner to validate that the design and operation of the organization's PKI system supports and implements the use of the nonce with OCSP.

Registration Authorities

Interactions between entities identified by certificates (sometimes called end entities) and CAs are an essential part of certificate management. These interactions include operations such as registration for certification, certificate retrieval, certificate renewal, certificate revocation, and key backup and recovery. In general, a CA must be able to authenticate the identities of end entities before responding to the requests. In addition, some requests need to be approved by authorized administrators or managers before being acted upon.

As previously discussed, the means used by different CAs to verify an identity before issuing a certificate can vary widely, depending on the organization and the purpose for which the certificate will be used. Interactions with end entities can be separated from the other functions of a CA and handled by a separate service called a Registration Authority (RA) to provide maximum operational flexibility.

An RA acts as a front end to a CA by receiving end entity requests, authenticating them, and forwarding them to the CA. After receiving a response from the CA, the RA notifies the end entity of the results. RAs can be helpful in scaling a PKI across different departments, geographical areas, or other operational units with varying policies and authentication requirements.

---

32 http://tools.ietf.org/html/rfc6960

Securing Network Components

In addition to providing throughput, a network's architecture should also help protect its assets. Listed below are the key concepts concerning isolating networks in different domains of trust that the security professional needs to be aware of.

Secure Routing/Deterministic Routing

While it is possible to establish corporate wide area networks (WANs) using the Internet and VPN technology, it is not desirable. Relying on the Internet to provide connectivity means that there is little ability to control the routes that traffic takes or to remedy performance issues. Deterministic routing means that WAN connectivity is supplied based upon a limited number of different routes, typically supplied by a large network provider. Deterministic routing means that traffic only travels by pre-determined routes that are known to be either secure or less susceptible to compromise. Similarly, deterministic routing from a large carrier will make it much easier to address performance issues and to maintain the service levels required by the applications on the WAN. If the WAN is supporting converged applications like voice (VOIP) or video (for security monitoring or video conferencing), then deterministic routing becomes even more essential to the assurance of the network.

Boundary Routers

Boundary routers primarily advertise routes that external hosts can use to reach internal ones. However, they should also be part of an organization's security perimeter by filtering external traffic that should never be allowed to enter the internal network. For example, boundary routers may prevent external packets from the Finger service from entering the internal network because that service is used to gather information about hosts.

A key function of boundary routers is the prevention of inbound or outbound IP spoofing attacks. In using a boundary router, spoofed IP addresses would not be routable across the network perimeter. Examples of IP spoofing attacks are:

Non-Blind Spoofing

This type of attack takes place when the attacker is on the same subnet as the victim. The sequence and acknowledgement numbers can be sniffed, eliminating the potential difficulty of calculating them accurately. The biggest threat of spoofing in this instance would be session hijacking. This is accomplished by corrupting the data stream of an established connection, then re-establishing it based on correct sequence and acknowledgement numbers with the attack machine.

Blind Spoofing

This is a more sophisticated attack because the sequence and acknowledgement numbers are unattainable. Several packets are sent to the target machine in order to sample sequence numbers. While not the case today, machines in the past used basic techniques for generating sequence numbers. It was relatively easy to discover the exact formula by studying packets and TCP sessions. Today, operating systems implement random sequence number generation, making it difficult to predict sequence numbers accurately. If, however, the sequence number was compromised, data could be sent to the target.

Man in the Middle Attack

Both types of spoofing are forms of a common security violation known as a man in the middle (MITM) attack. In these attacks, a malicious party intercepts a legitimate communication between two friendly parties. The malicious host then controls the flow of communication and can eliminate or alter the information sent by one of the original participants without the knowledge of either the original sender or the recipient.

Security Perimeter

The security perimeter is the first line of protection between trusted and untrusted networks. In general, it includes a firewall and router that help filter traffic. Security perimeters may also include proxies and devices, such as an intrusion detection system (IDS), to warn of suspicious traffic. The defensive perimeter extends out from these first protective devices to include proactive defense such as boundary routers, which can provide early warning of upstream attacks and threat activities.

It is important to note that while the security perimeter is the first line of defense, it must not be the only one. If there are not sufficient defenses within the trusted network, then a misconfigured or compromised device could allow an attacker to enter the trusted network.

Network Partitioning

Segmenting networks into domains of trust is an effective way to help enforce security policies. Controlling which traffic is forwarded between segments will go a long way to protecting an organization's critical digital assets from malicious and unintentional harm. See *Figure 4.5*.

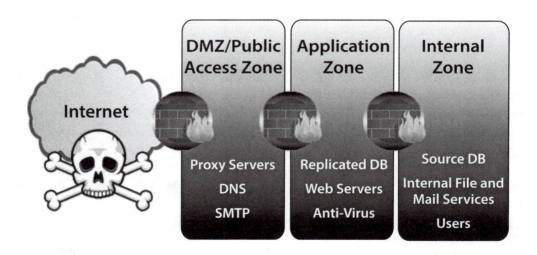

Figure 4.5 – **Network Partitioning**

Dual-Homed Host

A dual-homed host (*Figure 4.6*) has two network interface cards (NICs), each on a separate network. Provided that the host controls or prevents the forwarding of traffic between NICs, this can be an effective measure to isolate a network.

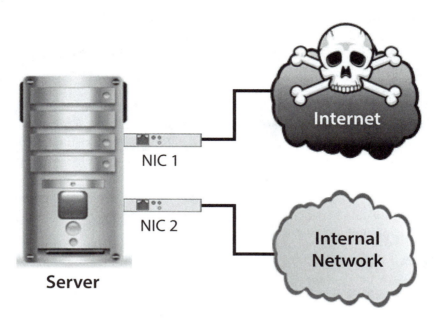

Figure 4.6 – **A Dual-Homed Host has two network interface cards (NICs), each on a separate network.**

Bastion Host

Bastion hosts serve as a gateway between a trusted and untrusted network that gives limited, authorized access to untrusted hosts. For instance, a bastion host at an Internet gateway could allow external users to transfer files to it via FTP. This permits files to be exchanged with external hosts without granting them access to the internal network in an uncontrolled manner.

If an organization has a network segment that has sensitive data, it can control access to that network segment by requiring that all access must be from the bastion host. In addition to isolating the network segment, users will have to authenticate to the bastion host, which will help audit access to the sensitive network segment. For example, if a firewall limits access to the sensitive network segment, allowing access to the segment from only the bastion host will eliminate the need for allowing many hosts access to that segment. For instance, terminal servers are a form of bastion host, which allow authenticated users deeper into the network.

A bastion host may also include functionality called a "data diode." In the world of electronics, a diode is a device that only allows current to flow in a single direction. A data diode only allows information to flow in a single direction; for instance, it enforces rules that allow information to be read, but nothing may be written (changed or created or moved).

A bastion host is a specialized computer that is deliberately exposed on a public network. From a secured network perspective, it is the only node exposed to the outside world and is therefore very prone to attack. It is placed outside the firewall in single firewall systems or, if a system has two firewalls, it is often placed between the two firewalls or on the public side of a demilitarized zone (DMZ).

The bastion host processes and filters all incoming traffic and prevents malicious traffic from entering the network, acting much like a gateway. The most common examples of bastion hosts are mail, domain name system, and Web and File Transfer Protocol (FTP) servers. Firewalls and routers can also become bastion hosts.

The bastion host node is usually a very powerful server with improved security measures and custom software. It often hosts only a single application because it needs to be very good at what it does. The software is usually customized, proprietary and not available to the public. This host is designed to be the strong point in the network to protect the system behind it. Therefore, it often undergoes regular maintenance and audit. Sometimes bastion hosts are used to draw attacks so that the source of the attacks may be traced.

To maintain the security of bastion hosts, all unnecessary software, daemons and users are removed. The operating system is continually updated with the latest security updates and an intrusion detection system is installed.[33]

Demilitarized Zone (DMZ)

A demilitarized zone (DMZ), also known as a screened subnet, allows an organization to give external hosts limited access to public resources, such as a company website, without granting them access to the internal network. See *Figure 4.7*. Typically, the DMZ is an isolated subnet attached to a firewall (when the firewall has three interfaces—internal, external, and DMZ—this configuration is sometimes called a three-legged firewall). Because external hosts by design have access to the DMZ (albeit controlled by the firewall), organizations should only place in the DMZ hosts and information that are not sensitive.

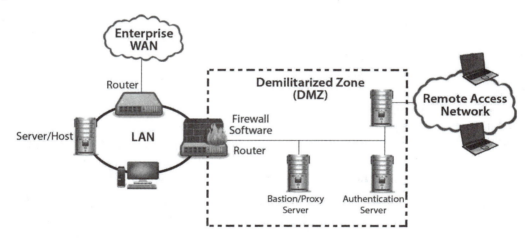

Figure 4.7 – **A Demilitarized Zone (DMZ) allows an organization to give external hosts limited access to public resources, such as a company website, without granting them access to the internal network.**
*(From Fung, K.T., **Network Security Technologies**, Auerbach Publications, Boston, MA, 2004. With permission.)*

---

33 "What is a Bastion Host?", by Cory Janssen, accessed January 15, 2015, http://www.techopedia.com/definition/6157/bastion-host

Hardware

Modems

Modems (modulator/demodulator) allow users remote access to a network via analog phone lines. Essentially, modems convert digital signals to analog and vice versa. A modem that is connected to the user's computer converts a digital signal to analog to be transmitted over a phone line. On the receiving end, a modem converts the user's analog signal to digital and sends it to the connected device, such as a server. Of course, the process is reversed when the server replies. The server's reply is converted from digital to analog and transmitted over the phone line, and so on.

Modems allow remote users to access a network from almost any analog phone line worldwide. While this provides easy access to telecommuters, road warriors, etc., it also provides easy access for intruders, who know they can sneak in an organization's backdoor while the security staff protects the Internet gateway. In fact, many organizations have implemented policies that forbid modems on the network for just this reason.

In order to mitigate some of the risks that exist from the legacy analogue work of communications, vendors have developed and taken to market "telephony firewalls," which act not unlike IP firewalls but are designed specifically to focus on analog signals. These firewalls will sit at the demarcation point between the Public Switched Telephone Network (PSTN) and the internal organizational network, whether it is an IP phone system or an analog phone system. Telephony firewalls will monitor both incoming and outgoing analog calls to enforce rule-sets. For instance, modem calls into the company phone exchange are only allowed from certain phone numbers. Or no modem communications are allowed—only voice and fax communications. In this way, even if rogue or forgotten modems exist on the analog phone network, they can be managed by the security practitioner.

Concentrators

Concentrators multiplex connected devices into one signal to be transmitted on a network. For instance, a Fiber Distributed Data Interface (FDDI) concentrator multiplexes transmissions from connected devices to a FDDI ring.

Front-End Processors

Input and output involve moving parts, such as fingers typing and disks spinning, which are quite slow compared to the speed of CPUs (central processing units). Servicing input and output, therefore, reduces a computer's throughput. Some hardware architectures employ a hardware front-end processor that sits between the input/output devices and the main computer. By servicing input/output on behalf of the main computer, front-end processors reduce the main computer's overhead.

Multiplexers

A multiplexer overlays multiple signals into one signal for transmission. Using a multiplexer is much more efficient than transmitting the same signals separately. Multiplexers are used in devices from simple hubs to very sophisticated dense-wave division multiplexers (DWDMs) that combine multi-optical signals on one strand of optical fiber.

Hubs and Repeaters

Hubs are used to implement a physical star topology. All of the devices in the star connect to the hub. Essentially, hubs retransmit signals from each port to all other ports. Although hubs can be an economical method to connect devices, there are several important disadvantages:

- All connected devices will receive each other's broadcasts, potentially wasting valuable resources processing irrelevant traffic.
- All devices can read and potentially modify the traffic of other devices.
- If the hub becomes inoperable, then the connected devices will not have access to the network.

Hubs are rarely used in current network architectures because they are both inefficient and insecure. Inefficient because they forward all traffic on to all hosts, which can severely tax networks that host many converged applications like voice, video, and business applications. Insecure because a network managed with hubs allows anyone with physical access to intercept all the traffic. To the extent that hubs are present in a network, they should be considered for replacement as legacy equipment.

As the distance between the sender and receiver increases, the signal's quality can degrade due to attenuation. To allow longer distances while preserving signal quality, repeaters are used to re-amplify signals. For example, a repeater can be used to increase the length of an Ethernet bus to accommodate a physically larger network.

Bridges and Switches

As Local Area Networks (LANs) grow in number of users, bandwidth utilization, and physical dimensions, they can reach thresholds that prevent the LAN from expanding. Bandwidth is exceeded, cable lengths cannot be increased because of signal attenuation, and the LAN can become too large to manage. On the other side of the coin, how would one interconnect LANs without reconfiguring the networks so that they can communicate?

One possible solution to both issues is to use bridges. Bridges are layer 2 devices that filter traffic between segments based on Media Access Control (MAC) addresses. In addition, they amplify signals to facilitate physically larger networks. A basic bridge filters out frames that are not destined for another segment. Consider the network shown in *Figure 4.8*.

When a client PC on segment A transmits to a server on segment A, the bridge will read the destination's MAC address and not forward the traffic to segments B and C, relieving them of the burden of traffic that is not destined for a device on these segments. In this example, if the segments had hundreds of devices on long network segments, the bridge would greatly reduce unnecessary traffic and allow the network to physically grow without signal attenuation.

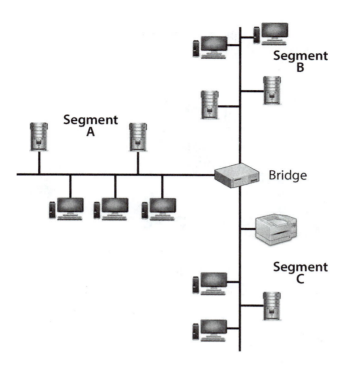

Figure 4.8 – **Network segments connected with a Bridge**

Bridges can connect LANs with unlike media types, such as connecting an Unshielded Twisted Pair (UTP) segment with a segment that uses coaxial cable. Bridges do not reformat frames, such as converting a Token Ring frame to Ethernet. This means that only identical layer 2 architectures can be connected with a simple bridge (e.g., Ethernet to Ethernet, etc.). Network administrators can use encapsulating bridges to connect dissimilar layer 2 architectures, such as Ethernet to Token Ring. These bridges encapsulate incoming frames into frames of the destination's architecture.

Other specialized bridges filter outgoing traffic based on the destination MAC address. In the network in *Figure 4.8*, suppose the bridge were a filtering bridge. When a user on segment A sends traffic to a server on segment B, the bridge will forward the transmission to segment B only, reducing unnecessary traffic on segment C.

Again, in the network in *Figure 4.8*, if a server on segment A sends out a broadcast on the wire, would segments B and C receive the broadcast? Because broadcasts are for all devices, the bridge will forward the broadcast. This is an important point to keep in mind about bridges: They do not filter broadcasts.

Bridges do not prevent an intruder from intercepting traffic on the local segment. A common type of bridge for many organizations is a wireless bridge based upon one of the IEEE 802.11 standards. While wireless bridges offer compelling efficiencies, they can pose devastating security issues to organizations by effectively making all traffic crossing the bridge visible to anyone connected to the LAN. Wireless bridges must absolutely apply link-layer encryption and any other available native security features, such as access lists, to ensure secure operation.

Switches solve the same issues posed at the beginning of this section, except the solutions are more sophisticated and more expensive. Essentially, a basic switch is a multiport device to which LAN hosts connect. Switches forward frames only to the device specified in the frame's destination MAC address, which greatly reduces unnecessary traffic. See *Figure 4.9*.

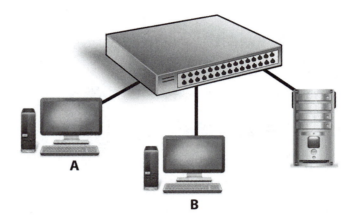

Figure 4.9 – **Simple switched network**

In this very simple LAN, client A transmits traffic to the server. When the switch receives the traffic, it relays it out of the port to which the server is connected. Client B does not receive any of the traffic. On the other hand, if the switch were a hub, client B would receive the traffic transmitted between client A and the server.

Because client B does not receive the traffic between the other client and server, the likelihood of client B intercepting the traffic is reduced (there are sophisticated attacks that could trick a switch, especially a poorly configured one, into sending traffic to client B).

Switches can perform more sophisticated functions to increase network bandwidth. Due to the increased processing speed of switches, models exist that can make forwarding decisions based on IP address and prioritization of types of network traffic. Like hubs and bridges, switches forward broadcasts.

Routers

Routers forward packets to other networks. They read the destination layer 3 address (e.g., destination IP address) in received packets, and based on the router's view of the network, it determines the next device on the network (the next hop) to send the packet. If the destination address is not on a network that is directly connected to the router, it will send the packet to another router.

Routers can be used to interconnect different technologies. For example, connecting a Token Ring and Ethernet networks to the same router would allow IP Ethernet packets to be forwarded to a Token Ring network.

4

Transmission Media

Wired

It is tempting to underestimate the importance of cables in a network. Yet without the cables, there would not be a network, just stand-alone components. One can think of cables as the glue that holds a network together.

Selecting proper cables in a network design is imperative. If inappropriate ones are used, the results can lead to network failures. Cables have to withstand much that threatens the confidentiality, integrity, and availability of the information on the network. Consider the risk of someone tapping into a cable to intercept its signal, electromagnetic interference from nearby devices, or simply the dangers of a cable breaking. This, considered with the technical parameters of cables, shows that the correct cable must be used for each application.

Here are some parameters that should be considered when selecting cables:

- **Throughput** – The rate that data will be transmitted. Certain cables, such as fiber optic, are designed for hauling an incredible amount of data at once.
- **Distance between Devices** – The degradation or loss of a signal (attenuation) in long runs of cable is a perennial problem, especially if the signal is at a high frequency. Also, the time required for a signal to travel (propagation delay) may be a factor. A bus topology that uses collision detection may not operate correctly if the cable is too long.
- **Data Sensitivity** – What is the risk of someone intercepting the data in the cables? Fiber optics, for example, makes data interception more difficult than copper cables.
- **Environment** – It is a cable-unfriendly world. Cables may have to be bent when installing, which contributes to degradation of conduction and signal distortion. The amount of electromagnetic interference is also a factor because cables in an industrial environment with a lot of interference may have to be shielded. Similarly, cables running through areas with wide temperature fluctuations and especially exposure to ultra-violet (sunlight) will degrade faster and be subject to degrading signals.

Twisted Pair [34]

Pairs of copper wires are twisted together to reduce electromagnetic interference and cross talk. Each wire is insulated with a fire-resistant material, such as Teflon. The twisted pairs are surrounded by an outer jacket that physically protects the wires. The quality of cable, and therefore its appropriate application, is determined by the number of twists per inch, the type of insulation, and conductive material. To help determine which cables are appropriate for an application or environment, cables are assigned into categories (*Table 4.11*).

---

34   TIA/EIA-568 is a set of telecommunications standards from the Telecommunications Industry Association (TIA), an offshoot of the Electronic Industries Alliance (EIA). The standards address commercial building cabling for telecommunications products and services. As of 2014, the standard is at revision C, replacing the 2001 revision B, the 1995 revision A, and the initial issue of 1991, which are now obsolete. Perhaps the best known features of TIA/EIA-568 are the pin/pair assignments for eight-conductor 100-ohm balanced twisted pair cabling. These assignments are named T568A and T568B. An IEC standard ISO/IEC 11801 provides similar standards for network cables.

Category 1	Less than 1 Mbps	Analog voice and basic interface rate (BRI) in Integrated Services Digital Network (ISDN)
Category 2	<4 Mbps	4 Mbps IBM Token Ring LAN
Category 3	16 Mbps	10 Base-T Ethernet
Category 4	20 Mbps	16 Mbps Token Ring
Category 5	100 Mbps	100 Base-TX and Asynchronous Transfer Mode(ATM)
Category 5e	1,000 Mbps	1000 Base-T Ethernet
Category 6	10,000 Mbps	1000 Base-T Ethernet

Table 4.11 – **Cable Categories**

Unshielded Twisted Pair (UTP)

UTP has several drawbacks. Because it does not have shielding like shielded twisted-pair cables, UTP is susceptible to interference from external electrical sources, which could reduce the integrity of the signal. Also, to intercept transmitted data, an intruder can install a tap on the cable or monitor the radiation from the wire. Thus, UTP may not be a good choice when transmitting very sensitive data or when installed in an environment with much electromagnetic interference (EMI) or radio frequency interference (RFI). Despite its drawbacks, UTP is the most common cable type. UTP is inexpensive, can be easily bent during installation, and, in most cases, the risk from the above drawbacks is not enough to justify more expensive cables.

Shielded Twisted Pair (STP)

Shielded twisted pair is similar to UTP. Pairs of insulated twisted copper are enclosed in a protective jacket. However, STP uses an electronically grounded shield to protect the signal. The shield surrounds each of the twisted pairs in the cable, surrounds the bundle of twisted pairs, or both. The shield protects the electronic signals from outside. Although the shielding protects the signal, STP has disadvantages over UTP. STP is more expensive and is bulkier and hard to bend during installation.

Coaxial Cable

Instead of a pair of wires twisted together, coaxial cable (or simply, coax) uses one thick conductor that is surrounded by a grounding braid of wire. A non-conducting layer is placed between the two layers to insulate them. The entire cable is placed within a protective sheath.

The conducting wire is much thicker than the twisted pair, and therefore it can support greater bandwidth and longer cable lengths. The superior insulation protects coaxial cable from electronic interference, such as EMI and RFI. Likewise, the shielding makes it harder for an intruder to monitor the signal with antennae or install a tap. Coaxial cable has some disadvantages. The cable is expensive and is difficult to bend during installation. For this reason, coaxial cable is used in specialized applications, such as cable TV.

Patch Panels

Even moderate-size data centers have many interconnected devices, such as switches, routers, servers, workstations, and even test equipment. It is a challenge for network administrators to organize the cables that connect these devices and to easily modify how they are connected.

As an alternative to directly connecting devices, devices are connected to the patch panel. Then, a network administrator can connect two of these devices by attaching a small cable, called a patch cord, to two jacks in the panel. To change how these devices are connected, network administrators only have to reconnect patch cords. Patch panels and wiring closets must be secured because they offer an excellent place to tap into the network and egress the product. Wiring must be well laid out and neat, and records should be kept in a secure location; otherwise, it is much easier to hide a tap in a mess of wires. Shared wiring closets should be avoided.

Fiber Optic

A fiber-optic system is similar to the copper wire system that fiber optics may be replacing. The difference is that fiber optics use light pulses to transmit information down fiber lines instead of using electronic pulses to transmit information down copper lines. Looking at the components in a fiber-optic chain will give the security professional a better understanding of how the system works in conjunction with wire based systems.

At one end of the system is a transmitter. This is the place of origin for information coming on to fiber-optic lines. The transmitter accepts coded electronic pulse information coming from copper wire. It then processes and translates that information into equivalently coded light pulses. A light-emitting diode (LED) or an injection-laser diode (ILD) can be used for generating the light pulses. Using a lens, the light pulses are funneled into the fiber-optic medium where they travel down the cable.

Think of a fiber cable in terms of a very long cardboard roll (from the inside roll of paper towels) that is coated with a mirror on the inside. If you shine a flashlight in one end, you can see light come out at the far end - even if it's been bent around a corner.

Light pulses move easily down the fiber-optic line because of a principle known as total internal reflection. This principle states that when the angle of incidence exceeds a critical value, light cannot get out of the glass; instead, the light bounces back in. When this principle is applied to the construction of the fiber-optic strand, it is possible to transmit information down fiber lines in the form of light pulses. The core must be made from a very clear and pure material. The core can be plastic (used for very short distances), but most are made from glass. Glass optical fibers are almost always made from pure silica, but some other materials, such as fluorozirconate, fluoroaluminate, and chalcogenide glasses, are used for longer-wavelength infrared applications.

There are three types of fiber-optic cable commonly used:

1. Single-mode
2. Multi-mode
3. Plastic Optical Fiber (POF).

Fiber-optic cable functions as a "light guide," guiding the light introduced at one end of the cable through to the other end. The light source can either be a light-emitting diode (LED) or a laser. The light source is pulsed on and off, and a light-sensitive receiver on the other end of the cable converts the pulses back into the digital ones and zeroes of the original signal.

Even laser light shining through a fiber-optic cable is subject to loss of strength, primarily through dispersion and scattering of the light, within the cable itself. The faster the laser fluctuates, the greater the risk of dispersion. Light strengtheners, called repeaters, may be necessary to refresh the signal in certain applications.

Fiber Types and Typical Specifications

Core/Cladding	Attenuation	Bandwidth	Applications/Notes
Multi-mode Graded-Index			
	@850/1300 nm	@850/1300 nm	
50/125 microns	3/1 dB/km	500/500 MHz-km	Laser-rated for GbE LANs
50/125 microns	3/1 dB/km	2000/500 MHz-km	Optimized for 850 nm VCSELs
62.5/125 microns	3/1 dB/km	160/500 MHz-km	Most common LAN fiber
100/140 microns	3/1 dB/km	150/300 MHz-km	Obsolete
Single-mode			
	@1310/1550 nm		
8-9/125 microns	0.4/0.25 dB/km	HIGH!	Telco/CATV/long high speed LANs
		~100 Terahertz	
Multi-mode Step-Index			
	@850 nm	@850 nm	
200/240 microns	4-6 dB/km	50 MHz-km	Slow LANs & links
POF (Plastic Optical Fiber)			
	@ 650 nm	@ 650 nm	
1 mm	~ 1 dB/m	~5 MHz-km	Short links & cars

Caution: You cannot mix and match fibers! Trying to connect Single-mode to Multimode fibers can cause 20 dB loss - that's 99% of the power. Even connections between 62.5/125 and 50/125 can cause loss of 3 dB or more - over half the power.

Network Access Control Devices

Firewalls

Firewalls are devices that enforce administrative security policies by filtering incoming traffic based on a set of rules. Often, firewalls are thought of as protectors of an Internet gateway only. While a firewall should always be placed at Internet gateways, there are also internal network considerations and conditions where a firewall would be employed, such as network zoning. Additionally, firewalls are also threat management appliances with a variety of other security services embedded, such as proxy services and Intrusion Prevention Services (IPS), which seek to monitor and alert proactively at the network perimeter.

Firewalls should be placed between entities that have different trust domains. For instance, if an engineering department LAN segment is on the same network as general LAN users, there would be two trust domains: general LAN users and engineers with the organization's intellectual property. Installing a firewall where the two trust domains meet would help the security practitioner to protect the intellectual property from the general LAN user population, as shown in *Figure 4.10*.

Firewalls will not be effective right out of the box. Firewall rules must be defined correctly in order to not inadvertently grant unauthorized access. Like all hosts on a network, administrators must install patches to the firewall and disable all unnecessary services. Also, firewalls offer limited protection against vulnerabilities caused by applications flaws in server software on other hosts. For example, a firewall will not prevent an attacker from manipulating a database to disclose confidential information.

Firewalls can be complex to administer and manage. The requirement to patch them frequently, monitor their logs, and alter their rules to accommodate internal business requirements can overwhelm security professionals and technical staff alike. For this reason, outsourcing of the complete management and maintenance of firewalls has become a significant and well established industry, with organizations from governments to banks to donut shops outsourcing this critical but complex and mundane security task.

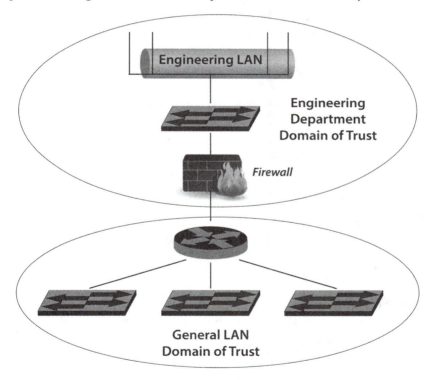

Figure 4.10 – **Firewall between two domains of trust**

Filtering

Firewalls filter traffic based on a rule set. Each rule instructs the firewall to block or forward a packet based on one or more conditions. For each incoming packet, the firewall will look through its rule set for a rule whose conditions apply to that packet, and it will block or forward the packet as specified in that rule. Below are two important conditions used to determine if a packet should be filtered.

By Address

Firewalls will often use the packet's source or destination address, or both, to determine if the packet should be filtered. For example, in the case shown in *Figure 4.10*, to grant a trusted user access to the engineering LAN segment, one can define a rule to forward a packet whose source address is from a trusted user's host on the general LAN.

By Service

Packets can also be filtered by service. The firewall inspects the service the packet is using (if the packet is part of the TCP or UDP, the service is the destination port number) to determine if the packet should be filtered. For example, firewalls will often have a rule to filter the Finger service to prevent an attacker from using it to gather information about a host.

Filtering by address and by service are often combined together in rules. If the engineering department wanted to grant anyone on the LAN access to its Web server, a rule could be defined to forward packets whose destination address is the Web server's and the service is HTTP (TCP port 80).

Network Address Translation (NAT)

Firewalls can change the source address of each outgoing (from trusted to untrusted network) packet to a different address. This has several applications, most notably to allow hosts with RFC 1918 addresses access to the Internet by changing their non-routable address to one that is routable on the Internet.[35] A non-routable address is one that will not be forwarded by an Internet router, and therefore remote attacks using non-routable internal addresses cannot be launched over the open Internet.

Anonymity is another reason to use NAT. Many organizations do not want to advertise their IP addresses to an untrusted host and thus unnecessarily give information about the network. They would rather hide the entire network behind translated addresses. NAT also greatly extends the capabilities of organizations to continue using IPv4 address spaces.

Port Address Translation (PAT)

An extension to NAT is to translate all addresses to one routable IP address and translate the source port number in the packet to a unique value. The port translation allows the firewall to keep track of multiple sessions that are using PAT.

Static Packet Filtering

When a firewall uses static packet filtering, it examines each packet without regard to the packet's context in a session. Packets are examined against static criteria, for example, blocking all packets with a port number of 79 (finger). Because of its simplicity, static packet filtering requires very little overhead, but it has a significant disadvantage. Static rules cannot be temporarily changed by the firewall to accommodate legitimate traffic. If a protocol requires a port to be temporarily opened, administrators have to choose between permanently opening the port and disallowing the protocol.

---

35 See the following: http://tools.ietf.org/html/rfc1918

4

Stateful Inspection or Dynamic Packet Filtering

Stateful inspection examines each packet in the context of a session, which allows it to make dynamic adjustments to the rules to accommodate legitimate traffic and block malicious traffic that would appear benign to a static filter. Consider FTP. A user connects to an FTP server on TCP port 21 and then tells the FTP server on which port to transfer files. The port can be any TCP port above 1023. So, if the FTP client tells the server to transfer files on TCP port 1067, the server will attempt to open a connection to the client on that port. A stateful inspection firewall would watch the interaction between the two hosts, and even though the required connection is not permitted in the rule set, it would allow the connection to occur because it is part of FTP.

Static packet filtering, in contrast, would block the FTP server's attempt to connect to the client on TCP port 1067 unless a static rule was already in place. In fact, because the client could instruct the FTP server to transfer files on any port above 1023, a static rule would have to be in place to permit access to the specified port.

Proxies

A proxy firewall mediates communications between untrusted end points (servers/hosts/clients) and trusted end points (servers/hosts/clients). From an internal perspective, a proxy may forward traffic from known, internal client machines to untrusted hosts on the Internet, creating the illusion for the untrusted host that the traffic originated from the proxy firewall, thus hiding the trusted internal client from potential attackers. A typical interaction with a server through a proxy is shown in *Figure 4.11*.

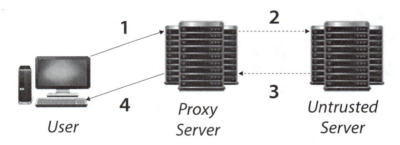

1. User's request goes to the proxy server.
2. Proxy server forwards the request to the untrusted host. To the untrusted host it will appear as if the request originated from the proxy server.
3. The untrusted host responds to the proxy server.
4. The proxy server forwards the response to the user.

Figure 4.11 – **Accessing a server through a proxy**

To the user, it appears that he or she is communicating directly with the untrusted server. Proxy servers are often placed at Internet gateways to hide the internal network behind one IP address and to prevent direct communication between internal and external hosts.

Circuit-Level Proxy

A circuit-level proxy creates a conduit through which a trusted host can communicate with an untrusted one. This type of proxy does not inspect any of the traffic that it forwards, which adds very little overhead to the communication between the user and untrusted server. The lack of application awareness also allows circuit-level proxies to forward any traffic to any TCP and UDP port. The disadvantage is that traffic will not be analyzed for malicious content.

Application-Level Proxy

An application-level proxy relays the traffic from a trusted end point running a specific application to an untrusted end point. The most significant advantage of application-level proxies is that they analyze the traffic that they forward for protocol manipulation and various sorts of common attacks such as buffer overflows. Application-level proxies add overhead to using the application because they scrutinize the traffic that they forward.

Web proxy servers are a very popular example of application-level proxies. Many organizations place one at their Internet gateway and configure their users' Web browsers to use the Web proxy whenever they browse an external Web server (other controls are implemented to prevent users from bypassing the proxy server). The proxies typically include required user authentication, inspection of URLs to ensure that users do not browse inappropriate sites, logging, and caching of popular webpages. In fact, Web proxies for internal users are one of the prime manners in which acceptable usage policies can be enforced because external sites can be blacklisted by administrators and logs of user traffic can be kept for later analysis if required for evidentiary purposes.

Personal Firewalls

What protects users from hosts that are behind a firewall? For example, the firewall in *Figure 4.10* does not protect a user on the engineering LAN segment from someone on the same segment.

Following the principle of security in depth, one should install personal firewalls on workstations, which protect the user from all hosts on the network. It is critical for home users with DSL or cable modem access to the Internet to have a personal firewall installed on every PC, especially if they do not have a firewall protecting their network.

Because personal firewalls are employed by general users, they are easy to install and configure. Firewall rules are created with a nontechnical interface that does not require expertise in networking or security. Although they do not provide the flexibility of the best enterprise firewalls, they provide all of the essential functions of a firewall, such as stateful inspection and logging.

End Point Security

End-users pose the biggest risk to security. They have access to the enterprise's most valuable information. And many of them ignore corporate security policies and do things they should not be doing, using all kinds of devices, applications, and networks. Plus, the cloud offers employees new ways to transport data on and off the endpoint, typically beyond the reach of monitoring systems. Because many of these devices and activities are out of the reach of the security practitioner, they are not likely to have the visibility necessary to protect against threats and data loss at the endpoint.

Worse yet, the sensitive data on users' endpoints is being targeted by attackers. Using the endpoint to establish an entry into the enterprise, attackers gain access to proprietary information and other systems from the compromised endpoint. Often they will simply execute a malicious software program. More often, they will use a blend of threat vectors to breach networks.

The end points of a network are often the most attractive targets as the rest of the network matures in defensive capabilities. Vulnerable workstations, printers, and other end points represent launching pads for numerous new attacks across the network. Workstations should be hardened, and users should be using limited access accounts whenever possible in accordance with the concept of "least privilege." Workstations should minimally have the following:

- Up-to-date anti-virus and anti-malware software
- A configured and operational host-based firewall
- A hardened configuration with unneeded services disabled
- A patched and maintained operating system

While workstations are clearly the end point most will associate with end point attacks, the landscape is changing. Mobile devices such as smartphones, tablets, and personal devices are beginning to make up more and more of the average organization's end points. With this additional diversity of devices, the security architect is required to also increase the diversity and agility of an organization's end point defenses. For mobile devices such as smartphones and tablets, security practitioners should consider the following:

- Encryption for the whole device or if not possible, then at least encryption for sensitive information held on the device
- Remote management capabilities including:
    - Remote wipe
    - Remote geo-locate
    - Remote update
    - Remote operation
- User policies and agreements that ensure an organization can manage the device or seize it for legal hold.

Content Distribution Networks

A content delivery network or content distribution network (CDN) is a large distributed system of servers deployed in multiple data centers across the Internet. The goal of a CDN is to serve content to end-users with high availability and high performance. CDNs serve a large fraction of the Internet content available today, including Web objects (text, graphics, and scripts), downloadable objects (media files, software, and documents), applications (e-commerce, portals), live streaming media, on-demand streaming media, and social networks.

Content delivery networks (CDNs) have been around for more than 15 years. CDNs are the key enabling technology behind successful consumer-facing sites in verticals such as media and entertainment, software download delivery, gaming, and ecommerce. CDNs give content owners and publishers the ability to rapidly scale to meet increasing user demand all over the world on multiple devices and on different platforms.

One example of a CDN is Amazon CloudFront, which is a content delivery network that lets developers get started creating hosted content quickly with a three-step process that utilizes either the Web-based AWS Management Console or Amazon CloudFront's programmable APIs. First, the customers store their content on an origin server. While

Amazon CloudFront is optimized to work with other AWS services—such as Amazon Elastic Compute Cloud (Amazon EC2), Amazon Elastic Load Balancing, and Amazon S3—customers can also use a Web server located outside of AWS, say in a customer's data center. Next, the location of the stored content is registered with AWS. Lastly, using the specified AWS domain name or your own personalized domain name, the content is added to your website code, media player, or application. When viewers access this content, the Amazon CloudFront service takes over and automatically re-directs them to the nearest edge server on Amazon's network.

The security architect, practitioner, and professional all have to spend time understanding the nature and potential of CDN technology. The ability to host content in the cloud and then have a distributed global network infrastructure available to provide almost instantaneous end point access across multiple platforms and form factors to any users on demand is a risk factor that has not been fully analyzed and accounted for by most architectures.

Secure Communication Channels

Voice

Modems and Public Switched Telephone Networks (PSTN)

The PSTN is a circuit-switched network that was originally designed for analog voice communication. When a person places a call, a dedicated circuit is created between the two phones. Although it appears to the callers that they are using a dedicated line, they are actually communicating through a complex network. As with all circuit-switched technology, the path through the network is established before communication between the two end points begins, and barring an unusual event, such as a network failure, the path remains constant during the call. Phones connect to the PSTN with copper wires to a central office (CO), which services an area of about 1 to 10 km.

The central offices are connected to a hierarchy of tandem offices (for local calls) and toll offices (toll calls), with each higher level of the hierarchy covering a larger area. Including the COs, the PSTN has five levels of offices. When both end points of a call are connected to the same CO, the traffic is switched within the CO. Otherwise, the call must be switched between a toll center and a tandem office. The greater the distance between the calls, the higher in the hierarchy the calls are switched. For example, in *Figure 4.12*, a call between callers 1 and 2 is switched within their central office. However, a call between callers 1 and 3 must be switched within the leftmost primary toll office. To accommodate the high volume of traffic, toll centers communicate with each other over fiber-optic cables.

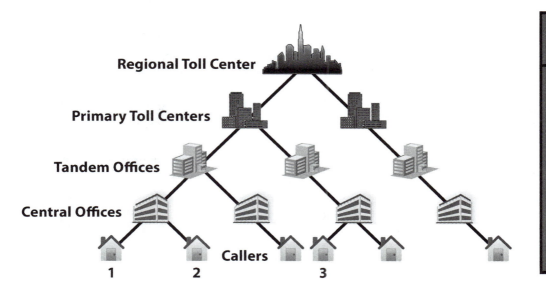

Figure 4.12 – **The Public Switched Telephone Network (PSTN)**

Previously, the PSTN was vulnerable to tone-frequency attacks. There was a subculture of phone hackers (phreaks) that attempted to make toll calls for free, manipulate public and private phone switches, gain unauthorized access to voicemail systems, etc. For example, in the 1960s, phone hackers discovered that AT&T signaled a 2600-Hz tone on all free toll lines and devised methods of reproducing that tone to make free long-distance calls. Phreaking as an art form has basically been made obsolete with the near ubiquitous deployment of digital switches and IP-based communications. To the extent phreaking exists, it is to exploit poorly configured company phone systems with key-pad commands to gain access to free long distance. However, most modern telecommunications carriers have entirely phased out analog (tone base) controls in favor of IP-based, digital controls, which are not available through public network entry points like phones.

War Dialing

Although modems allowed remote access to networks from almost anywhere, they could be used as a portal into the network by an attacker. Using automated dialing software, the attacker could dial the entire range of phone numbers used by the company to identify modems. If the host, to which the modem was attached, had a weak password, then the attacker would easily gain access to the network. Worse yet, if voice and data shared the same network, then both voice and data could be compromised.

The best defense against this attack is not to leave unattended modems turned on and keep an up-to-date inventory of all modems so none get orphaned and left to operate without the knowledge and oversight of the security professional. All modems should require some form of authentication, at least a single factor, although the industry standard has moved to two-factor authentication for modem connections due to the risks that the use of these devices poses. If modems are necessary, then organizations must ensure that the passwords protecting the attached host are strong, preferably with the help of authentication mechanisms, such as RADIUS, one-time passwords, etc.

POTS

Plain old telephone service (POTS) is commonly found in the "last mile" of most residential and business telephone services. Once called "Post Office Telephone Service" in some countries, the name has mostly been retired due to the proliferation of phones in homes and businesses. POTS typically represents a bidirectional analog telephone interface that was designed to carry the sound of the human voice. POTS lacks the mobility of cellular phones and the bandwidth of several competing products; however it is one of the most reliable systems available with an uptime close to or exceeding 99.999%. POTS is still often the telecom method of choice when high reliability is required and bandwidth is not. Typical applications include alarm systems and "out of band" command links for routers and other network devices.

PBX

A Private Branch Exchange (PBX) is an enterprise class phone system typically used in businesses or large organizations. A PBX often includes an internal switching network and a controller that is attached to telecommunications trunks. Many PBXs had default manufacturer configuration codes, ports, and control interfaces that could be exploited if the security professional did not reconfigure them prior to deployment. A PBX is often targeted by war dialers who can then use the PBX to route long distance calling or eavesdrop on the organization. Analog POTS PBXs have largely been replaced with VoIP based or VoIP enabled PBXs.

How Are Analog and Digital Phone Systems Different?

First, let's look at the basic differences between analog and digital telephone systems. Analog systems have supported businesses for decades. Built on standard copper wire and POTS (plain old telephone service) phones, they are reliable, boast good voice quality, and have the basic features you might find in a typical home phone such as hold, mute, redial, and speed dial. They may also be able to transfer calls between extensions. But their features end there. Because of their simplicity and limited potential for expansion, they are relatively inexpensive to purchase. However, analog systems can be expensive to support, configure, and upgrade because they use less-modular hardware. For example, changing the location of an extension requires rewiring a punchboard by a professional. Buying analog is cheaper in the short-term, but it will lock you into a closed system that requires adapters to integrate with common applications such as VoIP and customer relationship management (CRM) systems.

Digital telephone systems are more modern. Digital PBXs are designed with a proprietary bus structure for adding features and capabilities. Boards are added to the cabinets for analog, digital, or IP phones. Features such as music on hold, VoIP integration, and alarm systems can be supported with modular add-on boards. Today, most digital systems, even if they use proprietary hardware or protocol, offer an IP interface on the controller. The IP interface might allow unified messaging features such as voicemail delivery to email, fax delivery to email, voicemail transcription to SMS, click to dial, and a desktop client. These systems are considered "hybrid PBXs" because they use a combination of proprietary digital hardware and standards-based IP networking. A fully modern digital PBX is 100% IP and software based.

Because digital PBXs do not rely on simple copper wire circuits, you gain more flexibility for adds, moves, and changes. Often, those changes can be configured via point-and-click software. Voice clarity is the same or better than analog, and in addition to basic features such as extensions and transfers, digital PBXs offer advanced virtual auto attendants, voicemail, and call forwarding options. Digital PBX systems may also provide an interface to integrate with your call center and sales software as well.

Multimedia Collaboration

Peer-to-Peer Applications and Protocols

Peer-to-peer applications have gained popularity—or notoriety, depending on one's point of view—due to their controversial role in sharing of intellectual property, mainly multimedia files. For reasons of bandwidth consumption, unacceptable conduct, and legal implications, the auditing of peer-to-peer applications in a business environment is highly advisable.

Arguably, the first popular P2P application was Napster, whose demise was brought about by legal disputes that the company lost, based among other things on the fact that it was operating a set of servers through which intellectual property violations had been committed. Other more recent and popular P2P applications include Limewire, eMule, Kazaa, Shareaza, Morpheus, Bittorrent, MicroTorrent, and many others.

The security risks associated with P2P begin with applications for which they are generally intended and end with their adoption for propagation and management of massive botnets. Generally, P2P applications, while possessing many legitimate applications, are associated with piracy and abuse of copyright and other forms of intellectual property. Legal risks due to the nature of content that is often found in P2P networks can hit an organization even if it did not approve of the use of P2P applications.

P2P applications are often designed to open an uncontrolled channel through network boundaries (normally through tunneling). See *Figure 4.13*. They therefore provide a way for dangerous content, such as botnets, spyware applications, and viruses, to enter an otherwise protected network. Because P2P networks can be established and managed using a series of multiple, overlapping master and slave nodes, they can be very difficult to fully detect and shut down. If one master node is detected and shutdown, the "bot herder" who controls the P2P botnet can make one of the slave nodes a master and use that as a redundant staging point, allowing for botnet operations to continue unimpeded.

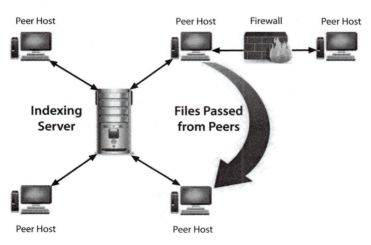

Figure 4.13 – **Peer-to-Peer (P2P) Architecture**

P2P usage, legitimate or otherwise, has become so popular that many ISP have taken the step of "throttling" traffic on their subscriber networks. Specifically, if P2P traffic is observed, usually based upon packet analysis or port usage, the bandwidth available to that IP address will be limited to whatever the ISP prescribes. Throttling is done in order to prevent a user address from consuming a disproportionate amount of bandwidth. What is "disproportionate" is a matter of opinion for the ISP, but a single user of P2P applications can easily consume 100 times the amount of bandwidth of a non-P2P user on any given day.

Remote Meeting Technology

Several technologies and services exist that allow organizations and individuals to meet "virtually." These applications are typically Web-based and either install extensions in the browser or client software on the host system. These technologies also typically allow "desktop sharing" as a feature. This feature not only allows the viewing of a user's desktop but also control of the system by a remote user.

Great care must be taken by the security professional when determining a provider for remote meeting technology and services (the provider's software and servers should be considered suspect until proven secure). Additionally, any options for encryption and authentication during the meeting should be considered by the participants as should the nature of the information being exchanged during the meeting itself.

Some organizations use dedicated equipment such as cameras, monitors, and meeting rooms to host and participate in remote meetings. These devices are often a combination of VoIP and in some cases POTS technology. They are also subject to the same risks including but not limited to:

- War dialing
- Vendor backdoors
- Default passwords
- Vulnerabilities in the underlying operating system or firmware

Instant Messaging

Instant messaging systems can generally be categorized in three classes: peer-to-peer networks, brokered communication, and server-oriented networks. See *Figure 4.14*. All these classes will support basic "chat" services on a one-to-one basis and frequently on a many-to-many basis. Most instant messaging applications do offer additional services beyond their text messaging capability, for instance, screen sharing, remote control, exchange of files, and voice and video conversation. Some applications even allow command scripting.

Instant messaging and chat is increasingly considered a significant business application used for office communications, customer support, and "presence" applications. Instant message capabilities will frequently be deployed with a bundle of other IP-based services such as VoIP and video conferencing support. It should be noted that many of the risks mentioned here apply also to online games, which today offer instant communication between participants. For instance, multiplayer role-playing games, such as multiuser domains (MUDs), rely heavily on instant messaging that is similar in nature to Internet Relay Chat (IRC), even though it is technically based on a variant of the TELNET protocol.

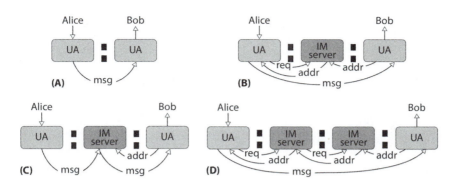

Figure 4.14 – **Setting up an instant-messaging connection:**

A) Directly
B) Through a central server
C) Centralized, including messaging
D) Through different servers

(From Wams, J.M.S and van Steen, M., Internet messaging, The Practical Handbook of Internet Computing, Singh, M.P., Ed., CRC Press, Boca Raton, FL, 2005. With permission.)

A large collection of real-time communication protocols and applications exists to support instant messaging. Originally, instant messaging required that client software be installed on the desktop, but current versions of instant messaging are based upon JavaScript and ActiveX—requiring only a modern Web browser for clients, which then connects to an instant messaging server through HTTP. In the next section, we will focus on applications based on open protocols.

Open Protocols, Applications, and Services

Extensible Messaging and Presence Protocol (XMPP) and Jabber

Jabber is an open instant messaging protocol for which a variety of open-source clients exist. A number of commercial services based on Jabber exist.

Ports	5222/TCP, 5222/UDP
Definition	RFC 3920
	RFC 3921

Table 4.12 – **XMPP Quick Reference**

Jabber has been formalized as an Internet standard under the name Extensible Messaging and Presence Protocol (XMPP), as defined in RFC 3920 and RFC 3921.[36]

Jabber is a server-based application. Its servers are designed to interact with other instant messaging applications. As with IRC, anybody can host a Jabber server. The Jabber server network can therefore not be considered trusted.

---

36 See the following: http://www.ietf.org/rfc/rfc3920
http://www.ietf.org/rfc/rfc3921

Although Jabber traffic can be encrypted via TLS, this does not prevent eavesdropping on the part of server operators. However, Jabber does provide an API to encrypt the actual payload data.[37]

Jabber itself offers a variety of authentication methods, including cleartext and challenge/response authentication. To implement interoperability with other instant messaging systems from the server, however, the server will have to cache the user's credentials for the target network, enabling a number of attacks, mainly on behalf of the server operator but also for anyone able to break into a server.

Internet Relay Chat (IRC)

Of the widely deployed chat systems on the Internet, IRC was arguably the first. IRC is still popular in academia but has lost its dominant position to commercial services; however, IRC channels and servers are still very much available and popular with people wishing to share information and files on an anonymous basis. IRC supported good anonymity because they typically operate through terminal or telnet connections, which leave no logs related to file transfers because the session is, in theory, just text on the screen.

Ports	194/TCP, 194/UDP
Definition	RFC 1459

Table 4.13 – **IRC Quick Reference Communication is organized in public discussion groups (channels) and private messaging between individual users.** [38]

IRC is a client/server-based network. IRC is unencrypted and therefore an easy target for sniffing attacks. The basic architecture of IRC, founded on trust among servers, enables special forms of denial-of-service attacks. For instance, a malicious user can hijack a channel while a server or group of servers has been disconnected from the rest (net split).

IRC is also a common platform for social engineering attacks, aimed at inexperienced or technically unskilled users.

Although original clients were UNIX based, IRC clients are now available for many platforms, including Windows, Apple Macintosh, and Linux. The security professionals will want to familiarize themselves with proprietary applications such as IBM Lotus Instant Messaging and Web Conferencing (Sametime), as well as commercial services such as:

- AOL Instant Messaging and ICQ, based on the proprietary Open System for Communication in Real-Time (OSCAR) protocol
- Google Talk, based on open Jabber/XMPP
- Microsoft MSN Messenger/Windows Messenger, based on the proprietary Mobile Status Notification Protocol (MSNP)
- Yahoo! Messenger, based on a proprietary protocol

All of these applications and services are server based. Interoperability between these services can be achieved through a server-based approach via XMPP or through multiple protocol clients. As usual, security of all of these applications rests in the strength of the protocol, quality

---

37   See the following for an overview of the Jabber development SDK and APIs: https://developer.cisco.com/site/collaboration/jabber/overview.gsp

38   http://www.ietf.org/rfc/rfc1439

of the implementation, trustworthiness of the operator, and behavior of the user. If these applications are to be used in a business context, stringent architectural and policy measures need to be put in place to prevent security gaps.

This is all the more important as many instant messaging applications by design support a variety of communication channels, offer the ability to tunnel through HTTP, and offer online awareness services that can be misused for technical or social attacks. While there are many business and personal benefits and efficiencies to be gained from adopting instant messaging/chat/IRC technologies, there are also many risks. These risks are faced both by private citizens and businesses trying to protect the integrity of their logical assets (networks, servers, workstations, data, and intellectual property):

Authenticity

User identification can be easily faked in instant messaging and chat applications by:

- Choosing a misleading identity upon registration or changing one's nickname while online.
- Manipulating the directory service if the application requires one.
- Manipulating either the attacker's or the target's client to send or display a wrong identity.

Although these risks are inherent to all kinds of communication networks (and are also common in email), they present an increased risk in real-time communication, where a user potentially has less time to analyze the communication presented to him or her. Similarly, the continued growth of social networking services and sites like Facebook, Vine, KiK, Twitter, LinkedIn, and others present ample opportunity to create false identity and try and dupe others for criminal purposes.

Confidentiality

Many chat systems transmit their information in cleartext. Similar to unencrypted email, information can be disclosed by sniffing on the network. A different form of confidentiality breach may occur based upon the fact that chat applications can generate an illusion and expectation of privacy, e.g., by establishing "closed rooms." Depending on the kind of infrastructure used, all messages can however be read in cleartext by privileged users such as the chat system's operators.

File transfer mechanisms embedded in instant messaging clients can be considered an uncontrolled channel for information— especially file—leakage. Due to the large number of other, similarly uncontrollable channels, the resulting additional risk should not be overestimated, while of course the overall risk may still be high.

Scripting

Certain chat clients, such as IRC clients, can execute scripts that are intended to simplify administration tasks, such as joining a chat channel. Because these scripts are executed with the user's privileges with relatively unsophisticated (no sandbox) or nonexistent protection, they are an attractive target for social engineering or other attacks. Once the victim has been tricked into executing commands, he can leave his computer wide open for other attacks.

Social Engineering

Related to spam and phishing email, in social engineering attackers can exploit human nature and goodwill to claim illicit legitimacy, for instance, by claiming to belong to a certain company or social group. Again, social networking applications and services provide many opportunities to masquerade as a legitimate member of a group for criminal and fraudulent purposes. As the social setting is informal and community oriented, there might even be social pressure to behave in an insecure manner, for instance, to demonstrate trust.

The lack of authenticity (and subsequently of non-repudiation) should be a concern, especially in business situations where instant messaging and chat systems can be used to give online support or enable other forms of customer interaction. Instant messaging is one of the primary avenues utilized by a person engaging in social engineering because it mixes the "live" nature of human communications with very little authentication and no tell-tale emotional indicators like body language or voice tonality.

Spam over Instant Messaging (SPIM)

With the proliferation of instant messaging clients and social networking sites, a particular form of SPIM through pop-up windows ran rampant for a while. The easiest countermeasure is to disable the service. A current scourge of the major social networking sites is SPIM and SPAM, which are propagated through the nominally internal messaging systems that are intended to mitigate Internet SPAM by keeping messaging services proprietary and internal to the service and its members. Unfortunately, as is always the case, con artists and criminals have learned to route around this defense by opening up thousands of bogus accounts within these social networking sites and bombarding members through the internal messaging systems directly.

Tunneling Firewalls and Other Restrictions

Similar to streaming audio and video applications, corporate firewalls were perceived as an obstacle in establishing direct contact with Internet peers. The easy, but arguably illegitimate, solution for developers was to enable tunneling through the protocol that would always be available, HTTP.

Depending on the client, it can even be possible to enable incoming connections by polling an external server. (This technique has been widely exploited in another type of application, a certain kind of remote-access software.) Control of HTTP tunneling can happen on the firewall or the proxy server. It should, however, be considered that in the case of peer-to-peer protocols, this would require a "deny by default" policy, and blocking instant messaging without providing a legitimate alternative is not likely to foster user acceptance and might give users incentive to utilize even more dangerous workarounds.

It should be noted that inbound file transfers can also result in circumvention of policy or restrictions in place, in particular for the spreading of viruses. An effective countermeasure can be found in on-access anti-virus scanning on the client, which should be enabled anyway.

Remote Access

VPN

Virtual Private Network (VPN)

A VPN (*Figure 4.15*) is an encrypted tunnel between two hosts that allows them to securely communicate over an untrusted network; e.g., the Internet. Remote users employ VPNs to access their organization's network, and depending on the VPN's implementation, they may have most of the same resources available to them as if they were physically at the office. As an alternative to expensive dedicated point-to-point connections, organizations use gateway-to-gateway VPNs to securely transmit information over the Internet between sites or even with business partners.

IPSec Authentication and Confidentiality for VPNs

IP Security (IPSec) is a suite of protocols for communicating securely with IP by providing mechanisms for authenticating and encryption. Implementation of IPSec is mandatory in IPv6, and many organizations are using it over IPv4. Further, IPSec can be implemented in two modes: one that is appropriate for end-to-end protection and one that safeguards traffic between networks.

Standard IPSec only authenticates hosts with each other. If an organization requires users to authenticate, they must employ a nonstandard proprietary IPSec implementation or use IPSec over L2TP (Layer 2 Tunneling Protocol). The latter approach uses L2TP to authenticate the users and encapsulate IPSec packets within an L2TP tunnel.

Because IPSec interprets the change of IP address within packet headers as an attack, NAT does not work well with IPSec. To resolve the incompatibility of the two protocols, NAT-Transversal (a.k.a. NAT-T) encapsulates IPSec within UDP port 4500 (see RFC 3948 for details).[39]

---

39   http://tools.ietf.org/html/rfc3948

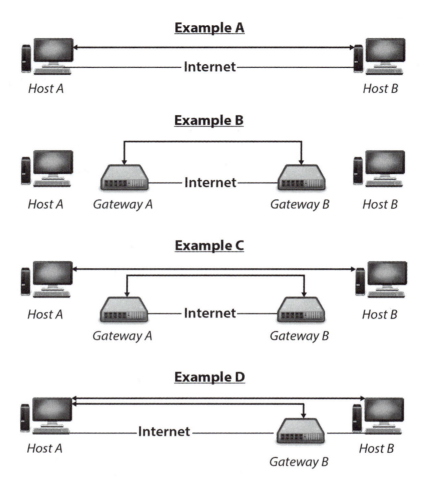

*Figure 4.15 – **VPN Types***

- **Example A:** *Two hosts establish secure peer communications over the Internet.*
- **Example B** *illustrates a typical gateway-to-gateway VPN with the VPN terminating at the gateways to provide connectivity for internal hosts.*
- **Example C** *combines Examples A and B to allow secure communications from host to host in an existing gateway-to-gateway VPN.*
- **Example D** *details the situation when a remote host connects to an ISP, receives an IP address, and then establishes a VPN with the destination network's gateway. A tunnel is established to the gateway, and then a tunnel- or transport- mode communication is established to the internal system. In this example, it is necessary for the remote system to apply the transport header prior to the tunnel header. Also, it will be necessary for the gateway to allow IPSec connectivity and key management protocols from the Internet to the internal system.*

(From Tiller, J.S., IPSec virtual private networks, Information Security Management Handbook, 6th edn., Tipton H.F., and Krause, M. Eds., Auerbach Publications, Boca Raton, FL, 2005. With permission.)

Authentication Header (AH)

The authentication header is used to prove the identity of the sender and ensure that the transmitted data has not been tampered with. Before each packet (headers + data) is transmitted, a hash value of the packet's contents (except for the fields that are expected to change when the packet is routed) based on a shared secret is inserted in the last field of the AH. The end points negotiate which hashing algorithm to use and the shared secret when they establish their security association. To help thwart replay attacks (when a legitimate session is retransmitted to gain unauthorized access), each packet that is transmitted during a security association has a sequence number, which is stored in the AH. In transport mode, the AH is shimmed between the packet's IP and TCP header. The AH helps ensure integrity, not confidentiality. Encryption is implemented through the use of encapsulating security payload (ESP).

Encapsulating Security Payload (ESP)

The encapsulating security payload encrypts IP packets and ensures their integrity. ESP contains four sections:

- ESP header: Contains information showing which security association to use and the packet sequence number. Like the AH, the ESP sequences every packet to thwart replay attacks.
- ESP payload: The payload contains the encrypted part of the packet. If the encryption algorithm requires an initialization vector (IV), it is included with the payload. The end points negotiate which encryption to use when the security association is established. Because packets must be encrypted with as little overhead as possible, ESP typically uses a symmetric encryption algorithm.
- ESP trailer: May include padding (filler bytes) if required by the encryption algorithm or to align fields.
- Authentication: If authentication is used, this field contains the integrity check value (hash) of the ESP packet. As with the AH, the authentication algorithm is negotiated when the end points establish their security association.

Security Associations

A security association (SA) defines the mechanisms that an end point will use to communicate with its partner. All SAs cover transmissions in one direction only. A second SA must be defined for two-way communication. Mechanisms that are defined in the SA include the encryption and authentication algorithms, and whether to use the AH or ESP protocol. Deferring the mechanisms to the SA, as opposed to specifying them in the protocol, allows the communicating partners to use the appropriate mechanisms based on situational risk.

Transport Mode and Tunnel Mode

End points communicate with IPSec using either transport or tunnel mode. In transport mode, the IP payload is protected. This mode is mostly used for end-to-end protection, for example, between client and server. In tunnel mode, the IP payload and its IP header are protected. The entire protected IP packet becomes a payload of a new IP packet and header. Tunnel mode is often used between networks, such as with firewall-to-firewall VPNs.

Internet Key Exchange (IKE)

Internet key exchange allows communicating partners to prove their identity to each other and establish a secure communication channel, and it is applied as an authentication component of IPSec. IKE uses two phases:

- **Phase 1** – In this phase, the partners authenticate with each other, using one of the following:
  - **Shared Secret** – A key that is exchanged by humans via telephone, fax, encrypted email, etc.
  - **Public Key Encryption** – Digital certificates are exchanged.
  - **Revised Mode of Public Key Encryption** – To reduce the overhead of public key encryption, a nonce (a Cryptographic function that refers to a number or bit string used only once, in security engineering) is encrypted with the communicating partner's public key, and the peer's identity is encrypted with symmetric encryption using the nonce as the key.

Next, IKE establishes a temporary security association and secure tunnel to protect the rest of the key exchange.

- **Phase 2** – The peers' security associations are established, using the secure tunnel and temporary SA created at the end of phase 1.

High Assurance Internet Protocol Encryptor (HAIPE)

Based on IPSec, HAIPE possesses additional restrictions and enhancements; for instance, the ability to encrypt multicast data using high-assurance hardware encryption, which requires that the same key be manually loaded on all communicating devices. HAIPE is an extension of IPSec that would be used for highly secure communications such as those employed by military applications.

Tunneling

Point-to-Point Tunneling Protocol (PPTP)

Point-to-Point Tunneling Protocol (PPTP) is a VPN protocol that runs over other protocols. PPTP relies on generic routing encapsulation (GRE) to build the tunnel between the end points. After the user authenticates, typically with Microsoft Challenge Handshake Authentication Protocol version 2 (MSCHAPv2), a Point-to-Point Protocol (PPP) session creates a tunnel using GRE. PPTP came under much fire in the 1990s. Cryptographers announced weaknesses in the protocol, including flaws with MSCHAPv1 (the authentication protocol) and the encryption implementation, and the use of user passwords as keys. Microsoft released PPTPv2, which addressed many of its predecessor's weaknesses, such as using an improved version of MSCHAP for authentication, but PPTPv2 is still vulnerable to offline password-guessing attacks.

A key weakness of PPTP is the fact that it derives its encryption key from the user's password. This violates the cryptographic principle of randomness and can provide a basis for attacks. Password-based VPN authentication in general violates the recommendation to use two-factor authentication for remote access. The security architect and practitioner both need to consider known weaknesses, such as the issues identified with PPTP, when planning for the deployment and use of remote access technologies.

Layer 2 Tunneling Protocol (L2TP)

Layer 2 Tunneling Protocol (L2TP) is a hybrid of Cisco's Layer 2 Forwarding (L2F) and Microsoft's PPTP. It allows callers over a serial line using PPP to connect over the Internet to a remote network. A dial-up user connects to his ISP's L2TP access concentrator (LAC) with a PPP connection. The LAC encapsulates the PPP packets into L2TP and forwards it to the remote network's layer 2 network server (LNS). At this point, the LNS authenticates the dial-up user. If authentication is successful, the dial-up user will have access to the remote network.

LAC and LNS may authenticate each other with a shared secret, but as RFC 2661 states, the authenticating is effective only while the tunnel between the LAC and LNS is being created.[40]

L2TP does not provide encryption and relies on other protocols, such as tunnel mode IPSec, for confidentiality.

Remote Authentication Dial-in User Service (RADIUS)

RADIUS is an authentication protocol used mainly in networked environments, such as ISPs, or for similar services requiring single sign-on for layer 3 network access, for scalable authentication combined with an acceptable degree of security. On top of this, RADIUS provides support for consumption measurement such as connection time. RADIUS authentication is based on provision of simple username/password credentials. These credentials are encrypted by the client using a shared secret with the RADIUS server.

Ports	1812/TCP, 1812/UDP
	1813/TCP, 1813/UDP
Definition	RFC 2865

Table 4.14 – **RADIUS Quick Reference** [41]

As the security architect considers whether to deploy RADIUS as part of a remote access architecture, he or she needs to consider the strengths and weaknesses of the system. An ISP, in particular, will want to balance the risk of unauthorized access (and theft of bandwidth) with the deployment cost of RADIUS. Fortunately, RADIUS is relatively easy to deploy and supported by a large number of devices in the market; its resulting cost reduction will offset the ISP's risk.

Conversely, RADIUS may not be sufficiently secure for higher security authentication and authorization requirements, such as access to a corporate network. In these cases, the added security offered by two-factor authentication in combination with RADIUS is clearly desirable.

---

40 http://tools.ietf.org/html/rfc2661

41 See the following for the complete set of RFCs pertaining to RADIUS: http://tools.ietf.org/html/rfc2865
http://tools.ietf.org/html/rfc3575
http://tools.ietf.org/html/rfc5080
http://tools.ietf.org/html/rfc6929

Overall, RADIUS has the following issues:

- RADIUS has become the victim of a number of cryptographic attacks and can be successfully attacked with a replay attack.
- RADIUS suffers from a lack of integrity protection.
- RADIUS transmits only specific fields using encryption.

Simple Network Management Protocol (SNMP)

SNMP is designed to manage network infrastructure.

Ports	161/TCP,161/UDP
	162/TCP,162/UDP
Definition	*RFC 1157*

Table 4.15 – **SNMP Quick Reference** [42]

SNMP architecture consists of a management server (called the manager in SNMP terminology) and a client, usually installed on network devices such as routers and switches called an agent. SNMP allows the manager to retrieve "get" values of variables from the agent, as well as "set" variables. Such variables could be routing tables or performance-monitoring information.

Although SNMP has proven to be remarkably robust and scalable, it does have a number of clear weaknesses. Some of them are by design; others are subject to configuration parameters.

Probably the most easily exploited SNMP vulnerability is a brute force attack on default or easily guessable SNMP passwords known as "community strings" often used to manage a remote device. Given the scale of SNMP v1 and v2 deployment, combined with a lack of clear direction from the security professional with regards to the risks associated with using SNMP without additional security enhancements to protect the community string, it is certainly a realistic scenario and a potentially severe but easily mitigated risk.

Until version 2, SNMP did not provide any degree of authentication or transmission security. Authentication consists of an identifier called a community string, by which a manager will identify itself against an agent (this string is configured into the agent), and a password sent with a command. As a result, passwords can be easily intercepted, which could then result in commands being sniffed and potentially faked.

---

42 See the following for the RFCs pertaining to SNMP: http://tools.ietf.org/html/rfc1157
  http://www.ietf.org/rfc/rfc3410
  http://www.ietf.org/rfc/rfc3411
  http://www.ietf.org/rfc/rfc3412
  http://www.ietf.org/rfc/rfc3413
  http://www.ietf.org/rfc/rfc3414
  http://www.ietf.org/rfc/rfc3415
  http://www.ietf.org/rfc/rfc3416
  http://www.ietf.org/rfc/rfc3417
  http://www.ietf.org/rfc/rfc3418
  http://www.ietf.org/rfc/rfc3584

Similar to the previous problem, SNMP version 2 did not support any form of encryption, so passwords (community strings) were passed as cleartext. SNMP version 3 addresses this particular weakness with encryption for passwords.[43]

Remote-Access Services

The services described under this section, TELNET, rlogin, and the X Window System (X11), while present in many UNIX operations and, when combined with NFS and NIS, provide the user with seamless remote working capabilities, do in fact form a risky combination if not configured and managed properly. Conceptually, because they are built on mutual trust, they can be misused to obtain access and to horizontally and vertically escalate privileges in an attack. Their authentication and transmission capabilities are insecure by design; they therefore have had to be retrofitted (as X11) or replaced altogether (TELNET and rlogin by SSH).

TCP/IP Terminal Emulation Protocol (TELNET)

TELNET is a command line protocol designed to give command line access to another host. Although implementations for Windows exist, TELNET's original domain was the UNIX server world, and in fact, a TELNET server is standard equipment for any UNIX server. (Whether it should be enabled is another question entirely, but in small LAN environments, TELNET is still widely used.)

- TELNET offers little security, and indeed, its use poses serious security risks in untrusted environments.
- TELNET is limited to username/password authentication.
- TELNET does not offer encryption.

Once an attacker has obtained even a normal user's credentials, he has an easy road toward privilege escalation because he can transfer data to and from a machine as well as execute commands. As the TELNET server is running under system privileges, it is an attractive target of attack in itself; exploits in TELNET servers pave the way to system privileges for an attacker.

Ports	23/TCP
Definition	RFC 854
	RFC 855

*Table 4.16 – **TELNET Quick Reference** [44]*

It is therefore recommended that security practitioners discontinue the use of TELNET over the Internet and on Internet facing machines. In fact, the standard hardening procedure for any Internet facing server should include disabling its TELNET service, which under UNIX systems would normally run under the name of telnetd, and using SSHv2 for remote administration and management where required.

---

43   See the following for a good overall reference for SNMP across all versions: http://www.ibr.cs.tu-bs.de/projects/snmpv3/

44   http://www.ietf.org/rfc/rfc854
     http://www.ietf.org/rfc/rfc855

Remote Log-in (rlogin), Remote Shell (rsh), Remote Copy (rcp)

In its most generic form, rlogin is a protocol used for granting remote access to a machine, normally a UNIX server. Similarly, rsh grants direct remote command execution, while rcp copies data from or to a remote machine.

Ports	*513/TCP*
Definition	*RFC 1258*

Table 4.17 – **RLogin Quick Reference** [45]

If an rlogin daemon (rlogind) is running on a machine, rlogin access can be granted in two ways, through the use of a central configuration file or through a user configuration. By the latter, a user may grant access that was not permitted by the system administrator. The same mechanism applies to rsh and rcp, although they are relying on a different daemon (rshd).

Authentication can be considered host/IP address based. Although rlogin grants access based on user ID, it is not verified; i.e., the ID a remote client claims to possess is taken for granted if the request comes from a trusted host. The rlogin protocol transmits data without encryption and is hence subject to eavesdropping and interception.

The rlogin protocol is of limited value. Its main benefit can be considered its main drawback: remote access without supplying a password. It should only be used in trusted networks, if at all. A more secure replacement is available in the form of SSHv2 for rlogin, rsh, and rcp.

Screen Scraper

A screen scraper is a program that can extract data from output on a display intended for a human. Screen scrapers are used in a legitimate fashion when older technologies are unable to interface with modern ones. In a nefarious sense, this technology can also be used to capture images from a user's computer, such as PIN pad sequences at a banking website, when implemented by a virus or malware.

Virtual Applications and Desktops

Virtual Network Terminal Services

Virtual terminal service is a tool frequently used for remote access to server resources. Virtual terminal services allow the desktop environment for a server to be exported to a remote workstation. This allows users at the remote workstation to execute desktop commands as though they were sitting at the server terminal interface in person. See *Table 4.18.*

Ports	*80/TCP*
	443/UDP
Definition	*Vendor Specific*

Table 4.18 – **VNTS Quick Reference**

---

45   http://www.ietf.org/rfc/rfc1258

The advantage of terminal services such as those provided by Citrix, Microsoft, or public domain VNC services is that they allow for complex administrative commands to be executed using the native interface of the server rather than a command-line interface, which might be available through SSHv2 or telnet. Terminal services also allow for the authentication and authorization services integrated into the server to be leveraged for remote users, in addition to all the logging and auditing features of the server as well.

Terminal services allow a remote user to manage a host without exposing that host to any potential malicious code that might be present on the remote machine; this is because only the terminal interface is exported; file systems are shared or joined between the system. While the various virtual terminal services run on different ports, most will also be available for tunneling through HTTP-SSL for security and to allow them to pass through zoning firewalls with a minimum of fuss and administration.

Like all sophisticated pieces of software, terminal services are subject to frequent vulnerability alerts from the vendors and must be patched as recommended. Unfortunately, patching virtual terminal services can be tricky because of interdependencies with native Web servers, which in turn will have interdependencies with the applications resident on the server.

Telecommuting

Especially in tech companies, having remote and virtual employees is not only a way to get things done round the clock, without commuting, and with hard-to-find skill sets, but it is also a way to meet the needs of employees who do not want to or cannot live near a corporate headquarters or main office hub. Red Hat is one example of a highly distributed, highly effective company; in addition to its corporate hub in Raleigh, NC and development center in Westford, MA, it employs many highly talented virtual employees. Red Hat's culture is friendly to remote workers. With a mobile mindset comes several unique challenges that the security professional must address. Common issues such as visitor control, physical security, and network control are almost impossible to address with teleworkers. Strong VPN connections between the teleworker and the organization need to be established, and full device encryption should be the norm for protecting sensitive information. If the user works in public places or a home office, the following should also be considered:

- Is the user trained to use secure connectivity software and methods such as a VPN?
- Does the user know which information is sensitive or valuable and why someone might wish to steal or modify it?
- Is the user's physical location appropriately secure for the type of work and type of information he or she is using?
- Who else has access to the area? While a child may seem trusted, the child's friends may not be.

Data Communications

A network's physical topology relates to how network components are connected with each other. The appropriate topology for a network can be determined by assessing the available protocols, how end nodes will be used, available equipment, financial constraints, and the importance of fault tolerance.

Analog Communication

Analog signals use electronic properties, such as frequency and amplitude, to represent information. Analog recordings are a classic example: A person speaks into a microphone, which converts the vibration from acoustical energy to an electrical equivalent. The louder the person speaks, the greater the electrical signal's amplitude. Likewise, the higher the pitch of the person's voice, the higher the frequency of the electrical signal.

Analog signals are transmitted on wires, such as twisted pair, or with a wireless device. In radio communication, for example, the electrical representation of the person's voice would be modulated with a carrier signal and broadcasted.

Digital Communication

Whereas analog communication uses complex waveforms to represent information, digital communication uses two electronic states (on and off). By convention, 1 is assigned to the on state and 0 to off. Electrical signals that consist of these two states can be transmitted over a cable, converted to light and transmitted over fiber optics, and broadcasted with a wireless device. In all of the above media, the signal would be a series of one of two states: on and off.

It is easier to ensure the integrity of digital communication because the two states of the signal are sufficiently distinct. When a device receives a digital transmission, it can determine which digits are 0s and which are 1s (if it cannot, then the device knows the signal is erroneous or corrupted). On the other hand, analog complex waveforms make ensuring integrity very difficult.

Network Topologies

Bus

A bus topology is a LAN with a central cable (bus) to which all nodes (devices) connect. All nodes transmit directly on the central bus. Each node listens to all of the traffic on the bus and processes only the traffic that is destined for it. This topology relies on the data-link layer to determine when a node can transmit a frame on the bus without colliding with another frame on the bus. A LAN with a bus topology is shown in *Figure 4.16*.

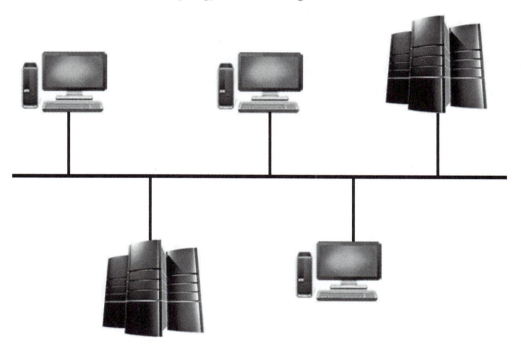

Figure 4.16 – **Network with a Bus topology**

Advantages of buses include:

■   Adding a node to the bus is easy.

■   A node failure will not likely affect the rest of the network.

Disadvantages of buses include:

■   Because there is only one central bus, a bus failure will leave the entire network inoperable.

Tree

A tree topology is similar to a bus. Instead of all of the nodes connecting to a central bus, the devices connect to a branching cable. Like a bus, every node receives all of the transmitted traffic and processes only the traffic that is destined for it. Furthermore, the data-link layer must transmit a frame only when there is not a frame on the wire. A network with a tree topology is shown in *Figure 4.17*.

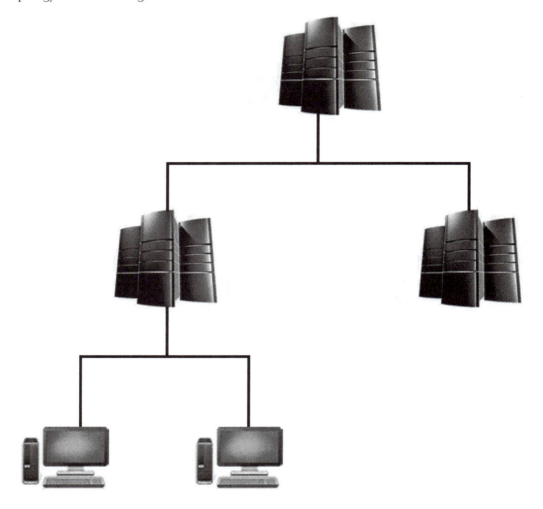

Figure 4.17 – **Network with a Tree topology**

Advantages of a tree include:
- Adding a node to the tree is easy.
- A node failure will not likely affect the rest of the network.
- Disadvantages of a tree include:
- A cable failure could leave the entire network inoperable.

Ring

A ring is a closed-loop topology. Data is transmitted in one direction only, based on the direction that the ring was initialed to transmit in, either clockwise or counter-clockwise. Each device receives data from its upstream neighbor only and transmits data to its downstream neighbor only. Typically, rings use coaxial cables or fiber optics. A Token Ring network is shown in *Figure 4.18*.

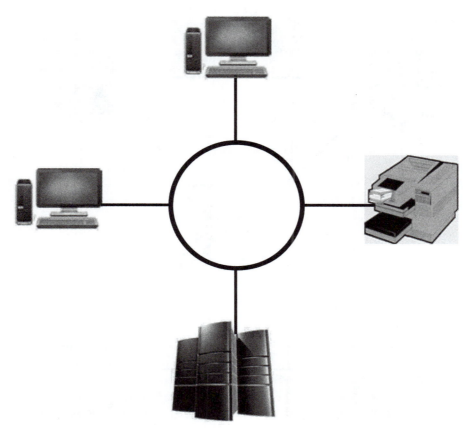

Figure 4.18 – **Network with a Ring topology**

Advantages of rings include:

- Because rings use tokens, one can predict the maximum time that a node must wait before it can transmit (i.e., the network is deterministic).
- Rings can be used as a LAN or network backbone.
- Disadvantages of rings include:
- Simple rings have a single point of failure. If one node fails, the entire ring fails. Some rings, such as fiber distributed data interface (FDDI), use dual rings for failover.

Mesh

In a mesh network, all nodes are connected to every other node on the network. A full mesh network is usually too expensive because it requires many connections. As an alternative, a partial mesh can be employed in which only selected nodes (typically the most critical) are connected in a full mesh, and the remaining nodes are connected to a few devices. As an example, core switches, firewalls, and routers and their hot standbys are often all connected to ensure as much availability as possible. A full mesh network is shown in *Figure 4.19*.

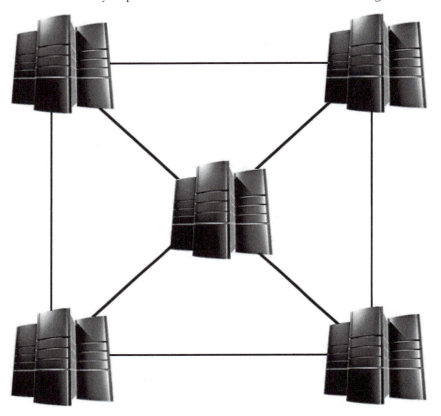

Figure 4.19 – **Network with a Mesh topology**

Advantages of a mesh include:
- Mesh networks provide a high level of redundancy.

Disadvantages of a mesh include:
- Mesh networks are very expensive because of the enormous amount of cables that are required.

Star

All nodes in a star network are connected to a central device, such as a hub, switch, or router. Modern LANs usually employ a star typology. A star network is shown in *Figure 4.20*.

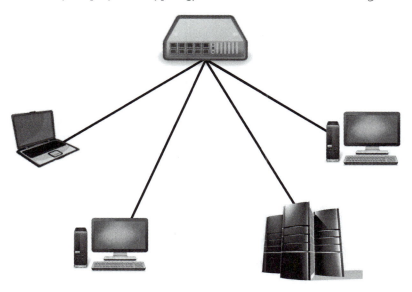

Figure 4.20 – **Network with a Star topology**

Advantages of a star include:

- Star networks require fewer cables than full or partial mesh.
- Star networks are easy to deploy, and nodes can be easily added or removed.

Disadvantages of a star include:

- The central connection device is a single point of failure. If it is not functional, all of the connected nodes lose network connectivity.

There are many points that the security architect and practitioner must consider about transmitting information from sender to receiver. For example, will the information be expressed as an analog or digital wave? How many recipients will there be? If the transmission media will be shared with others, how can one ensure that the signals will not interfere with each other?

Unicast, Multicast, and Broadcast Transmissions

Most communication, especially that directly initiated by a user, is from one host to another. For example, when a person uses a browser to send a request to a Web server, he or she sends a packet to the Web server. A transmission with one receiving host is called a unicast transmission.

A host can send a broadcast to everyone on its network or sub-network. Depending on the network topology, the broadcast could have anywhere from one to tens of thousands of recipients. Like a person standing on a soapbox, this is a noisy method of communication. Typically, only one or two destination hosts are interested in the broadcast; the other recipients waste resources to process the transmission. However, there are productive uses for broadcasts. Consider a router that knows a device's IP address but must determine the device's MAC address. The router will broadcast an Address Resolution Protocol (ARP) request asking for the device's MAC address.

Notice how one broadcast could result in hundreds or even thousands of packets on the network. Intruders often leverage this fact in denial-of-service attacks.

Public and private networks are used more often than ever for streaming transmissions, such as movies, videoconferences, and music. Given the intense bandwidth needed to transmit these streams, and the sender and recipients are not necessarily on the same network, how does one transmit the stream to only the interested hosts? The sender could send a copy of the stream via unicast to each receiver. Unless there is a very small audience, unicast delivery is not practical because the multiple simultaneous copies of the large stream on the network at the same time could cause congestion. Delivery with broadcasts is another possibility, but every host would receive the transmission, even if they were not interested in the stream.

Multicasting was designed to deliver a stream to only interested hosts. Radio broadcasting is a typical analogy for multicasting. To select a specific radio show, you tune a radio to the broadcasting station. Likewise, to receive a desired multicast, you join the corresponding multicast group.

Multicast agents are used to route multicast traffic over networks and administer multicast groups. Each network and sub-network that supports multicasting must have at least one multicast agent. Hosts use Internet Group Management Protocol (IGMP) to tell a local multicast agent that it wants to join a specific multicast group. Multicast agents also route multicasts to local hosts that are members of the multicast's group and relay multicasts to neighboring agents.

When a host wants to leave a multicast group, it sends an IGMP message to a local multicast agent. Multicasts do not use reliable sessions. Therefore, the multicasts are transmitted as best effort, with no guarantee that datagrams are received. As an example, consider a server multicasting a videoconference to desktops that are members of the same multicast group as the server (*Figure 4.21*). The server transmits to a local multicast agent. Next, the multicast agent relays the stream to other agents. All of the multicast agents transmit the stream to local hosts that are members of the same multicast group as the server.

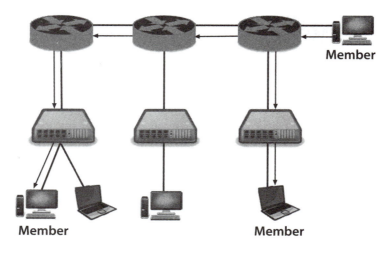

Member

Member   Member

Figure 4.21 – **Multicast transmission**

Circuit-Switched Networks

Circuit-switched networks establish a dedicated circuit between end points. These circuits consist of dedicated switch connections. Neither end point starts communicating until the circuit is completely established. The end points have exclusive use of the circuit and its bandwidth. Carriers base the cost of using a circuit-switched network on the duration of the connection, which makes this type of network only cost-effective for a steady communication stream between the end points. Examples of circuit-switched networks are the plain old telephone service (POTS), Integrated Services Digital Network (ISDN), and Point-to-Point Protocol (PPP).

Packet-Switched Networks

Packet-switched networks do not use a dedicated connection between end points. Instead, data is divided into packets and transmitted on a shared network. Each packet contains meta-information so that it can be independently routed on the network. Networking devices will attempt to find the best path for each packet to its destination. Because network conditions could change while the partners are communicating, packets could take different paths as they transverse the network and arrive in any order. It is the responsibility of the destination end point to ensure that the received packets are in the correct order before sending them up the stack.

Switched Virtual Circuits (SVCs) and Permanent Virtual Circuits (PVCs)

Virtual circuits provide a connection between end points over high-bandwidth, multiuser cable or fiber that behaves as if the circuit were a dedicated physical circuit. There are two types of virtual circuits, based on when the routes in the circuit are established. In a permanent virtual circuit, the carrier configures the circuit's routes when the circuit is purchased. Unless the carrier changes the routes to tune the network, respond to an outage, etc., the routes do not change. On the other hand, the routes of a switched virtual circuit are configured dynamically by the routers each time the circuit is used.

Carrier Sense Multiple Access (CSMA)

As the name implies, Carrier Sense Multiple Access (CSMA) is an access protocol that uses the absence/presence of a signal on the medium that it wants to transmit on as permission to speak. Only one device may transmit at a time; otherwise, the transmitted frames will be unreadable. Because there is not an inherent mechanism that determines which device may transmit, all of the devices must compete for available bandwidth. For this reason, CSMA is referred to as a contention-based protocol. Also, because it is impossible to predict when a device may transmit, CSMA is also nondeterministic.

There are two variations of CSMA based on how collisions are handled. LANs using Carrier Sense Multiple Access with Collision Avoidance (CSMA/CA) require devices to announce their intention to transmit by broadcasting a jamming signal. When devices detect the jamming signal, they know not to transmit; otherwise, there will be a collision. After sending the jamming signal, the device waits to ensure that all devices have received that signal, and then it broadcasts the frames on the media. CSMA/CA is used in the IEEE 802.11 wireless standard.

4

Communications &
Network Security

Devices on a LAN using Carrier Sense Multiple Access with Collision Detection (CSMA/CD) listen for a carrier before transmitting data. If another transmission is not detected, the data will be transmitted. It is possible that a station will transmit before another station's transmission had enough time to propagate. If this happens, two frames will be transmitted simultaneously, and a collision will occur. Instead of all stations simply retransmitting their data, which will likely cause more collisions, each station will wait a randomly generated interval before retransmitting. CSMA/CD is part of the IEEE 802.3 standard.[46]

Polling

A network that employs polling avoids contention by allowing a device (a slave) to transmit on the network only when it is asked to by a master device. Polling is used mostly in mainframe protocols, such as Synchronous Data Link. The point coordination function, an optional function of the IEEE standard, uses polling as well.

Token Passing

Token passing takes a more orderly approach to media access. With this access method, only one device may transmit on the LAN at a time, thus avoiding retransmissions.

A special frame, known as a token, circulates through the ring. When a device wishes to transmit on the network, it must possess the token. The device replaces the token with a frame containing the message to be transmitted and sends the frame to its neighbor. When each device receives the frame, it relays it to its neighbor if it is not the recipient. The process continues until the recipient possesses the frame. That device will copy the message, modify the frame to signify that the message was received, and transmit the frame on the network.

When the modified frame makes a trip back to the sending device, the sending device knows that the message was received. Token passing is used in Token Ring and FDDI networks. An example of a LAN using token passing can be seen in *Figure 4.22*.

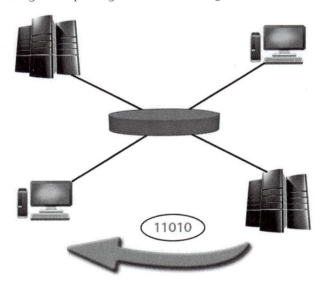

Figure 4.22 – **LAN token passing**

---

46   See the following to download the latest version for the IEEE 802.3 Standard: http://standards.ieee.org/about/get/802/802.3.html

Ethernet (IEEE 802.3)

Ethernet, which is defined in IEEE 802.3, played a major role in the rapid proliferation of LANs in the 1980s. The architecture was flexible and relatively inexpensive, and it was easy to add and remove devices from the LAN. Even today, for the same reasons, Ethernet is the most popular LAN architecture. The physical topologies that are supported by Ethernet are bus, star, and point to point, but the logical topology is the bus.

With the exception of full-duplex Ethernet (which does not have the issues of collisions), the architecture uses CSMA/CD. This protocol allows devices to transmit data with a minimum of overhead (compared to Token Ring), resulting in an efficient use of bandwidth. However, because devices must retransmit when more than one device attempts to send data on the medium, too many retransmissions due to collisions can cause serious throughput degradation.

The Ethernet standard supports coaxial cable, unshielded twisted pair, and fiber optics as transmission media.

Ethernet was originally rated at 10 Mbps, but like 10-megabyte disk drives, users quickly figured out how to use and exceed its capacity and needed faster LANs. To meet the growing demand for more bandwidth, 100 Base-TX (100 Mbps over twisted pair) and 100 Base-FX (100 Mbps over multimode fiber optics) were defined. When the demand grew for even more bandwidth over unshielded twisted pair, 1000 Base-T was defined, and 1000 Base-SX and 1000 Base-LX were defined for fiber optics. These standards support 1,000 Mbps.

Token Ring (IEEE 802.5):

Originally designed by IBM, Token Ring was adapted with some modification by the IEEE as IEEE 802.5. Despite the architecture's name, Token Ring uses a physical star topology. The logical topology, however, is a ring. Each device receives data from its upstream neighbor and transmits to its downstream neighbor. Token Ring uses ring passing to mediate which device may transmit. As mentioned in the section on token passing, a special frame, called a token, is passed on the LAN. To transmit, a device must possess the token.

To transmit on the LAN, the device appends data to the token and sends it to its next downstream neighbor. Devices retransmit frames whenever the token is not the intended recipient. When the destination device receives the frame, it copies the data, marks the frame as read, and sends it to its downstream neighbor. When the packet returns to the source device, it confirms that the packet has been read. It then removes the frame from the ring. Token ring is now considered a "legacy" technology that is rarely seen and on those rare occasions, it is only because there has been no reason for an organization to upgrade away from it. Token ring has almost entirely been replaced with Ethernet technology.

Fiber Distributed Data Interface (FDDI)

FDDI is a token-passing architecture that uses two rings. Because FDDI employs fiber optics, FDDI was designed to be a 100-Mbps network backbone. Only one ring (the primary) is used; the other one (secondary) is used as a backup. Information in the rings flows in opposite directions from each other. Hence, the rings are referred to as counter rotating. FDDI is also considered a legacy technology and has been supplanted by more modern transport technologies; initially Asynchronous Transfer Mode (ATM) but more recently Multiprotocol Label Switching (MPLS).

Multiprotocol Label Switching (MPLS) ⁴⁷

MPLS (*Figure 4.23*) has attained a significant amount of popularity at the core of the carrier networks as of late because it manages to couple the determinism, speed, and QoS controls of established switched technologies like ATM and Frame Relay, with the flexibility and robustness of the Internet Protocol world. (MPLS is developed and propagated through the Internet Engineering Task Force (IETF)) Additionally, the once faster and higher bandwidth ATM switches are being outperformed by Internet backbone routers. Equally important, MPLS offers simpler mechanisms for packet-oriented traffic engineering and multi-service functionality with the added benefit of greater scalability.

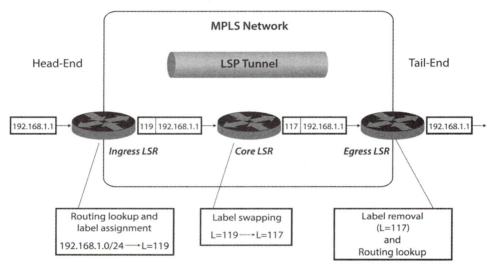

Figure 4.23 – **MPLS forwarding operation**

(From Tan, N.-K., **MPLS for Metropolitan Area Networks**, *Auerbach Publications, New York, 2004. With permission.)*

MPLS is often referred to as "IP VPN" because of the ability to couple highly deterministic routing with IP services. In effect, this creates a VPN-type service that makes it logically impossible for data from one network to be mixed or routed over to another network without compromising the MPLS routing device itself. MPLS does not include encryption services; therefore, any MPLS service called "IP VPN" does not in fact contain any cryptographic services. The traffic on these links would be visible to the service providers. The following guidelines should be considered by the network and security architects during the negotiation of MPLS bandwidth and associated service level agreements (SLAs) to ensure that services live up to the assurance requirements for the assets relying upon the network:

- **Site Availability** – Make certain MPLS is available for all desired locations; i.e., all the planned remote connections (offices) have MPLS service available in that area.
- **End-to-End Network Availability** – Inquire about peering relationships for MPLS for network requirements that cross Tier 1 carrier boundaries.
- **Provisioning** – How fast can new links in new sites be provisioned?

---

47 See the following for the IETF working Group on MPLS's homepage: http://datatracker.ietf.org/wg/ mpls/documents/

Local Area Network (LAN)

LANs service a relatively small area, such as a home, office building, or office campus. In general, LANs service the computing needs of their local users. LANs consist of most modern computing devices, such as workstations, servers, and peripherals connected in a star topology or internetworked stars. Ethernet is the most popular LAN architecture because it is inexpensive and very flexible. Most LANs have connectivity to other networks, such as dial-up or dedicated lines to the Internet, access to other LANs via WANs, and so on.

TLS/SSL

Secure Shell (SSH)

Secure Shell's (SSH) services include remote log-on, file transfer, and command execution. It also supports port forwarding, which redirects other protocols through an encrypted SSH tunnel. Many users protect less secure traffic of protocols, such as X Windows and VNC (virtual network computing), by forwarding them through an SSH tunnel. The SSH tunnel protects the integrity of communication, preventing session hijacking and other man-in-the-middle attacks.

There are two incompatible versions of the protocol, SSH-1 and SSH-2, though many servers support both. SSH-2 has improved integrity checks (SSH-1 is vulnerable to an insertion attack due to weak CRC-32 integrity checking) and supports local extensions and additional types of digital certificates such as Open PGP. SSH was originally designed for UNIX, but there are now implementations for other operating systems, including Windows, Macintosh, and OpenVMS.

SOCKS

SOCKS is a popular circuit proxy server with several commercial and freeware implementations. The heart of SOCKSv5 (the current version) is RFC 1928, which does not require that developers include encryption of traffic in their implementations. Users employ the SOCKS client to access a remote server. The client initiates a connection to the SOCKS proxy server, which accesses the remote server on behalf of the user. If the implementation supports encryption, then the server can act as a VPN, protecting the confidentiality of the traffic between the SOCKS and remote servers. Because SOCKS is concerned with maintaining a circuit, it can be used with almost any application.

A key advantage of SOCKS and SSL VPNs is the possibility to use proxy servers. This is a feature most other VPNs are lacking. A SOCKS server may require that a user authenticates before providing services.

SSL/TLS VPNs

SSL 3.0 (Secure Socket Layer) and TLS 1.2 (Transport Layer Security) are essentially fully compatible, with SSL being a session encryption tool originally developed by Netscape and TLS 1.2 being the open standard IETF version of SSL 3.0.[48]

SSL VPNs are another approach to remote access. Instead of building a VPN around the IPSec and the network layer, SSL VPNs leverage SSL/TLS to create a tunnel back to the home office. Remote users employ a Web browser to access applications that are in the organization's network. Even though users employ a Web browser, SSL VPNs are not restricted to applications that use HTTP. With the aid of plug-ins, such as Java, users can have access to back-end databases, and other non-Web-based applications.

SSL VPNs have several advantages over IPSec. They are easier to deploy on client workstations than IPSec because they require a Web browser only, and almost all networks permit outgoing HTTP. SSL VPNs can be operated through a proxy server. In addition, applications can restrict users' access based on criteria, such as the network that the user is on, which is useful for building extranets with several organizations.

IPSec VPNs, on the other hand, grant access directly to a network. A user is usually given access to applications and devices as if he or she were located at the office. Of course, this is a double-edged sword. Just as an authorized user has access to many devices on the internal network, so will an intruder who can steal IPSec VPN access. Currently, SSL VPNs do not support network-to-network tunnels. A significant disadvantage of IPSec VPNs is that a VPN client must be installed and updated on every workstation, while an SSL VPN can be established using just about any modern Web browser.

Virtual Local Area Networks (VLANs)

Virtual local area networks (VLANs) allow network administrators to use switches to create software-based LAN segments that can be defined based on factors other than physical location. Devices that share a VLAN communicate through switches, without being routed to other sub-

---

48   The 1996 draft of SSL 3.0 was published by IETF as a historical document in RFC 6101. See the following: http://tools.ietf.org/html/rfc6101
TLS 1.2 was defined in RFC 5246 in August 2008. It is based on the earlier TLS 1.1 specification. Major differences include:
  - The MD5-SHA-1 combination in the pseudorandom function (PRF) was replaced with SHA-256, with an option to use cipher suite specified PRFs.
  - The MD5-SHA-1 combination in the finished message hash was replaced with SHA-256, with an option to use cipher suite specific hash algorithms. However the size of the hash in the finished message is still truncated to 96-bits.
  - The MD5-SHA-1 combination in the digitally signed element was replaced with a single hash negotiated during handshake, defaults to SHA-1.
  - Enhancement in the client's and server's ability to specify which hash and signature algorithms they will accept.
  - Expansion of support for authenticated encryption ciphers, used mainly for Galois/Counter Mode (GCM) and CCM mode of Advanced Encryption Standard encryption.
  - TLS Extensions definition and Advanced Encryption Standard cipher suites were added.

All TLS versions were further refined in RFC 6176 in March 2011 removing their backward compatibility with SSL such that TLS sessions will never negotiate the use of Secure Sockets Layer (SSL) version 2.0.
See the following: http://tools.ietf.org/html/rfc5246
http://tools.ietf.org/html/rfc6176

networks, which reduces overhead due to router latency (as routers become faster, this is less of an advantage). Furthermore, broadcasts are not forwarded outside of a VLAN, which reduces congestion due to broadcasts.

Because VLANs are not restricted to the physical location of devices, they help make networks easier to manage. When a user or group of users changes their physical location, network administrators can simply change the membership of ports within a VLAN. Likewise, when additional devices must communicate with members of a VLAN, it is easy to add new ports to a VLAN. VLANs can be configured based on switch port, IP subnet, MAC address, and protocols.

It is important to remember that VLANs do not guarantee a network's security. At first glance, it may seem that traffic cannot be intercepted because communication within a VLAN is restricted to member devices. However, there are attacks that allow a malicious user to see traffic from other VLANs (so-called VLAN hopping). Therefore, a VLAN can be created so that engineers can efficiently share confidential documents, but the VLAN does not significantly protect the documents from unauthorized access. The following lists the most common attacks that could be launched against VLANs at the Data Link layer:

- ***MAC Flooding Attack*** – This is not properly a network "attack" but more a limitation of the way all switches and bridges work. They possess a finite hardware learning table to store the source addresses of all received packets. When this table becomes full, the traffic that is directed to addresses that cannot be learned anymore will be permanently flooded. Packet flooding however is constrained within the VLAN of origin, and therefore no VLAN hopping is permitted. This behavior can be exploited by a malicious user that wants to turn the switch he or she is connected to into a dumb pseudo-hub and sniff all the flooded traffic. This weakness can then be exploited to perform an actual attack, like the ARP poisoning attack. In particular, Port Security, 802.1x, and Dynamic VLANs are three features that can be used to constrain the connectivity of a device based on its user's login ID and based on the device's own MAC layer identification. With Port Security, for instance, preventing any MAC flooding attack becomes as simple as limiting the number of MAC addresses that can be used by a single port: The identification of the traffic of a device is thereby directly tied to its port of origin.

- ***802.1Q and Inter-Switch Link Protocol (ISL) Tagging Attack*** – Tagging attacks are malicious schemes that allow a user on a VLAN to get unauthorized access to another VLAN. For example, if a Cisco switch port were configured as Dynamic Trunking Protocol (DTP) auto and were to receive a fake DTP packet, it might become a trunk port and it might start accepting traffic destined for any VLAN. Therefore, a malicious user could start communicating with other VLANs through that compromised port. Sometimes, even when simply receiving regular packets, a switch port may behave like a full-fledged trunk port (for example, accept packets for VLANs different from the native), even if it is not supposed to. This is commonly referred to as "VLAN leaking." While the first attack can be prevented very easily by setting DTP to off on all non-trusted ports, the second attack can usually be addressed by following simple configuration guidelines or with software upgrades.

- ***Double-Encapsulated 802.1Q/Nested VLAN Attack*** – While internal to a switch, VLAN numbers and identification are carried in a special extended format that allows the forwarding path to maintain VLAN isolation from end to end without any loss of information. Instead, outside of a switch, the tagging rules are dictated by standards such as Cisco's ISL or 802.1Q. ISL is a Cisco proprietary technology and is in a sense a compact form of the extended packet header used inside the device. Because every packet always gets a tag, there is no risk of identity loss and therefore of security weaknesses. On the other hand, the IEEE committee that defined 802.1Q decided that because of backward compatibility it was desirable to support the so-called native VLAN, that is to say, a VLAN that is not associated explicitly to any tag on an 802.1Q link. This VLAN is implicitly used for all the untagged traffic received on an 802.1Q capable port. This capability is desirable because it allows 802.1Q capable ports to talk to old 802.3 ports directly by sending and receiving untagged traffic. However, in all other cases, it may be very detrimental because packets associated with the native VLAN lose their tags, for example, their identity enforcement as well as their Class of Service (802.1p bits) when transmitted over an 802.1Q link. For these sole reasons—loss of means of identification and loss of classification—the use of the native VLAN should be avoided. When double-encapsulated 802.1Q packets are injected into the network from a device whose VLAN happens to be the native VLAN of a trunk, the VLAN identification of those packets cannot be preserved from end to end since the 802.1Q trunk would always modify the packets by stripping their outer tag. After the external tag is removed, the internal tag permanently becomes the packet's only VLAN identifier. Therefore, by double-encapsulating packets with two different tags, traffic can be made to hop across VLANs. The idea is that if an attacker is connected to an access port that is in the 802.1q native VLAN (1, by default), he can cause traffic to hop VLANs by injecting double-tagged packets. The theory is that the attacker can inject double-tagged packets. The switch will strip off only the first tag and will fail to "notice" the second tag. When the packet is transmitted to another switch over an 802.1q trunk, no VLAN tag is applied because the packet belongs to a VLAN that is the native VLAN for the trunk (because the access port on which the packet was received is a member of the native VLAN). The packet reaches the other switch, which sees the remaining VLAN tag (i.e., the second tag that the attacker applied), and will forward the packet on the VLAN specified in that tag. The attacker has successfully caused a packet to hop into a different VLAN. The trick is that the "outer" tag that the attacker applies must identify the packet as belonging to the attacker's VLAN, the 802.1q native VLAN to be precise. In that case, the switch will accept the packet, even though it is arriving on an access port. The first tag is stripped off, but the second tag is unaffected. When the packet is transmitted on the 802.1q trunk, no tag is applied because the packet belongs to the native VLAN. This means that when that packet reaches another switch, the second tag applied by the attacker is still visible, and this causes the second switch to place the packet in the wrong VLAN. This scenario is to be considered a misconfiguration, since the 802.1Q standard does not necessarily force the users to use the native VLAN in these cases. As a matter of fact, the proper configuration that should always be used is to clear the native VLAN from all 802.1Q trunks. In cases where the native VLAN cannot be cleared, then always pick an unused VLAN as the native VLAN of all the trunks; do not allow use of this VLAN for any other purpose. Also, make sure that the commands "switchport mode access" and "switchport nonegotiate" are applied to all user-facing switch interfaces.

- **ARP Attacks** – In L2 devices that implement VLANs independently of MAC addresses, changing a device's identity in an ARP packet does not make it possible to affect the way it communicates with other devices across VLANs. As a matter of fact, any VLAN hopping attempts would be thwarted. On the other hand, within the same VLAN, the ARP poisoning or ARP spoofing attacks are a very effective way to fool end stations or routers into learning counterfeited device identities. This can allow a malicious user to pose as intermediary and perform a Man-In-the-Middle (MiM) attack. The MiM attack is performed by impersonating another device (for example, the default gateway) in the ARP packets sent to the attacked device: These packets are not verified by the receiver, and therefore they "poison" its ARP table with forged information. This type of attack can be prevented either by blocking the direct communication at L2 between the attacker and the attacked device or by embedding more intelligence into the network so that it can check the forwarded ARP packets for identity correctness. For example, the latter can be achieved by using ARP Inspection in Cisco products.

- **Multicast Brute Force Attack** – This attack tries to exploit switches' potential vulnerabilities, or bugs, against a storm of L2 multicast frames. The correct behavior should be to constrain the traffic to its VLAN of origin; the failure behavior would be to leak frames to other VLANs.

- **Spanning-Tree Attack** – Another attack that tries to leverage a possible switch weakness is the STP attack. The attack requires sniffing for STP frames on the wire to get the ID of the port STP is transmitting on. Then the attacker would begin sending out STP Configuration/Topology Change Acknowledgement BPDUs announcing that he was the new root bridge with a much lower priority.

- **Random Frame Stress Attack** – This last attack can have many incarnations, but in general it consists of a brute force attack that randomly varies several fields of a packet while keeping only the source and destination addresses constant.

While many of these attacks are old, and may not be effective unless certain circumstances or misconfiguration issues are allowed to go unchecked within the network, the security practitioner needs to be aware of these attack vectors and ensure that they understand how they operate and what appropriate countermeasures are available.

Integrated Services Digital Network (ISDN)

Before the days of DSL and cable modems, users wanted remote access with higher bandwidth than dial-up. ISDN provides such bandwidth by using a set of protocols and specialized equipment (see *Figure 4.24*). ISDN uses two types of channels: The B channel (bearer) is used for voice and data (at 64 kbps), and the D channel (delta) is used for signaling (at 16 kbps) and can also be used for data. The D channels are used to establish, maintain, and tear down connections with a remote site. Voice and data traffic are sent on the B channel. Each B channel can support a separate call or can be multiplexed (B channel bonding) to combine the bandwidth into a single channel.

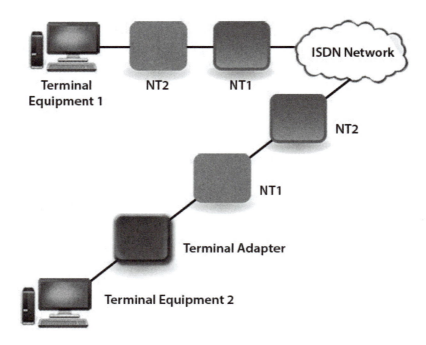

Figure 4.24 – **Integrated Services Digital Network (ISDN)**

ISDN comes in two varieties, basic rate interface (BRI) and primary rate interface (PRI). BRI supports two B channels and one D channel. Each B channel will support separate 64-kbps sessions or can be multiplexed into one 128-kbps session.

PRI is ISDN's high-end. When all of the B channels are bonded, the ISDN connection provides the bandwidth of a leased line. In North America, PRI supports 23 B channels and 1 D channel that can support as many as 23 sessions or, combined, a single 1.55-Mbps session (a full T1). In Europe and Australia, PRI supports 30 B channels and 1 D channel. The B channels can support 30 sessions or, bonded, 1 2.0-Mbps channel (a full E1). Some organizations use PRI ISDN as a low-cost backup for a leased line.

ISDN as a technology is at end-of-life and being decommissioned in many service locations; however, ISDN has been deployed for many remote connectivity applications that are not scheduled for de-commissioning for years to come. For this reason, ISDN will remain in service to support "legacy" applications for several more years.

Point-to-Point Lines
A point-to-point line connects two end points, most often over a WAN. In a wired WAN, point-to-point uses high-bandwidth fiber cable, but unlike FDDI, the traffic is dedicated to the end points. Point-to-point lines are an expensive option.

T1, T3, etc.
T1 carrier is a popular WAN method in North America and Japan. Using time division multiplexing, T1 multiplexes 24 channels over copper cable. In a 193-bit frame, each of the channels in a round-robin transmits 8 bits (seven data and one control bit). One bit for synchronization is appended to the beginning of the frame. A T1 frame is shown in *Figure 4.25.*

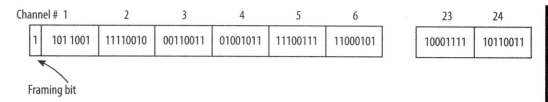

Figure 4.25 – **Structure of a T1 frame**

Eight thousand T1 frames are transmitted every second. Therefore, the transmission rate is 1.544 Mbps (8,000 frames/sec × 193 bits/frame).

A fractional T1 is available for organizations with a modest T1 budget. Customers may purchase fewer than 24 channels, which could be much less expensive than a full T1. Channels that are not purchased do not carry data. To meet the demand for additional WAN bandwidth, multiple T1 channels are multiplexed into technologies with more throughput. In general, customers use T1 and T3. A summary of T channels is shown in *Table 4.19.*

Channel	Multiplex Ratio	Bandwidth (Mbps)
T1	1 T1	1.544
T2	4xT1	6.312
T3	7xT2	44.736
T4	6xT3	274.176

Table 4.19 – **T-Carrier Bandwidth**

Fractional T3 is available at a reduced cost for organizations that do not need all T3 channels. As with fractional T1, fractional T3 channels that are not purchased do not carry data.

E1, E3, etc.
The E-carrier, used in Europe, employs a similar concept to the T-carrier. Using time division multiplexing, 32 channels take their turn transmitting 8 bits of data in a frame. E1 transmits 8,000 frames per second (the same rate as T1). The throughput for E1 is therefore 2.048 Mbps.

As with the T-carrier, E1 channels are multiplexed into E-carrier technology with more bandwidth. Each successive E-carrier level contains four times the channels as the previous one. *Table 4.20* shows the bandwidth of E1 to E4.

Channel	Bandwidth (Mbps)
E1	2.048
E2	8.848
E3	34.304
E4	139.264

Table 4.20 – **E-Carrier Bandwidth**

Customers typically use E1 and E3. In addition, fractional E-carrier lines are available for organizations that do not require the entire capacity of E1 or E3 line.

OC1, OC12, etc.

With SONET, like the T- and E-carriers, 8,000 frames are transmitted per second. However, a SONET (synchronous optical network) frame is larger and more complex, as shown in *Figure 4.26*.

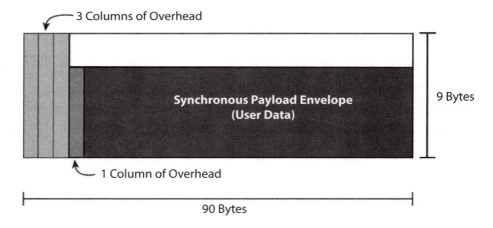

Figure 4.26 –**A SONET frame**

A SONET frame is a 90 × 9 byte matrix (810 bytes) with overhead in the first three columns. The overhead includes information for network management and the pointer to the start of user data. The rest of the frame is devoted to user data, known as the synchronous payload envelope (SPE), which can start at any byte within that area. However, the first column of the SPE is used as overhead.

SONET's basic transfer rate, optical carrier-1 (OC1) is 51.84 Mbps (810 bytes × 8 bits/byte × 8,000 bytes/s). Time division multiplexing of SONET signals is used to generate levels of SONET with a faster bandwidth. *Table 4.21* shows the potential speed of various OC levels.

OC Level	Bandwidth (Mbps)
OC-1	51.84
OC-3	155.52
OC-9	466.56
OC-12	622.08
OC-18	933.12
OC-24	1244.16
OC-36	1866.24
OC-48	2488.32
OC-192	9953.28

Table 4.21 – **E-Carrier Bandwidth**

Digital Subscriber Lines (DSL)

There are several methods of implementing DSL, including:

- **Asymmetric Digital Subscriber Line (ADSL)** – Downstream transmission rates are much greater than upstream ones, typically 256 to 512 kbps downstream and 64 kbps upstream.
- **Rate-Adaptive DSL (RADSL)** – The upstream transmission rate is automatically tuned based on the quality of the line.
- **Symmetric Digital Subscriber Line (SDSL)** – Uses the same rates for upstream and downstream transmissions.
- **Very High Bit Rate DSL (VDSL)** – Supports much higher transmission rates than other DSL technologies, such as 13 Mbps downstream and 2 Mbps upstream.

There are two significant issues with all variations of DSL:

1. There is a limit to the length of the phone line between the CO and the customer. The precise limit depends on several factors, including the quality of the cable and transmission rates. In other words, the customer cannot be too far from the CO.

2. DSL allows the users to be connected to the Internet for much longer time intervals. Certainly, this is very convenient for the user, but extended time exposed to the Internet greatly increases the risk of being attacked. To mitigate this serious risk, it is imperative that the host has a firewall, vendor security patches are installed, and dangerous and unused protocols are disabled.

Cable Modem

As with DSL, cable modems allow home users to enjoy high-speed Internet connectivity. Instead of sending data through the phone company, cable modems use their cable provider as an ISP. The user connects their PC Ethernet NIC to a cable modem, which is connected to the cable provider's network. Most major cable providers supply cable modems that comply with Data-Over-Cable Service Interface Specifications (DOCSIS), which helps ensure compatibility. See *Figure 4.27*.

At a high level, when a cable modem is powered on, it is assigned upstream and downstream channels. Next, it establishes timing parameters by determining how far it is from the head end (the core of the cable network). The cable modem makes a Dynamic Host Configuration Protocol (DHCP) request to obtain an IP address. To help protect the cable provider from piracy and its users from their data being intercepted by other cable users, the modem and head end exchange cryptography keys. From that point forward, all traffic between the two ends is encrypted.

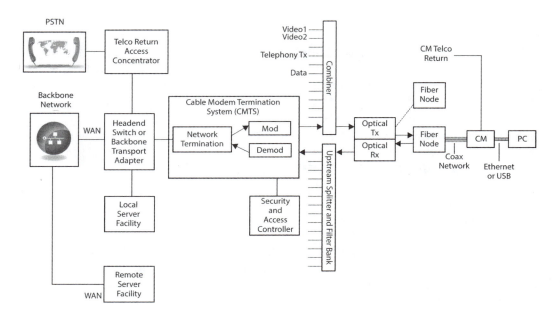

Figure 4.27 – **Data-Over-Cable reference architecture (after DOCSIS 2.0 RFI specification)**

*(From Howard, D. et al., Last mile HFC access, **Broadband Last Mile: Access Technologies for Multimedia Communications,** Jayant, N. Ed., Dekker, Boca Raton, FL, 2005. With permission.)*

Like DSL, cable modems make it practical for home users to remain connected to the Internet for an extended time, which exposes cable modem users to the same risks as DSL users. Cable modem users must take the same precautions as DSL users: Ensure that PCs on the home network have a personal firewall, install vendor security patches, and disable dangerous and unused protocols.

X.25

X.25 is a protocol from a very different era of networking. In the 1970s, when it was developed, users had dumb terminals (essentially a cathode ray tube monitor and keyboard) that were connected to a large computer. Also, networks were very unreliable, and a lot of resources had to be invested in error checking and correction.

X.25 allows users and hosts to connect through a modem to remote hosts via a packet-switched network. As with all packet-switched networks, the user's stream of data is subdivided into packets and forwarded through the X.25 network to the destination host. Although it may seem as if the user has a dedicated circuit over the WAN, actually, packets could take different paths along the way. Because networks were very unreliable when X.25 was developed, packets go through rigorous error checking, which adds much overhead—too much by today's standards. Most organizations now opt for newer technologies instead of X.25 for packet switching. Like ISDN, X.25 is largely de-commissioned now and available for the purposes of supporting legacy applications only.

4

Frame Relay

Frame relay is an economical alternative to circuit-switched networks and dedicated lines between networks that have significant idle time. Because frame relay uses packet-switching technology, organizations are charged for used bandwidth, which is less expensive than maintaining a dedicated line or the cost of a circuit that is based on the duration of the connection. A frame relay network is shown in *Figure 4.28*.

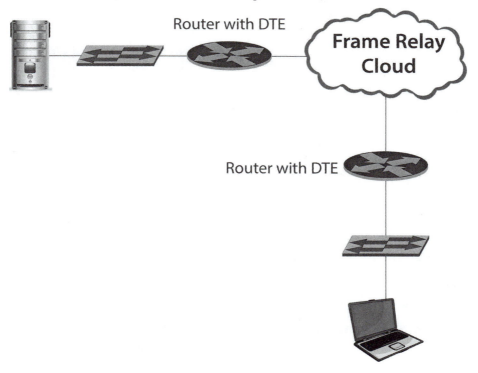

Figure 4.28 – **A Frame Relay network**

The heart of a frame relay network is the frame relay cloud of switches on the provider's premises. All frame relay customers share the resources in the cloud, which are assumed to be reliable, and do not require the intense error checking and correcting of X.25. This significantly increases the throughput over X.25. Devices within the cloud are considered data circuit-terminating equipment (DCE).

Devices that connect to the frame relay cloud, which are generally customer owned and on the customer's premises, are considered data terminal equipment (DTE). Communication between end points is connection oriented over permanent virtual circuits or switched virtual circuits. Organizations use a permanent virtual circuit when the connection between the DTEs will be active most of the time. For occasional connections, a switched virtual circuit is more cost-effective because the connection will be disconnected when it is completed.

Frame relay provides a mechanism that guarantees a customer-specified throughput through the cloud, called the committed information rate (CIR). For example, if 10 Kbps is specified, the provider will ensure that 10 Kbps will be available. In addition, the provider will permit bursts of higher throughput if the resources are available in the cloud. Naturally, higher CIRs are more expensive.

Asynchronous Transfer Mode (ATM)

ATM is a connection-oriented protocol designed to transmit data, voice, and video over the same network at very high speeds, such as 155 Mbps. This is facilitated by using small, fixed-length 53-byte cells for all ATM traffic.

Another hallmark of ATM is the use of virtual circuits. Cells transferred between circuit end points use the same path. To initiate a circuit, a cell is sent to the destination. As this cell transverses the network, all devices in the cell's path allocate necessary resources to prepare for the eventual transfer of data. As with IP, ATM does not guarantee the delivery of cells.

Virtual circuits can be either permanent or switched. Switched virtual circuits are torn down after the connection is terminated. Permanent virtual circuits, on the other hand, remain active.

Traffic engineering is an aspect of ATM. All virtual circuits are classified in one of the following categories:

- **Constant Bit Rate (CBR)** – The circuit's cells are transmitted at a constant rate.
- **Variable Bit Rate (VBR)** – The circuit's cells are transmitted within a specified range. This is often used for bursty traffic.
- **Unspecified Bit Rate (UBR)** – The circuit's cells receive bandwidth that has not been allocated by circuits in other categories. This is ideal for applications that are not interactive, such as file transfers.
- **Available Bit Rate (ABR)** – The circuit's throughput is adjusted based on feedback from monitoring the available network bandwidth.

Virtualized Networks

Software Defined Networking

OpenNetworking.org provides a definition of Software Defined Networking (SDN): "the physical separation of the network control plane from the forwarding plane, and where a control plane controls several devices." In the SDN architecture, the control and data planes are decoupled, network intelligence and state are logically centralized, and the underlying network infrastructure is abstracted from the application.[49]

The purpose of SDN is to separate traditional network traffic (this can apply to wired or wireless) into three components: raw data, how the data is sent, and what purpose the data serves. This involves a focus on data, control, and application (management) functions or "planes" that map to the infrastructure, control, and application layers. *Figure 4.29* shows a high level view of the three layers of the SDN architecture.

---

49   See the following: https://www.opennetworking.org/sdn-resources/sdn-definition

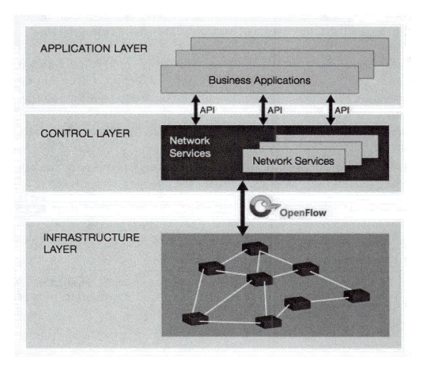

Figure 4.29 – **High-Level view of the three layers of the Software Defined Network**

- ■ ***Infrastructure Layer ("Data Plane")*** – Network switches and routers and the data itself as well as the process of forwarding data to the appropriate destination.
- ■ ***Control Layer ("Control Plane")*** – The intelligence in devices that works in true "middle-man" fashion, determining how traffic should flow based on the status of the infrastructure layer and the requirements specified by the application layer.
- ■ ***Application Layer ("Application Plane")*** – Network services, utilities, and applications that interface with the control level to specify needs and requirements.

The network hardware performs much or all these functions; the goal of SDN is to offload the handling of traffic and the way it meets the needs of the applications involved. For instance, the control layer might reside on a server and the application layer as a software-based application programming interface (API). This means the hardware that handles the network traffic does not need to direct it or deal with management, making the environment more flexible and adaptable.

The two trends that have the potential to greatly benefit from SDN are the cloud and virtualization. With both of these functions comes the need for better traffic management to handle scalability, delivery of critical data, increased bandwidth requirements, and faster provisioning of network services. SDN is intended to fit that need. SDN provides the ability to apply higher-level policies to shape and reorder network traffic based on users, devices, and applications to the networking and security professional. Some of the ways in which SDN will be able to address the growing needs of the cloud and virtualization are listed below:

- A cloud application might handle the direction of network traffic to ensure load balancing across servers or to deliver data via the fastest and most efficient routes.
- Automation can help enhance the reliability and simplify the network framework by implementing a more consistent, predictable environment.
- No longer are network resources limited to a device-by-device configuration with a weak link in the chain.
- Open-source SDN APIs can be used or written by networking staff to help further the capabilities.

SDN is based upon open standards. OpenFlow is one such example and has been defined by the Open Networking Forum.[50] It utilizes virtual device control and a standard instruction set. Policies can be applied to network traffic, and APIs are available for use or can be programmed by users.

A more technical view of the SDN architecture can be seen in *Figure 4.30.*

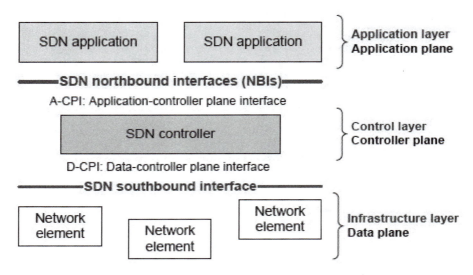

Figure 4.30 – **Technical view of the three layers of the Software Defined Network**

Architectural Components

The following list defines and explains the architectural components:

- ***SDN Application (SDN App)*** – SDN applications are programs that explicitly, directly, and programmatically communicate their network requirements and desired network behavior to the SDN Controller via a northbound interface (NBI). In addition, they may consume an abstracted view of the network for their internal decision making purposes. An SDN application consists of one SDN Application Logic and one or more NBI Drivers. SDN applications may themselves expose another layer of abstracted network control, thus offering one or more higher-level NBIs through respective NBI agents.

---

50   See the following: https://www.opennetworking.org/sdn-resources/onf-specifications/openflow

- **SDN Controller** – The SDN controller is a logically centralized entity in charge of translating the requirements from the SDN application layer down to the SDN datapaths and providing the SDN applications with an abstract view of the network, which may include statistics and events. An SDN controller consists of one or more NBI agents, the SDN Control Logic, and the Control to Data-Plane Interface (CDPI) driver. Definition as a logically centralized entity neither prescribes nor precludes implementation details such as the federation of multiple controllers, the hierarchical connection of controllers, communication interfaces between controllers, nor virtualization or slicing of network resources.

- **SDN Datapath** – The SDN datapath is a logical network device that exposes visibility and uncontended control over its advertised forwarding and data processing capabilities. The logical representation may encompass all or a subset of the physical substrate resources. An SDN datapath comprises a CDPI agent and a set of one or more traffic forwarding engines and zero or more traffic processing functions. These engines and functions may include simple forwarding between the datapath's external interfaces or internal traffic processing or termination functions. One or more SDN datapaths may be contained in a single (physical) network element—an integrated physical combination of communications resources, managed as a unit. An SDN datapath may also be defined across multiple physical network elements. This logical definition neither prescribes nor precludes implementation details such as the logical to physical mapping, management of shared physical resources, virtualization or slicing of the SDN datapath, interoperability with non-SDN networking, nor the data processing functionality, which can include layer 4-7 functions.

- **SDN Control to Data-Plane Interface (CDPI)** – The SDN CDPI is the interface defined between an SDN controller and an SDN datapath, which provides programmatic control of all forwarding operations, capabilities advertisement, statistics reporting, and event notification.

- **SDN Northbound Interfaces (NBI)** – SDN NBIs are interfaces between SDN applications and SDN controllers and typically provide abstract network views and enable direct expression of network behavior and requirements. This may occur at any level of abstraction (latitude) and across different sets of functionality (longitude).

Software Defined Storage and Virtual SAN

In its 2013 Storage Taxonomy Report, analyst group IDC describes SDS as any storage software stack that can be installed on any commodity resources (x86 hardware, hypervisors, or cloud) and/or off-the-shelf computing hardware.

An underlying premise of software-defined storage (SDS) is that the hypervisor is the new bare metal of the data center. In a software-defined data center (SDDC), all services are built on the virtualization layer, which not only explicitly decouples the data and control planes but also allows storage functionality to extend to the time of creation. Instead of depending on rigid hardware constructs to meet the needs of all workloads, features and policies can be applied via the hypervisor. The hypervisor and SDS work together by providing a menu of services (APIs) to learn about the capabilities of various hardware devices and apply the right capabilities and properties as needed, on a per-VM basis.

In SDS, the hardware is augmented with powerful software mechanisms that enable all x86 nodes to take part in a scale-out, distributed cluster that can scale in a linear fashion without much in the way of overall limits. In this scale-out storage model, each x86 node contains direct attached hard disks and solid-state storage that can be leveraged by all nodes and all workloads. Further, the scale-out applies to not only storage capacity but also to storage control logic to help avoid performance bottlenecks when scaling.

As is the case with SDN, SDS seeks to separate the physical storage hardware from the storage logic that determines data placement and what services are applied during read and write operations. The end result is a storage layer that is very flexible, which can adjust to meet shifting application needs. It also creates a unified and coherent data fabric that maintains full visibility of each virtual machine.

The storage services that have been traditionally available to the enterprise include:

- **Dynamic Tiering** – Today, storage systems generally support a combination of high-performance flash storage and slower, but larger capacity, hard disk drives. As a result, software-based dynamic tiering enables the storage layer to shift data between tiers of storage automatically to optimize performance. No administrator is required to deal with complex rule sets.

- **Caching** – Caching has become an increasingly important feature, primarily due to cost reductions for flash storage, and has enabled new classes of storage, such as server-side cache devices and hybrid storage arrays. But even though flash storage costs have come down, it is still much more expensive than traditional hard disk drives. As such, storage vendors are carefully leveraging flash in ways that enable faster performance by placing the most in-demand data in a higher speed cache.

- **Replication** – Storage replication creates a variety of data protection (local replication) and disaster recovery (replication across different locations) opportunities, which is why many organizations consider it to be an essential storage feature. With replication, organizations can copy production data between different storage systems located in geographically disparate data centers.

- **Quality of Service (QoS)** – The goal of QoS is to ensure predictable, consistent, high performance for each application. Historically, IT teams have avoided mixing different types of workloads (for example, Microsoft Exchange, SQL databases, and VDI) on a common platform because they compete for resources, thus jeopardizing performance SLAs. Having a distributed control plane, however, enables data to be stored locally to any specific VM so that performance is protected and performance characteristics can be easily observed and analyzed.

- **Snapshots** – Snapshots provide a point-in-time copy of the storage system, from which they can be recovered. Snapshots do not replace proper backups, but their ability to deliver a low recovery point objective has made them an important component for most recoveries.

- **Deduplication** – Although storage capacity costs continue to come down, even for flash storage, most people do not want to waste capacity when reasonable conservation opportunities are available. Deduplication is a popular way to achieve this goal. Deduplication can save organizations money, thanks to reduced capacity needs.

- **Compression** – Although data deduplication works at the block level, compression works at the file level and can crunch files down to a fraction of their original size.
- **Cloning** – Cloning is a sought-after feature because it helps administrators streamline and improve overall service.

Like virtualization and SDN, abstraction is a key element of SDS. Without virtualization, in fact, SDS would not be possible because SDS depends on the fact that storage resources are abstracted (or decoupled) away from hardware. When they are abstracted, those services are extended through additional software mechanisms. These attributes determine, for example, where to store data based on application need; they also provide important storage services, such as deduplication and thin provisioning. But these mechanisms are not part of the virtualization stack; they are additional services that provide additional functionality.

In an SDS system, the control plane enables policy-based management of storage services that is decoupled from the hardware environment. The importance of this decoupling becomes more apparent as multiple hardware systems are added to the environment. Given visibility into the full spectrum of hardware, data placement can extend beyond a single system or single location, leveraging cloud and even off-premises storage systems. An SDS system can have hardware present in many data centers, both public and private, and still be managed and controlled via a single, distributed control plane.

Besides being open from a hardware perspective, a key characteristic of the SDDC and SDS is interoperability facilitated by open application programming interfaces (APIs). Such APIs enable ongoing automation beyond direct storage management and enable provisioning that can be controlled by third-party extensions to the environment. A specific application may need a particular kind of storage, for example, and could use an SDS vendor's open API to provision that storage by using the knowledge of the environment that has been gleaned by the SDS management layer. Today, the most common API standard is called the representational state transfer (REST) API.

In SDS storage clusters, data availability is achieved through software resilience rather than through highly redundant hardware devices. In fact, the software layer is designed for a hardware infrastructure that is expected to have failures but can immediately detect and respond to unavailability of hardware resources to maintain overall storage SLAs. For example, rather than using expensive, slow, and increasingly unreliable RAID constructs, SDS systems may choose instead to take a replica-based approach to data protection by storing multiple copies of data at various locations in the cluster.

Further, with complete awareness of the other virtual elements in the infrastructure, the software layer can decide, based on administrator-defined policies, what storage is needed determined by what it sees taking place in the environment. For example, applications that need highly responsive storage can be serviced by flash-based capacity, while less time-critical workloads will tap into slower, but less expensive, hard disk drive-based storage. The abstraction layer offered by SDS and virtualization makes it possible to see every aspect of the environment, which provides automated workload management opportunities. SDS allows the storage fabric to be adaptive so that applications with high I/O demands are given access to storage resources with guaranteed SLAs. This ensures that the storage component of the data center is as flexible as other technologies.

SDS-based storage systems provide several types of protection and data availability mechanisms:

- **Intelligent Data Placement** – Data protection begins the second that data is written to a physical disk and acknowledged to the application workload. In an SDS storage system, data placement and protection are critical because no hardware-based RAID mechanism does the work of data protection. In SDS, data placement may happen several times.

- **Controllers** – In SDS, software-based controllers are responsible for making sure that data is read from and written to disk and remains available for use by applications and virtual machines. Software controllers are often redundant, helping the environment maintain a high level of availability, even in the event of a failure.

- **Software RAID** – Although SDS makes hardware-based RAID systems unnecessary, software-based RAID constructs may be used. To conform to the concepts of SDS, these RAID constructs must be fully supported by software-based controllers and must be able to scale to meet enterprise-class capacity and performance needs.

For the security professional to have a clear picture of the nature of SDS technology, we will briefly examine how it is implemented by VMware in their Virtual SAN offering. VMware® Virtual SAN™ is hypervisor-converged storage software that abstracts and pools server-side flash and disk to create a highly performant and resilient persistent storage tier at the hypervisor layer.

Hypervisor-Converged Storage

Virtual SAN is embedded into the vSphere kernel. This tight integration is important because it is uniquely positioned in the stack to understand the VMs and applications running above vSphere and the underlying storage infrastructure capabilities. It is Virtual SAN's unique positioning in the stack that allows it to optimize the I/O datapath to deliver better performance than a virtual appliance or external device.

VM-Centric Policy-Based Management and Automation

Storage requirements are tied to individual virtual machines or virtual disks in the form of policy statements. Virtual SAN provisions storage resources based on those policies governed by SLAs. Using Storage Policy Based Management (SPBM), server administrators are able to create storage policies based on each application or VM's performance, availability, and capacity needs. Those policies are then matched by Virtual SAN to underlying storage resources to deliver automation to storage resource provisioning and management. Virtual SAN automatically rebuilds and rebalances the storage to align with the designated QoS policy assigned to each virtual machine in the cluster.

Server-Side Read/Write Caching

Virtual SAN minimizes storage latency by accelerating read/write disk I/O traffic by leveraging enterprise-grade server side SSD flash. Virtual SAN dramatically improves the performance of virtual machines by leveraging the flash as both a write buffer and a read cache. The read cache keeps a list of commonly accessed disk blocks to reduce I/O read latency in the event of a cache hit. The write buffer is non-volatile and reduces latency for write operations by acknowledging writes significantly faster than writing to disk.

Built-in Failure Tolerance

Virtual SAN leverages distributed RAID and cache mirroring to ensure that data is never lost in case of disk, host, or network failures. Virtual SAN's SPBM feature lets administrators maximize resiliency by defining availability on a per-virtual machine basis: When setting the storage policy for each virtual machine, administrators can specify how many host, network, or disk failures it can tolerate in a Virtual SAN cluster.

Granular Non-Disruptive Scale-Up and Scale-Out

Capacity of the Virtual SAN data store can be easily and non-disruptively grown by adding disks to an existing host (scale-up) or by adding a new host to the cluster (scale-out). Performance can be boosted at the same time, by adding more flash drives (including PCIe cards) to new or existing hosts on the fly, and accelerate IO performance without interrupting service.

Hardware Independent

Virtual SAN is a hardware agnostic solution that can be deployed on hardware of all major server vendors. This provides the flexibility to run heterogeneous hardware with different configurations, operating systems, and magnetic disks.

PVLANs, Virtual Networks, and Guest Operating Systems

A private VLAN expands on the abilities of a standard VLAN, allowing traffic to be separated at another level allowing for a number of flexible options concerning design and security.

A Virtual Local Area Network, or VLAN, provides the ability to logically separate a LAN the same way that would be possible with multiple physical switches. For example, if we had four different physical switches, each of the switches could be connected to separate departments within a company. Without an interconnection or a routing device, the devices within each department would not be able to send traffic to each other and would typically be put into different subnets. A VLAN takes this ability to separate devices, but it does it logically instead of physically; a separate VLAN can be created for each department, and the physical ports that connect these devices can be configured into the correct VLAN. It is important to keep in mind however that the same rules apply to VLANs as physical LANs; that is, in order to communicate between them, a routing device is required and separate subnets should be assigned to the devices in each VLAN.

Private VLANs: Extending the Abilities of a VLAN

The private VLAN feature provides the ability to extend the capabilities of a "standard" VLAN. A Private VLAN is further divided into the groups:

- **Primary PVLAN –** The original VLAN that is being divided into smaller groups is called Primary, and all the secondary PVLANs exist only inside the primary.
- **Secondary PVLANs –** The secondary PVLANs exist only inside the primary. Each Secondary PVLAN has a specific VLAN ID associated to it, and each packet travelling through it is tagged with an ID as if it were a normal VLAN, and the physical switch associates the behavior (Isolated, Community, or Promiscuous) depending on the VLAN ID found in each packet.

It is important for the security professional to take note of the fact that depending upon the type of the groups involved, hosts are not able to communicate with each other, even if they belong to the same group.

Three Types of Secondary PVLANs

■ ***Promiscuous*** – A node attached to a port in a promiscuous secondary PVLAN may send and receive packets to any node in any other secondary VLAN associated to the same primary. Routers are typically attached to promiscuous ports.

■ ***Isolated*** – A node attached to a port in an isolated secondary PVLAN may only send to and receive packets from the promiscuous PVLAN.

■ ***Community*** – A node attached to a port in a community secondary PVLAN may send to and receive packets from other ports in the same secondary PVLAN, as well as send to and receive packets from the promiscuous PVLAN.

Figure 4.31 illustrates what a traffic flow for a Private VLAN would look like.

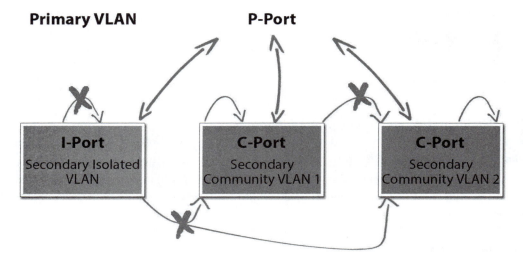

Figure 4.31 – **Private VLAN Traffic Flow**

Some additional things for the security professional to be aware of are listed below:

■ Promiscuous PVLANs have the same VLAN ID both for Primary and Secondary VLAN.

■ Community and Isolated PVLAN's traffic travels tagged as the associated Secondary PVLAN.

■ Traffic inside PVLANs is not encapsulated (no Secondary PVLAN encapsulated inside a Primary PVLAN Packet).

■ Traffic between virtual machines on the same PVLAN but on different hosts go through the Physical Switch. Therefore, the Physical Switch must be PVLAN aware and configured appropriately, to allow the secondary PVLANs to reach their destination.

■ Switches discover MAC addresses per VLAN. This can be a problem for PVLANs because each virtual machine appears to the physical switch to be in more than one VLAN, or at least, it appears that there is no reply to the request because the reply travels back in a different VLAN. For this reason, it is a requirement that each physical switch, where PVLANs are connected, must be PVLAN aware.

The security professional that has not worked with PVLANs before can check out the vendors listed below by category for product information, offerings, and demos.

Hardware Switches
- ■ ***Arista Networks*** – Data Center Switching
- ■ ***Cisco Systems*** – Catalyst 2960-XR, 3560, and higher product lines switches
- ■ ***Juniper Networks*** – EX switches
- ■ ***Brocade*** – BigIron, TurboIron, and FastIron switches

Software Switches
- ■ ***Cisco Systems*** – Nexus 1000V
- ■ ***VMWare*** – vDS switch
- ■ ***Microsoft*** – HyperV 2012R2

Other Private VLAN–Aware Products
- ■ ***Cisco Systems*** – FWSM firewall
- ■ ***Marathon Networks*** – PVTD Private VLAN deployment and operation appliance

Just What Is a Virtual Network Anyway?
(And why security professionals need to understand them)

A virtual network consists of one or more virtual machines that can send data to and receive data from one another. Each virtual machine represents a single computer within the network and resides on an ESXi server.

In VMware, switches are used to establish a connection between the virtual network and the physical network. With ESX and ESXi, two different kinds of switches can be used: standard switches and distributed switches.

Standard Switches

A network standard switch, virtual switch, or vSwitch, is responsible for connecting virtual machines to a virtual network. A vSwitch works similar to a physical switch, with some limitations, and controls how virtual machines communicate with one another.

The vSwitch uses the physical NICs (pNICs) associated with the host server to connect the virtual network to the physical network. In VMware, these pNICs are also called uplink adapters. Uplink adapters use virtual objects called vmnics, or virtual network adapters, to interface with the vSwitch.

Once the vSwitch has bridged the connection between the virtual network and the physical network, the virtual machines residing on the host server can begin transferring data to, and receiving data from, all of the network-capable devices connected to the physical network. That is to say, the virtual machines are no longer limited to communicating solely across the virtual network.

VMware can create a virtual network from a vSwitch mapped to one or more uplink adapters, or mapped to no uplink adapters at all. A vSwitch that lacks an assigned pNIC is called an internal vSwitch and cannot communicate with other virtual or physical machines outside of the ESXi host. Internal vSwitches are used whenever the host must remain isolated from the external network, such as when configuring a virtual appliance.

To connect to a vSwitch, a virtual machine must have a virtual NIC (vNIC) mapped to it, just like how physical machines cannot connect to a network without a working network adapter. In fact, if a physical machine residing outside the virtual environment were to receive

599

data from a vNIC associated with a virtual machine, the physical machine would not be able to tell that the information was coming from a virtualized network adapter. Like pNICs, vNICs have both a MAC address and an IP address.

Each virtual machine interfaces with the vSwitch via a port. vSwitches can consist of one or more port groups, which describe how the virtual switch should route traffic between the virtual network and the virtual machines connected to the specified ports. Administrators can use port groups to configure traffic shaping and bandwidth limitations, NIC failover, and other settings.

Distributed Switches

Distributed virtual switches, or DvSwitches, simplify the network management of multiple ESXi hosts. DvSwitches provide the same features and functions as do vSwitches, but with one major difference: While a standard virtual switch cannot be assigned to more than one host server at a time, a DvSwitch can. So, rather than create identical vSwitches for multiple hosts in a datacenter, you can instead create and associate a single DvSwitch with all the applicable ESXi servers.

Unlike vSwitches, which can be managed from the local host, due to its inherent architecture, DvSwitches must be created and controlled through a vCenter Server. A DvSwitch is made up of a control plane and an input/output (I/O) plane. The control plane resides in vCenter Server and is used to configure DvSwitches, NIC bonding, uplink adapters, and VLANs. The I/O plane, or data plane, on the other hand, is a "hidden" virtual switch built into each host server.

DvSwitches also support port groups, called distributed port groups, or dvport groups. dvport groups provide the same basic functionality as standard port groups, but they offer additional features such as allowing administrators to define not just outbound traffic shaping, but inbound traffic shaping as well, when working with dvPort groups.

Security professionals need to understand how virtual networks are set up and the components that make them up in order to be able to work with virtualized network infrastructure as well as incorporate it into existing security architectures and policies. Now that we have taken a look at how a virtual network is set up in VMware's ESXi operating system, it is time for you to try setting up a virtualized environment for yourself and configure basic networking connectivity for it. Because we have already examined VMware's approach to networking, this hands-on opportunity is set up to allow you to see Microsoft's approach to virtualization through the deployment of Windows Server 2012/2012R2 Hyper-V.

Please see **Appendix E** for the detailed tutorial.

Network Attacks

Attacks can be directed at the network itself, i.e., the network's availability or one of its other services—especially security services—is at risk. In the past, it was considered that the network itself was not the necessary objective of an attack (*Figure 4.32*), but this is no longer the case. Under IP convergence, the network has come to be the central nervous system of most organizations, controlling both physical and logical elements of the business. Physical elements can include the data and communications that control and manage massive productions systems and critical safety controls on pumps, furnaces, boilers, reaction chambers, and a wide range of other very "physical" elements that can cause serious property damage or loss of life. Physical elements can also include the access controls on buildings and the cameras and intercoms that monitor and record physical threats and alert security staff to emergencies. Logical elements include not only the data flowing around the network like email and files, but all telephony calls and information services like TV might also be relying completely on the same network. Crippling or controlling the network in modern organizations and businesses, without attacking a specific application, can have the same impact as successfully attacking all the resident applications.

The Network as an Enabler or Channel of Attack

One must distinguish between two subtly different situations here: where an attacker uses certain network characteristics to support his attack, for instance, by intelligence gathering, and where an attack is borne across the network. This section will focus primarily on attacks that can be borne through the network; however, it will also still discuss attacks against the network itself, which have cascading impacts to the applications and assets riding on the network.

Use of a network is not necessarily based on a breach of the network. For instance, in the case of a virus infection, the breach may have occurred on a user's laptop connected to the Internet. Although it is true that in such a case a deficiency in the network's architecture was exploited, its own infrastructure and the security services that were designed into it have not technically been breached.

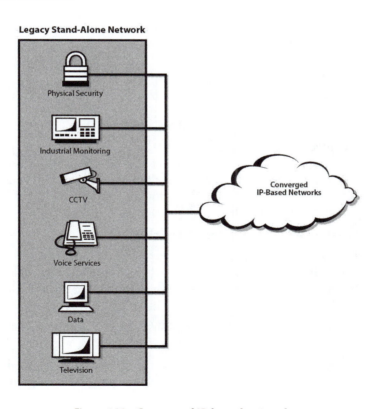

Figure 4.32 – **Converged IP-based networks**

The Network as a Bastion of Defense

The network is a key, if not the most valuable, strategic component supporting the objective of IT security: to protect the information and knowledge contained in the enterprise. It is therefore paramount to implement strong and coherent network security architecture across the entire enterprise. As described elsewhere, such measures will typically be built around a complete Information Security Management System (ISMS) including social, organizational, procedural, and technical activities and the supporting controls required to enforce them.

Measures will be based on the organization's security policy and typically include configuration and change management, monitoring and log reviews, vulnerability and compliance testing and scanning (including detection scans on the network), security reviews and audits, backup and recovery, as well as awareness and training measures. They need to be balanced, appropriate, and affordable to the organization and commensurate with its business objectives and level of risk acceptance and target assurance level. Key concepts for the security professional to consider include:

- **Definition of Security Domains** – This could be defined by level of risk or by organizational control. A prime example is the tendency of decentralized organizations to manage their IT—and thereby also their network security—locally and as a result, with different degrees of success.
- **Segregation of Security Domains** – Control of traffic flows according to risk/benefit assessment, and taking into account formal models, such as the Bell–La Padula model, the Biba integrity model, or the Clark–Wilson model.
- **Incident Response Capability** – Including but not limited to:
  - An inventory of business-critical traffic (this could, for instance, be email or file and print servers but also DNS and DHCP, telephony traffic—VOIP, building access control traffic and/or facilities management traffic. Remember, modern building controls, physical security controls, and process controls are converging onto IP).
  - An inventory of less critical traffic (such as HTTP or FTP).
  - A way to quickly contain breaches (for instance, by shutting off parts of the network or blocking certain types of traffic)
  - A process for managing the reaction.
  - Contingency or network "diversity" in case of overload or failure of the primary network connection; alternate network connections are in place to absorb the load/traffic automatically without loss of services to applications and users.

Network Security Objectives and Attack Modes

Although security objectives are specific to each organization, a number of key themes may be distinguished, which will be prioritized by each organization differently, but often the order in which they are listed here is the one chosen. A number of secondary objectives, such as interoperability and, in particular, ease of use, are undercurrents to these themes. A user expects the network (in particular, network security) to be fully transparent and not interfere with business processes and will not easily accept restrictions.

It is a common misperception that network security is the end point for all other security measures (i.e., that firewalls only will protect an organization). This is a flawed perception; perimeter defense (defending the edges of the network) is merely part of the overall solution set, or enterprise security architecture, that the security professional needs to ensure is in place in the enterprise. Perimeter defense is part of a wider concept known as "defense in depth," which simply holds that security must be a multi-layer effort including the edges but also the hosts, applications, network elements (routers, switches, DHCP, DNS, wireless access points), people, and operational processes. See *Figure 4.33*.

Furthermore, protective measures will not actually prevent an attack, which is far better than having to repel and attack with the subsequent risks of failure! Neither will detect, response, and recovery strategies stop an attack. Ideally, to counter an attack, network security must also be proactive—anticipate and oppose the attack against the infrastructure by interdicting and disrupting an attack preemptively or in self-defense. This requires intelligence on the threat, active surveillance at the perimeter and beyond, and the ability to intercede upstream or disable a threat agent's tools

Figure 4.33 – **Defense in Depth**

Techniques associated with proactivity can be undertaken independently by organizations with a willingness and resources to do so. Others such as upstream intercession (assuming an external source of the threat such as DDOS, spam/phish, or botnet attacks) can be accomplished fairly easily and affordably through cooperation with telecommunications suppliers and Internet service providers (ISP). Finally, the most effective proactive network defense (*Figure 4.34*) is related to the ability to disable attack tools before they can be deployed and applied against you. Such tactics have historically been considered too imprecise and legally dubious for use, but the level of risk to security associated with network-based attacks has led to the adoption of a counteroffensive doctrine by the United States Strategic Defense Command headed by the U.S. Air Force, as well as many other countries around the world.

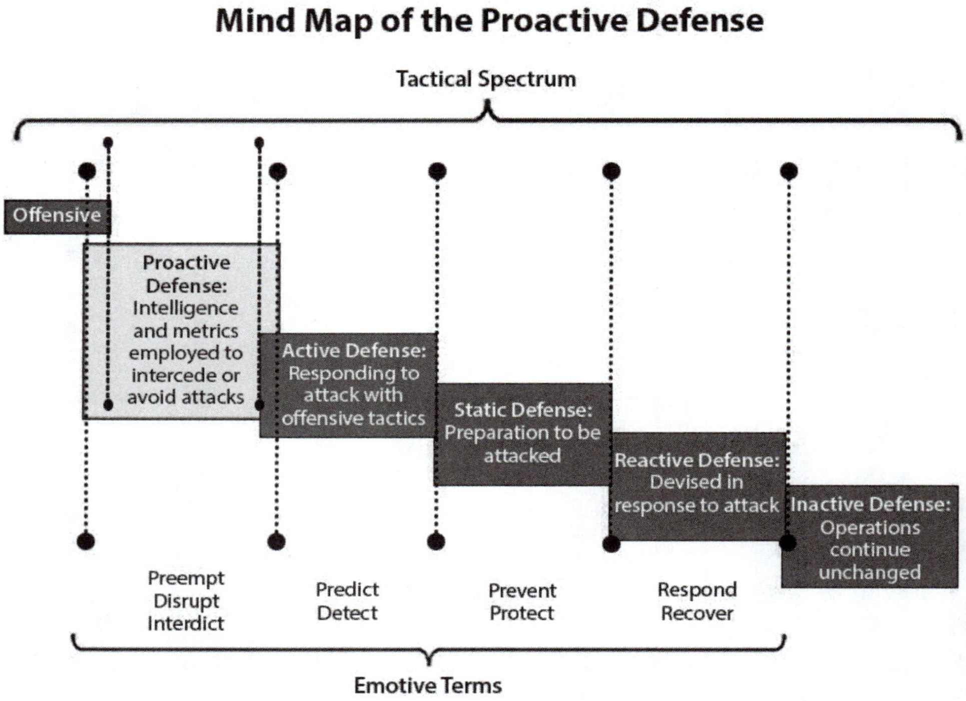

Mind Map of the Proactive Defense

Figure 4.34 – **Proactive Defense**

Confidentiality

In the context of telecommunications and network security, confidentiality is the property of nondisclosure to unauthorized parties. Attacks against confidentiality are by far the most prevalent today because information can be sold or exploited for profit in a huge variety of (mostly criminal) ways. The network, as the carrier of almost all digital information within the enterprise, provides an attractive target to bypass access control measures on the assets using the network and access information while it is in transit on the wire. Among the information that can be acquired is not just the payload information but also credentials, such as passwords. Conversely, an attacker might not even be interested in the information transmitted but simply in the fact that the communication has occurred. An overarching class of attacks carried out against confidentiality is known as "eavesdropping."

Eavesdropping (Sniffing)

To access information from the network, an attacker must have access to the network itself in the first place. An eavesdropping computer can be a legitimate client on the network or an unauthorized one. It is not necessary for the eavesdropper to become a part of the network (for instance, having an IP address); it is often far more advantageous for an attacker to remain invisible (and un-addressable) on the network. This is particularly easy in wireless LANs, where no physical connection is necessary.

Countermeasures to eavesdropping include encryption of network traffic on a network or application level, traffic padding to prevent identification of times when communication happens, rerouting of information to anonymize its origins and potentially split different parts of a message, and mandating trusted routes for data such that information is only traversing trusted network domains.

Integrity

In the context of telecommunications and network security, integrity is the property associated with corruption or change (intentional or accidental). A network needs to support and protect the integrity of its traffic. In many ways, the provisions taken for protection against interception and to protect confidentiality will also protect the integrity of a message. Attacks against integrity are often an interim step to compromising confidentiality or availability as opposed to the overall objective of the attack.

Although the modification of messages will often happen at the higher network layers (i.e., within applications), networks can be set up to provide robustness or resilience against interception and change of a message (man-in-the-middle attacks) or replay attacks. Ways to accomplish this can be based on encryption or checksums on messages, as well as on access control measures for clients that would prevent an attacker from gaining the necessary access to send a modified message into the network in the first place.

Conversely, many protocols, such as SMTP, HTTP, or even DNS, do not provide any degree of authentication. Consequently, it becomes relatively easy for the attacker to inject messages with fake sender information into a network from the outside through an existing gateway. The fact that no application can rely on the security or authenticity of underlying protocols has become a common design factor in networking.

Availability

In the context of telecommunications and network security, availability is the property of a network service related to its uptime, speed, and latency. Availability of the service is commonly the most obvious business requirement especially with highly converged networks, where multiple assets (data, voice, physical security) are riding on top of the same network. For this very reason, network availability has also become a prime target for attackers and a key business risk that security professionals need to be prepared to address. While a variety of availability threats and risks are addressed in this chapter, an overarching class of attack against availability is known as "denial of service".

Attacks on the transport layer of the OSI model (layer 4) seek to manipulate, disclose, or prevent delivery of the payload as a whole. This can, for instance, happen by reading the payload (as would happen in a sniffer attack) or changing it (which could happen in a man-in-the-middle attack). While disruptions of service can be executed at other layers as well, the transport layer has become a common attack ground via ICMP.

Domain Litigation

Domain names are subject to trademark risks, related to a risk of temporary unavailability or permanent loss of an established domain name. For the business in question, the consequences can be equivalent to the loss of its whole Internet presence in an IT-related disaster. Businesses should therefore put in place contingency plans if they are concerned with trademark disputes of any kind over a domain name used as their main Web and email address. Such contingency plans might include setting up a second domain unrelated to the trademark in question (based, for instance, on the trademark of a parent company) that can be advertised on short notice, if necessary.

Cyber-squatting and the illegitimate use of similar domains, containing common misspellings or representing the same second-level domain under a different top-level domain is occurring more frequently as the range of domains continues to expand. The only way to protect a business from this kind of fraud is the registration of the most prominent adjacent domains or by means of trademark litigation. A residual risk will always remain, relating not only to public misrepresentation but also to potential loss or disclosure of email.

Open Mail Relay Servers

An open mail relay server is an SMTP service that allows inbound SMTP connections for domains it does not serve (i.e., for which it does not possess a DNS MX record). An open mail relay is generally considered a sign of bad system administration. See *Figure 4.35.*

Open mail relays are a principal tool for the distribution of spam because they allow an attacker to hide his or her identity. A number of blacklists for open mail relay servers exist that can be used for blacklisting open mail relays; i.e., a legitimate mail server would not accept any email from this host because it has a high likelihood of being spam. Although using blacklists as one indicator in spam filtering has its merits, it is risky to use them as an exclusive indicator. Generally, they are run by private organizations and individuals according to their own rules, they are able to change their policies on a whim, they can vanish overnight for any reason, and they can rarely be held accountable for the way they operate their lists.

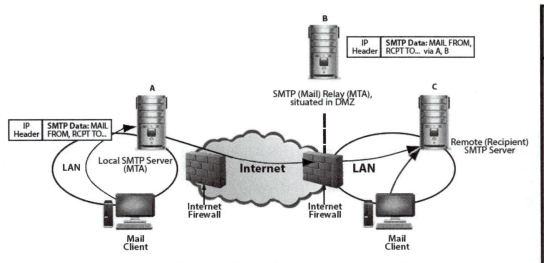

Figure 4.35 – **Representative SMTP exchange**

(From Young, S. and Aitel, D., ***Hacker's Handbook: The Strategy behind Breaking into and Defending Networks****, Auerbach Publications, Boca Raton, FL, 2004. With permission.)*

Spam

Spam benefits from the low cost of email, as opposed to phone calls or letters. It can be sent in massive amounts with little additional cost and a low risk of retribution. Over the years, sending spam has become a professional and highly profitable business. This means that spammers are highly organized and structured. In general, spam is not limited to email; it can also occur in newsgroups, Web logs (blogs), or through instant messaging (Spam over Instant Messaging (SPIM)) as well as over voice channels (Spam over Internet Telephony (SPIT)).

Spam often promotes illegitimate or fraudulent businesses and shady websites. It is often crafted in such a way as to trick the user into thinking that either he has been addressed personally, for instance, by inclusion of personal names or email addresses, or that he has accidentally received an important email intended for someone else. Spam relies on illegitimate means for its distribution.

Spam is almost always sent with invalid (faked) sender addresses or from addresses that have been compromised and are used for sending spam without the legitimate owner's knowledge or permission. Spam can be sent through open mail relays.

Spam appears to be increasingly sent via virus-infected, back-doored hosts (zombie networks). Where this is the case, a security breach is exploited and the spammer may be a party in executing it. The average amount of spam a user receives can easily outnumber his or her normal email on any given day. It has therefore become common practice to implement spam filters in email gateways to protect network and server capacity, save working time on behalf of the recipient, and reduce the risk of actual email accidentally being discarded.

By far, the most common way of suppressing spam is email filtering on an email gateway. A large variety of commercial products exists, based on a variety of algorithms. Filtering based on simple keywords can be regarded as technically obsolete because this method is prone to generating false-positives, and spammers are able to easily work around this type of filter simply by manipulating the content and key words in their messages. More sophisticated filters, based, for instance, upon statistical analysis or analysis of email traffic patterns, have come to market. Filtering can happen on an email server (mail transfer agent (MTA)) or in the client (mail user agent (MUA)).

The administrator of a mail server can configure it to limit or slow down an excessive number of connections (tar pit). A mail server can be configured to honor blacklists of spam sources either as a direct blocking list or as one of several indicators for spam. Organizations need to take precautions against becoming a spam haven; i.e., their mail servers and hosts need to be secured to avoid becoming a relay point for spam.

Organizations sending spam—whether deliberately or involuntarily— may face dire consequences and retribution, starting with being cut off from their own mail and Internet access partly or in its entirety.

Scanning Techniques

Port Scanning

Port scanning (*Figure 4.36*) is the act of probing for TCP services on a machine. It is performed by establishing the initial handshake for a connection. Although not in itself an attack, it allows an attacker to test for the presence of potentially vulnerable services on a target system.

Port scanning can also be used for fingerprinting an operating system by evaluating its response characteristics, such as timing of a response, details of the handshake. Protection from port scanning includes restriction of network connections (e.g., by means of a host-based or network-based firewall or by defining a list of valid source addresses on an application level).

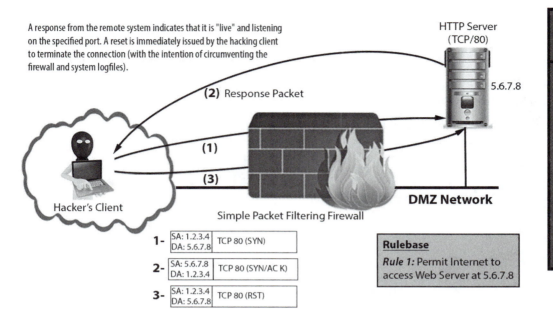

A response from the remote system indicates that it is "live" and listening on the specified port. A reset is immediately issued by the hacking client to terminate the connection (with the intention of circumventing the firewall and system logfiles).

HTTP Server
(TCP/80)

5.6.7.8

(2) Response Packet

(1)

(3)

Hacker's Client

DMZ Network

Simple Packet Filtering Firewall

1-	SA: 1.2.3.4 DA: 5.6.7.8	TCP 80 (SYN)
2-	SA: 5.6.7.8 DA: 1.2.3.4	TCP 80 (SYN/ACK)
3-	SA: 1.2.3.4 DA: 5.6.7.8	TCP 80 (RST)

Rulebase

Rule 1: Permit Internet to access Web Server at 5.6.7.8

Figure 4.36 – **Example of TCP port scan**
(From Young, S., and Aitel, D., **Hacker's Handbook: The Strategy Behind Breaking into and defending Networks**, *Auerbach Publications, Boca Raton, FL, 2004. With permission.)*

FIN, NULL, and XMAS Scanning

In FIN scanning, a stealth scanning method, a request to close a connection is sent to the target machine. If no application is listening on that port, a TCP RST or an ICMP packet will be sent. This attack commonly only works on UNIX machines, as Windows machines behave in a slightly different manner, deviating from RFC 793 (always responding to a FIN packet with an RST, thereby rendering recognition of open ports impossible) and thereby not being susceptible to the scan.[51] Firewalls that put a system into stealth mode (i.e., suppressing system responses to FIN packets) are available. In NULL scanning, no flags are set on the initiating TCP packet; in XMAS scanning, all TCP flags are set (or "lit," as in a Christmas tree). Otherwise, these scans work in the same manner as the FIN scan.

TCP Sequence Number Attacks

To detect and correct loss of data packets, TCP attaches a sequenced number to each data packet that is transmitted. If a transmission is not reported back as successful, a packet will be retransmitted. By eavesdropping on traffic, these sequence numbers can be predicted and fake packets with the correct sequence number can be introduced into the data stream by a third party. This class of attacks can, for instance, be used for session hijacking. Protection mechanisms against TCP sequence number attacks have been proposed based on better randomization of sequence numbers as described in RFC 1948.[52]

---

51   http://www.ietf.org/rfc/rfc793

52   http://www.ietf.org/rfc/rfc1948

Methodology of an Attack

Security attacks have been described formally as attack tree models. Attack trees are based upon the goal of the attacker, the risks to the defender, and the vulnerabilities of the defense systems. They are a specialized form of decision tree that can be used to formally evaluate system security (*Figure 4.37*). The following methodology describes not the attack tree itself (which is a defender's view) but the steps that an attacker would undergo to successfully traverse the tree toward his or her target.

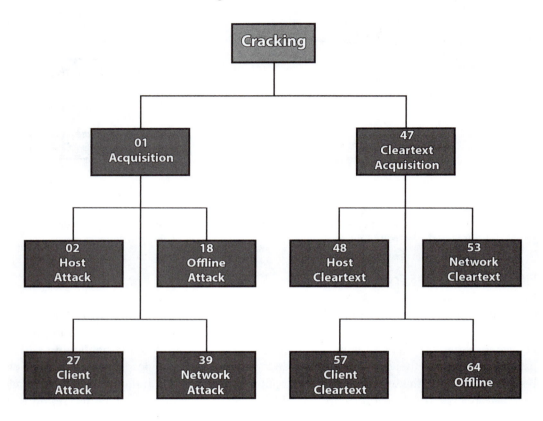

Figure 4.37 – **Attack Tree**

*(From Houser, D.D., Blended Threat Analysis: Passwords and Policy, in **Information Security Management Handbook**, 6th edition, Tipton, H.F. and Krause, M. Eds., Auerbach Publications, Boca Raton, FL, 2006. With permission.)*

Target Acquisition

An attack usually starts with intelligence gathering and surveillance to obtain a collection of possible targets, for instance, through evaluating directory services and network scanning. It is therefore important for the security architect and the security practitioner to work together to limit information available on a network and make intelligence gathering as difficult as possible for the attacker. This would include installation of split network security zones (internal nodes are only visible on the inside of a network), network address translation, limiting access to directories of persons and assets, using hidden paths, nonstandard privileged usernames, etc.

610

Importantly, not all of these obscurity measures have an inherent security value. They serve to slow the attacker down but will not in and of themselves provide any protection beyond this point; these measures are referred to as delaying tactics.

Target Analysis

In a second step, the identified target is analyzed for security weaknesses that would allow the attacker to obtain access. Depending on the type of attack, the discovery scan has already taken this into account, e.g., by scanning for servers susceptible to a certain kind of buffer overflow attack. Tools available for the target acquisition phase are generally capable of automatically performing a first-target analysis.

The most effective protection that the security professional can deploy is to minimize security vulnerabilities, for instance, by applying software patches at the earliest possible opportunity and practicing effective configuration management. In addition, target analysis should be made more difficult for the attacker. For example, system administrators should minimize the system information (e.g., system type, build, and release) that an attacker could glean, making it more difficult to attack the system.

Target Access

In the next step, an attacker will obtain some form of access to the system. This can be access as a normal user or as a guest. The attacker could be exploiting known vulnerabilities or common tools for this, or he or she could bypass technical security controls altogether by using social engineering attacks.

To mitigate the risk of unauthorized access, one should ensure that existing user privileges are well managed, access profiles are up to date, and unused accounts are either blocked or removed. Access should be monitored, and monitoring logs need to be regularly analyzed; however, most malware will come with root kits ready to subvert basic operating system privilege management.

Target Appropriation

At the last level of an attack, the attacker can then escalate his or her privileges on the system to gain system-level access. Again, exploitation of known vulnerabilities through existing or custom tools and techniques is the main technical attack vector; however, other attack vectors, such as social engineering, need to be taken into account.

Countermeasures against privilege escalation, by nature, are similar to the ones for gaining access. However, because an attacker can gain full control of a system through privilege escalation, secondary controls on the system itself (such as detecting unusual activity in log files) are less effective and reliable. Network (router, firewall, and intrusion detection system) logs can therefore prove invaluable to the security practitioner. Logs are so valuable, in fact, that an entire discipline within IT security has developed known as Security Event Management (SEM), or sometimes Security Event and Incident Management (SEIM).

For someone to detect the presence of unauthorized changes, which could indicate access from an attacker or backdoors into the system, the use of host-based or network-based intrusion detection systems can provide useful detection services. However, it is important to keep in mind that because an IDS relies on constant external input in the form of attack signature updates to remain effective, these systems are only as "good" as the quality and timeliness of the updates being applied to them. The output from the host-based IDS (such as regular snapshots or file hashes) needs to be stored in such a way that it cannot be overwritten from the source system in order to insure integrity.

Finally, yet importantly, the attacker may look to remotely maintain control of the system to regain access at a later time or to use it for other purposes, such as sending spam or as a stepping stone for other attacks. To such an end, the attacker could avail himself of prefabricated "rootkits" to sustain and maintain control over time. Such a rootkit will not only allow access but also hide its own existence from traditional cursory inspection methods.

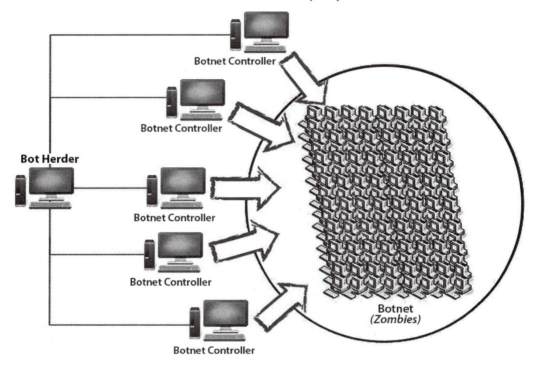

Figure 4.38 – **Architecture of a Botnet**

"Bots" and "botnets" are responsible for most of the activity leading to unauthorized, remote control of compromised systems today. Machines that have become infected, and are now considered to be "bots," are essentially zombies controlled by shadowy entities from the dark places on the Internet. Bots and botnets are the largest source of spam email and can be coordinated by "bot herders" to inflict highly effective denial of services attacks, all without the knowledge of the system owners. See *Figure 4.38*.

Network Security Tools and Tasks

Tools can make a security practitioner's job easier. Tools automate processes to save time and reduce error. Examples include scanners used to assess how well a server is configured and aids working to collect input for risk analysis. However, do not allow yourself to fall into the trap of reducing network security to collecting and using tools.

Intrusion Detection Systems

Intrusion detection systems (IDS) monitor activity and send alerts when they detect suspicious traffic. See *Figure 4.39*. There are two broad classifications of IDS: host-based IDS, which monitor activity on servers and workstations, and network-based IDS, which monitor network activity. Network IDS services are typically stand-alone devices or at least independent blades within network chassis. Network IDS logs would be accessed through a separate management console that will also generate alarms and alerts.

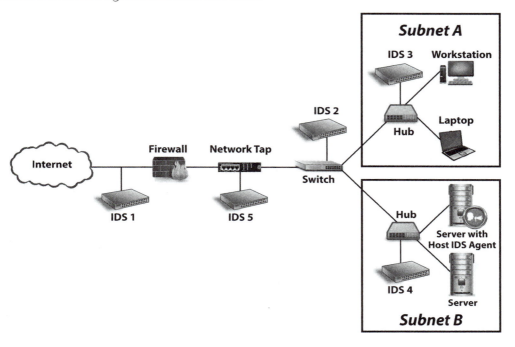

*Figure 4.39 – **Architecture of an Intrusion Detection System (IDS)***

Currently, there are two approaches to the deployment and use of intrusion detection systems. An appliance on the network can monitor traffic for attacks based on a set of signatures (analogous to anti-virus software), or the appliance can watch the network's traffic for a while, learn what traffic patterns are normal, and send an alert when it detects an anomaly. Of course, the IDS can be deployed using a hybrid of the two approaches as well.

Independent of the approach, how an organization uses an IDS determines whether the tool is effective. Despite its name, the IDS should not be used to detect intrusions because IDS solutions are not designed to be able to take preventative actions as part of their response. Instead, it should send an alert when it detects interesting, abnormal traffic that could be a prelude to an attack. For example, someone in the engineering department trying to access payroll information over the network at 3 a.m. is probably very interesting and not normal. Or perhaps a sudden rise in network utilization should be noted.

The above implies that an organization understands the normal characteristics of its network. When you consider modern networks' complexity and how much they change, that task is much easier said than done. Due to this complexity, it is fair to say that many IDS services deployed in enterprises today are merely "running" but not actually configured to be working the way that they were designed to. The security professional needs to decide whether he or she has the knowledge and resources necessary to operate the IDS correctly and for maximum effect or whether the best way to manage the IDS services would be to outsource to a qualified managed security service provider or integrate the IDS with a larger SEIM service such as splunk. "Snort" is a free and open-source intrusion detection system. In addition, a large number of commercial tools are available.

Security Event Management (SEM)

Security Event and Incident Management (SEIM)

SEM/SEIM is a solution that involves harvesting logs and event information from a variety of different sources on individual servers or assets and analyzing it as a consolidated view with sophisticated reporting. Similarly, entire IT infrastructures can have their logs and event information centralized and managed by large-scale SEM/SEIM deployments. SEM/SEIM will not only aggregate logs but will perform analysis and issue alerts (email, pager, audible, etc.) according to suspicious patterns.

SEM/SEIM solutions as concepts are not necessarily new. They have been around since shortly after 2000 at least; however, they are very complex technologies requiring significant skill on behalf of both the vendor (builder) and the integrator. This is because SEM/SEIM systems have to understand a wide variety of different applications and network element (routers/switches) logs and formats; consolidate these logs into a single database and then correlate events looking for clues to unauthorized behaviors that would be otherwise inconclusive if observed in a single log file.

Aggregation and consolidation of logs and events will also potentially require additional network resources to transfer log and event data from distinct servers and arrays to a central location. This transfer will also need to occur in as close to real time as possible if the security information is to possess value beyond forensics.

SEM/SEIM systems can benefit immensely from Security Intelligence Services (SIS). The output from security appliances is esoteric and lacks the real-world context required for predictive threat assessments. It falls short of delivering consistently relevant intelligence to businesses operating in a competitive marketplace. SIS uses all-source collection and analysis methods to produce and deliver precise and timely intelligence guiding not only the "business of security" but the "security of the business." SIS are built upon accurate security metrics (cyber and physical), market analysis, technology forecasting, and are correlated to real-world events, giving business decision makers time and precision. SIS provides upstream data from proactive cyber defense systems monitoring darkspace and darkweb.

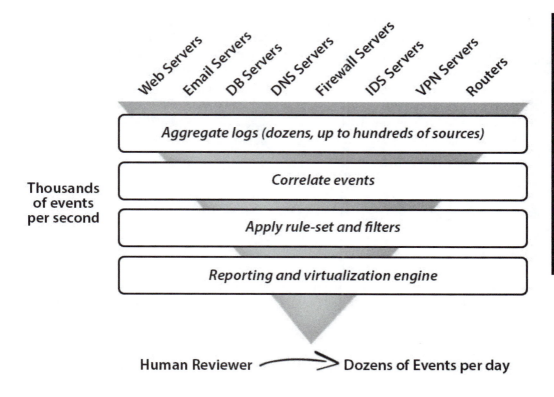

Figure 4.40 - SEIM services

Scanners

A network scanner can be used in several ways by the security practitioner:

■ Discovery of devices and services on a network, for instance, to establish whether new or unauthorized devices have been connected. Conversely, this type of scan can be used for intelligence gathering on potentially vulnerable services.

■ Test of compliance with a given policy, for instance, to ensure certain configurations (deactivation of services) have been applied.

■ Test for vulnerabilities, for instance, as part of a penetration test but also in preparation for an attack.

Discovery Scanning

A discovery scan can be performed with very simple methods, for example, by sending a ping packet (ping scanning) to every address in a subnet. More sophisticated methods will also discover the operating system and services of a responding device.

Compliance Scanning

A compliance scan can be performed either from the network or on the device (for instance, as a security health check). If performed on the network, it will usually include testing for open ports and services on the device.

Vulnerability Scanning and Penetration Testing

A vulnerability scan tests for vulnerability conditions generally by looking at responding ports and applications on a given server and determining patch levels. A vulnerability scan will infer a threat based upon what might be available as an avenue of attack. When new vulnerabilities have been published or are exploited, targeted scanner tools often become available from software vendors, anti-virus vendors, independent vendors, or the open-source community. Care must be taken when running scans in a corporate environment so that the load does not disrupt operations or cause applications and services to fail.

A penetration test is the follow-on step after a vulnerability scan, where the observed vulnerabilities are actually exploited or are attempted. It is often the case that an inferred vulnerability, when tested, is not actually a vulnerability. For instance, a service might be open on a port and appear un-patched, but upon testing it turns out that the security administrator has implemented a secure configuration that mitigates the vulnerabilities.

Penetration tests always have an elevated risk potential to bring down the asset against which they are being performed, and for this reason they should never be conducted on operational systems unless the risks associated with the tests have been assessed and accepted by the system's owner. In addition, a clear waiver from the asset owner should be obtained prior to testing.

Scanning Tools

This is not the place to describe the functionality of the many available scanning tools in detail. However the following tools are commonplace and worth understanding:

- **Nessus** – A vulnerability scanner
- **Nmap** – A discovery scanner that will allow for determining the services running on a machine, as well as other host characteristics, such as a machine's operating system

In addition, a large number of commercial tools exist.

Network Taps

A "network tap" or "span" is a device that has the ability to selectively copy all data flowing through a network in real time for analysis and storage. See *Figure 4.41*. Network taps may be deployed for the purposes of network diagnostics and maintenance or for purposes of forensic analysis related to incidents or suspicious events. Network taps will generally be fully configurable and will function at all layers from the physical layer up. In other words, a tap should be capable of copying everything from layer 1 (Ethernet, for instance) upward, including all payload information within the packets. Additionally, a tap can be configured to vacuum up every single packet of data or perhaps just focus on selected application traffic from selected sources.

Increasingly, network taps are being deployed for the purposes of compliance with legal requirements related to retaining records of transactions and detecting fraud. In a world of converged information assets with data, voice, instant messaging, and other communications assets all riding on top of the IP network, organizations might find themselves with little choice but to retain a complete copy of all traffic for later analysis if required. Network taps are available in a wide variety of forms and from a variety of commercial vendors.

4

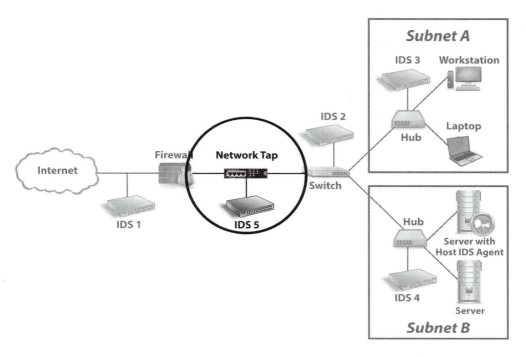

Figure 4.41 – **A network tap is a device that simply sits on a network in "monitor" or "promiscuous" mode and makes a copy of all the network traffic, possibly right down to the Ethernet frames.**

(From Macaulay, T., Securing Converged IP Networks, Auerbach Publications, Boca Raton, FL, 2006. With permission.)

IP Fragmentation Attacks and Crafted Packets

Teardrop
In this attack, IP packet fragments are constructed so that the target host calculates a negative fragment length when it attempts to reconstruct the packet. If the target host's IP stack does not ensure that fragment lengths are set within appropriate boundaries, the host could crash or become unstable. This problem is easily fixed with a vendor patch.

Overlapping Fragment Attack
Overlapping fragment attacks are used to subvert packet filters that only inspect the first fragment of a fragmented packet. The technique involves sending a harmless first fragment, which will satisfy the packet filter. Other packets follow that overwrite the first fragment with malicious data, thus resulting in harmful packets bypassing the packet filter and being accepted by the victim host. A solution to this problem is for TCP/IP stacks not to allow fragments to overwrite each other.

Source Routing Exploitation
Instead of only permitting routers to determine the path a packet takes to its destination, IP allows the sender to explicitly specify the path. An attacker can abuse source routing so that the packet will be forwarded between network interfaces on a multi-homed computer that is configured not to forward packets. This could allow an external attacker access to an internal network.

Source routing is specified by the sender of an IP datagram, whereas the routing path would normally be left to the router to decide. The best solution is to disable source routing on hosts and to block source-routed packets.

Smurf and Fraggle Attacks

Both attacks use broadcasts to create denial-of-service attacks. A Smurf attack misuses the ICMP echo request to create denial-of-service attacks.

In a Smurf attack, the intruder sends an ICMP echo request with a spoofed source address of the victim. The packet is sent to a network's broadcast address, which forwards the packet to every host on the network. Because the ICMP packet contains the victim's host as the source address, the victim will be overwhelmed by the ICMP echo replies, causing a denial-of-service attack.

The Fraggle attack uses UDP instead of ICMP. The attacker sends a UDP packet on port 7 with a spoofed source address of the victim. Like the Smurf attack, the packet is sent to a network's broadcast address, which will forward the packet to all of the hosts on the network. The victim host will be overwhelmed by the responses from the network.

NFS Attacks

NFS versions 2 and 3 have several drawbacks from a security perspective, due to their rather basic authentication mechanisms and to the fact that a file system protocol must possess some form of state management, for which some workarounds have to be introduced on top of the stateless protocol to enable, for instance, file locking. An attacker would have several opportunities to attack NFS, be it from a client, a server, or a network perspective.

The first step in setting up an NFS connection will be the publication (exporting) of file system trees from the server. These trees can be arbitrarily chosen by the administrator. Access privileges are granted based upon the client IP address and directory tree. Within the tree, the privileges of the server file system will be mapped to client users. Several points of risk exist:

- Export of parts of the file system that were not intended for publication or with inappropriate privileges (for instance, by accident or through the existence of UNIX file system hard links, which can be generated by the user). This is of particular concern if parts of the server root file system are made accessible. One can easily imagine scenarios where a password file can be accessed and the encrypted passwords contained therein are subsequently broken by an off-the-shelf tool. Regular review of exported file system trees is an appropriate mitigation.

- Using an unauthorized client. Because NFS identifies the client by its IP address or (indirectly) a host name, it is relatively easy to use a different client than the authorized one, by means of IP spoofing or DNS spoofing. At the very least, resolution of server host names should therefore happen via a file (/ etc/ hosts on UNIX), not through DNS.

- Incorrect mapping of user IDs between server and client. Any machine not controlled by the server administrator can be used to propagate an attack, as NFS relies on user IDs as the only form of authorization credential. An attacker, having availed himself of administrative access to a client, could generate arbitrary user IDs to match those on the server. It is paramount that user IDs on the server and the client are synchronized (e.g., through the use of NIS/NIS+).

■ Sniffing and access request spoofing. Because NFS traffic, by default, is not encrypted, it is possible to intercept it, either by means of network sniffing or by a man-in-the-middle attack. Because NFS does not authenticate each RPC call, it is possible to access files if the appropriate access token (file handle) has been obtained, for instance, through sniffing. NFS itself does not offer appropriate mitigation; however the use of secure NFS may. [53]

■ SetUID files. The directories accessed via NFS are used in the same way local directories are. On UNIX systems, files with the SUID bit can therefore be used for privilege escalation on the client. NFS should therefore be configured in such a way as to not respect SUID bits.

Network News Transport Protocol (NNTP) Security

From a security perspective, the main shortcoming in NNTP is authentication. Confidentiality of the message is much less of a concern, as the information is indeed intended for publication; however, the proper identification and authentication of the sender remains a strong concern.

One of the earlier solutions users found to this problem was signing messages with Pretty Good Privacy (PGP). However, this did not prevent impersonation or faked identities, as digital signatures were not a requirement, and indeed would be unsuitable for the repudiation problem implied. To make matters worse, NNTP offers a cancellation mechanism to withdraw articles already published. Naturally, the same authentication weakness applies to the control messages used for these cancellations, allowing users with even moderate skills to delete messages at will.

On a related note, NNTP feeds have been plagued with spam for more than a decade (in essence, since Usenet spam became economically viable). A number of mechanisms to deal with this problem have evolved. It can be safely said that all technical measures are just add-ons to what is mostly a social self-regulation mechanism. The original Usenet way of dealing with unwanted information was maintenance of client-based blacklists by the user, so-called killfiles.

Some newsgroups have been set up as moderated to prevent misuse, mostly by partisan participants, but naturally the mechanism also works against spam, even though it comes at an increased workload to the moderator of a newsgroup. Over time, a convention evolved, after which messages classified as spam by well-defined criteria (excessive repetitions or cross-posting of identical or highly similar messages) were legitimate targets for cancellations. The problem of authentication has never been adequately addressed in NNTP, and it might even be undesirable to do so: In a certain way, Usenet as a social construct may well depend on the ability to post anonymously or under pseudonyms.

Finger User Information Protocol

Finger is an identification service that allows a user to obtain information about the last log-in time of a user and whether he or she is currently logged into a system. The "fingered" user has the possibility to have information from two files in his or her home directory displayed (the .project and .plan files).

Developed as early as 1971, Finger is implemented as a UNIX daemon, fingerd. Finger has become less popular for several reasons:

---

53 Secure NFS (SNFS) offers secure authentication and encryption on the basis of secure RPC, which authenticates each RPC request.

- Finger has been the subject of a number of security exploits.
- Finger is raising privacy and security concerns; it can easily be abused for social engineering attacks.
- The user's self-actuation (an important social aspect in early UNIX networks) happens through webpages today.

For all practical purposes, the Finger protocol has become obsolete. Its use should be restricted to situations where no alternatives are available.

Ports	79/TCP
Definition	RFC 742
	RFC 1288

*Table 4.22 – **Finger Quick Reference** [54]*
Network Time Protocol (NTP)

NTP synchronizes computer clocks in a network. This can be extremely important for operational stability (for instance, under NIS) but also for maintaining consistency and coherence of audit trails, such as in log files. A variant of NTP exists in Simple Network Time Protocol (SNTP), offering a less resource intensive but also less exact form of synchronization. From a security perspective, our main objective with NTP is to prevent an attacker from changing time information on a client or a whole network by manipulating its local time server.

NTP can be configured to restrict access based upon IP address. From NTP version 3 onward, cryptographic authentication has become available, based upon symmetric encryption, but it is to be replaced by public key cryptography in NTP version 4.

To make a network robust against accidental or deliberate timing inaccuracies, a network should have its own time server and possibly a dedicated, highly accurate clock. As a standard precaution, a network should never depend on one external time server alone but synchronize with several trusted time sources. Thus, manipulation of a single source will have no immediate effect. To detect de-synchronization, one can use standard logging mechanisms with NTP to ensure synchronicity of time stamping.

Ports	123/TCP, 123/UDP
Definition	RFC 778
	RC 891
	RC 956
	RC 958
	RFC 1305

*Table 4.23 – **NTP Quick Reference***

---

54 http://www.ietf.org/rfc/rfc742
    http://www.ietf.org/rfc/rfc1288

Denial-of-Service (DoS) / Distributed-Denial-of Service (DDoS) Attacks

The easiest attack to carry out against a network, or so it may seem, is to overload it through excessive traffic or traffic that has been "crafted" to confuse the network into shutting down or slowing to the point of uselessness. See *Figure 4.42*.

Countermeasures include, but are not limited to, multiple layers of firewalls, careful filtering on firewalls, routers and switches, internal network access controls (NAC), redundant (diverse) network connections, load balancing, reserved bandwidth (quality of service, which would at least protect systems not directly targeted), and blocking traffic from an attacker on an upstream router. Bear in mind that malicious agents can and will shift an IP address or a DNS name to sidestep the attack, as well as employing potentially thousands of unique IP addresses during the execution of an attack. Enlisting the help of upstream service providers and carriers is ultimately the most effective countermeasure, especially if the necessary agreements and relationships have been established proactively or as part of agreed service levels.

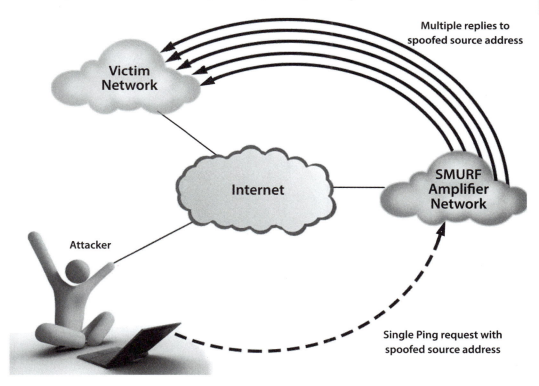

Figure 4.42 – **A Denial-of-Service attack. The attacker uses spoofed PING packets to floor a network by using a vulnerable intermediary network.**

It is instructive to note that many protocols contain basic protection from message loss that would at least mitigate the effects of denial-of-service attacks. This starts with TCP managing packet loss within certain limits, and it ends with higher level protocols, such as SMTP, that will provide robustness against temporary connection outages (store and forward). [55]

For the attacker, there are a number of ways to execute denial-of-service attacks while minimizing his own cost:

- **Distributed Denial-of-Service attack** – Using a network of remote-controlled hosts known as "botnets" (typically workstations that have been compromised by a virus or other form of "malware"), the target is subjected to traffic from a wide range of sources that are very hard to block. The downside of this type of attack to both the attacker and network service provider is that the attack may already throttle upstream network channels, taking out more than just its intended target.

  Distributed denial-of-service attacks have been used as a means of extortion but also as a political instrument (referred to by their initiators as online demonstration), where activists would instigate users to frequently reload a certain website at a certain point in time.

Countermeasures are similar to those of conventional denial-of-service attacks, but simple IP or port filtering might not work.

SYN Flooding

A SYN flood attack is a denial-of-service attack against the initial handshake in a TCP connection. Many new connections from faked, random IP addresses are opened in short order, overloading the target's connection table.

Countermeasures include tuning of operating system parameters such as the size of the backlog table according to vendor specifications. Another solution, which requires modification to the TCP/IP stack, is SYN cookies changing TCP numbers in a way that makes faked packets immediately recognizable. [56]

Daniel J. Bernstein, the primary inventor of this approach, defines them as "particular choices of initial TCP sequence numbers by TCP servers. The difference between the server's initial sequence number and the client's initial sequence number is:

- **Top 5 bits** – t mod 32, where t is a 32 bit time counter that increases every 64 seconds;
- **Next 3 bits** – An encoding of an MSS selected by the server in response to the client's MSS;
- **Bottom 24 bits** – A server-selected secret function of the client IP address and port number, the server IP address and port number, and t.

A server that uses SYN cookies does not have to drop connections when its SYN queue fills up. Instead it sends back a SYN+ACK, exactly as if the SYN queue had been larger. When the server receives an ACK, it checks that the secret function works for a recent value of t, and then rebuilds the SYN queue entry from the encoded MSS."

One of the most successful variants of SYN flooding can be carried out by the botnets discussed earlier. Botnets have the ability to direct potentially thousands of SYN requests to hosts at the same time, overwhelming not only the hosts but also the network connections that

---

55 The concept of store and forward allows for the reception of a data packet upstream from the end point and the queuing of that data for a period of time if necessary, in order to ensure delivery of the data to the end point once it is located.

56 Bernstein, Daniel J., "SYN cookies". N.P., 1996. Web. 30 June 2014. http://cr.yp.to/syncookies.html

they rest upon. Under such circumstances, there are no host-configuration countermeasures available because a host without a network is as good as dead anyway. While SYN flooding might be the mode of attack, it is not being employed in any cunning manner with spoofed IP addresses from possibly a single malicious host; it is being applied as a pure brute force form of attack.

Countermeasures include protecting the operating system through securing its network stack. This is not normally something the user or owner of a system has any degree of control over; it is a task for the vendor.

Finally, the network needs to be included in a corporation's disaster recovery and business contingency plans. For local area networks, one may set high recovery objectives and provide appropriate contingency, based upon the fact that any recovery of services is likely to be useless without at least a working local area network (LAN) infrastructure. As wide area networks are usually outsourced, contingency measures might include acquisition of backup lines from a different provider, procurement of telephone or Digital Subscriber Loop (DSL) lines, etc.

Spoofing

IP Address Spoofing and SYN-ACK Attacks

Packets are sent with a bogus source address so that the victim will send a response to a different host. Spoofed addresses can be used to abuse the three-way handshake that is required to start a TCP session. Under normal circumstances, a host offers to initiate a session with a remote host by sending a packet with the SYN option. The remote host responds with a packet with the SYN and ACK options. The handshake is completed when the initiating host responds with a packet with the ACK option.

An attacker can launch a denial-of-service attack by sending the initial packet with the SYN option with a source address of a host that does not exist. The victim will respond to the forged source address by sending a packet with the SYN and ACK options and then wait for the final packet to complete the handshake. Of course, that packet will never arrive because the victim sent the packet to a host that does not exist. If the attacker sends a storm of packets with spoofed addresses, the victim may reach the limit of uncompleted (half-open) three-way handshakes and refuse other legitimate network connections.

The above scenario takes advantage of a protocol flaw. To mitigate the risk of a successful attack, vendors have released patches that reduce the likelihood of the limit of uncompleted handshakes being reached. In addition, security devices, such as firewalls, can block packets that arrive from an external interface with a source address from an internal network.

Email Spoofing

As SMTP does not possess an adequate authentication mechanism, email spoofing is extremely simple. The most effective protection against this is a social one, whereas the recipient can confirm or simply ignore implausible email. Spoofing email sender addresses is extremely simple, and it can be done with a simple TELNET command to port 25 of a mail server and by issuing a number of SMTP commands. Email spoofing is frequently used as a means to obfuscate the identity of a sender in spamming, whereas the purported sender of a spam email is in fact another victim of spam, whose email address has been harvested by or sold to a spammer.

DNS Spoofing

To resolve a domain name query, such as mapping a Web server address to an IP address, the user's workstation will in turn have to undertake a series of queries through the Domain Name Server hierarchy. Such queries can be either recursive (a name server receiving a request will forward it and return the resolution) or iterative (a name server receiving a request will respond with a reference).

An attacker aiming to poison a DNS server's (name server) cache (information related to previous queries, which is stored for reuse in future queries for speed and efficiency) by injecting fake records, and thereby falsifying responses to client requests, will need to send a query to this very name server. The attacker now knows that the name server will shortly send out a query for resolution.

In the first case, the attacker has sent a query for a domain, whose primary name server he controls. The response from this query will contain additional information that was not originally requested, but which the target server will now cache. The second case is a dissimilar method that can also be used in iterative queries. Using IP spoofing, the attacker will send a response to his own query before the authoritative (correct) name server has a chance to respond.

In both cases, the attacker has used an electronic conversation to inject false information into the name server's cache. Not only will this name server now use the cached information, but the false information will propagate to other servers, making inquiries to this one. Due to the caching nature of DNS, attacks on DNS servers as well as countermeasures always have certain latency, determined by the configuration of a (domain) zone.

There are two principal vulnerabilities here, both inherent in the design of the DNS protocol: It is possible for a DNS server to respond to a recursive query with information that was not requested, and the DNS server will not authenticate information. Approaches to address or mitigate this threat have only been partly successful.

Later versions of DNS server software are programmed to ignore responses that do not correspond to a query. Authentication has been proposed, but attempts to introduce stronger (or even any) authentication into DNS (for instance, through the use of DNSSEC) have not found wide acceptance. Authentication services have been delegated upward to higher protocol layers. Applications in need of guaranteeing authenticity cannot rely on DNS to provide such but will have to implement a solution themselves.

The ultimate solution to DNS security issues for many organizations is to establish DNS servers dedicated to their domains and vigorously monitor them. An "internal" DNS server will also be established, which only accepts queries from internal networks and users, and therefore it is considered to be substantially more difficult for outsiders to compromise and use as a staging point for penetrating internal networks.

Manipulation of DNS Queries

Technically, the following two techniques are only indirectly related to DNS weaknesses. However, it is worth mentioning them in the context of DNS because they seek to manipulate name resolution in other ways.

"Pharming" is the manipulation of DNS records; for instance, through the "hosts" file on a workstation. A hosts file (*/etc/hosts* on many UNIX machines, *C:\Windows\System32\drivers\etc* on a Windows machine) is the resource first queried before a DNS request is issued. It will always contain the mapping of the host name local host to the IP address 127.0.0.1 (loopback interface, as defined in RFC 3330) and potentially other hosts.[57] A virus or malware may add addresses of anti-virus software vendors with invalid IP addresses to the hosts file to prevent download of virus pattern files. Alternately, Internet banking sites might have their IP addresses substituted for rogue, imposters' sites that will attempt to trick the user into providing login information. A further form of DNS pharming is to compromise a DNS server itself and thereby re-direct all users of the DNS server to imposter websites even though their workstation itself may be free from compromise.

Social engineering techniques will not try to manipulate a query on a technical level, but they can trick the user into misinterpreting a DNS address that is displayed to him in a phishing email or in his Web browser address bar. One way to achieve this in email or Hypertext Markup Language (HTML) documents is to display a link in text where the actual target address is different from what is displayed. Another way to achieve this is the use of non-ASCII character sets (for instance, Unicode—ISO/IEC 10646:2012—characters) that closely resemble ASCII (i.e., Latin) characters to the user.[58] This may become a popular technique with the popularization of internationalized domain names.

Information Disclosure

Smaller corporate networks do not split naming zones (i.e., names of hosts that are accessible only from an intranet are visible from the Internet). Although knowing a server name will not enable anyone to access it, this knowledge can aid and facilitate preparation of a planned attack as it provides an attacker with valuable information on existing hosts (at least with regard to servers), network structure, and, for instance, details such as organizational structure or server operating systems (if the OS is part of the host name, etc.).

An organization should therefore operate split DNS zones wherever possible and refrain from using telling naming conventions for their machines. In addition, a domain registrar's database of administrative and billing domain contacts (Whois database) can be an attractive target for information and email harvesting.

Namespace-Related Risks

Besides the technical risks described, a number of other risks exist that, although not strictly security related, can lead to equivalent exposure.

---

57   http://tools.ietf.org/html/rfc3330

58   See the following to download the ISO/IEC 10646:2012 Standard: http://standards.iso.org/ittf/
PubliclyAvailableStandards/index.html

625

Session Highjack

Session hijacking is the act of unauthorized insertion of packets into a data stream. It is normally based on sequence number attacks, where sequence numbers are either guessed or intercepted. Different types of session hijacking exist:

- ■ *IP Spoofing* – Based on a TCP sequence number attack, the attacker would insert packets with a faked sender IP address and a guessed sequence number into the stream. The attacker would not be able to see the response to any commands inserted.
- ■ *Man-in-the-Middle Attack* – The attacker would sniff or intercept packets, removing legitimate packets from the data stream and replacing them with his own. In fact, both sides of a communication would then communicate with the attacker instead of each other.

Countermeasures against IP spoofing can be executed at layer 3 (see IP Address Spoofing and Syn-Ack Attacks). As TCP sessions only perform an initial authentication, application layer encryption can be used to protect against man-in-the-middle attacks.

SYN Scanning

As traditional TCP scans became widely recognized and were blocked, various stealth scanning techniques were developed. In TCP half scanning (also known as TCP SYN scanning), no complete connection is opened; instead, only the initial steps of the handshake are performed. This makes the scan harder to recognize; for instance, it would not show up in application log files. However, it is possible to recognize and block TCP SYN scans with an appropriately equipped firewall.

Summary

Our discussions in the communication and network security domain have been focused on the structures, transmission methods, transport formats, and security measures used to provide confidentiality, integrity, and availability for transmissions over private and public communications networks and media. Network security, like all security controls and safeguards, is most effective when applied proactively. Waiting for impacts to materialize and applying controls and safeguards under crisis conditions will always cost more and be less effective than planned and managed deployments of network security policy, procedures, and technologies. The security professional has to be prepared to face crisis with as many options as possible available to apply the best possible solution at the point of contact.

As the disappearance of "traditional" network boundaries becomes a business requirement facilitated through hastened introduction of new technologies and the convergence of technologies onto an IP backbone, a constant struggle exists between ease of use and security. It is a fundamental tenet of secure design that the inside of a network must be as resilient as its perimeter, that tools alone are ineffective if not combined with proper process, and that the availability of a network is a critical measure of the success of its design. Increasingly, attacks on the network are aimed not only at disrupting availability but also at compromising the knowledge and "semantic" assets of the network through stealthy confidentiality and integrity attacks.

The security professional needs to continue to evolve his or her skills and abilities to match the threats that face the enterprise today. The ever shifting end point boundary for network security has made this a significant challenge in the face of a growing trend towards more access and more mobility for end-users. Coupled with the advanced nature of many of the attacks being launched against the enterprise today, the security professional must work harder and smarter to stay ahead and continue to safeguard the enterprise.

Domain 4: Review Questions

1. In the OSI reference model, on which layer can Ethernet (IEEE 802.3) be described?

    A.   Layer 1—Physical layer

    B.   Layer 2—Data-link layer

    C.   Layer 3—Network Layer

    D.   Layer 4—Transport Layer

2. A customer wants to keep cost to a minimum and has only ordered a single static IP address from the ISP. Which of the following must be configured on the router to allow for all the computers to share the same public IP address?

    A.   VLANs

    B.   PoE

    C.   PAT

    D.   VPN

3. Users are reporting that some Internet websites are not accessible anymore. Which of the following will allow the network administrator to quickly isolate the remote router that is causing the network communication issue, so that the problem can be reported to the appropriate responsible party?

    A.   Ping

    B.   Protocol analyzer

    C.   Tracert

    D.   Dig

4. Ann installs a new Wireless Access Point (WAP) and users are able to connect to it. However, once connected, users cannot access the Internet. Which of the following is the **MOST** likely cause of the problem?

    A.   The signal strength has been degraded and latency is increasing hop count.

    B.   An incorrect subnet mask has been entered in the WAP configuration.

    C.   The signal strength has been degraded and packets are being lost.

    D.   Users have specified the wrong encryption type and packets are being rejected.

5. What is the optimal placement for network-based intrusion detection systems (NIDS)?

    A.   On the network perimeter, to alert the network administrator of all suspicious traffic

    B.   On network segments with business-critical systems (e.g., demilitarized zones (DMZs) and on certain intranet segments)

    C.   At the network operations center (NOC)

    D.   At an external service provider

6. Which of the following end-point devices would **MOST** likely be considered part of a converged IP network?

    A.   file server, IP phone, security camera

    B.   IP phone, thermostat, cypher lock

    C.   security camera, cypher lock, IP phone

    D.   thermostat, file server, cypher lock

7. Network upgrades have been completed and the WINS server was shutdown. It was decided that NetBIOS network traffic will no longer be permitted. Which of the following will accomplish this objective?

    A.   Content filtering

    B.   Port filtering

    C.   MAC filtering

    D.   IP filtering

8. Which of the following devices should be part of a network's perimeter defense?

    A.   A boundary router, A firewall, A proxy Server

    B.   A firewall, A proxy server, A host based intrusion detection system (HIDS)

    C.   A proxy server, A host based intrusion detection system (HIDS), A firewall

    D.   A host based intrusion detection system (HIDS), A firewall, A boundary router

9. Which of the following is a principal security risk of wireless LANs?

    A.   Lack of physical access control

    B.   Demonstrably insecure standards

    C.   Implementation weaknesses

    D.   War driving

10. Which of the following is a path vector routing protocol?

    A. RIP

    B. EIGRP

    C. OSPF/IS-IS

    D. BGP

11. It can be said that IPSec

    A. provides mechanisms for authentication and encryption.

    B. provides mechanisms for nonrepudiation.

    C. will only be deployed with IPv6.

    D. only authenticates clients against a server.

12. A Security Event Management (SEM) service performs the following function:

    A. Gathers firewall logs for archiving

    B. Aggregates logs from security devices and application servers looking for suspicious activity

    C. Reviews access controls logs on servers and physical entry points to match user system authorization with physical access permissions

    D. Coordination software for security conferences and seminars.

13. Which of the following is the principal weakness of DNS (Domain Name System)?

    A. Lack of authentication of servers, and thereby authenticity of records

    B. Its latency, which enables insertion of records between the time when a record has expired and when it is refreshed

    C. The fact that it is a simple, distributed, hierarchical database instead of a singular, relational one, thereby giving rise to the possibility of inconsistencies going undetected for a certain amount of time

    D. The fact that addresses in e-mail can be spoofed without checking their validity in DNS, caused by the fact that DNS addresses are not digitally signed

14. Which of the following statements about open e-mail relays is incorrect?

    A. An open e-mail relay is a server that forwards e-mail from domains other than the ones it serves.

    B. Open e-mail relays are a principal tool for distribution of spam.

    C. Using a blacklist of open e-mail relays provides a secure way for an e-mail administrator to identify open mail relays and filter spam.

    D. An open e-mail relay is widely considered a sign of bad system administration.

15. A botnet can be characterized as

  A. An network used solely for internal communications
  B. An automatic security alerting tool for corporate networks
  C. A group of dispersed, compromised machines controlled remotely for illicit reasons.
  D. A type of virus

16. During a disaster recovery test, several billing representatives need to be temporarily setup to take payments from customers. It has been determined that this will need to occur over a wireless network, with security being enforced where possible. Which of the following configurations should be used in this scenario?

  A. WPA2, SSID enabled, and 802.11n.
  B. WEP, SSID enabled, and 802.11b.
  C. WEP, SSID disabled, and 802.11g.
  D. WPA2, SSID disabled, and 802.11a.

17. Which xDSL flavor delivers both downstream and upstream speeds of 1.544 Mbps over two copper twisted pairs?

  A. HDSL
  B. SDSL
  C. ADSL
  D. VDSL

18. A new installation requires a network in a heavy manufacturing area with substantial amounts of electromagnetic radiation and power fluctuations. Which media is best suited for this environment is little traffic degradation is tolerated?

  A. Coax cable
  B. Wireless
  C. Shielded twisted pair
  D. Fiber

19. Multi-layer protocols such as Modbus used in industrial control systems

  A. often have their own encryption and security like IPv6
  B. are used in modern routers as a routing interface control
  C. Are often insecure by their very nature as they were not designed to natively operate over today's IP networks
  D. Have largely been retired and replaced with newer protocols such as IPv6 and NetBIOS

20. Frame Relay and X.25 networks are part of which of the following?

    A.   Circuit-switched services

    B.   Cell-switched services

    C.   Packet-switched services

    D.   Dedicated digital services

4

Communications &
Network Security

Domain 5
Identity & Access Management

Before one can begin a comprehensive overview of the identity and access management domain, it is important to have an understanding of some key concepts that will be important throughout the chapter. These concepts form the basis for understanding how access management works, why it is a key security discipline, and how each individual component to be discussed in this chapter relates to the overall access management universe. The most fundamental and significant concept to master is a precise definition of what is meant by the term "access control." For the rest of this chapter and throughout this book, the following definition is used:

Access control is the process of allowing only authorized users, programs, or other computer systems (i.e., networks) to observe, modify, or otherwise take possession of the resources of a computer system. It is also a mechanism for limiting the use of some resources to authorized users.

In summary, access controls are the collection of mechanisms, processes, or techniques that work together to protect the assets of an organization. They help protect against threats and mitigate vulnerabilities by reducing exposure to unauthorized activities and providing access to information and systems to only authorized people, processes, or systems.

Although identity and access management is a single domain within the CISSP Common Body of Knowledge (CBK), it is the most pervasive and omnipresent aspect of information security. Access controls encompass all operational levels of an organization:

- **Facilities** – Access controls protect entry to, and movement around, an organization's physical locations to protect personnel, equipment, information, and other assets inside that facility.

- **Support Systems** – Access to support systems (such as power, heating, ventilation, and air conditioning (HVAC) systems; water; and fire suppression controls) must be controlled so that a malicious entity is not able to compromise these systems and cause harm to the organization's personnel or the ability to support critical systems.

- **Information Systems** – Multiple layers of access controls are present in most modern information systems and networks to protect those systems, and the information they contain, from harm or misuse.

- **Personnel** – Management, end-users, customers, business partners, and nearly everyone else associated with an organization should be subject to some form of access control to ensure that the right people have the ability to interface with each other and not interfere with the people with whom they do not have any legitimate business.

Additionally, almost all physical and logical entry points to the organization and its information systems need some type of access control. Given the pervasive nature and importance of access controls throughout the practice of security, it is necessary to understand the four key attributes of access control that enable good security management. Specifically, access controls enable management to:

- Specify which users can access a system or facility.

- Specify what resources those users can access.

- Specify what operations those users can perform.

- Enforce accountability for those users' actions.

Each of these four areas, although interrelated, represents an established and individual approach to defining an effective access control strategy. The information in this chapter will assist the security professional in determining the proper course of action to satisfy each of the attributes as it applies to a particular system, process, or facility.

The A-I-C triad: The common thread among information security objectives is that they address at least one (if not all three) of the core security principles: confidentiality, integrity, and availability (more commonly referred to as the C-I-A).

- **Confidentiality** – Refers to efforts made to prevent unauthorized disclosure of information to those who do not have the need, or right, to see it.

- **Integrity** – Refers to efforts made to prevent unauthorized or improper modification of systems and information. It also refers to the amount of trust that can be placed in a system and the accuracy of information within that system. For example, many systems and applications will check data that come into the system for syntactic and semantic accuracy to ensure that incoming data do not introduce operational or processing errors, thus affecting its overall integrity.

- **Availability** – Refers to efforts made to prevent disruption of service and productivity.

The goals of information security are to ensure the continued Confidentiality-Integrity-Availability of an organization's assets. This includes both physical assets (such as buildings, equipment, and, of course, people) and information assets (such as company data and information systems). Access controls play a key role in ensuring the confidentiality of systems and information. Managing access to physical and information assets is fundamental to preventing exposure of data by controlling who can see, use, modify, or destroy those assets. In addition, managing an entity's admittance and rights to specific enterprise resources ensures that valuable data and services are not abused, misappropriated, or stolen. It is also a key factor for many organizations that are required to protect personal information in order to be compliant with appropriate legislation and industry compliance requirements.

The act of controlling access inherently provides features and benefits that protect the integrity of business assets. By preventing unauthorized or inappropriate access, organizations can achieve greater confidence in data and system integrity. If an organization is without controls to manage who has access to specific resources, and what actions they are permitted to perform, there are a few alternate controls to ensure that information and systems are not modified by unwanted influences. Access controls (more specifically, records of access activity) also offer greater visibility into determining who or what may have altered data or system information, potentially affecting the integrity of those assets. Access controls can be used to match an entity (such as a person or a computer system) with the actions that entity takes against valuable assets, allowing organizations to have a better understanding of the state of their security posture.

Finally, access control processes go hand in hand with efforts to ensure the availability of resources within an organization. One of the most basic rules to embrace for any valuable asset, especially an asset whose criticality requires that it must be available for use over elongated periods of time, is that only people with a need to use that particular asset should be allowed access to that asset. Taking this stance ensures that the resource is not blocked or congested by people who have no business using it. This is why most organizations only allow their employees and other trusted individuals into their facilities or onto their corporate networks. In addition, restricting access to only those who need to use a resource reduces the likelihood that malicious agents can gain access and cause damage to the asset or that non-malicious individuals with unnecessary access can cause accidental damage.

5

Identity & Access Management

TOPICS

- Physical and logical access to assets
  - Information
  - Systems
  - Devices
  - Facilities
- Identification and authentication of people and devices
  - Identity management implementation (e.g., SSP, LDAP)
  - Single/ multi-factor authentication (e.g., factors, strength, errors)
  - Accountability
  - Session management (e.g., timeouts, screensavers)
  - Registration and proofing of identity
  - Federated identity management (e.g., SAML)
  - Credential management system
- Identity as a Service
- Third-party identity services
- Authorization mechanisms
  - Role-based access control (RBAC) methods
  - Rule-based access control methods
  - Mandatory access control (MAC)
  - Discretionary access control (DAC)
- Access control attacks
- The identity and access provisioning lifecycle

OBJECTIVES

According to the (ISC)² Candidate Information Bulletin (Exam Outline), a CISSP candidate is expected to be able to:

- Control physical and logical access to assets.

- Manage identification and authentication of people and devices.

- Integrate identity as a service.

- Integrate third-party identity services.

- Implement and manage authorization mechanisms.

- Prevent or mitigate access control attacks.

- Manage the identity and access provisioning lifecycle (e.g., provisioning, review).

5

Identity &
Access Management

Physical and Logical Access to Assets

Adequate security of information and information systems is a fundamental management responsibility. Nearly all applications that deal with financial, privacy, safety, or defense include some form of access control. Access control is concerned with determining the allowed activities of legitimate users, mediating every attempt by a user to access a resource in the system. In some systems, complete access is granted after successful authentication of the user, but most systems require more sophisticated and complex control. In addition to the authentication mechanism (such as a password), access control is concerned with how authorizations are structured. In some cases, authorization may mirror the structure of the organization, while in others it may be based on the sensitivity level of various documents and the clearance level of the user accessing those documents.

Access control systems are physical or electronic systems that are designed to control who, or what, has access to a network. The simplest example of a physical access control system is a door that can be locked, limiting people to one side of the door or the other. Electronic versions typically control network security, limiting which users are allowed to use resources on a computer system, for example. In some cases, physical access control systems are integrated with electronic ones. For example, a door may be unlocked with a swipe card, an RFID keyfob, or through some sort of biometric solution. A card access control system is one of the most common types of electronic door control, using a card with a magnetic stripe that can be swiped through a reader on the door. Hotels often use this system, which can be used to make temporary room keys. Laboratories and other facilities with areas requiring high security may also use a card control system, making the cards double as personnel identification.

Depending on the size of the organization and the varying levels of security that may be necessary, physical access control systems within a building may be linked or standardized, as is the case with a key that opens all of the doors in a building, or each access point may be controlled individually. The use of electronic systems allows an administrator to precisely define access privileges for each user and also instantly update them within the system, which is much more convenient than granting or revoking key privileges. Network security is also important, especially in a company that handles sensitive data. Access control systems that span computer networks are typically administered in a central location, with each user being given a unique identity. An administrator grants access privileges to personnel on a case by case basis, using settings within the administration software.

When installing these systems, the security professional should consider who will use the system and how it will be used. In a situation where numerous users, including guests, are entering the area, tiered levels of security may be advisable. For example, a bank with a large staff and customer base will undoubtedly employ multiple access control systems to ensure that the public cannot reach the safe and unauthorized staff cannot reach the automatic teller machines. On the other hand, a small business might be satisfied with a single key used to open all of the doors in the building, distributed to all employees.

Facility access control protects enterprise assets and provides a history of who gained access and when the access was granted. In some cases, the physical access control system also provides time and attendance functionality. And in truly integrated environments, physical access controls, time and attendance, and logical access control can be provided with a single set of credentials that work across all three applications.

5

Identity & Access Management

Logical access controls are protection mechanisms that limit users' access to information and restrict their forms of access on the system to only what is appropriate for them. Logical access controls are often built into the operating system, or they may be part of the "logic" of applications programs or major utilities, such as Database Management Systems. They may also be implemented in add-on security packages that are installed into an operating system; such packages are available for a variety of systems, including PCs and mainframes. Additionally, logical access controls may be present in specialized components that regulate communications between computers and networks. While logical access controls can be of great benefit to an organization, adding them to a system does not automatically make the system more secure. A poorly chosen or improperly configured control mechanism can have a detrimental effect, as can inadequate understanding of the complexities involved in implementing and managing the technology.

The concept of access modes is fundamental to logical access control. The effect of many types of logical access control is to permit or deny access by specific individuals to specific information resources in specific access modes. An overview of the common access modes follows.

- **Read Only** – This provides users with the capability to view, copy, and usually print information but not to do anything to alter it, such as delete from, add to, or modify it in any way.

- **Read and Write** – Users are allowed to view and print as well as add, delete, and modify information. Logical access control can further refine the read/write relationship such that a user has read-only ability for one field of information but the ability to write to a related field. An example would be a program that allows a user read-only ability for his or her assigned action items and permits responses to be written in the space below an action item for additional updates or information to be provided if needed.

- **Execute** – The most common activity performed by users in relation to applications programs on a system is to execute them. A user executes a program each time he or she uses a word processor, spreadsheet, database, etc. Users would not ordinarily be given read or write capabilities for an application, however, since it would appear in a format that is unintelligible to most users. On the other hand, it would be important for software developers to be able to have the ability to read and write for the code that they are working with.

Administration is the most complex and challenging aspect of logical access control. Administration of logical access controls involves implementing, monitoring, modifying, testing, and terminating user accesses on the system and can be a demanding task. Administration typically does not include making the actual decisions as to who may have access to what and be given which capabilities. Those decisions are usually the data owner's responsibility, perhaps made in conjunction with management. Decisions regarding accesses should be guided by organizational policy, employee job descriptions and tasks, information sensitivity, user "need to know" determinations, and many other factors. Procedures and forms for the request and approval process are also typically developed.

Regardless of how and at whose discretion the decisions on user accesses are made, implementation and management are accomplished through an administrative function. There are three basic approaches to administration: centralized, decentralized, or a hybrid.

Centralized administration means that one element is responsible for configuring access controls so that users can access data and perform the activities they need to. As users' information processing needs change, their accesses can be modified only through the central administration, usually after requests have been approved through an established procedure and by the appropriate authority.

The main advantage of centralized administration is that very strict control over information can be maintained because the ability to make changes resides with very few people. Each user's account can be centrally monitored, and closing all accesses for any user can be easily accomplished if that individual leaves the organization. Consistent and uniform procedures and criteria are usually not difficult to enforce because relatively few individuals oversee the process.

In contrast to centralized administration, decentralized administration means that access to information is controlled by the owners or creators of the files, whoever or wherever those individuals may be. An advantage of decentralized administration is that control is in the hands of the individuals most accountable for the information, most familiar with it, and best able to judge who should be able to do what in relation to it. One disadvantage, however, is that there may not be consistency among creators/owners as to procedures and criteria for granting user accesses and capabilities. Another is that when requests are not processed centrally, it may be much more difficult to form a system-wide view of all user accesses on the system at any given time. Different data owners may inadvertently implement combinations of accesses that introduce conflicts of interest or that are in some other way not in the organization's best interest. It may also be difficult to ensure that accesses are properly terminated when an employee transfers within or leaves an organization.

In a hybrid approach, centralized control is exercised for some information and decentralized is allowed for other information. One typical arrangement is that central administration is responsible for the broadest and most basic accesses, and the owners/creators of files control types of accesses or changes in users' abilities for the files under their control. For example, when a new employee is hired into a department, a central administrator might provide him with a set of accesses, perhaps based on the functional element he is assigned to, his job classification, and a specific task he was hired to work on. He might have read-only access to an organization-wide SharePoint document library and to project status report files but read and write privileges to his department's weekly activities report. Also, if he left a particular project, the project manager could close the employee's access to that file easily.

Physical Access Control is about accessibility of space. Granting or restricting access to buildings, rooms, and floors is controlling access to certain spaces. The accessibility of these spaces is usually controlled by a key or token, which is the something you have and can lend to someone else. Sometimes, you also have to know a password or username (something you know). A point of access may be set up so that during work hours a password will allow access, but after-hours access is dependent upon both the presentation of a valid token as well as either a password or PIN. These spaces may be subdivided into areas or cells so that access is further restricted by the system's knowledge of where a person should be allowed to go within the matrix of cells and areas. When a physical access control system is set up like this, it is important that individuals are not allowed to tailgate, or follow another person into or out of a door without providing their own credentials. If tailgating occurs, then the access control system will assume that the individual is still within an area and that he or she may have

5

Identity & Access Management

"passed back" his or her key, or access validator such as a token, a card, etc., to someone else when he or she entered and therefore will not allow that key to access any systems that it would otherwise be valid for. Hence this feature is called an Anti-Passback solution.

In high security installations, there is also a feature called Dual Custody or Dual Key Entry that may be part of the architecture of the access control system. This simply means that two valid keys have to be presented to the reader within a certain time for access to be granted. This solution is often used in vaults where there may be large quantities of cash, drugs, or evidence being stored. Sometimes as well as providing access to the physical space, there may be other elements that the access control system is designed to protect such as air conditioning, lighting, alarm arming and disarming panels, and CCTV control units. The access control solution may also change due to specific alarm events like fire, bomb threat, or other emergency conditions.

Access Control Tokens are available in many different technologies and in many different shapes. The information that is stored on the token is presented to a reader that reads the information and sends it on to the system for processing. The token may have to be swiped, inserted, or placed on or near a reader. The reader sends information to the system. This usually consists of something that identifies the token as belonging to the system as well as something unique that identifies the token itself. The system will then decide if access is to be granted or denied based upon the validity of the token for the point where it is read based upon time, date, day, holiday, or other condition that is used for controlling validation.

When biometric readers are used, then the token or key is your retina, fingerprint, hand geometry, voice, or whatever biological attribute is enrolled into the system. Again, this is something you are. Most biometric readers also require a PIN as this is used to index the stored data on the sample readings of your biological attribute. Biometric systems can also be used to determine whether or not a person is already in a database, such as for social service or national ID applications.

The operation of a biometric system can be described, in a simplified manner, by a three-step process. The first step in this process involves an observation, or collection, of the biometric data. This step uses various sensors, which vary between modality, to facilitate the observation. The second step converts and describes the observed data using a digital representation called a template. This step varies between modalities and also between vendors. In the third step, the newly acquired template is compared with one or more previously generated templates stored in a database. The result of this comparison is a "match" or a "non-match" and is used for actions such as permitting access, sounding an alarm, etc.

Declaring a match or non-match is based on the acquired template being similar, but not identical, to the stored template. A threshold determines the degree of similarity required to result in a match declaration. The acceptance or rejection of biometric data is dependent on the match score falling above or below the threshold. The threshold is adjustable so that the biometric system can be more or less strict, depending on the requirements of any given biometric application. Some biometric systems employ liveness detection mechanisms such as measuring finger warmth or blinking detection. Liveness detection is used to ensure that only characteristics from a living human being can be used in a biometric system and enables the detection of spoof attacks (e.g., submission of a fake biometric sample).

Physical Access Control is not restricted to humans. Vehicles often will have active access control devices fitted to them so that they are treated independently from the driver. This enables identification for parking, fuel, weight, and can even be used to check if the vehicle is being operated over the appropriate speed limit for a set of given conditions.

Organizations planning to implement an access control system should consider three abstractions: access control policies, models, and mechanisms. Access control policies are high-level requirements that specify how access is managed and who may access information under what circumstances. For instance, policies may pertain to resource usage within or across organizational units or may be based on need-to-know, competence, authority, obligation, or conflict-of-interest factors. At a high level, access control policies are enforced through a mechanism that translates a user's access request, often in terms of a structure that a system provides. An access control list is a familiar example of an access control mechanism. Access control models bridge the gap in abstraction between policy and mechanism. Rather than attempting to evaluate and analyze access control systems exclusively at the mechanism level, security models are usually written to describe the security properties of an access control system. Security models are formal presentations of the security policy enforced by the system and are useful for proving theoretical limitations of a system. Discretionary access control, which allows the creator of a file to delegate access to others, is one of the simplest examples of a model.

Physical Access Control Systems, or PACS, are used in many enterprises today. The United States Department of Homeland Security (DHS), Office of the Chief Security Officer (OCSO), Physical Access Control Division (PHYSD) operates the Physical Access Control System (PACS). PACS is a security technology integration application suite used to control and manage physical access devices, intrusion detection, and video surveillance at DHS Headquarters (HQ) facilities in the National Capital Region (NCR), primarily the Nebraska Avenue Complex (NAC).

According to DHS, "PACS allows authorized security personnel to simultaneously manage and monitor multiple entry points from a single, centralized location. PACS operates access control and intrusion detection functions at DHS HQ facilities in the NCR, primarily the NAC, and is comprised of a suite of applications which serve as a mechanism for the management of electronic access points and alarms. PACS produces automated transactional reports, documenting what activity took place, where and when.

PACS applications used at DHS HQ facilities in the NCR, primarily the NAC, are divided into four areas. All four applications and processes operate independently at the direction of the PACS Administrator:

1. **Identification** – PACS requires an individual's PII so it can authorize physical access to DHS facilities. PACS sensors read the information on an individual's Personal Identity Verification (PIV) card to verify if the individual is authorized access.

2. **Visitor Management** – Visitors and construction and service contractors who have not been issued a PIV card must be identified before being granted access. This is accomplished by having the individual provide the information requested on DHS Form 11000-13 "Visitor Process Information." OCSO personnel enter the information on the form into the PACS visitor management function. This information is then used to conduct a search of the National Crime Information Center (NCIC) to determine if there are any criminal records or outstanding arrest warrants for the individual. The results of the NCIC check are entered into PACS. If there is no disqualifying

information, such as an outstanding arrest warrant, the visitor is cleared for access. Access requests by foreign visitors (non-U.S. citizens and non-Legal Permanent Residents) are processed through the DHS Foreign National Visitor Management System (FNVMS).

3. **Parking Permit Management** – The Office of the Chief Administrative Officer (OCAO) uses PACS to issue and track parking permits for the NAC. OCAO personnel access PACS to determine if an individual is eligible to receive a parking permit. Once determined to be eligible, the individual must submit General Services Administration (GSA) Parking Application, Form 2941. Upon issuance of the parking permit, OCAO personnel enter into PACS the name and email address of the permit holder, the permit number and type, issue date, and expiration date.

4. **Alarm Monitoring and Intrusion Detection** – The PACS alarm monitoring application allows OCSO personnel to monitor the Intrusion Detection System (IDS). A record is created in PACS of all IDS alarm activations or other issues, such as communication and power failures for example. The IDS in PACS consists of sensors, lights, and other mechanisms through which OCSO can detect the unauthorized intrusion of persons or devices. The only PII collected by the PACS IDS suite is the first and last name of the individual authorized to turn the alarm system on and off and the corresponding PIN number which the individual inputs into the alarm keypad to activate or deactivate the alarm." [1]

The NIST Interagency Report 7316, Assessment of Access Control Systems, September 2006, can provide some very important guidance as planning is taking place to understand the requirements and capabilities that an access control system needs to be able to address.[2] The security professional may or may not implement a PACS system as detailed and robust as the one described above. However, the fact remains that the security professional will certainly need to have a thorough understanding of the following issues with regards to PACS systems:

1. The root cause(s) that they are being proposed to address
2. The security architecture that will support the deployment of such a solution into the enterprise
3. The policies needed to address the management and operation of such a system
4. The resources and metrics necessary to monitor and maintain such a system
5. The training and awareness programs required to allow such a system to be used effectively

As systems grow in size and complexity, access control is a special concern for systems that are distributed across multiple computers. These distributed systems can be a formidable challenge for developers because they may use a variety of access control mechanisms that must be integrated to support the organization's policy; for example, role-based access control that can enforce administrator-specified rules is often used. Popular database management system designs, such as Structured Query Language (SQL), incorporate many aspects of role- and rule-based access. Services that are particularly useful in implementing distributed access control include the Lightweight Directory Access Protocol (LDAP), capability-based

---

1   U.S. Department of Homeland Security, Privacy Impact Assessment for the Physical Access Control System. June 9, 2011: http://www.dhs.gov/xlibrary/assets/privacy/privacy_pia_dhs_pacs.pdf (Pages 1–2)

2   See the following: http://csrc.nist.gov/publications/nistir/7316/NISTIR-7316.pdf

Kerberos, and the Extensible Markup Language (XML)-based Extensible Access Control Markup Language (XACML).

The security professional needs to understand that an access control system is said to be safe if no permission can be leaked to an unauthorized or uninvited principal. To assure the safety of an access control system, the security professional must make certain that the access control configuration (e.g., access control model) will not result in the leakage of permissions to an unauthorized principal.

Identification and Authentication of People and Devices

To this point, the chapter has focused on access control principles and the design of the control environment. The section that follows covers details regarding specific access controls and essential control strategies. Areas include:

- Identification, authentication, and authorization
- Access control services
- Identity management
- Access control technologies

Identification, Authentication, and Authorization

Identification is the assertion of a unique identity for a person or system and is the starting point of all access control. Without proper identification, it is impossible to determine to whom or what to apply the appropriate controls. Identification is a critical first step in applying access controls because all activities and controls are tied to the identity of a particular user or entity.

The downstream effects of proper identification include accountability (with a protected audit trail) and the ability to trace activities to individuals. They also include the provisioning of rights and privileges, system profiles, and availability of system information, applications, and services. The objective of identification is to bind a user to the appropriate controls based on that unique user instance. For example, once the unique user is identified and validated through authentication, his or her identity within the infrastructure will be used to allocate resources based on predefined privileges.

Authentication is the process of verifying the identity of the user. Upon requesting access and presenting unique user identification, the user will provide some set of private data that only the user should have access to or knowledge of. The combination of the identity and information only known by, or only in the possession of, the user acts to verify that the user identity is being used by the expected and assigned entity (e.g., a person). This, then, establishes trust between the user and the system for the allocation of privileges.

Authorization is the final step in the process. Once a user has been identified and properly authenticated, the resources that user is allowed to access must be defined and monitored. Authorization is the process of defining the specific resources a user needs and determining the type of access to those resources the user may have. For example, Rae, Andy, and Matthew may all be identified and authenticated into the same system, but Rae is only authorized to access the payroll information, Andy is only authorized to access product source code, and Matthew is only authorized to view the company's internal websites.

5

Identity & Access Management

The relationship between these three important concepts is simple:

- Identification provides uniqueness
- Authentication provides validity
- Authorization provides control

Identification Methods

The most common form of identification is a simple username, user ID, account number, or Personal Identification Number (PIN). These are used as a point of assignment and association to a user entity within a system. However, identification may not be limited to human users and may include software and hardware services that may need to access objects, modules, databases, or other applications to provide a full suite of services. In an effort to ensure that the application is authorized to make the requests to potentially sensitive resources, the system can use digital identification, such as a certificate or one-time session identifier to identify the application. There are several common forms of identification used by organizations, and the type used may vary depending on the process or the situation.

Identification Badges

An identification badge is the most common form of physical identification and authorization in organizations. It represents that the badge holder is officially recognized and has some status within the organization. Most badges contain the name or logo of the organization, the name of the badge holder, and a picture of the holder printed on the face. In some cases, because of the cost of badge printing, organizations will print personalized badges only for employees. Visitors or temporary personnel will be given a generic badge, perhaps in a different color, to signify that they are permitted on the premises but do not belong to the organization.

The typical process behind an ID badge requires that the user wear the badge at all times while on company premises. Employees and security personnel will be able to observe the badge, check the picture on the badge against the badge wearer, and then make a determination as to whether the person legitimately belongs on the premises or not. If the name, picture, and badge holder do not all match, the employee should summon security or escort the badge holder off the premises.

Unfortunately, this process fails all too often. Most people, even security guards, fail to make a very close comparison of the badge against the holder. During the morning rush into a facility, most employees simply wave the badge in the air to indicate they have one and are allowed to pass. While this is not a universal problem—government and military facilities generally pay close attention to badge holders and their credentials—it is common enough to conclude that identification badges are not a foolproof security mechanism.

Another type of badge, the access badge, provides a much stronger security mechanism. Access badges are used to enter secured areas of a facility and are used in conjunction with a badge reader to read information stored on the badge. A central monitoring facility will read the badge information, match that information against a list of authorized personnel for that area, and make a determination for or against access. A failing of access badges is that because they are not physically tied with a specific person, employees often share their badges with others who may need temporary access to a secured area. While certainly not endorsed by the organization, and most often directly counter to security policy, this practice is widespread. To counter this problem, many organizations combine the identification badge with the access badge to provide a stronger tie between the badge holder and the individual ID card.

User ID

The common user ID—the standard entry point to most information systems—provides the system with a way of uniquely identifying a particular user amongst all the users of that system. No two users on a single system can have the same user ID, as that would cause confusion for the access control system and remove the ability to track any activity to an individual. It is important to note that the user ID should only be used as a system identifier, not an authenticator. The user ID simply tells the system that this user wants to be identified by that ID, not that this user has the legitimate right to access the system under that ID or be given access to any system resources. It is only when the user ID is combined with some other authentication mechanism, such as a password, security token, or a digital certificate, that a judgment can be made as to the legitimacy of the user, and access can be permitted or denied.

Account Number/PIN

Much like a user ID, an account number provides a unique identity for a particular user within a system or an enterprise. Most ordinary users will encounter account numbers as part of a financial services application or transaction. In such transactions, the personal identification number (PIN) provides the authentication information needed to determine whether the user has the legitimate right to use that account number and access the information under that account.

MAC Address

All computers that participate in a network must have some method of uniquely identifying themselves to that network so that information can be sent to and from the network connection associated with the proper computer. The most common form of machine address in use today is the media access control (MAC) address. The MAC address is a 48-bit number (typically represented in hexadecimal format) that is supposed to be globally unique, meaning that every network device in the world is supposed to have a unique MAC address. In the early days of network computing, the MAC address was embedded into the hardware of the device during its manufacture and was not changeable by end-users (or attackers). When that was the case, the MAC address was a good way to identify (and authenticate) particular devices with a high degree of certainty. Unfortunately, most modern network-enabled devices allow the MAC address to be set in software, meaning that anyone with administrative access to the device can alter the MAC address of that device to anything of his choosing.[3] Thus, the MAC address is no longer considered a strong identifier or authenticator.

IP Address

Computers using the TCP/IP network protocol are also assigned an Internet protocol (IP) address. Whereas the MAC address provides a way of identifying the physical location of a system, the IP address gives the logical location of a device on the IP network. IP addresses

---

3   See the following for some examples of software that can be used to change MAC Addresses:
     http://www.technitium.com/tmac/
     http://lizardsystems.com/change-mac-address/
     http://www.freewarefiles.com/Win7-MAC-Address-Changer_program_69175.html

are organized into logical groups called subnetworks or subnets. A device's IP address must be unique among all the systems on that device's same subnet, but there are circumstances where devices on different subnets can have identical IP addresses. As was the case with MAC addresses, a device's IP address is assigned in software by the administrator of a system. As such, IP address is not a very strong indicator of a system's identity. It is possible to use the IP address as one data point amongst many to narrow down a system's unique network location or identity, but it should not be used alone for such purposes.

Radio Frequency Identification (RFID)

Radio Frequency Identification (RFID) technology is a non-contact, automatic identification technology that uses radio signals to identify, track, sort, and detect a variety of objects including people, vehicles, goods, and assets without the need for direct contact (as found in magnetic stripe technology) or line of sight contact (as found in bar code technology). RFID technology can track the movements of objects through a network of radio-enabled scanning devices over a distance of several meters. A device called an RFID tag is a key component of the technology. An RFID tag usually has at least two components:

1. An integrated circuit for modulating and demodulating radio signals and performing other functions
2. An antenna for receiving and transmitting the signal

An RFID tag can perform a limited amount of processing and has small amount of storage. RFID tags are sometimes considered to be enhanced "electronic barcodes."

RFID tags that do not have any integrated circuit are called chipless RFID tags, and they are also known as RF fibers. These tags use fibers or materials that reflect a portion of the reader's signal back, and the unique return signal can be used as an identifier. Systems that make use of RFID technology are typically composed of three key elements:

1. An RFID tag, or transponder, that carries object-identifying data
2. An RFID tag reader, or transceiver, that reads and writes tag data
3. A back-end database that stores records associated with tag contents

Each tag contains a unique identity code. An RFID reader emits a low-level radio frequency magnetic field that energizes the tag. The tag responds to the reader's query and announces its presence via radio waves, transmitting its unique identification data. This data is decoded by the reader and passed to the local application system via middleware. The middleware acts as an interface between the reader and the RFID application system. The system will then search and match the identity code with the information stored in the host database or backend system. In this way, accessibility or authorization for further processing can be granted or refused, depending on results received by the reader and processed by the database.

Another adoption of RFID technology has been by governments, with the electronic passport project. In a number of countries, traditional paper passports are gradually being replaced with passports embedded with a small integrated circuit. Biometric information such as face recognition, fingerprints, or iris scans can be stored in the electronic passport, but many times they are stored as records in secure databases that are simply referenced by the information provided to the system by the RFID tag. The electronic passport project was originally initiated by the U.S., requesting all countries participating in the Visa Waiver Program (VWP) to issue e-passports with integrated circuits.[4] The main objectives of the program were for automated identity verification and for greater border protection and security.

RFID tags are considered "dumb" devices, in that they can only listen and respond, no matter who sends the request signal. This brings up risks of unauthorized access and modification of tag data that the security professional will need to be aware of and consider carefully before making a decision to deploy RFID technology within the enterprise. In other words, unprotected tags may be vulnerable to eavesdropping, traffic analysis, spoofing, or denial of service attacks.

- **Eavesdropping (or Skimming)** – Radio signals transmitted from the tag, and the reader, can be detected several meters away by other radio receivers. It is possible therefore for an unauthorized user to gain access to the data contained in RFID tags if legitimate transmissions are not properly protected. Any person who has their own RFID reader may interrogate tags lacking adequate access controls and eavesdrop on tag contents.

- **Traffic Analysis** – Even if tag data is protected, it is possible to use traffic analysis tools to track predictable tag responses over time. Correlating and analyzing the data could build a picture of movement, social interactions, and financial transactions. Abuse of the traffic analysis would have a direct impact on privacy.

- **Spoofing** – Based on the data collected from eavesdropping or traffic analysis, it is possible to perform tag spoofing. For instance, a software package known as "RFDump," which runs on a notebook computer or personal digital assistant, allows users to perform reading or writing tasks on most standard smart tags if they are not properly protected.[5] The software permits intruders to overwrite existing RFID tag data with spoofed data. By spoofing valid tags, the intruder could fool an RFID system and change the identity of tags to gain an unauthorized or undetected advantage.

- **Denial of Service Attack/Distributed Denial of Service Attack** – The problems surrounding security and trust are greatly increased when large volumes of internal RFID data are shared among business partners. A denial of service attack on RFID infrastructure could happen if a large batch of tags has been corrupted. For example, an attacker can use the "kill" command, implemented in RFID tags, to make the tags permanently inoperative if they gain password access to the tags. In addition, an attacker could use an illegal high power radio frequency (RF) transmitter in an attempt to jam frequencies used by the RFID system, bringing the whole system to a halt.

- **RFID Reader Integrity** – In some cases, RFID readers are installed in locations without adequate physical protection. Unauthorized intruders may set up hidden readers of a similar nature nearby to gain access to the information being transmitted by the readers or even compromise the readers themselves, thus affecting their integrity. Unauthorized readers may also compromise privacy by accessing tags without adequate access controls. As a result, information collected by readers and passed to the RFID application may have already been tampered with, changed, or stolen by unauthorized

---

4   See the following for more information on both the U.S. Visa Waiver Program (VWP) and e-passports: Visa Waiver program (VWP): http://travel.state.gov/content/visas/english/visit/visa-waiver-program.html e-passports: http://www.dhs.gov/e-passports

5   See the following: http://freecode.com/projects/rfdump?branch_id=61265&release_id=264928

persons. An RFID reader can also be a target for viruses. In 2006, researchers demonstrated that an RFID virus was possible. A proof-of-concept self-replicating RFID virus was written to demonstrate that a virus could use RFID tags to compromise backend RFID middleware systems via an SQL injection attack.[6]

■ **Personal Privacy –** As RFID is increasingly being used in the retailing and manufacturing sectors, the widespread item-level RFID tagging of products such as clothing and electronics raises public concerns regarding personal privacy. People are concerned about how their data is being used, whether they are subject to more direct marketing, or whether they can be physically tracked by RFID chips. If personal identities can be linked to a unique RFID tag, individuals could be profiled and tracked without their knowledge or consent. For instance, washing clothes with RFID tags embedded in them does not remove the chips because they are specially designed to withstand years of wear and tear. It is possible that everything an individual were to buy and own, if it had one or more embedded RFID tags, could be identified, numbered, and tracked. RFID readers can detect the presence of these RFID tags wherever they are close enough to receive a signal.

In the final analysis, RFID technology has been a big breakthrough in the manufacturing and consumer goods industries where it is helping to reduce inventory and product tracking costs. The values and risks to privacy and breach must be considered by the security professional when planning on deploying and using RFID badges.

Email Address

The use of a person's email address as an identification mechanism or user ID has become increasingly popular in recent years, particularly for Internet e-commerce and portal sites. Part of the reason for this is that an email address is globally unique. If a user's email address is sayge@smail.com, nobody else can legitimately use that address to send or receive email. Based on that assumption, many websites use the user's email address as the unique user ID and allow the user to select a password for authentication. Websites using this convention will additionally use that email address to send correspondence to the user for administrative or informational purposes. One common mechanism in current use is to have a new user register on the site by entering his email address as a user ID. The site will then send a confirmation email to that address and wait for a reply from the user before completing the registration process. The theory behind this process is that if a user has access to the email account specified by the entered address, there is a high degree of certainty that the user is legitimate.

However, this assumption may not be valid in many situations. The uniqueness of an email address is enforced solely by convention. There are no technical restrictions preventing the use of another person's email address as an identifier, and, the aforementioned verification mechanism notwithstanding, there is no way to formally verify the legitimacy of a particular email address or that a particular individual is the owner of that address. In addition, it is a simple matter to spoof (or falsify) the sender's email address in most common email systems in use today, and spammers, fraudsters, and phishing perpetrators regularly use this method as a way of masking the true origin of their attacks. It is convenient for a person to use an email address as identification because it is easy to remember, but if an organization wishes

---

6   See the following: http://www.rfidvirus.org/

to use this as an identification method, it should not place absolute trust in its legitimacy and should certainly use other authentication methods to tie the use of that address to a particular user. These methods should be carefully vetted by both the security architect as well as the security practitioner to ensure that wise choices are being made. For example, the reliance on a simple mechanism, such as a software based cookie that can "identify" a user upon return to a website, will typically offer no more protection or validation of identity than the email address discussed above would. However, on the other hand, the use of technology such as a SAML token to validate the user's identity could indeed offer additional security and protection that the previous mechanism would not be able to match.

User Identification Guidelines

There are three essential security characteristics regarding identities: uniqueness, non-descriptiveness, and secure issuance. First and foremost, user identification must be unique so that each entity on a system can be unambiguously identified. Although it is possible for a user to have many unique identifiers, each must be distinctive within an access control environment. In the event there are several disparate access control environments that do not interact, share information, or provide access to the same resources, duplication is possible. For example, a user's ID at work may be "mary_t," allowing her to be identified and authenticated within the corporate infrastructure. She may also have a personal email account with her Internet service provider (ISP) with the user ID of "mary_t." This is possible because the corporate access control environment does not interact with the ISP's access control environment. However, there are potential dangers with using the same ID on multiple systems. Users are prone to duplicating certain attributes, such as passwords, to minimize their effort. If an attacker discovers Mary's ISP ID and password, he or she may rightly conclude that she is using the same ID and password at work. Therefore, any duplication, although possible in certain circumstances, represents a fundamental risk to the enterprise.

User identification should generally be non-descriptive and should try as much as possible to disclose as little as possible about the user. The ID should also not expose the associated role or job function of the user. Common practice is to issue user IDs that are a variant of the user's name, for example, "agordon" or "adam.gordon." Once this scheme is identified by an attacker, it becomes easy to begin enumerating through possible variations on the theme to discover other valid user IDs in the organization. In addition, a person's job function should never be used as the basis for a user ID. If a user ID were to be named "CFO," an attacker would be able to focus energy on that user alone based on the assumption that he is the CFO of the company and would probably have privileged access to critical systems. However, this is practiced quite often. It is very common to have user IDs of "admin," "finance," "shipment," "Web master," or other representations of highly descriptive IDs. The naming of these IDs is voluntary and self-imposed by the organization.

There are some IDs, however, that cannot be easily changed. The most predominant is the username "root." It is the name given to the administrative account with unlimited access rights on a UNIX system. Everyone, including attackers, knows what the username "root" represents, and it is for this very reason that attaining root's password is so desirable. Unfortunately, in most UNIX systems, changing the user or masking that role is impossible. In Microsoft operating systems, it is possible to change the username of the default "administrator" account (nearly the equivalent of "root" in UNIX) to some other non-descriptive name, and this should be

5

Identity & Access Management

considered a best practice. The security professional needs to be aware of the additional "identifiers" that may be used to find accounts, the security identifier, or SID, and the relative identifier, or RID.

Every Windows user, computer, or service account has a unique alphanumeric identifier called the SID. Windows security-related processes, such as authentication, authorization, delegation, and auditing, use SIDs to uniquely identify security principals. Because SIDs are used by system processes, the format of a SID is not user or administrator-friendly. To illustrate, let's analyze an example SID retrieved from a test Active Directory (AD) system: S-1-5-21-4035617097-1094650281-2406268287-1981. All SID fields have a specific meaning; so, for the above sample SID:

- **S** – The initial S identifies the following string as a SID.
- **1** – The revision level, or version, of the SID specification. To date, this has never changed and has always been 1.
- **5** – The identifier authority value. This is a predefined identifier for the top-level authority that issued the SID. This is typically 5, which represents the SECURITY_NT_AUTHORITY.
- **21-4035617097-1094650281-2406268287** – This section is the domain or local computer identifier (in this example, a domain identifier). This is a 48-bit string that identifies the authority (the computer or domain) that created the SID.
- **1981** – The Relative ID (RID) is the last part of a SID. The RID uniquely identifies a security principal relative to the local or domain security authority that issued the SID. Any group or user that the Windows OS does not create has a RID of 1000 or greater by default.

The SID of an AD domain account is created by a domain's security authority that runs on every Windows domain controller (DC). The SID of a local account is created by the Local Security Authority (LSA) service that runs on every Windows box.

An important property of a SID is its uniqueness in time and place. A SID is unique in the environment where it was created (in a domain or on a local computer). It is also unique in time: If you create a user object, delete it, then recreate it with the same name, the new object will not have the same SID as the original object, nor will the SID of the original user object be used again in that Domain, as the domain security authority tracks all SIDs issued and revoked, and it does not allow SID reuse.

Well-known SIDs are a group of SIDs that identify generic users or generic groups. Their values remain constant across all operating systems. The following are well-known SIDs:[7]

SID:S-1-0

Name: Null Authority

Description: An identifier authority.

SID: S-1-0-0

Name: Nobody

Description: No security principal.

---

7   See the following for a complete listing of all published SIDs in Microsoft operating systems: http://support.microsoft.com/kb/243330/en-us

SID: S-1-1

Name: World Authority

Description: An identifier authority.

SID: S-1-1-0

Name: Everyone

Description: A group that includes all users, even anonymous users and guests. Membership is controlled by the operating system.

SID: S-1-5-21domain-500

Name: Administrator

Description: A user account for the system administrator. By default, it is the only user account that is given full control over the system.

SID: S-1-5-21domain-501

Name: Guest

Description: A user account for people who do not have individual accounts. This user account does not require a password. By default, the Guest account is disabled.

SID: S-1-5-21domain-502

Name: KRBTGT

Description: A service account that is used by the Key Distribution Center (KDC) service.

SID: S-1-5-21domain-512

Name: Domain Admins

Description: A global group whose members are authorized to administer the domain. By default, the Domain Admins group is a member of the Administrators group on all computers that have joined a domain, including the domain controllers. Domain Admins is the default owner of any object that is created by any member of the group.

Based on the well-known SID/RID combinations listed above, the security professional should be aware of the fact that the built-in administrator account is always identified with a RID of 500. Knowing this could be of value to the security professional/practitioner as they decide whether or not to rename the account to obfuscate its origin and true identity. This knowledge is also valuable to a hacker that may be attempting to identify the true identity of a renamed account.

Clearly, any highly privileged system account, such as "root" and "administrator," represents a target for attackers, and it can be difficult to mask its role. However, traditional users, who may have a broad set of privileges throughout the enterprise, can be more difficult for attackers to isolate as a target. Therefore, establishing a user ID that is independent of the user's name, job function, or role will act to mask the true privileges of the user. Ideally, user IDs should be randomly assigned or include some randomized elements to prevent ID guessing and enumeration by attackers. While renaming is a best practice and will prevent rudimentary attempts at access, it can be defeated by identifying the "Security IDs." Defense in depth must be practiced to ensure an appropriate level of defense is implemented vs. the burden to the user and risk.

Finally, the process of issuing identifiers must be secure and well documented. The quality of the identifier is in part based on the quality of how it is issued. If an identity can be inappropriately issued, the entire security system can break down. The identifier is the first, and arguably the most important, step in acquiring access. An organization must establish a secure process for issuing IDs, including the proper documentation and approval for all ID requests. The process must also account for notification of the user's management and any system owners for systems the user may have access to. The organization must deliver the user ID to the end-user in a secure manner. This can be as simple as delivery in a sealed envelope or as complicated as using digitally signed and encrypted communications channels. Finally, the entire process must be logged and documented properly to ensure that the process can be verified and audited.

Identity Management Implementation

Once the policies, standards, and processes for access control have been defined, the next step is to implement the various technology components that will support the organization's access control needs. This section describes the access control technology options that the security professional needs to deploy for an effective access control management service to be implemented as part of an enterprise security architecture.

Identity management technologies attempt to simplify the administration of distributed, overlapping, and sometimes conflicting data about the users of an organization's information technology systems. The foundation of a comprehensive identity management solution is the implementation of appropriate processes and technologies to consolidate and streamline the management of user IDs, authentication, and access information consistently across multiple systems. A typical enterprise will have many users with various access requirements for a diverse collection of data and application services. To bind the user to established policies, processes, and privileges throughout the infrastructure, several types of technologies are utilized to ensure consistency and oversight. Technologies utilized in identity management solutions include but are not limited to:

- Password management
- Account management
- Profile management
- Directory management
- Single sign-on

Password Management

Passwords are the most common authentication technology in use today, so password management should be a primary concern for the security professional. The policies, standards, and complexity associated with password use need to be managed in a consistent way throughout the enterprise. Because passwords may be compromised over time, it is prudent for users to periodically change their passwords. Most modern systems can be configured to require users to change their password at defined intervals. The reason for this is that if a password is compromised, this will limit the amount of damage that can be done through that compromised ID to the amount of time left before the next change interval. Most enterprise organizations enforce a password change interval ranging from 30 to 90 days. A shorter length is better for security reasons, but a longer period of time is more convenient for users and does not force them to re-memorize their password as often. As with most security issues, the optimal time to expire a password will be a compromise between business needs and security needs.

When users have multiple passwords, on multiple disparate systems, all expiring on different dates, they tend to write them down, store them insecurely (e.g., in a "password.txt" file on the desktop or on a sticky note underneath their keyboard), or replicate the same password across multiple systems. In the absence of a password management system incorporated into an enterprise-wide identity management solution, a user may set the same password for several systems as a matter of convenience or simply rotate a set of three or four, making it very easy to remember but equally easy for an attacker to guess and exploit. The security practitioner and the security professional can both work hand in hand here to educate the users and provide them the tools to be more proactive in their approach to password management.

For the security practitioners, they can choose password management software or an app that will be provided to the users for the purpose of managing their need to set and use multiple passwords that are unique. For the security professionals, they will need to craft the policies needed to manage the use of the software and apps that the security practitioner will provide. Both working together will be able to affect the desired change in the user's behavior vis-à-vis password use, reuse, and management.

To protect against an attacker trying to guess a password multiple times, many systems incorporate a password lockout mechanism for excessive invalid attempts. In such a system, if a user unsuccessfully tries to log into a system multiple times (three to five attempts are common), the ID is locked and the user has to contact support personnel to get it unlocked. The benefits of this process is that it limits the amount of damage password guessing can have on a user's login. The drawback is that users are notorious for forgetting their password and end up calling the help desk often, especially if they have been away from the computer for an extended period of time. In fact, password reset calls are almost always the single largest category of calls for most help desk services. Any process or technology that can dramatically reduce the number of password reset calls to the help desk will have the added benefit of saving a lot of money for the organization.

A password management system is designed to manage passwords consistently across the enterprise. This is usually achieved through the deployment of a central tool capable of synchronizing passwords across multiple systems. However, other features might include assisting users with routine password management tasks. For example, users who forget their password or trigger a lockout from too many failed attempts may be offered alternative authentication mechanisms to gain specific access to utilities to reset their password. It is not uncommon for an organization to issue multifactor authentication tokens to be used, in part, for providing access to utilities so users can self-manage their accounts and passwords on other, potentially older or nonintegrated systems. Other alternative methods include voice response units for resetting passwords, the use of personal questions to validate a user's identity, or in-person verification. In the event that an alternative authentication mechanism does not exist, password management systems typically allow administrators or support staff to quickly reset forgotten or disabled passwords.

Another common feature of a password management system, and regularly employed on large Internet sites, is a self-registration process that incorporates personal data questions whose answers are private to that user, allowing him or her to manage the account and reset the password without the intervention of an administrator or help desk staffer.

Account Management

One of most costly, time-consuming, and potentially risk-laden aspects of access control is the creation, modification, and decommissioning of user accounts. Many organizations consume inordinate amounts of resources to ensure the timely creation of new system access, the adjustments of user privileges to reflect changes in responsibilities, and the termination of access once a user leaves the organization.

Although Web-based access management tools can be used to address this problem for a Web-based environment, most enterprises are heterogeneous, with multiple types and versions of systems and applications, each with potentially different account management strategies, capabilities, and tools. For example, ERP systems, operating systems, network devices, mainframes, and database servers typically all have difficulty in interacting with a single centralized account directory. Moreover, for those that can achieve such integration, there may be limitations to the degree of control available within the system.

As a result, account management processes must typically be performed on each system directly. Account management systems attempt to streamline the administration of user identity across multiple systems. They normally include one or more of the following features to ensure a central, cross-platform security administration capability:

- A central facility for managing user access to multiple systems simultaneously. This ensures consistency between all systems and eases the administrative burden of managing access on these systems separately. This also reduces the risk of erroneous manual entry of user data, potentially resulting in the provisioning of inappropriate access.
- A workflow system where users can submit requests for new, changed, or terminated systems access, and these requests are automatically routed to the appropriate people for approval. Approved requests then trigger the creation of accounts and the allocation of other resources.
- Automatic replication of data, particularly user records, between multiple systems and directories. This ensures that user access permissions are propagated uniformly and promptly throughout the environment and reduces the likelihood of error through manual replication.
- A facility for loading batch changes to user directories. There are often occasions where large numbers of user changes need to be loaded in the database. This may come as a result of organizational restructuring, large employee hires, or large-scale employee terminations. The ability to load these changes in bulk will save time and increase accuracy over loading these changes individually.
- Automatic creation, change, or removal of access to system resources based on policies and triggered by changes to information elsewhere (e.g., in an HR system or corporate directory).Changes can happen more rapidly and reduce the window of opportunity for obsolete access permissions to be exploited when an organization eliminates human intervention and manual processing.

One of the biggest obstacles to the implementation of an account management system is the time and cost of full-scale deployment. Some systems can literally take years to deploy fully in a large enterprise environment. The complexity of account management systems can also overwhelm project teams as they struggle to determine the best method for deploying the system. Implementation teams should start small and gain experience and success on a smaller scale before proceeding to full-scale deployment.

Interface issues can also be a big project killer for many organizations. A fully automated account management system must interface with each system, application, and directory in the enterprise (sometimes numbering in the hundreds), each based on its own technology platform and almost none of which will be designed to interface with the account management service. The process of building all those interfaces will be a daunting, time-consuming, and costly task to overcome and will require the resources of a dedicated team of programmers.

The security practitioner needs to be focused on working with the security architect and the security professional to ensure that there is agreement about which repository for user information will be considered "THE" authoritative repository for the enterprise. Some organizations will consider their HR database to be the repository, while others will use the LDAP system. Still others may not have a formal thought process in place and a system designated. The challenge for the security actors in this regard comes in the form of user decommissioning. When a user leaves the organization, for whatever reasons, the need to have a central system designated that will be where ALL information pertaining to that user will be found and managed is critically important. Things such as group and role based memberships will need to be addressed through this system, as will system access across the enterprise. Without a central authoritative repository to rely on, the security practitioner will not be able to validate that the user has been decommissioned properly, according to the standing policy of the organization. In addition, the security professional will not be able to validate compliance with the security policies of the organization, as well as any overarching legal standards or regulatory requirements that may have to be adhered to.

Profile Management

Profiles are a collection of information associated with a particular identity or group. In addition to the user ID and password, a user profile may include personal information, such as name, telephone number, email address, home address, date of birth, etc. A profile can also contain information related to privileges and rights on specific systems. However, any information specific to a user is going to change over time, and the process to manage that change is an important component of an overall identity management process. When a change is required to a profile, the process should be easy to manage and be automatically propagated to key systems, such as the corporate directory and the individual systems a user logs into. Most customer relationship management (CRM) systems include some facility to manage user profiles, either administratively or using a self-service method. This capability is also available in some access management systems and password management systems. It is helpful to allow users to enter and manage those parts of their own profiles where new data are either not sensitive or do not have to be validated. This helps to reduce the cost and time to implement these changes and increase their accuracy.

Directory Management

A corporate directory is a comprehensive database designed to centralize the management of data about an assortment of company entities. A typical directory will contain a hierarchy of objects storing information about users, groups, systems, servers, printers, etc. The directory is stored on one or more servers that may replicate the data, in part or in whole, to other directory servers to ensure scalability and availability. Applications will normally access data stored in a directory by means of a standard directory protocol such as Lightweight Directory Access Protocol (LDAP).

The primary benefit of a directory service is that it provides a centralized collection of user data that can be used by many applications to avoid replication of information and simplify the architecture. When directories are used, it is possible to configure several applications to share data about users rather than having each system manage its own list of users, authentication data, etc. This simplifies the overall management of user data, improves the consistency of user data as it is used between systems, and promotes uniform security control in the environment.

A key limitation of directories and their role in simplifying identity management is the difficulty of integration with legacy systems. Mainframes, older applications, and outdated systems often do not natively support the use of an external system to manage their own users without the development of interface facilities or translation code. These interfaces can be difficult and expensive to develop and, in some cases, technically impossible, limiting their effectiveness and reducing the ability to use a directory service to manage enterprise-wide resources.

Directory Technologies

When someone is considering the use of a centralized directory service for the enterprise, there are a number of technologies that should be considered. These technologies are all supported by international standards, and most products that require directory services will be able to interface natively with one or more of them. The most common directory standards are X.500, the Lightweight Directory Access Protocol (LDAP), Active Directory, and X.400.

X.500: The X.500 set of communications protocols was developed by the International Telecommunications Union (ITU-T) in the late 1980s and early 1990s.[8] It is also known as ISO/IEC 9594-1:2008 originally, but it has been revised to ISO/IEC 9594-1:2014.[9] The X.500 protocol suite was developed by the telecommunications companies as a way to facilitate a standard method of developing electronic directories for use over telecommunications networks. The suite was originally developed to work with the OSI network communications model, although most current implementations allow it to operate over TCP/IP as well. X.500 actually consists of four separate protocols:

- The Directory Access Protocol (DAP). This is the primary protocol used in an X.500 directory.
- The Directory System Protocol (DSP)
- The Directory Information Shadowing Protocol (DISP)
- The Directory Operational Bindings Management Protocol (DOP)

---

8   The original work by the ITU-T was published as noted: ITU-T Rec. X.500, "The Directory: Overview of Concepts, Models and Service", 1993.

9   See the following:
New landing page for ISO/IEC 9594-1:2014: http://www.iso.org/iso/home/store/catalogue_ics/catalogue_detail_ics.htm?csnumber=64845
Original landing page for ISO/IEC 9594-1:2008: http://www.iso.org/iso/catalogue_detail.htm?csnumber=53364

Information in an X.500 directory is organized as a hierarchical database of information. The key field in the database is called the distinguished name (DN). The DN provides the full path through the X.500 database where a particular entry may be found. X.500 also supports the concept of a relative distinguished name (RDN). The RDN provides the name of a specific entry without the full path component attached.

LDAP

Although it is a comprehensive suite of protocols for managing directory information, X.500 can be complex to implement and complicated to administer. It also originally required the implementation of the OSI protocol stack for operation. For that reason, organizations wanted a simpler directory protocol that could operate in a TCP/IP environment. In the early 1990s, the lightweight directory access protocol (LDAP) was developed. Based on X.500's DAP, LDAP provides a simpler implementation of directory services for enterprises.

LDAP uses a hierarchical tree structure for directory entries. Like X.500, LDAP entries support the DN and RDN concepts. DN attributes are typically based on an entity's DNS name. Each entry in the database has a series of name/value pairs to denote the various attributes associated with each entry. Common attributes for an LDAP entry include the following:

- **DN** – Distinguished Name
- **CN** – Common Name
- **DC** – Domain Component
- **OU** – Organizational Unit

LDAP operates in a client/server architecture. Clients make requests for access to LDAP servers, and the server responds back to the client with results of that request. Standard requests the client can make include connecting and disconnecting to the LDAP service, searching a directory entry, comparing information in the directory, and adding, deleting, or modifying directory information. LDAP typically runs over unsecured network connections using TCP port 389 for communications. If advanced security is required, version 3 of the LDAP protocol supports the use of TLS to encrypt communications.[10]

Active Directory Domain Services (ADDS)

Active Directory Domain Services, commonly referred to simply as either the AD or ADDS, is an implementation of the LDAP protocol for Microsoft-based environments. Through the use of additional plug-in services, LDAP directories can also be utilized by many other systems, including UNIX, Linux, and even mainframe environments. ADDS provides central authentication and authorization capabilities for users and system services on an enterprise-wide level. ADDS implementations also have the ability to enforce organizational security and configuration policies across an enterprise. For that reason, many organizations use their ADDS implementations to enforce user and system-level security policies in a uniform and highly auditable manner.

ADDS uses LDAP for its naming structure. Like LDAP, ADDS uses a hierarchical framework to store information. ADDS directories are organized into forests and trees. A forest is a collection of all the objects and their associated attributes, and trees are logical groupings of one or more ADDS security domains within a forest. Domains in ADDS are identified by their DNS name. Objects in an ADDS database are grouped by Organizational Units.

---

10   See the following: http://tools.ietf.org/html/rfc4511

X.400

X.400 is a set of ITU-T guidelines for the exchange of email, known in parlance as Message Handling Systems (MHS). X.400 was originally developed in the early 1980s and designed to run on OSI-based networks. As with X.500, most X.400 systems currently in use have the ability to run in TCP/IP-based environments as well.

The X.400 protocol supports two primary functions: message transfer and message storage. X.400 addresses consist of a series of name/value pairs separated by semicolons. Typical elements of an address specification include:

- **O** – Organization name
- **OU** – Organizational Unit names
- **G** – Given name
- **I** – Initials
- **S** – Surname
- **C** – Country name

The implementation of security features was an early part of the X.400 specification, and early implementations included features related to message privacy and message integrity. These features were implemented in X.400 far earlier than in the next most common messaging protocol, SMTP. However, while X.400-based systems initially became popular in many parts of the world, they have been largely supplanted in recent years by SMTP-based email systems.

Single Sign-On

Single sign-on (SSO) is a term used to describe a unified login experience (from the viewpoint of the end-user) when accessing one or more systems. Single sign-on is often referred to as reduced sign-on or federated ID management. Some network enterprise systems provide users with access to many different computer systems or applications for their daily work. This wide range of access may require the user to have a user ID and password for each available resource. Users who often log into many systems will prefer to sign into one master system and thereafter be able to access other systems without being repeatedly prompted to identify and authenticate themselves. There are numerous technical solutions that offer SSO to users, but most are associated with the centralization of user data, such as a centralized directory service. As previously discussed, many legacy systems do not support an external means to identify and authenticate users. Therefore, an SSO solution for these systems will need to store the credentials outside of the various applications and have them automatically entered on behalf of the user when an application is launched. *Figure 5.1* shows the architecture for a typical SSO system.

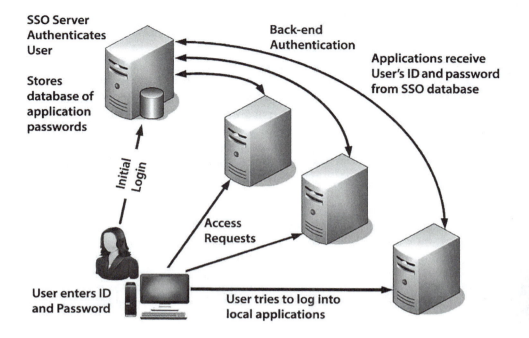

*Figure 5.1 – **Architecture for a typical single sign-on (SSO) system***

Classic single sign-on systems provide a central repository of user credentials, such as user IDs and passwords associated with a suite of applications. Users launch various applications through the SSO client software, which opens the appropriate application program and sends the appropriate keystrokes to that program, thus simulating the user to type his own user ID and password. However, there are some limitations and challenges presented by the use of a legacy SSO solution. First, given that the applications are completely unaware of the "sleight of hand" used by most SSO systems, when a user must change his or her password within the application, it must also be changed in the SSO system. The user must change the stored password in the application, but because the systems are not synchronized, the changed password must then be stored in the SSO system to maintain the synchronization between the two.

Today, many of these solutions utilize a smart card, secured by a PIN, to store the user's array of credentials in the memory of the card. The smart card loaded with user credentials is coupled with system software that detects when the user is prompted for authentication information. Upon detection, the user may be asked whether to learn the authentication data for the new application or ignore it in the future. If the system is told to learn it, it collects the identification and authentication information for that application from the user, stores it securely on the smart card, and populates the fields in the application on behalf of the user. From that point forward, the user must only remember the main SSO passphrase to unlock the smart card so that the system can gain access to the collection of identification and authorization materials for that application. There are also solutions that store the user's credentials on a central system or directory. Once authenticated to the primary SSO system, the user credentials are provided to the end system for downstream use.

There are many advantages to SSO solutions:

- ***Efficient log-on process*** – Users require fewer passwords to remember and are interrupted less when performing their job.
- ***No need for multiple passwords*** – The introduction of a SSO system translates into a single-use credential for users. While individual systems still require unique passwords, to the user there is only one master SSO password.
- ***Users may create stronger passwords*** – With the reduced number of passwords to remember, users can remember a single, very strong password or passphrase that can also be changed often.
- ***Standards can be enforced across entire SSO system*** – Access control policies and standards, such as inactivity time-outs and attempt thresholds, are easier to enforce through an SSO system because the system manages the enforcement across all applications. Inactivity time-outs are used to protect against a user being away from his workstation but still logged on for an extended period, thereby leaving the workstation available to an intruder to continue with the user's session. Attempt thresholds are used to protect against an intruder attempting to obtain an authentic user ID and password combination by brute force (trying all combinations). After a certain number of invalid access attempts (typically three to five), the account is locked.
- ***Centralized Administration*** – Most SSO solutions offer administrators a central administrative interface to support the enterprise.

Cost is a limiting factor in SSO development. The price of smart devices or simply the SSO software itself can become cost-prohibitive for a large or complex environment. If the solution is based on a centralized SSO system that users log into to collect their IDs and passwords, there are additional costs to ensure continuous availability of the system. If the entire user population utilizes the SSO system to gain access to enterprise applications and it was to fail (a classic single point of failure example), activity would come to a rapid halt.

One of the more prevalent concerns with centralized SSO systems is the fact that all of a user's credentials are protected by a single password: the SSO password. If someone was to crack that user's SSO password, he or she would effectively have all the keys to that user's kingdom. Likewise, many SSO systems store all the user credential and authentication information in a single database. Therefore, it is of critical importance that the SSO system be as hardened as possible against attack. In addition, strong monitoring and detection capabilities need to be implemented for the SSO systems to ensure that any problems are caught and addressed as quickly as possible.

Inclusion of unique platforms may also be challenging: enterprise level SSO architecture is complex and requires significant integration to be effective. It is not uncommon for a large enterprise to utilize hundreds, if not thousands, of applications running on a wide variety of operating systems, each with their own approach to user management. Therefore, the security professional will have to engage in significant planning and analysis prior to embarking on developing and deploying an SSO solution.

Script-Based Single Sign-On

If an integrated SSO solution is not available or practical, or if there are a lot of customized applications in use within the organization, an organization can implement its own solution by developing an array of customized scripts. These scripts manipulate the applications, interacting with them as if they were the user and injecting user ID, password, and other authentication information as needed. The scripts manage all the login and authentication interaction with the application on behalf of the user. This approach may be advantageous for an organization that wants, or needs, SSO functionality but whose options are limited by the pervasiveness of legacy technology or highly customized applications to which modern SSO systems will not interface. By developing its own system, the organization can create a highly customized service specifically tailored to its needs. Unfortunately the cost of developing such a system, as well as the ongoing maintenance of the system, can be extremely high. In addition, such systems become very complex to manage, adding to the maintenance problem. Further, the security practitioner needs to be aware of the potential security implications of allowing this kind of development to take place. The need to observe secure development practices has to be enforced. In addition, there is the possibility that Script-based SSO solutions can be implemented in an insecure fashion if care is not taken. As a result, they may allow for credential transmission or storage using insecure methods and mechanisms, potentially allowing for the confidentiality and integrity of the credentials to be compromised.

Kerberos

The name Kerberos comes from Greek mythology: It is the three-headed dog that guarded the entrance to Hades. The Kerberos security system guards a network with three elements: authentication, authorization, and auditing. Kerberos is essentially a network authentication protocol. It is designed to provide strong authentication for client/server applications by using secret key cryptography.

Kerberos is effective in open, distributed environments where users must have a unique ID for each application on a network. Kerberos verifies that users are who they claim to be and the network services they use are contained within their permission profile. It has four basic requirements for access control:

- **Security** – A network eavesdropper should not be able to obtain information that can be used to impersonate a user.
- **Reliability** – Resources must be available for users when they are needed.
- **Transparency** – Users should not be aware of the authentication process, and it should be as nonintrusive as possible.
- **Scalability** – The service must support a large number of clients and servers.

The Kerberos Process

Kerberos is based on the interaction between three systems: the requesting system (or the principal), the endpoint destination server (where the application or information resource resides), and the Kerberos or Key Distribution Center (KDC). A principal is any entity that interacts with the Kerberos server, such as a user workstation, an application, or a service. The KDC will serve two functions during the authentication transaction— as an authentication server (AS) and as a ticket-granting server (TGS).

5

Identity & Access Management

Kerberos is based on symmetrical encryption and a secret key shared amongst the participants: The KDC maintains a database of the secret keys of all the principals on the network. While acting as the AS, it will authenticate a principal via a pre-exchanged secret key. Once a principal is authenticated, the KDC operates as a TGS, providing a ticket—a piece of electronic data validated by the TGS—to the principal to establish trusted relationships between principals on the network. For example, a KDC maintains the secret keys for two principles on a network, a server and a workstation, both of which trust the KDC. When a user on the workstation authenticates to the AS and receives a ticket, that ticket will be accepted by the server because of the trust relationship between the server and the KDC.

Principals are preregistered with a secret key in the KDC, a process typically achieved through registration. When a user or system is added to the Kerberos realm, it is provided the realm key, a common key used for initial trusted communications. During the introduction into the realm, a unique key is created to support future communications with the KDC. For example, when a Windows workstation joins a domain, or a Linux workstation is joined to a realm, or a user joins the domain, a unique key is created and shared via the realm's key, which is managed by the KDC. In the case of a user, it is common for Kerberos to utilize a hash of the user's password as the unique user key.

Once the user is incorporated into the Kerberos realm, he or she can then be authenticated by the AS. At this point, the system authenticates the user, and the TGS provides him or her with a ticket-granting ticket (TGT). Possession of the TGT indicates that the client has successfully completed authentication and has the right to request service tickets (STs) on the KDC network. TGTs are valid for a certain period, typically between eight and ten hours, after which they expire and the user must re-authenticate to the KDC. However, once the TGT has been issued, there is no further use of passwords or other log-on factors when interacting with other systems within the Kerberos realm.

As demonstrated in *Figure 5.2*, a client (the workstation or application a user is working on) will request authentication from the AS. Once the client is authenticated, it will receive a TGT and a session encryption key. Later, the client may request access to an application server by requesting a ticket from the TGS. The client will need to produce the ticket received during the authentication process—the TGT—in order to receive a ticket to the application server. Upon validating the TGT, the TGS will generate a unique session key to be used between the client and the application server and will encrypt the session key with both the client's secret key and the application server's secret key. The KDC will pack up the data in an ST and send it to the client. If the client is legitimate, it will be able to decrypt the session key and send it, along with the encrypted application server's key, to the application server. The application server will receive the ticket from the client and decrypt the session key. Once all this is complete, the client and the application server are authenticated and now have the shared session key that can be used for encrypted communications between them.

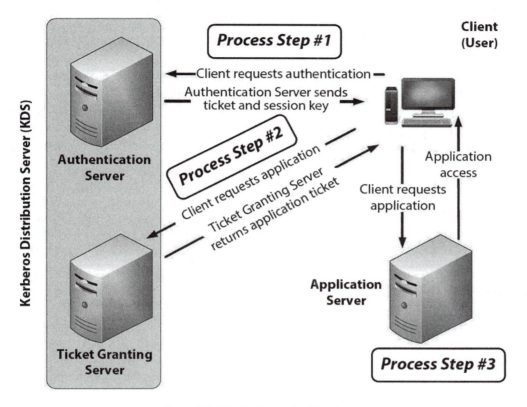

Figure 5.2 - **The Kerberos Architecture**

Given that the client and the application server have established secret keys with the KDC, the KDC can generate unique session keys and encrypt them with its stored secret keys from the systems requesting secure interactions. The client is sent the service ticket first to avoid DoS attacks against the application server; otherwise, the server could be overloaded with encrypted session requests. The session key is effectively encrypted twice, once with the client's secret key and once with application server's secret key. This forces both systems to authenticate themselves (by possession of the correct secret key) to obtain the unique session key. Once each has the session key, each now has matching key material that can be used in follow-on symmetrical encrypted communications.

There are a few key points to remember about Kerberos tickets:

- The user is authenticated once via a traditional log-on process and verified by means of message encryption to request and acquire service tickets. The user does not have to re-authenticate as long as the TGT is valid.

- When the user is authenticated to the AS, it simply receives a TGT. This, in and of itself, does not permit access. This is analogous to possession of a passport, which certifies that you are a legal citizen of your country but does not necessarily automatically grant you the ability to enter another country. Therefore, when the user obtains a TGT, it only allows him to legitimately request access to a resource. It does not automatically mean he will receive that access.

■ The TGT allows the user to request a service ticket from the TGS, authenticating the user through encryption processes and building an ST for the user to present to the target resource system.

■ The possession of the ST signifies that the user has been authenticated and can be provided access (assuming the user passes the application server's authorization criteria).

Kerberos processes are extremely time sensitive and often require the use of Network Time Protocol (NTP) Daemons to ensure times are synchronized. Failure to maintain a synchronized time infrastructure will lead to authentication failures. This can be an attractive vector for a DoS attack.

The primary goal of Kerberos is to ensure private communications between systems over a network. However, in managing the encryption keys, it acts to authenticate each of the principals in the communication based on the possession of the secret key, which allows access to the session key. Kerberos is an elegant solution and used in many platforms as the basis for broad authentication processes.

No solution is perfect, and there are some issues related to the use of Kerberos. For starters, the security of the whole system depends on careful implementation: Enforcing limited lifetimes for authentication credentials minimizes the threats of replayed credentials; the KDC must be physically secured, and it should be hardened, not permitting any non-Kerberos activity. More importantly, the KDC can be a single point of failure and therefore should be supported by backup and continuity plans. It is not uncommon for there to be several KDCs in a Kerberos architecture, each sharing principal information, such as keys, to support the infrastructure if one of the systems were to fail. In Microsoft Windows based ADDS environments, all Domain Controllers are KDCs, thus creating an architecture where there is no single point of failure due to a KDC being knocked offline or becoming unavailable.

The length of the keys (secret and session) is very important. For example, if the key is too short, it is vulnerable to brute force attacks. If it is too long, systems can be overloaded with encrypting and decrypting tickets and network data. Finally, the Achilles' heel of Kerberos is the fact that encryption processes are ultimately based on passwords. Therefore, it can fall victim to traditional password-guessing attacks.

One of the biggest roadblocks to implementing Kerberos in a processing environment is the need to embed Kerberos system calls into any application that needs to use the system. This process, known as "Kerberizing" an application, allows the application to attach to the Kerberos environment, exchange encryption keys and tickets, and communicate securely with other Kerberos-enabled devices and services. The system calls needed are part of the Kerberos library that must be compiled into every application, and that may cause a problem for some applications. While adding Kerberos library calls to source code may be possible with custom-developed applications, it is not practical in environments that rely on commercial, off-the-shelf (also known as COTS) software. If an organization does not have the ability to embed Kerberos calls into its applications, its ability to use Kerberos will be limited.

Perimeter-Based Web Portal Access

If an organization has a directory such as LDAP in place, it is possible to quickly leverage the directory data to manage user identity, authentication, and authorization data on multiple Web-based applications using a Web portal tied to a Web access management (WAM) solution. These solutions replace the sign-on process in affiliated Web applications, typically by using a plug-in service on the Web server hosting the portal to the member applications. When users authenticate for the first time into the Web portal environment, the portal (more specifically, the WAM) maintains that user's authentication state as the user navigates between applications. Moreover, these systems normally also allow for the definition of user groups and the ability to manage access privileges by group on the managed systems.

These systems provide effective user management and single sign-on in Web environments. They do not, in general, support comprehensive management of the entire access control environment or legacy systems. Nevertheless, WAM has offered a meaningful solution for Web environments to help organizations manage multiple Internet users accessing a collection of Web-based applications. For this reason, WAM tools have been rapidly adopted by organizations seeking more efficient methods for managing a large number of users for a select group of applications.

Federated Identity Management

Single sign-on services are a great productivity boon to both users and organizations. When implemented properly, they can also improve the application security of the organization implementing the service. However, most SSO implementations typically involve the management of users across multiple applications within a single enterprise, where the users are all part of the same organization and their identity and access privileges can be verified and managed by a single security infrastructure. A single organization manages the identity and authenticity information for each of its users and takes responsibility for the security and integrity of that process.

However, it is becoming more common that multiple organizations have the need to share the same applications and users between them. For example, an automobile manufacturer and a parts supplier may need to share each other's systems and information. Users from the manufacturer will need access to the supplier to check inventory levels, place orders, and check on order status. Users from the supplier will need to access the manufacturer's systems to check on part requirements, update order status information, and manage contract provisions. To provide this type of access, each company would normally have to manage the authentication and verification of the other company's users' identity before provisioning their access to internal systems. Unfortunately, each company does not have access to the other company's employee records (nor should they) and cannot easily track the employee lifecycle of the other company to determine whether or not the user is still a valid company employee.

The solution to problems such as this is the use of a federated identity management infrastructure. In a federated environment, each organization in the federation subscribes to a common set of policies, standards, and procedures for the provisioning and management of user identification, authentication, and authorization information, as well as a common process for access control for systems these users must access. Each participating organization then establishes a trust relationship with the other organizations such that users from any of the organizations—once authenticated—can access resources from any of the other organization's systems that participate in the federation. They can do this because all the organizations share an agreed-upon standard for security and access control provisioning. Each organization trusts that the other will hold up their end of the process and that users from a "foreign" organization go through the same rigorous vetting process that users from the "home" organization must go through.

Federated ID management systems use one of two basic processes for linking the member organizations' processes together. The first is a cross-certification model. In this model, each organization must individually certify that every other participating organization is worthy of its trust. The organizations review each other's processes and standards, and their due diligence efforts determine whether the other organizations meet or exceed their own standards. Once this verification and certification process is complete, the organizations can then begin to trust other organizations' users. *Figure 5.3* shows a graphical representation of a cross-certification trust model.

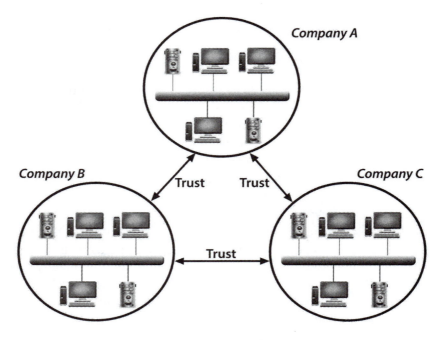

Figure 5.3 - **The Cross-Certification Trust model**

While the cross-certification model may be sufficient for some organizations, there are some drawbacks that must be considered before implementing such a plan. The first issue is that once the number of participating organizations goes beyond a few, the number of trust relationships that must be managed grows rapidly. For example, a cross-certification between two companies (A and B) requires that two trust relationships must be managed (A trusts B and B trusts A). If three companies participate (A, B, and C), the number of trust relationships grows to six (A trusts B, B trusts A, A trusts C, C trusts A, B trusts C, and C trusts B). Once the number of participants grows to five, there are twenty trust relationships that must be managed (the reason for this is left as a mathematical exercise for the reader). Along with this comes the process for verifying the trustworthiness of the other participating organizations. The process must be thorough and can take considerable time and resources to accomplish. Thus, once the number of participants in a cross-certification model grows beyond a small number, the complexity of the model may grow too burdensome or expensive to manage for many organizations.

An alternative to the cross-certification model is the trusted third party, or bridge model. In this model, each of the participating organizations subscribes to the standards and practices of a third party that manages the verification and due diligence process for all participating companies. Once that third party has verified the participating organization, they are automatically considered trustworthy by all the other participants. Later, when a user from one of the participants attempts to access a resource from another participant, that organization only needs to check that the user has been certified by the trusted third party before access is allowed. The third party, in effect, acts as a bridge between the participating organizations for identity verification purposes. The trusted third-party model is a good solution for organizations that need to enter into a federation with a large number of other organizations. *Figure 5.4* shows a diagram of a typical third-party certification model.

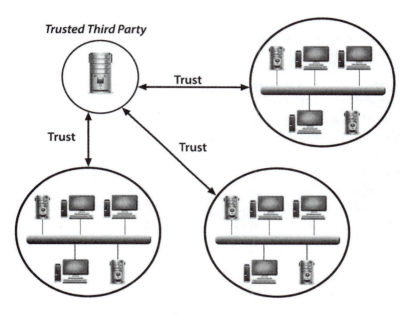

Figure 5.4 - **The Third-Party Certification Trust model**

Security Assertion Markup Language 2.0 is a version of the SAML OASIS standard for exchanging authentication and authorization data between security domains.[11] SAML 2.0 is an XML-based protocol that uses security tokens containing assertions to pass information about a principal (usually an end-user) between a SAML authority, that is an identity provider, and a Web service, that is a service provider. SAML 2.0 enables Web-based authentication and authorization scenarios including single sign-on (SSO).

The SAML specification defines three roles: the principal (typically a user), the identity provider (IdP), and the service provider (SP). When using SAML, the principal requests a service from the service provider. The service provider requests and obtains an identity assertion from the identity provider. On the basis of this assertion, the service provider can make an access control decision; in other words, it can decide whether to perform some service for the connected principal.

---

11   See the following for the Version 2 Standard Draft for SAML: https://www.oasis-open.org/committees/
     download.php/27819/sstc-saml-tech-overview-2.0-cd-02.pdf

Before delivering the identity assertion to the SP, the IdP may request some information from the principal – such as a username and password – in order to authenticate the principal. SAML specifies the assertions between the three parties: in particular, the messages that assert identity that are passed from the IdP to the SP. In SAML, one identity provider may provide SAML assertions to many service providers. Similarly, one SP may rely on and trust assertions from many independent IdPs. SAML is built upon a number of existing standards:

- **Extensible Markup Language (XML)** – Most SAML exchanges are expressed in a standardized dialect of XML, which is the root for the name SAML (Security Assertion Markup Language).
- **XML Schema** – SAML assertions and protocols are specified (in part) using XML Schema.
- **XML Signature** – Both SAML 1.1 and SAML 2.0 use digital signatures (based on the XML Signature standard) for authentication and message integrity.
- **XML Encryption** – Using XML Encryption, SAML 2.0 provides elements for encrypted name identifiers, encrypted attributes, and encrypted assertions (SAML 1.1 does not have encryption capabilities).
- **Hypertext Transfer Protocol (HTTP)** – SAML relies heavily on HTTP as its communications protocol.
- **SOAP** – SAML specifies the use of SOAP, specifically SOAP 1.1.

SAML is XML-based, which makes it a very flexible standard. Two federation partners can choose to share whatever identity attributes they want in a SAML assertion (message) payload as long as those attributes can be represented in XML. This flexibility led to pieces of the SAML standard, such as the SAML assertion format, being incorporated into other standards such as WS-Federation. Enterprise SAML identity federation use cases generally revolve around sharing identity between an existing Identity Management system and Web applications. There are two actors in the SAML scenario, the Identity Provider who "asserts" the identity of the user and the Service Provider who consumes the "assertion" and passes the identity information to the application. The interaction between the Identity Management system and the federation server is called "first mile" integration, and the interaction between the federation server and the application is called "last mile" integration.

For example, the Windows Azure Active Directory supports the SAML 2.0 Web browser single sign-on (SSO) profile. To request that Windows Azure Active Directory authenticate a user, the cloud service (the service provider) must use an HTTP Redirect binding to pass an **AuthnRequest** (authentication request) element to Windows Azure Active Directory (the identity provider). Windows Azure Active Directory uses an HTTP Post binding to post a **Response** element to the cloud service.

Once In-Unlimited Access

Some organizations do not need to tightly manage user access or restrict resources in a very granular manner. For example, a public service organization may have several services or websites that contributors are allowed to access. Alternatively, an organization may have a special area of their intranet that is available to all employees without the need to identify or authenticate to each application individually. Some of the affected applications may not require authentication at all. In such a circumstance, the organization may employ a once in-unlimited access (OIUA) model. In this model, the user authenticates once and then has access to all the resources participating in the model. This differs from a pure SSO model in that SSO typically manages authentication and access control behind the scenes from the user. In an OIUA model, the systems behind the initial authentication do not have any authentication mechanism to speak of. The fact that the user is able to access the system in the first place means that the user is authorized. How that initial authentication is managed varies with each implementation. In some cases, it is as simple as having access to the organization's intranet, the assumption being that if the user got on the network in the first place, he was authorized to be there.

The OIUA model suffers from one obvious drawback: the assumption on the part of each participating system that the user identification and authentication was properly handled before the user accesses the system. In many OIUA systems, there is no certificate or token that is passed between the authentication service and the back-end applications, and so true verification of the user's legitimacy is lacking. An unauthorized individual, such as a contractor or support person, accessing the organization's intranet can access the OIUA systems just as easily as a regular employee can. For some organizations, and depending on the type of systems affected by this model, that may not be a concern. Nevertheless, the security professional would be wise to thoroughly check the information contained in each participating system and the type of organizational resources those systems allow users to access before approving the use of an OIUA model. If the model serves a legitimate business purpose, the participating systems should be strongly isolated from the OIUA systems (logically and physically) before proceeding to offer this service to users.

Single/Multi-Factor Authentication
An authentication factor can be one of three types:

- ***Something You Know*** – A password or PIN
- ***Something You Have*** – A token or smart card
- ***Something You Are*** – Biometrics, such as a fingerprint

Single factor authentication involves the use of simply one of the three available factors solely in order to carry out the authentication process being requested. The subjects that want to be authenticated will have to provide their factor; in other words, they will have to present their password, or swipe their smart card, or scan their finger in order to validate their identity and authenticate into the system.

Multi-factor authentication ensures that a user is who he or she claims to be. The more factors used to determine a person's identity, the greater the trust of authenticity. Multi-factor authentication can be achieved using a combination of factors. Typically any combination of at least two factors is referred to as multi-factor authentication, although the most secure systems will require the use all three factors for a true multi-factor solution. One type of authentication may not be repeated in attempting to satisfy multi-factor authentication. For example, authenticating using two passwords does not constitute multi-factor. They are both part of "something you know" and can both only satisfy this category.

One example of how multi-factor authentication is being used in the enterprise today can be seen by examining what the Amazon Web Services (AWS) platform has architected for their customer facing solution. According to Amazon, AWS Multi-Factor Authentication (MFA) is a simple best practice that adds an extra layer of protection on top of your username and password. With MFA enabled, when users sign in to an AWS website, they will be prompted for their username and password (the first factor – what they know), as well as for an authentication code from their AWS MFA device (the second factor – what they have). Taken together, these multiple factors provide increased security for your AWS account settings and resources. The table in the following section lists the MFA form factors available for use.

MFA Form Factors

Virtual MFA Applications

Applications for your smartphone can be installed only from the application store that is specific for your phone type. In the list below are names of some applications for different smartphone types.

Android	AWS Virtual MFA; Google Authenticator
iPhone	Google Authenticator
Windows Phone	Authenticator
Blackberry	Google Authenticator

Another example of multi-factor authentication use can be found in the requirements of Homeland Security Presidential Directive-12, dated August 27, 2004:

"SUBJECT: Policies for a Common Identification Standard for Federal Employees and Contractors

■ Wide variations in the quality and security of forms of identification used to gain access to secure Federal and other facilities where there is potential for terrorist attacks need to be eliminated. Therefore, it is the policy of the United States to enhance security, increase Government efficiency, reduce identity fraud, and protect personal privacy by establishing a mandatory, Government-wide standard for secure and reliable forms of identification issued by the Federal Government to its employees and contractors (including contractor employees)." [12]

The directive calls for the establishment of a mandatory, Government-wide standard for secure and reliable forms of identification. The use of the authentication factors already discussed in some combination would certainly meet the specified requirements called for in the directive. The specific implementation of the "something you have" factor in this case will be a good case study for the security professional looking to better understand what a multi-factor authentication solution requires from beginning to end.

---

12 See the following: http://www.dhs.gov/homeland-security-presidential-directive-12

	Virtual MFA Device	*Hardware Keyfob MFA Device*	*Hardware Display Card MFA Device*
Device	See table below.	Purchase device.	Purchase device.
Physical Form Factor	Use your existing smartphone, tablet, or computer running any application that supports the open TOTP standard.[13]	Tamper-evident hardware keyfob device provided by Gemalto, a 3rd-party provider.	Tamper-evident hardware display card device provided by Gemalto, a 3rd-party provider.
Features	Support for multiple tokens on a single device.	The same type of device used by many financial services and enterprise IT organizations.	Similar to keyfob devices, but in a convenient form factor that fits in your wallet like a credit card

Tokens

Tokens are used by claimants to prove their identity and authenticate to a system or application, and they can be either software or hardware based. The token contains a secret that is used to prove the claimant is in control of the token. Token secrets are either based on asymmetric keys or symmetric (single) keys. In an asymmetric key model, the private key is stored on the token and used to prove possession when paired with the public key. Symmetric keys are shared directly between the claimant and the replying party for direct comparison over a secure channel (e.g., HTTPS).

Token input data, such as a challenge or nonce (number or bit string used only once), may be required to generate the token authenticator. Token input data may be supplied by the user or be a feature of the token itself (e.g., the clock in a One Time Password (OTP) device). Token activation data, such as a PIN, may be required to activate the token and permit generation of an authenticator.

An attacker would attempt to gain control of a token in order to impersonate the token owner and compromise the authentication protocol. Tokens may be lost, damaged, stolen from the owner, or cloned. For example, an attacker who gains access to the owner's computer might attempt to copy a software token. A hardware token might be stolen, tampered with, or duplicated.

Soft Token Implementation

Software tokens are stored on a general-purpose computer such as a desktop, laptop, or mobile device; and they require activation through a second factor of authentication (e.g., PIN, password, or biometric). Soft tokens are generally cheaper to implement and easier to manage than hard tokens, and they avoid some physical security risks that come with hard tokens. However, soft tokens are only as secure as the computer they are stored on and are susceptible to computer viruses, man-in-the-middle, phishing, and other software attacks. For remote access using multi-factor authentication, soft tokens are acceptable for the "something you have" factor with the following requirements implemented to protect the soft token software and the soft tokens for use with remote network authentication for access to secure information.

---

13   See the following for the Time Based One-Time Password Algorithm (TOTP) RFC: http://tools.ietf.org/html/rfc6238

- ■ **Private keys must be non-exportable** – Soft token software that utilizes encryption keys stored in a local key repository must mark the keys non-exportable. This helps prevent exportation of the key to be installed on an unauthorized system. Files of long-term private keys shall be protected by access controls that limit access to administrators and only to those applications that require access.

- ■ **Never store keys in plaintext (unencrypted) form** – If the soft token is using shared secret keys, the keys should not be stored in a format that can be read and copied outside of the application. Text files would have to be at least read only to the users of a system for the soft token software to function. This greatly increases the chance that the keys can be copied to another system.

- ■ **Distributing the seed record and initial passphrases requires a confidential channel to ensure that it is not duplicated in transit** – Installation of soft token software typically has two pieces of information (seed record, passphrase) to install and initialize the token generation engine. These two pieces of information, if captured by an unauthorized user, would allow unauthorized installations of the software, and they could be used by parties other than the authorized user.

- ■ **Activation of the token must occur every time user authenticates using the soft token software** – Each authentication shall require entry of the password or other activation data. Input of the other factor (password) must be strictly limited to manual user input when challenged by the relying party (system). Storing of the PIN or password allowing the software to generate a token without manual user input should not be implemented.

- ■ **Token time limit must be 2 minutes or less** – The token generated by the software must have a time limit for use. This small time window should be sufficient to initiate remote access, and it prevents the sharing of a token for other systems or theft of the token.

- ■ **Soft token software password should follow Password Management guidelines such as the IRS Publication 1075 Exhibit 8 Password Management Guidelines** – Password management requirements for soft token software should follow the complexity, size, change interval, and reuse guidelines stated in the Password Management guidelines. This will ensure that passwords used to generate tokens are not easily guessed and unique per user. [14]

- ■ **Audit all access to software tokens** – Audit logs must be captured for access to the soft token software when successful and unsuccessful remote access attempts have occurred. The audit trail should log attempts made to guess PIN numbers and passwords, and correlating software access with successful and unsuccessful remote access connections can show attempts to tamper or copy the soft token software.

- ■ **Always install the latest version of malware prevention software before using software tokens** – Malware prevention software must be installed to identify and prevent installation of key logging software or other malware that could capture the PIN or password used to access the soft token software.

---

14   See the following: http://www.irs.gov/pub/irs-pdf/p1075.pdf

■ ***Always use FIPS 140-2 validated cryptographic modules*** – The cryptographic module performing the encryption function must be validated to meet FIPS 140-2 Level 1.[15]

Additionally, the following security controls could be implemented by the security professional to decrease the likelihood that soft token software can be compromised.

■ ***PKI is the preferred key management platform*** – Public-key infrastructure (PKI) uses asymmetric (public/private) key pairs for all cryptographic operations. With PKI, the claimant can prove itself to the system without disclosing the private keys. Symmetric keys must be disclosed to authenticate, so they are more susceptible to compromise over time.

■ ***Use available Trusted Platform Modules (TPM)*** – A TPM is a local hardware encryption engine and secured storage for encryption keys. If you store the keys in the TPM key store, direct access to the key is interrupted by the TPM system asking for authentication to access keys.

■ ***Perform self-validation before issuing a token*** – Comparison of the software files, including the executable, DLL, and INI files, against a hash or any other mechanism that validates the software has not been altered must be performed before a token is given for remote access.

Hard Token Implementation

Hard tokens are non-software physical tokens that store credentials on hardened dedicated devices used to authenticate an identity. Hard tokens are susceptible to physical security attacks (i.e., direct physical access) if lost or stolen. For multi-factor authentication, the following types of hard tokens are acceptable for the "something you have" token. Each token type has associated implementation requirements for use with remote network authentication for access to secure information.

■ ***Look Up Secret Token*** – Can be a physical token that stores a set of secrets, and it is used to look up the secret based on a prompt from the authentication protocol. An example of this is a grid-card. The token authenticator must have at least 64 bits of entropy.

■ ***Out-of-Band Token*** – A one-time use token received over a separate channel from the primary authentication channel, and it is presented to the authentication protocol using the primary channel. An example of this is receiving an SMS message on a cell phone. The token authenticator must have at least 64 bits of entropy.

■ ***One-Time Password Device*** – A hardware device that provides generation of one-time use passwords (e.g., sequence based or time based). The one-time password is typically displayed on the device and manually inputs to the authentication protocol, and it may be activated by either "something you know" or "something you are." Examples of this are tokens that generate a code every 30-60 seconds or that have a button that, when pressed, generates a code. This could also include a one-time password generating application running on a cell phone or mobile device. The cryptographic module performing the verifier function shall be FIPS 140-2 validated, and the one-time password must be generated by using a FIPS-approved block cipher or hash function to combine a symmetric key stored on a personal hardware device with a nonce. The one-time password shall have a limited lifetime.

5

Identity &
Access Management

---

15   See the following: http://csrc.nist.gov/publications/fips/fips140-2/fips1402.pdf

■ ***Cryptographic Device*** – A hardware device that contains non-programmable logic and non-volatile storage dedicated to all cryptographic operations and protection of private keys. An example of this is a FIPS-201 smart card that contains several X.509 certificates and all processing of cryptographic functions. Each authentication requires entry of the activation data (e.g., password, PIN).[16]

Shared secret files shall also be encrypted so that the encryption key for the shared secret file is encrypted under a key held in a FIPS 140-2 validated hardware cryptographic module.

In order to build a secure token-based authentication module that is a part of a larger multi-factor authentication solution, the security professional would need to understand all of the guidance offered above and then be able to integrate that guidance into a formal enterprise security architecture encompassing at least one additional authentication factor to be able to deliver a true multi-factor authentication solution to the enterprise in support of the business requirements as outlined in the directive. Another good resource for the security professional to examine in this regard is the NIST SP800-63-1, Electronic Authentication Guideline, December, 2011.[17]

Biometrics

Biometric devices rely on measurements of biological characteristics of an individual, such as a fingerprint, hand geometry, voice, or iris patterns. Biometric technology involves data that is unique to the individual and is difficult to counterfeit. Selected individual characteristics are stored in a device's memory or on a card, from which stored reference data can be analyzed and compared with the presented template. A one-to-many or a one-to-one comparison of the presented template with the stored template can be made, and access can be granted if a match is found.

However, on the negative side, some biometric systems may periodically fail to perform or have a high rejection rate. The sensitivity of readers could make system readers susceptible to inadvertent reader damage or intentional sabotage. Some systems may be perceived by the user as a safety or health risk. Also, some of the systems may require a degree of skill on the part of the user for proper operation, and others may be perceived as unacceptable by management for a combination of reasons.

There are two types of failures in biometric identification:

■ ***False Rejection*** – Failure to recognize a legitimate user. While it could be argued that this has the effect of keeping the protected area extra secure, it is an intolerable frustration to legitimate users who are refused access because the scanner does not recognize them.

■ ***False Acceptance*** – Erroneous recognition, either by confusing one user with another or by accepting an imposter as a legitimate user.

Failure rates can be adjusted by changing the threshold ("how close is close enough") for declaring a match, but decreasing one failure rate will increase the other.

---

16 See the following for the latest FIPS-201 Draft: http://csrc.nist.gov/publications/drafts/fips201-2/Draft_NIST-FIPS-201-2.pdf

17 See the following: http://csrc.nist.gov/publications/nistpubs/800-63-1/SP-800-63-1.pdf

Biometric Readers

Biometric readers verify personal biological metrics of an individual. Biometric readers may be used in addition to credential devices or with a PIN code. This type of security technology is more likely found in high security areas such as a government Sensitive Compartmented Information Facility (SCIF) or a data center.

Current gains in large-scale production of some types of biometric readers have brought biometrics close in cost to conventional card readers. Although biometric scanners are typically not as fast as other readers, these technologies are still evolving.

Fingerprint

Fingerprint reader technology scans the loops, whorls, and other characteristics of a fingerprint and compares it with stored templates (*Figure 5.5*). When a match is found, access is granted. The advantage of fingerprint technology is that it is easily understood. The disadvantages are that the systems can be disrupted if cuts or sores appear on fingers or if grease or other medium contaminates the fingers and the scanning plates. Some systems create two templates for two different fingers, in the event that one finger is altered by injury or other means. Early fingerprint readers were compromised by picking up a valid fingerprint from a reader with a manufactured "finger." Sensors were equipped with the ability to sense a pulse and temperature to combat this shortcoming of the technology.

Figure 5.5 – **A Fingerprint Reader scans the loops, whorls, and other characteristics of a fingerprint and compares it with stored templates. When a match is found, access is granted.**

(Courtesy of Bosch Security Systems.)

Facial Image

This technology measures the geometric properties of the subject's face relative to an archived image. Specifically, the center of the subject's eyes must be located and placed at precise locations.

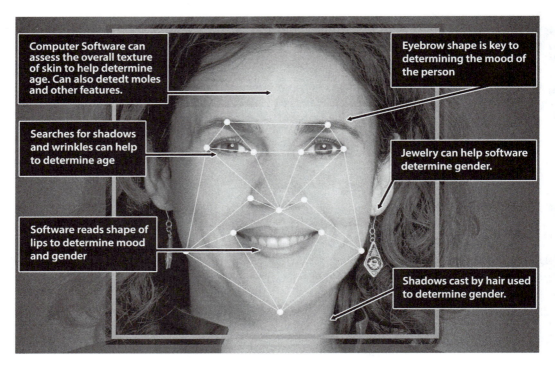

Computer Software can assess the overall texture of skin to help determine age. Can also detedt moles and other features.

Eyebrow shape is key to determining the mood of the person

Searches for shadows and wrinkles can help to determine age

Jewelry can help software determine gender.

Software reads shape of lips to determine mood and gender

Shadows cast by hair used to determine gender.

*Figure 5.6 –***Geometric properties of a subject's face used in Facial Imaging**

Hand Geometry

This technology assesses the hand's geometry: height, width, and distance between knuckle joints and finger length. Advantages of hand geometry are that the systems are durable and easily understood. The speed of hand recognition tends to be more rapid than fingerprint recognition. Hand recognition is reasonably accurate because the shape of all hands is unique. A disadvantage is that they tend to give higher false accept rates than fingerprint recognition. This technology cannot determine when fingernails have been applied, and it reads only geometric measurements of the hand.

Figure 5.7 – **Hand Geometry reader**

Voice Recognition

Voice recognition identifies the voice characteristics of a given phrase to that of one held in a template. Voice recognition is generally not performed as one function, and it is typically part of a system where a valid PIN must be entered before the voice analyzer is activated. An advantage of voice recognition is that the technology is less expensive than other biometric technologies. Additionally, it can be operated hands-free. A disadvantage is that the voice synthesizer must be placed in an area where the voice is not disturbed by background sounds. Often a booth or a security portal has to be installed to house the sensor in order to provide the system with an acceptable quiet background.

Iris Patterns

Iris recognition technology scans the surface of the eye and compares the iris pattern with stored iris templates. Iris scanning is the most accurate biometric technology. A benefit of iris recognition is that it is not susceptible to theft, loss, or compromise, and irises are less susceptible to wear and injury than many other parts of the body. Newer iris scanners allow scanning to occur from up to ten inches away. A disadvantage of iris scanning is that some people are timid about having their eye scanned. Throughput time for this technology should also be considered. Typical throughput time is two seconds. If a number of people need to be processed through an entrance in a short period of time, this can be problematic.

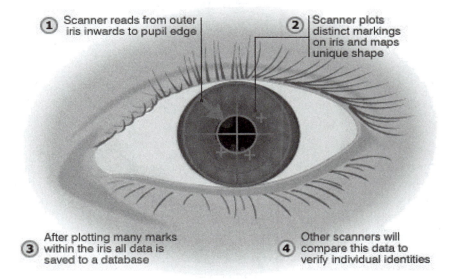

Figure 5.8 – **How Iris Scanners record identity**

(http://news.bbc.co.uk/2/shared/spl/hi/guides/456900/456993/html/nn3page1.stm)

Retinal Scanning

Retinal scanning analyzes the layer of blood vessels at the back of the eye, which is unique to each person. Scanning involves using a low-intensity LED light source and an optical coupler that can read the patterns with great accuracy. It does require the user to remove glasses, place his eye close to the device, and focus on a certain point. The user looks through a small

681

opening in the device and must keep his head still and eye focused for several seconds during which time the device will verify his identity. This process takes about 10 seconds.

Retina scan devices are probably the most accurate biometric available today. The continuity of the retinal pattern throughout life and the difficulty in fooling such a device also make it a great long-term, high-security option. Unfortunately, the cost of the proprietary hardware as well as the stigma of users thinking it is potentially harmful to the eye makes retinal scanning a bad fit for most situations. Typically, this application is used in high-end security applications, such as military bases and nuclear power plants.

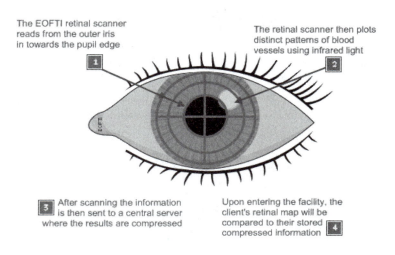

The EOFTI retinal scanner reads from the outer iris in towards the pupil edge

The retinal scanner then plots distinct patterns of blood vessels using infrared light

After scanning the information is then sent to a central server where the results are compressed

Upon entering the facility, the client's retinal map will be compared to their stored compressed information

Figure 5.9 – **How Retinal Scanners record identity**

(http://www.eofti.com/about/retinal-scan/)

Signature Dynamics

First, the signer writes out a handwritten signature on a special electronic pad, such as the ePad by Interlink or a Palm Pilot. The shape of the signature is then electronically read and recorded, along with such unique features as the pressure on the pen and the speed at which the signature was written in order to identify the signer's unique writing; for example, did the "t" get crossed from right to left and did the "i" get dotted at the very end?

The advantage of signature dynamics is that it works like a traditional signature. Signers do not need special knowledge of computers nor any unusual tools to make a signature. At the same time, the system allows the notary to record unique identifying features to help prevent and detect forged signatures. For example, if a forger attempted to copy the signature of another person and wrote slowly to try and create a visually identical style of writing, an analyst could compare it with the data to detect the slower writing speed and recognize it as a different signer.

Figure 5.10 – **Signature Dynamics pad**

(http://bit.ly/ePadAPIs)

Vascular Patterns

This is the ultimate palm reader. Vascular patterns are best described as a picture of the veins in a person's hand or finger. The thickness and location of these veins are believed to be unique enough to an individual to be used to verify a person's identity. The NTSC Subcommittee on Biometrics reports that researchers have determined that the vascular pattern of the human body is unique to the specific individual and does not change as people age. Claims for the technology include:

- ■ **Difficult to Forge** – Vascular patterns are difficult to recreate because they are inside the hand, and for some approaches, blood needs to flow to register an image.
- ■ **Contactless** – Users do not touch the sensing surface, which addresses hygiene concerns and improves user acceptance.
- ■ **Many and Varied Uses** – It is deployed at ATMs, hospitals, and universities in Japan. Applications include ID verification, high security physical access control, high security network data access, and POS access control.
- ■ **Capable of 1:1 and 1:Many Matches** – Users' vascular patterns are matched against personalized ID cards/smart cards or against a database of many scanned vascular patterns.

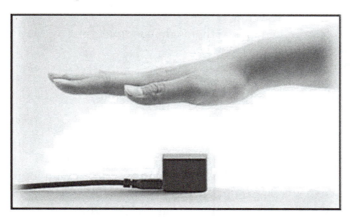

Figure 5.11 – **Vascular Pattern reader**

683

Keystroke Dynamics

Keystroke dynamics, also known as keyboard dynamics, looks at the way a person types at a keyboard. Specifically, the keystroke rhythms of a user are measured to develop a unique template of the users typing pattern for future authentication. Raw measurements available from most every keyboard can be recorded to determine dwell time (the amount of time you hold down a particular key) and flight time (the amount of time between the next key down and the next key up).

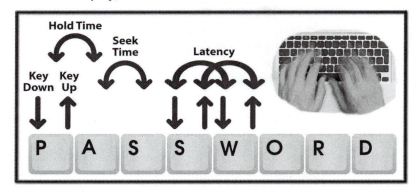

Figure 5.12 – **Sample Keystroke Dynamics measurements**
(http://bit.ly/typeprint_technology)

Accountability

Ultimately, one of the drivers behind strong identification, authentication, auditing, and session management is accountability. Accountability is fundamentally about being able to determine who or what is responsible for an action and can be held responsible. A closely related information assurance topic is non-repudiation. Repudiation is the ability to deny an action, event, impact, or result. Non-repudiation is the process of ensuring a user may not deny an action. Accountability relies heavily on non-repudiation to ensure users, processes, and actions may be held responsible for impacts. The following contribute to ensuring accountability of actions:

- Strong identification
- Strong authentication
- User training and awareness
- Comprehensive, timely, and thorough monitoring
- Accurate and consistent audit logs
- Independent audits
- Policies enforcing accountability
- Organizational behavior supporting accountability

Strong Identification

For accountability to be successful, an action must be attributable to a single individual, process, device, or object. Without the ability to directly associate an action with an individual, repudiation of the action can arise. One of the most prevalent examples of this is the use of shared accounts. When several people have access to a single account, the ability to directly associate an action performed through the account with an individual diminishes rapidly as users are able to blame others with plausible deniability.

Strong Authentication

Weak authentication not only makes it easier for an attacker to take control of an account with no accountability, but it also allows users to blame weak authentication on account abuses. Strong authentication such as biometrics helps ensure non-repudiation by strongly associating something only one individual has to an account. While not perfect, strong authentication with strong identification greatly increases accountability.

User Training and Awareness

Users need to be trained and have a basic awareness of the penalties for misuse of accounts, information, and systems. Informed users are less likely to intentionally or unintentionally abuse accounts, access, or information if they are aware of the consequences. A well-structured and repeated security awareness program is generally accepted as a baseline for ensuring users understand consequences and acceptable behaviors. The security professional may want to use login banners as one of many tools to reinforce the messages and behaviors that user training and awareness programs are designed to instill in users.

Monitoring

Monitoring must be sufficient to detect problems and violations with accounts, access, information egress, and system operation. If an organization does not have visibility into an information system, it is unlikely the organization will know when accountability issues surface. Monitoring technologies such as data loss prevention (DLP), intrusion detection systems (IDS), intrusion prevention systems (IPS), and firewalls can be implemented to increase visibility and therefore greatly strengthen accountability. It is up to the security architect and the security practitioner both to ensure that systems are designed and deployed that address the issues of monitoring from a bi-directional perspective across the enterprise. If the traditional bias and focus of these systems is maintained, and they only address perimeter-based external oriented monitoring, then they will be of limited use to the enterprise. The need to ensure that visibility is created with regards to internal activities and information flows is of equal importance.

Audit Logs

Audit logs are necessary in the event an action must be traced back to a user. Audit logs from DLP, IDS, servers, firewalls, and other network devices should be collected and consolidated as much as possible. Often these logs are collected into a Security Information and Event Management (SIEM) system. SIEMs are used in conjunction with analytical tools to correlate information and help "tell the story" of what happened. They are highly useful in helping ensure accountability.

Independent Audits

Independent audits help ensure accountability by bringing in an unbiased third party to review accounts, actions, and impacts. Independent audits, investigations, or reviews are required to establish accountability when collusion may have occurred between several parties. Routine independent audits can also set a tone throughout the organization that corrupt practices are not tolerated.

5

Identity & Access Management

Policy

An organization's policy must recognize the need for accountability and provide expectations of behavior and define sanctions and rewards for accountability related behaviors. Some organizations have an "integrity" award for outstanding acts of accountability in difficult situations. Without a policy, accountability cannot be enforced consistently and fairly throughout an organization.

Organizational Behavior

Arguably the most significant aspect of ensuring accountability is the culture of the organization. An organization that does not set the "tone at the top" for accountability expectations is unlikely to receive the support necessary to implement accountability controls throughout the organization. Additionally, if violations of accountability are not met with timely and consistent treatment, further instances of accountability violations can be expected.

Session Management

With the increase in Web-based applications and cloud computing, access controls must be viewed in light of session management. "Session management" is a term used to describe how a single instance of identification and authentication is applied to resources. For example a "desktop" session manager may allow a user to maintain a particular set of open applications, files, and functions while simultaneously starting another desktop session with a different set of applications, files, and functions. Many Unix and Linux operating systems offer this capability. Web browsers also rely on sessions to manage access to Web applications and resources often through the use of cookies or other session monitoring and tracking technologies. While session management provides ease of use and flexibility for the end-user, it also provides an avenue of attack.

Desktop Sessions

Desktop sessions can be controlled and protected through several means including but not limited to the following:

- Screensavers
- Timeouts
- Automatic Logouts
- Session/Login limitation
- Schedule Limitations

Screensavers

Most operating systems have a "screensaver" function. This function was originally designed to help prevent "burn in" of Cathode Ray Tube (CRT) display monitors. As technology has advanced, displays are subject to "burn in" of different types, and energy efficiency concerns have driven the screensaver to become an energy conservation tool. In addition to saving energy, many desktop screensavers can be configured to "lock" the session of the user. This is a form of a "timeout" session lock technology, which is designed to automatically lock the session of the user who may have left the session without locking it or logging out. This is helpful in preventing unauthorized access while ensuring the user can still access his or her session upon return.

Timeouts and Automatic Logouts

As noted prior, screensavers are a type of "timeout" control. Timeout controls can exist in many ways and are often cascaded to further restrict the access of an unattended session as time passes. For example, when an unattended desktop session has been ongoing for fifteen minutes, the screensaver may activate and require a username and password to access the system. After two hours, the system may automatically log off the user and close the session. After eight hours, the system may shut itself down. These are all forms of timeouts that must balance the risk of access and exposure with the impact to the user and mission.

Session/Logon Limitation

Session and logon limitation focus on usability and security trade-offs. For example, if a company has a highly mobile workforce, they may want to consider allowing multiple sessions from the same username. An example is if users have some work on their desktop they need to keep running over night, and they also need to work on a report using their laptop while in their home office. It is possible they will need two network sessions and perhaps two desktop sessions if virtual desktops are used. However, organizations must be cautious with regards to how multiple sessions are implemented because each session can provide an additional point of attack for an adversary and many more sessions to monitor for the security operations team and the end-user. The security practitioner needs to keep in mind that by monitoring sessions for behavior such as logins during non-business hours, he or she will be able to spot potentially suspicious behavior across any of the systems being observed.

Schedule Limitations

Some desktop sessions may be limited by time. For example, if a kiosk is available in the lobby of an organization for general use during normal hours, does it make sense to have it allow sessions during non-business hours? Or should cash registers allow the creation of sessions outside of normal operating hours? Typically, session management should follow the concept of "least privilege" and only allow the creation of sessions within the most restrictive schedule and resources required to meet the mission.

Logical Sessions

As more information systems become service-based through Web browsers, understanding Web-based sessions, their weaknesses, and how to protect them is critical for information security professionals to understand. Basic sessions are created between authenticated users, services, applications, and devices on a routine and regular basis in almost all information systems. For example, a typical online banking scenario may follow this sequence:

1. A user starts a Web browser and navigates to his or her bank's website.
   a. There is now a session created between the user's browser and the bank's Web server.
2. The user clicks on the "secure login" link to get to the bank login page.
   a. The user has now secured the session typically using Secure Sockets Layer (SSL).
3. The user enters a username and password and authenticates.
   a. This information is passed through the encrypted session where, if intercepted, it would be very difficult to decrypt.
4. The user conducts banking business and "logs off" of the banking website.

5

Identity & Access Management

687

    a. This will close the encrypted connection and ensure no other activities could occur under the user's credentials until another session is established.

If an attacker can hijack a session, he or she may be able to receive all the information the user expects be confidential. Session hijacking is common when sensitive information may be gained with little exposure and the attackers can easily insert themselves into the session establishment process. In general, here is how the attack would proceed:

1. A user starts a Web browser and navigates to his or her bank's website.
   - *a.* Attackers have inserted themselves between the user and the bank.
   - *b.* The attackers create a session between the user and themselves by passing the bank information to the user so it seems to be legitimate.
   - *c.* There is now a session created between the user's browser and the attacker and the bank's Web server.
2. The user clicks on the "secure login" link to get to the bank login page.
   - *a.* The attacker intercepts the request and sends a login page for the bank with invalid certificates. As many users are unaware of what invalid certificates represent, they often accept them.
   - *b.* The user has now secured a session between the attacker and the bank typically using Secure Sockets Layer (SSL).
3. The user enters a username and password and authenticates.
   - *a.* The attackers are able to view the user credentials as they are being decrypted at the attacker's session endpoint. The attacker is now able to pass those credentials to the bank impersonating the user.
4. The user conducts banking business and "logs off" of the banking website.
   - *a.* At this point, the attacker has the credentials of the user and may be able to log into the user's account and transfer money out of the account.

Session hijacking attacks are a form of "man-in-the-middle" attacks. There are several ways attacks such as this can be minimized and prevented. Logical sessions and session security will be explored in greater detail in the telecommunications and networking security chapter of this book.

Registration and Proof of Identity

Identity proofing is the process of collecting and verifying information about a person for the purpose of proving that a person who has requested an account, a credential, or other special privilege is indeed who he or she claims to be and establishing a reliable relationship that can be trusted electronically between the individual and said credential for purposes of electronic authentication. This process may include, for example, in-person evaluation of a driver's license, passport, birth certificate, or other government-issued identity, as well as other factors specified in the individual certificate policy of the organization issuing the certificate. Identity proofing is performed before the account is created (e.g., portal, email), the credential is issued (e.g., digital certificate), or the special privilege is granted. Identity proofing is more complex and lengthy the first time an account is created and in most cases needs not be repeated in its entirety during subsequent access, depending on the details of the relying party policy and the sensitivity and criticality of actions performed using the account.

Electronic authentication (e-authentication) is the process of establishing confidence in user identities electronically presented to an information system. It is the process of establishing confidence that an individual/organization using a credential that is known to the system (e.g., login name, digital certificate) is indeed the person/organization to whom the credential was issued. There are three types of authentication factors: something you know (e.g., password, PIN), something you have (e.g., smartcard, hard token, mobile phone), and something you are (e.g., biometric characteristic such as a fingerprint or voice pattern).

Authentication is performed each time a user logs into an account (e.g., portal, email) or otherwise uses a credential. Multi-factor authentication, which requires more than one type of authentication to be used at the point of system login, is sometimes used to achieve a higher level of assurance.

In the United States, each federal agency is responsible for verifying or validating the identity of individuals to whom it issues credentials. FIPS 201-2 establishes a specific level of trust in an individual's identity as part of a process that binds the ID card to an individual (e.g., employee or contractor).[18] Once that level of trust is established, it is possible to establish a chain of trust among government agencies. Establishing and binding a validated identity to a Personal Identity Verification (PIV) credential at the time the credential is issued is the foundation for a trusted common identity credential accepted throughout the federal enterprise.

FIPS 201-2 is composed of two major sections, PIV I and II. Both of these sections define requirements for the identity-proofing and registration process. In order to be in compliance with PIV I, agencies should implement a certified and accredited identity-proofing, registration, and issuance process for PIV cards across their enterprise.

A secure and robust identity-proofing process is the foundation for FIPS 201-2 compliance. A successful implementation of FIPS 201-2 is not contingent on technologies and systems only. If a PIV credential is issued based on a faulty identity-proofing process, the credential is compromised, no matter what technology it implements. FIPS 201-2 specifies an identity verification chain of trust for federal agencies. An identity verification chain of trust comprises a common set of identity vetting rules that are used by multiple entities so that they can accept and trust one another's credentials. The chain of trust assures all parties involved that each participating entity followed the vetting procedures to securely and accurately verify an individual's identity. One of the goals is to permit agencies other than the issuing agency to accept a credential and avoid the requirement to issue a separate credential.

The requirements for PIV I Identity Proofing and Registration are as follows:

1.   Agencies must use an approved identity proofing and registration process.
2.   The process must begin with the initiation of a National Agency Check with Written Inquiries (NACI) or an equivalent Office of Personnel Management (OPM) or National Security investigation required for federal employment. For current employees, this requirement is satisfied if the employee has a completed and successfully adjudicated NACI on file.

---

18   FIPS 201-2 incorporates three technical publications specifying several aspects of the required administrative procedures and technical specifications that may change as the standard is implemented and used. NIST Special Publication 800-73, "Interfaces for Personal Identity Verification" specifies the interface and data elements of the PIV card; NIST Special Publication 800-76, Biometric Data Specification for Personal Identity Verification" specifies the technical acquisition and formatting requirements for biometric data of the PIV system; and NIST Special Publication 800-78, "Cryptographic Algorithms and Key Sizes for Personal Identity Verification" specifies the acceptable cryptographic algorithms and key sizes to be implemented and used for the PIV system.

All of the relevant PIV supporting documents may be found here: http://csrc.nist.gov/groups/SNS/piv/standards.html

3.   Before PIV credential issuance occurs, the FBI National Criminal history fingerprint check portion of the National Agency Check with Written Inquiries (NACI) must be completed and properly adjudicated.

4.   The applicant must appear at least once in person in front of a PIV official before credential issuance can take place.

5.   During identity proofing, the applicant must provide two identity source documents in original form. The documents must be on the list of acceptable documents included in I-9, OMB No.1115-0136, Employment Eligibility. One of the documents must be a valid (not expired) picture ID issued by a state government or the federal government.

6.   The PIV identity-proofing, registration, and issuance process must adhere to the principle of separation of roles. No single individual may have the power to request issuance of a PIV credential without the approval of a second authorized person.

The identity proofing and registration process must be officially certified and accredited in accordance with NIST Special Publication 800-79-1: Guidelines for the Certification and Accreditation of PIV Card Issuing Organizations.

The role-based model assigns PIV identity-proofing responsibilities to individuals, based on the roles and functions they perform. In this model, one person cannot perform multiple roles, with one exception: The PIV Issuer and PIV Digital Signatory functions may be performed by the same entity. This requirement safeguards against the possibility of collusion between an applicant and the issuing authority.

The PIV role-based identity proofing process defines the following roles:

- Applicant
- PIV Sponsor
- PIV Registrar
- PIV Issuer
- PIV Digital Signatory
- PIV Authentication Certification Authority (CA)

The Applicant is the individual to whom a PIV card will be issued once the PIV Registrar approves the application and the appropriate background checks have taken place.

The PIV Sponsor is the individual who validates an Applicant's requirement for a PIV credential and sponsors the Applicant's request.

The PIV Registrar is the individual or entity that performs the identity-proofing process for the Applicant and ensures that the proper background checks have taken place with positive results. The PIV Registrar has final approval authority for issuance of a PIV credential to an Applicant. Once the background check is completed successfully, the PIV Registrar notifies the PIV Issuer that a PIV credential can be issued to the Applicant.

The PIV Issuer is the individual or entity that issues an identity credential to an Applicant following the positive completion of all identity proofing, background checks, and related approvals.

The PIV Digital Signatory is the entity that signs the PIV biometric and cardholder unique identifier (CHUID) of the Applicant.

The PIV Authentication Certification Authority (CA) is the CA that signs and issues the PIV Authentication Certificate of the Applicant.

The security professionals may not have to interact with a system as broad as the one described above unless they are doing work with a government entity. However, even in the private sector, the need for secure credentialing processes is a pressing one, and many enterprises are moving to adopt registration and proof of identity solution architectures that are robust and standards driven. It would make sense for the security professionals to become aware of the relevant standards and to also understand the scope of the architecture necessary to create and implement as well as manage such a system, based on the current needs of the enterprises that they interact with.

Credential Management Systems

A cornerstone of all security strategies is the organization's ability to control access to business systems and networks. Virtually all access controls rely on the use of credentials to validate the identities of users, applications, and devices. Organizations employ a variety of systems and technologies to convey identity and to attest to the claims and trust models that are associated with those identities. Some credentials are used to access the most valuable data in the organization, whereas others are used for more mundane tasks. Some are used thousands of times a second and others once a year. But as the number of credentials within an organization increases and the diversity of the security models and policies that they represent expands, the issue of credential management has emerged as a serious business challenge that goes way beyond traditional password management.

In the current online environment, individuals are asked to maintain dozens of different usernames and passwords, one for each website with which they interact. The complexity of this approach is a burden to individuals, and it encourages behavior—like the reuse of passwords— that makes online fraud and identity theft easier. At the same time, online businesses are faced with ever-increasing costs for managing customer accounts, the consequences of online fraud, and the loss of business that results from individuals' unwillingness to create yet another account. Moreover, both businesses and governments are unable to offer many services online because they cannot effectively identify the individuals with whom they interact. Spoofed websites, stolen passwords, and compromised accounts are all symptoms of inadequate authentication mechanisms.

Just as there is a need for methods to reliably authenticate individuals, there are many Internet transactions for which identification and authentication is not needed, or the information needed is limited. It is vital to maintain the capacity for anonymity in Internet transactions in order to enhance individuals' privacy and otherwise support civil liberties. Nonetheless, individuals and businesses need to be able to check each other's identity for certain types of sensitive transactions, such as online banking or accessing electronic health records.

As Information Technology (IT) continues to increase in complexity, many organizations struggle with the management headaches associated with an overabundance of application-specific user accounts and access controls. This problem is further complicated by today's mobile workforce and the need to access critical information anywhere and anytime. External threats such as malware, phishing, and vishing create an environment where proper selection of Identity and Access Management solutions is critical. Organizations are now working to establish unified, robust, and enterprise-wide user authorization and authentication frameworks to enable streamlined access without compromising the security that more sensitive applications and data demand.

5

Identity & Access Management

691

The security architect needs to be able to design secure credential management systems, the security practitioner needs to be able to deploy them in the enterprise, and the security professional needs to be able to manage them. The challenge for all is how to do this in a cost effective and mission appropriate manner. What does it take to achieve the business objective of secure credential management? The first step for the security architect is to understand the business requirements that need to be addressed. A high level summary of typical requirements can be found below:

- Privacy protections for individuals, who will be able trust that their personal data is handled fairly and transparently.
- Convenience for individuals, who may choose to manage fewer passwords or accounts than they do today.
- Efficiency for organizations, which will benefit from a reduction in paper-based and account management processes.
- Ease-of-use, by automating identity solutions whenever possible and basing them on technology that is simple to operate.
- Security, by making it more difficult for criminals to compromise online transactions.
- Confidence that digital identities are adequately protected, thereby promoting the use of online services.
- Innovation, by lowering the risk associated with sensitive services and by enabling service providers to develop or expand their online presence.
- Choice, as service providers offer individuals different—yet interoperable—identity credentials and media.

Once the requirements have been identified and understood, the security architect should then conduct a Business Impact Analysis (BIA) in order to understand the criticality of each of the business systems in production and how each business system will be impacted by the requirements. The results of the BIA can then be used by the architects to further narrow and refine their design as well as the scope of the deployment of the credential management system. When the architect has finalized his or her design and is ready to implement the system, the security practitioner takes over.

The security practitioner will be responsible for building and implementing the system that the architect has designed. This will entail following the plans laid out by the architect and ensuring that the system is built to specification. Many credential management systems will be built with the following features and capabilities:

Keep a History
A password archive allows for access to old passwords when needed and prevents future reuse.

Enforce Stronger Passwords
Use password policy templates to create strong passwords that meet the specific complexity requirements of the architecture.

Effortlessly Generate Passwords
Improve security by automatically generating complex passwords that are virtually impossible to guess or circumvent.

Find Passwords Fast

Save time searching and sorting through hundreds or thousands of passwords with a fast indexed search system.

Fine-Grained Access Control

- Control WHO has access. Manage access by user or the role(s) they are responsible for.
- Control WHAT they access. Apply security decisions on a per secured area basis.
- Control HOW they access. Determine what permissions are authorized when managing and accessing passwords.
- Control WHEN they access. Have people in authority decide if a requesting user can access a password for a period of time.

Limit Their Access

Permit certain people to run audit reports or use passwords without actually being able to see them.

Keep All Passwords Safe

Centrally store and encrypt credentials so they stay protected and available at all times.

Migrate passwords with ease: Use the built-in import and export tools to easily move credentials in and out of the credential management system.

Disaster Preparedness

Use the backup and restore tools to maintain the integrity of the data representing people, passwords, permissions, and policies.

Always On, Always Available

Ensure access to passwords is always available through configurable fail-over and redundancy capabilities, in addition to ensuring that all supporting processes and systems are accounted for in planning and management as well.

Keep Control of Credentials

Leverage built-in management capabilities to handle ownership and privilege changes, and seize back control of passwords as required.

Track and Audit Access

Collect the important information to build a timeline of activity and make informed decisions, all from one place.

Once the security practitioner has built the credential management system, it will be the responsibility of the security professional to oversee the operation of the system. The security practitioner may very well be the day to day custodian of the system, maintaining it and ensuring that it is functioning correctly, but he or she will typically partner with the security professional to manage the system. The security professional's role traditionally will take the form of an oversight function, ensuring that day to day operations are being carried out according to whatever policies and standards have been enacted to govern the system's use within the enterprise. The security professional will have to have a thorough understanding of the risks

5

Identity & Access Management

and benefits associated with implementing and maintaining a credential management system within the enterprise in order to do his or her job properly. Some common risks and benefits associated with credential management systems are listed below:

Risks

- Attackers that can gain control of the credential management system can issue credentials that make them an insider, potentially with privileges to compromise systems undetected.
- Compromised credential management processes result in the need to re-issue credentials, which can be an expensive and time-consuming process.
- Credential validation rates can vary enormously and can easily outpace the performance characteristics of a credential management system, jeopardizing business continuity.
- Business application owners' expectations around security and trust models are rising, and they can expose credential management as a weak link that may jeopardize compliance claims.

Benefits

- Add higher levels of assurance to maximize the value of the investment in credential management.
- Meet the highest security standards while ensuring state-of-the-art performance and resilience.
- Simplify administration, compliance, and auditing, with a common baseline for trust across the credential management system.
- Future-proof the enterprise to support more stringent trust models and policies as they emerge.

The partnership of the security architect, practitioner, and professional all working together in order to envision, design, build, deploy, and manage the credential management system is the key to a successful identity management lifecycle for the enterprise.

A practical example of a system architecture for credential management can be found by examining the way that the Microsoft Windows operating system addresses credential management.

Windows credentials management is the process by which the operating system receives the credentials from the service or user and secures that information for future presentation to the authenticating target. In the case of a domain-joined computer, the authenticating target is the domain controller. The credentials used in authentication are digital documents that associate the user's identity to some form of proof of authenticity, such as a certificate, a password, or a PIN.

By default, Windows credentials are validated against the Security Accounts Manager (SAM) database on the local computer or against Active Directory on a domain-joined computer, through the WinLogon service. Credentials are collected through user input on the logon user interface or coded through the API to be presented to the authenticating target.

Local security information is stored in the registry under HKEY_LOCAL_MACHINE\ SECURITY. Stored information includes policy settings, default security values, and account information, such as cached logon credentials. A copy of the SAM is also stored here, although it is write-protected.

Authentication Components for All Systems

Component	Description
User logon	Winlogon.exe is the executable file responsible for managing secure user interactions. The Winlogon service initiates the logon process for Windows operating systems by passing the credentials collected by user action on the secure desktop (Logon UI) to the Local Security Authority (LSA) through Secur32.dll.
Application logon	Application or service logons not requiring interactive logon. Most processes initiated by the user run in user mode by using Secur32.dll, whereas processes initiated at start up, such as services, run in kernel mode by using Ksecdd.sys.
Secur32.dll	The multiple authentication provider that forms the foundation of the authentication process.
Lsasrv.dll	The LSA Server service, which both enforces security policies and acts as the security package manager for the LSA. The LSA contains the Negotiate function, which selects either the NTLM or Kerberos protocol after determining which protocol will be successful.
Security Support Providers	A set of providers that can individually invoke one or more authentication protocols. The default set of providers can change with each version of Windows, and custom providers can be written.
Netlogon.dll	Some of the services that the Net Logon service performs include: - Maintains the computer's secure channel (not to be confused with Schannel) to a domain controller. - Passes the user's credentials through a secure channel to the domain controller and returns the domain SIDs and user rights for the user. - Publishes service resource records in the Domain Name System (DNS) and uses DNS to resolve names to the Internet Protocol (IP) addresses of domain controllers.
Samsrv.dll	The Security Accounts Manager (SAM), which stores local security accounts, enforces locally stored policies and supports APIs.
Registry	Contains a copy of the SAM database, local security policy settings, default security values, and account information that is only accessible to the system.

5

Identity &
Access Management

Two architectures exist for credential input in Windows. In Windows Server 2008 and Windows Vista, the Graphical Identification and Authentication (GINA) architecture was replaced with a credential provider model, which made it possible to enumerate different logon types through the use of logon tiles.

Graphical Identification and Authentication (GINA) Architecture

The GINA architecture applies to the Windows Server 2003, Windows 2000 Server, Windows XP, and Windows 2000 Professional operating systems. In these systems, every interactive logon session creates a separate instance of the Winlogon service. The GINA architecture is loaded into the process space used by Winlogon, receives and processes the credentials, and makes the calls to the authentication interfaces through LSALogonUser.

The instances of Winlogon for an interactive logon run in Session 0. Session 0 hosts system services and other critical processes, including the Local Security Authority (LSA) process.

The credential provider architecture applies to Windows Server 2008 R2, Windows Server 2008, Windows 7, and Windows Vista. In these systems, the credentials input architecture changed to an extensible design by using credential providers. These providers are represented by the different logon tiles on the secure desktop that permit any number of logon scenarios— different accounts for the same user and different authentication methods, such as password, smart card, and biometrics.

With the credential provider architecture, Winlogon always launches Logon UI after it receives a SAS event. Logon UI queries each credential provider for the number of different credential types the provider is configured to enumerate. Credential providers have the option of specifying one of these tiles as the default. After all providers have enumerated their tiles, Logon UI displays them to the user. The user interacts with a tile to supply his or her credentials. Logon UI submits these credentials for authentication.

Combined with supporting hardware, credential providers can extend Windows to enable users to log on through biometric (fingerprint, retinal, or voice recognition), password, PIN and smart card certificate, or any custom authentication package and schema that a third-party developer creates. The security architect can develop and deploy custom authentication mechanisms for all domain users and explicitly require users to use this custom logon mechanism.

Credential providers are not enforcement mechanisms. They are used to gather and serialize credentials. The Local Authority and authentication packages enforce security.

Credential providers can be designed to support single sign-on (SSO), authenticating users to a secure network access point (leveraging RADIUS and other technologies) as well as machine logon. Credential providers are also designed to support application-specific credential gathering and may be used for authenticating to network resources, joining machines to a domain, or providing administrator consent for User Account Control (UAC).

Credential providers are registered on the computer and are responsible for the following:

- Describing the credential information required for authentication
- Handling communication and logic with external authentication authorities
- Packaging credentials for interactive and network logon

Packaging credentials for interactive and network logon includes the process of serialization. Serialization of credentials allows multiple logon tiles to be displayed on the logon UI. Therefore, the security architect can control the logon display—such as users, target systems for logon, pre-logon access to the network, and workstation lock/unlock policies—through the use of customized credential providers. Multiple credential providers can co-exist on the same computer.

Single sign-on providers (SSOs) may be developed as a standard credential provider or as a Pre-Logon-Access provider. Each version of Windows contains one default credential provider and one default Pre-Logon-Access Provider (PLAP).

In Windows Server 2008, Windows Server 2003, Windows Vista, and Windows XP, Stored User Names and Passwords in Control Panel simplified the management and use of multiple sets of logon credentials, including X.509 certificates used with smart cards and Windows Live credentials. The credentials—part of the user's profile—are stored until needed. This can increase security on a per-resource basis by ensuring that if one password is compromised, it does not compromise all security.

After a user logs on and attempts to access additional password-protected resources, such as a share on a server, and if the user's default logon credentials are not sufficient to gain access, Stored User Names and Passwords is queried. If alternate credentials with the correct logon information have been saved in Stored User Names and Passwords, these credentials are used to gain access. Otherwise, the user is prompted to supply new credentials, which can then be saved for reuse, either later in the logon session or during a subsequent session. The following restrictions apply:

- If Stored User Names and Passwords contains invalid or incorrect credentials for a specific resource, access to the resource will be denied and the Stored User Names and Passwords dialog box will not appear.

- Stored User Names and Passwords stores credentials only for NTLM, Kerberos protocol, Windows Live ID, and SSL authentication. Some versions of Microsoft Internet Explorer maintain its own cache for basic authentication.

These credentials become an encrypted part of a user's local profile in the \Documents and Settings\Username\Application Data\Microsoft\Credentials directory. As a result, these credentials can roam with the user if the user's network policy supports Roaming Profiles. However, if the user has copies of Stored User Names and Passwords on two different computers and changes the credentials that are associated with the resource on one of these computers, the change will not be propagated to Stored User Names and Passwords on the second computer.

In Windows Server 2008 R2 and Windows 7, the storage and management of usernames and passwords were integrated into Credential Manager—a Control Panel feature. Credential Manager allows users to store credentials to other systems and websites in the secure Windows Vault. Some versions of Internet Explorer use this feature for authentication to websites.

Credential management by using Credential Manager is controlled by the user on the local computer. Users can save and store credentials from supported browsers and Windows applications to make it convenient when they need to sign in to these resources. Credentials are saved in special encrypted folders on the computer under the user's profile. Applications that support this feature (through the use of the Credential Manager APIs), such as Web browsers and apps, can present the correct credentials to other computers and websites during the logon process.

When a website, an application, or another computer requests authentication through NTLM or the Kerberos protocol, an Update Default Credentials or Save Password check box is presented to the user. This dialog to request the saving of credentials locally is generated by an application that supports the Credential Manager APIs. If the user selects the Save Password check box, Credential Manager keeps track of the user's name, password, and related information for the authentication service that is in use.

The next time the service is used, Credential Manager automatically supplies the credential that is stored in the Windows Vault. If it is not accepted, the user is prompted for the correct access information. If access is granted with the new credentials, Credential Manager overwrites the previous credential with the new one and then stores the new credential in the Windows Vault.

5

Identity & Access Management

Users may choose to save passwords in Windows by using an application or through the Credential Manager Control Panel applet. These credentials are stored on the hard disk drive and protected by using the Data Protection Application Programming Interface (DPAPI). Any program running as that user will be able to access credentials in this store.

Credential Manager can obtain its information in two ways:

1. **Explicit Creation** – When users enter a username and password for a target computer or domain, that information is stored and used when the users attempt to log on to an appropriate computer. If no stored information is available and users supply a username and password, they can save the information. If the user decides to save the information, Credential Manager receives and stores it.

2. **System Population** – When the operating system attempts to connect to a new computer on the network, it supplies the current username and password to the computer. If this is not sufficient to provide access, Credential Manager attempts to supply the necessary username and password. All stored usernames and passwords are examined, from most specific to least specific as appropriate to the resource, and the connection is attempted in the order of those usernames and passwords. Because usernames and passwords are read and applied in order, from most to least specific, no more than one username and password can be stored for each individual target or domain.

In Windows Server 2012 R2 and Windows 8.1, some of the new features implemented for credential protection and domain authentication controls to reduce credential theft are described below.

Restricted Admin mode provides a method of interactively logging on to a remote host server without transmitting the users credentials to the server. This prevents the user's credentials from being harvested during the initial connection process if the server has been compromised.

Using this mode with administrator credentials, the remote desktop client attempts to interactively log on to a host that also supports this mode without sending credentials. When the host verifies that the user account connecting to it has administrator rights and supports Restricted Admin mode, the connection succeeds. Otherwise, the connection attempt fails. Restricted Admin mode does not at any point send plain text or other re-usable forms of credentials to remote computers.

The Protected Users security group. This domain global group triggers new non-configurable protection on devices and host computers running Windows Server 2012 R2 and Windows 8.1. The Protected Users group enables additional protections for domain controllers and domains in Windows Server 2012 R2 domains. This greatly reduces the types of credentials available when users are signed in to computers on the network from a non-compromised computer.

Members of the Protected Users group are limited further by the following methods of authentication:

■ A member of the Protected Users group can only sign on using the Kerberos protocol. The account cannot authenticate using NTLM, Digest Authentication, or CredSSP. On a device running Windows 8.1, passwords are not cached, so the device that uses any one of these Security Support Providers (SSPs) will fail to authenticate to a domain when the account is a member of the Protected User group.

- The Kerberos protocol will not use the weaker DES or RC4 encryption types in the pre-authentication process. This means that the domain must be configured to support at least the AES cypher suite.

- The user's account cannot be delegated with Kerberos constrained or unconstrained delegation. This means that former connections to other systems may fail if the user is a member of the Protected Users group.

- The default Kerberos Ticket Granting Tickets (TGTs) lifetime setting of four hours is configurable using Authentication Policies and Silos accessed through the Active Directory Administrative Center (ADAC). This means that when four hours has passed, the user must authenticate again.

Virtual smart card technology from Microsoft offers comparable security benefits to physical smart cards by using two-factor authentication. Virtual smart cards emulate the functionality of physical smart cards, but they use the Trusted Platform Module (TPM) chip that is available on computers in many organizations rather than requiring the use of a separate physical smart card and reader. Virtual smart cards are created in the TPM, where the keys that are used for authentication are stored in cryptographically secured hardware.

By utilizing TPM devices that provide the same cryptographic capabilities as physical smart cards, virtual smart cards accomplish the three key properties that are desired for smart cards: non-exportability, isolated cryptography, and anti-hammering. Virtual smart cards are functionally similar to physical smart cards and appear in Windows as smart cards that are always inserted. Virtual smart cards can be used for authentication to external resources, protection of data by secure encryption, and integrity through reliable signing.

In the United States, the federal government has made progress regarding Identity Credential and Access Management (ICAM) in recent years. ICAM is the intersection of digital identities and associated attributes, credentials, and access controls into one comprehensive approach. The Homeland Security Presidential Directive 12 (HSPD-12) initiative provides a common, standardized identity credential that enables common physical access credentials and secure, interoperable online transactions.[19] Additional federal initiatives have resulted in the development of the following standards and guidelines that support ICAM strategies:[20]

- Smart Access Common ID Card: GSA, NIST (1998)
- Federal PKI Policy Authority (2002)
- OMB directive on smart ID cards: HSPD-12 (2004)
- Personal Identity Verification (PIV) of Federal Employees and Contractors:
- FIPS-201-1 (2006)
- FIPS-201-2 (2011)
- First Responder Authentication Credential (FRAC) (2006)
- Federal Identity, Credentialing and Access Management (FICAM) (2009)
- Cyberspace Policy Review (2009)
- Personal Identity Verification Interoperability for Non-Federal Issuers (PIV-I) (2009)

---

19 See the following: http://www.dhs.gov/homeland-security-presidential-directive-12

20 See the following for copies of all of the mentioned documents: http://www.idmanagement.gov/document-library

Nationally, in recognition of the rising cybersecurity risks as online transactions increase, the White House published the draft National Strategy for Trusted Identities in Cyberspace, Enhancing Online Choice, Efficiency, Security, and Privacy (NSTIC) in April 2011.[21] This strategy aims to reduce online fraud and identity theft by increasing the level of trust associated with identities in cyberspace. NSTIC outlines the needs of parties involved in electronic transactions (e.g., online banking, accessing electronic health records, accessing state benefits) to have a high degree of trust that they are interacting with known entities. The strategy presents a framework for raising the level of trust associated with the defined identities of individuals, organizations, services, and devices involved in certain types of online transactions.

The Office of the Chief Information Officer (OCIO) ICAM Division has created solutions that help the United States General Services Administration (GSA) meet federal mandates such as the NSTIC and the Office of Management and Budget (OMB) Memorandum 11-11 (M-11-11) to use the GSA Access Card for access to GSA facilities and information systems as noted below:[22]

GSA Credential and Identity Management System (GCIMS) is a GSA internal Web database that provides authoritative information on GSA personnel, work locations, and credentials. The GCIMS database streamlines the management and tracking of the background investigation and credentialing process and serves as a repository for personnel information. In addition, GSA personnel use GCIMS to update their contact information.

GSA Access Management System (GAMS) is a Logical Access Control System (LACS) that enables GSA employees and contractors to log into their computers at GSA work locations or remotely through a VPN using their GSA Access Card. The system provides shared identity and access management services for application business owners to verify and authorize user access requests. Benefits include:

- Offers Single Sign-On: Log on once with a GSA Access Card and Personal Identification Number (PIN) to access multiple IT applications.
- Provides Self-Service Capability: GAMS requests are routed through the approval chain and notifications sent to requestor when access request is complete.
- Protects Against Unauthorized Access: Application business owners customize policies based on user attributes to determine which resources a user can access.
- Reduces Audit Reporting Time: Query a single audit database for user access privileges, including successful and unsuccessful logon attempts.
- Enables the Reuse of Identity Data: User's access privileges are mapped to a single identity to avoid GSA collecting the same data multiple times.
- Expedites Employee and Contractor On-Boarding: Provides an automated approval process and access privileges for new staff and automated removal process for departing staff.

Physical Access System (PACS): The ICAM Division works with other GSA Offices to ensure that individuals accessing GSA facilities, both at the perimeter and at certain internal areas, have been properly cleared, authorized, and credentialed to do so. The most apparent application of the program is the issuance of the GSA Access Card and the underlying certification process. The GSA Access Card process supports an agency wide consistent application of

---

21 See the following: http://www.whitehouse.gov/sites/default/files/rss_viewer/NSTICstrategy_041511.pdf

22 See the following: http://www.whitehouse.gov/sites/default/files/omb/memoranda/2011/m11-11.pdf

Physical Access Standards. The program is consistently under review and development as the GSA and federal standards that govern access are developed, implemented, or revised. The program's dynamic nature is also driven by technology as hardware and software are upgraded and protocols are advanced.

The collection of preceding examples that describe credential management systems should be illustrative for the security architect as well as the practitioner and the professional. The discussion of the ways in which the various iterations of the Windows Server and client operating systems implement and manage credentialing processes within their architectures will help the architect to understand the varied options available to them for system design on the Windows platform. The security practitioner will also be able to glean a technical understanding of the system options available that will have to be addressed as part of the implementation, while the security professional will be able to have an understanding of the options available by platform and, as a result, the awareness of which options are being implemented based on the platform chosen. The discussion of the way in which the OCIO ICAM Division has helped the U.S. GSA to implement credential management across the GSA's operational geography should help the security architect to understand what a multi-level architecture may look like with regards to credential management in the enterprise. The inclusion of a centralized Web database, a logical access control system, and a physical access control system as part of the overall architectural design allows the security architect to see how all of these pieces can be designed to interact and mutually support and reinforce one another. The security practitioner and the security professional will both also be able to gain valuable insights into the design and implementation, as well as the management of this kind of an integrated architecture.

Identity as a Service (IDaaS)

Identity-as-Service (IDaaS) offerings are cloud-based services that broker identity and access management functions to target systems on customers' premises and in the cloud. IDaaS is described as a combination of administration and account provisioning, authentication and authorization, and reporting functions. Cloud-based IAM can be used to manage software-as-a-service (SaaS) applications and internal applications as well. According to Gartner, IDaaS functionality includes:[23]

- **Identity governance and administration (IGA)** — this includes the ability to provision identities held by the service to target applications.
- **Access** — this includes user authentication, single sign-on, and authorization enforcement.
- **Intelligence** — this includes logging events and providing reporting that can answer questions, such as who accessed what and when?

---

23 See the following: https://www.gartner.com/doc/2607617/market-trends-cloudbased-security-services

701

IDaaS offers management of identity (information) as a digital entity. This identity can be used during electronic transactions. Identity refers to a set of attributes associated with something and makes it recognizable. All objects may have same attributes, but their identity cannot be the same. This unique identity is assigned through the use of one or more unique identification attributes. Identity services can been deployed to validate services such as websites, transactions, transaction participants, clients, etc.

Features and benefits common to most cloud identity and access management systems include:

1. **Single Sign-on (SSO) Authentication** – One of the core services is the ability to authenticate users based on provided credentials and then allow each user to access multiple (internal and external) services without having to repeatedly supply credentials to each service.

2. **Federation** – Federated identity is where identity and authorization settings are collected from multiple identity management systems, enabling different systems to define user capabilities and access. Identity and authorization are a shared responsibility across multiple authoritative sources. Federated identity is a superset of authentication and single sign-on. Federation has made headway as a conveyance engine for SSO and Web Services. Its uptake in the cloud has been substantial because its core architecture helps companies navigate one of the thornier cloud issues: retaining in-house control of user accounts while leveraging cloud apps and data.

3. **Granular Authorization Controls** – Access is typically not an 'all-or-nothing' proposition; each user is allowed access to a subset of functions and data stored in the cloud. Authorization maps instruct applications about which resources to provide to each user. How much control the security professional has over each user's access depends, both on the capabilities of the cloud service provider and on the capabilities of the IAM system. The larger industry trends are a focus on finer-grained access control and removing access policy from code as much as possible. In other words, roles are necessary but not sufficient for authorization – you need attributes too.

4. **Administration** – Administrators generally prefer a single management pane for administering users and managing identity across multiple services. The goal of most cloud IAM systems is to do just that, but they need to offer granular adjustments to authorization across different applications while still pulling data from different identity authorities.

5. **Integration with Internal Directory Services** – Cloud IAM systems rely on integration with in-house LDAP, Active Directory, HR systems, and other services to replicate existing employee identity, roles, and groups into cloud services. In-house IAM services remain the central authority for in-house identity, but they delegate responsibility for cloud access management to the cloud IAM service.

6. **Integration with External Services** – One of the core benefits of a cloud IAM provider is it offers connectors to common cloud services so you do not need to write your own integration code. By offering pre-built connections to common SaaS, PaaS, and IaaS vendors, integration with new services is both easier and faster.

Additional capabilities may include multi-factor authentication support, mobile user integration, and support for multiple user personas. These features help tie traditional identity management into cloud services. But as vendors attempt to solve these issues, cloud IAM creates several new problems that do not get the same degree of attention:

1. **APIs –** While IAM vendors offer connectors to the most common cloud services, they are unlikely to provide all the connectors needed. The security architects will need to provide their own integration or contract with their IAM vendor to build a custom connector. This raises the additional challenge of onboarding third-party developers and giving them limited access rights.

2. **Authorization Mapping –** There are many possible ways to specify authorization rules, such as by role vs. by attribute. The existing access rules already in place in the enterprise may need to be rewritten for a cloud service provider.

3. **Audit –** In-house systems can be linked with log management and SIEM systems to produce compliance reports and provide monitoring and detection of security related events. Getting audit logs from cloud service providers remains problematic: Their multi-tenant models prevent most from providing full logs because the logs would necessarily disclose data on other customers.

4. **Privacy –** Users, user attributes, and other information are pushed outside the corporate network and into one or more cloud data repositories. The security and privacy controls for the external repositories are not fully under the control of the security practitioner, so the security architect needs to explore what the vendor does and does not provide.

5. **Latency –** Propagating rule changes from internal IAM to cloud IAM can take some time. For example, if an employee is terminated or has his or her access rights reduced, there may be a lag between the internal rule change and when the cloud service enforces the change. Latency is a subject to discuss with both the IAM provider and cloud service provider.

6. **App Identity –** Once you have the user logged in, you may still need to verify the application he or she is using – or maybe there is no user at all, just middleware. But where did the request come from? The answer for many apps today is that as long as you know how to call the service, they do not verify the client – even with medium-strength authentication.

7. **Mobile –** Security teams are still absorbing the implications of the cloud and mobile device waves, but technology does not sit still; there is yet another whole new paradigm to gear up for. The hybrid of mobile and cloud, or Bring Your Own Cloud (BYOC), is particularly relevant because cloud clients are very likely to be mobile. As a result, that means there is yet another account system and domain to manage for the security architect, practitioner, and professional.

IDaaS is a component of a larger layered security strategy. Its primary responsibility is administrative in terms of creating user credentials and assigning them to certain buckets of permission. This provisioning is based on the role, or roles, that a user holds within an organization. IDaaS also manages passwords and their synchronization across the enterprise as well as coordinating the federated connections between certain applications. It is Access Management (SaaS and Web single sign-on, multi-factor authorization) that enforces the rules set forth in identity management.

5

Identity &
Access Management

The security professional will need to consider IDaaS as part of the overall approach to identity management in the enterprise. IDaaS implementations can be seen as generally differentiating themselves across a series of core areas, as noted below.

- **Scope of Solution** – The security professional will need to consider the list of in-house technologies and processes that the proposed IDaaS offering will displace. Conceptually, IDaaS strives to offload as much of the identity management infrastructure that an enterprise would be required to install as possible. However, organizations with unique requirements may desire flexibility to keep some things in-house for a more hybrid model.

- **Intent** – The specific problem the implementation aims to solve. IDaaS products are generally developed to solve specific challenges faced by a customer or type of customer. Some take a general approach toward the size of a company for example, while others address specific market segments like healthcare. In general, vertically developed solutions will be less applicable to a mass audience but will be more powerful in the scenario for which they are intended. Some focus on ease of convergence, while others drive toward depth and flexibility.

- **Implementation** – The technology and execution used to achieve the proposed solution. Even though IDaaS categorically belongs in the cloud, each implementation may require the security architect and professional to take a tailored approach to setting it up, using it, and adopting preset policies. Additionally, how things integrate, how well they do so, and the third-party components that may or may not be hosted in their service can vary as well. It is key to completely develop solution requirements to determine which IDaaS offering will provide the best fit. In addition, the security actors need to have a full understanding of the impact of the additional complexity that IDaaS may introduce to existing system architectures, both traditional and cloud based.

- **Certification** – The level of attainment by recognized third parties. Perhaps the most common misunderstanding in the credentialing market is the assumption that certification automatically equates to a commensurate level of security. While certifications attest to a set of criteria being met, security is dynamic and certifications are typically narrow. The reality is that certifications should be viewed as a minimum starting point, not the overall achievement of security by the security architect.

- **Standards** – The adherence to standards from open and public domains. This is another area of significant variance. Standards can have significant implications on system operations. Thus, security architects should perform a diligent review as to which, if any, standards make sense for their business both short and long-term.

The security architect, practitioner, and professional will all need to familiarize themselves with the various aspects of an IDaaS offering in order for it to be implemented securely and cost effectively across the enterprise. The following recommendations will serve to help focus their activities:

Look beyond simple cost cutting. The size of the organization is key. For small to medium sized organizations, even the most expensive IDaaS solution is likely to be cheaper than an in-house solution to drive identity management. Also with IDaaS, costs are spread out per year rather than stacked up-front via perpetual licensing and backend infrastructure costs. However, for very large organizations with tens of thousands of users, these numbers start to reach parity. It is important to note that large organizations that could spend less on an in-house model may still choose IDaaS because it can have financial benefits in how services are accounted for as compared to depreciating purchased assets. It is important for the security architect to be aware of these issues and to address them during the initial planning phase of the identity management architecture.

Focus on both tangibles and intangibles. The whole point of IDaaS is to remove users and operators from the low-level components underneath so that most of what is going on cannot easily be seen. For example, the solution may have a key management function, but how does one know how the key material is being handled or even if the service uses a hardware security module at all? The architects cannot go by features alone; they will have to dig into to the intangibles to know what is included both visibly and out of sight with a specific offering in order to ensure that they understand the risks and benefits inherent in implementing the offering.

Avoid fixating on product comparisons. Comparing products against one another is a must, but too often security professionals become fixated on this aspect and lose sight of developing a clear definition of their requirements and benchmarking. Comparisons are relative but are fairly transparent against solid internal requirements.

Do not fall victim to the turnkey assumption. Architects often assume that because IDaaS eliminates a great deal of infrastructure deployment, they will be able to flip a switch and go. This is partially true if the service is truly an out-of-the-box, multi-tenant system. However, deciding on workflows, setting policies, pushing out to clients, ensuring quality assurance, building a notification and support process, and integrating the service into your infrastructure can all take time. Performing due diligence with regards to the service providers to ensure a complete understanding of how they secure their infrastructure takes time as well. Between scheduling, aligning resources, and acquiring approval to do these things, it can easily take several months before rolling out beyond an initial limited production environment is possible.

The following is an example of the use of IDaaS in a production environment:

WidePoint Corp., a McLean, Va.-based provider of secure, enterprise-wide solutions, launched a cloud-based, identity-as-a-service (IDaaS) capability that provides secure digital certificates to all types of mobile devices in January of 2014.[24] The company's IDaaS Certificate-on-Chip service provides a level of federally compliant assured information security beyond a simple username and password-based VPN solution. The service lets IT managers assign different levels of access to employees, consultants, and partners, based on the specific BYOD user device being used to establish connectivity. The service can enhance the information security of mobile transactions and access to government networks and databases by allowing agencies to:

- Create a secure VPN connection between the organization's network and the devices used by mobile or home-based employees without a proprietary software client.
- Ensure employees download sensitive data only to authorized, properly configured, and protected devices.
- Remotely revoke certificates of devices that were lost, stolen, or belong to an employee who has left the organization.

---

24 See the following: http://www.prnewswire.com/news-releases/widepoint-launches-secured-cloud-based-identity-as-a-service-certificate-on-chip-for-all-types-of-mobile-devices-239424101.html

Integrate Third-Party Identity Services

It is possible to manage user access to cloud computing resources in-house, but the architecture must take integration complexity and management costs into account. Most organizations – particularly enterprises – find that these inconveniences outweigh the benefits. For many of the same reasons (including on-demand service, elasticity, broad network access, reduction in capital expenditures, and total cost), companies adopt cloud computing services instead of in-house services, and they also leverage third-party cloud services to manage identity and access management.

Cloud computing services have turned identity management on its ear. The big shift has come in three main parts: IT no longer owns the servers and applications the organization relies upon, provider capabilities are not fully compatible with existing internal systems, and the ways users consume cloud services have changed radically. In fact, an employee may consume corporate cloud services without ever touching any in-house IT systems at all. Just about every enterprise uses Software as a Service (SaaS), and many use Platform and Infrastructure as a Service (PaaS and IaaS, respectively) as well – each with its own approaches to Identity and Access Management. Extending traditional corporate identity services outside the corporate environment is not a trivial effort; it requires integration of existing IAM systems with the cloud service provider(s). Most companies rely on many cloud service providers, each with a different set of identity and authorization capabilities, as well as different programmatic and Web interfaces. The time, effort, and cost to develop and maintain links with each service provider can be overwhelming for the security architect and practitioner.

A practical example of the challenges faced by the security architect in this area can be illustrated by examining any of the cloud service directory providers that offer services to the enterprise, such as Microsoft, Amazon, or Oracle. The first thing we need is a basic working definition of what a directory service is and what it provides the capability to do. Traditionally, your company directory can be defined as the list of users who can sign in to use applications and the users that you can look up so you can send an email or grant access to documents. Working from this definition, let us examine what the traditional methods of user account management are in the cloud-based enterprise.

There are three ways to manage user accounts within a cloud-based application and directory solution such as Microsoft's Office 365.

1. ***Cloud Identity*** – Users are created and managed in Office 365 and are stored in the Windows Azure Active Directory (AD). There is no connection to any other directory.

   Cloud identity has no integration requirements. Each user is created once in the cloud, and the account exists only in Windows Azure AD.

2. ***Directory Synchronization*** – Users are created and managed in an on-premises identity provider and are synchronized to Windows Azure AD, where they can be used for login to Office 365.

   Directory synchronization uses an existing on-premises directory and synchronizes it to Windows Azure AD. This synchronization can be done from an on-premises active directory using the Directory Synchronization tool, or it can be done from a non-AD on-premises directory using PowerShell and the Azure AD Graph APIs. Synchronization means that accounts are managed on-premises, and properties cannot be edited through the Office 365 cloud interface. If you are using the Directory Synchronization tool with Active Directory, then password hashes can also be synchronized so that users can log in with the same password on-premises and in the cloud.

3. ***Federated Identity*** – In addition to directory synchronization, login requests are handled by the on-premises identity provider. Federated identity is usually used to implement single sign-on.

Federation provides for a user to be signed in using the federated identity provider for the user's password check. Directory synchronization is also required as a prerequisite in order to populate the cloud-based directory. When using federated identity, many Office 365 customers use Active Directory Federation Services, which manages login password checks with the on-premises Microsoft Active Directory infrastructure. Some customers use third-party identity providers, and Microsoft supports Office 365 when it is connected with a variety of qualified third-party identity providers. Here are the federation options:

- Microsoft Active Directory using Active Directory Federation Services.
- Third-party WS-*-based identity providers that are qualified through the Works with Office 365-Identity program.
- The Shibboleth identity provider. Shibboleth is a SAML 2.0 identity provider.

In addition, administrators of a Microsoft cloud service who want to provide their Active Directory users with single sign-on experience by using third-party identity providers as their preferred Security Token Service (STS) can use the providers listed below:

- Optimal IDM Virtual Identity Server Federation Services
- PingFederate® 6.11
- Centrify
- IBM Tivoli Federated Identity Manager 6.2.2
- SecureAuth IdP 7.2.0
- CA SiteMinder 12.52
- RadiantOne CFS 3.0
- Okta
- OneLogin

Another example worth examining is the Amazon Web Service (AWS) Identity and Access Management (IAM) service. The service supports Amazon, Facebook, and Google Identity Federation, allowing developers to grant temporary authorization to people using these services. All the server-side code is managed without long-term credentials for the app. The service introduces a new AWS Security Token Service (STS) API that allows for temporary security credentials for customers who have been authenticated by Amazon.com, Facebook, or Google. According to the AWS blog, the "app can then use the temporary security credentials to access AWS resources such as Amazon Simple Storage Service (S3) objects, DynamoDB tables, or Amazon Simple Queue Service queues." [25]

---

25   See the following: http://aws.amazon.com/blogs/aws/aws-iam-now-supports-amazon-facebook-and-google-identity-federation/

Another example can be seen in the Oracle Identity Management platform, which enables organizations to effectively manage the end-to-end lifecycle of user identities across all enterprise resources, both within and beyond the firewall and into the cloud. The Oracle Identity Management platform delivers scalable solutions for identity governance, access management, and directory services. This modern platform helps organizations strengthen security, simplify compliance, and capture business opportunities around mobile and social access.

The example provided by the Australian government, and their lead agency approach to the provision of authentication services, which is an initiative to facilitate access to government services, is also of interest. This initiative minimizes investment in new authentication infrastructure and maximizes ease of use by reducing the number of authentication credentials required to access government services. In addition, there is an emerging commercial provider market for a range of online services such as personal data vaults, digital mailboxes, data verification, and authentication services in Australia. The Assurance Framework provides guidance for agencies to determine the Level of Assurance required to be demonstrated by Providers and the criteria to be satisfied by Providers to deliver the required Level of Assurance. The underlying premise of the Framework is that, based on an understanding of agency requirements, individuals will be able to choose to use the services offered by Accredited Service Providers in order to access online government services. Equally, a key premise is that individuals should not be forced to hold multiple credentials to access the range government services they require. The Assurance Framework is underpinned by existing Australian government security frameworks and informed by existing identity management policy frameworks and standards. The value of an individual's personal information must be recognized by Providers and reflected in the development of privacy and risk-based security controls that meet agency requirements.

Identity, and the ability to manage it, is becoming increasingly critical to the security of the enterprise across all systems. What's apparent is the need for third-party identity providers such as Ping Identity and services such as Forever, a personal cloud service that gives users control over their own personal data. Forever is provided by Kynetx, and it offers context-aware applications that can run on browsers, mobile phones, and desktops.[26] Other third-party services such as JanRain have prospered by serving as identity brokers. Enterprise app providers such as Symplified and Okta are SaaS providers that also offer identity services.[27] Whatever the source of identity information and whatever the services being used to access and manage it, whether they are cloud-based or on premise or a hybrid mix, is no longer as important as the need for the enterprise security architecture to be able to scale to address the concerns raised by this growing area of focus for the security professional.

---

26 See the following: https://www.pingidentity.com/
    http://www.kynetx.com/
    http://forevr.us/

27 See the following: http://janrain.com/
    http://www.symplified.com/
    https://www.okta.com/

Implement and Manage Authorization Mechanisms

Role-Based Access Control

A role-based access control (RBAC) model, as shown in *Figure 5.13*, bases the access control authorizations on the roles (or functions) that the user is assigned within an organization. The determination of what roles have access to a resource can be governed by the owner of the data, as with Discretionary Access Controls (DACs), or applied based on policy, as with Mandatory Access Controls (MACs).

Access control decisions are based on job function, previously defined and governed by policy, and each role (job function) will have its own access capabilities. Objects associated with a role will inherit privileges assigned to that role. This is also true for groups of users, allowing administrators to simplify access control strategies by assigning users to groups and groups to roles.

There are several approaches to RBAC. As with many system controls, there are variations on how they can be applied within a computer system. As demonstrated in *Figure 5.13*, there are four basic RBAC architectures:

1. ***Non-RBAC*** – Non-RBAC is simply a user-granted access to data or an application by traditional mapping, such as with ACLs. There are no formal "roles" associated with the mappings, other than any identified by the particular user.

2. ***Limited RBAC*** – Limited RBAC is achieved when users are mapped to roles within a single application rather than through an organization-wide role structure. Users in a limited RBAC system are also able to access non-RBAC-based applications or data. For example, a user may be assigned to multiple roles within several applications and, in addition, have direct access to another application or system independent of his or her assigned role. The key attribute of limited RBAC is that the role for that user is defined within an application and not necessarily based on the user's organizational job function.

3. ***Hybrid RBAC*** – Hybrid RBAC introduces the use of a role that is applied to multiple applications or systems based on a user's specific role within the organization. That role is then applied to applications or systems that subscribe to the organization's role-based model. However, as the term "hybrid" suggests, there are instances where the subject may also be assigned to roles defined solely within specific applications, complimenting (or, perhaps contradicting) the larger, more encompassing organizational role used by other systems.

4. ***Full RBAC*** – Full RBAC systems are controlled by roles defined by the organization's policy and access control infrastructure and then applied to applications and systems across the enterprise. The applications, systems, and associated data apply permissions based on that enterprise definition, and not one is defined by a specific application or system.

5

Identity & Access Management

Non-RBAC Management

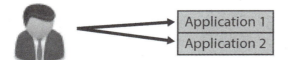

Users are mapped to applications

Limited RBAC Management

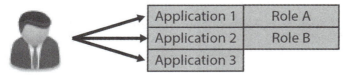

Users are mapped to application roles

Users ALSO mapped to applications that have not developed Role Based Access

Hybrid RBAC Management

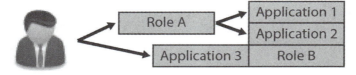

Users are mapped to multi-application roles

Only select application access rights are moved to the multi-application role

Full RBAC Management

Users are mapped to enterprise roles

Figure 5.13 – **Role-Based Access Control architecture**

The primary benefit of an RBAC-based access system is that it is easily modeled after the organization's own organization or functional structure. Just as employees have roles within the political hierarchy of the organization, so, too, do they have roles in the functional hierarchy of an information system. In addition, accounting for the movement of personnel around an organization and adjusting their information access accordingly is greatly simplified in an RBAC-based system. The administrator simply removes the old role designation from the user (instantly removing access to all information the old role required) and assigns that user to a new role, automatically granting that user access to all the information assigned to that new role.

Rule-Based Access Control

In a rule-based system, access is based on a list of predefined rules that determine what accesses should be granted. The rules, created or authorized by system owners, specify the privileges granted to users (e.g., read, write, and execute) when the specific condition of a rule is met. For example, a standard ACL may specify simply that user Bob is allowed to access the file labeled "Financial Forecast," but a rule-based system would additionally specify that Bob can only access that file between 9:00 AM and 5:00 PM Monday through Friday. A mediation mechanism enforces the rules to ensure only authorized access by intercepting every request, comparing it to user authorizations, and making a decision based on the appropriate rule. Rule-based controls are most commonly a form of DAC because the system owner typically develops the rules based on organization or processing needs.

Mandatory Access Controls (MACs)

Mandatory Access Control requires the system itself to manage access controls in accordance with the organization's security policies. MACs are typically used for systems and data that are highly sensitive and where system owners do not want to allow users to potentially contradict or bypass organizationally mandated access controls. Assigning the security controls of an object based on its classification and the clearance of subjects provides for a secure system that accommodates multilayered information processing.

MAC is based on cooperative interaction between the system and the information owner. The system's decision controls access, and the owner provides the need-to-know control. Not everyone who is cleared should have access, only those cleared and with a need to know. Even if the owner determines a user has the need to know, the system must ascertain that the user is cleared, or no access will be allowed. To accomplish this, data needs to be labeled as to its classification, allowing specific controls to be applied based on that classification.

Access Capabilities	
No Access	No access permission granted
Read (R)	Read but make no changes
Write (W)	Write to file. Includes change capability
Execute (X)	Execute a program
Delete (D)	Delete a file
Change (C)	Read, write, execute, and delete. May not change file permission
List (L)	List the files in a directory
Full Control (FC)	All abilities. Includes changing access control permissions

Access Permissions	
Public	R-L
Group	R-X
Owner	R-W-X-D
Admins	FC
System	FC

Figure 5.14 – **An example of access permissions. Access permissions are applied to an object based on the level of clearance given to a subject.**

As demonstrated in *Figure 5.14*, access permissions are applied to an object based on the level of clearance given to a subject. The example provided represents only a few of the possible permissions that can be assigned to an object. For example, "list" is a permission seen in common operating systems that permits users to only list the files in a directory, not read, delete, modify, or execute those files.

Moreover, a single object can have multiple access permissions depending on the user or group that needs to access that object. As demonstrated in *Figure 5.15*, users can be assigned to groups, such as administrators or printer users. Anyone in the group administrators has full control over the user directories for Bruce, Sally, and Bob. However, users in the printer users group can only access local printers but not any of the user directories.

```
┌─────────────────────────────────────┐  ┌─────────────────────────────────────┐
│ Access Control List (Users)         │  │ Access Control List (Groups)        │
├─────────────────────────────────────┤  ├─────────────────────────────────────┤
```

Access Control List (Users)

Mary:
  UserMaryDirectory - *Full Control*
  UserBobDirectory - *Write*
  UserBruceDirectory - *Write*
  Printer 001 - *Execute*

Bob:
  UserMaryDirectory - *Read*
  UserBobDirectory - *Full Control*
  UserBruceDirectory - *Write*
  Printer 001 - *Execute*

Bruce:
  UserMaryDirectory - *No Access*
  UserBobDirectory - *Write*
  UserBruceDirectory - *Full Control*
  Printer 001 - *No Access*

Bruce:
  UserMaryDirectory - *No Access*
  UserBobDirectory - *No Access*
  UserBruceDirectory - *No Access*
  Printer 001 - *No Access*

Access Control List (Groups)

Group Administrators:
Members - Ted, Alice
  UserBruceDirectory - *Full Control*
  UserSallyDirectory - *Full Control*
  UserBobDirectory - *Full Control*
  UserMaryDirectory - *Full Control*

Group Printer Users:
Members - Bruce, Sally, Bob
  UserBruceDirectory - *No Access*
  UserSallyDirectory - *No Access*
  UserBobDirectory - *No Access*
  PrinterDeviceP1 - *Print*
  PrinterDeviceP2 - *Print*
  PrinterDeviceP3 - *Print*

Figure 5.15 – **Access permissions and group roles. Users can be assigned to groups, such as Administrators or Printer Users. Anyone in the group Administrators has full control over the user directories for Bruce, Sally, and Bob. However, users In the Printer Users group can only access local printers but not any of the user directories.**

The third access control framework, nondiscretionary access control, is also based on the assignment of permissions to read, write, and execute files on a system. However, unlike discretionary access control, which allows the file owner to specify those permissions, nondiscretionary access control requires the administrator of a system to define and tightly control the access rules for files in the system.

Discretionary Access Controls (DACs)

Controls are placed on data by the owner of the data. The owner determines who has access to the data and what privileges they have. Discretionary controls represent a very early form of access control and were widely employed in VAX, VMS, UNIX, and other minicomputers in universities and other organizations prior to the evolution of personal computers. Today, DACs are widely employed to allow users to manage their own data and the security of that information, and nearly every mainstream operating system, from Microsoft and Apple to mobile operating systems and Linux, supports DAC. The advantage of a DAC-based system is that it is primarily user-centric. The data owner has the power to determine who can (and cannot) access that data based on the business requirements and constraints affecting that owner. While the owner never has the ability to ignore or contradict the organization's access control policies, he or she has the ability to interpret those policies to fit the specific needs of his or her system and his or her users.

Prevent or Mitigate Access Control Attacks

Most people have an intuitive understanding of the terms insiders and insider attacks. We all have seen spy movies in which agents and double agents exploit inside knowledge or privileged access to inflict damage on a hostile regime. The consequences of insider attacks can be extremely damaging. For example, in January 2008, Jerome Kerviel circumvented internal security mechanisms to place more than $70 billion in secret, unauthorized derivatives trades, which, according to his employer Societe Generale, resulted in a net loss of $7.2 billion to the bank.[28] Jerome Kerviel managed to launch his attack because, over time, he was able to take on two roles that should not have been held by any single individual, even at different points in time. But this role-based separation of duty was not implemented in any part of the IT system. Support for role-based access control (RBAC) within that IT system, in combination with proper identity management, may have prevented or at least detected this insider attack.

A massive data breach in April 2011 resulted in attackers stealing data from 77 million Sony PlayStation customer accounts.[29] In May 2011, 24.5 million Sony Online Entertainment accounts were compromised.[30] In June 2011, an attack on Sony Pictures compromised over one million user accounts, and the attackers bragged that they used a single SQL injection attack to retrieve data.[31] In October 2011, when Sony locked almost 100 thousand PlayStation accounts, it said the credentials were stolen from other sites and sent email messages to users encouraging them to "choose unique, hard-to-guess passwords," implying the problem was the customers' fault.[32]

In February of 2014, new details emerged revealing that hackers originally gained access to Target's network by stealing the access credentials, via a phishing attack, of a refrigeration contractor. The contractor said its electronic interaction with Target was limited to billing, contract submission, and project management (i.e., nothing related to the customer's personal or credit card data). Further details of the breach covered in the press revealed a sophisticated and prolonged attack at Target. Once the hackers infiltrated the Target network, they distributed malware to thousands of point-of-sale (PoS) machines designed to siphon off customer data, and then they set up a control server within Target's internal network that acted as the central repository for the stolen credit card data. The stolen data was later uploaded from the Target network to an FTP server.

---

28 The New York Times, French Bank Says Rogue Trader Lost $7 Billion, 25 January, 2008.

29 See the following: http://www.reuters.com/article/2011/04/26/us-sony-stoldendata-idUSTRE73P6WB20110426

30 See the following: http://www.theguardian.com/technology/blog/2011/may/03/sony-data-breach-online-entertainment

31 See the following: http://www.darkreading.com/attacks-and-breaches/lulzsec-attacker-pleads-guilty-to-sony-pictures-hack/d/d-id/1106852?
http://www.sonypictures.com/corp/press_releases/2011/06_11/060311_security.html

32 See the following: http://www.nytimes.com/2011/10/13/technology/sony-freezes-accounts-of-online-video-game-customers-after-hacking-attack.html?_r=0

Protecting the enterprise from such attacks requires a coordinated defense involving people, processes, and tools that span anti-malware, firewalls, application, server, and network access control, intrusion detection and prevention, security event monitoring, and more. But what about identity and access management (IAM)? As the security professional examines the Target scenario, he or she should see several areas where the right IAM preventive and detective controls could have helped to prevent, detect, or mitigate the attack:

- It all starts with getting visibility and control over user access privileges (who has access to what?) – Especially for highly sensitive data or applications. This means putting in place IAM tools to ensure the right access controls are in place and that user access privileges conform to policy.

- Next, you need detective controls such as periodic access certifications, which are designed to detect and revoke inappropriate access (e.g., an HVAC partner with access to credit card data) or access that does not map to a legitimate user (so-called "rogue" accounts). To ensure that potentially serious issues are detected promptly, the security architect and professional may choose to deploy "event-based" certifications that are triggered by any change in a user's privileges – requiring management review and approval.

- Access policy that can prevent or detect "toxic combinations" of access privileges. These types of policies are very useful in preventing risky scenarios. For example, the security practitioner can easily define policies that prevent partners from having access to PoS systems or systems storing customer data. Likewise, the security architect can enforce network segmentation by defining policies that prevent administrators on one network from having the same privileges on another.

- Lastly, to find cases where hackers are granting their own "rogue" privileges, the security professional can use automated account reconciliation to detect unauthorized changes to access privileges. Running a reconciliation process allows companies to detect access privileges that were granted outside of normal provisioning processes, without management approval. These rogue accounts can be detected in nightly scans and immediately reported to managers and application owners.

Implementing the right IAM controls can help the enterprise mitigate risks and more effectively protect critical resources and their customers' data.

Authentication attacks occur when a Web application authenticates users unsafely, granting access to Web clients that lack the appropriate credentials. Access control attacks occur when an access control check in the Web application is incorrect or missing, allowing users unauthorized access to privileged resources such as databases and files. Web applications are becoming increasingly prevalent because they allow users to access their data from any computer and to interact and collaborate with each other. However, exposing these rich interfaces to anyone on the Internet makes Web applications an appealing target for attackers who want to gain access to other users' data or resources. Web applications typically address this problem through access control, which involves authenticating users that want to gain access to the system and ensuring that a user is properly authorized to perform any operation the server executes on his or her behalf. In theory, this approach should ensure that unauthorized attackers cannot subvert the application.

5

Identity &
Access Management

Unfortunately, experience has shown that many Web applications fail to follow these seemingly simple steps, with disastrous results. Each Web application typically deploys its own authentication and access control framework. If any flaw exists in the authentication system, an authentication bypass attack may occur, allowing attackers to become authenticated as a valid user without having to present that user's credentials, such as a password. Similarly, a single missing or incomplete access control check can allow unauthorized users to access privileged resources. These attacks can result in the complete compromise of a Web application. [33]

Designing a secure authentication and access control system in a Web application is difficult. Part of the reason is that the underlying file system and database layers perform operations with the privileges of the Web application rather than with privileges of a specific Web application user. As a result, the Web application must have the superset of privileges of all of its users. However, much like a Unix setuid application, it must explicitly check if the requesting user is authorized to perform each operation that the application performs on his or her behalf; otherwise, an attacker could exploit the Web application's privileges to access unauthorized resources.

This approach is ad-hoc and weak because these checks must be sprinkled throughout the application code whenever a resource is accessed, spanning code in multiple modules written by different developers over a long period of time. It is hard for developers to keep track of all the security policies that have to be checked. Worse yet, code written for other applications or third-party libraries with different security assumptions is often reused without considering the security implications. In each case, the result is that it's difficult to ensure the correct checks are always performed.

Access control attacks attempt to bypass or circumvent access control methods. Access control starts with identification and authorization, and access control attacks often try to steal user credentials. After attackers have stolen a user's credentials, they can launch an online impersonation attack by logging in as the user and accessing the user's resources.

Access aggregation refers to collecting multiple pieces of non-sensitive information and combining (i.e., aggregating) them to learn sensitive information. In other words, a person or group may be able to collect multiple facts about a system and then use these facts to launch an attack.

Reconnaissance attacks are access aggregation attacks that combine multiple tools to identify multiple elements of a system, such as IP addresses, open ports, running services, operating systems, and more. Aggregation attacks are also employed against databases. Combining defense-in-depth, need-to-know, separation of duties, and least privilege principles helps prevent access aggregation attacks.

Protecting against access control attacks requires that the security professional implement numerous security precautions as well as rigid adherence to a strong security policy. The following list identifies many security precautions, but it is important to realize that this is not a comprehensive list of all proactive preventative steps that the security professional can take.

- ■ ***Control Physical Access to Systems.*** – The security architect needs to take into consideration in his or her designs that if an attacker has unrestricted physical access to a computer, the attacker owns it. If an attacker can gain physical access to an authentication server, he or she can often steal

---

33 Best Practices in securing IAM - https://stormpath.com/

the password file in a very short time. Once a password file is stolen, the attacker can crack the passwords offline. All passwords should be considered compromised, but the problem can be prevented by controlling physical access.

- **Control Electronic Access to Password Files** – The security practitioner needs to tightly control and monitor electronic access to password files. End-users and those who are not account administrators have no need to access the password database file for daily work tasks. Any unauthorized access to password database files should be investigated immediately.

- **Encrypt Password Files** – Protecting against access control attacks requires that the security professional implement numerous security precautions The security practitioner should encrypt password files with the strongest encryption available for the operating systems under management. One-way encryption (hashing) is commonly used for passwords instead of storing them in plain text. In addition, rigid control over all media containing a copy of the password database file, such as backup tapes or repair disks, should be maintained. Passwords should also be encrypted when transmitted over the network.

- **Create a Strong Password Policy** – The security professional needs to understand that a password policy can programmatically enforce the use of strong passwords and ensure that users regularly change their passwords. The longer and stronger a password, the longer it will take for it to be discovered in an attack. However, with enough time, all passwords can be discovered via brute force or other methods. Thus, changing passwords regularly is required to maintain security. More secure or sensitive environments require passwords to be changed more frequently. The security professional should use separate password policies for privileged accounts such as administrator accounts to ensure that they have stronger passwords and that the passwords are changed more frequently.

- **Use Password Masking** – The security practitioner should ensure that applications never display passwords in cleartext on any screen. Instead, mask the display of the password by displaying an alternate character such as an asterisk (*). This reduces shoulder surfing attempts, but users should be aware that an attacker may be able to watch the keystrokes to discover the password.

- **Deploy Multifactor Authentication** – The security architect should plan on deploying multifactor authentication, such as using biometrics or token devices. If passwords are not the only means used to protect the security of a network, their compromise will not automatically result in a system breach.

- **Use Account Lockout Controls** – Account lockout controls help prevent online password attacks. They lock an account after the incorrect password is entered a predefined number of times. It's common to allow a user to incorrectly enter the password as many as five times before the account is locked out. For systems and services that do not support account lockout controls, such as most FTP servers, the security practitioner should employ extensive logging and an intrusion detection system to look for evidence of password attacks.

- **Use Last Logon Notification** – Many systems display a message including the time, date, and location (such as the computer name or IP address) of the last successful logon. If users pay attention to this message, they might notice if their account has been accessed by someone else. For example, if the last time a user logged on was the previous Friday but a message indicates that the account was accessed on Saturday, it is apparent the account has been breached. Users who suspect that their account is under attack or has been compromised should report this to a system administrator.

- **Educate Users about Security** – The security professional needs to ensure that he or she properly trains users about the necessity of maintaining security and the use of strong passwords. Inform users that passwords should never be shared or written down; the only possible exception is that long, complex passwords for the most sensitive accounts, such as administrator or root accounts, can be written down and stored securely. In addition, the security professional should offer tips to users on how to create strong passwords and how to prevent shoulder surfing and inform users of the risk of using the same password for different accounts. For example, a user that uses the same password for banking accounts and an online shopping account can have all of his or her accounts compromised after a successful attack on a single system. Additionally, the security professional needs to inform users about social engineering tactics.

- **Audit Access Controls** – Regular reviews and audits of access control processes by the security practitioner will help assess the effectiveness of access controls. For example, auditing can track logon success and failure of any account. An intrusion detection system can monitor these logs and easily identify logon prompt attacks and notify administrators.

- **Actively Manage Accounts** – When an employee leaves an organization or takes a leave of absence, the account should be disabled as soon as possible by the security professional. Inactive accounts should be deleted when it is determined they are no longer needed. Regular user entitlement and access reviews can discover excessive or creeping privileges.

- **Use Vulnerability Scanners** – Vulnerability scanners can detect access control vulnerabilities and, when used regularly by the security practitioner, help an organization mitigate these vulnerabilities. Many vulnerability scanners include password cracking tools that will detect weak passwords in addition to tools that can verify that systems are kept up to date with patches.

TRY IT FOR YOURSELF

Below is a sampling of different activities and tools that the security professional can interact with to test out some of the approaches for mitigating access control attacks discussed in the previous section.

A – Control Electronic Access to Password Files

For Linux based environments, download Tripwire from here:

- http://sourceforge.net/projects/tripwire/

For Windows based environments, download Process Monitor from here:

- http://technet.microsoft.com/en-us/sysinternals/bb896645.aspx

B – Create a Strong Password Policy

A sample template that will allow the security practitioner to review in detail what a password policy statement and supporting documentation may look like is provided as Appendix F. The template will walk you through the stages of a password policy for a typical company. Defining a password policy documents clear responsibilities for all those involved with account management activities.

Download the template and go through the sections in order to understand how a password policy is structured.

C – Use Last Logon Notification, Use Account Lockout Controls, Audit Access Controls, and Actively Manage Accounts

Security practitioners can use the Active Directory Administration Center (ADAC) to perform common Active Directory object management tasks through both data-driven navigation and task-oriented navigation in Windows Server 2008 and Server 2012 based domains.

You can use the Active Directory Administrative Center to perform the following Active Directory administrative tasks:

- Create new user accounts or manage existing user accounts
- Create new groups or manage existing groups
- Create new computer accounts or manage existing computer accounts
- Create new organizational units (OUs) and containers or manage existing OUs
- Connect to one or several domains or domain controllers in the same instance of Active Directory Administrative Center, and view or manage the directory information for those domains or domain controllers
- Filter Active Directory data by using query-building search

Figure 5.16 shows the Windows Server 2012 version of the ADAC tool. When you open the Active Directory Administrative Center, the domain that you are currently logged on to on this server (the local domain) appears in the Active Directory Administrative Center navigation pane (the left pane). Depending on the rights of your current set of logon credentials, you can view or manage the Active Directory objects in this local domain.

You can also use the same instance of the Active Directory Administrative Center and the same set of logon credentials to view or manage Active Directory objects from any other domain. The domains that you view can belong to the same forest as the local domain. They can also *not* belong to the same forest as the local domain, as long as they have an established trust with the local domain. Both one-way trusts and two-way trusts are supported. In addition, you can open Active Directory Administrative Center by using a set of logon credentials that is different from your current set of logon credentials.

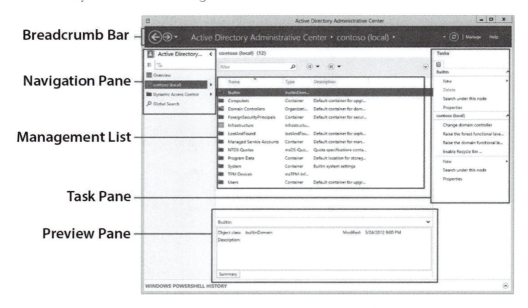

Figure 5.16 – **The Windows Server 2012 ADAC tool MMC**

The Windows Server 2008 operating system provides organizations with a way to define different password and account lockout policies for different sets of users in a domain. In Active Directory domains prior to Windows Server 2008, only one password policy and account lockout policy could be applied to all users in the domain. These policies were specified in the Default Domain Policy for the domain. As a result, organizations that wanted different password and account lockout settings for different sets of users had to either create a password filter or deploy multiple domains. Both are costly options that were cumbersome to manage effectively.

The security architect can use fine-grained password policies to specify multiple password policies within a single domain and apply different restrictions for password and account lockout policies to different sets of users in a domain. For example, you can apply stricter settings to privileged accounts and less strict settings to the accounts of other users. In other cases, the security practitioner might want to apply a special password policy for accounts whose passwords are synchronized with other data sources.

If you plan to use fine-grained password policies in Windows Server 2012, consider the following:

- Fine-grained password policies apply only to global security groups and user objects (or inetOrgPerson objects if they are used instead of user objects). By default, only members of the Domain Admins group can set fine-grained password policies. However, you can also delegate the ability to set these policies to other users. The domain functional level must be Windows Server 2008 or higher.

- You must use the Windows Server 2012 version of Active Directory Administrative Center to administer fine-grained password policies through a graphical user interface.

Fine-Grained Password Policy step-by-step: (try as little or as much as you would like)

In the following steps, you will use ADAC to perform the following fine-grained password policy tasks:

- *Step 1* – Raise the domain functional level
- *Step 2* – Create test users, group, and organizational unit
- *Step 3* – Create a new fine-grained password policy
- *Step 4* – View a resultant set of policies for a user
- *Step 5* – Edit a fine-grained password policy
- *Step 6* – Delete a fine-grained password policy

Please Note:

Membership in the Domain Admins group or equivalent permissions is required to perform the following steps.

Step 1 – Raise the Domain Functional Level

In the following procedure, you will raise the domain functional level of the target domain to Windows Server 2008 or higher. A domain functional level of Windows Server 2008 or higher is required to enable fine-grained password policies.

TO RAISE THE DOMAIN FUNCTIONAL LEVEL

1. Right click the Windows PowerShell icon, click Run as Administrator, and type dsac.exe to open ADAC.

2. Click Manage, click Add Navigation Nodes, and select the appropriate target domain in the Add Navigation Nodes dialog box and then click OK.

3. Click the target domain in the left navigation pane and in the Tasks pane, click Raise the domain functional level. Select a forest functional level that is at least Windows Server 2008 or higher and then click OK.

5

Identity & Access Management

721

Windows PowerShell Equivalent Commands

The following Windows PowerShell cmdlet or cmdlets perform the same function as the preceding procedure. Enter each cmdlet on a single line, even though they may appear word-wrapped across several lines here because of formatting constraints.

```
Set-ADDomainMode -Identity isc2.org -DomainMode 3
```

Step 2 – Create Test Users, Groups, and Organizational Units

To create the test users and group need for this step, follow the procedures located here: Step 3 – Create a New Fine-Grained Password Policy (you do not need to create the OU to demonstrate fine-grained password policy).

Step 3 – Create a New Fine-Grained Password Policy

In the following procedure, you will create a new fine-grained password policy using the UI in ADAC.

TO CREATE A NEW FINE-GRAINED PASSWORD POLICY

1. Right click the Windows PowerShell icon, click Run as Administrator, and type dsac.exe to open ADAC.
2. Click Manage, click Add Navigation Nodes, and select the appropriate target domain in the Add Navigation Nodes dialog box and then click OK.
3. In the ADAC navigation pane, open the System container and then click Password Settings Container.
4. In the Tasks pane, click New, and then click Password Settings.

Fill in or edit fields inside the property page to create a new Password Settings object. The Name and Precedence fields are required.

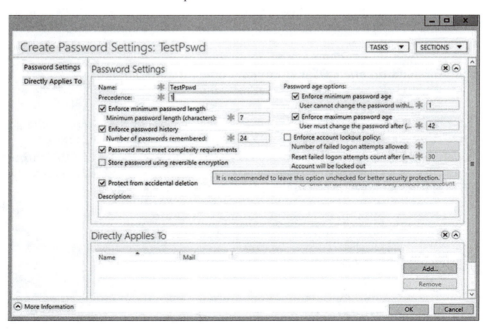

Under Directly Applies To, click Add, type group1, and then click OK.

This associates the Password Policy object with the members of the global group you created for the test environment.

1. Click OK to submit the creation.

Windows PowerShell Equivalent Commands

The following Windows PowerShell cmdlet or cmdlets perform the same function as the preceding procedure. Enter each cmdlet on a single line, even though they may appear word-wrapped across several lines here because of formatting constraints.

```
New-ADFineGrainedPasswordPolicy TestPswd -ComplexityEnabled:$true-
LockoutDuration:"00:30:00" -LockoutObservationWindow:"00:30:00"-
LockoutThreshold:"0" -MaxPasswordAge:"42.00:00:00"-
MinPasswordAge:"1.00:00:00" -MinPasswordLength:"7"-
PasswordHistoryCount:"24" -Precedence:"1"-
ReversibleEncryptionEnabled:$false-
ProtectedFromAccidentalDeletion:$true

Add-ADFineGrainedPasswordPolicySubject TestPswd -Subjects group1
```

Step 4 – View a Resultant Set of Policies for a User

In the following procedure, you will view the resultant password settings for a user that is a member of the group to which you assigned a fine-grained password policy in Step 3 – Create a New Fine-Grained Password Policy.

TO VIEW A RESULTANT SET OF POLICIES FOR A USER

1. Right click the Windows PowerShell icon, click Run as Administrator, and type dsac.exe to open ADAC.
2. Click Manage, click Add Navigation Nodes, and select the appropriate target domain in the Add Navigation Nodes dialog box and then click OK.
3. Select a user, test1 that belongs to the group, group1 that you associated a fine-grained password policy with in Step 3 – Create a New Fine-Grained Password Policy.
4. Click View Resultant Password Settings in the Tasks pane.
5. Examine the password setting policy and then click Cancel.

Windows PowerShell Equivalent Commands

The following Windows PowerShell cmdlet or cmdlets perform the same function as the preceding procedure. Enter each cmdlet on a single line, even though they may appear word-wrapped across several lines here because of formatting constraints.

```
Get-ADUserResultantPasswordPolicy test1
```

723

Step 5 – Edit a Fine-Grained Password Policy

In the following procedure, you will edit the fine-grained password policy you created in *Step 3 – Create a New Fine-Grained Password Policy*.

TO EDIT A FINE-GRAINED PASSWORD POLICY

1. Right click the Windows PowerShell icon, click Run as Administrator, and type dsac.exe to open ADAC.
2. Click Manage, click Add Navigation Nodes, and select the appropriate target domain in the Add Navigation Nodes dialog box and then click OK.
3. In the ADAC Navigation Pane, expand System and then click Password Settings Container.
4. Select the fine-grained password policy you created in Step 3: Create a New Fine-Grained Password Policy and click Properties in the Tasks pane.
5. Under Enforce password history, change the value of Number of passwords remembered to 30.
6. Click OK.

⊠ Windows PowerShell Equivalent Commands

The following Windows PowerShell cmdlet or cmdlets perform the same function as the preceding procedure. Enter each cmdlet on a single line, even though they may appear word-wrapped across several lines here because of formatting constraints.

```
Set-ADFineGrainedPasswordPolicy TestPswd -PasswordHistoryCount:"30"
```

Step 6 – Delete a Fine-Grained Password Policy

TO DELETE A FINE-GRAINED PASSWORD POLICY

1. Right click the Windows PowerShell icon, click Run as Administrator, and type dsac.exe to open ADAC.
2. Click Manage, click Add Navigation Nodes, and select the appropriate target domain in the Add Navigation Nodes dialog box and then click OK.
3. In the ADAC Navigation Pane, expand System and then click Password Settings Container.
4. Select the fine-grained password policy you created in Step 3: Create a New Fine-Grained Password Policy and in the Tasks pane, click Properties.
5. Clear the Protect from accidental deletion checkbox and click OK.
6. Select the fine-grained password policy and in the Tasks pane, click Delete.
7. Click OK in the confirmation dialog.

⊠ Windows PowerShell Equivalent Commands

The following Windows PowerShell cmdlet or cmdlets perform the same function as the preceding procedure. Enter each cmdlet on a single line, even though they may appear word-wrapped across several lines here because of formatting constraints.

```
Set-ADFineGrainedPasswordPolicy -Identity TestPswd -
ProtectedFromAccidentalDeletion $False
Remove-ADFineGrainedPasswordPolicy TestPswd -Confirm
```

The Active Directory Administrative Center enables you to create and manage Fine-Grained Password Policy (FGPP) objects. Windows Server 2008 introduced the FGPP feature, but Windows Server 2012 has the first graphical management interface for it. You apply Fine-Grained Password Policies at a domain level, and it enables overriding the single domain password required by Windows Server 2003. By creating different FGPP with different settings, individual users or groups get differing password policies in a domain.

In the Navigation pane, click Tree View, click your domain, click **System**, click **Password Settings Container**, and then in the Tasks pane, click **New** and **Password Settings**.

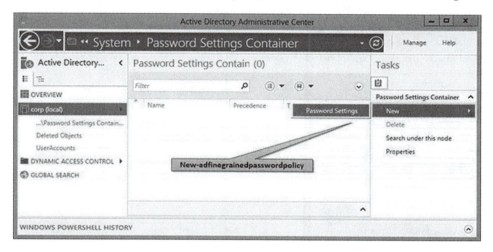

MANAGING FINE-GRAINED PASSWORD POLICIES

Creating a new FGPP or editing an existing one brings up the **Password Settings** editor. From here, you configure all desired password policies, as you would have in Windows Server 2008 or Windows Server 2008 R2, only now with a purpose-built editor.

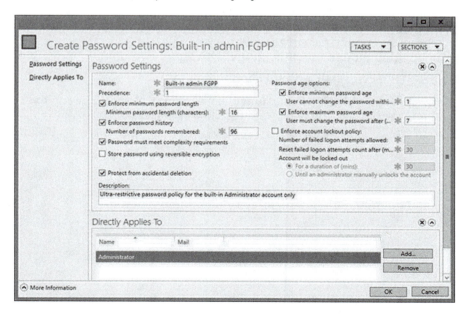

Fill out all required (red asterisk) fields and any optional fields, and then click **Add** to set the users or groups that receive this policy. FGPP overrides default domain policy settings for those specified security principals. In the figure above, an extremely restrictive policy applies only to the built-in Administrator account, to prevent compromise. The policy is far too complex for standard users to comply with, but it is perfect for a high-risk account used only by IT professionals.

You also set precedence and to which users and groups the policy applies within a given domain.

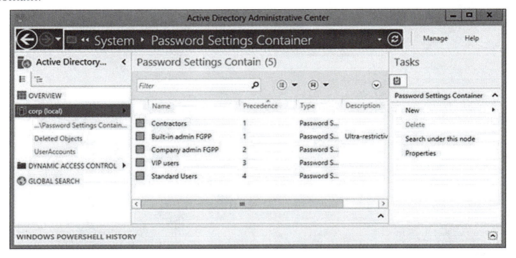

The Active Directory Windows PowerShell cmdlets for Fine-Grained Password Policy are:

- Add-ADFineGrainedPasswordPolicySubject
- Get-ADFineGrainedPasswordPolicy
- Get-ADFineGrainedPasswordPolicySubject
- New-ADFineGrainedPasswordPolicy
- Remove-ADFineGrainedPasswordPolicy
- Remove-ADFineGrainedPasswordPolicySubject
- Set-ADFineGrainedPasswordPolicy

Fine-Grained Password Policy cmdlet functionality did not change between the Windows Server 2008 R2 and Windows Server 2012. The following diagram illustrates the associated arguments for cmdlets:

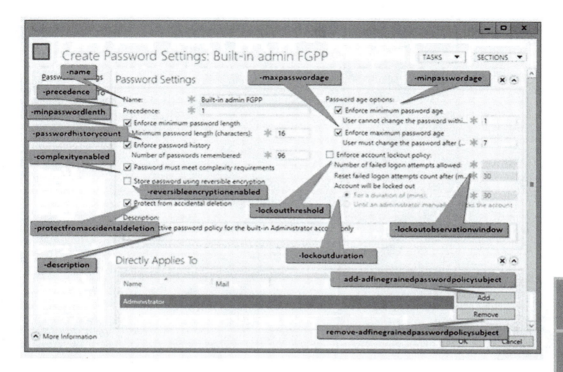

The Active Directory Administrative Center also enables you to locate the resultant set of applied FGPP for a specific user. Right click any user and click View resultant password settings… to open the Password Settings page that applies to that user through implicit or explicit assignment:

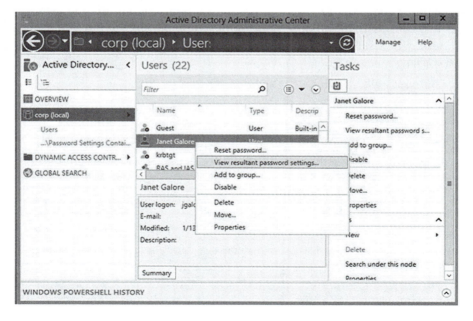

Examining the Properties of any user or group shows the Directly Associated Password Settings, which are the explicitly assigned FGPPs:

727

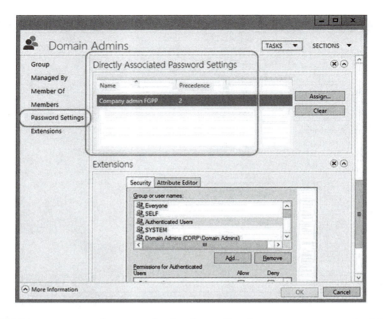

Implicit FGPP assignment does not display here; for that, you must use the View resultant password settings… option.

Hopefully the different options presented in this "**Try It For Yourself**" section will provide the security professional with a variety of opportunities to explore with regards to actions that can be taken to mitigate access control attacks.

Identity and Access Provisioning Lifecycle

Throughout this chapter, several aspects of access control and identity management have been discussed. Taken together, these concepts combine to form a "lifecycle" of access control with regards to resources. The lifecycle is the workflow of how a user obtains access, uses it, and finally loses it. The lifecycle is made up of the following phases:

1. Provisioning
2. Review
3. Revocation

Provisioning

When a new or an existing user requires additional access to a resource, the process that enables this access is called provisioning. Provisioning entails the security practitioner determining the organizational requirements for access to information and applying the appropriate access rights to the account of the user. When provisioning the elements of least privilege, one must consider separation of duties and access aggregation. The user should only be provided with access to information required to perform necessary functions. The provisioning of access should also determine if any aspect of new access would somehow violate a separation of duties process such as creation of a payment and authorization of a payment. Finally, the provisioning of resources should be considered in light of the access aggregation; does granting additional access mean access in another area should be revoked? Both the security architect and the security practitioner need to be involved in the access aggregation conversation, as the decisions made by one party can affect the other.

Review

Access rights and usage must be monitored on a basis commensurate with risk. Reviewing access can take the form of automated checks, manual audits, and several other methods. Access found to be excessive or inconsistent with a user's role or organizational function should be reviewed for modification or restriction. Access aggregation issues are often identified as part of the review process.

Revocation

At some point, access rights for most users typically will come to an end for one reason or another. For example, when a user leaves an organization, all access should be revoked. In some circumstances, such as an extended leave of absence, a revocation of access may only be temporary. Through the process of access review, revocation will typically be invoked when a user is found to have aggregated unnecessary access or access is not commensurate with the role of the user.

Across the identity and access provisioning lifecycle, the security architect needs to ensure that the design decisions being made are creating the appropriate environment for the security practitioner to implement access and identity systems that map to the business objectives that have been identified as being important to the enterprise. In addition, the ability of the security professional to manage these systems must also be ensured through the decisions made by the security architect at all levels of the system's design.

5

Identity &
Access Management

Summary 👍

As we end this comprehensive overview of the identity and access management domain, it is important to ensure that the security professional has an understanding of the key concepts that have been shown to be important throughout the chapter. These concepts form the basis for understanding how access management works, why it is a key security discipline, and how each individual component discussed in this chapter relates to the overall access management universe. The most fundamental and significant concept to master is a precise definition of what is meant by the term "access control." The following definition has been used:

Access control is the process of allowing only authorized users, programs, or other computer systems (i.e., networks) to observe, modify, or otherwise take possession of the resources of a computer system. It is also a mechanism for limiting the use of some resources to authorized users.

In summary, access controls are the collection of mechanisms, processes, or techniques that work together to protect the assets of an organization. They help protect against threats and mitigate vulnerabilities by reducing exposure to unauthorized activities and providing access to information and systems to only authorized people, processes, or systems.

Although identity and access management is a single domain within the CISSP Common Body of Knowledge (CBK), it is the most pervasive and omnipresent aspect of information security. Access controls encompass all operational levels of an organization:

- **Facilities** – Access controls protect entry to, and movement around, an organization's physical locations to protect personnel, equipment, information, and other assets inside that facility.

- **Support Systems** – Access to support systems (such as power, heating, ventilation, and air conditioning (HVAC) systems; water; and fire suppression controls) must be controlled so that a malicious entity is not able to compromise these systems and cause harm to the organization's personnel or the ability to support critical systems.

- **Information Systems** – Multiple layers of access controls are present in most modern information systems and networks to protect those systems, and the information they contain, from harm or misuse.

- **Personnel** – Management, end-users, customers, business partners, and nearly everyone else associated with an organization should be subject to some form of access control to ensure that the right people have the ability to interface with each other and not interfere with the people with whom they do not have any legitimate business.

Additionally, almost all physical and logical entry points to the organization and its information systems need some type of access control. Given the pervasive nature and importance of access controls throughout the practice of security, it is necessary to understand the four key attributes of access control that enable good security management. Specifically, access controls enable management to:

- Specify which users can access a system or facility.

- Specify what resources those users can access.

- Specify what operations those users can perform.

- Enforce accountability for those users' actions.

Each of these four areas, although interrelated, represents an established and individual approach to defining an effective access control strategy.

The goals of information security are to ensure the continued Confidentiality-Integrity-Availability of an organization's assets. This includes both physical assets (such as buildings, equipment, and, of course, people) and information assets (such as company data and information systems). Access controls play a key role in ensuring the confidentiality of systems and information. Managing access to physical and information assets is fundamental to preventing exposure of data by controlling who can see, use, modify, or destroy those assets. In addition, managing an entity's admittance and rights to specific enterprise resources ensures that valuable data and services are not abused, misappropriated, or stolen. It is also a key factor for many organizations that are required to protect personal information in order to be compliant with appropriate legislation and industry compliance requirements.

5

Identity &
Access Management

The act of controlling access inherently provides features and benefits that protect the integrity of business assets. By preventing unauthorized or inappropriate access, organizations can achieve greater confidence in data and system integrity. When an organization is without controls to manage who has access to specific resources, and what actions they are permitted to perform, there are a few alternate controls to ensure that information and systems are not modified by unwanted influences. Access controls (more specifically, records of access activity) also offer greater visibility into determining who or what may have altered data or system information, potentially affecting the integrity of those assets. Access controls can be used to match an entity (such as a person or a computer system) with the actions that entity takes against valuable assets, allowing organizations to have a better understanding of the state of their security posture.

Finally, access control processes go hand in hand with efforts to ensure the availability of resources within an organization. One of the most basic rules to embrace for any valuable asset, especially an asset whose criticality requires that it must be available for use over elongated periods of time, is that only people with a need to use that particular asset should be allowed access to that asset. Taking this stance ensures that the resource is not blocked or congested by people who have no business using it. This is why most organizations only allow their employees and other trusted individuals into their facilities or onto their corporate networks. In addition, restricting access to only those who need to use a resource reduces the likelihood that malicious agents can gain access and cause damage to the asset or that non-malicious individuals with unnecessary access can cause accidental damage.

 # Domain 5: Review Questions

1. Authentication is

    A.   the assertion of a unique identity for a person or system.

    B.   the process of verifying the identity of the user.

    C.   the process of defining the specific resources a user needs and determining the type of access to those resources the user may have.

    D.   the assertion by management that the user should be given access to a system.

2. Which best describes access controls?

    A.   Access controls are a collection of technical controls that permit access to authorized users, systems, and applications.

    B.   Access controls help protect against threats and vulnerabilities by reducing exposure to unauthorized activities and providing access to information and systems to only those who have been approved.

    C.   Access control is the employment of encryption solutions to protect authentication information during log-on.

    D.   Access controls help protect against vulnerabilities by controlling unauthorized access to systems and information by employees, partners, and customers.

3. _____ requires that a user or process be granted access to only those resources necessary to perform assigned functions.

    A.   Discretionary access control

    B.   Separation of duties

    C.   Least privilege

    D.   Rotation of duties

4. What are the seven main categories of access control?

    A.   Detective, corrective, monitoring, logging, recovery, classification, and directive

    B.   Directive, deterrent, preventative, detective, corrective, compensating, and recovery

    C.   Authorization, identification, factor, corrective, privilege, detective, and directive

    D.   Identification, authentication, authorization, detective, corrective, recovery, and directive

5

Identity & Access Management

5. What are the three types of access control?

    A. Administrative, physical, and technical

    B. Identification, authentication, and authorization

    C. Mandatory, discretionary, and least privilege

    D. Access, management, and monitoring

6. What are types of failures in biometric identification systems? (**Choose ALL that apply**)

    A. False reject

    B. False positive

    C. False accept

    D. False negative

7. What best describes two-factor authentication?

    A. Something you know

    B. Something you have

    C. Something you are

    D. A combination of two listed above

8. A potential vulnerability of the Kerberos authentication server is

    A. Single point of failure

    B. Asymmetric key compromise

    C. Use of dynamic passwords

    D. Limited lifetimes for authentication credentials

9. In mandatory access control the system controls access and the owner determines

    A. Validation

    B. Need to know

    C. Consensus

    D. Verification

10. Which is the least significant issue when considering biometrics?

    A. Resistance to counterfeiting

    B. Technology type

    C. User acceptance

    D. Reliability and accuracy

11. Which is a fundamental disadvantage of biometrics?

    A. Revoking credentials

    B. Encryption

    C. Communications

    D. Placement

12. Role-based access control

    A. Is unique to mandatory access control

    B. Is independent of owner input

    C. Is based on user job functions

    D. Can be compromised by inheritance

13. Identity management is

    A. Another name for access controls

    B. A set of technologies and processes intended to offer greater efficiency in the management of a diverse user and technical environment

    C. A set of technologies and processes focused on the provisioning and decommissioning of user credentials

    D. A set of technologies and processes used to establish trust relationships with disparate systems

14. A disadvantage of single sign-on is

    A. Consistent time-out enforcement across platforms

    B. A compromised password exposes all authorized resources

    C. Use of multiple passwords to remember

    D. Password change control

15. Which of the following is incorrect when considering privilege management?

    A. Privileges associated with each system, service, or application, and the defined roles within the organization to which they are needed, should be identified and clearly documented.

    B. Privileges should be managed based on least privilege. Only rights required to perform a job should be provided to a user, group, or role.

    C. An authorization process and a record of all privileges allocated should be maintained. Privileges should not be granted until the authorization process is complete and validated.

    D. Any privileges that are needed for intermittent job functions should be assigned to multiple user accounts, as opposed to those for normal system activity related to the job function.

5

Identity &
Access Management

16. The Identity and Access Provisioning Lifecycle is made up of which phases? (**Choose ALL that apply**)

    A.   Review

    B.   Developing

    C.   Provisioning

    D.   Revocation

17. When reviewing user entitlement the security professional must be **MOST** aware of

    A.   Identity management and disaster recovery capability

    B.   Business or organizational processes and access aggregation

    C.   The organizational tenure of the user requesting entitlement

    D.   Automated processes which grant users access to resources

18. A guard dog patrolling the perimeter of a data center is what type of a control?

    A.   Recovery

    B.   Administrative

    C.   Logical

    D.   Physical

CISSP®

Domain 6
Security Assessment & Testing

"Security Assessment and Testing" covers a broad range of ongoing and point-of-time based testing methods used to determine vulnerabilities and associated risk. Mature system development life cycles include security testing and assessment as part of the development, operations, and disposition phases of a system's life. The fundamental purpose of test and evaluation (T&E) is to provide knowledge to assist in managing the risks involved in developing, producing, operating, and sustaining systems and capabilities. T&E measures progress in both system and capability development. T&E provides knowledge of system capabilities and limitations for use in improving the system performance and for optimizing system use in operations. T&E expertise must be brought to bear at the beginning of the system lifecycle to provide earlier learning about the strengths and weaknesses of the system under development. The goal is early identification of technical, operational, and system deficiencies so that appropriate and timely corrective actions can be developed prior to fielding the system. The creation of the test and evaluation strategy involves planning for technology development, including risk, evaluating the system design against mission requirements, and identifying where competitive prototyping and other evaluation techniques fit in the process.

The content of a test and evaluation strategy is a function of where it is applied in the acquisition/development process, the requirements for the capability to be provided, and the technologies that drive the required capability. A test and evaluation strategy should lead to the knowledge required to manage risks, the empirical data required to validate models and simulations, the evaluation of technical performance and system maturity, and a determination of operational effectiveness, suitability, and survivability. In the end, the goal of the strategy is to identify, manage, and mitigate risk, which requires identifying the strengths and weaknesses of the system or service being provided to meet the end goal of the acquisition or development program. Ideally, the strategy should drive a process that confirms compliance with the Initial Capabilities Document (ICD), instead of discovering later that functional, performance, or non-functional goals are not being met. The discovery of problems late in the test and evaluation phase can have significant cost impacts as well as substantial operational repercussions.

Historically, test and evaluation consisted of testing a single system, element, or component, and it was carried out in a serial manner. One test would be performed, data would be obtained, and then the system would move to the next test event, often at a new location with a different test environment. Similarly, the evaluations themselves were typically performed in a serial manner, with determinations of how well the system met its required capabilities established through the combination of test results obtained from multiple sites with differing environments. The process was time consuming and inefficient, and with the advent of centralized collaboration strategies, it became insufficient. In large part, this was due to an approach to acquisition/development that did not easily accommodate the incremental addition of capabilities. Creating and maintaining an effective test and evaluation strategy under those conditions would have been difficult at best. A test and evaluation strategy is a necessity today because of the addition of capabilities via incremental upgrades, which is now the norm, and the shift to a network-centric construct where data is separated from the applications; data is posted and made available before it is processed; collaboration is employed to make data understandable; and a rich set of network nodes and paths provides the required supporting infrastructure.

When there is a need to deliver a set of capabilities as quickly as possible, further complexity in creating a test and evaluation strategy can be introduced, especially in cases where ICDs are largely nonexistent, ambiguous, inconsistent, or incomplete. In this situation, the development of a test and evaluation strategy represents a significant challenge, and in some cases it may be largely ignored to get a capability in the field as quickly as possible. However, this approach should not be carried out without the necessary attendant risk assessments and mitigation strategies – they are just accomplished at a high level very early in the process. Quick reaction capabilities (QRCs) of this sort are often followed by a more formal acquisition effort. Nonetheless, test and evaluation of QRCs cannot be completely ignored. At the outset, the critical capabilities must be identified, and their risks must be identified, managed, and mitigated through some level of test and evaluation.

TOPICS

- Assessment and Test Strategies
- Security Control Testing
  - Vulnerability Assessment
  - Penetration Testing
  - Log Reviews
  - Synthetic Transactions
  - Code Review and Testing
  - Negative Testing
  - Misuse Case Testing
  - Test Coverage Analysis
  - Interface Testing
- Collect Security Process Data
  - Account Management
  - Management Review
  - Key Performance and Risk Indicators
  - Backup Verification Data
  - Training and Awareness
  - Disaster Recovery and Business Continuity
- Test Output
  - Automated
  - Manual
- Conduct or Facilitate Internal and Third-Party Audits

OBJECTIVES

According to the (ISC)² Candidate Information Bulletin (Exam Outline), a CISSP candidate is expected to be able to:

- Design and validate assessment and test strategies.
- Conduct security control testing.
- Collect security process data (e.g., management and operational controls).
- Analyze and report test output.
- Conduct or facilitate internal and third-party audits.

Assessment and Test Strategies

A properly planned and executed test and evaluation strategy can provide information about risk and risk mitigation and empirical data to validate models and simulations, evaluate technical performance and system maturity, and determine whether systems are operationally effective, suitable, and survivable.

Systems engineers and security professionals should work with sponsors to create or evaluate test and evaluation strategies in support of acquisition/development programs. They may be asked to recommend test and evaluation approaches, which provide insights that can be used to manage risks. They also can monitor test and evaluation processes and recommend changes when they are warranted. They also should evaluate test plans and procedures that are applied during development testing and operational testing; occasionally, they may help to formulate the plans and procedures as a member or advisor to the test team. As a consequence, system engineers and security professionals are expected to understand the rationale behind the requirement for acquisition/development programs to create and execute a test and evaluation strategy. They are expected to understand where test and evaluation activities such as interoperability testing, information assurance testing, and modeling and simulation fit in the acquisition lifecycle and where they can be used most effectively to identify and mitigate risk. Finally, it should be expected that systems engineers and security professionals, in the course of their other activities such as requirements and design analysis, will include test and evaluation concerns in their analysis.

In many instances, the enterprise may seek to establish a working group to execute the test and evaluation strategy. This group is often referred to as a test and evaluation integrated product team, and it consists of test and evaluation subject matter experts, customer user representatives, and other stakeholders. The test and evaluation strategy is a living document, and this group is responsible for any updates that are required over time. The organization looks to this group to ensure that test and evaluation processes are consistent with the acquisition strategy and that the user's capability-based operational requirements are being met by the system. The organization's interest in and application of a test and evaluation strategy should be documented through the incorporation of test and evaluation into all of their acquisition and development contracts that are placed with partners and vendors if the work is to be done by third parties.

Software verification provides objective evidence that the design outputs of a particular phase of the software development lifecycle meet all of the specified requirements for that phase. Software verification looks for consistency, completeness, and correctness of the software and its supporting documentation, as it is being developed, and provides support for a subsequent conclusion that software is validated. Software testing is one of many verification activities intended to confirm that software development output meets its input requirements. Other verification activities include various static and dynamic analyses, code and document inspections, walkthroughs, and other techniques.

Security verification and validation are difficult because a developer cannot test forever, and it is hard to know how much evidence is enough. In large measure, validation is a matter of developing a "level of confidence" that the software or system meets all requirements and user expectations as documented. Measures such as defects found in specifications documents, estimates of defects remaining, testing coverage, and other techniques are all used to develop an acceptable level of confidence before deploying a product. The level of confidence, and therefore the level of software validation, verification, and testing effort needed, will vary depending upon the safety risk (hazard) posed by the system.

Software Development as Part of System Design

The decision to implement system functionality using software is one that is typically made during system design. Software requirements are typically derived from the overall system requirements and design for those aspects in the system that are to be implemented using software. There are user needs and intended uses for a finished system, but users typically do not specify whether those requirements are to be met by hardware, software, or some combination of both. Therefore, software validation must be considered within the context of the overall design validation for the system.

A documented requirements specification represents the user's needs and intended uses from which the system is developed. A primary goal of software validation is to then demonstrate that all completed software products comply with all documented software and system requirements. The correctness and completeness of both the system requirements and the software requirements should be addressed as part of the design validation process for the system. Software validation includes confirmation of conformance to all software specifications and confirmation that all software requirements are traceable to the system specifications. Confirmation is an important part of the overall design validation to ensure that all aspects of the system conform to user needs and intended uses.

Software is Different from Hardware

While software shares many of the same engineering tasks as hardware, it has some very important differences. For example: The vast majority of software problems are traceable to errors made during the design and development process. While the quality of a hardware product is highly dependent on design, development, and manufacture, the quality of a software product is dependent primarily on design and development with a tertiary concern for software manufacture. Software manufacturing consists of reproduction that can be easily verified. It is not difficult to manufacture thousands of program copies that function exactly the same as the original; the difficulty comes in getting the original program to meet all specifications.

One of the most significant features of software is branching, i.e., the ability to execute alternative series of commands, based on differing inputs. This feature is a major contributing factor for another characteristic of software - its complexity. Even short programs can be very complex and difficult to fully understand. Typically, testing alone cannot fully verify that software is complete and correct. In addition to testing, other verification techniques and a structured and documented development process should be combined to ensure a comprehensive validation approach.

Unlike hardware, software is not a physical entity and does not wear out. In fact, software may improve with age, as latent defects are discovered and removed. However, as software is constantly updated and changed, such improvements are sometimes countered by new defects introduced into the software during the change. Unlike some hardware failures, software failures can occur without advanced warning. The software's branching that allows it to follow differing paths during execution may hide some latent defects until long after a software product has been introduced into the marketplace.

Another related characteristic of software is the speed and ease with which it can be changed. This factor can cause both software and non-software professionals to believe that software problems can be corrected easily. Combined with a lack of understanding of software, it can lead managers to believe that tightly controlled engineering is not needed as much for software as it is for hardware. In fact, the opposite is true. Because of its complexity, the development process for software should be even more tightly controlled than for hardware in order to prevent problems that cannot be easily detected later in the development process.

Seemingly insignificant changes in software code can create unexpected and very significant problems elsewhere in the software program. The software development process should be sufficiently well planned, controlled, and documented to detect and correct unexpected results from software changes. Given the high demand for software professionals and the highly mobile workforce, the software personnel who make maintenance changes to software may not have been involved in the original software development. Therefore, accurate and thorough documentation is essential. Security impact assessments should be performed prior to new releases or changes to the software to ensure the program still meets the defined security and risk requirements.

Historically, software components have not been as frequently standardized and interchangeable as hardware components. However, many software developers are using component-based development tools and techniques. Object-oriented methodologies and the use of off-the-shelf software components hold promise for faster and less expensive software development. However, component-based approaches require very careful attention during integration. Prior to integration, time is needed to fully define and develop reusable software code and to fully understand the behavior of off-the-shelf components as well as the security concerns and risks that they may pose. For these and other reasons, software engineering needs an even greater level of managerial scrutiny and control than hardware engineering.

Log Reviews

A log is a record of the events occurring within an organization's systems and networks. Logs are composed of log entries; each entry contains information related to a specific event that has occurred within a system or network. Many logs within an organization contain records related to computer security. These computer security logs are generated by many sources, including security software, such as anti-virus software, firewalls, and intrusion detection and prevention systems; operating systems on servers, workstations, and networking equipment; and applications.

The number, volume, and variety of computer security logs have increased greatly, which has created the need for computer security log management—the process for generating, transmitting, storing, analyzing, and disposing of computer security log data. Log management is essential to ensuring that computer security records are stored in sufficient detail for an appropriate period. Routine log analysis is beneficial for identifying security incidents, policy violations, fraudulent activity, and operational problems. Logs are also useful when performing auditing and forensic analysis, supporting internal investigations, establishing baselines, and identifying operational trends and long-term problems.

6

Security Assessment & Testing

A fundamental problem with log management that occurs in many organizations is effectively balancing a limited quantity of log management resources with a continuous supply of log data. Log generation and storage can be complicated by several factors, including a high number of log sources; inconsistent log content, formats, and timestamps among sources; and increasingly large volumes of log data. Log management also involves protecting the confidentiality, integrity, and availability of logs. Another problem with log management is ensuring that security, system, and network administrators regularly perform effective analysis of log data.

The security architect, security practitioner, and security professional all have to play a part in establishing, operating, and managing a security culture within the enterprise that understands the importance of log management. Implementing the following recommendations should assist in facilitating more efficient and effective log management for the organization.

Policies and Procedures for Log Management

To establish and maintain successful log management activities, an organization should develop standard processes for performing log management. As part of the planning process, an organization should define its logging requirements and goals. Based on those, an organization should then develop policies that clearly define mandatory requirements and suggested recommendations for log management activities, including log generation, transmission, storage, analysis, and disposal. An organization should also ensure that related policies and procedures incorporate and support the log management requirements and recommendations. The organization's management should provide the necessary support for the efforts involving log management planning, policy, and procedures development.

Requirements and recommendations for logging should be created in conjunction with a detailed analysis of the technology and resources needed to implement and maintain them, their security implications and value, and the regulations and laws to which the organization is subject. Generally, organizations should require logging and analyzing of the data that is of greatest importance and also have non-mandatory recommendations for which other types and sources of data should be logged and analyzed if time and resources permit. In some cases, organizations choose to have all or nearly all log data generated and stored for at least a short period of time in case it is needed, which favors security considerations over usability and resource usage and also allows for better decision-making in some cases. When establishing requirements and recommendations, organizations should strive to be flexible because each system is different and will log different amounts of data than other systems.

The organization's policies and procedures should also address the preservation of original logs. Many organizations send copies of network traffic logs to centralized devices as well as use tools that analyze and interpret network traffic. In cases where logs may be needed as evidence, organizations may wish to acquire copies of the original log files, the centralized log files, and interpreted log data, in case there are any questions regarding the fidelity of the copying and interpretation processes. Retaining logs for evidence may involve the use of different forms of storage and different processes, such as additional restrictions on access to the records.

Prioritize Log Management

After an organization defines its requirements and goals for the log management process, it should then prioritize the requirements and goals based on the organization's perceived reduction of risk and the expected time and resources needed to perform log management functions. An organization should also define roles and responsibilities for log management for key personnel throughout the organization, including establishing log management duties at both the individual system level and the log management infrastructure level.

Create and Maintain a Log Management Infrastructure

A log management infrastructure consists of the hardware, software, networks, and media used to generate, transmit, store, analyze, and dispose of log data. Log management infrastructures typically perform several functions that support the analysis and security of log data. After establishing an initial log management policy and identifying roles and responsibilities, an organization should next develop one or more log management infrastructures that effectively support the policy and roles. Organizations should consider implementing log management infrastructures that include centralized log servers and log data storage. When designing infrastructures, organizations should plan for both the current and future needs of the infrastructures and the individual log sources throughout the organization. Major factors to consider in the design include the volume of log data to be processed, network bandwidth, online and offline data storage, the security requirements for the data, and the time and resources needed for staff to analyze the logs.

Provide Proper Support for All Staff with Log Management Responsibilities

To ensure that log management for individual systems is performed effectively throughout the organization, the administrators of those systems should receive adequate support. This should include disseminating information, providing training, designating points of contact to answer questions, providing specific technical guidance, and making tools and documentation available.

Standard Log Management Operational Processes

The major log management operational processes typically include configuring log sources, performing log analysis, initiating responses to identified events, and managing long-term storage. Administrators have other responsibilities as well, such as the following:

- Monitoring the logging status of all log sources
- Monitoring log rotation and archival processes
- Checking for upgrades and patches to logging software, and acquiring, testing, and deploying them
- Ensuring that each logging host's clock is synched to a common time source
- Reconfiguring logging as needed based on policy changes, technology changes, and other factors
- Documenting and reporting anomalies in log settings, configurations, and processes.
- Ensuring logs are consolidated to repositories such as Security Information and Event Management (SIEM) systems

Because of the widespread deployment of networked servers, workstations, and other computing devices and the ever-increasing number of threats against networks and systems, the number, volume, and variety of computer security logs have increased greatly. This has created the need for computer security log management, which is the process for generating, transmitting, storing, analyzing, and disposing of computer security log data.

6

Security Assessment & Testing

Most organizations use several types of network-based and host-based security software to detect malicious activity, protect systems and data, and support incident response efforts. Accordingly, security software is a major source of computer security log data. Common types of network-based and host-based security software include the following:

- **Anti-malware and Anti-virus Software** – The most common form of anti-malware software is anti-virus software, which typically records all instances of detected malware, file and system disinfection attempts, and file quarantines. Additionally, anti-virus software might also record when malware scans were performed and when anti-virus signature or software updates occurred. Anti-spyware software and other types of anti-malware software (e.g., rootkit detectors) are also common sources of security information.

- **Intrusion Detection and Intrusion Prevention Systems** – Intrusion detection and intrusion prevention systems record detailed information on suspicious behavior and detected attacks, as well as any actions intrusion prevention systems performed to stop malicious activity in progress. Some intrusion detection systems, such as file integrity checking software, run periodically instead of continuously, so they generate log entries in batches instead of on an ongoing basis.

- **Remote Access Software** – Remote access is often granted and secured through virtual private networking (VPN). VPN systems typically log successful and failed login attempts, as well as the dates and times each user connected and disconnected, and the amount of data sent and received in each user session. VPN systems that support granular access control, such as many Secure Sockets Layer (SSL) VPNs, may log detailed information about the use of resources.

- **Web Proxies** – Web proxies are intermediate hosts through which websites are accessed. Web proxies make webpage requests on behalf of users, and they cache copies of retrieved webpages to make additional accesses to those pages more efficient. Web proxies can also be used to restrict Web access and to add a layer of protection between Web clients and Web servers. Web proxies often keep a record of all URLs accessed through them.

- **Vulnerability Management Software** – Vulnerability management software, which includes patch management software and vulnerability assessment software, typically logs the patch installation history and vulnerability status of each host, which includes known vulnerabilities and missing software updates. Vulnerability management software may also record additional information about hosts' configurations. Vulnerability management software typically runs occasionally, not continuously, and is likely to generate large batches of log entries.

- **Authentication Servers** – Authentication servers, including directory servers and single sign-on servers, typically log each authentication attempt, including its origin, username, success or failure, and date and time.

- **Routers** – Routers may be configured to permit or block certain types of network traffic based on a policy. Routers that block traffic are usually configured to log only the most basic characteristics of blocked activity.

- **Firewalls** – Like routers, firewalls permit or block activity based on a policy; however, firewalls use much more sophisticated methods to examine network traffic. Firewalls can also track the state of network traffic and perform content inspection. Firewalls tend to have more complex policies and generate more detailed logs of activity than routers.

■ **Network Access Control (NAC)/Network Access Protection (NAP) Servers –** Some organizations check each remote host's security posture before allowing it to join the network. This is often done through a network quarantine server and agents placed on each host. Hosts that do not respond to the server's checks or that fail the checks are quarantined on a separate virtual local area network (VLAN) segment. Network quarantine servers log information about the status of checks, including which hosts were quarantined and for what reasons.

A sample of log data from the Security Log as viewed by the Windows Event Viewer is below. *Figure 6.1* shows the General view of the information presented to the security practitioner when the log is viewed. *Figure 6.2* shows the detailed view of the same information.

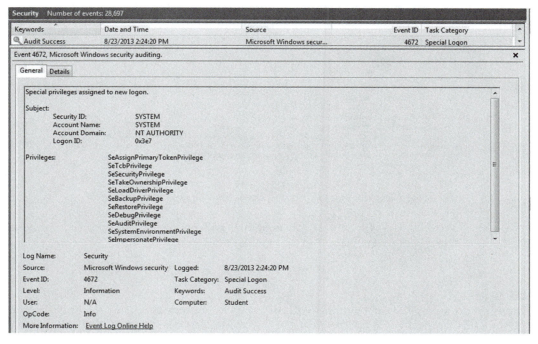

Figure 6.1 – **Security Log in Windows Event Viewer – General View**

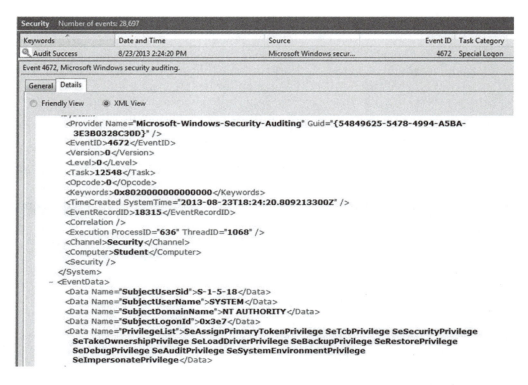

Figure 6.2 – **Security Log in Windows Event Viewer – Detailed XML View**

Operating systems (OS) for servers, workstations, and networking devices (e.g., routers, switches) usually log a variety of information related to security. The most common types of security-related OS data are as follows:

System Events

System events are operational actions performed by OS components, such as shutting down the system or starting a service. Typically, failed events and the most significant successful events are logged, but many OSs permit administrators to specify which types of events will be logged. The details logged for each event also vary widely; each event is usually time stamped, and other supporting information could include event, status, and error codes; service name; and user or system account associated with an event.

Audit Records

Audit records contain security event information such as successful and failed authentication attempts, file accesses, security policy changes, account changes (e.g., account creation and deletion, account privilege assignment), and use of privileges. OSs typically permit system administrators to specify which types of events should be audited and whether successful and/ or failed attempts to perform certain actions should be logged.

OS logs are most beneficial for identifying or investigating suspicious activity involving a particular host. After suspicious activity is identified by security software, OS logs are often consulted to get more information on the activity. For example, a network security device might detect an attack against a particular host; that host's OS logs might indicate if a user was logged into the host at the time of the attack and if the attack was successful. Many OS logs are created in syslog format. Other OS logs, such as those on Windows systems, are stored in proprietary formats.

Some applications generate their own log files, while others use the logging capabilities of the OS on which they are installed. Applications vary significantly in the types of information that they log. The following lists some of the most commonly logged types of information and the potential benefits of each:

- Client requests and server responses, which can be very helpful in reconstructing sequences of events and determining their apparent outcome. If the application logs successful user authentications, it is usually possible to determine which user made each request. Some applications can perform highly detailed logging, such as email servers recording the sender, recipients, subject name, and attachment names for each email; Web servers recording each URL requested and the type of response provided by the server; and business applications recording which financial records were accessed by each user. This information can be used to identify or investigate incidents and to monitor application usage for compliance and auditing purposes.

- Account information such as successful and failed authentication attempts, account changes (e.g., account creation and deletion, account privilege assignment), and use of privileges. In addition to identifying security events such as brute force password guessing and escalation of privileges, it can be used to identify who has used the application and when each person has used it.

- Usage information such as the number of transactions occurring in a certain period (e.g., minute, hour) and the size of transactions (e.g., email message size, file transfer size). This can be useful for certain types of security monitoring (e.g., a ten-fold increase in email activity might indicate a new email–borne malware threat; an unusually large outbound email message might indicate inappropriate release of information).

- Significant operational actions such as application startup and shutdown, application failures, and major application configuration changes. This can be used to identify security compromises and operational failures.

Much of this information, particularly for applications that are not used through unencrypted network communications, can only be logged by the applications, which makes application logs particularly valuable for application-related security incidents, auditing, and compliance efforts. However, these logs are often in proprietary formats that make them more difficult to use, and the data they contain is often highly context-dependent, necessitating more resources to review their contents.

The number of logs within an organization can be quite high because most hosts within an organization typically log some computer security-related information, often with multiple logs per host. Many logs record large volumes of data on a daily basis, so the total daily volume of log data within an organization is often overwhelming. This impacts the resources needed to store the data for the appropriate length of time and to perform reviews of the data. The distributed nature of logs, inconsistent log formats, and volume of logs all make the management of log generation and storage challenging.

6

Security Assessment & Testing

Logs need to be protected from breaches of their confidentiality and integrity. For example, logs might intentionally or inadvertently capture sensitive information such as users' passwords and the content of emails. This raises security and privacy concerns involving both the individuals that review the logs and others that might be able to access the logs through authorized or unauthorized means. Logs that are secured improperly in storage or in transit might also be susceptible to intentional and unintentional alteration and destruction. This could cause a variety of impacts, including allowing malicious activities to go unnoticed and manipulating evidence to conceal the identity of a malicious party. For example, many rootkits are specifically designed to alter logs to remove any evidence of the rootkits' installation or execution.

Organizations also need to protect the availability of their logs. Many logs have a maximum size, such as storing the 15,000 most recent events or keeping 250 megabytes of log data. When the size limit is reached, the log might overwrite old data with new data or stop logging altogether, both of which would cause a loss of log data availability. To meet data retention requirements, organizations might need to keep copies of log files for a longer period of time than the original log sources can support, which necessitates establishing log archival processes. Because of the volume of logs, it might be appropriate in some cases to reduce the logs by filtering out log entries that do not need to be archived. The confidentiality and integrity of the archived logs also need to be protected.

Within most organizations, network and system administrators have traditionally been responsible for performing log analysis—studying log entries to identify events of interest. It has often been treated as a low-priority task by administrators and management because other duties of administrators, such as handling operational problems and resolving security vulnerabilities, necessitate rapid responses. Administrators who are responsible for performing log analysis often receive no training on doing it efficiently and effectively, particularly on prioritization. Also, administrators often do not receive tools that are effective at automating much of the analysis process, such as scripts and security software tools (e.g., host-based intrusion detection products, security information and event management software). Many of these tools are particularly helpful in finding patterns that humans cannot easily see, such as correlating entries from multiple logs that relate to the same event. Log analysis is often treated as reactive—something to be done after a problem has been identified through other means—rather than proactive, to identify ongoing activity and look for signs of impending problems. Traditionally, most logs have not been analyzed in a real-time or near-real-time manner. Without sound processes for analyzing logs, the value of the logs is significantly reduced.

Despite the many challenges that the security professionals face in log management, there are a few key practices an organization can follow to avoid and even solve many of these obstacles it confronts. The following four measures give a brief explanation of these solutions:

- Prioritize log management appropriately throughout the organization. An organization should define its requirements and goals for performing logging and monitoring logs to include applicable laws, regulations, and existing organizational policies. The organization can then prioritize its goals based on balancing the organization's reduction of risk with the time and resources needed to perform log management functions.

- Establish policies and procedures for log management. Policies and procedures are beneficial because they ensure a consistent approach throughout the organization as well as ensuring that laws and regulatory requirements are being met. Periodic audits are one way to confirm that logging standards and guidelines are being followed throughout the organization. Testing and validation can further ensure that the policies and procedures in the log management process are being performed properly.

- Create and maintain a secure log management infrastructure. It is very helpful for an organization to create components of a log management infrastructure and determine how these components interact. This aids in preserving the integrity of log data from accidental or intentional modification or deletion and also in maintaining the confidentiality of log data. It is also critical to create an infrastructure robust enough to handle not only expected volumes of log data but also peak volumes during extreme situations (e.g., widespread malware incident, penetration testing, vulnerability scans). Organizations should consider using SIEM systems for storage and analysis.

- Provide adequate support for all staff with log management responsibilities. While defining the log management scheme, organizations should ensure that they provide the necessary training to relevant staff regarding their log management responsibilities as well as skill instruction for the needed resources to support log management. Support also includes providing log management tools and tool documentation, providing technical guidance on log management activities, and disseminating information to log management staff.

TRY IT FOR YOURSELF

The Sample Log Procedures Document will allow the security professional to examine the type of procedure documentation that will need to be created to properly implement and manage a log gathering, retention, and review process within his or her organization.

The Sample Log Policy Document will allow the security professional to examine what a security logging policy that will drive the proper implementation and management of a log gathering, retention, and review process within his or her organization will look like.

Synthetic Transactions

Real User Monitoring (RUM) is an approach to Web monitoring that aims to capture and analyze every transaction of every user of a website or application. Also known as real-user measurement, real-user metrics, or end-user experience monitoring (EUM), it's a form of passive monitoring, relying on Web-monitoring services that continuously observe a system in action, tracking availability, functionality, and responsiveness. While some bottom-up forms of RUM rely on capturing server-side information in order to reconstruct end-user experience, top-down client-side RUM can see directly how users interact with an application and what the experience is like for them. By using local agents or small bits of JavaScript to gauge site performance and reliability from the perspective of client apps and browsers, top-down RUM focuses on the direct relationship between site speed and user satisfaction, providing valuable insights into ways to optimize an application's components and improve overall performance.

Synthetic performance monitoring, sometimes called proactive monitoring, involves having external agents run scripted transactions against a Web application. These scripts are meant to follow the steps a typical user might use–search, view product, log in, and checkout–in order to assess the experience of a user. Traditionally, synthetic monitoring has been done with lightweight, low-level agents, but increasingly, it's necessary for these agents to run full Web browsers to process JavaScript, CSS, and AJAX calls that occur on pageload.

Unlike RUM, synthetics do not track real user sessions. This has a couple of important implications. First, because the script is executing a known set of steps at regular intervals from a known location, its performance is predictable. That means it's more useful for alerting than often-noisy RUM data. Second, because it occurs predictably and externally, it's better for assessing site availability and network problems than RUM is.

Many companies actually use this sort of monitoring before getting to production, in the form of integration tests with scripted browser simulations using automated tools such as Selenium.[1] Synthetic transactions in production can actually re-use these same scripts, as long as they do not change data. As applications get more complex, proxy metrics like load or server availability become less useful for measuring uptime. Running Selenium scripts against production is not a proxy measurement; it precisely measures uptime, providing full confidence that if the synthetic transactions are completing, the site is up and running.

Finally, because synthetics have full control over the client, unlike the sandboxed Java Script powering RUM, the detail that can be garnered is impressive. Full waterfall charts, resource-by-resource performance, and screenshots/videos of the pageload in action to determine paint times can be captured. This type of insight is currently the best way to understand the performance of state transitions in single page apps, as well.

A practical example of the use of synthetic transactions for monitoring can be found in Microsoft's System Center Operations Manager software. The software allows the security practitioner to create a variety of synthetic transactions that can be used to monitor across databases, website, and TCP port usage. Before you create the monitoring settings for Operations Manager to use in a synthetic transaction, you should plan the actions that you want the synthetic transaction to perform. For example, if you want to create a synthetic transaction that measures the performance of a website, you can plan actions that are typical for a customer, such as logging on, browsing webpages, and completing a transaction, such as placing an item in a shopping cart and making a purchase.

- **Website Monitoring** – Website monitoring uses synthetic transactions to perform HTTP requests to check availability and to measure performance of a webpage, website, or Web application.
- **Database Monitoring** – Database monitoring using synthetic transactions monitors the availability of a database.

---

1   http://docs.seleniumhq.org

- **TCP Port Monitoring –** A TCP port synthetic transaction measures the availability of your website, service, or application. You can specify the server and TCP port for Operations Manager to monitor.

The security architect and security practitioner both need to be involved in the decisions surrounding the use and deployment of RUM and Synthetic Transaction monitoring systems within the organization. Below is a list of the main reasons why using synthetic monitoring can add value:

- Monitor application availability 24 x 7.
- Know if a remote site is reachable.
- Understand the performance impact that third-party services have on business apps.
- Monitor performance availability of SaaS applications and supporting cloud infrastructure such as IaaS and PaaS.
- Test B2B Web services that use SOAP, REST, or other Web service technologies.
- Monitor critical databases queries for availability.
- Objectively measure service-level agreements (SLAs).
- Baseline and analyze performance trends across geographies.
- Complement real user monitoring by synthetically monitoring availability during periods of low traffic.

Code Review and Testing [2]

In software development, a small coding error can result in a critical vulnerability that ends up compromising the security of an entire system or network. Many times, a security vulnerability is not caused by a single error, however, but rather by a sequence of errors that occur during the course of the development cycle: A coding error is introduced, it goes undetected during the testing phases, and available defense mechanisms do not stop a successful attack.

Security must be a priority in all phases of software development. Effort should be aimed at preventing software vulnerabilities—detecting them before release, of course, but also limiting their practical impact, for example, by reducing the product's attack surface. Most security vulnerabilities are caused by one of the following four reasons:

- Bad programming patterns such as missing checks of user-influenced data that can cause, e.g., in SQL injections vulnerabilities,
- Misconfiguration of security infrastructures, e.g., too permissible access control or weak cryptographic configurations,
- Functional bugs in security infrastructures, e.g., access control enforcement infrastructures that inherently do not restrict system access,
- Logical flaws in the implemented processes, e.g., resulting in an application allowing customers to order goods without paying.

---

2   See the following for a listing of over 100 test types and their definitions: http://www.guru99.com/types-of-software-testing.html

The vast majority of successful attacks against IT applications do not attack core security primitives such as cryptographic algorithms. Attackers much more often exploit bad programming, interface problems, uncontrolled interconnections, or misconfigurations. From a high-level perspective, (security) testing techniques are often classified as follows:

- **Black-Box-Testing vs. White-Box-Testing** – In black-box-testing, the tested system is used as a black box, i.e., no internal details of the system implementation are used. In contrast, white-box-testing takes the internal system details (e.g., the source code) into account.
- **Dynamic Testing vs. Static Testing** – Traditionally, testing is understood as a dynamic testing, i.e., the system under test is executed and its behavior is observed. In contrast, static testing techniques analyze a system without executing the system under test.
- **Manual Testing vs. Automated Testing** – In manual testing, the test scenario is guided by a human, while in automated testing the test scenario is executed by a specialized application.

When selecting a security testing method or tool, the security practitioner needs to consider many different things, such as:

- **Attack Surface** – Different security testing methods find different vulnerability types.
- **Application Type** – Different security testing methods behave differently when applied to different application types.
- **Quality of Results and Usability** – Security testing techniques and tools differ in usability (e.g., fix recommendations) and quality (e.g., false positives rate).
- **Supported Technologies** – Security testing tools usually only support a limited number of technologies (e.g., programming languages), and if a tool supports multiple technologies, it does not necessarily support all of them equally well.
- **Performance and Resource Utilization** – Different tools and methods require different computing power or different manual efforts.

It is commonly accepted that fixing bugs and security vulnerabilities late in the software development is usually more costly compared to fixing them as early as possible. Therefore, security testing techniques should be applied as early as possible in a secure software development lifecycle and not as an afterthought.

During Planning and Design

Strictly speaking, a security review of the architecture and threat modeling are not security testing methods. Still, they are an important prerequisite for subsequent security testing efforts, and the security practitioner should be aware of the options available to them. The selection of security testing techniques is:

- **Architecture Security Reviews** – A manual review of the product architecture to ensure that it fulfils the necessary security requirements.
  - ¤ Prerequisites: Architectural model.
  - ¤ Benefit: Detecting architectural violations of the security standard.
- **Threat Modeling** – A structured manual analysis of an application specific business case or usage scenario. This analysis is guided by a set of precompiled security threats.

- Prerequisites: Business case or usage scenario.
- Benefits: Identification of threats, their impact, and potential countermeasures that are specific to the development of the software product.

These methods help to identify the attack surface and, thus, the most critical components. This allows a focusing of the security testing activities in order to ensure that they are as effective as possible.

During Application Development

In the development stages where an application is not yet sufficiently mature enough to be able to be placed into a test environment, the following techniques are applicable:

- **Static Source Code Analysis (SAST) and Manual Code Review** – Analysis of the application source code for finding vulnerabilities without actually executing the application.
  - Prerequisites: Application source code.
  - Benefits: Detection of insecure programming, outdated libraries, and misconfigurations.
- **Static Binary Code Analysis and Manual Binary Review** – Analysis of the compiled application (binary) for finding vulnerabilities without actually executing the application. In general, this is similar to the source code analysis but is not as precise and fix recommendations typically cannot be provided.

Executable in a Test Environment

At later stages of the development lifecycle, when the software can actually be executed, further security testing approaches can be applied, such as:

- **Manual or Automated Penetration Testing** – Simulates an attacker sending data to the application and observes its behavior.
  - Benefits: Identification of a wide range of vulnerabilities in a deployed application.
- **Automated Vulnerability Scanners** – Test an application for the use of system components or configurations that are known to be insecure. For this, pre-defined attack patterns are executed, and system fingerprints are analyzed.
  - Benefits: Detection of well-known vulnerabilities, i.e., detection of outdated frameworks and misconfigurations.
- **Fuzz Testing Tools** – Send random data, usually in larger chunks than expected by the application, to the input channels of an application to provoke a crashing of the application.
  - Benefits: Detection of application crashes (e.g., caused by buffer overflows) that might be security critical.

All these techniques require a deployed and configured application on an isolated test system, including back-ends or external services. While dynamic techniques usually do not achieve similar coverage of the analyzed application in relation to static approaches, they are particularly well suited for detecting vulnerabilities that involve data flows across system boundaries. The greater the parity between production and test environments, the higher the assurance of test results from the test environment reflecting what will happen in the production environment.

6

Security Assessment & Testing

System Operation and Maintenance

During the operation of an application, the security testing techniques discussed in the last section can be applied to ensure that the system configuration is still secure and that assumptions (e.g., a virus protection shall be installed, or a correct authorization concept is implemented) are not violated accidentally. Additionally, passive security testing techniques that monitor system behavior or analyze system logs (e.g., monitoring system, intrusion detection systems) are generally recommended.

From a software maintenance perspective, the security testing of patches is particularly important: Patches need to be security tested thoroughly (i.e., against all possible attacks and all system configurations the patch can be applied) to ensure that a customer that fixes bugs in his or her system is not, accidentally, exposed to new vulnerabilities.

Test plans and test cases should be created as early in the software development process as feasible. They should identify the schedules, environments, resources (personnel, tools, etc.), methodologies, cases (inputs, procedures, outputs, expected results), documentation, and reporting criteria. The magnitude of effort to be applied throughout the testing process can be linked to complexity, criticality, reliability, and safety issues (e.g., requiring functions or modules that produce critical outcomes to be challenged with intensive testing of their fault tolerance features).

Software testing has limitations that must be recognized and considered when planning the testing of a particular software product. Except for the simplest of programs, software cannot be exhaustively tested. Generally, it is not feasible to test a software product with all possible inputs, nor is it possible to test all possible data processing paths that can occur during program execution. There is no one type of testing or testing methodology that can ensure a particular software product has been thoroughly tested. Testing of all program functionality does not mean all of the program has been tested. Testing of all of a program's code does not mean all necessary functionality is present in the program. Testing of all program functionality and all program code does not mean the program is 100% correct! Software testing that finds no errors should not be interpreted to mean that errors do not exist in the software product; it may mean the testing was superficial or didn't cover the correct scenarios.

An essential element of a software test case is the expected result. It is the key detail that permits objective evaluation of the actual test result. This necessary testing information is obtained from the corresponding, predefined definition or specification. A software specification document must identify what, when, how, and why something is to be achieved with an engineering (i.e., measurable or objectively verifiable) level of detail in order for it to be confirmed through testing. The real effort of effective software testing lies in the definition of what is to be tested rather than in the performance of the test.

A software testing process should be based on principles that foster effective examinations of a software product. Applicable software testing tenets include:

- The expected test outcome is predefined.
- A good test case has a high probability of exposing an error.
- A successful test is one that finds an error.
- There is independence from coding.
- Both application (user) and software (programming) expertise are employed.
- Testers use different tools from coders.

- Examining only the usual case is insufficient.
- Test documentation permits its reuse and an independent confirmation of the pass/fail status of a test outcome during subsequent review.

Once the prerequisite tasks (e.g., code inspection) have been successfully completed, software testing begins. It starts with unit level testing and concludes with system level testing. There may be a distinct integration level of testing. A software product should be challenged with test cases based on its internal structure and with test cases based on its external specification. These tests should provide a thorough and rigorous examination of the software product's compliance with its functional, performance, and interface definitions and requirements.

Code-based testing is also known as structural testing or "white-box" testing. It identifies test cases based on knowledge obtained from the source code, detailed design specification, and other development documents. These test cases challenge the control decisions made by the program and the program's data structures including configuration tables. Structural testing can identify "dead" code that is never executed when the program is run. Structural testing is accomplished primarily with unit (module) level testing, but it can be extended to other levels of software testing.

The level of structural testing can be evaluated using metrics that are designed to show what percentage of the software structure has been evaluated during structural testing. These metrics are typically referred to as "coverage" and are a measure of completeness with respect to test selection criteria. The amount of structural coverage should be commensurate with the level of risk posed by the software. Use of the term "coverage" usually means 100% coverage. For example, if a testing program has achieved "statement coverage," it means that 100% of the statements in the software have been executed at least once. Common structural coverage metrics include:

- *Statement Coverage* – This criteria requires sufficient test cases for each program statement to be executed at least once; however, its achievement is insufficient to provide confidence in a software product's behavior.
- *Decision (Branch) Coverage* – This criteria requires sufficient test cases for each program decision or branch to be executed so that each possible outcome occurs at least once. It is considered to be a minimum level of coverage for most software products, but decision coverage alone is insufficient for high-integrity applications.
- *Condition Coverage* – This criteria requires sufficient test cases for each condition in a program decision to take on all possible outcomes at least once. It differs from branch coverage only when multiple conditions must be evaluated to reach a decision.
- *Multi-Condition Coverage* – This criteria requires sufficient test cases to exercise all possible combinations of conditions in a program decision.
- *Loop Coverage* – This criteria requires sufficient test cases for all program loops to be executed for zero, one, two, and many iterations covering initialization, typical running, and termination (boundary) conditions.
- *Path Coverage* – This criteria requires sufficient test cases for each feasible path, basis path, etc., from start to exit of a defined program segment, to be executed at least once. Because of the very large number of possible paths through a software program, path coverage is generally not achievable. The amount of path coverage is normally established based on the risk or criticality of the software under test.

6

Security Assessment & Testing

- **Data Flow Coverage** – This criteria requires sufficient test cases for each feasible data flow to be executed at least once. A number of data flow testing strategies are available.

Definition-based or specification-based testing is also known as functional testing or "black-box" testing. It identifies test cases based on the definition of what the software product (whether it be a unit (module) or a complete program) is intended to do. These test cases challenge the intended use or functionality of a program and the program's internal and external interfaces. Functional testing can be applied at all levels of software testing, from unit to system level testing.

The following types of functional software testing involve generally increasing levels of effort:

- **Normal Case** – Testing with usual inputs is necessary. However, testing a software product only with expected, valid inputs does not thoroughly test that software product. By itself, normal case testing cannot provide sufficient confidence in the dependability of the software product.
- **Output Forcing** – Choosing test inputs to ensure that selected (or all) software outputs are generated by testing.
- **Robustness** – Software testing should demonstrate that a software product behaves correctly when given unexpected, invalid inputs. Methods for identifying a sufficient set of such test cases include Equivalence Class Partitioning, Boundary Value Analysis, and Special Case Identification (Error Guessing). While important and necessary, these techniques do not ensure that all of the most appropriate challenges to a software product have been identified for testing.
- **Combinations of Inputs** – The functional testing methods identified above all emphasize individual or single test inputs. Most software products operate with multiple inputs under their conditions of use. Thorough software product testing should consider the combinations of inputs a software unit or system may encounter during operation. Error guessing can be extended to identify combinations of inputs, but it is an ad hoc technique. Cause-effect graphing is one functional software testing technique that systematically identifies combinations of inputs to a software product for inclusion in test cases.

Functional and structural software test case identification techniques provide specific inputs for testing rather than random test inputs. One weakness of these techniques is the difficulty in linking structural and functional test completion criteria to a software product's reliability. Advanced software testing methods, such as statistical testing, can be employed to provide further assurance that a software product is dependable. Statistical testing uses randomly generated test data from defined distributions based on an operational profile (e.g., expected use, hazardous use, or malicious use of the software product). Large amounts of test data are generated and can be targeted to cover particular areas or concerns, providing an increased possibility of identifying individual and multiple rare operating conditions that were not anticipated by either the software product's designers or its testers. Statistical testing also provides high structural coverage. It does require a stable software product. Thus, structural and functional testing are prerequisites for statistical testing of a software product.

Another aspect of software testing is the testing of software changes. Changes occur frequently during software development. These changes are the result of 1) debugging that finds an error and it is corrected, 2) new or changed requirements ("requirements creep"), and 3) modified designs as more effective or efficient implementations are found. Once a software product has been baselined (approved), any change to that product should have its own "mini life cycle," including testing. Testing of a changed software product requires additional effort. Not only should it demonstrate that the change was implemented correctly, testing should also demonstrate that the change did not adversely impact other parts of the software product. Regression analysis and testing are employed to provide assurance that a change has not created problems elsewhere in the software product. Regression analysis is the determination of the impact of a change based on review of the relevant documentation (e.g., software requirements specification, software design specification, source code, test plans, test cases, test scripts, etc.) in order to identify the necessary regression tests to be run. Regression testing is the rerunning of test cases that a program has previously executed correctly and comparing the current result to the previous result in order to detect unintended effects of a software change. Regression analysis and regression testing should also be employed when using integration methods to build a software product to ensure that newly integrated modules do not adversely impact the operation of previously integrated modules.

In order to provide a thorough and rigorous examination of a software product, development testing is typically organized into levels. As an example, a software product's testing can be organized into unit, integration, and system levels of testing.

Unit (module or component) level testing focuses on the early examination of sub-program functionality and ensures that functionality not visible at the system level is examined by testing. Unit testing ensures that quality software units are furnished for integration into the finished software product.

Integration level testing focuses on the transfer of data and control across a program's internal and external interfaces. External interfaces are those with other software (including operating system software), system hardware, and the users and can be described as communications links.

System level testing demonstrates that all specified functionality exists and that the software product is trustworthy. This testing verifies the as-built program's functionality and performance with respect to the requirements for the software product as exhibited on the specified operating platform(s). System level software testing addresses functional concerns and the following elements of a device's software that are related to the intended use(s):

- Security and privacy performance (e.g., function of encryption, security log reporting);
- Performance issues (e.g., response times, reliability measurements);
- Responses to stress conditions (e.g., behavior under maximum load, continuous use);
- Operation of internal and external security features;
- Effectiveness of recovery procedures, including disaster recovery;
- Usability;
- Compatibility with other software products;
- Behavior in each of the defined hardware configurations; and
- Accuracy of documentation.

Control measures (e.g., a traceability analysis) should be used to ensure that the intended coverage is achieved.

System level testing also exhibits the software product's behavior in the intended operating environment. The location of such testing is dependent upon the software developer's ability to produce the target operating environment(s). Test plans should identify the controls needed

6

Security Assessment & Testing

to ensure that the intended coverage is achieved and that proper documentation is prepared when planned system level testing is conducted at sites not directly controlled by the software developer.

Test procedures, test data, and test results should be documented in a manner permitting objective pass/fail decisions to be reached. They should also be suitable for review and objective decision making subsequent to running the test, and they should be suitable for use in any subsequent regression testing. Errors detected during testing should be logged, classified, reviewed, and resolved prior to release of the software. Software error data that is collected and analyzed during a development lifecycle may be used to determine the suitability of the software product for release for commercial distribution. Test reports should comply with the requirements of the corresponding test plans.

Enterprise software products are often complex. Software testing tools are frequently used to ensure consistency, thoroughness, and efficiency in the testing of such software products and to fulfill the requirements of the planned testing activities. These tools may include supporting software built in-house to facilitate unit (module) testing and subsequent integration testing (e.g., drivers and stubs) as well as commercial software testing tools. Such tools should have a degree of quality no less than the software product they are used to develop. Appropriate documentation providing evidence of the validation of these software tools for their intended use should be maintained.

As applied to software, the term maintenance does not mean the same as when applied to hardware. The operational maintenance of hardware and software are different because their failure/error mechanisms are different. Hardware maintenance typically includes preventive hardware maintenance actions, component replacement, and corrective changes. Software maintenance includes corrective, perfective, and adaptive maintenance but does not include preventive maintenance actions or software component replacement.

Changes made to correct errors and faults in the software are corrective maintenance. Changes made to the software to improve the performance, maintainability, or other attributes of the software system are perfective maintenance. Software changes to make the software system usable in a changed environment are adaptive maintenance.

When changes are made to a software system, either during initial development or during post release maintenance, sufficient regression analysis and testing should be conducted to demonstrate that portions of the software not involved in the change were not adversely impacted. This is in addition to testing that evaluates the correctness of the implemented change(s).

The specific validation effort necessary for each software change is determined by the type of change, the development products affected, and the impact of those products on the operation of the software. Careful and complete documentation of the design structure and interrelationships of various modules, interfaces, etc., can limit the validation effort needed when a change is made. The level of effort needed to fully validate a change is also dependent upon the degree to which validation of the original software was documented and archived. For example, test documentation, test cases, and results of previous verification and validation testing need to be archived if they are to be available for performing subsequent regression testing. Failure to archive this information for later use can significantly increase the level of effort and expense of revalidating the software after a change is made.

In addition to software verification and validation tasks that are part of the standard software development process, the following additional maintenance tasks should be addressed:

- ***Software Validation Plan Revision*** – For software that was previously validated, the existing software validation plan should be revised to support the validation of the revised software. If no previous software validation plan exists, it should be established to support the validation of the revised software.

- ***Anomaly Evaluation*** – Software organizations frequently maintain documentation, such as software problem reports that describe software anomalies discovered and the specific corrective action taken to fix each anomaly. Too often, however, mistakes are repeated because software developers do not take the next step to determine the root causes of problems and make the process and procedural changes needed to avoid recurrence of the problem. Software anomalies should be evaluated in terms of their severity and their effects on system operation and safety, but they should also be treated as symptoms of process deficiencies in the quality system. A root cause analysis of anomalies can identify specific quality system deficiencies. Where trends are identified (e.g., recurrence of similar software anomalies), appropriate corrective and preventive actions must be implemented and documented to avoid further recurrence of similar quality problems.

- ***Problem Identification and Resolution Tracking*** – All problems discovered during maintenance of the software should be documented. The resolution of each problem should be tracked to ensure it is fixed, for historical reference, and for trending.

- ***Proposed Change Assessment*** – All proposed modifications, enhancements, or additions should be assessed to determine the effect each change would have on the system. This information should determine the extent to which verification and validation tasks need to be iterated.

- ***Task Iteration*** – For approved software changes, all necessary verification and validation tasks should be performed to ensure that planned changes are implemented correctly, all documentation is complete and up to date, and no unacceptable changes have occurred in software performance.

- ***Documentation Updating*** – Documentation should be carefully reviewed to determine which documents have been impacted by a change. All approved documents (e.g., specifications, test procedures, user manuals, etc.) that have been affected should be updated in accordance with configuration management procedures. Specifications should be updated before any maintenance and software changes are made.

Negative Testing/Misuse Case Testing

There are two main testing strategies in software testing: positive testing and negative testing.

Positive testing determines that your application works as expected. If an error is encountered during positive testing, the test fails.

Negative testing ensures that your application can gracefully handle invalid input or unexpected user behavior. For example, if a user tries to type a letter in a numeric field, the correct behavior in this case would be to display the "Incorrect data type, please enter a number" message. The purpose of negative testing is to detect such situations and prevent applications from crashing. In addition, negative testing helps to improve the quality of the application and find its weak points. A core difference exists between positive testing and negative testing: Throwing an exception is expected in negative testing. When you perform negative testing, exceptions are expected – they indicate that the application handles improper user behavior correctly. It is generally considered a good practice to combine both the positive and the negative testing approaches. This strategy provides higher tested application coverage as compared to using only one of the specified testing methodologies.

Typical Negative Testing Scenarios

Negative testing is aimed at detecting possible application crashes in different situations. Below are several possible examples of such situations:

- **Populating Required Fields** – Some applications and webpages contain fields that are marked as required. To check an application's behavior, create a test that leaves the required fields empty and analyzes the tested application's response. For example, the application can show a message box requesting a user to populate an appropriate field. After that, your test must interpret the application's behavior as correct when working with invalid data.

- **Correspondence between Data and Field Types** – Typically, dialog boxes and forms contain controls that can accept data of a specific type (for example, numeric, date, text, etc.). To verify if the application functions properly, you can create a test that enters incorrect data into a control, for example, a test that enters a letter into an UpDown edit box or the value of 13/33/2016 to a date field.

- **Allowed Number of Characters** – Some applications and webpages contain fields allowing a limited number of characters to be entered; for example, the value of the User Name field for applications and webpages must contain less than 50 characters. To check the behavior of the application, create a test that enters more characters into the field than is allowed.

- **Allowed Data Bounds and Limits** – Applications can use input fields that accept data in a certain range. For example, there can be an edit box into which you enter an integer number from 10 to 50 or an edit box that accepts text of a specific length. To check the application's behavior, create a negative test that enters a value smaller than the lower bound or greater than the upper bound of the specified field. Another example of this negative test case is entering data that exceeds the data type limits. For instance, an integer value can normally contain values in the range of -2,132,4735,6231.. 4,147,4832,6475 (the size is limited by the number of bytes in memory). To check the application's behavior, you can create a negative test that enters a value exceeding the bounds. For instance, the test can enter a large number (100,000,000,000) into an integer field.

- **Reasonable Data** – Some applications and webpages include fields that have a reasonable limit; for example, entering 200 or a negative number as the value for the "Your age:" field is not allowed. To check the application's behavior, create a negative test that enters invalid data into the specified field.

- **Web Session Testing** – Some Web browsers require that you log in before the first webpage is opened. To check that these browsers function correctly, create a test that tries to open webpages in the tested application without logging in.

The security practitioner needs to have a general understanding of the uses of negative testing in order to ensure that the proper type of testing is being done against applications and systems that are in production and also for those being considered for production deployment.

Use cases are abstract episodes of interaction between a system and its environment. A use case characterizes a way of using a system or a dialog that a system and its environment may share as they interact. A scenario is a description of a specific interaction between particular individuals. A use case abstracts scenarios that are instances of the same kind of interaction between a system and its actors. A misuse case is simply a use case from the point of view of an actor hostile to the system under design. Misuse cases turn out to have many possible applications and to interact with use cases in interesting and helpful ways. Security requirements exist because people and agents that they create (such as computer viruses) pose real threats to systems. Security differs from all other specification areas as someone is deliberately threatening to break the system. Employing use and misuse cases to model and analyze scenarios in systems under design can improve security by helping to mitigate threats.

Some misuse cases occur in highly specific situations, whereas others continually threaten systems. For instance, a car is most likely to be stolen when parked and unattended, whereas a Web server might suffer a denial-of-service attack at any time. You can develop misuse and use cases recursively, going from system to subsystem levels or lower as necessary. Lower-level cases can highlight aspects not considered at higher levels, possibly forcing another analysis. The approach offers rich possibilities for exploring, understanding, and validating the requirements in any direction. Drawing the agents and misuse cases explicitly helps to focus the attention of the security practitioner on the elements of the scenario.

Interface Testing

Integration testing involves the testing of the different components of an application, e.g., software and hardware, in combination. This kind of combination testing is done to ensure that they are working correctly and conforming to the requirements based on which they were designed and developed.

Interface testing is different from integration testing in that interface testing is done to check that the different components of the application or system being developed are in sync with each other or not. In technical terms, interface testing helps determine that different functions like data transfer between the different elements in the system are happening according to the way they were designed to happen.

Interface testing is one of the most important software tests in assuring the quality of software products. Interface testing is conducted to evaluate whether systems or components pass data and control correctly to one another. It is usually performed by both testing and development teams. Interface testing helps to determine which application areas are accessed and their user-friendliness as well, and it can be used to check and verify:

- If all the interactions between the application and a server are executed properly.
- If errors are being handled properly.
- What happens if a user interrupts any transaction.
- What happens if a connection to a Web server is reset.

With regards to the server interface, testing can establish the following:

- Verify that communication is done correctly, Web server-application server to application server-database server, and vice versa.
- Compatibility of server software, hardware, network connections

Security Assessment & Testing

With regards to the external interface, testing can establish the following:

- Have all supported browsers been tested?
- Have all error conditions related to external interfaces been tested when the external application is unavailable or the server is inaccessible?

With regards to the internal interface, testing can establish the following:

- If the site uses plug-ins, can the site still be used without them?
- Can all linked documents be supported/opened on all platforms (e.g., can Microsoft Word be opened on Solaris)?
- Are failures handled if there are errors during download?
- Can users use copy/paste functionality?
- Are you able to submit unencrypted form data?
- If the system does crash, are the re-start and recovery mechanisms efficient and reliable?
- If we leave the site in the middle of a task, does it cancel?
- If we lose our Internet connection, does the transaction cancel?
- How is a browser crash handled?
- Has the development team implemented intelligent error handling?

A moderator is often tasked to undertake this quality assurance test. Throughout the process, he does not need to communicate anything to the end-user. Rather, he will only be documenting or recording the reaction of the user towards the application. At the session's end, he interviews the end-users and endorses their feedback to the software developer. This way, interface testing improves the software's overall acceptance and the consumer's user experience. Factors like functionality, performance speed, the time needed to use the program, the ease with which the user remembers using the program, user satisfaction, and the rate of user errors are the usual criteria that developers have for a well-designed user interface.

Common Software Vulnerabilities

"We don't know what we don't know."

That old adage sums up the biggest problem that the security professional faces. We do not know what it is that we are unaware of. More importantly, we usually only will become aware of the unknown directly after it has caused us harm.

The 2011 CWE/SANS Top 25 Most Dangerous Software Errors is a list of the most widespread and critical errors that can lead to serious vulnerabilities in software. They are often easy to find and easy to exploit. They are dangerous because they will frequently allow attackers to completely take over the software, steal data, or prevent the software from working at all.[3]

Category-Based View of the Top 25

This section sorts the entries into the following three high-level categories:

- Insecure Interaction between Components
- Risky Resource Management
- Porous Defenses

---

3   See the following for the main landing page for the listing: http://cwe.mitre.org/top25/

Insecure Interaction between Components

These weaknesses are related to insecure ways in which data is sent and received between separate components, modules, programs, processes, threads, or systems. For each weakness, its ranking in the general list is provided in square brackets.

Rank	CWE ID	Name
[1]	CWE-89	Improper Neutralization of Special Elements Used in an SQL Command ('SQL Injection')
[2]	CWE-78	Improper Neutralization of Special Elements Used in an OS Command ('OS Command Injection')
[4]	CWE-79	Improper Neutralization of Input during Webpage Generation ('Cross-site Scripting')
[9]	CWE-434	Unrestricted Upload of File with Dangerous Type
[12]	CWE-352	Cross-Site Request Forgery (CSRF)
[22]	CWE-601	URL Redirection to Untrusted Site ('Open Redirect')

Risky Resource Management

The weaknesses in this category are related to ways in which software does not properly manage the creation, usage, transfer, or destruction of important system resources.

Rank	CWE ID	Name
[3]	CWE-120	Buffer Copy without Checking Size of Input ('Classic Buffer Overflow')
[13]	CWE-22	Improper Limitation of a Pathname to a Restricted Directory ('Path Traversal')
[14]	CWE-494	Download of Code without Integrity Check
[16]	CWE-829	Inclusion of Functionality from Untrusted Control Sphere
[18]	CWE-676	Use of Potentially Dangerous Function
[20]	CWE-131	Incorrect Calculation of Buffer Size
[23]	CWE-134	Uncontrolled Format String
[24]	CWE-190	Integer Overflow or Wraparound

6

Security Assessment & Testing

Porous Defenses

The weaknesses in this category are related to defensive techniques that are often misused, abused, or just plain ignored.

Rank	CWE ID	Name
[5]	CWE-306	Missing Authentication for Critical Function
[6]	CWE-862	Missing Authorization
[7]	CWE-798	Use of Hard-coded Credentials
[8]	CWE-311	Missing Encryption of Sensitive Data
[10]	CWE-807	Reliance on Untrusted Inputs in a Security Decision
[11]	CWE-250	Execution with Unnecessary Privileges
[15]	CWE-863	Incorrect Authorization
[17]	CWE-732	Incorrect Permission Assignment for Critical Resource
[19]	CWE-327	Use of a Broken or Risky Cryptographic Algorithm
[21]	CWE-307	Improper Restriction of Excessive Authentication Attempts
[25]	CWE-759	Use of a One-Way Hash without a Salt

In addition to the Top 25 list, the SANS Critical Security Controls list is another valuable resource for the security professional in this area, specifically, Control number 6, Application Software Security. This control is designed to manage the security lifecycle of all in-house developed and acquired software in order to prevent, detect, and correct security weaknesses.[4]

How to Implement This Control

ID #	Description	Category
CSC 6-1 (NEW)	For all acquired application software, check that the version you are using is still supported by the vendor. If not, update to the most current version and install all relevant patches and vendor security recommendations.	Quick Win
CSC 6-2	Protect Web applications by deploying Web application firewalls (WAFs) that inspect all traffic flowing to the Web application for common Web application attacks, including but not limited to cross-site scripting, SQL injection, command injection, and directory traversal attacks. For applications that are not Web based, specific application firewalls should be deployed if such tools are available for the given application type. If the traffic is encrypted, the device should either sit behind the encryption or be capable of decrypting the traffic prior to analysis. If neither option is appropriate, a host-based Web application firewall should be deployed.	Quick Win
CSC 6-3	For in-house developed software, ensure that explicit error checking is performed and documented for all input, including for size, data type, and acceptable ranges or formats.	Visibility/ Attribution

---

4   See the following for the main landing page for the control: http://www.sans.org/critical-security-controls/control/6

ID #	Description	Category
CSC 6-4	Test in-house-developed and third-party-procured Web applications for common security weaknesses using automated remote Web application scanners prior to deployment, whenever updates are made to the application, and on a regular recurring basis. Include tests for application behavior under denial-of-service or resource exhaustion attacks.	Visibility/ Attribution
CSC 6-5	Do not display system error messages to end-users (output sanitization).	Visibility/ Attribution
CSC 6-6	Maintain separate environments for production and nonproduction systems. Developers should not typically have unmonitored access to production environments.	Visibility/ Attribution
CSC 6-7	Test in-house-developed Web and other application software for coding errors and potential vulnerabilities prior to deployment using automated static code analysis software as well as manual testing and inspection. In particular, input validation and output encoding routines of application software should be reviewed and tested.	Configuration/ Hygiene
CSC 6-8 (NEW)	For acquired application software, examine the product security process of the vendor (history of vulnerabilities, customer notification, patching/ remediation) as part of the overall enterprise risk management process.	Configuration/ Hygiene
CSC 6-9	For applications that rely on a database, use standard hardening configuration templates. All systems that are part of critical business processes should also be tested.	Configuration/ Hygiene
CSC 6-10	Ensure that all software development personnel receive training in writing secure code for their specific development environment.	Configuration/ Hygiene
CSC 6-11	For in-house developed applications, ensure that development artifacts (sample data and scripts; unused libraries, components, debug code; or tools) are not included in the deployed software or accessible in the production environment.	Configuration/ Hygiene

The security professional may also want to delve deeper into the specifics of how to implement and manage one or more of the aspects of the control discussed above. The following resources will assist in that effort:

- https://buildsecurityin.us-cert.gov/
- https://www.owasp.org/index.php/Main_Page

Collect Security Process Data

Information security continuous monitoring (ISCM) is defined as maintaining ongoing awareness of information security, vulnerabilities, and threats to support organizational risk management decisions. Any effort or process intended to support ongoing monitoring of information security across an organization must begin with senior leadership defining a comprehensive ISCM strategy encompassing technology, processes, procedures, operating environments, and people. This strategy:

- Is grounded in a clear understanding of organizational risk tolerance and helps officials set priorities and manage risk consistently throughout the organization;
- Includes metrics that provide meaningful indications of security status at all organizational tiers;
- Ensures continued effectiveness of all security controls;

6

Security Assessment & Testing

- Verifies compliance with information security requirements derived from organizational missions/business functions, federal legislation, directives, regulations, policies, and standards/guidelines;
- Is informed by all organizational IT assets and helps to maintain visibility into the security of the assets;
- Ensures knowledge and control of changes to organizational systems and environments of operation; and
- Maintains awareness of threats and vulnerabilities.

An ISCM program is established to collect information in accordance with pre-established metrics, utilizing information readily available in part through implemented security controls. Organizational officials collect and analyze the data regularly and as often as needed to manage risk as appropriate for each area of the enterprise. This process involves the entire organization, from senior leaders providing governance and strategic vision to individuals developing, implementing, and operating individual systems in support of the organization's core missions and business processes. Subsequently, determinations are made from an organizational perspective on whether to conduct mitigation activities or to reject, transfer, or accept risk.

Organizations' security architectures, operational security capabilities, and monitoring processes will improve and mature over time to better respond to the dynamic threat and vulnerability landscape. An organization's ISCM strategy and program are routinely reviewed for relevance and are revised as needed to increase visibility into assets and awareness of vulnerabilities. This further enables data-driven control of the security of an organization's information infrastructure and increases organizational resilience.

Organization-wide risk monitoring cannot be efficiently achieved through manual processes alone or through automated processes alone. Where manual processes are used, the processes are repeatable and verifiable to enable consistent implementation. Automated processes, including the use of automated support tools (e.g., vulnerability scanning tools, network scanning devices), can make the process of continuous monitoring more cost-effective, consistent, and efficient. Many of the technical security controls defined in NIST Special Publication (SP) 800-53r4, Security Controls for Federal Information Systems and Organizations, are good candidates for monitoring using automated tools and techniques.[5] Realtime monitoring of implemented technical controls using automated tools can provide an organization with a dynamic view of the effectiveness of those controls and the security posture of the organization. It is important to recognize that with any comprehensive information security program, all implemented security controls, including management and operational controls, must be regularly assessed for effectiveness, even if the monitoring of such controls cannot be automated or is not easily automated.

The process for developing an ISCM strategy and implementing an ISCM program is as follows:

- Define an ISCM strategy based on risk tolerance that maintains clear visibility into assets, awareness of vulnerabilities, up-to-date threat information, and mission/business impacts.
- Establish an ISCM program determining metrics, status monitoring frequencies, control assessment frequencies, and establish an ISCM technical architecture.

---

5   http://nvlpubs.nist.gov/nistpubs/SpecialPublications/NIST.SP.800-53r4.pdf

- Implement an ISCM program and collect the security-related information required for metrics, assessments, and reporting. Automate collection, analysis, and reporting of data where possible.
- Analyze the data collected and report findings, determining the appropriate response. It may be necessary to collect additional information to clarify or supplement existing monitoring data.
- Respond to findings with technical, management, and operational mitigating activities or acceptance, transference/sharing, or avoidance/rejection.
- Review and update the monitoring program, adjusting the ISCM strategy and maturing measurement capabilities to increase visibility into assets and awareness of vulnerabilities, further enable data-driven control of the security of an organization's information infrastructure, and increase organizational resilience.

Security architects, security professionals and security practitioners all need to work together to play a part in determining what metrics are to be used to evaluate and control ongoing risk to the organization. Metrics, which include all the security-related information from assessments and monitoring produced by automated tools and manual procedures, are organized into meaningful information to support decision-making and reporting requirements. Metrics should be derived from specific objectives that will maintain or improve security posture. Metrics are developed for system-level data to make it meaningful in the context of mission/business or organizational risk management.

Metrics may use security-related information acquired at different times and therefore with varying levels of data latency. Metrics may be calculated from a combination of security status monitoring, security control assessment data, and from data collected from one or more security controls. The following shows some examples of metrics:

- The number and severity of vulnerabilities revealed and remediated
- Number of unauthorized access attempts
- Configuration baseline information
- Contingency plan testing dates and results
- The number of employees who are current on awareness training requirements
- Risk tolerance thresholds for organizations
- The risk score associated with a given system configuration

The security professional needs to be aware of the fact that metrics are fundamentally flawed without assurance that all security controls are implemented correctly. Metrics are defined or calculated in accordance with output from the security architecture. Collecting metrics from a security architecture with security controls that have not been assessed is equivalent to using a broken or uncalibrated scale. The interpretation of metrics data presumes that controls directly and indirectly used in the metric calculation are implemented and working as anticipated. If a metric indicates a problem, the root cause could be any number of things. Without fundamental assurance of correct implementation and continued effectiveness of security controls that are not associated with the metric, the root cause analysis is going to be hampered, and the analysis may be inappropriately narrowed to a predetermined list, causing the security practitioner to overlook the true problem.

6

Security Assessment & Testing

According to NIST SP 800-137, Information Security Continuous Monitoring (ISCM) for Federal Information Systems and Organizations, the security practitioner needs to take the following criteria into consideration when establishing monitoring frequencies for metrics or assessment frequencies for security controls: [6]

- **Security Control Volatility** – Volatile security controls are assessed more frequently, whether the objective is establishing security control effectiveness or supporting calculation of a metric. Controls in the NIST SP 800-53 Configuration Management (CM) family are a good example of volatile controls. Information system configurations typically experience high rates of change. Unauthorized or unanalyzed changes in the system configuration can render the system vulnerable to exploits. Therefore, corresponding controls such as CM-6, Configuration Settings, and CM-8, Information System Component Inventory, may require assessment that is more frequent and monitoring, preferably using automated, SCAP-validated tools that provide alerts and status on demand. Conversely, controls such as PS-2, Position Categorization, or PS-3, Personnel Screening, (from the NIST SP 800-53 Personnel Security family of controls) are not volatile in most organizational settings. They tend to remain static over long periods and would therefore typically require less frequent assessment.

- **System Categorizations/Impact Levels** – In general, security controls implemented on systems that are categorized as high-impact are monitored more frequently than controls implemented on moderate-impact systems, which are in turn monitored more frequently than controls implemented on low-impact systems.

- **Security Controls or Specific Assessment Objects Providing Critical Functions** – Security controls or assessment objects that provide critical security functions (e.g., log management server, firewalls) are candidates for more frequent monitoring. Additionally, individual assessment objects that support critical security functions are deemed critical to the system (in accordance with the Business Impact Analysis).[7]

- **Security Controls with Identified Weaknesses** – Existing risks documented in security assessment reports (SARs) are considered for more frequent monitoring to ensure that risks stay within tolerance. Note that not all weaknesses require the same level of monitoring. For example, weaknesses deemed in the SAR to be of minor or low-impact risk to the system or organization are monitored less frequently than a weakness with a higher-impact risk to the system or organization.

- **Organizational Risk Tolerance** – Organizations with a low tolerance for risk (e.g., organizations that process, store, or transmit large amounts of proprietary and/or personally identifiable information (PII), organizations with numerous high-impact systems, organizations facing specific persistent threats) monitor more frequently than organizations with a higher tolerance for risk (e.g., organizations with primarily low- and moderate-impact systems that process, store, or transmit very little PII and/or proprietary information).[8]

---

6   http://csrc.nist.gov/publications/nistpubs/800-137/SP800-137-Final.pdf

7   See the following: http://csrc.nist.gov/publications/nistpubs/800-34-rev1/sp800-34-rev1_errata-Nov11-2010.pdf

8   See the following for an overview of how to address risk in the enterprise: http://csrc.nist.gov/publications/nistpubs/800-39/SP800-39-final.pdf

- **Threat Information** – Organizations consider current credible threat information, including known exploits and attack patterns.
- **Vulnerability Information** – Organizations consider current vulnerability information with respect to information technology products when establishing monitoring frequencies. For instance, if a specific product manufacturer provides software patches monthly, an organization might consider conducting vulnerability scans on that product at least that often.
- **Risk Assessment Results** – Results from organizational and/or system-specific assessments of risk (either formal or informal) are examined and taken into consideration when establishing monitoring frequencies. If a risk scoring scheme is in place at the organization, the risk scores may be used as justification to increase or decrease the monitoring frequencies of related controls.
- **Reporting Requirements** – Reporting requirements do not drive the ISCM strategy but may play a role in the frequency of monitoring. For instance, if the organizational policy requires quarterly reports on the number of unauthorized components detected and corrective actions taken, the organization would monitor the system for unauthorized components at least quarterly.

The security professional needs to establish a procedure for reviewing and modifying all aspects of the ISCM strategy, including relevance of the overall strategy, accuracy in reflecting organizational risk tolerance, accuracy/correctness of measurements, and applicability of metrics, reporting requirements, and monitoring and assessment frequencies. If any of the data collected is not required for reporting purposes or found to be not useful in maintaining or improving the organization's security posture, then the organization should consider saving resources by discontinuing that particular collection. Factors precipitating changes in the monitoring strategy may include but are not limited to:

- Changes to core missions or business processes;
- Significant changes in the enterprise architecture (including addition or removal of systems);
- Changes in organizational risk tolerance;
- Changes in threat information;
- Changes in vulnerability information;
- Changes within information systems (including changes in categorization/impact level);
- Trend analyses of status reporting output;
- New laws or regulations; and
- Changes to reporting requirements.

A robust ISCM program thus enables organizations to move from compliance-driven risk management to data-driven risk management providing organizations with information necessary to support risk response decisions, security status information, and ongoing insight into security control effectiveness. An ISCM program helps to ensure that deployed security controls continue to be effective and that operations remain within stated organizational risk tolerances in light of the inevitable changes that occur over time. In cases where security controls are determined to be inadequate, ISCM programs facilitate prioritized security response actions based on risk.

ISCM, a critical step in an organization's Risk Management Framework (RMF), gives organizational officials access to security-related information on demand, enabling timely risk management decisions, including authorization decisions. Frequent updates to security plans, security assessment reports, plans of action and milestones, hardware and software inventories, and other system information are also supported. ISCM is most effective when automated mechanisms are employed where possible for data collection and reporting. Effectiveness is further enhanced when the output is formatted to provide information that is specific, measurable, actionable, relevant, and timely.

Internal and Third-Party Audits

Some regulations require audits. For example, in the U.S., federal agencies are subject to the Federal Information Security Management Act (FISMA). FISMA requires agencies to self-audit and have an independent auditor review their information security implementation at least annually. The information security professional needs to understand that while the requirements outlined in laws and standards provide protection, they are rarely sufficient to ensure full protection or risk management of an information system. The information security professional must ensure proper scoping and tailoring get the appropriate number of controls at the correct level for the target system.

Organizations are increasingly outsourcing systems, business processes, and data processing to service providers in an effort to focus on core competencies, reduce costs, and more quickly deploy new application functionality. As a result, user organizations are updating their processes for monitoring their outsourced vendor relationships and managing the risks associated with outsourcing. Historically, many organizations have relied upon Statement on Auditing Standards (SAS) 70 reports to gain broad comfort over outsourced activities. However, SAS 70 was intended to focus specifically on risks related to internal control over financial reporting (ICOFR) and not broader objectives such as system availability and security. With the retirement of the SAS 70 report in 2011, a new breed of Service Organization Control (SOC) reports has been defined to replace SAS 70 reports and more clearly address the assurance needs of the users of outsourced services.

SOC Reporting Options

In the past, the SAS 70 report was intended to assist service organizations' users and their auditors in the context of a financial statement audit. Now, three types of SOC reports have been defined to replace SAS 70 and address a broader set of specific user needs—such as addressing security, privacy, and availability concerns. Additionally, service organizations are looking for better ways to provide assurance over their control environments.

SOC Report Types

SOC reports most commonly cover the design and effectiveness of controls for a 12-month period of activity with continuous coverage from year to year to meet user requirements from a financial reporting or governance perspective. In some cases, a SOC report may cover a shorter period of time, such as six months, if the system/service has not been in operation for a full year or if annual reporting is insufficient to meet user needs. A SOC report may also cover only the design of controls at a specified point in time for a new system/service or for the initial examination (audit) of a system/service.

Period of time reports covering design and operating effectiveness are generally referred to as "Type 2" reports, whereas point in time reports covering design are generally referred to as "Type 1" reports. For example, if an organization required a period of time report covering Security and Availability for a particular system, the organization would request a SOC 2 Type 2 Security and Availability report from the service provider. If the organization required a period of time report covering ICOFR controls for a particular system, the organization would request a SOC 1 Type 2 report of that system from the service provider. Table 6-1 compares and contrasts the required focus, scope, and control domains covered by SOC 2/SOC 3 versus SOC 1 reports.

	Internal Control Over Financial Reporting (ICOFR)	Operational Controls	
	SOC 1 *(Sometimes also referred to as an SSAE 16, AT 801, or ISAE 3402 report)*	**SOC 2**	**SOC 3** *(Sometimes also referred to as a SysTrust, WebTrust, or Trust Services report)*
Summary	Detailed report for users & their auditors.	Detailed report for users, their auditors, & specified parties.	Short report that can be more generally distributed, with the option of using a website seal.
Applicability	Focused on financial reporting risks and controls specified by the service provider. Most applicable when the service provider performs financial transaction processing or supports transaction processing systems.	Focused on: · Security · Availability · Confidentiality · Processing Integrity · Privacy	

Table 6-1 – **Required focus, scope, and control domains covered by SOC 2/SOC 3 versus SOC 1 reports**

SOC 2/SOC 3 Principles

SOC 2 and SOC 3 reports use the Trust Services Principles and Criteria, a set of specific requirements developed by the American Institute of Certified Public Accountants (AICPA) and Canadian Institute of Chartered Accountants (CICA) to provide assurance beyond ICOFR. Principles and criteria are specifically defined for security, availability, confidentiality, processing integrity, and privacy. This has been done in a modular way so that a SOC 2 or SOC 3 report could cover one or more of the principles depending on the needs of the service provider and its users.

In contrast, SOC 1 reports require a service organization to describe its system and define its control objectives and controls that are relevant to users' internal control over financial reporting. A SOC 1 report generally should not cover services or control domains that are not relevant to users from an ICOFR perspective, and it specifically cannot cover topics such as disaster recovery and privacy.

6

Security Assessment & Testing

775

SOC 2/SOC 3 Criteria

For first-time SOC 2 reports, starting with the security principle is often the most practical approach. Security is the most common area of user focus, and the security criteria in large part form the foundation for the other Trust Services Principles. In addition, the security criteria are relatively consistent with the requirements of other security frameworks such as ISO 27001. If the organization already has a security program based on a standard such as ISO 27001 or if it historically completed a SAS 70 examination that covered IT controls at a detailed level, many of the security criteria topics may already be addressed.

Security
- IT security policy
- Security awareness and communication
- Risk assessment
- Logical access
- Physical access
- Security monitoring
- User authentication
- Incident management
- Asset classification and management
- Systems development and maintenance
- Personnel security
- Configuration management
- Change management
- Monitoring and compliance

Building upon security, availability is also a frequent area of enterprise focus given increasing business dependencies on the availability of outsourced systems and the desire for assurance regarding system availability SLAs. The topics covered by the security and availability principles and criteria are:

Availability
- Availability policy
- Backup and restoration
- Environmental controls
- Disaster recovery
- Business continuity management

Principles and criteria are also established for confidentiality, processing integrity, and privacy with the covered topics summarized below. Whereas the security criteria provide assurance regarding the service provider's security controls, the confidentiality criteria can be used to provide additional detail regarding processes specifically for protecting confidential information.

Confidentiality

- Confidentiality policy
- Confidentiality of inputs
- Confidentiality of data processing
- Confidentiality of outputs
- Information disclosures (including third parties)
- Confidentiality of information in systems development

The processing integrity criteria can be used to provide assurance regarding a wide range of system processing beyond processing that would be relevant to users from purely an ICOFR perspective and where users cannot gain such assurance through other means, such as monitoring processes.

Processing Integrity

- System processing integrity policies
- Completeness, accuracy, timeliness, and authorization of inputs, system processing, and outputs
- Information tracing from source to disposition

The privacy criteria can be used to provide assurance regarding the effectiveness of a privacy program's controls. The security professional needs to be aware of the fact that this can be a complex area for organizations with multiple service offerings and geographically diverse users. Even more so than with the other criteria areas, significant preparation is typically required before completing a SOC 2 report including the privacy principle.

Privacy

- Management
- Notice
- Choice and consent
- Collection
- Use and retention
- Access
- Disclosure to third parties
- Quality
- Monitoring and enforcement

The security professional will also want to take note of the following:

- A cloud-based ERP service historically would have provided a SAS 70 report because it provided a core financial reporting service to users. It is likely that it would continue to provide a SOC 1 report for that same reason. However, it may also have a need to provide a SOC 2 or SOC 3 security and availability report to address user assurance needs specific to cloud services.
- Many data center colocation providers have historically completed SAS 70 examinations limited to physical and environmental security controls. However, most data center providers host much more than just customers' financial systems. As a result, leading providers are moving toward SOC 2 security reporting. Some service providers incorporate supporting environmental security controls within their SOC 2 security report, whereas others also address the availability criteria depending on the nature of their services.

6

Security Assessment & Testing

- For IT systems management, which can include general IT services provided to a portfolio of users as well as customized services provided to specific users, SOC 1 or SOC 2 reporting could be applicable, depending on whether users' assurance needs are more focused on ICOFR or security/availability.

At the other end of the spectrum, there are services that are operational and technology focused with very little, if any, direct connection to users' ICOFR. For example, these types of outsourced services are unlikely to be included within a public company's Sarbanes-Oxley (SOX) 404 scope. Users of these services are typically most concerned about security of their data, and availability of these systems, which can be addressed by a SOC 2 or SOC 3 report covering security and availability. Where applicable, SOC 2/SOC 3 reports can cover confidentiality, processing integrity, and privacy as well. SOC 2 is also potentially applicable for any organization that is storing and processing sensitive third-party data.

Where there is a need to demonstrate to third parties that effective security and confidentiality controls are in place to protect that information, SOC 2 and SOC 3 provide a mechanism for providing assurance. Through the system description in the report, the organization clearly describes the boundary of the "system", and the examination is then performed based on the defined Trust Services Criteria.

For service providers that have not previously completed an audit, there is typically a two-phase process to prepare for and complete the SOC 2/SOC 3 examination. The following listings summarize a phased approach for first-time audits. The security professionals should start with an Audit Preparation phase where they would collaborate with the service provider and provide guidance to set the stage for a successful audit. The Audit phase then builds upon the understanding of the service provider's architecture and controls that are established in the Audit Preparation phase.

Audit Preparation Phase
- Define audit scope and overall project timeline
- Identify existing or required controls through discussions with management, and review of available documentation
- Perform readiness review to identify gaps requiring management attention
- Communicate prioritized recommendations to address any identified gaps
- Hold working sessions to discuss alternatives and remediation plans
- Verify that gaps have been closed before beginning the formal audit phase
- Determine the most effective audit and reporting approach to address the service provider's external requirements

Audit Phase
- Provide overall project plan
- Complete advance data collection before on-site work to accelerate the audit process
- Conduct on-site meetings and testing
- Complete off-site analysis of collected information
- Conduct weekly reporting of project status and any identified issues
- Provide a draft report for management review and electronic and hard copies of the final report
- Provide an internal report for management containing any overall observations and recommendations for consideration

Point of View on the Use of SOC Reports

Historically, many organizations that use outsourced services have asked for SAS 70 reports. Few organizations understood or acknowledged that the SAS 70 report was designed for a specific purpose—to help users and their auditors to rely upon the controls over a service provider in the context of the users' financial statement and ICOFR audits. Many of these users were concerned about areas such as security, availability, and privacy with little or no regard for financial reporting implications. Despite the existence of other IT/security-focused assurance tools (e.g., WebTrust, SysTrust, ISO 27001, etc.) that were arguably better suited for the purpose, users continued to ask for SAS 70 reports, and service providers and their auditors accommodated.

With the replacement of the SAS 70 report with SOC reports, the professional guidance is now clear. The AICPA has also provided messaging to clearly explain the different types of SOC reports and where they are applicable. In the majority of cases, service providers that provide core financial processing services (e.g., payroll, transaction processing, asset management, etc.) moved to the SOC 1 report in 2011. IT service providers that have no impact or an indirect impact on users' financial reporting systems have started to move to the SOC 2 report. The SOC 3 report has been used where there is a need to communicate a level of assurance to a broad base of users without having to disclose detailed controls and test results. Some organizations may complete a combined SOC 2/SOC 3 examination with two reports geared for different constituencies.

Summary

The fundamental purpose of the "Security Assessment and Testing" domain is to provide the security architect, the security practitioner, and the security professional with the knowledge required by role to assist in managing the risks involved in developing, producing, operating, and sustaining systems and capabilities. Testing and Evaluation (T&E) measures progress in both system and capability development. T&E provides knowledge of system capabilities and limitations for use in improving the system performance and for optimizing system use in operations. T&E expertise must be brought to bear at the beginning of the system lifecycle to provide earlier learning about the strengths and weaknesses of the system under development. The goal is early identification of technical/system, operational, and managerial deficiencies so that appropriate and timely corrective actions can be developed prior to fielding the system. The creation of the test and evaluation strategy involves planning for technology development, including risk, evaluating the system design against mission requirements, and identifying where competitive prototyping and other evaluation techniques fit in the process.

In the end, the goal of the strategy is to identify, manage, and mitigate risk, which requires identifying the strengths and weaknesses of the system or service being provided to meet the end goal of the acquisition or development program. A test and evaluation strategy is a necessity today because of the addition of capabilities via incremental upgrades, which is now the norm, and the shift to a network-centric construct where data is separated from the applications; data is posted and made available before it is processed; collaboration is employed to make data understandable; and a rich set of network nodes and paths provide the required supporting infrastructure.

Domain 6: Review Questions

1. Real User Monitoring (RUM) is an approach to Web monitoring that?

    A. Aims to capture and analyze select transactions of every user of a website or application.

    B. Aims to capture and analyze every transaction of every user of a website or application.

    C. Aims to capture and analyze every transaction of select users of a website or application.

    D. Aims to capture and analyze select transactions of select users of a website or application.

2. Synthetic performance monitoring, sometimes called proactive monitoring, involves?

    A. Having external agents run scripted transactions against a web application.

    B. Having internal agents run scripted transactions against a web application.

    C. Having external agents run batch jobs against a web application.

    D. Having internal agents run batch jobs against a web application.

3. Most security vulnerabilities are caused by one? (**Choose ALL that apply**)

    A. Bad programming patterns

    B. Misconfiguration of security infrastructures

    C. Functional bugs in security infrastructures

    D. Design flaws in the documented processes

4. When selecting a security testing method or tool, the security practitioner needs to consider many different things, such as:

    A. Culture of the organization and likelihood of exposure

    B. Local annual frequency estimate (LAFE), and standard annual frequency estimate (SAFE)

    C. Security roles and responsibilities for staff

    D. Attack surface and supported technologies

6

Security Assessment & Testing

781

5. In the development stages where an application is not yet sufficiently mature enough to be able to be placed into a test environment, which of the following techniques are applicable: (**Choose ALL that apply**)

    A.   Static Source Code Analysis and Manual Code Review

    B.   Dynamic Source Code Analysis and Automatic Code Review

    C.   Static Binary Code Analysis and Manual Binary Review

    D.   Dynamic Binary Code Analysis and Static Binary Review

6. Software testing tenets include: (**Choose Two**)

    A.   Testers and coders use the same tools

    B.   There is independence from coding

    C.   The expected test outcome is unknown

    D.   A successful test is one that finds an error

7. Common structural coverage metrics include: (**Choose ALL that apply**)

    A.   Statement Coverage

    B.   Path Coverage

    C.   Asset Coverage

    D.   Dynamic Coverage

8. What are the two main testing strategies in software testing?

    A.   Positive and Dynamic

    B.   Static and Negative

    C.   Known and Recursive

    D.   Negative and Positive

9. What is the reason that an Information Security Continuous Monitoring (ISCM) program is established?

    A.   To monitor information in accordance with dynamic metrics, utilizing information readily available in part through implemented security controls

    B.   To collect information in accordance with pre-established metrics, utilizing information readily available in part through implemented security controls

    C.   To collect information in accordance with pre-established metrics, utilizing information readily available in part through planned security controls

    D.   To analyze information in accordance with test metrics, utilizing information readily available in part through implemented security controls

10. The process for developing an ISCM strategy and implementing an ISCM program is?

    A.   Define, analyze, implement, establish, respond, review and update

    B.   Analyze, implement, define, establish, respond, review and update

    C.   Define, establish, implement, analyze, respond, review and update

    D.   Implement, define, establish, analyze, respond, review and update

11. The NIST document that discusses the Information Security Continuous Monitoring (ISCM) program is?

    A.   NIST SP 800-121

    B.   NIST SP 800-65

    C.   NIST SP 800-53

    D.   NIST SP 800-137

12. A Service Organization Control (SOC) Report commonly covers a

    A.   6 month period

    B.   12 month period

    C.   18 month period

    D.   9 month period

6

Security Assessment & Testing

CISSP®

Domain 7
Security Operations

The Security Operations domain can be challenging. It is essentially two domains in one: operations security and security operations. Operations security is primarily concerned with the protection and control of information processing assets in centralized and distributed environments. Security operations are primarily concerned with the daily tasks required to keep security services operating reliably and efficiently. Operations security is a quality of other services and also a set of services in its own right. In addition, the concepts of business continuity planning (BCP) and disaster recovery planning (DRP) that address the preparation, processes, and practices required to ensure the preservation of the organization in the face of major disruptions to normal organization operations are discussed. BCP and DRP involve the identification, selection, implementation, testing, and updating of processes and specific prudent actions necessary to protect critical organization processes from the effects of major system and network disruptions and to ensure the timely restoration of organization operations if significant disruptions occur.

TOPICS

- ■ Investigations
  - ▫ Evidence collection handling
  - ▫ Reporting and documenting
  - ▫ Investigative techniques
  - ▫ Digital forensics
- ■ Investigation Types
  - ▫ Operational
  - ▫ Criminal
  - ▫ Civil
  - ▫ Regulatory
  - ▫ Electronic discovery (eDicsovery)
- ■ Logging and Monitoring
  - ▫ Intrusion detection and prevention
  - ▫ Security information and event management
  - ▫ Continuous monitoring
  - ▫ Egress monitoring
- ■ Provisioning of Resources
  - ▫ Asset inventory
  - ▫ Configuration management
  - ▫ Physical assets
  - ▫ Virtual assets
  - ▫ Cloud assets
  - ▫ Applications
- ■ Foundational Security Operations Concepts
  - ▫ Need-to-know/least privilege
  - ▫ Separation of duties and responsibilities
  - ▫ Monitor special privileges
  - ▫ Job rotation
  - ▫ Information lifecycle
  - ▫ Service-level agreements
- ■ Resource Protection Techniques
  - ▫ Media management
  - ▫ Hardware and software asset management
- ■ Incident Response
  - ▫ Detection
  - ▫ Response
  - ▫ Mitigation

- Reporting
- Recovery
- Remediation
- Lessons learned

- **Preventative Measures**
  - Firewalls
  - Intrusion detection and prevention systems
  - Whitelisting/Blacklisting
  - Third-party security services
  - Sandboxing
  - Honeypots/Honeynets
  - Anti-malware

- **Patch and Vulnerability Management**

- **Change Management Processes**

- **Recovery Strategies**
  - Backup storage strategies (e.g., offsite storage, electronic vaulting, tape rotating)
  - Recovery site strategies
  - Multiple processing sites (e.g., operationally redundant systems)
  - System resilience, high availability, quality of service, and fault tolerance

- **Disaster Recovery Processes**
  - Response
  - Personnel
  - Communications
  - Assessment
  - Restoration
  - Training and awareness

- **Disaster Recovery Plans**
  - Read through
  - Walk through
  - Simulation
  - Parallel
  - Full interruption

- **Business Continuity Planning and Exercising**

- **Physical Security**
  - Perimeter
  - Internal

- **Personnel Safety**

OBJECTIVES

According to the (ISC)² Candidate Information Bulletin (Exam Outline), a CISSP candidate is expected to be able to:

- Understand and support investigations.

- Understand requirements for investigation types.

- Conduct logging and monitoring activities.

- Secure the provisioning of resources.

- Understand and apply foundational security operations concepts.

- Employ resource protection techniques.

- Conduct incident response.

- Operate and maintain preventative measures.

- Implement and support patch and vulnerability management.

- Participate in and understand change management processes (e.g., versioning, baselining, security impact analysis).

- Implement recovery strategies.

- Implement disaster recovery processes.

- Test disaster recovery plan.

- Participate in business continuity planning and exercising.

- Implement and manage physical security.

- Participate in personnel safety (e.g., duress, travel, monitoring).

Investigations

One area that has traditionally been lacking in most organizations is proper evidence handling and management. The exact name given to this area ranges from computer forensics, digital forensics, and network forensics to electronic data discovery, cyber forensics, and forensic computing. For the sake of clarity, the term digital investigations will be used to encompass all the components expressed in the other terms mentioned; thus, no one definition will be provided. Instead, digital investigations will include all domains in which the evidence or potential evidence exists in a digital or electronic form, whether in storage or on the wire. We intentionally omit digital multimedia from the mix, as this is a related, yet highly differentiated, field within the umbrella of digital forensic science. Unlike the media depiction, computer forensics/digital investigations is not some piece of software or hardware. It is based on methodical, verifiable, and "auditable" sets of procedures and protocols.

Digital investigations fall under the larger domain of digital forensic science. In 2008, the American Academy of Forensic Sciences (AAFS) in the United States formally recognized digital forensic science as a discipline under the category of Digital and Multimedia Sciences; it was the first time in 28 years that a new section had been recognized by the AAFS. The Digital Forensic Science Research Workshop (DFRWS) defines digital forensic science as:

> *"The use of scientifically derived and proven methods toward the preservation, collection, validation, identification, analysis, interpretation, documentation and presentation of digital evidence derived from digital sources for the purpose of facilitating or furthering the reconstruction of events found to be criminal, or helping to anticipate unauthorized actions shown to be disruptive to planned operations." As a forensic discipline, this area deals with evidence and the legal system and is really the marriage of computer science, information technology, and engineering with law. The inclusion of the law introduces concepts that may be foreign to many security practitioners and security professionals. These include crime scene, chain of custody, best evidence, admissibility requirements, rules of evidence, etc. It is extremely important that anyone who may potentially be involved in an investigation is familiar with the basics of dealing with and managing evidence. There is nothing worse than finding the proverbial smoking gun only to learn that the evidence cannot be used, will be suppressed, or, even worse, the information security professional has violated the rights of the individuals in question and is now in worse trouble than the "bad guys." Although different countries and legal systems have slight variations in determining how evidence and the digital crime scene should be handled, there are enough commonalities that a general discussion is possible.[1]*

Like incident response, there are various computer forensics guidelines (e.g., International Organization of Computer Evidence (IOCE), Scientific Working Group on Digital Evidence (SWGDE), Association of Chief Police Officers (ACPO)). These guidelines formalize the computer forensic processes by breaking them into numerous phases or steps. A generic guideline would include the following areas of focus and practice:

---

1   http://www.dfrws.org/index.shtml

- **Identifying Evidence** – Correctly identifying the crime scene, evidence, and potential containers of evidence.
- **Collecting or Acquiring Evidence** – Adhering to the criminalistic principles and ensuring that the contamination and the destruction of the scene are kept to a minimum. Using sound, repeatable, collection techniques that allow for the demonstration of the accuracy and integrity of evidence or copies of evidence.
- **Examining or Analyzing the Evidence** – Using sound scientific methods to determine the characteristics of the evidence, conducting comparison for individuation of evidence, and conducting event reconstruction.
- **Presentation of Findings** – Interpreting the output from the examination and analysis based on findings of fact and articulating these in a format appropriate for the intended audience (e.g., court brief, executive memo, report).

The Crime Scene

Before the security professional can begin to identify evidence, the larger crime scene needs to be dealt with. A crime scene is nothing more than the environment in which potential evidence may exist. The same holds for a digital crime scene. The principles of criminalistics apply in both cases:

1. Identify the scene
2. Protect the environment
3. Identify evidence and potential sources of evidence
4. Collect evidence
5. Minimize the degree of contamination

With digital crime scenes, the environment consists of both the physical and the virtual, or cyber. The physical (e.g., server, workstation, laptop, smartphone, digital music device, tablet) is relatively straightforward to deal with; the virtual is more complicated because it is often more difficult to determine the exact location of the evidence (e.g., data on a cluster or GRID, or storage area networks (SANs)) or acquire the evidence, as is the case with "live" systems.

Live evidence is data that are dynamic and exist in running processes or other volatile locations (e.g., system/device RAM) that disappear in a relatively short time once the system is powered down. It is also more difficult for the security professional to protect the virtual scene. The crime scene can provide additional information related to whom or what might be responsible for the attack or incident.

Locard's exchange principle states that when a crime is committed, the perpetrators leave something behind and take something with them, hence the exchange.[2] This principle allows us to identify aspects of the persons responsible, even with a purely digital crime scene. As with traditional investigations, understanding the means, opportunity, and motives (MOM), as well as the modus operandi (MO [method of operation] or the way the crime was committed), allows for a more thorough investigation or root cause analysis. Identifying the root cause correctly and quickly is extremely important when dealing with an incident, whether it is criminal or not.

---

2   See the following for a full discussion of Dr. Edmond Locard and the Locard Principle:
      http://www.forensichandbook.com/locards-exchange-principle/

Criminologists, sociologists, and psychologists generally agree that behavior is intentional and serves to fulfill some purpose (e.g., need fulfillment). Criminal behavior is no different, and thus neither is criminal computer behavior. Computer criminals and hackers rarely have significant differences related to motivation for attacking systems. Like traditional criminals, computer criminals have specific MOs (e.g., hacking software, type of system or network attacked) and leave behind signature behaviors (e.g., programming syntax, email messages, bragging notices) that can be used to identify the attacker (or at least the tool), link other criminal behaviors together, and provide insight into the thought processes of the attackers. This information can be extremely useful in the event of an insider attack because it can be used during the interview process to solicit more accurate responses from the accused. With an external attack, the information can assist law enforcement in piecing together other offenses by the same individual, assist in the interview and interrogation process, and provide strategies at trial when the accused will be the most defensive.

Given the importance of the evidence that is available at a crime scene, only those individuals with knowledge of basic crime scene analysis should be allowed to deal with the scene. The logical choice will be members of the incident response or handling teams. The need for a formal approach to this task, coupled with very thorough documentation, is essential. So too is the ability to deal with a scene in a manner that minimizes the amount of disruption, contamination, or destruction of evidence. Once a scene has been contaminated, there is no undo or redo button to push; the damage is done. In many jurisdictions, the accused or opposing party has the right to conduct its own examination and analysis, requiring as original a scene as possible.

General Guidelines

Most seasoned digital investigators have mixed emotions regarding detailed guidelines for dealing with an investigation. The common concern is that too much detail and formalism will lead to rigid checklists and negatively affect the creative aspects of the analysis and examination. Too little formalism and methodology leads to sloppiness, difficulty in recreating the investigative process, and the lack of an "auditable" process that can be examined by the courts. In response to this issue, several international entities (e.g., Scientific Working Group on Digital Evidence (SWGDE)) have devised general guidelines that are based on the IOCE/Group of 8 Nations (G8) principles for computer forensics and digital/electronic evidence:[3]

- When dealing with digital evidence, one must apply all of the general forensic and procedural principles.
- Upon seizing digital evidence, actions taken should not change that evidence.
- When it is necessary for a person to access original digital evidence, that person should be trained for the purpose.
- All activity relating to the seizure, access, storage, or transfer of digital evidence must be fully documented, preserved, and available for review.
- An individual is responsible for all actions taken with respect to digital evidence while the digital evidence is in his possession.
- Any agency that is responsible for seizing, accessing, storing, or transferring digital evidence is responsible for compliance with these principles.

---

3   Read more about SWGDE here: https://swgde.org/

These principles form the foundation for the current international models most prominent today (e.g., United States National Institute of Standards and Technology (NIST), United States Department of Justice (DOJ)/ Federal Bureau of Investigations (FBI) Search and Seizure Manual, NIST SP 800-86: Computer Forensic Guidelines, SWGDE Best Practices for Computer Forensics, ACPO Good Practices Guide for Computer Based Evidence, IACIS forensic examination procedures). These models are also responsive to the prevailing requirements of the court systems and updated on a frequent basis.

The sagest advice that can be given to anyone involved in a computer forensics investigation or any form of incident response is to act ethically, in good faith, attempt to do no harm, and do not exceed one's knowledge, skills, and abilities. The following "rules of thumb" were developed by the Australian Computer Emergency Response Team (AusCERT) and should be a part of an investigator's methodology:

- Minimize handling/corruption of original data.
- Account for any changes and keep detailed logs of your actions.
- Comply with the five rules of evidence.
- Do not exceed your knowledge.
- Follow your local security policy and obtain written permission.
- Capture as accurate an image of the system as possible.
- Be prepared to testify.
- Ensure your actions are repeatable.
- Work fast.
- Proceed from volatile to persistent evidence.
- Do not run any programs on the affected system.

It is important for the security architect, the security practitioner, and the security professional to all stay up to date with the latest techniques, tools, processes, and requirements for admissibility of evidence. The entire area of computer forensics is coming under increased scrutiny by both the courts and the public and will undergo significant changes in the next few years as the field matures and develops, as did other more traditional forensic disciplines, such as DNA and latent fingerprint analysis.

For a more in-depth look at the world of Cyber Forensics and its impact on the Information Security Specialist, please see the *Official (ISC)² Guide to the CCFP CBK*. While this book targets the Certified Cyber Forensics Professional and candidates for the exam, it is also an authoritative reference and research book for all matters in the Cyber Forensics arena.

Policy, Roles, and Responsibilities

To have effective and efficient incident handling, an organization must possess a solid foundation of knowledge and policy. In this instance, the foundation is comprised of a corporate incident handling and response policy, clearly articulated procedures and guidelines that take into consideration the various legal implications of reacting to incidents, and the management and handling of evidence (digital, physical, and document based). The policy must be clear, concise, and provide a mandate for the incident response/handling team to deal with any and all incidents. The policy must also provide direction for employees on the escalation process to follow when a potential incident is discovered and how various notifications, contacts, and liaisons with third-party entities, the media, government, and law enforcement authorities are to be notified, by whom, and in what manner.

A properly staffed and trained response team is also required; the team can be virtual or permanent, depending on the requirements of the organization. Virtual teams usually consist of individuals that, while assigned to the response team, have other regular duties and are only called upon if there is some need to start the incident handling capability. Some organizations have teams whose members are permanently assigned to the incident team and work in this capacity on a full-time basis. A third model can be described as a hybrid of the virtual and permanent, with certain core members permanently assigned to the incident team and others called up as necessary. A fourth model that some organizations are using would involve outsourced resources that are available "on-demand" for participation in an investigation or as members of a response team. These outsourced resources are kept available to the organization through some sort of retainer fee, monthly subscription, or maintenance fees that are paid by the organization during the contract period for the services.

Although the actual makeup of the response team depends upon the structure of the organization, there are core areas that need to be represented: legal department (in lieu of in-house legal counsel, arrangements should be made with external counsel), human resources, communications, executive management, physical/corporate security, internal audit, IS security, and IT. In addition, there needs to be representation by other pertinent business units as well as systems administrators and anyone else that can assist in the recovery and investigation of an incident. Once the team has been established, it must be trained and stay current with its training. This sounds easy enough at first glance, but the initial and ongoing training requires a budget and resources to cover for team members who are away at training; more than one organization has been stymied in its attempt to establish a response team because of the failure to anticipate realistic costs associated with training and education.

What has yet to be discussed or even hinted at is dealing with the public or the media. This is not an oversight, as the whole domain of public relations and communications is an extremely sensitive issue at the best of times. When an event becomes an incident, the proper handling of public disclosure can either compound the negative impact or, if handled correctly, provide an opportunity to engender public trust in the organization. This is why communications, human resources, and only properly trained and authorized individuals should handle the communications and external notification responsibilities within the response function of the organization. In some countries or jurisdictions, legislation exists (or is being contemplated) that requires organizations to publicly disclose when they reasonably believe there has been an incident that may have jeopardized someone's private or financial information. Obviously, denial and "no comment" are not an effective public relations strategy in today's information culture.

Incident Response

Incident response, or more precisely incident handling, has become one of the primary functions of the security department in most organizations, and thus of those professionals working in this capacity. This increased importance is a direct result of the fact that attacks against networks and information systems are evolving – total volume of attacks appear to be decreasing, yet the sophistication and attack vectors are changing. Although statistics related to the exact increase in volumes of attacks and the corresponding economic costs are impossible to calculate given the lack of universal reporting, the gross trends indicate significant changes in the last few years. The types of attacks seem to undergo almost continuous modifications. Today, spam, phishing scams, worms, spyware, distributed denial-of-service attacks (DDoS), botnets, and other imaginative yet malicious attacks and mutations inundate personal computers, networks, and corporate systems on a daily basis.

Historically, incident response has been precisely that, a reaction to a trigger event. Incident response in its simplest form is the practice of detecting a problem, determining its cause, minimizing the damage it causes, resolving the problem, and documenting each step of the response for future reference. Although reactive controls are obviously necessary, lessons learned from the various attacks against information systems worldwide make it painfully obvious that preventive controls as well as detective controls are also required if we are to have any hope of recovering or maintaining business operations. Although various entities have developed detailed models for incident handling (e.g., Computer Emergency Response Team Coordination Center (CERT/CC), AusCERT, Forum of Incident Response Teams (FIRST), NIST, British Computing Society, and Canadian Communications Security Establishment (CSE)), there is a common framework to these models. The framework consists of the following components:

- Creation of a response capability
- Incident handling and response
- Recovery and feedback

Incident Handling and Response

If the appropriate groundwork has been laid, the next phase is the actual handling of an incident. Although there are various definitions of what constitutes an incident (usually any event that has the potential to negatively affect the business or its assets), it is ultimately up to the organization to categorize events that warrant the activation of the incident response escalation process. In most cases, this is described in some level of detail in various policies and guidelines.

When an event becomes an incident, it is essential that a methodical approach be followed. This is necessary given the complexities of dealing with the dynamics of an incident; several tasks must be carried out in parallel as well as serially. Often the output of one phase or stage in the handling of an incident produces input for a subsequent phase. In some cases, previous steps need to be revisited in light of new information obtained as the investigation develops; the process should be viewed as iterative in nature. CERT/CC at Carnegie Melon University, one of the foremost authorities on incident response and incident handling, depicts the incident handling model as a circular process that feeds back into itself, thus capturing the various dynamics and dependencies of the incident lifecycle. The incident response and the handling phase can be broken down further into triage, investigation, containment, and analysis and tracking.[4]

Triage Phase

Regardless of what actual model of incident handling is adhered to, there is usually some trigger event that kick-starts the process. The consensus of the various models is that the first step is some type of triage process. A good analogy here (and one that is mentioned in several models) is that of a hospital emergency department receiving a new patient. Once the patient arrives, he or she is examined to determine the urgency of care required. Patients with life-threatening conditions receive priority, patients with less life-threatening conditions are placed

---

4   http://www.cert.org/incident-management/

into a queue, and patients with minor conditions may be directed to their own physicians or neighborhood clinics.

Triage encompasses the detection, identification, and notification sub-phases. Following the medical model, once an incident has been detected, an incident handler is tasked with the initial screening to determine the seriousness of the incident and to filter out false-positives. One of the most time-consuming aspects of information security can be dealing with false-positives (events that are incorrectly deemed to be incidents based on rules or some other rubric). If during the initial phase of the triage it is determined that it is a false-positive, the event is logged and the process returns to the pre-incident escalation level of readiness. However, if it is a real incident, then the next step is identifying or classifying the type of incident. This classification is dependent on the organization, but it is commonly based on a hierarchy beginning with the general classifiers (e.g., apparent source = internal versus external) and progressing to more granular or specific characteristics (e.g., worm versus spam). This categorization is used to determine the level of potential risk or criticality of the incident, which in turn is used to determine what notifications are required. Here again, the policies, procedures, and guidelines that were developed before the incident provide direction for the incident handler to follow.

It is important to recognize that in the triage phase, the initial detection can come from automated safeguards or security controls, from employees, or some other third party (e.g., National CERT). Often, the end-users will notice that their system is behaving oddly or that they have received some type of suspicious email that was not blocked by the controls. If the end-user is well educated and informed about the policy and procedures to follow when he notices something unusual or suspicious, the entire response escalation process becomes far more efficient and effective.

Investigative Phase

The next major phase deals directly with the analysis, interpretation, reaction, and recovery from an incident. Regardless of the specific model that is followed, the desired outcomes of this phase are to reduce the impact of the incident, identify the root cause, get back up and running in the shortest possible time, and prevent the incident from occurring again. All of this occurs against the backdrop of adhering to company policy, applicable laws and regulations, and proper evidence management and handling. This last point cannot be stressed enough. Various countries have enacted privacy laws that protect employees and others from frivolous monitoring of network and online activities by employers. Potential evidence must also be handled correctly according to rules of evidence and a chain of custody documented and maintained, or it runs the risk of being inadmissible in the case of civil or criminal sanctions or even as grounds for terminating someone's employment (see the "Computer Forensics" section).

Containment

After the notification, the next task is to contain the incident, which can be described with a medical analogy yet again: It is similar to quarantining a patient until the exact nature of the disease or pathogen is determined. This quarantining prevents an outbreak if it turns out that the cause was some infectious agent, and it allows medical staff to conduct directed analysis of the cause of the malady. In our case, the patient is a system, device, or subset of systems on the network. The containment is used to reduce the potential impact of the incident by reducing the number of other systems, devices, or network systems that can become infected.

The method of containment can vary depending on the category of the attack (e.g., external, worm), the asset affected (e.g., Web server, router), and the criticality of the data or the risk of infection to the rest of the network. Strategies include removing the system from the network by disconnecting it, virtually isolating the systems by way of network segmentation (e.g., switch, virtual local area network (VLAN)), or implementing a firewall or filtering router with the appropriate rule sets. It should be noted that in some cases, complete isolation or containment may not be a viable solution, or if the ultimate goal of the exercise is to track the event or capture additional evidence of further wrongdoing, other alternatives such as sniffing traffic and honeypots can be used. However, depending on the incident or attack, the act of containing a system can alert the attacker that he or she has been detected. This can result in the attacker deleting any trails he or she has left or, in extreme cases, escalating the damage in an attempt to overwhelm the victim's resources, thus allowing the attacker to escape or obfuscate the source of the attack.

While one is dealing with the process of containment, proper documentation and handling of any potential sources of evidence must be maintained. It is very difficult at the beginning of an incident to anticipate the outcome (e.g., criminal attack, error, or omission); therefore, operating under the highest standard or "burden of proof" is prudent. If it turns out to be a false alarm or something not worth pursuing, the documentation and data can be used for training purposes as well as for postmortem or post-incident debriefing purposes.

Analysis and Tracking

The next logical step after isolation or containment is to begin to examine and analyze what has occurred, with a focus on determining the root cause. The idea of root cause goes deeper than identifying only symptoms. It looks at what is the initial event in the cause – effect chain. Root cause analysis also attempts to determine the actual source and the point of entry into the network. Different models portray this step in various forms, but the ultimate goal is to obtain sufficient information to stop the current incident, prevent future "like" incidents from occurring, and identify what or whom is responsible. This stage requires a well-trained team of individuals with heterogeneous or eclectic skills and a solid understanding of the systems affected, as well as system and application vulnerabilities. The ability to read and parse through large log files is also a skill that is in high demand during this phase because log files from routers, switches, firewalls, Web servers, etc. are often the primary source of initial information. Secondary sources of information are artifacts. An artifact is any file, object, or data directly related to the incident or left behind or created as part of the attack.

As with any form of analysis, the security practitioner will need a combination of formal training and sufficient real-world applied experience to make appropriate interpretations without the luxury of an unlimited timeframe. A side benefit of containment is that it "buys you time." By containing the potential spread, one can gain a bit of breathing room to continue with the analysis and tracking in a controlled manner as opposed to the complete state of chaos that may ensue at the beginning of the incident response and handling process. One of the biggest enemies to the tracking process is the dynamic nature of many of the logs, both internal and external. Log files tend to have a very limited life expectancy, and depending upon the organization, logs may be purged or overwritten in as little as 24 hours, unless the organization has put a Security Information and Event Management (SIEM) system in place centrally to gather and archive logs from multiple systems. The proverbial clock starts ticking the minute the attack, worm, virus, etc. is launched, not necessarily at the point when it is first detected.

Tracking often takes place in parallel with the analysis and examination. When information is obtained, it is fed into the tracking process to weed out false leads or intentionally spoofed sources. To have effective tracking or trackback capabilities, it is extremely important that the organization or team has a good working relationship with other entities, such as Internet Service Providers (ISP), other response teams, and law enforcement. These relationships can expedite the tracking process, and needless, time-consuming hiccups can be avoided (e.g., not knowing whom to notify at the ISP to request log information). Today, many law enforcement agencies have specialized units dedicated to high-tech crime investigations, and these agencies can be extremely helpful in assisting with the tracking and tracing.

An important point to consider, as part of developing the incident handling policy and guidelines, is what to do once the root cause has been both identified and traced back to the source. As an aside, some policies forbid tracking and traceback and direct the response team to focus on the recovery and future prevention aspects. An alarming trend deals with the suggestion of striking back at the source. The ramifications regarding this are huge, not only legally but also ethically. Source addresses can be spoofed, and often the source turns out to be a compromised machine, one that the owner had no idea was compromised and being used in an illegal manner. Although it is tempting to seek revenge after being wronged, it is better to take the moral high ground and seek redress through the proper legal channels.

Recovery Phase

The next major category deals with recovery, repair, and prevention of the affected systems and assets. The goal of this phase is to get the business back up and running (in a worst-case scenario) or, in the best case, bring the affected systems back into production, being sensitive to other activities that may be happening in unison (e.g., tracking and traceback).

Once the root cause analysis has provided sufficient information, the recovery process should begin. The exact strategy and techniques used are dependent on the type of incident and the characteristics of the "patient." The important consideration is to recover in a manner that has the maximum likelihood of withstanding another directed incident. For instance, if the incident was caused by human error, then training may be the best mitigation technique to apply to prevent the same error from being repeated. However, if the incident was caused due to a configuration error or another system design weakness, then there is little to be gained by simply recovering a system or device to the same level that it was at before the incident because the probability that it will be attacked again is quite high. If it did not survive the first attack, it is not likely to survive a subsequent attack. The more prudent approach is to delay putting the system or device back into production until it is at least protected from the incident that affected it in the first place. This can be accomplished by upgrading the operating system, updating service packs, applying the appropriate patches (after they are thoroughly tested, of course), or, in more drastic cases, rebuilding the entire system or replacing the original with a different or newer product. Once the system or device appears to be ready to be reintroduced back into production, it should be tested for vulnerabilities and weaknesses. It is not advisable to have the same members who worked on the recovery and repair conduct this activity, to ensure some independence and objectivity. There is an abundance of first-rate vulnerability testing software, both open-source and retail software, available that can be used to test the systems.

As was stated earlier, incident response is a dynamic process, with very fuzzy lines between the various phases; often, these phases are conducted in parallel, and each has some natural dependencies on the other. Incident response and handling can be thought of as an iterative process that feeds back into itself until there is some form of closure to the incident.

What exactly constitutes incident closure is dependent upon a number of variables, the nature or category of the incident, the desired outcome of the organization (e.g., business resumption, prosecution, system restoration), and the success of the team in determining the root cause and source of the incident. It is advisable that the enterprise policy or guidelines contain some sort of checklist or metric by which the team can determine when an incident is to be closed. The security professional needs to be focused on what "closure" is defined as for incidents with the organization, driving towards acceptable definitions and instantiating them within policies and procedures for all to follow. This is especially important as organizations may be faced with multiple, overlapping incidents that are not clear and distinct from one another, causing confusion for the organization and the security actors who are responding to them.

Evidence Collection and Handling

Chain of Custody

Two concepts that are at the heart of dealing effectively with digital/electronic evidence, or any evidence for that matter, are the chain of custody and authenticity/integrity. The chain of custody refers to the who, what, when, where, and how the evidence was handled – from its identification through its entire lifecycle, which ends with destruction or permanent archiving. Any break in this chain can cast doubt on the integrity of the evidence and on the professionalism of those directly involved in either the investigation or the collection and handling of the evidence. The chain of custody requires following a formal process that is well documented and forms part of a standard operating procedure that is used in all cases, with no exceptions.

Ensuring the authenticity and integrity of evidence is critical. If the courts feel the evidence or its copies are not accurate or lack integrity, it is doubtful that the evidence or any information derived from the evidence will be admissible. The current protocol for demonstrating authenticity and integrity relies on hash functions that create unique numerical signatures that are sensitive to any bit changes, e.g., SHA-256. Currently, if these signatures match the original or have not changed since the original collection, the courts will accept that integrity has been established.

Interviewing

A delicate component of any investigation is the actual interview of witnesses and suspects. Before someone conducts any interview, it is paramount that appropriate policies be reviewed, management is notified, and corporate legal counsel is contacted.

While interviewing witnesses may seem like a straightforward process, care must be taken to avoid invalidating the process. Interviewing (or interrogation) is both an art and a science, and success relies on proper training, experience, and preparation. Witnesses can be easily influenced (often unconsciously), intimidated, or become uncooperative. Therefore, only properly trained and experienced personnel should conduct a witness interview.

Suspect interviewing is fraught with potential legal "land mines," and investigators need to keep in mind such concerns as due process, the rights of the individual being questioned, and literally any other considerations that may be unique to the organization, jurisdiction, or country. Any violations of policy, law, or other charter or constitutionally protected right of the suspect can lead to charges against the investigator, legal redress by the suspect (e.g., lawsuits against the company and the individuals conducting the interview), and the possible suppression of any evidence derived from the interview (e.g., written or verbal confessions).

It is prudent to never conduct an interview alone, and when possible, videotape the entire interview for later corroboration of events and context of the meeting. Information security professionals are strongly advised to seek expert assistance before conducting interviews. All interviews should be conducted under the supervision of a legal counsel.

Reporting and Documenting

Once an incident has been deemed closed, the incident handling process is not yet complete. One of the most important, yet overlooked, phases is the debriefing and feedback phase. It would be utopian to believe that despite having the best policy, team, etc., there is nothing to be learned from every incident that is handled. Issues invariably arise; accidents happen, or some previously unexpected variable creeps into the mix. As the saying goes, organizations often learn more from their mistakes than from their successes. This is why it is vital to have a formal process in place to document what worked well, what did not work well, and what was totally unexpected. The debriefing needs to include all the team members, including representatives from the various business units that may have been affected by the incident. The output from the feedback process should also be used to adapt or modify policy and guidelines.

A side benefit to the formalism of the debriefing/feedback is the ability to start collecting meaningful data that can be used to develop or track performance metrics for the response team. Metrics (e.g., number and type of incidents handled, mean time from detection of incident to closure) can be used when determining budget allocations, personnel requirements, and baselines, demonstrating due diligence and reasonableness, and for numerous other statistical purposes. One of the biggest challenges faced by security professionals is the ability to produce meaningful statistics and metrics specific to the organization or, at the very least, the industry in general. By formalizing a process for capturing data specific to the organization, the incident team can finally reverse this trend.

Understand Forensic Procedures

The exact requirements for the admissibility of evidence vary across legal systems and between different cases (e.g., criminal versus tort). At a more generic level, evidence should have some probative value, be relevant to the case at hand, and meet the following criteria (often called the five rules of evidence):

- Be authentic
- Be accurate
- Be complete
- Be convincing
- Be admissible

Digital or electronic evidence, although more fragile or volatile, must meet these criteria as well. What constitutes digital/electronic evidence is dependent on the investigation; do not rule out any possibilities until they can be positively discounted. With evidence, it is better to have and not need than vice versa. Given the variance that is possible, the axiom to follow here is check with the respective judiciary, attorneys, or officer of the court for specific admissibility requirements.

The dynamic nature of digital electronic evidence bears further comment. Unlike more traditional types of evidence (e.g., fingerprints, hair, fibers, bullet holes), digital/electronic evidence can be very fragile and can be erased, partially destroyed, or contaminated very easily, and, in some circumstances, without the investigator knowing this has occurred. This type of evidence may also have a short life span and must be collected very quickly (e.g., cache memory, primary/random access memory, swap space) and by order of volatility (i.e., most volatile first). Sufficient care must also be taken not to disturb the timeline or chronology of events. Although time stamps are best considered relative and easily forged, the investigator needs to ensure that any actions that could alter the chronology (e.g., examining a live file system or accessing a drive that has not been write protected) are recorded or, if possible, completely avoided.

Media Analysis

Media analysis involves the recovery of information or evidence from information media such as hard drives, DVDs, CD-ROMs or portable memory devices. This media may have been damaged, overwritten, degaussed, or reused to aid in hiding evidence or useful information. Numerous tools and techniques exist that can recover information from the media with differing success. Should a forensic image be required, the information security professional may need to enlist the help of a media recovery specialist. These specialists often work in clean rooms and can rebuild a drive if needed and maintain a chain of custody while doing it if needed. However, they are very expensive, so unless a forensically sound image is required, several other tools and techniques should be considered. [5]

Network Analysis

The term network forensics (analysis) was coined in 1997 by Marcus Ranum and refers to the analysis and examination of data from network logs and network activity for use as potential evidence.[6] (The original definition used the term investigation, but later authors amended this to "evidence" to emphasize the forensic aspect.) Like software forensics/analysis, network analysis or network forensics is now encompassed under the larger category of digital evidence.

The analysis of network activity is an innate function of any incident response situation, and the process model is identical to what has been previously discussed in the "Incident Response" section of this chapter. The critical features are proper evidence management and handling (i.e., chain of custody) with the concern that any derived evidence will be admissible in a legal proceeding.

---

5   Read more about Media Analysis here: http://www.cscjournals.org/csc/manuscript/Journals/IJS/volume3/Issue2/IJS-13.pdf

6   Simson Farfinkel, and Gene Spafford, Web Security, Privacy & Commerce, (O'Reilly Media, 2001) http://www.oreillynet.com/network/2002/04/26/nettap.html (accessed July 14, 2014).

Software Analysis

With the move toward a more generic term for investigations related to digital evidence, many of the historical sub areas have been subsumed under the category of "Digital Evidence." However, the field of software analysis or software forensics bears further discussion.

Software analysis or forensics refers to the analysis and examination of program code. The code being analyzed can take the form of source code, compiled code (binaries), or machine code. Decompiling and reverse engineering techniques are often used as part of the process. Software analysis encompasses such investigative activities as malware analysis, intellectual property disputes, copyright infringements, etc. The objectives of the analysis include author identification, content analysis (payload), and context analysis.

Author identification, or more precisely author attribution, involves attempts to determine who created or authored the software/program in question (was it an individual or group effort?). The code is examined for clues to programming style, program language, development toolkits used, embedded comments and addresses, etc. The underlying theory here is that writing code is similar to writing prose, and each author has a unique style and eccentricities that allow the investigator to discriminate between various potential suspects. This is very similar to the scientific field of questioned document analysis, and both areas use many of the same techniques.

Content analysis involves the systematic analysis of the purpose of the code. In the case of Trojan horse programs, for example, the focus would be on determining what the actual attack was meant to do, what and where files were installed or altered on the infected systems, what communications channels were opened (ingress and egress), the identification of any upstream destination addresses, what information was being sent or stored locally for batch uploads, etc.

Content analysis is also used in cases related to intellectual property disputes. In these instances, a pain staking examination of the source code or decompiled binary is used to determine the similarity between two programs. The investigator is often asked to provide an expert opinion on how similar the programs are and on what basis the opinion is based.

Context analysis deals with developing a meta-view of the impact of the suspicious software relative to the case or the environment it was found in. Understanding context can assist with the analysis and can be used to develop a realistic rating of the risk to the organization or victim.

Hardware/Embedded Device Analysis

The analysis of hardware and embedded devices often involves the analysis of mobile devices such as smartphones or personal digital assistants (PDAs.) The standard hardware and firmware found in a laptop or a desktop computer's motherboard such as the CMOS chip used to control basic functions will also need to be forensically imaged and then examined. Special tools and techniques are required to image embedded devices. The information security professional must understand that many embedded devices cannot be read or copied without altering the very information they wish to obtain. The U.S. National Institute of Standards and technology recommends the following: [7]

---

7   Read more about hardware and embedded forensics here: http://csrc.nist.gov/publications/nistpubs/800-72/sp800-72.pdf (Published, November 2004) http://nvlpubs.nist.gov/nistpubs/SpecialPublications/NIST.SP.800-101r1.pdf (Published, May 2014)

- No actions performed by investigators should change data contained on digital devices or storage media.
- Individuals accessing original data must be competent to do so and have the ability to explain their actions.
- An audit trail or other record of applied processes, suitable for independent third-party review, must be created and preserved, accurately documenting each investigative step.
- The person in charge of the investigation has overall responsibility for ensuring the above mentioned procedures are followed and incompliance with governing laws.
- Upon someone seizing digital evidence, actions taken should not change that evidence.
- When it is necessary for a person to access original digital evidence, that person must be forensically competent.
- All activity relating to the seizure, access, storage, or transfer of digital evidence must be fully documented, preserved, and available for review.
- An individual is responsible for all actions taken with respect to digital evidence while the digital evidence is in his or her possession.

Any agency that is responsible for seizing, accessing, storing, or transferring digital evidence is responsible for compliance with these principles.

Requirements for Investigation Types

A requirement is an expression of desired behavior. A requirement deals with objects or entities, the states they can be in, and the functions that are performed to change states or object characteristics. For example, suppose we are building a system to generate paychecks for our customer's company. One requirement may be that the checks be issued every two weeks. Another may be that direct deposit of an employee's check be allowed for each employee at a certain salary level or higher. The customer may request access to the paycheck system from several different company locations. All of these requirements are specific descriptions of functions or characteristics that address the general purpose of the system: to generate paychecks. Thus, we look for requirements that identify key entities ("an employee is a person who is paid by the company"), limit entities ("an employee may be paid for no more than 40 hours per week"), or define relationships among entities ("employee X is supervised by employee Y if Y can authorize a change to X's salary").

Note that none of these requirements specify how the system is to be implemented. There is no mention of what database management system to use, whether a client-server architecture will be employed, how much memory the computer is to have, or what programming language must be used to develop the system. These implementation-specific descriptions are not considered to be requirements (unless they are mandated by the customer). The goal of the requirements phase is to understand the customer's problems and needs. Thus, requirements focus on the customer and the problem, not on the solution or the implementation. We often say that requirements designate what behavior the customer wants, without saying how that behavior will be realized. Any discussion of a solution is premature until the problem is clearly defined.

Computer crime has been defined as "any illegal act fostered or facilitated by a computer, whether the computer is an object of a crime, an instrument used to commit a crime, or a repository of evidence related to a crime" (Royal Canadian Mounted Police, 2000). Some of the most prominent types include e-commerce fraud, child pornography trafficking, software piracy, and network security breaches. Investigative difficulties are introduced when attempting to tackle computer crime because of its generally technologically advanced nature, the fact that it can occur almost instantaneously, and because it is extremely difficult to observe, detect, or track. These problems are compounded by the relative anonymity afforded by the Internet as well as the transcendence of geographical and physical limitations in cyberspace, both of which render difficult the detection of criminals who are able to take advantage of a virtually limitless pool of victims.

Role of the First-Responder

The role of the first responder in computer crime cases is of critical import because the evidence associated with a computer crime is often intangible in nature. Certain precautions must be taken to ensure that data stored on a system or on removable media is not modified or deleted - either intentionally or accidentally. Even the simple shutting-down of a computer can change the last-modified or last-accessed timestamp of certain system files, which introduces questions associated with the integrity of the data. In sum, to preclude vulnerabilities in the prosecutor's case and to adequately defend against any related challenges, care must be exercised by first responders during the search and seizure of computer equipment.

Information, Instrumentation, and Interviewing

There are three components of the criminal investigation: information, instrumentation, and interviewing. While technology and technique might change, these fundamentals persist across time.

Information accumulation will continue to be the "bread-and-butter" of the investigation of computer crimes. Even the most adept investigator will encounter difficulties if information culled during the course of the investigation is incomplete or generally inapplicable. With this in mind though, the investigator should execute instrumentation and interviewing, which are simply other methods to gather information, in a distinctively different manner from the traditional investigative practices used by law enforcement outside of the realm of computer crime.

Instrumentation in investigating financially related crimes involving computer systems primarily revolves around the tracking and analysis of records and logs to determine discrepancies or irregularities in the normal order. For example, money laundering with the use of computers concerns the process of concealing the source of illegally obtained money and often involves the creation, fabrication, or alteration of documents to create a legitimate paper trail and history. Financial institutions are presumed to keep detailed records of all transactions, currency exchanges, and the international transportation of funds exceeding a certain amount. Additionally, the Bank Secrecy Act of 1970 requires these institutions to maintain records that have a high degree of usefulness in criminal, tax, and regulatory investigations and proceedings, and it authorizes the Treasury Department to require the reporting of suspicious financial activity that might be related to a law violation.

Before the exponential growth of the Internet, the investigation of credit card fraud often involved accurate identification by witnesses and the collection and identification of condemning physical evidence. When an offender made a purchase at a retail establishment through the use of a fraudulent credit card for payment, sales clerks and store employees trained in accurately observing and remembering physical and behavioral details of perpetrators were able to assist in the investigation. Catching an offender in possession of the fraudulently acquired merchandise was also easier because purchases were made in a physical location. Finally, the handwriting sample obtained when the goods were signed for, and fingerprints left at the scene of the crime, also served as corroborating evidence.

With the advent and growth of electronic commerce, however, the assistive role of witnesses and physical evidence – sources of information previously (and even heavily) relied upon – has now been largely eliminated. Combined with inter-jurisdictional complications, a deficiency of available investigatory resources, and the fact that these crimes occur in such an unconstrained and unregulated manner in cyberspace, the problem is further compounded for the security professional seeking to conduct an investigation. Investigators of computer crime must consequently pursue other avenues of inquiry and learn to master information retrieval from these sources.

The third component - interviewing - appears to be less salient as a direct method to investigate computer crime, largely because the victim is often unaware (either immediately or even for a great length of time) that a crime has occurred and that harm has resulted. Information useful in the solving of these cases is sometimes only identified after examining data on a computer system, and often the victim's only role in these investigations is to report the crime and provide access to the system. Furthermore, witnesses in computer crime are relatively rare because these offenses tend to occur behind closed doors. The only witnesses in most cases are those who commit the crimes either individually or collectively, and therefore other techniques to gather information must be utilized.

Interviewing, then, may provide indirect utility for the investigator, such as insight into the motives and possibly the specific techniques employed, particularly if the offender was an "insider." Coworkers of a possible suspect may provide useful secondary information in this regard while also outlining the capabilities of (and methods potentially used by) the individual to bypass access controls to commit the crime.

The manner in which evidence is procured in computer crime cases remains a sizable challenge for law enforcement. Specific information related to the computer system requiring search and possible seizure must be detailed in the warrant in order to be approved and also so that the prosecutor can counter any evidentiary challenges brought by the defense staff. Due to the uniqueness of search warrant applications for computer crimes, some states within the United States are specifically designating individual judges to deal with these specialized requests. Nonetheless, requests must still be presented in a manner that allows ease of comprehension. The judge must not be confused by the technical details associated with the investigation but should understand the nuances of what is involved so that the court can make an informed decision. The goal is to clearly articulate probable cause that a crime has been committed and that the items described in the warrant are related to that crime. Likewise, victims often use technological jargon to communicate the specifics of the victimization and possible sources, which may uncover stronger evidence that would hold substantive weight in a court of law.

Evidence Collection and Processing

In terms of evidentiary issues, many police agencies are employing technicians who can assist responding officers or detectives in the proper preservation, collection, and processing of evidence, as well as with interpretation and presentation of the technological details of crime commission.

Once evidence associated with a computer crime is lawfully discovered, multiple safeguards should be instituted to preserve its continuity and integrity. Attention must be given to the specifications on the search warrant so that all relevant items are properly and legally seized. Moreover, it is paramount to protect physical and removable media because of their sensitive nature. Magnetic fields and even static electricity have the potential to render certain electronic equipment, such as data storage devices or disks, as unusable and unreadable. Another critical point is that suspects in a case should be restricted from the computing environment because of the possibility that digital evidence might be altered or deleted.

Jurisdiction

Since national boundaries effectively disappear when considering many computer crimes, jurisdiction is another complicated matter. While a complete examination of jurisdictional issues is beyond the scope of this work, it merits comment that countries differ in civil and criminal offense standards, substantive and procedural law, data collection and preservation practices, and other evidentiary and juridical factors. Moreover, it is often ambiguous as to whose responsibility it is to address a particular crime or spearhead an investigation, or how best to collaborate through extradition and mutual assistance policies. This plays out not only on an international level but also within nations where multiple law enforcement departments are implicated. For example, as computer crime originating in the United States often implicates interstate and international laws, many cases fall under federal jurisdiction. Federal collaboration with local law enforcement and prosecutors to share intelligence and efforts through teamwork is required to effectively investigate and prosecute these cases.

Logging and Monitoring Activities through Intrusion Detection and Prevention and Security Information and Event Management (SIEM)

In the classic defense-in-depth model, a complete and secure access control environment employs multiple layers of policy, technology, and process working together to ensure that the desired security posture is maintained. Although firewalls, remote-access devices, applications, and innumerable other technical solutions play an integral role in access control, intrusion detection and prevention systems provide another important layer in a defense-in-depth strategy.

An intrusion detection system (IDS) is a technology that alerts organizations to adverse or unwanted activity. An IDS can be implemented as part of a network device, such as a router, switch, or firewall, or it can be a dedicated IDS device monitoring traffic as it traverses the network. When used in this way, it is referred to as a network IDS, or NIDS. An IDS can also be used on individual host systems to monitor and report on file, disk, and process activity on that host. When used in this way, it is referred to as a host-based IDS, or HIDS.

IDS attempts to detect activities on the network or host that are evidence of an attack and warn administrators or incident-response personnel of the discovery, but it does not take any action on the problems found. An organization may want more proactive responses when unusual traffic or activity is identified. The automated response capabilities of an IDS may vary based on its placement in the infrastructure and the existence and integration of other access control technologies. An IDS is informative by nature and provides real time information when suspicious activities are identified. It is primarily a detective device and, acting in this traditional role, is not used to directly prevent the suspected attack.

In contrast, an intrusion prevention system (IPS) is a technology that monitors activity like an IDS but will automatically take proactive preventative action if it detects unacceptable activity. An IPS permits a predetermined set of functions and actions to occur on a network or system; anything that is not permitted is considered unwanted activity and blocked. The IPS is engineered specifically to respond in real time to an event at the system or network layer. By proactively enforcing policy, IPS can thwart not only attackers but also authorized users attempting to perform an action that is not within policy. Fundamentally, IPS is considered an access control and policy enforcement technology, whereas IDS is considered network monitoring and audit technology.

It is important to understand that the distinction between IDS and IPS is growing thinner. Some IDS solutions are adopting preventative capabilities that allow them to act more proactively in the event of policy infringement. IPS systems are incorporating detection techniques to augment the policy enforcement capabilities. In fact, for many of today's product offerings, the move from IDS functions to IPS capabilities is as simple as selecting the "block" option when specifying activities of interest in the device.

A critical operational requirement for establishing IDS capabilities is the need to tune the IDS to the unique traffic patterns generated by the organization. For example, without proper tuning, the activity associated with a company's custom-developed application may appear to an IDS as unwanted or suspicious activity, forcing the generation of multiple alerts. It is equally problematic if the IDS is not tuned to notice the difference between a custom application's activities and those of a real attack, producing no alerts. Tuning an IDS is somewhat of an art form and can become a significant gap in security if not performed correctly, potentially rendering the system worthless. It then becomes a noisy box people begin to ignore, or it sits quietly as networks and systems are attacked. Given the complexity that tuning represents and the potential for excessive false positives or false negatives, automated responses generated from IDS alerts represent an operational risk many organizations deem unacceptable.

Security Information and Event Management

Security Information and Event Management (SIEM) is a term used to describe a group of technologies that aggregate information about access controls and selected system activity to store for analysis and correlation. Logs and system information may be collected for a variety of reasons including but not limited to:

- Regulation or compliance requirements
- Internal accountability and non-repudiation
- Risk management functions
- Performance monitoring and trending
- Event correlation and root cause analysis
- Incident response
- Investigations

SIEMs and log analysis tools are two areas rapidly merging into one functional space. In general, a SIEM has the following characteristics:

- Store raw information from various systems logs
- Aggregate the information in a single repository
- Normalize the information to make comparisons more meaningful
- Analytical tools that can process, map, and extract target information
- Alerting and reporting tools

SIEMs and the functions they provide are becoming indispensable to many organizations as they offer the ability to get "near real time" reporting on events and incidents as they occur in network and information systems. In spite of the insight and reporting provided, SIEMs can be extremely complex and expensive to implement and maintain. They are often the central data system and decision support system for the security operation centers (SOC) of large organizations. SIEM's also present an attractive target for attackers because these systems are not only the repositories for current health information about the organization's information systems but also are the systems often first turned to when there is suspicion of an attack or infiltration. The security practitioner and the security professional need to work together in order to ensure that the definitions for what will be monitored and what will be examined as a result within the system is decided on ahead of the deployment and implementation of a SIEM system. The biggest obstacle the organization will face with regards to a SIEM system is the ability to narrowly define the mission objectives for the system and ensure alignment with the strategic imperatives for the organization. While SIEMs offer a great advantage, they also require extensive protection to ensure they do not become a liability.

Continuous and Egress Monitoring

The security architect and the security practitioner both bear responsibility for aspects of a continuous monitoring program. The security architect needs to be able to design a continuous monitoring system that will meet the needs of the organization. The security practitioner needs to be able to implement the design that the security architect provides and to do so correctly in order to ensure that the organization's critical infrastructure is protected. An area of interest with regards to continuous monitoring that the security architect should become familiar with is Continuous Monitoring as a Service (CMaaS). The initial need for this service has been driven by the United States federal government's focus on cyber-defense and the infrastructure that is being built to service that need.

The General Services Administration (GSA), Federal Acquisition Service (FAS), Assisted Acquisition Services (AAS), Federal Systems Integration and Management Center (FEDSIM) offers the Department of Homeland Security (DHS) and all Federal Departments and Agencies (D/As), State, Local, Regional, and Tribal (SLRT) Governments access to a multiple-award Blanket Purchase Agreement (BPA) that offers Continuous Monitoring as a Service (CMaaS) related products, services, and solutions with cumulative, stair step pricing discounts. These BPAs were established on behalf of the DHS Office of Cybersecurity and Communications (CS&C), Continuous Diagnostics and Mitigation (CDM) Program.

The CDM Program helps transform the way federal and other government entities manage their cyber networks through strategically sourced tools and services, and it enhances the ability of government entities to strengthen the posture of their cyber networks. The CDM Program brings an enterprise approach to continuous diagnostics and allows consistent application of best practices.

The CDM Program will provide specialized information technology (IT) tools and CMaaS to combat cyber threats in the civilian ".gov" networks. The CDM approach moves away from historical compliance reporting and toward combating threats to the nation's networks on a real time basis. The tools and services delivered through the CDM Program will provide DHS, other Federal D/As, and SLRT governments with the ability to enhance and automate their existing continuous network monitoring capabilities, correlate and analyze critical security-related information, and enhance risk-based decision making at the agency and federal enterprise level. Information obtained from the automated monitoring tools will allow for the correlation and analysis of security-related information across the federal enterprise.

BPAs were awarded to the following 17 industry partners:

- Booz Allen Hamilton
- CGI
- CSC
- DMI
- DRC
- GDIT
- HPES
- IBM
- KCG
- Kratos
- Lockheed-Martin
- ManTech
- MicroTech
- Northrop-Grumman
- SAIC
- SRA
- Technica

A security architect or security practitioner that is looking to leverage a CMaaS solution for his or her enterprise architecture can look to any number of cloud services providers to examine their wide range of offerings.

An in-depth discussion of continuous monitoring can be found in the "Security Assessment & Testing" domain, in the section entitled "Collect security process data (e.g., management and operational controls), Management review and Key performance and risk indicators." This section details the necessary steps and procedures that the security practitioner will need to follow to successfully implement a continuous monitoring system for his or her organization.

Some additional resources for the security practitioner can be found below:

1. http://csrc.nist.gov/groups/SMA/fisma/documents/faq-continuous-monitoring.pdf
2. http://csrc.nist.gov/publications/nistpubs/800-137/SP800-137-Final.pdf
3. http://www.govinfosecurity.com/continuous-monitoring-c-326
4. http://gsa.gov/graphics/staffoffices/Continuous_Monitoring_Strategy_Guide_072712.pdf
5. http://www.gsa.gov/portal/content/176671?utm_source=FAS&utm_medium=print-radio&utm_term=cdm&utm_campaign=shortcuts

Egress Monitoring

Egress filtering is the practice of monitoring and potentially restricting the flow of information outbound from one network to another. Typically, it is the information flow from a private computer network to the Internet that is being monitored and controlled. TCP/IP packets that are being sent out of the internal network are examined via a router, firewall, or similar edge device. Packets that do not meet security policies are not allowed to leave the network. Egress filtering helps ensure that unauthorized or malicious traffic never leaves the internal network.

SIP— Session Initiation Protocol
(Internet Telephony + Internet Messaging)

For the security practitioner, the typical recommendations are that all traffic except that emerging from a pre-identified and screened set of servers would be denied egress. In addition, only select protocols such as HTTP/HTTPS, SMTP, and SIP are typically allowed transit access out of the network as well. As a result, end-user workstations would need to be configured either manually or via proxy auto-config to use one of the allowed servers as a proxy gateway for Internet access. This configuration has several benefits for the security architecture of the organization. It will allow for the tight control, monitoring, and auditing of network traffic, which is important for governance and compliance issues. It will allow for the ability to attribute certain traffic to end points and to individual users, which is important for non-repudiation and data integrity mechanisms. It will allow for the use of physical as well as logical control mechanisms to shape and manage network traffic and bandwidth, such as VLANs, PVLANs, and Quality of Service (QOS). Also, the ability to control and interdict traffic flows based on monitoring in this system can mean that DoS and DDoS attack vectors can be removed due to malware infection because the command and control traffic required to manage the infected computers can be denied egress at the border of the network.

However, both the security architect and security practitioner need to be aware of the potential liabilities associated with this type of system as well. The issues of Single Point of Failure (SPOF) due to incorrect architecture of the egress filtering systems can be a problem. In addition, the potential for a DoS attack or a DDoS attack to be able to be successfully launched against the enterprise may be significantly increased if the architecture is not vetted properly, preventing and blocking the appropriate ports that could be used to communicate the command and control traffic required to organize and deploy one or more bots from within the borders of the enterprise.

Enterprise networks also typically have a limited number of internal address blocks in use. An edge device at the boundary between the internal corporate network and external networks (such as the Internet) is used to perform egress checks against packets leaving the internal network, verifying that the source IP address in all outbound packets is within the range of allocated internal address blocks. The purpose is to prevent computers on the internal network from IP address spoofing. Such "spoofing" is a common technique used in denial-of-service attacks.

Egress filtering may require policy changes and administrative work whenever a new application requires external network access. The security practitioner will need to partner with the security professional to ensure that the appropriate adjustments are made to the security policies and procedures of the organization to reflect any required changes. In addition, security awareness training materials may also have to be updated to reflect these changes.

The security architect and the security professional would also need to be aware of standards-based regulations regarding egress filtering. For instance, PCI DSS compliance requires egress filtering from any server in the card holder environment.

Data Leak/Loss Prevention (DLP)

Data leak prevention (DLP) is a suite of technologies aimed at stemming the loss of sensitive information that occurs in the enterprise. By focusing on the location, classification, and monitoring of information at rest, in use, and in motion, this solution can go far in helping an enterprise get a handle on what information it has and in stopping the numerous leaks of information that are potentially occurring daily. The successful implementation of this technology requires significant preparation and diligent ongoing maintenance on the part of the security architect and the security practitioner. Enterprises seeking to integrate and implement DLP should be prepared for a significant effort that, if done correctly, can greatly reduce risk to the organization. Those implementing the solution must take a strategic approach that addresses risks, impacts, and mitigation steps, along with appropriate governance and assurance measures.

Defining Data Leak Prevention

Most DLP solutions include a suite of technologies that facilitates three key objectives:

1. Locate and catalog sensitive information stored throughout the enterprise.
2. Monitor and control the movement of sensitive information across enterprise networks.
3. Monitor and control the movement of sensitive information on end-user systems.

These objectives are associated with three primary states of information: data at rest, data in motion, and data in use. Each of these three states of data is addressed by a specific set of technologies provided by DLP solutions:

Data at Rest

A basic function of DLP solutions is the ability to identify and log where specific types of information are stored throughout the enterprise. This means that the DLP solution must have the ability to seek out and identify specific file types, such as spreadsheets and word processing documents, whether they are on file servers, storage area networks (SANs), or even end-point systems. Once found, the DLP solution must be able to open these files and scan their contents to determine whether specific pieces of information are present, such as credit card or social security numbers. To accomplish these tasks, most DLP systems utilize crawlers, which are applications that are deployed remotely to log onto each end system and "crawl" through data stores, searching for and logging the location of specific information sets based on a set of rules that have been entered into the DLP management console. Collecting this information is a valuable step in allowing the enterprise to determine where its key information is located, whether its location is permitted within existing policies, and what paths these data might travel that would violate information policies.

Data in Motion (Network)

To monitor data movement on enterprise networks, DLP solutions use specific network appliances or embedded technology to selectively capture and analyze network traffic. When files are sent across a network, they are typically broken up into packets. To inspect the information being sent across the network, the DLP solution must be able to:

1. Passively monitor the network traffic
2. Recognize the correct data streams to capture
3. Assemble the collected packets
4. Reconstruct the files carried in the data stream
5. Perform the same analysis that is done on the data at rest to determine whether any portion of the file contents is restricted by its rule set

At the core of this ability is a process known as deep packet inspection (DPI), which enables the DLP data-in-motion component to accomplish these tasks. DPI goes beyond the basic header information of a packet to read the contents within the packet's payload.

This DPI capability allows the DLP system to inspect data in transit and determine contents, source, and destination. If sensitive data are detected flowing to an unauthorized destination, the DLP solution has the capability to alert and optionally block the data flows in real or near real time, again based on the rule set defined within its central management component. Based on the rule set, the solution may also quarantine or encrypt the data in question. An important consideration for network DLP is that the data must be decrypted before the DLP solution can inspect the data. Either the DLP solution must have the capability to do this itself (by having this feature and the necessary encryption keys), or there must be a device that will decrypt the traffic prior to its inspection by the DLP module and re-encrypt once the data have been inspected and allowed to pass.

Data in Use (End Point)

Data in use is perhaps the most challenging aspect of DLP. Data in use primarily refers to monitoring data movement stemming from actions taken by end-users on their workstations, whether that would entail copying data to a thumb drive, sending information to a printer, or even cutting and pasting between applications. DLP solutions typically accomplish this through the use of a software program known as an agent, which is ideally controlled by the same central management capabilities of the overall DLP solution. Implementing rule sets on an end-user system has inherent limitations, the most significant being that the end-user system must be able to process the rule sets applied. Depending on the number and complexity of the rules being enforced, it may be necessary to implement only a portion of the entire rule set, which can leave significant gaps in the overall solution.

The capability to address the three states of information must exist and be integrated by a centralized management function in order for something to be considered a full DLP solution. The range of services available in the management console varies between products, but many, if not most, have the following functions in common:

- **Policy Creation and Management** – Policies (rule sets) dictate the actions taken by the various DLP components. Most DLP solutions come with preconfigured policies (rules) that map to common regulations. It is just as important to be able to customize these policies or build completely custom policies.
- **Directory Services Integration** – Integration with directory services allows the DLP console to map a network address to a named end-user.
- **Workflow Management** – Most full DLP solutions provide the capacity to configure incident handling, allowing the central management system to route specific incidents to the appropriate parties based on violation type, severity, user, and other such criteria.
- **Backup and Restore** – Backup and restore features allow for preservation of policies and other configuration settings.
- **Reporting** – A reporting function may be internal or may leverage external reporting tools.

Organizational Data Classification, Location, and Pathways

Enterprises are often unaware of all of the types and locations of information they possess. It is important, prior to purchasing a DLP solution, to identify and classify sensitive data types and their flow from system to system and to users. This process should yield a data taxonomy, or classification system, that will be leveraged by various DLP modules as they scan for and take action on information that falls into the various classifications within the taxonomy. Analysis of critical business processes should yield the required information. Classifications can include categories such as private customer or employee data, financial data, and intellectual property. Once the data have been identified and classified appropriately, further analysis of processes should facilitate the location of primary data stores and key data pathways. Frequently, multiple copies and variations of the same data are scattered across the enterprise on servers, individual workstations, tape, and other media. Copies are frequently made to facilitate application testing without first cleansing the data of sensitive content. Having a good idea of the data classifications and location of the primary data stores proves helpful in both the selection and placement of the DLP solution. Once the DLP solution is in place, it can assist in locating additional data locations and pathways.

It is also important to understand the enterprise's data lifecycle. Understanding the lifecycle from point of origin through processing, maintenance, storage, and disposal will help uncover further data repositories and transmission paths.

Additional information should be collected by conducting an inventory of all data egress points because not all business processes are documented and not all data movement is a result of an established process. Analysis of firewall and router rule sets can aid these efforts.

Some of the Organizational benefits derived from deploying a DLP solution include:

- **Protect critical business data and intellectual property:** The primary benefit of DLP is the protection of information that is critical for the organization. Enterprises maintain many types of information that they must protect for competitive, regulatory, and reputational reasons.
- **Improve compliance:** DLP can help an enterprise meet regulatory requirements related to protecting and monitoring data containing private customer and financial information. DLP solutions typically come with preconfigured rules that address data types impacted by significant regulations such as payment card industry (PCI), GLBA, and HIPAA. Leveraging these rule sets can simplify efforts to protect data impacted by these regulations.
- **Reduce data breach risk:** When a DLP solution reduces the risk of data leaks, the financial risk to the enterprise decreases.
- **Enhance training and awareness:** While most enterprises have written policies, such policies may be forgotten over time. DLP solutions alert, and at times block, data movement that is in violation of policy and provide an ongoing education component to help ensure that users maintain an awareness of policies associated with sensitive data.
- **Improve business processes:** One of the key intangibles of DLP is the development of new policies, controls, and testing that help identify broken business processes. Often, the step of simply assessing and cataloging business processes in preparation for a DLP implementation can provide great insights to the security actors in the enterprise.

- **Optimize disk space and network bandwidth:** An important benefit of DLP solutions is the identification of stagnant files and streaming videos that consume a large amount of IT resources such as storage on file servers and network bandwidth. Purging stale files and preventing nonbusiness-related streaming video files can reduce storage, backup, and bandwidth requirements.

- **Detect rogue/malicious software:** Another key intangible of DLP is identifying malicious software that attempts to transmit sensitive information via email or an Internet connection. Network DLP can help reduce the damage of malicious software by detecting rogue transmission of sensitive information outside the enterprise. This is not always guaranteed because the transmissions may be encrypted. But even in that case, a system that has a rule set that will alert or block data streams it cannot decrypt can prove to be a strong addition to malware defenses.

Steganography and Watermarking

Steganography is the science of hiding information. Whereas the goal of cryptography is to make data unreadable by a third party, the goal of steganography is to hide the data from a third party. With computers and networks, there are many ways of hiding information, such as:

- Covert channels
- Hidden text within webpages
- Hiding files in "plain sight" (what better place to hide a file than with an important sounding name in the c:\winnt\system32 directory?)
- Null ciphers (e.g., using the first letter of each word to form a hidden message in an otherwise innocuous text)

Steganography is significantly more sophisticated than the examples above suggest, allowing a user to hide large amounts of information within image and audio files. These forms of steganography often are used in conjunction with cryptography so that the information is doubly protected; first it is encrypted and then hidden so that an adversary has to first find the information (an often difficult task in and of itself) and then decrypt it.

There are a number of uses for steganography. One of the most widely used applications is for so-called digital watermarking. A watermark, historically, is the replication of an image, logo, or text on paper stock so that the source of the document can be at least partially authenticated. A digital watermark can accomplish the same function; graphic artists, for example, might post sample images on their website complete with an embedded signature so that they can later prove their ownership in case others attempt to portray the work as their own.

Steganographic Methods

The following formula provides a very generic description of the pieces of the steganographic process: [8]

```
cover_medium + hidden_data + stego_key = stego_medium
```

In this context, the cover_medium is the file in which you will hide the hidden_data, which may also be encrypted using the stego_key. The resultant file is the stego_medium (which will, of course. be the same type of file as the cover_medium). The cover_medium (and, thus, the stego_medium) are typically image or audio files.

---

8   See the following for the original work Steganography: Hiding Data Within Data by Gary C. Kessler, September 2001: http://www.garykessler.net/library/steganography.html

Provisioning of Resources through Configuration Management

The purpose of configuration management is to establish and maintain the integrity of the product, system, or item that is being managed throughout its lifecycle within the organization. Software configuration management involves identifying configuration items for the software project, controlling these configuration items and changes to them, and recording and reporting status and change activity for these configuration items. Configuration management (CM) refers to a discipline for evaluating, coordinating, approving or disapproving, and implementing changes in artifacts that are used to construct and maintain software systems. An artifact may be a piece of hardware or software or documentation. CM enables the management of artifacts from the initial concept through design, implementation, testing, baselining, building, release, and maintenance.

At its heart, CM is intended to eliminate the confusion and error brought about by the existence of different versions of artifacts. Changes are made to correct errors, provide enhancements, or simply reflect the evolutionary refinement of a product's operational definition. CM is about keeping the inevitable change that happens under control. Without a well-enforced CM process, different team members (possibly at different sites) can use different versions of artifacts unintentionally; individuals can create versions without the proper authority; and the wrong version of an artifact can be used inadvertently. Successful CM requires a well-defined and institutionalized set of policies and standards that clearly define:

- The set of artifacts (configuration items) under the jurisdiction of CM
- How artifacts are named
- How artifacts enter and leave the controlled set
- How an artifact under CM is allowed to change.
- How different versions of an artifact under CM are made available and under what conditions each one can be used
- How CM tools are used to enable and enforce CM

These policies and standards are documented in a CM plan that informs everyone in the organization just how CM is to be carried out

The CMMI steps for CM

SEI Capability Maturity Model Integration, Version 1.1 for Systems Engineering and Software Engineering (CMMI-SE/SW, V1.1) lists the following practices as instrumental for a CM capability in an organization [SEI 2000a]: [9]

1. Identify the configuration items, components, and related work products that will be placed under configuration management.
2. Establish and maintain a configuration management and change management system for controlling work products.
3. Create or release baselines for internal use and for delivery to the customer.
4. Track change requests for the configuration items.
5. Control changes in the content of configuration items.
6. Establish and maintain records describing configuration items.
7. Perform configuration audits to maintain the integrity of the configuration baselines.

---

9   https://www.sei.cmu.edu/productlines/frame_report/config.man.htm

The security practitioner and the security professional should both become familiar with configuration management and the steps required to implement a full configuration management system within the enterprise.

There are many categories of organizational assets that will benefit from the establishment of a full configuration management system. These include:

- Physical assets (e.g., servers, laptops, tablets, smartphones)
- Virtual assets (e.g., Software Defined Networks (SDNs), virtual SAN (vSAN) systems, virtual machines (VMs))
- Cloud assets (e.g., services, fabrics, storage networks, tenants)
- Applications (e.g., workloads in private clouds, Web services, Software as a Service (SaaS))

From the security professional's perspective, whatever categories of assets from the previous list that need to be put under configuration management are not as important as the answers to the following questions:

1. What are the requirements (legal, regulatory, business, governance, etc.) for the assets in question to be managed to?
2. Are there specific issues or concerns to be addressed based on the implementation or architecture of the assets?
3. Will there be more than one owner of the asset? If so, how many?
4. Who is/are the intended customer(s) for the asset?
5. When does the asset have to be available? (24x7, 9 to 5, Monday – Thursday, etc.)
6. How is the asset to be accessed and made available to the organization's customers?
7. Where will the asset reside? On the LAN? On the WAN in the Cloud? Will it be outsourced as a third party supported and provided solution? Will it be owned and maintained "in-house"?
8. Why is the asset being provisioned in the first place? What business need(s) is it designed to address?

The unique tools and configuration choices to be made to manage a specific asset are beyond the scope of the discussion here, as they are as varied as the assets themselves. What the security professional needs to be focused on with regards to the configuration management of assets in the enterprise is the ability to develop a deep understanding of the reasons that the asset is being deployed into the organization in the first place. By understanding the business objectives that the asset is being deployed to address, the security professional will be able to align to support those objectives in all areas of the enterprise architecture, ensuring that the asset is deployed successfully, as well as being managed successfully throughout its lifecycle in the enterprise.

TRY IT FOR YOURSELF

Most security professionals are not configuration managers by training. The need to understand configuration management and how to build and implement a configuration management plan is very important to the success of any asset management program in the organization. The Sample Configuration Management Plan document in Appendix H can also be downloaded for you to work with

It will walk you through a mythical project from the beginning and illustrate each step involved in the creation and deployment of a complete Configuration Management Plan for the enterprise. The plan can be adjusted to fit any organization, and as a result, it can be used as a template to drive the deployment of Configuration Management into your organization if necessary.

Foundational Security Operations Concepts

Key Themes

There are four main themes discussed in this section: maintaining operational resilience, protecting valuable assets, controlling system accounts, and managing security services effectively. Each of these themes is fundamental to operations security.

1. ***Maintaining Operational Resilience*** – When it comes to day-to-day operations, few things are more important than maintaining the expected levels of service availability and integrity. Organizations require critical services to be resilient. When negative events affect the organization, the operations staff is expected to ensure minimal disruption to the organization's activities. This includes anticipating such disruptions and ensuring that key systems are deployed and maintained to help ensure continuity. They are also expected to maintain processes and procedures to help ensure timely detection and response.

2. ***Protecting Valuable Assets*** – Security operations are expected to provide day-to-day protection for a wide variety of resources, including human and material assets. They may not be responsible for setting strategy or designing appropriate security solutions. At a minimum, they will be expected to maintain the controls that have been put into place to protect sensitive or critical resources from compromise.

3. ***Controlling System Accounts*** – Under the current regulatory environment, there has been a renewed focus on maintaining control over users (subjects) that have access to key business systems. In many cases, these subjects have extensive or unlimited capabilities on a given system; these are privileges that could be misused or abused. Operations security will be expected to provide checks and balances against privileged accounts as well as maintain processes that ensure that there continues to be a valid business need for them.

4. ***Managing Security Services Effectively*** – No security operations will be effective without strong service management and the processes that are put into place to ensure service consistency. These include key service management processes common to most IT services such as change, configuration, and problem management. It will also include security-specific procedures such as user provisioning and Help/Service Desk procedures. In today's security operations, there is also considerable focus on reporting and continuous service improvement practices. These themes are discussed in the detailed sections below.

Key Operational Processes and Procedures

Security operations is expected to play a valuable role in supporting and leveraging a number of processes and procedures intended to provide for smooth operations. They help to ensure that changes are implemented with appropriate review and approval, that IT resources are configured to provide steady and reliable services, that incidents are addressed quickly and effectively, and that problems are fixed. The security professional should be able to describe these processes at a high level and identify his or her role in them.

Controlling Privileged Accounts

Security operations must maintain strong control over the number and types of accounts used on systems. This requires careful supervision over the management of accounts that are given privileges on IT systems, such as service accounts and accounts used to execute scripts. Identity management controls the lifecycle process for every account in a system, from the provisioning of the account through to its eventual removal from the system. Access management refers to the assignment of rights or privileges to those accounts that will allow them to perform their intended function. Identity and access management (IAM) solutions focus on harmonizing the provisioning of users and managing their access across multiple systems with different native access control systems.[10] Within the "Security Operations" domain, the focus is on using these solutions most effectively while also ensuring that privileged accounts are carefully controlled and audited.

Need to-Know/Least Privilege

The principle of least privilege is one of the most fundamental characteristics of access control for meeting security objectives. Least privilege requires that a user or process be given no more access privilege than necessary to perform a job, task, or function. The objective is to limit users and processes to access only resources and tools necessary to perform assigned functions. This often requires limits not only on what resources can be accessed but also includes limiting the actions that can be performed by the user even if he or she has authorized access to the resource. For example, a user may be assigned read-only, update, and execute permissions on a system without the ability to create or delete files and databases. Ensuring least privilege requires identifying what the user's job is, determining the minimum set of privileges required to perform that job, and restricting the user to a domain with those privileges and nothing more. Denying users access privileges that are not necessary for the performance of their duties ensures that those privileges cannot be used to circumvent the organization's security policy.

A companion concept to least privilege is the principle of need to know.

---

10   For further information on Identity and Access Management (IAM) solutions, please see the following:
     http://www.csoonline.com/article/2120384/identity-management/the-abcs-of-identity-management.html

If the goal of least privilege is reducing access to a bare minimum, need to know defines that minimum as a need for access based on job or business requirements. For example, although the CIO in an organization has the appropriate rank to view upcoming quarterly financial forecasts, the organization's comptroller may decide that the CIO does not have a need to know that information and, thus, restrict access to it. Need to know is also used heavily in situations where operational secrecy is a key concern, such as in military operations. Military leaders often keep operational plans on a need to know basis to reduce the number of people who know about the plans and reduce the risk that someone will leak that information to the enemy.

Managing Accounts Using Groups and Roles

Efficient management of users requires the assignment of individual accounts into groups or roles. This will allow rights and privileges to be assigned to groups or a role as opposed to individual accounts. Individual user accounts can then be assigned to one or more groups depending on the access and privileges they require. When groups can be set up according to job functions within the organization, role-based access control (RBAC) can be used. Under RBAC, individual users are assigned a single role that corresponds to the rights and privileges they require to do their jobs. These users are then assigned to that role, allowing them to execute the responsibilities of their job for the duration of their membership within the role group. When a user is transferred, or otherwise no longer should have access to the role, then the security practitioner can simply remove the user from the role group membership, thereby preventing them from continuing to have the access rights and permission associated with membership. Whether groups or roles are used, security administrators must devise the appropriate assignment of permissions and rights, depending on the access control strategy used.

Different Types of Accounts

On most systems, accounts with greater privilege are distinct from ordinary user accounts that require less privilege. Privileged entities possess extensive powers on a given system. While these privileges may be necessary, they could be misused by unscrupulous individuals or targeted by external attackers. The security practitioner is expected to maintain control and oversight of these privileged entities, including ensuring they are assigned for legitimate business use and that on-going continued need is being regularly examined. This requires a defined regimen for how privileged entities are created on various systems as well as the processes in place to confirm that they are still required. While ordinary user accounts have less privilege, they also need to be controlled through good account management practices.

Privileged Accounts

Traditionally, there are four types of accounts with different privilege levels identified as follows: root or built-in administrator accounts, service accounts, administrator accounts, and power user accounts.

- ***Root or Built-in Administrator Accounts*** – These accounts are the all-powerful default administrative accounts used to manage a device or system. These accounts are generally shared by administrators for performing specialized administrative tasks. However, administrators should refrain from using these accounts because a loss of accountability is possible when multiple individuals have access to an account password. These accounts should be renamed whenever possible and strictly controlled. Default passwords should be changed prior to adding the device or computer to the production network. Logs should be kept to record individual use of the root account and password as part of a change management and configuration management program. The logs should correlate with the system audit log regarding the account activity. In most modern systems, interactive login using the root or administrator account has been disabled in favor of individually assigned administrative accounts that can assume root powers when needed. If login as root is required, the administrators should log in at the device console in an area with restricted access. Remote login with root accounts should only occur when the session can be strongly encrypted and monitored. This prevents a compromise of the root password or session hijacking by a rogue node on the system. These accounts should always be considered for multi-factor authentication methods.

- **Service Accounts** – These accounts are used to provide privileged access used by system services and core applications. Systems use a variety of accounts to provide automated services, such as Web servers, email servers, and database management systems. Such services require accounts to perform actions on the local system. Services might also have multiple internal accounts. Database management systems, such as Oracle, can have 10 or more internal default accounts at the initial installation. Management of service accounts can become challenging in a distributed environment where administrators must perform administrative functions remotely. Passwords for service accounts should be complex and must be strictly controlled to mitigate the risks of attack. Developing a strategy for changing service account passwords on a routine basis is necessary to provide continued integrity for the system, as well as having a strategy to reclaim and turn off access for accounts that may have been compromised.

- **Administrator Accounts** – These accounts are assigned only to named individuals that require administrative access to the system to perform maintenance activities, and they should be different and separate from a user's normal account. Passwords for administrative accounts should be distributed in person or via a secure, trusted method that is designed to ensure both the confidentiality and integrity of the passwords. Administrators should acknowledge in writing receipt of their account and willingness to follow organizational usage policies for privileged accounts. Remove administrative accounts immediately from the system when individuals no longer require that level of access. It is common practice to revalidate continued business need on a regular basis to ensure that these accounts are still required. It is also important that all actions taken by an administrative account are audited. Given the power of these accounts, it is usually necessary to employ external logging systems because administrators may be able to tamper with log files. These accounts should always be considered for multi-factor authentication methods.

- **Power Users** – These accounts are granted greater privileges than normal user accounts when it is necessary for the user to have greater control over the system but where administrative access is not required. For example, it is common to allow power users to install software on their own desktop systems. These accounts must be controlled and should be revalidated regularly for continued business need. Power users should acknowledge in writing receipt of their account and willingness to follow organizational usage policies for privileged accounts. Remove power user accounts immediately from the system when individuals no longer require that level of access. It is common practice to revalidate continued business need on a regular basis to ensure that these accounts are still required. These accounts should always be considered for multi-factor authentication methods.

Ordinary or Limited User Accounts

Ordinary or limited user accounts are what most users are assigned. They should be restricted only to those privileges that are strictly required, following the principle of least privilege. Access should be limited to specific objects following the principle of need-to-know.

Separation of Duties and Responsibilities

Accounts are assigned to individuals with particular job roles. In this section, the security professional should be able to distinguish between the common types of job roles and how they are related in an operational environment.

System Administrators

System administrators enjoy the highest level of privilege on most systems, particularly in server environments. They are entrusted with managing system operations and maintenance, and helping ensure that the system is functioning properly for system users. They perform key maintenance and monitoring tasks on a wide range of systems, including workstations, servers, network devices, databases, and applications. Each of these components requires various levels of recurring maintenance to ensure continued operations. For example, system administrators require the ability to affect certain critical operations such as setting the time, boot sequence, system logs, and passwords.

System administrators may be responsible for managing different sorts of systems, including workstations, laptops, and servers. Specialized applications, such as database management systems, can be considered systems unto themselves. Sometimes an administrator is dedicated to the task of database management as the database administrator (DBA). The operational control concepts expressed for ordinary system administrators are also applicable to an individual's assigned administrative duties for specialized applications.

Given the impact systems administrators can have on an organization, special care should be used when hiring them. The security professional should ensure the following actions are considered for a system administrator role:

- **Least Privilege** – The system administrator often does not require access to every system and function in an organization. Determine what access is needed and apply accordingly.
- **Monitoring** – If possible, the system administrator's actions should be logged and sent to a separate system that the system administrator does not control. The logs should be reviewed with change or configuration management requests to determine if only authorized actions are taking place.
- **Separation of Duties** – An administrator should not have the ability to engage in malicious activities without collusion.
- **Background Investigation** – A background investigation should be conducted to determine if the system administrator has abused the role in the past or may be vulnerable to blackmail or extortion attempts.

■ **Job Rotation** – System administrators should be subject to job rotation. Job rotation ensures another individual must perform the original system administrator's duties and also review their work.

Operators

System operators represent a class of users typically found in data center environments where mainframe systems are used. They provide day-to-day operations of the mainframe environment, ensuring that scheduled jobs are running effectively and troubleshooting problems that may arise. They also act as the arms and legs of the mainframe environment, loading and unloading tape and results of job print runs. Operators have elevated privileges but less than those of system administrators. If misused, these privileges may be used to circumvent the system's security policy. As such, use of these privileges should be monitored through audit logs. Some of the privileges and responsibilities assigned to operators include:

■ **Implementing the Initial Program Load (IPL)** – This is used to start the operating system. The boot process or initial program load of a system is a critical time for ensuring system security. Interruptions to this process may reduce the integrity of the system or cause the system to crash, precluding its availability.

■ **Monitoring Execution of the System** – Operators respond to various events, to include errors, interruptions, and job completion messages.

■ **Volume Mounting** – This allows the desired application access to the system and its data.

■ **Controlling Job Flow** – Operators can initiate, pause, or terminate programs. This may allow an operator to affect the scheduling of jobs. Controlling job flow involves the manipulation of configuration information needed by the system. Operators with the ability to control a job or application can cause output to be altered or diverted, which can threaten the confidentiality.

■ **Bypass Label Processing** – This allows the operator to bypass security label information to run foreign tapes (foreign tapes are those from a different data center that would not be using the same label format that the system could run). This privilege should be strictly controlled to prevent unauthorized access.

■ **Renaming and Relabeling Resources** – This is sometimes necessary in the mainframe environment to allow programs to properly execute. Use of this privilege should be monitored because it can allow the unauthorized viewing of sensitive information.

■ **Reassignment of Ports and Lines** – Operators are allowed to reassign ports or lines. If misused, reassignment can cause program errors, such as sending sensitive output to an unsecured location. Furthermore, an incidental port may be opened, subjecting the system to an attack through the creation of a new entry point into the system.

Given the impact operators can have on an organization, special care should be used when hiring them. The security professional should ensure the following actions are considered for an operator role:

■ **Least Privilege** – The systems operator often does not require access to every system and function in an organization. Determine what access is needed and apply accordingly.

- **Monitoring** – If possible, the operator's actions should be logged and sent to a separate system that the operator does not control. The logs should be reviewed with change or configuration management requests to determine if only authorized actions are taking place.
- **Separation of Duties** – An operator should not have the ability to engage in malicious activities without collusion.
- **Background Investigation** – A background investigation should be conducted to determine if the operator has abused the role in the past or may be vulnerable to blackmail or extortion attempts.

Security Administrators

The role of security administrators is to provide oversight for the security operations of a system. The aspects of security operations in their purview include account management, assignment of file sensitivity labels, system security settings, and review of audit data. Operating systems and some applications, such as database management systems, and networking equipment contain a significant number of security settings. Security administrators are responsible for defining the security settings of a system. In some cases, the security administrator may also implement the settings in conjunction with the system administrator or appropriate application manager. It is necessary for the security administrator and system administrator to work together on security settings because an improper configuration can impact the proper operation of the system or network. These administrators usually have fewer rights than system administrators. This is necessary to ensure that separation of duties is enforced. Security administrators provide a check and balance of the power assigned to system administrators with the ability to audit and review their activities.

Help/Service Desk Personnel

Help/Service desk personnel are responsible for providing front line support for all users. While they may be supplemented by automated systems, they are typically responsible for some aspects of account management. For example, they often are responsible for resetting user passwords when needed. This requires that they have sufficient privileges on the system to perform these functions. As helpdesk personnel often have the ability to reset passwords, they should be subject to monitoring and background investigations as feasible and necessary.

Ordinary Users

Ordinary users are individuals requiring access to information technology resources. Their access is limited to normal user activities.

Monitor Special Privileges

A security professional is expected to ensure accounts and their privileges are assigned appropriately and reviewed on a regular basis. Only authorized users should be granted access and for only the period of time that they require that access. This means validating their trustworthiness and occasionally revalidating their privileges.

Clearances, Suitability, and Background Checks/Investigations

Individuals are granted clearances, suitabilities, and other types of acceptable personal background designations according to their past actions, history of trustworthiness, and the level of access to sensitive information needed for their assigned duties. Security administrators participate in the background investigation process by ensuring that individuals have had an appropriate background check completed and any requisite clearance, suitability, or designation assigned prior to providing the individual an account and password. Periodic background checks should also be conducted to ensure that the level of trust granted to an individual is appropriate for his or her assigned duty. Individuals should not be given access to areas of the system where they have demonstrated an unmitigated:

- Recent and relevant serious lack of judgment.
- Repeated patterns of high-risk behavior relevant to the performance of the role.
- Illegal activity relevant to the performance of the role.

For example, individuals convicted of committing financial fraud should not be granted access to financial systems and databases. On the other hand, a person convicted of reckless driving seven years ago may be suitable for the same position. A "whole person" concept viewed through the nexus of the role's responsibility is necessary to make sound and consistent background check decisions.[11] Background checks and investigations are a useful tool for determining the trustworthiness of an individual and the likelihood of his or her compliance with organization policy.

Account Validation

Reviews of account activity are necessary to determine the existence of inactive accounts. Those accounts found to be inactive due to the departure of an individual from the organization should be removed from the system. Accounts that are inactive due to extended leave or temporary duties should be disabled. Ideally, individuals or their supervisors would promptly report temporary or permanent departures of system users to the appropriate system or security administrator. However, this does not always occur, so the security practitioner must be vigilant in conducting periodic reviews of accounts for inactivity.

Job Rotation

Job rotations reduce the risk of collusion of activities between individuals. Companies with individuals working with sensitive information or systems where there might be the opportunity for personal gain through collusion can benefit by integrating job rotation with segregation of duties. Rotating the position may uncover activities that the individual is performing outside of the normal operating procedures, highlighting errors or fraudulent behavior. It may be difficult to implement in small organizations due to the particular skill set required for the position, and thus security controls and supervisory control will need to be relied upon. Rotating individuals in and out of jobs provides the ability to give backup coverage, succession planning, and job enrichment opportunities for those involved. It also provides diversity of skills to support separation of duties.

Manage the Information Lifecycle

Information has a life that consists of creation, use, and finally destruction. Several important information security activities surround the lifecycle of information to protect it, ensure it is available to only those who require access to it, and finally to destroy it when it is no longer needed. Several concepts of information ownership need to be understood by the information security professionals as part of their duties.

---

11   Read more about the United States Military's approach to the "whole person" concept and clearances here: http://www.dhra.mil/perserec/currentinitiatives.html#Guides

When information is created, someone in the organization must be directly responsible for it. Often this is the individual or group that created, purchased, or acquired the information to support the mission of the organization. This individual or group is considered the "information owner." The information owner typically has the following responsibilities:

- Determine the impact the information has on the mission of the organization.
- Understand the replacement cost of the information (if it can be replaced).
- Determine who in the organization or outside of it has a need for the information and under what circumstances the information should be released.
- Know when the information is inaccurate or no longer needed and should be destroyed.

Clearly, the information owner must work with the information security program and officer to ensure the protection, availability, and destruction requirements can be met. To standardize the types of information and protection requirements, many organizations use classification or categorization to sort and mark the information. Classification is concerned primarily with access, while categorization is primarily concerned with impact.

Classification is most often referred to when discussing military or government information. However, several organizations may use systems that are similar in function. The purpose of a classification system is to ensure information is marked in such a way that only those with an appropriate level of clearance can have access to the information. Many organizations will use the terms "confidential," "close hold," "restricted," or "sensitive" to mark information. These markings may limit access to specific members such as board members or possibly certain sections of an organization such as the Human Resources area.

Categorization is the process of determining the impact of the loss of confidentiality, integrity, or availability of the information to an organization. For example, public information on a webpage may be low impact to an organization as it requires only minimal uptime; it doesn't matter if the information is changed and it is globally viewable by the public. However, a startup company may have a design for a new clean power plant, which if it was lost or altered may cause the company to go bankrupt as a competitor may be able to manufacture and implement the design faster. This type of information would be categorized as "high" impact.

Several classification and categorization systems exist. The security professional should minimally be familiar with a few and understand which are common within the countries and industries that he or she may practice in. For an example of classification, see:

- Canada's "Security of Information Act" [12]
- China's Law on "Guarding State Secrets" [13]
- The United Kingdom's "Official Secrets Acts" [14]

An excellent example of categorization may be found in the United States' National Institute of Standards and Technology's (NIST) Federal Information Processing Standard 199 and NIST's Special Publication 800-60 Volume 1 Revision 1 "Guide for Mapping Types of

---

12   http://laws-lois.justice.gc.ca/eng/acts/O-5/

13   http://www.asianlii.org/cn/legis/cen/laws/gssl248/

14   http://www.legislation.gov.uk/ukpga/1989/6/section/8

Information and Information Systems to Security Categories." [15] The United States federal civilian government is required to categorize information using these standards and guidelines.

Classification and categorization is used to help standardize the defense baselines for information systems and the level of suitability and trust an employee may need to access information. By consolidating data of similar categorization and classification, organizations can realize economy of scale in implementing appropriate security controls. Security controls are then tailored for specific threats and vulnerabilities.

Finally, all information must eventually come to an end. Organizations often hoard old information assuming it will be valuable at some point when really most information outlives its value and usefulness in a matter of years or months. Organizations should document retention schedules for information in their administrative policies. These schedules should mandate the destruction of information after a set date, period, or non-use trigger. The advantages of taking this approach are:

- Storage costs are reduced.
- Only relevant information is kept and this can speed up searching and indexing.
- Litigation holds and eDiscovery is less likely to encounter erroneous, pre-decisional or deliberative information.

Service Level Agreements (SLAs)

Many security architects, security professionals, and security practitioners have SLAs in place in their organizations, but they have never stopped to really understand these documents and what they represent to the enterprise with regards to risk management and the Business Impact Analysis (BIA). Below is a "primer" on SLAs for all three security actors.

What is an SLA?

A service-level agreement (SLA) is simply a document describing the level of service expected by a customer from a supplier, laying out the metrics by which that service is measured, and the remedies or penalties, if any, should the agreed-upon levels not be achieved. Usually, SLAs are between companies and external suppliers, but they may also be between two departments within a company (these are referred to as Operational Level Agreements, or OLAs).

Why Do I Need SLAs?

An SLA pulls together information on all of the contracted services and their agreed-upon expected reliability into a single document. It clearly states metrics, responsibilities, and expectations so in the event of issues with the service, neither party can plead ignorance. It ensures both sides have the same understanding of requirements. Any significant contract without an associated SLA (reviewed by legal counsel) is open to deliberate or inadvertent misinterpretation. The SLA protects both parties in the agreement.

Who Provides the SLA?

Most service providers have standard SLAs – sometimes several, reflecting various levels of service at different prices – that can be a good starting point for negotiation. These should be reviewed and modified by the organization's legal counsel because they are usually slanted in

---

15   **FIPS:** http://csrc.nist.gov/publications/fips/fips199/FIPS-PUB-199-final.pdf
   NIST: http://csrc.nist.gov/publications/nistpubs/800-60-rev1/SP800-60_Vol1-Rev1.pdf

favor of the supplier. When sending out an RFP, the organization should include expected service levels as part of the request; this will affect supplier offerings and pricing and may even influence the supplier's decision to respond. For example, if you demand 99.999 percent availability for a system, and the supplier is unable to accommodate this requirement with your specified design, it may propose a different, more robust solution.

What's in an SLA?

The SLA should not only include a description of the services to be provided and their expected service levels but also metrics by which the services are measured, the duties and responsibilities of each party, and the remedies and penalties for breach. Metrics should be designed so bad behavior by either party is not rewarded. For example, if a service level is breached because the client did not provide information in a timely manner, the supplier should not be penalized.

What Are Key Components of an SLA?

The SLA should include components in two areas: services and management.

Service elements include specifics of services provided (and what is excluded, if there is room for doubt), conditions of service availability, standards such as time window for each level of service (prime time and non-prime time may have different service levels, for example), responsibilities of each party, escalation procedures, and cost/service tradeoffs.

Management elements should include definitions of measurement standards and methods, reporting process, contents and frequency, a dispute resolution process, an indemnification clause protecting the customer from third-party litigation resulting from service level breaches (this should already be covered in the contract, however), and a mechanism for updating the agreement as required. This last item is critical; service requirements and vendor capabilities change, so there must be a way to make sure the SLA is kept up to date.

What about Indemnification?

The SLA should include a provision in which the service provider agrees to indemnify the customer company for any breaches of its warranties. Indemnification means that the provider will have to pay the customer for any third-party litigation costs resulting from its breach of the warranties. If you use a standard SLA provided by the service provider, it is likely this provision will be absent; ask your in-house counsel to draft a simple provision to include it, although the service provider may want further negotiation of this point.

Is an SLA Transferable?

Should the service provider be acquired by or merge with another company, the customer may expect that its SLA will continue to be in force, but this may not be the fact. The agreement may have to be renegotiated. Make no assumptions!

How Can I Verify Service Levels?

Most service providers make statistics available, often on a Web portal. There, customers can check whether SLAs are being met and whether they are entitled to service credits or other penalties as laid out in the SLA.

However, for mission-critical services where the business itself is at risk if service levels are not met, it may be worth considering using a third-party monitoring organization or an SLA management tool to supplement the vendor's data. The extra expense of these additional methods can be worthwhile for critical services.

What Kind of Metrics Should Be Monitored?

Many items can be monitored as part of an SLA, but the scheme should be kept as simple as possible to avoid confusion and excessive cost on either side. In choosing metrics, examine your operation and decide what is most important. The more complex the monitoring (and associated remedy) scheme, the less likely it is to be effective because no one will have time to properly analyze the data. When in doubt, opt for ease of collection of metric data; automated systems are best because it is unlikely that a costly manual collection of metrics will be reliable.

Depending on the service, the types of metric to monitor may include:

- **Service Availability** – the amount of time the service is available for use. This may be measured by time slot, with, for example, 99.5 percent availability required between the hours of 8 am and 6 pm, and more or less availability specified during other times. E-commerce operations typically have extremely aggressive SLAs at all times; 99.999 percent uptime is a not uncommon requirement for a site that generates millions of dollars an hour.
- **Defect Rates** – counts or percentages of errors in major deliverables. Production failures such as incomplete backups and restores, coding errors/ rework, and missed deadlines may be included in this category.
- **Technical Quality** – in outsourced application development, measurement of technical quality by commercial analysis tools that examine factors such as program size and coding defects.
- **Security** – In these hyper-regulated times, application and network security breaches can be costly. Measuring controllable security measures such as anti-virus updates and patching is key in proving all reasonable preventive measures were taken, in the event of an incident.

What Uptime Provisions Are Typical for Network Service Providers?

Hosted network services offer various levels of uptime guarantees, at escalating prices. The customer should expect to pay less for 99 percent availability (which allows for over 7 hours of unplanned downtime per month) than for 99.9 percent (43.8 minutes per month) or 99.99 percent (4.4 minutes per month). For mission-critical applications, providers will offer near 100 percent availability, but it will be more expensive.

The operative word here is unplanned; service providers will have predetermined windows for network maintenance, although network redundancy should prevent customer outages.

When Should We Review Our SLAs?

As businesses change, so do its service requirements. An SLA should not be viewed as a static document: It should be reviewed periodically, specifically if:

- The client's business needs have changed (for example, establishing an e-commerce site increases availability requirements).
- The technical environment has changed (for example, more reliable equipment makes a higher availability guarantee possible).
- Workloads have changed.
- Metrics, measurement tools, and processes have improved.

The SLA is a critical part of any supplier agreement, and it will pay off in the long-term if the SLA is properly thought-out and codified at the beginning of a relationship. It protects both parties and, should disputes arise, will specify remedies and avoid misunderstandings. That can save considerable time and money for both the customer and supplier. The security professional should seek the advice of the legal counsel within the organization with regards to the SLAs being considered and should have them reviewed by the legal counsel prior to acceptance and implementation.

Resource Protection

It may seem obvious that security operations are focused on protecting valuable assets. It is never practical to protect all assets equally because the cost to protect them may exceed their value. The real challenge is finding out which assets are truly valuable to the organization. In most cases, security functions depend on asset owners to identify valuable assets and help ensure that they are being protected appropriately.

Tangible versus Intangible Assets

Assets may be either tangible or intangible. Tangible assets are physical and fall under the category of traditional property. Intangible assets are not physical and fall under the categories of intellectual property. Some assets may include both tangible and intangible elements. For example, a physical server box is a tangible asset, while the information stored on that server is intangible. They are valued and protected in very different ways.

Protecting Physical Assets

Physical assets are easier to value because they have a declared value on the organization's financial statements. Such assets in an IT setting include all types of IT systems from end-user equipment (such as desktops and laptops) to high-end server equipment. These assets must be protected from potential theft and damage.

In the case of physical assets, the IT department is often playing both an owner and custodian role. It depends on who is ultimately paying for the gear and who is bearing the cost associated with maintenance and licensing. It is frequently the role of the security professional to confirm asset ownership and to consult with those owners to verify the declared value of those assets. It would then be the responsibility of security operations to ensure that the physical asset was being protected appropriately.

Facilities

Facilities require appropriate systems and controls to sustain the IT operation environment. Various utilities and systems are necessary to support operations and provide continuous protection. Fire detection and suppression systems are necessary for resource protection and worker safety. Heating, ventilation, and air conditioning systems provide appropriate temperature and humidity controls for user comfort and acceptable environmental operating ranges for equipment. Water and sewage systems are an integral part of any facility. IT systems cannot provide adequate availability without a reliable power supply and distribution system. Power should also be conditioned to remove spikes and fluctuations. Stable communications are a vital aspect of geographically distributed systems. Finally, an integrated facility access control and intrusion detection system forms the first line of defense regarding the IT operations security. Facilities should be marked plainly when possible to make identification of a data center more difficult.

Hardware

System hardware requires appropriate physical security measures to maintain the desired confidentiality, integrity, and availability. Physically secure data center facilities and locked server rooms are used to protect critical computing systems at common locations.

Access to these facilities should be limited to named individuals with a requirement for physical access following the principle of least privilege. Individuals who do not require frequent physical access to physical systems should not receive access to the facility. If occasional access is required, then temporary access should be granted and revoked when it is no longer required.

Operator consoles and workstations should also have limited access whenever possible. Users performing sensitive data operations should have their workstations located in a separate room with access limited to the individuals authorized to work in the room. Providing physical security to sensitive workstations can reduce the likelihood of an unauthorized individual from tampering with a workstation to bypass logical controls, remove media, or install malicious code or devices.

There are also a number of assets that will need to be protected outside of physically secure data center facilities or server rooms. Mobile assets such as laptops, smartphones, and tablets need to be protected. This can include solutions such as cable locking devices.

Printing devices should be located near the authorized users. System policies should be established that prevent users from producing output to printers outside of their immediate area unless absolutely necessary. Users should be required through policy and instructed through training to immediately retrieve their output from printing devices to preclude unauthorized access to sensitive information. Where possible, users may also be required to authenticate to the printer prior to receiving output.

Network devices are also key hardware assets that need to be protected from compromise or misuse. They are usually stored in secure data center facilities with other IT assets as well as secured utility closets and riser rooms. Strong physical security controls including cameras should be considered for these areas.

Media Management

Organizational information resides on various media types. Security practitioners should keep in mind that media includes soft copy as well as hard copy. Soft-copy media can be found as magnetic, optical, and solid state. Magnetic media includes floppy disks, tapes, and hard drives. CD-ROMs and DVDs are examples of optical media. Solid-state media includes flash drives and memory cards. Hard-copy examples include paper and microfiche.

Media containing sensitive or confidential information should be encrypted. There are a wide variety of encryption options for media available, depending on what type of media is being used. Many hard drive manufacturers now support on-disk encryption, which automatically encrypts data when it is being written to the hard disk. Backup tape drives from some manufacturers also support encryption, mitigating some of the risk associated with lost or stolen tapes. Many programs that are used to burn DVDs or CDs provide similar functions. Even portable USB flash drives can support encryption solutions. The security professional should help select an appropriate solution for the media being used.

In some cases, sensitive information is transmitted between media storage locations. Electronic transport strategies such as system snapshots, shadowing, network backups, and electronic vaulting send bulk information from one part of a network to another. The information may travel a significant distance and pass many network segments before reaching the intended storage area. The data can be viewed by network sniffing devices within any segment where the traffic passes. For this reason, the data should be protected through the use of encryption to mitigate a compromise.

Particular types of media may require special protections. For example, product software must be carefully controlled. Original copies and installed versions of system and application software require appropriate protection and management for information assurance purposes. Weak controls on software can subject a system to compromise through the introduction of backdoors and malicious code such as Trojan horses, viruses, and worms. Protecting the integrity of system code is necessary to defend against these types of threats. The process of handling software from original media through installation, use, modification, and removal should follow the concepts of least privilege and separation of duties. The types of controls necessary include access control, change control management, and library maintenance.

Original copies of software media should be controlled through a software librarian. Establishing a software library where original copies of software are strictly controlled provides accountability and a form of integrity control. A librarian is necessary to catalog and securely store the original copies of test data, binaries, object files, and source code.

Installed software should have appropriate access controls in place to prevent unauthorized access or modification. Ordinary users should have read and execute permissions for executable content and other system binaries and libraries. Setting this level of access control can prevent accidental or unauthorized modification to system binaries. For example, some viruses infect executable content through modification of the binary. If the user does not have write, modify, or delete permissions to system binaries, then the virus will be unable to affect these files when executing in the context of an ordinary user.

Removable Media

Portable devices such as thumb drives and external hard drives are a growing threat to organizations in terms of data loss. Organizations that do not provide secure means of providing users encrypted removable media often find users will purchase their own and use it without encryption. This leads to several problems:

- The organization does not know when information is leaving the enterprise.
- The organization does not know if the information is breached.
- The user has little incentive to report breaches.

To mitigate these situations, the security professional should advise:

- The organization implement data loss prevention capability, which includes:
  - Monitoring and restriction of USB and other external ports
  - Monitoring of DVD, Blu-ray, and other writable disk drives
- A secure removable media solution, which includes
  - Mandatory encryption with strong authentication
  - Monitoring and logging of information transferred to the media
  - An inventory capability
  - A remote wipe capability if required
  - A geo-locate capability if required

7

Providing users with a secure removable media solution has many benefits. The security professional can provide assurance to management that data is protected. Should removable media be lost, the security professional can mitigate the impact of data loss. The implementation of an enterprise secure removable media may also enhance the productivity of the workforce.

Archival and Offline Storage

Backups and archives are two different types of methods used to store information. Backups are conducted on a regular basis and are useful in recovering information or a system in the event of a disaster. Backups contain information that is regularly processed by the system users. Information that is needed for historical purposes, but not in continual use, should be saved and removed from the system as an archive. Each type of record retention requires appropriate management to include strong physical access controls and periodic reviews for the relevance of the stored records.

Data stored in a backup or archive may need to be reloaded into the main production environment. In this case, it is not only appropriate that a suitable technical solution be in place but that there are procedures in place to ensure that recovery can be done quickly and effectively.

Recovery from backups, for example, may need to have well-defined and documented procedures to ensure that restorations are done in the right order. When one is using these procedures, it is possible to determine how long it will take to recover a system given particular backup solutions. It is also important, however, that all backup and archival media is tested regularly to see if it can still be used for restorations. For longer term retention purposes, it may be necessary to migrate backups and archives to new media on a regular basis depending on the viability of the media. The security professional should ensure the drives, media, software, and support required to restore media is available or advise moving legacy archives and backups to modern and supported media if necessary.

Cloud and Virtual Storage

Cloud storage is a data storage model where the digital data is stored in logical pools, the physical storage spans across multiple servers (and often locations), and the physical environment is typically owned and managed by a hosting company. These cloud storage providers are responsible for keeping the data available and accessible and the physical environment protected and running. People and organizations buy or lease storage capacity from the providers to store end-user, organization, or application data. Cloud storage services may be accessed through a co-located cloud compute service, a Web service application programming interface (API), or by applications that utilize the API, such as cloud desktop storage, a cloud storage gateway, or Web-based content management systems.

From the security practitioner's perspective, cloud storage is:

- Made up of many distributed resources, but it still acts as one.
- Highly fault tolerant through redundancy and distribution of data.
- Highly durable through the creation of versioned copies.

There are several concerns that the security practitioner needs to consider with regards to cloud based storage in the enterprise:

1. When data is distributed, it is stored at more locations, increasing the risk of unauthorized physical access to the data. The risk of unauthorized access to data can be mitigated through the use of encryption, which can be applied to

831

data as part of the storage service or by on-premises equipment that encrypts data prior to uploading it to the cloud.

2. The number of people with access to the data who could be compromised (i.e., bribed or coerced) increases dramatically. Encryption keys that are kept by the service user, as opposed to the service provider, limit the access to data by service provider employees.

3. It increases the number of networks over which the data travels. Instead of just a local area network (LAN) or storage area network (SAN), data stored on a cloud requires a WAN (wide area network) to connect them both.

4. When you are sharing storage and networks with many other users/customers, it is possible for other customers to access your data, sometimes because of erroneous actions, faulty equipment, a bug, or because of criminal intent. This risk applies to all types of storage and not only cloud storage. The risk of having data read during transmission can be mitigated through encryption technology. Encryption in transit protects data as it is being transmitted to and from the cloud service. Encryption at rest protects data that is stored at the service provider. Encrypting data in an on-premises cloud service on-ramp system can provide both kinds of encryption protection.

Virtual storage is the pooling of physical storage from multiple network storage devices into what appears to be a single storage device that is managed from a central console. Storage virtualization software converts a server into a storage controller and the storage inside the server into the storage system. The benefit of virtualization is that commodity hardware or less expensive storage can be used to provide enterprise-class functionality. Storage virtualization also helps the storage administrator perform the tasks of backup, archiving, and recovery more easily and in less time by disguising the actual complexity of a storage area network (SAN).

Within the context of a storage system, there are two primary types of virtualization that can occur:

- Block virtualization refers to the abstraction (separation) of logical storage (partition) from physical storage so that it may be accessed without regard to physical storage or heterogeneous structure. This separation allows the administrators of the storage system greater flexibility in how they manage storage for end-users.

- File virtualization eliminates the dependencies between the data accessed at the file level and the location where the files are physically stored. This provides opportunities to optimize storage use and server consolidation and to perform non-disruptive file migrations.

Different Types of Virtualized Storage

Host-based

Host-based virtualization requires additional software running on the host, as a privileged task or process. In some cases, volume management is built into the operating system, and in other instances it is offered as a separate product. Volumes (LUNs) presented to the host system are handled by a traditional physical device driver. However, a software layer (the volume manager) resides above the disk device driver, intercepts the I/O requests, and provides the meta-data lookup and I/O mapping. Most modern operating systems have some form of logical volume management built-in (in Linux, it is called the Logical Volume Manager or LVM; in

Solaris and FreeBSD, ZFS's zpool layer; in Windows, the Logical Disk Manager or LDM) that performs virtualization tasks.

Storage Device-based
A primary storage controller provides the virtualization services and allows the direct attachment of other storage controllers. Depending on the implementation, these may be from the same or different vendors. The primary controller will provide the pooling and meta-data management services. It may also provide replication and migration services across those controllers that it is virtualizing.

Network-based
Network based storage is storage virtualization operating on a network-based device (typically a standard server or smart switch) and using iSCSI or Fibre Channel (FC) networks to connect as a SAN. These types of devices are the most commonly available and implemented form of virtualization. The virtualization device sits in the SAN and provides the layer of abstraction between the hosts performing the I/O and the storage controllers providing the storage capacity.

The security practitioner should become familiar with the basic concepts surrounding both cloud and virtualized storage technologies. The continuing evolution of both of these technology areas means that there will be new architecture and security elements that may have to be examined and considered for deployment within the enterprise security architecture at some point in the future.

Hard Copy Records
Information generated by an organization in the course of business – especially hard-copy records – should be protected. Records and information management (RIM) programs, as defined by ARMA International (www.arma.org), are essential activities to protect business information and can be established in compliance with laws, regulations, or corporate governance. Such a program ensures that critical information is protected and available to an organization during, or after, a crisis. From a disaster recovery perspective, output from a Business Impact Analysis (BIA) can help identify critical information in either physical or electronic forms. By identifying critical business functions, a BIA can help identify what information (e.g., vital records) is needed to restore organizational functions and to assist in business resumption. Once the vital hard-copy records are identified, they can be protected using a vital records plan (which can be made a part of a business continuity and/or disaster recovery plan).

Protecting Hard-Copy Records
Loss of or damage to paper records can occur from fires, floods, hurricanes and tornadoes, explosions, smoke, mold and microbial contamination, water pipes bursting, accidental sprinkler discharges, and freezing temperatures. Strategies for protecting vital hard-copy documents include storing them in secure, clean, and environmentally stable containers; making backup copies and storing the backups in secure off-site areas with stabilized temperature and humidity; making microfiche copies; and scanning documents into PDF or other data formats. Specialized document storage companies like Iron Mountain (www.ironmountain.com), BMS CAT (www.bmscat.com), and GRM Document Management (www.grmdocumentmanagement.com) can provide a range of document protection services.

Document scanning service companies like IPS (www.ipsservices.com), Royal Imaging Services, LLC (www.royalimaging.com), and Docufree Corporation (www.docufree.com) can scan thousands of documents for less than five cents apiece. That service includes scanning, conversion to a specific format, and storing the scanned documents electronically. If the original documents can be shredded or destroyed once they have been scanned, there may also be a charge for that option. Fire-resistant storage containers may be advisable for storing particularly important documents such as historical documents like company organization papers, deeds, court records, and early stock certificates.

Additional resources for the security professional to use are:

- ANSI/ARMA 5-2010, Vital Records Programs: Identifying, Managing, and Recovering Business-Critical Records sets the requirements for establishing a vital records program; ISBN: 978-1-931786-87-4
- ARMA Guideline for Evaluating Offsite Records Storage Facilities (PDF); ISBN: 978-1-931786-31-7

Disposal/Reuse

When media is to be reassigned (a form of object reuse), it is important that all residual data is carefully removed. Simply deleting files or formatting media does not actually remove the information. File deletion and media formatting often simply remove the pointers to the information. Providing assurance for object reuse requires specialized tools and techniques according to the type of media on which the data resides.

Specialized hardware devices known as degaussers can be used to erase data saved to magnetic media.[16] The measure of the amount of energy needed to reduce the magnetic field on the media to zero is known as coercivity. It is important to make sure that the coercivity of the degausser is of sufficient strength to meet object reuse requirements when erasing data. If a degausser is used with insufficient coercivity, then a remanence of the data will exist. Remanence is the measure of the existing magnetic field on the media; it is the residue that remains after an object is degaussed or written over. Data is still recoverable even when the remanence is small. While data remanence exists, there is no assurance of safe object reuse. Some degaussers can destroy drives. The security professional should exercise caution when recommending or using degaussers on media for reuse.

Software tools also exist that can provide object reuse assurance. These tools overwrite every sector of magnetic media with a random or predetermined bit pattern. Overwrite methods are effective for all forms of electronic media with the exception of read-only optical media. There exists a drawback to using overwrite software. During normal write operations with magnetic media, the head of the drive moves back and forth across the media as data is written. The track of the head does not usually follow the exact path each time. The result is a miniscule amount of data remanence with each pass. With specialized equipment, it is possible to read data that has been overwritten. To provide higher assurance in this case, it is necessary to overwrite each sector multiple times. Security practitioners should keep in mind that a one-time pass may be acceptable for noncritical information, but sensitive data should be overwritten with multiple passes. Overwrite software can also be used to clear the sectors within solid-state media such

---

16 For more information on degaussing, please see the following resource: http://www.nsa.gov/ia/_files/government/MDG/NSA_CSS-EPL-9-12.pdf

as USB thumb drives. It is suggested that physical destruction methods such as incineration or secure recycling should be considered for solid-state media that is no longer used.

The last form of preventing unauthorized access to sensitive data is media destruction. Shredding, burning, grinding, and pulverizing are common methods of physically destroying media. Degaussing can also be a form of media destruction. High-power degaussers are so strong in some cases that they can literally bend and warp the platters in a hard drive. Shredding and burning are effective destruction methods for non-rigid magnetic media. Indeed, some shredders are capable of shredding some rigid media such as an optical disk. This may be an effective alternative for any optical media containing non-sensitive information due to the residue size remaining after feeding the disk into the machine. However, the residue size might be too large for media containing sensitive information. Alternatively, grinding and pulverizing are acceptable choices for rigid and solid-state media. Specialized devices are available for grinding the face of optical media that either sufficiently scratches the surface to render the media unreadable or actually grinds off the data layer of the disk. Several services also exist that will collect drives, destroy them on site if requested, and provide certification of completion. It will be the responsibility of the security professional to help, select, and maintain the most appropriate solutions for media cleansing and disposal.

Incident Response

Security professionals manage the day-to-day operations of key security services as well as participate in cross-enterprise processes. The security professional must understand the many types of security technologies that are deployed. The security professional should also understand the role that security plays in operational processes such as change, configuration, incidet, and problem management.

Incident Management

When bad things happen, it is important they are detected quickly and addressed effectively. While it is ideal that all potential incidents be prevented from happening in the first place, organizations cannot prevent all possible threats, particularly those involving human threat agents. Security operations must have strong processes in place that allow security analysts to quickly detect and respond to security-related incidents.

A successful incident management program combines people, processes, and technology. For security-related incidents, this will require trained individuals who have experience dealing with security-related incidents, processes that will guide the response, and technologies that will enable the response to be performed quickly and efficiently.

For example, consider a security-related incident involving a single system that has become unreliable. The system is now continuously rebooting itself, declaring that the security kernel is not available. Network operations detects the outage, and since it is security-related, security operations is called in. It turns out that the system in question is highly critical to the organization and that it will need to be backed up and running in a very short time frame.

In this case, the priority is clear: Get the system back up and running. At the same time, the security professional wants to preserve as much information as possible for investigative purposes. The system has been attempting to perform an emergency system restart (by rebooting itself), but it has been unable to return itself to normal service. While a warm reboot (or graceful reboot) is not likely going to work, perhaps a cold reboot, which shuts the system down completely, may be most suitable.

Will restoration from backup be required? Is there a redundant server available that can be brought online? What about the evidence of a potential attack that may be lost if we shut down the system? The possible questions and avenues of response are almost endless.

Incident management procedures are intended to guide all activities related to the incident and guide the security practitioner down a pre-defined and (where possible) pre-approved path for resolution. They describe the actions that should be taken during the incident, roles and responsibilities of the various parties that may be involved, and who gets to make decisions around what will be done. These procedures are in constant development and must incorporate the lessons learned from previous incidents.

Security Measurements, Metrics, and Reporting

Security services also need to provide the ability to measure the effectiveness of security controls deployed in the enterprise. Such measurements provide a point-in-time gauge of the current state. They form the basis for metrics, which combine measurement with goals to be measured against. Such metrics can be used to determine if technology deployments are successful just as they can be used to determine if manual processes can be improved.

Most security technologies support measurements and metrics. Intrusion detection and prevention systems can provide information on attacks that were detected or blocked and provide trending over time. Firewalls can identify common sources of attacks through IP addresses and other means. Email security services can provide information on the amount of malware or spam that is being detected and blocked. Of course, all platforms can be measured according to their availability and reliability.

Many things can be used to drive metrics within the organization. The key to using them is to focus on the metrics that mean the most to the organization's executives and to their overall mission. For example, one large retail organization focused their entire IT mission on a straightforward availability target. They had come to the conclusion that nothing was more important than ensuring that systems were available when they needed to be. All departments and their systems were measured against it. It drove technology investment and was the foundation for their incentive programs, both with internal staff and with their external partners.

Reporting is also fundamental to successful security operations. It can take a variety of forms depending on the intended audience. Technical reporting tends to be designed for technical specialists or managers with direct responsibility for service delivery. Management reporting will provide summaries of multiple systems as well as key metrics for each of the services covered by the report. Executive dashboards are intended for the executive who is interested in seeing only the highlights across multiple services, and they provide simple summaries of the current state, usually in a highly visual form like charts and graphs.

Reporting frequency will also vary. At an operational level, some measurements and metrics may be required yearly, monthly, weekly, or even daily, depending on how closely management wishes to monitor service delivery.

Managing Security Technologies

There is a large number of technical controls deployed at most enterprises. These controls need to be maintained and managed effectively if they are to be trusted to protect the enterprise. They will also be necessary to quickly alert the security professional when security incidents occur and assist them to respond more effectively. In security operations, the focus is less on the technologies themselves and more on the ways that they are managed in an operational environment.

Boundary Controls

An important technology for the security professional to understand is boundary controls. Boundary controls may be placed wherever there is a necessary division between more trusted and less trusted environments. Such boundaries may be deployed within the enterprise network using firewalls, routers, proxies, and other technologies to control the boundary between more trusted and less trusted network segments. Similar technologies can be deployed within individual systems. For example, the boundaries between kernel functions and end-user processes may be enforced through common anti-malware systems, ring protection, and various process isolation techniques.

Security operations will focus on ensuring that these technologies have been deployed effectively and monitoring their use over time to ensure that they are still effective. Changes to firewall rules and router Access Control Lists (ACLs) need to be carefully examined to determine if they accomplish their intended purpose without affecting other rules or the stability of the platform. Secured systems will need to be examined regularly to ensure that system boundaries remain intact.

Detection

Intrusion detection and prevention systems are used to identify and respond to suspected security-related events in real time or near real time. Intrusion detection systems (IDS) will use available information to determine if an attack is underway, send alerts, and provide limited response capabilities. Intrusion prevention systems (IPS) will use available information to determine if an attack is underway, send alerts, but it will also block the attack from reaching its intended target.

Network-based intrusion systems focus on the analysis of network traffic, while host-based intrusion systems focus on audit logs and processes inside a single system.

The distinction between IDS and IPS is very important because it materially affects both how the system must be deployed and its effect on the systems it is monitoring. If an IDS is used, it may be deployed out-of-band, meaning that it is not deployed in the middle of the communications path, and will not affect normal processing or cause latency. Any attacks, however, will likely reach their intended target. If an IPS is used, it must be deployed in-line (also known as in-band), meaning that it is deployed in the middle of the communications path. Because it is in-line, it will cause some latency and slow down normal processing to a slight extent. Detected attacks, however, will not likely reach their intended targets. On many modern systems, both IDS and IPS techniques can be used within the same device, allowing the security practitioner to decide whether to use one technique or the other.

Intrusion systems use a number of techniques to determine whether an attack is underway:

- **Signature- or Pattern-Matching systems** – Examine the available information (logs or network traffic) to determine if it matches a known attack.

- **Protocol Anomaly-Based systems** – Examine network traffic to determine if what it sees conforms to the defined standard for that protocol, for example, as it is defined in a Request for Comment or RFC.

- **Statistical-Anomaly-Based systems** – Establish a baseline of normal traffic patterns over time and detect any deviations from that baseline. Some also use heuristics to evaluate the intended behavior of network traffic to determine if it intended to be malicious or not. Most modern systems combine two or more of these techniques together to provide a more accurate analysis before it decides whether it sees an attack or not.

In most cases, there will continue to be problems associated with false-positives as well as false-negatives. False-positives occur when the IDS or IPS identifies something as an attack, but it is in fact normal traffic. False-negatives occur when the IPS or IDS fails to interpret something as an attack when it should have. In these cases, intrusion systems must be carefully "tuned" to ensure that these are kept to a minimum.

An IDS requires frequent attention; it requires the response of a human who is knowledgeable enough with the system and types of normal activity to make an educated judgment about the relevance and significance of the event. Alerts need to be investigated to determine if they represent an actual event or if they are simply background noise.

Anti-Malware Systems

Today, anti-malware systems may be deployed at various points throughout the enterprise. They are installed on individual hosts, on systems such as email servers, and even at key points in the network in email and Web gateways as well as Unified Threat Management (UTM) devices, which combine anti-malware with other functions (such as firewall, intrusion detection/prevention, and content filtering).

To remain effective, anti-malware solutions require continual updates and must be monitored to ensure they are still active and effective. Each implementation should be monitored to ensure that updates are received and active. Likewise, the anti-malware engines should be configured to take advantage of automatic scanning for new media and email attachments. Scanning should be scheduled and accomplished on a regular basis. It is best for the scanning to be done automatically during nonpeak usage times.

Security Event Information Management (SEIM)

Few solutions tools are more important to security operations than one that provides the ability to get a view into security-related events in real time. System audit logs collect valuable information on the operation of the system, but logs do not alert security professionals. They also do not provide ways to collate audit logs across multiple systems.

Security-related audit logs will typically log access attempts (including successes and failures), the use of privileges, service failures, and the like. Even on a single system, these logs can get to be very large. They may need to be tuned to ensure that you are only collecting the logs that you want using appropriate clipping levels. For example, successful login attempts may not be required for analysis and may be filtered out.

One disadvantage of system logs is that they provide a view into that single system. They do not provide a view into events that may be affecting multiple systems or where multiple systems have some information that may be required to detect an incident and track it back to its sources. Security Event Information Management (SEIM) solutions products are intended to provide a common platform for log collection, collation, and analysis in real time to allow for more effective and efficient responses.

They can also provide reports on historical events using log information from multiple sources.

Log management systems are similar: They also collect logs and provide the ability to report against them, although their focus tends to be on historical analysis of log information rather than real time analysis. They may be combined with SEIM solutions to provide both historical and real time functions.

In both cases, log information must be carefully managed, and security operations must maintain a disciplined practice of log storage and archiving. For most SEIM or log management systems, there is a practical limit to the amount of information they can analyze at once or generate reports against. For most systems, only a fraction of the logs will be stored online with the remaining logs moved into longer term storage or archival solutions. These solutions store online logs for 30 to 180 days, shift them into an online or near-line archive for up to a year, and then move any logs into longer term backup to cover the remainder of the retention period. At the end of that period, security operations are responsible for ensuring that old log information is properly disposed of using defined data disposal procedures and tools.

Modern reporting tools can also be used to transform security event information into useful business intelligence. Rather than focusing on basic log analysis, they tend to focus on higher level reporting on service metrics as well as reporting for compliance purposes.

Response

When an incident is detected, a containment strategy must be decided. Containment may include disconnecting devices from the network, shutting systems down, or redirecting traffic around an affected area of the network. The containment strategy should be driven by several criteria including:

- The need to preserve forensic evidence for possible legal action.
- The availability of services the affected component provides.
- The potential damage that leaving the affected component in place may cause.
- The time required for the containment strategy to be effective.
- The resources required to contain the affected component.

Delaying containment when a system is compromised by a suspected attacker is often a poor choice because it can lead to further attacks on more information systems. Arguments may be made that the security professional could observe the attacker to learn more about what is happening; however that is best left to honeypots and experienced security engineers. There may also be legal implications if the organization knows about the compromised system and then the compromised system is used to attack another system.

The team should instead focus on obtaining a forensic image of the RAM and hard drive of the compromised system and then determine how to mitigate the vulnerability that caused the compromise. The security professional should consult an organization's legal team to determine if the image gathered must be suitable for law enforcement or be admissible in court. If needed for law enforcement or court, the security professional must avoid violating the chain of custody and is best assisted by law enforcement or an experienced forensics team while creating an image.

The initial incident and as much relevant information as possible should be documented in an incident management system. The incident should be updated as more information becomes available until the incident is deemed resolved by the security operations team. The documented incident is often one of the most important parts of reconstructing the attack and explaining what happened to third parties.

Reporting

Some organizations are required to report incidents that meet certain conditions. For example, United States civilian government agencies are required to report any breach of personally identifiable information to the U.S. Computer Emergency Readiness Team (US-CERT) within an hour of discovery.[17] Security professionals must be aware of when an incident must be reported to upper management or law enforcement. Policies and procedures must be defined to determine how an incident is routed when criminal activity suspected. Additionally, policies and procedures need to be in place to determine how an incident escalates and should address:

- Does the media or an organization's external affairs group need to be involved?
- Does the organization's legal team need to be involved in the review?
- At what point does notification of the incident rise to the line management, middle management, senior management, the board of directors, or the stakeholders?
- What confidentiality requirements are necessary to protect the incident information?
- What methods are used for the reporting? If email is attacked, how does that impact the reporting and notification process?

Recovery

Recovery can range from the very basic of restoring an image to a machine to no recovery situations that involve the loss of sensitive information. The first step of recovery is eradication if possible. Eradication is the process of removing the threat. For example, if an unpatched system were infected with malware, removal of the malware would be the eradication. Recovery is primarily interested in restoring or repairing a system back to a known good state. Recovery can be extremely complicated if the last known image or "good" state actually contained the vulnerability that caused the incident. In those cases, a new image may need to be created and tested prior to application in the production environment.

Remediation and Review (Lessons Learned)

Perhaps the most important part of incident response is the lesson learned. Organizations have an opportunity to analyze and understand what failed and try to ensure it does not happen again. There are various degrees of rigor an organization can take when reviewing an incident with a trade off in the time required for analysis and the impact of the results.

---

17   http://www.whitehouse.gov/sites/default/files/omb/memoranda/fy2006/m06-19.pdf

Root Cause Analysis

Fundamentally, Root Cause Analysis (RCA) is asking "why?" until there is only one answer. RCA is an intensive process involving numerous individuals from across different disciplines to determine why something happened and how to prevent it in the future. RCA involves reviewing system logs, policies, procedures, security documentation, and network traffic capture if available to first piece together the history of the event that caused the incident. Once the event is understood, the RCA team can work backwards to determine what allowed the event to happen in the first place. Did a system not get patched? If this is true, why did the system not get patched? If the answer is "the patch management team could not patch it because the system was off, " the next question is "why was it off?" If the answer is "the new Green IT policy mandates all systems be shut down and powered off when not in use," then the question needs to be "can we turn systems on when patching through Wake-on-LAN (WoL), and have all systems check for patches on boot before connected to the Internet?" If the answer is "yes," then a solution is reached. If not, then the team needs to keep asking "why?"

While this is a very simple example of patching missing a machine, it helps to illustrate the process. When incidents involve motivated attackers and multiple vulnerabilities and systems, this process gets extremely complicated fast. Further complicating matters, individuals whose areas are targets for the analysis may resist providing information or cooperating for fear of appearing weak or mismanaged. RCA can quickly cross boundaries between technical, cultural, and organizational. The security professional should work through the consensus of the RCA team and ensure senior management is supporting the analysis. Remediation actions from RCA are then reviewed by management for adoption and implementation, or management may decide to accept the risk if the proposed recommendation costs more than the exposure or the likelihood of the event happening again is extremely small.

Problem Management

Incident and problem management are intimately related. While incident management is concerned primarily with managing an adverse event, problem management is concerned with tracking that event back to a root cause and addressing the underlying problem.

Problem management is seen as distinct from incident management for a number of reasons. First, their goals are slightly different. While incident management is focused on limiting the effect of an incident, problem management is about addressing defects that made the incident possible or more successful. Second, problem management tends to have a longer term view of incidents as they occur in the operational environment. It can take longer periods of time to track down the underlying defect because it may take specific conditions to be in place that may not occur frequently. For example, a defect associated with insufficient resources may only manifest when system load is particularly high.

Security Audits and Reviews – The Precursor to Mitigation

A security audit is typically performed by an independent third party to the management of the system. The audit determines the degree with which the required controls are implemented. A security review is conducted by the system maintenance or security personnel to discover vulnerabilities within the system. A vulnerability occurs when policies are not followed, misconfigurations are present, or flaws exist in the hardware or software of the system. System reviews are sometimes referred to as a vulnerability assessment.

Penetration testing is a form of security review where an attempt is made to gain access or compromise a system. Penetration tests can be conducted with physical access to the system or from the outside of the system and facility.

Security audits can be divided between internal and external reviews. Internal reviews are conducted by a member of the organization's staff that does not have management responsibility for the system. External reviews involve outside entities that evaluate the system based on the organizational security requirements. Entities performing an external review provide an independent assessment of the system. Security practitioners may find this review particularly appealing if the assessment supports prior security concerns that have been avoided by management. Managers should invite an independent review as a fresh perspective that may uncover unknown weaknesses within the system or associated processes.

The outcome of the security audit and review process should be a list of items and issues that have to be addressed by the security actors in the organization. Depending on the issues identified, the security architect may be called on to design or re-design one or more elements of the enterprise security architecture in order to comply with the audit findings. The security practitioner may need to change the configuration of one or more system components to ensure that they have been re-configured according to the recommendations of the audit team. The security professional may need to craft new policies and procedures to allow for the changes in system architecture and implementation to be managed going forward. Whatever the outcomes, the process that one or more of these security actors will be engaging in is mitigation. The minimizing of the potential for a risk or a vulnerability or a threat to be exploited is at the heart of what mitigation seeks to do. The impact that mitigation can have is in direct proportion to the amount of activities that are engaged in as part of the mitigation strategy being deployed.

Preventative Measures against Attacks

Operations can be impacted by a variety of threats. These threats may be caused by individuals or environmental factors. A security practitioner who is aware of common threats will be more prepared to propose or implement controls to mitigate or limit the potential damage. Just as most security requirements can be summed up by the AIC (or CIA) triad (availability, integrity, and confidentiality), most threats are associated with their opposites: disclosure, corruption, and destruction.

Unauthorized Disclosure

The unauthorized release of information is a considerable threat. Disclosure may result when a hacker or cracker penetrates a system that contains confidential information. Sensitive information may be leaked through malware infection. It may also be intentionally disclosed by disgruntled employees, contractors, or partners. From an operations perspective, technical solutions intended to protect sensitive information need to be maintained and privileged users monitored to detect any potential disclosure.

Destruction, Interruption, and Theft

Malicious activity on the part of malware and malicious users can cause the loss of a significant amount of information. Errors on the part of users can cause the accidental deletion of important data. The concept of secure operations is intended to prevent destruction of sensitive assets, except of course when done intentionally as part of an information retention program.

Interruptions in service can also be extremely disruptive to normal business operations. Failure of equipment, services, and operational procedures can cause system components to become unavailable. Denial-of-Service (DoS) attacks and malicious code can also interrupt operations. Any loss of availability will need to be dealt with appropriately, either automatically through technology or manually through strong processes and procedures.

Theft is also a common threat. While large-scale thefts within a secure operation may be less likely, component theft is often common in many environments. The security professional may be expected to help prevent these sorts of thefts as well as coordinate investigations into such problems.

Corruption and Improper Modification

Environmental factors as well as the acts of individuals can cause damage to systems and data. Sporadic fluctuations in temperature or line power can cause systems to make errors while writing data. Inappropriate or accidental changes to file or table permissions can cause unintended data corruption. The security practitioner may be expected to help implement and maintain integrity protections on key systems as well as provide appropriate procedures to ensure that privileged access to high-integrity resources is tightly controlled and monitored.

Network Intrusion Detection System Architecture

NIDS are usually incorporated into the network in a passive architecture, taking advantage of promiscuous mode access to the network. This means that it has visibility into every packet traversing the network segment. This allows the system to inspect packets and monitor sessions without impacting the network or the systems and applications utilizing the network.

Typically, a passive NIDS is implemented by installing a network tap, attaching it to a hub, or mirroring ports on a switch to a NIDS dedicated port. Given that the NIDS is monitoring all the traffic traveling through that device, the NIDS must be able to handle traffic throughput equivalent to (or greater than) the combined traffic load for all the ports on that device, or it will begin to drop packets. For example, if a 100-MB, 10-port switch is used and all the ports are mirrored to a single-GB port for the NIDS, the NIDS device must have the capacity to monitor and investigate GB traffic or else it will begin to lose information.

NIDS can also fail to provide adequate monitoring if the traffic it is monitoring is encrypted. The same encryption employed to ensure confidentiality of communication greatly reduces the ability for IDS to inspect the packet. The amount and granularity of information that can be investigated from an encrypted packet is related to the way the packet is encrypted. In most cases, only the data portion of a packet is encrypted, leaving the packet headers in cleartext. Therefore, the IDS can gain some visibility into the communication participants, session information, protocol, ports, and other basic attributes. However, if the IDS needs to dig deeper into the packet to perform data analysis, it will eventually fail due to the encryption.

Many technologies now exist that can break session encryption and then re-establish it. Using these technologies, it is possible for an organization to get greater insight into network packets. Organizations must be careful though as user training and privacy concerns must be taken into consideration and at times balanced with security requirements.

Because a NIDS analyzes a copy of each packet to analyze the contents and its role in a session, it does not interfere with existing communications and can perform various investigative functions against the collected data. On those occasions when an IDS detects an unwanted communication stream and is enabled to perform automated responses, it can attempt to terminate the connection.

This can be accomplished in a multitude of ways. For example, it can start blocking any packets coming from the source of the traffic, or it can utilize features of the TCP protocol and inject reset packets into the network, forcing the remote system to cancel the communications. In lieu of directly terminating the session, many IDS solutions can be integrated with firewalls, routers, and switches to facilitate dynamic rule changes to block specific protocols, ports, or IP addresses associated with the unwanted communications.

Host-Based Intrusion Detection System (HIDS)

HIDS is the implementation of IDS capabilities at the host level. Its most significant difference from NIDS is that related processes are limited to the boundaries of a single-host system. However, this presents advantages in effectively detecting objectionable activities because the IDS process is running directly on the host system, not just observing it from the network. This offers unfettered access to system logs, processes, system information, and device information, and it virtually eliminates limits associated with encryption. The level of integration represented by HIDS increases the level of visibility and control at the disposal of the HIDS application.

There are also multihost IDSs that identify and respond to data from multiple hosts. The multihost HIDS architecture allows systems to share policy information and real time attack data. For example, if a system were to experience an attack, the signature of the attack and associated remediation actions can be shared with other systems automatically in an attempt to establish a defensive posture.

The biggest drawback of HIDS, and the reason many organizations resist its use, is that it can be very invasive to the host operating system. HIDS must have the capability to monitor all processes and activities on the host system, and this can sometimes interfere with normal system processing. HIDS can consume inordinate amounts of CPU and memory to function effectively, especially during an event. Although today's server platforms are powerful, diminishing some of these performance issues, workstations, and laptops (good candidates for HIDS) may suffer from the overhead of performing analysis on all system activities.

IDS Analysis Engine Methods

Several analysis methods can be employed by an IDS, each with its own strengths and weaknesses, and their applicability to any given situation should be carefully considered. There are two basic IDS analysis methods: pattern matching (also called signature analysis) and anomaly detection. Some of the first IDS products used signature analysis as their detection method and simply looked for known characteristics of an attack (such as specific packet sequences or text in the data stream) to produce an alert if that pattern was detected. For example, an attacker manipulating an FTP server may use a tool that sends a specially constructed packet. If that particular packet pattern is known, it can be represented in the form of a signature that IDS can then compare to incoming packets. Pattern-based IDS will have a database of hundreds, if not thousands, of signatures that are compared to traffic streams. As new attack signatures are produced, the system is updated, much like anti-virus solutions.

There are drawbacks to pattern-based IDS. Most importantly, signatures can only exist for known attacks. If a new or different attack vector is used, it will not match a known signature and, thus, slip past the IDS. Additionally, if an attacker knows that the IDS is present, he or she can alter his or her methods to avoid detection. Changing packets and data streams, even slightly, from known signatures can cause an IDS to miss the attack. As with some anti-virus systems, the IDS is only as good as the latest signature database on the system. Therefore, regular updates are required to ensure that the IDS has the most recent signatures. This is especially critical for newly discovered attacks.

Alternately, anomaly detection uses behavioral characteristics of a system's operation or network traffic to draw conclusions on whether the traffic represents a risk to the network or host. Anomalies may include but are not limited to:

- Multiple failed logon attempts
- Users logging in at strange hours
- Unexplained changes to system clocks
- Unusual error messages
- Unexplained system shutdowns or restarts
- Attempts to access restricted files

An anomaly-based IDS tends to produce more data because anything outside of the expected behavior is reported. Thus, they tend to report more false positives as expected behavior patterns change. An advantage to anomaly-based IDS is that because they are based on behavior identification and not specific patterns of traffic, they are often able to detect new attacks that may be overlooked by a signature-based system. Often, information from an anomaly-based IDS may be used to create a pattern for a signature-based IDS.

Stateful Matching Intrusion Detection

Stateful matching takes pattern matching to the next level. It scans for attack signatures in the context of a stream of traffic or overall system behavior rather than the individual packets or discrete system activities. For example, an attacker may use a tool that sends a volley of valid packets to a targeted system. Because all the packets are valid, pattern matching is nearly useless. However, the fact that a large volume of the packets was seen may, itself, represent a known or potential attack pattern. To evade attack, then, the attacker may send the packets from multiple locations with long wait periods between each transmission to either confuse the signature detection system or exhaust its session timing window. If the IDS service is tuned to record and analyze traffic over a long period of time, it may detect such an attack. Because stateful matching also uses signatures, it too must be updated regularly and, thus, has some of the same limitations as pattern matching.

Statistical Anomaly-Based Intrusion Detection

The statistical anomaly-based IDS analyzes event data by comparing it to typical, known, or predicted traffic profiles in an effort to find potential security breaches. It attempts to identify suspicious behavior by analyzing event data and identifying patterns of entries that deviate from a predicted norm. This type of detection method can be very effective and, at a very high level, begins to take on characteristics seen in IPS by establishing an expected baseline of behavior and acting on divergence from that baseline. However, there are some potential issues that may surface with a statistical IDS. Tuning the IDS can be challenging, and if not performed regularly, the system will be prone to false positives. Also, the definition of normal traffic can be open to interpretation and does not preclude an attacker from using normal activities to penetrate systems. Additionally, in a large, complex, dynamic corporate environment, it can be difficult, if not impossible, to clearly define "normal" traffic.

The value of statistical analysis is that the system has the potential to detect previously unknown attacks. This is a huge departure from the limitation of matching previously known signatures. Therefore, when combined with signature matching technology, the statistical anomaly-based IDS can be very effective.

Protocol Anomaly-Based Intrusion Detection

A protocol anomaly-based IDS identifies any unacceptable deviation from expected behavior based on known network protocols. For example, if the IDS is monitoring an HTTP session and the traffic contains attributes that deviate from established HTTP session protocol standards, the IDS may view that as a malicious attempt to manipulate the protocol, penetrate a firewall, or exploit a vulnerability.

The value of this method is directly related to the use of well-known or well-defined protocols within an environment. If an organization primarily uses well-known protocols (such as HTTP, FTP, or telnet), this can be an effective method of performing intrusion detection. In the face of custom or nonstandard protocols, however, the system will have more difficulty or be completely unable to determine the proper packet format. Interestingly, this type of method is prone to the same challenges faced by signature-based IDSs. For example, specific protocol analysis modules may have to be added or customized to deal with unique or new protocols or unusual use of standard protocols. Nevertheless, having an IDS that is intimately aware of valid protocol use can be very powerful when an organization employs standard implementations of common protocols.

Traffic Anomaly-Based Intrusion Detection

A traffic anomaly-based IDS identifies any unacceptable deviation from expected behavior based on actual traffic structure. When a session is established between systems, there is typically an expected pattern and behavior to the traffic transmitted in that session. That traffic can be compared to expected traffic conduct based on the understandings of traditional system interaction for that type of connection.

Like the other types of anomaly-based IDS, traffic anomaly-based IDS relies on the ability to establish "normal" patterns of traffic and expected modes of behavior in systems, networks, and applications. In a highly dynamic environment, it may be difficult, if not impossible, to clearly define these parameters.

Intrusion Response

Upon detection of an adverse event or suspicious activity, the IDS or IPS can begin, if permitted to and configured accordingly, to interact with the system (or systems) to restrict or block traffic and collaborate with other IDS devices or logical access control systems.

Early versions of IDS integration for automated intrusion responses tied the IDS to the firewall, allowing it to instruct the firewall to implement specific rules targeted at the questionable traffic. This practice is still employed today and used when the attack can be clearly quantified and the proposed rules do not conflict with normal business operations. On the surface, injecting a rule in a firewall to stop an attack seems logical. However, firewalls may have hundreds of rules, and the positioning of the new rule in the rule set can have a negative impact on normal, mission-critical communications. Moreover, some firewall platforms will share all or portions of their rules with other firewalls in the organization. Therefore, an attack affecting the Internet connection to headquarters may be blocked without affecting local traffic, but when that change is replicated to firewalls at remote sites, the results can be catastrophic.

Much like firewall rule set modification, the IDS can also inject new access control lists in routers, VPN gateways, or VLAN switches to block or restrict traffic. Again, the placement of the rule in the system's existing ACL can have repercussions to other communications. Nevertheless, in some cases these concerns can be quelled by tuning the interaction between the IDS and other filtering devices and predefining acceptable rules and default placement. Finally, because an attack can potentially cause large losses to confidentiality, integrity, and availability, as well as lost productivity or revenue, temporary loss of other communications may be deemed an acceptable risk in the face of an aggressive attack.

Finally, in some cases, the IDS can be used in combination with custom applications to enact changes in systems logically distant from the attack. For example, a script can be activated by an alert from an IDS that temporarily disables a user account, increases the level of auditing on certain systems, or suspends an application from accepting new connections.

Alarms and Signals
The impetus for the use of IDS is to gain visibility into the activities on the network and alert administrators to potentially harmful behavior. The core capability of IDS is to produce alarms and signals that work to notify people and systems to adverse events. There are three fundamental components of an alarm capability:

1. Sensor
2. Control and communication
3. Enunciator

A sensor is the detection mechanism that identifies an event and produces the appropriate notification. The notification can be informational, simply alerting an administrator of the event, or it can be active, triggering a specific response activity to deal with the problem. Tuning sensors to the appropriate sensitivity is important. If it is not sensitive enough, events will be missed, and if it is too sensitive, there will be too many false alarms. In addition, there may be different types of sensors used for different purposes. A sensor tuned to monitor network traffic will be different than one monitoring CPU activity on a server.

Control and communication refers to the mechanism of handling alert information. For example, an alert may be sent as an email, instant message, pager message, text message, or even an audible message to a phone or voicemail.

The enunciator is essentially a relay system. It may be necessary to notify local resources immediately and remote resources later. Also, the enunciator is the system that can employ business logic, such as determining the specific business unit that is affected by an event and alerting the management of that unit. In addition, the enunciator can construct the message to accommodate different delivery mechanisms. For example, it may have to truncate the message to send to a pager, format to support a specific type of email system, compile a special text-to-voice message, or send a fax.

Establishing who within an organization receives an alert, as well as the timing and delivery mechanism, is critical. Once the appropriate people are identified, determining what types of alerts they should receive and the level of urgency for those alerts must be determined. For example, if an alert occurs and a message containing sensitive material needs to be delivered to the CSO, the security of that information must be considered. Therefore, the type of technology used for delivery can have a bearing on the amount and type of data sent. To further complicate the issue of secure delivery, when one communication transaction fails and a secondary method is attempted, the message format as well as the information it contains may need to be changed. For example, the CSO may determine that the most secure mode of notification during working hours is his or her private fax machine in his or her office. If acknowledgment is not received in a predetermined time frame, the next mode of communication is a message to his or her cell phone. Given this, the format of the message must be adjusted to accommodate not only the receiving device but the security of that device as well.

IDS Management

As IDS became an accepted enterprise security technology and adopted more readily, it began to suffer from ill-founded perceptions. Many organizations felt that it was simply a technology investment that needed little or no ongoing maintenance. Nothing is further from the truth. The success of an effective IDS or IPS service depends as much on the implementation and maintenance of the service as on the technology used. IDS and IPS are real time devices that require ongoing operational support.

An IDS is designed to alert an administrator in the event something is detected. If it is not implemented properly, tuned accordingly, and if the appropriate personnel is not trained, the organization will get little or no value from its investment. In a typical corporate IDS implementation, what at first appears as simply a product investment quickly turns into a full technology management process, including the services of a full time IDS administrator.

Soon after, investments are needed for managing the data output from the systems, and technology for storage, retention, and security. Finally, with added awareness of what is occurring on the network, many organizations are motivated to acquire additional technology, such as more IDSs, correlation engines, and other security controls to address the onslaught.

If not properly managed, an IDS or IPS system can quickly become a gravity well of time, effort, and money. An IDS requires expert administration and overall management of the solution, and the technology's success within the enterprise is directly proportional to the support of management to maximize the value of their investment. Upon implementing IDS, organizations must ensure they have a knowledgeable resource to select, install, configure, operate, and maintain the system. Management processes and procedures must be developed and employed to ensure that the system is regularly updated with signatures, evaluated for suspicious activities, and the IDS itself is not vulnerable to direct attack.

One of the more important, but overlooked, aspects of IDS is managing the output from the system. Many organizations employ IDS to gain a better understanding of what may be occurring on their networks and systems. Once the IDS detects an event, it is necessary for the organization to have an incident response process. Although an IDS can be configured to perform some automated functions to thwart an attack, complete reliance on the system is not realistic. IDS is designed to detect and, if possible, identify an attack. It is up to the people in the organization to work within their environment to follow through with the process of managing an incident. Therefore, though it is an effective technology, IDS is simply the tip of the security management and incident response spear.

Physically implementing an IDS is the first step in orchestrating a comprehensive incident management infrastructure designed to deal with potentially harmful events. In summary, the following are needed to ensure an effective IDS:

- Employ a technically knowledgeable person to select, install, configure, operate, and maintain the IDS.
- Regularly update the system with new signature attacks and evaluate expected behavior profiles.
- Be aware that the IDS may be vulnerable to attacks and protect it accordingly.

Finally, the security practitioner needs to be aware of the fact that intruders may try to disable the IDS or IPS with false information or overload the system through a DoS or DDoS attack. In addition, the security architect and the security professional both need to work together to ensure that from a design and a policy perspective, the IDS or IPS system is aligned to support the needs of the organization.

Whitelisting, Blacklisting, and Greylisting... Oh My!

A whitelist is a list of email addresses and/or Internet addresses that someone knows as "good" senders. A blacklist is a corresponding list of known "bad" senders. Greylisting is an approach that says, "I don't know who you are, so I'm going to make your email message jump through some extra hoops before I accept it." So an email from an unrecognized sender is neither on the whitelist or the blacklist and therefore is treated differently. Greylisting works by telling the sending email server to resend the message sometime soon. Many spammers set their software to blindly transmit their spam email, and the software does not understand the "resend soon" message. Thus, the spam would never actually be delivered.

The security practitioner needs to be aware of the different spam filtering tools that are available to them. One of the most important is The Spamhaus Project. The Spamhaus Project is an international nonprofit organization whose mission is to track the Internet's spam operations and sources, to provide dependable real time anti-spam protection for Internet networks, to work with law enforcement agencies to identify and pursue spam and malware gangs worldwide, and to lobby governments for effective anti-spam legislation. Spamhaus maintains a number of security intelligence databases and real time spam-blocking databases ('DNSBLs') responsible for keeping back the vast majority of spam and malware sent out on the Internet. These include the Spamhaus Block List (SBL), the Exploits Block List (XBL), the Policy Block List (PBL), and the Domain Block List (DBL). In addition, Spamhaus maintains The Register of Known Spam Operations (ROKSO) database, which collates information and evidence on known professional spam operations that have been terminated by a minimum of 3 Internet Service Providers for spam offenses.[18]

Third-party Security Services, Sandboxing, Anti-malware, Honeypots and Honeynets

Sandboxing is a form of software virtualization that lets programs and processes run in their own isolated virtual environment. Typically, programs running within the sandbox have limited access to your files and system, and they can make no permanent changes. That means that whatever happens in the sandbox stays in the sandbox. Sandboxing, one alternative to

---

18   http://www.spamhaus.org/rokso/

traditional signature-based malware defense, is seen as a way to spot zero-day malware and stealthy attacks in particular.

Malware uses a variety of techniques and approaches to evade detection. One of these techniques delays the execution of malicious code so that a sandbox times out. However, to do this, the malware does not simply sleep. Instead, the malware performs some useless computations that give the appearance of activity. The stalling technique by the malware works because it appears to the sandbox as if the malware is simply executing functions that any normal program would, and from the point of view of the malware analysis system, everything is normal.

To monitor malware, a sandbox introduces hooks. These hooks can be inserted directly into a program to get notifications (callbacks) for function or library calls. The problem with direct hooks is that the program code needs to be modified, and this can be detected by malware or interfere with dynamic code generation. But the main problem with hooking system calls is that the sandbox cannot see any instruction that the malware executes between calls. This is a significant blind spot that malware authors can target; and they do so with code that runs between system calls. Another evasive method is carried out through environmental checks. Malware authors can add novel, zero-day environmental checks related to the operating system and manipulate the return value as an evasive maneuver that forces vendors to patch their sandbox to catch it.

The security practitioner needs to rely on third-party services and systems in order to find and detect these kinds of threats within the enterprise. In addition, there may be other threats that go undetected from third-party software and services that are being consumed by users in the organization as well. The use of different technology vendors scanning tools for malware and virus mitigation is one area that the security practitioner can act upon fairly easily. The need to contract with a third-party company to help provide Dynamic Application Security Testing (DAST) services may be a brand new thought process for many security practitioners.

Dynamic application security testing (DAST) technologies are designed to detect conditions indicative of a security vulnerability in an application in its running state. Most DAST solutions test only the exposed HTTP and HTML interfaces of Web-enabled applications; however, some solutions are designed specifically for non-Web protocol and data malformation (for example, remote procedure call, Session Initiation Protocol [SIP], and so on).

The following are several areas where DAST solutions are providing interesting and innovative approaches to the security issues that face the enterprise today:

- Dynamic application security testing as a service. The market for dynamic testing as a service is growing, and some of the DAST solution vendors such as Qualys, Veracode, and WhiteHat only offer their solution as a service. The security professional may prefer to use a product and a service from the DAST vendor: For example, they may want to perform testing on their more sensitive applications on-premises using a DAST product, testing on their less-sensitive applications via DAST as a service, or testing on deployed applications as a service, with testing of applications in the QA phase of the development process using on-premises DAST products.
- The ability to crawl and test Rich Internet Applications (RIA). A hallmark of Web 2.0 applications is the use of RIA, mostly in the form of JavaScript and Ajax frameworks. In addition, many applications include large amounts of client-side logic in the form of Adobe Flash, Flex, and Microsoft's Silverlight.

The use of client-side RIA logic complicates how applications are crawled and how traditional DAST testing is performed because the JavaScript and other types of code are rendered at the client, not at the server.

■ HTML5. HTML5 is not a single standard, and the multiple standards that collectively represent HTML5 are at different levels of maturity and adoption. Testing HTML5 and keeping up with the fluid standards is an emerging requirement for all DAST solutions.

■ The ability to crawl and test applications that use other types of interfaces carried over Web protocols. For example, many DAST solutions test Web services using protocols and formats, such as Simple Object Access Protocol (SOAP), representational state transfer (REST), Extensible Markup Language (XML), and JavaScript Object Notation (JSON).

■ Static application testing capabilities (SAST). For comprehensive application security testing, applications should be able to be tested from the "inside out" using static analysis and from the "outside in" using dynamic analysis.

■ Interactive Security Testing. Some of the testing providers enable interaction between their static and dynamic security testing techniques. One of the most common ways is to instrument the application while it is being tested dynamically. This provides more detailed information (such as identifying the line of code where a vulnerability occurs and assessing the code coverage of testing). While this may not be suitable for production applications, this approach is quite useful in QA testing in order to provide more meaningful results to developers.

■ Comprehensive fuzz testing. Some DAST solutions are designed specifically to expand well beyond Web protocols to include non-Web protocols (for example, remote procedure calls, Server Message Block, Session Initiation Protocol [SIP], and so on) as well as data input malformation. This is especially critical for the dynamic security testing of applications used within embedded devices, such as storage appliances, telecommunications and networking equipment, directories, automated teller machines, medical devices, and so on.

■ Testing mobile and cloud-based applications. Ideally, mobile applications would be tested with SAST and DAST; however, pure DAST testing can add value. Beyond the use of RIA and HTML5 discussed previously, most Android and iOS applications are Web-like in nature and communicate over Web or RESTful HTTP-based protocols. At a minimum, the exposed interfaces of the applications should be testable using DAST. Many of the mobile applications communicate with cloud-based applications on the back end, which must also be tested. In addition, many applications have specific code paths for supporting mobile devices. In order to test these properly, DAST solutions must emulate a number of mobile browsers.

In addition to the use of DAST services, the security practitioner needs to consider the value of a honeypot or honeynet deployment within a secured area of the enterprise for testing and evaluation purposes. Honeypot systems are decoy servers or systems set up to gather information regarding an attacker or intruder into your system. It is important to remember that honeypots do not replace other traditional Internet security systems; they are an additional level or system. Honeypots can be set up inside, outside, or in the DMZ of a firewall design or even in all of the locations; although they are most often deployed inside of a firewall for control purposes. In a sense, they are variants of standard intruder detection systems (IDS) but with more of a focus on information gathering and deception. Two or more honeypots on a network form a honeynet. Typically, a honeynet is used for monitoring a larger and more diverse network in which one honeypot may not be sufficient. Honeynets and honeypots are usually implemented as parts of larger network intrusion detection systems. A honeyfarm is a centralized collection of honeypots and analysis tools. Some common honeypots are:

- **Glastopf** – A low-interaction, open source honeypot that emulates a vulnerable Web server. Running on Python, PHP, and MySQL, Glastopf can emulate literally thousands of vulnerabilities and is intended to be Web crawled, a recognition that today's attackers frequently use search engines to find innocent websites to infect. Glastopf has GUI management and reporting features, and it's actively maintained and updated.[19]

- **Specter** – A commercial honeypot, is GUI-based and has a few interesting features (it updates its own content, has "marker" files that can be used to trace hackers, and more) that make it a honeypot to check out.[20]

- **Ghost USB** – Is a free USB emulation honeypot that mounts as a fake USB drive to enable easier capture and analysis of malware that uses USB drives to replicate.[21]

- **KFSensor** – A Windows based honeypot intrusion detection system (IDS). It acts as a honeypot to attract and detect hackers and worms by simulating vulnerable system services and trojans. By acting as a decoy server, it can divert attacks from critical systems and provide a higher level of information than can be achieved by using firewalls and NIDS alone. KFSensor is designed for use in a Windows based corporate environment and contains many innovative and unique features such as remote management, a Snort compatible signature engine, and emulations of Windows networking protocols.[22]

The security practitioner has a difficult job in general, and when it comes to malware protection for the organization, that job can be even tougher due to the proliferation of mobile and handheld devices, as well as cloud based storage and collaboration technologies. While the standard anti-malware technologies exist and can be deployed to prevent some infections, the ability to protect varied end points and access points within the enterprise is difficult to scale as rapidly as the proliferation of these devices and access mechanisms. One of the interesting tools that the security professional can leverage is the Anti-Malware Testing Standards Organization (AMTSO). AMTSO's charter focuses on the following four areas:

1. Providing a forum for discussions related to the testing of anti-malware and related products.

2. Developing and publicizing objective standards and best practices for testing of anti-malware and related products.

3. Promoting education and awareness of issues related to the testing of anti-malware and related products.

4. Providing tools and resources to aid standards-based testing methodologies.

---

19 http://glastopf.org/

20 http://www.specter.com/default50.htm

21 https://code.google.com/p/ghost-usb-honeypot/

22 http://www.keyfocus.net/kfsensor/

AMTSO supports two "Feature Settings Check" webpages that allow anyone to check his or her favorite anti-malware solutions.[23] One page is designed to test Windows desktops, while the other tests Android devices. With the different checks, you can verify if the corresponding feature is configured properly within your anti-malware solution. The checks provided for Windows desktops are listed below:

1. Test if my protection against the manual download of malware (EICAR.COM) is enabled.
2. Test if my protection against a drive-by download (EICAR.COM) is enabled.
3. Test if my protection against the download of a Potentially Unwanted Application (PUA) is enabled.
4. Test if protection against accessing a Phishing Page is enabled.
5. Test if my cloud protection is enabled.

The checks provided for Android devices are listed below:

1. Test if my protection against the manual download of malware is enabled.
2. Test if my protection against a drive-by download is enabled.
3. Test if my protection against the download of a Potentially Unwanted Application (PUA) is enabled.
4. Test if protection against accessing a Phishing Page is enabled.

NOTE – None of the files downloaded nor pages visited are malicious by any means. It is only by industry-agreement that these innocent files are detected, solely for the purpose for the users to verify that their Android based anti-malware solution is configured correctly and reacting as expected.

Patch and Vulnerability Management

A key part of configuration and change management involves the deployment of software updates, which is also known as patch management. Flaws in vendor products are continuously discovered. The development and distribution of vendor patches results in a never-ending cycle of required updates to production systems. Managing these updates is not a trivial task for any organization. The patch management process must be formalized through change and configuration management to ensure that changes to existing configurations are carefully controlled.

The main objective of a patch management program is to create a consistently configured environment that is secure against known vulnerabilities in operating systems and application software. Unfortunately, as with many technology-based problems, good, practical solutions are not as apparent. Managing updates for all the applications and operating system versions used in a small company is fairly complicated, and the situation only becomes more complex when additional platforms, availability requirements, and remote offices and workers are factored in as the organization grows in size.

Security-related patches will typically be issued following the discovery or disclosure of a security vulnerability. Vendors will frequently fix security problems in software or firmware through version updates. They may not specify the reason for the version change or what flaws were addressed in a given update. In this case, it is important to obtain vulnerability

---

23   http://www.amtso.org/feature-settings-check-main.html

information from third-party services. Several sources of vulnerability and patch availability information can be obtained from resource centers such as:

- ***http://cve.mitre.org*** – The Common Vulnerability and Exposures database that provides the standard naming and numbering convention for disclosed vulnerabilities
- ***http://nvd.nist.gov*** – An online database of known vulnerabilities managed by the U.S. National Institute of Standards and Technology (NIST)
- ***http://www.us-cert.gov*** – An online resource for a wide variety of information on known vulnerabilities and remediation options

Given the large number of vulnerabilities found each year, the security practitioner must be able to examine systems for known vulnerabilities and recommend action. There are a variety of automated and manual tools that test devices, systems, and applications for known flaws. They work by probing the target environment and examining it against a database of known vulnerabilities. While many of these systems are highly automated, they must be kept up to date and may not contain all vulnerabilities being exploited in the wild. Additionally, these systems may produce false positives. The security practitioner must be able to determine if the finding is truly a vulnerability or simply a mistake by the tool.

Once a discovery is made of a flawed item in the target system, a determination should be made whether to patch the item. A risk-based decision is required to determine the necessity of patching the problem. What will be the risk if the flaw is not patched? Is the system likely to be exposed to threats that may exploit the vulnerability? Will special privileges be required for the vulnerability to be exploited? Can the vulnerability be used to gain administrative privileges on the target? How easy is it to exploit the vulnerability? Will it require physical access to the system or can it be exploited remotely? The answers to these questions will influence how critical it will be to patch the system. The security professional is expected to evaluate the level of risk and determine if and when a suitable patch (or workaround) should be applied.

Upon determining the level of potential exposure, the security practitioner should consult with the management and the owners of the system to determine the chosen course of action. The security professional should work with administrators to determine if the update causes any undesirable affects. For example, some updates can change system configurations or security settings. Some vendor patches have been known to reset access control lists on various sensitive files, creating a subsequent vulnerability. In this regard, patch testing should address not only the proper functioning of the system but also the effect the update may have on the overall security state and policy of the system.

Once the update is tested and residual issues addressed, a schedule should be established for system deployment. It is important that users be notified of system updates prior to deployment. This way, if an unanticipated error occurs, it can be corrected more readily. When possible, it is best to schedule updates during periods of low productivity, such as evenings or weekends. Again, this is primarily accomplished to accommodate unforeseen system crashes.

Prior to deploying updates to production servers, make certain that a full system backup is conducted. In the event of a system crash due to the update, the server and data can be recovered without significant loss of data. Additionally, if the update involved propriety code, it will be necessary to provide a copy of the server or application image to the media librarian.

Deploy the update in stages, when possible, to accomplish a final validation of the update in the production environment. This may not always be possible given the network configuration, but it is desirable to limit unforeseen difficulties.

After the deployment, it is necessary to confirm that the updates are deployed to all of the appropriate machines. System management tools and vulnerability scanners can be used to automate the validation. Continue checking the network until every network component scheduled for the change has been validated. Redeploy updates as necessary until all systems receive the update.

The last step in the patch management process is to document the changes. This provides a record of what was accomplished, the degree of success, and issues discovered. Documentation should also be conducted when decisions are made to not patch a system. The reasons for the decision and the approving authority should be recorded. This serves the dual purpose of providing external auditors with evidence that the organization is practicing due diligence regarding system maintenance and imparting a history of uniqueness within the system.

Security and Patch Information Sources

A key component of patch management is the intake and vetting of information regarding both security issues and patch release: The security practitioner needs to know which security issues and software updates are relevant to their environment. An organization needs a point person or team that is responsible for keeping up to date on newly released patches and security issues that affect the systems and applications deployed in their environment. This team can also take the lead in alerting administrators and users of security issues or updates to the applications and systems they support and use. A comprehensive and accurate asset management system can help determine whether all existing systems are accounted for when researching and processing information on patches and updates.

An organization should also have relationships with their key operating system, network device, and application vendors that facilitate the timely release and distribution of information on product security issues and patches. These relationships can range from monthly calls with the account manager to simple subscriptions to the vendor's security announcement list.

Patch Prioritization and Scheduling

Several scheduling guidelines and plans should exist in a comprehensive patch management program. First, a patch cycle must exist that guides the normal application of patches and updates to systems. This cycle does not specifically target security or other critical updates. Instead, this patch cycle is meant to facilitate the application of standard patch releases and updates. This cycle can be time or event based; for example, the schedule can mandate that system updates occur monthly, or a cycle may be driven by the release of service packs or maintenance releases. In either instance, modifications and customizations can and should be made based on availability requirements, system criticality, and available resources.

The second scheduling plan deals more with critical security and functionality patches and updates. This plan helps the organization deal with the prioritization and scheduling of updates that, by their nature, must be deployed in a more immediate fashion. A number of factors are routinely considered when determining patch priority and scheduling urgency. Vendor-reported criticality (e.g., high, medium, and low) is a key input for calculating a patch's significance and priority, as is the existence of a known exploit or other malicious code that uses the vulnerability being patched as an attack vector. Other factors that should be taken into account when scheduling and prioritizing patches are system criticality (e.g., the relative importance of the applications and data the system supports to the overall business) and system exposure (e.g., DMZ systems vs. internal file servers vs. client workstations).

Patch Testing

Ideally, the breadth and detail of an organization's patch testing will relate directly to the criticality of systems and data handled and the complexity of the environment (e.g., number of supported platforms and applications, number of remote offices). The patch testing process begins with the acquisition of the software updates and continues through acceptance testing after production deployment. The first component of patch testing will thus be the verification of the patch's source and integrity. This step helps ensure that the update is valid and has not been maliciously or accidentally altered. Digital signatures or some form of checksum or integrity verification should be a component of patch validation. This signature should be regularly verified, especially as an update is passed through an organization's technology operations (e.g., on the update server, in build images, in software repositories).

Once a patch has been determined valid, it is typically placed in a test environment. While the perfect test environment will mirror production as closely as possible, it is important to at least account for the majority of critical applications and supported operating platforms in your patch testing infrastructure. Many organizations will use a subset of production systems as an ad hoc test environment; department-level servers and IT employee systems are typically used in these cases. Regardless of the available test equipment and systems, exposing the update to as many variations of production-like systems as possible will help ensure a smooth and predictable rollout.

The actual mechanics of testing a patch vary widely by organization. This testing could be simply installing a patch and making sure the system reboots, or the test procedure could involve the execution of a battery of detailed and elaborate test scripts that validate continued system and application functionality. In the end, a suitable approach toward detailed patch testing will be dictated by system criticality and availability requirements, available resources, and patch severity.

The initial phases of production rollout can be considered an additional component of the testing process. Rollouts are often done in tiers, with the initial tiers often involving less critical systems. Based on the performance of these stages of the patch deployment process, the entire environment will be updated, and the testing process can be considered finished with the completion of final acceptance testing.

Change Management

Change management is vital to every stage of the patch management process. As with all system modifications, patches and updates must be performed and tracked through the change management system. It is highly unlikely that an enterprise-scale patch management program can be successful without proper integration with the change management system and organization.

Like any environmental changes, patch application plans submitted through change management must have associated contingency and backout plans. What are the recovery plans if something goes wrong during or as a result of the application of a patch or update? Also, information on risk mitigation should be included in the change management solution. For example, how are desktop patches going to be phased and scheduled to prevent mass outages and support desk overload? Monitoring and acceptance plans should also be included in the change management process. How will updates be certified as successful? There should be specific milestones and acceptance criteria to guide the verification of the patches' success and to allow for the closure of the update in the change management system (e.g., no reported issues within a week of patch application).

Patch Installation and Deployment

The deployment phase of the patch management process tends to be where administrators and engineers have the most experience. Installation and deployment is where the actual work of applying patches and updates to production systems occurs. And, while this stage is the most visible to the organization as a whole, the effort expended throughout the entire patch management process is what dictates the overall success of a given deployment and the patch management program in total.

The most important technical factor affecting patch deployment is likely the choice of tools used. One key distinction between patch tools is a common system development issue - to buy or to build? Historically, many organizations have created custom solutions using scripting languages combined with available platform tools to distribute and apply patches. As the industry has matured and the need for comprehensive and automated updates has increased, many tools have become available to help manage the patch application process. These tools are often classified as being either agent-based or agentless systems, depending on whether they rely on software being installed on the target systems that are to be patched. Additionally, many existing system management tools have the capability to perform software and system updates. The correct choice of patch management tools for any organization depends on a number of issues, including the number of platforms supported, the number of systems to be patched, existing expertise and personnel involved, and the availability of existing system management tools.

While applying patches, and especially security updates, in a timely manner is critical, these updates must be made in a controlled and predictable fashion. Without an organized and controlled patch application process, system state will tend to drift rather quickly from the norm, and compliance with mandated patch and update levels will diminish. In general, users and even administrators should not be permitted to apply patches arbitrarily. While this should be addressed initially at a policy and procedure level (e.g., with acceptable use policies, change management, and established maintenance windows), it may also be appropriate to apply additional technical controls to limit when and by whom patches can be applied. The type of controls enforced will vary by organization and requirement but include items such as restricted user rights (the user does not have sufficient permissions to update the system) and network-based access controls (the system cannot access the resources needed to perform an update; for example, Windows Update). In smaller organizations, automated, user-driven tools such as Windows Update may be acceptable. However, groups that use these update methods will likely need to rely heavily on policy guidance and enforcement along with regular assessment to ensure that organizational goals for patch and configuration compliance are met.

Audit and Assessment

Regular audit and assessment helps gauge the success and extent of patch management efforts. In this phase of the patch management program, you are essentially trying to answer two questions:

- What systems need to be patched for any given vulnerability or bug?
- Are the systems that are supposed to be updated actually patched?

The audit and assessment component will help answer these questions, but there are dependencies. Two critical success factors are accurate and effective: asset and host management. Often, these related goals of asset and host management are addressed by a single product, such as with Tivoli, UnicenterTG, or System Center Configuration Manager (SCCM). The major requirement for any asset management system is the ability to accurately track deployed hardware and software throughout the enterprise, including remote users and office locations. Ideally, host management software will allow the administrator to generate reports (e.g., all clients without a given hot fix, all versions of particular applications) that will be used to drive the effort toward consistent installation of patches and updates across the organization.

System discovery and auditing are also components of the audit and assessment process. While asset and host management systems can help you administer and report on known systems, there are likely a number of systems that have been either unknowingly or intentionally excluded from inventory databases and management infrastructures. System discovery tools can help uncover these systems and assist in bringing them under the umbrella of formal system management and patch compliance. Organizations typically use either their own discovery and assessment mechanisms or one of the various managed vulnerability assessment tools. Regardless of the tools used, the goal is to discover unknown systems within your environment and assess their compliance with organization update and configuration guidelines.

Consistency and Compliance

While the audit and assessment element of the patch management program will help identify systems that are out of compliance with organizational guidelines, additional work is required to reduce non-compliance. Audit and assessment efforts can be considered "after the fact" evaluation of compliance because the systems being evaluated will typically be already deployed into production. To supplement post-implementation assessment, one should put controls in place to ensure that newly deployed and rebuilt systems are up to spec with regard to patch levels.

System build tools and guidelines are the primary enforcement means of ensuring compliance with patch requirements at installation time. As new patches are approved and deployed, build images and scripts should be updated so that all newly built systems are appropriately patched, and associated build documentation should be updated to reflect these changes. In addition to updates to build tools and documentation, operational procedures must exist to facilitate ongoing compliance of newly built systems. If an engineering team typically builds servers (e.g., with the base operating system and applications) and a separate operations team then assumes management of the system, a process must exist to funnel operational changes back to the build and engineering stage of the system lifecycle. These modifications are most ideally and suitably handled via an enterprise-wide change management system. Any new patches and updates that are approved and installed by operations should also be integrated by the engineering team into new builds, with the change management system providing both an appropriate audit trail and suitable procedural guidelines for this implementation.

While the issue of patch management has technology at its core, it's clear that focusing only on technology to solve the problem is not the answer. Installing patch management software or vulnerability assessment tools without supporting guidelines, requirements, and oversight will be a wasted effort that will further complicate the situation. Instead, solid patch management programs will team technological solutions with policy and operationally based components that work together to address each organization's unique needs.

Vulnerability Management Systems

Sun Tzu once wrote, "If you know the enemy and know thyself, then you need not fear the result of a hundred battles." The two principal factors needed for an organization to "know thyself" involve configuration management and vulnerability scanning. Configuration management provides an organization with knowledge about all of its parts, while vulnerability scanning identifies the weakness present within the parts. Knowing what composes the system is the first critical step in understanding what is needed to defend it. Identifying vulnerabilities of a known system provides the security practitioner with the necessary knowledge to defend against the onslaught of all types of attackers.

Vulnerabilities arise from flaws, misconfigurations (also known as weaknesses), and policy failures. Flaws result from product design imperfections. The most common type of flaw in software is the buffer overflow. Flaws are usually fixed with a security patch, new code, or a hardware change. Misconfigurations represent implementation errors that expose a system to attack. Examples of misconfigurations include weak access control lists, open ports, and unnecessary services. Policy failures occur when individuals fail to follow or implement security as required. This includes weak passwords, unauthorized network devices, and unapproved applications. Vulnerability scanning is conducted against network, host system, and application resources. Each type of scan is used to detect vulnerabilities specific to the type of scan. Network scans look for vulnerabilities on the network. Flaws in devices are found with scanning tools designed to perform tests that simulate an attack. Misconfigured network settings such as unauthorized services can be found during network scans.

Policy violations, which include unauthorized devices, workstations, and servers, are also found with a comprehensive network scanning tool. Host-based scans are conducted at the system console or through the use of agents on servers and workstations throughout the network. Host-based scans are critical for identifying missing security updates on servers and workstations. This type of scan can also identify when local policy or security configurations, such as audit log settings, are not implemented correctly. A good host-based scanner can also identify unauthorized software or services that might indicate a compromised system or a blatant violation of configuration management within the organization. The last type of vulnerability scanning involves specialized application security scanners. These tools check for patch levels and implementations of applications. For instance, some application scanning tools can identify vulnerabilities in Web-based applications. Other tools are designed to work with large applications, such as a database management system, to identify default settings or improper rights for sensitive tables.

Change and Configuration Management

Systems experience frequent changes. Software packages are added, removed, or modified. New hardware is introduced, while legacy devices are replaced. Updates due to flaws in software are regular business activities for system managers. The rapid advancement of technology, coupled with regular discovery of vulnerabilities, requires proper change control management to maintain the necessary integrity of the system. Change control management is embodied in policies, procedures, and operational practices.

Maintaining system integrity is accomplished through the process of change control management. A well-defined process implements structured and controlled changes necessary to support system integrity and accountability for changes. Decisions to implement changes should be made by a committee of representatives from various groups within the organization such as ordinary users, security, system operations, and upper-level management. Each group provides a unique perspective regarding the need to implement a proposed change. Users have a general idea of how the system is used in the field. Security can provide input regarding the possible risks associated with a proposed change. System operations can identify the challenges associated with the deployment and maintenance of the change. Management provides final approval or rejection of the change based on budget and strategic directions of the organization. Actions of the committee should be documented for historical and accountability purposes.

The change management structure should be codified as an organization policy. Procedures for the operational aspects of the change management process should also be created. Change management policies and procedures are forms of directive controls. The following subsections outline a recommended structure for a change management process.

- **Requests** – Proposed changes should be formally presented to the committee in writing. The request should include a detailed justification in the form of a business case argument for the change, focusing on the benefits of implementation and costs of not implementing.
- **Impact Assessment** – Members of the committee should determine the impacts to operations regarding the decision to implement or reject the change.
- **Approval/Disapproval** – Requests should be answered officially regarding their acceptance or rejection.
- **Build and Test** – Subsequent approvals are provided to operations support for test and integration development. The necessary software and hardware should be tested in a non-production environment. All configuration changes associated with a deployment must be fully tested and documented. The security team should be invited to perform a final review of the proposed change within the test environment to ensure that no vulnerabilities are introduced into the production system. Change requests involving the removal of a software or a system component require a similar approach. The item should be removed from the test environment and have a determination made regarding any negative impacts.
- **Notification** – System users are notified of the proposed change and the schedule of deployment.
- **Implementation** – The change is deployed incrementally, when possible, and monitored for issues during the process.

- **Validation** – The change is validated by the operations staff to ensure that the intended machines received the deployment package. The security staff performs a security scan or review of the affected machines to ensure that new vulnerabilities are not introduced. Changes should be included in the problem tracking system until operations has ensured that no problems have been introduced.
- **Documentation** – The outcome of the system change, to include system modifications and lessons learned, should be recorded in the appropriate records. This is the way that change management typically interfaces with configuration management.

Configuration Management

Organizational hardware and software require proper tracking, implementation testing, approvals, and distribution methods. Configuration management is a process of identifying and documenting hardware components, software, and the associated settings. A well-documented environment provides a foundation for sound operations management by ensuring that IT resources are properly deployed and managed. The security professional plays an important role in configuration management through the identification and remediation of control gaps in current configurations.

Detailed hardware inventories are necessary for recovery and integrity purposes. Having an inventory of each workstation, server, and networking device is necessary for replacement purposes in the event of facility destruction. All devices and systems connected to the network should be in the hardware list. At a minimum, configuration documentation should include in the hardware list the following information about each device and system:

1. Make
2. Model
3. MAC addresses
4. Serial number
5. Operating system or firmware version
6. Location
7. BIOS and other hardware-related passwords
8. Assigned IP address if applicable
9. Organizational property management label or bar code

Software is a similar concern, and a software inventory should minimally include:

1. Software name
2. Software vendor (and reseller if appropriate)
3. Keys or activation codes (note if there are hardware keys)
4. Type of license and for what version
5. Number of licenses
6. License expiration
7. License portability
8. Organizational software librarian or asset manager
9. Organizational contact for installed software
10. Upgrade, full or limited license

The inventory is also helpful for integrity purposes when attempting to validate systems, software, and devices on the network. Knowing the hardware versions of network components is valuable from two perspectives. First, the security professional will be able to quickly find and mitigate vulnerabilities related to the hardware type and version. Most hardware vulnerabilities are associated with a particular brand and model of hardware. Knowing the type of hardware and its location within the network can substantially reduce the effort necessary to identify the affected devices. Additionally, the list is invaluable when performing a network scan to discover unauthorized devices connected to the network. A new device appearing on a previously documented network segment may indicate an unauthorized connection to the network.

A configuration list for each device should also be maintained. Devices such as firewalls, routers, and switches can have hundreds or thousands of configuration possibilities. It is necessary to properly record and track the changes to these configurations to provide assurance for network integrity and availability. These configurations should also be periodically checked to make sure that unauthorized changes have not occurred.

Operating systems and applications also require configuration management. Organizations should have configuration guides and standards for each operating system and application implementation. System and application configuration should be standardized to the greatest extent possible to reduce the number of issues that may be encountered during integration testing. Software configurations and their changes should be documented and tracked with the assistance of the security practitioner. It is possible that server and workstation configuration guides will change frequently due to changes in the software baseline.

Develop a Recovery Strategy

Recovery strategies are driven by the recovery time frame required by the function or application to be recovered. Some strategies the security professional may consider for organization operations are as follows:

- **Surviving Site** – A surviving site strategy is implemented so that while service levels may drop, a function never ceases to be performed because it operates in at least two geographically dispersed buildings that are fully equipped and staffed.
- **Self-Service** – An organization can transfer work to another of its own locations, which has available facilities and/or staff to manage the time sensitive workload until the interruption is over.
- **Internal Arrangement** – Training rooms, cafeterias, conference rooms, etc. may be equipped to support organization functions while staff from the impacted site travels to another site and resumes organization.
- **Reciprocal Agreements/Mutual Aid Agreements** – Other similar organizations may be able to accommodate those affected. For example, one law firm may be able to provide office space to another in the event of an outage. This could involve the temporary suspension of non-time sensitive functions at the organization operations not affected by the outage.
- **Dedicated Alternate Sites** – Built by the company to accommodate organization function or technology recovery.
- **Work from Home** – Many organizations today have the capability to have employees work from locations that are remote from a physical office environment.

- **External Suppliers** – A number of external organizations offer facilities covering a wide range of organization recovery needs from full data centers with a wide range of platforms, alternate site space in physical facilities, mobile units that can be transported to the company site, and temporary staff to provide services when the employees cannot.

- **No Arrangement** – For low-priority business functions or applications, it may not be cost justified to plan at a detailed level. The minimum requirement would be to record a description of the functions, the maximum allowable lapse time for recovery, and a list of the resources required.

Each of these strategies can be considered for the organization and technology recovery. Those that are recommended need to have a cost/benefit analysis (CBA) performed to determine if the costs of the strategy being recommended fits within the amount of risk or loss the organization is trying to avoid. The company should not spend $1,000,000 a year on a recovery strategy to protect $100,000 of income. Every organization does not need a dual data center recovery strategy. The strategy selected must fit the organizational need.

The cost of implementing the recovery strategy recommended needs to include the initial costs associated with building out the strategy as well as ongoing costs to maintain the recovery solution, and where applicable, the cost of periodic testing of the solution to ensure it remains viable, as well as the costs associated with communication, to ensure that all users in the organization are aware of the plans.

Once the strategy has been agreed to and funded, the security professional must then implement the various strategies approved. This may involve negotiating with vendors to provide recovery services for organization or technology, doing site surveys of existing sites to determine excess capacity, wiring conference rooms or cafeterias to support organization functions, buying recovery technology, installing remote replication software, installing networks for voice and data recovery, assigning alternate site seats to the various organization areas, and the like. The security professional also needs to ensure that communication systems are in place to allow the organization to be able to reach all employees during and immediately after an event and to allow for on-going information and status updates to be disseminated to the employees throughout the duration of an event.

Implement a Backup Storage Strategy

Backup strategies for data used to restore technology are varied and are driven by the Recovery Time Objective (RTO) and the Recovery Point Objective (RPO) needed to support the organizational requirements. Some organizations have begun tiering data based on its importance to the organization and frequency of use. The more time sensitive data is replicated offsite either synchronously or asynchronously to ensure its availability and its currency. Other data is backed up to tape and sent offsite once or more a day.

If the backup tapes are stored somewhere else besides an alternate site, then the time it takes to pack and transport those tapes must be included in the RTO. Depending on how many tapes are required, this could increase the time to recovery by hours or even days. To reduce the recovery time from 3 to 5 days minimum to 24 hours or less, the data that will be used to recover systems and applications must be stored at the recovery site.

It is vital that the data that is stored offsite include not only the application data but also the application source code, hardware and software images for the servers and end-user desktops, utility software, license keys, etc.

863

Most organizations, no matter what strategy they employ for storing data offsite, start by performing full backups of all their data followed by periodic incremental backups. Incremental backups take copies of only the files that have changed since the last full or incremental backup was taken and then set the archive bit to "0." The other common option is to take a differential backup. A differential backup copies only the files that have had their data change since the last full backup and does not change the archive bit value.

If a company wants the backup and recovery strategy to be as simple as possible, then they should only use full backups. They take more time and hard drive space to perform, but they are the most efficient in recovery. If that option is not viable, a differential backup can be restored in just two steps; by first laying down the full backup then the differential backup on top of it. Remember that a differential backup records every piece of data in a file that has changed since the last full backup.

An incremental backup takes the most time in restoration because the full backup must be performed first and then every incremental backup taken since the last full backup. If daily incremental backups are taken but only monthly full backups, and a recover is needed on the 26th day of the month, the full backup restore must be performed first and then 26 incremental backups must be laid on top in the same order that they were taken in.

Interdependencies, both internal and external, need to be understood and documented. Interdependencies include all the inputs to a function or application and where they come from as well as all the outputs to a function or application and where they go to. They include external dependencies such as network service providers and the post office for mail delivery and internal dependencies such as firewalls and local area networks.

The RTO or Maximum Tolerable Downtime (MTD) for a business process or for an application is going to determine the recovery strategy for the process or application. The more time that can elapse before the recovery needs to occur, the more recovery options are available. The more time sensitive an application or function is, the fewer options an organization will have in selecting a recovery strategy.

Recovery Site Strategies

Depending on how much downtime an organization has before the technology recovery must be complete, recovery strategies selected for the technology environment could be any one of the following:

- ■ **Dual Data Center** – This strategy is employed for applications that cannot accept any downtime without negatively impacting the organization. The applications are split between two geographically dispersed data centers and either load balanced between the two centers or hot swapped between the two centers. The surviving data center must have enough head room to carry the full production load in either case.

- ■ **Internal Hot Site** – This site is standby ready with all the technology and equipment necessary to run the applications positioned there. The administrator will be able to effectively restart an application in a hot site recovery without having to perform any bare metal recovery of servers. If this is an internal solution, then often the organization will run non-time sensitive processes there, such as development or test environments, which will be pushed aside for recovery of production when needed. When employing this strategy, one must keep the two environments as close to identical as possible to avoid problems with O/S levels, hardware differences, capacity differences, etc. from preventing or delaying recovery.

- **External Hot Site** – This strategy has equipment on the floor waiting, but the environment must be rebuilt for the recovery. These are services contracted through a recovery service provider. Again, it is important that the two environments be kept as close to identical as possible to avoid problems with O/S levels, hardware differences, capacity differences, etc. from preventing or delaying recovery. Hot site vendors tend to have the most commonly used hardware and software products to attract the largest number of customers to utilize the site. Unique equipment or software would generally need to be provided by the organization either at time of disaster or stored there ahead of time.

- **Warm Site** – A leased or rented facility that is usually partially configured with some equipment but not the actual computers. It will generally have all the cooling, cabling, and networks in place to accommodate the recovery, but the actual servers, mainframe, etc. equipment are delivered to the site at the time of disaster.

- **Cold Site** – A cold site is a shell or empty data center space with no technology on the floor. All technology must be purchased or acquired at the time of disaster.

There are advantages and disadvantages for each of these recovery strategies.

Advantages of a dual data center:
- Little or no downtime
- Ease of maintenance
- No recovery required

Disadvantages of a dual data center:
- Most expensive option
- Requires redundant hardware, networks, staffing
- Distance limitations

Advantages of internal or external hot site:
- Allows recovery to be tested
- Highly available
- Site can be operational within hours

Disadvantages of internal or external hot site:
- Expensive – Internal solution more expensive than external
- Hardware and software compatibility issues in external sites

Advantages of warm and cold site:
- Less expensive
- Available for longer recoveries

Disadvantages of warm and cold site:
- Not immediately available
- Not fully testable without extensive work

Mobile Sites

Another option available is the *mobile site*, meaning the data center of an organization is housed in a mobile trailer or possibly a standard sea cargo shipping container. Should disaster strike, an organization can simply load up the cargo container data center and move it to another location that has the power, resources, and connectivity required to continue operations. *Figure 7.1* shows what a container based mobile solution may look like:

Figure 7.1 – **An example of a Container Data Center module with a cutout of a typical interior layout.** [24]

The advantages to this approach include:

- Highly mobile and relatively easy to transport
- Modular approach to building data centers
- Buildings are not required to house equipment

The disadvantages include:

- "Cold site" capability must be built at determined locations
- The density and design of the container make upgrading and customizing challenging
- Maintaining a shipping contract or equipment to move the container in times of disaster can be expensive

---

24   http://www.nasa.gov/offices/ocio/ittalk/06-2010_cloud_computing.html

7

Security Operations

Processing Agreement

Organizations may also choose to create different processing agreements with other organizations. This can take many forms, but typically they can be viewed as reciprocal agreements or outsourced agreements.

Reciprocal Agreements

Reciprocal agreements are between organizations who choose to share the risk of an outage with each other. Each organization commits to host the data and processing of each other in the event of a disaster. While this seems like a logical solution, it is fraught with problems.

The reality of the situation is both organizations must agree to either maintain spare capacity for the other or agree to a reduced processing capability should one fail. Additionally, if there is a disparity in the number of outages affecting one party, the other party could request compensation. There is also a concern regarding the other organization's ability to comply with all the requirements of the first. For example, if the first organization is a healthcare provider in the U.S., they will be subject to the requirements of the Health Insurance Portability and Accountability Act (HIPAA). Whoever is the partner for a reciprocal agreement must also agree to adhere to the rules of HIPAA even if that is not their core business. This leads organizations seeking to be in reciprocal agreements often searching for partners in their own industry. If competition is a concern then it may be very difficult to find a willing partner for a reciprocal agreement.

Outsourcing

To avoid the problems with reciprocal agreements and the cost of building alternative sites, some organizations may choose to outsource their contingency operations and disaster recovery. This can be cost effective as the business may only incur major costs if a plan is activated, but it also carries risks in the form of unknown capabilities and the ability to ensure compliance with requirements. For example, while a service level agreement (SLA) may state a service will only be down for a certain period of time, it does not provide assurance the provider can actually meet the SLA during a disaster.

The benefits of outsourcing include:

- Service as needed
- All requirements and execution responsibilities are on a third party
- Little to no capital costs
- Greater geographical options for continuity and recovery

The disadvantages include:

- More proactive testing and assessment to ensure capability is ready
- Contract disputes should the vendor be unable to perform
- Vendor lock-in if proprietary systems are deployed
- Can cost more than building the capability if frequent outages occur

Multiple Processing Sites

Multiple processing sites can be a solution for an organization if the organization's facilities separated throughout a country or the world. Multiple processing sites can be an advantage if numerous locations are required to conduct business and there is sufficient bandwidth and latency between the locations. If multiple processing sites are used for the production environment, they should be treated as an organizational "reciprocal" agreement. This means workloads must be categorized based on criticality to the organization, and each location must be able to process, store, and transmit another's workload. While this can be a very cost efficient arrangement, it takes careful planning and coordination to ensure success.

System Resilience and Fault Tolerance Requirements

A large number of potential dangers cause systems to be unreliable. Thankfully, there are also a large number of ways that the security and reliability of key computing systems can be maintained.

The best way to ensure that systems are resilient is to ensure that they are designed to be resilient in the first place and that you are selecting resilient solutions. Most systems are designed to accommodate common threats to smooth operations and provide some ability to prevent common threats from being successful, or if they are, responding quickly to them to minimize disruption to the organization.

For example, systems are examined carefully during design and development to determine where common system failures will likely occur and to calculate the mean time to failure (MTTF) for key system components. Components with moving parts such as fans, power supplies, and hard drives will most likely fail sooner than components with fewer moving parts. This is one of the main reasons why critical systems are deployed with redundant fans and power supplies or why we use drive configurations that take drive failure into account. The key principle is to avoid single points of failure where practical and provide for automated and manual means to address any problems that can disrupt normal service.

It is also vital that systems have some ability to react automatically to common failures and do what they can to address the problem without human intervention. This will limit that amount of disruption. The following sections discuss some common ways by which systems can provide greater resilience to common threats.

Trusted Paths and Fail Secure Mechanisms

While there are a number of system security mechanisms that aid in protecting systems, there are a number of them that could be compromised and must be maintained by operations. Trusted paths provide trustworthy interfaces into privileged user functions and are intended to provide a way to ensure that any communications over that path cannot be intercepted or corrupted. For example, when a user logs in locally to a system, it is important that his credentials can be shared safely and securely through the paths taken from the user interface to the access control subsystem. Many attacks, however, are designed to specifically attack such trusted paths by redirecting input down an alternative channel where it can be intercepted, disclosed, or manipulated. The success of such attacks increases with the level of privilege, making attacks using privileged user accounts very dangerous.

Operations security must include measures to validate that trusted paths continue to operate as intended. Typical countermeasures include log collection and analysis, vulnerability scanning, patch management, and system integrity checking on a regular basis. A combination of these techniques is used to limit or detect any changes in the behavior of trusted paths.

Similarly, operations will be expected to ensure that fail-safe and fail-secure mechanisms are working correctly. While both are concerned with how a system behaves when it fails, they are often confused with each other. It is important for the security professional to distinguish between them:

- **Fail-Safe** – Mechanisms focus on failing with a minimum of harm to personnel or systems.
- **Fail-Secure** – Focuses on failing in a controlled manner to block access while the systems is in an inconsistent state.

For example, data center door systems will fail safe to ensure that personnel can escape the area when the electrical power fails. A fail-secure door would prevent personnel from using the door at all, which could put personnel in jeopardy. Fail-safe and fail-secure mechanisms will need to be maintained and tested on a regular basis to ensure that they are working as designed.

Redundancy and Fault Tolerance

Redundant items are said to provide fault tolerance within a system. This means that a system can continue to operate in the event of a component failure. This can involve the use of spare components, leveraging redundant servers or networks, and redundant data storage.

Spares are components that are available in case that the primary component is damaged or becomes unavailable for some reason. Depending on how the spare is used will determine if it is a cold, warm, or hot spare:

- **Cold Spare** – A cold spare is s a spare component that is not powered up but is a duplicate of the primary that can be inserted into the system if needed. Typically, cold spares will be stored near the system in question and will require someone to manually unpack it and insert it into the affected system.
- **Warm spares** – Are normally already inserted in the system but do not receive power unless they are required.
- **Hot spares** – Are not only inserted into the system but are powered on and waiting to be called upon as needed. In many cases, the system will be able to work with warm or hot spares automatically and without much human intervention required.

Spares may present their own problems. Cold spares are obviously not going to be much use in an unmanned facility, and they will typically require that the system be shut down to be brought online. Cold and warm spares may not successfully start up when needed and cause further disruption. Hot spares may also fail more rapidly than cold or warm spares because they are powered up and will wear down like any powered equipment.

These are some of the reasons why most facilities do not rely solely on redundant components but make use of redundant systems instead. In a typical redundant configuration such as an active–passive pair, the primary system will provide all services while the passive system monitors the primary for any problems. If the primary fails for some reason, the secondary system can take over. Ideally, this means that there is little or no disruption in service caused by system failure. Assuming that the passive system is a duplicate of the primary, there is not even degradation in service.

Redundant networks are similar. In the case that the primary network is unavailable, a secondary path is available. For example, it is common to use a redundant connection to an alternate service provider to deal with the failure of the primary connection. It is also common to deploy core enterprise networks to allow for portions of the core to fail while still providing service. However, duplicate systems often come at over twice the price! The security professional must assure the cost of the system is less than the benefit derived.

Clustering may also be used, although it should not be confused with redundancy. In clustering, two or more members are joined into the cluster and may all provide service at the same time. For example, in an active–active pair, both systems may provide services at any time. In the case of a failure, the remaining partners may continue to provide service but at a decreased capacity.

That degradation in service may not be acceptable in some environments, so often clusters will be deployed with "passive partners" that are intended to join into the active cluster in the case that one of the active systems fails. Naturally, a wide variety of components, systems, and networks can be configured with appropriate levels of fault tolerance and redundancy where needed and where the additional cost is justified.

Power Supplies

If the power fails or becomes unreliable, then systems will obviously fail or become unreliable. Redundant (or dual) power supplies are common in systems where such failures cannot be tolerated (such as in core network switches, for example). Alternatively, failures that occur outside of an individual system can be dealt with using appropriate uninterruptible power supply (UPS) systems and alternative sources of power from the main grid (such as diesel-based generators common to many data center facilities).

Drives and Data Storage

One of the most common types of failure is drive failure. Normal hard drives consist of many rotating and moving parts that will eventually fail. Even the newer solid state disk (SSD) will eventually fail after so many write operations. To help address drive failure and minimize disruption of service or loss of data, a number of options have been developed over the years. The most appropriate solution will depend largely on where the data is stored and what type of media is being used.

In the simplest configuration, all data is stored on a hard drive or multiple hard drives housed within the system itself. In more complex situations, the data may be stored in large storage networks connected to the systems using controllers or in common storage attached to the network. The data may also be mirrored across multiple systems or portions of it stored on different systems and shared equally.

The security professional is expected to understand the common ways that data is stored and identify the most common ways that data can be protected. This includes understanding the basics of how hard disk storage is used in single systems, in storage area networks (SANs), and network attached storage (NAS). Each of these will require different approaches to providing system resilience.

A SAN consists of dedicated block level storage on a dedicated network. They can be made of numerous storage devices such as tape libraries, optical drives, and disk arrays. They utilize protocols like iSCSI to appear to operating systems as locally attached devices.

A NAS is similar to a SAN but with a few very important distinctions. A NAS operates at the file level instead of the block level. A NAS is generally designed to simply store and serve files. Common uses of a NAS include FTP servers and other types of file servers. They are typically on a shared network and cannot be mounted as local drives on a system, but they can often be mapped as network drives. If performance enhancements and redundancy is required within a single system, it is very common to use multiple drives to accomplish this. On systems with multiple drives, these drives may be configured in a number of different ways, depending on what the system needs to do.

If all that is required is basic data storage, then a just-a-bunch-of-drives (JBOD) configuration may be most appropriate. If the disks are configured in this way, each disk may be used independently and in isolation from one another. In this case, data is stored on discrete disks and is not stored across multiple disks. Partitions are usually stored on single disks (and not across multiple disks). In the case that a drive fails, all the data from that drive is lost, but the other drives will continue to be available.

Where it may be desirable to use multiple disks for a single partition, this is referred to as concatenation. Concatenated disks will appear to the operating system as a single, continuous drive. This may be most appropriate where exceptionally large partitions are desirable, but drive failures may cause considerable problems because all the data on the failed drive would be lost.

To help systems use multiple drives in concert, redundant array of independent disk (RAID) levels have been standardized. RAID levels describe various ways that multiple disks can be configured to work together. Some RAID levels will provide enhanced performance, while others provide enhanced reliability. Some are intended to provide both. The security professional should know each of these different levels as well as their advantages and disadvantages.

- **RAID 0** – Writes files in stripes across multiple disks without the use of parity information. This technique allows for fast reading and writing to disk because all of the disks can be accessed in parallel. However, without the parity information, it is not possible to recover from a hard drive failure. This technique does not provide redundancy and should not be used for systems with high availability requirements. It does, however, represent the fastest RAID configuration and may be suitable in scenarios where resilience is not required. For example, it is common to use RAID 0 to store temporary data that will only be required for a short period of time.

- **RAID 1** – This level duplicates all disk writes from one disk to another to create two identical drives. This technique is also known as data mirroring. Redundancy is provided at this level; when one hard drive fails, the other is still available. This mirroring may even happen between drives on different hard drive controllers (which is called duplexing). RAID 1 is very costly from a drive space perspective because half of the available disk is given to the mirroring and is typically only used between pairs of drives. It is commonly used to provide redundancy for system disks where the core operating system files are found.

- **RAID 2** – This RAID level is more or less theoretical and not used in practice. Data is spread across multiple disks at the bit level using this technique. Redundancy information is computed using a Hamming error correction code, which is the same technique used within hard drives and error- correcting memory modules. Due to the complexity involved with this technique (and the number of drives required to make it work), it is not used.

- **RAID 3 and 4** – These levels require three or more drives to implement. In these raid levels, we get striping of data like in RAID 0, but now we also get redundancy in the form of a dedicated parity drive. Parity information is written to a dedicated disk. If one of the data disks fails, then the information on the parity disk may be used to reconstruct the drive. The difference between RAID 3 and RAID 4 is in how the data is striped: Data is striped across multiple disks at the byte level for RAID 3 and at the block level for RAID 4. It is a minor difference, but it does mean that RAID 3 is more efficient with disk space but that RAID 4 is a little faster. In both cases, the parity drive is the Achilles' heel because it can become a bottleneck and will typically fail sooner than the other drives.

- **RAID 5** – This level also requires three or more drives to implement and is similar to RAID 4 is many respects. The big difference is in how parity information is stored. Rather than using a dedicated parity drive, data and parity information is striped together across all drives. This level is the most popular and can tolerate the loss of any one drive because the parity information on the other drives can be used to reconstruct the lost one. It is most commonly used for general data storage.

- **RAID 6** – This level extends the capabilities of RAID 5 by computing two sets of parity information. The dual parity distribution accommodates the failure of two drives. However, the performance of this level is slightly less than that of RAID 5. This implementation is not frequently used in commercial environments as it is usually possible to reconstruct a single failed drive before a second one fails.

- **RAID 0+1 and RAID 1+0** – These are examples of nested RAID levels, combining two different RAID types together to try to get the advantages of both. In RAID 0+1, two different arrays of disk are at play. The first set of disks stripes all of the data across the available drives (the RAID 0 part) and those drives are mirrored to a different set of disks (the RAID 1 part). In RAID 1+0 (also known as RAID 10), two different arrays of disk are at play, but they are used a little differently. In this case, each drive in the first set is mirrored to a matching drive in the second set. When data is striped to one drive, it is immediately striped to another. In general, RAID 1+0 is considered to be superior to RAID 0+1 in all respects, both in terms of speed and redundancy.

Redundancy can also be provided for tape media. This is known as redundant array of independent tapes (RAIT). A RAIT is created with the use of robotic mechanisms to automatically transfer tapes between storage and the drive mechanisms. RAIT utilizes striping without redundancy. It is also common to use tape vaulting to make multiple copies of tapes that are used for backup and recovery.

Storage Area Networks (SANs) also provide additional options for performance, capacity, and redundancy. In SANs, large banks of disks are made available to multiple systems connecting to them via specialized controllers or via Internet Protocol (IP) networks. They offer the same RAID levels described above but with some additional advantages. For example, SANs may be used to provide warm or hot spares for a variety of systems in a central location. They may also be used to provide additional drive capacity that can be allocated or reallocated on the fly. They can also provide additional redundancy by providing mechanisms to mirror data to separate drive arrays, speeding up any recovery, and may even allow for such mirroring to occur over long distances. This technique is commonly used by organizations with multiple data centers that wish to be able to serve equally from two or more locations.

NAS may also be used to provide storage for multiple systems across the network. They also generally support the same RAID levels above and may be servers in their own right. There are also additional redundancy options available within application and database software platforms. For example, database shadowing may be used where a database management system updates records in multiple locations. This technique updates an entire copy of the database at a remote location.

Backup and Recovery Systems

Not all problems can be solved using fault tolerance and redundancy. In many cases, the only solution will be to restore the system to a previous state, presumably before the system became damaged or unreliable. Backup and recovery systems focus on copying data from one location to another so that it can be restored if it is needed. These backups typically include both critical system files as well as user data. Normally, backups occur at times of day when normal use is lower so that the backup processes do not impact normal use. This requires the planning of backups around selected backup windows where they will be least disruptive. If the backup window is large enough, a full backup, where all the files are backed up, may be chosen.

In some cases, the window may not be long enough to back up all the data on the system during each backup. In that case, differential or incremental backups may be more appropriate. In an incremental backup, only the files that changed since the last backup will be backed up. In a differential backup, only the files that changed since the last full backup will be backed up. In general, differentials require more space than incremental backups while incremental backups are faster to perform. On the other hand, restoring data from incremental backups requires more time than differential backups. To restore from incremental backups, the last full backup and all of the incremental backups performed are combined. In contrast, restoring from a differential backup requires only the last full backup and the latest differential.

Usually, a backup involves copying data from the production system to removable media, such as high-density tapes that can be transported and stored in different locations. It is common for at least three bulk copies of backup tapes to be available. The original will be stored on-site and can be used to quickly restore individual failed systems. Tape stored in a near-site facility (close by but in a different building) is typically used only when the primary facility has suffered a more general failure and where the local tapes have been damaged.

An off-site facility (typically a disaster recovery site) is a secure location at some distance from the primary facility. This provides assurance of a recovery in the event that the facility is destroyed in a catastrophe. The off- site location should be far enough away to preclude mutual destruction in the event of a catastrophe but not so far away as to introduce difficulties in transporting the media or retrieving it for recovery purposes. Unfortunately, the answer to off-site storage is a difficult challenge in areas prone to natural catastrophes. Geographical areas prone to natural disasters such as forest fires, earthquakes, tornados, typhoons, or hurricanes make it difficult to decide on an appropriate off-site location.

Electronic vaulting is accomplished by backing up system data over a network. The backup location is usually at a separate geographical location known as the vault site. Vaulting can be used as a mirror or a backup mechanism using the standard incremental or differential backup cycle. Changes to the host system are sent to the vault server in real time when the backup method is implemented as a mirror. If vaulting updates are recorded in real time, then it will be necessary to perform regular backups at the off-site location to provide recovery services due to inadvertent or malicious alterations to user or system data.

873

Vault servers can also be configured to act in a similar fashion as a backup device. As opposed to performing real time updates, file changes can be transferred to the vault using an incremental or differential method. Off-line backups of the vault server may not be necessary if there is sufficient storage space for multiple backup cycles.

Journaling is a technique used by database management systems to provide redundancy for their transactions. When a transaction is completed, the database management system duplicates the journal entry at a remote location. The journal provides sufficient detail for the transaction to be replayed on the remote system. This provides for database recovery in the event that the database becomes corrupted or unavailable.

Staffing for Resilience

Technical solutions will only get you so far, and there is only so much that a system can do automatically without requiring human assistance. An important part of maintaining resilient operations is ensuring adequate and trained staff is available to keep everything running smoothly. An adequate level of staffing will depend on the individual organization. In general, the principle is to avoid single points of failure associated with critical individuals on the operations team. If two or more individuals are capable of providing similar services, then the operation will be less influenced by the unavailability of single individuals. Adequate staffing levels can also depend on when staff will be required. In a 24 × 7 operation, larger numbers of staff will be required to cover all shifts and services than would be required in a business-hours-only operation.

In any case, training and education is critical to successful operations. Operations staff need to have the appropriate skills to perform their duties effectively and maintain those skills as technologies and processes change over time. Cross-training can also be used to encourage multiple individuals to be able to cover for each other. While mandatory vacations and job rotation have other security advantages, they also encourage skills to be shared between multiple individuals.

The Disaster Recovery Process

Disaster recovery is the process of restoring services from a contingency state. DR is typically performed and described in several areas including response, personnel, communications, assessment, restoration, and training. The process must be documented. During adverse events personnel should rely on documented plans and not on ad hoc solutions because judgment may be impaired during stressful events such as natural disasters.

An enterprise-wide business continuity testing policy should be established by the board and senior management and should set expectations for business lines and support functions to follow in implementing testing strategies and test plans. The policy should establish a testing cycle that increases in scope and complexity over time. As such, the testing policy should continuously improve by adapting to changes in business conditions and supporting expanded integration testing.

The testing policy should incorporate the use of a BIA and risk assessment for developing enterprise-wide and business line continuity testing strategies. The policy should identify key roles and responsibilities and establish minimum requirements for the organization's business continuity testing, including baseline requirements for frequency, scope, and reporting test results.

Testing policies will vary depending on the size and risk profile of the organization. While all organizations should develop testing policies on an enterprise-wide basis and involve essential employees in the testing process, some considerations differ depending on whether the organization relies on service providers or whether it manages its systems internally.

A serviced organization's testing policy should include guidelines addressing tests between the organization and its service provider. Serviced organizations should participate in tests with their critical service providers to ensure that organization employees fully understand the recovery process.

The testing policy for in-house systems should address the active involvement of personnel when systems and data files are tested. Organizations often send their backup media to a recovery site to be processed by the backup service provider's employees. This is not a sufficient test of an organization's BCP and is considered ineffective because the organization's employees are not directly involved in the testing process. As a result, the organization cannot verify that tests were conducted properly, and organization personnel may not be familiar with recovery procedures and related logistics in the event of a true disaster.

Once an organization develops the testing policy, this policy is typically implemented through the development of testing strategies that include the testing scope and objectives and test planning using various scenarios and testing methods.

Documenting the Plan

Once recovery strategies have been developed and implemented for each area, the next step is to document the plan itself. The plan includes plan activation procedures, the recovery strategies to be used, how recovery efforts will be managed, how human resource issues will be handled, how recovery costs will be documented and paid for, how recovery communications to internal and external stakeholders will be handled, and detailed action plans for each team and each team member. The plan then needs to be distributed to everyone who has a role.

The documentation for recovery of the technology environment needs to be detailed enough that a person with a similar skill set, having never executed the procedures before, could use them to perform the recovery. Documentation tends to be a task put off until it is too late; however, there is no guarantee that the people who perform this function in the production environment or the person who restored the infrastructure and application at the last test is going to be available at the time of disaster. In addition, disasters tend to be chaotic times where many demands are happening at once. Without the proper documentation, a practiced recovery strategy can fall apart and add to the chaos. Restoring an application can be challenging; restoring an entire data center just destroyed by a tornado can be overwhelming if not impossible without good documentation.

Event Management Requirements

- Strategy must be consistent regardless of event
- Need to establish an assessment process
- Event ownership needs to be defined
- Management teams identified
- Response teams identified
- Process for gathering of key decision makers
- Methods of communication need to be defined

Figure 7.2 – **The requirements of an event management process**

The documentation needs to be stored at the recovery facility, and every time the recovery is tested, the documentation should be used by the recovery participants and updated as needed. Once the level of confidence is high on the documentation, have someone who has never performed the procedure attempt it with the subject matter expert observing them. It may slightly delay the recovery time at that particular test, but once it is complete, confidence in the documentation will be strong.

Goals of Event Management

- Single source of information
- Triage
- Rapid Escalation
- Consistent Problem Management
- Rumor control
- Make sure *everyone* who need to know does
- Allow the problem solvers room to solve
- Playbook which documents key roles and reponsibilities

Figure 7.3 – **The goals of an event management process**

In addition to the actual recovery procedures, the security professional also needs to document the process that will be used to manage the recovery in any type of event. Documentation version control also has to be a point of focus for the security professional. The need to ensure that the correct and accurate version of the documentation is available at all times is a key responsibility for the security professional in this area. See *Figure 7.2* for the requirements of an event management process and *Figure 7.3* for the goals of an event management process. Event management is about communication and response and because those two things are needed even when the problem is not to the level of a disaster; event management can become part of the fabric of an organization and how it manages problems that arise.

The event management process has to have a trigger, something that causes the process to begin. The trigger is an event. An event is defined as anything that either already has or has the potential to cause a significant organization interruption. A hardware failure, a power outage, a network failure, and a building evacuation are all examples of events.

Response

Once an event is identified, it must be reported to a central communications group who will then be responsible for initiating the communications to those who must respond to the event and to those who are impacted by the event. The group that gets this initial report from the problem finder needs to operate twenty-four hours a day and seven days a week (24x7) because problems happen 24x7. Everyone in the organization should have this central number available to them to report problems. Commonly, these communications would go to an organization's help desk, technology operations center, physical security staff, or whoever in the organization is responsible for alarm monitoring.

In support of this communication, emergency notification lists are built by event type because different events have different event owners. A facility event such as a power failure, a water leak, or a fire would be owned by the facility staff, whereas a network outage would be owned by the network communication staff. In addition, each event would impact different organization people depending on their physical location or the technology they used.

Any event that occurs would first be reported to an assessment team. The assessment team's sole purpose is to determine if the problem requires further escalation and if so, who else needs to know about this event and who else needs to help fix the problem.

If it is determined that the event requires further escalation and communication, the first escalation team for that event type would be contacted. The first escalation team consists of the event owner, the event responders, and anyone else who has determined that when this type of disruption occurs, it directly and immediately affects their ability to execute the business or mission performed in that environment.

Many organizations manage this communication with a conference call. The conference call acts as a virtual command center to manage the communications and response to the event. One conference bridge should be for managing the responders, the people responsible for fixing the problem, and another conference bridge meeting is held where the event owner can communicate to those impacted by the event. They communicate what the problem is, the current status of the problem, how long it should be before it is resolved, what is impacted, and if necessary, when the next update will be provided and how. However, do not forget the conference bridge or the phone systems may be affected by an event. In those situations, plan for alternate communications. Internal and external communications are often the processes that determine if a contingency plan is successful.

The organization's senior leadership team generally does not need to be a part of the initial response to an issue. However, at some point they need to be made aware that the issue exists, and if the problem persists or has a significant impact, they may be called in to make decisions on how to manage the organizational impacts and to coordinate the larger scale response if needed.

Every event that the firm has should be managed through this process, from a small event such as a plumbing leak that has impacted workstations on the floor below to large events such as typhoons, hurricanes, and tornadoes. If an organization will design and use a graduated contingency plan, it will be used and understood on a frequent basis. Everyone understands how he or she will be communicated to and where to go to get the right information or help needed when a catastrophic disaster occurs. Event management takes practice.

The event management plan is part of the BC and DR plan. Making a decision to execute the BCP or DR plan is one possible response to an event. The event management plan needs to identify who is authorized to declare a disaster, how a declaration is done, and when the decision to "declare" is made, how it will be communicated to the teams that need to respond.

The executive emergency management team is a team that consists of the senior executives within the organization who have an overall responsibility for the recovery of the organization and services to others. As needed during the emergency, these individuals will participate in the command centers, virtual or physical, established for the recovery efforts and in the execution of the plan. The plan documents both a formal integrated response process for management and on-site coverage and support in emergencies.

The executive team does not directly manage the day-to-day operations of the organization under normal circumstances and is not expected to have day-to-day responsibilities in managing the recovery efforts from the emergency. However, the executive team will respond to and assist in the resolution of issues that need their direction. They will be the spokesperson for the organization to the media and make decisions on how the organization will manage the business impacts of the event.

The executives of most organizations are concerned with strategic issues, not with tactical delivery. While the next team, the emergency management team, needs to be held accountable for the tactical response from the event, the executive team needs to focus on the strategic response. It is the executive team that will lead the organization through the crisis, not manage the crisis itself. *Figure 7.4* shows the difference between crisis management and crisis leadership.

Crisis Management vs. Crisis Leadership

Managing	vs.	Leading
React		Anticipate
Short-term		Long-term
Process		Principles
Narrow		Wide Focus
Tactical		Strategic

*Figure 7.4 – **Crisis Management vs. Crisis Leadership***

The emergency management team is comprised of individuals who report directly to the command center and have responsibility to oversee the recovery and restoration process being executed by the emergency response teams. They are responsible for communicating the recovery status to the executive management team and making the necessary management decisions to support the recovery efforts. The emergency management team leader has overall responsibility for the recovery team and communications with the executive management team. The objectives and the functions of the executive management team are:

- Make a preliminary assessment of the damage.
- Notify senior management on the current status, impact to organization, and plan of action.
- Declare the disaster if necessary.
- Initiate the plan during the emergency situation.
- Organize and control the command centers as a central point of control of the recovery efforts.
- Organize and provide administrative support to the recovery effort.
- Administer and direct the problem management function.

Emergency response teams are comprised of individuals who are responsible for executing the recovery processes necessary for the continuity or recovery of critical organization functions in that site. These individuals report to the alternate sites for their critical functions to execute the recovery process. They report to the emergency management team through emergency response team leaders who have overall responsibility for the response teams' efforts in those locations. The response teams may be broken into sub-teams, each with their own leader to facilitate the recovery effort.

The primary responsibilities of the members of these teams are as follows:

- Retrieve offsite records and recovery information from offsite storage.
- Report to the alternate site identified in their procedures.
- Execute the organization recovery procedures for their area of responsibilities in the order of priority identified.
- Communicate the status of the recovery to the command centers as needed.
- Identify issues or problems to be escalated to the management team for resolution.
- Establish shifts for recovery team members to support the recovery effort 24x7.
- Establish liaison with alternate site personnel if needed.
- Support efforts to return to normal operations.
- Reestablish support operations affected by the disaster.
- Identify replacement equipment/software needed for the recovery effort and to return to normal operations.

Command centers are set up as a central location for communications and decision making during an emergency situation. Command centers are set up in response to the disaster and are equipped with a copy of the plan document and other resources that may be needed in a disaster. For insurance purposes, it is important that costs associated with the recovery effort be tracked as well as payment for purchases of needed supplies and replacement equipment be expedited. Procedures for handling finance issues must also be included in the plan.

If there are multiple locations for the organization, there needs to be an initial response plan for each site where the organization conducts business. That plan will document the following:

- What organization or technology operates at that site
- The recovery strategy in place for the organization or technology
- Who the decision makers are
- Where everyone should go if they cannot get back into the building
- The declaration process for declaring a disaster for that site
- The location of the alternate site
- Travel directions to get to the alternate site
- Seat assignments at the alternate site
- Hotels, transportation services, and supply options near the alternate site

For each recovery strategy, detail execution procedures need to be documented on how to execute the recovery strategy at the time of disaster. Again, these procedures need to be written in such a way that someone with a similar skill set or background, having never done them before, would be able to pick up the procedure and execute it.

When documenting the plan, do not forget some of the simple things often taken for granted when business is normal. Some areas to consider are actions such as planning for delivery of office supplies to the alternate site, setting up a package delivery account for the alternate site like UPS or Airborne, having a postage meter for the alternate site, and knowing where the post office is located.

If the organization uses some type of mail zone for internal delivery of mail between sites, make sure the plan sets one up for the alternate site as well. Be prepared to have a "switchboard operator" or an automated service at the alternate site until the company can publish a new phone directory for the employees working from the alternate site. This operator or service would manage a central phone number that can be published quickly to the appropriate stakeholders until the new phone numbers for individuals can be published.

Personnel

One common factor left out of many plans is human resource issues. Disasters are events that can greatly impact humans, and it is important that the plan documents the responsibility of the firm to the employees participating in the recovery. Organizations need to recognize that to respond to the organization's needs in a disaster situation, it must also recognize the hardships placed on the families of its response team. To be able to give the best to the company at the time when it is needed most, employees need to have a level of comfort that their family members are safe and the employee's absence during the recovery effort will not place undue hardship on them.

The level of support to team members will be clearly defined by the nature of the disaster itself. In the case of natural disaster where the employee's family may be at risk, it may provide for a temporary relocation of family members or allowing the family to accompany the employee to the recovery site. It may range from facilitating dependent care services, company-paid travel for employees to return home for a visit or for family members to travel to recovery locations, or cash advances to provide for family needs. This section of the plan also needs to document how the company will handle the injury or death of an employee that occurs during an event.

Do not forget to include administrative support as part of the recovery team. Planners do not often think of administrative support staff as being "time sensitive," but they are welcome additions in a recovery. They do things no one else has the time to do – answering phones, sending communications as requested to communicate to recovery staff, making travel arrangements for recovery staff, ordering food at recovery locations, keeping minutes of the status meetings, making copies, arranging courier service, keeping track of the locations of employees, and similar administrative and personnel related functions.

Communications

Employee Notification

Employees who are members of an emergency notification list will be contacted directly in the event of an emergency situation by the responsible management team member. The security professional will need to document the process of how the organization will communicate with the remaining employees about the event and the recovery efforts.

A common method of doing this is having a contingency information line established for the general employee population to get information about what happened and the progress of the recovery. To keep this number handy, many organizations put it on a sticker on the back of their employee badges and on a magnet the employee is supposed to take home and put on his or her refrigerator. This same number can be used by the company to communicate office closures and early release or late start notifications in the event of severe weather.

The plan needs to document how the organization communications to all the stakeholders will be managed (*Figure 7.5*).

Potential Stakeholders

☑ Employees and their families   ☑ Customers

☑ Contractors and business partners   ☑ Goverment Regulators and Politicians

☑ Facility and Site Managers   ☑ Competitors

☑ Staff Managers (HR, IT, etc.)   ☑ Media representatives

☑ Senior Managers; Board of Directors   ☑ Unions

☑ Institutional investors and shareholders ☑ Communities

☑ Insurance representatives   ☑ Internet users or bloggers

☑ Suppliers and Distributors   ☑ Industry activist groups

Figure 7.5 – **Potential Stakeholders**

Employees who talk with customers or clients as a part of their normal organization day should be provided with a statement or list of statements regarding the recovery effort. It is important that EVERYONE tell the same story. Any customer or vendor not satisfied with the response provided should be referred to management or the organizational communications staff.

As the recovery progresses, the company will need to provide recovery status updates to all the stakeholders. It is important that the statements be honest and concise. It is also important to consider each stakeholder's various needs and concerns. Employees may be worried about their jobs, where stockholders may be more worried about the impact to the company stock, and customers just want to know that their product or service will be there when they need it.

The security professional will need to document a process for reporting and managing problems that will occur during the recovery. Even if the plan was tested yesterday and everything worked perfectly, unexpected problems may happen during the recovery. There needs to be a process in the plan to document them, triage them, escalate them, fix them, and report on them. If the company already has a formal problem management/change management process, use that in the plan. If not, invent one to use in a recovery and test the problem management process while testing recovery.

If the process for managing problems day to day is to have the problem reported to a central group and a ticket opened and assigned to a responder, use that process in recovery. Even during alternate site tests when organization users come to validate alternate site readiness or during a data center recovery exercise, make people call in a ticket before a problem is addressed.

During the course of the recovery efforts, it may be helpful to establish conference bridges to communicate recovery issues and to coordinate communications between the different recovery locations. Multiple conference bridges can be used for different parts of the recovery. Often, it is best to keep the discussions between the technical groups and the organization partners separate because technical language barriers can cause confusion.

Assessment

During an event, a decision will need to be made regarding the severity of the event. A person or process within the contingency team will need to determine the impact of the event on the organization and its mission and determine the appropriate response. This is done by using tiers or categorizations of such as the following:

- ■ **Non-Incident** – These events are typically caused by system malfunctions or human errors, which result in limited to minor disruptions of service. There is a short period of downtime and alternate processing or storage facilities are not required.
- ■ **Incident** – Events that cause an entire facility or service to be inoperative for a significant amount of time. These events require the enactment of the disaster recovery plan and reporting of information and status to senior management and may involve crisis management.
- ■ **Severe Incident** – Significant destruction or interruption to an organization's mission, facility, and personnel. These events require the enactment of the DR plan and may involve the building of a new primary facility. These events require senior management reporting and crisis management.

Restoration

The final parts of the documented plan are about restoration of the primary environment and transition back to normal operations. While other parts of the organization are focusing on the resumption of organization in the alternate site, part of the staff needs to focus on what needs to be done to restore the production environment of the primary facility.

Ownership of this process is dependent on what was impacted by the event. In most cases, it will be a coordinated effort between the facilities staff to restore the building to its original state or acquire and build out new space, the technology staff to repair or replace technology hardware, software or network components affected, and records management to recover lost or damaged records.

The organization's legal staff and insurance agent will play a role in the restoration and recovery from the event. No recovery efforts should begin until both have been contacted, but the area of impact should be secured from further loss and, where possible, pictures taken of the damage before anything is removed, repaired, or replaced.

The transition back to normal operations is easier than the recovery for the simple fact that it is a planned event. The plan can be to return all at once or the plan can move operations back over time to control issues that may arise from the transition and prevent yet another event. General transition plans should be documented about the process to move back, but detailed plans will need to be written to respond to the specific issues of the transition that results from the type of event that the organization is in recovery for. Moving an organizational operation back to its primary space is challenging but is usually easier than moving a data center. If the data center was impacted by this event, then the organization needs to manage the transition project like a data center move.

For example, an organization may be located in alternate sites for 15 months following the events of an earthquake and for two months following the events of a hurricane. After 9 weeks in the earthquake alternate site, an interim transition plan was executed where employees were distributed between two interim sites while the primary site was repaired and built out. The interim sites used spare equipment and furniture from storage and other sites to populate the space. When it was time to re-populate the data center, asset swaps were used instead of moving the technology that was used in the alternate sites.

Assets swaps involve negotiating with a vendor to provide the equipment to populate the new or restored data center. This allows the ability to burn-in and test the new equipment and the building infrastructure before the actual move. After the move back is completed, the equipment in the alternate site was given back to the appropriate vendor, moved back to storage, or sold. In the event equipment is sold or traded, the organization must ensure proper decommission and sanitation processes are followed.

Provide Training

It does not matter how good the plan is if no one knows what is in it. It is important that every single person in the firm be able to know what to do in an emergency. Business continuity needs to be imbedded in the culture of the organization. To accomplish that, the security professional must introduce training and awareness programs that involve all the stakeholders.

The type of training needed is different for different populations of the organization. The leadership team needs crisis management training. Their role in a recovery is not to execute the recovery but to lead the organization back to organization as normal. The technical teams need to know not just the procedures for executing the recovery but also the logistics of where they are going and how they will get there.

The security professional will need to design awareness programs for different audiences. Various vehicles for the delivery of training and awareness programs can be utilized depending on the audience that needs to hear the message. The intranet portion of the organizational website is a good vehicle for communicating the plan to the general employee population.

The customers of an organization may want to know that the company has a plan and will be there for them no matter what. They should be aware of the planned course of action in the event of a disaster, alternate contact numbers, and any changes in operational procedures they may expect. The organizational website available to the public may be a good means of communicating information to the customers of an organization.

The employees need to know basic information about the plan and their role in the plan. This includes assembly areas following evacuation, who the leadership team is, how they will be communicated to after an event, alternate site location including directions to get there and when they should report to the alternate site.

Conducting exercises is also a form of training for those who have a direct role in the recovery. Whether the exercise is a tabletop exercise, an actual exercise at the alternate site, or just a call notification exercise, the team will practice their role during the exercises. The more the plan is exercised, the more confident the recovery team will be if or when it happens for real.

Putting a section on the BCP program in a new employee orientation session is a great vehicle for introducing the program when an employee starts with the organization. The information provided can explain the overall scope of the plan, what they should expect if a disaster were to happen, and where they can go to get additional information on the program.

Exercise, Assess, and Maintain the Plan

Once the plan has been completed and the recovery strategies fully implemented, it is important to test all parts of the plan to validate that it would work in a real event. The testing policy should include enterprise-wide testing strategies that establish expectations for individual business lines. Business lines include all internal and external supporting functions, such as IT and facilities management, across the testing lifecycle of planning, execution, measurement, reporting, and test process improvement. The testing strategy should include the following:

- Expectations for business lines and support functions to demonstrate the achievement of business continuity test objectives consistent with the BIA and risk assessment;
- A description of the depth and breadth of testing to be accomplished;
- The involvement of staff, technology, and facilities;
- Expectations for testing internal and external interdependencies; and
- An evaluation of the reasonableness of assumptions used in developing the testing strategy.

Testing strategies should include the testing scope and objectives, which clearly define what functions, systems, or processes are going to be tested and what will constitute a successful test. The objective of a testing program is to ensure that the business continuity planning process is accurate, relevant, and viable under adverse conditions. Therefore, the business continuity planning process should be tested at least annually, with more frequent testing required when significant changes have occurred in business operations. Testing should include applications and business functions that were identified during the BIA. The BIA determines the recovery point objectives and recovery time objectives, which then help determine the appropriate recovery strategy. Validation of the RPOs and RTOs is important to ensure that they are attainable.

Testing objectives should start simply and gradually increase in complexity and scope. The scope of individual tests can be continually expanded to eventually encompass enterprise-wide testing and testing with vendors and key market participants. Achieving the following objectives provides progressive levels of assurance and confidence in the plan. At a minimum, the testing scope and objectives should:

- Not jeopardize normal business operations;
- Gradually increase the complexity, level of participation, functions, and physical locations involved;

- Demonstrate a variety of management and response proficiencies under simulated crisis conditions, progressively involving more resources and participants;
- Uncover inadequacies so that testing procedures can be revised;
- Consider deviating from the test script to interject unplanned events, such as the loss of key individuals or services; and
- Involve a sufficient volume of all types of transactions to ensure adequate capacity and functionality of the recovery facility.

The testing policy should also include test planning, which is based on the predefined testing scope and objectives established as part of management's testing strategies. Test planning includes test plan review procedures and the development of various testing scenarios and methods. Management should evaluate the risks and merits of various types of testing scenarios and develop test plans based on identified recovery needs. Test plans should identify quantifiable measurements of each test objective and should be reviewed prior to the test to ensure they can be implemented as designed. Test scenarios should include a variety of threats, event types, and crisis management situations and should vary from isolated system failures to wide-scale disruptions. Scenarios should also promote testing alternate facilities with the primary and alternate facilities of key counterparties and third-party service providers. Comprehensive test scenarios focus attention on dependencies, both internal and external, between critical business functions, information systems, and networks. Integrated testing moves beyond the testing of individual components, to include testing with internal and external parties and the supporting systems, processes, and resources. As such, test plans should include scenarios addressing local and wide-scale disruptions, as appropriate. Business line management should develop scenarios to effectively test internal and external interdependencies, with the assistance of IT staff members who are knowledgeable regarding application data flows and other areas of vulnerability. Organizations should periodically reassess and update their test scenarios to reflect changes in the organization's business and operating environment.

Test plans should clearly communicate the predefined test scope and objectives and provide participants with relevant information, including:

- A master test schedule that encompasses all test objectives;
- Specific description of test objectives and methods;
- Roles and responsibilities for all test participants, including support staff;
- Designation of test participants;
- Test decision makers and succession plans;
- Test locations; and
- Test escalation conditions and test contact information.

Test Plan Review

Management should prepare and review a script for each test prior to testing to identify weaknesses that could lead to unsatisfactory or invalid tests. As part of the review process, the testing plan should be revised to account for any changes to key personnel, policies, procedures, facilities, equipment, outsourcing relationships, vendors, or other components that affect a critical business function. In addition, as a preliminary step to the testing process, management should perform a thorough review of the BCP (checklist review). A checklist review involves distributing copies of the BCP to the managers of each critical business unit and requesting that they review portions of the plan applicable to their department to ensure that the procedures are comprehensive and complete.

It is often wise to stop using the word "test" for this and begin to use the word exercise. The reason to call them exercises is that when the word "test" is used, people think pass or fail. In fact, there is no way to fail a contingency test. If the security professionals knew that it all worked, they would not bother to test it. The reason to test is to find out what does not work so it can be fixed before it happens for real.

Testing methods can vary from simple to complex, depending on the preparation and resources required. Each bears its own characteristics, objectives, and benefits. The type or combination of testing methods employed by an organization should be determined by, among other things, the organization's age and experience with business continuity planning, size, complexity, and the nature of its business.

Testing methods include both business recovery and disaster recovery exercises. Business recovery exercises primarily focus on testing business line operations, while disaster recovery exercises focus on testing the continuity of technology components, including systems, networks, applications, and data. To test split processing configurations, in which two or more sites support part of a business line's workload, tests should include the transfer of work among processing sites to demonstrate that alternate sites can effectively support customer-specific requirements and work volumes and site-specific business processes. A comprehensive test should involve processing a full day's work at peak volumes to ensure that equipment capacity is available and that RTOs and RPOs can be achieved.

More rigorous testing methods and greater frequency of testing provide greater confidence in the continuity of business functions. While comprehensive tests do require greater investments of time, resources, and coordination to implement, detailed testing will more accurately depict a true disaster and will assist management in assessing the actual responsiveness of the individuals involved in the recovery process. Furthermore, comprehensive testing of all critical functions and applications will allow management to identify potential problems; therefore, management should use one of the more thorough testing methods discussed in this section to ensure the viability of the BCP before a disaster occurs.

There are many different types of exercises that the security professional can conduct. Some will take minutes, others hours or days. The amount of exercise planning needed is entirely dependent on the type of exercise, the length of the exercise, and the scope of the exercise the security professional will plan to conduct. The most common types of exercises are call exercises, walkthrough exercises, simulated or actual exercises, and compact exercises.

Tabletop Exercise/Structured Walk-Through Test

A tabletop exercise/structured walk-through test is considered a preliminary step in the overall testing process and may be used as an effective training tool; however, it is not a preferred testing method. Its primary objective is to ensure that critical personnel from all areas are familiar with the BCP and that the plan accurately reflects the organization's ability to recover from a disaster. It is characterized by:

- Attendance of business unit management representatives and employees who play a critical role in the BCP process;
- Discussion about each person's responsibilities as defined by the BCP;

- Individual and team training, which includes a walk-through of the step-by-step procedures outlined in the BCP; and
- Clarification and highlighting of critical plan elements, as well as problems noted during testing.

Walk-Through Drill/Simulation Test

A walk-through drill/simulation test is somewhat more involved than a tabletop exercise/structured walk-through test because the participants choose a specific event scenario and apply the BCP to it. It includes:

- Attendance by all operational and support personnel who are responsible for implementing the BCP procedures;
- Practice and validation of specific functional response capabilities;
- Focus on the demonstration of knowledge and skills, as well as team interaction and decision-making capabilities;
- Role playing with simulated response at alternate locations/facilities to act out critical steps, recognize difficulties, and resolve problems in a non-threatening environment;
- Mobilization of all or some of the crisis management/response team to practice proper coordination without performing actual recovery processing; and
- Varying degrees of actual, as opposed to simulated, notification and resource mobilization to reinforce the content and logic of the plan.

Functional Drill/Parallel Test

Functional drill/parallel testing is the first type of test that involves the actual mobilization of personnel to other sites in an attempt to establish communications and perform actual recovery processing as set forth in the BCP. The goal is to determine whether critical systems can be recovered at the alternate processing site and if employees can actually deploy the procedures defined in the BCP. It includes:

- A full test of the BCP, which involves all employees;
- Demonstration of emergency management capabilities of several groups practicing a series of interactive functions, such as direction, control, assessment, operations, and planning;
- Testing medical response and warning procedures;
- Actual or simulated response to alternate locations or facilities using actual communications capabilities;
- Mobilization of personnel and resources at varied geographical sites, including evacuation drills in which employees test the evacuation route and procedures for personnel accountability; and
- Varying degrees of actual, as opposed to simulated, notification and resource mobilization in which parallel processing is performed and transactions are compared to production results.

Full-Interruption/Full-Scale Test

Full-interruption/full-scale test is the most comprehensive type of test. In a full-scale test, a real life emergency is simulated as closely as possible. Therefore, comprehensive planning should be a prerequisite to this type of test to ensure that business operations are not negatively affected. The organization implements all or portions of its BCP by processing data and transactions using backup media at the recovery site. It involves:

- Enterprise-wide participation and interaction of internal and external management response teams with full involvement of external organizations;
- Validation of crisis response functions;
- Demonstration of knowledge and skills as well as management response and decision-making capability;
- On-the-scene execution of coordination and decision-making roles;
- Actual, as opposed to simulated, notifications, mobilization of resources, and communication of decisions;
- Activities conducted at actual response locations or facilities;
- Actual processing of data using backup media; and
- Exercises generally extending over a longer period of time to allow issues to fully evolve as they would in a crisis and to allow realistic role-playing of all the involved groups.

After every exercise the security professional conducts, the exercise results need to be published and action items identified to address the issues that were uncovered by the exercise. Action items should be tracked until they have been resolved and, where appropriate, the plan updated. It is very unfortunate when an organization has the same issue in subsequent tests simply because someone did not update the plan.

Update and Maintenance of the Plan

All team members have an obligation to participate in the change control process. The plan document and all related procedures will need to be updated on an on-going basis such as after each exercise and after each material change to the production, IT, or organization environment. The procedures should be reviewed every three months, and the formal audit of the procedures should be conducted annually. The exercise reports produced following each exercise should be provided to internal audit, and internal audit should include a review of the plan documentation and test results as part of their regular audit cycle. A sample data center exercise report is included in *Figure 7.6*.

Note the data center exercise report contains the following information on each platform and application recovered:

- The name of the technology or application restored
- The RTO for the application
- The date last tested
- Whether the application was recovered in the RTO during that test
- Whether the application was recovered at all even if it did not meet the RTO
- Whether current documented repeatable processes for recovery are stored offsite
- If the application had a batch cycle, was it run and was it successful?
- Application owner

September through December 2014 – *Disaster Recovery Exercise Report*

Application/ Platform	RTO	Last Tested	Documented Plan Offsite	Recovery met RTO	Recovered Successfully	End-User Validation	Batch 1 Success	Batch 2 Success	Support Team
Applications									
Call Center Application	24 Hours	8-Jun					N/A	N/A	Joe Smith
Corp. Fin. - ABC	72 Hours	8-Jun					N/A	N/A	Dave Brown
Corp. Fin. - Peoplesoft GL	72 Hours	8-Jun					N/A	N/A	Linda Jones
Corp. Fin. - Peoplesoft AP	72 Hours	8-Jun					N/A	N/A	Mark Swain
Corp. Fin. - Treasury Ops	72 Hours	8-Jun					N/A	N/A	Scott Gray
Account Applications	24 Hours	8-Jun							Mike Beta
Corp. Serv. - Employee DB	72 Hours	8-Jun					N/A	N/A	Michael Green
Infrastructure									
AS400	24 Hours	7-Nov				N/A	N/A	N/A	Joe Myer
CAT Switch	12 Hours	7-Nov				N/A	N/A	N/A	Bob Gerang
CICS	12 Hours	7-Nov				N/A	N/A	N/A	Chris Alpha
Cisco Routers	12 Hours	7-Nov				N/A	N/A	N/A	John Crank
Cleartrust	24 Hours	7-Nov				N/A	N/A	N/A	Tom Skye
DB2	12 Hours	7-Nov				N/A	N/A	N/A	Lucy James
DNS/DHCP Gateway	12 Hours	7-Nov				N/A	N/A	N/A	Ned Young
DS3	12 Hours	7-Nov				N/A	N/A	N/A	Dave Anderson
LAN	12 Hours	7-Nov				N/A	N/A	N/A	Sam Okra
Linux	24 Hours	7-Nov				N/A	N/A	N/A	Frank Perry
Mainframe IPL	12 Hours	7-Nov				N/A	N/A	N/A	Mike Night
RS6000	24 Hours	7-Nov				N/A	N/A	N/A	Jim Dyer
SUN	24 Hours	7-Nov				N/A	N/A	N/A	Liz Harris
Alt Site Network	2 Hours	7-Nov				N/A	N/A	N/A	Mike O'Toole
Windows	24 Hours	7-Nov				N/A	N/A	N/A	Lucas Kerry

Figure 7.6 – **Sample data center exercise report**

The plan needs to have version control numbers on it to make sure everyone is using the current version of the plan. The plan needs to be published to everyone who has a role and also needs to be stored in a secure offsite location that not only survives the disaster but is accessible immediately following the disaster.

Transitioning from Project to Program

The contingency planning program is an ongoing process. All of the tasks defined to originally build the program need to be repeated on a regular basis to ensure that the plan stays current with the organization and technology environment of the company through the years. In support of that, the program has annual requirements that need to be completed by the planning team in order to remain in compliance with the program. See the sample report card in *Figure* 7.7.

Business Continuity Program Status Report

Home Office Business Area	BCP Contact	ENL	Identity Functions	Alt Site Require-ments	Technology Review	Inter-Dependencies	Published Plan	Call Test	Walk-through Test	Alter-nate Site Test
DC Operations	Dave Caster									
Help Desk	Mike Lamp									
Facilities	Priscilla Jones									
Finance	Jen Kato									
Operations	Pam Halpern									
Process Support	Jennifer Potts									
Mail Room	Joe Kalyn									
Office General Council	Linda Logan									
Human Resources	Steve Riley									
Audit	Mary French									

Figure 7.7 – **Sample report card**

The following is a brief explanation of the contingency planning program and its components.

The contingency planning program is designed to serve as an aid in developing and maintaining viable organization function contingency plans.

The organizational contingency planning program provides for the continuation of the company's critical organization functions in the event of an organization interruption. The organizational program assists and prepares the various areas of the company to document and exercise emergency response and recovery plans.

The senior manager of each operating area has the responsibility for ensuring the organization's survival. To help facilitate this, each senior manager will appoint a business continuity planner to coordinate the contingency planning and response efforts of the organization functions performed by that functional area.

The emergency management organization (EMO) is formed to provide both a formal response process for management and on-site coverage, support, and expertise during large-scale emergencies. The EMO ensures that all locations and operating areas will receive an appropriate, coordinated response in the event of a serious outage of any type.

The EMO management team is the decision-making body of the EMO and is usually comprised of areas within the company that play a key role in responding to emergency situations, including the following areas:

- Security
- Real estate
- Systems
- Human resources
- Organizational communications
- Compliance
- Risk and insurance management
- Organizational contingency planning

Each of these groups has specific responsibilities in the event of an emergency, including:

- Responding to incidents and emergencies
- Determining the extent of the impending or actual emergency situation
- Establishing and maintaining communication with senior management
- Communicating with employees and customers
- Managing media communications, security, systems, facilities
- Coordinating and integrating business continuity planners

The organizational emergency operations center (EOC) has been established to provide a location, equipped with all of the necessary resources to manage the organization resumption process whenever the EMO is activated.

Roles and Responsibilities

The organizational contingency planning group develops, implements, and maintains a worldwide business contingency planning program for the company. This group provides leadership and guidance in maintaining integrated continuity of critical organization functions, and it assists management in achieving timely recovery of organization operations in the event of organization interruption. The roles and responsibilities of the group are:

- Setting strategic direction and plans for all organization units to ensure BC and effective emergency management.
- Integrating the contingency planning process across organization units when the nature of the organization requires it.
- Providing consulting services and direction to senior level contingency managers.
- Coordinating and integrating the activation of emergency response organizations with the organization units.
- Providing periodic management reporting and status.
- Ensuring executive management compliance with the contingency planning program.
- Ensuring the identification and maintenance of all critical organization functions and requirements.

- Procuring and managing the alternate sites used to support recovery of the operations of the company whether technical or organization.
- Developing, implementing, and maintaining policy and guidelines for all organization units to follow.
- Developing and maintaining testing and maintenance programs for all contingency planning organizations.
- Providing training, maintenance, and support for approved contingency planning tools.

The business continuity planners act as a focal point for their company in any situation involving contingency planning or emergency response. The security professional plans the integration of a series of tasks, procedures, and information that direct actions at the time of an organization interruption in order to reduce confusion, improve communications, and achieve a timely continuation/resumption of organization. The roles and responsibilities of the business continuity planner include:

- Provide primary contact for their functional area to handle coordination response during an organization interruption.
- Act as a resource for contingency planning efforts within their area of responsibility.
- Secure appointment, training, and backup of all contingency planning and response teams.
- Assist in the design and maintenance of alternate sites.
- Maintain currency of all contingency planning documentation, including all deliverables listed in *Figure 7.8*.
- Program Requirements

	Current BCP Deliverable	*Description/Specifics*	*Due Date*
1	Management Engagement	- Appoint BCP	Ongoing
		- Established Goal for BCP	
		- Present to President	
2	BCP Engagement	- Attend monthly BCP meetings	Ongoing
		- Participates in training conferences	
		- Actively work BCP deliverables list	
3	Cell phones for key employees	- Maintain event management listings	Ongoing
4	Published ENL	- Publish and distribute emergency conference call in number and procedure to key personnel	Quarterly
5	Conference Bridge Procedures	- Establish and distribute emergency conference call in number and procedure to key personnel	Annually
6	Identify business functions and time sensitivity	- ID all functions the group performs	Semi Annually
		- ID on core or mission critical function although the rating may be below "A"	
7	Alternate site requirements defined	- Document systems and personnel needed to perform functions	Semi Annually

	Current BCP Deliverable	Description/Specifics	Due Date
8	Perform technology review	- Inventory and assess hardware and software used by the business function - Participate in validating technology recovery	Annually
9	Interdependencies defined	- ID any internal or external dependencies	Annually
10	Published Plan	- Signed off by leadership	Annually
11	Call Notification exercise	- Report results	Semi Annually
12	Walkthrough/Tabletop exercise	- Report results	Annually
13	Alternate site exercise	- Report results	Semi Annually

Figure 7.8 – **List of contingency planning documentation**

Business Continuity and Other Risk Areas

There is a significant interrelationship between information security and BC and other risk management areas such as physical security, records management, vendor management, internal audit, financial risk management, operational risk management, and regulatory compliance (legal/regulatory risk) in the context of an overall risk management framework.

It does not matter how strong the firewall is or how good the password enforcement is if the physical security practices are so poor that unauthorized individuals can easily gain access to the company space. It does not matter if the company has an alternate site if the records management practices are so poor that the data needed to recover the organization is not available offsite. All of these efforts are enterprise-wide in scope; they intersect each other at various points, and the extent to which we do one well and another area poorly can impact all the other areas. Each of these areas needs to work collaboratively to effectively manage risk.

Implementation and Operation of Perimeter Security

The primary goal of a physical protection program is to control access into the facility. In the concept of defense-in-depth, barriers are arranged in 10 layers with the level of security growing progressively higher as one comes closer to the center or the highest protective area. Defending an asset with a multiple posture can reduce the likelihood of a successful attack; if one layer of defense fails, another layer of defense will hopefully prevent the attack, and so on. (*Figure 7.9*) This design requires the attacker to circumvent multiple defensive mechanisms to gain access to the targeted asset. Implementing defense in depth requires that the security practitioner understands the goals of security. Essentially, security can be distilled down to three basic elements: availability, integrity, and confidentiality. Availability addresses the fact that legitimate users require resources, which should be available to the users as needed. Integrity relates to the concept that information is whole, complete, and remains unchanged from its true state. Confidentiality can be defined as ensuring that data is available to only those individuals that have legitimate access to it.

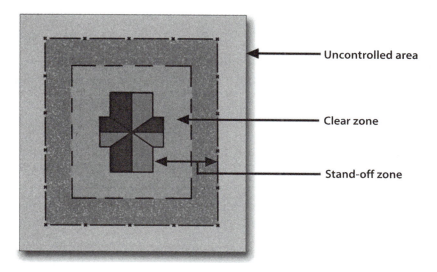

Uncontrolled area

Clear zone

Stand-off zone

7

Security Operations

Figure 7.9 – **Defending an asset with a multiple posture can reduce the likelihood of a successful attack; if one layer of defense fails, another layer of defense will hopefully prevent the attack, and so on.**
(Courtesy of Bosch Security Systems)

Consider, for example, the layers of security at a local bank, which employs many redundant measures to protect personnel and assets. The fortress-like appearance and protective reputation that is synonymous with banking is likely a deterrent factor to some would be bank robbers, but of course not all. The next line of defense that serves as both a deterrent and as a means for suspect apprehension and asset recovery are security cameras. This layer of security obviously has a level of failure; how many times have we seen video of bank robberies showing a suspect who was never caught. If the cameras are considered ineffective, the next layer is an armed security guard present both as a deterrent factor and to physically defend the bank. This too is not 100% effective because the security guard can be neutralized by the intruder.

If the security guard is overpowered, the next layer involves hardware such as bulletproof glass and electronically locked doors. Of course, not all branch offices are fortified in this manner, leaving the bank tellers vulnerable. In this case, the teller must rely on the silent alarm button, dye packs, and robbery training. Some branches also have double time-release doors where people are slightly delayed during ingress and egress. The vault itself has defense-in-depth through multiple layers of defense such as opening only at certain controlled times, its heavy metal construction, and multiple compartments that require further access.

The defense-in-depth principle may seem contradictory to the "secure the weakest link" principle because we are essentially saying that defenses taken as a whole can be stronger than the weakest link. However, there is no contradiction; the principle "secure the weakest link" applies when components have security functionality that does not overlap. But when it comes to redundant security measures, it is indeed possible that the sum protection offered is far greater than the protection offered by any single component.

Of course, all of these defenses collectively do not ensure that the bank will never be successfully robbed, even at banks with this much security. If the attacker wants to rob the bank, he is going to give it his best effort.

Nonetheless, it is quite obvious that the sum total of all these defenses results in a far more effective security system than any one of these defenses alone. This does not mean that every known defensive measure should be indiscriminately applied in every situation. Using risk, vulnerability, and threat assessment, one must find a balance between security provided by the defense-in-depth approach and the financial, human, and organizational resources the management is willing to expend.

The key to a successful system is the integration of people, procedures, and equipment into a system that protects the targets from the threat. A well-designed system provides defense-in-depth, minimizes the consequences of component failures, and exhibits balanced protection. Physical protection is no different from information security, and in fact, it is a dovetail of the processes: An organization performs a threat analysis, then designs a system that involves equipment and procedures, and then tests it. The system itself typically has a number of elements that fall into the essence of deter–detect – delay–respond.

Deter is meant to render a facility as an unattractive target so that an adversary abandons attempts to infiltrate or attack. Examples of deterrence are the presence of security guards, adequate lighting at night, signage, and the use of barriers such as fencing or bars on windows. While deterrence can be very helpful in discouraging attacks by adversaries, it cannot stop an adversary who chooses to attack regardless of defenses. Similar to the bank robber who is dead set on robbing the bank, nothing is going to stop him from attempting to rob the bank. The deterrent value of a true physical protection system can be very high while at the same time providing protection for assets in the event of an attack.

Detect involves the use of appropriate devices, systems, and procedures to signal that an attempted or actual unauthorized access has occurred. It will have one or more layers of barriers and sensors, which will be utilized to keep out casual intruders, detect deliberate intruders, and make it difficult for them to defeat your defensive security easily. Delay involves having a perpetrator delayed by the use of layered defenses. It will delay the attack for a sufficient period to allow a response force time to confront and intercept.

Response requires communication to a response force that an unauthorized person is attempting to or has entered the facility. The response force is required to intercept the adversary before an attack has occurred or has been completed.

Security systems are best designed utilizing multiple barriers – "rings of protection" – encircling the protected asset. Layered barrier designs are advantageous when they require increased knowledge, skill, and talent to circumvent them. A group of attackers with the necessary skills must be assembled, and since group secrecy is hard to maintain, the likelihood of being discovered is increased. Layered barriers also afford a greater time delay because each layer requires time to be circumvented. This helps to provide the necessary delay in the event that the response time is relatively slow.

The following critical building components should be located away from main entrances, vehicle circulation, parking, and maintenance areas. If this is not possible, harden as appropriate:

- Emergency generator, including fuel systems, day tank, fire sprinkler, and water supply
- Fuel storage
- Telephone distribution and main switchgear

- Fire pumps
- Building control centers
- Uninterrupted power supply (UPS) systems controlling critical functions
- HVAC systems if critical to building operation
- Elevator machinery and controls
- Shafts for stairs, elevators, and utilities
- Critical distribution feeders for emergency power

Gates and Fences

Barriers

Barriers can be comprised of natural or manufactured elements. The idea is to define an area that is designated to impede or deny access. A natural barrier can be a river, dense growth, a culvert, or a ditch. Fabricated or structural barriers can be a wall, a fence, doors, or the building itself. Walls, fences, and gates have long been designated as the first line of defense for a facility. There are a multitude of barriers, and they provide the same objective: Keep intruders out, delay them, and keep them at a safe distance. However, with sufficient time and effort, any barrier can be breached. Thus, the principle objective is to delay the intruder until law enforcement or a security team can respond.

Fences

As shown in *Figure 7.10*, fences are a perimeter identifier that is designed and installed to keep intruders out. However, most organizations do not like the feeling of a fenced-in compound and look for other remedies to secure their property. Depending on the organization, location, and funding, a fence can consist of many variations and levels of protection.

The most commonly used fence is the chain linked fence, and it is the most affordable. The standard is a six-foot high fence with two-inch mesh square openings. The material should consist of nine-gauge vinyl or galvanized metal. Nine-gauge is a typical fence material installed in residential areas. Additionally, it is recommended to place barbed wire strands angled out from the top of the fence at a 45° angle and away from the protected area with three strands running across the top. This will provide for a seven-foot fence. There are several variations of the use of "top guards" using V-shaped barbed wire or the use of concertina wire as an enhancement, which has been a replacement for more traditional three strand barbed wire "top guards."

The fence should be fastened to ridged metal posts set in concrete every six feet with additional bracing at the corners and gate openings.

Figure 7.10 – **From left to right: Ornamental fence, security fence with 3 strands of barb wire, high-security fence with 3 rolls of razor wire, and another view of rolled razor wire**

(Courtesy of Bosch Security Systems)

The bottom of the fence should be stabilized against intruders crawling under by attaching posts along the bottom to keep the fence from being pushed or pulled up from the bottom. If the soil is sandy, the bottom edge of the fence should be installed below ground level.

For maximum security design, the use of double fencing with roles of concertina wire positioned between the two fences is the most effective deterrent and cost-efficient method. In this design, an intruder is required to use an extensive array of ladders and equipment to breach the fences.

Most fencing is largely a psychological deterrent and a boundary marker rather than a barrier because in most cases, such fences can be rather easily penetrated unless added security measures are taken to enhance the security of the fence. Sensors attached to the fence to provide electronic monitoring of cutting or scaling the fence can be used.

Gates

Gates exist to facilitate and control access. Gates need to be controlled to ensure that only authorized persons and vehicles pass through. A variety of controls are used. It is best to minimize the number of gates and access points because any opening is always a potential vulnerability. Each gate requires resources whether it uses electronic access control or a guard. The fewest number of entry points, the better the control of the facility.

Walls

Walls serve the same purpose as fences. They are manufactured barriers but generally are more expensive to install than fences. Common types of walls are block, masonry, brick, and stone. Walls tend to have a greater aesthetic value, appealing to those who prefer a more gentle and subtle look. Regardless of the type of wall used, its purpose as a barrier is the same as a fence. To be most effective, walls ought to be 7 feet high with 3 to 4 strands of barbed wire on top. This will help deter scaling. Walls also have a disadvantage in that they obstruct the view of an area. Chain link and wire fencing allow for visual access from both sides.

Perimeter Intrusion Detection

Depending on the extent of security required to protect the facility, exterior or perimeter sensors will alert an organization to any intruders attempting to gain access across open space or attempting to breach the fence line. These may provide security ample opportunity to evaluate and intercept any threat. In general, open terrain sensors work best on flat, cleared areas. Heavily or irregularly contoured areas are not conducive to open terrain sensing systems. Open terrain sensors include infrared, microwave systems, combination (dual technology), vibration sensors, video content analysis, and motion path analysis (CCTV) systems.

Infrared Sensors

Passive infrared sensors are designed for human body detection, so they are great for detecting when someone approaches. Passive-infrared sensors detect the heat emitted by animate forms. Because all living things emit heat, a system of recording measurable changes in a specific area provides a means of detecting unauthorized intrusions. When the unit registers changes in temperature in its area of detection, it relays the information to a processor, which measures the change according to detection parameters. If the change falls outside the parameters, the processor sends a signal to the unit's alarm. Active infrared sensors transmit an infrared signal via a transmitter. The location for reception is at a receiver. Interruption of the normal IR signal indicates an intruder or object has blocked the path. The beam can be narrow in focus, but it should be projected over a cleared path.

Microwave

Microwave sensors come in two configurations: bistatic and monostatic. With both bistatic and monostatic sensors, the sensors operate by radiating a controlled pattern of microwave energy into the protected area. The transmitted microwave signal is received, and a base level "no intrusion" signal is established. Motion by an intruder causes the received signal to be altered, setting off an alarm. Microwave signals pass through concrete and steel and must be applied with care if roadways or adjacent buildings are near the area of coverage. Otherwise, nuisance alarms may occur due to reflected microwave patterns. A bistatic sensor (*Figure 7.11*) sends an invisible volumetric detection field that fills the space between a transmitter and receiver. Monostatic microwave sensors use a single sensing unit that incorporates both transmitting and receiving functions. It generates a beam radiated from the transceiver and creates a well-controlled, three-dimensional volumetric detection pattern with adjustable range. Many monostatic microwave sensors feature a cutoff circuit, which allows the sensor to be tuned to cover only the area within a selected region. This helps to reduce nuisance alarms.

Figure 7.11 – **Bistatic Microwave Sensor**
(Courtesy of Bosch Security Systems)

Coaxial Strain-Sensitive Cable

These systems use a coaxial cable woven through the fabric of the fence (*Figure 7.12*). The coaxial cable transmits an electric field. As the cable moves due to strain on the fence fabric caused by climbing or cutting, changes in the electric field are detected within the cable, and an alarm condition occurs. Coaxial strain-sensing systems are readily available and are highly tunable to adjust for field conditions due to weather and climate characteristics. Some coaxial cable systems are susceptible to electromagnetic interference and radio frequency interference.

Figure 7.12 – **Coaxial Strain-Sensitive Cable**
(Courtesy of Bosch Security Systems)

Time Domain Reflectometry (TDR) Systems

Time Domain Reflectometry (TDR) systems send induced radio frequency (RF) signals down a cable that is attached to the fence fabric. Intruders climbing or flexing a fence create a signal path flaw that can be converted to an alarm signal. When the conductor cable is bent or flexed, a part of the signal returns to the origination point. This reflected signal can be converted to an intrusion point by computing the time it takes for the signal to travel to the intrusion point and return. The cable can be provided in an armored cable, which requires more than a bolt cutter to sever the sensing cable. These systems require their own processor unit and can be configured in a closed loop, such that if the cable is cut, it can be detected by the other return path.

Video Content Analysis and Motion Path Analysis

Video content analysis and motion path analysis intrusion detection is sophisticated software analysis of the camera images. CCTV camera systems are increasingly being used as intrusion detection systems. Application of complex algorithms to digital CCTV camera images allows CCTV systems to detect intruders. The software programming is smart enough to detect pixel changes and differentiate and filter out normal video events (leaves blowing, snow falling) from true alarm events. The application of software rules can further evolve to differentiate between a rabbit hopping across a parking lot to a person trespassing through the parking lot, which needs to be addressed. The application of complex software algorithms to CCTV digital images takes on the aspect of an artificial camera, whereby the camera and processors become "smart video" and start to emulate a human operator. The difference between a smart camera and a human operator is that it takes complex software programming and associated rules to allow the camera to differentiate and assess video events compared to the processing ability of the human mind.

The advantage of video content analysis and motion path analysis is that the camera systems do not get tired. They remain "alert" after monitoring hundreds of video events during a shift. Video content analysis systems can monitor more cameras, more effectively, with fewer operators at a reduced cost. This allows for the use of less dispatch center/command staff while letting technology assist with the human factor.

Lighting

Security lighting can be provided for overall facility illumination along with the perimeter to allow security personnel to maintain a visual assessment during times of darkness. It may provide both a real and psychological deterrent against intruders who will attempt to use the cover of darkness as a means of entry into a compound, parking lot, or facility. Lighting should enable security personnel and employees to notice individuals at night at a distance of 75 feet or more and to identify a human face at about 33 feet. These distances will allow the security personnel to avoid the individuals or take defensive action while still at a safe distance. Security lighting increases the effectiveness of guard forces and CCTV by increasing the visual range of the guards or CCTV during periods of darkness. It also provides increased illumination of an area where natural light does not reach or is insufficient. Lighting also has value as a deterrent to individuals looking for an opportunity to commit crime. Normally, security lighting requires less intensity than lighting in working areas. An exception is at doorways where increased illumination is required.

Lighting is relatively inexpensive to maintain and may reduce the need for security personnel while enhancing personal protection by reducing opportunities for concealment and surprise by potential attackers. Overall, it will be required to provide sufficient lighting at entry control points to ensure adequate identification of personnel. Also, wherever practical, place lighting devices as high as possible to give a broader and more natural light distribution. This requires fewer poles and is more aesthetically pleasing than standard lighting.

Types of Lighting Systems

The type of site lighting system used depends on the overall security requirements. Four types of lighting are used for security lighting systems:

- **Continuous lighting** is the most common security lighting system. It consists of a series of fixed lights arranged to flood a given area continuously during darkness with overlapping cones of light.
- **Standby lighting** has a layout similar to continuous lighting; however, the lights are not continuously lit but are either automatically or manually turned on when suspicious activity is detected or suspected by the security personnel or alarm systems.
- **Movable lighting** consists of manually operated, movable searchlights that may be lit during hours of darkness or only as needed. The system normally is used to supplement continuous or standby lighting.
- **Emergency lighting** is a backup power system of lighting that may duplicate any or all of the above systems. Its use is limited to times of power failure or other emergencies that render the normal system inoperative. It depends on an alternative power source such as installed or portable generators or batteries. Consider emergency/backup power for security lighting as determined to be appropriate.

Depending on the nature of the facility, protective lighting will be deployed to illuminate the perimeter of the facility along with any outside approaches. It will also be utilized in order to concentrate on the inner area and the buildings within the perimeter. The United States Code of Federal Regulations lists a specific requirement of 0.2 foot-candles (fc) for lighting protected areas within a perimeter.

Isolation zones and all exterior areas within the protected area shall be provided with illumination sufficient for the monitoring and observation requirements, but not less than 0.2 fc measured horizontally at ground level. 0.5 fc is acceptable for side landscapes and roadways. But from the standpoint of a regular security profession, who can determine what exactly an fc is? The basic idea for perimeter lighting (0.5 fc) will equate to using a 40W bulb in a 12×12 foot room. It gives off enough light to see, as it is a soft amber glow, but it will not totally illuminate the entire room.

Types of Lights
There are several types of lights that can be used within the protected area. They include fluorescent, mercury vapor, sodium vapor, and quartz lamps.

- **Fluorescent lights** are highly efficient and cost effective. However, they are temperature sensitive and while improving are not considered an effective outdoor lighting system. This light is better suited inside buildings and facilities.
- **Mercury vapor lights** are the preferred security light that disperses a strong white-bluish cast. They have an extended lamp life; however the downside is they take an amount of time to full light when activated – typical to the lights at a stadium.
- **Sodium vapor lights** provide a soft yellow light and is more efficient than mercury vapor. This light is used in areas where fog can be a problem.
- **Quartz lamps** emit a very bright white light and comes on immediately. They typically provide high wattage from 1500 to 2000 and can be used on perimeters and troublesome areas where high visibility and a daylight scene is required.

According to the American Institute of Architects, interior lighting levels for elevators, lobbies, and stairwell range from 5 to 10 fc; exterior lighting requirements vary for different locations. Common lighting levels include the following:

- Building entrances (5 fc)
- Walkways (1.5 fc)
- Parking garages (5 fc)
- Site landscape (0.5 fc)
- Areas immediately surrounding the building (1 fc)
- Roadways (0.5 fc)

Adequate lighting for monitoring activities is important. In addition, lighting serves as a crime deterrent and discourages unwanted visitors while giving the building occupants a sense of security and safety. Lights used for CCTV monitoring generally require at least 1 to 2 fc of illumination, whereas the lighting needed for safety considerations in exterior areas such as parking lots or garages is substantially greater (at least 5 fc).

Infrared Illuminators

The human eye cannot see infrared (IR) light. Most monochrome CCTV (black/white) cameras can. Thus, invisible infrared light can be used to illuminate a scene, which allows night surveillance without the need for additional artificial lighting. See *Figure 7.13*. IR beam shapes can be designed to optimize CCTV camera performance and can provide covert surveillance, which allows for no visible lighting to alert or annoy neighbors. This is extremely effective in low-light areas and can provide the monitoring guard the ability to see in the dark.

Figure 7.13 – **An infrared camera is extremely effective in low-light areas and can provide the monitoring guard the ability to see in the dark.**

(Courtesy of Bosch Security Systems)

Access Control

The primary function of an access control system (ACS) is to ensure that only authorized personnel are permitted inside the controlled area. This can also include the regulation and flow of materials into and out of specific areas. Persons subject to control can include employees, visitors, customers, vendors, and the public. Access control measures should be different for each application to fulfill specific security, cost, and operational objectives.

Control can begin at the facility property line to include such areas as parking lots. Exterior building entrances can then be controlled. Within the facility, any area can be controlled at the discretion of management. However, control is normally applied to be consistent with identified risk and the protective value that is desired. Protected areas include street level entrances, lobbies, loading docks, elevators, and sensitive internal areas containing assets such as customer data, proprietary information, and classified information.

The goal of an access control program is to limit the opportunity for a crime to be committed. If the potential perpetrator of a crime cannot gain access to financial assets, data files, computer equipment, programs, documentation, forms, operating procedures, and other sensitive material, the ability to commit a crime against the institution is minimized. Thus, only identified, authorized personnel should be permitted access to restricted areas. The basic components of an ACS include card readers, electric locks, alarms, and computer systems to monitor and control the ACS (*Figure 7.14*).

In order for the system to identify an authorized employee, an ACS needs to have some form of enrollment station used to assign and activate an access control device. Most often, a badge is produced and issued with the employee's identifiers with the enrollment station giving the employee specific areas that will be accessible. In general, an ACS compares an individual's badge against a verified database. If authenticated, the ACS sends output signals that allow authorized personnel to pass through a controlled area such as a gate or door. The system has the capability of logging and archiving entry attempts (authorized and unauthorized).

Figure 7.14 – **A card reader is one of the basic components of an access control system.**

Card Types

Magnetic stripe (mag stripe) cards consist of a magnetically sensitive strip fused onto the surface of a PVC material, like a credit card. A magnetic stripe card is read by swiping it through a reader or by inserting it into a position in a slot. This style of card is old technology; it may be physically damaged by misuse, and its data can be affected by magnetic fields. Magnetic stripe cards are easily duplicated.

Proximity cards (prox cards) use embedded antenna wires connected to a chip within the card. The chip is encoded with the unique card identification. Distances at which proximity cards can be read vary by the manufacturer and installation. Readers can require the card to be placed within a fraction of an inch from the reader to six inches away. This will then authenticate the card and will release the magnetic lock on the door.

Smart cards are credential cards with a microchip embedded in them. Smart cards can store data such as access transactions, licenses held by individuals, qualifications, safety training, security access levels, and biometric templates. This card can double as an access card for doors and be used as an authenticator for a computer. The U.S. federal government has mandated smart cards to provide personal identity verification (PIV) to verify the identity of every employee and contractor in order to improve data and facility security. The card will be used for identification, as well as for facility and data access.

Additional security measures can be employed using keypads with PIN Codes or biometric readers. Coded devices use a series of assigned numbers commonly referred to as a PIN. This series of numbers is entered into a keypad and is matched to the numbers stored in the ACS. This provides additional security because if a badge is lost or stolen, it will not activate a control area without the proper PIN number, similar to an ATM bank card. Biometrics provides the same support because even if the card is stolen, the reader must match a biometric to the biometric on the card to be successful.

Access Control Head End

The application software housed in the CPU provides the intelligent controller where all ACS activity is monitored, recorded, commanded, and controlled by the operator. Current state-of-the-art access systems allow each local security panel to hold the system logic for its associated devices. The CPU retains the system-specific programming to allow entry (access) for authorized personnel and deny access to unauthorized personnel.

Communication failure between the CPU and the local access control panels could result in new users not being permitted entry; however, the system is set so that the panel will recognize personnel already installed and will grant access to an authorized badge holder. These systems have advances that can integrate with CCTV and provide instant visual recognition along with visual alarm activation in order to provide the security console operator visual information before dispatching a security response team.

Closed Circuit TV

Closed circuit television (CCTV) is a collection of cameras, recorders, switches, keyboards, and monitors that allow viewing and recording of security events. The CCTV system is normally integrated into the overall security program and centrally monitored at the security central station.

Within the past several years, there have been enhanced developments in the CCTV industry, particularly better picture resolution, microprocessor-based video switchers, and the ability to transmit video over networks with a compressed bandwidth ratio.

CCTV provides a highly flexible method of surveillance and monitoring. One advantage is its immediate output. There is never a question of whether the equipment works properly or not. In addition, it can be adapted through the use of remote control devices, recorders, and computer imaging to guard against virtually any crime including burglary, unauthorized entrance, and employee theft. Uses of CCTV systems for security services include several different functions as described below:

- **Surveillance** – CCTV cameras can be used to give a viewer the capability to be made aware of or view visual events at multiple locations from a centralized remote viewing area. CCTV camera technology makes visual information available that would normally only be available through multiple (possibly roving) human resources.
- **Assessment** – When alerted by an alarm notification, CCTV cameras allow the security control center operators or other viewers to assess the situation and make a determination as to what type of response may or may not be required. An example would be an intrusion alarm at a remote facility. Visual assessment may indicate an unannounced maintenance crew at work. This situation will be handled differently than if the operator viewed an unknown individual removing a laptop from the facility.

- **Deterrence** – While more effective against unsophisticated burglars, as opposed to trained covert insurgents, CCTV cameras may deter burglary, vandalism, or intrusion due to fear of discovery and prosecution.
- **Evidentiary Archives** – Retrieval of archived images may be helpful in the identification and prosecution of trespassers, vandals, or other intruders.

Cameras

Color cameras offer more information, such as the color of a vehicle or a subject's clothing. Some ultra-low-light color cameras are able to automatically sense the ambient light conditions and switch from color to black and white in low-light conditions. Cameras must have auto-white balance to adjust for the changing color temperature of daylight and artificial lighting needed for night-time viewing. Black and white cameras are more sensitive under low-light or darkness conditions. Color cameras require a higher illumination level than black and white cameras to be effective. Typically, a high-quality color camera will work well down to fc illumination, whereas a standard black and white camera might only require 0.5 fc. These lighting level requirements vary with the camera model and manufacturer, so be sure to specify the necessary illumination level that is required for camera observation, and coordinate carefully with the lighting levels for the particular area to be viewed. In addition, placement of cameras to allow for capturing and viewing of all activities in the remotely observed area is also an important consideration for the security professional.

Outdoor Cameras

Outdoor camera installations cost more than indoor cameras due to the need to environmentally house, heat, and ventilate the camera. When mounting a camera outdoors, the lighting requirements change depending on the time of day and the weather. Because of this, consider the following for outdoor cameras:

- Shrubs, trees, and other vegetation in a camera's line of sight may cause obstructed views. Security professionals need to be aware of this when determining where to place cameras. Also, motion detector systems can register a false positive when plants in the field of view move in windy conditions.
- Provide heater blower packages for cold weather applications.
- Always use auto-iris lenses with outdoor cameras. The iris automatically adjusts the amount of light reaching the camera and thereby optimizes its performance. The iris also protects the image sensor from getting damaged by strong sunlight.
- Always set the focus in low light with an auto-iris lens. If the adjustment is made in sunlight, it is very easy to focus, but at night the iris diameter increases and the image is not in focus anymore.
- Special dark focus filters called "neutral density" (ND) filters help reduce lighting by one or more stops of exposure. These filters do not affect the color of the image.
- Always try to avoid direct sunlight in an image. Direct sunlight blinds the camera and may permanently bleach the small color filters on the sensor chip, causing stripes in the image. If possible, position the camera so that it is looking away from the sun.
- When using a camera outdoors, avoid viewing too much sky. Due to the large contrast, the camera will adjust to achieve a good light level for the

sky, and the landscape and objects that must be assessed might appear too dark. One way to avoid these problems is to mount the camera high above ground (*Figure 7.15*). Use a pole if needed. Given mounting choices, mount cameras facing away from the rising or setting sun, but realize that this varies by season. This is especially important with a long focal length lens. These lenses amplify even the smallest movement of the mount. Building mounts are generally more stable than pole mounts.

Fixed Position Cameras

A fixed position camera cannot rotate or pan. A good application for fixed cameras is detection surveillance because video motion detection can be more readily applied to the static field of view. The installation and cost of fixed cameras is lower because there is no associated motor/control wiring.

Figure 7.15 – **A Wall-Mounted Camera**

Fixed cameras are good for review of pre-alarm conditions because there is a static view of the alarm area. Pre-alarm allows the review of video information for the time period immediately before the alarm occurred. Due to the static view, fixed cameras are not as well suited for tracking a dynamic event.

Pan/Tilt/Zoom (PTZ) Cameras

PTZ camera mounts allow the camera to rotate, pan, tilt, and zoom (*Figure 7.16*). Because of the drive motor, housing, and wiring for controls, PTZ cameras are typically three to four times more expensive than fixed cameras. However, the operator gets a much better view of the overall area than with a fixed camera. PTZ cameras are often used to view and assess alarm conditions. PTZ cameras are not well suited for pre-alarm assessment because they may not be focused on the alarm area at all times. When designing CCTV surveillance, consider the lost coverage within the camera sweep field of view when the camera zooms to a fixed location.

Figure 7.16 – **A Pan/Tilt/Zoom (PTZ) Camera**

Dome Cameras

Dome cameras (*Figure 7.17*) are actually a cheaper version of the PTZ camera when the total cost is considered (installation, parts, and maintenance). Dome cameras are mounted in a hardened plastic lower dome, which is commonly smoke colored to conceal the camera. The use of smoke-colored domes provides covert lens positioning, while the use of clear domes provides for better low-light performance. Dome cameras are a good design solution for applications where the camera needs to be protected from the environment or it is desired to conceal the axis and field of view of a scanning camera. A common application of dome cameras is in office buildings with suspended ceilings. The dome camera is more aesthetic looking than a standard camera unit. Improvements in product design have reduced the packing to integral units that now fit in the space of a quarter ceiling tile. PTZ features within dome cameras move substantially quicker than conventional cameras with a separate PTZ drive unit on them.

Figure 7.17 – **A Dome Camera**

Internet Protocol (IP) Cameras

An IP camera captures a video image digitally. The IP camera resides on a local area network (LAN). Video data is transmitted via the LAN to a video server that routes the video to end-users and a mass storage server. While this may sound advantageous, there are pros and cons. IP cameras are the least secure CCTV system, but they may have applications where remote viewing over a network is desired or where a high bandwidth and low latency network may exist. With an IP camera system, a network connection between the sites is all that is required to view any camera image on the system. One drawback to IP cameras is that they cost more than a standard analog (non-IP) camera. Due to the security concerns with the Internet, IP cameras will generally not be used on high-risk projects. The possible exception would be CCTV surveillance of low priority assets at remote locations.

Lens Selection

Another important consideration during installation of a CCTV system is the proper choice of lenses. Focal length is the distance from the surface of the lens to the point of focus measured in millimeters. Lenses either have a fixed or variable focal length. Manually variable focal length lenses are called "Vari-Focal Camera Lenses." The focal length of a lens is usually given in millimeters (mm). Focal lengths of most CCTV camera lenses vary from 3.6mm to 16mm for fixed focal length lenses to well over 70mm for zoom lenses. For a security camera in a warehouse with a high visibility requirement, a 2.8 or 4mm lens (makes wide, somewhat distant view) is the best choice. If the requirement is to positively identify people 25 feet away from a camera, a short focal length lens, 3.6mm, would give such a large field of view (37 feet × 26 feet) that recognition would be uncertain. An 8mm or even 12mm lens would be far better (see *Figure 7.18*).

7

Security Operations

Figure 7.18 – **Camera view with 3.6 mm lens (top left), 4.3 mm lens (top right), 6 mm lens (middle left), 12 mm lens (middle right), and 25 mm lens (bottom)**

(Courtesy of Bosch Security Systems)

Lighting Requirements

One design parameter of CCTV systems is specification of a proper light-to-dark ratio in the space viewed. "Light-to-dark" ratio refers to the light intensity (as measured in foot-candles or LUX) of the lightest (most reflective surface) to the darkest (least reflective surface). A proper light-to-dark ratio for good CCTV picture clarity is 4:1. The maximum ratio is 8:1. When the ratio is too high, the shadows appear black and the viewer cannot distinguish any shapes in the shadows. While not always achievable, the designer should strive for a light-to-dark ratio of 4:1.

Some cameras will automatically switch from color during daytime to black/white at night, which permits viewing under low-light conditions. This can be an effective solution in situations where the existing illumination levels are too low during night conditions to permit color camera use, but color camera use is desired during daytime conditions. Numerous CCTV camera manufacturers offer auto switching cameras.

Resolution

Resolution refers to the "graininess" of an image. The clearer the picture, the more pixels it will have. In addition, the larger the file, the more bandwidth it will consume. 352×288, which is the default frame rate for CCTV digital video recorder (DVR) systems, will generate a satisfactory image that can help with transmission costs because it is a quarter of the data associated with a 640 by 480 image. While several high definition (HD) cameras exist, which can operate at 720 and 1080 lines, the security professional must understand the bandwidth, storage, and processing resources that HD gear requires.

Frames Per Second (FPS)

CCTV cameras transmit video in image frames. The measure of the "smoothness" of the playback of the video is quantified in frames per second (fps). The more frames per second you choose, the more network capacity each camera will require and the more data storage you will need. For most security applications, 30 fps is higher than needed for evidentiary and investigative purposes. Additionally, CCTV cameras have the option to transmit video at two image rates: alarm condition and non-alarm condition. Making use of a lower non-alarm fps can reduce project cost by allowing a lower bandwidth transmission and storage recording of the CCTV system. The idea is to increase the frame rate to actual motion when an alarm or the operator wants to capture images in real time compared to having the DVR record an image every 2 seconds at a reduced frame rate. In general, the bandwidth required will be increased with the frame rate used.

Compression

Digital images and digital video can be compressed in order to save space on hard drives and make transmission faster. Typically, the compression ratio is between 10 and 100. There are several standard commercial compression algorithms, but the most common is MPEG-4. Moving Picture Experts Group (MPEG) is a compression technique for audio and video that balances compression against loss of detail in the image.

The greater the compression, the more information is lost. MPEG can be provided in any resolution size. MPEG-4 allows a style of transmission where an "anchor" image is transmitted and then another image is not transmitted until something in the image changes. This minimizes the number of images transmitted when there is no movement. MPEG-4 is a proven compression standard because it is economical and has all the clarity and ease of use.

Digital Video Recorder (DVR)

In current CCTV systems, the DVR has become the central focus of the CCTV system. The DVR is used principally for the download of camera images onto a hard drive for recording and storage of historical information. Older systems used VHS tapes but have largely been phased out. This system required tapes to be changed every day for storage, and when an incident occurred, you had to sit in front of the monitor and review the entire tape. DVRs currently have memory storage capability starting at tens of gigabytes to several terabytes with options to expand using additional hardware to increase storage. DVRs typically come in an 8 port or 16 port version, meaning that 8 or 16 cameras can be recorded at one time. Most DVRs are provided with self-contained DVD burners for archiving or removal of stored data. Many security specifications require a CCTV system to be able to retain a minimum of 45 days of camera images. The amount of storage required for 45 days is dependent on a number of factors, including number of cameras, compression ratio, resolution, and frame rate. Most systems can be configured to motion detections and will not fill up the database with useless images. For example, is it necessary for the DVR to record the loading dock area from midnight until 4 am if there is no activity? Once there is motion in front of the camera, then the system will begin recording. This does not mean that the monitoring officer cannot see the real time images; it just will not store images that have no significant reason for maintaining. Again, this is a feature that each security professional can determine whether or not he or she wishes to utilize.

Monitor Displays

Single Image Display

A single CCTV camera image is displayed. It is typical for a receptionist or a guard to monitor an entry door position where they are assigned duties.

Split Screen

Split screen is most commonly used to describe displaying multiple CCTV camera images on a single display. The display screen is typically split into a square pattern. Typically, if a 16 port DVR is used, then the screen can be installed to monitor 16 specific views. It is recommended that a second screen be utilized to allow the officer, guard, or receptionist to pull one view off the split screen for specific viewing or allow a flip sequencing of selected views to change every second in a larger view.

Matrix Displaying for Large Format Displays

LCD and flat-screen plasma displays (*Figure 7.19*) lend themselves to programming to show several camera images. The configuration is best done in a square matrix. A square matrix avoids distorting or stretching the camera image in one direction or the other, as would occur in a 5 by 7 matrix configuration for "alarm call-up" with additional monitors for a fixed view or switching images.

Figure 7.19 – **Large format displays in a power facility**

Guards

Security officers are the physical presence and the deterrence to unauthorized entry into a facility along with being the response force to an alarm activation. With all the alarm technology, it still requires human intervention to respond to an alarm, make contact with an intruder, interact with employees, and provide first aid when necessary.

Security officers are required to conduct foot patrols of building interiors, exteriors, and parking areas. Some officers are assigned a fixed or stationary position at entrances and other designated areas in order to prevent unauthorized entrance or the introduction of prohibited items. Another security officer responsibility is to control access into the facility by checking employee identification badges, issuing temporary badges, and registering visitors. Officers are required to respond to fire, security, and medical emergencies, and they also render assistance when needed as well as submit written or verbal reports regarding significant events to security management. They also escort designated visitors, usually construction or maintenance contractors, who require nonbusiness hour access to facilities or access to areas where classified or proprietary information is accessible. They must report potentially hazardous conditions and items in need of repair, including inoperative lights, leaky sprinkler heads, leaky faucets, toilet stoppages, broken or slippery floor surfaces, trip hazards, etc.

Proprietary

The advantages of proprietary security include the quality of personnel, degree of control over the security program, employee loyalty to the company, and prestige for both the employee and the company. A proprietary security force would be provided better training, which would be more specific to the operation, and better training equates to better performance. There would be a sense of employee loyalty, which will create a stronger sense of ownership. Officers see themselves as a part of the team and are willing to go the extra mile for the benefit of the company and other employees. They see themselves with a stake in the long-term success of the company. Proprietary guards benefit from esprit de corps and a sense of community. Because it is possible to pay better wages to proprietary employees, turnover might be lower in proprietary guard organizations.

Utilizing proprietary security allows companies to design, field, and manage a security program to meet its particular needs. Many managers feel that they have a much greater degree of control over personnel when they are directly on the firm's payroll. Employee loyalty is often much greater in a proprietary system. Contract security personnel are often moved around between different clients, making it hard for them to develop relationships and a sense of loyalty to a particular client. In the end, it is the contract company, not the client whom they protect, that signs their paychecks.

However, proprietary security operations have their disadvantages, including cost, administration, staffing, impartiality, and expertise. The administration required to operate a proprietary security operation includes recruiting, screening, and training security personnel, as well as maintaining logs, audits, and other security program components. There is little question that the administrative workload is substantially decreased when a contract service is employed.

A considerable disadvantage of a proprietary service is the time it would take a firm to establish its own program, from selecting a head of security, filling of numerous positions, and the specific training that would be needed. Businesses would spend a considerably larger amount of money and time on in-house services where they would have to offer competitive wages and benefits to compete with other businesses and security firms. Another disadvantage is the possibility that more permanent in-house guards have the potential to form friendships and become somewhat partial to other employees, which could result in favoritism and a lack in their performance of duty.

Contract

Contract security can adapt staffing levels more easily than a proprietary system, as the need for staff rises and falls due to sudden or unexpected circumstances. The cost of hiring, training, and equipping proprietary staff makes rapidly increasing or decreasing staff levels more cumbersome than if contract services were used. With contract guard services, the cost for salary, insurance, administrative costs, uniforms, and benefits are all rolled up in one hourly price. This is helpful for budgeting purposes, and there are no hidden costs.

Contract security employees are seen as impartial because they are paid by an outside company to enforce a set of policies and are not as likely to deviate from procedures due to personal relationships or pressure. There is no bond between the employees and the guard company, and if there is found to be a quid pro quo system starting to develop, a phone call to the account manager can replace the guard easily.

Contract security companies focus on security as a business, not a supporting function of business. This gives them an advantage over proprietary operations. When clients hire a security service, they also hire the management of that service to guide them in their overall security program. It may take time for a company to develop a proprietary security organization with the wide-ranging level of experience that comes with a contract security company.

When it comes to staffing needs, guard companies already have a process established for the recruitment and hiring of staff. Their business is to have bodies available for assignment. This relieves the company of paying overtime when proprietary employees leave or take vacation. With a contract guard service, when you need three guards, you ask for three guards. When you do not need three anymore, you ask for two. Another big benefit is that if a contract officer does not work out, he or she can easily be replaced. You just call your account manager and ask for a replacement.

Contract security costs less than proprietary security because, typically, proprietary personnel earn more than contract personnel, due to the prevailing wage at their company. Contract personnel generally have fewer benefits than proprietary personnel do. Start-up costs for proprietary systems also make contract security services cheaper.

Hybrid

Sometimes, contract security officers make sense. Sometimes, proprietary guards make sense. Sometimes, mixing both together at the same institution makes better sense. The hybrid system allows an organization to maintain more control over its security program while achieving the cost savings and administration reduction associated with contract security. The use of hybrid systems is considered a workable solution because it affords the benefits of both contract and proprietary security while possibly mitigating the downsides of both.

Alarm Monitoring

After all the cameras, alarm systems, and locks are installed throughout a facility, the question remains: "Who will monitor and respond to the alarms?" All alarm, CCTV, and access control signals are tied into a central station. An organization will typically have a central station located on their property and monitored by a proprietary or contract guard service.

The central center (*Figure 7.20*), also known as the security console center, security control center, or dispatch center, is an area that serves as a central monitoring and assessment space for access control, CCTV, and intrusion detection systems. In this space, operators assess alarm conditions and determine the appropriate response, which may entail dispatching of security forces. Normally, the central station is staffed by trained personnel 24 hours a day, seven days a week.

Maintaining a 24/7 security control center requires at the minimum two officers per shift. They are responsible for monitoring alarms, access control, CCTV, and fire. They will be required to dispatch officers to investigate alarms, disturbances, and unknown events.

Figure 7.20 – **The central center, also known as the security console center, security control center, or dispatch center, is an area that serves as a central monitoring and assessment space for access control, CCTV, and intrusion detection systems.**

(Courtesy of Bosch Security Systems)

In this circumstance, a hybrid scenario is a practical application in the use of proprietary officers within the security control center and contract officers out on the floor. Inside the control center, an organization needs a higher level of commitment to the company and performance continuity in knowledge and action. The contract officers can be crossed trained for times when there is a staffing issue dealing with the control center propriety staff. This would be a support element that could be counted on for vacation, sickness, or temporary duties. While the contractor management does not like being an employment warehouse, the contracted officer can be viewed as a potential replacement in the event a proprietary position becomes available.

Many organizations utilize the UL 1981 standard when dealing with high security facilities for designating staffing levels at a central station. UL 1981 requires monitoring facility staffing be such that all alarm signals be acknowledged and the appropriate dispatch or verification action be initiated not more than a defined period after the monitoring facility receiver acknowledges to the alarm panel at the protected site that the alarm signal has been received.[25]

Design Requirements

The control center will be located on the main floor or in the basement of the facility, as long as the area is not below ground level and there is no chance of flooding. Entry will be controlled, and only authorized personnel will be allowed inside the center. The control center will be provided with primary and secondary sources of power. The secondary power should consist of a battery backup or UPS system that will provide for a normal load of at least 24 hours. It is also recommended that an engine drive generator system be used as a complement to the rechargeable battery system in order to keep uninterrupted power to the control center.

Internal Security

Interior Intrusion Detection Systems

Within the facility, it is still necessary to maintain levels of security. The layered approach provides for additional security measures while inside the perimeter of the facility. Specifically, not all employees need access to the sensitive areas, such as the phone closets, or need access into the data center. It is not practical or economical to have guards stationed at every security point within the facility; however, an access control system can provide the necessary security controls throughout the building.

A card reader can control access into a specific room. This can be controlled through the access control software, which will be maintained within the security control center. If the individual has access to the room, the employee will place his badge up to the reader and it will release the electric lock and allow entry. Other elements necessary for this control of interior access are as follows:

- **Balanced Magnetic Switch (BMS)** – This device uses a magnetic field or mechanical contact to determine if an alarm signal is initiated. One magnet will be attached to the door and the other to the frame; when the door is opened, the field is broken. A BMS differs from standard magnetic status switches in that a BMS incorporates two aligned magnets with an associated reed switch. If an external magnet is applied to the switch area, it upsets the balanced magnetic field such that an alarm signal is received. Standard magnetic switches can be defeated by holding a magnet near the switch. Mechanical contacts can be defeated by holding the contacts in the closed position with a piece of metal or by taping them closed. Balanced magnetic switches are not susceptible to external magnetic fields and will generate an alarm if tampering occurs. These switches are used on doors and windows (*Figure 7.21*).

---

25 http://ulstandardsinfonet.ul.com/scopes/scopes.asp?fn=1981.html

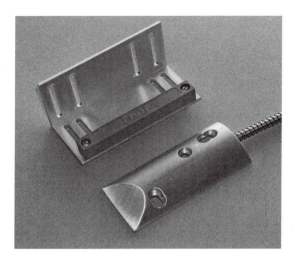

Figure 7.21 – **Balanced Magnetic Switch (BMS), used on doors and windows, uses a magnetic field or mechanical contact to determine if an alarm signal is initiated.**

(Courtesy of Bosch Security Systems)

■ ***Motion Activated Cameras*** – A fixed camera with a video motion feature can be used as an interior intrusion point sensor. In this application, the camera can be directed at an entry door and will send an alarm signal when an intruder enters the field of view. This device has the added advantage of providing a video image of the event, which can alert the security officer monitoring the camera, and he can make a determination of the need to dispatch a security force. Typically one camera can be associated with several doors along a hallway. If a door is forced open, the alarm will trigger the camera to begin recording and can give the monitoring officer a video view starting one minute before the alarm was tripped, so as to allow the operator all the possible information before dispatching a security response. This system uses technology to supplement the guard force. It can activate upon motion and can give a control center operator a detailed video of actual events during alarm activation.

■ ***Acoustic Sensors*** – This device uses passive listening devices to monitor building spaces. An application is an administrative building that is normally only occupied in daylight working hours. Typically, the acoustic sensing system is tied into a password-protected building entry control system, which is monitored by a central security monitoring station. When someone has logged into the building with a proper password, the acoustic sensors are disabled. When the building is secured and unoccupied, the acoustic sensors are activated. After hours, intruders make noise, which is picked up by the acoustic array, and an alarm signal is generated. The downside is the false alarm rate from picking up noises such as air conditioning and telephone ringers. This product must be deployed in an area that will not have any noise. Acoustic sensors act as a detection means for stay-behind covert intruders. One way to use the system is as a monitoring device, when it goes into alarm, the system will open up an intercom and the monitoring officer can listen to the area. If no intruder is heard then the alarm is cancelled.

- ***Infrared Linear Beam Sensors*** – Many think of this device from spy movies, where the enduring image of secret agents and bank robbers donning their special goggles to avoid triggering an active infrared beam is recalled. This is the device found in many homes on garage doors. A focused infrared (IR) light beam is projected from an emitter and bounced off of a reflector that is placed at the other side of the detection area (*Figure 7.22*). A retroreflective photoelectric beam sensor built into the emitter detects when the infrared beam is broken by the passing of a person or the presence of an object in the path of the infrared beam. If the beam is broken, the door will stop or the light will come on. This device can also be used to notify security of individuals in hallways late at night, when security is typically at its reduced coverage.

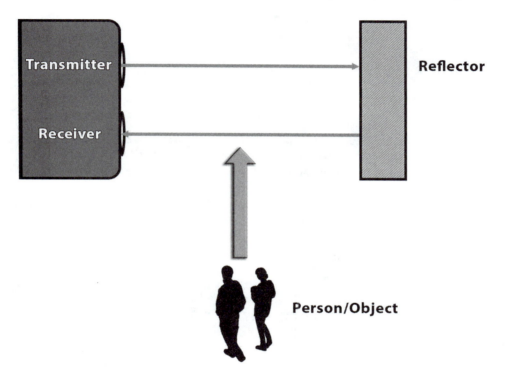

Figure 7.22 – **Infrared Linear Beam Sensors**

- ***Passive Infrared (PIR) Sensors*** – A PIR sensor (*Figure 7.23*) is one of the most common interior volumetric intrusion detection sensors. It is called passive because there is no beam. A PIR picks up heat signatures (infrared emissions) from intruders by comparing infrared receptions to typical background infrared levels. Infrared radiation exists in the electromagnetic spectrum at a wavelength that is longer than visible light. It cannot be seen, but it can be detected. Objects that generate heat also generate infrared radiation, and those objects include animals and the human body. The PIR is set to determine a change in temperature, whether warmer or colder, and distinguish an object that is different from the environment that it is set in. Typically, activation differentials are three degrees Fahrenheit. These devices work best in a stable, environmentally controlled space.

Figure 7.23 – **A passive infrared (PIR) sensor is one of the most common interior volumetric intrusion detection sensors. Because there is no beam, it is called passive.**

(Courtesy of Bosch Security Systems)

A PIR is a motion detector and will not activate for a person who is standing still because the electronics package attached to the sensor is looking for a fairly rapid change in the amount of infrared energy it is seeing. When a person walks by, the amount of infrared energy in the field of view changes rapidly and is easily detected. The sensor should not detect slower changes, like the sidewalk cooling off at night.

PIRs come in devices that project out at a 45° angle and can pick up objects 8 to 15 meters away. There are also 360° PIRs, which can be used in a secured room, so when there is entry, the PIR will activate. These motion detection devices can also be programmed into an alarm key pad located within the protected space. When motion is detected, it can be programmed to wait for a prescribed time while the individuals swipe their badge or enter their pass code information into the keypad. If identification is successful, the PIR does not send an intruder notification to the central station.

While not only a security application, PIRs are often used as an automatic request to exit (REX) device for magnetically locked doors. In this application, the REX (*Figure 7.24*) acts as the automatic sensor for detecting an approaching person in the exit direction for magnetically locked doors and deactivates the alarm.

Figure 7.24 – **An automatic Request to Exit (REX) device [located over the Exit sign] provides for magnetically locked doors, acting as an automatic sensor for detecting an approaching person in the exit direction and deactivates the alarm as the person exits.**

■ ***Dual-Technology Sensors*** – These provide a common sense approach for the reduction of false alarm rates. For example, this technology uses a combination of microwave and PIR sensor circuitry within one housing. An alarm condition is only generated if both the microwave and the PIR sensor detect an intruder. Since two independent means of detection are involved, false alarm rates are reduced when configured into this setting. Integrated, redundant devices must react at the same time to cause an alarm. More and more devices are coming with dual-technology that will reduce the need for multiple devices and will significantly reduce the false alarm rates.

Escort and Visitor Control

All visitors entering the facility should sign in and sign out on a visitor's log to maintain accountability of who is in the facility, the timeframe of the visit, who they visited, and in the case of an emergency, have accountability of everyone for safety purposes.

All visitors should be greeted by a knowledgeable receptionist who in turn will promptly contact the employee that they are there to visit or meet with. There should be some type of controlled waiting area within the lobby so the receptionist can keep track of the visitor and can direct the employee to them, in the event they have never met previously.

Visitors are given temporary badges, but this badge does not double as an access card. The temporary badge will be issued at an entry control point only after the visitor identifies the purpose of the visit and receives approval by the employee being visited. In some organizations, only certain employees may approve visitor access along with the day and time of the visit. In many operations, the visitor is escorted at all times while inside the facility. When the visitor arrives, he will present a form of photo identification, such as a driver's license, to the receptionist for verification. Some visitor badges are constructed of paper and may have a feature that causes a void line to appear after a preset time period. Typically, the pass is dated and issued for a set period, usually one day. In most cases, a visitor will wear a conspicuous badge that identifies him or her as a visitor and clearly indicates whether an escort is required (often done with color-coded badges). If an escort is required, the assigned person should be identified by name and held responsible for the visitor at all times while on the premises. A visitor management system can be a pen and paper system that records basic information about visitors to the facility. Typical information found in an entry includes the visitor's name, reason for the visit, date of visit, and the check in and check out times.

Other types of visitor management systems use a computer-based system or specific visitor software product. They can either be manually inserted into the system by the receptionist or, on a higher-end visitor management system, the visitor provides the receptionist with identification, such as a driver's license or a government or military ID. The receptionist then swipes the person's identification through a reader. The system automatically populates the database with ID information and recognizes whether the ID is properly formatted or false. The receptionist who is registering the guest identifies the group to which the person belongs – guest, client, vendor, or contractor. Then the badge is printed.

It is best for the employee to come to the lobby area and greet the visitor personally. This is more than a common courtesy because it provides the necessary security in proper identification, escorting, and controlling the movement of the visitor. Some companies initiate a sound security practice by properly identifying the visitor and signing him or her into a visitor management system, but then they allow the visitor to wander the halls of the company trying to find his or her contact. This completely defeats the prior work of identifying and badging the visitor.

Building and Inside Security

Doors

Door assemblies include the door, its frame, and anchorage to the building. As part of a balanced design approach, exterior doors should be designed to fit snugly in the doorframe, preventing crevices and gaps, which also helps prevent many simple methods of gaining illegal entry. The doorframe and locks must be as secure as the door in order to provide good protection.

Perimeter doors should consist of hollow steel doors or steel-clad doors with steel frames. Ensure the strength of the latch and frame anchor equals that of the door and frame. Permit normal egress through a limited number of doors, if possible, while accommodating emergency egress. Ensure that exterior doors into inhabited areas open outward. Locate hinges on the interior of restricted areas. Use exterior security hinges on doors opening outward to reduce their vulnerability.

If perimeter doors are made of glass, make sure that the material is constructed of a laminate material or stronger. Ensure that glass doors only allow access into a public or lobby area of the facility. High security doors will then need to be established within the lobby area where access will be controlled. All doors that are installed for sensitive areas such as telephone closets, network rooms, or any area that has access control will require the door to have an automatic door closing device.

Door Locks

Electric Locks

The electric lock is a secure method to control a door. An electric lock actuates the door bolt. For secure applications, dual locks can be used. In some cases, power is applied to engage the handle, so the user can retract the bolt instead of the electric lock door operator actually retracting the bolt. Most electric locks can have built-in position switches and request-to-exit hardware. Although offering a high security level, electric locks are expensive. A special door hinge that can accommodate a wiring harness and internal hardware to the door is required. For retrofit applications, electric locks usually require the purchase of a new door.

Electric Strikes

The difference between an electric strike and an electric lock is in the mechanism that is activated at the door. In an electric-lock door, the bolt is moved. In an electric-strike, door the bolt remains stationary and the strike is retracted. As in electric locks, electric strikes can be configured for fail-safe or fail-secure operation. The logic is the same. In fail-safe configuration, the strike retracts when de-energized on loss of power. This allows the door to be opened from the public side. In fail-secure configuration, the strike remains in place, causing the door to be locked from the public side requiring manual key entry to unlock the door from the public side. Again, as with electric locks, unimpeded access is allowed for in the direction of exit by manual activation of the door handle or lever when exiting from the secure side. For retrofit situations, electric strikes rarely require door replacement and can often be done without replacing the doorframe.

Magnetic Locks

The magnetic lock is popular because it can be easily retrofitted to existing doors (*Figure 7.25*). The magnetic lock is surface-mounted to the door and doorframe. Power is applied to magnets continuously to hold the door closed. Magnetic locks are normally fail-safe, but do have a security disadvantage. In requirements for the

*Figure 7.25 – **Magnetic Lock***

U. S. Life Safety Codes, doors equipped with magnetic locks are required to have one manual device (emergency manual override button) and an automatic sensor (typically a passive infrared sensor (PIR) or request to exit (REX) device) to override the door lock signal when someone approaches the door in the exit direction.[26] All locks are controlled by a card reader that, when activated, will release the secured side portion of the door and allow entry into the facility. While enhancing overall building safety, the addition of these extra devices allows possible compromise of the door lock. In the scenario, where a REX is used with magnetic locks, it not only turns off the alarm when the individual exits but also deactivates the locking device. This can be a problem if an adversary can get something through or under the door to cause the REX to release the magnetic lock.

Anti-Passback

In high security areas, a card reader is utilized on both entry and exit sides of the door. This keeps a record of who went in and out. Anti-passback is a strategy where a person must present a credential to enter an area or facility and then again use the credential to "badge out." This makes it possible to know how long a person is in an area and to know who is in the area at any given time. This requirement also has the advantage of instant personnel accountability during an emergency or hazardous event. Anti-passback programming prevents users from giving their cards or PIN number to someone else to gain access to the restricted area. In a rigid anti-passback configuration, a credential or badge is used to enter an area and that same

---

26 http://www.nfpa.org/codes-and-standards/document-information-pages?mode=code&code=101&DocN um=101&cookie_test=1

credential must be used to exit. If a credential holder fails to properly "badge-out," entrance into the secured area can be denied.

Turnstiles and Mantraps

A common and frustrating loophole in an otherwise secure ACS can be the ability of an unauthorized person to follow through a checkpoint behind an authorized person, called "piggybacking" or "tailgating."

The traditional solution is an airlock-style arrangement called a "mantrap," in which a person opens one door and waits for it to close before the next door will open (*Figure 7.26*). A footstep-detecting floor can be added to confirm there is only one person passing through. A correctly constructed mantrap or portal will provide for tailgate detection while it allows roller luggage, briefcases, and other large packages to pass without causing nuisance alarms. People attempting to enter side-by-side are detected by an optional overhead sensing array. The mantrap controller prevents entry into secured areas if unauthorized access is attempted.

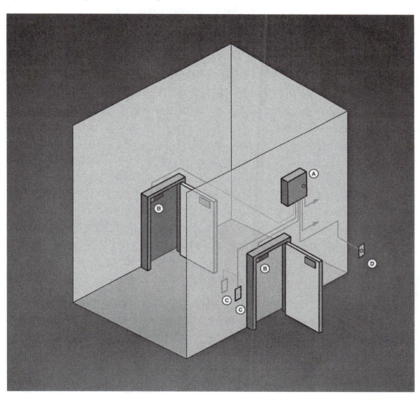

Figure 7.26 – **A Mantrap**
(Courtesy of Bosch Security Systems)

Another system that is available is a turnstile, which can be used as a supplemental control to assist a guard or receptionist while controlling access into a protected area. Anyone who has gone to a sporting event has gone through a turnstile. In this approach, the individual's badge is used to control the turnstile arm and allow access into the facility. See *Figure 7.27*.

Figure 7.27 – **A turnstile can be used as a supplemental control to assist a guard or receptionist while controlling access into a protected area.**

A higher end turnstile is an optical turnstile, which is designed to provide a secure access control in the lobby of a busy building. This system is designed as a set of parallel pedestals that form lanes, which allow entry or exit. Each barrier is equipped with photoelectric beams, guard arms, and a logic board. See *Figure 7.28*.

To gain access to the interior of the building, an authorized person uses his access card at the optical turnstile. When the access card is verified, the guard arm is dropped, the photoelectric beam is temporarily shut off, and the cardholder passes without creating an alarm. The concept behind these options is to create a secure perimeter just inside the building to ensure only authorized people proceed further into the building, thereby creating the secure working environment.

Figure 7.28 – **A higher end turnstile is an optical turnstile, which is designed to provide a secure access control in the lobby of a busy building.**

(Courtesy of Boeing Canada)

Keys, Locks, and Safes

Types of Locks

Key locks are one of the basic safeguards in protecting buildings, personnel, and property and are generally used to secure doors and windows. According to UL standard 437, door locks and locking cylinders must resist attack through the following testing procedures: the picking test, impression test (a lock is surreptitiously opened by making an impression of the key with a key blank of some malleable material – wax or plastic – which is inserted into the keyway and then filed to fit the lock), forcing test, and salt spray corrosion test for products intended for outdoor use. The door locks and locking cylinders are required by UL standards to resist picking and impression for ten minutes.[27]

Rim Lock

A rim lock, shown in *Figure 7.29*, is a lock or latch typically mounted on the surface of a door. It is typically associated with a dead bolt type of lock.

Figure 7.29 – A rim lock is a lock or latch typically mounted on the surface of a door.
(Courtesy of Bosch Security Systems)

Mortise Lock

A mortise lock, shown in *Figure 7.30*, is a lock or latch that is recessed into the edge of a door rather than being mounted to its surface. This configuration has a handle and locking device all in one package.

---

27   http://ulstandardsinfonet.ul.com/tocs/tocs.asp?doc=s&fn=0437.toc

Figure 7.30 – **A mortise lock is a lock or latch that is recessed into the edge of a door rather than being mounted to its surface.**

(Courtesy of Bosch Security Systems)

Locking Cylinders

The pin tumbler cylinder is a locking cylinder that is composed of circular pin tumblers that fit into matching circular holes on two internal parts of the lock (*Figure 7.31*). The pin tumbler functions on the principle that the pin tumblers need to be placed into a position that is entirely contained with the plug. Each pin is of a different height, thus accounting for the varying ridge sizes of the key. When the pins are properly aligned, the plug can be turned to unlock the bolt.

Figure 7.31 – **A pin tumbler cylinder is a locking cylinder that is composed of circular pin tumblers that fit into matching circular holes on two internal parts of the lock.**

(Courtesy of Bosch Security Systems)

7

Security Operations

Cipher Lock

A cipher lock, shown in *Figure 7.32*, is controlled by a mechanical key pad, typically 5 to 10 digits. When it is pushed in the right combination, the lock will release and allow entry. The drawback is someone looking over a shoulder can see the combination. However, an electric version of the cipher lock is in production in which a display screen will automatically move the numbers around, so if someone is trying to watch the movement on the screen, they will not be able to identify the number indicated unless they are standing directly behind the victim.

Remember locking devices are only as good as the wall or door that they are mounted in, and if the frame of the door or the door itself can be easily destroyed, then the lock will not be effective. A lock will eventually be defeated, and its primary purpose is to delay the attacker.

Figure 7.32 – **A cipher lock is controlled by a mechanical key pad with digits that when pushed in the right combination will release the lock and allow entry.**

(Courtesy of Bosch Security Systems)

Hi-Tech Keys

Not all lock and key systems are standard metal composite. There have been developments in key technology that offer convenient, reliable access control.

"Intelligent keys" are keys with a built-in microprocessor, which is unique to the individual key holder and identifies the key holder specifically (*Figure 7.33*). The lock, which also contains a minicomputer, and the key exchange data, allowing the lock to make valid access decisions based on the parameters established for the key holder. For example, the key will know if the employee is allowed access into the facility after normal business hours; if not, the key will not work. Also, it will keep track of whose key is being used to access specific locked doors and when the attempts are taking place. When an employee resigns from the organization, the relevant key is disabled.

"Instant keys" provide a quick way to disable a key by permitting one turn of the master key to change a lock. This method of changing a lock can save both time and money in the event a master key is lost. According to a manufacturer, a 50-story bank building can be rekeyed in six hours by two security guards. The system can go through 10 to 15 changes before having to be re-pinned.

Figure 7.33 – **"Intelligent keys" have a built-in microprocessor that is unique to the individual key holder and identifies the key holder specifically**

Safes

Safes are often the last bastion of defense between an attacker and an asset. Several types of safes not only protect against theft but also fire and flood. A safe (*Figure 7.34*) is defined as a fireproof and burglarproof iron or steel chest used for the storage of currency, negotiable securities, and similar valuables.

Figure 7.34 – **A safe is a fireproof and burglarproof iron or steel chest used for the storage of currency, negotiable securities, and similar valuables.**

(Courtesy of Bosch Security Systems)

The categories for safes depend on the amount of security needed. Underwriters Laboratories lists several classifications of safe; the following is one such classification:

Tool-Resistant Safe Class TL-15. This type of combination lock safe is designed to meet the following requirements:

- It must be resistant to entry (by opening the door or making a six-inch hand hole through the door) for a net working time of 15 minutes using any combination of the following tools:
  - ☐ Mechanical or portable electric hand drills not exceeding one-half-inch size
  - ☐ Grinding points, carbide drills (excluding the magnetic drill press and other pressure-applying mechanisms, abrasive wheels, and rotating saws)
  - ☐ Common hand tools such as chisels, drifts, wrenches, screwdrivers, pliers, and hammers and sledges not to exceed the eight-pound size, pry bars and ripping tools not to exceed five feet in length
  - ☐ Picking tools that are not specially designed for use against a special make of safe.

A TL-15 safe must:

- Weigh at least 750 pounds or be equipped with anchors and instructions for anchoring in larger safes, in concrete blocks, or to the floor of the bank premises.
- Have metal in the body that is solid cast or fabricated open-hearth steel at least 1 inch thick with a tensile strength of 50,000 pounds per square inch (psi) and that is fastened to the floor in a manner equal to a continuous 1/4-inch penetration weld of open-hearth steel having an ultimate tensile strength of 50,000psi.
- Have the hole to permit insertion of electrical conductors for alarm devices not exceeding a 1/4-inch diameter and be provided in the top, side, bottom, or back of the safe body, but it must not permit a direct view of the door or locking mechanism.
- Be equipped with a combination lock meeting UL Standard No. 768 requirements for Group 2, 1, or 1R locks.
- Be equipped with a relocking device that will effectively lock the door if the combination lock is punched.

The UL classifications mean that a Tool-Resistant Safe Class TL-30 will take 30 minutes to break into the safe using tools. A TRTL-30 safe means it will take 30 minutes for a combination of tools and torches to break into the safe. The categories go up to a safe that can resist tools, torches, and explosives.

Vaults

A vault (*Figure* 7.35) is defined as a room or compartment designed for the storage and safekeeping of valuables and has a size and shape that permits entrance and movement within by one or more persons. Vaults generally are constructed to withstand the best efforts of man and nature to penetrate them.

The UL has developed standards for vault doors and vault modular panels for use in the construction of vault floors, walls, and ceilings. The standards are intended to establish the burglary-resistant rating of vault doors and modular vault panels according to the length of time they withstand attack by common mechanical tools, electric tools, cutting torches, or any combination thereof. The ratings, based on the net working time to affect entry, are as follows:

- **Class M** – One quarter hour
- **Class 1** – One half hour
- **Class 2** – One hour
- **Class 3** – Two hours

Figure 7.35 – **A vault is a room or compartment designed for the storage and safe-keeping of valuables and has a size and shape that permits entrance and movement within by one or more persons.**

Containers

A container is a reinforced filling cabinet that can be used to store proprietary and sensitive information. The standards for classified containers are typically from a government. For example, the U.S. government lists a class 6 container (*Figure 7.36*) as approved for the storage of secret, top secret, and confidential information. The container must meet the protection requirements for 30 man-minutes against covert entry and 20 hours against surreptitious entry with no forced entry.

7

Figure 7.36 – **A class 6 container is approved for the storage of secret, top secret, and confidential information.**

(Courtesy of Bosch Security Systems)

Key Control

Key control, or more accurately the lack of key control, is one of the biggest risks that businesses and property owners face. Strong locks and stronger key control are the two essentials in a high security locking system. In most cases, master and sub-master keys are required for most building systems so that janitorial and other maintenance personnel may have access. Thus, the control of all keys becomes a critical element of the key lock system: All keys need to be tightly controlled from the day of purchase by designated personnel responsible for the lock system.

Without a key control system, an organization cannot be sure who has keys or how many keys may have been produced for a given property. Not having a patent-controlled key system leads to unauthorized key duplication, which can lead to unauthorized access or employee theft. Most key control systems utilize patented keys and cylinders. These lock cylinders employ very precise locking systems that can only be operated by the unique keys to that system. Because the cylinders and the keys are patented, the duplication of keys can only be done by factory-authorized professional locksmiths.

The key blanks and lock cylinders are made available only to those same factory authorized professional locksmiths. Procedures may be in place to allow the organization to contract another security professional should the need arise.

All high-security key control systems require specific permission to have keys originated or duplicated. These procedures assure the property owner or manager that they will always know who has keys and how many they possess. If an employee leaves and returns the keys, the organization can be reasonably assured that no copies of the keys were made. Most systems have cylinders that will retrofit existing hardware, keeping the cost of acquisition lower. Some systems employ different levels of security within the system, still giving patented control, but not requiring ultra-high security where it is not needed. These measures are again aimed at cost control.

Most systems can be master keyed; some will coordinate with existing master key systems. There are systems available that allow interchangeable core cylinders for retrofitting of existing systems.

Locks, keys, doors, and frame construction are interconnected and all must be equally effective. If any single link is weak, the system will break down. The Medeco Guide for Developing and Managing Key Control states: [28]

The following represents the basic and most critical elements of key control and shall be included, as a minimum, in the key control specification.

2.1. Facility shall appoint a Key Control Authority or Key Control Manager to implement, execute, and enforce key control policies and procedures.

2.2. A policy and method for the issuing and collecting of all keys shall be implemented.

2.3. Keys and key blanks shall be stored in a locked cabinet or container, in a secured area.

2.4. A key control management program shall be utilized. A dedicated computer software application is preferred.

2.5. All keys shall remain the property of the issuing facility.

2.6. A key should be issued only to individuals who have a legitimate and official requirement for the key.

2.6.1. A requirement for access alone, when access can be accomplished by other means (such as unlocked doors, request for entry, intercoms, timers, etc.), shall not convey automatic entitlement to a key.

2.7. All keys shall be returned and accounted for.

2.8. Employees must ensure that keys are safeguarded and properly used.

Personnel safety (e.g., duress, travel, monitoring)

---

28   http://www.medeco.com/Other/Medeco/Downloads/Key_Control/Key_Control.pdf (Page 3)

Personnel Safety

Personnel are often the greatest assets when designing physical and environmental security. Personnel are becoming more mobile and more concerned regarding their privacy. An information security professional must be aware of privacy laws and expectations that can influence environmental monitoring and ensure personnel are aware of physical concerns when traveling. Finally, personnel under duress represent a special situation that requires forethought and training.

Privacy

All individuals have an expectation of privacy. This expectation varies by culture and people, but the security professional must understand the limits of monitoring individuals within the law of a country. While it is generally considered acceptable to place CCTV cameras in public parking lots, most of the world would not approve of CCTV cameras in a private area such as a shower or locker room. While these examples are extreme, others fall into a "grey" area. Such examples include a home office. Does an organization have a right to monitor any space work is performed on their behalf including a private home? Most privacy experts would side with a "no" answer for this question, but some security professionals or investigators may say "yes." This is largely due to a difference in perspective. The investigator is interested in collecting evidence and the security professional is interested in ensuring the safety of the individual and security of the organization's information.

In most instances communication about the organization's privacy policies is key to ensuring privacy related complaints are minimized. Many organizations place conspicuous signs that state CCTV or other types of monitoring are being conducted in an area. While some may argue this is alerting an attacker, in reality the attackers already assume or know there are cameras in the area. If they did not, a notice may very will deter or dissuade them. Either way, notifying or being conspicuous about monitoring can have advantages.

Travel

Monitoring employees and trying to ensure their safety with the safety of the organization's information while abroad can be challenging. Many of the controls available in an organization's facility are not available while abroad, so the information security professional must compensate with better personnel training and technical controls. The United States National Counterintelligence Executive provides the following tips for overseas travelers: [29]

YOU SHOULD KNOW

- In most countries, you have no expectation of privacy in Internet cafes, hotels, offices, or public places. Hotel business centers and phone networks are regularly monitored in many countries. In some countries, hotel rooms are often searched.
- All information you send electronically – by fax machine, personal digital assistant (PDA), computer, or telephone – can be intercepted. Wireless devices are especially vulnerable.

---

29 http://www.ncix.gov/publications/reports/docs/traveltips.pdf
Another site for the security professional to look at is: http://www.nationsonline.org/oneworld/travel_warning.htm

- Security services and criminals can track your movements using your mobile phone or PDA and can turn on the microphone in your device even when you think it's off. To prevent this, remove the battery.
- Security services and criminals can also insert malicious software into your device through any connection they control. They can also do it wirelessly if your device is enabled for wireless. When you connect to your home server, the "malware" can migrate to your business, agency, or home system, can inventory your system, and can send information back to the security service or potential malicious actor.
- Malware can also be transferred to your device through thumb drives (USB sticks), computer disks, and other "gifts."
- Transmitting sensitive government, personal, or proprietary information from abroad is therefore risky.
- Corporate and government officials are most at risk, but do not assume you are too insignificant to be targeted.
- Foreign security services and criminals are adept at "phishing" – that is, pretending to be someone you trust in order to obtain personal or sensitive information.
- If a customs official demands to examine your device or if your hotel room is searched while the device is in the room and you are not, you should assume the device's hard drive has been copied.

BEFORE YOU TRAVEL

- If you can do without the device, don't take it.
- Do not take information you do not need, including sensitive contact information. Consider the consequences if your information were stolen by a foreign government or competitor.
- Backup all information you take; leave the backed-up data at home. If feasible, use a different mobile phone or PDA from your usual one and remove the battery when not in use. In any case, have the device examined by your agency or company when you return.
- Seek official cybersecurity alerts from:
- www.onguardonline.gov *and*
- www.us-cert.gov/cas/tips

Prepare your device:

- Create a strong password (numbers, upper and lowercase letters, special characters – at least 8 characters long). Never store passwords, phone numbers, or sign-on sequences on any device or in its case.
- Change passwords at regular intervals (and as soon as you return).
- Download current, up-to-date anti-virus protection, spyware protection, OS security patches, and a personal firewall.
- Encrypt all sensitive information on the device. (But be warned: In some countries, customs officials may not permit you to enter with encrypted information.)
- Update your Web browser with strict security settings.
- Disable infrared ports and features you don't need.
- Use a virtual machine to run your desktop while travelling in order to ensure all changes made to the system are isolated within the virtual environment.

7

Security Operations

WHILE YOU'RE AWAY

- Avoid transporting devices in checked baggage.
- Use digital signature and encryption capabilities when possible.
- Do not leave electronic devices unattended. If you have to stow them, remove the battery and SIM card and keep them with you.
- Do not use thumb drives given to you; they may be compromised. Do not use your own thumb drive in a foreign computer for the same reason. If you're required to do it anyway, assume you have been compromised; have your device cleaned as soon as you can.
- Shield passwords from view. Do not use the "remember me" feature on many websites; retype the password every time.
- Be aware of who is looking at your screen, especially in public areas.
- Terminate connections when you're not using them.
- Clear your browser after each use: Delete history files, caches, cookies, URL, and temporary Internet files.
- Do not open emails or attachments from unknown sources. Do not click on links in emails. Empty your "trash" and "recent" folders after every use.
- Avoid Wi-Fi networks if you can. In some countries, they are controlled by security services; in all cases, they are insecure.
- If your device or information is stolen, report it immediately to your home organization and the local U.S. embassy or consulate.

WHEN YOU RETURN

- Change your password. Have your company or agency examine the device for the presence of malicious software.
- For general travel alerts and information, see:
- http://travel.state.gov/content/passports/english/alertswarnings.html

These tips represent sound considerations for anyone traveling for business or anyone with access to sensitive information traveling for any reason. Personnel should be gently reminded through awareness and training that they can be targeted when abroad and even though they may be on vacation, they should remain vigilant while enjoying themselves.

Duress

Duress is a topic that relates to the concept of a person doing something or divulging something they normally would not under threat of harm. For example, an intruder may break into a data center and demand the receptionist cancel the alarm and tell the police it is a false alarm or the attacker will harm the receptionist. These situations can occur quite quickly, and proper training is crucial for ensuring personnel safety.

Bank tellers offer an excellent example of a position that is possibly subject to duress. During a bank robbery, the teller is forced to commit an act (giving away the bank's money) he or she normally wouldn't perform to avoid harm. The key to understanding duress situations is knowing the assets, access, and the alternatives of the organization. The assets of an organization should be identified to ensure the security professional understands where a duress situation may occur. This may be at a corporate building or with an executive on travel with special patents. Regardless of where the asset is, the security professional must remember the protection and risk of duress follows the asset and the access to the asset. Personnel with access to the assets are typically the targets of duress situations. They can be the victims of verbal, physical, and emotional abuse and harassment while the attacker attempts to access the asset. In all cases, the life and safety of the individual must be paramount when working with duress situations.

Scenario analysis can assist in determining the alternatives available and ensuring appropriate training and education can be conducted for individuals subject to duress. Scenario analysis is a type of risk analysis where assets, access, and alternatives are mapped out in different "stories" to determine how a situation can play out. The more scenarios reviewed and the more knowledgeable the participants, the better the results of the exercise. The results should be used to train personnel with access to assets. For example, bank tellers are often trained to put a dye pack with the money they give to the robber. This pack explodes, rendering the money worthless, and marks the robber with indelible ink for identification. Additionally, a receptionist told to turn off a sounding alarm may enter a special duress code, which not only turns off the alarm but silently alerts the police that there is a duress situation and to come immediately!

Duress situations are extremely challenging with sometimes deadly or life altering consequences. The information security professional should always seek the assistance of law enforcement or other professionals who specialize in this area when working through the design and implementation of duress training or mitigation controls.

Summary

Operations security and security operations are two halves of the same coin. Operations security is primarily concerned with the protection and control of information processing assets in centralized and distributed environments. Security operations are primarily concerned with the daily tasks required to keep security services operating reliably and efficiently. Operations security refers to a quality of other services that must be maintained. Security operations are a set of services in its own right.

7

Security Operations

 # Domain 7: Review Questions

1. Assuming a working IDS is in place, which of the following groups is **BEST** capable of stealing sensitive information due to the absence of system auditing?

    A.   Malicious software (malware)

    B.   Hacker or cracker

    C.   Disgruntled employee

    D.   Auditors

2. Which of the following provides controlled and un-intercepted interfaces into privileged user functions?

    A.   Ring protection

    B.   Anti-malware

    C.   Maintenance hooks

    D.   Trusted paths

3. The doors of a data center spring open in the event of a fire. This is an example of

    A.   Fail-safe

    B.   Fail-secure

    C.   Fail-proof

    D.   Fail-closed

4. Which of the following ensures constant redundancy and fault-tolerance?

    A.   Cold spare

    B.   Warm spare

    C.   Hot spare

    D.   Archives

5. If speed is preferred over resilience, which of the following RAID configuration is the most suited?

    A.   RAID 0

    B.   RAID 1

    C.   RAID 5

    D.   RAID 10

6. Updating records in multiple locations or copying an entire database on to a remote location as a means to ensure the appropriate levels of fault-tolerance and redundancy is known as

    A. Data mirroring

    B. Shadowing

    C. Backup

    D. Archiving

7. When the backup window is not long enough to backup all of the data and the restoration of backup must be as fast as possible. Which of the following type of high-availability backup strategy is **BEST**?

    A. Full

    B. Incremental

    C. Differential

    D. Increase the backup window so a full backup can be performed

8. At a restricted facility, visitors are requested to provide identification and verified against a pre-approved list by the guard at the front gate before being let in. This is an example of checking for

    A. Least privilege

    B. Separation of duties

    C. Fail-safe

    D. Psychological acceptability

9. When sensitive information is no longer critical but still within scope of a record retention policy, that information is **BEST**

    A. Destroyed

    B. Re-categorized

    C. Degaussed

    D. Released

10. Which of the following **BEST** determines access and suitability of an individual?

    A. Job rank or title

    B. Partnership with the security team

    C. Role

    D. Clearance level

11. Which of the following can help with ensuring that only the needed logs are collected for monitoring?

    A. Clipping level

    B. Aggregation

    C. XML Parsing

    D. Inference

12. The main difference between a Security Event Information Management (SEIM) system and a log management system is that SEIM systems are useful for log collection, collation and analysis

    A. In real time

    B. For historical purposes

    C. For admissibility in court

    D. In discerning patterns

13. The best way to ensure that there is no data remanence of sensitive information that was once stored on a DVD-R media is by

    A. Deletion

    B. Degaussing

    C. Destruction

    D. Overwriting

14. Which of the following processes is concerned with not only identifying the root cause but also addressing the underlying issue?

    A. Incident management

    B. Problem management

    C. Change management

    D. Configuration management

15. Before applying a software update to production systems, it is **MOST** important that

    A. Full disclosure information about the threat that the patch addresses is available

    B. The patching process is documented

    C. The production systems are backed up

    D. An independent third party attests the validity of the patch

16. Computer forensics is the marriage of computer science, information technology, and engineering with

    A. Law

    B. Information systems

    C. Analytical thought

    D. The scientific method

17. What principal allows an investigator to identify aspects of the person responsible for a crime when, whenever committing a crime, the perpetrator leaves traces while stealing assets?

    A. Meyer's principal of legal impunity

    B. Criminalistic principals

    C. IOCE/Group of 8 Nations principals for computer forensics

    D. Locard's principle of exchange

18. Which of the following is part of the five rules of evidence?

    A. Be authentic, be redundant and be admissible.

    B. Be complete, be authentic and be admissible.

    C. Be complete, be redundant and be authentic.

    D. Be redundant, be admissible and be complete

19. What is not mentioned as a phase of an incident response?

    A. Documentation

    B. Prosecution

    C. Containment

    D. Investigation

20. Which BEST emphasizes the abstract concepts of law and is influenced by the writings of legal scholars and academics.

    A. Criminal law

    B. Civil law

    C. Religious law

    D. Administrative law

21. Which of the following are computer forensics guidelines?

    A.   IOCE, MOM and SWGDE.

    B.   MOM, SWGDE and IOCE.

    C.   IOCE, SWGDE and ACPO.

    D.   ACPO, MOM and IOCE.

22. Triage encompasses which of the following incident response subphases?

    A.   Collection, transport, testimony

    B.   Traceback, feedback, loopback

    C.   Detection, identification, notification

    D.   Confidentiality, integrity, availability

23. The integrity of a forensic bit stream image is determined by:

    A.   Comparing hash totals to the original source

    B.   Keeping good notes

    C.   Taking pictures

    D.   Encrypted keys

24. When dealing with digital evidence, the crime scene:

    A.   Must never be altered

    B.   Must be completely reproducible in a court of law

    C.   Must exist in only one country

    D.   Must have the least amount of contamination that is possible

25. When outsourcing IT systems

    A.   all regulatory and compliance requirements must be passed on to the provider.

    B.   the outsourcing organization is free from compliance obligations.

    C.   the outsourced IT systems are free from compliance obligations.

    D.   the provider is free from compliance obligations.

26. When dealing with digital evidence, the chain of custody:

    A.   Must never be altered

    B.   Must be completely reproducible in a court of law

    C.   Must exist in only one country

    D.   Must follow a formal documented process

27. To ensure proper forensics action when needed, an incident response program must:

    A. avoid conflicts of interest by ensuring organization legal council is not part of the process.

    B. routinely create forensic images of all desktops and servers.

    C. only promote closed incidents to law enforcement.

    D. treat every incident as though it may be a crime.

28. A hard drive is recovered from a submerged vehicle. The drive is needed for a court case. What is the best approach to pull information off the drive?

    A. Wait for the drive to dry and then install it in a desktop and attempt to retrieve the information via normal operating system commands.

    B. Place the drive in a forensic oven to dry it and then use a degausser to remove any residual humidity prior to installing the drive in a laptop and using the OS to pull off information.

    C. While the drive is still wet use a forensic bit to bit copy program to ensure the drive is preserved in its "native" state.

    D. Contact a professional data recovery organization, explain the situation and request they pull a forensic image.

29. To successfully complete a vulnerability assessment, it is critical that protection systems are well understood through:

    A. Threat definition, target identification and facility characterization

    B. Threat definition, conflict control and facility characterization

    C. Risk assessment, threat identification and incident review

    D. Threat identification, vulnerability appraisal and access review

30. The strategy of forming layers of protection around an asset or facility is known as:

    A. Secured Perimeter

    B. Defense-in-Depth

    C. Reinforced Barrier Deterrent

    D. Reasonable Asset Protection

31. The key to a successful physical protection system is the integration of:

    A. people, procedures, and equipment

    B. technology, risk assessment, and human interaction

    C. protecting, offsetting, and transferring risk

    D. detection, deterrence, and response

32. For safety considerations in perimeter areas such as parking lots or garages what is the advised lighting?

    A. 3 fc

    B. 5 fc

    C. 7 fc

    D. 10 fc

33. What would be the most appropriate interior sensor used for a building that has windows along the ground floor?

    A. infrared glass-break sensor

    B. ultrasonic glass-break sensors

    C. acoustic/shock glass-break sensors

    D. volumetric sensors

34. Which of the following BEST describe three separate functions of CCTV?

    A. surveillance, deterrence, and evidentiary archives

    B. intrusion detection, detainment and response

    C. optical scanning, infrared beaming and lighting

    D. monitoring, white balancing and inspection

35. What is the BEST means of protecting the physical devices associated with the alarm system?

    A. Tamper protection

    B. Target hardening

    C. Security design

    D. UL 2050

Domain 8
Security in the Software Development Life Cycle

Although information security has traditionally emphasized system-level access controls, the security professional needs to ensure that the focus of the enterprise security architecture includes applications because many information security incidents now involve software vulnerabilities in one form or another. Application vulnerabilities also allow an entry point to attack systems, sometimes at a very deep level. (Web application vulnerabilities have been frequently used in this manner.) Malware is much more than a mere nuisance: It is now a major security risk faced by every enterprise that connects to external networks and allows external data to be ported to their internal systems in some form.

Development of in-house systems, commercial and off-the-shelf software, and controls on the choice, maintenance, and configuration of applications must be given greater attention than has been the case in the past. Unfortunately, at the same time, too few security professionals have a significant programming or systems development background. In addition, training in programming and development tends to emphasize speed and productivity over quality, let alone considerations of security. From the perspective of many developers, security is an impediment and a roadblock. This perception is changing, and in the current development environment, the security professional needs to take care not to be seen as a problem to be avoided.

When examined, most major incidents, breaches, and outages will be found to involve software vulnerabilities. Software continues to grow increasingly larger and more complex with each release. In addition, software is becoming standardized, both in terms of the programs and code used as well as the protocols and interfaces involved. Although this provides benefits in training and productivity, it also means that a troublesome characteristic may affect the computing and business environment quite broadly. Also, legacy code and design decisions taken decades ago are still involved in current systems and interact with new technologies and operations in ways that may open up additional vulnerabilities that the security professional may, or may not, even be aware of.

949

TOPICS

- ■ Security in the software development life cycle
  - □ Development lifecycle methodologies
  - □ Maturity models
  - □ Operation and maintenance
  - □ Change management
  - □ Integrated product team
- ■ Security controls in the development environment
  - □ Security of the software environments
    - – Program languages
    - – Libraries
    - – Toolsets
    - – Integrated development environments
    - – Runtime
  - □ Security weaknesses and vulnerabilities at source code level
  - □ Configuration management as an aspect of secure coding
  - □ Security of code repositories
  - □ Security of application programming interfaces
- ■ The effectiveness of software security
  - □ Auditing and logging of changes
  - □ Risk analysis and mitigation
    - – Corrective actions (e.g., rollback planning)
    - – Testing and verification (e.g., code signing)
    - – Regression testing
  - □ Acceptance testing
- ■ Assess software acquisition security

OBJECTIVES

According to the (ISC)[2] Candidate Information Bulletin (Exam Outline), a CISSP candidate is expected to:

- Understand and apply security in the software development life cycle
- Enforce security controls in the development environment
- Assess the effectiveness of software security
- Assess software acquisition security

8

Security in the Software
Development Life Cycle

Software Development Security Outline

The security professional needs to be aware of the important security concepts that apply during software development, operation, and maintenance processes. Software includes both operating system software and application software. The computing environment is layered. The foundation is the hardware of the computer system and the functions that are built into that hardware. In some cases, a layer of microcode or firmware is implemented to generate or ease the use of certain common operations. The operating system provides management of all computer hardware resources, as well as a number of software and data resources required for proper operation. In addition, the operating system manages a variety of utilities and functions that are necessary for overall system security and audit. The applications sit on top of the operating system and associated utilities. The user interacts with data and the network resources through these applications. In some cases, there are additional layers, very often in terms of the interface either with the user or between systems. In addition, these systems may now be built on a distributed basis, with portions or aspects of the programming running on a variety of different machines.

When examining applications security, one must consider the applications that users use to do their jobs and interact with the operating system. However, also be aware that the fundamental concepts of application development also apply to operating system software development, even though most users purchase an existing operating system. Thus, although most enterprises do not develop operating system code, they do design, develop, operate, and maintain proprietary applications relevant to their business needs. Analysis and mitigation of software vulnerabilities uses similar concepts in both cases, although the significance of vulnerabilities in operating system software is greater.

The information security professionals must thoughtfully apply these concepts to the specifics of their own company or situation. Software must be considered both an asset, to be assessed early in the risk management process, and a tool, with vulnerabilities that may require the addition of mitigation or specific controls and safeguards to the system.

Operating system and application software consist of increasingly complex computer programs. Without this software, it would be impossible to operate the computer for the purposes required of it. In the early days of computers, users had to write code for each activity to be undertaken using a language native to the specific machine. To improve productivity, sets or libraries of code were developed that would implement many of the more common instructions. These standard files of functions, along with utilities to ease their use, became the forerunners of what is known as programming languages. In that early environment, the programmers would have been intimately familiar with those standard libraries and likely would have created most of them themselves. In the current situation, developers frequently use utilities and libraries with functionality that exceeds what is immediately required, and programmers may not fully understand the internal structure and operations of the tools, utilities, and modules that comprise a given structure.

8

Security in the Software Development Life Cycle

The development of programming languages is referred to in terms of generations. There are specific concerns at each level of this progression but particularly in more recent environments, where the tendency has been to have functions and operations masked from the user and handled by the operating system in the background. Reliance on the programming environment and code libraries may prevent the developer from fully understanding the dependencies and vulnerabilities included in the final structure.

It should be noted that the security professional is not required to be an expert programmer or know the inner workings of developing application software code, like the C# programming language, or how to develop web applet code using Java. It is not even necessary that the security professional know detailed security-specific coding practices such as the major divisions of buffer overflow exploits or the reason for preferring str(n)cpy to strcpy in the C language (although all such knowledge is, of course, helpful). Because the security professional may be the person responsible for ensuring that security is included in such developments, the security professional should know the basic procedures and concepts involved during the design and development of software programming. That is, in order for the security professional to monitor the software development process and verify that security is included, the security professional must understand the fundamental concepts of programming developments and the security strengths and weaknesses of various application development processes.

Development Life Cycle

A project management tool that can be used to plan, execute, and control a software development project is the systems development life cycle (SDLC). The SDLC is a process that includes systems analysts, software engineers, programmers, and end-users in the project design and development. Because there is no industry-wide SDLC, an organization can use any one or a combination of SDLC methods. The SDLC simply provides a framework for the phases of a software development project from defining the functional requirements to implementation. Regardless of the method used, the SDLC outlines the essential phases, which can be shown together or as separate elements. The model chosen should be based on the project. For example, some models work better with long-term, complex projects, while others are more suited for short-term projects. The key element is that a formalized SDLC is utilized.[1]

The number of phases can range from three basic phases (concept, design, and implement) on up to several phases. The basic phases of SDLC are:

- Project initiation and planning
- Functional requirements definition
- System design specifications
- Development and implementation
- Documentation and common program controls
- Testing and evaluation control (certification and accreditation)
- Transition to production (implementation)

The system life cycle (SLC) extends beyond the SDLC to include two additional phases:

- Operations and maintenance support (post-installation)
- Revisions and system replacement

---

1   See the following for some examples of System Development Life Cycles: Open SDLC:
    http://opensdlc.org/mediawiki/index.php?title=Main_Page
    IT Solutions Life Cycle Management (ITSCLM): http://www.pbgc.gov/itslcm/index.html

Projects start out with one or more ideas, a vision, and the goal or the objective. These may address particular business needs (functional requirements) along with a proposed technical solution. This information is contained in a document that outlines the project's objectives, scope, strategies, and other factors, such as an estimate of cost or schedule. Management approval for the project is based on this project plan document. During this phase, security must also be considered. Note that security activities should be done in parallel with project initiation activities and, indeed, with every task throughout the project.

The security professional's mental checklist during the project initiation phase should include topics such as:

- Does particular information have special value or sensitivity, and therefore require special protection?
- Does the application or software package being used to access the data itself have proprietary functionality or intellectual property that will need to be safeguarded separate from the data it is processing?
- Even if the original data is of low sensitivity, does the resultant information have higher value?
- Has the information owner determined the information's value?
- Are there any special regulatory or compliance requirements to be addressed?
- What are the assigned classifications or categorizations?
- Will application operation risk exposure of sensitive information?
- Will control of output displays or reports require special measures?
- Will data be processed, stored, or transmitted through public or semipublic networks?
- Are controlled areas required for operation?
- What systems and data sources interconnect with this system?
- What will this system do to the operations and culture of the organization?
- Could the company become dependent upon it, and will the system require special support in terms of the business's continuity of operations?

These questions should be readily recognizable as forming the basis of the risk management process, and all of the answers to these questions should have been determined during that procedure.

Functional Requirements Definition

The project management and systems development teams will conduct a comprehensive analysis of current and possible future functional requirements to ensure that the new system will meet end-user needs. The teams also review the documents from the project initiation phase and make any revisions or updates as needed. For smaller projects, this phase is often subsumed in the project initiation phase. At this point, security requirements should be formalized as well.

System Design Specifications

This phase includes all activities related to designing the system and software. In this phase, the system architecture, system outputs, and system interfaces are designed. Data input, data flow, and output requirements are established and security features are designed, generally based on the overall security architecture for the company.

Development and Implementation

During this phase, the source code is generated, test scenarios and test cases are developed, unit and integration testing is conducted, and the program and system are documented for maintenance and for turnover to acceptance testing and production. As well as general care for software quality, reliability, and consistency of operation, particular care should be taken to ensure that the code is analyzed to eliminate common vulnerabilities that might lead to security exploits and other risks.

Documentation and Common Program Controls

These are controls used when editing the data within the program, the types of logging the program should be doing, and how the program versions should be stored. A large number of such controls may be needed, including tests and integrity checks for:

- Program/application
- Operating instructions/procedures
- Utilities
- Privileged functions
- Job and system documentation
- Components – hardware, software, files, databases, reports, users
- Restart and recovery procedures
- Common program controls
- Edits such as syntax, reasonableness (sanity), range checks, and check digits
- Logs (who, what, when)
- Time stamps
- Before and after images
- Counts – useful for process integrity checks; includes total transactions, batch totals, hash totals, and balances.
- Internal checks – checks for data integrity within the program from when it gets the data to when it is done with the data.
- Parameter ranges and data types
- Valid and legal address references
- Completion codes
- Peer review – the process of having peers of the programmer review the code
- Program or data library when developing software applications:
  - Automated control system
  - Current versions – programs and documentation
  - Record of changes made
- By whom, when authorized by, what changed
  - Test data verifying changes
  - User sign-offs indicating correct testing
- A librarian ensures a program or data library is controlled in accordance with policy and procedures:
  - Controls all copies of data dictionaries, programs, load modules, and documentation and can provide version controls.
- Change control/management – ensures no programs are added unless properly tested and authorized.
- Erroneous/invalid transactions detected are written to a report and reviewed by developers and management.

Acceptance

In the acceptance phase, preferably an independent group develops test data and tests the code to ensure that it will function within the organization's environment and that it meets all the functional and security requirements. It is essential that an independent group test the code during all applicable stages of development to prevent a separation of duties issue. The goal of security testing is to ensure that the application meets its security requirements and specifications. The security testing strives to uncover all design and implementation flaws that would allow a user to violate the software security policy and requirements. To ensure test validity, one should test the application in an environment that simulates the production environment. This should include a security certification package and any user documentation. This is the first phase of what is commonly referred to as the certification and accreditation (C&A) process, or the security authorization process, which will be detailed shortly.

Testing and Evaluation Controls

During the test and evaluation phase, the following guidelines can be included as appropriate to the environment:

- Test data should include data at the ends of the acceptable data ranges, various points in between, and data beyond the expected and allowable data points. Some data should be chosen randomly to uncover off-the-wall problems. However, some data should specifically be chosen on a fuzzy basis (that is, close to expected proper or problem values) to concentrate on particular areas.
- Test with known good data, although never with live production data. * If testing with live production data cannot be avoided, then the data owner needs to be consulted, and he or she will have to sign off on the usage of the data for testing. Further, usage controls that are strictly regulating what can be done with the data during testing will need to be negotiated between the data owner and the testing coordinator to ensure that the exposure and risk to the data is managed properly.
- **Data Validation:** Before and after each test, review the data to ensure that data has not been modified inadvertently.
- **Bounds Checking:** Field size, time, date, etc. Bounds checking prevents buffer overflows.
- **Sanitize** test data to ensure that sensitive production data is not exposed through the test process. Test data should not be production data until one is preparing for final user acceptance tests, at which point special precautions should be taken to ensure that actions are not taken as a result of test runs.

When designing testing controls, make sure to test all changes. The program or media librarian should maintain implementation test data used to test modifications and should retain copies that are used for particular investigations. Testing done in parallel with production requires that a separate copy of production data be utilized for the assessment. Clear and adequate segregation between testing and production environments must be maintained at all times, with test ID's being clearly distinguishable from production ID's. Use copies of master files, not production versions, and ensure either that the data has been sanitized or that the output of the test cannot generate production transactions. Management should be informed of, and acknowledge, the results of the test.

Certification and Accreditation (Security Authorization)

Certification is the process of evaluating the security stance of the software or system against a predetermined set of security standards or policies. Certification also examines how well the system performs its intended functional requirements. The certification or evaluation document should contain an analysis of the technical and nontechnical security features and countermeasures and the extent to which the software or system meets the security requirements for its mission and operational environment. A certifying officer then verifies that the software has been tested and meets all applicable policies, regulations, and standards for securing information systems. Any exceptions are noted for the accreditation or authorizing official.

Security activities verify that the data conversion and data entry are controlled, and only those who need to have access are allowed on the system. Also, an acceptable level of risk is determined. Additionally, appropriate controls must be in place to reconcile and validate the accuracy of information after it is entered into the system. It should also test the ability to substantiate processing. The acceptance of risk is based on the identified risks and operational needs of the application to meet the organization's mission.

Management, after reviewing the certification, authorizes the software or system to be implemented in a production status, in a specific environment, for a specific period. There are two types of accreditation: provisional and full. Provisional accreditation is for a specific period and outlines required changes to the applications, system, or accreditation documentation. Full accreditation implies that no changes are required for making the accreditation decision. Note that management may choose to accredit a system that has failed certification or may refuse to accredit a system even if it has been certified correct. Certification and accreditation are related, but they are not simply two steps in a single process.

Transition to Production (Implementation)

During this phase, the new system is transitioned from the acceptance phase into the live production environment. Activities during this phase include obtaining security accreditation; training the new users according to the implementation and training schedules; implementing the system, including installation and data conversions; and, if necessary, conducting any parallel operations.

Revisions and System Replacement

As systems are in production mode, the hardware and software baselines should be subject to periodic evaluations and audits. In some instances, problems with the application may not be defects or flaws, but rather they may be additional functions not currently developed in the application. Any changes to the application must follow the same SDLC and be recorded in a change management system.

Revision reviews should include security planning and procedures to avoid future problems. Periodic application audits should be conducted and include documenting security incidents when problems occur. Documenting system failures is a valuable resource for justifying future system enhancements.

Maturity Models

While there are a number of useful technologies in this regard, possibly the best protection to use is to recall the lessons taught in pretty much every course in programming and software development. The best tools are those requiring attention and thought to the process, such as using an SDLC methodology, or structured programming.

System Life Cycle and Systems Development

Software development and maintenance is the dominant expenditure in information systems. Because of the expenses associated with early software development, industry research began to provide the best methods for reducing costs, which subsequently led to the discipline of software engineering. Software engineering stated that software products had to be planned, designed, constructed, and released according to engineering principles. It included software metrics, modeling, methods, and techniques associated with the designing of the system before it was developed, tracking project progress through the entire development process.

Software development faces numerous problems that could result in higher costs and lower quality. Budget and schedule overruns are two of the largest problems for software development. Remember that Windows 95 was released about 18 months late, and it is estimated that the budget was exceeded by 25%. Software projects continue to escalate. Subsequent to Windows 95, Windows NT required 4 million lines of code, whereas Windows XP contained about 39 million. Compare that with Windows 7, which contained about 40 million lines of code, Office 2013, which contained about 45 million lines of code, Facebook, which uses approximately 61 million lines of code, and Mac OS X 'Tiger', which used about 85 million lines of code.

On the other side, if software development is rushed and software developers are expected to complete projects within a shortened time frame, the quality of the software product could be reduced. In its 4 million lines of code, Windows NT was estimated to contain approximately 64,000 bugs, many of which had security implications. IT industry analysts have focused on software vulnerabilities as the greatest current issue to be addressed in the whole field of information security. These days, software development is treated as a project - more often than not, a large project. Like any other large project, software development benefits from a formal project management structure: a lifecycle of systems development. A great many such structures have been proposed. No single management structure will equally benefit all possible programming projects, but the common elements of organization, design, communications, assessment, and testing will aid any project.

The Software Engineering Institute released the Capability Maturity Model for Software (CMM or SW-CMM) in 1991.[2] The CMM focuses on quality management processes and has five maturity levels that contain several key practices within each maturity level. The five levels describe an evolutionary path from chaotic processes to mature, disciplined software

---

2   See the following: http://cmmiinstitute.com/cmmi-solutions/
    The CMM has been used to address a variety of fields, including security and systems integration. When followed, the CMM provides a means of determining the current maturity of an organization, and key practices to improve the ability of organizations to meet goals for cost, schedule, functionality, and product quality in order to move to the next level. The model establishes a yardstick against which it is possible to judge, in a repeatable way, the maturity of an organization's software process and also compare it to the state of the practice of the industry. The model can also be used by an organization to plan improvements to its software development processes.

processes. The results of using CMM are intended to be higher quality software products produced by more competitive companies.

The CMM framework establishes a basis for evaluation of the reliability of the development environment. At an initial level, it is assumed that good practices can be repeated. If an activity is not repeated, there is no reason to improve it. Organizations must commit to having policies, procedures, and practices and to using them so that the organization can perform in a consistent manner. Next, it is hoped that best practices are repeatable and can be rapidly transferred across groups. Practices need to be defined in such a manner as to allow for transfer across project boundaries. This can provide for standardization across the entire organization. At the penultimate level, quantitative objectives are established for tasks. Measures are established, done, and maintained to form a baseline from which an assessment is possible. This can ensure that the best practices are followed and deviations are reduced. At the final level, practices are continuously improved to enhance capability (optimizing).

The International Organization for Standardization (ISO) has included software development in its ISO 9000 quality standards as the ISO/IEC 90003:2004 standard.[3] ISO/IEC 90003:2004 provides guidance for organizations in the application of ISO 9001:2000 to the acquisition, supply, development, operation, and maintenance of computer software and related support services. ISO/IEC 90003:2004 does not add to or otherwise change the requirements of ISO 9001:2000.

The application of ISO/IEC 90003:2004 is appropriate to software that is:

- Part of a commercial contract with another organization,
- A product available for a market sector,
- Used to support the processes of an organization,
- Embedded in a hardware product, or
- Related to software services

ISO/IEC 90003:2004 identifies the issues that should be addressed and is independent of the technology, lifecycle models, development processes, sequence of activities, and organizational structure used by an organization.

Both the ISO and SEI efforts are intended to reduce software development failures, improve cost estimates, meet schedules, and produce a higher quality product.

Operation and Maintenance

During this phase, the system is in general use throughout the organization. The activities involve monitoring the performance of the system and ensuring continuity of operations. This includes detecting defects or weaknesses, managing and preventing system problems, recovering from system problems, and implementing system changes. The operating security activities during this phase include testing backup and recovery procedures, ensuring proper controls for data and report handling, and ensuring the effectiveness of security processes.

During the maintenance phase, periodic risk analysis and recertification of sensitive applications are required when significant changes occur. Significant changes include a change in data sensitivity or criticality, relocation or major change to the physical environment,

---

3   ISO/IEC 90003 was prepared by Joint Technical Committee ISO/IEC JTC 1, Information technology, Subcommittee SC 7, Software and system engineering. ISO/IEC 90003 cancels and replaces ISO 9000-3:1997, which has been updated for conformity with ISO 9001:2000. ISO 9000-3:1997 was under the responsibility of ISO/TC 176/SC 2.

new equipment, new external interfaces, new operating system software, and new application software. Throughout the operation and maintenance phase, it is important to verify that any changes to procedures or functionality do not disable or circumvent the security features. Also, someone should be assigned the task of verifying compliance with applicable service-level agreements according to the initial operational and security baselines.

Change Management

To ensure the integrity of applications, one should take care to ensure that the application is not changed in an unauthorized and/or undocumented manner during maintenance and patching cycles. Most particularly, there must be controls in place to ensure that users cannot request changes that will breach security policies and that developers cannot implement modifications to the software with unknown effects. Change controls must be sufficient to protect against accidental or deliberate introduction of variations in code that would allow system failures, security intrusions, corruption of data, or improper disclosure of information.

Successful change management is more likely to occur if the following are included:

- Utilize benefits management and realization to define measurable stakeholder aims, create a business case for their achievement (which should be continuously updated), and monitor assumptions, risks, dependencies, costs, return on investment, and cultural issues affecting the progress of the associated work
- Employ effective communication that informs various stakeholders of the reasons for the change (why?), the benefits of successful implementation (what is in it for us and you?) as well as the details of the change (when? where? who is involved? how much will it cost? etc.)
- Devise an effective education, training, and/or skills upgrading scheme for the organization (if appropriate based on type of change)
- Counter resistance from employees and align them to the overall strategic direction of the organization
- Ensure that monitoring of the implementation and fine-tuning occurs as required

The change management process should have a formal cycle in the same manner as the SDLC. There should be a formal change request, an assessment of impact and resource requirements and approval decision, implementation (programming) and testing, implementation in production, and a review and verification within the production environment. The key points of change management are that there is a rigorous process that addresses quality assurance, changes must be submitted, approved, tested, and recorded, and there should be a back-out plan in case the change is not successful.

The same process should be applied to patch management, when vendors supply patches, hot fixes, and service packs to commercial software. In addition, it should be noted that patches are frequently released to address security vulnerabilities, so they should be applied in a timely manner. This is particularly important given the evidence that black hat groups study released patches to craft new exploits. A strategy should be developed for patch management and should be kept in place as part of the software maintenance infrastructure. A team, responsible for the patch management process, should research (and authenticate) announcements and related information from vendor websites.

8

Security in the Software Development Life Cycle

Research should also be conducted in other areas, such as user groups, where other experiences with patches may be reported. This requirement may need to be addressed for various systems and applications. Analysis should be conducted to balance the implications of the vulnerability addressed, the need for timely application, and the need for thorough testing. Test the patch and then deploy it into production. The test environment should mirror the production environment as far as possible. A fallback position should be prepared so that the patch or system can be "rolled back" to a previous stage if the patch creates unforeseen problems. Patch less sensitive systems first to ensure that an error in the patch does not immediately affect critical systems.

 TRY IT FOR YOURSELF

A sample template that will allow the security professional to review in detail what a change management request, and supporting documentation may look like, is provided as Appendix I. The template will walk you through the stages of a change management request. Defining a change management policy, and the supporting procedures necessary to implement change management, documents clear responsibilities for all those involved with life cycle activities.

Download the template and go through the sections in order to understand how a change request is structured.

Integrated Product Team (e.g., DevOps)

Integrated Product and Process Development (IPPD) is a management technique that simultaneously integrates all essential acquisition activities through the use of multidisciplinary teams to optimize the design, manufacturing, and supportability processes. IPPD facilitates meeting cost and performance objectives from product concept through production, including field support. One of the key IPPD tenets is multidisciplinary teamwork through Integrated Product Teams (IPTs).

IPTs are composed of representatives from all appropriate functional disciplines working together with a Team Leader to build successful and balanced programs, identify and resolve issues, and make sound and timely decisions. Team members do not necessarily commit 100% of their time to an IPT, and a person may be a member of more than one IPT.

The purpose of IPTs is to make team decisions based on timely input from the entire team (e.g., program management, engineering, manufacturing, test, logistics, financial management, procurement, and contract administration) including customers and suppliers.[4] IPTs are generally formed at the Program Manager level and may include members from both the enterprise and the system/subsystem contractor. A typical IPT at the program level, for example, may be composed of the following functional disciplines: design engineering,

---

4   See the following for a good overview of Integrated Product Teams and managing them for maximum success: https://www.cna.org/sites/default/files/research/2796004910.pdf

manufacturing, systems engineering, test and evaluation, subcontracting, quality assurance, training, finance, reliability, maintainability, supportability, procurement, contract administration, suppliers, and customers.

In broad terms, DevOps is an approach based on lean and agile principles in which business owners and the development, operations, and quality assurance departments collaborate to deliver software in a continuous manner that enables the business to more quickly seize market opportunities and reduce the time to include customer feedback. When implemented holistically, DevOps can become a business-driven software delivery approach, an approach that takes a new or enhanced business capability from an idea all the way to production, providing business value to customers in an efficient manner and capturing feedback as customers engage with the capability. To do this, you need participation from stakeholders beyond just the development and operations teams. A true DevOps approach includes lines of business, practitioners, executives, partners, suppliers, and so on.

There are many variants on the DevOps concept that exist today based on the "localized" flavor that the enterprise implementing the DevOps framework may choose to apply. Companies such as Google, IBM, Amazon, and Microsoft all have DevOps constructs that they use to drive elements of their business. Regardless of the variations, there are core common principles that underlie the DevOps construct. These principles are:

- Develop and test against production-like systems
  - The goal is to allow development and quality assurance (QA) teams to develop and test against systems that behave like the production system, so that they can see how the application behaves and performs well before it's ready for deployment.
- Deploy with repeatable, reliable processes
  - This principle allows development and operations to support an iterative software development process all the way through to production. Automation is essential to create processes that are iterative, frequent, repeatable, and reliable, so the organization must create a delivery pipeline that allows for continuous, automated deployment and testing. Frequent deployments also allow teams to test the deployment processes themselves, thereby lowering the risk of deployment failures at release time.
- Monitor and validate operational quality
  - This principle moves monitoring earlier in the lifecycle by requiring that automated testing be done early and often to monitor functional and non-functional characteristics of the application. Whenever an application is deployed and tested, quality metrics should be captured and analyzed. Frequent monitoring provides early warning about operational and quality issues that may occur in production.
- Amplify feedback loops
  - This principle calls for organizations to create communication channels that allow all stakeholders to access and act on feedback.

Environment and Security Controls

Software Development Methods

Several software development methods have evolved to satisfy different requirements.

Waterfall

The traditional waterfall lifecycle method is the oldest method for developing software systems. It was developed in the early 1970s and provided a sense of order to the process.[5] Each phase – concept, requirements definition, design, etc. – contains a list of activities that must be performed and documented before the next phase begins. From the perspective of business in general, the disadvantage of the waterfall model is that it demands a heavy overhead in planning and administration, and it requires patience in the early stages of a project. These same factors are considered an advantage in the security community because they force deliberate consideration and planning. Because each phase must be completed before the next, it can inhibit a development team from pursuing concurrent phases or activities. This limit slows initial development, but it ensures that ad hoc additions are minimized. Usually, this method is not good for projects that must be developed in quick turnaround time periods (generally less than 6 months). The waterfall model is considered the paradigm for the following styles, known as non-iterative models. From the perspective of security, non-iterative models are preferred for systems development.

- **Structured Programming Development** – A method that programmers use to write programs allowing considerable influence on the quality of the finished products in terms of coherence, comprehensibility, freedom from faults, and security. It is one of the most widely known programming development models, and versions are taught in almost all academic systems development courses. The methodology promotes discipline, allows introspection, and provides controlled flexibility. It requires defined processes and modular development, and each phase is subject to reviews and approvals. It also allows for security to be added in a formalized, structured approach.

- **Spiral Method** – A sort of nested version of the waterfall method. The development of each phase is carefully designed using the waterfall model. A distinguishing feature of the spiral model is that in each phase of the waterfall there are four sub-stages, based on the common Deming PDCA (Plan-Do-Check-Act) model, in particular, a risk assessment review (Check).[6] The estimated costs to complete and the schedules are revised each time the risk assessment is performed. Based on the results of the risk assessment, a decision is made to continue or cancel the project.

- **Cleanroom** – Developed in the 1990s as an engineering process for the development of high-quality software, it is named after the process of cleaning electronic wafers in a wafer fabrication plant. (Instead of testing for and cleaning contaminants from the wafer after it has been made, the objective is to prevent pollutants from getting into the fabrication environment.) In software application development, it is a method of controlling defects (bugs) in the software. The goal is to write the code correctly the first time

---

5   Royce, Winston (1970), "Managing the Development of Large Software Systems", Proceedings of IEEE WESCON 26 (August): 1–9, http://www.cs.umd.edu/class/spring2003/cmsc838p/Process/waterfall.pdf

6   Moen and Norman. "Evolution of the PDCA Cycle". http://pkpinc.com/files/ NA01MoenNormanFullpaper.pdf Retrieved 26 May 2014.

rather than trying to find the problems once they are there. Essentially, cleanroom software development focuses on defect prevention rather than defect removal. In order to achieve this, one should spend more time in the early phases, relying on the assumption that the time spent in other phases, such as testing, is reduced. (Quality is achieved through design rather than testing and remediation.) Because testing can often consume the majority of a project timeline, the time saved during the testing phase can be substantial. In terms of security, if risk considerations are addressed up front, security becomes an integral part of the system rather than an add-on.

Iterative Development [7]

The pure waterfall model is highly structured and does not allow for changes once the project is started or revisiting a stage in light of discoveries made in a later phase. Iterative models allow for successive refinements of requirements, design, and coding. Allowing refinements during the process requires that a change control mechanism be implemented. Also, the scope of the project may be exceeded if clients change requirements after each point of development. Iterative models also make it very difficult to ensure that security provisions are still valid in a changing environment.

- **Prototyping** – Prototyping was formally introduced in the early 1980s to combat the perceived weaknesses of the waterfall model with regard to the speed of development. The objective is to build a simplified version (prototype) of the application, release it for review, and use the feedback from the users' review to build a second, better version. This is repeated until the users are satisfied with the product. It is a four-step process: initial concept, design and implement initial prototype, refine prototype until acceptable, and complete and release final version.

- **Modified Prototype Model (MPM)** – A form of prototyping that is ideal for web application development. It allows for the basic functionality of a desired system or component to be formally deployed in a quick time frame. The maintenance phase is set to begin after the deployment. The goal is to have the process be flexible enough so the application is not based on the state of the organization at any given time. As the organization grows and the environment changes, the application evolves with it rather than being frozen in time.

- **Rapid Application Development (RAD)** – A form of rapid prototyping that requires strict time limits on each phase and relies on tools that enable quick development. This may be a disadvantage if decisions are made so rapidly that it leads to poor design.

- **Joint Analysis Development (JAD)** – Originally invented to enhance the development of large mainframe systems. Recently, JAD facilitation techniques have become an integral part of RAD, web development, and other methods. It is a management process that helps developers to work directly with users to develop a working application. The success of JAD is based on having key players communicating at critical phases of the project. The focus is on having the people who actually perform the job (they usually have the best knowledge of the job) work together with those who have the best understanding of the technologies available to design a solution.

---

7   See the following for a good overview of the various methods described in this section:
    http://www.ctg.albany.edu/publications/reports/survey_of_sysdev/survey_of_sysdev.pdf

JAD facilitation techniques bring together a team of users, expert systems developers, and technical experts throughout the development life cycle. While input from the users may result in a more functional program, the involvement of large numbers may lead to political pressures that militate against security considerations.

■ ***Exploratory Model*** – This is a set of requirements built with what is currently available. Assumptions are made as to how the system might work, and further insights and suggestions are combined to create a usable system. Because of the lack of structure, security requirements may take second place to enhancements, which may be added on an ad hoc basis.

Other Methods and Models

There are other software development methods that do not rely on the "iterate/do not iterate" division, such as the following:

■ ***Computer-Aided Software Engineering (CASE)*** [8] – The technique of using computers and computer utilities to help with the systematic analysis, design, development, implementation, and maintenance of software. It was designed in the 1970s but has evolved to include visual programming tools and object-oriented programming. It is most often used on large, complex projects involving multiple software components and many people. It may provide mechanisms for planners, designers, code writers, testers, and managers to share a common view of where a software project is at each phase of the lifecycle process. If a team has an organized approach, code and design can be reused, which can reduce costs and improve quality. The CASE approach requires building and maintaining software tools and training for the developers who use them.

■ ***Component-Based Development*** [9] – The process of using standardized building blocks to assemble, rather than develop, an application. The components are encapsulated sets of standardized data and standardized methods of processing data, together offering economic and scheduling benefits to the development process. From a security perspective, the advantage is (or can be) that components have previously been tested for security. This is similar to object-oriented programming (OOP) where objects and classes may be designed with security methods initially and then instantiated.

■ ***Reuse Model*** [10] – In this model, an application is built from existing components. The reuse model is best suited for projects using object-oriented development because objects can be exported, reused, or modified. Again, the components may be chosen on the basis of known security characteristics.

■ ***Extreme Programming*** [11] – This is a discipline of software development that is based on values of simplicity, communication, and feedback. Despite the name, extreme programming is a fairly structured approach, relying on subprojects of limited and defined scope and programmers working in pairs. The team produces the software in a series of small, fully integrated releases

---

8   See the following: http://ithandbook.ffiec.gov/it-booklets/development-and-acquisition/development-procedures/software-development-techniques/computer-aided-software-engineering.aspx

9   See the following: http://www.users.globalnet.co.uk/~rxv/CBDmain/cbdfaq.htm

10   See the following: http://www.ctg.albany.edu/publications/reports/survey_of_sysdev?chapter=10

11   See the following: http://www.extremeprogramming.org/

that fulfill the customer-defined needs for the software. Those who have worked with the method say that it works best with small teams: around a dozen programmers in total.

Model Choice Considerations and Combinations

Depending on the application project and the organization, models can be combined to fit the specific design and development process. For example, an application may need a certain set of activities to take place to achieve success, or the organization may require certain standards or processes to meet industry or government requirements. When someone is deciding on the programming model, security must be a consideration. Many developers focus on functionality and not security; thus, it is important to educate those individuals responsible for the development and the managers who oversee the projects. If developers are brought into the project knowing there is a focus on security, they may better understand the importance of coding both functionality and security.

The Database and Data Warehousing Environment

Database systems have always been a major class of computer applications and have specific security requirements all their own. Indeed, some aspects of database security have proven quite intractable and still present unique challenges.

In the early history of information systems, data processing occurred on stand-alone systems that used separate applications that contained their own sets of data files. As systems expanded and more applications were run on the same machine, redundant files were gathered. Several complexities and conflicts also arose, mainly the possibility of having duplicate information within each application contained on the same system. For example, an employee's address might be duplicated in several application systems within the organization, once in the payroll system and again in the personnel system. This duplication of information not only wasted storage space, but it also led to the possibility of inconsistency in the data. If an employee moved and notified payroll (to make sure the payroll check still arrived), only the database in payroll would be updated. If the personnel department needed to send something to the employee, the address contained within its application would not show the change. Another danger might occur if the personnel department saw the change in the payroll system, considered it to be an error, and overwrote the newer payroll data with data from the personnel files.

Databases were developed to incorporate the information from multiple sources to resolve the potential inconsistencies of having information replicated in several files on a system. They are an attempt to integrate and manage the data required for several applications into a common storage area that will support an organization's business needs.

DBMS Architecture

Organizations tend to collect data from many separate databases into one large database system, where it is available for viewing, updating, and processing by either programs or users. A database management system (DBMS) is a suite of application programs that typically manage large structured sets of persistent data. It stores, maintains, and provides access to data using *ad hoc* query capabilities. The DBMS provides the structure for the data and some type of language for accessing and manipulating the data. The primary objective is to store data and allow users to view the data. DBMSs have transformed greatly since their introduction in the late 1960s. The earliest file access systems were limited based on the storage technology of the time: primarily tape. These later evolved into network databases in the 1970s. In the 1980s, relational databases became dominant. In the 1990s, object-oriented databases emerged. Because companies have become increasingly dependent upon the successful operation of the DBMS, it is anticipated that future demands will drive more innovations and product improvements.

Typically, a DBMS has four major elements: the database engine itself, the hardware platform, application software (such as record input interfaces and prepared queries), and users. The database element is one (or more) large, structured sets or tables of persistent data. Databases are usually associated with another element: the software that updates and queries the data. In a simple database, a single file may contain several records that contain the same set of fields, and each field is a certain fixed width. The DBMS uses software programs that allow it to manage the large, structured sets of data and provide access to the data for multiple, concurrent users while at the same time maintaining the integrity of the data. The applications and data reside on hardware and are displayed to the user via some sort of display unit, like a monitor.

The major elements may be supported by a number of additional components. These may include virtual machine platforms, interfaces or middleware between the applications and the database engine itself, utilities in support of applications, and, increasingly, Web access as a front end. Remember that increasing the items involved increases complexity, at a possible cost to security. The data consists of individual entities and entities with relationships linking them together. The mapping or organization of the data entities is based on a database model. The database model describes the relationship between the data elements and provides a framework for organizing the data. The data model is fundamental to the design because it provides a mechanism for representing the data and any correlations between the data.

The database model should provide for:

- **Transaction Persistence** – The state of the database is the same after a transaction (process) has occurred as it was prior to the transaction, and the transaction should be durable.
- **Fault Tolerance and Recovery** – In the event of a hardware or software failure, the data should remain in its original state. Two types of recovery systems available are rollback and shadowing. Rollback recovery is when incomplete or invalid transactions are backed out. Shadow recovery occurs when transactions are reapplied to a previous version of the database. Shadow recovery requires the use of transaction logging to identify the last good transaction.
- **Sharing by Multiple Users** – The data should be available to multiple users at the same time without endangering the integrity of the data; that is the locking of data.
- **Security Controls** – Examples include access controls, integrity checking, and view definitions.

DBMSs may operate on hardware that has been implemented to run only databases and often only specific database systems. This allows hardware designers to increase the number and speed of network connections, incorporate multiple processors and storage disks to increase the speed of searching for information, and also increase the amount of memory and cache.

When an organization is designing a database, the first step is to understand the requirements for the database and then design a system that meets those requirements. This includes what information will be stored, who is allowed access, and estimating how many people will need to access the data at the same time. The structuring of the database may also depend upon minimizing duplication of attributes and keys, maximizing flexibility, and balancing those demands against the need to reduce accesses in order to increase performance.

In most database developments, the database design is usually done by either a database design specialist or a combination of database administrators and software analysts. The database designers produce a schema that defines what the data is and how the data is stored, how it relates to other data, and who can access, add, and/or modify the data. The data in a database can be structured in several different ways, depending upon the types of information stored. Different data storage techniques can exist on practically any machine level, from a PC to mainframe, and in various architectures, such as stand-alone, distributed, or client/server.

Hierarchical Database Management Model

The hierarchical model is the oldest of the database models and is derived from the information management systems of the 1950s and 1960s. Even today, there are hierarchical legacy systems that are still being operated by banks, insurance companies, government agencies, and hospitals. This model stores data in a series of records that have field values attached. It collects all the instances of a specific record together as a record type. These record types are the equivalent of tables in the relational model, with the individual records being the equivalent of rows. To create links between the record types, the hierarchical model uses parent/child relationships through the use of trees. A weakness is that the hierarchical model is only able to cope with a single tree and is not able to link between branches or over multiple layers. For example, an organization could have several divisions and several subtrees that represent employees, facilities, and products. If an employee worked for several divisions, the hierarchical model would not be able to provide a link between the two divisions for one employee. The hierarchical model is no longer used in current commercially available DBMS products; however, these models still exist in legacy systems.

Network Database Management Model

The network database management model, introduced in 1971, is an extended form of the hierarchical data structure. It does not refer to the fact that the database is stored on the network, but rather it refers to the method of how data is linked to other data. The network model represents its data in the form of a network of records and sets that are related to each other, forming a network of links. Records are sets of related data values and are the equivalent of rows in the relational model. They store the name of the record type, the attributes associated with it, and the format for these attributes. For example, an employee record type could contain the last name, first name, address, etc., of the employee. Record types are sets of records of the same type. These are the equivalent of tables in the relational model. Set types are the relationships between two record types, such as an organization's division and the employees in that division. The set types allow the network model to run some queries faster; however, it does not offer the flexibility of a relational model. The network model is not commonly used today to design database systems; however, there are some legacy systems remaining.

Relational Database Management Model

The majority of organizations use software based on the relational database management model. The relational database has become so dominant in database management systems that many people consider it to be the only form of database. (This may create problems when dealing with other table-oriented database systems that do not provide the integrity functions required in a true relational database.) The relational model is based on set theory and predicate logic and provides a high level of abstraction.[12] The use of set theory allows data to be structured in a series of tables that have columns representing the variables and rows that contain specific instances of data. These tables are organized using normal forms. The relational model outlines how programmers should design the DBMS so that different database systems used by the organization can communicate with each other.

For our purposes, the basic relational model consists of three elements:

1. Data structures that are called either tables or relations
2. Integrity rules on allowable values and combinations of values in tables
3. Data manipulation agents that provide the relational mathematical basis and an assignment operator

Each table, or relation, in the relational model consists of a set of attributes and a set of tuples (rows) or entries in the table. Attributes correspond to a column in a table. Attributes are unordered left to right and thus are referenced by name and not by position. All data values in the relational model are atomic. Atomic values mean that at every row/ column position in every table, there is always exactly one data value and never a set of values. There are no links or pointers connecting tables; thus, the representation of relationships is contained as data in another table.

A tuple of a table corresponds to a row in the table. Tuples are unordered top to bottom because a relation is a mathematical set and not a list. Also, because tuples are based on tables that are mathematical sets, there are no duplicate tuples in a table (sets in mathematics by definition do not include duplicate elements). The primary key is an attribute or set of attributes that uniquely identifies a specific instance of an entity. Each table in a database must have a primary key that is unique to that table. It is a subset of the candidate key. Any key that could be a primary key is called a candidate key. The candidate key is an attribute that is a unique identifier within a given table. One of the candidate keys is chosen to be the primary key, and the others are called alternate keys.

Primary keys provide the sole tuple-level addressing mechanism within the relational model. They are the only guaranteed method of pinpointing an individual tuple; therefore, they are fundamental to the operation of the overall relational model. Because they are critical to the relational model, the primary keys cannot contain a null value and cannot change or become null during the life of each entity. When the primary key of one relation is used as an attribute in another relation, it is the foreign key in that relation.

The foreign key in a relational model is different from the primary key. The foreign key value represents a reference to an entry in some other table. If an attribute (value) in one table matches those of the primary key of some other relation, it is considered the foreign key. The link (or matches) between the foreign and primary keys represents the relationships between tuples. Thus, the matches represent references and allow one table to be referenced to another table. The primary key and foreign key links are the binding factors that hold the database together. Foreign keys also provide a method for maintaining referential integrity in the data and for navigating between different instances of an entity.

---

12 See the following:
   Set Theory: http://plato.stanford.edu/entries/set-theory/
   Predicate Logic: http://i.stanford.edu/~ullman/focs/ch14.pdf

Integrity Constraints in Relational Databases

To solve the problems of concurrency and security within a database, the database must provide some integrity. The user's program may carry out many operations on the data retrieved from the database, but the DBMS is only concerned about what data is read/written from or to the database – the transaction. Users submit transactions and view each transaction as occurring by itself. Concurrency occurs when the DBMS interleaves actions (reads/writes of database objects) of various transactions. For concurrency to be secure, each transaction must leave the database in a consistent state if the database is consistent when the transaction begins.

The DBMS does not really understand the semantics of the data; that is, it does not understand how an operation on data occurs, such as when interest on a bank account is computed. A transaction might commit after completing all its actions, or it could abort (or be aborted by the DBMS) after executing some actions. A very important property guaranteed by the DBMS for all transactions is that they are atomic. Atomicity implies that a user can think of X as always executing all its actions in one step or not executing any actions at all. To help with concurrency, the DBMS logs all actions so that it can undo the actions of aborted transactions. The security issues of concurrency can occur if several users who are attempting to query data from the database interfere with each other's requests.

The two integrity rules of the relational model are entity integrity and referential integrity. The two rules apply to every relational model and focus on the primary and foreign keys. These rules actually derive from the Clark and Wilson integrity model.

In the entity integrity model, the tuple must have a unique and non-null value in the primary key. This guarantees that the tuple is uniquely identified by the primary key value.

The referential integrity model states that for any foreign key value, the referenced relation must have a tuple with the same value for its primary key. Essentially, every table relation or join must be accomplished by coincidence of the primary keys or of a primary key and the foreign key that is the primary key of the other table. Each table participating in the join must demonstrate entity integrity and in the referenced relation must have a similar primary key/foreign key relationship. Another example of the loss of referential integrity is to assign a tuple to a nonexistent attribute. If this occurs, the tuple could not be referenced, and with no attribute, it would be impossible to know what it represented.

Note that null values in non-key attributes are not a formal matter of integrity for relational databases, even though semantically they may be a problem for the database itself.

Structured Query Language (SQL)

The relational model also has several standardized languages.[13] One is called the Structured Query Language (SQL), in which users may issue commands. An advantage of having a standard language is that organizations can switch between different database engine vendor systems without having to rewrite all of its application software or retrain staff.

SQL was developed by IBM and is an International Organization for Standardization (ISO) and American National Standards Institute (ANSI) standard. (ANSI is a private, nonprofit organization that administers and coordinates the U.S. voluntary standardization and conformity assessment system.) Because SQL is a standard, the commands for most systems

---

13   See the following for an overview of all three sublanguages discussed: http://databases.about.com/od/
     Advanced-SQL-Topics/a/Data-Control-Language-Dcl.htm

are similar. There are several different types of queries, such as those for predesigned reports (included in applications) and *ad hoc* queries (usually done by database experts).

The main components of a database using SQL are:

- **Schemas** – Describes the structure of the database, including any access controls limiting how the users will view the information contained in the tables.
- **Tables** – The columns and rows of the data are contained in tables.
- **Views** – Defines what information a user can view in the tables – the view can be customized so that an entire table may be visible or a user may be limited to only being able to see just a row or a column. Views are created dynamically by the system for each user and provide access control granularity.

The simplicity of SQL is achieved by giving the users a high-level view of the data. A view is a feature that allows for virtual tables in a database; these virtual tables are created from one or more real tables in the database. A view can be set up for each user (or group of users) on the system so that the user can then only view those virtual tables (or views). In addition, access can be restricted so that only rows or columns are visible in the view. The value of views is to have control over what users can see. For example, a database administrator can allow users to see their information in an employee database but not the other employee salaries unless they have sufficient authorization.

This view removes many of the technical aspects of the system from the users and instead places the technical burden on the DBMS software applications. As an example, assume that all employees in the personnel department have the same boss, the director of personnel. This type of data would be stored in a separate table to avoid repeating the data for each employee. This saves storage space and reduces the time it would take for queries to execute.

SQL actually consists of three sublanguages. The data definition language (DDL) is used to create databases, tables, views, and indices (keys) specifying the links between tables. Because it is administrative in nature, users of SQL rarely use DDL commands. DDL also has nothing to do with the population of use of the database, which is accomplished by data manipulation language (DML), used to query and extract data, insert new records, delete old records, and update existing records. System and database administrators utilize data control language (DCL) to control access to data. It provides the security aspects of SQL and is therefore our primary area of concern. Some of the DCL commands are:

- **COMMIT** – Saves work that has been done
- **SAVEPOINT** – Identifies a location in a transaction to which you can later roll back, if necessary
- **ROLLBACK** – Restores the database to its state at the last COMMIT
- **SET TRANSACTION** – Changes transaction options such as what rollback segment to use

There are other scripting and query languages that can be used in similar ways to create database interface applications that rely on an underlying database engine for function.

Object-Oriented Database Model

The object-oriented (OO) database model is one of the most recent database models. Similar to object-oriented programming languages, the OO database model stores data as objects. The OO objects are a collection of public and private data items and the set of operations that can be executed on the data. Because the data objects contain their own operations, any call to data potentially has the full range of database functions available. The object-oriented model does not necessarily require a high-level language like SQL because the functions (or methods) are contained within the objects. An advantage of not having a query language is that it allows the object-oriented DBMS to interact with applications without the language overhead.

Relational models are starting to add object-oriented functions and interfaces, to create an object-relational model. An object-relational database system is a hybrid system: a relational DBMS that has an object-oriented interface built on top of the original software. This can be accomplished either by a separate interface or by adding additional commands to the current system. The hybrid model allows organizations to maintain their current relational database software and, at the same time, provide an upgrade path for future technologies.

Database Interface Languages

The existence of legacy databases has proven a difficult challenge for managing new database access requirements. To provide an interface that combines newer systems and legacy systems, several standardized access methods have evolved, such as:

- Open Database Connectivity (ODBC)
- Java Database Connectivity (JDBC)
- eXtensible Markup Language (XML)
- Object Linking and Embedding Database (OLE DB)
- ActiveX Data Objects (ADO)

These systems provide a gateway to the data contained in the legacy systems as well as the newer systems.

Open Database Connectivity (ODBC)

ODBC is the dominant means of standardized data access. It is a standard developed and maintained by Microsoft. Almost all database vendors use it as an interface method to allow an application to communicate with a database either locally or remotely over a network. It is an API that is used to provide a connection between applications and databases. It was designed so that databases could connect without having to use specific database commands and features.

ODBC commands are used in application programs, which translate them into the commands required by the specific database system. This allows programs to be linked between DBMSs with a minimum of code changes. It allows users to specify which database is being used, and it can be easily updated as new database technologies enter the market. ODBC is a powerful tool; however, because it operates as a system entity, it can be exploited. The following are issues with ODBC security:

- The username and password for the database are stored in plaintext. The files should be protected to prevent disclosure of this information,. For example, if an HTML document was calling an ODBC data source, the HTML source must be protected to ensure that the username and password in plaintext cannot be read. (The HTML should call a common gateway interface (CGI) that has the authentication details because HTML can be viewed in a browser.)
- The actual call and the returned data are sent as cleartext over the network.
- Verification of the access level of the user using the ODBC application may be substandard.

- Calling applications must be checked to ensure they do not attempt to combine data from multiple data sources, thus allowing data aggregation.
- Calling applications must be checked to ensure they do not attempt to exploit the ODBC drivers and gain elevated system access.

Java Database Connectivity (JDBC)

JDBC is an API from Sun Microsystems used to connect Java programs to databases. It is used to connect a Java program to a database either directly or by connecting through ODBC, depending on whether the database vendor has created the necessary drivers for Java. Regardless of the interface used to connect the user to the database, security items to consider include how and where the user will be authenticated, controlling user access, and auditing user actions. Fortunately, Java has a number of provisions for security, but these must be deliberately implemented in order to secure the database calls and applications.

eXtensible Markup Language (XML)

XML is a World Wide Web Consortium (W3C) standard for structuring data in a text file so that both the format of the data and the data can be shared on intranets and the Web. A markup language, such as the Hypertext Markup Language (HTML), is simply a system of symbols and rules to identify structures (format) in a document. XML is called extensible because the symbols are unlimited and can be defined by the user or author. The format for XML can represent data in a neutral format that is independent of the database, application, and the underlying DBMS.

XML became a W3C standard in 1998, and many believe it is the *de facto* standard for integrating data and content. It offers the ability to exchange data and bridge different technologies, such as object models and programming languages. Because of this advantage, XML is expected to transform data and documents of current DBMSs and data access standards (e.g., ODBC, JDBC, etc.) by web-enabling these standards and providing a common data format. Another, and probably more important, advantage is the ability to create one underlying XML document and display it in a variety of different ways and devices. The Wireless Markup Language (WML) is an example of an XML-based language that delivers content to devices such as cell phones, tablets, and other mobile devices. As with any of program used to make database interface calls, an XML application must also be reviewed for how authentication of users is established, access controls are implemented, auditing of user actions is implemented and stored, and confidentiality of sensitive data can be achieved.

Object Linking and Embedding Database (OLE DB)

Object Linking and Embedding (OLE) is a Microsoft technology that allows an object, such as an Excel spreadsheet, to be embedded or linked to the inside of another object, such as a Word document. The Component Object Model (COM) is the protocol that allows OLE to work.

OLE allows users to share a single source of data for a particular object. The document contains the name of the file containing the data, along with a picture of the data. When the source is updated, all the documents using the data are updated as well. On the other hand, with object embedding, one application (the source) provides data or an image that will be contained in the document of another application (the destination). The destination application contains the data or graphic image, but it does not understand it or have the ability to edit it. It simply displays, prints, or plays the embedded item. The embedded object must be opened in the source application that created it for someone to edit or update it. This occurs automatically when you double-click the item or choose the appropriate edit command while the object is highlighted.

OLE DB is a low-level interface designed by Microsoft to link data across various DBMSs. It is an open specification that is designed to build on the success of ODBC by providing an open standard for accessing all kinds of data. It enables organizations to easily take advantage of information contained not only in data within a DBMS but also when accessing data from other types of data sources. (Note, however, that because it is based on OLE, OLE DB is restricted to Windows interface applications.)

Essentially, the OLE DB interfaces are designed to provide access to all data, regardless of type, format, or location. For example, in some enterprise environments, the organization's critical information is located outside of traditional production databases and instead is stored in containers such as Microsoft Access, spreadsheets, project management planners, or web applications. The OLE DB interfaces are based on the Component Object Model (COM), and they provide applications with uniform access to data regardless of the information source. The OLE DB separates the data into interoperable components that can run as middleware on a client or server across a wide variety of applications. The OLE DB architecture provides for components such as direct data access interfaces, query engines, cursor engines, optimizers, business rules, and transaction managers.

When developing databases and determining how data may be linked through applications, whether through an ODBC interface or an OLE DB interface, one must consider security during the development stage. If OLE DB is considered, there are optional OLE DB interfaces that can be implemented to support the administration of security information. OLE DB interfaces allow for authenticated and authorized access to data among components and applications. The OLE DB can provide a unified view of the security mechanisms that are supported by the operating system and the database components.

Accessing Databases through the Internet

Many database developers are supporting the use of the Internet and corporate intranets to allow users to access the centralized back-end servers. Several types of Application Programming Interfaces (APIs) can be used to connect the end-user applications to the back-end database. Although a couple of APIs that are available are covered, ActiveX Data Objects (ADO) and Java Database Connectivity (JDBC), there are several security issues about any of the API technologies that must be reviewed. These include authentication of users, authorizations of users, encryption, protection of the data from unauthorized entry, accountability and auditing, and availability of current data.

One approach for Internet access is to create a tiered application approach that manages data in layers. There can be any number of layers; however, the most typical architecture is to use a three-tier approach: presentation layer, business logic layer, and data layer. This is sometimes referred to as the Internet computing model because the browser is used to connect to an application server that then connects to a database.

Depending on the implementation, it can be good or bad for security. The tier approach can add to security because the users do not connect directly to the data. Instead, they connect to a middle layer, the business logic layer, which connects directly to the database on behalf of the users. The bad side of security is that if the database provides security features, they may be lost in the translation through the middle layer. Thus, when someone is looking at providing security, it is important to analyze not only how the security features are implemented but also where they are implemented and how the configuration of the application with the back-end database affects the security features. Additional concerns for security are user authentication, user access control, auditing of user actions, protecting data as it travels between the tiers, managing identities across the tiers, scalability of the system, and setting privileges for the different tiers.

ActiveX Data Objects (ADO)

ADO is a Microsoft high-level interface for all kinds of data. It can be used to create a front-end database client or a middle-tier business object using an application, tool, or Internet browser. Developers can simplify the development of OLE DB by using ADO. Objects can be the building blocks of Java, JavaScript, Visual Basic, and other object-oriented languages. When common and reusable data access components (Component Object Model (COM)) are utilized, different applications can access all data regardless of data location or data format. ADO can support typical client/server applications, HTML tables, spreadsheets, and mail engine information. Note that many security professionals are concerned about the use of ActiveX because there are no configurable restrictions on its access to the underlying system. Newer browsers implement sandboxing and stronger ActiveX controls to help mitigate this vulnerability.

Metadata

The information about the data, called metadata (literally data about data or knowledge about data), provides a systematic method for describing resources and improving the retrieval of information. The objective is to help users search through a wide range of sources with better precision. It includes the data associated with either an information system or an information object for the purposes of description, administration, legal requirements, technical functionality, usage, and preservation. It is considered the key component for exploiting and using a data warehouse.

Metadata is useful because it provides:

- Valuable information about the unseen relationships between data
- The ability to correlate data that was previously considered unrelated
- The keys to unlocking critical or highly important data inside the data warehouse

Note that the data warehouse is usually at the highest classification or categorization level possible. However, users of the metadata are usually not at that level, and therefore, any data that should not be publicly available must be removed from the metadata. Generally, this involves abstracting the correlations but not the underlying data that the correlations came from.

The Dublin Core metadata element set was developed during the first metadata workshop in Dublin, OH in 1995 and 1996. It was a response to the need to improve retrieval of information resources, especially on the Web. It continues to be developed by an international working group as a generic metadata standard for use by libraries, archives, governments, and publishers of online information. The Dublin Core standard has received widespread acceptance among the electronic information community and has become the *de facto* Internet metadata standard.

The Dublin Core website posts several proposals that are open for comment and review from the community.[14] A former security proposal that the Dublin Core metadata group was working on was for access controls. The proposal states that security classification and access rights are not the same. Security classification deals with any official security stamp to give a particular status to the resource.[15] Only some resources will have such a stamp. Access rights do not need official stamps and can be used more loosely for the handling of the resource; for example, a resource marked "public" in a content management system can be published, and a resource marked "not public" will not be published, although metadata about the resource could be published. The nature of the two qualifiers is different, but the values could be related; for example, if the security classification is "top secret," then access rights should contain a value reflecting this. The difference between access rights and audience is that audience contains values stating which segment of the user group the information in the resource is created for. Access rights state which user group has permission to access the resource; it does not say anything about the content (whereas the audience does).

The proposed solution: "For full implementation of this refinement, a namespace is needed. Inclusion in DC will mean the availability of a practical, usable namespace." For further information, refer to the Dublin Core metadata website.[16] Data contained in a data warehouse is typically accessed through front-end analysis tools such as online analytical processing (OLAP), data mining, or knowledge discovery in databases (KDD) methods.

Online Analytical Processing (OLAP)

OLAP technologies provide an analyst with the ability to formulate queries and, based on the outcome of the queries, define further queries. The analyst can collect information by roaming through the data. The collected information is then presented to management. Because the data analyst interprets aspects of the data, the data analyst should possess in-depth knowledge about the organization and also what type of knowledge the organization needs to adequately retrieve information that can be useful for decision making.

For example, a retail chain may have several locations that locally capture product sales. If the management decided to review data on a specific promotional item without a data warehouse, there would be no easy method of capturing sales for all stores on the one item. However, a data warehouse could effectively combine the data from each store into one central repository. The analyst could then query the data warehouse for specific information on the promotional item and present the results to those people in the management who are responsible for promotional items.

Data Mining

In addition to OLAP, data mining is another process (or tool) for discovering information in data warehouses by running queries against the data. A large repository of data is required to perform data mining. Data mining is used to reveal hidden relationships, patterns, and trends in the data warehouse. Data mining is a decision-making technique that is based on

---

14   See the following: http://dublincore.org/documents/usageguide/qualifiers.shtml

15   See the following: http://dublincore.org/groups/government/securityClassification.shtml

16   See the following: http://dublincore.org/

a series of analytical techniques taken from the fields of mathematics, statistics, cybernetics, and genetics. The techniques are used independently and in cooperation with one another to uncover information from data warehouses.

There are several advantages to using data-mining techniques, including the ability to provide better information to managers that outlines the organization's trends, its customers, and the competitive marketplace for its industry. There are also disadvantages, especially for security. The detailed data about individuals obtained by data mining might risk a violation of privacy. The danger increases when private information is stored on the Web or an unprotected area of the network, and thus it becomes available to unauthorized users. In addition, the integrity of the data may be at risk. Because a large amount of data must be collected, transformed and loaded, the chance of errors through human data entry may result in inaccurate relationships or patterns. These errors are referred to as data contamination.

One positive security function of data mining is to use the tools to review audit logs for intrusion attempts. Because audit logs usually contain thousands of entries, data-mining tools can help to discover abnormal events by drilling down into the data for specific trends or unusual behaviors. Information system security officers can use a data-mining tool in a testing environment to try to view unauthorized data. For example, testers could log in with the rights assigned to a general user, then use a data-mining tool to access various levels of data. If during this test environment, they are able to successfully view sensitive or unauthorized data, appropriate security controls, such as limiting views, could be implemented. Note that these tools and utilities should be used carefully for the purposes of audit log reduction or the establishment of clipping levels; make attempts to ensure that valuable information is not lost as a result. Data mining is still an evolving technology; thus, standards and procedures need to be formalized so that organizations will be able to use their data for a variety of business decisions and uses. The challenge will be to address the business need while still complying with security requirements that will protect the data from unauthorized users.

Database Vulnerabilities and Threats

One of the primary concerns for the DBMS is the confidentiality of sensitive data. A major concern for most people is that many databases contain health and financial information, both of which are protected by privacy laws in many countries. Another primary concern for the DBMS is enforcing the controls to ensure the continued integrity of the data. A breach of data integrity through an invalid input or an incorrect definition could jeopardize the entire viability of the database. In such an instance, the work required to restore the database or manually write queries to correct the data could have a serious impact on operations. The threats to a DBMS include:

- **Aggregation** – The ability to combine non-sensitive data from separate sources to create sensitive information. For example, a user takes two or more unclassified pieces of data and combines them to form a classified piece of data that then becomes unauthorized for that user. Thus, the combined data sensitivity can be greater than the classification of individual parts. For years, mathematicians have been struggling unsuccessfully with the problem of determining when the aggregation of data results in data at a higher classification.

- **Bypass Attacks** – Users attempt to bypass controls at the front end of the database application to access information. If the query engine contains security controls, the engine may have complete access to the information; thus, users may try to bypass the query engine and directly access and manipulate the data.

- **Compromising Database Views Used for Access Control** – A view restricts the data a user can see or request from a database. One of the threats is that users may try to access restricted views or modify an existing view. Another problem with view-based access control is the difficulty in verifying how the software performs the view processing. Because all objects must have a security label identifying the sensitivity of the information in the database, the software used to classify the information must also have a mechanism to verify the sensitivity of the information. Combining this with a query language adds even more complexity. Also, the view just limits the data the user sees; it does not limit the operations that may be performed on the views. An additional problem is that the layered model frequently used in database interface design may provide multiple alternative routes to the same data, not all of which may be protected. A given user may be able to access information through the view provided, through a direct query to the database itself, or even via direct system access to the underlying data files. Further, any standard views set up for security controls must be carefully prepared in terms of the granularity of the control. Views can restrict access to information down to a field, and even content-based, level, and modifications to these regulations can significantly change the degree of material provided.

- **Concurrency** – When actions or processes run at the same time, they are said to be concurrent. Problems with concurrency include running processes that use old data, updates that are inconsistent, or having a deadlock occur.

- **Data Contamination** – The corruption of data integrity by input data errors or erroneous processing. This can occur in a file, report, or a database.

- **Deadlocking** – Occurs when two users try to access the information at the same time and both are denied. In a database, deadlocking occurs when two user processes have locks on separate objects, and each process is trying to acquire a lock on the object that the other process has. (Deadlock is also sometimes referred to as a deadly embrace.) When this happens, the database should end the deadlock by automatically choosing and aborting one process, allowing the other process to continue. The aborted transaction is rolled back, and an error message is sent to the user of the aborted process. Generally, the transaction that requires the least amount of overhead to roll back is the transaction that is aborted. Deadlock can be viewed as a special issue of concurrency.

- **Denial of Service** – Any type of attack or actions that could prevent authorized users from gaining access to the information. Often this can happen through a poorly designed application or query that locks up the table and requires intensive processing (such as a table scan where every row in the table must be examined to return the requested data to the calling application). This can be partially prevented by limiting the number of rows of data returned from any one query.

- **Improper Modification of Information** – Unauthorized or authorized users may intentionally or accidentally modify information incorrectly.

- **Inference** – The ability to deduce (infer) sensitive or restricted information from observing available information. Essentially, users may be able to determine unauthorized information from what information they can access and may never need to directly access unauthorized data. For example, if a user is reviewing authorized information about patients, such as the medications they have been prescribed, the user may be able to determine the illness. Inference is one of the hardest threats to control.

- **Interception of Data** – If dial-up or some other type of remote access is allowed, the threat of interception of the session and modification of the data in transit must be controlled.

- **Query Attacks** – Users try to use query tools to access data not normally allowed by the trusted front end (e.g., those views controlled by the query application). Malformed queries using SQL or Unicode in such a way as to bypass security controls are also popular. There are many other instances where improper or incomplete checks on query or submission parameters can be used in a similar way to bypass access controls.

- **Server Access** – The server where the database resides must be protected not only from unauthorized logical access but also from unauthorized physical access to prevent the disabling of logical controls.

- **Time of Check/Time of Use (TOC/TOU)** – TOC/TOU can also occur in databases. An example is when some type of malicious code or privileged access could change data between the time that a user's query was approved and the time the data is displayed to the user.

- **Web Security** – Many DBMSs allow access to data through Web technologies. Static webpages (HTML or XML files) are methods of displaying data stored on a server. One method is when an application queries information from the database and the HTML page displays the data. Another is through dynamic webpages that are stored on the Web server with a template for the query and HTML display code, but no actual data is stored. When the webpage is accessed, the query is dynamically created and executed, and the information is displayed within the HTML display. If the source for the page is viewed, all information, including restricted data, may be visible. Providing security control includes measures for protecting against unauthorized access during a log-in process, protecting the information while it is transferred from the server to the Web server, and protecting the information from being stored on or downloaded to the user's machine.

- **Unauthorized Access** – Allowing the release of information either intentionally or accidentally to unauthorized users. Examples may include error messages or system prompts that provide the unauthorized user with information about the nature or function of the system.

DBMS Controls

The future of the database environment is becoming more technically complex. Organizations must find solutions to easily and quickly support their end-users' requirements. This includes user-friendly interfaces to access data stored in different DBMSs, from many different locations, and on a variety of platforms. Additionally, users want to manipulate the data from their own workstation using their own software tools and then transmit updates to other locations in the network environment.

Database security is a very specific and esoteric field of study. The challenge for both the security and database managers is to retain control over the organization's data and ensure business rules are consistently applied when core data is accessed or manipulated. The DBMS provides security controls in a variety of forms – both to prevent unauthorized access and to prevent authorized users from accessing data simultaneously or accidentally or intentionally overwriting information.

As a first line of security to prevent unauthorized users from accessing the system, the DBMS should use identification, authentication, authorization, and other forms of access controls. Most databases have some type of log-on and password authentication control that limits access to tables in the database based on a user account. Another initial step is to assign permissions to the authorized users, such as the ability to read, write, update, query, and delete data in the database.

Typically, there are fewer users with add or update privileges than users with read and query privileges. For example, in an organization's personnel database, general users would be allowed to change their own mailing address, office number, etc., but only personnel officers would be allowed to change an employee's job title or salary.

Lock Controls

The DBMS can control who is able to read and write data through the use of locks. Locks are used for read and write access to specific rows of data in relational systems or objects in object-oriented systems.

In a multiuser system, if two or more people wish to modify a piece of data at the same time, a deadlock occurs. A deadlock is when two transactions try to access the same resource; however, the resource cannot handle two requests simultaneously without an integrity problem. The system will not release the resource to either transaction, thereby refusing to process both of the transactions. To prevent a deadlock so that no one can access the data, the access controls lock part of the data so that only one user can access the data. Lock controls can also be more granular so that locking can be accomplished by table, row, record, or even field.

By using locks, only one user at a time can perform an action on the data. For example, in an airline reservation system, there may be two requests to book the last remaining seat on the airplane. If the DBMS allowed more than one user (or process) to write information to a row at the same time, then both transactions could occur simultaneously. To prevent this, the DBMS takes both transactions and gives one transaction a write lock on the account. Once the first transaction has finished, it releases its lock, and then the other transaction, which has been held in a queue, can acquire the lock and make its action or, in this example, be denied the action.

These and related requirements are known as the ACID test, which stands for atomicity, consistency, isolation, and durability. These terms are defined below:[17]

- **Atomicity** – Is when all the parts of a transaction's execution are either all committed or all rolled back – do it all or not at all. Essentially, all changes take effect, or none do. Atomicity ensures there is no erroneous data in the system or data that does not correspond to other data as it should.
- **Consistency** – Occurs when the database is transformed from one valid state to another valid state. A transaction is allowed only if it follows user-defined integrity constraints. Illegal transactions are not allowed, and if an integrity constraint cannot be satisfied, the transaction is rolled back to its previously valid state, and the user is informed that the transaction has failed.

---

17   See the following for a good overview of the ACID test: http://www.lynda.com/Access-tutorials/
Transactions-ACID-test/112585/121201-4.html

- **Isolation** – Is the process guaranteeing the results of a transaction are invisible to other transactions until the transaction is complete.
- **Durability** – Ensures the results of a completed transaction are permanent and can survive future system and media failures; that is, once they are done, they cannot be undone. Again, this is similar to transaction persistence.

For access control, the relational and object-oriented database models use either discretionary access control (DAC) or mandatory access control (MAC). Refer to the Identity and Access Management domain for more information about discretionary and mandatory access control.

Other DBMS Access Controls

Security for databases can be implemented either at the user level, by restricting the operations (views) available to a user or placing permissions on each individual data item, or within an object-oriented database, the object itself. Objects can be tables, views of tables, and the columns in those tables, or views. For example, in the SQL 92 standard, rights to objects can be individually assigned. However, not all databases provide this capability, as outlined in SQL 92. The types of actions available in SQL include select (allows the reading of data), insert (allows adding new data to a table), delete (allows removing data from a table), and update (allows changing data in a table). Thus, it is possible to grant a set of actions to a particular table for a specific object.[18]

View-Based Access Controls

In some DBMSs, security can be achieved through the appropriate use and manipulation of views. A trusted front end is built to control assignment of views to users. View-based access control allows the database to be logically divided into pieces that allow sensitive data to be hidden from unauthorized users. It is important that controls are in place so that a user cannot bypass the front end and directly access and manipulate the data. The database manager can set up a view for each type of user, and then each user can only access the view that is assigned to that user. Some database views allow the restriction of both rows and columns, while others allow for views that can write and update data as well as read (not just read-only).

Grant and Revoke Access Controls

Grant and revoke statements allow users who have "grant authority" permission to grant permission and revoke permission to other users. In a grant and revoke system, if a user is granted permission without the grant option, the user should not be able to pass grant authority to other users. This is, in a sense, a modification of discretionary access control. However, the security risk is that a user granted access, but not grant authority, could make a complete copy of the relation and subvert the system. Because the user, who is not the owner, created a copy, the user (now the owner of the copy) could provide grant authority over the copy to other users, leading to unauthorized users being able to access the same information contained in the original relation. Although the copy is not updated with the original relation, the user making the copy could continue making similar copies of the relation and continue to provide the same data to other users. The revoke statement functions like the grant statement. One of the characteristics of the revoke statement is its cascading effect. When the rights previously granted to a user are subsequently revoked, all similar rights are revoked for all users who may have been granted access by the newly revoked user.

---

18 See the following for the original SQL 92 standard draft paper: http://www.contrib.andrew.cmu. edu/~shadow/sql/sql1992.txt

Security for Object-Oriented (OO) Databases

Most of the models for securing databases have been designed for relational databases. Because of the complexity of object-oriented databases, the security models for object-oriented databases are also more complex. The views of the object-oriented model differ, which adds to this complexity; therefore, each security model has to make some assumptions about the object-oriented model used for its particular database.

Metadata Controls

In addition to facilitating the effective retrieving of information, metadata can also manage restricted access to information. Metadata can serve as a gatekeeper function to filter access and thus provide security controls. One specialized form of metadata is the data dictionary, a central repository of information regarding the various databases that may be used within an enterprise. The data dictionary does not provide direct control of the databases or access control functions, but it does give the administrator a full picture of the various bodies of information around the company, potentially including the sensitivity and classification of material held in different objects. Therefore, the data dictionary can be used in risk management and direction of protective resources.

Data Contamination Controls

There are two types of controls that ensure the integrity of data: input and output controls. Input controls consist of transaction counts, dollar counts, hash totals, error detection, error correction, resubmission, self-checking digits, control totals, and label processing. Output controls include the validation of transactions through reconciliation, physical-handling procedures, authorization controls, verification with expected results, and audit trails.

Online Transaction Processing (OLTP)

OLTP is designed to record all of the business transactions of an organization as they occur. It is a data processing system facilitating and managing transaction-oriented applications. These are characterized as a system used by many concurrent users who are actively adding and modifying data to effectively change real-time data. OLTP environments are frequently found in the finance, telecommunications, insurance, retail, transportation, and travel industries. For example, airline ticket agents enter data in the database in real-time by creating and modifying travel reservations, and these are increasingly joined by users directly making their own reservations and purchasing tickets through airline company websites as well as discount travel website portals. Therefore, millions of people may be accessing the same flight database every day, and dozens of people may be looking at a specific flight at the same time.

The security concerns for OLTP systems are concurrency and atomicity. Concurrency controls ensure that two users cannot simultaneously change the same data or that one user cannot make changes before another user is finished with it. In an airline ticket system, it is critical for an agent processing a reservation to complete the transaction, especially if it is the last seat available on the plane. Atomicity ensures that all of the steps involved in the transaction complete successfully. If one step should fail, then the other steps should not be able to complete. Again, in an airline ticketing system, if the agent does not enter a name into the name data field correctly, the transaction should not be able to complete.

8

**Security in the Software
Development Life Cycle**

OLTP systems should act as a monitoring system and detect when individual processes abort, automatically restart an aborted process, back out of a transaction if necessary, allow distribution of multiple copies of application servers across machines, and perform dynamic load balancing.

A security feature uses transaction logs to record information on a transaction before it is processed and then mark it as processed after it is done. If the system fails during the transaction, the transaction can be recovered by reviewing the transaction logs. Checkpoint restart is the process of using the transaction logs to restart the machine by running through the log to the last checkpoint or good transaction. All transactions following the last checkpoint are applied before allowing users to access the data again.

Knowledge Management

Knowledge management involves several existing research areas tied together by their common application environment: that is, the enterprise. Some topics listed under the knowledge management category are workflow management, business process modeling, document management, databases and information systems, knowledge-based systems, and several methodologies to model diverse aspects relevant to the knowledge in an enterprise environment. A key feature of knowledge management is application of artificial intelligence techniques to decision support.

A key term for knowledge management is *corporate memory* or *organizational memory* because knowledge management systems frequently make use of data warehousing. The memory serves to store the accumulated enterprise knowledge that has to be managed. Corporate memory contains several kinds of information stored in databases, including employee knowledge, lists of customers, suppliers, and products, and specific documents relating to the organization. Essentially, it is all of the information, data, and knowledge about an organization that can be obtained from several different sources.

For data to be helpful, it must have meaning. The interpretation of the data into meaning requires knowledge. This knowledge is an integral aspect of interpreting the data. When an organization tries to understand the raw data from various sources, it can have a knowledgeable employee attempt to interpret the data into some meaning for the organization. To automate this process, knowledge-based systems (KBSs) are used along with problem-solving methods for inference. In the first case, the user knows or learns something, whereas in the KBS, the system contains the knowledge.

Knowledge discovery in databases (KDD) is a mathematical, statistical, and visualization method of identifying valid and useful patterns in data.

It is an evolving field of study to provide automated analysis solutions. The knowledge discovery process takes the data from data mining and accurately transforms it into useful and understandable information. This information is usually not retrievable through standard retrieval techniques, but it is uncovered through the use of artificial intelligence (AI) techniques.

There are many approaches to KDD. A probabilistic method uses graphical representation models to compare different knowledge representations. The models are based on probabilities and data independencies. The probabilistic models are useful for applications involving uncertainty, such as those used in planning and control systems. A statistical approach uses rule discovery and is based on data relationships. A learning algorithm can automatically select useful data relationship paths and attributes. These paths and attributes are then used to construct rules for discovering meaningful information. This approach is used to generalize patterns in the data and to construct rules from the noted patterns. An example of the statistical approach is OLAP. Classification groups data according to similarities. One example is a pattern discovery and data-cleaning model that reduces a large database to only a few specific records.

By eliminating redundant and non-important data, one simplifies the discovery of patterns in the data. Deviation and trend analysis uses filtering techniques to detect patterns. An example is an intrusion detection system that filters a large volume of data so that only the pertinent data is analyzed.

Neural networks are specific AI methods used to develop classification, regression, association, and segmentation models based on the way neurons work in the human brain. A neural net method organizes data into nodes that are arranged in layers, and links between the nodes have specific weighting classifications. The neural net is helpful in detecting the associations among the input patterns or relationships. It is also considered a learning system because new information is automatically incorporated into the system. However, the value and relevance of the decisions made by the neural network are only as good as the experience it is given. The greater the experience, the better the decision. Note that neural nets have a specific problem in terms of an individual's ability to substantiate processing, in that the neural nets are subject to superstitious knowledge, which is a tendency to identify relations when no relations actually exist.

More sophisticated neural nets are less subject to this problem. The expert system uses a knowledge base (a collection of all the data, or knowledge, on a particular matter) and a set of algorithms or rules that infer new facts from knowledge and incoming data. The knowledge base could be the human experience that is available in an organization. Because the system reacts to a set of rules, if the rules are faulty, the response will also be faulty. Also, because human decision is removed from the point of action, if an error were to occur, the reaction time from a human would be longer. As always, a hybrid approach could combine more than one system, which provides a more powerful and useful system.

Security controls include:

- Protecting the knowledge base as you would any database.
- Routinely verifying the decisions based on what outcomes are expected from specific inputs.
- If using a rule-based approach, changes to the rules must go through a change control process.
- If the data output seems suspicious or out of the ordinary, perform additional and different queries to verify the information.
- Making risk management decisions because decisions that are based on data warehouse analysis techniques may be incorrect.
- Developing a baseline of expected performance from the analytical tool.

8

Security in the Software Development Life Cycle

Web Application Environment

Webpages are the most visible part of the enterprise because they are designed to be seen from the outside. Therefore, they attract vandals, who delight in the manifest defacement of a public website. Even if the webpages are not modified, it is possible that the invader can execute a Denial of Service (DoS) attack against the website.

Because websites are also the primary interface for e-commerce, there is also the potential for fraud or even outright theft. In some cases, this may simply be access to information or resources that should have a charge associated with their use, but some situations may allow attackers to order goods without payment or even transfer funds. In some cases, transaction data is kept on the Web server, thus allowing the attacker direct access to information that may contain details about either the activities of the company or customer particulars, such as credit card numbers.

Because Web-based systems are tied to production or internal systems (or both) for ease of maintenance, access to database information, or transaction processing, websites may also offer a vector for intrusion into the private networks themselves. If the Web server can be compromised, it offers the attacker a semi-trusted platform from which to mount probes or other activities. Again, such access may provide the interloper with intelligence about corporate sales and projects, but it can also provide an avenue to the enterprise's proprietary intellectual property.

Most attacks are conducted at the application level, either against the Web server application itself, in-house scripts, or the common front-end applications that are used for e-commerce. The pace of change is quite rapid for this type of software, and quality checks do not always uncover vulnerabilities and security problems. Therefore, attacks on the application software are much more likely to succeed than attacks on the underlying platforms. (Once the application has been breached, an attack on the operating system is generally also possible.)

There are additional factors common to websites that make them vulnerable. For one thing, websites are designed to be widely accessible, and are usually heavily advertised as well. Therefore, a very large number of people will have information about the site's addresses. Web server software does make provisions for logging of traffic, but many administrators either turn off logging altogether or reduce the logging to minimal levels. The standard security tools of firewalls and intrusion detection systems can be applied, but they are not particularly well suited to protecting such public sites. In the case of firewalls, a website must have a standard port or ports open for requests to be made. Intrusion detection systems (IDS) must be tuned and maintained to provide any useful information out of a flood of data. Websites will see all kinds of traffic, from all kinds of sites, requesting connections, webpages, submitting form information, or even updating search engine facts.

Web Application Threats and Protection

Specific protections that may be helpful include having a particular assurance sign-off process for Web servers, hardening the operating system used on such servers (removing default configurations and accounts, configuring permissions and privileges correctly, and keeping up to date with vendor patches), extending Web and network vulnerability scans prior to deployment, passively assessing IDS and advanced intrusion prevention system (IPS) technology, using application proxy firewalls, and disabling any unnecessary documentation and libraries.

In regard to administrative interfaces, ensure that they are removed or secured appropriately. Only allow access from authorized hosts or networks, and then use strong (possibly multifactor) user authentication. Do not hard code the authentication credentials into the application itself, and ensure the security of the credentials using certificates or similar high trust authenticators. Use account lockout and extended logging and audit, and protect all authentication traffic with encryption. Ensure that the interface is at least as secure as the rest of the application, and most often secure it at a higher level.

Because of the accessibility of Web systems and applications, input validation is critical. Application proxy firewalls are appropriate in this regard, but ensure that the proxies are able to deal with problems of buffer overflows, authentication issues, scripting, submission of commands to the underlying platform (which includes issues related to database engines, such as SQL commands), encoding issues (such as Unicode), and URL encoding and translation. In particular, the proxy firewall may have to address issues of data submission to in-house and custom software, ensuring validation of input to those systems. (This level of protection will have to be custom programmed for the application.)

In regard to sessions, remember that HTTP (Hypertext Transfer Protocol) is a stateless technology, and, therefore, periods of apparent attachment to the server are controlled by other technologies, such as cookies or URL data, which must be both protected and validated. If using cookies, always encrypt them. You may wish to have time validation included in the session data. Do not use sequential, calculable, or predictable cookies, session numbers, or URL data for these purposes; use random and unique indicators.

Again, protection for web applications is the same as for other programming. Use the same protections; validate all input and output, fail secure (closed), make your application or system as simple as possible, use secure network design, use penetration testing to validate secure designs and to identify potential vulnerabilities and threats to be mitigated, and use defense in depth. Specific points to consider in a Web system are not to cache secure pages; confirm that all encryption used meets industry standards, monitor your code vendors for security alerts, log any and all critical transactions and milestones, handle exceptions properly, do not trust any data from the client, and do not automatically trust data from other servers, partners, or other parts of the application.

Several organizations have developed frameworks for secure Web development. One of the most common is the Open Web Application Security Project (OWASP).[19] OWASP has several guides available for Web application development including:

- Development Guide
- Code Review Guide
- Testing Guide
- Top ten Web application security vulnerabilities
- OWASP Mobile

Given the prevalence of Web-based and cloud-based solutions, OWASP provides an accessible and thorough framework with processes for Web application security. The security professional should be familiar with the "top ten" Web application vulnerabilities and also how to mitigate them.

---

19   See the following: https://www.owasp.org/index.php/Main_Page

Security of the Software Environment

Applications Development and Programming Concepts

The security of data and information is one of the most important elements of information system security. It is through software mechanisms that users process and access the data on the system. In addition, almost all technical controls are implemented in software, and the interfaces to all technical countermeasures are managed through software. The objective of information security is to make sure that the system and its resources are available when needed, that the integrity of the processing of the data and the data itself is ensured, and that the confidentiality of the data is protected. All of these purposes rely upon secure, consistent, reliable, and properly operating software.

Application development procedures are absolutely vital to the integrity of systems. If applications are not developed properly, data may be processed in such a way that the integrity of either the original data or the processed results is corrupted. In addition, the integrity of both application and operating system software itself must be maintained, in terms of both change control and attack from malicious software such as viruses. If special protection requirements (such as confidentiality) for the data controlled by a system are required, protective mechanisms and safeguards (like encryption) should be designed and built into the system and coded from the beginning, and not added on as an afterthought. Because operating system software is also responsible for many of the controls on access to data and systems, it is vital that these areas of programming be tightly protected.

Current Software Environment

Information systems are becoming more distributed, with a substantial increase in the use of open protocols, interfaces, and source code, as well as sharing of resources. Increased sharing requires that all resources be protected against unauthorized access. Many of these safeguards are provided through software controls, especially operating system mechanisms. The operating system must offer controls that protect the computer's resources. In addition, the relationship between applications and the operating system is also important. Controls must be included in operating systems so that applications cannot damage or circumvent the operating system controls. A lack of software protection mechanisms can leave the operating system and critical computer resources open to corruption and attack.

Note also that information systems are becoming much more complex. Originally a given application might have been the only application running on a specific machine, aside from the hardwired functions resident in the central processing unit (CPU). Today, an application may involve the hardware platform, CPU microcode, virtual machine server, operating system, network operating system and utilities, remote procedure calls, object request broker, engine servers (such as database and Web servers), engine application, multiple interface applications, interface utilities, API libraries, and multiple entities involved in a remote client interface. While many of these levels have been added in the name of interoperability and standardization, the complexity introduced does make assurance of security and compliance more difficult.

Some of the main security requirements for applications and databases are to ensure that only valid, authorized, and authenticated users can access the data; that permissions related to use of the data can be controlled and managed; that the system or software provides some type of granularity for controlling such permissions; that encryption or other appropriate logical controls are available for protecting sensitive information such as password storage; and that audit trails, sufficient to provide assurance of the functional security controls, can be implemented and reviewed.

It is becoming increasingly evident that many problems in access control, networking, and operations security are related to the development of software and systems. Whether the problems are caused by improper system development, sloppy programming practices, or a lack of rigorous testing, it is clear that a number of vulnerabilities are present, and continue to be created, in the software that is in widespread use. Essentially, security in operating systems, applications, and databases focuses on the ability of the software to enforce controls over the storage and transfer of information in and between objects. Remember that the underlying foundation of the software security controls is the organization's security policy. The security policy reflects the security requirements of the organization. Therefore, if the security policy requires that only one set of users can access information, the software must have the capability to limit access to that specific group of users. Keep in mind that the ability to refer to a system as secure is based upon the reliable enforcement of the organization's security policy.

Open Source

The term *open source* has a number of competing definitions. However, most advocates would agree to the basic condition that the vendor releases the software source code so that users may modify the software either to suit their own situation or for further development. When the source is open, this also means that others can comment on or assist in debugging the code. Traditionally, vendors have relied on the secrecy of their proprietary code to protect the intellectual property of their product by hiding the source code and releasing only an executable version in machine or object code. There is a trend toward open-source codes in commercial software houses, and many successful business models support this activity, but most software companies still keep their source code secret, relying on proprietary code to prevent others from producing competing products.

Advocates of open-source software believe that security can be improved when the source code is available to the public. This is expressed in Linus's law: With sufficiently many eyeballs looking at the code, all bugs will become apparent.[20] Let other developers and programmers review the code and help to find the security vulnerabilities. The idea is that this openness will lead to quick identification and repair of any issues, including those involved with security.

Other developers disagree. Will other programmers be able to find all of the security vulnerabilities? Just releasing the source code does not ensure that all security bugs will be found, and the automatic assumption of reliability can lead to a false sense of security. Devotees of proprietary systems note that dishonest programmers may find security vulnerabilities but not disclose the problem, or at least not until they have exploited it. There have been instances where those in the black hat community tried to blackmail software vendors when they found problems.

---

20   See the following: http://www.catb.org/~esr/writings/cathedral-bazaar/cathedral-bazaar/index.html

A final determination on this issue has not yet been made. However, in general, it is known that "security by obscurity" – the idea that if a system is little known, there is less likelihood that someone will find out how to break into it – does not work. Whether programs are available in source or only executable versions, it is known that observation, reverse engineering, disassembly, trial and error, and random chance may be able to find security vulnerabilities.

Full Disclosure

A related issue, frequently tied to the idea of the open-source model, is full disclosure. Full disclosure means that individuals who find security vulnerabilities will publicly disseminate the information, possibly including code fragments or programs that might exploit the problem. Many models of partial disclosure exist, such as first contacting the vendor of the software and asking that the vulnerability and a subsequent fix be released to the public or the release only of information of the vulnerability and possible workaround solutions.

For security purposes, it may be better to look at how the software was designed rather than making policy regarding the purchase of open-source or proprietary software. Was security included as an initial consideration when decisions were made about such issues as programming languages, features, programming style, and tests and evaluations?

The Software Environment

The situation in which software operates is fundamental to computer operations. This environment begins with the standard model of hardware resources, with items such as the central processing unit (CPU), memory, input/output (I/O) requests, and storage devices. The operating system is responsible for controlling these resources and providing security mechanisms to protect them, as well as providing resource access permissions and safeguards against misuse. The applications employed by the end-users make requests or calls to the operating system, or sometimes directly to devices, to provide the required computer services. In some applications, security features are built into the software that allow the users more control over their information, such as access controls or auditing capabilities.

Vulnerabilities can be introduced in the application, such as when a buffer overflow attack takes advantage of improper parameter checking within the application. Note that because of layering in the software, protections imposed at one level may be bypassed by functions at another.

In addition, many applications now include some form of distributed computing. There are many varieties, levels, and forms of distribution you may encounter, ranging from simple cooperation of programs to standard interfacing, message passing (in object environments), layering (as noted above, in more extensive forms), middleware (particularly in database applications), clustering, or virtual machines. Distributed applications provide a particular challenge in terms of security due to the complexity of the information flow model.

Security Issues of Programming Languages

In the development phase, programmers have the option of writing code in several different programming languages. A programming language is a set of rules telling the computer what operations to perform. Programming languages have evolved in generations, and each language is characterized into one of the generations. Those in the lower level are closer in form to the binary language of the computer. Both machine and assembly languages are considered low-level languages. As the languages become easier and more similar to the language people use to communicate, they become higher level. High-level languages are easier to use than low-level languages and can be used to produce programs more quickly. In addition, high- level languages may be said to be beneficial because they enforce coding standards and can provide more security. On the other hand, higher level languages automate certain functions, and provide complicated operations for the program, implemented by the programming environment or tool, the internal details of which may be poorly understood by the programmer. Therefore, it is possible that high-level languages may introduce security vulnerabilities in ways that are not apparent to the developer.

Programming languages are frequently referred to by generations. The first generation is generally held to be the machine language, opcodes (operating codes), and object code used by the computer itself. These are very simple instructions that can be executed directly by the CPU of a computer. Each type of computer has its own machine language. However, the hexadecimal or binary code is difficult for people to understand, and so a second generation of assembly language was created, which uses symbols as abbreviations for major instructions. The third generation, usually known as high-level language, uses meaningful words (generally English) as the commands. COBOL, FORTRAN, BASIC, Java and C are examples of this type.

Above this point, there may be disagreement on definitions. Fourth-generation languages, sometimes known as very high-level languages, are represented by query languages, report generators, and application generators. Fifth-generation languages, or natural language interfaces, require expert systems and artificial intelligence. The intent is to eliminate the need for programmers to learn a specific vocabulary, grammar, or syntax. The text of a natural language statement very closely resembles human speech.

Process and Elements

Most of those working in the information systems security profession are not experienced programmers. Therefore, the following is a very quick and simplistic explanation of the concepts and processes of different types of programming. It is provided purely for background understanding for the other material in this domain.

Machine language does not consist of the type of commands seen in higher level languages. Higher level languages use words from normal human languages, and so, while a given program probably looks odd to the nonprogrammer, nevertheless, programmers see recognizable words such as *print*, *if*, *load*, *case*, and so forth, which give some indication of what might be going on in the program. This is not true of machine language.

Machine language is all just ones and zeroes. The patterns of ones and zeroes are directions to the computer. The directive patterns, called opcodes, are the actual commands that the computer uses. Opcodes are very short – in most desktop microcomputers, they are generally only a single byte (8 bits) in length or possibly two. Opcodes may also have a byte or two of data associated with them, but the entire string of command and argument is usually no more than 4 bytes, or 32 bits, altogether. This is the equivalent of a word of no more than four letters.

Almost all computers in use today are based on what is termed the von Neumann architecture (named after John von Neumann).[21] One of the fundamental aspects of von Neumann architecture is that there is no inherent difference between data and programming in the memory of the computer. Therefore, one cannot tell whether the pattern 4Eh (00101110) is the letter N or a decrement opcode. Similarly, the pattern 72h (01110010) may be the letter r or the first byte of the "jump if below" opcode. Therefore, when viewing the contents of a program file, as seen in *Figure 8.1*, the viewer will be faced with an initially confusing agglomeration of random letters and symbols and incomprehensible garbage.

```
–d ds:100 11f
B8 19 06 BA CF 03 05 FA-0A 3B 06 02 00 72 1B B4
..........;...r..
09 BA 18 01 CD 21 CD 20–4E 6F 74 20 65 6E 6F 75   .....!. Not enou
–u ds:100 11f
0AEA:0100 B81906 MOV AX,0619
0AEA:0103 BACF03 MOV DX,03CF
0AEA:0106 05FA0A ADD AX,0AFA
0AEA:0109 3B060200 CMP AX,[0002]
0AEA:010D 721B JB 012A
0AEA:010F B409 MOV AH,09
0AEA:0111 BA1801 MOV DX,0118
0AEA:0114 CD21 INT 21
0AEA:0116 CD20 INT 20
0AEA:0118 4E DEC SI
0AEA:0119 6F DB 6F
0AEA:011A 7420 JZ 013C
0AEA:011C 65 DB 65
0AEA:011D 6E DB 6E
0AEA:011E 6F DB 6F
0AEA:011F 7567 JNZ 0188
```

Figure 8.1 - **Display of the same section of a program file, first as data and then as an assembly language listing**

Ultimately, understanding this chaotic blizzard of symbols is going to be of the greatest use to machine language programmers or software forensic specialists. Source code may be available, particularly in cases dealing with script, macro, or other interpreted programming. To explain some of those objects, one must examine the process of programming.

The Programming Procedure

In the beginning, programmers created object (machine or binary) files directly. (Some programmers have retained this skill. It is possible to enter data directly from the keyboard of a common desktop computer, using only printable characters, and create a usable program. However, this activity is now relegated to the level of a game and has little relation to modern, commercial software development.) The operating instructions (opcodes) for the computer and any necessary arguments or data were presented to the machine in the form that was needed to

---

21 See the following for the 1946 paper, written with Arthur W. Burks and Hermann H. Goldstine, which was titled "Preliminary Discussion of the Logical Design of an Electronic Computing Instrument", that was to become the basis for the development of the modern computer: https://www.fdi.ucm.es/profesor/mozos/EC/burks.pdf

get it to process properly. Assembly language was produced to help with this process. Although there is a fairly direct correspondence between the assembly mnemonics and specific opcodes, at least the assembly files are formatted in a way that is relatively easy for humans to read rather than being strings of hexadecimal or binary numbers. You will notice in the second part of *Figure 8.1*, a column of codes that might almost be words: MOV (move), CMP (compare), DEC (decrement), and ADD. Assembly language added these mnemonics because "MOV to register AX" makes more sense to a programmer than simply B8h or 10111000. An assembler program also takes care of details regarding addressing in memory so that every time a minor change is made to a program, all the memory references and locations do not have to be manually changed.

With the advent of high-level (or at least higher level) languages (the so-called third generation), programming language systems split into two types. High-level languages are those where the source code is somewhat more comprehensible to people. Those who work with C may dispute this assertion, of course. These languages, in the hands of skilled programmers, can produce highly functional programs from very little source code but at the expense of legibility. The much maligned COBOL is possibly the best example. As you can see in *Figure 8.2*, the general structure of a COBOL program should be evident from the source code, even for those not trained in the language.

```
OPEN INPUT RESPONSE-FILE
    OUTPUT REPORT-FILE
    INITIALIZE SURVEY-RESPONSES
    PERFORM UNTIL NO-MORE-RECORDS
    READ RESPONSE-FILE
    AT END
    SET NO-MORE-RECORDS TO TRUE
    NOT AT END
    PERFORM 100-PROCESS-SURVEY
    END-READ
    END-PERFORM
    begin.
    display "My parents went to Vancouver and all they got"
    display "for me was this crummy COBOL program!".
```

Figure 8.2 - **Two sections of code from different COBOL programs. Note that the intention of the program is reasonably clear, as opposed to** *Figure* **8.1.**

Compiled languages involve two separate processes before a program is ready for execution. The application must be programmed in the source (the text or human-readable) code, and then the source must be compiled into object code that the computer can understand: the strings of opcodes. Those who actually do programming will know that this is an overly simplified picture of a process that generally involves linkers and a number of other utilities, but the point is that the source code for languages like FORTRAN and Modula cannot be run directly; it must be compiled first.

993

```
<html>
<head>
<title>
Adding input
</title>
<!-- This script writes three lines on the page -->
<script>
document.write ("Hello, ");
document.write ("class.<br>This line ");
document.write ("is written by the JavaScript in the  header.");
document.write ("<br>but appears in the body of the  page,");
</script>
<body>
<!-- The following line is HTML, giving a line break and text -->
<br>This line is the first line that is written by HTML itself.<p>
Notice that this is the last line that appears until after the new
input is obtained.<p>
<!-- This script asks for input in a new window -->
<!-- Note that window, like document, is an object with methods -->
<script>
// Note that within scripts we use C++ style comments
// We declare a variable, studentName
var studentName;
// Then we get some input
studentName = window.prompt ("What is your name?", "student  name");
/* Although we can use C style
multi-line comments */
</script>
<!-- This script writes a single line of text -->
<script>
document.write ("Thank you for your input, " +  studentName);
</script>
</body>
</html>
```

Figure 8.3 - **A JavaScript applet that will work in all browsers. Note that this script uses much more internal commenting than is usually the case.**

Interpreted languages shorten the process. Once the source code for the program has been written, it can be run, with the help of the interpreter. The interpreter translates the source code into object code "on the fly," rendering it into a form that the computer can use. There is a cost in performance and speed for this convenience; compiled programs are native, or natural, for the CPU to use directly (with some mediation from the operating system) and so run considerably faster. In addition, compilers tend to perform some level of optimization on the programs, choosing the best set of functions for a given situation. However, interpreted languages have an additional advantage. Because the language is translated on the machine where the program is run, a given interpreted program can be run on a variety of different computers, as long as an interpreter for that language is available. Scripting languages, used on a variety of platforms, are of this type.

JavaScript is a language most commonly used in webpages. However, it is not Java and has no relation to Java. It was originally named LiveScript and was renamed as a marketing strategy. It is interpreted by the user's Web browser and allows control over most of the features of the Web browser. It has access to most of the contents of the Hypertext Markup Language (HTML) document and has full interaction with the displayed content. Depending upon the browser, it may have significant access to the system itself. As opposed to Java, which has sandbox restrictions for applets and an extensive security model, security management in JavaScript is minimal; it is either enabled or disabled.

JavaScript applets, such as the example in *Figure 8.3*, may be embedded in webpages and then run in browsers that support the language regardless of the underlying computer architecture or operating system. (JavaScript is probably a bad example to use when talking about cross-platform operation because a given JavaScript program may not even run on a new version of the same software company's browser, let alone one from another vendor or for another platform. But it is supposed to work across platforms.) As with most other technologies where two options are present, there are hybrid systems that attempt to provide the best of both worlds. Java, for example, compiles source code into a sort of pseudo-object code called bytecode. The bytecode is then processed by the interpreter (called the Java Virtual Machine, or JVM) for the CPU to run. Because the bytecode is already fairly close to object code, the interpretation process is much faster than for other interpreted languages. And because bytecode is still undergoing an interpretation, a given Java program will run on any machine that has a JVM. (Java does have a provision for direct compilation into object code, as do a number of implementations for interpreted languages such as BASIC.)

Java Security

Java provides examples of a number of other points related to the security of software and development. At the time the bytecode is interpreted, Java checks the use of variables and memory by the application. This check can be a good thing for security or a bad thing. In general, it is good because programs use memory properly and do not exceed set bounds. However, overreliance on such functions (if developers do not use additional security checks in their code) may result in sloppy practices that lead to other security problems.

For example, Java is usually held to be very good at garbage collection, the automatic review of memory locations, and the de-allocation of memory areas that are no longer required. This is good in that it ensures the program does not fill all available memory and then run into problems. However, the language has no way of determining the sensitivity of the information that might be stored in those memory locations. Therefore, it may be possible for sensitive information to be improperly disclosed. Languages that do not provide this garbage collection service require that the programmer make a conscious choice about memory allocation, and this choice may prompt the programmer to consider overwriting the memory location before returning it to the pool of available memory.

The Java programming language implements some specific security provisions. Some of these have been added to subsequent programming languages.

The three parts (sometimes referred to as layers) of the Java security approach are:

1. ***Verifier (or Interpreter)*** – Helps to ensure type safety. It is primarily responsible for memory and bounds checking.

2. **Class Loader** – Loads and unloads classes dynamically from the Java runtime environment.

3. **Security Manager** – Acts as a security gatekeeper protecting against rogue functionality.

The verifier is responsible for scrutinizing the bytecode (regardless of how it was created) before it can run on a local Java VM. Because many programs written in Java are intended to be downloaded from the network, the Java verifier acts as a buffer between the computer and the downloaded program. Because the computer is actually running the verifier, which is executing the downloaded program, the verifier can protect the computer from dangerous actions that can be caused by the downloaded program. The verifier is built into the Java VM and by design cannot be accessed by programmers or users.

The verifier can check bytecode at a number of different levels. The simplest check ensures that the format of a code fragment is correct. The verifier also applies a built-in theorem prover to each code fragment. The theorem prover can ensure that the bytecode does not have rogue code, such as the ability to forge pointers, violate access restrictions, or access objects using incorrect type information. If the verifier discovers rogue code within a class file, it executes an exception and the class file is not executed.

A criticism of the Java verifier is the length of time it takes to verify the bytecodes. Although the delay time is minimal, Web business owners thought that any delay, such as 10 to 20 seconds, would prevent customers from using their sites. This could be viewed as an example of a technology that is not quite ready for the argument (trade-off) between functionality and security. In most Java implementations, when the bytecode arrives at the Java VM, the class loader forms it into a class, which the verifier automatically examines. The class loader is responsible for loading the mobile code and determining when and how classes can be added to a running Java environment. For security purposes, the class loaders ensure that important parts of the Java runtime environment are not replaced by impostor code (known as class spoofing). Also for security purposes, class loaders typically divide classes into distinct namespaces according to origin. This is an important security element – to keep local classes distinct from external classes. However, a weakness was discovered in the class loader – in some instances, it was possible for the namespaces to overlap. This has subsequently been protected with an additional security class loader.

The third part of the model is the security manager, which is responsible for restricting the ways an applet uses visible interfaces (Java API calls). It is a single Java object that performs runtime checks on dangerous operations. Essentially, code in the Java library consults the security manager whenever a potentially dangerous operation is attempted. The security manager has veto authority and can generate a security exception. A standard browser security manager will disallow most operations when they are requested by untrusted code and will allow trusted code to perform all of its operations. It is the responsibility of the security manager to make all final decisions as to whether a particular operation is permitted or rejected.

Java was originally designed for a distributed application environment, and so the security model implemented a sandbox that imposed strict controls on what distributed Java programs can and cannot do. An alternative to the sandbox approach of handling mobile code is to run only the code that is trusted. For example, ActiveX controls should be run only when you completely trust the entity that signed the control. Unfortunately, there have been problems with both the design and implementation of the ActiveX system. ActiveX has no sandbox restrictions on the activity of an ActiveX control; it can perform any action or function available to any executable program. There is no runtime check on the reliability or bounds restriction of the program.

In the Java sandbox model, the Web browser defines and implements a security policy for running downloaded Java code, such as an applet. A Java-enabled Web browser includes a Java verifier and runtime library along with classes (in Java, all objects belong to classes) to implement a security manager. The security manager controls the access to critical system resources and ensures that the Web browser's version of the security manager is implemented correctly. In the extreme, if a Java-enabled Web browser did not install a system security manager, an applet would have the same access as a local Java application. The sandbox is not the only example of the operation of the security manager. Any Java application or environment can implement, and tune, a specific security manager and particular restrictions, making additional controls possible for specialized environments or applications.

A weakness of the three-part model is that if any of the three parts fail to operate, the security model may be completely compromised. Since Java's introduction, several additional security features have been released, including the Java security package. This package is an API that includes both a cryptographic provider interface and APIs for common cryptographic algorithms. It provides the ability to implement cryptography and manage or modify default security protections for a specific application. This provides additional application security, but only if the developer chooses to implement it.

Other new Java releases focusing on security include:

- Java Certification Path API for building and validating certification paths and managing certificate revocation lists.
- Java GSS-API for securely exchanging messages between communication applications using Kerberos. Support for single sign-on using Kerberos is also included.
- Java Authentication and Authorization Service (JASS), which enables services to authenticate and enforce access controls upon users.
- Java Cryptography Extension (JCE) provides a framework and implementation for encryption, key generation, key agreement, and message authentication code (MAC) algorithms.
- Java Secure Socket Extension (JSSE) enables secure Internet connections. It implements a Java version of the Secure Sockets Layer (SSL) and Transport Layer Security (TLS) protocols and includes functionality for data encryption, server authentication, message integrity, and optional client authentication.

Object-Oriented Technology and Programming

Object-oriented programming (OOP) is considered by some to be a revolutionary concept that changed the rules in computer program development. It is organized around objects rather than linear procedures. OOP is a programming method that makes a self-sufficient object. The object is a block of preassembled programming code in a self-contained module, although it operates differently, and more independently, than a function or procedure in a procedural language. The module encapsulates both data and the processing instructions that may be called to process the data. Once a block of programming code is written, it can be reused in any number of programs. Examples of object-oriented languages are Eiffel, Smalltalk (one of the first), Ruby, Java (one of the most popular today), C++ (also one of the most popular today), Python, Perl, and Visual Basic. A number of recent object-oriented languages are, themselves, built on top of other, previous object-oriented languages, and they may extend them in specialized ways.

When we are defining an object-oriented language, the following are some of the key characteristics:

Encapsulation (Also Known as Data Hiding)

A class defines only the data it needs to be concerned with. When an instance of that class (i.e., an object) is run, the code will not be able to accidentally access other data, which is generally seen as positive in terms of security.

Inheritance

The concept of a data class makes it possible to define subclasses of data objects that share some or all of the main (or super) class characteristics. If security is properly implemented in the high-level class, then subclasses should inherit that security. The same is true of objects derived not from a class but from another object.

Polymorphism

Objects may be processed differently depending on their data type. Instantiating an object from a prior object ensures that the new object inherits attributes and methods from the original. Changing attributes and aspects of an object created in such a way may change the operation of the modified object. Unfortunately, this has implications for security that must be carefully assessed because secure methods may be lost through polymorphism.

Polyinstantiation -(Why Dogs Go WOOF and Cats Go MEOW) [22]

Specific objects, instantiated from a higher class, may vary their behavior depending upon the data they contain. Therefore, it may be difficult to verify that inherited security properties are valid for all objects. However, polyinstantiation can also be used to prevent inference attacks against databases because it allows different versions of the same information to exist at different classification levels.

Within an OOP environment, all predefined types are objects. A data type in a programming language is a set of data with values having predefined characteristics, such as integer, character, string, and pointer. In most programming languages, a limited number of such data types are built into the language. The programming language usually specifies the range of values for a given data type, how the values are processed by the computer, and how they are stored. In OOP, all user-defined types are also objects.

The first step in OOP is to identify all the objects you want to manipulate and how they relate to each other; this is often known as data modeling. Once the object is identified, it is generalized as a class of objects and defined as the kind of data it contains and as any

---

22 The "simple" definition of polyinstantiation is as follows:
  Imagine that you have both a cat and a dog in front of you.
  Both are given the command to "speak" (same command given to both objects).
  What happens?
  Dog = WOOF
  Cat = MEOW
  Polyinstantiation: Different Objects + Same Command = Different Outcome

logic sequences that can manipulate it. Each distinct logic sequence is known as a method. A real instance of a class is called an object or an instance of a class, and this is what is run in the computer. The object's methods provide computer instructions, and the class object characteristics provide relevant data. Communication with objects, and objects communication with each other, is established through interfaces called messages.

When building traditional programs, the programmers must write every line of code from the beginning. With OOP, programmers can use the predetermined blocks of code (objects). Consequently, an object can be used repeatedly in different applications and by different programmers. This reuse reduces development time and thus reduces programming costs.

Object-Oriented Security

In object-oriented systems, objects are encapsulated. Encapsulation protects the object by denying direct access to view or interact with what is located inside the object – it is not possible to see what is contained in the object because it is encapsulated. Encapsulation of the object does provide protection of private data from outside access. For security purposes, no object should be able to access another object's internal data. On the other hand, it could be difficult for system administrators to apply the proper policies to an object if they cannot identify what the object contains.

Polyinstantiation allows for iteratively producing a more defined version of an object by replacing variables with values (or other variables). Thus, multiple distant differences between data within objects are done to discourage low-level objects from gaining information at a high level of security. It is also the technique used to avoid covert channels based on inference by causing the same information to exist at different classification levels. Therefore, users at a lower classification level do not know of the existence of a higher classification level.

In object-oriented programming, polymorphism refers to a programming language's ability to process objects differently depending on their data type. The term is sometimes used to describe a variable that may refer to objects whose class is not known at compile time but will respond at runtime according to the actual class of the object to which they refer. Even though polymorphism seems straightforward, if used incorrectly, it can lead to security problems. The problems stem from the data driving the object and a malicious user taking advantage of the feature.

One of the basic activities of an object-oriented design is establishing relationships between classes. One fundamental way to relate classes is through inheritance. This is when a class of objects is defined; any subclass that is defined can inherit the definitions of the general (or super) class. Inheritance allows a programmer to build a new class similar to an existing class without duplicating all the code. The new class inherits the old class's definitions and adds to them. Essentially, for the programmer, an object in a subclass does not need to have its own definitions of data and methods that are generic to the class it is a part of. This can help decrease program development time – what works for the superclass will also work for the subclass.

Multiple inheritances can introduce complexity and may result in security breaches for object accesses. Issues such as name clashes and ambiguities must be resolved by the programming language to avoid a subclass inheriting inappropriate privileges from a superclass.

8

Security in the Software Development Life Cycle

Distributed Object-Oriented Systems

As the age of mainframe-based applications began to wane, the new era of distributed computing emerged. Distributed development architectures allow applications to be divided into pieces that are called components, and each component can exist in different locations. This development paradigm allows programs to download code from remote machines onto a user's local host in a manner that is seamless to the user.

Applications today are constructed with software systems that are based on distributed objects, such as the Common Object Request Broker Architecture (CORBA), Java Remote Method Invocation (JRMI), Enterprise JavaBean (EJB), and Distributed Component Object Model (DCOM, restricted to Microsoft Windows). A distributed object-oriented system allows parts of the system to be located on separate computers within an enterprise network. The object system itself is a compilation of reusable, self-contained objects of code designed to perform specific business functions.

How objects communicate with one another is complex, especially because objects may not reside on the same machine, but they may be located across machines on the network. To standardize this process, the Object Management Group (OMG) created a standard for finding objects, initiating objects, and sending requests to the objects. The standard is the Object Request Broker (ORB), which is part of the Common Object Request Broker Architecture (CORBA).

Common Object Request Broker Architecture (CORBA)

Common Object Request Broker Architecture (CORBA) is a set of standards that address the need for interoperability between hardware and software products. CORBA allows applications to communicate with one another regardless of where they are stored. The ORB is the middleware that establishes a client–server relationship between objects. Using an ORB, a client can transparently locate and activate a method on a server object either on the same machine or across a network. The ORB operates regardless of the processor type or programming language.

Not only does the ORB handle all the requests on the system, but it also enforces the system's security policy. The policy describes what the users (and the system) are allowed to do and also what user (or system) actions will be restricted. The security provided by the ORB should be transparent to the user's applications. The CORBA security service supports four types of policies: access control, data protection, non-repudiation, and auditing.

The client application (through an object) sends a request (message) to the target object.

1. The message is sent through the ORB security system. Inside the ORB security system is the policy enforcement code, which contains the organization's policy regarding objects.
2. If the policy allows the requester to access the targeted object, the request is then forwarded to the target object for processing.

When reviewing CORBA implementations, consider the following:

- The specific CORBA security features that are supported
- The implementation of CORBA security building blocks, such as cryptography blocks or support for Kerberos systems
- The ease by which system administrators can use the CORBA interfaces to set up the organization's security policies

- Types of access control mechanisms that are supported
- Types, granularity, and tools for capturing and reviewing audit logs
- Any technical evaluations (i.e., Common Criteria)

CORBA is not the only method for securing distributed application environments. Java's Remote Method Invocation (JRMI) and Enterprise JavaBean (EJB) are similar.

EJB is a Sun Microsystems model providing an API specification for building scalable, distributed, multitier, component-based applications. EJB uses Java's RMI implementations for communications. The EJB server provides a standard set of services for transactions, security, and resource sharing. One of the security advantages is the EJB allows the person assembling the components to control access. Instead of a component developer hard coding the security policies, the end-user (i.e., system administrator or security officer) can specify the policy. Other security features are also available to the end-user. A vulnerability of EJB is the noted weakness of the RMI. For example, the RMI is typically configured to allow clients to download code automatically from the server when it is not present. Thus, before the client can make a secure connection, it can still download code, or a malicious attacker could masquerade as the client to the server and download code. Although improvements have been made to increase the security of RMI, all implementations must be reviewed for security features.

Libraries & Toolsets

A software library consists of pre-written code, classes, procedures, scripts, and configuration data. A developer might manually add a software library to a program to achieve more functionality or to automate a process without writing the code for it from scratch. This allows the developers to "create" the functionality that they want to use, or call, within the application, but to do so without having to write all of the code necessary to provide the functionality, as it is contained within the code library. For example, when developing a mathematical program or application, a developer may add a mathematics software library to the program to eliminate the need for writing complex functions. All of the available functions within a software library can just be called/used within the program body without defining them explicitly.

When built correctly with safe coding practices, implemented properly, and kept up to date with security patches and an iterative feedback mechanism to address bugs and faults as they are identified, software libraries can have the following positive benefits:

- ***Increased Dependability*** – Reused software that has been tried and tested in working systems should be more dependable than new software. The initial use of the software reveals any design and implementation faults. These are then fixed, thus reducing the number of failures when the software is reused.
- ***Reduced Process Risk*** – If software exists, there is less uncertainty in the costs of reusing that software than in the costs of development. This is an important factor for project management because it reduces the margin of error in project cost estimation. This is particularly true when relatively large software components such as sub-systems are reused.
- ***Effective Use of Specialists*** – Instead of developers doing the same work on different projects, these specialists can develop reusable software that encapsulate their knowledge.

- **Standards Compliance** – Some standards, such as user interface standards, can be implemented as a set of standard reusable components. For example, if menus in a user interfaces are implemented using reusable components, all applications present the same menu formats to users. The use of standard user interfaces improves dependability as users are less likely to make mistakes when presented with a familiar interface.
- **Accelerated Development** – Bringing a system to market as early as possible is often more important than overall development costs. Reusing software can speed up system production because both development and validation time should be reduced.

A standard library in computer programming is the library made available across implementations of a programming language. Standard libraries typically include definitions for commonly used algorithms, data structures, and mechanisms for input and output. Depending on the constructs made available by the host language, a standard library may include:

- Subroutines
- Macro definitions
- Global variables
- Class definitions
- Templates

Most standard libraries include definitions for at least the following commonly used facilities:

- Algorithms (such as sorting algorithms)
- Data structures (such as lists, trees, and hash tables)
- Interaction with the host platform, including input/output and operating system calls

Examples of common programming language libraries that the security professional may interact with include:

- The C standard library, for the C programming language
- The C++ standard library, for the C++ programming language
- The Framework Class Library (FCL), for the .NET Framework
- The Java Class Library (JCL), for the Java programming language and Java Platform
- The Ruby standard library, for the Ruby programming language

A programming tool or software development tool is a program or application that software developers use to create, debug, maintain, or otherwise support other programs and applications.

Software tools come in many forms:

- Binary compatibility analysis tools
- Bug databases
- Build tools
- Code coverage
- Compilation and linking tools
- Debuggers
- Disassemblers

- Documentation generators
- GUI interface generators
- Library interface generators
- Integration tools
- Memory debuggers
- Parser generators
- Performance analysis or profiling tools
- Revision control tools
- Scripting languages
- Search tools
- Source code editors
- Source code generation tools
- Static code analysis tools
- Unit testing tools

Not all security professionals have the background and necessary skills to undertake software development and to use code libraries or software development and testing tools as described above. The focus of the security professional needs to be on awareness of the existence and availability of these items as they pertain to the security of the systems that the security professional is being asked to manage and maintain. The ability for the security professional to call on experts in this area as needed to help to better understand the impact of the use of one or more of these items in a production system is paramount to the success of the security professional and to his or her ability to build and maintain defense in depth architectures that seek to address the enterprise's strategic goals and objectives.

Integrated Development Environments (IDEs) & Runtime

Integrated development environments combine the features of many tools into one software program for use by the developer. Integrated development environments are designed to maximize programmer productivity by providing tight-knit components with similar user interfaces. IDEs present a single program in which all development is done. An IDE normally consists of a source code editor, build automation tools, and a debugger. Many modern IDEs also have a class browser, an object browser, and a class hierarchy diagram for use in object-oriented software development. Sometimes, versioning control is included to help computer programmers manage the development of a graphical user interface (GUI). An integrated development environment (IDE) for object-oriented programming (OOP) usually features a class browser, tools to produce class hierarchy diagrams, and an object inspector.

By using such a comprehensive toolset, coders can perform less mode-switching and access more system resources. Programmers can also compile code as it is written and review any syntax errors. Graphical IDEs with windowing features can enhance programmer productivity. Visual IDEs enable software developers to arrange building blocks and code nodes to produce structure diagrams and flowcharts. Often, these flowcharts are based on unified modeling language (UML), a standardized general-purpose platform for creating visual models called UML diagrams. Computer programmers who work with Fortran, Java or JavaScript, Pascal or Object Pascal, Perl, PHP, Python, Ruby, or Smalltalk may use an integrated development environment (IDE) for a specific language or use an IDE for multiple languages.

A runtime system exhibits the behavior of the constructs of a computer language. Every programming language has some form of a runtime system, whether the language is a compiled language, interpreted language, embedded domain-specific language, or is invoked via an API. In addition to the behavior of the language constructs, a runtime system may also perform support services such as type checking, debugging, or code generation and optimization. For instance, the Java Runtime Environment (JRE) is what you get when you download Java software. The JRE consists of the Java Virtual Machine (JVM), Java platform core classes, and supporting Java platform libraries. The JRE is the runtime portion of Java software, which is all you need to run it in your Web browser.

The runtime system is also the gateway by which a running program interacts with the runtime environment, which contains state values that are accessible during program execution, as well as active entities that can be interacted with during program execution. Environment variables are features of many operating systems and are part of the runtime environment; a running program can access them via the runtime system. Beginning with SQL Server 2005, SQL Server features the integration of the common language runtime (CLR) component of the .NET Framework for Microsoft Windows. This means that you can now write stored procedures, triggers, user-defined types, user-defined functions, user-defined aggregates, and streaming table-valued functions using any .NET Framework language, including Microsoft Visual Basic .NET and Microsoft Visual C#.

Security Issues in Source Code

There are many threats to software during design, development, and operation. Most of these fall into standard patterns; the most common ones are mentioned here. Note that the threats are not mutually exclusive and that many overlap to a greater or lesser extent. A given threat may belong to more than one category, and it is important to identify all relevant characteristics. This is particularly important with regards to malware.

Buffer Overflow

The buffer overflow problem is one of the oldest and most common problems in software development and programming, dating back to the introduction of interactive computing. It can result when a program fills up the assigned buffer of memory with more data than its buffer can hold. When the program begins to write beyond the end of the buffer, the program's execution path can be changed, or data can be written into areas used by the operating system itself. This can lead to the insertion of malicious code that can be used to gain administrative privileges on the program or system.

Buffer overflows can be created or exploited in a wide variety of ways, but the following is a general example of how a buffer overflow works. A program that is the target of an attack is provided with more data than the application was intended to handle. This can be done by diverse means such as entering too much text into a dialog box, submitting a Web address that is far too long, or creating a network packet much larger than is necessary. The attacked program (target) overruns the memory allocated for input data and writes the excess data into the system memory. The excess data can contain machine language instructions so that when the next step is executed, the attack code, like a Trojan horse or other type of malicious code, is run. (Frequently, the early part of the excess data contains characters that are read by the CPU as "perform no operation," forming a "no-op sled." The malicious code is usually at the end of the excess data.)

An actual attack method is far more detailed and is highly dependent on the target operating system and hardware architecture. The desired result is to put the attack instructions into memory. These instructions usually do something such as patch the kernel in such a way as to execute another program at an elevated privilege level. Sometimes the malicious code will call other programs or even download them over the network.

Citizen Programmers

Because desktop and personal computers (and even applications, now) come equipped with scripting and programming tools, allowing all computer users to create their own utilities is a common practice that can have extremely harmful consequences and may violate the principle of separation of duties. If this type of unsupervised programming is allowed, then a single user may have complete control over an application or process. While programmers traditionally have little or no training in security requirements, they will at least have basic understandings of issues of software quality, reliability, and interoperability. Casual users have no such training, and they may create applications with both security and reliability problems. Visual Basic, included in the Microsoft Office suite, is often used by citizen programmers to develop their applications or extend existing ones. Citizen, or casual, programmers are unlikely to be trained in, or bound by, system development practices that involve proper application design, change control, and support for the application. Therefore, application development in such a manner is likely to be chaotic and lack any form of assurance in regard to security. It should be addressed as a matter of policy, enforcement, awareness, and sanctions when needed.

Covert Channel

A covert channel or confinement problem is an information flow issue. It is a communication channel that allows two cooperating processes to transfer information in such a way that it violates the system's security policy. Even though there are protection mechanisms in place, if unauthorized information can be transferred using a signaling mechanism via entities or objects not normally considered to be able to communicate, then a covert channel may exist. In simplified terms, it is any flow of information, intentional or inadvertent, that enables an observer not authorized to have the information to infer what it is or that it exists. This is primarily a concern in systems containing highly sensitive information.

There are two commonly defined types of covert channels: storage and timing. A covert storage channel involves the direct or indirect reading of a storage location by one process and a direct or indirect reading of the same storage location by another process. Typically, a covert storage channel involves a finite resource, such as a memory location or sector on a disk that is shared by two subjects at different security levels.

A covert timing channel depends upon being able to influence the rate that some other process is able to acquire resources, such as the CPU, memory, or I/O devices. The variation in rate may be used to pass signals. Essentially, the process signals information to another by modulating its own use of system resources in such a way that this manipulation affects the real response time observed by the second process. Timing channels are normally considerably less efficient than storage channels because they have a reduced bandwidth, but they are usually harder to detect and control.

These examples relate only to a situation in which an insider is attempting to provide information to an outsider and is very restricted in application. In order to have a complete view of covert channels, one should envisage a broader concept that includes, for example, unintentional covert channels that enable an un-cleared or unauthorized person to observe a system activity that enables the inference of facts of which that person should not be aware.

Malicious Software (Malware)

Malware comes in many varieties and is written for different operating systems and applications, as well as for different machines. Malware also uses a variety of attacks when attempting to compromise a system or exfiltrate sensitive information.

Malformed Input Attacks

A number of attacks employing input from the user are currently known, and various systems detect and protect against such attacks. Therefore, a number of new attacks rely on configuring that input in unusual ways. For example, an attack that redirected a Web browser to an alternate site might be caught by a firewall through the detection of the Uniform Resource Locator (URL) of an inappropriate site. If, however, the URL was expressed in a Unicode format, rather than ASCII, the firewall would likely fail to recognize the content, whereas the Web browser would convert the information without difficulty. In another case, many websites allow query access to databases, but they place filters on the requests to control access. When requests using the Structure Query Language (SQL) are allowed, the use of certain syntactical structures in the query can fool the filters into seeing the query as a comment, whereupon the query may be submitted to the database engine and retrieve more information than the owners intended. In another instance, a site that allows users to input information for later retrieval by other users, such as a blog, may fail to detect when such input comes in the form of active scripting. This is the basis of cross-site scripting attacks. (Buffer overflows are also a form of malformed input.)

Memory Reuse (Object Reuse)

Memory management involves sections of memory allocated to one process for a while, then de-allocated, then reallocated to another process. Because residual information may remain when a section of memory is reassigned to a new process after a previous process is finished with it, a security violation may occur. When memory is reallocated, the operating system should ensure that memory is zeroed out completely or overwritten completely before it can be accessed by a new process. Thus, there is no residual information in memory carrying over from one process to another. While memory locations are of primary concern in this regard, developers should also be careful with the reuse of other resources that can contain information, such as disk space. The paging or swap file on the disk is frequently left unprotected and may contain an enormous amount of sensitive information if care is not taken to prevent this occurrence. (Note that memory or object reuse may be a form of covert channel, as discussed earlier.)

Executable Content/Mobile Code

Executable content, or mobile code, is software that is transmitted across a network from a remote source to a local system and is then executed on that local system. The code is transferred by user actions and, in some cases, without the explicit action of the user. The code can arrive to the local system as attachments to email messages or through webpages.

Mobile code has been called by many names: mobile agents, mobile code, downloadable code, executable content, active capsules, remote code, etc. Even though the terms seem the same, there are slight differences. For example, mobile agents are programs that can migrate from host to host in a network, at times and to places of their own choosing. They have a high degree of autonomy rather than being directly controlled from a central point. Mobile agents differ from applets, which are programs downloaded as the result of a user action, then executed from beginning to end on one host. Examples include ActiveX controls, Java applets, and scripts run within the browser. All of these deal with the local execution of remotely sourced code.

One way of looking at mobile code is in terms of current security architectures. Typically, security in the operating system could answer the question "Can subject X use object Y?" The challenge with mobile code is how to resolve when one subject may be acting on behalf of another or may be acting on its own behalf. Thus, security mechanisms must be put into place that resolve whether these requests should be allowed or denied. Many of the issues of mobile code are tightly connected to problems of malware.

Social Engineering

One method of compromising a system is to befriend users to gain information; individuals with system administrator access are especially vulnerable. Social engineering is the art of getting people to divulge sensitive information to others either in a friendly manner, as an attempt to be "helpful," or through intimidation. It is sometimes referred to as people hacking because it relies on vulnerabilities in people rather than those found in software or hardware. While social engineering has many proper uses in management and training, in regard to information security, social engineering is really only a fancy name for lying.

Social engineering comes in many forms, but they are all based on the principle of representing oneself as someone who needs or deserves the information to gain access to the system. For example, one method is for attackers to pretend they are new to the system and need assistance with gaining access. Another method is when attackers pretend to be a system staff member and try to gain information by helping to fix a computer problem, even though there is not a problem. Typically, therefore, social engineering is not considered to be a concern of software development and management. However, there are two major areas where social engineering should be considered in system development and management.

- The first is in regard to the user interface and human factors. It has frequently, and sadly, been the case where users have misunderstood the intent of the programmer with regard to the operation of certain commands or buttons, and sometimes the misunderstanding has had fatal results. (In one famous case, a correction to dosage levels on the input screen of a medical radiation treatment machine did not change the radiation-level settings, and dozens of patients suffered fatal overdoses before the problem was found and rectified.)
- The second is in regard to its use in malicious software. Most malware will have some kind of fraudulent component, in an attempt to get the user to run the program so that the malicious payload can perform undetected.

Time of Check/Time of Use (TOC/TOU)

This is a common type of attack that occurs when some control changes between the time the system security functions check the contents of variables and the time the variables actually are used during operations. For instance, a user logs on to a system in the morning and later is fired. As a result of the termination, the security administrator removes the user from the user database. Because the user did not log off, he still has access to the system and might try to get even.

In another situation, a connection between two machines may drop. If an attacker manages to attach to one of the ports used for this link before the failure is detected, the invader can hijack the session by pretending to be the trusted machine. (A way to prevent this is to have some form of authentication performed constantly on the line.)

Between-the-Lines Attack

Another similar attack is a between-the-lines entry. This occurs when the telecommunication lines used by an authorized user are tapped into and data is falsely inserted. To avoid this, the telecommunication lines should be physically secured, and users should not leave telecommunication lines open when they are not being used.

Trapdoor/Backdoor

A trapdoor or backdoor is a hidden mechanism that bypasses access control measures. It is an entry point into a program that is inserted in software by programmers during the program's development to provide a method of gaining access into the program for modification if the access control mechanism malfunctions and locks them out. (In this situation, it may also be called a maintenance hook.) They can be useful for error correction, but they are dangerous opportunities for unauthorized access if left in a production system. A programmer or someone who knows about the backdoor can exploit the trapdoor as a covert means of access after the program has been implemented in the system. An unauthorized user may also discover the entry point while trying to penetrate the system.

This list of software threats is to be used as a reminder of the types of threats that developers and managers of software development should be aware. It is not intended to be an inclusive list, as there are new threats developed every day.

Source Code Analysis Tools

Source code analysis tools are designed to analyze source code and/or compiled versions of code in order to help find security flaws. Ideally, such tools would automatically find security flaws with such a high degree of confidence that what's found is indeed a flaw. However, this is beyond the state of the art for many types of application security flaws. Thus, such tools frequently serve as aids for analysts to help them zero in on security relevant portions of code so they can find flaws more efficiently.

The software development phase is one of the best phases within the development life cycle to employ such tools, as they can provide immediate feedback to the developer on issues they might be introducing into the code during code development itself. This immediate feedback is very useful, especially when compared to finding vulnerabilities much later in the development cycle. The security professional needs to work closely with the developer to ensure that testing is done throughout the SDLC as appropriate, and that the results of the testing are documented and acted upon as necessary to ensure that all vulnerabilities identified are addressed prior to the release of the software.

Strengths of Source Code Analysis Tools:

■ **Scale well** – can be run on lots of software and can be run repeatedly (as with nightly builds).

- Useful for things that such tools can automatically find with high confidence, such as buffer overflows, SQL Injection Flaws, etc.
- **Output is good for developers** – highlights the precise source files and line numbers that are affected.

Weaknesses of Source Code Analysis Tools:

- Many types of security vulnerabilities are very difficult to find automatically, such as authentication problems, access control issues, insecure use of cryptography, etc. The current state of the art only allows such tools to automatically find a relatively small percentage of application security flaws. Tools of this type are getting better, however.
- High numbers of false positives.
- Frequently cannot find configuration issues because they are not represented in the code.
- Difficult to prove that an identified security issue is an actual vulnerability.
- Many of these tools have difficulty analyzing code that cannot be compiled. Analysts frequently cannot compile code because they do not have the right libraries, all the compilation instructions, all the code, etc.

Open Source or Free Tools of This Type:

- **Google CodeSearchDiggity** – Utilizes Google Code Search to identify vulnerabilities in open source code projects hosted by Google Code, MS CodePlex, SourceForge, Github, and more. The tool comes with over 130 default searches that identify SQL injection, cross-site scripting (XSS), insecure remote and local file includes, hard-coded passwords, and much more. Essentially, Google CodeSearchDiggity provides a source code security analysis of nearly every single open source code project in existence – simultaneously.
- **FindBugs** – Find bugs (including some security flaws) in Java Programs.
- **FxCop (Microsoft)** – FxCop is an application that analyzes managed code assemblies (code that targets the .NET Framework common language runtime) and reports information about the assemblies, such as possible design, localization, performance, and security improvements.
- **PMD** – PMD scans Java source code and looks for potential code problems (this is a code quality tool that does not focus on security issues).
- **PreFast (Microsoft)** – PREfast is a static analysis tool that identifies defects in C/C++ programs.
- **RATS (Fortify)** – Scans C, C++, Perl, PHP, and Python source code for security problems like buffer overflows and TOCTOU (Time of Check, Time of Use) race conditions.
- **OWASP SWAAT Project** – Languages: Java, JSP, ASP .Net, and PHP
- **Flawfinder** – Scans C and C++
- **RIPS** – RIPS is a static source code analyzer for vulnerabilities in PHP Web applications.
- **Brakeman** – Brakeman is an open source vulnerability scanner specifically designed for Ruby on Rails applications.
- **Codesake Dawn** – Codesake Dawn is an open source security source code analyzer designed for Sinatra, Padrino, and Ruby on Rails applications. It can work also for non-Web applications written in Ruby programming language.

8

Security in the Software Development Life Cycle

1009

- **VCG** – Scans C/C++, Java, C# and PL/SQL for security issues and for comments that may indicate defective code. The config files can be used to carry out additional checks for banned functions or functions that commonly cause security issues.

Commercial tools of this type:
- IBM Security AppScan Source Edition (formerly Ounce)
- Insight (KlocWork)
- Parasoft Test
- Seeker: Seeker performs code security without actually doing static analysis. Seeker does Interactive Application Security Testing (IAST), correlating runtime code and data analysis with simulated attacks. It provides code level results without actually relying on static analysis.
- Source Patrol (Pentest)
- Static Source Code Analysis with CodeSecure (Armorize Technologies)
- Static Code Analysis (Checkmarx)
- Security Advisor (Coverity)
- Veracode

Malicious Software (Malware)

Malware is a term created to address the need to discuss software or programs that are intentionally designed to include functions for penetrating a system, breaking security policies, or carrying malicious or damaging payloads. Because this type of software has started to develop a bewildering variety of forms – such as backdoors, data diddlers, DDoS, hoax warnings, logic bombs, pranks, RATs, Trojans, viruses, worms, zombies, etc. – the term *malware* has come to be used for the collective class of malicious software. However, the term is often used very loosely simply as a synonym for virus in the same way that virus is often used simply as a description of any type of computer problem.

Viruses are the largest class of malware, in terms of both numbers of known entities and impact in the current computing environment. Viruses will therefore be given primary emphasis in this discussion, but they will not be the only malware type examined.

Programming bugs or errors are generally not included in the definition of malware, although it is sometimes difficult to make a hard and fast distinction between malware and bugs. For example, if a programmer left a buffer overflow in a system and it creates a loophole that can be used as a backdoor or a maintenance hook, did he do it deliberately? The answer to this question is not easily discerned, and the security professional would have to guess as to the intentions of the programmer, without necessarily knowing for sure what the intent of the programmer truly was.

In addition, it should be noted that malware is not just a collection of utilities for the attacker. Once launched, malware can continue an attack without reference to the author or user and in some cases will expand the attack to other systems. There is a qualitative difference between malware and the attack tools, kits, or scripts that have to operate under an attacker's control, and which are not considered to fall within the definition of malware. There are gray areas here as well because RATs and DDoS zombies provide unattended access to systems, but they need to be commanded to deliver a payload.

Malware can attack and destroy system integrity in a number of ways. Viruses are often defined in terms of their ability to attach to programs (or to objects considered to be programmable) and so must, in some way, compromise the integrity of applications. Many viruses or other forms of malware contain payloads (such as data diddlers) that may either erase data files or interfere with application data over time in such a way that data integrity is compromised and data may become completely useless.

When considering malware, one should be aware of an additional type of attack on integrity. As with attacks where the intruder takes control of your system and uses it to explore or assail further systems, to hide his own identity, malware (viruses and DDoS zombies in particular) are designed to use your system as a platform to continue further assaults, even without the intervention of the original author or attacker. This can create problems within domains and intranets where equivalent systems "trust" each other, and it can also create "badwill" when organizations doing business with each other find out one is sending viruses to the other.

As noted, malware can compromise programs and data to the point where they are no longer available. In addition, malware generally uses the resources of the system it has attacked and can, in extreme cases, exhaust CPU cycles, available processes (process numbers, tables, etc.), memory, communications links and bandwidth, open ports, disk space, mail queues, and so forth. Sometimes this can be a direct DoS attack, and sometimes it is a side effect of the activity of the malware. Malware such as backdoors and RATs are intended to make intrusion and penetration easier. Viruses such as Goner, Klez, and SirCam send data files from your system to others (in these particular cases, seemingly as a side effect of the process of reproduction and spread). Malware can be written to do directed searches and send confidential data to specific parties and can also be used to open covert channels of other types.

The fact that you are infected with viruses, or compromised by other types of malware, can become quite evident to others. This compromises confidentiality by providing indirect evidence of your level of security, and it may also create public relations problems. It has long been known that the number of variants of viruses or other forms of malware is directly connected to the number of instances of a given platform. The success of a given piece of malware is also related to the relative proportion of a given platform in the overall computing environment.

The modern computing environment is one of consistency. The Intel platform has achieved dominance in hardware, and Microsoft has a near monopoly on the desktop. In addition, compatible application software (and the addition of functional programming capabilities in those applications) can mean that malware from one hardware and operating system environment can work perfectly well in another. The functionality added to application macro and script languages has given them the capability to either directly address computer hardware and resources or easily call upon utilities or processes that have such access. This means that objects previously considered to be data, and therefore immune to malicious programming, must now be checked for malicious functions or payloads.

In addition, these languages are very simple to learn and use, and the various instances of malware carry their own source codes, in plaintext and sometimes commented, making it simple for individuals wanting to learn how to craft an attack to gather templates and examples of how to do so, without even knowing how the technology actually works. This expands the range of authors of such software enormously.

8

Security in the Software Development Life Cycle

Malware Types

Viruses are not the only form of malicious software. Other forms include worms, Trojans, zombies, logic bombs, and hoaxes. Each of these has its own characteristics. Some forms of malware combine characteristics of more than one class, and it can be difficult to draw hard and fast distinctions with regard to individual examples or entities, but it can be important to keep the specific attributes in mind. Viruses and Trojans are being used to spread and plant Remote Access Trojans (RATs), and RATs are being used to install zombies. In some cases, hoax virus warnings are being used to spread viruses. Virus and Trojan payloads may contain logic bombs and data diddlers.

Viruses

A computer virus is a program written with functions and intent to copy and disperse itself without the knowledge and cooperation of the owner or user of the computer. A final definition has not yet been agreed upon by all researchers. A common definition is "a program that modifies other programs to contain a possibly altered version of itself." This definition is generally attributed to Fred Cohen from his seminal research in the mid-1980s, although Dr. Cohen's actual definition is in mathematical form. The term *computer virus* was first defined by Dr. Cohen in his graduate thesis in 1984.[23] Cohen credits a suggestion from his advisor, Leonard Adleman (of RSA fame), for the use of the term.

Cohen's definition is specific to programs that attach themselves to other programs as their vector of infection. However, common usage now holds viruses to consist of a set of coded instructions that are designed to attach to an object capable of containing the material, without knowledgeable user intervention. This object may be an email message, program file, document, thumb drive, CD-ROM, short message system (SMS) message on cellular telephones, or any similar information medium.

A virus is defined by its ability to reproduce and spread but to do so with the aid of the user in some form. Just as a cold or flu spreads after one person gets sick and interacts with others, leaving behind the virus, the computer virus spreads after a sick person helps by exposing uninfected people to it.

A worm, which is sometimes seen as a specialized type of virus, is currently distinguished from a virus because a virus generally requires an action on the part of the user to trigger or aid reproduction and spread, while a worm spreads on its own. The action on the part of the user is generally a common function, and the user generally does not realize the danger of the action or the fact that he or she is assisting the virus. The only requirement that defines a program as a virus is that it reproduces. There is no necessity that the virus carries a payload, although a number of viruses do. In many cases (in most cases of successful viruses), the payload is limited to some kind of message.

A deliberately damaging payload, such as erasure of the disk or system files, usually restricts the ability of the virus to spread because the virus uses the resources of the host system. In some cases, a virus may carry a logic bomb or time bomb that triggers a damaging payload on a certain date or under a specific, often delayed, condition.

---

23 See the following: http://all.net/books/Dissertation.pdf

Types of Viruses

There are a number of functionally different types of viruses, such as a file infector, boot sector infector (BSI), system infector, email virus, multipartite, macro virus, and script virus. These terms do not necessarily indicate a strict division. A file infector may also be a system infector. A script virus that infects other script files may be considered a file infector, although this type of activity, while theoretically possible, is unusual in practice. There are also difficulties in drawing a hard distinction between macro and script viruses.

- **File Infectors** – A file infector infects program (object) files. System infectors that infect operating system program files (such as COMMAND.COM in DOS) are also file infectors. File infectors can attach to the front of the object file (prependers), attach to the back of the file and create a jump at the front of the file to the virus code (appenders), or overwrite the file or portions of it (overwriters). A classic example of this type of behavior is the file infector Jerusalem. A bug in early versions caused it to add itself over and over again to files, making the increase in file length detectable. (This has given rise to the persistent myth that it is characteristic of a virus to eventually fill up all disk space: by far, the majority of file infectors add minimally to file lengths.)

- **Boot Sector Infectors** – Boot sector infectors (BSIs) attach to or replace the master boot record, system boot record, or other boot records and blocks on physical disks. (The structure of these blocks varies, but the first physical sector on a disk generally has some special significance in most operating systems and usually is read and executed at some point in the boot process.) BSIs usually copy the existing boot sector to another unused sector and then copy themselves into the physical first sector, ending with a call to the original programming. Examples are Brain, Stoned, and Michelangelo.

- **System Infectors** – System infector is a somewhat vague term. The phrase is often used to indicate viruses that infect operating system files, or boot sectors, in such a way that the virus is called at boot time and has or may have preemptive control over some functions of the operating system. (The Lehigh virus infected only COMMAND.COM on MS-DOS machines; recent viruses in the Windows environment sometimes preferentially infect utility files in the system directory.) In other usage, a system infector modifies other system structures, such as the linking pointers in directory tables or the MS Windows system registry, in order to be called first when programs are invoked on the host computer. An example of directory table linking is the DIR virus family. Many email viruses target the registry. MTX and Magistr can be very difficult to eradicate.

- **Companion Virus** – Some viral programs do not physically touch the target file at all. One method is quite simple and may take advantage of precedence in the system. In MS-DOS, for example, when a command is given, the system checks first for internal commands, then .COM, .EXE, and .BAT files, in that order. .EXE files can be infected by writing a .COM file in the same directory with the same filename. This type of virus is most commonly known as a companion virus, although the term spawning virus is also used.

- **Email Virus** – An email virus specifically, rather than accidentally, uses the email system to spread. Although virus-infected files may be accidentally sent as email attachments, email viruses are aware of email system functions. They generally target a specific type of email system, harvest email addresses from various sources, and may append copies of themselves to all email sent, or may generate email messages containing copies of themselves as attachments. Some email viruses may monitor all network traffic and follow up legitimate messages with messages that they generate. Most email viruses are technically considered to be worms because they often do not infect other program files on the target computer, but this is not a hard and fast distinction. There are known examples of email viruses that are file infectors, macro viruses, script viruses, and worms. Melissa, Loveletter, Hybris, and SirCam are all examples of the same type of activity.

Email viruses have made something of a change to the epidemiology of viruses. Traditionally, viruses took many months to spread, but they stayed around for many years in the computing environment. Many email viruses have become "fast burners" that can spread around the world, infecting hundreds of thousands or even millions of machines within hours. However, once characteristic indicators of these viruses become known, they die off almost immediately as users stop running the attachments.

- **Multipartite** – The term multipartite was originally used to indicate a virus that was able to infect both boot sectors and program files. (This ability is the origin of the alternate term dual infector.) Current usage tends to mean a virus that can infect more than one type of object or that infects or reproduces in more than one way. Examples of traditional multipartites are Telefonica, One Half, and Junkie, but these programs have not been very successful. In contrast, Nimda was quite successful, spreading as a classic worm, a file infector, using network shares and other means.

- **Macro Virus** – A macro virus uses macro programming of an application such as a word processor. (Most known macro viruses use Visual Basic for Applications in Microsoft Word; some are able to cross between applications and function in, for example, a PowerPoint presentation and a Word document, but this ability is rare.) Macro viruses infect data files and tend to remain resident in the application itself by infecting a configuration template such as MS Word's NORMAL.DOT. Although macro viruses infect data files, they are not generally considered file infectors; a distinction is made between program and data files. Macro viruses can operate across hardware or operating system platforms as long as the required application platform is present. (For example, many MS Word macro viruses can operate on both the Windows and Macintosh versions of MS Word.) Examples are Concept and CAP. Melissa is also a macro virus, in addition to being an email virus: It mailed itself to potential victims as an infected document.

- **Script Virus** – Script viruses are generally differentiated from macro viruses in that they are usually stand-alone files that can be executed by an interpreter, such as Microsoft's Windows.

- **Script Host (.vbs files)** – A script virus file can be seen as a data file in that it is generally a simple text file, but it usually does not contain other data and often has some indicator (such as the.vbs extension) that it is executable. Loveletter is an example of a script virus found on the Microsoft platform. Another example would be the ALS.Bursted.C virus, which is written in AutoLisp, a scripting language used by AutoCAD.

Worms

A worm reproduces and spreads like a virus and unlike other forms of malware. Worms are distinct from viruses, though they may have similar results. Most simply, a worm may be thought of as a virus with the capacity to propagate independent of user action. In other words, they do not rely on (usually) human-initiated transfer of data between systems for propagation, but instead they spread across networks of their own accord, primarily by exploiting known vulnerabilities in common software. The lack of requirement for user involvement means that worms have a significant speed advantage when spreading. Even fast burner viruses have required times measured in days to spread around the world, where worms can travel worldwide in hours or even minutes.

Originally, the distinction was made that worms used networks and communications links to spread and that a worm, unlike a virus, did not directly attach to an executable file. In early research into computer viruses, the terms *worm* and *virus* tended to be used synonymously, it being felt that the technical distinction was unimportant to most users. The first worm to garner significant attention was the Morris Internet Worm of 1988. Recently, many of the most prolific virus infections have not been strictly viruses but have used a combination of viral and worm techniques to spread more rapidly and effectively. LoveLetter was an example of this convergence of reproductive technologies. Although infected email attachments were perhaps the most widely publicized vector of infection, LoveLetter also spread by actively scanning attached network drives, infecting a variety of common file types. This convergence of technologies will be an increasing problem in the future. Code Red and a number of Linux programs (such as Lion) are modern examples of worms. (Nimda is an example of a worm, but it also spreads in a number of other ways, so it could be considered to be an email virus and multipartite as well.)

Hoaxes

Hoaxes are usually warnings about new viruses: new viruses that do not, of course, exist. Hoaxes generally carry a directive to the user to forward the warning to all addresses available to him. Thus, these descendants of chain letters form a kind of self-perpetuating spam. Hoaxes use an odd kind of social engineering, relying on people's desire to communicate and on a sense of urgency and importance, using the ambition that people have to be the first to provide important new information.

It is wisest, in the current environment, to doubt all virus warnings, unless they come from a known and historically accurate source, such as a vendor with a proven record of providing reliable and accurate virus alert information or preferably an independent researcher or group. It is best to check any warnings received against known virus encyclopedia sites and to check more than one such site. In the initial phases of a fast burner attack, some sites may not have had time to analyze samples to their own satisfaction, and the better sites will not post information they are not sure about.

An older example of a hoax, referring to SULFNBK.EXE, got a number of people to clear this legitimate utility off their machines. The origin was likely the fact that the Magistr virus targets Windows system software, and someone with an infection did not realize that the file is actually present on all Windows 98 systems. Thus, a new class of malicious hoax message has started to appear, attempting to make users actually cripple their own machines.

Trojans

Trojans, or Trojan horse programs, are the largest class of malware, aside from viruses. However, use of the term is subject to much confusion, particularly in relation to computer viruses.

A Trojan is a program that pretends to do one thing while performing another unwanted action. The extent of the pretense may vary greatly. Many of the early PC Trojans merely used the filename and a description on a bulletin board. Log-in Trojans, popular among university student mainframe users, mimicked the screen display and the prompts of the normal log-in program and could in fact pass the username and password along to the valid log-in program at the same time as they stole the user data. Some Trojans may contain actual code that does what it is supposed to while performing additional acts not clearly documented or defined.

Some data security writers consider a virus to simply be a specific example of the class of Trojan horse programs. There is some validity to this usage because a virus is an unknown quantity that is hidden and transmitted along with a legitimate disk or program, and any program can be turned into a Trojan by infecting it with a virus. However, the term *virus* more properly refers to the added, infectious code rather than the virus/target combination. Therefore, the term *Trojan* refers to a deliberately misleading or modified program that does not reproduce itself.

An additional confusion with viruses involves Trojan horse programs that may be spread by email. In years past, a Trojan program had to be posted on an electronic bulletin board system or a file archive site. Because of the static posting, a malicious program would soon be identified and eliminated. More recently, Trojan programs have been distributed by mass email campaigns, by posting on Usenet newsgroup discussion groups, through downloads on infected websites, or through automated distribution agents (bots) on Internet Relay Chat (IRC) channels. Because source identification in these communications channels can be easily hidden, Trojan programs can be redistributed through a number of channels, and specific identification of a malicious program has become much more difficult as a result.

Social Engineering

A major aspect of Trojan design is the social engineering component. A recent email virus, in generating its messages, carried a list of a huge variety of subject lines, promising pornography, humor, virus information, an antivirus program, and information about abuse of the recipient's email account. Sometimes the message is simply vague and relies on curiosity. It is instructive to examine some classic social engineering techniques. Formalizing the problem makes it easier to move on to working toward effective solutions, making use of realistic, pragmatic policies. Effective implementation of such policies, however good they are, is not possible without a considered user education program and cooperation from management.

Social engineering can range from simple lying (such as a false description of the function of a file), to bullying and intimidation (to pressure a low-level employee into disclosing information), to association with a trusted source (such as the username from an infected machine), to dumpster diving (to find potentially valuable information people have carelessly discarded), to shoulder surfing (to find out personal identification numbers and passwords).

A recent entry to the list of malicious attacks aimed at computer users is the practice of phishing. Phishing attempts to get the user to provide information that will be useful for identity theft-type frauds. Although phishing messages frequently use websites and try to confuse the origin and ownership of those sites, very little programming, malicious or otherwise, may be involved. Phishing is unadulterated social engineering or deception. However, some recent phishing attacks have incorporated technical aspects, such as the creation of unframed browser windows in order to overlay areas in the browser frame and recreate "browser chrome," such as the padlock symbol denoting a site certificate and authentication/encryption via the SSL protocol.[24]

Remote-Access Trojans (RATs)

Remote-access Trojans are programs designed to be installed, usually remotely, after systems are in production and not in development, as is the case with logic bombs and backdoors. Their authors would generally like to have the programs referred to as remote administration tools to convey a sense of legitimacy. All networking software can, in a sense, be considered remote-access tools: file transfer sites and clients, World Wide Web servers and browsers, and terminal emulation software that allows a microcomputer user to log on to a distant computer and use it as if he were on-site. The RATs considered to be in the malware camp tend to fall somewhere in the middle of the spectrum. Once a client, such as W32.Shadesrat, FAKEM, BlackShades, Back Orifice, Netbus, Bionet, or SubSeven, is installed on the target computer, the controlling computer is able to obtain information about the target computer. The master computer will be able to download files from and upload files to the target. The control computer will also be able to submit commands to the victim, which basically allows the distant operator to do pretty much anything to the prey. One other function is quite important: all of this activity goes on without any alert being given to the owner or operator of the targeted computer.

When a RAT program has been run on a computer, it will install itself in such a way as to be active every time the computer is started subsequent to the installation. Information is sent back to the controlling computer (sometimes via an anonymous channel such as IRC) noting that the system is active. The user of the command computer is now able to explore the target, escalate access to other resources, and install other software, such as DDoS zombies, if so desired.

Once more, it should be noted that remote-access tools are not viral. When the software is active, the master computer can submit commands to have the installation program sent on, via network transfer or email, to other machines. In addition, RATs can be installed as a payload from a virus or Trojan. Many RATs now operate in very specialized ways, making the affected computer part of a botnet (robot network). Botnets use large numbers of computers to perform functions such as distributing spam messages, increasing the number of messages that can be sent, and isolating the actual sender from the targets of the messages. Recently, it has been demonstrated that certain viruses have carried RAT programming payloads to set up spam botnets and that such spam botnets have also been used to seed the release of new viruses. Rootkits, containing software that can subvert or replace normal operating system software, have been around for some time. RATs differ from rootkits in that a working account must be either subverted or created on the target computer to use a rootkit. RATs, once installed by a virus or Trojan, do not require access to an account.

---

24   See the following: http://www.pcmag.com/encyclopedia/term/38972/browser-chrome

DDoS Zombies

DDoS (distributed denial of service) is a modified DoS attack. DoS attacks do not attempt to destroy or corrupt data, but they attempt to use up a computing resource to the point where normal work cannot proceed. The structure of a DDoS attack requires a master computer to control the attack, a target of the attack, and a number of computers in the middle that the master computer uses to generate the attack. These computers in between the master and the target are variously called agents or clients, but they are usually referred to as running zombie programs. As you can see, DDoS is a specialized type of RAT or botnet.

Again, note that DDoS programs are not viral, but checking for zombie software not only protects your system but also prevents attacks on others. However, it is still in your best interest to ensure that no zombie programs are active. If your computers are used to launch an assault on some other system, you could be liable for damages. The efficacy of this platform was demonstrated in early 2000, when a couple of teenagers successfully paralyzed various prominent online players in quick succession, including Yahoo, Amazon, and eBay. It is also important for the security professional to be aware of the DDoS tactic that is often used as a "bait and switch" to distract and confuse the security apparatus of an enterprise into focusing their attentions on the DDoS attack, when in fact the DDoS attack is simply a ruse being used by the bad actors to draw attention away from their real attacks taking place elsewhere in the network. DDoS is generally considered to be the first instance of the botnet concept to work in an effective manner.

Logic Bombs

Logic bombs are software modules set up to run in a dormant state and to monitor a specific condition or set of conditions and to activate their payload under those conditions. A logic bomb is generally implanted in or coded as part of an application under development or maintenance. Unlike a RAT or Trojan, it is difficult to implant a logic bomb after the fact. There are numerous examples of this type of activity, usually based upon actions taken by a programmer to deprive a company of needed resources if employment was terminated. A Trojan or a virus may contain a logic bomb as part of the payload. A logic bomb involves no reproduction and no social engineering.

A variant on the concept of logic bombs involves what is known as the salami scam. The basic idea involves the siphoning off of small amounts of money (in some versions, fractions of a cent) credited to a specific account, over a large number of transactions. In most discussions of this type of activity, it is explained as the action of an individual, or small group, defrauding a corporation. However, a search of the RISKS-FORUM archives, for example, will find only one story about a fast food clerk who diddled the display on a drive-through window and collected an extra dime or quarter from most customers. Other examples of the scheme are cited, but it is instructive to note that these narratives, in opposition to the classic salami scam anecdote, almost always are examples of fraudulent corporate activity, typically collecting improper amounts from customers.

Spyware and Adware

It is extremely difficult to define which spyware and adware entities are malicious and which are legitimate marketing tools. Originally, many of the programs now known as spyware were intended to support the development of certain programs by providing advertising or marketing services. These were generally included with shareware, but they were installed as a separate function or program that generated advertising screens or reported on user activities, such as other installed programs and user Web-surfing activities. Over time, a number of these programs became more and more intrusive, and frequently now have functions that will install without the user's knowledge and in the absence of any other utility being obtained.

Companies involved with spyware and adware have been quite active in promoting the confusion of definitions and terms. Vendors and developers of anti-spyware programs have frequently found themselves targets of lawsuits alleging that the identification of programs as spyware is defamation.

Pranks

Pranks are very much a part of the computer culture, so much so that anyone can now buy commercially produced joke packages that allow you to perform "stupid Mac (or PC or Windows) tricks." There are numerous pranks available as shareware. Some make the computer appear to insult the user; some use sound effects or voices; some use special visual effects. A fairly common thread running through most pranks is that the computer is, in some way, nonfunctional. Many pretend to have detected some kind of fault in the computer (and some pretend to rectify such faults, of course making things worse). One entry in the virus field is PARASCAN, the paranoid scanner. It pretends to find large numbers of infected files, although it does not actually check for any infections.

Generally speaking, pranks that create some kind of announcement are not malware; viruses that generate a screen or audio display are actually quite rare. The distinction between jokes and Trojans is harder to make, but pranks are intended for amusement. Joke programs may, of course, result in a DoS if people find the prank message frightening. One specific type of joke is the Easter egg, a function hidden in a program and generally accessible only by some arcane sequence of commands. These may be seen as harmless, but note that they do consume resources, even if only disk space, and also make the task of ensuring program integrity much more difficult. Repeated pranks may also serve to dissuade the end-user from seeking help from the helpdesk when legitimately needed for a security reason.

Botnets

A botnet is a network of automated systems or processes (robots or bots) performing a specific function. A botnet is also dedicated to some form of malicious activity. Botnets have greatly magnified the power and speed of malicious operations and have allowed for tuning and directing of operations in a way that was not possible with viral programs alone. The distributed nature of botnets, and related technologies such as fast-flux domain and IP (Internet Protocol) address reassignment (rapidly rotating domain names and IP addresses), has made it much more difficult to detect, analyze, and remove botnets and botnet activity.

Bot agent software can be installed on user machines in any number of ways. Trojan horse programs may be mailed, and the user may be incited, or socially engineered, to infect his or her own machine. This may or may not be associated with a virus carrier. Worms may examine machines for server software with specific vulnerabilities. Drive-by downloads, peer-to-peer file sharing software, and instant messaging clients all have functions that may allow remote submission of files and invocation of commands or programs. Once any of these methods can be made to work, any further desired software may be placed on the user machine and set in operation. Generally speaking, once botnet software has been installed on the infected machine, it no longer requires personal intervention by the bot herder, but it will respond to automated communications through the command and control channel directed at a number of computers in the botnet. This includes promotion into, and demotion out of, the control channel itself.

In the earliest days of botnets, IRC was the command and control channel of choice. IRC provided a one-to-many communications channel that did not require either that the attacker contact each machine individually or that the infected computers regularly establish a connection with a central location, such as a Web server, for instructions. IRC also provided a measure of anonymity for the attacker or bot herder. A system of codes or passwords could be used to ensure that the bot herder retained control of the botnet without losing it to someone else.

IRC is far from the only control channel that can be used. Peer-to-peer (P2P) networking and file transfer systems have the same decentralization and anonymization functions that made IRC so suitable, as well as built-in functions that can be used for updating and access to new systems. Instant messaging (IM) is another highly functional means that can be used for malicious control, generally with means to evade normal firewall restrictions. Even basic Internet management protocols, such as the Domain Name System (DNS), can be used to pass information in a distributed and generally anonymous manner.

Malware Protection

In almost any recent work on security, there will be a list of signs to watch for to determine if a system has been infected by a virus. Unfortunately, all such catalogs seem to have extremely limited utility. The characteristics mentioned tend to refer to older malware instances, and they may also relate to a number of conditions that do not involve any malicious programming.

Training and explicit policies can greatly reduce the danger to users. Some guidelines that can really help in the current environment are:

- Do not double-click on attachments.
- When sending attachments, provide a clear and specific description as to the content of the attachment.
- Do not blindly use the most widely used products as a company standard.
- Disable Windows Script Host, ActiveX, VBScript, and JavaScript. Do not send HTML-formatted email.
- Use more than one scanner, and scan everything.

Whether these guidelines are acceptable in a specific environment is a business decision based upon the level of acceptable risk. But remember, whether risks are evaluated and whether policies are explicitly developed, every environment has a set of policies (some are explicit, while some are implicit) and every business accepts risk. The distinction is that some companies are aware of the risks that they choose to accept.

All antivirus software is essentially reactive: That is, it exists only because viruses and other programmed threats existed first. It is common to distinguish between virus-specific scanning or known virus scanning (KVS) on the one hand and generic measures on the other. The technological aspects of antivirus software can be described in terms of three main approaches.

Protective tools in the malware area are generally limited to antivirus software. To this day there are three major types, first discussed by Fred Cohen in his research: known signature scanning, activity monitoring, and change detection. These basic types of detection systems can be compared with the common intrusion detection system (IDS) types, although the correspondence is not exact. A scanner is like a signature-based IDS. An activity monitor is like a rule-based IDS or an anomaly-based IDS. A change detection system is like a statistical-based IDS.

Scanners

Scanners, also known as signature scanners or known virus scanners, look for search strings whose presence is characteristic of a known virus. They frequently have capabilities to remove the virus from an infected object. However, some objects cannot be repaired. Even where an object can be repaired, it is often preferable (in fact, safer) to replace the object rather than repair it, and some scanners are very selective about which objects they repair.

Heuristic Scanners

A recent addition to scanners is intelligent analysis of unknown code, currently referred to as heuristic scanning. It should be noted that heuristic scanning does not represent a new type of antiviral software. More closely akin to activity monitoring functions than traditional signature scanning, this looks for suspicious sections of code that are generally found in viral programs. Although it is possible for normal programs to try to "go resident," look for other program files, or even modify their own code, such activities are telltale signs that can help an informed user come to some decision about the advisability of running or installing a given new and unknown program. Heuristics, however, may generate a lot of false alarms and may either scare novice users or give them a false sense of security after "wolf" has been cried too often.

Activity Monitors

An activity monitor performs a task very similar to an automated form of traditional auditing: It watches for suspicious activity. It may, for example, check for any calls to format a disk or attempts to alter or delete a program file while a program other than the operating system is in control. It may be more sophisticated and check for any program that performs direct activities with hardware, without using the standard system calls.

It is very hard to tell the difference between a word processor updating a file and a virus infecting a file. Activity monitoring programs may be more trouble than they are worth because they can continually ask for confirmation of valid activities. The annals of computer virus research are littered with suggestions for virus-proof computers and systems that basically all boil down to the same thing: If the operations that a computer can perform are restricted, viral programs can be eliminated. Unfortunately, so is most of the usefulness of the computer.

Change Detection

Change detection software examines system or program files and configuration, stores the information, and compares it against the actual configuration at a later time. Most of these programs perform a checksum or cyclic redundancy check (CRC) that will detect changes to a file even if the length is unchanged. Some programs will even use sophisticated encryption techniques to generate a signature that is prohibitively expensive, in processing terms, from the point of view of a piece of malware to execute an attack against.

Change detection software should also note the addition of completely new entities to a system. It has been noted that some programs have not done this and allowed the addition of virus infections or malware. Change detection software is also often referred to as integrity-checking software, but this term may be somewhat misleading. The integrity of a system may have been compromised before the establishment of the initial baseline of comparison.

A sufficiently advanced change detection system, which takes all factors including system areas of the disk and the computer memory into account, has the best chance of detecting viral strains. However, change detection also has the highest probability of false alarms because it will not know whether a change is viral or valid. The addition of intelligent analysis of the changes detected may assist with this failing.

Reputation Scoring

Cyber criminals know that the weakest link in most organizations is not the technology but (in the majority of cases) the person sitting in front of a computer. These criminals, often out for financial gain, exploit the popularity of high traffic sites such as YouTube, Facebook, and Twitter to distribute malicious links and payloads. Very often users are not even aware that by clicking on links they may be exposing their machine and the network to a number of threats. This 'attack surface' grew considerably with the introduction of short URLs (e.g., http://bit.la/w5AcJm) – all URLs look practically the same.

The attackers also know that few users think about risk when they visit a new website, and they use this behavior to their advantage, riding piggy-back on the success of high traffic sites that are used to initiate the transmission of malicious content.

This content however requires a host, i.e. a website from where the content can be distributed. There are two ways to create malicious content on the Web:

1. Create a new website or use an existing website to host the malicious content.
2. Compromise (hack) a legitimate site and inject malicious content.

Cybercriminals and security organizations are playing a constant cat-and-mouse game – one side creating new malicious content, the other designing protective measures to block it. The best weapon for criminals is an ever-changing malware host. Effective attacks require a website or malware strain that is currently not recognized by antivirus engines. So the best means of attack is to actually deploy new websites or website hosts as often as possible. This ensures that these websites have not been recognized by security organizations and consequently blocked. Once a website is 'caught' by antivirus engines or other security measures, it loses its effectiveness and would need to be taken down and replaced by another.

Zero-Day/Zero-Hour

0-day/0-hour is defined as the period of time from when a new malware hosting website is created until it is recognized as malicious. During this period, activity on these sites is considered high risk.

In the zero-hour period, no matter how many antivirus engines you have deployed, anybody visiting a website hosting new malicious content is at risk and his or her machine will probably be infected. So how do we mitigate this problem? Reputation is the answer. Certain types of websites, including those that have not been seen before, are immediately classified as "Suspicious". Applying a reputation score to websites and classifying them as "Suspicious" is a proactive approach to security: You are addressing a risk before it can become a serious threat.

Web Reputation is a method that can be used to boost protection against current to future malicious content on the Web for those browsing the Internet. When one is using Web Reputation, websites are assessed for immediate and potential threats, malicious content, and risky characteristics, and a score (0 – 100) is given.

In a similar way that Content Categorization places websites into different categories and classifies them based on their content, Web Reputation scores are used to determine the risk factor of each website. Once the score for a website has been determined, this will help an administrator to take action: block or proceed with caution and allow access to those websites.

Although a good antivirus engine offers significant threat coverage, and multiple antivirus engines provide greater protection than you get with a single antivirus engine, it is very difficult to achieve total protection in a very dynamic threat environment. Web Reputation fills a void left by traditional protection engines by giving a "safety" rating to websites and where necessary, allowing proactive blocking of risky sites.

It gives each URL a score (0-100) – the lower the score, the greater the risk that website poses to users. Broadly speaking, Web Reputation scores typically fall into five risk bands:

- High Risk (1 – 20)
- Suspicious (21 – 40)
- Moderate Risk (41 – 60)
- Low Risk (61 – 80)
- Trustworthy (81 – 100)

Why Use Web Reputation Technology?

To better understand the benefits of Web Reputation, review the following real world example. Let's say you are going on vacation. While you are planning your holiday, you check the reviews of the hotel where you would like to stay before you actually take a decision to book or not. Unless you confirm that the hotel, which you have never stayed in before, has been given a good rating in various categories (price, cleanliness, location, family friendly, etc.), you would not book your stay there.

The same concept applies to the Web. The Web Reputation Index is calculating a score for a website for the end-users to proactively determine, on the basis of various 'safety variables', whether they should visit that site or not.

With the growing number of malware threats and an ever-changing security landscape, it is increasingly difficult for traditional antivirus engines to be constantly up to date and protect users from ALL the latest threats. Different antivirus vendors have different response times to different types of emerging threats – some focus on speed and all the latest threats, while others focus on complete coverage with threat signatures going back many years.

Therefore, having additional defense mechanisms in place to protect against new zero-hour and zero-day threats is a must. Malware authors are constantly changing their techniques and use various tricks to outsmart antivirus engines. The ability to assess websites and domains on the basis of reputation radically boosts the antivirus software's capability to protect users and organizations against new and unknown threats.

Anti-Malware Policies

Creating policies or educating users in safe practices can reduce the risk of becoming infected, even when a virus enters the organization. There are many possible preemptive measures, such as avoiding the use of applications that are particularly vulnerable and denying entry to mail attachments that are likely to be vectors for inbound viruses. Such measures can be very effective at addressing aspects of antivirus damage that reactive antivirus software does not deal with very well.

Organizations can use access control software suites to minimize the possibility of a virus or Trojan gaining entry by enforcing authentication of program files, disks, users, or any combination of the three. This approach is sometimes combined with virus-specific or generic scanning. Applying such a multilayered strategy can be much more effective than using only one of these approaches, but the strategy's success in avoiding threats has to be balanced against the probable impairment of performance that multi-layering entails.

It should be noted that a significant difference exits between access control as it is used in malware control and access control as it is often understood by systems administrators. Access control systems determine the appropriate allocation of access privileges to individuals and grant systems access to authenticated individuals. In other words, if the system recognizes an individual, he or she is allowed to use that system to the extent that the user's privileges allow. Authenticating the individual is not enough in the malware arena because viruses and worms are usually spread (unwittingly) by trusted individuals. Confirming the identity of the individual does not disclose anything about his or her good intentions, though most would usually hope that the human resources department has applied the appropriate checks. It tells less about the individual's competence at following security guidelines or the currency and acuity of his or her antivirus measures.

Some software places the user at higher risk of virus infection. This is a simple fact. As has been noted, the more widely an operating system is used, the more likely it is that someone has written a virus for it. The same is true for application platforms, such as email programs or word processors. There are other factors that can increase or decrease risk. Certain software designs are more dangerous than others. Specific strategic factors render Windows more vulnerable than it needs to be. Many users resent the restrictions that a highly secure environment imposes on the pursuit of business or personal aims. Management often pays lip service to the importance of security in meetings and reports but cuts corners on implementation. Computer users frequently resent the obtrusiveness of most security measures. (In this regard, it should also be noted that draconian security policies, without good reason, will frequently be ignored or circumvented.)

The basic types of antivirus programs have a great many variations. There are hundreds of thousands of PC viruses and variants known. When a scanner checks for those viruses and variants, checking for every byte of viral code each time would impose a huge processing overhead. To keep this overhead to a minimum, scanners check for the shortest search strings they can afford and deduce the presence of a given virus accordingly. Scanners may apply a number of heuristics according to the virus type. Therefore, on-access scanners, as well as those based on firewalls and network gateways, always have poorer detection capabilities than their on-demand, or manual, counterparts, and this difference sometimes accounts for as much as a 20% disparity in performance and accuracy. The memory resident and on-demand components of a modern antivirus suite may use the same definitions database and still not score identical results with the identical test set.

Malware Assurance

In order to facilitate protecting against malware, as well as raising user awareness, one should put policies in place that will effectively protect against common malware and malware vectors, without unduly restricting operations. Explain to users the reasons for the control measures and the specific exploits that they protect against. Policies and education are useful protections against malware, regardless of scanning and restriction technologies.

For technical antimalware systems, regularly review their effectiveness. If the organization uses on-demand or server-based scanners, have regular check scans with a manual scanner in addition to the automated scanning. Note that disinfection is not always effective or possible, and have a policy to prefer deletion of malware and replacement of infected items from an uncompromised backup.

Monitor activity, especially communications. Check for open ports and scan outgoing, as well as incoming, email. This will not protect your system from infection, but it will provide a means of detecting various malware-related activities should some problem get past your defenses. It also acts as a check on botnet activities and is not affected by rootkit or stealth capabilities in malware.

Software Protection Mechanisms

Security Kernels, Reference Monitors, and the TCB

A term associated with security kernels and the reference monitor is the trusted computing base (TCB).[25] The TCB is the collection of all of the hardware, software, and firmware within a computer system that contains all elements of the system responsible for supporting the security policy and the isolation of objects. When the TCB is enabled, the system is considered to have a trusted path along with a trusted shell. The trusted path is a communication channel between the user or program and the TCB. The TCB is responsible for providing the protection mechanisms necessary to ensure that the trusted path cannot be compromised in any way. The trusted shell implies that any activity taking place within the shell, or communication channel, is isolated to that channel and cannot be interacted with either from inside or outside by an untrusted party or entity.

The reference monitor is an abstraction, but there may be a reference validator, which usually runs inside the security kernel and is responsible for performing security access checks on objects, manipulating privileges, and generating any resulting security audit messages. In other words, the reference monitor is considered to be an abstract machine that mediates, or controls, all access that subjects (users) have to objects (data or resources). The reference monitor acts in order to ensure that any subject attempting to access any object has the appropriate rights to do so in order to protect the object from unauthorized access attempts by bad actors. The reference monitor is a conceptual idea, or an abstraction as noted above. As a result of being an idea, it must be implemented or enacted in some way in order to actually perform the functions that it represents. The security kernel is what actually implements the reference monitor concept.

The security kernel is made up of all of the components of the TCB (the software, hardware, and firmware), and it is responsible for implementing and enforcing the reference monitor. A security kernel is responsible for enforcing a security policy. It is a strict implementation of a reference monitor mechanism. The architecture of a kernel operating system is typically layered, and the kernel should be at the lowest and most primitive level. It is a small portion of the operating system through which all references to information and all changes to

---

25 See the following: http://www.princeton.edu/~achaney/tmve/wiki100k/docs/Trusted_computing_base.html

authorizations must pass. The kernel implements access control and information flow control between implemented objects according to the security policy.

To be secure, the kernel must meet three basic conditions: [26]

1. **Completeness** – All accesses to information must go through the kernel
2. **Isolation** – The kernel itself must be protected from any type of unauthorized access
3. **Verifiability** – The kernel must be proven to meet design specifications

The security capabilities of products for use in the TCB can be verified through various evaluation criteria, such as the earlier Trusted Computer System Evaluation Criteria (TCSEC) and the current Common Criteria standards.[27]

Processor Privilege States

The processor privilege states protect the processor and the activities that it performs. The earliest method of doing this was to record the processor state in a register that could only be altered when the processor was operating in a privileged state. Instructions such as I/O requests were designed to include a reference to this register. If the register was not in a privileged state, the instructions were aborted. The hardware typically controls entry into the privilege mode. For example, the Intel vPro processor prevents system code and data from being overwritten, although these protections are seldom directly used. The privilege-level mechanism should prevent memory access (programs or data) from less privileged to more privileged levels, but only if the controls are invoked and properly managed in software. The privileged levels are typically referenced in a ring structure.

To illustrate this point, many operating systems use two processor access modes: user (or process, problem, or program) mode and kernel (or supervisor) mode. User application code runs in user mode, and operating system code runs in kernel mode. The privileged processor mode is called kernel mode. The kernel mode allows the processor access to all system memory, resources, and all CPU instructions.

The application code should run in a non-privileged mode (the user mode) and have a limited set of interfaces available, limited access to system data, and no direct access to hardware resources. An advantage of the operating system having a higher privilege level than the application software is that problematic application software cannot disrupt the system's functioning. A major security failure in modern desktop processing is that operating systems and applications may be most effective if run in supervisor or kernel mode at all times.

When a user mode program calls a system service (such as reading a document from storage), the processor catches the call and switches the calling request to kernel mode. When the call is complete, the operating system switches the call back to user mode and allows the

---

26 The three conditions stipulated for the kernel are actually the requirements of the reference monitor. The security kernel implements the reference monitor, and as a result, draws its architectural references from the design requirements of the monitor.

27 See the following:
TCSEC: http://csrc.nist.gov/publications/history/dod85.pdf
Common Criteria: https://www.commoncriteriaportal.org/
See the following for the ISO/IEC 15408:2009 standard: http://standards.iso.org/ittf/PubliclyAvailableStandards/index.html
TCSEC & Common Criteria compared together: https://www.cs.purdue.edu/homes/ninghui/courses/526_Fall12/handouts/526_topic18.pdf

user mode program to continue. Under the most secure operating policy, the operating system and device drivers operate at ring level 0, also known as kernel-level or system-level privilege.[28] At this privilege level, there are no restrictions on what a program can do. Because programs at this level have unlimited access, users should be concerned about the source of device drivers for machines that contain sensitive information.

Applications and services should operate at ring level 3, also known as user-level or application-level privilege. Note that if an application or service fails at this level, a trap screen will appear (also known as a general protection fault) that can be dismissed, and the operating system does not care. The decision to have services run at the same privilege level as regular applications is based on the idea that if the service traps, the operating system should continue to operate.

A monolithic operating system exists as a large program consisting of a set of procedures; there are no restrictions on what procedures may be called by any other procedures. This means that the majority of the operating system and device driver codes share the kernel mode protected memory space. Once in kernel mode, the operating system and the device driver code have complete access to system space memory and can bypass security to access objects. Because most of the operating system code runs in kernel mode, it is critical that kernel mode components be carefully designed to ensure they do not violate security features. If a system administrator installs a third-party device driver, it operates in kernel mode and then has access to all operating system data. If the device driver installation software also contains malicious code, that code will also be installed and could open the system to unauthorized accesses.

A privileged state failure can occur if an application program fails. The safest place for an application to fail is to a system halt. For example, if an application has an error, it will fail to the operating system program, and the user can then use the operating system to recover the application and data. This vulnerability could also be exploited by allowing an attacker to crash an application to get to the operating system with the identity and privileges of the person who started the application.

Security Controls for Buffer Overflows

Another issue with privilege states is called ineffective parameter checking, which causes buffer overflows. A buffer overflow is caused by improper (or lacking) bounds checking on input to a program. Essentially, the program fails to see if too much data is provided for an allocated space of memory. Because programs are loaded into memory when run, when there is an overflow, the data has to go somewhere. If that data happens to be executable malicious code that is loaded, it may run as if it were the program or make other changes to the execution environment that can be exploited by an attacker.

Buffer overflows must be corrected by the programmer or by directly patching system memory. They can be detected and fixed by reverse engineering (disassembling programs) and looking at the operations of the application. Hardware states and other hardware controls can make buffer overflows impossible, although enterprises seldom specify hardware at this level. Bounds enforcement and proper error checking will also stop buffer overflows.

---

28 See the following for an overview discussion and historical background on where the concept of protection ring levels come from:
Short version: http://www.osronline.com/article.cfm?article=224
Long version: http://duartes.org/gustavo/blog/post/cpu-rings-privilege-and-protection/

Controls for Incomplete Parameter Check and Enforcement

A security risk exists when all parameters have not been fully checked for accuracy and consistency by the operating systems. The lack of parameter checking can lead to buffer overflow attacks. A recent parameter check attack involved an email attachment with a name longer than 64 K in length. Because the application required attachment names to be less than 64 K, attachments that had longer names would overwrite program instructions.

To counter the vulnerability, operating systems should offer some type of buffer management. Parameter checking is implemented by the programmer and involves checking the input data for disallowed characters, length, data type, and format. Certain programming commands or styles are preferable and should be encouraged or mandated. Other technologies to protect against buffer overflows include canaries (the use and monitoring of indicator data values at the end of buffer areas).

Process Isolation and Memory Protection

A process can be defined as the instance of a computer program being executed in memory. Computers are capable of running multiple processes at the same time. In order for the processes to coexist, they must be managed in such a way that they are able to access resources as needed to successfully carry out their missions, but at the same time, they need to do so without getting in each other's way. However, this can become complicated at times because processes can share memory, data, and system resources. In order to maintain the integrity of the operating system, and the integrity of the process and the data that it is accessing at all times, one should ensure that multiple processes do not attempt to access the same system resources at the same time.

This need to isolate processes from one another within the computer has to be managed to ensure that it is happening effectively and thoroughly, without exceptions. The operating system is the program that acts to ensure that this process isolation takes place, and it partners with the CPU to enforce the process isolation through the use of interrupts and time slicing. The use of interrupts allows the operating system to ensure that a process is given enough time to access the CPU when necessary to carry out its required functions, but it also ensures that the process does not overstay its welcome and lock up resources that are necessary for other processes to execute as well. In order to enforce the concept of process isolation, use any of the following methods that can be used by the operating system:

- Encapsulation of objects
- Time multiplexing of shared resources
- Naming distinctions
- Virtual memory mapping

Encapsulating a process means that no other process is able to understand or interact with the internal programming code of the process. The act of encapsulating forces processes to interact with each other through well-defined interfaces that allow for the exchange of information in a structured and controlled manner. Encapsulation provides the process with the ability to cloak, or stealth its internal workings from other processes, effectively allowing it to engage in data hiding. Data hiding provides the process with an integrity mechanism that allows it to maintain control over its function and execution in a controlled way, and it also provides the ability to enforce the concept of modularity in the programming of the processes and the operating system overall.

Time multiplexing allows the operating system to provide well-defined and structured access to processes that need to use resources according to a controlled and tightly managed schedule. This schedule is defined as a micro period of time, a time slice, which will grant access to the system resource required by the process and then terminate that access once the time period has expired. Multi-processor computing systems create an additional layer of performance, but they also add complexity with regards to time multiplexing. Due to the fact that each CPU in a computer can have more than one core or more than one processor, the ability for the computer to process multiple requests for access to resources from processes simultaneously continues to increase. This increase in overall ability to handle multiple requests at the same time, or multitasking, has led to the sustained growth in computing power and ability that Gordon Moore predicted.[29]

Naming distinctions are used to ensure that each process is assigned a unique identity within the context of the operating system. This means that each process will be given a unique name and Process ID, or PID, ensuring that when it is referenced by the operating system, there is no confusion as to which process is being accessed by which resources. In *Figure 8.4*, the use of the PID column to expose the Process ID for running processes in the Windows Task Manager is shown. When the user selects the PID check box, the PID column is added to the Processes tab view, allowing the PID to be seen and cross-referenced with the process name by the user. The operating system does this matching automatically as the process executes, or it is called by another process to provide information. In a Linux operating system, the user could use either Top or Proc from a command shell to access the same information.

Virtual address memory mapping allows each process to have access to its own memory space as it executes. This is enforced through the operating system's use of the memory manager. The memory manager is used to ensure that processes do not access each other's memory areas in improper ways that can lead to loss of integrity and confidentiality or corruption of information.

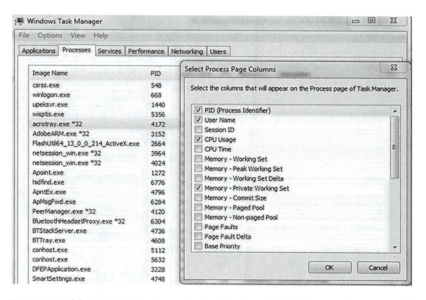

*Figure 8.4 –***Adding the PID column to the Windows Task Manager Processes tab**

29   See the following: http://en.wikipedia.org/wiki/Moore's_law

Memory management is used by the operating system to achieve the following goals:
1. Provide an abstraction level for programmers
2. Maximize performance with the limited amount of memory available to the system (Physical RAM)
3. Protect the operating system and applications once they are loaded into memory

The memory manager is the function of the operating system that keeps track of how different types of memory are used. It allocates and deallocates the different memory types as needed by running processes, enforces access control to ensure that processes are only able to interact with their own memory segments, and manages the swapping of memory contents from RAM to the hard drive when needed.

In addition, the memory manager has five responsibilities:
1. **Relocation** – Move, or swap, content between RAM and the hard drive as needed and provide pointers to applications if their information has been moved to a different location in memory.
2. **Protection** – Provide access control for memory segments and limit processes to interacting only with the memory segments assigned to them.
3. **Sharing** – Allow for multiple users with different access levels to interact with an application or process while running and enforce integrity and confidentiality controls between processes while using shared memory segments.
4. **Logical organization** – Segmentation of all memory types, providing an addressing scheme at an abstraction level and allowing for the sharing of software modules such as DLL procedures.
5. **Physical organization** – Segmentation of the physical memory space for allocation.

There is one additional part of the memory management process that needs to be discussed, which is the use of registers. Registers allow the operating system to make sure that a process is only able to interact with the defined memory segments assigned to it by the memory manager. There are two types of registers used by the CPU to identify memory addresses. A base register is used to identify the beginning address assigned to the process. A limit register is used to identify the ending address assigned to the process. A CPU will create one or more threads to execute a process. A thread is the set of instructions generated by a process to allow it to carry out the specific activity it has been requested to execute. The CPU will use the threads to allow the process to execute actions by referencing the address of where the instructions and the data needed for execution reside in memory. The CPU will compare the address to the base and limit registers to ensure that the access being requested by the process is within the allowed memory space assigned to that process and not outside or in some other memory space that is protected.

Memory protection is concerned with controlling access to main memory. When several processes are running at the same time, it is necessary to protect the memory used by one process from unauthorized access by another. Thus, it is necessary to partition memory to ensure processes cannot interfere with each other's local memory and to ensure common memory areas are protected against unauthorized access. This extends beyond applications executing in the main computer memory. An operating system may use secondary memory (storage devices) to give the illusion of a larger main memory pool, or it may partition the main memory among users so that each user sees a virtual machine that has memory smaller than that on the real machine. Additional controls may be required in these situations.

The memory used by the operating system needs to be protected to maintain the integrity and confidentiality of privileged code and data. Because memory protection deals with addressing, many protection mechanisms protect memory by placing it outside the address space available to a process. The main memory protection issues to be addressed are address reference validation, access rights to memory segments, protection levels assigned to data types in memory, and access by processes through unpermitted address creation or manipulation.

There are four methods used to provide memory protection so that no user process can inadvertently or deliberately corrupt the address space of another process or the operating system itself.

The first method ensures all system-wide data structures and memory pools used by kernel mode system components can be accessed only while in kernel mode. Thus, user mode requests cannot access these pages. If they attempt to do so, the hardware will generate a fault, and then the memory manager will create an access violation. In early Windows operating systems, such as Windows 95 and Windows 98, some pages in the system address space were writable from user mode, thus allowing an errant application to corrupt key system data structures and crash the system. The implementation of a Hardware Abstraction Layer (HAL) along with improved memory management techniques has eliminated this behavior, and as a result, more recent Windows based operating systems do not experience this same kind of behavior for these reasons. This has led to more stable and secure operating system implementations, such as Windows 7 and 8 on the desktop and Windows Server 2008 and 2012 on the server side.

Second, each process has a separate, private address space protected from being accessed by any request belonging to another process, with a few exceptions. Each time a request references an address, the virtual memory hardware, in conjunction with the memory manager, intervenes and translates the virtual address into a physical one. This control mechanism is referred to as Address Space Layout Randomization (ASLR). ASLR is implemented in many operating system platforms, and it allows the memory manager to effectively change, or randomize, the memory space addressing used by a process to execute within on a continuous basis. Because operating systems such as Windows 7, Windows 8/8.1, and OpenBSD control how virtual addresses are translated, requests running in one process do not inappropriately access a page belonging to another process.

Third, most modern processors provide some form of hardware or software controlled memory protection, such as read or write access. While this protection mechanism is implemented differently depending on manufacturer, it is commonly referred to as Data Execution Prevention (DEP). The type of protection offered depends on the processor. For example, a memory protection option is page_noaccess. If an attempt is made to read from, write to, or execute the code in this region, an access violation will occur. DEP has the ability to make certain areas of the system memory unavailable to processes for execution by marking them as unavailable. This has the dual benefit of reducing the usable memory areas to be managed by the memory manager as well as reducing the available areas of memory that can be made available to a process to execute within. This allows the operating system to further optimize performance, speeding up transactions as well as reducing the usable memory space that attackers may be able to get access to in order to execute attacks.

The fourth protection mechanism uses access control lists to protect shared memory objects, forcing them to undergo a security check when processes attempt to open them. Another security feature involves access to mapped files. To map to a file, the object (or user) performing the request must have at least read access to the underlying file object, or the operation will fail.

Covert Channel Controls

A covert channel or confinement problem is an information flow that is not controlled by a security control. It is a communication channel allowing two cooperating processes to transfer information in a way that violates the system's security policy. Even though there are protection mechanisms in place, if unauthorized information can be transferred using a signaling mechanism or other objects, then a covert channel may exist. The standard example used in application security is a situation where a process can be started and stopped by one program, and the existence of the process can be detected by another application. Thus, the existence of the process can be used, over time, to signal information.

The only channels of interest are those breaching the security policy; those channels that parallel legitimate communications paths are not of concern. Although there are differences for each type of covert channel, there is a common condition – the transmitting and receiving objects over the channel must have access to a shared resource.

The first step is to identify any potential covert channels; the second is to analyze these channels to determine whether a channel actually exists. The next steps are based on manual inspection and appropriate testing techniques to verify if the channel creates security concerns.

Cryptography

Cryptographic techniques protect information by transforming the data through encryption schemes. They are used to protect the confidentiality and integrity of information. Most cryptographic techniques are used in telecommunications systems; however, because of the increase in distributed systems, they are becoming increasingly used in operating systems. Encryption algorithms can be used to encrypt specific files located within the operating system. For example, database files that contain user information, such as group rights, are encrypted using one-way hashing algorithms to ensure a higher protection of the data.

Password Protection Techniques

Operating system and application software use passwords as a convenient mechanism to authenticate users. Typically, operating systems use passwords to authenticate the user and establish access controls for resources, including the system, files, or applications. Password protections offered by the operating system include controls on how the password is selected and how complex the password is, password time limits, and password length.

Password files stored within a computer system must be secured by the protection mechanisms of the operating system. Because password files are prone to unauthorized access, the most common solution is to encrypt password files using one-way encryption algorithms (hashing). These, however, are very susceptible to a dictionary attack if the passwords chosen appear in any dictionary. Another feature offered by an operating system for password security involves an overstrike or password-masking feature. This prevents others from reading the typed password through shoulder surfing.

Inadequate Granularity of Controls

If there is not enough granularity of security, users may be able to gain more access permission than needed. If the user is unable to access object A, but the user has access to a program that can access object A, then the security mechanisms could be bypassed. If the security controls are granular enough to address both program and user, then the disclosure may be prevented. Inadequate granularity of controls can be addressed by properly implementing the concept of least privilege, setting reasonable limits on the user. Also, the separation of duties and functions should be covered. Programmers should never be system administrators or users of the application. Grant users only those permissions necessary to do their job.

Users should have no access to server rooms or legacy programs; programmers and system analysts should not have write access to production programs, allowing them to change the installed program code. Programmers should have no ongoing direct access to production programs. Access to fix crashed applications should be limited to the time required to repair the problem causing the failure. Mainframe operators should not be allowed to do programming. Maintenance programmers should not have access to programs under development. Assignment of system privileges must be tightly controlled and a shared responsibility.

More specifically, granularity addresses the issue of a finely tuned access control mechanism. As far as the operating system is concerned, an object is a file, not a structure within that file. Therefore, users granted access to a file can read the whole file. To restrict access to certain parts of the file, such as records or fields within a database, one must build additional controls into the database access application that will ensure that areas of concern are protected.

Control and Separation of Environments

The following environmental types can exist in software development:

- Development environment
- Quality assurance environment
- Application (production) environment

The security issue is to control how each environment can access the application and the data and then provide mechanisms to keep them separate. For example, systems analysts and programmers write, compile, and perform initial testing of the application's implementation and functionality in the development environment. As the application reaches maturity and moves toward production readiness, users and quality assurance people perform functional testing within the quality assurance environment. The quality assurance configuration should simulate the production environment as closely as possible. Once the user community has accepted the application, it is moved into the production environment. Blended environments combine one or more of these individual environments and are generally the most difficult to control.

Control measures protecting the various environments include physical isolation of environment, physical or temporal separation of data for each environment, access control lists, content-dependent access controls, role-based constraints, role definition stability, accountability, and separation of duties.

Race Conditions vs. Time of Check/Time of Use (TOC/TOU) Attacks [30]

If there are multiple threads of execution occurring at the same time, a TOC/TOU attack is possible. A TOC/TOU attack takes advantage of the dependency on the timing of events that takes place in a multitasking operating system. An example of a TOC/TOU attack may involve the use of two processes and two files as follows. Process 1 is used to validate the credentials of a user to allow the user to open a standard text file called "File A", and process 2 is used to call and access the file once process 1 authorizes the user access. If an attacker can manage to redirect process 2 to open a secure file such as a payroll file after process1 authorizes the user access but before process 2 executes the handed off request to retrieve and access the non-secure file called "File-A", then the attacker has performed a TOC/TOU attack. Flaws in the programming code of the operating system are what can allow this kind of attack to take place.

To avoid TOC/TOU attacks, the operating system should use the concept of software locking. Software locking applies a lock, or a blocking mechanism, to the file or resource being accessed by the process. This enables the operating system to ensure that the file cannot be substituted out for another file while access is being validated, thus ensuring that only the file initially requested by the process will be accessed by the user as the process completes.

Very often, race conditions will be used as an example of TOC/TOU attacks. A race condition occurs when two processes need to carry out their tasks against one resource. The trick is that the processes need to execute in the correct order: process 1 first and process 2 second. If that order can be disrupted by an attacker, then the attacker can manipulate the output of the results of the combined action of the two processes and potentially create a different outcome than the one intended.

For example, what would happen if the operating system were to allow the security functions for authentication and authorization to be handled by two different processes? The outcome may be perfectly normal and acceptable almost all of the time, meaning, that when a user attempts to log into a system, he or she is first authenticated, then authorized to access system resources as required based on his or her group memberships and resource permissions. However, what if an attacker were able to force the authorization process to execute before the authentication process? The outcome would be a user that is granted access to resources in the system without authentication of his or her identity taking place.

To protect against a race condition attack from taking place within a system, the security professional needs to ensure that the architecture and design of the operating system, and the programs that run on top of it, are not allowing critical tasks to be split up for execution. The use of atomic operations needs to be enforced within the system to ensure this does not happen

The difference between race conditions and TOC/TOU attacks is subtle but important for the security professional to understand. A race condition implies that two processes will be forced to execute out of sequence, allowing the attacker to control or manipulate the outcome. While a TOC/TOU attack happens as a result of the attackers inserting themselves in between two processes as they are executing, causing a redirection of the second process in some way to control or manipulate the outcome.

---

30   See the following: http://cwe.mitre.org/data/definitions/367.html

Social Engineering

Some of the ways in which attackers can try to use social influence over users in order to subvert normal processes and technical controls for their own gain include subtle intimidation, bluster, pulling rank, exploiting guilt, pleading for special treatment, exploiting a natural desire to be helpful, or appealing to an underling's subversive streak. Social engineering in software, particularly malicious software, tends to be more simplistic, but all forms should be noted.

In regard to protection against social engineering attacks, users and help desk staff need a proper framework to work. The staff needs a good understanding of what the rules actually are, what their responsibilities are, and what recourse they have in the event of a grievance or problem. They also need to know that when they have a run-in with a difficult user, they will have the backing of management, as long as they conform to policy.

Social engineering attracts such a range of definitions, covering such a variety of activities (from password stealing to scavenging through garbage and waste for useful information to spreading malicious misinformation) as to be confusing at best. The question is, do accepted definitions of social engineering meet the needs of those tasked with addressing this class of threat? Some examples of the use of social engineering in malware may be instructive for the security professional.

The Swen worm passed itself off as a message that had been sent from Microsoft. It claimed that the attachment was a patch that would remove Windows vulnerabilities. This led many people to take the claim seriously and try to install the bogus 'patch' – even though it was really a worm. The Nimda and Aliz mail worms exploited Microsoft Outlook's vulnerabilities. When the victims opened an infected message – or even placed their cursor on the message in the preview window – the worm file launched, infecting the system. Another example was the Trojan virus that was sent to email addresses that were taken from a recruitment website. People that had registered on the site received fake job offers – but the offers included a Trojan virus. The attack mainly targeted corporate email addresses, and the cybercriminals knew that the staff that received the Trojan would not want to tell their employers that they had been infected while they were looking for alternative employment.

The best method of preventing social engineering attacks is to make users aware of the threat and give them the proper procedures for handling unusual or what may seem like usual requests for information. For example, if users were to receive a phone call from a "system administrator" asking for their password, they should be aware of social engineering threats and ask that the system administrator come to their office to discuss the problems in a face-to-face format. Even if the user is 100% sure that the person on the phone is the system administrator and the phone line could not be tampered with, it is almost impossible to imagine a situation under which a user should give a password to anyone else, particularly using the phone lines.

Backup Controls

Backing up operating system and application software is a method of ensuring productivity in the event of a system crash. Operation copies of software should be available in the event of a system crash. Also, storing copies of software in an off-site location can be useful if the building is no longer available. Data, programs, documentation, computing, and communications equipment redundancy can ensure that information is available in the event of an emergency. Requiring that the source code for custom-designed software is kept in escrow ensures that if the software vendor were to go out of business, the source code would be available to use or give to another vendor in the event upgrades or assistance is needed. Contingency planning documents help to provide a plan for returning operations to normal in the event of an emergency. Disk mirroring, redundant array of independent disks (RAID), etc., provide protection for information in the event of a production server crashing.

Software Forensics

Software, particularly malicious software, has traditionally been seen in terms of a tool for the attacker. The only value that has been seen in the study of such software is in regard to protection against malicious code. However, experience in the virus research field, and more recent studies in detecting plagiarism, indicates that evidence of intention can be gained, and cultural and individual identity, from the examination of software itself. Although most would see software forensics strictly as a tool for assurance, in software development and acquisition, it has a number of uses in protective procedures. Outside of virus research, forensic programming is a little known field. However, the larger computer science world is starting to take note of software forensics. It involves the analysis of program code, generally object or machine language code, to make a determination of or provide evidence for the intent or authorship of a program.

Software forensics has a number of possible uses. In analyzing software suspected of being malicious, it can be used to determine whether a problem is a result of carelessness or was deliberately introduced as a payload. Information can be obtained about authorship and the culture behind a given programmer and the sequence in which related programs were written. This can be used to provide evidence about a suspected author of a program or to determine intellectual property issues. The techniques behind software forensics can sometimes also be used to recover source code that has been lost.

Software forensics generally deals with two different types of code. The first is source code, which is relatively legible to people. Analysis of source code is often referred to as code analysis and is closely related to literary analysis. The second; analysis of object, machine, or code, is generally referred to as forensic programming.

Literary analysis has contributed much to code analysis and is an older and more mature field. It is referred to, variously, as authorship analysis, stylistics, stylometry, forensic linguistics, or forensic stylistics. Stylistic or stylometric analysis of messages and text may provide information and evidence that can be used for identification or confirmation of identity.

Physical fingerprint evidence frequently does not help identify a perpetrator in terms of finding the person that a fingerprint is obtained from. However, a fingerprint can confirm an identity or place a person at the scene of a crime once a suspect is determined. In the same way, the evidence gathered from analyzing the text of a message, or a body of messages, may help to confirm that a given individual or suspect is the person who created the fraudulent postings. Both the content and the syntactical structure of text can provide evidence that relates to an individual.

Some of the evidence discovered may not relate to individuals. Some information, particularly that relating to the content or phrasing of the text, may relate to a group of people who work together, influence each other, or are influenced from a single outside source. This data can still be of use to us, in that it will provide clues in regard to a group that the author may be associated with, and may be helpful in building a profile of the writer.

Groups may also use common tools. Various types of tools, such as word processors or databases, may be commonly used by groups and provide similar evidence. In software analysis, indications of languages, specific compilers, and other development tools can be found. Compilers leave definite traces in programs and can be specifically identified. Languages leave indications in the types of functions and structures supported. Other types of software development tools may contribute to the structural architecture of the program or the regularity and reuse of modules.

In regard to programming, it is possible to trace indications of cultures and styles in programming. A very broad example is the difference between design of programs in the Microsoft Windows environment and the UNIX environment. Windows programs tend to be large and monolithic, with the most complete set of functions possible built into the main program, large central program files, and calls to related application function libraries. UNIX programs tend to be individually small, with calls to a number of single-function utilities.

Evidence of cultural influences exists right down to the machine-code level. Those who work with assembler and machine code know that a given function can be coded in a variety of ways, and that there may be a number of algorithms to accomplish the same end. For example, it is possible to note, for a given function, whether the programming was intended to accomplish the task in a minimum amount of memory space (tight code), a minimum number of machine cycles (high-performance code), or a minimal effort on the part of the programmer (sloppy code).

The syntax of text tends to be characteristic. Does the author always use simple sentences? Always use compound sentences? Have a specific preference when a mix of forms is used? Syntactical patterns have been used in programs that detect plagiarism in written papers. The same kind of analysis can be applied to source code for programs, finding identity between the overall structure of code even when functional units are not considered. A number of such plagiarism detection programs are available, and the methods that they use can assist with this type of forensic study. Errors in the text or program can be extremely helpful in our analysis and should be identified for further study.

"It may be important to distinguish between issues of style and stylometry when we are dealing with authorship analysis. Literary critics, and anyone with a writing background, may be prejudiced against technologies that ignore content and concentrate on other factors. Although techniques such as cusum analysis have been proven to work in practice, they still engender unreasoning opposition from many who fail to understand that material can contain features quite apart from the content and meaning.

It may seem strange to use meaningless features as evidence. However, Richard Forsyth reported on studies and experiments that found that short substrings of letter sequences can be effective in identifying authors. Even a relative count of the use of single letters can be characteristic of authors.

Certain message formats may provide additional information. A number of Microsoft email systems include a data block with every message that is sent. To most readers, this block contains meaningless garbage. However, it may include a variety of information, such as part of the structure of the file system on the sender's machine, the sender's registered identity, programs in use, and so forth.

Other programs may add information that can be used. Microsoft's word processing program, Word, for example, is frequently used to create documents sent by email. Word documents include information about file system structure, the author's name (and possibly company), and a global user ID. This ID was analyzed as evidence in the case of the Melissa virus. MS Word can provide even more data. Comments and "deleted" sections of text may be retained in Word files and simply marked as hidden to prevent them from being displayed. Simple utility tools can recover this information from the file itself.

Mobile Code Controls

The concept of attaching programs to webpages has very real security implications. However, through the use of appropriate technical controls, the user does not have to consider the security consequences of viewing the page. Rather, the controls determine if the user can view the page. Secured systems should limit mobile code (applets) access to system resources such as the file system, the CPU, the network, the graphics display, and the browser's internal state. Additionally, the system should garbage-collect memory to prevent both malicious and accidental memory leakage. The system must manage system calls and other methods that allow applets to affect each other as well as the environment beyond the browser.

Fundamentally, the issue of safe execution of code comes down to a concern with access to system resources. Any running program has to access system resources to perform its task. Traditionally, that access has been given to all normal user resources. Mobile code must have restricted access to resources for safety. However, it must be allowed some access to perform its required functions.

It is important to identify the resources the program needs and then provide certain types of limited access to these resources to protect against threats when creating a secure environment for an executable program, such as mobile code. Examples of threats to resources include:

- Disclosure of information about a user or the host machine
- Denial-of-service (DoS) attacks that make a resource unavailable for legitimate purposes
- Damaging or modifying data
- Annoyance attacks, such as displaying obscene pictures on a user's screen

Some resources are clearly more dangerous to give full access to than others. For example, it is hard to imagine any security policy where an unknown program should be given full access to the file system. On the other hand, most security policies would not limit a program from almost full access to the monitor display. Thus, one of the key issues in providing for safe execution of mobile code is determining which resources a particular piece of code is allowed access. That is, there is a need for a security policy that specifies what type of access any mobile code can have. Two basic mechanisms can be used to limit the risk to the user:

- Attempt to run code in a restricted environment where it cannot do harm, such as in a sandbox.
- Cryptographic authentication can be used to attempt to show the user who is responsible for the code.

Sandbox

One of the control mechanisms for mobile code is the sandbox. The sandbox provides a protective area for program execution. Limits are placed on the amount of memory and processor resources the program can consume. If the program exceeds these limits, the Web browser terminates the process and logs an error code. This can ensure the safety of the browser's performance. In the Java sandbox security model, there is an option to provide an area for the Java code to do what it needs to do, including restricting the bounds of this area. A sandbox cannot confine code and its behavior without some type of enforcement mechanism. The Java security manager makes sure all restricted code stays in the sandbox. Trusted code resides outside the sandbox; untrusted code is confined within it. By default, Java applications live outside the sandbox and Java applets are confined within.

Applets are either sandbox applets or privileged applets. Sandbox applets are run in a security sandbox that allows only a set of safe operations. Privileged applets can run outside the security sandbox and have extensive capabilities to access the client.

Applets that are not signed are restricted to the security sandbox, and they run only if the user accepts the applet. Applets that are signed by a certificate from a recognized certificate authority can either run only in the sandbox, or they can request permission to run outside the sandbox. In either case, the user must accept the applet's security certificate; otherwise the applet is blocked from running.

Sandbox applets are restricted to the security sandbox and can perform the following operations:

- They can make network connections to the host they came from.
- They can easily display HTML documents using the showDocument method of the java.applet.AppletContext class.
- They can invoke public methods of other applets on the same page.
- Applets that are loaded from the local file system (from a directory in the user's CLASSPATH) have none of the restrictions that applets loaded over the network do.
- They can read secure system properties.
- When launched by using the Java Network Launch Protocol (JNLP), sandbox applets can also perform the following operations:
  - They can open, read, and save files on the client.
  - They can access the shared system-wide clipboard.
  - They can access printing functions.
  - They can store data on the client, decide how applets should be downloaded and cached, and much more.

Sandbox applets cannot perform the following operations:

- They cannot access client resources such as the local filesystem, executable files, system clipboard, and printers.
- They cannot connect to or retrieve resources from any third-party server (any server other than the server it originated from).
- They cannot load native libraries.
- They cannot change the SecurityManager.
- They cannot create a ClassLoader.
- They cannot read certain system properties.

Privileged applets do not have the security restrictions that are imposed on sandbox applets and can run outside the security sandbox. The sandbox aims to ensure that an untrusted application cannot gain access to system resources. Newer malware is capable of detecting sandboxes and some can break out of them.

Programming Language Support

A method of providing safe execution of programs is to use a type-safe programming language (also known as strong typing), such as Java. A type-safe language or safe language is a program that will never go wrong in certain ways. These ensure that arrays stay in bounds, the pointers are always valid, and code cannot violate variable typing (such as placing code in a string and then executing it). From a security perspective, the absence of pointers is important. Memory access through pointers is one of the main causes for weaknesses (bugs) and security problems in C or C++. Java does an internal check, called static type checking, which examines whether the arguments an operand may get during execution are always of the correct type. The process of verifying and enforcing the constraints of types – type checking – may occur either at compile-time (a static check) or run-time (a dynamic check). If a language specification requires its typing rules strongly (i.e., more or less allowing only those automatic type conversions that do not lose information), then the process can be referred to as being strongly typed, if not, it is then considered as being weakly typed.

Configuration Management

For software, configuration management (CM) refers to monitoring and managing changes to a program or documentation. The goal is to guarantee integrity, availability, and usage of the correct version of all system components such as the software code, design documents, documentation, and control files.

Configuration management consists of reviewing every change made to a system. This includes identifying, controlling, accounting for, and auditing all changes. The first step is to identify any changes that are made. The control task occurs when every change is subject to some type of documentation that must be reviewed and approved by an authorized individual. Accounting refers to recording and reporting on the configuration of the software or hardware throughout any change procedures. Finally, the auditing task allows the completed change to be verified, especially ensuring that any changes did not affect the security policy or protection mechanisms that are implemented.

The best method of controlling changes is to have a configuration management plan that ensures that changes are performed in an agreed upon manner. Any deviations from the plan could change the configuration of the entire system and could essentially void any certification that it is a secure, trusted system. In a project, configuration management often refers to the controlling of changes to the scope or requirements of the project. Scope creep caused by a lack of configuration management can lead to a project never being completed or structured because its requirements are continuously changing.

At its heart, CM is intended to eliminate the confusion and error brought about by the existence of different versions of artifacts. An artifact may be a piece of hardware or software or documentation. Changes are made to correct errors, provide enhancements, or simply reflect the evolutionary refinement of product definition. Without a well-enforced CM process, different team members can use different versions of artifacts unintentionally; individuals can create versions without the proper authority; and the wrong version of an artifact can be used inadvertently. Successful CM requires a well-defined and institutionalized set of policies and standards that clearly define:

- The set of artifacts (configuration items) under the jurisdiction of CM
- How artifacts are named
- How artifacts enter and leave the controlled set
- How an artifact under CM is allowed to change
- How different versions of an artifact under CM are made available and under what conditions each one can be used
- How CM tools are used to enable and enforce CM

These policies and standards are documented in a CM plan that informs everyone in the organization just how CM is carried out.

Information Protection Management

If software is shared, it should be protected from unauthorized modification by ensuring that policies, developmental controls, and lifecycle controls are in place. In addition, users should be trained in security policies and procedures. Software controls and policies should require procedures for changing, accepting, and testing software prior to implementation. These controls and policies require management approval for any software changes and compliance with change control procedures.

Security of Code Repositories

The security professional needs to be concerned with how to ensure the safety of code while it is being developed, as well as during usage and while at rest in the enterprise. The security of code repositories can pose a challenge for the security professional for several reasons. With the move to offshoring application development, the code being developed may not be available to the enterprise directly, and the development environment may likewise be unavailable for management and inspection. The following is a summary of the security measures that GitHub has put in place to safeguard code hosted through it:

Physical Security

Data center access limited to data center technicians and approved GitHub staff. Biometric scanning for controlled data center access. Security camera monitoring at all data center locations. 24/7 onsite staff that provides additional protection against unauthorized entry Unmarked facilities to help maintain low profile. Physical security audited by an independent firm.

System Security

System installation using hardened, patched OS. Dedicated firewall and VPN services to help block unauthorized system access. Dedicated intrusion detection devices to provide an additional layer of protection against unauthorized system access. Distributed Denial of Service (DDoS) mitigation services powered by industry-leading solutions.

Operational Security

Our primary data center operations are regularly audited by independent firms against an ISAE 3000/AT 101 Type 2 Examination standard. Systems access logged and tracked for auditing purposes. Secure document-destruction policies for all sensitive information. Fully documented change-management procedures.

Software Security
We employ a team of 24/7/365 server specialists at GitHub to keep our software and its dependencies up-to-date eliminating potential security vulnerabilities. We employ a wide range of monitoring solutions for preventing and eliminating attacks to the site.

Communications
All private data exchanged with GitHub is always transmitted over SSL (which is why your dashboard is served over HTTPS, for instance). All pushing and pulling of private data is done over SSH authenticated with keys, or over HTTPS using your GitHub username and password.

The SSH login credentials used to push and pull cannot be used to access a shell or the filesystem. All users are virtual (meaning they have no user account on our machines) and are access controlled through the peer reviewed, open source git-shell.

File System and Backups
Every piece of hardware we use has an identical copy ready and waiting for an immediate hot-swap in case of hardware or software failure. Every line of code we store is saved on a minimum of three different servers, including an off-site backup just in case a meteor ever hits our data centers (we'll keep our fingers crossed that doesn't happen). We do not retroactively remove repositories from backups when deleted by the user, as we may need to restore the repository for the user if it was removed accidentally.

We do not encrypt repositories on disk because it would not be any more secure. The website and git back-end would need to decrypt the repositories on demand, slowing down response times. Any user with shell access to the file system would have access to the decryption routine, thus negating any security it provides. Therefore, we focus on making our machines and network as secure as possible.

Employee Access
No GitHub employees ever access private repositories unless required to for support reasons. Staff working directly in the file store access the compressed Git database. Your code is never present as plaintext files like it would be in a local clone. Support staff may sign into your account to access settings related to your support issue. In rare cases, staff may need to pull a clone of your code; this will only be done with your consent. Support staff does not have direct access to clone any repository. They will need to temporarily attach their SSH key to your account to pull a clone. When working a support issue, we do our best to respect your privacy as much as possible; we only access the files and settings needed to resolve your issue. All cloned repositories are deleted as soon as the support issue has been resolved.

Maintaining Security
We protect your login from brute force attacks with rate limiting. All passwords are filtered from all our logs and are one-way encrypted in the database using bcrypt. Login information is always sent over SSL.

We also allow you to use two-factor authentication, or 2FA, as an additional security measure when accessing your GitHub account. Enabling 2FA adds security to your account by requiring both your password as well as access to a security code on your phone to access your account.

We have full time security staff to help identify and prevent new attack vectors. We always test new features in order to rule out potential attacks, such as XSS-protecting wikis, and ensuring that Pages cannot access cookies.

We also maintain relationships with reputable security firms to perform regular penetration tests and ongoing audits of GitHub and its code. These firms include ^Lift Security and Matasano Security.

We're extremely concerned and active about security, but we're aware that many companies are not comfortable hosting code outside their firewall. For these companies we offer GitHub Enterprise, a version of GitHub that can be installed to a server within the company's network.

Credit Card Safety

When you sign up for a paid account on GitHub, we do not store any of your card information on our servers. It's handed off to Braintree Payment Solutions, a company dedicated to storing your sensitive data on PCI-Compliant servers." [31]

Based on the security precautions outlined above, it is clear that GitHub has a strong security architecture to ensure the safety of the code being hosted through it. The architecture is comprised of multiple layers, and it meets or exceeds all standards that could be used to measure its effectiveness. The security professionals would be well advised to carefully study the measures outlined above and to understand which ones may be of value to them in their enterprise architectures. However, not all concerns and issues that the security professional will be asked to address may fit under the broad umbrella of an enterprise security architecture such as the one in use by GitHub.

What if we approach the problem from a different perspective? What if the following scenario is more in line with the issues that you may be asked to address as a security professional with regards to code security and visibility? Take the following example:

Company X's source code repository is currently hosted at its offshore development site, and there is no external access to it, either through the Internet or via a VPN. While this is certainly desirable from a security standpoint, it provides no visibility into what the developers are actually working on.

Aidan, the security professional, has asked the director of the offshore development site to put her on the mailing list for commits. The director has replied that they do not have such a system since all the developers sit in the same room. In addition, the developers are not very thrilled about getting a bunch of commit mails in their inbox every day.

Aidan asks him how long it would take to set up mail notifications, and he said he would look into it. Several days later, the director tells Aidan that it would not be so straightforward to implement, and he wants to know what Aidan's real reason for wanting this information is anyways.

---

31   See the following: https://help.github.com/articles/github-security

To resolve this, Aidan decides to create her own Subversion repository and migrate the source code from the offshore site. This way, Aidan will have complete control of the code then, and she will be able to set up permissions, branches, and email notifications. Plus, the new server will double as a continuous integration server when they are ready for that step at some point later on. The next big challenge is how to do it. How does Aidan set up her own subversion repository securely?

There are many options, such as commercial hosting solutions like GitHub, beanstalk, unfuddle, and SVNRepository.com. In addition, Aidan could setup and maintain her own Subversion repository within the enterprise directly.

Apache Subversion is a full-featured version control system originally designed to be a better Concurrent Versions System (CVS). According to the subversion.apache.org website, Subversion exists to be universally recognized and adopted as an open-source, centralized version control system characterized by its reliability as a safe haven for valuable data, the simplicity of its model and usage, and its ability to support the needs of a wide variety of users and projects, from individuals to large-scale enterprise operations.

Some of the main features of Apache Subversion are as follows:

- **Directories are versioned** – Subversion versions directories as first-class objects, just like files.
- **Copying, deleting, and renaming are versioned** – Copying and deleting are versioned operations. Renaming is also a versioned operation.
- **Free-form versioned metadata ("properties")** – Subversion allows arbitrary metadata ("properties") to be attached to any file or directory. These properties are key/value pairs, and they are versioned just like the objects they are attached to. Subversion also provides a way to attach arbitrary key/value properties to a revision (that is, to a committed changeset). These properties are not versioned because they attach metadata to the version-space itself, but they can be changed at any time.
- **Atomic commits** – No part of a commit takes effect until the entire commit has succeeded. Revision numbers are per-commit, not per-file, and commit's log message is attached to its revision, not stored redundantly in all the files affected by that commit.
- **File locking** – Subversion supports (but does not require) locking files so that users can be warned when multiple people try to edit the same file. A file can be marked as requiring a lock before being edited, in which case Subversion will present the file in read-only mode until a lock is acquired.
- **Symbolic links can be versioned** – Unix users can place symbolic links under version control. The links are recreated in Unix working copies but not in win32 working copies.
- **Executable flag is preserved** – Subversion notices when a file is executable, and if that file is placed into version control, its executability will be preserved when it is checked out to other locations. (The mechanism Subversion uses to remember this is simply versioned properties, so executability can be manually edited when necessary, even from a client that does not acknowledge the file's executability, e.g., when having the wrong extension under Microsoft Windows).

- **Apache network server option, with WebDAV/DeltaV protocol** – Subversion can use the HTTP-based WebDAV/DeltaV protocol for network communications and the Apache Web server to provide repository-side network service. This gives Subversion an advantage over CVS in interoperability, and it allows certain features (such as authentication and wire compression) to be provided in a way that is already familiar to administrators.

- **Standalone server option (svnserve)** – Subversion offers a standalone server option using a custom protocol because not everyone wants to run an Apache HTTPD server. The standalone server can run as an inetd service or in daemon mode, and it offers the same level of authentication and authorization functionality as the HTTPD-based server. The standalone server can also be tunnelled over ssh.

- **Repository read-only mirroring** – Subversion supplies a utility, svnsync for synchronizing (via either push or pull) a read-only slave repository with a master repository.

- **Bindings to programming languages** – The Subversion APIs come with bindings for many programming languages, such as Python, Perl, Java, and Ruby. (Subversion itself is written in C.)

- **Changelists** – Subversion 1.5 introduces changelists, which allow a user to put modified files into named groups on the client side and then commit by specifying a particular group. For those who work on logically separate changesets simultaneously in the same directory tree, changelists can help keep things organized.

How Do I Do It?

If you are not familiar with Subversion, you may be better served by a graphical client. (The Subversion project only maintains a command-line-based clients, but a number of third parties maintain graphical clients that build on their API's.) **Do a Web search for Subversion GUI client**.

How to Make an Existing Directory a Working Copy of a New Repository

Step 1 will be to download the latest working build of Apache Subversion. Use the following URL:

http://subversion.apache.org/download/

The following commands will convert a ./my-directory/ containing files into a working copy of a newly-created repository:

On Unix:

```
$ mkdir -p $HOME/.svnrepos/
$ svnadmin create ~/.svnrepos/my-repos
$ svn mkdir -m "Create directory structure." file://$HOME/.
svnrepos/my-repos/trunk file://$HOME/.svnrepos/my-repos/
branches file://$HOME/.svnrepos/my-repos/tags
$ cd my-directory
$ svn checkout file://$HOME/.svnrepos/my-repos/trunk ./
$ svn add --force ./
$ svn commit -m "Initial import"
$ svn up
```

On Windows:

```
> set REPOS_DIR=C:\repos\my-repos
> mkdir C:\repos
> svnadmin create %REPOS_DIR%
> svn mkdir -m "Create directory structure." "file:///%REPOS_DIR%/
trunk" "file:///%REPOS_DIR%/branches" file:///%REPOS_DIR%/tags"
> cd my-directory
> svn checkout "file:///%REPOS_DIR%/trunk" ./
> svn add --force ./
> svn commit -m "Initial import"
> svn up
```

Security of Application Programming Interfaces (API)

Many supposedly secure devices have some kind of application programming interface, or API, that untrustworthy people and processes can call in order to get some task performed. For instance, if you enable Javascript, then your browser exposes an application programming interface – Javascript – that the owners of websites you visit can use to do various things. A secure operating system may limit the calls that an application program can make, using a reference monitor or other wrapper to enforce a policy such as preventing information flow from high to low.

Application Programming Interfaces are the connectors for the Internet of Things (IoT), allowing our devices to speak to each other. At the same time however, APIs are the "unknown, unseen force" of the Internet because end-users are not aware that they are there. Yet, APIs are everywhere: When a fitness wristband sends your jogging time to a website, that uses an API; when you remotely unlock a car with a mobile app, that uses an API; when you remotely change the temperature in your home thermostat from your office, that uses an API. These APIs must be managed and secured. So the challenge for IT organizations is securely exposing functionality to be consumed by developers and partners, some of whom are unknown to the enterprise. At the same time, IT still needs to fulfill its primary mandate: to provide security and protection for a company's systems and for company and user data. Comprehensive data security has to protect the whole digital value chain, from apps to APIs to back-end services. API security, and the security of the infrastructures the APIs are running on, is critical to an enterprise that is exposing digital assets.

Another example can be found by looking at what Microsoft described as its Next Generation Secure Computing Base (NGSCB), or 'Trusted Computing'. This initiative has been somewhat responsible for putting a Trusted Platform Module (TPM) chip for secure crypto key storage on most of the PC and Mac motherboards shipping today. The plan, according to Microsoft, is that future applications would have a traditional 'insecure' part running on top of Windows as before and also a 'secure' part or Nexus Computing Agent (NCA) that would run on top of a new security kernel known as the Nexus, which would be formally verified and thus much more resistant to software attacks. The Nexus and the NCA would guard crypto keys and other critical variables for applications. The question this raises, however, is how the interface between the application and the NCA is to be protected. In short, whenever a trusted computer talks to a less trusted one, the language it uses is critical. You have to expect that the less trusted device will try out all sorts of unexpected combinations of commands in order to trick the more trusted one into revealing information it is not supposed to make available.

With increasing levels of personal data flying around the Internet, and now between devices, security is a greater cause for concern for the security professional than ever before. Aside from issues of ownership, there are problems determining who is responsible for ensuring that data arrives safely where it is needed, without interruption. The security professional needs to understand API security at many levels. The overarching framework that can link those various levels together is the concept of data governance, allowing for the structured and controlled development and deployment of APIs that will be used to manage and secure all data exchanges straight from the very beginning of the lifecycle of a system, ensuring that data is protected at every step of the process.

Late in 2013, it came to light that Tesla had created a security issue through the use of a custom developed Representational State Transfer (REST) API to allow access to their Model S cars. Tesla offers Android and iPhone apps for Model S owners, which can be used to check the vehicle's battery, track its location and status, and tweak several other settings, like climate control and the sunroof. It can also be used to unlock the doors on the Model S. The problem is that the REST API used by Tesla to provide access for Android and iPhone apps has several fairly serious security flaws, which could offer a way in for unscrupulous hackers. According to an article written by George Reese for O'Reilly, Tesla appears to have broken from accepted best practice when designing the API for the Model S.

"It's flawed in a way that makes no sense. Tesla ignored most conventions around API authentication and wrote their own. As much as I talk about the downsides to OAuth (a standard for authenticating consumers of REST APIs–Twitter uses it), this scenario is one that screams for its use," he wrote.[32]

REST is a means of expressing specific entities in a system by URL path elements; REST is not an architecture, but it is an architectural style to build services on top of the Web. REST allows interaction with a Web-based system via simplified URLs rather than complex request body or POST parameters to request specific items from the system.

The widespread use of REST APIs is really at the heart of the key challenge to the security professional with regards to API security. REST APIs are used everywhere today. With regards to Web services, APIs that adhere to the REST constraints are called RESTful. RESTful APIs are defined with these aspects:

- Base URI, such as http://example.com/resources/
- An Internet media type for the data. This is often JSON but can be any other valid Internet media type (e.g., XML, Atom, microformats, images, etc.)
- Standard HTTP methods (e.g., GET, PUT, POST, or DELETE)
- Hypertext links to reference state
- Hypertext links to reference related resources

REST-based APIs can be secured, but the security professional needs to work at it to get the security implemented correctly and consistently across the enterprise, as well as within all of the systems that touch, consume, and/or offer up data through REST-based APIs in way. The following recommendations, with regards to things that API developers need to do in order to ensure REST-based API security, will be helpful to the security professional:

1. Employ the same security mechanisms for your APIs as any web application your organization deploys. For example, if you are filtering for XSS on the Web front end, you must do it for your APIs, preferably with the same tools.

---

32   See the following: http://programming.oreilly.com/2013/08/tesla-model-s-rest-api-authentication-flaws.html

2. Do not create and implement your own security solutions. Use a framework or existing library that has been peer-reviewed and tested. Developers not familiar with designing secure systems often produce flawed security implementations when they try to do it themselves, and they leave their APIs vulnerable to attack as a result (remember the Tesla discussion).

3. Unless your API is a free, read-only public API, do not use single key-based authentication. It is not enough. You should add a password requirement.

4. Do not pass unencrypted static keys. If you are using HTTP and sending it across the wire, then make sure that you always encrypt it.

5. Ideally, use hash-based message authentication code (HMAC) because it is the most secure. Use SHA-2 and up; avoid SHA and MD5 because of known vulnerabilities and weaknesses.

In addition, the security professional may need to provide guidance on the use of authentication protocols with regards to REST APIs in the enterprise. There are three main paths that the security professional should be familiar with, as well as many additional variations depending on the business requirements needing to be addressed.

Basic Authentication w/ TLS

Basic authentication is the easiest of the three to implement because the majority of the time, it can be implemented without additional libraries. Everything needed to implement basic authentication is usually included in your standard framework or language library. The problem with basic authentication is that it is basic, and it offers only the absolute lowest security options of the available common protocols. There are no advanced options for using this protocol, so you are just sending a username and password that is Base64 encoded. Basic authentication should never be used without Transport Layer Security (TLS) (formerly known as SSL) encryption because the username and password combination can be easily decoded otherwise.

Oauth1.0a

Oauth 1.0a is the most secure of the three common protocols. The protocol uses a cryptographic signature, (usually HMAC-SHA1) value that combines the token secret, nonce, and other request-based information. The great advantage of OAuth 1 is you never directly pass the token secret across the wire, which completely eliminates the possibility of anyone seeing a password in transit. This is the only one of the three protocols that can be safely used without SSL, although you should still use SSL if the data transferred is sensitive. However, this level of security comes with a price: Generating and validating signatures can be a complex process. You have to use specific hashing algorithms with a strict set of steps. This is really not an issue anymore though because every major programming language has a library to handle this for you.

Oauth2

Oauth2's current specification removes signatures, so you no longer need to use cryptographic algorithms to create, generate, and validate signatures. All the encryption is now handled by TLS, which is required. There are not as many Oauth2 libraries as there are Oauth1a libraries, so integrating this protocol into your API may be more challenging.

The security professional could also examine the use of such solutions as Key Management Interoperability Protocol (KMIP) V1.1.[33] Client certificates and HTTP Digest could also be examined as possible options for creating a secure solution.

Another resource for the security professional to consider when examining REST API based security needs and concerns will be the Open Web Application Security Project OWASP REST Security Cheat Sheet.[34] One example of the guidance offered by the OWASP REST Security Cheat Sheet:

> "RESTful web services should use session based authentication, either by establishing a session token via a POST, or using an API key as a POST body argument or as a cookie. Usernames and passwords, session tokens and API keys should not appear in the URL, as this can be captured in web server logs and makes them intrinsically valuable.

OK:

```
https://example.com/resourceCollection/<id>/action
https://twitter.com/vanderaj/lists
```

NOT OK:

```
https://example.com/controller/<id>/
action?apiKey=a53f435643de32 (API Key is in URL)
http://example.com/controller/<id>/action?apiKey=a53f435643de32
(transaction not protected by TLS and API Key is in URL)"
```

Assess the Effectiveness of Software Security

Certification and Accreditation

In the United States, federal agencies are mandated to conduct security certification of systems that process, store, or transmit information on behalf of the government. Certification is the technical evaluation or assessment of security compliance of the information system within its operational environment; it is the endorsement by the users and managers that the system/application meets their functional requirements and in most cases the independent verification of the endorsement. The certification process is followed by accreditation or authorization. The accreditation or authorization process reviews the certification (or the assessment) information and grants the official authorization to place the information system into operational use; it is the formal approval by senior management. The U.S. National Institute of Standards and Technology (NIST) has developed a document, SP 800-37 Revision 1: Guide for Applying the Risk Management Framework to Federal Information Systems that recommends a security authorization process and procedures.[35] Every U.S. federal executive government system and application that goes into production must go through a process of certification and accreditation prior to implementation.

1. The NIST SP 800-37 Revision 1 guidance has sought to create a change in the traditional thought process surrounding Certification and Accreditation. The revised process emphasizes:

33　See the following: http://docs.oasis-open.org/kmip/spec/v1.1/os/kmip-spec-v1.1-os.pdf

34　See the following: https://www.owasp.org/index.php/REST_Security_Cheat_Sheet

35　See the following: http://csrc.nist.gov/publications/nistpubs/800-37-rev1/sp800-37-rev1-final.pdf

2. Building information security capabilities into federal information systems through the application of state-of-the-practice management, operational, and technical security controls; Maintaining awareness of the security state of information systems on an ongoing basis though enhanced monitoring processes; and

3. Providing essential information to senior leaders to facilitate decisions regarding the acceptance of risk to organizational operations and assets, individuals, other organizations, and the Nation arising from the operation and use of information systems.

The traditional Certification and Accreditation process has been transformed into a six step Risk Management Framework (RMF). The risk management process changes the traditional focus of C&A as a static, procedural activity to a more dynamic approach that provides the capability to more effectively manage information system-related security risks in highly diverse environments of complex and sophisticated cyber threats, ever-increasing system vulnerabilities, and rapidly changing missions.

The RMF has the following characteristics:

- Promotes the concept of near real-time risk management and ongoing information system authorization through the implementation of robust continuous monitoring processes;
- Encourages the use of automation to provide senior leaders the necessary information to make cost-effective, risk-based decisions with regard to the organizational information systems supporting their core missions and business functions;
- Integrates information security into the enterprise architecture and system development life cycle;
- Provides emphasis on the selection, implementation, assessment, and monitoring of security controls, and the authorization of information systems;
- Links risk management processes at the information system level to risk management processes at the organization level through a risk executive (function); and
- Establishes responsibility and accountability for security controls deployed within organizational information systems and inherited by those systems (i.e., common controls).

While the U.S. government and its business associates are required to undergo a formal authorization process, there are several reasons a private organization may choose to as well:

- A certification and accreditation process ensures a control framework has been selected and is consistently being applied across the organization.
- If implemented as part of a change management program, the system authorization process is relatively low overhead.
- Security authorization standards mandate the use of standards. Standardization across an organization can lead to gains in efficiency and lower unexpected changes.
- If implemented properly, a security authorization program includes all aspects of a system's security including physical, training, environment, and interconnections that could be missed by purely technical approaches.

Auditing and Logging of Changes

Systems and network device reporting is important to the overall health and security of systems. Every network device, operating system, or application provides some form of logging capabilities. Logs provide a clear view of who owns a process, what action was initiated, when it was initiated, where the action occurred, and why the process ran. A log is a record of actions and events that have taken place on a computer system. Logs are the primary record keepers of system and network activity. When security controls experience failures, logs are particularly helpful in capturing the pertinent information that will help the security professional understand what has happened and why. It is in the best interest of the enterprise to have appropriate auditing policies in place that effectively and efficiently collect information regarding critical events occurring in the network and systems in the form of logs and to manage them appropriately. This information regarding events, available in the form of logs, would enable all interested parties such as senior level executives as well as network and system administrators to understand and assess:

- The need for establishing baselines
- The performance of various servers and systems
- An application's functional and operational problems
- Effective detection of intrusion attempts
- Forensic analysis
- Compliance with various regulatory laws

The security professional needs to understand change and change management as integral elements in any successful enterprise security architecture. The ability to plan for change, manage it through a well-defined lifecycle, document it, and roll it back if required are all critical skills that the security professional must be comfortable with. There is best practice guidance of all sorts out there for the security professional to look to depending on what systems are deployed and what technologies may be in use in the enterprise. Technology platforms such as VMware, Microsoft, Oracle, and Cisco all have published guidance on the specifics of how to set up logging and auditing securely on their technology platforms.[36] NIST has included aspects of guidance and best practice recommendations on auditing and logging in many of their published guides. The NIST SP 880-92 Guide to Computer Security Log Management specifically speaks to these issues directly.[37] In addition, the NIST SP 800-137 Information Security Continuous Monitoring (ISCM) for Federal Information Systems and Organizations also provides oversight and guidance.[38]Among the many Computer and Emergency Response Teams (CERT) guidance that is available in a wide variety of areas, the CERT-In Indian Computer Emergency Response Team has published the Guidelines for Auditing and Logging, as CERT-IN Security Guidance CISG-2008-01.[39]

---

36   See the following for examples: http://blogs.vmware.com/vsphere/2011/04/ops-changes-part-8-log-files.html
       http://technet.microsoft.com/en-us/library/ff459262(v=exchg.150).aspx
       http://www.cisco.com/c/en/us/td/docs/voice_ip_comm/cucm/service/7_1_2/admin/Serviceability/saaulog.html
       http://docs.oracle.com/cd/E27559_01/admin.1112/e27152/basic_logging.htm

37   See the following: http://csrc.nist.gov/publications/nistpubs/800-92/SP800-92.pdf

38   See the following: http://csrc.nist.gov/publications/nistpubs/800-137/SP800-137-Final.pdf

39   See the following: http://delhi.gov.in/wps/wcm/connect/d3a5c00049d901a59e9bff034753160e/CISG-
       2008-01.pdf?MOD=AJPERES&lmod=-190487169&CACHEID=d3a5c00049d901a59e9bff034753160e

Information Integrity

Procedures should be applied to compare or reconcile what was processed against what was supposed to be processed. For example, controls can compare totals or check sequence numbers. This would check whether the right operation was performed on the right data.

Information Accuracy

To check input accuracy, one should incorporate data validation and verification checks into appropriate applications. Character checks compare input characters against the expected type of characters, such as numbers or letters. This is sometimes also known as sanity checking. Range checks verify input data against predetermined upper and lower limits. Relationship checks compare input data to data on a master record file. Reasonableness checks compare input data to an expected standard, another form of sanity checking. Transaction limits check input data against administratively set ceilings on specified transactions.

Information Auditing

Because vulnerabilities exist in the software life cycle, there is a likelihood that attacks will occur. Auditing procedures assist in detecting any abnormal activities. A secure information system must provide authorized personnel with the ability to audit any action that can potentially cause access to, damage to, or in some way affect the release of sensitive information. The level and type of auditing is dependent on the auditing requirements of the installed software and the sensitivity of data that is processed or stored on the system. The key element is that the audit data provides information on what types of unauthorized activities have taken place and who or what processes took the action.

The system resources should be protected when they are available for use. If security software or security features of software are disabled in any way, notification should be given to appropriate individuals. The ability to bypass security features must be limited to only those individuals who need that level of access, such as system administrators or information system security officers. Hardware and software should be evaluated for compatibility with existing or complementary systems.

Risk Analysis and Mitigation

Risk is defined as an event that has a probability of occurring and could have either a positive or negative impact to a project should that risk occur. A risk may have one or more causes and, if it occurs, one or more impacts. For example, a cause may be having limited personnel assigned to design the project. The risk event is that the assigned personnel available may not be adequate for the activity. If that event occurs, there may be an impact on the project cost, schedule, or performance. All projects assume some element of risk, and it is through risk management where tools and techniques are applied to monitor and track those events that have the potential to impact the outcome of a project.

Risk management is an ongoing process that continues through the life of a project. It includes processes for risk management planning, identification, analysis, monitoring, and control. Many of these processes are updated throughout the project lifecycle as new risks can be identified at any time. It is the objective of risk management to decrease the probability and impact of events adverse to the project. On the other hand, any event that could have a positive impact should be exploited.

The identification of risk normally starts before the project is initiated, and the number of risks increases as the project matures through the lifecycle. When a risk is identified, it is first assessed to ascertain the probability of occurring, the degree of impact to the schedule, scope, cost, and quality, and then it is prioritized. Risk events may impact only one or multiple impact categories. The probability of occurrence, number of categories impacted, and the degree (high, medium, low) to which they impact the project will be the basis for assigning the risk priority. All identifiable risks should be entered into a risk register and documented as part of a risk statement.

As part of documenting a risk, two other important items need to be addressed.

The first is mitigation steps that can be taken to lessen the probability of the event occurring. The second is a contingency plan, or a series of activities that should take place either prior to or when the event occurs. Mitigation actions frequently have a cost. Sometimes, the cost of mitigating the risk can exceed the cost of assuming the risk and incurring the consequences. It is important to evaluate the probability and impact of each risk against the mitigation strategy cost before deciding to implement a contingency plan. Contingency plans implemented prior to the risk occurring are pre-emptive actions intended to reduce the impact or remove the risk in its entirety. Contingency plans implemented after a risk occurs can usually only lessen the impact.

Identifying and documenting events that pose a risk to the outcome of a project is just the first step. It is equally important to monitor all risks on a scheduled basis through the use of a risk management team and report on them in the project status report.

As part of the Software Development Life Cycle (SDLC), an ongoing or continuous approach to risk assessment, analysis and mitigation is advisable. A vast majority of vulnerabilities are either developed into the software at its inception or as a part of changing the software's configuration over time. Standard risk analysis tools from a variety of industries and academia may be useful in helping a person understand and document processes and systems. These tools include Ishikawa Diagrams, P-Diagrams, Preliminary Hazard Analysis (PHA), Failure Modes and Effect Analysis (FMEA), Failure Modes and Effect Criticality Analysis (FMECA), and Hazard Analysis of Critical Control Points (HACCP).

A well-designed risk analysis and mitigation strategy will:

- Be integrated into the overall SDLC and the change management process of an organization.
- Use standardized methods of accessing risk and reporting risk to stakeholders:
  - ¤ Qualitative versus quantitative or hybrid approaches should be considered.
  - ¤ Standards such as those provided by the ISO, NIST, ANSI, and ISACA should be considered for frameworks to be comprehensive in risk coverage and focus not just on the technology but also the operational and managerial controls related to the system.
- Track and manage weaknesses discovered during assessment, change management, and continuous monitoring.
- Memorialize resultant risk decisions for prosperity and due diligence.

8

Security in the Software Development Life Cycle

Corrective Actions

Software is frequently delivered with vulnerabilities that are not discovered until after the software has been installed and is operational. All major software products have numerous security weaknesses that have been discovered only after their release. Because this is an ongoing problem, organizations must implement policies and procedures to limit the vulnerabilities that are inherent in the software by implementation of applicable vendor patches.

The security professional needs to ensure that a patch management solution is architected and implemented that addresses the needs of the enterprise. There are many places to look for guidance and best practices regarding patch management. The United States Department of Homeland Security, under the Control Systems Security Program and as part of the National Cyber Security Division, published the Recommended Practice for Patch Management of Control Systems in December 2008.[40] NIST Special Publication 800-40 Revision 3, Guide to Enterprise Patch Management Technologies is also a good reference.[41] Symantec has a Patch Management Best Practices How To article available as well.[42]

Regardless of the initial guidance that the security professional uses to help with the architecture of a patch management program, there are some general best practices and guidelines that should always be a part of any solution deployed to protect the enterprise. These generic best practices include the following:

Use a Change Control Process

A good change control procedure has an identified owner, a path for customer input, an audit trail for any changes, a clear announcement and review period, testing procedures, and a well-understood back-out plan. Change control will manage the process from start to finish. If your current procedure is lacking any of the above, please reconsider carefully before using it for deployment of updates.

Read All Related Documentation

Before applying any service pack, hotfix or security patch, one should read and peer-review all relevant documentation. The peer review process is critical as it mitigates the risk of a single person missing critical and relevant points when evaluating the update. Reading all associated documentation is the first step in assessing whether:

- The update is relevant and will resolve an existing issue.
- Its adoption will not cause other issues resulting in a compromise of the production system.
- There are dependencies relating to the update (i.e., certain features being enabled or disabled for the update to be effective).
- Potential issues will arise from the sequencing of the update, as specific instructions may state or recommend a sequence of events or updates to occur before the service pack, hotfix, or security patch is applied.

Apply updates on a needs only basis.

---

40 See the following: http://ics-cert.us-cert.gov/sites/default/files/recommended_practices/
    PatchManagementRecommendedPractice_Final.pdf

41 See the following: http://nvlpubs.nist.gov/nistpubs/SpecialPublications/NIST.SP.800-40r3.pdf

42 See the following: http://www.symantec.com/business/support/index?page=content&id=HOWTO3124

Testing

Service packs and hotfixes must be tested on a representative non-production environment prior to being deployed to production. This will help to gauge the impact of such changes.

Have a Working Backup and Schedule Production Downtime

Server outages should be scheduled, and a complete set of backup tapes and emergency repair disks should available, in case a restoration is required.

Make sure that you have a working backup of your system. The best method of restoring your server to a previous working installation is typically from a backup.

Always Have a Back-Out Plan

A back-out plan will allow the system and enterprise to return to their original state, prior to the failed implementation. It is important that these procedures are clear, and that contingency management has tested them, because in the worst case, a faulty implementation can make it necessary to activate contingency options.

Enterprises may need to exercise their back-out plan in the event of the update not having an uninstall process or the uninstall process failing. The back-out plan can be as simple as restoring from tape or may involve many lengthy manual procedures.

Forewarn Helpdesk and Key User Groups

You need to notify helpdesk staff and support agencies of the pending changes so they may be ready for arising issues or outages. It is also a good idea to prepare key user groups of proposed updates in order to minimize the user impact because this will assist in managing user expectations.

Target Non-Critical Servers First

If all tests in the lab environment are successful, start deploying on non-critical servers first, if possible, and then move to the primary servers once the service pack has been in production for 10-14 days.

In addition to patch management, other risks will need to be addressed by the security professional throughout the SDLC. Findings must be reviewed and prioritized. Not all findings may need to be mitigated. For example, if a low risk finding has an extremely high cost or will not have a major impact on the operations of an organization, it should be accepted. Although it may seem obvious that a high risk finding with a low corrective cost should be the first to be mitigated. However, often this is not the case. Many times, high risk findings may have substantial costs associated with implementing the corrective action(s) recommended or required for mitigation. In these circumstances, senior management must make difficult decisions regarding either the acceptance of the risk or the reprogramming of funds to cover the cost of the mitigation of the high risk items identified.

The information security professional must be in a position to provide:

- The finding with supporting details as to how it was discovered.
- How the risk was determined and any supplemental information regarding threats, vulnerabilities, likelihood, and impact.
- The remediation cost details and what exactly the mitigation will buy and how it will affect threats, vulnerabilities, likelihood, or impacts.

■ Be ready to define the impact of not remediating the weakness with scenarios, stories, and examples of what could happen. Remember to include impacts in the public space and the reputation of the organization.

Testing and Verification

When mitigations are implemented, they must be tested. In mature SDLC environments, this is often done as part of the promotion between development environments by the quality assurance and testing teams. Security findings should be addressed by the development team the same as any other change request: with the condition that the security assessor or another independent entity verify and validate the flaw has indeed been remediated. Typically, in large organizations, independent verification and validation (IV&V) teams work to determine if security findings and flaws are truly resolved. An internal audit group or information assurance team may also perform the IV&V function. Most importantly, the developer or system owner does not authoritatively declare the risk mitigated without the concurrence of an independent party. In addition to testing of mitigations, the developer should be encourage to use code signing as another integrity check for the code he or she is producing.

Code signing is a security technique that can be used to ensure code integrity, to determine who developed a piece of code, and to determine the purposes for which a developer intended a piece of code to be used. Although the code signing system performs policy checks based on a code signature, it is up to the caller to make policy decisions based on the results of those checks. When it is the operating system that makes the policy checks, whether your code will be allowed to run in a given situation depends on whether you signed the code and on the requirements you included in the signature.

Code signing certificates are digital certificates that will help protect users from downloading compromised files or applications. When a file or application signed by a developer is modified or compromised after publication, a popup browser warning will appear to let users know that the origin of the file or application cannot be verified.

When a piece of code has been signed, it is possible to determine reliably whether the code has been modified by someone other than the signer. The system can detect such alternation whether it was intentional (by a malicious attacker, for example) or accidental (as when a file gets corrupted). In addition, through signing, a developer can state that an app update is valid and should be considered by the system as the same app as the previous version.

For example, suppose a user grants the CISSP CERT app permission to access a file. Each time CISSP CERT attempts to access that item, the system must determine whether it is indeed the same app requesting access. If the app is signed, the system can identify the app with certainty. If the developer updates the app and signs the new version with the same unique identifier, the system recognizes the update as the same app and gives it access without requesting verification from the user. On the other hand, if CISSP CERT is corrupted or hacked, the signature no longer matches the previous signature; the system detects the change and refuses access to the file. Similarly, if you use Parental Controls to prevent your child from running a specific game, and that game has been signed by its manufacturer, your child cannot circumvent the control by renaming or moving files. Parental Controls uses the signature to unambiguously identify the game regardless of its name, location, or version number.

All sorts of code can be signed, including tools, applications, scripts, libraries, plug-ins, and other "code-like" data. Code signing has three distinct purposes. It can be used to:

- Ensure that a piece of code has not been altered
- Identify code as coming from a specific source (a developer or signer)
- Determine whether code is trustworthy for a specific purpose (for example, to access a specific item)

To enable signed code to fulfill these purposes, a code signature consists of three parts:

1. A seal, which is a collection of checksums or hashes of the various parts of the code, such as the identifier, the main executable, the resource files, and so on. The seal can be used to detect alterations to the code and to the app identifier.

2. A digital signature, which signs the seal to guarantee its integrity. The signature includes information that can be used to determine who signed the code and whether the signature is valid.

3. A unique identifier, which can be used to identify the code or to determine to which groups or categories the code belongs. This identifier can be provided explicitly by the signer.

Note that code signing deals primarily with running code. Although it can be used to ensure the integrity of stored code, that is a secondary use. To fully appreciate the uses of code signing, the security professional should be aware of some things that signing cannot do:

- It cannot guarantee that a piece of code is free of security vulnerabilities.
- It cannot guarantee that an app will not load unsafe or altered code – such as untrusted plug-ins – during execution.
- It is not a digital rights management (DRM) or copy protection technology. Although the system could determine that a copy of your app had not been properly signed by you or that its copy protection had been hacked, thus making the signature invalid, there is nothing to prevent a user from running the app anyway.

Regression and Acceptance Testing

Whenever developers change or modify their software, even a small tweak can have unexpected consequences. Testing existing software applications to make sure that a change or addition has not broken any existing functionality is called regression testing. Its purpose is to catch bugs that may have been accidentally introduced into a new build or release candidate and to ensure that previously eradicated bugs continue to stay dead. By re-running testing scenarios that were originally scripted when known problems were first fixed, the developer or security professional can make sure that any new changes to an application have not resulted in a regression or caused components that formerly worked to fail. Adequate coverage without wasting time should be a primary consideration when conducting regression tests. Some strategies and factors to consider during this process include the following:

- Test fixed bugs promptly. The programmer might have handled the symptoms but not have gotten to the underlying cause.
- Watch for side effects of fixes. The bug itself might be fixed, but the fix might create other bugs.
- Write a regression test for each bug fixed.
- If two or more tests are similar, determine which is less effective and get rid of it.
- Identify tests that the program consistently passes and archive them.

- Focus on functional issues, not those related to design.
- Make changes (small and large) to data and find any resulting corruption.
- Trace the effects of the changes on program memory.

The most effective approach to regression testing is based on developing a library of tests made up of a standard battery of test cases that can be run every time a new version of the program is built. The most difficult aspect involved in building a library of test cases is determining which test cases to include. Automated tests as well as test cases involving boundary conditions and timing definitely belong in your library.

As with most forms of automated testing, setting a regression-testing program on autopilot is not a surefire solution, and some conscious oversight and input is generally still needed to ensure that the tests catch all the bugs they should. When you have the exact same suite of tests running repeatedly, night after night, the testing process itself can become static. Over time, developers may learn how to pass a fixed library of tests, and then your standard array of regression tests can inadvertently end up not testing much of anything at all.

For regression testing to be effective, it needs to be seen as one part of a comprehensive testing methodology that is cost-effective and efficient while still incorporating enough variety, such as well-designed frontend UI automated tests alongside targeted unit testing, based on smart risk prioritization, to prevent any aspects of your software applications from going unchecked. Many Agile work environments employing workflow practices such as XP (Extreme Programming), RUP (Rational Unified Process), or Scrum use regression testing as an essential aspect of a dynamic, iterative development and deployment schedule.

Acceptance testing is a formal test conducted to determine whether or not a system satisfies its acceptance criteria and to enable the customer to determine whether or not to accept the system. Originally called functional tests because each acceptance test tries to test the functionality of a user story, acceptance tests are different from unit tests in that unit tests are modeled and written by the developer of each class, while the acceptance test is at least modeled and possibly even written by the customer.

Testing generally involves running a suite of tests on the completed system. Each individual test, known as a case, exercises a particular operating condition of the user's environment or feature of the system, and it will result in a pass or fail outcome. There is generally no degree of success or failure. The test environment is usually designed to be identical, or as close as possible, to the anticipated user's environment. These test cases must each be accompanied by test case input data and/or a formal description of the operational activities to be performed. The intentions are to thoroughly elucidate the specific test case and description of the expected results.

In agile software development, acceptance tests/criteria are usually created by business customers and expressed in a business domain language. These are high-level tests to verify the completeness of a user story or stories that are 'played' during any sprint/iteration. These tests are created ideally through collaboration between business customers, business analysts, testers, and developers. It's essential that these tests include both business logic tests as well as UI validation elements. The business customers (product owners) are the primary project stakeholder of these tests. As the user stories pass their acceptance criteria, the business owners can be reassured the developers are progressing in the right direction.

Assess Software Acquisition Security

Software vulnerabilities, malicious code, and software that does not function as promised pose a substantial risk to an enterprise's software-intensive critical infrastructure that provides essential information and services. Minimizing these risks is the function of software assurance (SwA). According to the United States Committee on National Security Systems *National Information Assurance (IA) Glossary*, CNSS Instruction No. 4009, 26 April, 2010, page 69: "Software assurance is the level of confidence that software is free from vulnerabilities, either intentionally designed into the software or accidentally inserted at any time during its lifecycle, and that it functions in the intended manner." [43]

SwA is critical because dramatic increases in business and mission risks are attributable to software that does not perform as intended and is exploitable. Exploitable software is vulnerable to attack. Software vulnerabilities jeopardize intellectual property, consumer trust, business operations and services, and a broad spectrum of critical infrastructure, including everything from process control systems to commercial software products. To ensure the integrity of business operations and key assets within critical infrastructure, one should confirm that the software is reliable and secure.

SwA can be organized around the major phases of a generic acquisition process. The major phases are:

1. **Planning Phase** – This phase begins with:
   a. Needs determination for acquiring software services or products, identifying potential alternative software approaches, and identifying risks associated with those alternatives. This set of activities is followed by
   b. Developing software requirements to be included in work statements;
   c. Creating an acquisition strategy and/or plan that includes identifying risks associated with various software acquisition strategies; and
   d. Developing evaluation criteria and an evaluation plan.

2. **Contracting Phase** – This phase includes three major activities:
   a. Creating/issuing the solicitation or RFP with a work statement, instructions to offerors, terms and conditions (including conditions for acceptance), prequalification considerations, and certifications;
   b. Evaluating supplier proposals submitted in response to the solicitation or RFP; and
   c. Finalizing contract negotiation to include changes in terms and conditions and awarding the contract. Software risks are addressed and mitigated through terms and conditions, certifications, evaluation factors for award, and risk mitigation requirements in the work statement.

3. **Monitoring and Acceptance Phase** – This phase involves monitoring the supplier's work and accepting the final service or product delivered under a contract. This phase includes three major activities:
   a. Establishing and consenting to the contract work schedule;
   b. Implementing change (or configuration) control procedures; and

---

43   See the following: http://www.ncix.gov/publications/policy/docs/CNSSI_4009.pdf

    c. Reviewing and accepting software deliverables. During the monitoring and acceptance phase, software risk management and assurance case deliverables must be evaluated to determine compliance in accepted risk mitigation strategies as stated in the requirements of the contract.

4. ***Follow-on*** – This phase involves maintaining the software (the process is often called sustainment). This phase includes two major activities:

    a. Sustainment (includes risk management, assurance case management, and change management) and

    b. Disposal or decommissioning.

    c. During the follow-on phase, software risks must be managed through continued analysis of the assurance case and should be adjusted to mitigate changing risks.

The security professional needs to ensure that a well-documented SwA policy and process is in place in the enterprise. Without the benefits of an SwA policy, the dangers faced by the enterprise range from potentially acquiring for use and deployment software with errors or other vulnerabilities to the unknowing acceptance of software that contains malicious code. Vulnerable software may permit the following:

- Unintentional errors leading to faulty operations that result in destruction of information or major disruption of operations
- Intentional insertion of malicious code intent on loss of life, destruction of information, major disruption of operations, or even destruction of critical infrastructure
- Theft of vital information that is sensitive or classified
- Theft of personal information
- Changed product, inserted agents, or corrupted information

The security professional needs to understand that the acquisition process can be leveraged to promote good software development practices and to facilitate the delivery of trustworthy software. All final software security requirements decisions are made during the acquisition process, in addition to acceptance and implementation decisions. Security must be engineered in from the beginning, as security cannot be "bolted on" after the product is delivered.

According to the ISO/IEC JTC1 SC7 Software and systems engineering technical committee, "System and software assurance focuses on the management of risk and assurance of safety, security, and dependability within the context of system and software life cycles". Many suppliers use capability maturity models (CMMs) to guide process improvement and assess capabilities; yet most of the CMMs do not explicitly address safety and security. As such, suppliers claiming mature process capabilities can fail to exercise practices critical to software assurance. Therefore, the security professional should be prepared to ask questions to determine how SwA has been factored into suppliers' process capabilities. Some of the following questions may prove to be of value for the security professional to consider asking, depending on the circumstances.

How does the supplier ensure that an infrastructure for safety and security is established and maintained? What evidence can be presented to demonstrate that the supplier:

- Ensures safety and security competency within the workforce?
- Established a qualified work environment (including the use of qualified tools)?

- Ensures integrity of safety and security information?
- Monitors operations and report incidents (relative to the environment in which the software will be deployed)?
- Ensures business continuity?

How does the supplier ensure safety and security risks are identified and managed? What evidence can be presented to demonstrate that the supplier:

- Identifies safety and security risks?
- Analyzes and prioritizes risks relative to safety and security?
- Determines, implements, and monitors the associated risk mitigation plan?

How does the supplier ensure safety and security requirements are satisfied? What evidence can be presented to demonstrate that the supplier:

- Determines regulatory requirements, laws, and standards?
- Develops and deploys safe and secure products and services?
- Objectively evaluates products?
- Establishes safety and security assurance arguments?

How does the supplier ensure that activities and products are managed to achieve safety and security requirements and objectives? What evidence can be presented to demonstrate that the supplier:

- Establishes independent safety and security reporting?
- Establishes a safety and security plan?
- Selects and manages suppliers, products, and services using safety and security criteria?
- Monitors and controls activities and products relative to safety and security requirements?

Summary

Software Development Security covers a wide range of topics focused on designing security into software and across IT services throughout the enterprise. The security professional is expected to understand a number of key security concepts and apply them against a number of common scenarios. The use of a SDLC to create more secure systems and software is a key objective that the security professional needs to ensure is incorporated into the enterprise by choosing frameworks and development methodologies that support its use. The need to understand security and ensure that it is built in at every phase of the development lifecycle is the security professional's main focus in this domain.

A short list of resources for the security professional with regards to some websites and standards to become familiar with:

More to Know

» The United States Department of Homeland Security's *Build Security In* website:

https://buildsecurityin.us-cert.gov/

» The United States Department of Homeland Security's Office of Cyber Security and Communications and NIST's *SAMATE – Software Assurance Metrics and Tool Evaluation* website:

http://samate.nist.gov/Main_Page.html

» The Mitre *Common Weakness Enumeration* website:

http://cwe.mitre.org/

» ISO/IEC 15408–3:2009. Information technology – Security techniques – Evaluation criteria for IT security – Part 3, Security assurance requirements, available at:

https://www.sabs.co.za/content/uploads/files/SANS15408-3.pdf

http://standards.iso.org/ittf/PubliclyAvailableStandards/index.html

» Common Criteria for Information Technology Security Evaluation, Part 3: Security assurance components, available at:

https://www.commoncriteriaportal.org/files/ccfiles/CCPART3V3.1R3.pdf

» ISO/IEC 27001:2013. Information technology – Security techniques – Information security management systems – Requirements, available at:

https://www.iso.org/obp/ui/#iso:std:iso-iec:27001:ed-2:v1:en

8

Security in the Software
Development Life Cycle

 # Domain 8: Review Questions

1. The key objective of application security is to ensure

    A.   that the software is hacker proof

    B.   the confidentiality, integrity and availability of data

    C.   accountability of software and user activity

    D.   prevent data theft

2. For an application security program to be effective within an organization, it is critical to

    A.   identify regulatory and compliance requirements.

    B.   educate the software development organization the impact of insecure programming.

    C.   develop the security policy that can be enforced.

    D.   properly test all the software that is developed by your organization for security vulnerabilities.

3. Which of the following architectures states: "There is no inherent difference between data and programming representations in computer memory" which can lead to injection attacks, characterized by executing data as instructions.

    A.   Von Neumann

    B.   Linus' Law

    C.   Clark and Wilson

    D.   Bell LaPadula

4. An important characteristic of bytecode is that it

    A.   has increased secure inherently due to sandboxing

    B.   manages memory operations automatically

    C.   is more difficult to reverse engineer

    D.   is faster than interpreted languages

5. Two cooperating processes that simultaneously compete for a shared resource, in such a way that they violate the system's security policy, is commonly known as

- A.   Covert channel
- B.   Denial of Service
- C.   Overt channel
- D.   Object reuse

6. An organization has a website with a guest book feature, where visitors to the web site can input their names and comments about the organization. Each time the guest book web page loads, a message box is prompted with the message 'You have been P0wnd' followed by redirection to a different website. Analysis reveals that the no input validation or output encoding is being performed in the web application. This is the basis for the following type of attack?

- A.   Denial of Service
- B.   Cross-site Scripting (XSS)
- C.   Malicious File Execution
- D.   Injection Flaws

7. The art of influencing people to divulge sensitive information about themselves or their organization by either coercion or masquerading as a valid entity is known as

- A.   Dumpster diving
- B.   Shoulder surfing
- C.   Phishing
- D.   Social engineering

8. An organization's server audit logs indicate that an employee that was terminated in the morning was still able to access certain sensitive resources on his system, on the internal network, that afternoon. The logs indicate that the employee had logged on successfully before he was terminated but there is no record of him logging off before he was terminated. This is an example of this type of attack?

- A.   Time of Check/Time of Use (TOC/TOU)
- B.   Logic Bomb
- C.   Remote-Access Trojans (RATS)
- D.   Phishing

9. The most effective defense against a buffer overflow attack is

    A.   disallow dynamic construction of queries

    B.   bounds checking

    C.   encode the output

    D.   forced garbage collection

10. It is extremely important that as one follows a software development project, security activities are performed

    A.   before release to production, so that the project is not delayed

    B.   if a vulnerability is detected in your software

    C.   in each stage of the life cycle

    D.   when management mandates it

11. Software Acquisition (SwA) can be organized around the major phases of a generic acquisition process. The major phases are:

    A.   Planning, contracting, monitoring and acceptance, follow on

    B.   Contracting, planning, monitoring and acceptance, follow on

    C.   Planning, contracting, monitoring and certification, follow on

    D.   Planning, contracting, monitoring and accreditation, follow on

12. Who can ensure and enforce the separation of duties by ensuring that programmers don't have access to production code?

    A.   Operations personnel

    B.   Software librarian

    C.   Management

    D.   Quality assurance personnel

13. Technical evaluation of assurance to ensure that security requirements have been met is known as?

    A.   Accreditation

    B.   Certification

    C.   Validation

    D.   Verification

8

Security in the Software Development Life Cycle

14. Defect prevention rather than defect removal is characteristic of which of the following software development methodology?

    A. Computer Aided Software Engineering (CASE)

    B. Spiral

    C. Waterfall

    D. Cleanroom

15. A security protection mechanism in which untrusted code, which is not signed, is restricted from accessing system resources is known as?

    A. Sandboxing

    B. Non-repudiation

    C. Separation of Duties

    D. Obfuscation

16. A program that does not reproduce itself but pretends to be performing a legitimate action, while acting performing malicious operations in the background is the characteristic of which of the following?

    A. Worms

    B. Trapdoor

    C. Virus

    D. Trojan

17. A plot to take insignificant pennies from a user's bank account and move them to the attacker's bank account is an example of

    A. Social Engineering

    B. Salami Scam

    C. Pranks

    D. Hoaxes

18. Role-based access control to protect confidentiality of data in databases can be achieved by which of the following?

    A. Views

    B. Encryption

    C. Hashing

    D. Masking

19. The two most dangerous types of attacks against databases containing disparate non-sensitive information are

    A. Injection and scripting

    B. Session hijacking and cookie poisoning

    C. Aggregation and inference

    D. Bypassing authentication and insecure cryptography

20. A property that ensures only valid or legal transactions that do not violate any user-defined integrity constraints in DBMS technologies is known as?

    A. Atomicity

    B. Consistency

    C. Isolation

    D. Durability

21. Expert systems are comprised of a knowledge base comprising modeled human experience and which of the following?

    A. Inference engine

    B. Statistical models

    C. Neural networks

    D. Roles

22. The best defense against session hijacking and man-in-the-middle (MITM) attacks is to use the following in the development of your software?

    A. Unique and random identification

    B. Use prepared statements and procedures

    C. Database views

    D. Encryption

8

Security in the Software Development Life Cycle

Appendix A
Answers to Domain Review Questions

Domain 1 – **Security and Risk Management**

1. Within the realm of IT security, which of the following combinations best defines risk?

    A.   Threat coupled with a breach

    B.   Threat coupled with a vulnerability

    C.   Vulnerability coupled with an attack

    D.   Threat coupled with a breach of security

Answer: **B**

A vulnerability is a lack of a countermeasure or a weakness in a countermeasure that is in place. A threat is any potential danger that is associated with the exploitation of a vulnerability. The threat is that someone, or something, will identify a specific vulnerability and use it against the company or individual. A risk is the likelihood of a threat agent exploiting a vulnerability and the corresponding business impact.

2. When determining the value of an intangible asset which is be **BEST** approach?

    A.   Determine the physical storage costs and multiply by the expected life of the company

    B.   With the assistance of a finance of accounting professional determine how much profit the asset has returned

    C.   Review the depreciation of the intangible asset over the past three years.

    D.   Use the historical acquisition or development cost of the intangible asset

Answer: **B**

Intangible asset value is challenging to determine. While there are several ways to determine the value of an intangible asset, the best approach involves seeking assistance from finance or accounting professionals to determine the impact of the asset to the organization.

3. Qualitative risk assessment is earmarked by which of the following?

    A. Ease of implementation and it can be completed by personnel with a limited understanding of the risk assessment process

    B. Can be completed by personnel with a limited understanding of the risk assessment process and uses detailed metrics used for calculation of risk

    C. Detailed metrics used for calculation of risk and ease of implementation

    D. Can be completed by personnel with a limited understanding of the risk assessment process and detailed metrics used for the calculation of risk

Answer: **A**

Qualitative risk assessments are a form of risk assessments that use stratified forms of risk such as "high, moderate and low." This simplified approach allows for those not as familiar with risk assessments the ability to perform risk assessments, which while not as specific as quantitative assessments are still meaningful.

4. Single loss expectancy (SLE) is calculated by using:

    A. Asset value and annualized rate of occurrence (ARO)

    B. Asset value, local annual frequency estimate (LAFE), and standard annual frequency estimate (SAFE)

    C. Asset value and exposure factor

    D. Local annual frequency estimate and annualized rate of occurrence

Answer: **C**

The formula for calculating SLE is SLE = asset value (in $) × exposure factor (loss in successful threat exploit, as %).

5. Consideration for which type of risk assessment to perform includes all of the following:

    A. Culture of the organization, likelihood of exposure and budget

    B. Budget, capabilities of resources and likelihood of exposure

    C. Capabilities of resources, likelihood of exposure and budget

    D. Culture of the organization, budget, capabilities and resources

Answer: **D**

It is expected that an organization will make a selection of the risk assessment methodology, tools, and resources (including people) that best fit its culture, personnel capabilities, budget, and timeline.

6. Security awareness training includes:

    A.   Legislated security compliance objectives

    B.   Security roles and responsibilities for staff

    C.   The high-level outcome of vulnerability assessments

    D.   Specialized curriculum assignments, coursework and an accredited institution

Answer: **B**

Security awareness training is a method by which organizations can inform employees about their roles, and expectations surrounding their roles, in the observance of information security requirements. Additionally, training provides guidance surrounding the performance of particular security or risk management functions, as well as providing information surrounding the security and risk management functions in general.

7. What is the minimum and customary practice of responsible protection of assets that affects a community or societal norm?

    A.   Due diligence

    B.   Risk mitigation

    C.   Asset protection

    D.   Due care

Answer: **D**

Due diligence is the act of investigating and understanding the risks the company faces. A company practices due care by developing security policies, procedures, and standards. Due care shows that a company has taken responsibility for the activities that take place within the corporation and has taken the necessary steps to help protect the company, its resources, and employees from possible risks. So due diligence is understanding the current threats and risks and due care is implementing countermeasures to provide protection from those threats. If a company does not practice due care and due diligence pertaining to the security of its assets, it can be legally charged with negligence and held accountable for any ramifications of that negligence.

8. Effective security management:

    A.   Achieves security at the lowest cost

    B.   Reduces risk to an acceptable level

    C.   Prioritizes security for new products

    D.   Installs patches in a timely manner

Answer: **B**

There will always be residual risk accepted by an organization, and effective security management will minimize this risk to a level that fits within the organization's risk tolerance or risk profile.

9. Availability makes information accessible by protecting from:

    A.   Denial of services, fires, floods, hurricanes, and unauthorized transactions

    B.   Fires, floods, hurricanes, unauthorized transactions and unreadable backup tapes

    C.   Unauthorized transactions, fires, floods, hurricanes and unreadable backup tapes

    D.   Denial of services, fires, floods, and hurricanes and unreadable backup tapes

Answer: **D**

Availability is the principle that information is available and accessible by users when needed. The two primary areas affecting the availability of systems are (1) denial of service attacks and (2) loss of service due to a disaster, which could be man-made or natural.

10. Which phrase best defines a business continuity/disaster recovery plan?

    A.   A set of plans for preventing a disaster.

    B.   An approved set of preparations and sufficient procedures for responding to a disaster.

    C.   A set of preparations and procedures for responding to a disaster without management approval.

    D.   The adequate preparations and procedures for the continuation of all organization functions.

Answer: **D**

Business continuity planning (BCP) and Disaster recovery planning (DRP) address the preparation, processes, and practices required to ensure the preservation of the business in the face of major disruptions to normal business operations.

11. Which of the following steps should be performed first in a business impact analysis (BIA)?

    A.   Identify all business units within an organization

    B.   Evaluate the impact of disruptive events

    C.   Estimate the Recovery Time Objectives (RTO)

    D.   Evaluate the criticality of business functions

Answer: **A**

The four cyclical steps in the BIA process are:

1. Gathering information;
2. Performing a vulnerability assessment;
3. Analyzing the information; and
4. Documenting the results and presenting the recommendations.

The initial step of the BIA is identifying which business units are critical to continuing an acceptable level of operations.

12. Tactical security plans are **BEST** used to:

    A.   Establish high-level security policies

    B.   Enable enterprise/entity-wide security management

    C.   Reduce downtime

    D.   Deploy new security technology

Answer: **D**

Tactical plans provide the broad initiatives to support and achieve the goals specified in the strategic plan. These initiatives may include deployments such as establishing an electronic policy development and distribution process, implementing robust change control for the server environment, reducing vulnerabilities residing on the servers using vulnerability management, implementing a "hot site" disaster recovery program, or implementing an identity management solution. These plans are more specific and may consist of multiple projects to complete the effort. Tactical plans are shorter in length, such as 6 to 18 months to achieve a specific security goal of the company.

13. Who is accountable for implementing information security?

    A.   Everyone

    B.   Senior management

    C.   Security officer

    D.   Data owners

Answer: **C**

The security officer must work with the application development managers to ensure that security is considered in the project cost during each phase of development (analysis, design, development, testing, implementation, and post implementation). To facilitate this best from an independence perspective, the security officer should not report to application development.

14. Security is likely to be most expensive when addressed in which phase?

    A.   Design

    B.   Rapid prototyping

    C.   Testing

    D.   Implementation

Answer: **D**

Security is much less expensive when it is built into the application design versus added as an afterthought at or after implementation.

15. Information systems auditors help the organization:

    A. Mitigate compliance issues

    B. Establish an effective control environment

    C. Identify control gaps

    D. Address information technology for financial statements

Answer: **C**

Auditors provide an essential role for maintaining and improving information security. They provide an independent view of the design, effectiveness, and implementation of controls. The results of audits generate findings that require management response and corrective action plans to resolve the issue and mitigate the risk.

16. The Facilitated Risk Analysis Process (FRAP)

    A. makes a base assumption that a broad risk assessment is the most efficient way to determine risk in a system, business segment, application or process.

    B. makes a base assumption that a narrow risk assessment is the most efficient way to determine risk in a system, business segment, application or process.

    C. makes a base assumption that a narrow risk assessment is the least efficient way to determine risk in a system, business segment, application or process.

    D. makes a base assumption that a broad risk assessment is the least efficient way to determine risk in a system, business segment, application or process.

Answer: **B**

The Facilitated Risk Analysis Process (FRAP) makes a base assumption that a narrow risk assessment is the most efficient way to determine risk in a system, business segment, application or process. The process allows organizations to prescreen applications, systems, or other subjects to determine if a risk analysis is needed. By establishing a unique prescreening process, organizations will be able to concentrate on subjects that truly need a formal risk analysis. The process has little outlay of capital and can be conducted by anyone with good facilitation skills.

17. Setting clear security roles has the following benefits:

    A. Establishes personal accountability, reduces cross-training requirements and reduces departmental turf battles

    B. Enables continuous improvement, reduces cross-training requirements and reduces departmental turf battles

    C. Establishes personal accountability, establishes continuous improvement and reduces turf battles

    D. Reduces departmental turf battles, Reduces cross-training requirements and establishes personal accountability

Answer: **C**

Establishing clear, unambiguous security roles has many benefits to the organization beyond providing information as to the responsibilities to be performed and who needs to perform them.

18. Well-written security program policies are **BEST** reviewed:

    A.   At least annually or at pre-determined organization changes

    B.   After major project implementations

    C.   When applications or operating systems are updated

    D.   When procedures need to be modified

Answer: **A**

Policies should survive two or three years even though they should be reviewed and approved at least annually.

19. An organization will conduct a risk assessment to evaluate

    A.   threats to its assets, vulnerabilities not present in the environment, the likelihood that a threat will be realized by taking advantage of an exposure, the impact that the exposure being realized will have on the organization, the residual risk

    B.   threats to its assets, vulnerabilities present in the environment, the likelihood that a threat will be realized by taking advantage of an exposure, the impact that the exposure being realized will have on another organization, the residual risk

    C.   threats to its assets, vulnerabilities present in the environment, the likelihood that a threat will be realized by taking advantage of an exposure, the impact that the exposure being realized will have on the organization, the residual risk

    D.   threats to its assets, vulnerabilities present in the environment, the likelihood that a threat will be realized by taking advantage of an exposure, the impact that the exposure being realized will have on the organization, the total risk

Answer: **C**

An organization will conduct a risk assessment (the term *risk analysis* is sometimes interchanged with risk assessment) to evaluate:

- Threats to its assets
- Vulnerabilities present in the environment
- The likelihood that a threat will be realized by taking advantage of an exposure (or probability and frequency when dealing with quantitative assessment)
- The impact that the exposure being realized will have on the organization
- Countermeasures available that can reduce the threat's ability to exploit the exposure or that can lessen the impact to the organization when a threat is able to exploit a vulnerability
- The residual risk (e.g., the amount of risk that is left over when appropriate controls are properly applied to lessen or remove the vulnerability)

An organization may also wish to document evidence of the countermeasure in a deliverable called an exhibit or in some frameworks this is called "evidence." An exhibit can be used to provide an audit trail for the organization and, likewise, evidence for any internal or external auditors that may have questions about the organization's current state of risk. Why undertake such an endeavor? Without knowing what assets are critical and which would be most at risk within an organization, it is not possible to protect those assets appropriately.

20. A security policy which will remain relevant and meaningful over time includes the following:

    A. Directive words such as shall, must, or will, technical specifications and is short in length

    B. Defined policy development process, short in length and contains directive words such as shall, must or will

    C. Short in length, technical specifications and contains directive words such as shall, must or will

    D. Directive words such as shall, must, or will, defined policy development process and is short in length

Answer: **D**

Technical implementation details do not belong in a policy. Policies must be written technology independent. Technology controls may change over time as an organization's risk profile changes and new vulnerabilities are found.

21. The ability of one person in the finance department to add vendors to the vendor database and subsequently pay the vendor violates which concept?

    A. A well-formed transaction

    B. Separation of duties

    C. Least privilege

    D. Data sensitivity level

Answer: **B**

Separation of duties ensures fraud or other undesirable behavior cannot occur without collusion between two or more parties. In this example, individuals could add himself or herself as a vendor and then pay themselves.

22. Collusion is best mitigated by:

    A. Job rotation

    B. Data classification

    C. Defining job sensitivity level

    D. Least privilege

Answer: **A**

Collusion involves multiple parties conspiring to perform an act harmful to the organization. By rotating jobs, collusion becomes more difficult as an increasing number of individuals must agree to harm the organization.

23. Data access decisions are best made by:

    A.   User managers

    B.   Data owners

    C.   Senior management

    D.   Application developer

Answer: **B**

Data owners are ultimately responsible for the information and therefore should determine access decisions.

24. Which of the following statements BEST describes the extent to which an organization should address business continuity or disaster recovery planning?

    A.   Continuity planning is a significant organizational issue and should include all parts or functions of the company.

    B.   Continuity planning is a significant technology issue and the recovery of technology should be its primary focus.

    C.   Continuity planning is required only where there is complexity in voice and data communications.

    D.   Continuity planning is a significant management issue and should include the primary functions specified by management.

Answer: **A**

Business continuity planning and Disaster recovery planning involve the identification, selection, implementation, testing, and updating of prudent processes and specific actions necessary to protect critical business processes from the effects of major system and network disruptions and to ensure the timely restoration of business operations if significant disruptions occur.

25. Business impact analysis is performed to BEST identify:

    A.   The impacts of a threat to the organization operations.

    B.   The exposures to loss to the organization.

    C.   The impacts of a risk on the organization.

    D.   The cost efficient way to eliminate threats.

Answer: **B**

The business impact analysis is what is going to help the company decide what needs to be recovered and how quickly it needs to be recovered.

26. During the risk analysis phase of the planning, which of the following actions could BEST manage threats or mitigate the effects of an event?

    A.   Modifying the exercise scenario.

    B.   Developing recovery procedures.

    C.   Increasing reliance on key individuals

    D.   Implementing procedural controls.

Answer: **D**

The third element of risk is mitigating factors. Mitigating factors are the controls or safeguards the planner will put in place to reduce the impact of a threat.

27. The BEST reason to implement additional controls or safeguards is to:

    A.   deter or remove the risk.

    B.   identify and eliminate the threat.

    C.   reduce the impact of the threat.

    D.   identify the risk and the threat.

Answer: **C**

Preventing a disaster is always better than trying to recover from one. If the planner can recommend controls to be put in place to prevent the most likely of risks from having an impact on the organization's ability to do business, then the planner will have fewer actual events to recover from.

28. Which of the following statements BEST describes organization impact analysis?

    A.   Risk analysis and organization impact analysis are two different terms describing the same project effort.

    B.   A organization impact analysis calculates the probability of disruptions to the organization.

    C.   A organization impact analysis is critical to development of a business continuity plan.

    D.   A organization impact analysis establishes the effect of disruptions on the organization.

Answer: **D**

All business functions and the technology that supports them need to be classified based on their recovery priority. Recovery time frames for business operations are driven by the consequences of not performing the function. The consequences may be the result of business lost during the down period; contractual commitments not met resulting in fines or lawsuits, lost goodwill with customers, etc.

29. The term "disaster recovery" refers to the recovery of:

      A.   organization operations.

      B.   technology environment.

      C.   manufacturing environment.

      D.   personnel environments.

Answer: **B**

Once computers became part of the business landscape, it quickly became clear that we could not return to our manual processes if our computers failed. If those computer systems failed, there were not enough people to do the work nor did the people in the business still have the skill to do it manually anymore. Th is was the start of the disaster recovery industry. Still today, the term "disaster recovery" or "DR" commonly means recovery of the technology environment.

30. Which of the following terms BEST describes the effort to determine the consequences of disruptions that could result from a disaster?

      A.   Business impact analysis.

      B.   Risk analysis.

      C.   Risk assessment.

      D.   Project problem definition

Answer: **A**

The BIA is what is going to help the company decide what needs to be recovered and how quickly it needs to be recovered.

31. The elements of risk are as follows:

      A.   Natural disasters and manmade disasters

      B.   Threats, assets and mitigating controls

      C.   Risk and business impact analysis

      D.   business impact analysis and mitigating controls

Answer: **B**

There are three elements of risk: threats, assets, and mitigating factors.

32. Which of the following methods is not acceptable for exercising the business continuity plan?

    A.   Table-top exercise.

    B.   Call exercise.

    C.   Simulated exercise.

    D.   Halting a production application or function.

Answer: **D**

The only difference between a simulated and an actual exercise is that the first rule of testing is the planner will never create a disaster by testing for one. The planner must make every effort to make certain that what is being tested will not impact the production environment whether business or technical.

33. Which of the following is the primary desired result of any well-planned business continuity exercise?

    A.   Identifies plan strengths and weaknesses.

    B.   Satisfies management requirements.

    C.   Complies with auditor's requirements.

    D.   Maintains shareholder confidence

Answer: **A**

After every exercise the planner conducts, the exercise results need to be published and action items identified to address the issues that were uncovered by the exercise. Action items should be tracked until they have been resolved and, where appropriate, the plan updated. It is very unfortunate when an organization has the same issue in subsequent tests simply because someone did not update the plan.

34. A business continuity plan is best updated and maintained:

    A.   Annually or when requested by auditors.

    B.   Only when new versions of software are deployed.

    C.   Only when new hardware is deployed.

    D.   During the configuration and change management process.

Answer: **D**

The plan document and all related procedures will need to be updated after each exercise and after each material change to the production, IT, or business environment.

35. Which of the following is MOST important for successful business continuity?

    A.   Senior leadership support.

    B.   Strong technical support staff.

    C.   Extensive wide area network infrastructure.

    D.   An integrated incident response team.

Answer: **A**

Without senior leadership support it is unlikely a business continuity program will succeed.

36. A service's recovery point objective is zero. Which approach BEST ensures the requirement is met?

    A.   RAID 6 with a hot site alternative.

    B.   RAID 0 with a warm site alternative

    C.   RAID 0 with a cold site alternative

    D.   RAID 6 with a reciprocal agreement.

Answer: **A**

RAID 6 will provide a highly redundant storage situation while the hot site will stand ready to fail over should the primary site fail.

37. The (ISC)² code of ethics resolves conflicts between canons by:

    A.   there can never be conflicts between canons.

    B.   working through adjudication.

    C.   the order of the canons.

    D.   vetting all canon conflicts through the board of directors.

Answer: C

Conflicts are resolved through the order of the canons.

Domain 2 – **Asset Security**

1. In the event of a security incident, one of the primary objectives of the operations staff is to ensure that

    A.   the attackers are detected and stopped.

    B.   there is minimal disruption to the organization's mission.

    C.   appropriate documentation about the event is maintained as chain of evidence.

    D.   the affected systems are immediately shut off to limit to the impact.

Answer: **B**

While the operations staff may be able to detect the attack and in some cases the attackers, there is very little that the operations staff can do to stop them.

All actions taken by the operations staff as they respond to handle the security incident must follow established protocols and documented, but this is not their primary objective. The affected systems must only be shut off after necessary data or evidence that will be admissible in court is collected. The best answer choice is that the operations staff must maintain operational resilience.

2. Good data management practices include:

    A.   Data quality procedures at all stages of the data management process, verification and validation of accuracy of the data, adherence to agreed upon data management practices, ongoing data audit to monitor the use and assess effectiveness of management practices and the integrity of existing data.

    B.   Data quality procedures at some stages of the data management process, verification and validation of accuracy of the data, adherence to agreed upon data management practices, ongoing data audit to monitor the use and assess effectiveness of management practices and the integrity of existing data.

    C.   Data quality procedures at all stages of the data management process, verification and validation of accuracy of the data, adherence to discussed data management practices, ongoing data audit to monitor the use and assess effectiveness of management practices and the integrity of existing data.

    D.   Data quality procedures at all stages of the data management process, verification and validation of accuracy of the data, adherence to agreed upon data management practices, intermittent data audit to monitor the use and assess effectiveness of management practices and the integrity of existing data.

Answer: **A**

Data management is a process involving a broad range of activities from administrative to technical aspects of handling data. Good data management practices include:

- A data policy that defines strategic long-term goals and provides guiding principles for data management in all aspects of a project, agency, or organization.
- Clearly defined roles and responsibilities for those associated with the data, in particular of data providers, data owners, and custodians.

- Data quality procedures (e.g., quality assurance, quality control) at all stages of the data management process. Verification and validation of accuracy of the data.
- Documentation of specific data management practices and descriptive metadata for each dataset.
- Adherence to agreed upon data management practices.
- Carefully planned and documented database specifications based on an understanding of user requirements and data to be used.
- Defined procedures for updates to the information system infrastructure (hardware, software, file formats, storage media), data storage and backup methods, and the data itself.
- Ongoing data audit to monitor the use and assess effectiveness of management practices and the integrity of existing data. Data storage and archiving plan and testing of this plan (disaster recovery).
- Ongoing and evolving data security approach of tested layered controls for reducing risks to data.
- Clear statements of criteria for data access and, when applicable, information on any limitations applied to data for control of full access that could affect its use.
- Clear and documented published data that is available and useable to users, with consistent delivery procedures.

3. Issues to be considered by the security practitioner when establishing a data policy include:

    A.   Cost, Due Care and Due Diligence, Privacy, Liability, Sensitivity, Existing Law & Policy Requirements, Policy and Process

    B.   Cost, Ownership and Custodianship, Privacy, Liability, Sensitivity, Future Law & Policy Requirements, Policy and Process

    C.   Cost, Ownership and Custodianship, Privacy, Liability, Sensitivity, Existing Law & Policy Requirements, Policy and Procedure

    D.   Cost, Ownership and Custodianship, Privacy, Liability, Sensitivity, Existing Law & Policy Requirements, Policy and Process

Answer: **D**

A sound data policy defines strategic long-term goals for data management across all aspects of a project or enterprise. A data policy is a set of high-level principles that establish a guiding framework for data management. A data policy can be used to address strategic issues such as data access, relevant legal matters, data stewardship issues and custodial duties, data acquisition, and other issues. Because it provides a high-level framework, a data policy should be flexible and dynamic. This allows a data policy to be readily adapted for unanticipated challenges, different types of projects, and potentially opportunistic partnerships while still maintaining its guiding strategic focus. Issues to be considered by the security practitioner when establishing a data policy include:

- **Cost** – Consideration should be given to the cost of providing data versus the cost of providing access to data. Cost can be both a barrier for the user to acquire certain datasets, as well as for the provider to supply data in the format or extent requested.

- **Ownership and Custodianship** – Data ownership should be clearly addressed. Intellectual property rights can be owned at different levels; e.g. a merged dataset can be owned by one organization, even though other organizations own the constituent data. If the legal ownership is unclear, the risk exists for the data to be improperly used, neglected, or lost.
- **Privacy** – Clarification of what data is private and what data is to be made available in the public domain needs to occur. Privacy legislation normally requires that personal information be protected from others. Therefore clear guidelines are needed for the inclusion, usage, management, storage, and maintenance of personal information in datasets.
- **Liability** – Liability involves how protected an organization is from legal recourse. This is very important in the area of data and information management, especially where damage is caused to an individual or organization as a result of misuse or inaccuracies in the data. Liability is often dealt with via end-user agreements and licenses. A carefully worded disclaimer statement can be included in the metadata and data retrieval system so as to free the provider, data collector, or anyone associated with the dataset of any legal responsibility for misuse or inaccuracies in the data.
- **Sensitivity** – There is a need to identify any data which is regarded as sensitive. Sensitive data is any data which if released to the public, would result in an adverse effect (harm, removal, destruction) on the attribute in question or to a living individual. A number of factors need to be taken into account when determining sensitivity, including type and level of threat, vulnerability of the attribute, type of information, and whether it is already publicly available.
- **Existing Law and Policy Requirements** – Consideration should be given to laws and policies related to data and information as they apply. Existing legislation and policy requirements may have an effect on the enterprise's data policy.
- **Policy and Process** – Consideration should be given to legal requests for data and policies that may need to be put in place to allow for the timely processing of, and if appropriate, response to the request. In addition, if one or more policies already exist, then they have to be examined and assessed to decide whether they will be sufficient, or if they may need to be modified in some way to be fully integrated with any new processes being created. The policy and process used to provide access to data based on a legal request have to be designed and implemented in such a way that they do not violate access controls and/or any existing policies that mandate how secure access may be granted under such circumstances, ensuring that only the data subject to the request is made available, and not exposing any unrelated data.

4. The information owner typically has the following responsibilities:

    A.   Determine the impact the information has on the mission of the organization, understand the replacement cost of the information, determine who in the organization or outside of it has a need for the information and under what circumstances the information should be released, know when the information is inaccurate or no longer needed and should be archived.

    B.   Determine the impact the information has on the mission of the organization, understand the replacement cost of the information, determine who in the organization or outside of it has a need for the information and under what circumstances the information should be released, know when the information is inaccurate or no longer needed and should be destroyed.

    C.   Determine the impact the information has on the policies of the organization, understand the replacement cost of the information, determine who in the organization or outside of it has a need for the information and under what circumstances the information should not be released, know when the information is inaccurate or no longer needed and should be destroyed.

    D.   Determine the impact the information has on the mission of the organization, understand the creation cost of the information, determine who in the organization or outside of it has a need for the information and under what circumstances the information should be released, know when the information is inaccurate or no longer needed and should be destroyed.

Answer: **B**

When information is created someone in the organization must be directly responsible for it. Often this is the individual or group which created, purchased or acquired the information to support the mission of the organization. This individual or group is considered the "information owner." The information owner typically has the following responsibilities:

- Determine the impact the information has on the mission of the organization.
- Understand the replacement cost of the information (if it can be replaced).
- Determine who in the organization or outside of it has a need for the information and under what circumstances the information should be released.
- Know when the information is inaccurate or no longer needed and should be destroyed.

5. QA/QC mechanisms are designed to prevent data contamination, which occurs when a process or event introduces either of which two fundamental types of errors into a dataset: (**choose TWO**)

    A. Errors of commission

    B. Errors of insertion

    C. Errors of omission

    D. Errors of creation

Answer: **A | C**

QA/QC mechanisms are designed to prevent data contamination, which occurs when a process or event introduces either of two fundamental types of errors into a dataset:

- Errors of commission include those caused by data entry or transcription, or by malfunctioning equipment. These are common, fairly easy to identify, and can be effectively reduced up front with appropriate QA mechanisms built into the data acquisition process, as well as QC procedures applied after the data has been acquired.
- Errors of omission often include insufficient documentation of legitimate data values, which could affect the interpretation of those values. These errors may be harder to detect and correct, but many of these errors should be revealed by rigorous QC procedures.

6. Some typical responsibilities of a data custodian may include: (**Choose ALL that apply**)

    A. Adherence to appropriate and relevant data policy and data ownership guidelines.

    B. Ensuring accessibility to appropriate users, maintaining appropriate levels of dataset security.

    C. Fundamental dataset maintenance, including but not limited to data storage and archiving.

    D. Assurance of quality and validation of any additions to a dataset, including periodic audits to assure ongoing data integrity.

Answer: **A | B | C | D** *(all of the above)*

Data custodians are established to ensure that important datasets are developed, maintained, and are accessible within their defined specifications. Designating a person or role as being charged with overseeing these aspects of data management helps to ensure that datasets do not become compromised. How these aspects are managed should be in accordance with the defined data policy applicable to the data, as well as any other applicable data stewardship specifications. Some typical responsibilities of a data custodian may include:

- Adherence to appropriate and relevant data policy and data ownership guidelines
- Ensuring accessibility to appropriate users, maintaining appropriate levels of dataset security
- Fundamental dataset maintenance, including but not limited to data storage and archiving
- Dataset documentation, including updates to documentation
- Assurance of quality and validation of any additions to a dataset, including periodic audits to assure ongoing data integrity

7. The objectives of data documentation are to: (**Choose ALL that apply**)

    A. Ensure the longevity of data and their re-use for multiple purposes

    B. Ensure that data users understand the content context and limitations of datasets

    C. Facilitate the confidentiality of datasets

    D. Facilitate the interoperability of datasets and data exchange

Answer: **A | B | D**

Data documentation is critical for ensuring that datasets are useable well into the future. Data longevity is roughly proportional to the comprehensiveness of their documentation. All datasets should be identified and documented to facilitate their subsequent identification, proper management and effective use, and to avoid collecting or purchasing the same data more than once. The objectives of data documentation are to:

- Ensure the longevity of data and their re-use for multiple purposes
- Ensure that data users understand the content context and limitations of datasets
- Facilitate the discovery of datasets
- Facilitate the interoperability of datasets and data exchange

8. Benefits of data standards include:

    A. more efficient data management, decreased data sharing, higher quality data, improved data consistency, increased data integration, better understanding of data, improved documentation of information resources

    B. more efficient data management, increased data sharing, higher quality data, improved data consistency, increased data integration, better understanding of data, improved documentation of information resources

    C. more efficient data management, increased data sharing, medium quality data, improved data consistency, decreased data integration, better understanding of data, improved documentation of information resources

    D. more efficient data management, increased data sharing, highest quality data, improved data consistency, increased data integration, better understanding of data, improved documentation of information metadata

Answer: **B**

Data standards describe objects, features, or items that are collected, automated, or affected by activities or the functions of organizations. In this respect, data need to be carefully managed and organized according to defined rules and protocols. Data standards are particularly important in any situations where data and information need to be shared or aggregated. Benefits of data standards include:

- more efficient data management (including updates and security)
- increased data sharing
- higher quality data
- improved data consistency
- increased data integration
- better understanding of data
- improved documentation of information resources

9. When classifying data, the security practitioner needs to determine the following aspects of the policy: (**Choose ALL that apply**)

    A. who has access to the data

    B. what methods should be used to dispose of the data

    C. how the data is secured

    D. whether the data needs to be encrypted

Answer: **A | B | C | D** *(all of the above)*

Data classification entails analyzing the data that the organization retains, determining its importance and value, and then assigning it to a category. Data that is considered "secret" whether contained in a printed report or stored electronically needs to be classified so that it can be handled properly. IT administrators and security administrators can guess how long data should be retained and how it should be secured, but unless the organization has taken the time to classify its data, it may not be secured correctly or retained for the required time period.

When classifying data, the security practitioner needs to determine the following aspects of the policy:

    1) Who has access to the data? Define the roles of people who can access the data. Examples include accounting clerks who are allowed to see all accounts payable and receivable but cannot add new accounts, and all employees who are allowed to see the names of other employees (along with managers' names, and departments, and the names of vendors and contractors working for the company). However, only HR employees and managers can see the related pay grades, home addresses, and phone numbers of the entire staff. And only HR managers can see and update employee information classified as private, including Social Security numbers (SSNs) and insurance information.

    2) How the data is secured. Determine whether the data is generally available or, by default, off limits. In other words, when defining the roles that are allowed to have access, you also need to define the type of access—view only or update capabilities—along with the general access policy for the data. As an example, many companies set access controls to deny database access to everyone except those who are specifically granted permission to view or update the data.

    3) How long the data is to be retained. Many industries require that data be retained for a certain length of time. For example, the finance industry requires a seven-year retention period. Data owners need to know the regulatory requirements for their data, and if requirements do not exist, they should base the retention period on the needs of the business.

    4) What method(s) should be used to dispose of the data? For some data classifications, the method of disposal will not matter. But some data is so sensitive that data owners will want to dispose of printed reports through cross-cut shredding or another secure method. In addition, they may require employees to use a utility to verify that data has been removed fully from their PCs after they erase files containing sensitive data to address any possible data remanence issues or concerns.

    5) Whether the data needs to be encrypted. Data owners will have to decide whether their data needs to be encrypted. They typically set this requirement when they must comply with a law or regulation such as the Payment Card Industry Data Security Standard (PCI-DSS).

6) What use of the data is appropriate? This aspect of the policy defines whether data is for use within the company, is restricted for use by only selected roles, or can be made public to anyone outside the organization. In addition, some data has legal usage definition associated with it. The organization's policy should spell out any such restrictions or refer to the legal definitions as required.

Proper data classification also helps the organization comply with pertinent laws and regulations.

10. The major benefit of information classification is to

    A.   map out the computing ecosystem

    B.   identify the threats and vulnerabilities

    C.   determine the software baseline

    D.   identify the appropriate level of protection needs

Answer: **D**

Information classification refers to the practice of differentiating between different types of information assets and providing some guidance as to how classified information will need to be protected. Vulnerability scans can be used to map out the computing ecosystem. Threat modeling is used to identify threats and vulnerabilities. Configuration management can be used to determine the software baseline.

11. When sensitive information is no longer critical but still within scope of a record retention policy, that information is **BEST**

    A.   Destroyed

    B.   Re-categorized

    C.   Degaussed

    D.   Released

Answer: **B**

Information categorization also includes the processes and procedures to lower the sensitivity label of information. For example, declassification may be used to downgrade the sensitivity of information. Over the course of time, information once considered sensitive may decline in value or criticality. In these instances, declassification efforts should be implemented to ensure that excessive protection controls are not used for non-sensitive information. When declassifying information, marking, handling, and storage requirements will likely be reduced. Organizations should have categorization or declassification practices well documented for use by individuals assigned with the task. Information may still be needed and so it cannot be destroyed, degaussed, or deleted.

12. What are the FOUR phases of the equipment lifecycle?

    A. Defining requirements, acquiring and implementing, operations and maintenance, disposal and decommission

    B. Acquiring requirements, defining and implementing, operations and maintenance, disposal and decommission

    C. Defining requirements, acquiring and maintaining, implementing and operating, disposal and decommission

    D. Defining requirements, acquiring and implementing, operations and decommission, maintenance and disposal

Answer: **A**

The following illustrates common activities that the information security professional should engage in throughout the equipment lifecycle:

- ### Defining Requirements
  - ¤ Ensure relevant security requirements are included in any specifications for new equipment
  - ¤ Ensure appropriate costs have been allocated for security features required
  - ¤ Ensure new equipment requirements fits into the organizational security architecture

- ### Acquiring and Implementing
  - ¤ Validate security features are included as specified
  - ¤ Ensure additional security configurations, software and features are applied to the equipment
  - ¤ Ensure the equipment is followed through any security certification or accreditation process as required
  - ¤ Ensure the equipment is inventoried

- ### Operations and Maintenance
  - ¤ Ensure the security features and configurations remain operational
  - ¤ Review the equipment for vulnerabilities and mitigate if discovered
  - ¤ Ensure appropriate support is available for security related concerns
  - ¤ Validate and verify inventories to ensure equipment is in place as intended
  - ¤ Ensure changes to the configuration of the system are reviewed through a security impact analysis and vulnerabilities are mitigated

- ### Disposal and Decommission
  - ¤ Ensure equipment is securely erased and then either destroyed or recycled depending on the security requirements of the organization
  - ¤ Ensure inventories are accurately updated to reflect the status of decommissioned equipment

13. Which of the following **BEST** determines the employment suitability of an individual?

    A. Job rank or title
    B. Partnership with the security team
    C. Role
    D. Background investigation

Answer: **D**

A background investigation relevant to the role, job or access is the best approach for minimal security problems. While a background investigation will not guarantee the integrity or honesty of an individual it will give the organization a glimpse into the history of an individual and references.

14. The best way to ensure that there is no data remanence of sensitive information that was once stored on a DVD-R media is by

    A. Deletion
    B. Degaussing
    C. Destruction
    D. Overwriting

Answer: **C**

Optical media such as CDs and DVD must be physically destroyed to make sure that there is no residual data that can be disclosed. Since the media mentioned in this context is a read-only media (burn-once) DVD, the information on it cannot be overwritten or deleted. Degaussing can reduce or remove data remanence in magnetic non-optical media.

15. Which of the following processes is concerned with not only identifying the root cause but also addressing the underlying issue?

    A. Incident management
    B. Problem management
    C. Change management
    D. Configuration management

Answer: **B**

While incident management is concerned primarily with managing an adverse event, problem management is concerned with tracking that event back to a root cause and addressing the underlying problem. Maintaining system integrity is accomplished through the process of change control management. Configuration management is a process of identifying and documenting hardware components, software, and the associated settings.

16. Before applying a software update to production systems, it is **MOST** important that

    A. Full disclosure information about the threat that the patch addresses is available

    B. The patching process is documented

    C. The production systems are backed up

    D. An independent third party attests the validity of the patch

Answer: **C**

Prior to deploying updates to production servers, make certain that a full system backup is conducted. In the regrettable event of a system crash, due to the update, the server and data can be recovered without a significant loss of data. Additionally, if the update involved propriety code, it will be necessary to provide a copy of the server or application image to the media librarian. The presence or absence of full disclosure information is good to have but not a requirement as the patching process will have to be a risk-based decision as it applies to the organization. Documentation of the patching process is the last step in patch management processes. Independent third-party assessments are not usually related to attesting patch validity

Domain 3 – Security Engineering

1. A holistic lifecycle for developing security architecture that begins with assessing business requirements and subsequently creating a 'chain of traceability' through phases of strategy, concept, design, implementation and metrics is characteristic of which of the following frameworks?

    A. Zachman

    B. SABSA

    C. ISO 27000

    D. TOGAF

Answer: **B**

SABSA (Sherwood Applied Business Security Architecture) is a holistic lifecycle for developing security architecture that begins with assessing business requirements. It generates a "chain of traceability" of security requirements to business functionality, through the phases of strategy, concept, design, implementation, and metrics. It represents any architecture using six layers, each representing a different perspective for the design and construction and use of the target system.

2. While an Enterprise Security Architecture (ESA) can be applied in many different ways, it is focused on a few key goals. Identify the proper listing of the goals for the ESA:

    A. It represents a simple, long term view of control, it provides a unified vision for common security controls, it leverages existing technology investments, it provides a fixed approach to current and future threats and also the needs of peripheral functions

    B. It represents a simple, long term view of control, it provides a unified vision for common security controls, it leverages new technology investments, it provides a flexible approach to current and future threats and also the needs of core functions

    C. It represents a complex, short term view of control, it provides a unified vision for common security controls, it leverages existing technology investments, it provides a flexible approach to current and future threats and also the needs of core functions

    D. It represents a simple, long term view of control, it provides a unified vision for common security controls, it leverages existing technology investments, it provides a flexible approach to current and future threats and also the needs of core functions

Answer: **D**

    While ESA can be applied in many different ways, it is focused on a few key goals:

- **It represents a** simple, long-term view of control: With the heterogeneity of possible solutions, duplications and inefficiencies are endemic to many security architectures. To ensure that the organization gets the right level of control to address the most common risks, a good architecture must be comprehensive but also simple. It must also avoid unnecessary duplication of services or complexities that could compromise the business benefits of the security services. It must be able to address control requirements as they evolve over time.

- It provides a unified vision for common security controls: By providing this common services model, the architecture looks at security controls from a holistic view, identifying potential gaps in those controls, and providing a long-term plan for improvement. As such, it is a fundamental part of good security management practices.

- It leverages existing technology investments: Any proposed security should reuse existing technologies that are already deployed in the enterprise whenever practical. By focusing on what the organization has already deployed, the architecture can take full advantage of the internal skill sets, licensing and agreements to minimize the need for training or staff augmentation.

- It provides a flexible approach to current and future threats and also the needs of core functions: If done well, the implementation of the architecture should be flexible enough to provide safeguards and countermeasures for current and emerging threats. It also, however, has to be flexible enough to allow the core applications within the organization to operate and integrate as intended.

The result should be an architecture that supports and integrates with:

1) An effective security program that recognizes that all information is not equal or constant in terms of value and risk over time.

2) An efficient security program that applies the right technology to protect the most critical assets combined with quality processes that reduce the risks to acceptable business levels. This is achieved through some form of evaluation process.

3) A high quality security program that includes regular management reviews and technology assessments to ensure controls are working as intended and providing feedback so that technology and processes can adapt to changes in value and risks over time. This is measured and monitored as part of a system assurance program.

3. Which of the following can **BEST** be used to capture detailed security requirements?

    A. Threat modeling, covert channels, and data classification

    B. Data classification, risk assessments, and covert channels

    C. Risk assessments, covert channels, and threat modeling

    D. Threat modeling, data classification, and risk assessments

Answer: **D**

Threat modeling can be used to determine the threats to your system or software, which can be used to generate detailed countermeasure requirements. Data classification can be used to determine appropriate levels of protection for the data that is transmitted or stored and this can be used to determine confidentiality, integrity or availability requirements. Determining residual and acceptable risk thresholds can be used to generate security requirements as well.

4. Which of the following security standards is internationally recognized as the standards for sound security practices and is focused on the standardization and certification of an organization's Information Security Management System (ISMS)?

    A. ISO 15408

    B. ISO 27001

    C. ISO 9001

    D. ISO 9146

Answer: **B**

ISO 27000 series will assist organizations of all types to understand the fundamentals, principles, and concepts to improve the protection of their information assets. ISO 15408 is the common criteria which includes the evaluation criteria for IT security. ISO 9001 provides the requirements for quality management system. ISO 9126 is an international standard for the evaluation of software quality.

5. Which of the following describes the rules that need to be implemented to ensure that the security requirements are met?

    A. Security kernel

    B. Security policy

    C. Security model

    D. Security reference monitor

Answer: **B**

Security policy documents the security requirements of an organization. Subsequently, a security model is a specification that describes the rules to be implemented to support and enforce the security policy. While the security policy provides the "What" requirements needs to be met, the security model provides "HOW" (the rules by which) the requirements will be met. The part of the operating system where security features are located is the security kernel. Security reference monitor is the tamperproof module that controls the access request of software to either the data or the system.

6. A two-dimensional grouping of individual subjects into groups or roles and granting access to groups to objects is an example of which of the following types of models?

    A. Multilevel lattice

    B. State machine

    C. Non-interference

    D. Matrix-based

Answer: **D**

While lattice-based models tend to treat similar subjects and objects with similar restrictions, matrix-based models focus on one-to-one relationships between subjects and objects. The best known example is the organization of subjects and objects into an access control matrix. An access control matrix is a two-dimensional table that allows for individual subjects and objects to be related to each other. A state machine model, describes the behavior of a system as it moves between one state and another, from one moment to another. A noninterference model maintains activities at different security levels to separate these levels from each other. In this way, it minimizes leakages that may happen through covert channels, because there is complete separation between security levels

7. Which of the following models ensures that a subject with clearance level of 'Secret' has the ability to write only to objects classified as 'Secret' or 'Top Secret' but is prevented from writing information classified as 'Public'?

    A. Biba-Integrity

    B. Clark–Wilson

    C. Brewer–Nash

    D. Bell–LaPadula

Answer: **D**

Bell–LaPadula is a confidentiality model that deals with the prevention of information disclosure.

8. Which of the following is unique to the Biba Integrity Model?

    A.   Simple property

    B.   * (star) property

    C.   Invocation property

    D.   Strong * property

Answer: **C**

Both Biba and Bell–LaPadula have the simple and * (star) property and the strong * property is part of the confidentiality Bell–LaPadula model. The Invocation property is unique to the Biba integrity model, which considers a situation where corruption may occur because a less trustworthy subject was allowed to invoke the powers of a subject with more trust.

9. Which of the following models is **BEST** considered in a shared data-hosting environment so that the data of one customer is not disclosed to a competitor or other customers sharing that hosted environment?

    A.   Brewer–Nash

    B.   Clark–Wilson

    C.   Bell–LaPadula

    D.   Lipner

Answer: **A**

While the other models listed can provide confidentiality assurance, it is only the Brewer–Nash Model, which is also known as the Chinese wall model, which has a clear separation of access rights. The principle of Brewer–Nash model is that users should not be able to access the confidential information of both a client organization and one or more of its competitors. It is called the Chinese wall model because, like the Great Wall of China, once you are on one side of the wall, you cannot get to the other side.

10. Which of the following security models is primarily concerned with how the subjects and objects are created and how subjects are assigned rights or privileges?

    A.   Bell–LaPadula

    B.   Biba-Integrity

    C.   Chinese Wall

    D.   Graham–Denning

Answer: **D**

The Graham–Denning access control model has three parts: a set of objects, a set of subjects, and a set of rights. Bell–LaPadula is a confidentiality model. Biba is an integrity model. The Chinese Wall Model is also a confidential assurance model that deals with the about separation of access.

11. Which of the following ISO standards provides the evaluation criteria that can be used to evaluate security requirements of different products with different functions?

    A.   15408

    B.   27000

    C.   9100

    D.   27002

Answer: **A**

ISO/IEC 15408 is commonly referred to as the common criteria. It is an internationally recognized standard provided the first truly international product evaluation criteria. It has largely superseded all other criteria, although there continue to be products in general use that were certified under TCSEC, ITSEC, and other criteria. It takes a very similar approach to ITSEC by providing a flexible set of functional and assurance requirements, and like ITSEC, it is not very proscriptive as TCSEC had been. Instead, it is focused on standardizing the general approach to product evaluation and providing mutual recognition of such evaluations all over the world.

12. In the Common Criteria, the common set of functional and assurance requirements for a category of vendor products deployed in a particular type of environment are known as

    A.   Protection Profiles

    B.   Security Target

    C.   Trusted Computing Base

    D.   Ring Protection

Answer: **A**

Protection profiles are the common set of functional and assurance requirements while security target is the specific functional and assurance requirements that the author of the security target wants a given product to fulfill. Trusted computing base and ring protection are not concepts of the common criteria.

13. Which of the following evaluation assurance level that is formally verified, designed and tested is expected for high risk situation?

    A.   EAL 1

    B.   EAL 3

    C.   EAL 5

    D.   EAL 7

Answer: **D**

EAL 7 is the only one that given after the product is formally verified, designed, and tested. All the other levels of assurances are not formally verified.

14. Formal acceptance of an evaluated system by management is known as

    A. Certification

    B. Accreditation

    C. Validation

    D. Verification

Answer: **B**

In the accreditation phase, management evaluates the capacity of a system to meet the needs of the organization. If management determines that the needs of the system satisfy the needs of the organization, they will formally accept the evaluated system, usually for a defined period of time. During the certification phase, the product or system is tested to see whether it meets the documented requirements (including any security requirements). Validation and verification are usually part of the certification phase.

15. Which stage of the Capability Maturity Model (CMM) is characterized by having organizational processes that are proactive?

    A. Initial

    B. Managed

    C. Defined

    D. Optimizing

Answer: **C**

In the initial stage, the processes are unpredictable, poorly ¬controlled, and reactive. During the managed stage, the processes are characterized for projects (not the entire organization) and it is often reactive. In the defined stage, the processes are characterized for the entire organization and are proactive. In the optimizing stage the organization focuses on continuous process improvement.

16. Which of the following **BEST** provides a method of quantifying risks associated with information technology when validating the abilities of new security controls and countermeasures to address the identified risks?

    A. Threat/risk assessment

    B. Penetration testing

    C. Vulnerability assessment

    D. Data classification

Answer: **A**

Penetration testing, vulnerability assessments, and data classification may help with the identification of threats and countermeasures, but do not necessarily always translate or quantify the threats and vulnerabilities to risk.

17. The TCSEC identifies two types of covert channels, what are they? (**Choose TWO**)

    A. Storage

    B. Boundary

    C. Timing

    D. Monitoring

Answer: **A | C**

Explanation: Covert channels are communications mechanisms hidden from the access control and standard monitoring systems of an information system. Covert channels may use irregular methods of communication such as the free space sections of a disk or even the timing of processes to transmit information. The TCSEC identifies two types of covert channels:

- Storage channels that communicate via a stored object.
- Timing channels that modify the timing of events relative to each other.

The only way to mitigate covert channels is through the secure design of an information system. The security architect must understand how covert channels function and strive to eliminate them in any design which has associated requirements.

18. Which of the following is the main reason for security concerns in mobile computing devices?

    A. The 3G/4G protocols are inherently insecure

    B. Lower processing power

    C. Hackers are targeting mobile devices

    D. The lack of anti-virus software.

Answer: **B**

These devices share common security concerns with other resource-constrained devices. In many cases, security services have been sacrificed to provide richer user interaction when processing power is very limited. Also, their mobility has made them a prime vector for data loss since they can be used to transmit and store information in ways that may be difficult to control.

19. In decentralized environments device drivers that enable the OS to control and communicate with hardware need to be securely designed, developed and deployed because they are

    A. typically installed by end-users and granted access to the supervisor state

    B. typically installed by administrators and granted access to user mode state

    C. typically installed by software without human interaction.

    D. integrated as part of the operating system.

Answer: **A**

Device drivers that control input/output devices are typically installed by end-users (not necessarily administrators) and are often granted access to supervisor state to help them run faster. This may allow a malformed driver to be used to compromise the system unless other controls are in place to mitigate this risk. Drivers are not add-ons to the operating system and usually require human interaction for installation.

20. A system administrator grants rights to a group of individuals called "Accounting" instead of granting rights to each individual. This is an example of which of the following security mechanisms?

    A. Layering
    B. Data hiding
    C. Cryptographic protections
    D. Abstraction

Answer: **D**

In computer programming, layering is the organization of programming into separate functional components that interact in some sequential and hierarchical way, with each layer usually having an interface only to the layer above it and the layer below it. Data hiding maintains activities at different security levels to separate these levels from each other. Cryptography can be used in a variety of ways to protect sensitive system functions and data. By encrypting sensitive information and limiting the availability of key material, data can be hidden from less privileged parts of the system. Abstraction involves the removal of characteristics from an entity in order to easily represent its essential properties.

21. Asymmetric key cryptography is used for the following:

    A. Encryption of data, Access Control, Steganography
    B. Steganography, Access control, Nonrepudiation
    C. Nonrepudiation, Steganography, Encryption of Data
    D. Encryption of Data, Nonrepudiation, Access Control

Answer: **D**

Steganography is the hiding of a message inside of another medium.

22. Which of the following supports asymmetric key cryptography?

    A. Diffie–Hellman
    B. Rijndael
    C. Blowfish
    D. SHA-256

Answer: **A**

The Diffie–Hellman asymmetric algorithm was the first of its kind and still one of the most commonly used today.

23. What is an important disadvantage of using a public key algorithm compared to a symmetric algorithm?

    A.   A symmetric algorithm provides better access control.

    B.   A symmetric algorithm is a faster process.

    C.   A symmetric algorithm provides nonrepudiation of delivery.

    D.   A symmetric algorithm is more difficult to implement.

Answer: **B**

Processing efficiency of asymmetric cryptography is less than symmetric cryptography due to relative computational processing resources needed. Its lower performance is a disadvantage of asymmetric cryptography.

24. When a user needs to provide message integrity, what option is **BEST**?

    A.   Send a digital signature of the message to the recipient

    B.   Encrypt the message with a symmetric algorithm and send it

    C.   Encrypt the message with a private key so the recipient can decrypt with the corresponding public key

    D.   Create a checksum, append it to the message, encrypt the message, and then send to recipient

Answer: **D**

The use of a simple error detecting code, checksum, or frame check sequence is often used along with symmetric key cryptography for message integrity. A is meaningless without sending the message itself to compare hash results. B has a weakness if the attacker ever gets the symmetric key used to encrypt the message. C, while providing privacy, is, by itself, computationally inefficient relative to the objective of message integrity.

25. A Certificate Authority (CA) provides which benefits to a user?

    A.   Protection of public keys of all users

    B.   History of symmetric keys

    C.   Proof of nonrepudiation of origin

    D.   Validation that a public key is associated with a particular user

Answer: **D**

A Certificate Authority (CA) "signs" an entities digital certificate to certify that the certificate content accurately represents the certificate owner. A is not a CA function because public keys are not meant to be secret. B is a function of key management. C is a function of a digital certificate.

26. What is the output length of a RIPEMD-160 hash?

    A.   160 bits

    B.   150 bits

    C.   128 bits

    D.   104 bits

Answer: **A**

The output for RIPEMD-160 is 160 bits.

27. ANSI X9.17 is concerned primarily with

    A.   Protection and secrecy of keys

    B.   Financial records and retention of encrypted data

    C.   Formalizing a key hierarchy

    D.   The lifespan of key-encrypting keys (KKMs)

Answer: **A**

Protection and secrecy of keys is the primary concern of ANSI 9.17. ANSI X9.17 was developed to address the need of financial institutions to transmit securities and funds securely using an electronic medium. Specifically, it describes the means to ensure the secrecy of keys.

28. When a certificate is revoked, what is the proper procedure?

    A.   Setting new key expiry dates

    B.   Updating the certificate revocation list

    C.   Removal of the private key from all directories

    D.   Notification to all employees of revoked keys

Answer: **B**

When a key is no longer valid, the certificate revocation list should be updated. A certificate revocation list (CRL) is a list of non-valid certificates that should not be accepted by any member of the PKI.

29. Which is true about link encryption?

> A. Link encryption is advised for high-risk environments, provides better traffic flow confidentiality, and encrypts routing information.
>
> B. Link encryption is often used for Frame Relay or satellite links, is advised for high-risk environments and provides better traffic flow confidentiality.
>
> C. Link encryption encrypts routing information, is often used for Frame Relay or satellite links, and provides traffic flow confidentiality.
>
> D. Link encryption provides better traffic flow confidentiality, is advised for high-risk environments and provides better traffic flow confidentiality.

Answer: **C**

Link encryption is not suitable for high-risk environments due to possible privacy weakness at each node. It is possible that an attacker could view decrypted data as encrypt decrypt function is performed at each node along the data path.

30. NIST identifies three service models that represent different types of cloud services available, what are they?

> A. Software as a Service (SaaS), Infrastructure as a Service (IaaS) and Platform as a Service (PaaS)
>
> B. Security as a Service (SaaS), Infrastructure as a Service (IaaS) and Platform as a Service (PaaS)
>
> C. Software as a Service (SaaS), Integrity as a Service (IaaS) and Platform as a Service (PaaS)
>
> D. Software as a Service (SaaS), Infrastructure as a Service (IaaS) and Process as a Service (PaaS)

Answer: **A**

Explanation: NIST identifies three service models that represent different types of cloud services available:

- Software as a Service (SaaS): The capability provided to the consumer is to use the provider's applications running on a cloud infrastructure. The applications are accessible from various client devices through either a thin client interface, such as a web browser (e.g., web-based email), or a program interface. The consumer does not manage or control the underlying cloud infrastructure including network, servers, operating systems, storage, or even individual application capabilities, with the possible exception of limited user-specific application configuration settings.

- Platform as a Service (PaaS): The capability provided to the consumer is to deploy onto the cloud infrastructure consumer-created or acquired applications created using programming languages, libraries, services, and tools supported by the provider. The consumer does not manage or control the underlying cloud infrastructure including network, servers, operating systems, or storage, but has control over the deployed applications and possibly configuration settings for the application-hosting environment.

- Infrastructure as a Service (IaaS): The capability provided to the consumer is to provision processing, storage, networks, and other fundamental computing resources where the consumer is able to deploy and run arbitrary software, which can include operating systems and applications. The consumer does not manage or control the underlying cloud infrastructure but has control over operating systems, storage, and deployed applications; and possibly limited control of select networking components (e.g., host firewalls)".

31. The process used in most block ciphers to increase their strength is

    A. Diffusion

    B. Confusion

    C. Step function

    D. SP-network

Answer: **D**

The SP-network is the process described by Claude Shannon used in most block ciphers to increase their strength. SP stands for substitution and permutation (transposition), and most block ciphers do a series of repeated substitutions and permutations to add confusion and diffusion to the encryption process.

32. Which of the following BEST describes fundamental methods of encrypting data:

    A. Substitution and transposition

    B. 3DES and PGP

    C. Symmetric and asymmetric

    D. DES and AES

Answer: **C**

Data encryption relies on either symmetric or asymmetric designs to ensure the confidentiality of data. The vast majority of all encryption products algorithms or processes fall into one or the other methods.

33. Cryptography supports all of the core principles of information security except

    A. Availability

    B. Confidentiality

    C. Integrity

    D. Authenticity

Answer: **D**

Cryptography supports all three of the core principles of information security. Authenticity is not one of the cove principles.

34. A way to defeat frequency analysis as a method to determine the key is to use

    A. Substitution ciphers

    B. Transposition ciphers

    C. Polyalphabetic ciphers

    D. Inversion ciphers

Answer: **C**

The use of several alphabets for substituting the plaintext is called polyalphabetic ciphers. It is designed to make the breaking of a cipher by frequency analysis more difficult.

35. The running key cipher is based on

    A. Modular arithmetic

    B. XOR mathematics

    C. Factoring

    D. Exponentiation

Answer: **A**

The use of modular mathematics and the representation of each letter by its numerical place in the alphabet are the key to many modern ciphers including running key ciphers.

36. The only cipher system said to be unbreakable by brute force is

    A. AES

    B. DES

    C. One-time pad

    D. Triple DES

Answer: **C**

One-time pad is a key that is only used once and that must be as long as the plaintext but never repeats.

37. The main types of implementation attacks include: (**Choose ALL that apply**)

    A. Fault analysis

    B. Known plaintext

    C. Probing

    D. Linear

Answer: **A | C**

Implementation attacks are some of the most common and popular attacks against cryptographic systems due to their ease and reliance on system elements outside of the algorithm. The main types of implementation attacks include:

- Side-channel analysis
- Fault Analysis
- Probing Attacks

Side-channel attacks are passive attacks that rely on a physical attribute of the implementation such as power consumption/emanation. These attributes are studied to determine the secret key and the algorithm function. Some examples of popular side-channels include timing analysis and electromagnetic differential analysis.

Fault analysis attempts to force the system into an error state to gain erroneous results. By forcing an error, gaining the results and comparing it with known good results, an attacker may learn about the secret key and the algorithm.

Probing attacks attempt to watch the circuitry surrounding the cryptographic module in hopes that they complementary components will disclose information about the key or the algorithm. Additionally new hardware may be added to the cryptographic module to observe and inject information.

38. Which is the **BEST** choice for implementing encryption on a smart card?

    A.   Blowfish

    B.   Elliptic Curve Cryptography

    C.   TwoFish

    D.   Quantum Cryptography

Answer: **B**

Smart cards have limited processing power and memory and therefore should use an approach which is light on processor demands. Elliptic Curve Cryptography is the only option provided which is highly efficient and therefore relies on little processing power.

39. An e-mail with a document attachment from a known individual is received with a digital signature. The e-mail client is unable to validate the signature. What is the **BEST** course of action?

    A.   Open the attachment to determine if the signature is valid.

    B.   Determine why the signature can't be validated prior to opening the attachment.

    C.   Delete the e-mail

    D.   Forward the e-mail to another address with a new signature.

Answer: **B**

When a digital signature cannot be validated, there may be several reasons. A system may not be able to reach a CA, but also the certificate used to sign the document may have been self-generated or worse forged.

40. The vast majority of Virtual Private Networks use

    A. SSL/TLS and IPSec.

    B. El Gamal and DES.

    C. 3DES and Blowfish

    D. TwoFish and IDEA.

Answer: **A**

Two major tools assist in both VPN and e-commerce secure networking. IPSec and SSL/TLS have become synonymous with network security. These protocols form the vast majority of secure network traffic and e-commerce enablement.

Domain 4 – **Communications and Network Security**

1. In the OSI reference model, on which layer can Ethernet (IEEE 802.3) be described?

    A. Layer 1—Physical layer

    B. Layer 2—Data-link layer

    C. Layer 3—Network Layer

    D. Layer 4—Transport Layer

Answer: **B**

Layer 2, the data-link layer, describes data transfer between machines, for instance, by an Ethernet.

2. A customer wants to keep cost to a minimum and has only ordered a single static IP address from the ISP. Which of the following must be configured on the router to allow for all the computers to share the same public IP address?

    A. VLANs

    B. PoE

    C. PAT

    D. VPN

Answer: **C**

Port Address Translation (PAT), is an extension to network address translation (NAT) that permits multiple devices on a local area network (LAN) to be mapped to a single public IP address. The goal of PAT is to conserve IP addresses.

3. Users are reporting that some Internet websites are not accessible anymore. Which of the following will allow the network administrator to quickly isolate the remote router that is causing the network communication issue, so that the problem can be reported to the appropriate responsible party?

    A. Ping

    B. Protocol analyzer

    C. Tracert

    D. Dig

Answer: **C**

The Tracert utility will attempt to trace the route to the target address over a maximum of 30 hops. As a result, it will tell the user which routes are valid, and where the packets are being dropped, allowing them to quickly diagnose connectivity problems.

4. Ann installs a new Wireless Access Point (WAP) and users are able to connect to it. However, once connected, users cannot access the Internet. Which of the following is the MOST likely cause of the problem?

    A. The signal strength has been degraded and latency is increasing hop count.

    B. An incorrect subnet mask has been entered in the WAP configuration.

    C. The signal strength has been degraded and packets are being lost.

    D. Users have specified the wrong encryption type and packets are being rejected.

Answer: **B**

The subnet mask is broken into two parts, the Network ID and the Host ID. The Network ID represents the network that the device is connected to. If, for example, the subnet mask in question was supposed to be 255.255.240.0, but instead was entered as 255.240.0.0, then the device would only be able to see other computers in the 255.240.0.0 subnet, and the default gateway of the subnet. When the wrong subnet mask is entered for a network configuration, the device will not be able to communicate with any other devices outside of the subnet until the right subnet mask is entered, allowing them to be able to interact with the devices on the network that the subnet mask represents.

5. What is the optimal placement for network-based intrusion detection systems (NIDS)?

    A. On the network perimeter, to alert the network administrator of all suspicious traffic

    B. On network segments with business-critical systems (e.g., demilitarized zones (DMZs) and on certain intranet segments)

    C. At the network operations center (NOC)

    D. At an external service provider

Answer: **A**

Intrusion detection systems (IDS) monitor activity and send alerts when they detect suspicious traffic. There are two broad classifications of IDS: host-based IDS, which monitor activity on servers and workstations, and network-based IDS, which monitor network activity. Placing an IDS on the network perimeter monitors all traffic into an organization.

6. Which of the following end-point devices would **MOST** likely be considered part of a converged IP network?

    A.   file server, IP phone, security camera

    B.   IP phone, thermostat, cypher lock

    C.   security camera, cypher lock, IP phone

    D.   thermostat, file server, cypher lock

Answer: **A**

See *Figure 4.32* on Converged IP Networks

7. Network upgrades have been completed and the WINS server was shutdown. It was decided that NetBIOS network traffic will no longer be permitted. Which of the following will accomplish this objective?

    A.   Content filtering

    B.   Port filtering

    C.   MAC filtering

    D.   IP filtering

Answer: **B**

TCP/IP port filtering is the practice of selectively enabling or disabling Transmission Control Protocol (TCP) ports and User Datagram Protocol (UDP) ports on computers or network devices. When used in conjunction with other security practices, such as deploying firewall software at your Internet access point, applying port filters to intranet and Internet servers insulates those servers from many TCP/IP-based security attacks, including internal attacks by malicious users.

8. Which of the following devices should be part of a network's perimeter defense?

    A.   A boundary router, A firewall, A proxy Server

    B.   A firewall, A proxy server, A host based intrusion detection system (HIDS)

    C.   A proxy server, A host based intrusion detection system (HIDS), A firewall

    D.   A host based intrusion detection system (HIDS), A firewall, A boundary router

Answer: **B**

The security perimeter is the first line of protection between trusted and untrusted networks. In general, it includes a firewall and router that helps filter traffic. Security perimeters may also include proxies and devices, such as an intrusion detection system (IDS), to warn of suspicious traffic. The defensive perimeter extends out from these first protective devices, to include proactive defense such as boundary routers which can provide early warning of upstream attacks and threat activities. HIDS are associated with hosts behind the perimeter.

A

Answers to Domain Review Questions

9. Which of the following is a principal security risk of wireless LANs?

    A. Lack of physical access control

    B. Demonstrably insecure standards

    C. Implementation weaknesses

    D. War driving

Answer: **A**

Wireless networks allow users to be mobile while remaining connected to a LAN. Unfortunately, this allows unauthorized users greater access to the LAN as well. In fact, many wireless LANs can be accessed off of the organization's property by anyone with a wireless card in a laptop, which effectively extends the LAN where there are no physical controls.

10. Which of the following is a path vector routing protocol?

    A. RIP

    B. EIGRP

    C. OSPF/IS-IS

    D. BGP

Answer: **D**

A path vector protocol is a computer network routing protocol which maintains the path information that gets updated dynamically. Updates which have looped through the network and returned to the same node are easily detected and discarded. It is different from the distance vector routing and link state routing. Each entry in the routing table contains the destination network, the next router and the path to reach the destination. BGP is an example of a path vector protocol. In BGP the routing table maintains the autonomous systems that are traversed in order to reach the destination system.

IPv4 routing protocols are classified as follows:

- RIPv1 (legacy): IGP, distance vector, classful protocol
- IGRP (legacy): IGP, distance vector, classful protocol developed by Cisco
- RIPv2: IGP, distance vector, classless protocol
- EIGRP: IGP, distance vector, classless protocol developed by Cisco
- OSPF: IGP, link-state, classless protocol
- IS-IS: IGP, link-state, classless protocol
- BGP: EGP, path-vector, classless protocol

11. It can be said that IPSec

    A.   provides mechanisms for authentication and encryption.

    B.   provides mechanisms for nonrepudiation.

    C.   will only be deployed with IPv6.

    D.   only authenticates clients against a server.

Answer: **A**

IP Security (IPSec) is a suite of protocols for communicating securely with IP by providing mechanisms for authenticating and encryption. Standard IPSec authenticates only hosts with each other.

12. A Security Event Management (SEM) service performs the following function:

    A.   Gathers firewall logs for archiving

    B.   Aggregates logs from security devices and application servers looking for suspicious activity

    C.   Reviews access controls logs on servers and physical entry points to match user system authorization with physical access permissions

    D.   Coordination software for security conferences and seminars.

Answer: **B**

SEM/SEIM systems have to understand a wide variety of different applications and network element (routers/switches) logs and formats; consolidate these logs into a single database and then correlate events looking for clues to unauthorized behaviors that would be otherwise inconclusive if observed in a single log file.

13. Which of the following is the principal weakness of DNS (Domain Name System)?

    A.   Lack of authentication of servers, and thereby authenticity of records

    B.   Its latency, which enables insertion of records between the time when a record has expired and when it is refreshed

    C.   The fact that it is a simple, distributed, hierarchical database instead of a singular, relational one, thereby giving rise to the possibility of inconsistencies going undetected for a certain amount of time

    D.   The fact that addresses in e-mail can be spoofed without checking their validity in DNS, caused by the fact that DNS addresses are not digitally signed

Answer: **A**

Authentication has been proposed but attempts to introduce stronger authentication into DNS have not found wider acceptance. Authentication services have been delegated upward to higher protocol layers. Applications in need of guaranteeing authenticity cannot rely on DNS to provide such but will have to implement a solution themselves

14. Which of the following statements about open e-mail relays is incorrect?

    A. An open e-mail relay is a server that forwards e-mail from domains other than the ones it serves.

    B. Open e-mail relays are a principal tool for distribution of spam.

    C. Using a blacklist of open e-mail relays provides a secure way for an e-mail administrator to identify open mail relays and filter spam.

    D. An open e-mail relay is widely considered a sign of bad system administration.

Answer: **C**

Although using blacklists as one indicator in spam filtering has its merits, it is risky to use them as an exclusive indicator. Generally, they are run by private organizations and individuals according to their own rules, they are able to change their policies on a whim, they can vanish overnight for any reason, and they can rarely be held accountable for the way they operate their lists.

15. A botnet can be characterized as

    A. An network used solely for internal communications

    B. An automatic security alerting tool for corporate networks

    C. A group of dispersed, compromised machines controlled remotely for illicit reasons.

    D. A type of virus

Answer: **C**

"Bots" and "botnets" are most insidious implementations of unauthorized, remote control of compromised systems. Such machines are essentially zombies controlled by ethereal entities from the dark places on the Internet.

16. During a disaster recovery test, several billing representatives need to be temporarily setup to take payments from customers. It has been determined that this will need to occur over a wireless network, with security being enforced where possible. Which of the following configurations should be used in this scenario?

    A. WPA2, SSID enabled, and 802.11n.

    B. WEP, SSID enabled, and 802.11b.

    C. WEP, SSID disabled, and 802.11g.

    D. WPA2, SSID disabled, and 802.11a.

Answer: **D**

WPA2 is a security technology commonly used on Wi-Fi wireless networks. WPA2 (Wi-Fi Protected Access 2) replaced the original WPA technology on all certified Wi-Fi hardware since 2006 and is based on the IEEE 802.11i technology standard for data encryption. WPA was used to replace WEP, which is not considered a secure protocol for wireless systems due to numerous issues with its implementation. Disabling the SSID will further enhance the security of the solution, as it requires the user that wants to connect to the WAP to have the exact SSID, as opposed to selecting it from a list.

17. Which xDSL flavor delivers both downstream and upstream speeds of 1.544 Mbps over two copper twisted pairs?

    A. HDSL

    B. SDSL

    C. ADSL

    D. VDSL

Answer: **A**

High-Data-Rate Digital Subscriber Line. One of four DSL technologies. HDSL delivers 1.544 Mbps of bandwidth each way over two copper twisted pairs. Because HDSL provides T1 speed, telephone companies have been using HDSL to provision local access to T1 services whenever possible. The operating range of HDSL is limited to 12,000 feet (3658.5 meters), so signal repeaters are installed to extend the service. HDSL requires two twisted pairs, so it is deployed primarily for PBX network connections, digital loop carrier systems, interexchange POPs, Internet servers, and private data networks.

18. A new installation requires a network in a heavy manufacturing area with substantial amounts of electromagnetic radiation and power fluctuations. Which media is best suited for this environment if little traffic degradation is tolerated?

    A. Coax cable

    B. Wireless

    C. Shielded twisted pair

    D. Fiber

Answer: **D**

Since fiber relies on light, electromagnetic and source power-based distortions do not affect it. Coax, wireless and shielded twisted pair rely and electromagnetic principles to operate and are therefore susceptible to electromagnetic interference.

19. Multi-layer protocols such as Modbus used in industrial control systems

    A. often have their own encryption and security like IPv6

    B. are used in modern routers as a routing interface control

    C. Are often insecure by their very nature as they were not designed to natively operate over today's IP networks

    D. Have largely been retired and replaced with newer protocols such as IPv6 and NetBIOS

Answer: **C**

Industrial control systems and their multi-layer protocols are largely insecure due to the original designs used to implement them. Given the life expectancy of the control systems, many are in use with inherently insecure designs, protocols and configurations.

20. Frame Relay and X.25 networks are part of which of the following?

    A. Circuit-switched services

    B. Cell-switched services

    C. Packet-switched services

    D. Dedicated digital services

Answer: **C**

Packet-Switched Technologies include:

- X.25
- Link Access Procedure-Balanced (LAPB)
- Frame Relay
- Switched Multimegabit Data Service (SMDS)
- Asynchronous Transfer Mode (ATM)
- Voice over IP (VoIP)

Domain 5 – **Identity and Access Management**

1. Authentication is

    A. the assertion of a unique identity for a person or system.

    B. the process of verifying the identity of the user.

    C. the process of defining the specific resources a user needs and determining the type of access to those resources the user may have.

    D. the assertion by management that the user should be given access to a system.

Answer: **B**

Identification is the assertion of a unique identity for a person or system and is the starting point of all access control. Without proper identification it is impossible to determine to whom or what to apply the appropriate controls. Identification is a critical first step in applying access controls because all activities and controls are tied to the identity of a particular user or entity.

Authentication is the process of verifying the identity of the user. Upon requesting access and presenting unique user identification, the user will provide some set of private data that only the user should have access to or knowledge of. The combination of the identity and information only known by, or only in the possession of, the user acts to verify that the user identity is being used by the expected and assigned entity (e.g., a person). This, then, establishes trust between the user and the system for the allocation of privileges.

Authorization is the final step in the process. Once a user has been identified and properly authenticated, the resources that user is allowed to access must be defined and monitored. Authorization is the process of defining the specific resources a user needs and determining the type of access to those resources the user may have.

2. Which best describes access controls?

    A.   Access controls are a collection of technical controls that permit access to authorized users, systems, and applications.

    B.   Access controls help protect against threats and vulnerabilities by reducing exposure to unauthorized activities and providing access to information and systems to only those who have been approved.

    C.   Access control is the employment of encryption solutions to protect authentication information during log-on.

    D.   Access controls help protect against vulnerabilities by controlling unauthorized access to systems and information by employees, partners, and customers.

Answer: **B**

Access controls are the collection of mechanisms that work together to protect the assets of the enterprise. They help protect against threats and vulnerabilities by reducing exposure to unauthorized activities and providing access to information and systems to only those who have been approved.

3. _____ requires that a user or process be granted access to only those resources necessary to perform assigned functions.

    A.   Discretionary access control

    B.   Separation of duties

    C.   Least privilege

    D.   Rotation of duties

Answer: **C**

The principle of least privilege is one of the most fundamental characteristics of access control for meeting security objectives. Least privilege requires that a user or process be given no more access privilege than necessary to perform a job, task, or function.

4. What are the seven main categories of access control?

    A.   Detective, corrective, monitoring, logging, recovery, classification, and directive

    B.   Directive, deterrent, preventative, detective, corrective, compensating, and recovery

    C.   Authorization, identification, factor, corrective, privilege, detective, and directive

    D.   Identification, authentication, authorization, detective, corrective, recovery, and directive

Answer: **B**

The seven main categories of access control are directive, deterrent, compensating, detective, corrective, and recovery.

5. What are the three types of access control?

    A.   Administrative, physical, and technical

    B.   Identification, authentication, and authorization

    C.   Mandatory, discretionary, and least privilege

    D.   Access, management, and monitoring

Answer: **A**

For any of the access control categories, the controls in those categories can be implemented in one of three ways: administrative controls, technical (logical) controls, and physical controls

6. What are types of failures in biometric identification systems? (**Choose ALL that apply**)

    A.   False reject

    B.   False positive

    C.   False accept

    D.   False negative

Answer: **A | C**

There are two types of failures in biometric identification:

- ***False Rejection*** – Failure to recognize a legitimate user. While it could be argued that this has the effect of keeping the protected area extra secure, it is an intolerable frustration to legitimate users who are refused access because the scanner does not recognize them.
- ***False Acceptance*** – Erroneous recognition, either by confusing one user with another or by accepting an imposter as a legitimate user.

7. What best describes two-factor authentication?

    A.   A hard token and a smart card

    B.   A user name and a PIN

    C.   A password and a PIN

    D.   A PIN and a hard token

Answer: **D**

There are three fundamental types of authentication: authentication by knowledge— something a person knows, authentication by possession— something a person has, and authentication by characteristic—something a person is. Technical controls related to these types are called "factors." Something known can be a password or PIN, something physically possessed can be a token fob or smart card, and something a person is can usually be some form of biometrics. Single-factor authentication is the employment of one of these factors, two-factor authentication is using two of the three factors, and three-factor authentication is the combination of all three factors. The general term for the use of more than one factor during authentication is multifactor authentication.

8. A potential vulnerability of the Kerberos authentication server is

    A.   Single point of failure

    B.   Asymmetric key compromise

    C.   Use of dynamic passwords

    D.   Limited lifetimes for authentication credentials

Answer: **A**

There are some issues related to the use of Kerberos. For starters, the security of the whole system depends on careful implementation: enforcing limited lifetimes for authentication credentials minimizes the threats of replayed credentials, the KDC must be physically secured, and it should be hardened, not permitting any non-Kerberos activity. More importantly, the KDC can be a single point of failure, and therefore should be supported by backup and continuity plans.

9. In mandatory access control the system controls access and the owner determines

    A.   Validation

    B.   Need to know

    C.   Consensus

    D.   Verification

Answer: **B**

MAC is based on cooperative interaction between the system and the information owner. The system's decision controls access and the owner provides the need-to-know control.

10. Which is the least significant issue when considering biometrics?

    A.   Resistance to counterfeiting

    B.   Technology type

    C.   User acceptance

    D.   Reliability and accuracy

Answer: **B**

In addition to the access control elements of a biometric system, there are several other considerations that are important to the integrity of the control environment. These are resistance to counterfeiting, data storage requirements, user acceptance, reliability and accuracy, and target user and approach.

11. Which is a fundamental disadvantage of biometrics?

    A. Revoking credentials

    B. Encryption

    C. Communications

    D. Placement

Answer: **A**

When considering the role of biometrics, its close interactions with people, and the privacy and sensitivity of the information collected, the inability to revoke the physical attribute of the credential becomes a major concern. The binding of the authentication process to the physical characteristics of the user can complicate the revocation or decommissioning processes.

12. Role-based access control

    A. Is unique to mandatory access control

    B. Is independent of owner input

    C. Is based on user job functions

    D. Can be compromised by inheritance

Answer: **C**

A role-based access control (RBA) model bases the access control authorizations on the roles (or functions) that the user is assigned within an organization. The determination of what roles have access to a resource can be governed by the owner of the data, as with DACs, or applied based on policy, as with MACs.

13. Identity management is

    A. Another name for access controls

    B. A set of technologies and processes intended to offer greater efficiency in the management of a diverse user and technical environment

    C. A set of technologies and processes focused on the provisioning and decommissioning of user credentials

    D. A set of technologies and processes used to establish trust relationships with disparate systems

Answer: **B**

Identity management is a much-used term that refers to a set of technologies intended to offer greater efficiency in the management of a diverse user and technical environment.

14. A disadvantage of single sign-on is

    A.   Consistent time-out enforcement across platforms

    B.   A compromised password exposes all authorized resources

    C.   Use of multiple passwords to remember

    D.   Password change control

Answer: **B**

One of the more prevalent concerns with centralized SSO systems is the fact that all of a user's credentials are protected by a single password: the SSO password. If someone were to crack that user's SSO password, they would effectively have all the keys to that user's kingdom.

15. Which of the following is incorrect when considering privilege management?

    A.   Privileges associated with each system, service, or application, and the defined roles within the organization to which they are needed, should be identified and clearly documented.

    B.   Privileges should be managed based on least privilege. Only rights required to perform a job should be provided to a user, group, or role.

    C.   An authorization process and a record of all privileges allocated should be maintained. Privileges should not be granted until the authorization process is complete and validated.

    D.   Any privileges that are needed for intermittent job functions should be assigned to multiple user accounts, as opposed to those for normal system activity related to the job function.

Answer: **D**

An authorization process and a record of all privileges allocated should be maintained. Privileges should not be granted until the authorization process is complete and validated. If any significant or special privileges are needed for intermittent job functions, these should be performed using an account specifically allocated for such a task, as opposed to those used for normal system and user activity. This enables the access privileges assigned to the special account to be tailored to the needs of the special function rather than simply extending the access privileges associated with the user's normal work functions.

16. The Identity and Access Provisioning Lifecycle is made up of which phases? (**Choose ALL that apply**)

    A. Review

    B. Developing

    C. Provisioning

    D. Revocation

Answer: **A | C | D**

The lifecycle is the workflow of how a user obtains access, uses it and finally loses it. The lifecycle is made up of the following phases:

■   Provisioning

■   Review

■   Revocation

17. When reviewing user entitlement the security professional must be **MOST** aware of

    A. Identity management and disaster recovery capability

    B. Business or organizational processes and access aggregation

    C. The organizational tenure of the user requesting entitlement

    D. Automated processes which grant users access to resources

Answer: **B**

Business and organizational processes and access aggregation are the most significant concerns with user entitlement. As individuals move through the organization, they accumulate access unless deliberately revoked. Additionally, the business process should always drive the need for entitlement and revocation of access.

18. A guard dog patrolling the perimeter of a data center is what type of a control?

    A. Recovery

    B. Administrative

    C. Logical

    D. Physical

Answer: **D**

A guard dog is an operational component of physical security.

Domain 6 – **Security Assessment and Testing**

1. Real User Monitoring (RUM) is an approach to Web monitoring that?

   A. Aims to capture and analyze select transactions of every user of a website or application.

   B. Aims to capture and analyze every transaction of every user of a website or application.

   C. Aims to capture and analyze every transaction of select users of a website or application.

   D. Aims to capture and analyze select transactions of select users of a website or application.

Answer: **B**

Real User Monitoring (RUM) is an approach to Web monitoring that aims to capture and analyze every transaction of every user of a website or application. Also known as real-user measurement, real-user metrics, or end-user experience monitoring (EUM), it's a form of passive monitoring, relying on Web-monitoring services that continuously observe a system in action, tracking availability, functionality, and responsiveness. While some bottom-up forms of RUM rely on capturing server-side information in order to reconstruct end-user experience, top-down client-side RUM can see directly how users interact with an application and what the experience is like for them. By using local agents or small bits of JavaScript to gauge site performance and reliability from the perspective of client apps and browsers, top-down RUM focuses on the direct relationship between site speed and user satisfaction, providing valuable insights into ways to optimize an application's components and improve overall performance.

2. Synthetic performance monitoring, sometimes called proactive monitoring, involves?

   A. Having external agents run scripted transactions against a web application.

   B. Having internal agents run scripted transactions against a web application.

   C. Having external agents run batch jobs against a web application.

   D. Having internal agents run batch jobs against a web application.

Answer: **B**

Synthetic performance monitoring, sometimes called proactive monitoring, involves having external agents run scripted transactions against a web application. These scripts are meant to follow the steps a typical user might–search, view product, log in and checkout in order to assess the experience of a user. Traditionally, synthetic monitoring has been done with lightweight, low-level agents, but increasingly, it's necessary for these agents to run full web browsers to process JavaScript, CSS, and AJAX calls that occur on pageload.

3. Most security vulnerabilities are caused by one? (**Choose ALL that apply**)

     A.   Bad programming patterns

     B.   Misconfiguration of security infrastructures

     C.   Functional bugs in security infrastructures

     D.   Design flaws in the documented processes

Answer: **A | B | C**

Most security vulnerabilities are caused by one of the following four reasons:

- Bad programming patterns such as missing checks of user-influenced data that can cause, e.g., SQL injections vulnerabilities,
- Misconfiguration of security infrastructures, e.g., too permissible access control or weak cryptographic configurations,
- Functional bugs in security infrastructures, e.g., access control enforcement infrastructures that inherently do not restrict system access,
- Logical flaws in the implemented processes, e.g., resulting in an application allowing customers to order goods without paying.

4. When selecting a security testing method or tool, the security practitioner needs to consider many different things, such as:

     A.   Culture of the organization and likelihood of exposure

     B.   Local annual frequency estimate (LAFE), and standard annual frequency estimate (SAFE)

     C.   Security roles and responsibilities for staff

     D.   Attack surface and supported technologies

Answer: **D**

When selecting a security testing method or tool, the security practitioner needs to consider many different things, such as:

- Attack Surface: Different security testing methods find different vulnerability types.
- Application type: Different security testing methods behave differently when applied to different application types.
- Quality of Results and Usability: Security testing techniques and tools differ in usability (e.g., fix recommendations) and quality (e.g., false positives rate).
- Supported Technologies: Security testing tools usually only support a limited number of technologies (e.g., programming languages) and if a tool supports multiple technologies, it does not necessary support all of them equally well.
- Performance and Resource Utilization: different tools and methods require different computing power or different manual efforts.

5. In the development stages where an application is not yet sufficiently mature enough to be able to be placed into a test environment, which of the following techniques are applicable: (**Choose ALL that apply**)

    A.   Static Source Code Analysis and Manual Code Review

    B.   Dynamic Source Code Analysis and Automatic Code Review

    C.   Static Binary Code Analysis and Manual Binary Review

    D.   Dynamic Binary Code Analysis and Static Binary Review

Answer: **A | C**

In the development stages where an application is not yet sufficiently mature enough to be able to be placed into a test environment, the following techniques are applicable:

- Static Source Code Analysis (SAST) and Manual Code Review: Analysis of the application source code for finding vulnerabilities without actually executing the application.

  - ✓ **Prerequisites:** Application source code.

  - ✓ **Benefits:** Detection of insecure programming, outdated libraries, and misconfigurations.

- Static Binary Code Analysis and Manual Binary Review: Analysis of the compiled application (binary) for finding vulnerabilities without actually executing the application. In general, this is similar to the source code analysis but is not as precise and fix recommendations typically cannot be provided.

6. Software testing tenets include: (**Choose Two**)

    A.   Testers and coders use the same tools

    B.   There is independence from coding

    C.   The expected test outcome is unknown

    D.   A successful test is one that finds an error

Answer: **B | D**

A software testing process should be based on principles that foster effective examinations of a software product. Applicable software testing tenets include:

- The expected test outcome is predefined;
- A good test case has a high probability of exposing an error;
- A successful test is one that finds an error;
- There is independence from coding;
- Both application (user) and software (programming) expertise are employed;
- Testers use different tools from coders;
- Examining only the usual case is insufficient;
- Test documentation permits its reuse and an independent confirmation of the pass/fail status of a test outcome during subsequent review.

7. Common structural coverage metrics include: (**Choose ALL that apply**)

    A.   Statement Coverage

    B.   Path Coverage

    C.   Asset Coverage

    D.   Dynamic Coverage

Answer: **A | B**

Common structural coverage metrics include:

- ***Statement Coverage*** – This criteria requires sufficient test cases for each program statement to be executed at least once; however, its achievement is insufficient to provide confidence in a software product's behavior.

- ***Decision (Branch) Coverage*** – This criteria requires sufficient test cases for each program decision or branch to be executed so that each possible outcome occurs at least once. It is considered to be a minimum level of coverage for most software products, but decision coverage alone is insufficient for high-integrity applications.

- ***Condition Coverage*** – This criteria requires sufficient test cases for each condition in a program decision to take on all possible outcomes at least once. It differs from branch coverage only when multiple conditions must be evaluated to reach a decision.

- ***Multi-Condition Coverage*** – This criteria requires sufficient test cases to exercise all possible combinations of conditions in a program decision.

- ***Loop Coverage*** – This criteria requires sufficient test cases for all program loops to be executed for zero, one, two, and many iterations covering initialization, typical running and termination (boundary) conditions.

  Path Coverage – This criteria requires sufficient test cases for each feasible path, basis path, etc., from start to exit of a defined program segment, to be executed at least once. Because of the very large number of possible paths through a software program, path coverage is generally not achievable. The amount of path coverage is normally established based on the risk or criticality of the software under test.

  Data Flow Coverage – This criteria requires sufficient test cases for each feasible data flow to be executed at least once. A number of data flow testing strategies are available.

8. What are the two main testing strategies in software testing?

    A.   Positive and Dynamic

    B.   Static and Negative

    C.   Known and Recursive

    D.   Negative and Positive

Answer: **D**

There are two main testing strategies in software testing: positive testing and negative testing.

- Positive testing determines that your application works as expected. If an error is encountered during positive testing, the test fails.

- Negative testing ensures that your application can gracefully handle invalid input or unexpected user behavior. For example, if a user tries to type a letter in a numeric field, the correct behavior in this case would be to display the "Incorrect data type, please enter a number" message. The purpose of negative testing is to detect such situations and prevent applications from crashing. In addition, negative testing helps to improve the quality of the application and find its weak points. A core difference exists between positive testing and negative testing: throwing an exception is expected in negative testing. When you perform negative testing, exceptions are expected – they indicate that the application handles improper user behavior correctly. It is generally considered a good practice to combine both the positive and the negative testing approaches. This strategy provides higher tested application coverage as compared to using only one of the specified testing methodologies.

9. What is the reason that an Information Security Continuous Monitoring (ISCM) program is established?

    A.   To monitor information in accordance with dynamic metrics, utilizing information readily available in part through implemented security controls

    B.   To collect information in accordance with pre-established metrics, utilizing information readily available in part through implemented security controls

    C.   To collect information in accordance with pre-established metrics, utilizing information readily available in part through planned security controls

    D.   To analyze information in accordance with test metrics, utilizing information readily available in part through implemented security controls

Answer: **B**

Information security continuous monitoring (ISCM) is defined as maintaining ongoing awareness of information security, vulnerabilities, and threats to support organizational risk management decisions. Any effort or process intended to support ongoing monitoring of information security across an organization must begin with senior leadership defining a comprehensive ISCM strategy encompassing technology, processes, procedures, operating environments, and people. This strategy:

- Is grounded in a clear understanding of organizational risk tolerance and helps officials set priorities and manage risk consistently throughout the organization;

- Includes metrics that provide meaningful indications of security status at all organizational tiers;
- Ensures continued effectiveness of all security controls;
- Verifies compliance with information security requirements derived from organizational missions/business functions, federal legislation, directives, regulations, policies, and standards/guidelines;
- Is informed by all organizational IT assets and helps to maintain visibility into the security of the assets;
- Ensures knowledge and control of changes to organizational systems and environments of operation; and
- Maintains awareness of threats and vulnerabilities.

An ISCM program is established to collect information in accordance with pre-established metrics, utilizing information readily available in part through implemented security controls. Organizational officials collect and analyze the data regularly and as often as needed to manage risk as appropriate for each area of the enterprise. This process involves the entire organization, from senior leaders providing governance and strategic vision to individuals developing, implementing, and operating individual systems in support of the organization's core missions and business processes. Subsequently, determinations are made from an organizational perspective on whether to conduct mitigation activities or to reject, transfer, or accept risk.

10. The process for developing an ISCM strategy and implementing an ISCM program is?

    A.   Define, analyze, implement, establish, respond, review and update

    B.   Analyze, implement, define, establish, respond, review and update

    C.   Define, establish, implement, analyze, respond, review and update

    D.   Implement, define, establish, analyze, respond, review and update

Answer: C

The process for developing an ISCM strategy and implementing an ISCM program is as follows:

- Define an ISCM strategy based on risk tolerance that maintains clear visibility into assets, awareness of vulnerabilities, up-to-date threat information, and mission/business impacts.
- Establish an ISCM program determining metrics, status monitoring frequencies, control assessment frequencies, and an ISCM technical architecture.
- Implement an ISCM program and collect the security-related information required for metrics, assessments, and reporting. Automate collection, analysis, and reporting of data where possible.
- Analyze the data collected and Report findings, determining the appropriate response. It may be necessary to collect additional information to clarify or supplement existing monitoring data.
- Respond to findings with technical, management, and operational mitigating activities or acceptance, transference/sharing, or avoidance/rejection.

- Review and Update the monitoring program, adjusting the ISCM strategy and maturing measurement capabilities to increase visibility into assets and awareness of vulnerabilities, further enable data-driven control of the security of an organization's information infrastructure, and increase organizational resilience.

11. The NIST document that discusses the Information Security Continuous Monitoring (ISCM) program is?

    A. NIST SP 800-121

    B. NIST SP 800-65

    C. NIST SP 800-53

    D. NIST SP 800-137

Answer: **D**

NIST SP 800-137, Information Security Continuous Monitoring (ISCM) for Federal Information Systems and Organizations.

http://csrc.nist.gov/publications/nistpubs/800-137/SP800-137-Final.pdf

12. A Service Organization Control (SOC) Report commonly covers a

    A. 6 month period

    B. 12 month period

    C. 18 month period

    D. 9 month period

Answer: **B**

SOC reports most commonly cover the design, and effectiveness of controls for a 12-month period of activity with continuous coverage from year to year to meet user requirements from a financial reporting or governance perspective. In some cases, a SOC report may cover a shorter period of time, such as six months, if the system/service has not been in operation for a full year or if annual reporting is insufficient to meet user needs. A SOC report may also cover only the design of controls at a specified point in time for a new system/service or for the initial examination (audit) of a system/service.

Domain 7 – **Security Operations**

1. Assuming a working IDS is in place, which of the following groups is **BEST** capable of stealing sensitive information due to the absence of system auditing?

    A.   Malicious software (malware)

    B.   Hacker or cracker

    C.   Disgruntled employee

    D.   Auditors

Answer: **C**

Insiders (employees, contractors, etc.) can have access to ¬information that they should not be allowed to and in the absence of auditing (logging) their actions can go unnoticed. Encryption can provide controls over unauthorized disclosure. External attacker (hacker or cracker) activity and malware usually raise alerts on intrusion detection systems (IDS). Auditors may have the need and authorization for the disclosure of sensitive information and this access is often monitored.

2. Which of the following provides controlled and un-intercepted interfaces into privileged user functions?

    A.   Ring protection

    B.   Anti-malware

    C.   Maintenance hooks

    D.   Trusted paths

Answer: **D**

Ring protection can be used to enforce boundary control between kernel functions and end-user controls. Anti-malware software is used to protect against malicious software. Maintenance hooks are coding constructs written by the software developer for troubleshooting and impersonation purposes, but can be a potential backdoor for malicious software. Trusted paths provide trustworthy interfaces into privileged user functions and are intended to provide a way to ensure that any communications over that path cannot be intercepted or corrupted

3. The doors of a data center spring open in the event of a fire. This is an example of

    A.   Fail-safe

    B.   Fail-secure

    C.   Fail-proof

    D.   Fail-closed

Answer: **A**

Fail-safe mechanisms focuses on failing with a minimum of harm to personnel while fail-secure focuses on failing in a controlled manner to block access while the systems is in an inconsistent state. For example, data center door systems will fail safe to ensure that personnel can escape the area when the electrical power fails. A fail-secure door would prevent personnel from using the door at all, which could put personnel in jeopardy. Fail-open and fail-closed are fail safe mechanisms

4. Which of the following ensures constant redundancy and fault-tolerance?

    A.   Cold spare

    B.   Warm spare

    C.   Hot spare

    D.   Archives

Answer: **C**

A cold spare is a spare component that is not powered up but is a duplicate of the primary component that can be inserted into the system if needed. Warm spares are those that are already inserted in the system but do not receive power unless they are required. Hot spares stay powered on and waiting to be called upon as needed. Archives are data backups stored for historical purposes. To ensure constant redundancy and fault-tolerance, hot spare is the best option.

5. If speed is preferred over resilience, which of the following RAID configuration is the most suited?

    A.   RAID 0

    B.   RAID 1

    C.   RAID 5

    D.   RAID 10

Answer: **A**

In a RAID 0 configuration, files are written in stripes across multiple disks without the use of parity information. This technique allows for fast reading and writing to disk since all of the disks can typically be accessed in parallel. However, without the parity information, it is not possible to recover from a hard drive failure. This technique does not provide redundancy and should not be used for systems with high availability requirements.

6. Updating records in multiple locations or copying an entire database on to a remote location as a means to ensure the appropriate levels of fault-tolerance and redundancy is known as

    A.   Data mirroring

    B.   Shadowing

    C.   Backup

    D.   Archiving

Answer: **B**

Data mirroring is a RAID technique that duplicates all disk writes from one disk to another to create two identical drives. Database shadowing is the technique in which updates are shadowed in multiple locations. It is like copying the entire database on to a remote location. Backups are to be conducted on a regular basis and are useful in recovering information or a system in the event of a disaster. Archiving is the storage of data that is not in continual use for historical purposes.

7. When the backup window is not long enough to backup all of the data and the restoration of backup must be as fast as possible. Which of the following type of high-availability backup strategy is **BEST**?

    A.   Full

    B.   Incremental

    C.   Differential

    D.   Increase the backup window so a full backup can be performed

Answer: **C**

Full backup would not be possible since the backup window is not long ago for all the data to be backed up. Additionally, it is less likely that the backup window can be increased to allow for a full backup, which is both time consuming and costly from a storage perspective. In an incremental backup, only the files that changed since the last backup will be backed up. In a differential backup, only the files that changed since the last full backup will be backed up. In general, differentials require more space than incremental backups while incremental backups are faster to perform. On the other hand, restoring data from incremental backups requires more time than differential backups. To restore from incremental backups, the last full backup and all of the incremental backups performed are combined. In contrast, restoring from a differential backup requires only the last full backup and the latest differential.

8. At a restricted facility, visitors are requested to provide identification and verified against a pre-approved list by the guard at the front gate before being let in. This is an example of checking for

    A.   Least privilege

    B.   Separation of duties

    C.   Fail-safe

    D.   Psychological acceptability

Answer: **A**

Access to facilities should be limited to named individuals with a requirement for physical access following the principle of least privilege. Individuals who do not require frequent physical access to physical systems should not receive access to the facility. If occasional access is required, then temporary access should be granted and revoked when it is no longer required. It is recommended that you are familiar with the other principles mentioned.

9. When sensitive information is no longer critical but still within scope of a record retention policy, that information is **BEST**

   A. Destroyed

   B. Re-categorized

   C. Degaussed

   D. Released

Answer: **B**

Information categorization also includes the processes and procedures to lower the sensitivity label of information. For example, declassification may be used to downgrade the sensitivity of information. Over the course of time, information once considered sensitive may decline in value or criticality. In these instances, declassification efforts should be implemented to ensure that excessive protection controls are not used for non-sensitive information. When declassifying information, marking, handling, and storage requirements will likely be reduced. Organizations should have categorization or declassification practices well documented for use by individuals assigned with the task. Information may still be needed and so it cannot be destroyed, degaussed, or deleted.

10. Which of the following **BEST** determines access and suitability of an individual?

   A. Job rank or title

   B. Partnership with the security team

   C. Role

   D. Background investigation

Answer: **D**

A background investigation relevant to the role, job or access is the best approach for minimal security problems. While a background investigation will not guarantee the integrity or honesty of an individual it will give the organization a glimpse into the history of an individual and references.

11. Which of the following can help with ensuring that only the needed logs are collected for monitoring?

   A. Clipping level

   B. Aggregation

   C. XML Parsing

   D. Inference

Answer: **A**

Clipping levels are used to ensure that only needed logs are collected. This is mainly used, because even on a single system, logs can get to be very large. An example of a clipping level is that only failed access attempts are logged.

12. The main difference between a Security Event Information Management (SEIM) system and a log management system is that SEIM systems are useful for log collection, collation and analysis

    A.   In real time

    B.   For historical purposes

    C.   For admissibility in court

    D.   In discerning patterns

Answer: **A**

Security event information management (SEIM) solutions are intended to provide a common platform for log collection, collation, and analysis in real-time to allow for more effective and efficient response. Log management systems are similar in that, they also collect logs and provide the ability to report against them, although their focus tends to be on the historical analysis of log information, rather than real-time analysis. They may be combined with SEIM solutions to provide both historical and real-time functions. Evidence collections for admissibility in court and pattern discernment are not real-time functions.

13. The best way to ensure that there is no data remanence of sensitive information that was once stored on a DVD-R media is by

    A.   Deletion

    B.   Degaussing

    C.   Destruction

    D.   Overwriting

Answer: **C**

Optical media such as CDs and DVD must be physically destroyed to make sure that there is no residual data that can be disclosed. Since the media mentioned in this context is a read-only media (burn-once) DVD, the information on it cannot be overwritten or deleted. Degaussing can reduce or remove data remanence in magnetic non-optical media.

14. Which of the following processes is concerned with not only identifying the root cause but also addressing the underlying issue?

    A.   Incident management

    B.   Problem management

    C.   Change management

    D.   Configuration management

Answer: **B**

While incident management is concerned primarily with managing an adverse event, problem management is concerned with tracking that event back to a root cause and addressing the underlying problem. Maintaining system integrity is accomplished through the process of change control management. Configuration management is a process of identifying and documenting hardware components, software, and the associated settings.

15. Before applying a software update to production systems, it is **MOST** important that

    A. Full disclosure information about the threat that the patch addresses is available

    B. The patching process is documented

    C. The production systems are backed up

    D. An independent third party attests the validity of the patch

Answer: **C**

Prior to deploying updates to production servers, make certain that a full system backup is conducted. In the regrettable event of a system crash, due to the update, the server and data can be recovered without a significant loss of data. Additionally, if the update involved propriety code, it will be necessary to provide a copy of the server or application image to the media librarian. The presence or absence of full disclosure information is good to have but not a requirement as the patching process will have to be a risk-based decision as it applies to the organization. Documentation of the patching process is the last step in patch management processes. Independent third-party assessments are not usually related to attesting patch validity.

16. Computer forensics is the marriage of computer science, information technology, and engineering with

    A. Law

    B. Information systems

    C. Analytical thought

    D. The scientific method

Answer: **A**

As a forensic discipline, this area deals with evidence and the legal system and is really the marriage of computer science, information technology, and engineering with law.

17. What principal allows an investigator to identify aspects of the person responsible for a crime when, whenever committing a crime, the perpetrator leaves traces while stealing assets?

    A. Meyer's principal of legal impunity

    B. Criminalistic principals

    C. IOCE/Group of 8 Nations principals for computer forensics

    D. Locard's principle of exchange

Answer: **D**

Locard's principle of exchange states that when a crime is committed, the perpetrators leave something behind and take something with them, hence the exchange. This principle allows an investigator to identify aspects of the persons responsible, even with a purely digital crime scene.

18. Which of the following is part of the five rules of evidence?

    A. Be authentic, be redundant and be admissible.

    B. Be complete, be authentic and be admissible.

    C. Be complete, be redundant and be authentic.

    D. Be redundant, be admissible and be complete

Answer: **B**

At a more generic level, evidence should have some probative value, be relevant to the case at hand, and meet the following criteria (often called the five rules of evidence): be authentic, be accurate, be complete, be convincing, and be admissible.

19. What is not mentioned as a phase of an incident response?

    A. Documentation

    B. Prosecution

    C. Containment

    D. Investigation

Answer: **B**

The incident response and handling phase can be broken down further into triage, investigation, containment, and analysis and tracking.

20. Which BEST emphasizes the abstract concepts of law and is influenced by the writings of legal scholars and academics.

    A. Criminal law

    B. Civil law

    C. Religious law

    D. Administrative law

Answer: **B**

Civil law emphasizes the abstract concepts of law and is influenced by the writings of legal scholars and academics, more so than common law systems.

21. Which of the following are computer forensics guidelines?

    A. IOCE, MOM and SWGDE.

    B. MOM, SWGDE and IOCE.

    C. IOCE, SWGDE and ACPO.

    D. ACPO, MOM and IOCE.

Answer: **C**

Like incident response, there are various computer forensics guidelines (e.g., International Organization of Computer Evidence (IOCE), Scientific Working Group on Digital Evidence (SWGDE), Association of Chief Police Officers (ACPO)). These guidelines formalize the computer forensic processes by breaking them into numerous phases or steps. MOM stands for means, opportunity, and motives.

22. Triage encompasses which of the following incident response sub-phases?

    A.   Collection, transport, testimony

    B.   Traceback, feedback, loopback

    C.   Detection, identification, notification

    D.   Confidentiality, integrity, availability

Answer: **C**

Triage encompasses the detection, identification, and notification sub-phases.

23. The integrity of a forensic bit stream image is determined by:

    A.   Comparing hash totals to the original source

    B.   Keeping good notes

    C.   Taking pictures

    D.   Encrypted keys

Answer: **A**

Ensuring the authenticity and integrity of evidence is critical. If the courts feel the evidence or its copies are not accurate or lack integrity, it is doubtful that the evidence or any information derived from the evidence will be admissible. The current protocol for demonstrating authenticity and integrity relies on hash functions that create unique numerical signatures that are sensitive to any bit changes. Currently, if these signatures match the original or have not changed since the original collection, the courts will accept that integrity has been established.

24. When dealing with digital evidence, the crime scene:

    A.   Must never be altered

    B.   Must be completely reproducible in a court of law

    C.   Must exist in only one country

    D.   Must have the least amount of contamination that is possible

Answer: **D**

Given the importance of the evidence that is available at a crime scene, the ability to deal with a scene in a manner that minimizes the amount of disruption, contamination, or destruction of evidence. Once a scene has been contaminated, there is no undo or redo button to push; the damage is done.

25. When outsourcing IT systems

    A.   all regulatory and compliance requirements must be passed on to the provider.

    B.   the outsourcing organization is free from compliance obligations.

    C.   the outsourced IT systems are free from compliance obligations.

    D.   the provider is free from compliance obligations.

Answer: **A**

An organization's obligations for due care extend to its business partners.

26. When dealing with digital evidence, the chain of custody:

    A.   Must never be altered

    B.   Must be completely reproducible in a court of law

    C.   Must exist in only one country

    D.   Must follow a formal documented process

Answer: **D**

The chain of custody must explain evidence from origin to destruction.

27. To ensure proper forensics action when needed, an incident response program must:

    A.   avoid conflicts of interest by ensuring organization legal council is not part of the process.

    B.   routinely create forensic images of all desktops and servers.

    C.   only promote closed incidents to law enforcement.

    D.   treat every incident as though it may be a crime.

Answer: **D**

An incident may be harmless but it may also be the start of an investigation. Therefore all incidents must be handled with care until proven benign.

28. A hard drive is recovered from a submerged vehicle. The drive is needed for a court case. What is the best approach to pull information off the drive?

A. Wait for the drive to dry and then install it in a desktop and attempt to retrieve the information via normal operating system commands.

B. Place the drive in a forensic oven to dry it and then use a degausser to remove any residual humidity prior to installing the drive in a laptop and using the OS to pull off information.

C. While the drive is still wet use a forensic bit to bit copy program to ensure the drive is preserved in its "native" state.

D. Contact a professional data recovery organization, explain the situation and request they pull a forensic image.

Answer: **D**

For heavily damaged media, professional data recovery services are the best chance for recovery.

29. To successfully complete a vulnerability assessment, it is critical that protection systems are well understood through:

A. Threat definition, target identification and facility characterization

B. Threat definition, conflict control and facility characterization

C. Risk assessment, threat identification and incident review

D. Threat identification, vulnerability appraisal and access review

Answer: **A**

At the beginning, a good assessment requires the security professional to determine specific protection objectives. These objectives include threat definition, target identification, and facility characteristics.

30. The strategy of forming layers of protection around an asset or facility is known as:

A. Secured Perimeter

B. Defense-in-Depth

C. Reinforced Barrier Deterrent

D. Reasonable Asset Protection

Answer: **B**

In the concept of defense-in-depth, barriers are arraigned in layers with the level of security growing progressively higher as one comes closer to the center or the highest protective area. Defending an asset with a multiple posture can reduce the likelihood of a successful attack; if one layer of defense fails, another layer of defense will hopefully prevent the attack, and so on.

31. The key to a successful physical protection system is the integration of:

    A. people, procedures, and equipment

    B. technology, risk assessment, and human interaction

    C. protecting, offsetting, and transferring risk

    D. detection, deterrence, and response

Answer: **A**

The key to a successful system is the integration of people, procedures and equipment into a system that protects the targets from the threat. A well-designed system provides protection-in-depth, minimizes the consequences of component failures and exhibits balanced protection.

32. For safety considerations in perimeter areas such as parking lots or garages what is the advised lighting?

    A. 3 fc

    B. 5 fc

    C. 7 fc

    D. 10 fc

Answer: **B**

Lights used for CCTV monitoring generally requires at least one to two footcandles of illumination, whereas the lighting needed for safety considerations in exterior areas such as parking lots or garages substantially greater (at least 5 fc).

33. What would be the most appropriate interior sensor used for a building that has windows along the ground floor?

    A. infrared glass-break sensor

    B. ultrasonic glass-break sensors

    C. acoustic/shock glass-break sensors

    D. volumetric sensors

Answer: **C**

Glass-break sensors are a good intrusion detection device for buildings with a lot of glass windows and doors with glass panes. The use of ¬dual-technology glass break sensors—acoustic and shock wave—is most effective. The reason is that if only acoustic is used and an employee pulls the window blinds up, it can set off a false alarm; but if it is set to a dual-alarm system both acoustic and shock sensors will need to be activated before an alarm is triggered.

34. Which of the following BEST describe three separate functions of CCTV?

    A.   surveillance, deterrence, and evidentiary archives

    B.   intrusion detection, detainment and response

    C.   optical scanning, infrared beaming and lighting

    D.   monitoring, white balancing and inspection

Answer: **A**

Uses of CCTV systems for security services include several different functions: surveillance, assessment, deterrence, and evidentiary archives.

35. What is the BEST means of protecting the physical devices associated with the alarm system?

    A.   Tamper protection

    B.   Target hardening

    C.   Security design

    D.   UL 2050

Answer: **A**

Tamper protection is the means of protecting the physical devices associated with the alarm system through line supervision, encryption, or tamper alarming of enclosures and components.

Domain 8 – **Software Development Security**

1. The key objective of application security is to ensure

    A.   that the software is hacker proof

    B.   the confidentiality, integrity and availability of data

    C.   accountability of software and user activity

    D.   prevent data theft

Answer: **B**

The objective of application security is to make sure that the system and its resources are available when needed, that the integrity of the processing of the data and the data itself are ensured, and that the confidentiality of the data is protected. All of these purposes rely upon secure, consistent, reliable, and properly operating software. Ensuring confidentiality, integrity, and availability will mitigate the chances and impact of a hacking incident or data theft, but it must be recognized that total hacker proof software is utopian. Auditing (logging) functionality in software can help with detecting software and user activity, but this is not the key objective of application security. Software security controls can reduce the likelihood of data theft but they are not necessarily preventative.

2. For an application security program to be effective within an organization, it is critical to

    A. identify regulatory and compliance requirements.

    B. educate the software development organization the impact of insecure programming.

    C. develop the security policy that can be enforced.

    D. properly test all the software that is developed by your organization for security vulnerabilities.

Answer: **C**

The underlying foundation of software security controls is the organization's security policy. The security policy reflects the security requirements of the organization. The identification of regulatory and compliance requirements such as Sarbanes–Oxley (SOX), payment card industry data security standard (PCIDSS) are essential and must be factored into the security policy. Without a clear understanding of what the security requirements are, as defined in the security policy, educating software development teams may potentially be still inadequate. Testing for security vulnerability can provide some degree of software assurance, but with newer kinds of attacks against software being discovered, security testing does not directly indicate the effectiveness of an application security program.

3. Which of the following architectures states: "There is no inherent difference between data and programming representations in computer memory" which can lead to injection attacks, characterized by executing data as instructions.

    A. Von Neumann

    B. Linus' Law

    C. Clark and Wilson

    D. Bell LaPadula

Answer: **A**

One of the fundamental aspects of von Neumann architecture is that there is no inherent difference between data and programming in the memory of the computer. Therefore, one cannot tell whether the pattern 4Eh (00101110) is the letter N or a decrement opcode. Similarly, the pattern 72h (01110010) may be the letter r or the first byte of the "jump if below" opcode.

4. An important characteristic of bytecode is that it

    A.   has increased secure inherently due to sandboxing

    B.   manages memory operations automatically

    C.   is more difficult to reverse engineer

    D.   is faster than interpreted languages

Answer: **D**

A programming language like Java compiles source code into a sort of pseudo-object code called bytecode. The bytecode is then processed by the interpreter (called the Java Virtual Machine, or JVM) for the CPU to run. Because the bytecode is already fairly close to object code, the interpretation process is much faster than for other interpreted languages. And because bytecode is still undergoing an interpretation, a given Java program will run on any machine that has a JVM. Memory management and sandboxing are important security aspects that apply to the programming language Java, but not to bytecode itself. The debate over whether a pseudo-object (bytecode) representation can be easily reverse engineered is debatable and inconclusive. Because bytecode is more pseudo-object representation of the source code, reversing to source code is in fact considered less difficult than from object or executable code.

5. Two cooperating processes that simultaneously compete for a shared resource, in such a way that they violate the system's security policy, is commonly known as

    A.   Covert channel

    B.   Denial of Service

    C.   Overt channel

    D.   Object reuse

Answer: **A**

A covert channel or confinement problem is an information flow issue. It is a communication channel allowing two cooperating processes to transfer information in such a way that it violates the system's security policy. There are two types of covert channels: storage and timing. A covert storage channel involves the direct or indirect reading of a storage location by one process and a direct or indirect reading of the same storage location by another process. Typically, a covert storage channel involves a finite resource, such as a memory location or sector on a disk that is shared by two subjects at different security levels. This scenario is a description of a covert storage channel. A covert timing channel depends upon being able to influence the rate that some other process is able to acquire resources, such as the CPU, memory, or I/O devices. Covert channels as opposed to what should be the case (overt channels) could lead to denial of service and object reuse has to do with disclosure protection when objects in memory are reused by different processes.

6. An organization has a website with a guest book feature, where visitors to the web site can input their names and comments about the organization. Each time the guest book web page loads, a message box is prompted with the message 'You have been P0wnd' followed by redirection to a different website. Analysis reveals that the no input validation or output encoding is being performed in the web application. This is the basis for the following type of attack?

    A.   Denial of Service

    B.   Cross-site Scripting (XSS)

    C.   Malicious File Execution

    D.   Injection Flaws

Answer: **B**

A Web site that allows users to input information for later retrieval by other users, such as a guestbook comment page or blog, without proper input validation, may fail to detect when such input comes in is in the form of active scripting. Without appropriate output encoding, the script can be actively read and executed by the browser causing denial of service (Web site defacement) or other serious impacts. This is the basis of cross-site scripting attacks.

7. The art of influencing people to divulge sensitive information about themselves or their organization by either coercion or masquerading as a valid entity is known as

    A.   Dumpster diving

    B.   Shoulder surfing

    C.   Phishing

    D.   Social engineering

Answer: **D**

Social engineering is the art of getting people to divulge sensitive information to others either in a friendly manner, as an attempt to be "helpful," or through intimidation. Phishing is the form of social engineering using electronic means such as e-mail. Shoulder surfing is a disclosure attack wherein, an attacker stands over the shoulders of someone and reads the sensitive information they are viewing. Masking of information (asterisking password) can mitigate shoulder surfing. Dumpster diving is another disclosure attack in which dumpsters are searched to glean sensitive information.

8. An organization's server audit logs indicate that an employee that was terminated in the morning was still able to access certain sensitive resources on his system, on the internal network, that afternoon. The logs indicate that the employee had logged on successfully before he was terminated but there is no record of him logging off before he was terminated. This is an example of this type of attack?

    A.   Time of Check/Time of Use (TOC/TOU)

    B.   Logic Bomb

    C.   Remote-Access Trojans (RATS)

    D.   Phishing

Answer: **A**

TOC/TOU is a common type of attack that occurs when some control changes between the time that the system security functions check the contents of variables and the time the variables actually are used during operations. For instance, a user logs on to a system in the morning and later is fired. As a result of the termination, the security administrator removes the user from the user database. Because the user did not log off, he or she still has access to the system and might try to get even. Logic bombs are software modules set up to run in a quiescent state, but to monitor for a specific condition or set of conditions and to activate their payload under those conditions. Remote access trojans are malicious programs designed to be installed, usually remotely, after systems are installed and working. Phishing attempts to get the user to provide information that will be useful for identity theft-type frauds.

9. The most effective defense against a buffer overflow attack is

    A.   disallow dynamic construction of queries

    B.   bounds checking

    C.   encode the output

    D.   forced garbage collection

Answer: **B**

Buffer overflows can result when a program fills up the assigned buffer of memory with more data than its buffer can hold. When the program begins to write beyond the end of the buffer, the program's execution path can be changed, or data can be written into areas used by the operating system itself. A buffer overflow is caused by improper (or lacking) bounds checking on input to a program. By checking for the bounds (boundaries) of allowable input size, buffer overflow can be mitigated. Disallowing dynamic construction of queries is a defense against injection attacks and encoding the output mitigates scripting attacks. The collection of dangling objects in memory (garbage) can be requested but not necessarily forced and proper memory management can help mitigate buffer overflow attacks, but the most effective defenses against buffer overflow is bounds checking and proper error checking.

10. It is extremely important that as one follows a software development project, security activities are performed

      A. before release to production, so that the project is not delayed

      B. if a vulnerability is detected in your software

      C. in each stage of the life cycle

      D. when management mandates it

Answer: **C**

Security activities should be done in parallel with project initiation activities and, indeed, with every task throughout the project.

11. Software Acquisition (SwA) can be organized around the major phases of a generic acquisition process. The major phases are:

      A. Planning, contracting, monitoring and acceptance, follow on

      B. Contracting, planning, monitoring and acceptance, follow on

      C. Planning, contracting, monitoring and certification, follow on

      D. Planning, contracting, monitoring and accreditation, follow on

Answer: **A**

SwA can be organized around the major phases of a generic acquisition process. The major phases are:

- **Planning Phase** – This phase begins with
  - ▢ Needs determination for acquiring software services or products, identifying potential alternative software approaches, and identifying risks associated with those alternatives. This set of activities is followed by
  - ▢ Developing software requirements to be included in work statements;
  - ▢ Creating an acquisition strategy and/or plan that includes identifying risks associated with various software acquisition strategies; and
  - ▢ Developing evaluation criteria and an evaluation plan.
- **Contracting Phase** – This phase includes three major activities: (1) creating/issuing the solicitation or RFP with a work statement, instructions to offerors, terms and conditions (including conditions for acceptance), prequalification considerations, and certifications; (2) evaluating supplier proposals submitted in response to the solicitation or RFP; (3) and finalizing contract negotiation to include changes in terms and conditions and awarding the contract. Software risks are addressed and mitigated through terms and conditions, certifications, evaluation factors for award, and risk mitigation requirements in the work statement.
- **Monitoring and Acceptance Phase** – This phase involves monitoring the supplier's work and accepting the final service or product delivered under a contract. This phase includes three major activities: (1) establishing and consenting to the contract work schedule; (2) implementing change (or configuration) control procedures; and (3) reviewing and accepting software deliverables. During the monitoring and acceptance phase, software risk management and assurance case deliverables must be evaluated to determine compliance in accepted risk mitigation strategies as stated in the requirements of the contract.

■ ***Follow-on*** – This phase involves maintaining the software (the process is often called sustainment). This phase includes two major activities: (1) sustainment (includes risk management, assurance case management, and change management) and (2) disposal or decommissioning. During the follow-on phase, software risks must be managed through continued analysis of the assurance case and should be adjusted to mitigate changing risks.

12. Who can ensure and enforce the separation of duties by ensuring that programmers don't have access to production code?

    A.   Operations personnel

    B.   Software librarian

    C.   Management

    D.   Quality assurance personnel

Answer: **B**

A software librarian ensures program or data library is controlled in accordance with policy and procedures.

13. Technical evaluation of assurance to ensure that security requirements have been met is known as?

    A.   Accreditation

    B.   Certification

    C.   Validation

    D.   Verification

Answer: **B**

Certification is the process of evaluating the security stance of the software or system against a predetermined set of security standards or policies. Management, after reviewing the certification, authorizes the software or system to be implemented in a production status, in a specific environment, for a specific period. Management authorization is known as accreditation.

14. Defect prevention rather than defect removal is characteristic of which of the following software development methodology?

        A. Computer Aided Software Engineering (CASE)

        B. Spiral

        C. Waterfall

        D. Cleanroom

Answer: **D**

In cleanroom software development methodology, the goal is to write code correctly the first time, rather than trying to find the problems once they are there. Essentially, it focuses on defect prevention rather than defect removal. The waterfall methodology is extremely structured and its key distinguishing characteristic is that each phase (stage) must be completed before moving on to the next, in order to prevent ad hoc scope creep. A distinguishing feature of the spiral model is that in each phase of the waterfall there are four substages, based on the common Deming PDCA (Plan-Do-Check-Act) model; in particular, a risk assessment review (Check). CASE is the technique of using computers and computer utilities to help with the systematic analysis, design, development, implementation, and maintenance of software.

15. A security protection mechanism in which untrusted code, which is not signed, is restricted from accessing system resources is known as?

        A. Sandboxing

        B. Non-repudiation

        C. Separation of Duties

        D. Obfuscation

Answer: **A**

One of the control mechanisms for mobile code is the sandbox. The sandbox provides a protective area for program execution. Limits are placed on the amount of memory and processor resources the program can consume. If the program exceeds these limits, the Web browser terminates the process and logs an error code. This can ensure the safety of the browser's performance. Non-repudiation is a security control mechanism in which the user or process cannot deny its action. Separation of duties is about ensuring that a security policy cannot be violated by a single user or process. Obfuscation is the process of rendering source code to be unreadable and unintelligible as a protection against reversing and IP issues.

16. A program that does not reproduce itself but pretends to be performing a legitimate action, while acting performing malicious operations in the background is the characteristic of which of the following?

    A. Worms

    B. Trapdoor

    C. Virus

    D. Trojan

Answer: **D**

A Trojan is a program that pretends to do one thing while performing another, unwanted action. A Trojan does not reproduce itself as do worms and viruses in order to spread. A trapdoor or backdoor is a hidden mechanism that bypasses access control measures. It is an entry point into a program that is inserted in software by programmers during the program's development to provide a method of gaining access into the program for modification if the access control mechanism malfunctions and locks them out. Developers often refer to them as maintenance hooks.

17. A plot to take insignificant pennies from a user's bank account and move them to the attacker's bank account is an example of

    A. Social Engineering

    B. Salami Scam

    C. Pranks

    D. Hoaxes

Answer: **B**

A variant on the concept of logic bombs involves what is known as the salami scam. The basic idea involves siphoning off small amounts of money (in some versions, fractions of a cent) credited to a specific account, over a large number of transactions. Pranks are very much a part of the computer culture, so much so that you can now buy commercially produced joke packages that allow you to perform "stupid Mac (or PC or Windows) tricks." Hoaxes use an odd kind of social engineering, relying on people's naturally gregarious nature and desire to communicate, and on a sense of urgency and importance, using the ambition that people have to be the first to provide important new information.

18. Role-based access control to protect confidentiality of data in databases can be achieved by which of the following?

    A. Views

    B. Encryption

    C. Hashing

    D. Masking

Answer: **A**

A view is a feature that allows for virtual tables in a database; these virtual tables are created from one or more real tables in the database. For example, a view can be set up for each user (or group of users) on the system so that the user can then only view those virtual tables (or views). Encryption, hashing, and masking can all provide confidentiality as well, but for databases, views based access control which is a content dependent access control mechanism is the best answer.

19. The two most dangerous types of attacks against databases containing disparate non-sensitive information are

    A. Injection and scripting

    B. Session hijacking and cookie poisoning

    C. Aggregation and inference

    D. Bypassing authentication and insecure cryptography

Answer: **C**

Aggregation is the ability to combine non-sensitive data from separate sources to create sensitive information. For example, a user takes two or more unclassified pieces of data and combines them to form a classified piece of data that then becomes unauthorized for that user. Thus, the combined data sensitivity can be greater than the classification of individual parts. Inference is the ability to deduce (infer) sensitive or restricted information from observing available information. Essentially, users may be able to determine unauthorized information from what information they can access and may never need to directly access unauthorized data. For example, if a user is reviewing authorized information about patients, such as the medications they have been prescribed, the user may be able to determine the illness. Inference is one of the hardest threats to control. All of the other attacks are primarily attacks on Web applications.

20. A property that ensures only valid or legal transactions that do not violate any user-defined integrity constraints in DBMS technologies is known as?

    A. Atomicity

    B. Consistency

    C. Isolation

    D. Durability

Answer: **B**

ACID test, which stands for atomicity, consistency, isolation, and durability, is an important DBMS concept.

- Atomicity is when all the parts of a transaction's execution are either all committed or all rolled back—do it all or not at all. Essentially, all changes take effect, or none do

- Consistency occurs when the database is transformed from one valid state to another valid state. A transaction is allowed only if it follows user-defined integrity constraints. Illegal transactions are not allowed, and if an integrity constraint cannot be satisfied, the transaction is rolled back to its previously valid state and the user is informed that the transaction has failed.

- Isolation is the process guaranteeing the results of a transaction are invisible to other transactions until the transaction is complete.

- Durability ensures the results of a completed transaction are permanent and can survive future system and media failures, that is, once they are done, they cannot be undone. This is similar to transaction persistence.

21. Expert systems are comprised of a knowledge base comprising modeled human experience and which of the following?

    A. Inference engine

    B. Statistical models

    C. Neural networks

    D. Roles

Answer: **A**

The expert system uses a knowledge base (a collection of all the data, or knowledge, on a particular matter) and a set of algorithms or rules that infer new facts from knowledge and incoming data. The knowledge base could be the human experience that is available in an organization. Because the system reacts to a set of rules, if the rules are faulty, the response will also be faulty. Also, because human decision is removed from the point of action, if an error were to occur, the reaction time from a human would be longer.

22. The best defense against session hijacking and man-in-the-middle (MITM) attacks is to use the following in the development of your software?

    A.   Unique and random identification

    B.   Use prepared statements and procedures

    C.   Database views

    D.   Encryption

Answer: **A**

Prepared statements and procedures protect against SQL injection. Data base views protect against unauthorized modification. Encryption protects the confidentiality of information but may not protect against a session hijacking attempt. Unique and random identifiers present a challenge for the attacker to guess what the next identifier may be.

Appendix B
Domain 1 Materials

The following templates and forms are referenced in *Domain 1 – Security and Risk Management*, and include the following:

- Risk Assessment Template
- Potential Breach Reporting Form
- Breach Register Template
- Risk Management Log Procedures
- Risk Management Plan

You can download the materials from this appendix for free by going to the following link:

https://learning.isc2.org/content/cissp-textbook-appendices

Risk Assessment Template

Step 1: Risk Identification	Step 2: Risk Assessment		Step 3: Risk Management				
List of Possible Risks	Likelihood H/M/L	Impact H/M/L	What are we already doing about it? (mitigating factors)	What more can we do about it?	Timescale	Person Responsible	Reviewed Level of Risk

Date to be reviewed	
Person/Group responsible for review	

Potential Breach Reporting Form

Business Unit:		Breach Report Completed by:	
Identified by:		Date Identified:	

PART 1

Summary of Potential Breach:	
Assessment of Potential Breach: (Very Low, Low, Medium, High, or Very High)	
Justification of Assessment: (Describe the rationale behind the assessment rating)	
Breach Investigation Team Members:	
Breach Investigation Response Time:	
Assessment Signed-off by Executive Management:	

PART 2

Investigation of Breach	
Internal Investigation: (Describe results of internal investigation)	
Legal or Other External Consultation: (Describe interaction with lawyers or other external advisors and the advice received)	
Conclusion: (Was the breach confirmed?)	
Final Rating of Breach:	

B

Domain 1 Materials

Resolution Steps at Date of Initial Assessment (Including ongoing process improvements)	
Already Implemented	Still to be Implemented
Executive Review and Approval	
Breach Closed by: (Include breach register update) **Date Closed:**	
Reviewed/Approved by: **Date Reviewed:**	

Breach Register Template

The (fill in name of responsible party) will own the breach register and will use the potential breach reporting form template to source information about the breach. This register is to be used for confirmed breaches only.

Date Breach Discovered	Date(s) of Breach	Description of Breach	Responsible Person	How was the breach identified?	Process & Responsibilities for Handling Breach	Date Breach Rectified and Closed

Risk Management Log Procedures

Document Revision History

Version Number	Date	Description

Introduction

A risk management log needs to be developed to help with the identification, management, and ranking of risks throughout the organization. Below are the types of fields that are contained within the worksheet. Following is an example of a risk management worksheet.

General Risks

General Risks are risks that can occur but do not have a specific date that can be associated with it.

Specific Risks

Specific Risks are risks that can be associated with a particular date when it may occur.

Number

A sequential number is assigned to the risk for identification purposes. Example of number scheme - 1, 2... for general risks, and 1, 2... for specific risks.

Risk/Threat

Risk identification consists of determining risks that are likely to affect the organization and documenting the characteristics of those risks. Risks to both the internal and external areas of the organization should be tracked. Internal risks are those items the security professional can directly control, and external risks are those events that happen outside the direct influence of the security professional.

Business Priority

Determining the business priority can be simplified by using the following table. This table can be modified to fit the needs of a particular organization, or business unit. For most organizations, this table works well just as it is.

Risk Category Descriptions			Impact	Occurrence Probability	Exposure (rank)
Category	Level	Value			
Resources	High	3	Assessed by the security professional against the context of the risk identified	Very likely: Greater than 70% probability	Impact x Occurrence
	Med	2		Probable:30-70% probability	Probability =Rank
	Low	1		Unlikely: Less than 30% probability	
Schedule	High	3		Very likely: Greater than 70% probability	
				Probable: 30-70% probability	
	Med	2			
				Unlikely: Less than 30% probability	
	Low	1			

Risk Category

The risk category identifies the type of risk impact you are working with.

Impact

Based on the expected impact from the previous table, enter the value into the impact field on the worksheet.

Occurrence Probability

Based on the expected occurrence probability from the table above enter the value into the occurrence probability field on the worksheet.

Exposure (Rank)

Exposure or Rank is determined by multiplying the impact times the probability occurrence. The higher the resulting number, the greater the risk is.

Risk Management Strategy

Mitigation Activities
Enter the mitigation activities that can be accomplished to prevent the risk from happening. For example, if you are having a birthday party and you are purchasing pizza and want to make sure that the pizza is ready when you go to pick it up, call the pizza shop the day before to verify the order and the pickup time.

Contingency
Contingency plans are developed as a result of a risk being identified. Contingency plans are pre-defined action plans that can be implemented if identified risks actually occur. For example, even though you called to verify your pizza order and the time of pickup when you get there, the pizza shop is closed. Your contingency plan is to go to the market and buy frozen pizza that you can heat up and serve at the party.

Trigger
A trigger is an event that occurs that marks the time the risk turns into a problem.

Condition
Enter the event that causes the risk to become a problem.

Date
Enter the date that the condition will occur.

Schedule
Enter the schedule line number when the trigger will occur. (A trigger task has been included in the schedule.)

Activities
Identify the activities that will be done if the risk occurs.

Status
Enter a short description of status on the risk.

\<Name of Organization\>

Risk Management Plan

Document Revision History

Version Number	Date	Description

Statement

Describe the purposes and importance to the organization of identifying and tracking risks.

Objectives

State the objectives of the risk management plan.

Roles and Responsibilities

Use a table like the following to depict the roles and responsibilities of all participants in the Risk Management process.

Process Task Name	System Support Staff	IT Manager	User	Project Manager	Project Team	Steering Committee	Executive Sponsor

Risk Process

Describe the stages of the risk management process and provide a process diagram.

Risk Management Worksheets

Use a Risk Management Log to help with the assessment and control of risks throughout the life of the project. Access the Risk Management Log Procedures for assistance in completing the log.

Appendix C
Domain 2 Materials

The following sample Record Retention and Destruction and Security Approach policies are referenced in *Domain 2 – Asset Security*. You can download the materials from this appendix for free by going to the following link:

https://learning.isc2.org/content/cissp-textbook-appendices

Record Retention and Destruction Policy

"Company X" recognizes that the firm's engagement and administrative files are critical assets. As such, the firm has established this formal written policy for record retention and destruction in accordance with applicable state and federal laws. Compliance with this policy is mandatory for all employees.

Engagement Files

Engagement files are defined, for purposes of this policy, as all records related to the engagement, including work papers and other documents that form the basis of the services rendered by the firm. For example, all documentation reflecting the procedures applied, evidence obtained, and conclusions reached in the engagement. In order to adequately address the needs of the firm and meet the current regulatory requirements established by the profession and the regulatory agencies, this policy will address separately the document retention requirements for engagement files by the categories indicated below.

Audit/Review/Compilation Services

"Company X" will retain all records related to the audit, review, or compilation (including electronic records) for a period of five years from the conclusion of the audit, review, or compilation that meet the following two criteria:

1. The records have been created, sent, or received in connection with the audit, review, or compilation.

And

2. The records contain conclusions, opinions, analyses, financial data related to the audit, review, or compilation, or significant information that is inconsistent with the final conclusions, opinions, or analyses (e.g., significant differences in professional judgment or differences of opinion on issues that are material to the financial statements or to the final conclusions).

Records for purposes of this subsection include work papers and other documents that form the basis of the financial statement engagement; and memoranda, correspondence, communications, and other documents and records that meet both of the criteria stated above.

It is the firm's position that all documents (whether hard copy or electronic) that do not meet the specified criteria above would not be considered substantive in nature and thus would not have to be retained in accordance with this policy. The firm, however, acknowledges the following exception to this rule:

- All significant information that is inconsistent with the final conclusions, opinions, or analyses (e.g., significant differences in professional judgment or differences of opinion on issues that are material to the financial statements or to the final conclusions) must be considered substantive in nature and appropriately retained in accordance with this policy.

Although this list is not meant to be all inclusive, the following are examples of those items that generally would not meet the criteria for retention and should be destroyed at the completion of the engagement:

- Superseded drafts of memoranda, financial statements, or regulatory filings
- Notes on superseded drafts of memoranda, financial statements, or regulatory filings that reflect incomplete or preliminary thinking
- Duplicates of documents

- Copies of client records (unless the client records contain evidence of audit or other procedures applied by the firm.)
- Review notes
- To-do lists (which have been completed)
- Documents that contain typographical errors or other minor errors that result from the normal business/learning process or from preliminary views based on incomplete information or data
- Voicemail messages (It is the firm's policy that all significant voicemail messages that would record or support the firm's professional services should be documented as a memo to file and retained in accordance with the terms of this policy.)

Questions arising in connection with applying the rules set forth in this section should be referred immediately to the partner on the engagement. The Quality Control Partner must approve any exceptions to this policy.

Other Services (Includes Tax and Consulting Services)

"Company X" will retain sufficient records (whether hard copy or electronic) to reflect services performed by and substantive information provided to the firm for the engagement for five years after it completes such services. Records, for the purposes of this subsection, mean final work papers and any other documents, including correspondence and copies of client records, that are necessary for a reasonable person to understand the services performed by and substantive information provided to "Company X" for the engagement but do not include the firm's billing records.

Administrative Files

It is the firm's policy that all administrative files (including but not limited to billing and collecting activities, accounts payable, loans, leases, fixed assets, and personnel files) will be maintained for no less than the current legal or regulatory requirements for such items or longer if they serve a useful purpose as determined by the Executive Assistant and with the approval of the Quality Control Partner. The Executive Assistant will be responsible for maintaining and annually updating a summary of the legal and regulatory requirements for all administrative files and keeping the Quality Control Partner updated of any changes to such requirements.

Physical Security

It is company protocol to protect all hard copy files, electronic files, computer hardware, software, data, and documentation from misuse, theft, unauthorized access, and environmental hazards. As such, the firm has adopted procedures for information maintained in both hard copy form and electronic form to ensure physical security.

Hard Copy Form

- The firm will store all of its on-site hard copy client files in file cabinets. File cabinets are restricted to those employees authorized to have such access.
- The Executive Assistant will have the responsibility for establishing filing procedures to ensure that files can be easily located and retrieved as necessary.

Electronic Form

The firm has established back-up procedures on electronic files to minimize the risk that data may be destroyed, modified, or disclosed without authorization. These procedures include, but are not limited to, the following:

- The Information Technology Partner will be responsible for ensuring that all data files will be backed up daily to an off-site backup facility administered by Info Secure, 123 NE. Chapman Street., Blue Bird, WI 94837.
- The Information Technology Partner will be responsible for ensuring also that all software applications used in storing the files are retained or available (including all updated or superseded applications) so that the electronic files can continue to be accessed for the retention periods stated in this policy.

Access controls have been established to maintain the confidentiality and integrity of data stored on the firm's computer systems. Access shall be restricted to only those actions that are appropriate to each employee's specific job duties. The Information Technology Partner will have the responsibility for the administration of access controls and will ensure that all additions, deletions, and changes are processed appropriately upon written request from the applicable supervisor and/or partner. Employees will have individual access codes and passwords to the firm's computer network systems. These systems are accessible at all times by the firm, and the Information Technology Partner will maintain a complete list of access codes and passwords in a secured place. Employees are prohibited from the unauthorized use of the access codes and passwords belonging to other employees.

Confidentiality

All of the documents and records relating to clients are the property and proprietary interest of "Company X" to the extent it is consistent with applicable laws. All original documents are the property of the client and should be returned to the client upon request or at the end of the engagement. The firm's documents and records relating to clients are confidential and may not be disclosed without express written permission from the client or unless required by law. All employees of the firm must ensure that privacy will be maintained for client information.

> In consideration of the firm's size and complexity, the nature and scope of the professional services we render to our clients, and the sensitivity of the information we collect, the firm has determined that compliance with this policy appears to satisfy the current regulatory requirements under the Federal Trade Commission Safeguards Rule (www. ftc.gov/privacy/glbact).

Destruction of Records

The Quality Control Partner has the responsibility for ensuring compliance with this policy for the destruction of records, files, and electronic data. It is the firm's policy that all engagement letters issued on or after the effective date of this policy should contain language regarding the firm's applicable record retention period. Refer to Exhibit A for sample language. For engagements prior to the effective date of this policy, or for engagements that did not have engagement letter language addressing the record retention policy, the Executive Assistant will make a reasonable attempt to contact the client or former client to inform them of the intent to destroy the records. Notice shall be deemed to be reasonable if given by U.S. mail postage prepaid to the client's last known address, whether actually received or not. The firm will conduct on an annual basis an inventory of all records, files, and electronic data subject to destruction based on the retention periods outlined in Exhibit B attached. The Executive Assistant will review this list with the Quality Control Partner for approval prior to the actual destruction of such records.

> *Under no circumstances will any records, files, or electronic data be destroyed, regardless of the retention periods identified in this policy, if there is any pending regulatory investigation, disciplinary action, legal action, or if the firm has knowledge of the intent by a regulatory agency to launch an inquiry or knowledge of a potential legal claim.*

Roles and Responsibilities

Quality Control Partner	■ Enforce this security policy. ■ Annually review and update this policy as needed to ensure compliance with regulatory requirements. ■ Approve and document exceptions to this policy on an as needed basis.
Partners	■ Enforce this security policy. ■ Annually review and update this policy as needed to ensure compliance with regulatory requirements.
Engagement Partner/Manager	■ Responsible for ensuring, in accordance with the terms of this policy, that all required documentation (including electronic records) is maintained at the end of the client engagement. ■ Confirms with others as necessary that all documentation not required to be retained in accordance with this policy is appropriately destroyed at the end of the client engagement.
Executive Assistant	■ Maintain and annually update the legal and regulatory requirements for all administrative files, including but not limited to personnel documents and payroll records. ■ Responsible for establishing and maintaining filing procedures and for limiting the access as appropriate to prevent breaches in security in accordance with the terms of this policy. ■ Responsible for ensuring compliance with this policy for the destruction of records, files, and electronic data. ■ Notify employees of the policy and updates, as appropriate.
Information Technology Partner	■ Ensure that back-up procedures are in place on all electronic files in accordance with the terms of this policy. ■ Ensure that appropriate access controls are maintained to protect and maintain the confidentiality and integrity of the data stored on the firm's computer systems in accordance with all legal and regulatory requirements.
Managers/Supervisors/Seniors	■ Ensure that all personnel are aware of and comply with this policy. ■ Develop and apply appropriate performance standards, control practices, and procedures designed to provide reasonable assurance that all employees observe this policy.
All employees and Independent Contractors	■ Adhere to this policy at all times.

Employees should notify their immediate supervisor or any member of management upon learning of violations of this policy. Employees who violate this policy will be subject to disciplinary action, up to and including termination of employment.

Exhibit A

Sample Engagement Letter Language Re: Record Retention

It is our policy to keep records related to this engagement for five years. However, "Company X" does not keep any original client records, so we will return those to you at the completion of the services rendered under this engagement. When records are returned to you, it is your responsibility to retain and protect your records for possible future use, including potential examination by any government or regulatory agencies. By your signature below, you acknowledge and agree that upon the expiration of the five year period "Company X" shall be free to destroy our records related to this engagement.

C

Domain 2 Materials

Exhibit B

Record Retention Periods—Engagement Files

	Retention Period	
	Current Client	**Former Client**
Billing Files	5 years	5 years
Correspondence Files	5 years	5 years
Audit/Review/Compilation Statements & Reports	5 years	5 years
Tax Returns	5 years	5 years
Special Reports	5 years	5 years

Work Paper Files:		
Audit/Review/Compilation Work Papers	5 years	5 years
Tax Return Work Papers	5 years	5 years
All Other Services	5 years	5 years
Permanent/Carry-Forward Files (Audit/Review/Compilation Services)	Permanently	5 years
Permanent/Carry-Forward Files (Other Services)	Permanently	5 years

Note: If a client at any time becomes a former client, the former client retention policy will be in effect. If they return as a current client, the current client retention procedures will go into effect from that point forward.

<Project Name>

Security Approach

Version Number: <1.0>

Version Date: <mm/dd/yyyy>

<u>*Notes to the Author*</u>

- *Blue italicized text enclosed in square brackets ([text]) provides instructions to the document author, or describes the intent, assumptions, and context for content included in this document.*

- *Blue italicized text enclosed in angle brackets (<text>) indicates a field that should be replaced with information specific to a particular project.*

- *Text and tables in black are provided as boilerplate examples of wording and formats that may be used or modified as appropriate to a specific project.*

When using this template, refer to the following recommended steps:

1. *Replace all text enclosed in angle brackets (e.g., <Project Name>) with the correct field document values. These angle brackets appear in both the body of the document and in headers and footers. To customize fields in Microsoft Word (which display a gray background when selected) select File->Properties->Summary and fill in the appropriate fields within the Summary and Custom tabs.*

   After clicking OK to close the dialog box, update all fields throughout the document by selecting Edit>Select All (or Ctrl-A) and pressing F9. Or you can update each field individually by clicking on it and pressing F9.

   These actions must be done separately for any fields contained within the document's Header and Footer.

2. *Modify boilerplate text as appropriate for the specific project.*

3. *To add any new sections to the document, ensure that the appropriate header and body text styles are maintained. Styles used for the Section Headings are Heading 1, Heading 2, and Heading 3. The style used for boilerplate text is Body Text.*

4. *To update the Table of Contents, right-click on it and select "Update field" and choose the option - "Update entire table."*

5. *Before submission of the first draft of this document, delete this instruction section "Notes to the Author" and all instructions to the author throughout the entire document.*

VERSION HISTORY

[Provide information on how the development and distribution of the Security Approach will be controlled and tracked. Use the table below to provide the version number, the author implementing the version, the date of the version, the name of the person approving the version, the date that particular version was approved, and a brief description of the reason for creating the revised version.]

Version Number	Implemented By	Revision Date	Approved By	Approval Date	Description of Change
1.0	<Author name>	<mm/dd/yy>	<name>	<mm/dd/yy>	<description of change>

TABLE OF CONTENTS

1 INTRODUCTION

1.1. Purpose of the Security Approach

Defining a security approach for a project provides a line of site from business requirements through team members and components all the way to implemented security controls. It documents clear responsibilities for implementation, certification, and accreditation of the system security and provides a framework for communicating security based impacts on other development and project management activities. This security approach defines from a security perspective how systems associated with the *<Project Name>* project will be characterized, categorized, and managed.

2 SECURITY APPROACH

2.1 Process Overview

[Summarize the steps necessary for establishing the security approach.]

The project manager, working in collaboration with the security team, developed a preliminary assessment of the system's FIPS 199 categorization, and using the proposed project goals defined the following approach to securing the IT system in development. The approach seeks the most cost effective and efficient approach to meeting technical, operational, and managerial security requirements. The approach seeks to ensure that security considerations are effectively integrated with other critical processes such as requirements analysis and risk management throughout the life of the project and that an early assessment of system classification and boundary definitions is appropriately considered to facilitate development and certification efforts later in the project lifecycle.

2.2 Security Approach Summary

[Summarize the overall system approach here. The description should reflect decisions that guided how the system boundaries have been defined and the relative maturity of the systems being developed or modified as well as any system interconnections and dependencies. The relationship with existing systems, internal and external, is critical to defining how to approach the overall security of this system. Identifying a security manager for each system and certifying an accreditation authority early in the process ensures that both development and ongoing maintenance are cost effective and efficient.]

<Provisional High-Level Diagram of Systems with FIPS 199 classification and interconnections identified>

C

Domain 2 Materials

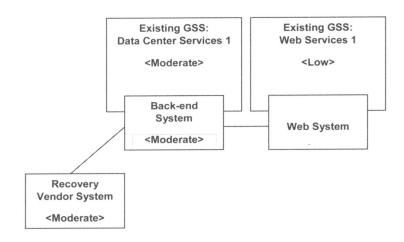

3 TEAM MEMBERS

3.1 Certification and Accreditation Team

Project Role	Name
Chief Information Officer	*<name>*
Information System Owner	*<name>*
Senior Information Security Officer	*<name>*
Chief Information Security Officer	*<name>*
Authorizing Official	*<name>*

3.2 Security Team

[Define the security stakeholders in this section. Include names, roles, and contact information]

Name	Project Role	Security
<name>	System Security Manager	*<system name(s) within scope of responsibility if applicable>*
	Developer	
	Security Critical Partner	
	C&A Authority	

4 SYSTEM CATEGORIZATION

4.1 Core Systems

Description – *<System Name>* is a new system under development intended to *[describe system purpose]*.

Security Manager – *[Identify the security manager for this system]*

Characterization – *<System Name>* is characterized as a *<GSS, MA, or Other>*.

Categorization – Based on an estimate of FIPS 199 impact, this system is provisionally defined as a *<LOW, MODERATE, or HIGH>*.

Boundaries – *[Describe at a high level what security services or components are to be included in the part of the system]*

Dependencies – *[Describe the security services or components being inherited from a GSS or MA]*

Interconnections – *[Describe other system interconnections established for data sharing, business continuity, or backup]*

4.2 Sub-Systems

Description – *<System Name>* is a new system under development intended to *<describe system purpose>*.

Security Manager – *[Identify the security manager for this system]*

Characterization – *<System Name>* is characterized as a *<GSS, MA, or Other>*.

Categorization – Based on an estimate of FIPS 199 impact, this system is provisionally defined as a *<LOW, MODERATE, or HIGH>*.

Boundaries – *[Describe at a high level what security services or components are to be included in the part of the system]*

Dependencies – *[Describe the security services or components being inherited from a GSS or MA]*

Interconnections – *[Describe other system interconnections established for data sharing, business continuity, or backup]*

4.3 Interconnected Systems

Description – *<System Name>* is a new system under development intended to *<describe system purpose>*.

Security Contact – *[Include contact information for this system]*

Interconnections – *[Describe other system interconnections established for data sharing, business continuity, or backup]*

5 PROGRAMMATIC ACTIVITIES

[Use this section to define administrative and management activities that support the overall security approach. These include activities such as training, configuration management, risk management, and communication plans.]

5.1 Team Training

[Outline specific training related to security. Include any database or developer training that applies to development activities. Include any specific rules of behavior or special security considerations on which team members need to be educated.]

5.2 Requirements Management

Baseline security requirements for each system have been integrated into the Requirements Management process documented in *<Project Management or Requirements Management document name>* located on *<full network path location>*.

5.3 Configuration Management

Baseline security requirements for each system have been integrated into the Configuration Management process documented in *<Project Management or Configuration Management document name>* located on *<full network path location>*.

5.4 Risk Management

Baseline security requirements for each system have been integrated into the Risk Management process documented in *<Project Management or Risk Management document name>* located on *<full network path location>*.

5.5 Change Management

Baseline security requirements for each system have been integrated into the Change Management process documented in *<Project Management or Change Management document name>* located on *<full network path location>*.

APPENDIX A: SECURITY APPROACH APPROVAL

The undersigned acknowledge that they have reviewed the *<Project Name>* **Security Approach** and agree with the information presented within this document. Changes to this **Security Approach** will be coordinated with, and approved by, the undersigned or their designated representatives.

[List the individuals whose signatures are desired. Examples of such individuals are Business Owner, Project Manager (if identified), Designated Approving Authorities, and any appropriate stakeholders. Add additional lines for signature as necessary.]

Signature: _____   Date: _____

Print Name: _____

Title: _____

Role: _____

Signature: _____   Date: _____

Print Name: _____

Title: _____

Role: _____

Signature: _____   Date: _____

Print Name: _____

Title: _____

Role: _____

APPENDIX B: REFERENCES

[Insert the name, version number, description, and physical location of any documents referenced in this document. Add rows to the table as necessary.]

The following table summarizes the documents referenced in this document.

Document Name	Description	Location
<Document Name and Version Number>	*<Document description>*	*<URL or network path where document is located>*

APPENDIX C: KEY TERMS

The following table provides definitions and explanations for terms and acronyms relevant to the content presented within this document.

Term	Definition
[Insert Term]	*<Provide definition of term and acronyms used in this document.>*

APPENDIX D: RELATED DOCUMENTS

- FIPS 199, *Standards for Security Categorization of Federal Information and Information Systems*
- FIPS 200, *Minimum Security Requirements for Federal Information and Information Systems*
- SP 800-18, *Guide for Developing Security Plans for Federal Information Systems*
- SP 800-30, *Risk Management Guide for Information Technology Systems*
- SP 800-37, *Guide for the Security Certification and Accreditation of Federal Information Systems*
- SP 800-53, *Recommended Security Controls for Federal Information Systems*
- Draft SP 800-53A, *Guide for Assessing the Security Controls in Federal Information Systems*
- SP 800-55, *Security Metrics Guide for Information Technology Systems*
- SP 800-60, *Guide for Mapping Types of Information and Information Systems to Security Categories*
- SP 800-70, *Security Configuration Checklists Program for IT Products: Guidance for Checklists Users and Developers*
- SP 800-100, *Information Security Handbook: A Guide for Managers*

Appendix D
Domain 3 Materials

The following example mobile device security policy is referenced in *Domain 3 – Security Engineering*. You can download the materials from this appendix for free by going to the following link:

https://learning.isc2.org/content/cissp-textbook-appendices

Example Mobile Device Security Policy

Using this Policy

One of the challenges facing IT departments today is securing both privately owned and corporate mobile devices, such as smartphones and tablet computers. This example policy is intended to act as a guideline for organizations looking to implement or update their mobile device security policy.

Where required, adjust, remove, or add information according to your needs and your attitude to risk. This is not a comprehensive policy but rather a pragmatic template intended to serve as the basis for your own policy.

Background to this Policy

This policy provides a framework for securing mobile devices and should be linked to other policies that support your organization's posture on IT and data security.

D

Example Policy

1. *Introduction*

Mobile devices, such as smartphones and tablet computers, are important tools for the organization, and their use is supported to achieve business goals.

However, mobile devices also represent a significant risk to information security and data security because, if the appropriate security applications and procedures are not applied, they can be a conduit for unauthorized access to the organization's data and IT infrastructure. This can subsequently lead to data leakage and system infection.

<Company X> has a requirement to protect its information assets in order to safeguard its customers, intellectual property, and reputation. This document outlines a set of practices and requirements for the safe use of mobile devices.

2. *Scope*

2.1. This policy applies to all mobile devices, whether owned by <Company X>, or owned by employees, that have access to corporate networks, data, and systems (not including corporate IT-managed laptops). This includes smartphones and tablet computers.

2.1. *Exemptions:* Where there is a business need to be exempted from this policy (too costly, too complex, adversely impacting other business requirements), a risk assessment must be conducted prior to being authorized by security management.

3. *Policy*

3.1. Technical Requirements

3.1.1. Devices must use the following Operating Systems: Android 2.2 or later, IOS 4.x or later. **<add or remove as necessary>**

3.1.2. Devices must store all user-saved passwords in an encrypted password store.

3.1.3. Devices must be configured with a secure password that complies with <Company X>'s password policy. This password must not be the same as any other credentials used within the organization.

3.1.4. With the exception of those devices managed by IT, devices are not allowed to be connected directly to the internal corporate network

3.2. User Requirements

3.2.1. Users must only load data essential to their role onto their mobile device(s).

3.2.2. Users must report all lost or stolen devices to <Company X> IT immediately.

3.2.3. If a user suspects that unauthorized access to company data has taken place via a mobile device, the user must report the incident in alignment with **<Company X>**'s incident handling process.

3.2.4. Devices must not be "jailbroken"* or have any software/firmware installed that is designed to gain access to functionality not intended to be exposed to the user.

3.2.5. Users must not load pirated software or illegal content onto their devices.

3.2.6. Applications must only be installed from official platform-owner approved sources. Installation of code from un-trusted sources is forbidden. If you are unsure if an application is from an approved source, contact **<Company X>** IT.

3.2.7. Devices must be kept up to date with manufacturer or network provided patches. As a minimum, patches should be checked for weekly and applied at least once a month.

3.2.8. Devices must not be connected to a PC that does not have up-to-date and enabled anti-malware protection and that does not comply with corporate policy.

3.2.9. Devices must be encrypted in line with **<Company X>**'s compliance standards.

3.2.10. Users must be cautious about the merging of personal and work email accounts on their devices. They must take particular care to ensure that company data is only sent through the corporate email system. If a user suspects that company data has been sent from a personal email account, either in body text or as an attachment, they must notify **<Company X>** IT immediately.

3.2.11. **(If applicable to your organization)** Users must not use corporate workstations to backup or synchronize device content such as media files unless such content is required for legitimate business purposes.

Note – To jailbreak a mobile device is to remove the limitations imposed by the manufacturer. This gives access to the operating system, thereby unlocking all its features and enabling the installation of unauthorized software.

Appendix E
Domain 4 Materials

The following instructions on installing Hyper V are referenced in *Domain 4 – Communication and Network Security*. You can download the materials from this appendix for free by going to the following link:

https://learning.isc2.org/content/cissp-textbook-appendices

Installing Hyper-V

The following assumptions are being made as we start this tutorial:

- You have installed Windows Server 2012/2012R2
- Applied the most recent patches
- Connected to storage
- Renamed your network adapters to enable easy identification (and teamed them, if required)
- Configured IP addresses

The next step is to enable the Hyper-V role. This task can be performed graphically, through Server Manager, using the same process that you use to add any other role or feature. Or you can use Windows PowerShell:

NOTE: In Windows PowerShell, unlike in the Add Roles and Features Wizard, management tools and snap-ins for a role are not included by default. To include management tools as part of a role installation, add the -IncludeManagementTools parameter to the cmdlet. If you are installing roles and features on a server that is running the Server Core installation option of Windows Server 2012, and you add a role's management tools to an installation, you are prompted to change the installation option to a minimal-shell option that allows the management tools to run. Otherwise, management tools and snap-ins cannot be installed on servers that are running the Server Core installation option of Windows Server.

Do one of the following to open a Windows PowerShell session with elevated user rights.

- On the Windows desktop, right-click Windows PowerShell on the taskbar, and then click Run as Administrator.
- On the Windows Start page, type any part of the name Windows PowerShell. Right-click the shortcut for Windows PowerShell when it is displayed on the Start page in the Apps results, click Advanced, and then click Run as Administrator. To pin the Windows PowerShell shortcut to the Start page, right-click the shortcut, and then click Pin to Start.

Type the following, and then press Enter, where computer_name represents a remote computer on which you want to install Hyper-V.

To install Hyper-V directly from a console session, do not include -ComputerName <computer_name> in the command.

```
Install-WindowsFeature –Name Hyper-V –ComputerName
<computer_name> -IncludeManagementTools -Restart
```

The benefit of using the Server Manager GUI is that it also prompts you to create a virtual switch on a selected network adapter in the server. The virtual network adapters that you configure on your VMs connect to this switch to access the external network. By default, a virtual network adapter is also created on the host OS so that the OS can use that adapter for VM traffic. If you have a dedicated management network adapter, disable the shared adapter after you complete the installation process.

The Following are the Basic Steps for Using Server Manager:

1. Log on, as an account with administrative credentials, to the server that will be the Hyper-V host and launch Server Manager, or remotely launch Server Manager with an account that has administrative credentials on the server that will be the Hyper-V host.

2. Select Add Roles and Features from the Manage menu.

3. Click Next on the Before You Begin page.

4. On the Installation Type page, choose the Role-based installation type and click Next.

5. On the Server Selection page, from the list of servers in the server pool, choose the server on which to install the Hyper-V role and click Next.

6. Under Server Roles, select Hyper-V and accept the option to automatically install the management tools.

7. On the Create Virtual Switches page, select the network adapter that you want to use for VM traffic and click Next.

8. Leave the check box for the option to enable live migrations cleared and click Next. Live migration can easily be added later.

9. Choose new locations for VM storage, or accept the defaults, and click Next.

10. Select the check box to enable automatic restart of the server if required, and click Yes in the displayed confirmation box. Click the Install button.

Congratulations!!! You have successfully installed the Hyper-V Role. Once the Windows Server restarts, log back in. Once you have logged in, Server Manager will start. From within Server Manager, under Tools, choose Hyper-V Manager and navigate to your server. Note that there are no VMs. However, if you click the Virtual Switch Manager action, you'll see a single virtual switch that has the name of the network adapter controller; for example, Realtek PCIe GBE Family Controller.

You should consider renaming the virtual switch to something more descriptive, such as External Switch, to represent the network to which it connects. Using consistent naming for switches across your Hyper-V hosts is important: If you move VMs between hosts, a switch of the same name must exist on both the target and source hosts if the VM is to maintain its network connectivity. Also, clear the check box for the Allow management operating system to share this network adapter option. That option is needed only if you do not have a separate network adapter for management of the host or if you have only one network adapter that is shared for VM and host traffic. You can also use this interface to create additional switches, as required.

You are now ready to start creating VMs on your standalone host.

To Create a Virtual Machine:

1. Open Hyper-V Manager.

2. From the navigation pane of Hyper-V Manager, select the computer running Hyper-V.

3. From the Actions pane, click New and then click Virtual Machine.

4. The New Virtual Machine wizard opens. Click Next.

5. On the Specify Name and Location page, type an appropriate name.

6. On the Assign Memory page, specify enough memory to start the guest operating system.

7. On the Configure Networking page, connect the virtual machine to the switch you created when you installed Hyper-V.

8. On the Connect Virtual Hard Disk and Installation Options pages, choose the option that is appropriate for how you plan to install the guest operating system:

> ¤ If you will install the guest operating system from a DVD or an image file (an .ISO file), choose Create a virtual hard disk. Click Next, and then click the option that describes the type of media you will use. For example, to use an .iso file, click Install an operating system from a boot CD/DVD and then specify the path to the .iso file.
>
> ¤ If the guest operating system is already installed in a virtual hard disk, choose Use an existing virtual hard disk and click Next. Then, choose Install an operating system later.

9. On the Summary page, verify your selections and then click Finish.

Windows PowerShell Equivalent Commands

The following Windows PowerShell cmdlet or cmdlets perform the same function as the preceding procedure. Enter each cmdlet on a single line, even though they may appear word-wrapped across several lines here because of formatting constraints.

Run the following command to create a virtual machine named web server with 1 GB of startup memory and use an existing virtual hard disk in which a guest operating system has already been installed.

```
New-VM –Name "web server" –MemoryStartupBytes 1GB –
                VHDPath d:\vhd\BaseImage.vhdx
```

To Install the Guest Operating System into the VM:

1. From Hyper-V Manager, in the Virtual Machines section of the results pane, right-click the name of the virtual machine and click Connect.

2. The Virtual Machine Connection tool opens.

3. From the Action menu in the Virtual Machine Connection window, click Start.

4. The virtual machine starts, searches the startup devices, and loads the installation package.

5. Proceed through the installation.

Appendix F
Domain 5 Materials

The following Password Security Policy is referenced in *Domain 5 – Identity and Access Management*. You can download the materials from this appendix for free by going to the following link:

https://learning.isc2.org/content/cissp-textbook-appendices

Section x	**IS Security Policies**	mm/dd/yy	-Effective
		mm/dd/yy	-Revised
Policy x.xx	**Password**	Information Services	-Author

Introduction

User authentication is a means to control who has access to an Information Resource system. Controlling the access is necessary for any Information Resource. Access gained by a non-authorized entity can cause loss of information confidentiality, integrity, and availability that may result in loss of revenue, liability, loss of trust, or embarrassment to [COMPANY NAME].

Three factors, or a combination of these factors, can be used to authenticate a user. Examples are:

- Something you know – Password, Personal Identification Number (PIN)

- Something you have – Smartcard

- Something you are – Fingerprint, iris scan, voice

- A combination of factors – Smartcard and a PIN

Purpose

The purpose of the [COMPANY NAME] Password Policy is to establish the rules for the creation, distribution, safeguarding, termination, and reclamation of the [COMPANY NAME] user authentication mechanisms.

Audience

The [COMPANY NAME] Password Policy applies equally to all individuals who use any [COMPANY NAME] information resource.

Definitions

Information Resources (IR): Any and all computer printouts, online display devices, magnetic storage media, and all computer-related activities involving any device capable of receiving email, browsing websites, or otherwise capable of receiving, storing, managing, or transmitting electronic data including, but not limited to, mainframes, servers, personal computers, notebook computers, hand-held computers, personal digital assistant (PDA), pagers, smartphones, tablets, distributed processing systems, network attached and computer controlled medical and laboratory equipment (i.e., embedded technology), telecommunication resources, network environments, telephones, fax machines, printers, and service bureaus. Additionally, it is the procedures, equipment, facilities, software, and data that are designed, built, operated, and maintained to create, collect, record, process, store, retrieve, display, and transmit information.

Information Security Officer (ISO): Responsible to the executive management for administering the information security functions within the enterprise. The ISO is the enterprise's internal and external point of contact for all information security matters.

Information Services (IS): The name of the company department responsible for computers, networking, and data management.

Password: A string of characters that serves as authentication of a person's identity, which may be used to grant, or deny, access to private or shared data.

Strong Passwords: A strong password is a password that is not easily guessed. It is normally constructed of a sequence of characters, numbers, and special characters, depending on the capabilities of the operating system. Typically the longer the password, the stronger it is. It should never be a name, dictionary word in any language, an acronym, a proper name, a number, or be linked to any personal information about you such as a birth date, social security number, and so on.

F

Domain 5 Materials

Password Policy

- All passwords, including initial passwords, must be constructed and implemented according to the following [COMPANY NAME] rules:
  - ❖ It must be routinely changed.
  - ❖ It must adhere to a minimum length as established by [COMPANY NAME] IS.
  - ❖ It must be a combination of alpha and numeric characters.
  - ❖ It must not be anything that can be easily tied back to the account owner such as: username, social security number, nickname, relative's names, birth date, etc.
  - ❖ It must not be dictionary words or acronyms.
  - ❖ Password history must be kept to prevent the reuse of a password.
- Stored passwords must be encrypted.
- User account passwords must not be divulged to anyone. [COMPANY NAME] IS and IS contractors will not ask for user account passwords.
- Security tokens (i.e., smartcard) must be returned on demand or upon termination of the relationship with [COMPANY NAME].
- If the security of a password is in doubt, the password must be changed immediately.
- Administrators must not circumvent the Password Policy for the sake of ease of use.
- Users cannot circumvent password entry with auto logon, application remembering, embedded scripts, or hardcoded passwords in client software. Exceptions may be made for specific applications (like automated backup) with the approval of the [COMPANY NAME] ISO. In order for an exception to be approved, there must be a procedure to change the passwords.
- Computing devices must not be left unattended without enabling a password protected screensaver or logging off of the device.
- IS help desk password change procedures must include the following:
  - ❖ Authenticate the user to the help desk before changing password
  - ❖ Change to a strong password
  - ❖ The user must change password at first login
- In the event passwords are found or discovered, the following steps must be taken:
  - ❖ Take control of the passwords and protect them.
  - ❖ Report the discovery to the [COMPANY NAME] Help Desk.
  - ❖ Transfer the passwords to an authorized person as directed by the [COMPANY NAME] ISO.

Password Guidelines

- Passwords must be changed at least every 60 days.
- Passwords must have a minimum length of 8 alphanumeric characters.
- Passwords must contain a mix of upper and lowercase characters and have at least 2 numeric characters. The numeric characters must not be at the beginning or the end of the password. Special characters should be included in the password where the computing system permits. The special characters are (!@#$%^&*_+=?/~`;:,<>|\).
- Passwords must not be easy to guess and they:
  - ❖ must not be your username
  - ❖ must not be your employee number
  - ❖ must not be your name
  - ❖ must not be family member names
  - ❖ must not be your nickname
  - ❖ must not be your social security number
  - ❖ must not be your birthday
  - ❖ must not be your license plate number
  - ❖ must not be your pet's name
  - ❖ must not be your address
  - ❖ must not be your phone number
  - ❖ must not be the name of your town or city
  - ❖ must not be the name of your department
  - ❖ must not be street names
  - ❖ must not be makes or models of vehicles
  - ❖ must not be slang words
  - ❖ must not be obscenities
  - ❖ must not be technical terms
  - ❖ must not be school names, school mascot, or school slogans
  - ❖ must not be any information about you that is known or is easy to   learn (favorite food, color, sport, etc.)
  - ❖ must not be any popular acronyms
  - ❖ must not be words that appear in a dictionary
  - ❖ must not be the reverse of any of the above

- Passwords must not be reused for a period of one year.
- Passwords must not be shared with anyone.
- Passwords must be treated as confidential information.

F

Domain 5 Materials

Creating a Strong Password	• Combine short, unrelated words with numbers or special characters. For example: eAt42peN
	• Make the password difficult to guess but easy to remember.
	• Substitute numbers or special characters for letters. (But do not just substitute) For example:
	❖ livefish - is a bad password.
	❖ L1veF1sh - is better and satisfies the rules, but setting a pattern of 1st letter capitalized, and i's substituted by 1's can be guessed.
	❖ l!v3f1Sh - is far better; the capitalization and substitution of characters is not predictable.

Disciplinary Actions	Violation of this policy may result in disciplinary action, which may include termination for employees and temporaries; a termination of employment relations in the case of contractors or consultants; dismissal for interns and volunteers; or suspension or expulsion in the case of a student. Additionally, individuals are subject to loss of [COMPANY NAME] Information Resources access privileges, civil, and criminal prosecution.

Supporting Information Reference #	***This Security Policy is supported by the following Security Policy Standards***
	Policy Standard detail
1.	IR Security controls must not be bypassed or disabled.
2.	Security awareness of personnel must be continually emphasized, reinforced, updated, and validated.
3.	All personnel are responsible for managing their use of IR and are accountable for their actions relating to IR security. Personnel are also equally responsible for reporting any suspected or confirmed violations of this policy to the appropriate management.
4.	Passwords, Personal Identification Numbers (PIN), Security Tokens (i.e., smartcard), and other computer systems security procedures and devices shall be protected by the individual user from use by, or disclosure to, any other individual or organization. All security violations shall be reported to the custodian, data/program owner, or department management.
5.	Access to, change to, and use of IR must be strictly secured. Information access authority for each user must be reviewed on a regular basis, as well as each job status change such as a transfer, promotion, demotion, or termination of service.
6.	On termination of the relationship with the company, users must surrender all property and IR managed by the agency. All security policies for IR apply to and remain in force in the event of a terminated relationship until such surrender is made. Further, this policy survives the terminated relationship.

Appendix G
Domain 6 Materials

The following are samples of the Log Management Policies and Procedure documents that are referenced in *Domain 6 – Security Assessment and Testing*. You can download the materials from this appendix for free by going to the following link:

https://learning.isc2.org/content/cissp-textbook-appendices

Sample Log Management Policy

Revisions

V2.0 8.13.2014

Purpose:

The purpose of this policy is to establish a requirement to enable and review logs on ABC Corp. IT resources that store, access, or transmit data classified by ABC Corp. as Confidential or Private.

Scope:

This policy covers all ABC Corp. data that is available currently or that may be created and used in the future. This policy applies to all individuals who maintain affected systems or data.

Policy:

IT resources that store, access, or transmit data classified, by ABC Corp., as Confidential or Private shall be electronically logged. Logging shall include system, application, database, and file activity whenever available or deemed necessary.

- Logging shall include creation, access, modification, and deletion activities.
- Log files shall be regularly examined for access control discrepancies, breaches, and policy violations.
- Data custodians or device managers are responsible for developing appropriate processes for monitoring and analyzing their logs.
- Individuals shall not be assigned to be the sole reviewers of their own user activity.
- System activity review cycles shall include review of audit logs minimally every 30 days and may include daily exception reporting.

Definitions:

Confidential Data – A class of data whereby its unauthorized disclosure, alteration, or destruction could result in significant risk to the mission, safety, or integrity of ABC Corp. and its constituents.

Private Data – A class of data whereby its unauthorized disclosure, alteration, or destruction could result in moderate risk to the mission, safety, or integrity of ABC Corp. and its constituents.

Device Managers – Entity responsible for maintaining or managing a class of information systems.

Data Custodian – Those who are authorized by the Data Owner to use or manipulate data. Data Custodians have the responsibility to adhere to all policies applicable to the data entrusted to them.

Responsibilities:

Data Owners are responsible for assigning the classifications categories to their data, and they have the primary responsibility for ensuring the appropriate use and security of the data.

Data Custodians are responsible for identifying the systems that must be reviewed based on the classification assigned by the data owners, the information on these systems that must be reviewed, the types of access reports that are to be generated, and the individual(s) responsible for reviewing all logs and reports. The data custodians are also responsible for ensuring appropriate evidence of regular log review is happening in accordance with this policy.

The Information Security Officer is responsible for verifying that a review process has been implemented in an effective manner.

Administration and Interpretations:

This policy shall be administered by Information Security. Questions regarding this policy should be directed to the Information Security Officer.

Amendment/Termination of this Policy:

ABC Corp. reserves the right to modify, amend, or terminate this policy at any time. This policy does not constitute a contract between ABC Corp. and its employees.

References to Applicable Policies/Standards:

Data Classification Policy

Exceptions:

None

Violations/Enforcement:

Any known violations of this policy should be reported to ABC Corp's Information Security Officer at 302-189-3286 or via email to security_team@ABCCorp.com

Violations of this policy can result in immediate withdrawal or suspension of system and network privileges and/or disciplinary action in accordance with ABC Corp's procedures.

ABC Corp. may advise law enforcement agencies when a criminal offense may have been committed.

Sample Log Procedures Document

ABC Corp. Information Technology Services

Log Procedures

Introduction:

Log collection and review is an important component of an information security program. The following provides guidance regarding types of logs that should be enabled and reviewed, frequency of review, and escalation procedures.

See the ABC Corp. Information Security Log Policy for requirements that apply to electronic information resources that contain, access, or transmit data classified by ABC **Corp.** as confidential or restricted.

ABC Corp's Information Security Officer (ISO) reviews and updates these procedures periodically in response to changes in industry standards, law, regulation, or ABC Corp. policy.

----

1. ***Enable logging and auditing at the OS, application/database, system, and workstation level. Enable logs for the following as available and technically feasible:***

    a. Failed and successful logins

    b. Modification of security settings

    c. Privileged use or escalation of privileges

    d. System events

    e. Modification of system-level objects

    f. Session activity

    g. Account management activities including password changes (success and failure)

    h. Policy change

    i. Workstation firewalls

    j. Anti-virus/anti-malware product

    k. Applications such as Web servers

The following information should be captured for each of the above items as feasible:

2. ***Date and time of activity***

    a. For connection logs: peer IP address

    b. Identification of user performing activity

    c. Description of attempted or completed activity

    d. Application logs: client requests and server responses

    e. Abnormal usage, e.g., number of transactions, usage spikes, etc.

    f. Abnormal application behavior, including repeated application restart

    g. Data modification where required for regulatory compliance

3. ***Check the following when reviewing logs:***

      a.   All information collected in (1) above

      h.   Other indicators of suspicious activity, such as configuration changes, successful and failed access attempts, and the presence of threats identified by vendor databases or signatures.

Examples include:

- ***Remote Management tools*** – Review patch logs, installation history, and vulnerability status, including known vulnerabilities and missing patches.
- ***Routers*** – Review configuration changes, login attempts, interface usage, and error events for evidence of anomalous activity.
- ***Firewalls*** – Check for abnormalities, failed inbound and outbound connection attempts; additional investigation upon detection of abnormalities/ compromises.
- ***Intrusion Detection System (IDS)*** – Look for abnormalities such as suspicious behavior and detected attacks. Investigate or escalate for investigation as appropriate.
- ***Configuration Control Applications, e.g., Tripwire*** – Review application configuration changes.

4. ***Frequency of review***

The System Steward is responsible for defining and ensuring appropriate log monitoring. Available logs should be reviewed in response to suspected or reported security problems. See the ABC **Corp.** Information Security Log Policy for specific requirements.

5. ***Retention***

Default retention for logs is 90 days. The retention period may be shortened or lengthened according to business need, law, regulations, ABC **Corp.** policy, or technical constraints such as capacity limitations.

6. ***Escalate security-related issues, questions, or concerns to IT Security via IT Request ticket (see "Getting help" below)***

      a.   See Security Incident Reporting Procedures for details. ITS staff are to follow ITS' Response Procedures for Compromised Computers for issues potentially involving compromised computers.

      b.   Indicate whether restricted data is involved.

      c.   When escalating to Security, save logs until you receive further instructions from Security. If relevant logs may expire, make a static copy to preserve them. Small log extracts may be attached directly to the IT Request ticket if they do not contain restricted data.

7. *Appropriate use and protection of log information*

Logs must be accessed, secured, and protected according to the nature of the information they may contain. While it is necessary for the organization to perform regular collection and monitoring of logs, this activity must be consistent with the provisions of information protection described in ITS' Routine System Monitoring Practices and the ABC **Corp.** Electronic Communications Policy.

8. *Additional information*

      a. ABC Corp's IT Group's Routine System Monitoring Practices

      b. ABC Corp's Information Security Log Policy

9. *Getting help*

For questions or assistance with these procedures, or to escalate issues to IT Security, contact the ITS Support Center:

    E-Mail: itrequest@ABCCorp.com or help@ABCCorp.com

    Voice: (205) 123-HELP

    In Person: M-F 8AM-5PM, Room 291 Central Headquarters Bldg.

Appendix H
Domain 7 Materials

The following sample Configuration Management Plan is referenced in *Domain 7 – Security Operations*. You can download the materials from this appendix for free by going to the following link:

https://learning.isc2.org/content/cissp-textbook-appendices

Configuration Management Plan
<Project Name>

COMPANY NAME

STREET ADDRESS

CITY, STATE ZIP CODE

DATE

TABLE OF CONTENTS

INTRODUCTION

The purpose of the Configuration Management Plan is to describe how configuration management (CM) will be conducted throughout the project lifecycle. This includes documenting how CM is managed, roles and responsibilities, how configuration item (CI) changes are made, and communicating all aspects of CM to project stakeholders. Without a documented configuration management plan, it is likely that CIs may be missed, incomplete, or unnecessary work is done because of a lack of version and document control. While a configuration management plan is important for all projects, this is especially so for software and other information technology (IT) projects.

The Azmith Project will utilize existing TP Company network infrastructure and add numerous capabilities in order to allow for remote access, direct ability to modify LAN/WAN environments, and improved monitoring of network tools and devices. As a result, TP Company's ability to perform network maintenance and updates will be significantly improved. Additionally, TP Company will improve its ability to monitor all network diagnostics in real time and streamline workforce efficiency. Cost savings will be realized by greatly reducing the amount of time associated with competing network tasks and allowing TP Company employees to perform work that was previously outsourced.

In order to effectively manage the Azmith Project, one will need a coordinated Configuration Management (CM) Plan. This plan will establish CM roles and responsibilities and describe how the Azmith Project team will track, implement, and communicate configuration items (CIs) and changes throughout the project lifecycle.

ROLES AND RESPONSIBILITIES

Roles and responsibilities are an important part of any plan. In order to communicate a clear understanding of expectations, one must clearly define these roles and responsibilities. Any work that will be performed as part of the plan must be assigned to someone, and this section allows us to illustrate who owns these tasks and to communicate them to all project stakeholders.

The following roles and responsibilities pertain to the CM Plan for TP Company's Azmith Project.

Configuration Control Board (CCB)

The CCB is comprised of the Azmith Project Sponsor, Project Manager, Configuration Manager, and the Lead Engineer for the configuration item (CI) under consideration. The CCB is responsible for the following:

- Review and approve/reject configuration change requests.
- Ensure all approved changes are added to the configuration management database (CMDB).
- Seek clarification on any CIs as required.

Project Sponsor

The Project Sponsor is responsible for:

- Chairing all CCB meetings.
- Providing approval for any issues requiring additional scope, time, or cost.

Project Manager

The Project Manager is responsible for:

- Overall responsibility for all CM activities related to the Azmith project.
- Identification of CIs.
- All communication of CM activities to project stakeholders.
- Participation in CCB meetings.
- Re-baselining, if necessary, any items affected by CM changes.

Configuration Manager

The Configuration Manager will be appointed by the Program Management Office (PMO). The Configuration Manager is responsible for:

- Overall management of the CMDB.
- Identification of CIs.
- Providing configuration standards and templates to the project team.
- Providing any required configuration training.

Lead Engineers

All identified CIs will be assigned to a Lead Engineer. The assigned Lead Engineer is responsible for:

- Designating a focus group to develop the change request.
- Ensuring all change requests comply with organizational templates and standards prior to the CCB.
- Identification of CIs.

Engineers

Each CI will be assigned to a focus group consisting of several engineers. Each member of the focus group will provide input to the change request prior to submitting the change request to the lead engineer for review and presentation at the CCB.

CONFIGURATION CONTROL

Configuration Control is the process of systematically controlling and managing all steps of configuration throughout the project lifecycle. In order to effectively handle project CM, one should use a process that ensures only necessary configuration changes are made. Additionally, like any change management efforts, configuration change decisions must be made with the understanding of the impact of the change.

The Azmith Project will use a standardized configuration control process throughout the project lifecycle in order to ensure all CIs are handled in a consistent manner and any approved changes are fully vetted regarding impact and communicated to stakeholders.

As CIs are identified by the project team, the Configuration Manager will assign a CI name, and the CI will be entered into the CMDB in an "initiate" status. The CI will then be assigned to an engineer focus group. Each member of a CI's focus group will have the ability to access the CI through the CMDB, make changes and edits, and enter the CI back into the CMDB with a description of the change/edit annotated in the CMDB log.

It is imperative that for any software changes, testing is conducted by the focus group in order to validate any changes made. The Lead Engineer assigned to manage the focus group is responsible for ensuring that testing has been conducted, changes are entered into the CMDB log, and that all changes/edits are saved properly into the CMDB. The Lead Engineer is also responsible for assigning new version numbers and CMDB status for any changes made by his or her assigned focus group.

Many times, a CI will have a relationship with one or more other CIs within a project. The Lead Engineer, CM, and Project Manager will work together to ensure these relationships are fully understood. The Lead Engineer and CM will then be responsible for illustrating these relationships and co-dependencies in the CMDB to ensure a full understanding of each CI and how they relate to one another.

Any configuration changes that are identified by the project team or stakeholders must be captured in a configuration change request (CCR) and submitted to the CCB. The CCB will review, analyze, and approve/deny the request based on the impact, scope, time, and cost of the proposed change. If the change is approved, the project requirements will be re-baselined (if necessary), and all changes will be communicated to the project team and stakeholders by the Project Manager. Denied CCRs may be re-submitted with additional or new information for re-consideration by the CCB.

H

Domain 7 Materials

CONFIGURATION MANAGEMENT DATABASE (CMDB)

A Configuration Management Database (CMDB) is where the organization's configuration information is stored. CMDB is a term that originates from the Information Technology Infrastructure Library (ITIL), which provides a framework for best practices in IT services management. The CMDB contains not only the configuration information for assets but also information about the assets such as physical location, ownership, and its relationship to other configurable items (CIs).

A key component to configuration management is having a well-defined and followed process for both document and data management.

The CMDB will be the centralized repository for all configuration information for the Azmith project. The CMDB provides a common platform for the project team to edit, change, revise, and review CIs and also to ensure all documents and data are updated with the latest revision and release formats.

Access to the CMDB will be granted and governed by standard UNIX permissions. Two types of CMDB access will be granted for the Azmith project:

1. Full read and write access will be granted to the CM, Project Manager, Lead Engineers, and Engineers. These individuals will be authorized to access the CMDB to make changes, edit documents and data, and review and approve versions and CI status.

2. Read only access will be granted to the Project Sponsor and all other stakeholders. This access will allow these individuals to view all CIs and CI data, but they will not be authorized to make any changes. If these individuals identify the need for a change or edit, they will notify the CM who will review the notification and provide feedback.

The CMDB will provide assurance that members of the project team are always working off of the latest version of software, data, and documentation. However, it is important to maintain the history of these assets throughout the project lifecycle. As these assets are changed and updated, the Lead Engineer of the CI's assigned focus group will be responsible for updating the status of the CI and providing new revision numbering. This numbering will be done in accordance with TP Company's standard revision control numbering process wherein higher version numbers indicate more recent versions of the software, data, or documentation.

CONFIGURATION STATUS ACCOUNTING

Accounting for the status of the configuration involves the collection, processing, and reporting of the configuration data for all CIs at any given time. This also includes management stored configuration information held in the Configuration Management Database (CMDB). This may include approved configuration documents, software, data, and their current version numbers; build reports; status of any submitted changes; or any discrepancies and status identified through configuration audits.

It is important that for the Azmith Project, the Project Sponsor and Vice President of Technology have the ability to review configuration status at any given time. The Project Manager will also submit weekly reports, to include configuration status, every Friday. These reports will consist of the following information as part of the configuration status section:

1. Change requests

    a. Aging - How long change requests have been open

    b. Distribution – number of change requests submitted by owner/group

    c. Trending – what area(s) are approved changes occurring in

2. Version Control

    a. Software

    b. Hardware

    c. Data

    d. Documentation

3. Build Reporting

    a. Files

    b. CI relationships

    c. Incorporated Changes

4. Audits

    a. Physical Configuration

    b. Functional Configuration

Prior to any new software releases, the CM will work with each Lead Engineer to ensure all CIs are updated with latest release versions.

CONFIGURATION AUDITS

Audits are an important part of project and configuration management. The purpose of an audit is to ensure that established processes are being followed as intended and to provide an opportunity to correct any deviations from these processes. Many people hold a negative view of audits; however, when used appropriately, audits are an effective management and quality assurance tool.

Configuration audits will be an ongoing part of the Azmith project lifecycle. The purpose of the configuration audit is to ensure all team members are following the established procedures and processes for configuration management. Project audits for the Azmith Project will occur prior to any major software release or at the Project Manager's or Sponsor's discretion if they determine the need for one.

All Azmith configuration audits will be performed by the CM. Throughout the project, the CM works closely with Lead Engineers to ensure that all configuration processes and procedures are being followed. As part of the configuration audit, the CM will perform the following tasks:

1. Establish an audit environment in the CMDB.

2. The CM will copy all of the latest software, data, and document versions into the audit environment.

3. The CM will ensure all versions are correctly numbered and that version control has been performed properly.

4. The CM will analyze historical versions and time stamps of all software, data, and documents to ensure all changes/edits were properly recorded and captured.

5. The CM will copy latest software versions and conduct software testing to ensure requirements are being met.

6. The CM will ensure all required artifacts are present and current in the CMDB.

7. The CM will ensure all approved CCRs have been incorporated into the project and are recorded in the CMDB.

Once the audit has been performed, the CM will compile his or her audit findings. For each finding, the CM must work with the Project Manager/Team to identify the corrective action(s) necessary to resolve the discrepancy and assign responsibility for each corrective action.

Upon completion of the project audit and findings, the CM will note all discrepancies and compile a report to be presented to the Project Manager, Sponsor, and VP of Technology.

SPONSOR ACCEPTANCE

Approved by the Project Sponsor:

_____ Date:_____-

<Project Sponsor>
<Project Sponsor Title>

Domain 7 Materials

Appendix I
Domain 8 Materials

The following sample Change Management Plan is referenced in *Domain 8 – Software Development Security*. You can download the materials from this appendix for free by going to the following link:

https://learning.isc2.org/content/cissp-textbook-appendices

<PROJECT NAME>

CHANGE MANAGEMENT PLAN

Version <Type Version #>

My signature indicates approval of this Change Management Plan.

Prepared by:

_____
Project Manager

Approved by:

_____
CIO

Approved by:

_____
Project Sponsor

Table of Contents

Revision History

Date	Version	Description	Author
<MM/DD/YYYY>	<0.00>	<Type brief description here>	<First Initial & Last Name>

Template Overview and Instructions:

The Change Management Plan documents how changes will be proposed, accepted, monitored, and controlled. Edit this document to establish the process to manage change. Instructional text in this document is bracketed and has a grey background. Other text may be used in your actual plan. **Please remove the instructions when the document is finalized**.>

Domain 8 Materials

1   PURPOSE

The Change Management Plan establishes how changes will be proposed, accepted, monitored, and controlled. The change control procedures identified in the Change Management Plan will govern changes to the baseline project scope including changes to the work breakdown structure and requirements from project inception to completion. In addition, the change control procedures will govern changes to the baseline schedule and cost. This Change Management Plan addresses the following activities:

- Identification and inventory of change requests

- Analysis and documentation of the complete impact of requested changes

- Approval or rejection of change requests

- Tracking changes and updating of project documentation to account for approved changes

2   PROCEDURES FOR CHANGE IDENTIFICATION

<Describe the procedures to be used to identify and document change requests to project baselines (e.g., approved scope baseline, cost baseline, and schedule baseline). Describe who is authorized to submit change requests. The following is sample language that may be included in change identification procedures.>

Any project team member can submit a change request to the Project Manager. When the need for a change to the approved baseline is identified, the change will be clearly defined using the Change Request Form (See Attachment A: Change Request Form).

- The Requestor completes Section 1 of the Change Request Form and submits it to the Project Manager for review.

- The Project Manager records the request in the Change Control Log (Attachment B: Change Control Log) and assigns a change request number to the change request.

3   PROCEDURES FOR CHANGE ANALYSIS

<Describe the procedures to be used to analyze and assess the impact of the proposed change. The change should be assessed relative to the project's baseline scope (additions or deletions), schedule (impact on established schedule milestones), and total project costs.

Also, describe the process to be used by the project team to evaluate and approve a proposed change to be forwarded to the Project Sponsor, Executive Sponsor, and/or the Change Control Board (CCB) for final review and approval. A CCB is a group of individuals assigned to control identified project changes, review impacts, and grant approvals or rejections of proposed changes. The CCB comprises project stakeholders or their representatives. In many projects, the Steering Committee functions as the CCB.

To fully evaluate and accept or reject the change request, the project team should provide the approver(s) with the impact that the change will have on the project. The Project Manager and the approver(s) are most interested in the impact of change to the project scope, schedule, cost, quality, and risk. The following is sample language that may be included in change analysis procedures.>

Page 4 of 7

- The Project Manager will assign a project team member to complete Section 2 of the Change Request Form, which details the work to complete the change and the impact of the change to the project and deliverables.

- The Project Manager will determine if the request is viable and decide whether the request merits consideration by the Project Sponsor, Executive Sponsor, and/or CCB.

4   CHANGE REQUEST APPROVAL PROCESS

<Document the process to be used to evaluate, approve, and communicate changes to the project scope, schedule, and cost baseline. Within this section, define what members of the project team are needed to assess changes, maintain change records, present proposed changes to management, and review and approve or reject changes. The following is sample language that may be used in the Change Request Approval Process.>

- When the impact of the change has been recorded, the Project Manager forwards the Change Request Form to the Project Sponsor, Executive Sponsor, and/or CCB for acceptance or rejection.

- The Project Sponsor, Executive Sponsor, and/or CCB will review the change request and indicate their decisions by completing Section 3 of the Change Request Form and returning it to the Project Manager.

- If it is approved, the Project Manager will update the appropriate project documentation to reflect the change. For example, if the scope is changed, the Project Scope Statement should reflect the updated scope. Corresponding contract modifications may also be required if the approved change impacts the contractual scope, schedule, costs, or other terms.

- If it is rejected, the Project Manager will update the Change Control Log.

5   CHANGE TRACKING

<Describe the process for maintaining a master log of all changes submitted, approved, and rejected for the project so that clear traceability of all proposed changes is evident. The following is sample language that may be used.>

- The Project Manager will maintain a master log of all change requests and the resolution of each request. All requests will be maintained in a Change Control Log. A sample Change Control Log is included in Attachment B.

- For approved changes, the Project Manager will complete Section 4 of the Change Request Form to indicate completion of project document updates and will file the form with other project artifacts.

ATTACHMENT A: SAMPLE PROJECT CHANGE REQUEST FORM

Project Information		
Project Title:		**Project Number:**
Project Manager:		

Section 1: Change Request		
Requestor Name: **Requestor Phone:**	**Date of Request:**	**Change Request Number:** *Supplied by (PM)*
Item to be Changed:		**Priority:**
Description of Change:		
Estimated Cost & Time:		

Section 2: Change Evaluation	
Evaluated by:	**Work Required:**
What is Affected:	
Impact to Cost, Schedule, Scope, Quality, and Risk:	

Section 3: Change Resolution			
Accepted ☐ **Rejected** ☐	**Approved by (Print):**	**Signature:**	**Date:**
Comments:			

Section 4: Change Tracking			
Completion Date:	**Completed by (Print):**	**Signature:**	**Date:**

My signature above indicates that the project documentation has been updated to accurately and comprehensively reflect the approved changes.

ATTACHMENT B: SAMPLE CHANGE CONTROL LOG

Project Information								
Project Title:					**Project Number:**			
Project Manager:								
Change Number	**Description of Change**	**Priority**	**Date Requested**	**Requested By**	**Status:** (Evaluating, Pending, Approved, Rejected)	**Date Resolved**	**Resolution/Comments**	

Appendix J
Glossary

6to4 – Transition mechanism for migrating from IPv4 to IPv6. It allows systems to use IPv6 to communicate if their traffic has to transverse an IPv4 network.

A Checklist Test – Copies of the plan are handed out to each functional area for examination to ensure the plan properly deals with the area's needs and vulnerabilities.

A Cold Site – Is just a building with power, raised floors, and utilities. No devices are available. This is the cheapest of the three options, but can take weeks to get up and operational.

A Full-Interruption Test – One in which regular operations are stopped and processing is moved to the alternate site.

A Hot Site – Fully configured with hardware, software, and environmental needs. It can usually be up and running in a matter of hours. It is the most expensive option, but some companies cannot be out of business longer than a day without very detrimental results.

A Parallel Test – One in which some systems are actually run at the alternate site.

A Reciprocal Agreement – One in which a company promises another company it can move in and share space if it experiences a disaster, and vice versa. Reciprocal agreements are very tricky to implement and are unenforceable.

A Simulation Test – A practice execution of the plan takes place. A specific scenario is established, and the simulation continues up to the point of actual relocation to the alternate site.

A Structured Walk-Through Test – Representatives from each functional area or department get together and walk through the plan from beginning to end.

A Warm Site – Does not have computers, but it does have some peripheral devices, such as disk drives, controllers, and tape drives. This option is less expensive than a hot site, but takes more effort and time to become operational.

Absolute Addresses – Hardware addresses used by the CPU.

Abstraction – The capability to suppress unnecessary details so the important, inherent properties can be examined and reviewed.

Accepted Ways for Handling Risk – Accept, transfer, mitigate, avoid.

Access – The flow of information between a subject and an object.

Access Control Matrix – A table of subjects and objects indicating what actions individual subjects can take upon individual objects.

Access Control Model – An access control model is a framework that dictates how subjects access objects.

Access Controls – Are security features that control how users and systems communicate and interact with other systems and resources.

Accreditation – Formal acceptance of the adequacy of a system's overall security by management.

Active Attack – Attack where the attacker does interact with processing or communication activities.

ActiveX – A Microsoft technology composed of a set of OOP technologies and tools based on COM and DCOM. It is a framework for defining reusable software components in a programming language–independent manner.

Address Bus – Physical connections between processing components and memory segments used to communicate the physical memory addresses being used during processing procedures.

Address Resolution Protocol (ARP) – A networking protocol used for resolution of network layer IP addresses into link layer MAC addresses.

Address Space Layout Randomization (ASLR) – Memory protection mechanism used by some operating systems. The addresses used by components of a process are randomized so that it is harder for an attacker to exploit specific memory vulnerabilities.

Algebraic Attack – Cryptanalysis attack that exploits vulnerabilities within the intrinsic algebraic structure of mathematical functions.

Algorithm – Set of mathematical and logic rules used in cryptographic functions.

Analog Signals – Continuously varying electromagnetic wave that represents and transmits data.

Analytic Attack – Cryptanalysis attack that exploits vulnerabilities within the algorithm structure.

Annualized Loss Expectancy (ALE) – Annual expected loss if a specific vulnerability is exploited and how it affects a single asset. SLE × ARO = ALE.

Application Programming Interface (API) – Software interface that enables process-to-process interaction. Common way to provide access to standard routines to a set of software programs.

Arithmetic Logic Unit (ALU) – A component of the computer's processing unit, in which arithmetic and matching operations are performed.

AS/NZS 4360 – Australia and New Zealand business risk management assessment approach.

Assemblers – Tools that convert assembly code into the necessary machine-compatible binary language for processing activities to take place.

Assembly Language – A low-level programming language that is the mnemonic representation of machine-level instructions.

Assurance Evaluation Criteria – Check-list and process of examining the security-relevant parts of a system (TCB, reference monitor, security kernel) and assigning the system an assurance rating.

Asymmetric Algorithm – Encryption method that uses two different key types, public and private. Also called public key cryptography.

Asymmetric Mode Multiprocessing – When a computer has two or more CPUs and one CPU is dedicated to a specific program while the other CPUs carry out general processing procedures.

Asynchronous Communication – Transmission sequencing technology that uses start and stop bits or similar encoding mechanism. Used in environments that transmit a variable amount of data in a periodic fashion.

Asynchronous Token Generating Method – Employs a challenge/response scheme to authenticate the user.

Attack Surface – Components available to be used by an attacker against the product itself.

Attenuation – Gradual loss in intensity of any kind of flux through a medium. As an electrical signal travels down a cable, the signal can degrade and distort or corrupt the data it is carrying.

Attribute – A column in a two-dimensional database.

Authentication Header (AH) Protocol – Protocol within the IPSec suite used for integrity and authentication.

Authenticode – A type of code signing, which is the process of digitally signing software components and scripts to confirm the software author and guarantee that the code has not been altered or corrupted since it was digitally signed. Authenticode is Microsoft's implementation of code signing.

Availability – Reliable and timely access to data and resources is provided to authorized individuals.

Avalanche effect – Algorithm design requirement so that slight changes to the input result in drastic changes to the output.

1229

Base registers – Beginning of address space assigned to a process. Used to ensure a process does not make a request outside its assigned memory boundaries.

Baseband transmission – Uses the full bandwidth for only one communication channel and has a low data transfer rate compared to broadband.

Bastion host – A highly exposed device that will most likely be targeted for attacks, and thus should be hardened.

Behavior blocking – Allowing the suspicious code to execute within the operating system and watches its interactions with the operating system, looking for suspicious activities.

Birthday attack – Cryptographic attack that exploits the mathematics behind the birthday problem in the probability theory forces collisions within hashing functions.

Block cipher – Symmetric algorithm type that encrypts chunks (blocks) of data at a time.

Blowfish – Block symmetric cipher that uses 64-bit block sizes and variable-length keys.

Border Gateway Protocol (BGP) – The protocol that carries out core routing decisions on the Internet. It maintains a table of IP networks, or "prefixes," which designate network reachability among autonomous systems.

Bots – Software applications that run automated tasks over the Internet, which perform tasks that are both simple and structurally repetitive. Malicious use of bots is the coordination and operation of an automated attack by a botnet (centrally controlled collection of bots).

Broadband transmission – Divides the bandwidth of a communication channel into many channels, enabling different types of data to be transmitted at one time.

Buffer overflow – Too much data is put into the buffers that make up a stack. Common attack vector used by attackers to run malicious code on a target system.

Bus topology – Systems are connected to a single transmission channel (i.e., network cable), forming a linear construct.

Business Continuity Management (BCM) – is the overarching approach to managing all aspects of BCP and DRP.

Business Continuity Plan (BCP) – A business continuity action plan is a document or set of documents that contains the critical information a business needs to stay running in spite of adverse events. A business continuity plan is also called an emergency plan.

Business Impact Analysis (BIA) – An exercise that determines the impact of losing the support of any resource to an organization, establishes the escalation of that loss over time, identifies the minimum resources needed to recover, and prioritizes the recovery of processes and supporting systems.

J

Cable Modem – A device that provides bidirectional data communication via radio frequency channels on cable TV infrastructures. Cable modems are primarily used to deliver broadband Internet access to homes.

Cache memory – Fast memory type that is used by a CPU to increase read and write operations.

Caesar Cipher – Simple substitution algorithm created by Julius Caesar that shifts alphabetic values three positions during its encryption and decryption processes

Capability Maturity Model Integration (CMMI) – A process improvement methodology that provides guidance for quality improvement and point of reference for appraising existing processes developed by Carnegie Mellon.

Capability Maturity Model Integration (CMMI) model – A process improvement approach that provides organizations with the essential elements of effective processes, which will improve their performance.

Capability Table – A capability table specifies the access rights a certain subject possesses pertaining to specific objects. A capability table is different from an ACL because the subject is bound to the capability table, whereas the object is bound to the ACL.

Carrier Sense Multiple Access with Collision Avoidance (CSMA/CA) – LANs using carrier sense multiple access with collision avoidance require devices to announce their intention to transmit by broadcasting a jamming signal.

Carrier Sense Multiple Access with Collision Detection (CSMA/CD) – Devices on a LAN using carrier sense multiple access with collision detection listen for a carrier before transmitting data.

CBC-MAC – Cipher block chaining message authentication code uses encryption for data integrity and data origin authentication.

Cell – An intersection of a row and a column.

Cell suppression – A technique used to hide specific cells that contain sensitive information.

Central Processing Unit (CPU) – The part of a computer that performs the logic, computation, and decision-making functions. It interprets and executes instructions as it receives them.

Certificate – Digital identity used within a PKI. Generated and maintained by a certificate authority and used for authentication.

Certificate Revocation List (CRL) – List that is maintained by the certificate authority of a PKI that contains information on all of the digital certificates that have been revoked.

Certification – Technical evaluation of the security components and their compliance to a predefined security policy for the purpose of accreditation.

Certification Authority – Component of a PKI that creates and maintains digital certificates throughout their life cycles.

Change control – The process of controlling the changes that take place during the life cycle of a system and documenting the necessary change control activities.

Channel Service Unit (CSU) – A line bridging device for use with T-carriers, and that is required by PSTN providers at digital interfaces that terminate in a Data Service Unit (DSU) on the customer side. The DSU is a piece of telecommunications circuit terminating equipment that transforms digital data between telephone company lines and local equipment.

Chosen-ciphertext attack – Cryptanalysis attack where the attacker chooses a ciphertext and obtains its decryption under an unknown key.

Chosen-plaintext attack – Cryptanalysis attack where the attacker can choose arbitrary plaintexts to be encrypted and obtain the corresponding ciphertexts.

Cipher – Another name for algorithm.

Ciphertext-only attack – Cryptanalysis attack where the attacker is assumed to have access only to a set of ciphertexts.

Classless Interdomain Routing (CIDR) – A method for using the existing 32-bit Internet Address Space efficiently.

Client-side validation – Input validation is done at the client before it is even sent back to the server to process.

Clipping Level – A threshold.

Closed system – Designs are built upon proprietary procedures, which inhibit interoperability capabilities.

Cloud computing – The delivery of computer processing capabilities as a service rather than as a product, whereby shared resources, software, and information are provided to end users as a utility. Offerings are usually bundled as an infrastructure, platform, or software.

CMAC – Cipher message authentication code that is based upon and provides more security compared to CBC-MAC.

CMM – Block cipher mode that combines the CTR encryption mode and CBC-MAC. One encryption key is used for both authentication and encryption purposes.

CobiT – Set of control objectives used as a framework for IT governance developed by Information Systems Audit and Control Association (ISACA) and the IT Governance Institute (ITGI).

Cognitive passwords – Fact or opinion based information used to verify an individual's identity.

Cohesion – A measurement that indicates how many different types of tasks a module needs to carry out.

Collision – (1) A condition that is present when two or more terminals are in contention during simultaneous network access attempts. (2) In cryptography, an instance when a hash function generates the same output for different inputs.

Collusion – Two or more people working together to carry out fraudulent activities.

Common Criteria – International standard used to assess the effectiveness of the security controls built into a system from functional and assurance perspectives.

Compilers – Tools that convert high-level language statements into the necessary machine-level format (.exe, .dll, etc.) for specific processors to understand.

Compression viruses – Another type of virus that appends itself to executables on the system and compresses them by using the user's permissions.

Concealment Cipher – Encryption method that hides a secret message within an open message.

Confidentiality – A security concept that assures the necessary level of secrecy is enforced and unauthorized disclosure is prevented.

Confusion – Substitution processes used in encryption functions to increase randomness.

Content-based access – Bases access decisions on the sensitivity of the data, not solely on subject identity.

Context-based access – Bases access decisions on the state of the situation, not solely on identity or content sensitivity.

Control – Safeguard that is put in place to reduce a risk, also called a countermeasure.

Control functions –
- *Deterrent*: Discourage a potential attacker
- *Preventive*: Stop an incident from occurring
- *Corrective*: Fix items after an incident has occurred
- *Recovery*: Restore necessary components to return to normal operations
- *Detective*: Identify an incident's activities after it took place
- *Compensating*: Alternative control that provides similar protection as the original control"

Control types – Administrative, technical (logical), and physical

Control unit – Part of the CPU that oversees the collection of instructions and data from memory and how they are passed to the processing components of the CPU.

Cookies – Data files used by web browsers and servers to keep browser state information and browsing preferences.

Cooperative multitasking – Multitasking scheduling scheme used by older operating systems to allow for computer resource time slicing.

Copyright – A form of protection granted by law for original works of authorship fixed in a tangible medium of expression.

COSO – Internal control model used for corporate governance to help prevent fraud developed by the Committee of Sponsoring Organizations (COSO) of the Treadway Commission.

Cost/benefit analysis – An estimate of the equivalent monetary value of proposed benefits and the estimated costs associated with a control in order to establish whether the control is feasible.

Coupling – A measurement that indicates how much interaction one module requires for carrying out its tasks.

CRAMM – Central Computing and Telecommunications Agency Risk Analysis and Management Method.

Cross-Site Scripting (XSS) attack – An attack where a vulnerability is found on a web site that allows an attacker to inject malicious code into a web application.

Crosstalk – A signal on one channel of a transmission creates an undesired effect in another channel by interacting with it. The signal from one cable "spills over" into another cable.

Cryptanalysis – Practice of uncovering flaws within cryptosystems.

Cryptography – Science of secret writing that enables an entity to store and transmit data in a form that is available only to the intended individuals.

Cryptology – The study of both cryptography and cryptanalysis.

Cryptosystem – Hardware or software implementation of cryptography that contains all the necessary software, protocols, algorithms, and keys.

Data bus – Physical connections between processing components and memory segments used to transmit data being used during processing procedures.

Data custodian – Individual responsible for implementing and maintaining security controls to meet security requirements outlined by data owner.

Data dictionary – Central repository of data elements and their relationships.

Data diddling – The act of willfully modifying information, programs, or documentation in an effort to commit fraud or disrupt production.

Data Execution Prevention (DEP) – Memory protection mechanism used by some operating systems. Memory segments may be marked as non-executable so that they cannot be misused by malicious software.

Data hiding – Use of segregation in design decisions to protect software components from negatively interacting with each other. Commonly enforced through strict interfaces.

Data mining – A methodology used by organizations to better understand their customers, products, markets, or any other phase of the business.

Data modeling – Considers data independently of the way the data are processed and of the components that process the data. A process used to define and analyze data requirements needed to support the business processes.

Data owner – Individual responsible for the protection and classification of a specific data set.

Data structure – A representation of the logical relationship between elements of data.

Data warehousing – Combines data from multiple databases or data sources into a large database for the purpose of providing more extensive information retrieval and data analysis.

Database – A cross-referenced collection of data.

Database Management System (DBMS) – Manages and controls the database.

Decipher – Act of transforming data into a readable format.

Defense-in-depth – Implementation of multiple controls so that successful penetration and compromise is more difficult to attain.

Delphi method – Data collection method that happens in an anonymous fashion.

Differential cryptanalysis – Cryptanalysis method that uses the study of how differences in an input can affect the resultant difference at the output.

Diffie-Hellman algorithm – First asymmetric algorithm created and is used to exchange symmetric key values. Based upon logarithms in finite fields.

Diffusion – Transposition processes used in encryption functions to increase randomness.

Digital Rights Management (DRM) – Access control technologies commonly used to protect copyright material.

Digital signals – Binary digits are represented and transmitted as discrete electrical pulses.

Digital signature – Ensuring the authenticity and integrity of a message through the use of hashing algorithms and asymmetric algorithms. The message digest is encrypted with the sender's private key.

Digital Subscriber Line (DSL) – A set of technologies that provide Internet access by transmitting digital data over the wires of a local telephone network. DSL is used to digitize the "last mile" and provide fast Internet connectivity.

Distance-Vector routing protocol – A routing protocol that calculates paths based on the distance (or number of hops) and a vector (a direction).

DNS zone transfer – The process of replicating the databases containing the DNS data across a set of DNS servers.

DNSSEC – A set of extensions to DNS that provide to DNS clients (resolvers) origin authentication of DNS data to reduce the threat of DNS poisoning, spoofing, and similar attack types.

DoDAF – U.S. Department of Defense architecture framework that ensures interoperability of systems to meet military mission goals.

Domain Name System (DNS) – A hierarchical distributed naming system for computers, services, or any resource connected to an IP based network. It associates various pieces of information with domain names assigned to each of the participating entities.

Dual-homed firewall – This device has two interfaces and sits between an untrusted network and trusted network to provide secure access.

Dumpster diving – Refers to going through someone's trash to find confidential or useful information. It is legal, unless it involves trespassing, but in all cases it is considered unethical.

Dynamic Host Configuration Protocol (DHCP) – DHCP is an industry standard protocol used to dynamically assign IP addresses to network devices.

Dynamic link libraries (DLLs) – A set of subroutines that are shared by different applications and operating system processes.

El Gamal algorithm – Asymmetric algorithm based upon the Diffie-Hellman algorithm used for digital signatures, encryption, and key exchange.

Elliptic curve cryptosystem algorithm – Asymmetric algorithm based upon the algebraic structure of elliptic curves over finite fields. Used for digital signatures, encryption, and key exchange.

E-mail spoofing – Activity in which the sender address and other arts of the e-mail header are altered to appear as though the e-mail originated from a different source. Since SMTP does not provide any authentication, it is easy to impersonate and forge e-mails.

Encapsulating Security Payload Protocol (ESP) – Protocol within the IPSec suite used for integrity, authentication, and encryption.

EncipherK – Act of transforming data into an unreadable format.

End-to-End encryption – The encryption of information at the point of origin within the communications network and postponing of decryption to the final destination point.

Ethernet – Common LAN media access technology standardized by IEEE 802.3. Uses 48-bit MAC addressing, works in contention-based networks, and has extended outside of just LAN environments.

Exposure – Presence of a vulnerability, which exposes the organization to a threat.

Facilitated Risk Analysis Process (FRAP) – A focused, qualitative approach that carries out pre-screening to save time and money.

Failure Modes and Effect Analysis (FMEA) – Approach that dissects a component into its basic functions to identify flaws and those flaw's effects.

Fault tree analysis – Approach to map specific flaws to root causes in complex systems.

Federated identity – A portable identity, and its associated entitlements, that can be used across business boundaries.

Fiber Distributed Data Interface (FDDI) – Ring-based token network protocol that was derived from the IEEE 802.4 token bus timed token protocol. It can work in LAN or MAN environments and provides fault tolerance through dual-ring architecture.

File – A basic unit of data records organized on a storage medium for convenient location, access, and updating.

Foreign key – An attribute of one table that is related to the primary key of another table.

Fraggle attack – A DDoS attack type on a computer that floods the target system with a large amount of UDP echo traffic to IP broadcast addresses.

Frequency analysis – Cryptanalysis process used to identify weaknesses within cryptosystems by locating patterns in resulting ciphertext.

Frequency-Division Multiplexing (FDM) – An older technique in which the available transmission bandwidth of a circuit is divided by frequency into narrow bands, each used for a separate voice or data transmission channel, which many conversations can be carried on one circuit.

Functionality versus Effectiveness of Control – Functionality is what a control does, and its effectiveness is how well the control does it.

Fuzzing – A technique used to discover flaws and vulnerabilities in software.

Garbage collector – Tool that marks unused memory segments as usable to ensure that an operating system does not run out of memory.

General registers – Temporary memory location the CPU uses during its processes of executing instructions. The ALU's "scratch pad" it uses while carrying out logic and math functions.

Guideline – Suggestions and best practices.

H.323 – A standard that addresses call signaling and control, multimedia transport and control, and bandwidth control for point-to-point and multipoint conferences.

Hardware segmentation – Physically mapping software to individual memory segments.

Hashed Message Authentication Code (HMAC) – Cryptographic hash function that uses a symmetric key value and is used for data integrity and data origin authentication.

Hierarchical data model – Combines records and fields that are related in a logical tree structure.

High Availability – Refers to a system, component, or environment that is continuously operational.

High-Level languages – Otherwise known as third-generation programming languages, due to their refined programming structures, using abstract statements.

Honeypots – Systems that entice with the goal of protecting critical production systems. If two or more honeypots are used together, this is considered a honeynet.

HTTPS – A combination of HTTP and SSL\TLS that is commonly used for secure Internet connections and e-commerce transactions.

Hybrid cryptography – Combined use of symmetric and asymmetric algorithms where the symmetric key encrypts data and an asymmetric key encrypts the symmetric key.

Hybrid Microkernel architecture – Combination of monolithic and microkernel architectures. The microkernel carries out critical operating system functionality, and the remaining functionality is carried out in a client\server model within kernel mode.

Hypervisor – Central program used to manage virtual machines (guests) within a simulated environment (host).

IEEE 802.1AE (MACSec) – Standard that specifies a set of protocols to meet the security requirements for protecting data traversing Ethernet LANs.

IEEE 802.1AR – Standard that specifies unique per-device identifiers (DevID) and the management and cryptographic binding of a device (router, switch, access point) to its identifiers.

Immunizer – Attaches code to the file or application, which would fool a virus into "thinking" it was already infected.

Information gathering – Usually the first step in an attacker's methodology, in which the information gathered may allow an attacker to infer additional information that can be used to compromise systems.

Information Technology Security Evaluation Criteria (ITSEC) – European standard used to assess the effectiveness of the security controls built into a system.

Initialization vectors (IVs) – Values that are used with algorithms to increase randomness for cryptographic functions.

Instruction set – Set of operations and commands that can be implemented by a particular processor (CPU).

Integrated Services Digital Network (ISDN) – A circuit-switched telephone network system technology designed to allow digital transmission of voice and data over ordinary telephone copper wires.

Integrity – Accuracy and reliability of the information and systems are provided and any unauthorized modification is prevented.

International Data Encryption Algorithm (IDEA) – Block symmetric cipher that uses a 128-bit key and 64-bit block size.

Internet Control Message Protocol (ICMP) – A core protocol of the IP suite used to send status and error messages.

Internet Group Management Protocol (IGMP) – Used by systems and adjacent routers on IP networks to establish and maintain multicast group memberships.

J

Internet Message Access Protocol (IMAP) – A method of accessing electronic mail or bulletin board messages that are kept on a (possibly shared) mail server. IMAP permits a client e-mail program to access remote message stores as if they were local. For example, e-mail stored on an IMAP server can be manipulated from a desktop computer at home, a workstation at the office, and a notebook computer while traveling, without the need to transfer messages of files back and forth between these computers. IMAP can be regarded as the next-generation POP.

Internet Protocol (IP) – Core protocol of the TCP/IP suite. Provides packet construction, addressing, and routing functionality.

Internet Security Association and Key Management Protocol (ISAKMP) – Used to establish security associates and an authentication framework in Internet connections. Commonly used by IKE for key exchange.

Interpreters – Tools that convert code written in interpreted languages to the machine-level format for processing.

Interrupt – Software or hardware signal that indicates that system resources (i.e., CPU) are needed for instruction processing.

Interrupts – Values assigned to computer components (hardware and software) to allow for efficient computer resource time slicing.

Intra-Site Automatic Tunnel Addressing Protocol (ISATAP) – An IPv6 transition mechanism meant to transmit IPv6 packets between dual-stack nodes on top of an IPv4 network.

IPSec – Protocol suite used to protect IP traffic through encryption and authentication. De facto standard VPN protocol.

IPv6 – IP version 6 is the successor to IP version 4 and provides 128-bit addressing, integrated IPSec security protocol, simplified header formats, and some automated configuration.

ISO/IEC 27000 series – Industry-recognized best practices for the development and management of an information security management system.

ISO/IEC 27005 – International standard for the implementation of a risk management program that integrates into an information security management system (ISMS).

ITIL – Best practices for information technology services management processes developed by the United Kingdom's Office of Government Commerce.

Java applets – Small components (applets) that provide various functionalities and are delivered to users in the form of Java bytecode. Java applets can run in a web browser using a Java Virtual Machine (JVM). Java is platform independent; thus, Java applets can be executed by browsers for many platforms.

Kerckhoffs' Principle – Concept that an algorithm should be known and only the keys should be kept secret.

Kernel mode (supervisory state, privilege mode) – Mode that a CPU works within when carrying out more trusted process instructions. The process has access to more computer resources when working in kernel versus user mode.

Key – Sequence of bits that are used as instructions that govern the acts of cryptographic functions within an algorithm.

Key clustering – A weakness that would exist in a cryptosystem if two different keys would generate the same ciphertext from the same plaintext.

Key Derivation Functions (KDFs) – Generation of secret keys (subkeys) from an initial value (master key).

Keyspace – A range of possible values used to construct keys.

Keystream generator – Component of a stream algorithm that creates random values for encryption purposes.

Known-plaintext attack – Cryptanalysis attack where the attacker is assumed to have access to sets of corresponding plaintext and ciphertext.

Layered operating system architecture – Architecture that separates system functionality into hierarchical layers.

Limit registers – Ending of address space assigned to a process. Used to ensure a process does not make a request outside its assigned memory boundaries.

Linear cryptanalysis – Cryptanalysis method that uses the study of affine transformation approximation in encryption processes.

Link encryption – Technology that encrypts full packets (all headers and data payload) and is carried out without the sender's interaction.

Link-state routing protocol – A routing protocol used in packet-switching networks where each router constructs a map of the connectivity within the network and calculates the best logical paths, which form its routing table.

Logic bomb – Executes a program, or string of code, when a certain event happens or a date and time arrives.

Logical addresses – Indirect addressing used by processes within an operating system. The memory manager carries out logical-to-absolute address mapping.

Machine language – A set of instructions in binary format that the computer's processor can understand and work with directly.

Macro virus – A computer virus that spreads by binding itself to software such as Word or Excel.

Maintenance hooks – Code within software that provides a back door entry capability.

Mandatory vacation – Detective administrative control used to uncover potential fraudulent activities by requiring a person to be away from the organization for a period of time.

Maskable interrupt – Interrupt value assigned to a non-critical operating system activity.

Mean Time Between Failures (MTBF) – The predicted amount of time between inherent failures of a system during operation.

Mean Time To Repair (MTTR) – A measurement of the maintainability by representing the average time required to repair a failed component or device.

Media access control (MAC) – Data communication protocol sub-layer of the data link layer specified in the OSI model. It provides hardware addressing and channel access control mechanisms that make it possible for several nodes to communicate within a multiple-access network that incorporates a shared medium.

Meet-in-the-middle attack – Cryptanalysis attack that tries to uncover a mathematical problem from two different ends.

Meme viruses – These are not actual computer viruses, but types of e-mail messages that are continually forwarded around the Internet.

Memory card – Holds information but cannot process information.

Mesh topology – Network where each system must not only capture and disseminate its own data, but also serve as a relay for other systems; that is, it must collaborate to propagate the data in the network.

Message authentication code (MAC) – Keyed cryptographic hash function used for data integrity and data origin authentication.

Metro Ethernet – A data link technology that is used as a metropolitan area network to connect customer networks to larger service networks or the Internet.

Metropolitan area network (MAN) – A data network intended to serve an area approximating that of a large city or college campus. Such networks are being implemented by innovative techniques, such as running fiber cables through subway tunnels.

Microarchitecture – Specific design of a microprocessor, which includes physical components (registers, logic gates, ALU, cache, etc.) that support a specific instruction set.

Microkernel architecture – Reduced amount of code running in kernel mode carrying out critical operating system functionality. Only the absolutely necessary code runs in kernel mode, and the remaining operating system code runs in user mode.

Mobile code – Code that can be transmitted across a network, to be executed by a system or device on the other end.

MODAF – Architecture framework used mainly in military support missions developed by the British Ministry of Defence.

Mode transition – When the CPU has to change from processing code in user mode to kernel mode.

Monolithic operating system architecture – All of the code of the operating system working in kernel mode in an ad-hoc and non-modularized manner.

Multilevel security policies – Outlines how a system can simultaneously process information at different classifications for users with different clearance levels.

Multipart virus – Also called a multipartite virus, this has several components to it and can be distributed to different parts of the system. It infects and spreads in multiple ways, which makes it harder to eradicate when identified.

Multiplexing – A method of combining multiple channels of data over a single transmission line.

Multiprogramming – Interleaved execution of more than one program (process) or task by a single operating system.

Multi-protocol Label Switching (MPLS) – A networking technology that directs data from one network node to the next based on short path labels rather than long network addresses, avoiding complex lookups in a routing table.

Multipurpose Internet Mail Extension (MIME) – The standard for multimedia mail contents in the Internet suite of protocols.

Multitasking – Simultaneous execution of more than one program (process) or task by a single operating system.

Multi-threading – Applications that can carry out multiple activities simultaneously by generating different instruction sets (threads).

Natural languages – Otherwise known as fifth-generation programming languages, which have the goal to create software that can solve problems by themselves. Used in systems that provide artificial intelligence.

Network address translation (NAT) – The process of modifying IP address information in packet headers while in transit across a traffic routing device, with the goal of reducing the demand for public IP addresses.

Network convergence – The combining of server, storage, and network capabilities into a single framework, which decreases the costs and complexity of data centers. Converged infrastructures provide the ability to pool resources, automate resource provisioning, and increase and decrease processing capacity quickly to meet the needs of dynamic computing workloads.

NIST SP 800-30 – Risk Management Guide for Information Technology Systems A U.S. federal standard that is focused on IT risks.

NIST SP 800-53 – Set of controls that are used to secure U.S. federal systems developed by NIST.

Noise and perturbation – A technique of inserting bogus information in the hopes of misdirecting an attacker or confusing the matter enough that the actual attack will not be fruitful.

Non-Maskable interrupt – Interrupt value assigned to a critical operating system activity.

J

Object – Can be a computer, database, file, computer program, directory, or field contained in a table within a database.

Object-Oriented database – Designed to handle a variety of data (images, audio, documents, video), which is more dynamic in nature than a relational database.

Object-Relational Database (ORD) – Uses object-relational database management system (ORDBMS) and is a relational database with a software front end that is written in an object-oriented programming language.

One-Time Pad – A system that randomly generates a private key, and is used only once to encrypt a message that is then decrypted by the receiver using a matching one-time pad and key. One-time pads have the advantage that there is theoretically no way to break the code by analyzing a succession of messages.

One-Way Hash – Cryptographic process that takes an arbitrary amount of data and generates a fixed-length value. Used for integrity protection.

Online Certificate Status Protocol (OCSP) – Automated method of maintaining revoked certificates within a PKI.

Open Mail relay – An SMTP server configured in such a way that it allows anyone on the Internet to send e-mail through it, not just mail destined to or originating from known users.

Open system – Designs are built upon accepted standards to allow for interoperability.

Open Systems Interconnection (OSI) model – International standardization of system-based network communication through a modular seven-layer architecture.

Operationally Critical Threat, Asset, and Vulnerability Evaluation (OCTAVE) – Team-oriented approach that assesses organizational and IT risks through facilitated workshops.

Out-of-band method – Sending data through an alternate communication channel.

Packages—EALs – Functional and assurance requirements are bundled into packages for reuse. This component describes what must be met to achieve specific EAL ratings.

Parameter validation – The values that are being received by the application are validated to be within defined limits before the server application processes them within the system.

Passive attack – Attack where the attacker does not interact with processing or communication activities, but only carries out observation and data collection, as in network sniffing.

Patent – Grants ownership and enables that owner to legally enforce his rights to exclude others from using the invention covered by the patent.

Personally Identifiable Information (PII) – Data that can be used to uniquely identify, contact, or locate a single person or can be used with other sources to uniquely identify a single individual.

Phishing – Phishing is a scam in which the perpetrator sends out legitimate-looking e-mails, in an effort to phish (pronounced fish) for personal and financial information from the recipient.

Ping of Death – A DoS attack type on a computer that involves sending malformed or oversized ICMP packets to a target.

Plaintext – A message before it has been encrypted or after it has been decrypted using a specific algorithm and key; also referred to as cleartext. (Contrast with ciphertext.)

Plenum cables – Cable is jacketed with a fire-retardant plastic cover that does not release toxic chemicals when burned.

Policy – High-level document that outlines senior management's security directives.

Polymorphic virus – Produces varied but operational copies of itself. A polymorphic virus may have no parts that remain identical between infections, making it very difficult to detect directly using signatures.

Polymorphism – Two objects can receive the same input and have different outputs.

Ports – Software construct that allows for application- or service-specific communication between systems on a network. Ports are broken down into categories; well known (0–1023), registered (1024–49151), and dynamic (49152–65535).

Post Office Protocol (POP) – An Internet standard protocol used by e-mail clients to retrieve e-mail from a remote server and supports simple download-and-delete requirements for access to remote mailboxes.

Preemptive multitasking – Multitasking scheduling scheme used by operating systems to allow for computer resource time slicing. Used in newer, more stable operating systems.

Pretty Good Privacy (PGP) Cryptosystem – used to integrate public key cryptography with e-mail functionality and data encryption, which was developed by Phil Zimmerman.

Primary key – Columns that make each row unique. (Every row of a table must include a primary key.)

Private Branch Exchange (PBX) – A small version of the phone company's central switching office. Also known as a private automatic branch exchange. A central telecommunications switching station that an organization uses for its own purposes.

Private key – Value used in public key cryptography that is used for decryption and signature creation and known to only key owner.

Procedures – Step-by-step implementation instructions.

Process – Program loaded in memory within an operating system.

Process isolation – Protection mechanism provided by operating systems that can be implemented as encapsulation, time multiplexing of shared resources, naming distinctions, and virtual memory mapping.

Process states (ready, running, blocked) – Processes can be in various activity levels. Ready = waiting for input. Running = instructions being executed by CPU. Blocked = process is "suspended."

Program counter – Holds the memory address for the following instructions the CPU needs to act upon.

Program Status Word (PSW) – Condition variable that indicates to the CPU what mode (kernel or user) instructions need to be carried out in.

Protection profile – Description of a needed security solution.

Proxy server – A system that acts as an intermediary for requests from clients seeking resources from other sources. A client connects to the proxy server, requesting some service, and the proxy server evaluates the request according to its filtering rules and makes the connection on behalf of the client. Proxies can be open or carry out forwarding or reverse forwarding capabilities.

Public key – Value used in public key cryptography that is used for encryption and signature validation that can be known by all parties.

Public key cryptography – An asymmetric cryptosystem where the encrypting and decrypting keys are different and it is computationally infeasible to calculate one form the other, given the encrypting algorithm. In public key cryptography, the encrypting key is made public, but the decrypting key is kept secret.

Public-Switched Telephone Network (PSTN) – The public circuit-switched telephone network, which is made up of telephone lines, fiber-optic cables, cellular networks, communications satellites, and undersea telephone cables and allows all phone-to-phone communication. It was a fixed-line analog telephone system, but is now almost entirely digital and includes mobile as well as fixed telephones.

Qualitative risk analysis – Opinion-based method of analyzing risk with the use of scenarios and ratings.

Quantitative risk analysis – Assigning monetary and numeric values to all the data elements of a risk assessment.

Quantum cryptography – Use of quantum mechanical functions to provide strong cryptographic key exchange.

Race condition – Two or more processes attempt to carry out their activity on one resource at the same time. Unexpected behavior can result if the sequence of execution does not take place in the proper order.

RAM – Hardware inside a computer that retains memory on a short-term basis and stores information while the computer is in use.

It is the working memory of the computer into which the operating system, startup applications and drivers are loaded when a computer is turned on, or where a program subsequently started up is loaded, and where thereafter, these applications are executed.

RAM can be read or written in any section with one instruction sequence. It helps to have more of this working space installed when running advanced operating systems and applications. RAM content is erased each time a computer is turned off. RAM is the most common type of memory found in computers and other devices, such as printers. There are two basic types of RAM: dynamic RAM (DRAM) and static RAM (SRAM).

Random Number Generator – Algorithm used to create values that are used in cryptographic functions to add randomness.

RC4 – Stream symmetric cipher that was created by Ron Rivest of RSA. Used in SSL and WEP.

RC5 – Block symmetric cipher that uses variable block sizes (32, 64, 128) and variable-length key sizes (0–2040).

RC6 – Block symmetric cipher that uses a 128-bit block size and variable length key sizes (128, 192, 256). Built upon the RC5 algorithm.

Real-time Transport Protocol (RTP) – Used to transmit audio and video over IP-based networks. It is used in conjunction with the RTCP. RTP transmits the media data, and RTCP is used to monitor transmission statistics and QoS, and aids synchronization of multiple data streams.

Record – A collection of related data items.

Recovery Point Objective (RPO) – A measurement of the point prior to an outage to which data are to be restored.

Recovery Time Objective (RTO) – The earliest time period and a service level within which a business process must be restored after a disaster to avoid unacceptable consequences.

Reference monitor – Concept that defines a set of design requirements of a reference validation mechanism (security kernel), which enforces an access control policy over subject's (processes, users) ability to perform operations (read, write, execute) on objects (files, resources) on a system.

Register – Small, temporary memory storage units integrated and used by the CPU during its processing functions.

Registration Authority (RA) – The primary purpose of an RA is to verify an end entity's identity and determine whether it is entitled to have a public key Certificate issued.

Relational database model – In a relational database, data is organized in two-dimensional tables or relations.

Remote Access Trojans (RATs) – Malicious programs that run on systems and allow intruders to access and use a system remotely.

J

Remote Authentication Dial-In User Service (RADIUS) – A network protocol that provides client/server authentication and authorization, and audits remote users.

Remote Journaling – Involves transmitting the journal or transaction log offsite to a backup facility.

Replay attack – This type of attack occurs when an attacker intercepts authentication information through the use of network monitoring utilities. The attacker then "replays" this information to the security system in an effort to gain access to the system.

Residual risk – Risk that remains after implementing a control. Threats × vulnerabilities × assets × (control gap) = residual risk.

Restricted interface – Limits the user's environment within the system, thus limiting access to objects.

Rijndael – Block symmetric cipher that was chosen to fulfil the Advanced Encryption Standard. It uses a 128-bit block size and various key lengths (128, 192, 256).

Ring topology – Each system connects to two other systems, forming a single, unidirectional network pathway for signals, thus forming a ring.

Risk – The probability of a threat agent exploiting a vulnerability and the associated impact.

Rollback – An operation that ends a current transaction and cancels all the recent changes to the database until the previous checkpoint/ commit point.

ROM – Computer memory chips with preprogrammed circuits for storing such software as word processors and spreadsheets. Information in the computer's ROM is permanently maintained even when the computer is turned off

Rootkit – Set of malicious tools that are loaded on a compromised system through stealthy techniques. The tools are used to carry out more attacks either on the infected systems or surrounding systems.

Rotation of duties – Detective administrative control used to uncover potential fraudulent activities.

Rule-based access – Access is based on a list of rules created or authorized by system owners that specify the privileges granted to users.

Running Key Cipher – Substitution cipher that creates keystream values, commonly from agreed-upon text passages, to be used for encryption purposes.

SABSA – Framework Risk-driven enterprise security architecture that maps to business initiatives, similar to the Zachman framework.

Sandbox – A virtual environment that allows for very fine-grained control over the actions that code within the machine is permitted to take. This is designed to allow safe execution of untrusted code from remote sources.

Schema – Defines the structure of the database.

Screened host – A firewall that communicates directly with a perimeter router and the internal network. The router carries out filtering activities on the traffic before it reaches the firewall.

Screened Subnet architecture – When two filtering devices are used to create a DMZ. The external device screens the traffic entering the DMZ network, and the internal filtering device screens the traffic before it enters the internal network.

Scytale Cipher – A simple transposition cipher system that employs a rod of a certain thickness around which was wrapped a long, thin strip of parchment.

Secure Electronic Transaction (SET) – The SET specification has been developed by Visa and MasterCard to allow for secure credit card and offline debit card (check card) transactions over the World Wide Web.

Secure MIME (S/MIME) – Secure/Multipurpose Internet Mail Extensions, which outlines how public key cryptography can be used to secure MIME data types.

Secure Shell (SSH) – Network protocol that allows for a secure connection to a remote system. Developed to replace Telnet and other insecure remote shell methods.

Security Assertion Markup Language (SAML) – An XML standard that allows the exchange of authentication and authorization data to be shared between security domains.

Security assurance requirements – Measures taken during development and evaluation of the product to assure compliance with the claimed security functionality.

Security domain – Resources within this logical structure (domain) are working under the same security policy and managed by the same group.

Security functional requirements – Individual security functions which must be provided by a product.

Security kernel – The central part of a computer system (hardware, software, or firmware) that implements the fundamental security procedures for controlling access to system resources.

Security perimeter – Mechanism used to delineate between the components within and outside of the trusted computing base.

Security policy – Strategic tool used to dictate how sensitive information and resources are to be managed and protected.

Security Target – Vendor's written explanation of the security functionality and assurance mechanisms that meet the needed security solution.

Security through Obscurity – Relying upon the secrecy or complexity of an item as its security, instead of practicing solid security practices.

Self-Garbling virus – Attempts to hide from anti-virus software by modifying its own code so that it does not match predefined signatures.

Sender Policy Framework (SPF) – An e-mail validation system designed to prevent e-mail spam by detecting e-mail spoofing, a common vulnerability, by verifying sender IP addresses.

Separation of Duties – Preventive administrative control used to ensure one person cannot carry out a critical task alone.

Server Side Includes (SSI) – An interpreted server-side scripting language used almost exclusively for web-based communication. It is commonly used to include the contents of one or more files into a web page on a web server. Allows web developers to reuse content by inserting the same content into multiple web documents.

Service Provisioning Markup Language (SPML) – Allows for the automation of user management (account creation, amendments, revocation) and access entitlement configuration related to electronically published services across multiple provisioning systems.

Session hijacking – An intruder takes over a connection after the original source has been authenticated.

Session Initiation Protocol (SIP) – The signaling protocol widely used for controlling communication, as in voice and video calls over IP based networks.

Session keys – Symmetric keys that have a short lifespan, thus providing more protection than static keys with longer lifespans.

Shielded twisted pair (STP) – Twisted-pair cables are often shielded in an attempt to prevent RFI and EMI. This shielding can be applied to individual pairs or to the collection of pairs.

Shoulder surfing – Viewing information in an unauthorized manner by looking over the shoulder of someone else.

Side-channel attack – Non-Intrusive Attack that uses information (timing, power consumption) that has been gathered to uncover sensitive data or processing functions. Often tries to figure out how a component works without trying to compromise any type of flaw or weakness.

Simple Mail Transfer Protocol (SMTP) – An Internet standard protocol for electronic mail (e-mail) transmission across IP-based networks.

Simple Network Management Protocol (SNMP) – Provides remote administration of network device; simple because the agent requires minimal software.

Simple Object Access Protocol (SOAP) – A lightweight protocol for exchange of information in a decentralized, distributed environment.

Single loss expectancy (SLE) – One instance of an expected loss if a specific vulnerability is exploited and how it affects a single asset. Asset Value × Exposure Factor = SLE.

Six Sigma – Business management strategy developed by Motorola with the goal of improving business processes.

Smart card – Plastic cards, typically with an electronic chip embedded, that contain electronic value tokens. Such value is disposable at both physical retail outlets and online shopping locations.

Smurf attack – A DDoS attack type on a computer that floods the target system with spoofed broadcast ICMP packets.

Social Engineering – Gaining unauthorized access by tricking someone into divulging sensitive information.

Social Engineering Attack – Manipulating individuals so that they will divulge confidential information, rather than by breaking in or using technical cracking techniques.

Software Configuration Management (SCM) – Identifies the attributes of software at various points in time, and performs a methodical control of changes for the purpose of maintaining software integrity and traceability throughout the software development life cycle.

Software deadlock – Two processes cannot complete their activities because they are both waiting for system resources to be released.

Software escrow – Storing of the source code of software with a third-party escrow agent. The software source code is released to the licensee if the licensor (software vendor) files for bankruptcy or fails to maintain and update the software product as promised in the software license agreement.

Source Routing – Allows a sender of a packet to specify the route the packet takes through the network versus routers determining the path.

Spanning Tree Protocol (STP) – A network protocol that ensures a loop-free topology for any bridged Ethernet LAN and allows redundant links to be available in case connection links go down.

Special Registers – Temporary memory location that holds critical processing parameters. They hold values as in the program counter, stack pointer, and program status word.

Stack Memory – Construct that is made up of individually addressable buffers. Process-to-process communication takes place through the use of stacks.

Standard – Compulsory rules that support the security policies.

Star topology – Network consists of one central device, which acts as a conduit to transmit messages. The central device, to which all other nodes are connected, provides a common connection point for all nodes.

Statement of Work (SOW) – Describes the product and customer requirements. A detailed-oriented SOW will help ensure that these requirements are properly understood and assumptions are not made.

Static analysis – A debugging technique that is carried out by examining the code without executing the program, and therefore is carried out before the program is compiled.

J

Statistical attack – Cryptanalysis attack that uses identified statistical patterns.

Statistical Time-Division Multiplexing (STDM) – This form of multiplexing uses all available time slots to send significant information and handles inbound data on a first-come, first-served basis.

Stealth virus – A virus that hides the modifications it has made. The virus tries to trick anti-virus software by intercepting its requests to the operating system and providing false and bogus information.

Steganography – (1) The method of concealing the existence of a message or data within seemingly innocent covers. (2) A technology used to embed information in for example, audio and graphical material. The audio and graphical materials appear unaltered until a steganography tool is used to reveal the hidden message.

Stream cipher – An encryption method in which a cryptographic key and an algorithm are applied to each bit in a datastream, one bit at a time.

Subject – An active entity that requests access to an object or the data within an object.

Subnet – Logical subdivision of a network that improves network administration and helps reduce network traffic congestion. Process of segmenting a network into smaller networks through the use of an addressing scheme made up of network and host portions.

Substitution Cipher – Encryption method that uses an algorithm that changes out (substitutes) one value for another value.

Symmetric algorithm – Encryption method where the sender and receiver use an instance of the same key for encryption and decryption purposes.

Symmetric Mode Multiprocessing – When a computer has two or more CPUs and each CPU is being used in a load-balancing method.

SYN flood – DoS attack where an attacker sends a succession of SYN packets with the goal of overwhelming the victim system so that it is unresponsive to legitimate traffic.

Synchronous communication – Transmission sequencing technology that uses a clocking pulse or timing scheme for data transfer synchronization.

Synchronous Optical Networking (SONET) and Synchronous Digital Hierarchy (SDH) – Standardized multiplexing protocols that transfer multiple digital bit streams over optical fiber and allow for simultaneous transportation of many different circuits of differing origin within a single framing protocol.

Synchronous Token Device – Synchronizes with the authentication service by using time or a counter as the core piece of the authentication process. If the synchronization is time-based, the token device and the authentication service must hold the same time within their internal clocks.

System Development Life Cycle (SDLC) – The scope of activities associated with a system, encompassing the system's initiation, development and acquisition, implementation, operation and maintenance, and, ultimately, its disposal, which instigates another system initiation.

Target of Evaluation (TOE) – Product proposed to provide a needed security solution.

T-carriers – Dedicated lines that can carry voice and data information over trunk lines.

TCP/IP model – Standardization of device-based network communication through a modular four-layer architecture. Specific to the IP suite, created in 1970 by an agency of the U.S. Department of Defense (DoD).

Teredo – Transition mechanism for migrating from IPv4 to IPv6. It allows systems to use IPv6 to communicate if their traffic has to transverse an IPv4 network, but also performs its function behind NAT devices.

Thread – Instruction set generated by a process when it has a specific activity that needs to be carried out by an operating system. When the activity is finished, the thread is destroyed.

Threat – The danger of a threat agent exploiting a vulnerability.

Threat agent – Entity that can exploit a vulnerability.

Threat modeling – A systematic approach used to understand how different threats could be realized and how a successful compromise could take place.

Time Multiplexing – Technology that allows processes to use the same resources.

Time-Division Multiplexing (TDM) – A type of multiplexing in which two or more bit streams or signals are transferred apparently simultaneously as sub-channels in one communication channel, but are physically taking turns on the single channel.

Time-of-Check/Time-of-Use (TOC/TOU) attack – Attacker manipulates the "condition check" step and the "use" step within software to allow for unauthorized activity.

TOGAF – Enterprise architecture framework used to define and understand a business environment developed by The Open Group.

Token ring – LAN medium access technology that controls network communication traffic through the use of token frames. This technology has been mostly replaced by Ethernet.

Total risk – Full risk amount before a control is put into place. Threats × vulnerabilities × assets = total risk.

Trade secrets – Proprietary business or technical information, processes, designs, practices, etc. that are confidential and critical to the business.

Trademark – Protect words, names, product shapes, symbols, colors, or a combination of these used to identify products or a company. These items are used to distinguish products from the competitors' products.

J

Transmission Control Protocol (TCP) – The major transport protocol in the Internet suite of protocols providing reliable, connection-oriented, full-duplex streams.

Transport mode – Mode that IPSec protocols can work in that provides protection for packet data payload.

Transposition – Encryption method that shifts (permutation) values.

Triple DES (3-DES) – Symmetric cipher that applies DES three times to each block of data during the encryption process.

Trojan Horse – A program that is disguised as another program with the goal of carrying out malicious activities in the background without the user knowing.

Trusted Computer System Evaluation Criteria (TCSEC) – U.S. DoD standard used to assess the effectiveness of the security controls built into a system. Replaced by the Common Criteria. Also known as the Orange Book.

Trusted Computing Base (TCB) – A collection of all the hardware, software, and firmware components within a system that provide security and enforce the system's security policy.

Trusted path – Trustworthy software channel that is used for communication between two processes that cannot be circumvented.

Tunnel mode – Mode that IPSec protocols can work in that provides protection for packet headers and data payload.

Tuple – A row in a two-dimensional database.

Two-Phase Commit – A mechanism that is another control used in databases to ensure the integrity of the data held within the database.

Type I error – When a biometric system rejects an authorized individual (false rejection rate).

Type II error – When the system accepts impostors who should be rejected (false acceptance rate).

Uncertainty Analysis – Assigning confidence level values to data elements.

Unshielded Twisted Pair (UTP) – Cabling in which copper wires are twisted together for the purposes of canceling out EMI from external sources. UTP cables are found in many Ethernet networks and telephone systems.

User Datagram Protocol (UDP) – Connectionless, unreliable transport layer protocol, which is considered a "best effort" protocol.

User mode (problem state) – Protection mode that a CPU works within when carrying out less trusted process instructions.

User provisioning – The creation, maintenance, and deactivation of user objects and attributes as they exist in one or more systems, directories, or applications, in response to business processes.

Validation – Determines if the product provides the necessary solution for the intended real-world problem.

Verification – Determines if the product accurately represents and meets the specifications.

Very high-level languages – Otherwise known as fourth-generation programming languages and are meant to take natural language-based statements one step ahead.

View – A virtual relation defined by the database administrator in order to keep subjects from viewing certain data.

Virtual Local Area Network (VLAN) – A group of hosts that communicate as if they were attached to the same broadcast domain, regardless of their physical location. VLAN membership can be configured through software instead of physically relocating devices or connections, which allows for easier centralized management.

Virtual memory – Combination of main memory (RAM) and secondary memory within an operating system.

Virtualization – Creation of a simulated environment (hardware platform, operating system, storage, etc.) that allows for central control and scalability.

Virus – A small application, or string of code, that infects host applications. It is a programming code that can replicate itself and spread from one system to another.

Vishing (Voice and Phishing) – Social engineering activity over the telephone system, most often using features facilitated by VoIP, to gain unauthorized access to sensitive data.

VLAN hopping – An exploit that allows an attacker on a VLAN to gain access to traffic on other VLANs that would normally not be accessible.

Voice over IP (VoIP) – The set of protocols, technologies, methodologies, and transmission techniques involved in the delivery of voice data and multimedia sessions over IP-based networks.

Vulnerability – Weakness or a lack of a countermeasure.

War dialing – When a specialized program is used to automatically scan a list of telephone numbers to search for computers for the purposes of exploitation and hacking.

Wave-Division Multiplexing (WDM) – Multiplying the available capacity of optical fibers through use of parallel channels, with each channel on a dedicated wavelength of light. The bandwidth of an optical fiber can be divided into as many as 160 channels.

Web proxy – A piece of software installed on a system that is designed to intercept all traffic between the local web browser and the web server.

Wide Area Network (WAN) – A telecommunication network that covers a broad area and allows a business to effectively carry out its daily function, regardless of location.

J

Wiretapping – A passive attack that eavesdrops on communications. It is only legal with prior consent or a warrant.

Work Breakdown Dtructure (WBS) – A project management tool used to define and group a project's individual work elements in an organized manner.

Wormhole attack – This takes place when an attacker captures packets at one location in the network and tunnels them to another location in the network for a second attacker to use against a target system.

Worms – These are different from viruses in that they can reproduce on their own without a host application and are self-contained programs.

Zachman framework – Enterprise architecture framework used to define and understand a business environment developed by John Zachman.

Zero Knowledge Proof – One entity can prove something to be true without providing a secret value.

CISSP®

Appendix K
Index

K

Index

K

Index

K

Index

K

Index

K

Index

K

Index

K

Index

A. RAMIREZ FALL 2015